Base Ball Founders

Base Ball Founders

*The Clubs, Players and
Cities of the Northeast
That Established the Game*

Edited by Peter Morris, William J. Ryczek,
Jan Finkel, Leonard Levin *and*
Richard Malatzky

McFarland & Company, Inc., Publishers
Jefferson, North Carolina, and London

Library of Congress Cataloguing-in-Publication Data

Base ball founders : the clubs, players and cities of the Northeast
that established the game / edited by Peter Morris, William J. Ryczek, Jan Finkel,
Leonard Levin and Richard Malatzky.
p.   cm.
Includes bibliographical references and index.

ISBN 978-0-7864-7430-1
softcover : acid free paper ∞

1. Baseball—Northeastern States—History—19th century.
2. Baseball teams—Northeastern States—History—19th century.
3. Baseball players—Northeastern States—History—19th century.
I. Morris, Peter, editor of compilation.   II. Title: Baseball founders.
GV863.N72B37 2013   796.357097409034—dc23   2013017959

British Library cataloguing data are available

On the cover: The Excelsiors of Brooklyn, 1860 (A. G. Spalding Baseball
Collection, New York Public Library); (background)
lithograph of New York City by Charles Parsons, 1856

Manufactured in the United States of America

*McFarland & Company, Inc., Publishers
Box 611, Jefferson, North Carolina 28640
www.mcfarlandpub.com*

To the memory of
Fred Ivor-Campbell, Bob McConnell and David Ball,
three stellar baseball historians who didn't live
to see the completion of this project.

Table of Contents

Introduction (William J. Ryczek)   1

Timeline of the Pioneer Era (Robert Tholkes)   3

Note on Sources and Usage (Peter Morris)   5

❖ CHAPTER ONE: NEW YORK CITY AND VICINITY ❖

Introduction (William J. Ryczek)   7

Knickerbocker Base Ball Club (John Thorn, William J. Ryczek and Peter Morris)   10

New York Base Ball Club (a.k.a. Washington BBC, Gotham BBC) (John Thorn)   46

Magnolia Base Ball Club (John Thorn)   62

Active Base Ball Club (Gregory Christiano)   65

Eagle Base Ball Club (Gregory Christiano)   69

Empire Base Ball Club (Gregory Christiano)   76

Mutual Base Ball Club (William J. Ryczek)   80

Union Base Ball Club of Morrisania (Aaron W. Miller)   93

❖ CHAPTER TWO: BROOKLYN ❖

Introduction (Peter Morris)   98

Excelsior Base Ball Club (William J. Ryczek and Peter Morris)   101

Putnam Base Ball Club (William J. Ryczek)   111

Atlantic Base Ball Club (Craig B. Waff and William J. Ryczek)   117

Pastime Base Ball Club (Peter Morris)   140

Star Base Ball Club (Craig B. Waff, William J. Ryczek and Peter Morris)   144

Eckford Base Ball Club (William J. Ryczek and Peter Morris)   167

Contest Base Ball Club (Peter Morris)   187

❖ CHAPTER THREE: NEW JERSEY ❖

Introduction (John G. Zinn)   191

Pioneer Base Ball Club of Jersey City (John G. Zinn)   194

Excelsior Base Ball Club of Jersey City (John G. Zinn)   197

Liberty Base Ball Club of New Brunswick (John G. Zinn)   199

Nassau Base Ball Club of Princeton (John G. Zinn)   202

Eureka Base Ball Club of Newark (John G. Zinn)   207

Irvington Base Ball Club (John G. Zinn)   214

Olympic Base Ball Club of Paterson (John G. Zinn) 218
Champion Base Ball Club of Jersey City (John G. Zinn) 222

❖ CHAPTER FOUR: PHILADELPHIA ❖

Introduction (John Shiffert) 226
Olympic Base Ball Club (Richard Hershberger) 228
Athletic Base Ball Club (Richard Hershberger) 234
Equity Base Ball Club (Peter Morris) 241
Keystone Base Ball Club (Peter Morris) 246
Pythian Base Ball Club (Jared Wheeler) 251
Chester Base Ball Club (Peter Morris) 254
Marion Base Ball Club (Richard Hershberger) 257

❖ CHAPTER FIVE: MASSACHUSETTS ❖

Introduction (Peter Morris) 260
Lowell Base Ball Club (Benjamin Dettmar) 264
Pioneer Base Ball Club of Springfield (Peter Morris) 270
Lawrence Base Ball Club of Harvard (Peter Morris) 281
Harvard Class of '66 Base Ball Club (Peter Morris) 284
Eagle Base Ball Club of Florence (Brian Turner and John S. Bowman) 296
Lightfoot Base Ball Club of North Brookfield (Peter Morris) 299
Chemung Base Ball Club of Stoughton (Peter Morris) 302
Kearsarge Base Ball Club of Stoneham (Peter Morris) 304
Clipper Base Ball Club of Lowell (Peter Morris) 307
Cummaquid Base Ball Club of Barnstable (Peter Morris) 315

General Bibliography 321
About the Contributors 323
Index 325

Introduction
William J. Ryczek

In April 2012, *Base Ball Pioneers, 1850–1870*, chronicling the spread of baseball beyond the areas of its birth, appeared in print from McFarland. It included an eloquent introduction by Peter Morris that described the origin of the concept of the Pioneer Project, the basic outline of that volume and this one, and the various contributions that brought both to fruition.

Peter Morris specializes in people, almost exclusively dead people. The former director of our local historical society had a sign posted on her office door that read, "If you're not dead, we're not interested." So it is with Peter. His indefatigable thirst for genealogical data provided the backbone for most of the player profiles contained in both volumes, and his delight in finding the missing and the intriguing added immeasurably to the value of the work. In contradiction of the common adage, Morris's dead people told many tales. Some, like William Wheaton, were meaningful contributors to the development of the game; some, like Alexander Cartwright, led very interesting lives after their baseball days were over; and others, like Joseph Vanderbilt, catcher of the Eckford Base Ball Club of Brooklyn and grandfather of advice columnist Amy Vanderbilt, spawned prominent descendants.

As they did for the first volume, Jan Finkel and Len Levin copy edited the entire manuscript and their tactful craftsmanship again produced proper grammar, style and usage in the text and intact self-esteem on the part of the contributors. Roger Erickson and Skip McAfee likewise volunteered their expertise in indexing.

In addition to Peter, Jan and Len, the material for this work is the product of many authors, all authorities on the clubs they covered and all working on a voluntary basis, fueled by intellectual curiosity, a desire to share with the reading public what they have learned about early baseball, and the relentless prodding of the editorial team.

The clubs profiled in *Base Ball Founders* are those that played in the areas of the United States in which baseball originated: New York, Boston, Philadelphia and the surrounding regions. Those three cities were the most populous in the United States during the time of baseball's birth, and it is nat-ural that the game would have been begun there. It did not arise in similar form in all three cities, however. During the 1850s, for the most part, the game played in Boston was the "Massachusetts Game," which yielded to the New York version in popularity after the Civil War. Early ball games in Philadelphia were the old game of "town ball," which also gave way to the New York game.

Every year, new information regarding baseball's earliest days is discovered, some of which is in conflict with what we thought we knew, some of which confirms and expands upon our existing knowledge, and some of which raises even more questions that we hope can be answered by further research. John Thorn discovered the virtually unknown Magnolia Base Ball Club of the 1840s, and his chapter on the New York Base Ball Club (also known as the Washington and Gotham base ball club) contains much new information about the early days of the organization, a period coincident with the birth of New York baseball.

Some club histories, notably those of the Atlantics and the New York clubs, are much longer than others. Baseball began in New York, and soon spread to Brooklyn; therefore, clubs in those cities had a longer history than those that adopted the game later. More significantly, those clubs, and the Knickerbockers, had a major influence on the development of the game, and their members were among the most prominent figures in early baseball. The New York and Knickerbocker clubs were instrumental in the formalization of the game and the transformation of the sport from an informal recreational activity to a structured business venture. The Atlantics, although they were formed much later than the former two organizations, were the dominant nine on the playing field from the late 1850s through 1870. We hope the reader will indulge us the relatively large amount of space devoted to these leading pioneers.

We hope this book will be a "page turner" not in the sense of a dramatic mystery novel, in which one races through the text to see the mystery unraveled, but in a way that will make you flip both forward and back to see the inter-relationships of the clubs and players. Early baseball clubs were often fluid, and the names of William Wheaton, Doc Adams, and others appear in the histories of more than one pioneer club. We have treated the two volumes as complementary, to be read as one; therefore, if a player is profiled in *Base Ball Pioneers, 1850–1870*, we have referred the reader to it rather than repeat the information here.

When looking back on a project after it is finished, one must determine whether it has achieved its planned objectives. As Peter stated in his introduction to the first volume, our primary purpose in producing this work, which took several years to finalize, was to set forth the heretofore untold story of the clubs and players who played the game prior to 1870. An ancillary purpose was to provide a comprehensive reference source for those who want to learn more about baseball's earliest days, and who may undertake further research and build upon the data we've presented. The standard contemporary source on the history of early baseball was *The Book of American Pastimes*, published in 1866 by Charles A. Peverelly. A century and a half after its appearance, Peverelly's work still serves as a valuable research tool, but we now know much more than Peverelly knew in 1866, and there is much additional information presented in these pages. The final judgment as to whether we have achieved our goals rests, of course, with our readers, and we hope you will find both volumes interesting and useful.

Timeline of the Pioneer Era
Robert Tholkes

Base Ball Founders, like its companion volume, *Base Ball Pioneers*, focuses on what we have referred to as the pioneer era. Beginning with the earliest inter-club matches and ending with the advent of professional baseball, the period includes all of the 1850s and 1860s. Viewed with 150 years' hindsight, the events of the period unspool in a logical sequence of inevitable steps.

1850: Five years after the Knickerbocker Base Ball Club of New York drew up the ancestor of today's rules, the "New York Rules," the Washington Base Ball Club of New York became the second to adopt them for play. Interclub matches began in 1851. Both were social clubs, collecting dues and sponsoring amateur teams in multiple skill grades from among their members for the purposes of healthful exercise and friendly competition. The social club format, at least, would endure throughout the Pioneer Period and into the first years of professional baseball as the pattern for organized adult play, and emulated by an uncounted number of junior clubs.

1853: The *New York Sunday Mercury* begins publication of game accounts. Other publications shortly follow suit and together spread word from Maine to California of the benefits of the game, information about the playing rules, accounts of match play, and a record of the game's spread.

1857: Several other clubs playing various forms of base ball (then still two words) having also agreed to adopt the Knickerbocker rules, a meeting is held in New York in January to standardize play.

1858: Formation in March of the National Association of Base Ball Players (NABBP) to further regulate play and relationships among the clubs and to promote the expansion of the game. The conventions continue on an annual basis, but NABBP remains entirely a volunteer group, with no paid staff. Its effectiveness against the gambling and professionalism that accompany the game's growth is limited.

1858: The NABBP Rules Committee acts to curb the rising number of pitches thrown in a game, which is making game times too long. Pitchers sought to deceive and exhaust the patience of hitters and to curb base-stealing, while hitters in turn ignored good balls to both exhaust pitchers and to give their mates a chance to steal, to the extent that combined pitch counts ran to hundreds per game. Umpires were directed to begin calling strikes when in their judgment such tactics were being employed. Five years later the ability to call balls was added. Frequently ignored by umpires, who were usually players from other clubs, these were only the first of a series of steps, taken at intervals over the next twenty years, toward the eventual calling of balls and strikes on every pitch.

1858: Admission to matches is charged for the first time, for a series of Brooklyn–New York City all-star games at the Fashion Race Course in Queens. The proceeds are donated to New York's and Brooklyn's fire companies, with which clubs and players were frequently associated. Attendance for the three games was estimated to be in the tens of thousands.

1860: *Beadle's Dime Base Ball Player*, the first guide to rules, regulations, and play, appears, making available authoritative annotations explaining the rules.

1860: The Excelsior Base Ball Club of South Brooklyn takes the game on the road, traveling to western New York State, Baltimore, and Philadelphia, while dazzling the locals with their caliber of play. The Excelsior roster includes the first reputed professional, pitcher Jim Creighton. With prestige and the attraction of dues-paying members at stake, various forms of surreptitious compensation are devised as the 1860s progress: payment of club dues, "benefit" games, side jobs requiring varying degrees of actual work, and an outright salary as an employee of the club.

1860: The "conquering" (rubber) game of the three-game match between the Excelsiors and the Atlantic Base Ball Club of Brooklyn ends in unprecedented fashion when the Excelsiors leave the field in protest against the rowdy behavior of the crowd.

1860: Teams composed of compositors employed by two New York newspapers, the *World* and the *Times*, play a game. Teams sponsored by companies and corporations would become a major source of opportunity for organized play by adults and juniors alike over the next several decades.

1861–1865: The War Between the States significantly reduces participation in and public attention to the game, but also to an unknowable degree assists its spread, as it is frequently played in army camps. The United States government assists by distributing equipment. Baseball writers such as William Cauldwell of the *Sunday Mercury* point out as a precedent the games of cricket played in British camps during the recently completed Crimean War.

1862: The for-profit Union Grounds, the first enclosed playing grounds, opens in Brooklyn. Admission is charged on a regular basis. The effect is to further promote professionalism, as funding shifts from reliance on volunteerism to reliance on selling tickets to the public.

1865: Culminating a six-year struggle, the most contentious rules question of the period is settled after the 1864 season when the "bound rule," whereby fair balls caught on the first bounce put out the batter, is dropped in favor of the "fly rule," which calls for putouts on fair balls only when the ball is caught before touching the ground. The fly rule's proponents have for years criticized the bound rule as "boyish," and a detriment to the game's contest with cricket for the allegiance of young sportsmen.

1865: Paid by a gambler, three Mutual Base Ball Club of New York players "heave" a September game against the Eckford Base Ball Club of Williamsburg (Brooklyn), are caught, and are expelled from the club. It is regarded as a sign of the times in baseball rather than an isolated incident; the players were later reinstated.

1866: The 10th annual NABBP convention, exceeding pre-war levels, attracts 202 clubs from 17 states and the District of Columbia.

1867: Post-war "base ball fever" peaks, with clubs in virtually every state in the Union. The Nationals of Washington make the first trans–Allegheny tour, traveling as far west as St. Louis.

1868: Several top clubs are demonstrably of "semi-pro" status, with several gradations along the continuum from avowedly amateur social sporting clubs on the Knickerbocker model to clubs pursuing (and paying) top players for the pursuit of prestige, members, and profit.

1869: Open recognition of the existence of professional clubs and players by the NABBP, as a response to the sham amateurism and gambling influences by then felt to be damaging the status of the game. At the time, it was estimated that of the thousand or more clubs playing nationwide, fewer than twenty were fully professional, and about fifty paid one or more players.

1869: The Cincinnati Base Ball Club fields the most immediately successful, openly full-time, all-professional team, the Red Stockings, seeking and employing the best players available regardless of location, for a group of civic-minded investor "members." They are essentially, though not in name, stockholders. The team firmly establishes professional dominance of the sport by touring nationally and going undefeated.

1870: Cincinnati's bitter rival for Western supremacy, Chicago, ups the ante, dropping the social-club format and selling enough stock in the Chicago Base Ball Club to reportedly pay $10,000 in salaries to the all-professional White Stockings.

1870–1871: The professionals break away from the NABBP, forming the National Association of Professional Base Ball Players, and plan the first intercity "pennant race" for the 1871 season. A separate amateur association is formed and struggles to mid-decade before fading out of sight.

Note on Sources and Usage
Peter Morris

A general bibliography at the end of this work lists key sources on the pioneer era of baseball. Contributors were invited to include their own note on sources used or a selected bibliography at the end of their entry, but were encouraged not to be exhaustive and not to duplicate the books that appear in the general bibliography unless the works were of direct use. In particular, the research done to identify and trace club members was likely to involve the use of dozens of city directory listings, census records, and other genealogical sources. Exhaustive lists of these sources would be more likely to exhaust readers than enlighten them, so every effort has been made to keep these to a minimum.

Contemporaneous newspaper accounts are the primary source for most of these entries, so a few words about their use are in order for those who have not experienced the joys and sorrows of perusing them. Chief among the joys is that reporters of the era were lively and engaging writers, as will be clear from the many excerpts that are reprinted in these pages. Less pleasantly, the concepts of journalistic ethics and plagiarism had only begun to emerge, which meant that some nineteenth-century American newspapers abounded in blatant libel and stolen material.

The latter issue makes accurate acknowledgment of sources difficult, since all newspapers of the era borrowed liberally from one another, but only some of them were meticulous about acknowledging such debts (and many of the ones that did were not very accurate in their attributions).[1] In 1885 *Sporting Life*'s Cleveland correspondent grumbled: "The gentleman who is in charge of [the sporting] department of the [Cleveland] *Leader* evidently has a pair of long scissors, with which he completely cuts up the *Sporting Life* and Cincinnati papers, but fails to credit the source for the news stolen. Nothing original in the sporting line emanates from the *Leader*."[2] It is a state of affairs that makes it impossible to be confident that a note originated in the source cited. So while every effort has been made to cite sources in as precise and helpful a form as possible, there is no way to be certain of the original source. Bylines were very rarely attached to articles,

so are included when given in the original, but it is often necessary to refer vaguely to their author as a reporter or writer.

An issue that is more likely to catch readers' attention is that quoted material often contains differences from current standards of spelling, punctuation and capitalization. Until the 1880s the term "base ball" was almost exclusively written as two words and only in the twentieth century did it become common to spell it as a single word. Other terms, such as "short stop," "team mate," "some one," "every one," and "to-day," also took time to become recognized as compound words. "Innings" with an *s* was used where we would now expect "inning," while British/Canadian spellings of words such as center ("centre"), practice ("practise"), and criticize ("criticise") remained common in the United States. The spelling of city names that ended in "burgh" (e.g., Pittsburgh, Newburgh, Lansingburgh) is too involved an issue to get into here, but suffice it to say that it was not until the twentieth century that the *h* became permanent.

Similarly, placement of commas also varied greatly from today's usage, while capitalization was based on very different principles; "Main Street" was then "Main street" and "Allegheny County" usually "Allegheny county," to cite only a couple of examples. Great care has been taken to ensure that all quoted material has been reproduced verbatim, especially passages that look odd to the modern eye. Rather than regularly interrupting these quotations with the indicator of [*sic*], use of this label has been kept to a minimum, generally only when there was an obvious mistake of fact or grammar or a deviation from the spelling conventions of the day.

The format of club names is also likely to puzzle baseball fans who are accustomed to having the city name come first ("Philadelphia Phillies"). Throughout the pioneer era, formal club names almost always took the following form: the Ontario Base Ball Club of Oswego, or when the city name stood alone, the Utica Base Ball Club. For simplicity's sake, these names were often abbreviated: the Ontario Club of Oswego, the Ontarios of Oswego, the Ontarios; the Utica Club, the Uticas. (Singular construction — the Ontario of Oswego — was sometimes used as well, but was less common, so for consistency's sake the plural form has been given preference.) The modern formulation of "the Oswego Ontarios" did not become common until the 1870s, so the original version has been used. Making things more difficult to follow, two of the best clubs of the pioneer era became known by unofficial nicknames — the Cincinnati Base Ball Club (the "Red Stockings") and the Union Base Ball Club of Lansingburgh (Troy "Haymakers").

Finally, the term "National Association" is likely to prove a source of confusion because it was used to refer to two very different entities. From 1857 to 1870, the game's governing body was known as the National Association of Base Ball Players or NABBP. This entity disbanded prior to the 1871 season and was replaced by separate bodies for the professional and amateur clubs: the National Association of Professional Base Ball Players and the National Association of Amateur Base Ball Players. The latter body was not very active, but the former became the first major league, lasting from 1871 until the formation of the National League in 1876, and it soon came to be known simply as the National Association. Unfortunately, articles from the 1860s often referred to the NABBP as the National Association. To try to keep things as simple as possible, references to the NABBP generally use either the full name or the acronym, and clarification is provided when it seems likely to be helpful.

Notes

1. The profile of Henry Mason Scovell in the Franklins of Detroit entry in *Base Ball Pioneers, 1850–1870* explains some of the reasons attribution was erratic.

2. *Sporting Life*, May 13, 1885.

CHAPTER ONE

NEW YORK CITY AND VICINITY

❖ *Introduction* (William J. Ryczek) ❖

The most prevalent brand of baseball played in the United States during the 1860s was referred to as the "New York game" in deference to its origin in the nation's largest city. For many years, the origin of New York baseball was attributed to the Knickerbockers, who left an exhaustive trail of documentation, including scorebooks, minutes of their many meetings, and endless detail of their petty arguments and mundane tasks. In recent years many scholars, most prominently the indefatigable John Thorn, have proved to us that there were New York clubs that preceded the Knickerbockers but lacked their propensity to painstakingly record their deeds for posterity.

As early as the 1830s, nearly ten years before the formation of the Knickerbockers, there were clubs playing a bat and ball game nearly identical to that played by Alexander Cartwright and his associates. William Wheaton and Daniel (Doc) Adams, both of whom gained prominence with the early Knickerbockers, were members of a group called the New York Club, which established a set of rules and played during the late 1830s. Other clubs formed prior to the Knickerbockers included the Washington Club, the Eagle, which originally played a brand of ball a little different from the eventual New York version, and the little known Magnolia Club. The information recently unearthed regarding the latter organization is tantalizing in that it indicates that the Magnolias were a baseball club whose members were a colorful group that had a number of interesting connections to working–class social life. Tantalization leads to frustration, however, in that very little else can be found about that potentially interesting club. With John Thorn hot on the trail, however, we remain hopeful that a broader portrait of the enigmatic Magnolias can be painted in the near future. Despite all of the new information unearthed during the past few years, one fact remains undisputed. The origin of baseball remains firmly rooted in New York.[1]

The heyday of early New York baseball lasted through the mid–1850s. The Washington Club became the Gothams, the Eagles converted to the standardized New York game and the Knickerbockers met religiously to play games among themselves. Even though there were three active teams in the city, interclub matches were rare. The primary purpose of a baseball club was to meet on a regular basis, divide into teams, and play for exercise and the health of its members. A perusal of the minutes and club books of the Knickerbockers might also convince one that a secondary purpose was to rival legislative bodies in their thirst for administrative minutiae. There was sport, there was exercise, and there were minutes, but the heated competition that would soon envelop the world of baseball was lacking in the early 1850s.

The first recorded matches between two clubs took place in the fall of 1845 when a team from New York defeated one from Brooklyn in two straight matches. The following June 19, the game that was long celebrated as the first match game featured the Knickerbockers losing ingloriously to the New York Club at Hoboken, New Jersey.

If New York was Mesopotamia, Brooklyn was Greece and Rome combined, as the heart of the baseball world soon left Manhattan for the City of Churches. The Atlantics, Eckfords, and Excelsiors were the dominant clubs of the late 1850s and early 1860s, with New York having only the Mutuals and Unions of Morrisania capable of competing on equal footing with the Brooklyn clubs. Several of the teams that were based in New York did not even play in the city, having moved across the Hudson to the Elysian Fields in Hoboken. The real-estate boom in Manhattan had consumed much of the city's open land, and there were far more profitable uses for urban parcels than playing fields for the Eagles and Knickerbockers. Central Park was one of the most luxurious open spaces in the United States, but despite numerous efforts by the ball playing community, the city refused to allow baseball to be played within its confines. In 1862 the Union Grounds were constructed in Brooklyn, and the Capitoline Grounds followed two years later. There were no enclosed grounds in New York City, nor would there be for several years.

By the early 1860s the only New York clubs that played competitive baseball with the Brooklyn nines were the aforementioned Mutuals and Unions. The Mutuals had a long and

Top: Cricket at the Red House Grounds in Harlem. The grounds were a frequent site of baseball games in the 1850s, home of the Tiger, Baltic, Harlem and Gotham clubs. *Bottom:* The Elysian Fields were located in Hoboken, a short ferry ride across the Hudson from New York City. The property was an extensive recreational retreat for city dwellers, with picnic grounds, a merry-go-round and a ferris wheel. There were also a number of ball fields used for cricket and baseball. Until the enclosed Union Grounds were constructed in 1862, the Elysian Fields were the center of baseball activity in the New York area.

Top: Before the Civil War, when cricket and baseball vied for the title of national pastime, many athletes played both games. Here is the St. George Cricket Club at the Elysian Fields of Hoboken in 1861, featuring 14-year-old George Wright (standing fifth from left)—son of the club's professional, Sam Wright—destined to become baseball's greatest player of the post–Civil War era. *Bottom:* Another view of the Elysian Fields. The facility was developed by Colonel John Stevens, who also owned the ferry concession and wanted to increase traffic across the Hudson. Edgar Allan Poe based "The Mystery of Marie Rogêt" on an event that occurred at the Elysian Fields.

storied history, beginning with their formation in 1857 and ending with their expulsion from the National League following its inaugural 1876 season. Perhaps the most intriguing feature of the Mutuals was their close affiliation with Tammany Hall. Many Mutual players worked for the city of New York, particularly in the street cleaning and coroner's departments, and William (Boss) Tweed was present at club events.

The Unions of Morrisania were the first team from outside Brooklyn to win the national championship. The Unions were the champions of 1867, although by that time the selection process had become somewhat muddled. The following year, the Mutuals became the second New York nine to win the championship.

The Mutuals and Unions fought alone for the honor of New York, for the early clubs like the Gothams, Eagles, Empires, and Knickerbockers continued to play mainly for recreation. When professionalism became widespread after the end of the Civil War, the Knickerbockers and the other old amateur organizations had no intention of competing with clubs that employed professional players.

New York City was the birthplace of modern baseball and remained the focus of the small baseball world through the mid–1850s. By the middle of the 1880s New York was represented by the Metropolitans of the American Association and the New York Club of the National League, and in the twentieth century its Yankees and Giants played in many World Series, making New York again the sport's premier city. In the interim, however, New York played a secondary role, hampered by a lack of suitable playing sites. Yet, without the Knickerbockers, Eagles, and Gothams, there might never have been Atlantics, Eckfords, Athletics, and Red Stockings. For its role in baseball's beginnings, New York will forever hold a valued place in the history of early baseball.

Notes

1. An excellent source on the origin of baseball in New York is John Thorn, *Baseball in the Garden of Eden: The Secret History of the Early Game* (New York: Simon & Schuster, 2011). Chapters two and three describe the New York genesis of the sport in terrific detail.

❖ *Knickerbocker Base Ball Club* ❖
(John Thorn, William J. Ryczek and Peter Morris)

CLUB HISTORY

For more than 150 years the Knickerbocker Base Ball Club of New York (KBBC) has been accepted as the pioneer club of the national pastime. One of its principal members, Alexander Joy Cartwright, Jr., has been credited, by those unwilling to credit the Abner Doubleday legend, with inventing the game. Even as A.G. Mills was reluctantly anointing Doubleday as the inventor of baseball in his 1908 report on the origins of baseball, he declared:

> Then, and ever since, I have heard cricket spoken of as the essentially English game, and, until my perusal of this testimony, my own belief had been that our game of Base Ball, substantially as played to-day, originated with the Knickerbocker club of New York, and it was frequently referred to as the "New York Ball Game."[1]

Recent scholarship has indicated that the Knickerbockers were not the first to play the game, or the first to be organized as a formal club, or the first to govern its play with a formal set of rules. Moreover, Cartwright did not invent the game any more than Doubleday did. All the same, it may not be too much to call the Knickerbockers the pioneer club, or to support their historic claim to significance. If they were not the first baseball club, they were the most important in shaping the game that would be embraced by other clubs, and in short order all America.

There is no overestimating Americans' love and fear of organization, then as now. It is certain that variants of the Massachusetts Game were older than variants of the New York Game. No matter; the Knickerbockers brought in *system* before the New Englanders did. And finally — has the obvious eluded us all this time? — New York may have won out because of a skillful publicity campaign in which its game of baseball, held up as a paragon of manliness, was in fact easier for unathletic clerks to play. For common men of sedentary habits who would, if they had their wish, be leisured gentlemen — such as the Knickerbockers — it was more important to comport themselves well than to play well. Did the New York Game surmount all challenges because it allowed more chance to exhibit skill and nerve? In sport as in war, perhaps, the first casualty is truth.

Several groups of young men began to play ball at Madison Square in the 1830s. It was a game they understood to be baseball, no matter what its rules and field configuration may have been. Some would go on to form the New York (a.k.a. Gotham) Base Ball Club in 1837. Several of these players split off from the NYBBC to become Knickerbockers, and were joined by others who were not previously attached to the Eagle or Magnolia clubs — which, like the New York, preceded the KBBC.

By mid–1845 the ur-Knickerbockers, as yet unformed and unnamed, had seen their playing grounds, first at Madison

Square and then at Murray Hill, give way to the needs of the railroad. Charles A. Peverelly, in his 1866 *Book of American Pastimes,* described their situation:

> At a preliminary meeting, it was suggested that as it was apparent they would soon be driven from Murray Hill, some suitable place should be obtained in New Jersey, where their stay could be permanent; accordingly, a day or two afterwards, enough to make a game assembled at Barclay street ferry, crossed over, marched up the road, prospecting for ground on each side, until they reached the Elysian Fields, where they "settled." Thus it occurred that a party of gentlemen formed an organization, combining together health, recreation, and social enjoyment, which was the nucleus of the now great American game of Base Ball so popular in all parts of the United States, than which there is none more manly or more health-giving.[2]

The Knickerbocker party of course did not wander about northern New Jersey looking for a place to play. In selecting the Elysian Fields they had been preceded by other clubs, both baseball and cricket. The New York Ball Club, for one, celebrated its second anniversary in Hoboken with an intramural game in the fall of 1845 in which many nominal Knickerbockers and Gothams played.[3] The Magnolias had established there sometime in 1843 as well. The "prospecting" Knicks knew to come to the Elysian Fields because in this, as in so many other things, they were not truly the first.

The Knickerbockers organized on September 23, 1845, and codified their playing rules in a document of that date which does not survive; their first printed booklet of rules and by-laws was published in 1848. The two-man committee that produced the rules consisted of attorney William R. Wheaton and tobacconist William H. Tucker. It seems likely that Wheaton was the more important of the two, as he had devised the rules for the Gothams eight years earlier. Those rules, he said 50 years later, were only barely changed for the Knickerbockers' use: "After the Gotham club had been in existence a few months it was found necessary to reduce the rules of the new game to writing. This work fell to my hands, and the code I then formulated is substantially that in use to-day." Further, he observed, "The new game quickly became very popular with New Yorkers [c. 1845], and the numbers of the club soon swelled beyond the fastidious notions of some of us, and we decided to withdraw and found a new organization, which we called the Knickerbocker...."[4]

Indeed, Wheaton, who was named vice president of the club — Duncan F. Curry was president and Tucker was both secretary and treasurer — might fairly be regarded as the most important Knickerbocker as well as the most important member of its predecessor organization. Cartwright was not one of the original officers of the club but became treasurer in May 1846. By that time, perhaps owing to a dispute, Wheaton was no longer a Knick and returned to cricket play.

Long before the relocation of New York ballclubs to Hoboken, the optimal sides had been figured at eight, which included a "pitch," a "behind," three infielders, and three men positioned in the outfield. In fact, baseball as played by the Knicks or any other club in New York up to 1849 was almost never a nine-man game. On the rare occasions when nine or more fielding positions might have arisen due to a surfeit of players, the "extras" were put into the outfield, or a second catcher was added, or the surplus men were held in reserve. In an intramural game in May 1847, for example, when 11 men were available to each side, the Knickerbockers' response was to play with nine, including four outfielders, while holding two men out as substitutes.[5]

Daniel L. "Doc" Adams was not an original Knick, but joined about a month after the club formed. By 1847 he had replaced Curry as president and became the club's most important figure, serving as president through 1849 and again in 1856, 1857, and 1861. An excellent player who continued to take to the field until 1859, when he was 44, Adams made many contributions to the game, including the creation of the position of shortstop. The advent of the short fielder, or shortstop, unlike so much else that is claimed for the Knickerbockers, is a genuine innovation. "I used to play shortstop," he reminisced,"and I believe I was the first one to occupy that place, as it had formerly been left uncovered."[6]

Historians previously credited the Knickerbockers as the pioneer club for these reasons: first, they were organized as a ballclub; second, they created a written set of by-laws and rules for play; third, they eliminated the practice of retiring a runner by plugging him with the ball between bases; and fourth, they devised the important feature of foul territory. It appears today, however, that they were neither the first club to organize nor the first to write down their rules, and that the concepts of tagging, forced outs, and boundaries were likewise not original with them. John Ward had it right when he stated in his 1888 book that the Knicks were consolidators rather than innovators:

> They drew up a Constitution and By-laws, and scattered through the latter are to be found the first written rules of the game. They little thought that that beginning would develop into the present vast system of organized base-ball. They were guilty of no crafty changes of any foreign game; there was no incentive for that. They recorded the rules of the game as they remembered them from boyhood and as they found them in vogue at that time.[7]

As to 90 feet, nine men, and nine innings, the accomplishments engraved on Alexander Cartwright's plaque in the Baseball Hall of Fame, it may be said with certainty that neither he nor the Knickerbockers originated any of those central features in 1845. "Carried baseball to Pacific Coast and Hawaii in pioneer days," the plaque goes on to read, but recent scholarship by Monica Nucciarone has debunked that too.[8]

The KBBC played their first recorded game under their new rules on October 6, 1845. In this intrasquad game, seven Knickerbockers won 11–8 over an equal number of their fellows in three innings; clearly, nine men to the side and nine innings were not part of the 1845 rules, and the rulebook requirement that a game be played to 21 aces could be shelved if so desired. Although they commenced formal play in brisk weather, the

Scorecard from the first game played by the Knickerbockers at the Elysian Fields after changing their playing site from Manhattan. The club gathered twice a week and divided into teams for intramural competition. As seen from the scorecard, the number of players was not always nine to a side and the game did not always consist of nine innings or end when a club scored 21 runs.

Knickerbockers managed to squeeze in 14 games before shutting down to await the opening of a new season.

In 1846, the Knickerbockers played for the first time against another club, meeting the New York Club on June 19, 1846, in a match that was until recently believed to be the first interclub match. The Knickerbockers were defeated 23–1, and did not play another club for five years.

The Knickerbockers played relatively few games with other clubs, even when interclub matches became increasingly popular, and were quite particular as to which clubs they would play. They declined challenges from the Eckford and Mutual clubs, up-and-coming organizations with strong playing talent, and in 1857 decided they would play against only those clubs

that occupied the Elysian Fields.[9] In both 1857 and 1860 the club held spirited debates on whether there should be *any* games against other clubs.[10] The Eagles and Gothams were the Knickerbockers' most frequent opponents, and there was little enthusiasm for greatly expanding the field. Brooklyn was the hotbed of baseball in the late 1850s, but it was not until 1858 that the Knicks accepted an invitation to play the Excelsiors, the first Brooklyn nine they faced. The pioneers appeared more interested in shaping the game than in playing it at a high competitive level. Through the 1856 season, the Knicks played 21 games, mostly against the Gothams and Eagles, winning 13, losing 6, and tying 2.[11]

The principal purpose of the Knickerbockers, like that of most early clubs, was to gather regularly for exercise. They typically met about 50 times per year, each Monday and Thursday during the playing season. When the club was organized, the competitive spirit that was to predominate by the late 1850s was not prevalent, and baseball ability was not required in order to become a Knickerbocker. The criteria for admission were a recommendation from an existing member and a ballot of the members that included no more than one negative vote. Once admitted, a member was required to pay a $2 initiation fee and dues of 50 cents per month.

Alexander Cartwright, for years the member best known to the public, was a strapping 6-feet-1 and by all accounts relatively skilled at the new game. It was not until several years after they were formed, however, that the Knickerbockers asked prospective members to appear on a playing day to determine whether they could hit, field, and throw a baseball.[12] Even very good players, however, were accepted only on referral, for it was important that a new member be the right kind of man. Most of the prominent Knickerbockers achieved prominence for their influence in club matters or in the development of the game of baseball rather than for their skill on the playing field. Charles De Bost was a talented catcher, and Harry Wright played with the club early in his career, and both, along with James Whyte Davis, played for the New York nine in at least one of the three games of the Fashion Race Course series. Most of the Knickerbocker players, however, were outclassed when the level of competition increased in the late 1850s.

In 1848 Adams, as Knickerbocker president, headed the Committee to Revise the Constitution and By-Laws. His interest in refining the rules of the game, already evident, was further piqued by the formation of additional clubs, beginning with the Washington Base Ball Club in 1850, which like the Knickerbockers was constructed around several former New York and Gotham Ball Club members (these men had surely continued to play among themselves since 1846). In 1851 the Washingtons took up the old name of Gothams and embraced additional players, while the venerable Eagle Ball Club, which dated to 1840, reconstituted itself as the Eagle *Base* Ball Club. "The playing rules remained very crude up to this time," Adams recalled in later years,

> but in 1853 the three clubs united in a revision of the rules and regulations. At the close of 1856 there were twelve clubs in existence, and it was decided to hold a convention of delegates from all of these for the purpose of establishing a permanent code of rules by which all should be governed. A call was therefore issued, signed by the officers of the Knickerbocker Club as the senior organization, and the result was the assembling of the first convention of baseball players in May 1857. I was elected presiding officer.[13]

At that 1856 KBBC meeting, Doc Adams — along with Louis F. Wadsworth, who had come to the Knickerbockers from the Gothams just as they and the Eagles conformed their rules for the 1854 season — backed a motion to permit nonmembers to take part in Knickerbocker intramural games if fewer than 18 Knicks were present (nine men to the side had become the *de facto* standard for match play by this point, though it still was not mandated by the rules of the game). These two, along with their allies among the Knickerbockers, thought it more important to preserve the quality of the game than to exclude those who were not club members. Duncan F. Curry countermoved that if 14 Knickerbockers were available, the game should admit no outsiders and be played shorthanded, as had been their practice since 1845. The Curry forces, or "Old Fogies," prevailed, 13–11. The Knicks, thus resolved among themselves upon an acceptable standard of seven men to the side, also settled upon a seven-inning game to replace the old custom of playing to 21 runs, which had recently produced a highly unsatisfactory

The scorecard from the first interclub match played by the Knickerbockers. They were soundly defeated by the New York Club 23–1 and did not play another match game for five years. The 1846 game was long celebrated as the first match between two clubs, but further research determined that other games had been played previously.

12–12 tie game, called on account of darkness. Because this matter of seven vs. nine had been one of the most heated and divisive votes in club history, William F. Ladd suggested that a committee be formed to cooperate with other clubs to decide upon the proper number of players for a match, leaving each club to decide for itself what was acceptable for intramural

Above and opposite page: **The Knickerbockers kept meticulous records of their games and meetings, one of the reasons they were recognized for years as baseball's pioneer club. If they didn't always take their baseball seriously, they spared no effort in preserving their activities for posterity.**

thus placing one seven-inning advocate (Curry) alongside a nine-inning advocate (Adams), as the Knicks pointed toward their next meeting, at Smith's Hotel at 462 Broome Street on December 6, 1856. The purpose of this Knickerbocker-only meeting was to issue a call for a convention of all the clubs.

The hotheaded Wadsworth had offered his resignation to the Knicks on July 31, 1856, then had withdrawn it a month later (he had previously rebelled while a member of the committee to revise the player uniform, resigning and unresigning within two days in August 1855).[14] Curry resigned on December 6, 1856, the very day of the meeting at Smith's. The Knicks proceeded to endorse a universal concord with the other clubs on this vexing point of how many innings should constitute a match game and other issues, such as settling the "doubtful point, as to the position of the Pitcher," and debating the merits of the fly out vs. the bound catch. The Knickerbockers also established a three-man commission to enlist the attendance of metropolitan area clubs at a convention for the purpose of standardizing the rules. The three were Wadsworth, Adams, and William Henry Grenelle.

In the Knickerbockers' Report on the Convention of January 31, 1857, Wadsworth was named the club's representative on the "Committee to Draft a Code of Laws on the Game of Base Ball, to be Submitted to the Convention." Prior to the convention of

games. This motion carried unanimously, and Wadsworth moved that the chairman of the gathering, Alexander Drummond, appoint the committee. The committee appointed was Curry and Ladd; Ladd declined, and Adams took his place,

February 25, 1857, which later came to be termed the first National Association meeting, Section 26 of the rules was adopted by the Committee, on the recommendation of the Knickerbockers, making the game "seven innings." In the convention, however, on Wadsworth's motion, the assembled delegates modified the Knickerbockers' recommendation to "nine innings."[15] Clearly, by enlisting the support of other clubs, Wadsworth was bucking the Knickerbocker majority.

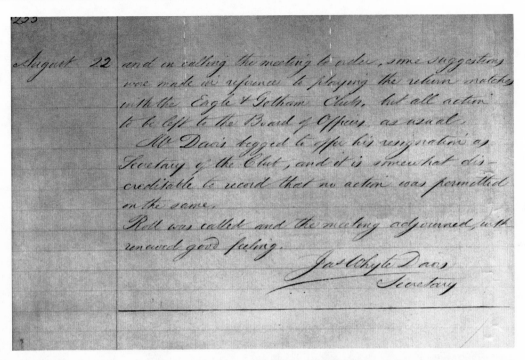

Ten days later, on March 7, the Knicks held their regular club meeting. They voted to adopt the by-laws of the convention but to accept the new playing rules only for matches with other clubs. On March 14 the rules were formally adopted, upon which the dyspeptic Daniel S. Stan(s)bury[16] moved that the Knicks play no more matches with other clubs. His motion was tabled. Last, Wadsworth moved to alter the Knickerbocker rules and by-laws to incorporate all the new changes from the convention. His motion carried, and the Old Fogy or exclusionary clique of the Knicks, as originally headed by Curry, was finished.

In a way, so were the Knickerbockers (although they lingered until 1882), as a club whose stature gave prominence to its views. Many of their proposed revisions were adopted by the convention's rules committee in its meeting of January 22, 1857, but on all three key changes the Knicks tried to enact, they were foiled: number of innings; minimum number of players to constitute a side; and the institution of the manly fly game, which went down to defeat because the newer clubs were concerned that the players might hurt their hands.[17]

One of the reasons the Knickerbockers received so much credit as the pioneer club of baseball was that its members left behind them voluminous documentation of their activity. Both the scorebook and the club books survive to this day, and each contains nearly complete records of the action on the field and in the meeting room, the latter generally being more contentious and divisive than the former. The score of every intraclub match, including the performance of each player, was memorialized, and the resolutions, debates, fines, and expulsions that were such a material component of the early clubs' activities were recorded. Each play date was listed, along with the names of the members who attended.

Fines and discipline were a major part of Knickerbocker life. Four consecutive unexcused absences from play days drew a 50-cent fine and eight warranted expulsion. There were fines for the use of improper language, with the offending words put in the minutes, tempered by appropriate blanks in the interest of decency. Fines sometimes came unexpectedly. At an 1860 meeting Treasurer David Keeler stood up and announced that several members were delinquent with their dues. Two of the nonpayers said they had never been billed, a transgression for which Keeler was immediately fined $2.[18]

The position of treasurer was a taxing one, and the Knicks often had difficulty filling the post. Elected candidates sometimes declined to serve, and a second choice had to be convinced, often reluctantly, to take on the job.

For a group that prided itself on its gentlemanly pedigree, the meeting minutes reveal an unseemly number of petty quarrels, bruised feelings, and long discussions on matters that bore limited relevance to baseball. Members worried that comrades would open their lockers and remove items, that they would leave their lockers in disorderly condition, and that monetary obligations would not be honored. James Whyte Davis was once fined for going into another man's locker to get a ball that was needed to play a game.[19]

Davis, a member for so many years, was involved in a number of incidents. In 1860 he accused Norman Welling of using abusive language at a meeting. When Welling failed to appear at the meeting during which Davis brought a formal charge, Davis insisted that Welling, like himself a prominent member, be expelled. Other members calmed the accuser and persuaded him to agree to let Welling present a defense at a future meeting. At that time, Welling admitted to using offensive language but apologized and said he meant no harm, and the matter was dropped.[20]

Social activity was a very important component of the Knickerbocker routine. With interclub matches relatively rare, the wealthier clubs could afford to entertain the opposition after nearly every match, and the Knickerbockers generally did so in liberal fashion. Victuals, libations, speeches, and the presentation of the ball to the winning club constituted the program, and a failure to provide a pleasant entertainment was considered an inexcusable breach of etiquette.

When Adams withdrew from the Knickerbocker Base Ball Club in the spring of 1862 (he would retire from his New York medical practice not long thereafter and move with his new wife to Connecticut), his associates awarded him an honorary membership and passed a resolution naming him the "Nestor of Ball Players." Davis, who had joined the club in 1850, wrote in a letter to Adams, "I indulge the hope that the 'spirit' you express of being with us always, may be accompanied by the *body* on the old Play Grounds."[21] Adams indeed returned to Hoboken one last time to play his final formal game of baseball on September 27, 1875, in an old-timers' contest (the first such) that was staged in conjunction with Davis's 25th anniversary of Knickerbocker membership.

A few years ago an unusual item came up for auction: a trophy presentation of a silver baseball and miniature bats that had been given to Davis that day.[22] The award presentation had taken place at a banquet following the game, played at Hoboken's Elysian Fields between the Knicks of 1850, including Adams and William H. Tucker, and those of 1860, for whom Davis pitched. The Knickerbocker pennant—with a blue "K" in a white circle surmounting a red horizontal panel and a blue one—was also presented to Davis, who had designed it in 1855. "Worn to ribbons by long service," reported the *New York Sun,* the banner afterwards was draped over Davis's dresser until his death. He was wrapped in it upon his burial in 1899.[23]

Whether one viewed the

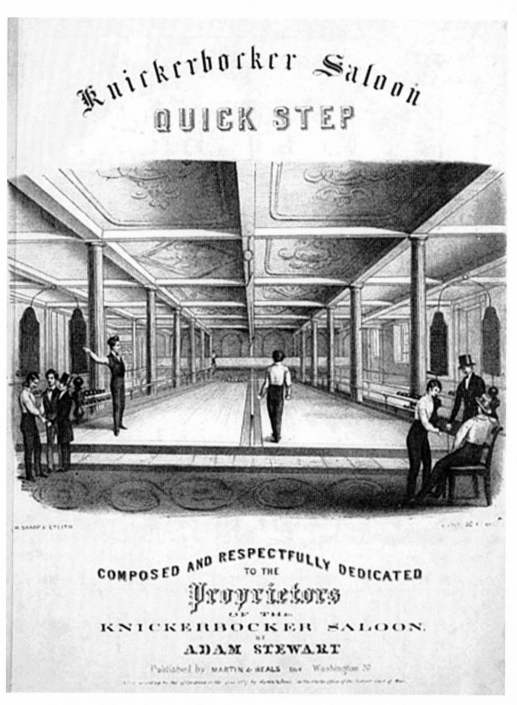

The Knickerbocker name was everywhere in New York. Washington Irving wrote in 1849, "I find, after a lapse of nearly forty years, this haphazard production of my youth ... become a 'household word,' and used to give the home stamp to everything recommended for popular acceptance, such as Knickerbocker societies, Knickerbocker insurance companies, Knickerbocker steamboats, Knickerbocker omnibuses, Knickerbocker bread, and Knickerbocker ice...."

This composite photograph shows some early KBBC members in 1862. Left to right standing: Duncan Curry; Walter T. Avery; Henry T. (Tiebout) Anthony; Charles H. Birney; William H. Tucker. Seated: Charles Schuyler DeBost; Daniel Lucius "Doc" Adams; James W. Davis; Ebenezer R. Dupignac, Jr.; Fraley C. Niebuhr.

Knickerbockers as kindly shepherds or as would-be dictators of the developing game, the locus of change had already begun to shift by the late 1850s from Hoboken, where the early New York clubs played, to Brooklyn, where workingmen created clubs, notably the Eckford and the Atlantic, to rival them. The Excelsior and Putnam clubs of Brooklyn would emulate the Knickerbockers in their fastidiousness, but like them were mere footnotes to professional baseball as it would evolve in the 1870s.

In its later years the Knickerbocker Club was not a part of the baseball mainstream. Professionalism had taken hold, and the institution that played such a major part in the early years of baseball gradually evolved into a social club whose baseball activity was more a pleasant memory than an active pastime. The KBBC played some games each season against other clubs, but when the schedules of the professional teams expanded to 60 or 70 games a season, the Knickerbockers played just a handful, scarcely more than in the mid–1850s. They withdrew from the National Association in 1869, then rejoined the newly configured all-amateur NABBP for 1871, as the professionals formed their own association and league. At their apogee, the Knickerbockers had never played for gate

receipts, as dues and assessments on the members covered their operating expenses, and by 1871 it is doubtful many would have paid to watch them play. The game they nurtured and developed had passed them by. "We pioneers," said Adams in 1896,"never expected the game so universal as it has now become."[24] By that time Adams, Wheaton, Davis, Curry, and their comrades were long removed from the baseball scene and few enthusiasts remembered that they had at one time been connected with the game.

CLUB MEMBERS

"In looking over the early history of baseball," Albert Spalding observed in 1905,"I find the names of eleven New York gentlemen who were the founders of the original Knickerbocker club, names that should be honored and remembered as the founders of the national game by the million baseball players of the present day. They are as follows: Col. James Lee, Dr. Ransom, Abraham Tucker, James Fisher, W. Vail, Alexander J. Cartright [sic], William R. Wheaton, Duncan F. Curry, E.R. Dupignac, Jr., William H. Tucker and Daniel L. Adams [who was actually not an original member; see above]. Are not some of these gentlemen still living? Or possibly some of their heirs might throw some light on the early history and especially the origin of baseball."[25]

By then, all of those men were indeed in their graves and the members of Spalding's commission on baseball's origins do not appear to have tried to contact those Knickerbockers who were alive in 1905. As a result, General Abner Doubleday, deceased since 1893, was anointed as baseball's inventor—a conclusion that would have amazed that distinguished gentleman—and the game's true pioneers slipped into undeserved obscurity. Fortunately, that has begun to change in recent years and the sketches that follow are the result:

Daniel (Doc) Adams, circa 1865. Adams was a physician who was an early New York player credited with developing the position of shortstop. A long-time officer of the Knickerbockers, he played a significant role in the development of the early rules of baseball.

Dr. Daniel Lucius Adams: No member of the 1845 Knickerbockers was more overshadowed than Dr. Daniel Adams. John Thorn began the process of giving Adams his due in "The True Father of Baseball," *Elysian Fields Quarterly*, Winter 1992, vol. 11, no. 1, 85–91, and then in several of the eight editions of the encyclopedia *Total Baseball* (eds. John

Thorn, Pete Palmer, et al., various publishers, 1989–2004). Thorn's detailed profile of Adams is now part of the SABR BioProject: *http://sabr.org/bioproj/person/14ec7492*. For this reason, this sketch will be fairly brief. Daniel L. Adams was born in Mont Vernon, New Hampshire, on November 1, 1814, one of two sons of Dr. Daniel Adams and the former Nancy Mulliken. The elder Dr. Adams, a Dartmouth College graduate, was the author of *The Scholar's Arithmetic, Or, Federal Accountant*, a standard mathematics primer of the era; it was often referred to simply as *Adams' Arithmetic*. The younger Daniel Adams graduated from Yale in 1835 and earned a medical degree from Harvard three years later. He soon settled in New York City and for two decades was a leading figure in the Knickerbocker Club and the emerging baseball scene. Adams married in 1861 and resigned from the Knickerbocker Club in the following year. Three years later, citing poor health, he gave up his medical practice and moved to Connecticut, where he and his wife raised their four children. Baseball remained a part of his life, and he played in a Knickerbockers' reunion game in 1875 and enjoyed backyard games with his two sons.[26] Adams also gave a key interview about the pioneer era, "Dr. D. L. Adams; Memoirs of the Father of Base Ball; He Resides in New Haven and Retains an Interest in the Game," which appeared in *The Sporting News* on February 29, 1896. Daniel Lucius Adams died in New Haven, Connecticut, on January 3, 1899.

David Haight Anthony: Two men with the surname of Anthony played in the Knickerbockers' celebrated June 19, 1846, game against the New York Club. One was Henry T. Anthony, later a club officer. The other is listed as "D. Anthony" by Charles A. Peverelly, so is presumed to be Henry's brother David, a grocer who did not remain involved in the club's activities. David Anthony was born in Manhattan on December 12, 1821, and died in Hackensack, New Jersey. A third brother, Edward Anthony (b. January 31, 1819, New York City; d. December 14, 1888, New York City) was Henry Anthony's business partner and may also have been involved in the Knickerbockers. Yet another brother, Jacob Anthony, Jr., who was born in New York City on October 24, 1816, and died there on May 25, 1872, was also a club member. Harold Peterson believed that the father, Jacob Anthony, Sr., was also a club member, but the basis for this conclusion is not known.[27]

Henry Tiebout Anthony: While his brothers appear to have had only limited involvement with the Knickerbocker Club, Henry T. Anthony served several terms as a club officer during the 1850s. In an 1865 letter Alexander Cartwright mentioned "Harry Anthony" as one of the Knickerbockers whom he remembered fondly.[28] Henry was born in New York City on September 18, 1814, into a distinguished family that had come over from Holland in the 1620s. His father, Jacob Anthony, Sr., held prominent positions at the United States Branch Bank and the Bank of the State of New York. Henry

Anthony studied at Columbia College and graduated in 1832 along with fellow Knickerbocker Walter Avery.[29] Like Avery, he became a civil engineer and worked on several major projects, including the Croton Aqueduct. Meanwhile his brother Edward had been studying the new art of daguerreotyping under Samuel Morse and in 1841 opened his own studio. By 1852 the business's success enabled Henry Anthony to become Edward's partner in the firm, which eventually became known as E. & H.T. Anthony. Henry T. Anthony concentrated his efforts on improvement of the colloidal and paper printing processes. He also edited an annual bulletin that reported on new inventions within the field. The company remained at the center of the American photographic scene for decades and the Anthony brothers enjoyed a close relationship with Mathew Brady. "Anthony's Instantaneous Stereoscope Views," in particular, caused a sensation when introduced in 1859 by demonstrating that photographs did not have to be staged. Henry T. Anthony died in New York City on October 11, 1884.[30]

Walter Titus Avery: Walter T. Avery played in the Knickerbockers' historic 1846 game and, after some years spent in California, was reelected to membership in 1857, serving four terms as vice president. Born in New York City on January 18, 1814, the only child of John Smith Avery and the former Amelia Titus, Avery was a classmate of Henry T. Anthony in Columbia's Class of 1832. He and Anthony both became civil engineers and took part in the construction of the Croton Aqueduct. Like several other club members, Avery was moved by the California Gold Rush to head west in 1849.[31] He arrived in San Francisco on June 6, 1850, after a voyage of 114 days.[32] Biographical sketches indicated that he remained in California for about seven years, which corresponds perfectly with his absence from the Knickerbocker Club's roles. Curiously, however, he is listed on the 1850 census as living with his parents in New York City. His name also appears on the 1852 California census, so if he did indeed return to New York in 1850 his stay there was very brief. It seems more likely that his parents assumed that the takers of the 1850 census would not locate him in California, so chose to report him as a member of their household. In any event, while in California Avery was part owner of Avery and Hewlett, a Stockton wholesale firm specializing in groceries, dry goods, and produce. He returned to New York around 1855, perhaps motivated by the failing health of his aged father, who died in the spring of 1857. Upon his return, he rejoined the Knickerbockers and became a successful Front Street commission merchant in the firm of Avery & Lockwood, Importers. A lifelong bachelor, Avery retired in the early 1880s to East Moriches, on Long Island, where he became known as an "enthusiastic lover of aquatic sports [who] kept a sloop yacht and an East Bay catboat, and was a member of the Moriches Yacht Club." In addition, he indulged a passion for history, tracing his family back for several centuries. An obituary also noted that Avery "was the last one of the original members of the Knickerbocker Baseball Club."[33]

Avery had recently celebrated his 90th birthday when he died in East Moriches on June 10, 1904.[34]

Louis J. Belloni, Jr.: Born in New York City on December 9, 1827, Belloni was the son and namesake of an immigrant from Genoa, Italy.[35] His mother, a New York native named Ann Sang, died when he was very young.[36] Her name suggests the possibility of an exotic ethnic background, but unfortunately nothing is known about her. The elder Louis Belloni soon remarried, to Mary G. Morris, a great-granddaughter of Lewis Morris, one of the signers of the Declaration of Independence.[37] Louis Belloni, Jr., was the Knickerbockers' treasurer in 1859 and, like so many club members, he was active in the volunteer fire department (Engine Company 52). He was also involved in numerous other civic activities, including the Lafayette Fusileers. He married Kate Havemeyer, the daughter of Frederick C. Havemeyer, who had made a fortune in the sugar industry. (Frederick Havemeyer was the cousin and business partner of William F. Havemeyer, who served three separate terms as mayor of New York.) Belloni became the senior member of Belloni & Co., a firm that had extensive shipping and coal interests in Pennsylvania and Nova Scotia. He also was active in numerous trade organizations, serving as president of the Harlem Building and Mutual Loan Association, as treasurer of the Firemen's Benevolent Fund and as chairman of the Commission of Estimate and Assessment. Like many of the city's businessmen, he experienced financial troubles during the turbulent 1870s.[38] But he appears to have recovered and been a very wealthy man by the time of his death in New York City on December 20, 1898.[39]

William P. Bensel: William P. Bensel served as president of the Knickerbockers from 1862 through 1864 and appeared in several games for the club in 1865. A cooper by profession, Bensel received two patents for inventions to be used for chiming and jointing staves. Bensel also found time to enlist in the 7th Regiment of the National Guard of the State of New York in 1856. His service continued during the Civil War and he earned promotion to captain. In later life, Bensel was also a member of the Produce Exchange, but in 1878 a reversal of fortunes forced him into bankruptcy. He died on March 8, 1883, at the age of 64.[40]

Edward Apthorpe Bibby: Edward A. Bibby was a club member in 1848, but did not remain active after that. Born in New York City around 1821, Bibby was the grandson of Thomas Bibby, a British army officer during the Revolutionary War who was captured at the Battle of Saratoga. After being exchanged, Thomas Bibby became assistant adjutant-general of the English troops in New York and married into the Gouverneur family, relatives of President James Monroe. Edward A. Bibby began his career as a government customs officer and his popularity among New York merchants enabled him to become a broker in the Broad Street firm of Grenelle, Talman, Bibby & Co. Both of his partners, William Grenelle and William Talman, were also members of the Knickerbocker

Club. Edward Bibby died on June 30, 1879, and his death led a longtime friend to offer this eulogy: "In his youth and middle age Mr. Bibby was a model of masculine beauty and distinguished for grace of bearing and a finished courtesy of manner of the old school.... It has been recently said that in the death of [Evert A.] Duyckinck the last of the Knickerbockers passed away. So with Mr. Bibby passes away the last of that cheerful race of Old New York which once made her name famous for generous warm-hearted hospitality. A more liberal, warm-hearted man never breathed than this courteous gentleman."[41]

E.H. Birdsall: This man, a club director in 1854, can only be Edward H. Birdsall, whose father, Samuel, represented New York's 25th District in the U.S. House of Representatives from 1837 to 1839. Edward H. Birdsall was born in Waterloo, New York, around 1827 and moved to New York City in the early 1850s along with his young wife to accept a position in the Coin Department of the U.S. Sub-Treasury. Samuel Birdsall had studied law in the office of President Martin Van Buren and no doubt that connection helped his son obtain this post. He kept it, however, because "his services were recognized as almost invaluable, and his wonderful power of detecting spurious and light-weight coin, together with his faithful and exceptional accuracy in the discharge of the duties of his most responsible trust, as the head of the coin department of the office, gave him a wide reputation. In consequence he retained his position among all the changes of parties for nearly thirty years."[42] It was said that Birdsall "could, in emptying a $5000 bag, at the first dip of his hands into the glittering mass, pick out all the spurious coins."[43] Birdsall also raised his son after being widowed in 1870. Eventually he left the civil service and opened a successful brokerage. Edward Birdsall died in Manhattan on April 11, 1882, and is buried at Green-Wood Cemetery.[44]

Charles H. Birney: Charles Birney played for the Knickerbockers in their historic 1846 game against the New York Club and was chosen as club treasurer one year later. Henry Chadwick referred to him as "Barney" but identified him as the secretary of the East River Insurance Company, so there can be no doubt about his identity. Charles H. Birney was born in Ireland around 1811 and worked his way up the ranks of the East River Insurance Company, finally being elected president in 1857.[45] Birney also served as an officer of the New York Board of Fire Insurance Companies from 1858 to 1866. During the Civil War, he was the treasurer of the Friendly Sons of St. Patrick, a benevolent society for impoverished Irish immigrants; he was also involved in several other Irish-American societies. By 1860 he and his family were living in Mamaroneck, New York, in Westchester County, and after retiring from business in the 1870s he served several terms as the town's supervisor, including winning reelection in 1874 without opposition. In 1877, however, Birney was defeated and an audit of his records determined that he was a "defaulter to the town." Birney forfeited his home and his friends paid

the balance of $6,000.[46] The Birneys returned to New York City and finally settled in Montclair, New Jersey, where Charles H. Birney died on February 12, 1892.

Bogert/Bogart: Several people with this surname were connected to the Knickerbockers: Charles De Bost was the son of the former Ann S. Bogart, William H. Westervelt was the son of the former Rachel Bogert or Bogart, and a man named Horatio Bogert graduated from Columbia in 1832 along with Henry Anthony and Walter Avery.[47] Given all these connections, it is not surprising that the name Bogert or Bogart appears in the box score of one of the Knickerbockers' 1845 practice games. Unfortunately, this man's first name is unknown and is likely lost to history.

John A. Boyle: John Boyle, a club member in 1854, was a custom house clerk who was born around 1826. In 1863 Boyle was found dead of a fractured skull at the basement door of his home at 138 West 17th Street. The coroner did not believe that his injuries could have been sustained by an accidental fall, yet his watch and pocketbook were undisturbed, which seemed to rule out robbery. The result was a mystery that does not appear to have been solved.[48]

Brodhead: A player listed as "Brodhead" took part in the first practice game recorded in the Knickerbockers' scorebook in the fall of 1845. Harold Peterson identified this man as "George Broadhead, a Wall Street broker."[49] While the basis of this identification is unknown, it certainly seems plausible that the man in question was George Hamilton Brodhead, a broker who later became president of the New York Stock Exchange. Brodhead was the grandson of Captain Luke Brodhead, who served on Lafayette's staff during the American Revolution, and the son of the Rev. John Brodhead, who was credited with introducing Methodism to New Hampshire. Born Epaphras Kibby Brodhead in Newfield, New Hampshire, on January 1, 1814, Brodhead can hardly be blamed for having his name changed. He studied at Phillips Exeter Academy and Harvard, but left school after losing an eye while playing shinny with his friend Benjamin F. Butler (later a Civil War general, congressman, and the governor of Massachusetts). No doubt this injury also accounted for his limited involvement with the Knickerbockers. Brodhead then worked for a bank in Pontiac, Michigan, before arriving in New York City around 1841 and joining the Stock Exchange.[50] In the early 1850s Brodhead became secretary of the New York Stock Exchange and retained that position for many years. His ascension to the presidency, however, came under unusual circumstances. As explained in 1874, when he was elected as president of the stock exchange, "for over 20 years [Brodhead] occupied the position of Secretary, to which he was elected unanimously year after year, notwithstanding he frequently requested the Board to accept his resignation. Finally, some years since he was forced to retire by failing health and it was only with the greatest reluctance that the members consented to his retirement."[51] Brodhead was a popular president until finally retiring for good at the end of the decade. One of his sisters, Mary R. Pike, was born on September 11, 1815, and was reported to be the oldest person in New Hampshire when she died in 1922 at the age of 106 years, 8 months and 4 days.[52] Her brother didn't live that long, but he was 89 when he died at his New York City home on March 1, 1903.[53] One of his daughters married Joseph Smith Harris, the president of the Reading Railroad.

Brodie: An 1887 reminiscence by an unnamed Knickerbocker mentioned that one of the members was Brodie, who was identified as a cloak maker on Canal Street.[54] This can only mean George Brodie, identified in city directories as the proprietor of a "cloaks and mantillas" establishment, first at 51 Canal and later at 300 Canal. Brodie was born in Scotland around 1818 and married the Irish-born Sarah Campbell in New York City in 1845. Brodie died in 1866 and is buried at Green-Wood Cemetery. The extent of his involvement with the Knickerbockers is not known, so it's possible that the 1887 informant confused him with George Brodhead, but given the specificity of details that seems unlikely.

Benjamin K. Brotherson: Benjamin K. Brotherson had been a member of the Knickerbockers for at least eight years when he was elected club secretary in 1856. Born in Charlton, Schenectady County, New York, on March 8, 1819, Brotherson was the son of Philip Brotherson (1780–1854) and the former Catherine Kissam (1781–1822), who was the aunt of fellow club member Samuel Kissam. According to the *Albany Knickerbocker*, Brotherson began his career in 1836 as a clerk in the Albany dry-goods store of James Winne.[55] Two years later he moved to New York City to take a position with the Union Bank. His Kissam family connections were probably responsible for this good fortune, as several members of that family worked at the bank. Still a "mere child" when he was hired, Brotherson gradually "worked himself up from the lowest station in the bank to the position of head bookkeeper," in the meantime gaining the complete trust of his superiors. By 1858 there was mounting evidence of a massive embezzlement at the bank and the evidence pointed to Brotherson's involvement. The bank's president and cashier refused to believe the allegations, even after a detective followed Brotherson "every afternoon from Wall street to various gambling saloons in the lower part of the city, witnessed his extravagant play at faro, noted down each and every amount lost and won, and then presented his case once more," explaining "that a man with a salary of scarce $2,000 per year could not conveniently spend two or three hundred dollars a night at the gaming table."[56] That changed when Brotherson left work early claiming a toothache and fled New York, reportedly bound for either California or South America. It soon became clear that Brotherson and one of the bank's clients, a stockbroker named Jacob Mott, had perpetrated an embezzlement scheme that netted them $145,000. The magnitude of the fraud made it front-page news all across the state and journalists scrambled to come up with the most lurid stories. A *New York Times* reporter vis-

ited a gambling den at 214 Broadway and described it as "one of the most notorious 'day-game' establishments in the City, and one of the places which Brotherson ... used to frequent after 'banking hours,' and 'buck' with the proceeds of his day's embezzlement."[57] Back in Albany, the *Knickerbocker* informed its readers that Brotherson was a former resident but blamed his downfall on his move to the big city: "During his residence in Albany he was looked upon as a model young man, being steady, industrious and of unquestioned morals. His residence in New York, it appears, has undermined his virtue. He has indulged in splurge, late hours, woodcock, gambling, & c. These have produced the usual results — felony and disgrace to be soon followed by suicide or imprisonment. When Mr. Brotherson left Albany there was no man who placed a higher value on personal honor. In his fall, the young man may see the danger of 'the first false move.' It is the first crime which leads to all the rest. Our virtues are like so many bricks standing on their ends — overturn one and down go the whole."[58] Brotherson had married a young woman named Anna Robinson in 1855 and one reporter claimed that she had admitted that "many years ago, previous to her marriage, [Brotherson] told her that there was a defalcation in the Union Bank of $100,000, and asked her if she would marry him knowing this fact! She consented, and has faithfully kept his secret, but she says that it has worried him night and day, and that he has repeatedly resolved to make a confession to the President, but could not raise sufficient courage. She says that B. asked for his pistol when he left, but seeing his excitement she refused to let him have it, and he went away without it, telling her that she would not see him again for many years."[59] The search for the embezzler continued to make headlines for the next week, with the public being counseled to be on the alert for man about 5-feet-8 with a "slight form," "sandy hair and whiskers," and "a peculiar habit of carrying his arm extended from his body."[60] Then Brotherson's name vanished from newspaper coverage, while Mott was prosecuted in 1861 but acquitted.[61] So what had happened to Brotherson? His name appears in the New York census in both 1860 and 1870 and in at least one city directory, so the most likely supposition is that bank officials made it clear that they did not want to prosecute Brotherson and he faded out of the limelight. But it was not unheard of for the wife of a disgraced man to report him as still living with her rather than admit to his guilt, so it's conceivable that he did indeed flee and never returned to New York. In any event, Brotherson died in obscurity in Santa Barbara, California, on October 28, 1878.[62]

George A. Brown: George A. Brown served several terms as a club director or officer in the early 1850s. He was later described as a custom-house entry clerk, so it seems very likely that he was a man by that name who remained in New York City and became a successful stockbroker. The man in question was born around 1827, raised a large family, and died on September 4, 1897. A man with the same surname played first base for the Knickerbockers in 1868, but it seems logical to assume that this was a different man.

Bunker: A man by this surname was involved with the Knickerbockers, but contemporaneous sources do not include a first name. Harold Peterson reported that his first name was William and there was indeed a William J. Bunker who was the proprietor of the Mansion House hotel at 39 Broadway during the 1830s and 1840s. Given the location, it would be logical for him to have been involved in the club.

H.L. Butler: A Knickerbocker identified only as "H.L. Butler" is probably Henry L. Butler, a prominent Manhattan dry-goods merchant. Butler was born in Baltimore on December 9, 1822, and entered the dry-goods business after arriving in New York in 1847. He soon founded the firm of Butler, Broome, and Clapp and remained in the business until retiring around 1890. He died in New Brighton, Staten Island, on December 21, 1895, and is buried at Green-Wood Cemetery.[63] The waistcoat worn by Butler at his 1848 wedding was later donated to the Staten Island Historical Society and may be viewed online at *http://statenisland.pastperfect-online.com/ 00039cgi/mweb.exe?request=record;id=95DA1E7A-60B5-44F7-91CA-218369322477;type=101.*

Andrew J. Carl: Andrew J. Carl's involvement with the Knickerbocker Club appears to have been limited. He is thought to be a Manhattan clerk by that name who was born in New Jersey around 1827 and later returned there, working as a jeweler and bartender. After spending much of his life in Millburn, this man died in Newark on April 7, 1896, within hours of the death of his wife. The couple had been ill for only two days.[64]

Alexander Joy Cartwright, Jr.: Alexander Cartwright was inducted into the Baseball Hall of Fame in 1938 for his contributions to the Knickerbocker Club and to baseball. He was undoubtedly an important figure during the club's early years but recent historians have established that he received more credit than was due to him. In particular, Cartwright headed west during the 1849 Gold Rush and never returned to New York, yet his Hall of Fame plaque credits him with several innovations that occurred after his departure. The result is a complex legacy that was recently explored in a well-researched biography: Monica Nucciarone's *Alexander Cartwright: The Life Behind the Baseball Legend* (Lincoln: University of Nebraska Press, 2009). Nucciarone's book makes a detailed retelling of Cartwright's life unnecessary, but here is a brief summary. Cartwright was born in New York City on April 17, 1820, the son of Captain Alexander Cartwright, a veteran of the War of 1812, and the former Esther Burlock. As a young man he worked as a clerk in the office of a Wall Street stockbroker, as a clerk and bank teller at the Union Bank, and as co-owner of a Wall Street bookstore. Like so many of the Knickerbockers, he was also active in the volunteer fire department. Cartwright married Eliza Van Wie in 1842 and by the end of the decade they were the parents of three children. In

1849 he headed west and ended up in Hawai'i, where he became a successful shipping agent and commission merchant. Eliza joined him two years later and they had two more children in Hawai'i. Alexander Cartwright died in Honolulu on September 9, 1892.

Alfred DeForest Cartwright: Alexander Cartwright's brother Alfred umpired one of the Knickerbockers' 1846 games, but does not otherwise seem to have been involved in the club's activities.[65] Born in New York City in 1822, Alfred Cartwright headed to San Francisco in January 1849 and it took him over half of the year to get there.[66] He soon followed his brother to Hawai'i and operated a number of businesses there. In the late 1860s, he relocated to Oakland, California, where he died on February 6, 1891.[67]

George D. Cassio: George D. Cassio was the brother-in-law of Alexander Cartwright, having married Cartwright's sister Catherine on October 25, 1838. He made his debut with the Knickerbockers on November 15, 1845. Cassio was born around 1813 and as a young man he taught bookkeeping in New York University's Commercial Department and at Goldsmith's Writing and Bookkeeping Academy, located at 189 Broadway. According to an advertisement for the latter institution, "The system of instruction pursued by Mr. Cassio ... is not derived from any PRINTED WORK, but is the result of a thorough practical knowledge of the subject. The exercises being so arranged as to render familiar to the student every department of mercantile business, *which certainly cannot be acquired by balancing one sett* [sic] *of books.*"[68] Cassio later became a Broadway wine and liquor dealer. He took his own life in 1869.[69]

John Clancy: Service as a volunteer New York fireman during the turbulent 1840s and '50s, historian Sean Wilentz explained, became "an apprenticeship for a career in the party clubhouse."[70] Nobody exemplified that better than John Clancy, who was listed as a member of the Knickerbockers in 1854. Born to Irish immigrants in New York City's Sixth Ward on March 4, 1828, Clancy "was emphatically a self-made man and rose by the force of his own energy of character and some considerable natural ability from a very humble position to be one of the most influential Democrats in this State."[71] No doubt these traits were the important factor in his ascendance, but Clancy also was greatly aided by the fraternal bonds he made along the way. As a young man, Clancy worked as a clerk in the law office of Peter Sweeney and also "occupied himself with commercial pursuits of various descriptions."[72] In addition, he served as foreman of two volunteer hose companies and was a member of the Knickerbocker Club. His most important ties were probably made at the Ivy Green, a watering hole on the corner of Elm Street near Franklin that was the headquarters of the Empire Club, then "the strongest and most popular Democratic organization in the state."[73] Clancy was said to have "presided over" the Ivy Green and the mixed reputation of its clientele — which ranged from prostitutes to

Democratic Party bigwigs like Mike Walsh, Matt Brennan, General Dan Sickles, and Joe Dowling — probably accounting for the tactful wording of the later comment that Clancy operated "commercial pursuits of various descriptions."[74] John Clancy's own political career began in 1854 when he was elected a councilman. The Know-Nothings were in such firm control of the Board of Councilmen during Clancy's two-year tenure that in 1855 he did not serve on a single committee. More importantly, however, he established a reputation as "an active partisan" Democrat and a trusted ally of Mayor Fernando Wood. With Wood's assistance, Clancy was elected an alderman from the "Bloody Sixth Ward" in 1856 and served in that position for three eventful years.[75] During his first year in office, the Democrats were in the minority but Clancy was nonetheless elected its president.[76] He soon "became the head of a compact clique, who were strong enough to have their own way in most things, backed, as they were, by the two-thirds power of the Mayor's veto."[77] Clancy also served as ex officio mayor when the elected mayor was absent from the city.[78] According to his political opponents, the result was a series of wasteful expenditures designed to enrich Wood's friends in the political machine that became known as Tammany Hall. During the passage of all of these controversial measures, Clancy was said to have been the mayor's "obsequious friend." The *New York Tribune* charged that Clancy also took advantage of his office to make himself a rich man. When the *New York Leader* received a lucrative printing contract from the city, the *Tribune* alleged that Clancy "is the editor and, we believe, chief proprietor of a newspaper, and as soon as his party got into power, a resolution was passed, for which he voted himself, making that a Corporation paper at its own charges, although the Charter makes it a misdemeanor for any Alderman to be thus interested in work done at the city's cost."[79] Clancy maintained that he had "*no interest, direct or remote, in the publication of any newspaper, and never had any,*" but the *Tribune* wasn't satisfied with this explanation, pointing out that the masthead of the *Leader* listed Clancy as one of its editors.[80] Mayor Wood was defeated for reelection in 1857 but Clancy remained a major force in city politics over the next two years. At the end of his term as an alderman, Clancy secured the well-paying position of county clerk. This post and his stake in the *Leader* enabled him to report a wealth of $25,000 when the 1860 census was taken. In 1862 Clancy stepped down as county clerk and began to devote all of his time to the newspaper. Many of Clancy's old cronies became involved with the newspaper, with Jack Leveridge as "fire editor" and former Empire Club secretary George Wooldridge using the pen name of Tom Quick to write a column on "The Old Sports of New York."[81] Though now out of politics, he remained an influential figure within the party and it seemed safe to assume that sooner or later he would return to public life. Instead John Clancy suffered a severe case of sunstroke during a visit to the countryside in the summer of 1864. He was rushed back to his home but died there on July 1, 1864. Clancy, who had never married, was reported to have been "in pleasant circumstances politically and financially" when he met his untimely death.[82]

Clare: A man listed as either Clare or Clair took part in two of the Knickerbockers' 1845 games, but no first name was provided. Harold Peterson listed this man as a Wall Street broker named Joseph Clare, probably on the basis that his occupation would have made him a good fit for the club.[83] The problem with this is that Joseph Clare was 69 when he died on October 23, 1859, meaning that he would have been in his mid–50s when the 1845 contests were played. So was Joseph Clare unusually hardy and adventurous or was the Knickerbocker player somebody else? That's a mystery that may never be solved.

Beverly Clarke: Someone by the name of Clarke manned third base for the Knickerbockers in both 1858 and 1868, though the two are not necessarily one and the same. A man named Beverly Clarke was club secretary in 1858, so it seems likely that he was the 1858 player and at least possible that he was also the 1868 player. Beverly Clarke is a very unusual name, so it seems likely that the Knickerbocker was a Civil War veteran by that name. Born in New York around 1830, Beverly Clarke was a postal clerk who served in the 71st Regiment of the New York State Militia. After the war, Clarke became the "Blank agent of the Post Office Department of the Second District, comprising the New England and middle States." In 1868 he was arrested and charged with being part of a conspiracy to defraud the Post Office.[84] The arrest received considerable press attention, but nothing is known about Clarke's doings thereafter.

Herman Cohen: Herman Cohen's only known Knickerbocker activity was his 1867 resignation from the club. There are at least two men by that name of appropriate age and we can only guess as to which one was a Knickerbocker.

E.W. Cone: A man by this name played in one of the Knickerbockers' 1845 intrasquad games. Harold Peterson identified him as a Wall Street lawyer named Edward W. Cone, which certainly makes sense. Cone was born in Baltimore on March 4, 1814, the son of a prominent Baptist minister, graduated in the first class of the City University of New York in 1833, and died in New York City on January 23, 1871.

Richard S. Conover: The player named Conover who appeared in one of the Knickerbockers' 1857 games is believed to be Richard Stevens Conover, the nephew of Elysian Fields proprietor John Cox Stevens. Stevens died in 1857 and bequeathed a house and lot to the recently married Conover, which would explain why his name disappears from the club's rolls. Conover was born on April 25, 1832, in Hoboken and became a wealthy farmer in Middlesex County; by 1870, the value of his real estate holdings was estimated at $100,000. Conover died in Princeton, New Jersey, on April 3, 1912.

Duncan Fraser Curry: Born in Brooklyn on November

28, 1812, Duncan F. Curry became the first president of the Knickerbockers in 1845 and was again selected to fill that position in the following year. Though older than most of the

New York April 4, 1862

D. L. Adams Esq.

Dr Sir

I beg to acknowledge receipt of your note of 26 ult tendering your resignation as a member of the old Knickerbocker B B Club, and that it was reluctantly accepted with great regret and you was unanimously elected an Honorary Member.

Permit me to add my personal regret of the necessity that induced such a course and tendering you my best wishes for your health and prosperity, & indulge the hope that the 'spirit' you express of being with us always, may be accompanied by the body on the old Play Grounds

Yours very truly

Jas Whyte Davis

Secretary.

Playing commences on the 21st.

Correspondence from James Whyte Davis to Daniel Adams. Davis joined the Knickerbockers in 1850 and was one of the club's most enthusiastic members. He served as an officer of the club and was buried wrapped in the Knickerbocker flag.

playing members of the club, he continued to be active in its activities for several years, taking part in a married/single game in 1854. Perhaps most significantly, he served on committees to codify the game's rules in both 1848 and 1853. After the mid–1850s, Curry's involvement with the Knickerbockers di-

minished significantly and may have ended entirely. No doubt the reason was that the man who had played on the bachelor side in the 1854 game had finally gotten married and started a family. Curry was an insurance man by profession, working as secretary of the City Fire Insurance Company from 1843 to 1852 and then filling the same office for the Republic Fire Insurance Company for another 25 years before retiring. After his retirement, he had several conversations about the origins of the Knickerbocker Club with sportswriter William Rankin. Unfortunately, Rankin's later accounts of those conversations paint a contradictory picture, suggesting that the memory of one of those men was faulty.[85] Duncan Curry died in Brooklyn on April 18, 1894, and is buried at Green-Wood Cemetery.[86] His tombstone proclaims him the "Father of Baseball."

James Whyte Davis: Left fielder James Whyte Davis was (along with Samuel Kissam) one of only two players to be regular players for the Knickerbockers both before and after the Civil War. Described by one reporter as the "life of the Knickerbocker nine," Davis was also quite a character.[87] "He was a somewhat excitable man," recalled one of Davis's fellow club members, "and found much pleasure in calling for judgment."[88] "He ought to go down to history as the first base ball fiend," Daniel Adams confirmed. "Indeed, we used to call him a fiend in the old days because of his enthusiasm."[89] Davis's desire to be buried in the Knickerbocker Club's flag was a particular source of bemusement. One reporter explained that Davis "was an enthusiast on the subject of base ball. He had been a member of the Knickerbocker Base Ball Club for 25 years. Hanging over the bed was the old original worn and tattered flag of the club, which he said was to be used as his shroud when he died. In a glass case, that looked like a handsome aquarium, were stowed away a piece of an old style base-ball shirt, a blue sash, with 'Poor Old Davis' embroidered on it, a silver ball, and crossed bats, presented to him last September by the other members of the Knickerbocker Club, and a blue base-ball belt. Two immense straw hats hung on the wall by the altered flag which was to be buried with him. 'I have been married twice,' said Mr. Davis, 'but the happiest day of my life was when I got that ball and sash.'"[90] James

Whyte Davis was born in New York on March 2, 1826, the son of Connecticut natives John and Harriet Davis. Like so many of the Knickerbockers, he was a volunteer firefighter, in his case with No. 36 Hose Company (Oceana). To earn a living, he worked as a broker successively of fruit, produce, general merchandise, and, finally, stock certificates, earning along the way "the distinction of being the champion dancer of the Stock Exchange."[91] It was on September 16, 1850, however, that he found the great passion of his life when he joined the Knickerbocker Club. In the ensuing years, "his humorous antics on the diamond always caused much amusement."[92] He also served as club secretary three times, as treasurer twice and as president three times. On August 27, 1855, the club unveiled its first pennant—a triangular pennant with a blue "K" in a white circle surmounting horizontal panels of red and blue. Naturally it was Davis who had designed it. Other members meant more to the Knickerbocker Club than James Whyte Davis, but to none did the club mean more. That was brought home with especial force by his celebrations of the anniversaries of his Knickerbocker membership. In 1875, though the club had long since ceased to field a competitive nine, there was a large turnout of familiar names to commemorate his 25th anniversary as a Knickerbocker. To the applause of the assemblage, his daughter presented him with a belt of blue ribbon embroidered with the name of the club. Hanging from the belt were two blue silk ribbons, one of which was inscribed with the words, "To Poor Old Davis" while the other read, "For his 25th ball birthday."[93] Five years later another impressive crowd was on hand to mark Davis's 30th anniversary as a member of his beloved club.[94] The Knickerbocker Club formally disbanded in 1882 and Davis's last years do not appear to have been happy ones. Both of the marriages Davis alluded to appear to have been to the same woman, the former Maria Harwood, and while the couple had three children, their marriage seems to have remained turbulent until Maria's early death. In 1893 Davis wrote to Edward B. Talcott, one of the owners of the New York Giants, requesting help in raising money for a fitting burial. Davis reiterated his longstanding desire to be "buried in my baseball suit, and wrapped in the original flag of the old Knickerbockers" and requested this inscription on his tombstone: "Wrapped in the Original Flag/Of the Knickerbocker Base Ball Club of N.Y.,/Here lies the body of James Whyte Davis,/A member for thirty years./He was not 'Too Late,'/Reaching the 'Home Plate.'/Born March 2, 1826./Died _____."[95] Sadly, the request fell on deaf ears and when he died in New York City on February 15, 1899, James Whyte Davis was buried in an unmarked grave at Green-Wood Cemetery.[96]

Charles Schuyler De Bost: Born on August 4, 1826, Charles Schuyler De Bost was the son of Charles De Bost and the former Ann Schuyler Bogart. Orphaned at a young age, Charles and his siblings were raised by their maternal grandparents in Southampton, Long Island. A cloakmaker by pro-

fession, De Bost was only 19 when he played his first game for the Knickerbockers on October 31, 1845. He resigned his membership in 1847 but rejoined the club on June 14, 1850, and later served as a club director. His work as the catcher of the first nine impressed one onlooker so much that he declared, "Debost, as behind man, has no equal."[97] Another reporter, however, expressed reservations about his demeanor on the playing field. After an 1859 contest, he remarked, "We think that the Knickerbockers were defeated, through the foolishness, fancy airs and smart capers of De Bost. Like a clown in a circus, he evidently plays for the applause of the audience at his 'monkey shines,' instead of trying to win the game. This is reprehensible, especially when playing against a Brooklyn club, where the reputation of the New Yorkers as players is at stake. But so long as the spectators applaud his tom-foolery, just so long will he exert the part of a clown."[98] Nevertheless, De Bost's playing ability was held in high regard within the ballplaying fraternity and he was one of only three New York players to take part in all three of the 1858 Fashion Race Course games. He last played for the club's first nine in 1859, but was an enthusiastic participant in the 1875 celebrations of James Whyte Davis's 25th anniversary as a club member.[99] De Bost was 68 when he died in Mohegan, Westchester County, New York. He is buried in Brooklyn's Green-Wood Cemetery. De Bost's son, also named Charles, inherited two baseballs from the Fashion Race Course Games of 1858 (the two games won by New York) and in 1909 he claimed these to be perhaps the oldest baseballs in existence.[100]

George W. Devoe: George W. Devoe appeared on the 1854 list of club members and played for the married side in a married/single intrasquad game that year. Otherwise his involvement with the club seems to have been limited, which no doubt was the result of his many responsibilities and 1853 marriage. Born in New York City around 1824, George Devoe was a member of the family that formed the first paint brand in America, Devoe Paint, in the mid–18th century. He and his brother Frederick took over the business and expanded it considerably, establishing an office at 117 Fulton Street. George Devoe obtained numerous patents for labor-saving devices by which a specified amount of paint could be transferred from tanks to cans. In 1868 he merged his business with a large paint wholesaler and formed the Devoe & Pratt Manufacturing Company. George Devoe subsequently moved to New Brunswick, New Jersey, where he founded and served as president of the People's National Bank. He died there on November 28, 1890.[101]

DeWitt: A man by this name played on the same side as Alexander Cartwright in the club's first recorded game, on October 6, 1845, and also played for the club in the spring of 1846. Harold Peterson identified this player as Peter DeWitt, Jr., a 25-year-old lawyer and friend of Cartwright. Yet no first name or initial was recorded in the club's annals, so it is just as likely that "DeWitt" was either Peter's older brother, Alfred (born 1818), or younger brother Theodore (born 1821). (A fourth brother, Henry, was born in 1828, so is too young to be a plausible candidate.) Cartwright's first child was born at the home of Peter DeWitt, Sr., in 1843 and was named DeWitt Robinson Cartwright in tribute to the close connection between the two families. Intriguingly, Alfred DeWitt subsequently moved to San Francisco and his success as a dry goods merchant may have had something to do with Cartwright's decision to head west. In the end, however, we can only speculate as to which of the DeWitts took part in these games.[102]

E. Dick: E. Dick, a peripheral club member, is presumably Thomas W. Dick, Jr.'s, brother Enoch. Born on November 24, 1827, Enoch Dick grew up in White Plains and began working at the Bowery Bank while still a teenager. When that bank failed, he was hired by the Chatham National Bank where he earned a series of promotions and became the receiving and paying teller. Enoch Dick enlisted in the Union Army in June 1863 but was discharged five weeks later. He was at work at the bank when he dropped dead on August 14, 1886.[103]

Thomas W. Dick, Jr.: Thomas W. Dick, Jr., was a club member in 1854 and is believed to be the man by that name who served in the Eighth Company of the Seventh Regiment during the Civil War. Knickerbocker member William B. Eager, Jr., was the surgeon of that Company, and numerous other Knickerbockers served in other companies of the Seventh Regiment. The son and namesake of a Scottish immigrant, Thomas W. Dick, Jr., was born around 1826 and grew up in White Plains. In the late 1840s, Dick and partner James D. Merritt opened a coal business in Manhattan but it seems to have closed after Merritt's 1858 death. Dick then joined the Union Army, serving both in the Seventh Regiment and in the New York Heavy Artillery, in which he saw action at the battles of Petersburg and Manassas. Only two years after being discharged, Dick passed away on October 16, 1866.[104] His wife of sixteen years later married Major Edward Owen, a veteran of the Confederate Army.

John D. Dixon: A club member by this name is believed to have been a sash maker who represented New York City's Fifth Ward in the New York State Assembly from 1855 to 1857. Born around 1815, this man was described as follows during his time in the assembly: "a master mechanic (a sash-maker) and a thorough business man. He was born in the ward he represents; thus contradicting the sentiment that a man has no honor in his own country among his own kindred; attends the Methodist church; is a married man; has been connected with the fire department. Mr. Dixon is a tall, finely formed man, with dark hair, somewhat bald, has large magnetic eyes, a full, fresh, jovial face, the index to a generous nature which is one of his striking characteristics. He is on the committee of banks, internal affairs of towns and counties, and the sub-committee of sixteen. Mr. Dixon seldom speaks, but votes always — according to the instructions he received from his constituents."[105] After leaving the Senate to go into the assembly, Dixon seems

to have kept a low profile, though he did continue to serve as an election inspector.[106] Dixon died on July 5, 1868.[107]

Robert Dorsett: Robert Dorsett, age 53, played in the 1875 old-timers' game to celebrate James Whyte Davis's twenty-fifth anniversary as a club member, though his name is not previously known to have appeared on the club's rolls. This pretty much has to be a Manhattan fancy goods dealer by that name and age who died on March 23, 1893, age 70.

Alexander H. Drummond: Alex Drummond functioned as a Knickerbocker officer for nine consecutive years, serving as club secretary in 1847, as a director from 1848 to 1850, as vice president from 1851 to 1854, and finally as president in 1855. He continued to be involved in club activities, refereeing the Putnam–Excelsior match that concluded the 1856 season and playing a major role in the post-game festivities. According to his passport application, Drummond was born in Edinburgh, Scotland, around 1820 and immigrated to New York along with his father John at a young age. He was a partner with fellow Knickerbockers William L. Talman, William H. Grenelle, and Edward A. Bibby in a brokerage at 4 Broad Street until it dissolved in 1860.[108] Drummond's name continued to appear in the city directory until 1864, at which point he and his wife of thirteen years vanished. In 1887, a fellow member recalled Drummond as a "fat, good-natured broker" but did not shed any light onto what happened to him.[109]

Ebenezer R. Dupignac, Jr.: Ebenezer R. Dupignac, Jr., was one of the five men who formed the club's informal "board of recruiting officers" in 1845. He subsequently served as a club officer in 1849 and 1855. Born in New York City around 1821, Dupignac's mother was an Avery. He was a relative of fellow Knickerbocker Walter Avery, but not a particularly close one; Dupignac's great-great-grandparents Ephraim Avery and Deborah Lothrop were Avery's grandparents. The elder Ebenezer Dupignac was a chair maker and merchant who eventually made the sale of varnish his primary business. His son followed him into the business, operating stores at several Manhattan locations. Ebenezer Dupignac, Jr., married in the late 1840s and named his first son Henry Clay, but this was not a statement of his political sympathies — his wife's maiden name had been Clay. He died in Manhattan on March 16, 1885, of Bright's disease.[110]

Dr. William Blake Eager, Jr.: William B. Eager, Jr., was a club director in 1855 and 1856 and seems to have been quite active in the club during those years. Eager was born on December 11, 1824, in Neely Town, a rural community in Orange County, New York. (Today in Hamptonburgh, New York, Neelytown Road intersects with Eager Road.) After apprenticing with an Orange County doctor, Eager earned his medical degree from the College of Physicians and Surgeons in New York City in 1848. He began his medical practice there, serving as chief of staff at Blackwell's Island and as Professor of Gynecology at Bellevue Hospital. According to a fellow physician, Eager's "ability to inspire a personal trust and faith in him on the part of his patients, was most wonderful, and amounted almost to personal magnetism. Fertility of resource in every branch of both medicine and surgery, and especially in gynecology, made him the consultant most sought after throughout the section in which he lived."[111] Having already started a family, he was also very active in the Fifth Ward school board and was credited with playing a major role in revising the school laws for the entire state. During the Civil War, Eager served as a surgeon for three years until failing health forced him to accept an honorable discharge. He returned to New York City and resumed his medical practice, while also operating a successful drug store. In 1874, however, severe rheumatism forced him to give up his practice and move to Middletown, New York, near his boyhood home. By then he was a wealthy man, but failed investments and the need to support an invalid wife and two widowed daughters took a heavy toll. Dr. Eager practiced medicine whenever his health permitted, but by 1887 he was also suffering from cataracts and in grave financial straits. Fortunately, successful cataract surgery in that year enabled him to begin working again and by the time of his death in Middletown on January 18, 1890, his finances were much improved.[112]

Arthur Mercein Ebbets: Brothers Arthur M. and Edward A. Ebbets were involved with the Knickerbocker Club during its formative years. Their surname still resonates with baseball fans because their first cousin once removed, Charles H. Ebbets, became the president of the Brooklyn Dodgers and the namesake of Ebbets Field. (Arthur and Edward Ebbets were the grandsons of Elizabeth Kip and Daniel Ebbets, Sr., who were the great-grandparents of Charles Ebbets.) The two brothers were the sons of Daniel Ebbets, Jr., whose position as cashier of the Union Bank made him one of New York City's most important financiers. He was also one of Wall Street's most enduring figures, representing the Union Bank from 1805 to 1855 with the exception of a brief period upstate in the aftermath of the great fire of 1835.[113] Arthur was the younger brother, having been born in New York City on January 18, 1830. His involvement with the Knickerbockers was brief because the Gold Rush led him to set sail for San Francisco on August 5, 1849. He made the arduous journey around the Horn on the sailing vessel *Pacific* and it was not a pleasant trip. During the voyage, Ebbets published a newspaper full of criticisms of ship captain Hall J. Tibbits, who was so unpopular that when the ship docked in Rio de Janeiro the American consul had him replaced. Ebbets at last arrived safely in San Francisco and was able to sell, at extraordinary prices, a number of useful articles that he had had the forethought to bring with him. This success led him to abandon his original intention of searching for gold and instead to focus his energies on selling goods and providing to the new arrivals. He established himself as a general merchant on Broadway, near Sansome, and invested in real estate. Before long, he was a wealthy man and, like fellow Knickerbocker William R. Wheaton, became deeply

involved in the vigilance committees that sought to preserve law and order. He also built San Francisco's first notable mansion, a two-story house on the northwest corner of Jones and Washington streets for which all of the lumber was brought around Cape Horn. Arthur Ebbets's fortunes took a dramatic turn for the worse during the 1857 financial panic. A lucky speculation in a mine briefly restored his previous status but then more bad fortune followed and he was forced into bankruptcy in 1858. Leaving behind his wife and young family, Ebbets then traveled to British Columbia to take part in that year's Fraser Canyon Gold Rush. As he had done in San Francisco, he opened a store and became involved in a number of other successful businesses that catered to the needs of a group of gold rushers. By 1859, most of the Fraser Canyon gold mines were panned out and Ebbets returned to San Francisco. He opened a wholesale and retail coal business on Sacramento Street, between Drum and Davis streets, and remained in business at that location for more than forty years. During those years, he remained active in civic affairs, serving as county recorder in 1861, as chairman of the finance committee in 1874–75, and helping to organize the Fireman's Fund and Insurance companies. By the time of his retirement in 1901, Ebbets was one of only a few San Franciscans who still recalled the 1849 Gold Rush. He remained active in the Society of California Pioneers until his death in Alameda on May 5, 1903. His papers chronicling his many adventures are now housed at the Huntington Digital Library.[114]

Edward A. Ebbets: Edward A. Ebbets was the older brother of Arthur Ebbets, having been born at No. 43 Frankfort Street in New York City on January 4, 1821. He seems to have been more active in the Knickerbocker Club than his brother, but his involvement ended abruptly when he followed his brother to San Francisco, where he pursued commercial and shipping enterprises. Less than two months after his arrival on April 22, 1850, he was one of the organizers of the Sansome Hook and Ladder Company, No. 3. One of the other founders was Alfred DeWitt, a close friend of Alexander Cartwright who, as discussed in an earlier profile, may have been a Knickerbocker.[115] After the death of his father in 1855, Edward Ebbets returned to New York and began a paper collars business. He returned to San Francisco in 1888, but his stay there was brief and he spent the remainder of his life in Huntington, Long Island, where he died on March 17, 1909.[116]

Henry C. Ellis: Henry C. Ellis was the name of a Knickerbocker Club member who does not seem to have been very active. While there is no way to identify him with certainty, there is a man by that name whose life intersected with club members in numerous ways and it seems a safe assumption that this is the Knickerbocker. This summary of Ellis's life reveals the extent of the parallels: "He was born in New-York in 1831 and received the education of young men of his time. He entered the firm of David Babcock & Co., furnishers of naval supplies, as a clerk, but finally became a member of the firm.... Before the War he was a member of the 7th Regiment, but left it to enter active service as a private in the 65th Zouaves, better known as the 1st United States Chasseurs. He passed through the various ranks up to the captaincy, which he held at the close of the War." Ellis continued to work as a naval supplier until his death in Brooklyn on June 19, 1886.[117]

Fanning: Harold Peterson reports that a man by this name played in the Knickerbockers' game of April 10, 1846, that opened the new season.[118] There are several men with that last name in the New York City directory of 1846 and there's no way to be sure which one of them was the Knickerbocker. It's also possible that this man was Fanning C. Tucker (c. 1790–1856), president of the Leather Manufacturers Bank. Tucker's age makes that seem implausible, but perhaps for one game he was willing to exert himself.

Francis, Jules, and Charles Fijux: Several members of the Fijux family were honorary Knickerbockers, which is appropriate because of the significant role they played in the club's all-important banquets. Family patriarch Francis Fijux was born around 1811 and worked as a milliner and as proprietor of a fancy-goods store before opening his own restaurant, hotel, and bar at 11 Barclay Street. The establishment soon earned a reputation as "an eating house that rare gastronomers in the fashionable society of the time lauded to the skies." The name Fijux, however, proved less palatable, so "[a]rtists and men of letters, puzzled by his unpronounceable name, called the proprietor 'Fish Hooks,' and thus the name is printed in old-time newspapers and in reminiscences of New-York's literary Bohemians."[119] The Knickerbockers held several important events at Fijux's, including the 1854 season-ending banquet for all of the city's ballclubs and the club's annual meeting in the spring of 1855.[120] Later in 1855, Francis Fijux moved his business to Nos. 42 and 44 Murray Street and the Knickerbockers continued to use it for club meetings. At one of those gatherings, Francis Fijux's newborn son was nominated for membership and "was duly brought forward and received a kiss from all present. He was then placed in the center of the table and duly christened Charles Knickerbocker Fijux and the Secretary directed to place his name on the Roll."[121] He thus became the game's first mascot. Sadly, Charles Knickerbocker Fijux did not live to see his second birthday, dying in Newark on June 29, 1859.[122] His father died less than a year later, on April 28, 1860.[123] His widow sold the restaurant after his death, but his son Jules subsequently revived the restaurant and continued to run it until the mid–1870s, this time at 10 Waverly Place. Jules Fijux died in New York City on January 4, 1894, age 53.[124]

James Fisher: See New York Base Ball Club (a.k.a. Washington BBC, Gotham BBC).

Henry C. Flender: Club member Henry C. Flender was born in New York around 1815, the son of Prussian-born Thomas Flender and the former Miriam Pell, a direct descendant of Sir John Pell, the First Lord of Pelham Manor. He lived at 50 Thomas in the Fifth Ward and was the foreman of New York City fire engine No. 6. Flender was generally listed in the city directory as a wheelwright or "hoistwheel." He married Adelaide Orange in 1851 and later moved to Jersey City, where he ran a grocery store. He died in Jersey City on August 15, 1882.

Edwin Constantine Fronk: Born in New York City on November 7, 1828, Edwin C. Fronk worked as a Wall Street broker during the early 1850s. By 1854, he had moved to Hoboken, where he married Catherine Reynolds Avery in 1857. When Fronk applied for a passport in 1858, fellow Knickerbocker George A. Brown attested to his being a citizen. Fronk was only 44 when he died suddenly on November 29, 1872.[125] He is buried at Green-Wood Cemetery.

William Benson Goodspeed: William B. Goodspeed's involvement with the Knickerbockers was recorded only because of the coincidence that he died on the same day as Daniel Adams. As a result, a tribute to Adams in *Sporting Life* also mentioned the death of Goodspeed, who was described as having been "well known thirty years ago as an amateur second baseman, he having filled that position at one time for the old Knickerbocker Club."[126] The claim appears questionable, since Goodspeed was only 53 when he died and his name does not appear in the Knickerbockers scorebooks of the 1850s and '60s, but there is indeed confirmation of its essential accuracy: Marshall Wright lists a man named William Goodspeed as playing second base for the Gotham Club in the late 1860s, and during a brief revival of the Knickerbockers in 1873, the second baseman of the nine was a man named Goodspeed.[127] So who was this latter-day Knickerbocker? It turns out that he would have fit right in with Adams and the other club founders. Born in Hyannis, Massachusetts, on June 15, 1845, Goodspeed was a member of a very old New England family, with one of his mother's ancestors having come over on the *Mayflower*. The family moved to Hoboken when William was an infant; while he was still a teenager he went to work at the First National Bank of Hoboken as a messenger. He worked his way up the ranks and in 1880 was named a teller. Along the way, he married the daughter of the bank's president, which couldn't have hurt his chances. By the time Goodspeed died at his home in Summit, New Jersey, on January 3, 1899, he was the bank's cashier and one of its directors.[128]

Archibald T. Gourlie: Archibald T. Gourlie played in the first game recorded in the Knickerbocker scorebooks, on October 6, 1845. During the game, Gourlie was fined "six pence" for disputing one of the umpire's rulings, making him the first known player to be penalized on the ballfield. After that promising beginning, however, his career seems to have faltered. Born around 1815, Gourlie joined the cotton brokerage of Merle & Bright in 1844 and had an office at 5 Hanover. The 1860 census shows him with a wealth of $35,000, so the umpire's fine obviously was not a big deterrent. Gourlie died in Yonkers on May 5, 1864, and is buried at Green-Wood Cemetery.[129]

William Henry Grenelle: William H. Grenelle was elected to club membership on June 14, 1850, and played a significant role in the 1857 formation of the National Association of Base Ball Players. A Knickerbocker Club director in 1857, Grenelle joined Daniel Adams and Louis Wadsworth on a committee formed to arrange a convention of the "various base ball clubs of this city and vicinity."[130] He also played at least one game for the Knickerbockers' first nine in both 1857 and 1858 and represented the club at several NABBP conventions. His name was "erased" from the club's membership roll on February 1, 1868, presumably for nonpayment of his annual dues. Born in New York City around 1819, Grenelle worked as a Wall Street broker. For a time he was in partnership with fellow Knickerbockers William H. Talman, Edward A. Bibby, and Alexander H. Drummond, until the firm broke up in 1860. Grenelle died in Brooklyn on December 21, 1890.

Thomas Grierson: Thomas Grierson was secretary of the Knickerbocker Club in 1865, but that name did not appear in the city directories of the era, nor has a strong candidate been identified on any census.

David Hart: David Hart was an early Knickerbocker who umpired one of the club's 1846 contests. It seems likely that the club member was a Pacific Bank teller named David Davids Hart who was born in New York City on March 19, 1819. David Davids Hart came from a distinguished family; his father, Bernard Hart (1763–1855), was a wealthy New York City brewer and Jewish civic leader; his brother, Emanuel Bernard Hart (1809–1897), was a U.S. congressman; and his nephew, Bret Harte (1836–1902), was one of the best-known American writers of the 19th century, now best remembered for the stories "The Luck of Roaring Camp" and "The Outcasts of Poker Flat." (Bret Harte's father, David's half-brother, changed the spelling of his surname.)[131] David D. Hart had a long involvement with the New York City Guard. Despite his age, he enlisted in the Civil War and was severely wounded at the First Battle of Bull Run, being shot in the head with a Minié ball. The injury left Captain Hart deaf and prevented him from being promoted to cashier, but he returned to work at the Pacific Bank and had been there for nearly half a century when he retired at the end of December 1887. He died at his New York City home a few days later, on January 2, 1888. His funeral was "conducted under the strict regulations of the Hebrew faith," with Rabbi Henry Pereira Mendes on hand to "consign the remains of the deceased captain to the earth at Cypress Hills, where rest the remains of so many old Holland and English Hebrews who have been foremost among New York's citizens."[132]

Abner Hayward: Club member Abner Hayward was born in Pennsylvania around 1828 and worked on Wall Street as the secretary of the Fireman's Insurance Company. In 1872 Hayward disappeared under mysterious circumstances and an investigation revealed that he had "recently been living a fast, irregular life, and he was discharged on account of neglect of

duty." An audit discovered that the sum of $2,100 was missing.[133] Hayward died in Boston on September 27, 1894, and his body was brought back to New York for burial. His death certificate reports that he was the president of an insurance company, but that seems to have been a flight of fancy as the Boston city directories listed him without an occupation.

Peter S. Henderson: A club director in 1852, Peter S. Henderson was, like so many of his fellow club members, a clerk and bank teller. His 1850 marriage to Charlotte Pell produced five children, but he had the misfortune to outlive all of them. When the 1910 census was taken, the 88-year-old Henderson was living with a grandchild in Milford, Connecticut. Presumably nobody informed him of the Mills Commission; Henderson might have had some valuable memories to share.

Richard H. Hinsdale: Richard H. Hinsdale played for the Knickerbockers' first nine in the years immediately following the Civil War and served two terms as club treasurer beginning in 1865. Born in Connecticut around 1825, he was a grandson of Stephen Hosmer, chief justice of the Connecticut Supreme Court, and the great-grandson of Titus Hosmer, who signed the Articles of Confederation as a Connecticut delegate at the 1778 Continental Congress. After moving to New York, Hinsdale married the daughter of Epenetus Doughty, a prominent volunteer firefighter, and became a dry-goods dealer. He died in Manhattan on February 6, 1895.[134]

George Ireland, Jr.: The name of George Ireland, Jr., appeared in an April 10, 1846, intrasquad game and on the Knickerbocker Club's rolls in 1848 and '54. Ireland's father was the president of the Mutual Insurance Company, which was later renamed the Knickerbocker Insurance Company. Born on April 23, 1813, he graduated from Columbia College in 1830 and then began studying law in the office of Daniel Lord. In 1837 Ireland married Anna Mary Brown, the only daughter of General Aaron Brown, and they raised a large family.[135] Ireland practiced law from offices on Nassau Street and Broadway and specialized in legal titles. According to a family history, Ireland "was not a member of any secret society or club; but was a member of the old Knickerbocker Base Ball Club, which was an amateur association composed of professional men of the city who played ball for their own amusement, having their grounds in Hoboken. That was in the days before base ball had become the sport of professionals."[136] George Ireland, Jr., died in New Canaan, Connecticut, on August 24, 1873.

Francis Upton Johnston: There can be no doubt about the given names of Dr. F.U. Johnston, a club member whose name entered the rolls in 1845. But the Johnstons' were part of "a long line of physicians," making it difficult to be sure whether the Knickerbocker Club member was Dr. Francis Upton Johnston, Sr., (1796–1858) or his son, Dr. Francis Upton Johnston, Jr., (1826–1892).[137] While the elder Johnston seems a bit old for membership, the younger Johnston was still a teenager in 1845 and seems even less plausible. Daniel Adams reported having played the game with several medical fellows by 1840, so on the whole it appears more likely that Francis Upton Johnston, Sr., was the Knickerbocker.

D.B. Keeler, Jr.: A man by this name was club treasurer in 1860 and there can be little doubt that he was David B. Keeler, Jr., who was born on February 17, 1835, on Shelter Island, Suffolk County, New York. A volunteer fireman before the war, Keeler served on the staff of General George B. Buchanan during the Civil War. Later he was successful in real estate, playing a major role in the development of Seabright, New Jersey, the future home of Albert Goodwill Spalding. Keeler died in New York on September 6, 1915.[138]

W.H. Kirby: A club member by this name cannot be identified with absolute confidence. The best candidate in the city directories is a dry-goods merchant at 35 and 37 Vesey Street named William H. Kirby. Sportswriter and early-baseball expert Frank Menke referred to Kirby as a "businessman."

Peter Rutgers Kissam: "Among the deaths on Tuesday was that of Mr. P.R. Kissam, a member of the New York Stock Exchange since July 22, 1864," reported the *Brooklyn Eagle* in 1889. "He was a veteran of the old Knickerbocker Base Ball Club and one of its most esteemed members."[139] It's an intriguing note because Peter Rutgers Kissam (1834–1889) was the younger brother of Knickerbocker mainstay Samuel Hamilton Kissam, profiled below. No confirmation of Peter's involvement with the club has been found, but it's possible that he played some role in their activities; perhaps he even took part in some of the games credited to his brother, though if so one would expect to find an initial next to his name. Peter Kissam was a banker and broker, working at the Union Bank along with his kinsman Benjamin Brotherson, and had to testify in the legal proceedings that proceeded from Brotherson's embezzlement.

Samuel Hamilton Kissam: Samuel H. Kissam joined James Whyte Davis as the only Knickerbockers to play for the first nine both before and after the Civil War. Primarily an outfielder, Kissam joined the club on April 1, 1854, after being nominated by Charles De Bost, and was still a regular in 1868. By then, he was "one of the very few left of the old members" but was still "one of the most active and attentive" and faithful in his "love of the sport and attachment to the old Club."[140] Kissam and Davis were also involved in an 1871 effort to form a lily-white amateur association to succeed the NABBP. In 1879 Kissam celebrated his silver anniversary as a club member and was honored with a silver ball with an inscription that read: "Presented to Samuel H. Kissam by a fellow member to commemorate his twenty-fifth anniversary of membership in the Knickerbocker Base Ball Club. And as a remembrance of an unbroken and warm friendship on 1854, the green fields of Hoboken 1879. And also attesting his many sacrifices and kindnesses which will be cherished forever, by your loving and

grateful friends. God be with you."[141] Born in December of 1830, Kissam came from a distinguished family. His father, the Rev. Samuel Kissam, was a Dutch Reformed minister. His great-grandfather Benjamin Kissam was a lawyer who played a prominent role in the First and Second Provincial Congresses. Benjamin Kissam also mentored John Jay, the first chief justice of the United States Supreme Court, while Jay was a legal apprentice in his office; Jay later described Kissam as "the best friend I ever had, and the best man I ever knew." Yet while the family included noteworthy attorneys and ministers, it was in the field of medicine that the name Kissam was best known. "Twenty-two members of the family actually practiced medicine," reported Paul Cushman, Jr., "The accumulation of such a large number of physicians in one family is unique in American medicine to my knowledge. Further, the tendency of the medical Kissams to concentrate in the New York City area is remarkable. Seventeen Kissams were actively engaged in the practice of medicine at one time or another in the New York City area. Therefore the history of the medical Kissams largely parallels the history of medicine in New York City.... The relation of the Kissam family to the Columbia University College of Physicians and Surgeons or to its predecessors is unique in American medicine. Twenty-three members of the family were associated with the college in a variety of ways during almost every decade of its first century of existence."[142] Samuel Kissam, however, chose a different career. Starting as a bank clerk at the age of 18, he eventually headed a brokerage and became one of the best-known figures on the New York Stock Exchange. His brokerage handled much of the business of William H. Vanderbilt, who had married Kissam's sister. Kissam was a longtime member of the Stock Exchange's Board of Governors and also served as one of the administrators of its Gratuity Fund. In addition, Kissam was an active member of the Brooklyn City Guard. He retired from business in the 1890s but lived to a ripe old age and was one of the last surviving Knickerbockers when he died at his Manhattan home on April 18, 1915.[143]

William F. Ladd: Although older than most of the playing members of the club, William F. Ladd took part in an 1852 game played to celebrate the Fourth of July and then served as a club director for several years. In 1857, perhaps in acknowledgment of his age, he was elected an honorary member. Ladd was born in England on September 2, 1807, and followed his older brother to New York around 1822. Four years later he opened a watch and jewelry store that was a fixture on Wall Street until 1891. Ladd's ties to his fellow club members were further strengthened by his involvement in the Columbia Fire Insurance Company. The club member who reminisced to a *New York Sun* reporter in 1887 commented that Ladd had "disappeared," but in fact Ladd was still alive and in town.[144] Indeed, Ladd even shared his memories of the Knickerbockers with Johnny Ward, who relied on them in *How to Become a Base-Ball Player*.[145] He was also a fellow of the American Geographical Society and one of the founders of the Mechanics' Library. When William F. Ladd died at his home on West Thirty-Sixth Street on September 14, 1889, he was described in one obituary as having been "the official time-keeper of the Stock Exchange."[146] He is buried in Green-Wood Cemetery.

James P. Landsdown: Club member James P. Landsdown (also spelled Landsdowne, Lansdowne, or Lansdown) was born in Deptford, Kent, England, on May 1, 1815. After immigrating to the United States, he lived in Philadelphia before settling in New York City, where he became a hatter. He served in the Union Army during the Civil War. Landsdown was only 41 when he died on October 27, 1866. He is buried in Green-Wood Cemetery.

Langworthy: The first name of this club member is not known with certainty, but it is a sufficiently unusual surname that we can hazard a reasonable guess. The only male Langworthy to appear in the city directory between 1840 and 1860 was John Langworthy, who lived in New York City's Fourth Ward and was in the artificial-flower business. Born in England around 1795, Langworthy later relocated to Jersey City and was in the same business there when the 1870 census was taken.

Edgar Francis Lasak: Edgar F. Lasak was the son of Francis Lasak, a partner of John Jacob Astor, and was born around 1824. He joined his father in the fur business, operating a store on Broadway. As a young man, he was active in both the fire department and the Knickerbocker Club. Lasak died on January 29, 1881.

Benjamin C. Lee: Benjamin C. Lee, the son of James Lee (profiled in the New York Base Ball Club entry) was active in the Knickerbocker Club during its early years, serving as a club director from 1848 to 1850. Born around 1828, Lee had joined his father's business by 1846 and also served as a director of the Bank of the Commonwealth and the Gebhard Fire Insurance Company. He was only 31 when he died at the home of his father-in-law, Cornelius Smith, on July 27, 1859.[147]

James Lee: See New York Base Ball Club (a.k.a. Washington BBC, Gotham BBC).

James H. Leggett: A member by this name was elected on August 26, 1858, and subsequently reported as having "Gone to California and not heard from." The city directories and censuses do not yield a strong candidate.

W. Lippincott: The name of this 1846 club member is too common for positive identification, but the most likely candidate is William H. Lippincott, a commercial dealer at 60 West Washington Market. This man died on March 21, 1882, at the age of 64.[148]

Gershom Lockwood: Gershom Lockwood was born into an old Connecticut family in New Canaan, Connecticut, on March 3, 1819, and worked as a tailor in New York City. By 1850 he had moved his residence to Newark but continued in business on Fifth Avenue well into the 1880s. Lockwood died in Stamford, Connecticut, on December 11, 1893.

William Davenport Maltbie, Jr.: William D. Maltbie's father and namesake worked in Manhattan and was secretary of the Chatham Fire Insurance Company.[149] The younger Maltbie, born on September 21, 1816, was working on Wall Street as a cotton broker by 1846 and played in the Knickerbockers' game on October 6, 1845 (recorded as "Maltby"). In 1853 he helped to organize the New York Cotton Brokers' Association.[150] But Maltbie's fortunes later turned and after moving to Suffern, in Rockland County, New York, he was forced into bankruptcy in 1868.[151] On the 1875 state census he is living with his daughter's family with no occupation listed. Little is known about Maltbie's later years and family trees give contradictory information about when he died. In fact, he died in Suffern on April 29, 1889.[152]

Michael McCarty: Michael McCarty played in one of the Knickerbockers' games in the fall of 1847 and as the proprietor of the Colonnade Hotel at the Elysian Fields had frequent interactions with club members. The Colonnade was erected in the middle of the grounds in 1834 and its white front and Doric pillars made it an impressive edifice.[153] Though still in his early 20s, the Irish-born McCarty became its proprietor in 1841 and took out advertisements urging New Yorkers to escape the "noise, bustle and confinement" of the city and visit the "pure air, shady walks, green fields, delightful prospects, and refreshing breezes of Hoboken."[154] Over the next decade he became so closely associated with the Colonnade that it often was referred to as McCarty's Hotel. For special events, he set up stages or pavilions around the hotel so that patrons could eat or drink to their heart's content while enjoying the scenery. The Knickerbockers often availed themselves of his hospitality. The State of Hawai'i Archives has a receipt in McCarty's handwriting acknowledging the payment of $30 in exchange for dinner for 20 members of the Knickerbocker Base Ball Club on December 5, 1845. On May 5, 1846, the club's officers were elected at a meeting at McCarty's Hotel. That fall, club members voted to give a prize of $10 to McCarty. Then on June 17, 1851, following a match game against the Washington Club, "an entertainment was given after play at McCarty's Hotel, Elysian Fields."[155] A few weeks earlier, the Colonnade had been the scene of a much more ominous scene when a dispute between German and Irish youths escalated into a riot. McCarty fired into the crowd and shot either one or two Germans, depending upon the paper consulted. The day of the riot had been one of the Knickerbockers' regular play days, but after four innings the record of play ends abruptly and the bottom of the scoresheet bears this terse notation: "Broke up by the Dutch [German] Fight."[156] One year later, on March 3, 1852, Michael McCarty fatally shot himself while hunting.[157]

William F. McCutcheon: William F. McCutcheon, who became a club member in 1854, was described when nominated for membership as a "bookkeeper at bank." He was later reported by Henry Chadwick to have been affiliated with the Mechanics' Bank. Based on this, he pretty much has to be the son of Hugh McCutcheon or McCutchen, a longtime bank clerk for the Mechanics' Bank. The 1850 census listed a 23-year-old son named William living with Hugh McCutcheon and working as a clerk. This man seems to disappear for many years, but then the 1892 census of Brooklyn has a William F. McCutcheon, age 65 and working as a clerk, without any family members living with him. On April 15, 1900, William Frere McCutcheon, age 74, died at the Brooklyn Home for Aged Men.[158] This man is buried at Green-Wood Cemetery along with Hugh McCutcheon and other family members, so there can be little doubt that he is our man.

McDonald: A man with this surname took part in the 1852 game the Knickerbockers played to celebrate the Fourth of July holiday. With no other clues, the task of identifying him seems hopeless but there is one intriguing candidate. One of the participants in the 1875 old-timers' game played to celebrate James Whyte Davis's 25th anniversary as a club member was Dr. William Ogden McDonald. Dr. McDonald was only 40 in 1875 so would still have been a teenager in 1852, making it seem implausible that he was the player in question. McDonald, however, graduated from the New York Medical College in 1855, which would mean that he was already a student there in the summer of 1852. Since both Dr. Adams and James Whyte Davis took part in the 1852 game, it is entirely possible that McDonald joined the Knickerbockers that day, perhaps at Adams's suggestion, and that his old acquaintance with Davis led him to play in the 1875 contest. William Ogden McDonald was born in Waddington, St. Lawrence County, New York, around 1835 and graduated from the New York Medical College in 1855. During the war, he served as a surgeon in the 61st New York, the 27th Connecticut, and the 2nd Kentucky Cavalry. He then was the medical officer of the 6th Army Corps until the close of the war, at which point he resigned with the rank of lieutenant colonel. McDonald subsequently was on the faculty of the New York Homeopathic Medical College for more than 20 years, where he taught gynecology. Dr. McDonald died in Brooklyn on March 25, 1918.[159]

Charles Follen McKim: Charles F. McKim was a renowned architect who played for the Knickerbockers during an 1874 effort to keep the club alive. Born in Isabella Furnace, Chester County, Pennsylvania, on August 24, 1847, McKim was the son of a Presbyterian minister who was an outspoken Abolitionist. After completing his public schooling in Philadelphia, he enrolled at Harvard's Lawrence Scientific School as a member of the Class of '70. He ended up spending only one year at Harvard before his father elected to withdraw him from the school and send him to Paris's École des Beaux-Arts. During that year in Cambridge, McKim played four games for the school's baseball nine.[160] Nevertheless, baseball played a significant role in his time at Harvard. As discussed in another entry in this volume, Harvard's Class of '67 had formed the first permanent nine and had established baseball as a promi-

nent part of campus life. Soon after arriving on campus, McKim wrote to his father, "I get an hr. and sometimes more to play ball during the day and this so far has been my only exercise; soon, however, I hope to get to the gymnasium regularly. I have had offers to join the Scientific base ball club and boat club, but have refused both from want of time. Gracious! if study were secondary what a time I could have. They are talking of making the 'Harvard' nine University (hitherto it has been devoted to undergraduates) and I understand my name is being considered among the great powers as one of the players. This would be a great honor here, the nine being looked up to as oracles, and the chances of 'getting on' being very few and far between. However, nothing has been determined on, as the season is already at its close and the ball must be buried until next Spring."[161] By the spring of 1867, Rev. McKim had decided to withdraw his son from Harvard and send him to Paris. However, James Russell Lowell, the celebrated poet who was then a professor of languages at Harvard, wrote to Rev. McKim as follows: "We hear that you are inclined to play the Roman father and not let Charles stay here to play the next ball-match with the Lowell Club. This must be some of the old leaven of Presbyterianism. I can testify from the evidence of my own eyes that he is essential to the success of our nine who are really the muses, only disguised. Now do be a good fellow and let him stay for it is of great consequence that we beat the Lowell Club, who are a little stuck up."[162] McKim stayed for the game and played a starring role in Harvard's victory. Upon his return to the United States in 1872, McKim was hired by New York architect Henry Hobson Richardson and it was during this time that he was briefly involved with the Knickerbocker Club. In 1879, McKim joined with William Mead and Stanford White to form the McKim, Mead & White architectural firm, which soon became one of the country's most successful and influential architectural firms. McKim was personally involved in such important projects as the second Madison Square Garden, the Agricultural building at the Chicago World's Columbian Exposition, the Boston Public Library, the renovation of the White House, and the original plan for the uptown campus of Columbia College, now known as Columbia University. By the time of his death in St. James, New York, on September 14, 1909, he had received many prestigious awards, including the Paris Exhibition's royal gold medal for his contributions to architecture.

Napoleon Bonaparte McLaughlen: Napoleon B. McLaughlen, who was the secretary of the Knickerbocker Club in 1857, was born in Chelsea, Vermont, on December 8, 1823. He entered the 2nd U.S. Dragoons in 1850 and it was while based in New York City that he became a member of the Knickerbocker Club. In 1955 McLaughlen's daughter donated the belt that he wore while playing with his fellow Knickerbockers to the Hall of Fame, making it the only known surviving item of clothing to have been used by a Knickerbocker on the baseball diamond. (Recent hints from the family of Doc

Adams indicate that his monogrammed jersey-front buttons may survive as well.)[163] During the Civil War, McLaughlen was a colonel in the 1st Massachusetts Infantry and led his troops into battle at Fredericksburg, Chancellorsville, Gettysburg, the Wilderness, and Spottsylvania. He had attained the rank of brigadier general by the time of his retirement in 1882. McLaughlen's name was spelled with an E but was misspelled as McLaughlin during his time with the Knickerbockers and in numerous ways during his military career. In an 1864 telegram, Ulysses S. Grant referred to him first as "Capt N B McLaugher" and later as "Capt McLaughter." Yet the error could not have been intended as a sign of disrespect, since Grant's telegram requested authority to muster McLaughlen in as colonel of a regiment "said to be in a wretched condition for want of a commander."[164] McLaughlen died in Middletown, New York, on January 27, 1887.[165]

James Moncrief: James Moncrief began playing for the Knickerbockers in the contest on October 6, 1845, and remained active for several more years, serving as a club director in 1850. His involvement in the club's doings was extensive enough for Daniel Adams to mention him as an earlier member in an 1896 interview.[166] Born in Harrison County, Ohio, on September 16, 1822, James Moncrief was of Scottish descent. He lost his father at a young age and by 1837 he was living in New York City and working as a law clerk in the office of General Philip S. Crooke. He proved a diligent student of the law and was still a very young man when he began a legal partnership with Daniel B. Tallmadge. In 1858, Moncrief was elected as a judge of the Superior Court. He was only 47 when he died on February 1, 1870. An obituary credited him with having had "those rare and high qualifications for usefulness in these degenerate times, and added, "Possessing talent of a high order, with a well balanced mind, great clearness of comprehension, a fine discriminating judgment, retentive memory and a highly-cultivated and well-stored intellect, with the strictest honesty and morality, noblest generosity, coupled with fine conversational powers and great natural ease and grace of manner, rendered him at once a model Judge, an able and learned lawyer and wise counselor."[167] He was buried at Green-Wood Cemetery.

James L. Montgomery: The Knickerbockers were meticulous about recording the middle initials of club members, making it possible, at the very least, to identify likely candidates. For example, there are several men named James Montgomery in the New York City directories but only one with the correct middle initial, so the presumption is that the club member was a man who began teaching gymnastics at Ottignon's Gymnasium on Crosby Street in 1856. Montgomery's partner, Charles F. Ottignon, had been a familiar figure in the city as a boxing instructor and operator of gymnasiums for more than a decade. At a time when boxing was struggling to achieve respectability, Ottignon had a stellar reputation and the city's best citizens were willing to let him teach their sons

the "manly art of self-defense." Montgomery became his partner in May 1856 and brought to the gymnasium a new emphasis on weight-lifting. Montgomery, according to one account, "introduced the fashion of using dumb bells, and when he curled and put up the 100 pound bell all New York wondered."[168] A cast of one of Montgomery's biceps was even reproduced in *The American Phrenological Journal and Repository of Science* in 1858, along with an explanation of how "judicious practice" in the gymnasium had turned a slender teenager into a man capable of extraordinary feats of strength.[169] The new partners placed a great emphasis on respectability, "tastefully decorating" the gymnasium with "patriotic and appropriate emblems." Apt mottos were also on prominent display, including "Dryden's famous maxim, 'The Wise for Cure on Exercise Depend' and the slogan 'From Labor Health, From Health Contentment Springs.'" As a result, the gymnasium was reported to be "attended by our most fashionable and intellectual assemblages, and have won the unqualified approval of the ladies." To underscore this message, in December of 1856 a public exhibition was held at the gymnasium. With a band playing, the pupils of the gymnasium "made their appearance in single file with Professor Jas. L. Montgomery as corporal of the guard" and gave exhibitions of their proficiency in tumbling and fencing and with the use of dumb bells, swinging rings, perpendicular poles, trapeze, parallel bars and the like."[170] Despite the success of the exhibition, Montgomery soon withdrew from the partnership with Ottignon and worked at a gymnasium in Albany before fading into obscurity. In 1865, the death of a 34-year-old James L. Montgomery was reported in the *New York Tribune*. The dead man was reported to be the nephew of Isaac M. Woolley, a successful Manhattan merchant who had died a few years earlier, and is buried at Green-Wood Cemetery. Under the circumstances, we can't be certain that this decedent was the former professor of gymnastics, but it seems likely.[171]

Henry T. Morgan: Henry T. Morgan, a club member in 1848, was born in Lee, Massachusetts, in 1816. He was a member of the illustrious banking family that included J.P. Morgan and was a very successful Wall Street commission broker in his own right. Morgan began his career at the age of 15 as a bank clerk in Norwalk, Connecticut, and soon earned promotion to teller. In 1836 he moved to New York and, along with three of his brothers, opened the stockbroking business that made him a very wealthy man. Morgan died on January 27, 1883, after collapsing at Delmonico's restaurant. He is buried at Green-Wood Cemetery.[172]

Augustus C. Morrill: Augustus C. Morrill, a club member in 1848, was listed in the 1850 New York City directory as a lawyer at 9 Chambers with a home on 125th Street, which would have been a country estate at that time. Morrill was born around 1824 in New York City and was the son of Elisha Morrill, also a lawyer and an active member of the volunteer fire department, and the former Mary Lyon Tucker. After his parents died in the 1850s, he seems to have devoted most of his attention to the management of their estate. Morrill was only 36 when he died on March 28, 1861.[173]

John Paige Mumford: J. Paige Mumford began playing for the Knickerbockers in 1846 and also took part in a September 16, 1847, contest that was denoted as a "match game" in the club's game book. One year later, he sat on the club's Committee to Revise Constitution and By-Laws along with Adams, Cartwright, Curry, and Eugene Plunkett. J. Paige Mumford was born around 1823 into the closest thing to an aristocracy that New York City could then boast; his grandfathers, John P. Mumford and Anthony L. Underhill, were among the city's most successful merchants. "In the old times," reported one contemporary, "there was no name more eminent among the merchants of New York city than that of Mumford."[174] However, John Paige Mumford's father, John I. Mumford, was a different story. After being educated at Princeton, he began a coffee business in partnership with his brother-in-law, Henry Underhill. But he dissolved the business and in 1828 launched a new career as a newspaper editor. His *Daily Standard* was the city's only staunch Democratic organ, and a grateful President Andrew Jackson sought to reciprocate by feeding Mumford advance copies of key addresses. But, "Alas! there is no use of disguising the fact, John I. Mumford loved liquor, and it had the same effect upon him as it does upon many other clever people. If he drank one glass, fifty followed. A tremendous reckless spree was sure to follow."[175] The scoops naturally dried up and John I. Mumford was soon back in business in New York City, where he experienced only limited success. His son, John Paige Mumford, worked as a clerk at a Manhattan hotel and at the Custom House as a young man. He was also active in the state militia. After marrying Frances Charlotte Aspinwall in 1852, Mumford began studying the law and in 1857 he relocated to Minnesota to start a law practice there.[176] Like his father, however, Mumford proved a bit of a dilettante. He returned to New York to serve in the Civil War and over the next few decades popped up in numerous Minnesota cities with a baffling array of occupations. By the mid–1880s Mumford, now remarried, turned up in Winona, Minnesota, and convinced the city council that he "was for many years on the construction of the Erie and other railroads."[177] He was appointed the city's sanitary engineer, but within a few years he was back in St. Paul. In the early 1890s he returned to New York City, where he died on December 10, 1898. He is buried in the Underhill Family Vault at Trinity Churchyard.

John Murphy: See New York Base Ball Club (a.k.a. Washington BBC, Gotham BBC).

John Murray, Jr.: There are at least four references to players with the surname of Murray in the Knickerbockers' annals. One of the participants in the club's 1852 Fourth of July game was a player named Murray, no first game given. Two years later, the name John Murray, Jr., was reported to

be on the club's rolls. Several years after that, John Murray, Jr., was listed as an honorary member. Then at the 1875 reunion game to celebrate James Whyte Davis's silver anniversary as a club member, the left fielder for one of the sides was identified as John Murray, age 47. While these are not necessarily all the same man, the evidence suggests that they were. John Murray, Jr., was born in New York City on December 26, 1827, into a remarkable Quaker family. His great-grandfather Robert Murray (1721–1786) came over from Ireland as a boy and became a very successful New York City shipping merchant. His 29-acre farm became known as Murray Hill and was the site of one of the Knickerbockers' first baseball fields; the name remains a recognized Manhattan neighborhood to this day. During the American Revolution, Robert Murray's wife, Mary Lindley Murray (1726–1782), is said to have delayed British General William Howe at her home after a British victory and thereby allowed the American troops to retreat safely. Robert and Mary Murray's children included Lindley Murray (1745–1826), who wrote a book of grammar that was a standard school primer during the early 19th century, and John Murray, Jr., apparently so named in honor of Robert's brother. This John Murray, Jr., (1758–1819) was a successful New York merchant and brewer who retired from business at a young age and devoted the remainder of his life to philanthropy. He was active in the Abolitionist movement, served as governor of New York Hospital, and helped to found the New York Historical Society. It was at his home in Franklin Square that the New York public school system originated in 1805 with the founding of the New York Free School Society.[178] The children of John Murray, Jr., included Lindley Murray (1790–1847), a drugstore owner and the father of 11 children. One of them bore the logical name of Lindley Murray, Jr., and another, in an apparent attempt to drive future researchers to distraction, was named John Murray, Jr., the future Knickerbocker. Unlike his distinguished forbears, the whereabouts of John Murray, Jr., are not always easy to trace. There's a builder by that name in the New York City directories in the late 1850s and early '60s who may be him, but that's far from clear. A Civil War service record may also belong to him, but that too may belong to somebody else. We do at least know that he wed Mary Stacy Collins on October 2, 1862, and that their only son was born in New Jersey on November 27, 1865. Naturally, they named him John Murray, Jr. The 1870 census finds the Murrays living in Orange, New Jersey, with the elder John working as a bank clerk in New York City and possessing a net wealth of only $800. His wife died in 1875, the year of the reunion game, and John Murray again becomes difficult to trace until he appears in the 1900 census in Los Angeles, where he worked as a teacher and was living with his son. City directory listings suggest that he was still living in Los Angeles until at least 1904, though he was never listed as a teacher and appears to have been working as a carpenter. His exact date of death remains unknown. John Murray of the Knickerbockers was the first cousin several generations removed of Robert Lindley Murray, two-time U.S. Open tennis champion.

Samuel Nichols: Samuel Nichols was a prominent English-born New York newspaperman and member of the St. George Cricket Club who died in 1854. Two years later, at a postgame banquet, a reporter from the rival *Porter's Spirit of the Times* declared that during Nichols's tenure as editor of the *Sunday Mercury*, the newspaper had been a "special organ for cricket." Alexander Drummond, however, jumped to Nichols's defense, noting that Nichols had been a member of the Knickerbocker Club and had once told him "that where three had a fair chance to play cricket, twenty had a fair chance to play base ball."[179] Nichols was born in Hampstead, England, on March 30, 1810, and became a lawyer. He continued to practice law after immigrating to New York, but in the late 1830s he switched professions and soon became editor of the *Sunday Mercury*. During his tenure, the *Sunday Mercury* was indeed a leader in the coverage of baseball. Nichols was still in that position on September 18, 1854, when he attempted to board a moving Third Avenue Railway car but fell and slipped under the wheels. He died from his injuries the next morning, leaving a widow and seven children.[180]

Fraley C. Niebuhr: Fraley C. Niebuhr was a dedicated club officer, serving as treasurer in 1848 and '49, vice president in 1850, president for four years beginning in 1851, and finally as a director in 1857 and '58. Niebuhr also took part in several games during the club's early years and, in addition, attested to the citizenship of Alexander Cartwright, Charles De Bost, and James Whyte Davis when they applied for passports. Born in Philadelphia on November 11, 1820, Niebuhr moved to New York at the age of 14 and began a long career on Wall Street at the Custom House brokerage. His was a life filled with success, but when he died in Brooklyn on December 10, 1901, his obituary found room to mention his affiliation with the Knickerbockers. Niebuhr is buried at Green-Wood Cemetery.[181]

Walter Oakley: Walter Oakley was a Knickerbocker club member by 1846 and took part in at least one of their contests. Born in New York around 1817, Oakley worked at the Merchants' Exchange Bank on Greenwich Street in the late 1840s and then as a cashier for the Central Bank, located at 88 Chambers Street, during the early 1850s. In 1856, he became a deputy tax collector for the city, but two years later he was removed from the position and accused of failing to remit all of the money he had collected. The allegations at first received considerable attention in the press, but the coverage soon ended.[182] Nonetheless, the issue must not have been resolved, and for decades the city continued to list Oakley as being in default in an amount exceeding $36,000.[183] Meanwhile, Walter Oakley continued to work in New York City as a broker. He died on December 6, 1889.[184]

Thomas J. O'Brien: Thomas J. O'Brien, the club treasurer in 1862, was not a brother of John and William, and his common name makes it impossible to pinpoint his identity.

William O'Brien, Jr., John O'Brien, and possibly one or more of their brothers: "Many others were [Knickerbocker Club] members at one time or another," Daniel Adams recalled in 1896. "Besides those named in the list I remember two brothers named O'Brien, who were brokers and afterward became very wealthy."[185] The two men in question are undoubtedly brothers William and John O'Brien, whose participation in a November 18, 1845, Knickerbocker practice game was later confirmed by Henry Chadwick (though Chadwick gave their names as W. and I. O'Brien).[186] John O'Brien also was one of the first Knickerbockers to be disciplined "for improper language," earning a fine of six-and-a-quarter cents (a "half-bit") for swearing in an intramural contest in October 1845. The O'Briens came from a family of 11 children, so it is possible that other brothers also took part in the Knickerbockers' activities, but there is no solid evidence that this was the case. The family patriarch, William O'Brien, Sr., (1768?–1846), fled Dublin in 1798 after taking part in that year's Irish Rebellion. After settling in New York City, he became a prominent Wall Street insurance adjuster and raised a large family. His two oldest sons, William and John, followed him into important positions on Wall Street, William as the cashier of the Mechanics' Bank and John in the same position at the Manhattan Bank. In 1842, the two brothers established their own banking and brokerage firm; the partnership of William & John O'Brien soon became "one of the landmarks of Wall Street." It eventually employed their three younger brothers, Robert, Charles, and Joseph. William O'Brien, who never married, was 72 when he died on January 3, 1885.[187] John O'Brien was a very wealthy man by the time he died at his summer home in Newport, Rhode Island, on October 1, 1899. Survivors included his widow and a stepdaughter who was married to a French baron, the Baron de Sellière.[188]

Henry Moscrop Onderdonk: Henry M. Onderdonk was a member of the Knickerbockers in 1848, though his involvement with the club seems to have ended after his young wife's death the following year. Born in New York City on March 26, 1818, Onderdonk was the son of the Rev. Benjamin T. Onderdonk, a member of a prominent Hempstead family who became bishop of the Episcopal Diocese of New York in 1830. His mother was the daughter of the Rev. Henry Moscrop, young Henry's namesake. In 1835, the 17-year-old Henry Onderdonk was convicted of check forgery and sentenced to prison, only to be granted clemency by Governor William L. Marcy, a decision that stirred public controversy. Reportedly, Onderdonk had agreed to go into exile by embarking on a three-year whaling voyage.[189] By the end of the decade, Onderdonk was back in New York and working as a civil engineer. On July 18, 1841, he married Justine Bibby, the sister of fellow Knickerbocker Edward A. Bibby (whose distinguished family is discussed in his entry). According to a friend of Onderdonk's bride, the wedding was a "runaway match," suggesting that the 1835 scandal had not been forgotten.[190] After his marriage,

Onderdonk established a printing and publishing business on John Street that specialized in religious literature. He also published his father's written defense against charges that he had made sexual advances toward a number of female parishioners. Bishop Onderdonk adamantly denied the charges, but was suspended from performing his duties after a trial before the House of Bishops. He remained the nominal bishop of the Episcopal Diocese of New York until his death in 1861, but provisional bishops performed his duties. During these years a regular visitor to Onderdonk's shop was his friend Clement C. Moore. In 1848, Onderdonk published the first book version of Moore's iconic poem "A Visit From St. Nicholas," accompanied with illustrations by Theodore C. Boyd, a wood engraver who had a nearby shop. One year later, Justine Onderdonk gave birth to a pair of twins who would have been the couple's fifth and sixth children. There were complications and she died, along with both of the twins. A grief-stricken Henry Onderdonk moved to Virginia's Kanawha River Valley (later to become part of West Virginia), where he went back to civil engineering and served as a postmaster. He also remarried and began a new family. When the Civil War broke out, Onderdonk moved to Gallipolis, Ohio, where he operated a bookstore and served in the State Senate. In 1870 he bought the *Hempstead Inquirer* and returned to New York. After settling his family on a large estate, Onderdonk also helped to found the New York & Hempstead Railroad. He was still operating the newspaper and participating in a wide range of civic activities when he died on September 2, 1885. He was survived by his second wife, six children and his nonagenarian mother.[191]

Anson S. Palmer: Anson S. Palmer was the secretary of the Knickerbocker Club in 1861. Born around 1835, Palmer was still a very young man when he became secretary of the newly formed Lafayette Fire Insurance Company in 1856. Palmer married in 1862 and around that time he began a new career as a confectioner and chocolate dealer. Palmer was only 44 when he died in New York on June 11, 1879.

C.H. Parisen: This name, or something closely resembling it, appears in the Knickerbockers' club books, but no candidate with those precise initials has been identified. Possibly the man in question was Samuel H. Parisen (born April 19, 1836; died August 25, 1915), a Civil War veteran from New Jersey.

Otto William Parisen, Jr.: Otto W. Parisen was a club member in 1854 and likely played in the July 5, 1853, contest that was the first Knickerbocker game recorded by the press, although this could conceivably be the other club member with the same surname. Parisen was born in New York around 1825 and lost his father and namesake when he was an infant. The 1847 New York City directory finds him working as a dancing master. He married in 1853, apparently for the second time, and by this time had settled in Hoboken, though he continued to work in New York City as a bookkeeper. He was

also active in Hoboken's Highwood Guard during these years. Sensing that civil war was inevitable, Parisen helped to organize a company of Zouaves in New York City in 1860. When the Civil War did indeed break out in April 1861, "Hawkins' Zouaves" was formed and officially sworn into service on May 4 as the 9th New York Volunteer Infantry. Parisen became a captain in Company C. After seeing combat duty in at least half a dozen battles, he was wounded in the knee at Antietam and had to be hospitalized.[192] Eventually he was sent home to recuperate and, while there, his proud comrades in the Highwood Guard presented him with "a gold medal ... which represents a Shield, [and] is of massive gold, surmounted by an American eagle. On one side is the following inscription: 'Highwood Guard to Captain Otto W. Parisen, esteemed as our Orderly Sergeant, a valorous and chivalric soldier, Captain Company C, New York Ninth regiment Volunteers.' On the reverse side were inscribed the names of the various battles he was engaged in, which are the following: Hatteras, Roanoke, Winton, Camden, Gatesville, South Mountain, and Antietam. Captain Parisen is now home on account of ill health, he having been confined to the hospital ever since the battle of Antietam. He has borne the reputation of being one of the best officers in the regiment, and he will soon return to again add his weight in the defense of the Union and the constitution."[193] Parisen indeed soon rejoined the 9th Regiment and participated in several more battles before being mustered out in May 1863. He then re-enlisted in the 122nd New York Infantry and served as a first lieutenant until the end of the war. Intriguingly, Parisen was stationed in Johnson's Island, Ohio, in March 1864, just four months before Ohio's earliest recorded New York-rules match game was played there in July, though there is no evidence that he played any role in it.[194] Less than five years after completing his Civil War service, Parisen died suddenly at his Hoboken home.[195]

Paulding: A man with this surname took part in two of the Knickerbockers' 1846 games, and the umpire's signature line for one of those games bears the name "J. Paulding." That suggests that this Knickerbocker was John Paulding, a lawyer and a Kings County delegate to the 1862 New York State Democratic convention who died at his home in Gravesend, Long Island, on April 8, 1871, age 52.[196]

Charles H. Peirson: Charles H. Peirson, often spelled as Pierson, is believed to have been a man by that name who began a long and successful partnership with John A. Ubsdell in 1837 by opening a dry-goods firm at the corner of Canal and Mercer Streets. Born in England around 1812, Peirson married an American and became a U.S. citizen in 1844. In 1849 Ubsdell, Peirson & Company opened a St. Louis branch, which eventually became a successful business in its own right. In an intriguing coincidence, the employees of this firm formed one of St. Louis's pioneer ball clubs. New Yorker Merritt Griswold moved to St. Louis shortly before the Civil War and taught the Knickerbockers' version of baseball to members of the townball-playing Morning Star Club. As Jeffrey Kittel reported in an entry in the first volume of this book, the Morning Star Club went on to play two of the earliest match games in St. Louis baseball history. Seven of the 14 known members of the club worked for Ubsdell, Peirson & Co. as clerks, salesmen, or cashiers.[197] As for Charles Peirson, he sold his share in the business in 1864 and eventually returned to England. He died in East Grimstead, Sussex, on June 24, 1880.[198]

Eugene Plunkett: Eugene Plunkett was elected secretary of the Knickerbocker Club in 1848 and served as an officer for the next five years. Born around 1820 in New York, he was the vice president of the Excelsior Fire Insurance Company. Two years later, Plunkett ascended to the company's presidency.[199] By the time the 1870 census was taken, Plunkett was living in South Orange, New Jersey, and had amassed a wealth of $30,000 in real estate and $20,000 in personal property. Plunkett died in San Antonio, Texas, on December 7, 1883.[200]

Purdy: At least one and perhaps two men with this surname were members of the club. R.F. Purdy, described as being 56, was one of the participants in the 1875 Davis 25th anniversary game, playing on the same side as Daniel Adams, William H. Tucker, William Avery, and other grizzled veterans.[201] Five years later, Richard F. Purdy's death warranted an obituary in the *Clipper* and a mention of his association with the Knickerbocker Club.[202] So there can be little doubt that this Purdy, a clothier who died on June 12, 1880, was a club member. Henry Chadwick, however, reported that "Dr. James R. Purdy" was a club member. He undoubtedly meant Dr. James W. Purdy, a physician who died in Brooklyn on June 20, 1908, at the age of 76. It is certainly possible that he too was a club member, though there is no other evidence that such was the case.

Charles A. Righter, Jr.: Charles A. Righter, Jr., who was born around 1839, served as the secretary of the Knickerbocker Club in 1866. During the Civil War, Righter procured a draft substitute and instead took part in the United States Christian Commission, doing humanitarian work in Petersburg and City Point, Virginia.[203] Righter was also the corresponding secretary of the Brooklyn Young Men's Christian Association and became its acting president in 1864. Employed by George A. Clark & Bro. of New York, Righter became a "familiar figure in the importing and jobbing trade" of the city and also made frequent trips to Europe. In addition, he remained active in the New York social scene, being described in an obituary as having been "one of the originators of the social organization now known on the Hill as 'The Park Club,' a member of Altair Lodge, F. and A.M., the American Model Yacht Club, the old time Knickerbocker Base Ball Club and the Consolidated Stock and Petroleum Exchanges of New York." Righter died in March of 1888.[204]

Rutherford: A man with this surname was a club member. Lacking a first name, we can only make an educated guess that he may have been an attorney named Walter Rutherford who practiced on Nassau Street and lived in Hudson County, New Jersey. Walter Rutherford was 55 when he died in Newark on January 10, 1868. Two of his sons later formed the Broad Street brokerage firm of John A. Rutherford & Co.[205]

John Simpkins: The Knickerbocker by this name is presumed to be a Wall Street stockbroker who was born in Yarmouth, Massachusetts, on February 18, 1831, the son of Nathaniel Stone Simpkins, Sr., longtime editor of the *Barnstable Journal* and the *Yarmouth Register*. Simpkins was only 39 when he died in Brooklyn on November 6, 1870.[206] Despite his early death, Simpkins and his brother Nathaniel, Jr. also a Wall Street stockbroker, had made a small fortune as the selling agents for the Calumet and Hecla Mining Company. He was survived by a wife and a large number of children, including John Simpkins, Jr., (1862–1898), a congressman from Cape Cod.[207]

Alonzo Slote: Alonzo Slote was vice president of the Knickerbockers in 1862 and '63. He may have been the Slote brother who played for the first nine in 1868, but we don't know which one is in the box score. Born on the corner of Orchard and Broome Streets, in New York's Tenth Ward, on September 13, 1830, Slote was the son of Daniel Slote, Sr., a well-known New York City merchant. He began his career as a clerk for his uncle and risked his uncle's disapproval in 1851 by joining his older brother Daniel Slote, Jr., as a member of Oceana Hose Company No. 36. (Daniel Slote, Jr., later became famous for being Mark Twain's roommate on a tour of Europe and the Holy Land and providing the basis for one of the characters in Twain's *The Innocents Abroad*, the "one who was frankly American, and saw no good in anything unless it was useful according to his own standards.")[208] The Oceana was made up primarily of merchants and their clerks and earned a reputation as the "dudes" of the volunteer fire department, with some of their jealous rivals sarcastically referring to them as "the quills." Other members included Knickerbockers William A. Woodhull and James Whyte Davis. Slote continued his involvement with the hose company for 11 years and later had very fond memories of those days. "We did everything up in style regardless," he recalled, "on the principle that what was worth doing at all was worth doing well. At a parade we sought to excel, and we contended in a manly way for superiority in the line of duty. I liked the business. Even now I am full of it. Afraid that I might miss a fire I would not leave the hose house evenings to go to the theater or other place of amusement. Yet I never missed a day from business. I was a fireman in opposition to my uncle's wishes — in whose house I was a clerk — and my pride would not allow me to offer fire duty as an excuse for absence from business. I was enthusiastic and liked to be where the pipe was — nearest the fire, where the hardest work was."[209] Despite his uncle's concerns, Alonzo Slote had a very successful career as a partner in the clothing firm of Tredwell, Slote & Co., located at the corner of Broadway and Chambers Street. His business partner, Alanson Tredwell, had also been a member of the Oceana Hose Company. Slote had many other business interests, serving as president of the Coney Island Elevated Railway Company, vice president of the Wallabout Bank, a trustee of the People's Trust Company, and a director of the Brooklyn Insurance Company and several other businesses.[210] He died in Lake George, New York, on July 29, 1901.[211] His mother had died only six months earlier at the age of 100—born in County Armagh, Ireland, in the final year of the 18th century, she had lived long enough to witness the dawn of the 20th century.[212]

Henry L. Slote: Alonzo Slote's brother Henry was also a club member, though his involvement does not appear to have been extensive. It is conceivable that he was the Slote who played for the first nine in 1868, but since he was older than Alonzo, it is more likely that the 1868 player was a third brother. Henry L. Slote was born in November 1825 and served as a volunteer fireman before beginning a successful career as a Manhattan stationer in 1854. Slote died in Brooklyn on January 21, 1906, and is buried at Green-Wood Cemetery, as are his brother Alonzo and many other family members.

D.D. Smith: Club member D.D. Smith, who umpired a game on October 17, 1845, is presumed to be Daniel Drake Smith. Born in New York City on August 29, 1818, Smith began his career at the age of 14 in the Beaver Street dry-goods firm Babcock & Suydam. In 1838 he took a job as a clerk for the Atlantic Mutual Insurance Company, beginning a long career in the insurance business. His expertise in underwriting became well known throughout the city and by 1852 he was a trustee of the Republic Fire Insurance Company, of which fellow Knickerbocker Duncan F. Curry was the secretary.[213] In that same year, Smith became the president of the newly formed Commercial Mutual Insurance Company, a position he held until his retirement in 1879. During those years, he also "took an active part in every movement that concerned the welfare" of New York City, serving on the Chamber of Commerce, as a director of the Bank of the State of New York, and as president of the Marine Board of Underwriters and the Rapid Transit Commission. Smith died at his home in Englewood, New Jersey, on February 8, 1887, and was remembered as "one of the fast-disappearing types of the grand old-fashioned gentleman."[214]

Smith(s): At least one additional man named Smith was involved with the Knickerbockers, perhaps more. Henry Chadwick compiled a list of Knickerbockers in 1903 that included "I.C. Smith," described as being affiliated with the Bank of Commerce along with Samuel H. Kissam. No doubt he meant J. Connor Smith, who was born in New York in June of 1825 and began working for the Phoenix Bank in 1844. He went to California with the '49ers but returned to New York in 1855 and began a long career as the general bookkeeper of the Metropolitan National Bank.[215] By 1875, he was living in New Jersey and was also treasurer of the city of Bergen.[216] Smith eventually returned to Manhattan and continued to work for the

Metropolitan National Bank until his death on November 22, 1900. An obituary in the *New York Times* described him as the "oldest banking officer in point of service in the United States."[217] J. Connor Smith is buried at Green-Wood Cemetery.

Daniel Stan(s)bury: On March 7, 1857, shortly after the formation of the National Association of Base Ball Players, the Knickerbockers adopted the bylaws of the convention but decided to use the new playing rules only when playing matches against other clubs. At a follow-up meeting one week later, a member named Daniel Stansbury earned his place in club lore by moving that the Knickerbockers play no more matches with other clubs. His motion was tabled and Stansbury played at least one game for the Knickerbockers' first nine that year. Identifying this opponent of change, however, is surprisingly difficult. New York City directories of the 1830s listed both a Daniel Stansbury and a Daniel Stanbury, both successful businessmen but unquestionably different people despite their nearly identical names. Daniel Stansbury does not appear to have had a namesake and the name Daniel Stansbury disappears from the city directory in the early 1840s. Daniel Stanbury did have a namesake, however, and his son's 1826 year of birth makes him a strong candidate to have been the Knickerbocker. When he died in Manhattan on September 5, 1895, an obituary reported that, "Mr. Stanbury was a member of an old New York family. His father and grandfather were born in this city. Forty years ago he was engaged in the wholesale grocery business with John Fox under the firm name of Stanbury & Fox. He held a responsible post in the Tax Department when his brother-in-law, Congressman John Wheeler, was President of the Board of Tax Commissioners. Mr. Stanbury was a bachelor."[218] It seems likely that Daniel Stanbury was the Knickerbocker.

John Stanton: One of the players in the 1875 game to celebrate James Whyte Davis's anniversary was identified as John Stanton, age 44.[219] It is likely that he was a man born in England on February 25, 1830 who, like John Simpkins, became associated with the development of a very successful copper mining company in Michigan's Upper Peninsula. John Stanton was still affiliated with the Three Lake Copper Mining Company when he died in Manhattan on February 23, 1906.

Richard Fowler Stevens: See Equity Base Ball Club.

John G. Storm: Club member John G. Storm was president of the Lenox Fire Insurance Company during the 1850s. He was only 38 when he died on February 6, 1863.[220]

Lambert Suydam, Jr.: Club member Lambert Suydam, Jr., a "descendant of the oldest Knickerbocker families," was born "in the family homestead on Broome Street, then part of the fashionable residence section of old New York," around 1829.[221] He went to Sacramento with the Gold Rush of 1849 along with his older brother James. While in Sacramento, he advertised for sale a "dysentery cordial" known as "Cherry Bounce," which was said to be "a preventative, as well as a cure, for the diseases incident to this climate."[222] Upon his return to New York in 1852, he went into real estate and became very prosperous. Suydam, who never married, died on January 18, 1916, at the age of 86, and is buried at Green-Wood Cemetery.[223]

Talmadge: We have no first name for this club member, so can only make educated guesses. One intriguing possibility is Thomas Goyn Talmadge (1801–1863), a New York state assemblyman, county judge, president of the Broadway Railroad Company, and mayor of Brooklyn in 1845. If so, it's safe to assume that he had little time to devote to the Knickerbocker Club. Early club member James Moncrief was the law partner of Daniel B. Tallmadge (1793–1847), so Tallmadge and members of his family are also possibilities. There are several other men named Talmadge or Talmage in New York at the time who also might be the club member in question.

Edward W. Talman: Edward W. Talman was vice president of the Knickerbocker Club in 1849 and its president one year later. Born on December 17, 1810, Talman spent most of his working life in the vicinity of Wall Street as a bank teller or clerk. As of 1873, he was affiliated with the Empire City Fire Insurance Company, 102 Broadway. Talman was related by marriage to the Audubons and spent his final years at Audubon Park, which is where he died on January 13, 1878.[224]

William L. Talman: Edward Talman's brother William was a club director in 1851 and took part in one of the club's married/single games three years later. Born around 1820, William L. Talman married into the Van Nortwick family in 1844 and by that same year was employed as a custom-house broker. He later worked as the paying teller of the Continental Bank and formed a short-lived brokerage with fellow Knickerbockers William H. Grenelle and Edward A. Bibby. He died on July 8, 1876, and is buried at Green-Wood Cemetery.[225]

Asa Potter Taylor: Born in South Kingstown, Rhode Island, on March 7, 1822, early club member Asa P. Taylor graduated from Brown University and in 1845 began a law practice at 7 Nassau Street. He was only 35 when he died at his home in Jersey City on January 12, 1858.[226]

William Lamont Taylor: William L. Taylor was treasurer of the Knickerbocker Club for two years beginning in 1863 and then served for two more years as club president. Born in New York City on September 22, 1825, to Scottish immigrants, William L. Taylor joined his brothers, Alexander and Peter B. Taylor, to form the Wall Street banking and brokerage firm of Taylor Brothers in the 1840s. He spent long enough on Wall Street eventually to form a brokerage with one of his sons and to earn recognition as the oldest living member of the Stock Exchange. Taylor died in Manhattan on March 23, 1900, at the age of 74.[227]

Henry A. Thomas: Henry A. Thomas was the club treasurer in 1861. His identity cannot be determined with certainty, but it seems likely that the Knickerbocker was a broker by that name who was born in 1832 and later worked as a merchant.

This man was living in Jersey City when the 1900 census was taken but died the following year and is buried at Green-Wood Cemetery.

Austin D. Thompson: See New York Base Ball Club (a.k.a. Washington BBC, Gotham BBC).

Thorne: A man with this surname umpired one of the club's 1845 games and participated in another. His initials in the club book appear to be "W.L." but no plausible candidate with those initials can be found, so it is more likely that the "L" was in fact a script "S" and that the member was William S. Thorne, a broker and the longtime president of the National Fire Insurance Company. William S. Thorne died on April 19, 1869, at the age of 59.[228]

Cadwallader Gilbert Colden Tracy: The name of G. Colden Tracy appears on the club's membership role in 1854 and this has to be a man whose full name was Cadwallader Gilbert Colden Tracy but who frequently dispensed with one or more of his given names. The surplus of names reflected a distinguished heritage. His paternal grandfather, Uriah Tracy (1755–1807), was a U.S. senator from Connecticut during George Washington's administration and one of the president's personal friends. On his mother's side, he was a descendant of Cadwallader Colden (1688–1776), lieutenant governor of the Province of New York in the years immediately preceding the American Revolution. Born around 1830, Colden Tracy worked in Manhattan as a broker during the years that he was a member of the Knickerbocker Club. In 1860, he married a South Carolinian named Harriet Ruth Brisbane. Two years later, with the birth of his first child imminent, Tracy was arrested and charged with complicity in fraud against the government, then taken to Washington as a prisoner. The details of the case were shrouded in mystery but press coverage gave the impression that, with the country in the midst of civil war, a charge of treason was at least under consideration. Tracy's first cousin, a judge named George Gould, was outraged by the proceedings and wrote an angry letter to President Lincoln that was later reprinted in the press. "The young man is the grandson of that Uriah Tracy, who lived and died a Senator of the United States, from Connecticut; who was the first man buried in the Congressional burying-ground at Washington; and whose ashes are insulted, by this atrocious invasion of the liberties of the people, in the person of his grandson," declared Judge Gould. "We know, and we acknowledge, the rules of war, where the necessity of the case requires the existence of martial law. But we know also the common law of liberty, and the broad, great charter of the Constitution."[229] Press coverage ended there, suggesting that the charges were quietly dropped. Yet it seems a safe assumption that the Tracys didn't find the episode as easy to forget, and perhaps it played a role in their decision to spend much of the remainder of their lives in Europe. At any rate, they never lost their love of their native land. When Harriet Tracy died in Isleworth, Middlesex County, England, on May 30, 1918, an obituary reported that "Mrs. Tracy was indirectly a victim of the war, her house in London having been damaged in the March raid and despite wonderful fortitude and self-control, the shock and exposure to cold hastened her end. She was an intensely loyal American and at the memorial service held at Isleworth on June 1 her body was surrounded by her beloved soldiers and sailors of the United States army and navy to whom her house was ever open, and the coffin was covered by them with the American flag, so dear to her heart."[230] She was survived by her husband, who appears to have been the last living member of the Knickerbocker Club. One family genealogy indicates that he died in 1924, but provides no details. Another one reports that he died in Paddington, England, on October 6, 1921, which fits the documented record of a Cadwallader C. Tracy dying in that place in the last quarter of that year.[231]

Tryon/Tyron/Tyson: In 1845 and 1846 a man with this surname was active in the Knickerbocker Club, taking part in several contests, including the match played against the New York Club at Hoboken on June 19, 1846. Then in 1854, the name Frank W. Tryon appears on the club's membership rolls and he plays on the single side in a married/single game. While it has generally been assumed that these two men are one and the same, the evidence suggests otherwise. Francis W. Tryon, the 1854 club member, was born around 1830 and during the 1850s was living in Hoboken and working in Manhattan. On July 7, 1857, he married Lelia Clark, but she died only two days after their first wedding anniversary. At the outbreak of the Civil War, Tryon enlisted as a sergeant in the 83rd New York Infantry Regiment, where he earned a promotion to full lieutenant and a transfer to the 51st New York Infantry. One of the soldiers under his command was George Washington Whitman, brother of poet Walt Whitman.[232] After the war Tryon remarried and returned to working as a commission merchant and later as a clerk. In the mid–1890s, suffering from rheumatism, heart disease and the effects of a bullet wound, Tryon was admitted to a veterans home and spent more than 20 years in a variety of veterans homes. He died at a home in Bath, New York, on May 19, 1918, and is buried in Bath National Cemetery. Yet while Frank Tryon's long life makes him one of the last surviving Knickerbockers, he is too young to be a plausible candidate to have been the 1845–46 club member. Harold Peterson concluded that the earlier player was Daniel Tryon, a merchant who was born around 1804 and who died in Brooklyn on November 15, 1861.[233] This is certainly possible, but he is a bit older than might be expected and there is no conclusive evidence of his membership. A better bet would be William Tyson, also listed as Tyron, proprietor of an omnibus line named the Telegraph Line that employed 40 men in 1850. Tyson had been nominated for the State Assembly in 1846 by the Whig party. His company was linked with the great Kipp & Brown Stage Line.

Abraham W. Tucker: See New York Base Ball Club (a.k.a. Washington BBC, Gotham BBC).

William H. Tucker: See New York Base Ball Club (a.k.a. Washington BBC, Gotham BBC).

Francis H. Turk: Frank Turk began playing in the Knickerbockers' intrasquad games in the fall of 1845. He did not take part in the historic match game versus the New York Club on June 19, 1846, but did play in the fun contest that followed. He was born in Stamford, Connecticut. There is conflicting information about his date of birth but it seems most likely that he was born around 1817. By the 1840s he was working in New York City as a post-office clerk and studying the law. In early 1849 fellow New Yorker John W. Geary was appointed San Francisco's postmaster and Turk was named his assistant. The two men traveled to their new home by way of Mexico, arriving in San Francisco on the U.S. revenue cutter *Edith* on May 29, 1849.[234] By that summer, Turk had resigned his position at the post office and advertisements began to appear in the *Alta California* for the services of "Frank Turk: Attorney At Law, Parker House."[235] Soon he was making a name for himself by prosecuting a gang of thugs who had been terrorizing the city. On August 1, 1849, while the trials were still in progress, Turk was elected second alcalde of San Francisco, essentially the vice mayor, while Geary was elected alcalde, or mayor. Turk was the acting alcalde on at least one occasion when Geary was out of town.[236] Over the next 15 years Turk formed law practices with several different partners and amassed significant landholdings that included most of Nob Hill and a ranch in San Mateo County. He also briefly renewed his interest in baseball, being elected to the Committee on By Laws of the Knickerbocker Club of San Francisco on January, 6, 1851.[237] Around the end of the Civil War, Turk relocated to Washington, D.C., where he continued to practice law. In 1879, with his health failing and his fortunes in severe decline, he returned to San Francisco. Frank Turk, who never married, died at the city's almshouse on July 15, 1887. San Francisco's Turk Street is named in his honor.[238]

Turney: A man with this surname took part in the Knickerbockers' June 19, 1846, game against the New York Club. His first name is unknown, but there's a reasonable chance that he was James Turney, Jr., a member of a family of printers and stereotypers who printed one of the first American editions of Charles Dickens's *The Pickwick Papers*. Born around 1814, Turney died in Brooklyn on January 27, 1895.

William A. Tyson: Club member William A. Tyson cannot be identified with any confidence. The best-known New Yorker by that name was an African American who was born in the late 1790s and who was prominent in the crusade against slavery. It's conceivable that the Knickerbockers granted him an honorary membership — he was a cook, like Fijux — but it doesn't seem very likely. A more promising candidate is another William A. Tyson who was born around 1828 and was the son of a New York City leather merchant.

James Everett Vail: A man named James E. Vail was club secretary in 1865–66 and in one of those years his name is listed as James E. Vail, Jr. He is not to be confused with W. Vail, who was prominent in the doings of the Knickerbocker and New York clubs two decades earlier. The club secretary pretty much has to be James Everett Vail, who was born in June of 1834. Despite the fact that "Jr." was sometimes appended to his name, he was the son of Henry Vail, president of the Bank of Commerce — he had an uncle named James E. Vail and the "Jr." was apparently used to avoid confusion, even appearing in one of his father's obituaries.[239] In 1858 Vail married Redelia Brainard, sister of Asa Brainard, the pitcher of the 1869 Red Stockings of Cincinnati, and the two men were neighbors in Brooklyn's Tenth Ward on the 1860 census. Vail was then just getting started in his professional career, but he soon became a prominent manufacturer's agent and commission merchant in Manhattan's dry-goods district. He also was a familiar figure in Brooklyn's social circles, where he lived for much of his life. James E. Vail died at his daughter's home in Manhattan on January 19, 1907.[240]

William Vail: See New York Base Ball Club (a.k.a. Washington BBC, Gotham BBC).

Van Nortwick: A man with this surname makes several appearances in the Knickerbockers' annals and then appears as a guest player in a game on October 24, 1845. Harold Peterson identifies this member as William Van Nortwick, a Manhattan merchant.[241] It's very plausible that this man, whose middle name was Bruce, was a club member, since his daughter married Knickerbocker William L. Talman in 1844. But since he was born in 1775, it seems unlikely that he took part in an 1845 game, leaving the identity of that man a mystery.

Alfred Vredenburgh: Alfred Vredenburgh was the club's vice president in 1858 and that year was instrumental in reaching a compromise by which the Knickerbockers used the bound rule against other clubs but the fly rule in their own games.[242] He also played for the first nine in 1857 and 1858. The "scion of a prominent Knickerbocker family," Vredenburgh was born in New York City on October 16, 1823, and belonged to the city's volunteer fire department. He spent 35 years as deputy receiver or chief clerk of the New York City tax bureau. Vredenburgh died in Bayonne, New Jersey, on October 11, 1892.[243]

Lewis/Louis F. Wadsworth: See New York Base Ball Club (a.k.a. Washington BBC, Gotham BBC).

Waller: A man with this surname appears in several of the Knickerbockers' games between 1845 and 1853 and one notation in the club's record appears to give his first initial as "G." But no strong candidate with that first initial has been identified, suggesting that the Knickerbocker may have had a first name beginning with another letter. There are quite a few such candidates.

Norman M. Welling: Norman M. Welling was a club director in 1858 and in that year he nominated Harry Wright for membership. He was also one of the mainstays of the first nine before the war, playing second base, outfield, and pitcher. In 1887 a club member recalled that Welling "kept the club house at the Elysian Fields. He was afterward a partner of Tom Hyer and is now chief caterer at old Glass's Prospect House."[244] Obviously word had not reached this member of Welling's death, which had occurred on January 1, 1885, in Gravesend (which is now part of Brooklyn). Welling was 53.[245]

James Fowler Wenman: James F. Wenman may have been the most representative Knickerbocker of them all. Born on March 7, 1824, in Manhattan — "at Fulton and Church streets in the days when Canal street was regarded as the end of the city" — he was the son of Uzziah Wenman and the former Anne Fowler.[246] His father soon became the chief engineer of the volunteer fire department, so James's boyhood was immersed in the world of the fire engine. As an infant, he paid daily visits to the firehouse of Franklin Engine Company 39 and one of his earliest recollections was of wearing a fire cap and sitting on the front box of the engine as he was given instructions about how to give orders through the trumpet. During New York's Great Fire of 1835, James's father spent three days leading the firefighting efforts and was credited with a major role in saving the building that housed the Bank of America. Upon his return home, however, Uzziah Wenman was furious when he learned that young James and one of his brothers had been out all night watching the blaze and had nearly frozen to death. At the age of 14, James became a member of Victory Hose Company No. 15 and he subsequently served in Hose Companies 5, 19, and 35, and Engine 38. He was credited with saving lives during the Kipp & Brown blaze of 1848 and the W.T. Jennings & Co. fire of 1854.[247] Wenman later looked back on his years as a volunteer firefighter as "the happiest days I ever spent in my life."[248] It was also during this period that Wenman joined the Knickerbocker Base Ball Club. The extent of his involvement is difficult to be sure of, and he was either greatly exaggerating or pulling the reporter's leg when he later claimed to have "organized a nine called the Knickerbocker Club" and to have made a spectacular game-saving catch in a game against the Excelsiors.[249] Yet he certainly was a club member and no doubt there is some truth in his later recollections about playing shortstop for the club at the Elysian Fields. The later claim that Wenman "put the base in base ball" was undoubtedly another exaggeration, but perhaps the 5-foot-4 ballplayer did help put the short in shortstop.[250] Wenman also served in the 7th Regiment of the state guard, along with several other Knickerbockers, and was active in the Masons and numerous civic organizations. He remained especially active in the Veteran Firemen's Association and in 1885 was presented with an oil painting of himself in tribute to his many years of service.[251] But all of these were avocations and he also found plenty of time to pursue a successful vocation. At the age of 13 he became a clerk in the office of Thomas Stewart, a cotton broker with an office at the corner of Wall and Water Streets. In time he took over the business and then founded the New York Board of Cotton Brokers in 1861, which subsequently became the Cotton Exchange. Eventually the "father of the Cotton Exchange" became "known to every banker, broker, policeman, and messenger boy in the vicinity of the New York Cotton Exchange as 'Old Captain Wenman.'"[252] In addition, Wenman served as president of New York City's Department of Public Parks in the late 1870s, a demanding position in which he attracted his share of critics.[253] A man who started work at such a young age might be expected to retire as soon as possible, but Wenman was still reporting to work at the Cotton Exchange three-quarters of a century after being hired as a clerk (though by then he was taking the afternoon off if the Giants were playing a home game). "I have been in the vicinity of Old Slip for seventy-two years," he reminisced. "From the window of this little office I have watched the old sailing ships come up this street and depart again, but now the street is filled in and the river is two blocks away. They are running up a skyscraper across the way, and down at the corner the subway workers are digging a tube to Brooklyn. It was a beautiful scene from here fifty years ago to see the sunlight playing on the water, and the ships under full sail." Wenman also had many fond memories of his days on the baseball diamond; the wall over his desk featured "a painting much the worse for age, but treasured as if it were a government bond" depicting a scene at the Elysian Fields. "Grouped under the elm trees are eighteen players ranging in age all the way from nineteen to forty. In the distance the Hudson River sparkles in the sunshine, a fitting background to a memorable scene." Wenman's souvenirs of his ballplaying days also included a set of twisted fingers that he proudly displayed as proof of his claim that "there is nothing hard about baseball as they play it now. Seventy years ago we had no gloves, masks, chest protectors or shin guards."[254] In 1915 New York City's paid fire department celebrated its 50th anniversary and Wenman, "the 'living link' between the old volunteer fire department and the first organized paid department," led the parade.[255] Even at that advanced age, Wenman kept up a pace that astonished younger men. "There is no denying the fact that the Captain looks the picture of good health," marveled one reporter. "His blue eyes are as clear and bright as those of a man of sixty, he walks erect and fairly bubbles over with good humor and optimism, although his hair and Van Dyke beard are a silvery white."[256] Wenman celebrated his 93rd birthday in 1917 by making plans to "take a long walk, or go to a dance, or do something else to prove that years mean nothing whatever in his life. Captain Jimmy — he hasn't been called anything else in years — is almost as spry as he was in the old days when he played shortstop on New York's first ball club."[257] As late as 1919, the old shortstop remained in such robust health that amazed onlookers saw him "literally skipping across Beaver street to avoid an oncoming automobile. Knowing his age, we congratulated him on his activity and he answered, 'Men are only old when they admit it.'"[258] He again marched in several parades that year, including leading "a parade of the Exempt Firemen's Association on a two mile hike on Washington's Birthday." After the excursion, Wenman "felt none the worse for it," though he did complain that his picture in the next day's paper "makes me look as if I were near a hundred."[259] The following month, he marched with his son and grandson in a parade to honor the 7th Regiment with "a step as spry as a man half his years."[260] But nobody goes on forever, and on May 29, 1919, James Fowler Wenman's long life came to an end.[261]

William Henry Westervelt: William H. Westervelt, an early club member, was born in New York City on October 25 or 26, 1822, the son of James W. Westervelt and the former Rachel Bogart/Bogert. As a young man he was a member of the Amity Hose Company. After beginning his career working for his uncle, a flour merchant, he joined the firm of Motz & Pollitz, a drug and general merchandise store that offered a wide range of imported medicinal products. He eventually became a junior partner in the firm, which became known as O.W. Pollitz & Co. In 1847, he married Susan M. Tallman and they named their first son Otto Wilhelm Pollitz Westervelt in honor of his partner. The partnership was dissolved in 1859 and Westervelt then opened a storage business on Beaver Street. Three years later Westervelt and his brother opened a business importing Mediterranean fruits that proved very successful. They eventually opened a branch store in New Orleans and, when it came time for Westervelt's brother to retire, his son Otto became his partner. William H. Westervelt died in East Orange, New Jersey, on April 2, 1891.[262]

William Rufus Wheaton: See New York Base Ball Club (a.k.a. Washington BBC, Gotham BBC).

A.H. Winslow: A.H. Winslow was nominated for club membership by Charles De Bost and elected on April 1, 1854. He played with the Knickerbockers against the Gotham Club in a game on October 26, 1854, but he was not present at roll call after May 10, 1855, and his name was erased. He is believed to be Albert H. Winslow, Jr., who was born in New York City in 1828, the son of a grocer. By 1860, he was married and living in Branford, Connecticut, which explains why his name was erased from the club's rolls. Frequent references to him as Colonel Winslow indicate that he served in the Civil War, but a matching service record has not been located. Winslow died of typhoid pneumonia in Manhattan on December 30, 1874, and is buried in Branford.[263]

William A. Woodhull: William A. Woodhull was the treasurer of the Knickerbocker Club in 1857 and 1858. Born in 1826, Woodhull joined First Ward Hose Company No. 8 in 1847. After 3½ years, he switched to the Oceana Hose Company, joining Knickerbockers Alonzo Slote and James Whyte Davis. After three years as foreman Woodhull resigned to become secretary of the volunteer fire department, at which point his colleagues in the Oceana Hose Company presented him with an inscribed rosewood bookcase.[264] Woodhull's father had established a wholesale grocery store at 207 Front Street early in the century. It was passed down to Woodhull and two of his brothers, who turned it into a local landmark that remained in the family until close to the end of the century. William A. Woodhull died at Roosevelt Hospital on January 11, 1904, and was remembered as "one of the few surviving members of the old Volunteer Fire Department."[265]

Harry Wright: See the entries for the New York Base Ball Club (in this volume) and the Cincinnati Base Ball Club (in *Base Ball Pioneers, 1850–1870*).

Sam Yates: See Eagle Base Ball Club.

Other Club Members: Arthur, Benson, Churchill, Coe, De Mott, Dillon, Greenleaf, Hatfield, Homans, A. and B. Kirkland, John Lalor (of the New York Base Ball Club), Marshall, Moore, Morrow, Robinson, Rogers, Schack, Stephens, Van Zandt, Walston, Watson, Wood.

Notes

1. Mills to Sullivan, December 30, 1907. This letter was published in the 1908 *Spalding Guide* under the heading "Final Decision of the Special Base Ball Commission," 45–48.

2. Charles A. Peverelly, *The Book of American Pastimes, Containing a History of the Principal Base Ball, Cricket, Rowing, and Yachting Clubs of the United States* (New York: Published by the Author, 1866), 340.

3. "Sporting Intelligence," *New York Herald*, November 11, 1845, 2.

4. "How Baseball Began: A Member of the Gotham Club of Fifty Years Ago Tells About It," *San Francisco Daily Examiner*, November 27, 1887, 14.

5. This assertion is supported by a complete review of each game played by the Knickerbocker Base Ball Club of New York, 1845–1854. Albert Spalding Baseball Collections, Knickerbocker Base Ball Club of New York Game Books, October 6, 1845–1856, New York Public Library.

6. "Dr. D. L. Adams; Memoirs of the Father of Base Ball; He Resides in New Haven and Retains an Interest in the Game," *The Sporting News*, February 29, 1896, 3. Thorn's extensive biography of Adams appeared as "The True Father of Baseball," first in *Elysian Fields Quarterly*, vol. 11, no. 1, (Winter 1992), 85–91, and then in several of the eight editions of the encyclopedia *Total Baseball* (eds. John Thorn, Pete Palmer, et al., various publishers, 1989–2004).

7. John Ward, *Base-Ball: How to Become a Player* (Philadelphia: Athletic Publishing Company, 1888), 24.

8. Monica Nucciarone, *Alexander Cartwright: The Life Behind the Baseball Legend* (Lincoln: University of Nebraska Press, 2009).

9. Knickerbocker Club Books, Minutes of May 21, 1857.

10. Knickerbocker Club Books, Minutes of March 14, 1857, and June 18, 1860.

11. Marshall D. Wright, *The National Association of Base Ball Players, 1857–1870* (Jefferson, N.C.: McFarland, 2000).

12. Knickerbocker Club Books, Minutes of April 4, 1857.

13. "Dr. D. L. Adams; Memoirs of the Father of Base Ball; He Resides in New Haven and Retains an Interest in the Game," *The Sporting News*, February 29, 1896, 3.

14. He resigned twice from the Knickerbocker Base Ball Club, only to rejoin the club within days. The third time he resigned it was for good. It was not uncommon for members of the Knickerbockers to tender their resignation in a moment of pique, and withdraw same when placated by their comrades. Albert Spalding Baseball Collections, Knickerbocker Base Ball Club of New York Club Books, 1854–1868, New York Public Library.

15. "City Intelligence," *New York Herald*, March 2, 1857, 8.

16. See the player profiles for a discussion of the correct spelling of the surname of Stansbury/Stanbury.

17. "Base Ball Convention," *New York Herald*, March 2, 1857; *Porter's Spirit of the Times*, March 7, 1857, 5.

18. Knickerbocker Club Books, Minutes of July 5, 1860.

19. Knickerbocker Club Books, Minutes of September 6, 1860.

20. Knickerbocker Club Books, Minutes of July 5, 1860.

21. Letter from Davis to Adams of April 4, 1862. This letter resides unremarked within a folder of 14 letters from the distinguished scholar Daniel Adams to his son, Daniel Lucius Adams, when the latter was a student at Yale, 1833–1835. Yale Miscellaneous Manuscripts Collection, Manuscripts and Archives, Yale University Library, Misc MSS A, Box 1, Folder 4.

22. The award was referenced in a report of the day's old-timers' game in "The Knickerbocker Club: Baseball in the Olden Time," *New York Clipper*, October 9, 1875 ("Then Mr. Taylor presented him with an elegant silver ball and two silver bats in morocco cases. The ball was inscribed… .").

23. *New York Sun*, July 27, 1893.

24. "Dr. D. L. Adams; Memoirs of the Father of Base Ball; He Resides in New Haven and Retains an Interest in the Game," *The Sporting News*, February 29, 1896, 3.

25. *Salt Lake Tribune*, April 2, 1905, 4.

26. "The Knickerbocker Club: Baseball in the Olden Time," *New York Clipper*, October 9, 1875, 221.

27. Harold Peterson, *The Man Who Invented Baseball* (New York: Scribner, 1973), 71–72.

28. Monica Nucciarone, *Alexander Cartwright*, 78.

29. *New York American*, September 18, 1832, 1.

30. *The British Journal of Photography*, September 26, 1884.

31. Louis J. Rasmussen, *San Francisco Ship Passenger Lists*, vol. 1 (Colma, CA: Louis J. Rasmussen, 1965; reprint Baltimore: Genealogical Publishing Co., 1978), 35.

32. Angus Macfarlane, "The Knickerbockers: San Francisco's First Baseball Team?" *Base Ball* 1:1 (Spring 2007), 14.

33. *Suffolk County News*, June 17, 1904.

34. For more on Avery's life, see J. M. Arms Sheldon, *Walter Titus Avery* (Greenfield, MA: T. Morey & Son, 1912), which is primarily devoted to the Avery genealogy.

35. *New York Tribune*, May 2, 1864, 5.

36. New York marriage record of Charles Belloni, brother of Louis, Jr.

37. *New York Herald*, February 24, 1909, 9.

38. *New York Times*, November 9, 1878.

39. The *New York Tribune, New York Herald, New York Sun* and *New York Times* all published similar obituaries on December 21, 1898.

40. *New York Times*, March 10, 1883; *New York Herald*, March 11, 1883, 11.

41. *New York Evening Post*, July 2, 1879.

42. *Geneva Gazette*, April 21, 1882.

43. *Harper's Weekly*, September 30, 1865, 610.

44. *New York Evening Telegram*, April 13, 1882, 5; *Geneva Gazette*, April 21, 1882.

45. *New York Times*, March 25, 1857.

46. *Poughkeepsie Eagle*, August 2, 1877.

47. *New York American*, September 18, 1832, 1.

48. *New York Times*, February 22, 1863.

49. Harold Peterson, *The Man Who Invented Baseball*, 72.

50. *New York Tribune*, March 3, 1903, 9.

51. *New York Evening Express*, May 9, 1874.

52. *Oswego Palladium*, May 17, 1922.

53. *New York Tribune*, March 3, 1903, 9.

54. *New York Sun*, January 16, 1887, 10.

55. *Albany Knickerbocker*, quoted in the *New York Herald*, March 15, 1858, 5.

56. *New York Herald*, March 11, 1858, 1.

57. *New York Times*, March 15, 1858.

58. *Albany Knickerbocker*, quoted in the *New York Herald*, March 15, 1858, 5.

59. *New York Evening Express*, March 11, 1858.

60. *New York Herald*, March 14, 1858, 8.

61. *New York Times*, August 3, 1861.

62. *New York Herald*, November 9, 1878.

63. *New York World*, December 21, 1895; *New York Times*, December 24, 1895.

64. *New York Times*, April 8, 1896; *New York Herald*, April 9, 1896, 7.

65. Harold Peterson, *The Man Who Invented Baseball*, 75.

66. Angus Macfarlane, "The Knickerbockers: San Francisco's First Baseball Team?" *Base Ball* 1:1 (Spring 2007), 12.

67. Monica Nucciarone, *Alexander Cartwright*, 48–49, 59, 136.

68. *New York Tribune*, December 18, 1843, italics in original.

69. *New York Herald*, January 31, 1869.

70. Sean Wilentz, *Chants Democratic: New York City and the Rise of the American Working Class, 1788–1850* (1984; reprint New York: Oxford University Press, 2004), 262.

71. *Irish American Weekly*, July 9, 1864.

72. Ibid.

73. *National Police Gazette*, September 11, 1880, 14.

74. Timothy J. Gilfoyle, *City of Eros: New York City, Prostitution, and the Commercialization of Sex, 1790–1920* (New York: W. W. Norton, 1992), 88; *National Police Gazette*, September 11, 1880, 14.

75. *New York Tribune*, October 28, 1858, 4.

76. *New York Herald*, January 6, 1857.

77. *New York Tribune*, October 28, 1858, 4.

78. *Irish American Weekly*, July 9, 1864.

79. *New York Tribune*, October 28, 1858, 4.

80. *New York Tribune*, February 19, 1857, 5.

81. J. Frank Kernan, *Reminiscences of the Old Fire Laddies and Volunteer Fire Departments of New York* (New York: M. Crane, 1885), 487; Patricia Cline Cohen, Timothy J. Gilfoyle, Helen Lefkowitz Horowitz, *The Flash Press: Sporting Male Weeklies in 1840s New York* (Chicago: University of Chicago Press, 2008), 112–113.

82. *New York Evening Express*, July 2, 1864; *Brooklyn Eagle*, July 2, 1864.

83. Harold Peterson, *The Man Who Invented Baseball*, 71–72.

84. *New York Evening Express*, September 8, 1868, 1.

85. Monica Nucciarone, *Alexander Cartwright*, 171–173.

86. *New York Herald*, April 19, 1894; *New York Tribune*, April 19, 1894; "Diamond Field Gossip," *New York Clipper*, April 28, 1894, 122; "The Obituary Record," *New York Times*, April 19, 1894, 2.

87. *Brooklyn Eagle*, August 3, 1889, 2.

88. *New York Sun*, January 16, 1887, 10.

89. "Dr. D. L. Adams; Memoirs of the Father of Base Ball; He Resides in New Haven and Retains an Interest in the Game," *The Sporting News*, February 29, 1896, 3.

90. *New York Sun*, January 16, 1876, 1.

91. *New York Clipper*, February 25, 1899, 882.

92. Ibid.

93. "Poor Old Davis," *New York Sun*, September 28, 1875, 1.

94. *New York Clipper*, October 28, 1880, 228.

95. *New York Sun*, July 27, 1893.

96. *New York Times*, February 17 and 18, 1899; Green-Wood Cemetery records.

97. *Spirit of the Times*, September 22, 1855.

98. *New York Atlas*, July 3, 1859, 5.

99. "Poor Old Davis," *New York Sun*, September 28, 1875, 1.

100. *New York Times*, January 21, 1909.

101. *New York Herald*, November 29, 1890.

102. Angus Macfarlane, "The Knickerbockers: San Francisco's First Baseball Team?" *Base Ball* 1:1 (Spring 2007), 10–12.

103. *New York Tribune*, August 16, 1886; *New York Tribune*, July 29, 1896.

104. *New York Herald* and *New York Times*, October 19, 1866.

105. George Washington Bungay, *Pen and Ink Portraits of the Senators, Assemblymen, and State Officers, of the State of New York* (Albany: J. Munsell, Printer, 1857), 23.

106. *New York Times*, October 14, 1865.

107. *New York Herald*, July 6, 1868.

108. *New York Evening Express*, March 3, 1860, 1.

109. *New York Sun*, January 16, 1887, 10.

110. *New York Herald*, March 19, 1885.

111. Milton C. Conner, M.D., "Memoir of William B. Eager, M.D.," *Transactions of the New York State Medical Association* (1891), 491.

112. *Boston Medical and Surgical Journal*, January 30, 1890, 120; *New York Times*, March 29, 1887; Milton C. Conner, M.D., "Memoir of William B. Eager, M.D.," *Transactions of the New York State Medical Association* (1891), 491.

113. Edward E. Steele, "The Ebbets Family of New York City," *New York Genealogical and Biographical Record* 132:92 (2001–2002).

114. "Call Comes for Pioneer A.M. Ebbets; Prominent Settler of Early Days Passes Away," *San Francisco Call*, May 6, 1903; Bailey Millard, *History of the San Francisco Bay Region* (Chicago: American Historical Society, 1924), vol. 3, 256–257; Finding Aid for Rosario Curletti Collection of A.M. Ebbets Papers, Huntington Digital Library, San Marino, California.

115. Frank Soulé, John H. Gihon, M.D., and James Nisbet, *The Annals of San Francisco* (San Francisco, 1855), 624.

116. *The Long Islander*, March 19, 1909, 1; Edward E. Steele, "The Ebbets Family of New York City," *New York Genealogical and Biographical Record* 132:92 (2001–2002).

117. *New York Herald*, June 21, 1886.

118. Harold Peterson, *The Man Who Invented Baseball*, 75.

119. *New York Times*, January 5, 1894.

120. *New York Times*, December 19, 1854, and April 7, 1855.

121. Peter Nash, *Baseball Legends of Brooklyn's Green-Wood Cemetery* (Charleston, S.C.: Arcadia, 2003), 29.

122. *New York Herald*, July 1, 1859.

123. *New York Times*, April 30, 1860.

124. *New York Times*, January 5, 1894.

125. *New York Tribune*, December 2, 1879.

126. "Veterans Done For," *Sporting Life*, January 20, 1899, 9.

127. *Spirit of the Times*, September 20, 1873.

128. *Syracuse Evening Telegram*, January 3, 1899, 1; *New York Times*, January 4, 1899; Weston Arthur Goodspeed, *History of the Goodspeed Family* (Chicago: Weston Arthur Goodspeed, 1907), 435.

129. *New York Tribune*, May 6, 1864, 5.

130. *Spirit of the Times*, December 6, 1856.

131. Henry Childs Merwin, *The Life of Bret Harte: With Some Account of the California Pioneers* (New York: Houghton Mifflin, 1911), 4–6. Bret Harte was the son of his father's first wife, a Christian, while David and all of his other children were the products of a second marriage to a Jewish woman.

132. *New York Herald*, January 4, 1888, 10.

133. *New York Herald*, September 22, 1872.

134. *New York Sun*, February 7, 1895, 2.

135. *New York Evening Post*, November 11, 1837.

136. William Richard Cutter and William Frederick Adams, eds., *Genealogical and Personal Memoirs Relating to the Families of the State of Massachusetts* (New York: Lewis Historical Publishing Company, 1910), vol. 2, 779–780.

137. *New York Evening Post*, November 21, 1892.

138. *New York Times*, September 7, 1915.

139. *Brooklyn Eagle*, March 28, 1889, 1.

140. Charles A. Peverelly, *The Book of American Pastimes*, 348.

141. John Thorn, *Treasures of the Baseball Hall of Fame: The Official Companion to the Collection at Cooperstown* (New York: Villard, 1998), 19.

142. Paul Cushman, Jr., "The Kissam Family: Its Importance in New

York Medicine," *Bulletin of the New York Academy of Medicine* 45:7 (July 1969), 689–701.

143. *New York Herald*, April 19, 1915, 7; *New York Times*, April 19, 1915; *Brooklyn Daily Eagle*, April 19, 1915, 3.

144. *New York Sun*, January 16, 1887, 10.

145. John Ward, *How to Become a Base-Ball Player* (New York, 1888), 13.

146. *New York Evening Post*, September 16, 1889, 8; *New York World*, September 15, 1889, 3.

147. *New York Evening Post*, July 27, 1859.

148. *New York Tribune*, March 24, 1882, 5; *New York Herald*, March 23, 1882, 5.

149. *New York Evening Post*, May 30, 1825.

150. *New Orleans Times Picayune*, November 11, 1853.

151. *Rockland County Journal*, September 12, 1868, 3.

152. *New York Tribune*, April 30, 1889.

153. "'Elysian Fields' of Years Ago," *New York Times*, February 17, 1895.

154. *New York Herald*, June 14, 1841.

155. Charles A. Peverelly, *The Book of American Pastimes*, 342, 345.

156. John Thorn, *Baseball in the Garden of Eden*, 98; *Trenton State Gazette*, May 28 and June 2, 1851.

157. *Brooklyn Eagle*, March 4, 1852.

158. *Brooklyn Eagle*, April 16, 1900.

159. *New York Herald*, March 27, 1918, 6.

160. *Base Ball at Harvard* (privately published by the 1903 Harvard baseball team), 6.

161. Quoted in Charles Moore, *The Life and Times of Charles Follen McKim* (Boston: Houghton Mifflin, 1929), 18–19.

162. Ibid., 20.

163. John Thorn, *Treasures of the Baseball Hall of Fame*, 18.

164. Ulysses S. Grant, *The Papers of Ulysses S. Grant: August 16–November 15, 1864*, vol. 12, ed. John Y. Simon (Carbondale: Southern Illinois University Press, 1984), 145.

165. *The National Cyclopaedia of American Biography*, vol. 12 (New York: James T. White & Co., 1904).

166. "Dr. D. L. Adams; Memoirs of the Father of Base Ball; He Resides in New Haven and Retains an Interest in the Game," *The Sporting News*, February 29, 1896, 3.

167. *New York Tribune*, February 4, 1870.

168. *New York Daily Reformer*, August 8, 1865.

169. *The American Phrenological Journal and Repository of Science* XXVIII: 5 (November 1858), 65.

170. *New York Clipper*, December 27, 1856, 282.

171. *New York Tribune*, June 7, 1865.

172. *New York Herald*, January 28, 1883, 14; *New York Truth*, January 28, 1883; *New York Sun*, January 28, 1883, 1.

173. *New York Herald*, March 30, 1861.

174. Joseph Alfred Scoville, *The Old Merchants of New York City, Volume 5* (New York, 1885), 190.

175. Ibid., 194–196.

176. *New York Herald*, February 10, 1857; *St. Paul Daily Pioneer*, March 2, 1857.

177. *Winona Daily Republican*, April 21, 1885, 3.

178. *New York Evening Post*, February 20, 1905, 1.

179. *Porter's Spirit of the Times*, November 8, 1856.

180. *Semi-Weekly Courier and New York Enquirer*, September 23, 1854; *New York Tribune*, September 20, 1854, 6; *New York Times*, September 20, 1854.

181. *New York Times*, December 12, 1901.

182. *New York Times*, November 26 and 30, 1858; *New York Commercial Advertiser*, November 16, 1858; *New York Herald*, July 22, 1859, 8.

183. *Report of the Comptroller of the City of New York for the Fiscal Year ending December 31, 1904*.

184. *New York Herald*, December 7, 1889.

185. "Dr. D. L. Adams; Memoirs of the Father of Base Ball; He Resides in New Haven and Retains an Interest in the Game," *The Sporting News*, February 29, 1896, 3.

186. *National Daily Base Ball Gazette*, April 24, 1887.

187. *New York Herald*, January 4, 1885.

188. *New York Times*, October 4, 1899; *New York Herald*, October 6, 1899, 16; "Mrs. Livermore Weds Baron Sellière," *New York Herald*, April 23, 1892, 4.

189. *Albany Evening Journal*, August 13 and 18, 1835; *Chittenango Herald*, November 24, 1835; *New York Evening Post*, August 14 and November 14, 1835.

190. Marian Campbell Gouverneur, *As I Remember: Recollections of American Society During the Nineteenth Century* (New York: D. Appleton, 1911), 371.

191. *New York Herald*, September 3, 1885; *New York Times*, September 3, 1885; "Hempstead Now and Then" blog, http://westhempstead-nowandthen.blogspot.com/2011/07/henry-m-onderdonk-editor-of-hempstead.html.

192. J.H.E. Whitney, *The Hawkins' Zouaves: (Ninth N. Y. V.) Their Battles and Marches* (New York, 1866), 198.

193. *New York Herald*, October 12, 1862, 2.

194. John Richmond Husman, "Ohio's First Baseball Game: Played by Confederates and Taught to Yankees" *Base Ball* 2:1 (Spring 2008), 58–65.

195. *Jersey Journal*, January 22, 1870; *New York Herald*, January 22, 1870.

196. *New York Herald*, April 10, 1871.

197. Alfred H. Spink, *The National Game* (1911; reprint Carbondale: South Illinois University Press, 2000), 406; *Sporting News*, November 2, 1895, 5.

198. *New York Herald*, June 26, 1880.

199. *New York Evening Post*, May 24, 1858.

200. *New York Herald*, December 9, 1883; *New York Evening Telegram*, December 19, 1883.

201. "Poor Old Davis," *New York Sun*, September 28, 1875, 1.

202. *New York Clipper*, June 19, 1880.

203. *Brooklyn Union*, September 18, 1863.

204. *Brooklyn Eagle*, March 21, 1888; *New York Tribune*, March 22, 1888.

205. *New York Sun*, July 29, 1903, 2.

206. *New York Herald*, November 7 and 10, 1870.

207. *Memorial Addresses on the Life and Character of John Simpkins (Late a Representative from Massachusetts), Delivered in the House of Representatives and Senate, Fifty-Fifth Congress, Second and Third sessions* (Washington, D.C.: GPO, 1899)

208. "Centenarian Died at Century's Dawn," *New York Herald*, January 3, 1901.

209. Augustine Costello, *Our Firemen: The History of the New York Fire Departments* (New York, 1887), chapter 27.

210. *New York Tribune*, May 4, 1880; *New York Times*, July 30, 1901.

211. *New York Times*, July 30, 1901.

212. *New York Herald*, December 30, 1900; "Centenarian Died at Century's Dawn," *New York Herald*, January 3, 1901.

213. *Irish American Weekly*, November 27, 1852.

214. *New York Tribune*, February 10, 1887.

215. *New York Times*, November 23, 1900.

216. *Jersey Journal*, April 10, 1875.

217. *New York Times*, November 23, 1900.

218. *New York Sun*, September 8, 1895, 3.

219. "Poor Old Davis," *New York Sun*, September 28, 1875, 1.

220. *New York Herald*, February 7, 1863.

221. *New York Times*, January 19, 1916.

222. *Sacramento Transcript*, February 27, 1851.

223. *New York Times*, January 19, 1916.

224. *New York Herald*, January 15, 1878.

225. *New York Herald*, July 11, 1876.

226. *New York Times*, January 13, 1858.

227. *New York Times*, March 25, 1900.

228. *New York Herald*, April 20, 1869.

229. *Cattaraugus Union*, December 19, 1862.

230. "Passes Away in England," *Charleston News & Courier*, July 17, 1918, 8.

231. England & Wales, Death Index: 1916–2005.

232. Letter from George Washington Whitman to Louisa Van Velsor Whitman, September 30, 1862, in Jerome M. Loving, ed., *The Civil War Letters of George Washington Whitman* (Durham: Duke University Press, 1975).

233. Harold Peterson, *The Man Who Invented Baseball*, 76.

234. Angus Macfarlane, "The Knickerbockers: San Francisco's First Baseball Team?" *Base Ball* 1:1 (Spring 2007), 11.

235. *Daily Alta California*, July 10, 1849.

236. *Daily Alta California*, December 12, 1849.

237. Angus Macfarlane, "The Knickerbockers: San Francisco's First Baseball Team?" *Base Ball* 1:1 (Spring 2007), 12.

238. "Death of a Pioneer: Frank Turk, the Last of the City's Alcaldes, Passes Away," *San Francisco Examiner*, July 16, 1887, 8; "Death of Frank Turk," *Daily Alta California*, July 16, 1887; Angus Macfarlane, "The Knickerbockers: San Francisco's First Baseball Team?" *Base Ball* 1:1 (Spring 2007), 7–21.

239. *New York Herald*, September 23, 1881.

240. *Brooklyn Eagle*, January 19, 1907, 2.

241. Harold Peterson, *The Man Who Invented Baseball*, 75.

242. William J. Ryczek, *Baseball's First Inning* (Jefferson, N.C.: McFarland), 175.

243. *New York Herald*, October 12, 1892; *New York Times*, October 12, 1892.

244. *New York Sun*, January 16, 1887, 10.

245. *Brooklyn Eagle*, January 3, 1885, 5.

246. "Scooped 'Em With a Net When Mr. Wenman Played Ball," *New York Evening Telegram*, March 9, 1915; *New York Herald*, May 30, 1919, 4.

247. Augustine Costello, *Our Firemen: The History of the New York Fire Departments*, chapter 26.

248. "The Old Fire Department," *New York Herald*, March 2, 1884, 8.

249. "James F. Wenman, At 85, Still Active Cotton Trader," *New York Evening Telegram*, November 17, 1908, 15; "Scooped 'Em With a Net When Mr. Wenman Played Ball," *New York Evening Telegram*, March 9, 1915.

250. "Scooped 'Em With a Net When Mr. Wenman Played Ball," *New York Evening Telegram*, March 9, 1915. Wenman's height comes from his passport application.

251. *New York Times*, October 15, 1885.

252. "Scooped 'Em With a Net When Mr. Wenman Played Ball," *New York Evening Telegram*, March 9, 1915.

253. *New York Evening Telegram*, June 18, 1879, 2.

254. "Scooped 'Em With a Net When Mr. Wenman Played Ball," *New York Evening Telegram*, March 9, 1915.

255. *Brooklyn Daily Eagle*, June 12, 1915, 2; *New York Sun*, June 13, 1915, 7.

256. "Scooped 'Em With a Net When Mr. Wenman Played Ball," *New York Evening Telegram*, March 9, 1915.

257. *New York Sun*, March 7, 1917, 11.

258. *Commerce and Finance* 8:1 (1919), 744.

259. *New York Sun*, March 6, 1919; *New York Herald*, February 23, 1919, 14.

260. *New York Herald*, March 25, 1919, part 2, 2.

261. *New York Herald*, May 30, 1919, 4.

262. *Genealogy of the Westervelt Family*, comp. Walter Tallman Westervelt and ed. Wharton Dickinson (New York: 1905), 117; *New York Herald*, April 4, 1891.

263. *New York Herald*, December 31, 1874.

264. Augustine Costello, *Our Firemen: The History of the New York Fire Departments*, chapter 32.

265. *New York Evening Post*, January 12, 1904; *New York Tribune*, January 12, 1904.

❖ *New York Base Ball Club (a.k.a. Washington BBC, Gotham BBC)* ❖
(John Thorn)

CLUB HISTORY

Recent study has revealed the claim of the Knickerbocker Base Ball Club of New York to pioneer status, as well as that of Alexander Cartwright to be the game's inventor, to be suspect if not altogether baseless. I have taken up the latter claim at length in *Baseball in the Garden of Eden* and will not do so here, except to reiterate my view that baseball was not invented but instead evolved. All the same, however, it had many fathers — prime among them William Rufus Wheaton, Daniel Lucius "Doc" Adams, and Louis F. Wadsworth — each of whom may be credited with specific innovations that were previously credited to Cartwright.[1]

Adams played ball as early as 1839, the year he came to New York after earning his M.D. at Harvard.[2] As he declared to an interviewer in 1896, when he was 81:

> I was always interested in athletics while in college and afterward and soon after going to New York I began to play base ball just

for exercise, with a number of other young medical men. Before that [i.e., before 1839] there had been a club called the New York Base Ball Club, but it had no very definite organization and did not last long. Some of the younger members of that club got together and formed the Knickerbocker Base Ball Club, September 24, 1845 [actually September 23].... About a month after the organization of this club, several of us medical fellows joined it, myself among the number.[3]

Wheaton testified to an interviewer in 1887, when he was 73, that he had written the rules for that New York Base Ball Club in 1837.[4] And Wadsworth, who in 1857 gave to baseball the key features of nine innings and nine men to the side, began to play baseball with the Gotham Club, successor to the New Yorks, in 1852 or 1853.[5]

While the Knickerbocker was the most enduringly influential of the baseball clubs that sprang up prior to the Civil War, it was not the first to play the game, or the first to be organized, or the first to play a "match game" (one contested between two distinct clubs), or the first to play by written rules that we might regard as governing the "New York Game." This regional variant, in which we may detect the seeds of baseball as we know it today, was distinct from the Massachusetts or New England Game, also called round ball or, with justice, simply "base ball," a descriptive name that applies, in my view, to all games of bat and ball with bases that are run in the round — and thus not only to the New York Game but also to the versions played in Massachusetts, Philadelphia, and elsewhere.

If the Knickerbockers were not the first to play the New York Game, what clubs preceded them? Perhaps it was the Gymnastics and the Sons of Diagoras, clubs associated with Columbia College who played a game of "Bace" in 1805, which the former won by a score of 41–34.[6] Perhaps it was the unnamed clubs that contested at Jones' Retreat in New York's Greenwich Village in 1823.[7] It may have been the men of the Eagle Ball Club, organized in 1840 to play by rules similar if not identical to those of the KBBC.[8] Or it may have been the Magnolia Ball Club or the New York Club, each of which played baseball among themselves at the Elysian Fields of Hoboken in the autumn of 1843 and, like Doc Adams' medical fellows, had played in New York City before then.

So, it must be said, had many other men who would become Knickerbockers. They were playing ball at Madison Square and Murray Hill in the early 1840s. Charles A. Peverelly, in his *Book of American Pastimes* (1866), wrote:

> At a preliminary meeting, it was suggested that as it was apparent they would soon be driven from Murray Hill, some suitable place should be obtained in New Jersey, where their stay could be permanent; accordingly, a day or two afterwards, enough to make a game assembled at Barclay street ferry, crossed over, marched up the road, prospecting for ground on each side, until they reached the Elysian Fields, where they "settled." Thus it occurred that a party of gentlemen formed an organization, combining together health, recreation, and social enjoyment, which was the nucleus of the now great American game of Base Ball so popular in all parts of the United States, than which there is none more manly or more health-giving.[9]

The Knickerbocker party of course did not wander about northern New Jersey looking for a place to play. They had been preceded by other clubs, both baseball and cricket, in selecting the Elysian Fields; proprietor Edwin Augustus Stevens (in conjunction with his brothers) had already donated the use of his grounds to the New York Cricket Club and the New York Yacht Club, and had offered liberal lease terms to the Magnolia and New York baseball clubs.[10]

In this support of sport, Stevens was of course encouraging traffic to the Elysian Fields: he controlled the ferries as well as the resort, which included the Beacon Course, a horse-racing track opened in 1834. By encouraging play (and gambling) on his turf and along his waters he created a long-standing model for "traction magnates" to own baseball clubs.

William Rufus Wheaton asserted that the rules he and William H. Tucker drafted for the Knickerbockers in 1845 were scarcely different from those he had created for the Gotham Club eight years earlier.

Of less interest to scholars have been the naming precedents from clubs in sports that captured the public fancy earlier than baseball, but these provide archaeological hints at how baseball developed within pre-established models.

Both the Knickerbocker and New York names were attached to boating clubs in the early years of the century. Rowing was America's first modern sport, in that competitions were marked by record-keeping, prizes, and wagers, yet also provided spectator interest for those with no pecuniary interest. The first boat club to be organized in the United States was named the Knickerbocker, in 1811.[11] As reported in the *New-York Mirror* of July 15, 1837, by boating veteran "Jacob Faithful," who borrowed his *nom de plume* from an 1834 novel by Frederick Marryat:

> This club suffered a suspension during the war [that of 1812], and for many years subsequently the boat which bore its name was hung up in the New-York Museum, as a model of the finest race-boat ever launched in this port. Subsequent attempts to

revive the association fell through; and though many exertions to form new ones were made, yet the first effort that succeeded in establishing the clubs upon their present footing — viz., building their own boats, wearing a regular uniform, and observing rigid navy discipline, was made in the year 1830, by the owners of the barge *Sea-drift*, a club consisting of one hundred persons, which could boast of one no less distinguished in aquatick and sporting matters than Robert L. Stevens for its first president, with Ogden Hoffman, Charles L. Livingston, Robert Emmet, John Stevens, and other good men and true for his successors. To this club the rudder of the old Knickerbocker was bequeathed, with the archives thereto pertaining: nor was anything spared by the members, during the first years of their existence as a club, to give spirit to its doings.[12]

Baseball historians, take note. Jacob Faithful was attempting to counter a recent assertion in the *New York Evening Star* that the Wave Club had been the first "to introduce the amusement." The new organization of 1830 referenced above was named the "New York Boat Club."[13] The Knickerbocker Boat Club — whose very existence had already, by 1837, been cast into oblivion — did not disappear immediately after the War of 1812. It was still conducting boat races and theatrical benefits in 1820. For its celebrated race of November 1820 against the British-born boat builder John Chambers' *American Star*, the Knickerbocker Club's John Baptis built a replacement for his dry-docked Knickerbocker rowboat of 1811 and called it the *New York*. The *New York* was characterized in the press as "having the real Knickerbocker [i.e., American] stamp."[14]

Boat racing was nothing short of a craze in the 1820s and '30s, as recalled by Colonel Thomas Picton in *Spirit of the Times*, July 7, 1883:

After them [the *New York* and *American Star*] came the *Atalanta*, manned by dry-goods clerks; the *Seadrift*, by bakers; the *Neptune*, by Fulton Market butchers; the *Fairy*, by law students; the *Columbia* and the

Both the Knickerbocker and New York names were attached to boating clubs in the early years of the century. The first boat club to be organized in the United States was named the Knickerbocker, in 1811; the New York Club was the second.

The boating craze of the 1830s parallels intriguingly the baseball craze of the 1850s and '60s. The New York Boat Club began in 1830, the New York Yacht Club in 1844.

Halcyon, by city collegians; the *Water Witch*, by engine runners; the *Red Rover*, by Ninth Ward firemen, and so on to the end of a miraculous chapter, utterly exhausting the catalogue of sea-gods, nereids and hamadryads, deified in pagan mythology. Boat-builders toiled night and day in the production of racing novelties, and one fair of the American Institute, appropriately held at Castle Garden, was almost entirely consecrated to specimens of their art, painted in all the colors of the rainbow, and in others, emanating from overtaxed imaginations, any man inventing a previously-unknown hue being tolerably certain of immediate canonization.

To my eyes, the boating craze, with its attachment of clubs to specific occupations and classes, parallels intriguingly the baseball craze of the 1850s and '60s.

The New York Cricket Club that has come down in history was organized at McCarty's Hotel (the Colonnade) in Hoboken on October 11, 1843, as an American-based answer to the St. George Cricket Club, which filled its playing ranks with English nationals. The first 12 members of the NYCC were drawn from the staff of William T. Porter's *Spirit of the Times*, with elected members coming from the sporting set that swirled about that weekly journal, including Edward Clark, a lawyer; William Tylee Ranney, a celebrated painter who lived in Hoboken; and James F. Cuppaidge, an accountant

who played as "Cuyp the bowler."[15] Some have speculated on a connection between the New York Cricket Club and the New York Base Ball Club, founded in the same year, but firm evidence has not yet emerged. Picton, the NYCC secretary, wrote in the *Clipper*: "The New York, with commendable foresight ... established their grounds at Hoboken, to the rear of the Elysian Fields. For a couple of years they played upon a section of the domain of Mr. Edwin A. Stevens but subsequently they removed to a more spacious and accessible locality [the Fox Hill Cricket Ground], just beyond the upper end of the old race track [the Beacon, which closed after the 1845 season]."[16]

The NYCC continued until 1873, but it had stood on the shoulders of earlier cricket clubs bearing the same name. A club of that name had formed in 1837, the same year as the Gotham or New York Base Ball Club, as referenced in the Wheaton reminiscences below. In 1838 it played a match with the Long Island Cricket Club for $500. One year later it played an anniversary match at its grounds on 42nd Street, near the Bloomingdale Road (today's Broadway). Coexisting with the St. George Cricket Club for a while, ultimately the NYCC merged with it under the latter's name, a move that inspired Porter to a nationalistic response in 1843.[17]

According to Chadwick, a "New York Cricket Club" had

been founded in 1808 at the Old Shakespeare in Nassau Street; it lasted but one year. But another one predated that by at least six years, meeting at the Bunch of Grapes, at No. 11 Nassau (corner of Cedar and Pine) in 1802.[18] A bit of newspaper digging for this essay has revealed an even earlier New York Cricket Club, going back to 1788.[19]

A New York Sporting Club for the preservation of game within city limits had been created in 1806.[20] Members of the

The Hoboken Turtle Club was New York's first social club, founded at Fraunces Tavern at the corner of Broad and Pearl streets in 1796.

Hoboken Turtle Club — New York's first club, founded at Fraunces Tavern at the corner of Broad and Pearl streets in 1796 — were called to order in June 1820 for "Spoon Exercise." In sum, the notion of a New York Club devoted to *baseball* did not arise from nothing.

Accordingly, a series of questions confronts us. If baseball was played by organized clubs prior to the Knickerbockers, which of these might lay fair claim to being the true first — that is, first to organize, first to draft rules for play, and first not only to play a match game but also to endure long enough to influence the game's development? Reflect that the Knickerbockers are credited with playing the first match game, on June 19, 1846 ... yet history has not accorded an equivalent laurel to their opponents, the New Yorks, who defeated the "pioneers" by a score of 23–1. If the Knicks could not defeat them on the field, however, they were more successful in eradicating them from the historical record, dismissing the victors as unfairly advantaged "cricketers" or, even worse, "disorganized," a slap at any purposeful aggregation in the rising age of system.

Peverelly offered this capsule portrait of the New York

Nine: "It appears that this was not an organized club, but merely a party of gentlemen who played together frequently, and styled themselves the New York Club."[21] Henry Chadwick, who may have fed Peverelly his line, had written in the *Beadle Guide* in 1860,"we shall not be far wrong if we award to the [Knickerbockers] the honor of being the pioneer of the present game of Base Ball."[22]

In fact, the New York Club not only preceded the Knickerbocker in every innovation cited above, but was also its progenitor. The process by which they became two separate clubs may not have been an altogether amicable split. The understanding of veteran baseball players at the turn of the 20th century was exceedingly hazy as to who had been a Knickerbocker and who a member of the New Yorks. A widely syndicated article by Albert G. Spalding (it appeared in the *Akron Beacon Journal* on April 1, 1905) announced the formation of an investigative body to examine the origins of baseball; this has come to be known as the Mills Commission. (This article was read by Abner Graves, who responded to the editor of the newspaper and lifted Abner Doubleday to inventor status.) Extracting from the materials he had received from Chadwick, Spalding named 11 men as Knickerbocker Base Ball Club founders, including: "Colonel James Lee, Dr. Ransom, Abraham Tucker, James Fisher, W. Vail, Alexander J. Cartwright, William R. Wheaton, Duncan F. Curry, E. R. Dupignac, Jr., William H. Tucker, and Daniel L. Adams." The first four of these played with the New York or Gotham club, as did Wheaton and Tucker. The last named, Adams, did not join the Knickerbocker until one month after its founding.

Known as the New York or Gotham or Washington from the 1830s through the 1860s, these clubs were lineally the same, and appear to have gone by several names at the same time. The murky relationship between the original Gothams of 1837, the Washingtons, the New Yorks, the Knickerbockers, and the later Gothams may be summarized below.

Because they regarded themselves as the first organized club, the Gotham Club was also called the Washington. A matter of custom, this practice was said to denote that they were, like the father of our country, first. Another explanation, personally alluring but not yet proved, is that the Gotham's alternative name referred to its origins with the influential merchant class — mostly butchers and produce brokers — of Washington Market, founded in 1812. Some of these men organized in 1818 as New York City's first target company (for archery and riflery), which they named the Washington Market Chowder Club.[23] It survived all the way through the Mexican War into the next decade. The *Tribune* reported on November 29, 1850:

> Washington Market Chowder Club. A company bearing the above name, composed, we understand of the butchers of Washington Market, passed our office yesterday morning on a target excursion, accompanied by Dodsworth's Band. They were very numerous, and fine looking body of men. And it would be in-

deed surprising that any company composed of butchers should be anything else than fine looking; that occupation embraces the most robust and hardy men in the city.

Many in the meat trade went on to become political wheeler-dealers and sporting men (not sportsmen), from Bill "the Butcher" Poole — whose father had been a Washington Market butcher before him, with his stand occupying the same place — to James McCloud, the butcher and pool-seller who facilitated the Louisville game-fixing scandal of 1877.

The weekly *New York Illustrated* offered a colorful capsule of the Washington Market in 1870:

> Flour, meal, butter, eggs, cheese, meats, poultry, fish, cram the tall warehouses and rude sheds, teeming at the water's edge, to their fullest capacity. Fruit-famed, vegetable-renowned Jersey pours four-fifths of its products into this lap of distributive commerce; the river-hugging counties above contribute their share, and car-loads come trundling in from the West to feed this perpetually hungry maw of the Empire City. The concentration of this great and stirring trade is to be met with at Washington Market. This vast wooden structure, with its numerous outbuildings and sheds, is an irregular and unsightly one, but presents a most novel and interesting scene within and without. The sheds are mainly devoted to smaller stands and smaller sales. Women with baskets of fish and tubs of tripe on their heads, lusty butcher-boys lugging halves and quarters of beef or mutton into their carts, pedlars of every description, etc., tend to amuse and bewilder at the same time. Some of the produce dealers and brokers, who occupy the little box-like shanties facing the market from the river, do a business almost as large as any of the neighboring merchants boasting their five-story warehouses.[24]

At some point in the early 1840s the Gotham club was renamed the New York Ball Club, retaining most if not all of its Gotham members. The New Yorks then spun off the Knickerbockers, as Wheaton relates in the 1887 interview offered verbatim below. The Gotham, meanwhile, continued to play ball among themselves from 1845 to 1849, just as the Knickerbocker and Eagle clubs appear to have done. In 1850 those Gotham and New York members who had not attached to the Knickerbockers in Hoboken reconstituted themselves as, yet again, the Washingtons, playing at the Red House Grounds ("a most comfortable 'asylum for distressed husbands,'" offered *Spirit of the Times*) at Second Avenue and 105th Street in New York.

In 1851 this Washington Base Ball Club challenged the Knickerbockers to match games that have been preserved in the historical record. In 1852 the club reverted to its old name of Gothams, "consolidating with" the Washingtons.[25]

Admittedly, this is a serpentine path. Let me now bring in William Rufus Wheaton to help fill in the story. Born in 1814, Wheaton attended New York's Union Hall Academy, at the corner of Prince and Oliver streets, near Chatham Square and the racket court and handball alley at Allen Street, which he appears to have frequented. He read law with the notable

attorney John Leveridge, passed the bar in 1836, was active in the New York 7th Regiment, and in 1841 was admitted to practice in the Court of Chancery and the Supreme Court of New York. His legal training, more than that of any other original Knick mentioned as a "father of baseball," equipped him to codify the venerable if still anecdotal playing rules.

The ball was presented to the winning team and often preserved as a symbol of victory. This ball was won by the Gotham Club in 1869. The Gothams were one of the earliest clubs, but by 1869 had been surpassed in importance by professional clubs like the Atlantics and Mutuals.

Wheaton was a solid cricketer as well as a baseballist. He umpired two baseball games played between the New York and Brooklyn clubs on October 21 and 24, 1845, both of which were played eight to the side and reported in the press, with accompanying box scores. He recruited members for the Knickerbocker Base Ball Club, as Peverelly noted. He was the club's first vice president. Although paired with the tobacconist William H. Tucker as the entirety of the Knickerbocker Committee on By-Laws, Wheaton appears to have been the one who truly wrote the rules that were formalized on September 23, 1845. Before that, by his own account, he drew up the rules for the Gotham club of the 1830s, which the Knickerbockers adopted with little change aside from repealing the Gotham provision for an out to be recorded by a catch on the fly.

By the spring of 1846, however, barely six months after the founding of the Knickerbocker Club, Wheaton resigned. We do not know the circumstances. On June 5 of that year, the Knickerbockers, not yet one year old, elected their first honorary members, 49-year-old James Lee and 53-year-old

The Washington Market Chowder Club arose in 1818 from the butcher stalls on New York's west side, which may also have spawned the city's first ball clubs.

Abraham Tucker, both of whom had been Gothams. Wheaton was not accorded such an honor.[26] He left the Knickerbockers and returned to active play at cricket, going on to win a trophy bat for highest score in a match of the New York Cricket Club in October 1848.[27]

On January 28, 1849, a month before Alexander Cartwright's departure from New York, Wheaton embarked for California in a speculative venture called the New York Mining Company, in which he was one of a hundred gold-besotted souls who purchased and outfitted a ship, the *Strafford*, for what would be a 213-day journey to San Francisco around Cape Horn. Although he returned east upon occasion, he made his substantial business and political career in the West.

On Sunday, November 27, 1887, an "interesting history" appeared on page 14 of the *San Francisco Examiner*. It was entitled "How Baseball Began — a Member of the Gotham Club of Fifty Years Ago Tells About It." This interview with an unnamed "old pioneer," undoubtedly Wheaton, lay buried in the microfilm archives until 2004, when Randall Brown published extensive excerpts from it in his landmark article, "How Baseball Began," in SABR's *National Pastime*.[28] Here is the entirety of the *Examiner* piece, with variant spellings and styles intact.

HOW BASEBALL BEGAN
A Member of the Gotham Club of Fifty Years Ago Tells About It.
PLAYED FOR FUN THEN.
The Game Was the Outgrowth of Three-Cornered Cat, Which Had Become Too Tame.
Baseball to-day is not by any means the game from which it

sprang. Old men can recollect the time when the only characteristic American ball sport was three-cornered cat, played with a yarn ball and flat paddles.

The game had an humble beginning. An old pioneer, formerly a well-known lawyer and politician, now living in Oakland, related the following interesting history of how it originated to an EXAMINER reporter:

"In the thirties I lived at the corner of Rutgers street and East Broadway in New York. I was admitted to the bar in '36, and was very fond of physical exercise. In fact we all were in those days, and we sought it wherever it could be found. There were at that time two cricket clubs in New York city, the St. George and the New York, and one in Brooklyn called the 'Star,' of which Alexander Campbell, who afterwards became well known as a criminal lawyer in 'Frisco, was a member. There was a racket club in Allen street with an enclosed court. [A note in the *Clipper* on October 23, 1880 evokes the period: "In olden times Chatham square used to be an open meadow or common, and was the play-ground of the boys of this city. Baseball was the favorite game played on the square, but it was then a simple pastime, with flat sticks or axe-handles for bats, and yarn balls. Occasionally a boy, more lucky than the rest, would bring on the ground a ball made of a sturgeon's nose, procured from the racket court in Allen street, where it had been driven over the wall by a rash blow."]

["]Myself and intimates, young merchants, lawyers and physicians, found cricket to[o] slow and lazy a game. We couldn't get enough exercise out of it. Only the bowler and the batter had anything to do, and the rest of the players might stand around all the afternoon without getting a chance to stretch their legs. Racket was lively enough, but it was expensive and not in an open field where we could have full swing and plenty of fresh air with a chance to roll on the grass. Three-cornered cat was a boy's game, and did well enough for slight youngsters, but it was a dangerous game for powerful men, because the ball was thrown to put out a man between bases, and it had to hit the runner to put him out. The ball was made of a hard rubber center, tightly wrapped with yarn, and in the hands of a strong-armed man it was a terrible missile, and sometimes had fatal results when it came in contact with a delicate part of the player's anatomy."

THE GOTHAM BASEBALL CLUB.

"We had to have a good outdoor game, and as the games then in vogue didn't suit us we decided to remodel three-cornered cat and make a new game. We first organized what we called the Gotham Baseball Club. This was the first ball organization in the United States, and it was completed in 1837. Among the members were Dr. John Miller, a popular physician of that day; John Murphy, a well-known hotel-keeper; and James Lee, President of the New York Chamber of Commerce. To show the difference between times then and now, it is enough to say that you would as soon expect to find a Bishop or Chief Justice playing ball as the present President of the Chamber of Commerce. Yet in old times everybody was fond of outdoor exercise, and sober merchants and practitioners played ball till their joints got so stiff with age they couldn't run. It is to the oft-repeated and vigorous open-air exercise of my early manhood that I owe my vigor at the age of 73.

"The first step we took in making baseball was to abolish the rule of throwing the ball at the runner and order that it should be thrown to the baseman instead, who had to touch the runner with it before he reached the base. During the regime of three-cornered cat there were no regular bases, but only such permanent objects as a bedded boulder or an old stump, and often the diamond looked strangely like an irregular polygon. We laid out the ground at Madison square in the form of an accurate diamond, with home-plate and sand-bags for bases. You must remember that what is now called Madison square, opposite the Fifth Avenue Hotel, in the thirties was out in the country, far from the city limits. We had no short-stop, and often played with only six or seven men on a side. The scorer kept the game in a book we had made for that purpose, and it was he who decided all disputed points. The modern umpire and his tribulations were unknown to us."

HOW THEY PLAYED THEN.

"We played for fun and health, and won every time. The pitcher really pitched the ball and underhand throwing was forbidden. Moreover he pitched the ball so the batsman could strike it and give some work to the fielders. The men outside the diamond always placed themselves where they could do the most good and take part in the game. Nowadays the game seems to be played almost entirely by the pitcher and catcher. The pitcher sends his ball purposely in a baffling way, so that the batsman half the time can't get a strike [meaning "a hit"] or reach a base. After the Gotham club had been in existence a few months it was found necessary to reduce the rules of the new game to writing. This work fell to my hands, and the code I then formulated is substantially that in use to-day. We abandoned the old rule of putting out on the first bound and confined it to fly catching. The Gothams played a game of ball with the Star Cricket Club of Brooklyn and beat the Englishmen out of sight, of course. That game and the return were the only two matches [i.e., games with other clubs] ever played by the

first baseball club. [NOTE: These undoubtedly refer to the contests of October 1845.]"

"The new game quickly became very popular with New Yorkers, and the numbers of the club soon swelled beyond the fastidious notions of some of us, and we decided to withdraw and found a new organization, which we called the Knickerbocker. For a playground we chose the Elysian fields of Hoboken, just across the Hudson river. And those fields were truly Elysian to us in those days. There was a broad, firm, greensward, fringed with fine shady trees, where we could recline during intervals, when waiting for a strike [i.e., a turn at bat], and take a refreshing rest."

LOTS OF EXERCISE AND FUN.

"We played no exhibition or match games, but often our families would come over and look on with much enjoyment. Then we used to have dinner in the middle of the day, and twice a week we would spend the whole afternoon in ball play. We were all mature men and in business, but we didn't have too much of it as they do nowadays. There was none of that hurry and worry so characteristic of the present New York. We enjoyed life and didn't wear out so fast. In the old game when a man struck out[,] those of his side who happened to be on the bases had to come in and lose that chance of making a run. We changed that and made the rule which holds good now. The difference between cricket and baseball illustrates the difference between our lively people and the phlegmatic English. Before the new game was made we all played cricket, and I was so proficient as to win the prize bat and ball with a score of 60 in a match cricket game in New York of 1848, the year before I came to this Coast. But I never liked cricket as well as our game. When I saw the game between the Unions and the Bohemians the other day, I said to myself if some of my old playmates who have been dead forty years could arise and see this game they would declare it was the same old game we used to play in the Elysian Fields, with the exception of the short-stop, the umpire, and such slight variations as the swift underhand throw, the masked catcher and the uniforms of the players. We started out to make a game simply for safe and healthy recreation. Now, it seems, baseball is played for money and has become a regular business, and, doubtless, the hope of beholding a head or limb broken is no small part of the attraction to many onlookers."

The scorebook that Wheaton referenced, along with the Gotham bylaws and playing rules, was not a figment of his aged imagination. Gotham shortstop Charles C. Commerford wrote to Henry Chadwick in 1905 that the first baseball game he saw (he played in the 1840s and 1850s) was played by the New York Club, which "had its grounds on a field bounded by 23rd and 24th streets and 5th and 6th avenues." Commerford would have seen this game just prior to the fall of 1843, when the New York Ball Club moved its playing grounds to Hoboken. "There was a roadside resort nearby [the Madison Cottage] and a trotting track in the locality. I remember very well that the constitution and by-laws of the old Gotham club, of which I became a member in 1849, stated that the Gotham Club was the successor of the old New York City Club."[29]

Commerford added, in a 1911 letter to the *New York World*: "There was always some little contention between the

Knickerbocker Club and the Gotham Club as to the date of organization. The Knickerbockers claimed that they were the first to organize and the Gothams claimed priority, as the New York Club was merged into the Gotham and the former (New York) always insisted that they were the first to organize as such."[30]

To provide additional gloss on Wheaton's reminiscence, the games cited above, in which the Gothams "beat the Englishmen out of sight," were the very same games recorded in the press as pitting New York against Brooklyn in late October 1845. These were the last two of three games played between representatives of the two cities in that month, although we cannot say for certain that the first game was played by the same clubs as the latter two, as no box score survives to identify its contestants.

The Knickerbockers played *their* first recorded game, an intrasquad contest, in that month as well. On October 6, seven Knicks won by a count of 11–8 over seven of their fellows in three innings. Wheaton was the umpire. William H. Tucker scored three of the losing squad's eight runs.[31] Like Wheaton and other Knickerbockers, he had been a player with the New York Base Ball Club and maintained his tie to them, indeed playing in the two formal matches of the New Yorks with the Brooklyn Club on October 21 and 24 of 1845, a month after he had helped to form the Knicks. In *The Tented Field: A History of Cricket in America*, author Tom Melville pointed to an even earlier contest between Brooklyn and New York clubs, played on October 10 and reported in the *New York Morning News*.[32] Research more than a decade later has revealed a somewhat fuller account in the obscure and short-lived newspaper the *True Sun*:

> The Base Ball match between eight Brooklyn players, and eight players of New York, came off on Friday on the grounds of the Union Star Cricket Club. The Yorkers were singularly unfortunate in scoring but one run in their three innings. Brooklyn scored 22 and of course came off winners.[33]

Many of the early New York baseballists had cut their teeth on cricket, and this was true of the Brooklyn players as well. In the game of October 21, conducted at the Elysian Fields, the eight players of the New York club won handily. They did so again in the game three days later, played at the grounds of the Union Star Cricket Club, opposite Sharp's Hotel, at the corner of Myrtle and Portland avenues near Fort Greene. The scores were, respectively, 24–4 and 37–19. On both these occasions the Brooklyn baseballists included established cricketers John Hines, William Gilmore, John Hardy, William H. Sharp, and Theodore Forman.[34] Their lineup appears to have been identical for the two games, as the Ayers in the October 21 box score and the Meyers of October 24 may be alternative renderings of the same individual. The other seven Brooklynites match up.

For me, the New York Base Ball Club second-anniversary game of November 10, 1845, reported in the *New York Herald*

on the following day, has much in common with the purported "first match game" of June 19, 1846, while the games of October 1845, particularly the latter two, seem to be true match games between wholly differentiated clubs. It could be argued—I certainly would—that the Knickerbockers played *no* match games until they met the Washington club on June 3, 1851, a game the Knicks won by a count of 21–11. Look at the cast of characters in the *Herald*'s account of the game.

NEW YORK BASE BALL CLUB:—The second Anniversary of this Club came off yesterday, on the ground in the Elysian fields. The game was as follows:

	Runs		Runs
Murphy	4	Winslow	4
Johnson	4	Case	4
Lyon	3	Granger	1
Wheaton	3	Lalor	3
Sweet	3	Cone	1
Seaman	1	Sweet	4
Venn	2	Harold	3
Gilmore	1	Clair	2
Tucker	3	Wilson	1
	24		23

J.M. Marsh, Esq., Umpire and Scorer

After the match, the parties took dinner at Mr. McCarty's, Hoboken, as a wind up for the season. The Club were honored by the presence of representatives from the Union Star Cricket Club, the Knickerbocker Clubs, senior and junior, and other gentlemen of note. [35]

Several interesting things emerge from this notice of the game. Prominent Knickerbocker names are present—Wheaton, Tucker, Cone, Clair (Clare). So too are Gotham players of prominence—Lalor, Murphy, Johnson, Winslow, Case. The Davis who plays here and in the game of June 19, 1846, is not the Knickerbocker James Whyte Davis, who played opposite him in at least one contest after J.W. Davis's entrance on the scene in 1850. Venn is Harry Venn, celebrated Bowery icon and proprietor of the Gotham Cottage (a billiard and bowling saloon) at 298 Bowery, longtime clubhouse to the Gotham BBC. Gilmore may well be the Union Star cricketer who played baseball with the Brooklyns on October 21 and 24.

The game of November 10 was played nine to the side, clearly to 21 runs or more in equal innings, a rule that may have been invoked only for formalized contests. The two sides were unnamed. While the New Yorks were celebrating their second year as an organized club, on another field in Hoboken, that very same day, the Knickerbockers were playing an intramural match all their own, eight to the side.

So who were these mysterious NYBBC players, so important to baseball's development yet nearly invisible in the shadow of the Knickerbocker Club? Let me supply a brief record with identifications for a few major figures. An addendum to this essay will portray, in a more perfunctory manner than it deserves, the reconstituted Gotham Club from 1852 until it drifted into inconsequence after the professionals formed their league in 1871. Someone ought to write a book.

The Gotham Inn at 298 Bowery, also known as the Gotham Saloon or Cottage, was built in the 1770s. It became the clubhouse for the venerable Gotham Base Ball Club and the site of several annual conventions of the National Association of Base Ball Players.

According to Peverelly, the Gotham Base Ball Club of New York was organized early in 1852, with a mysterious Mr. Tuche as its first president. In his *Book of American Pastimes* he treated the Washington Base Ball Club as a separate entity, supplying slim details of their two matches with the Knickerbockers on June 3 and 17, 1851. For the first, which the Knicks won by a count of 21–11 in eight innings at the Red House Grounds, all that he had was a line score (both games went unreported in the press). For the second game, which the Knicks won 22–20 in ten innings, he listed the Washington players, several of whom we recognize as New York Base Ball Club players from the 1845 anniversary game and the purported match game of June 19, 1846: William. H. Van Cott, Trenchard, Barnes, William Burns, C[harles] Davis, Robert Winslow, Charles L. Case, Jackson, Thomas Van Cott. Peverelly also lists the officers of the Gotham Club since 1856 and describes the club uniform of ten years after as "a blue merino cap, with a white star in the centre; white flannel shirt, with red cord binding; blue flannel pants, red belt, and white buckskin shoes."

When the Gothams met the Knicks on July 1, 1853, a game interrupted by rain and resumed on the 5th, their players included (William) Vail, W.H. Van Cott, Thomas Van Cott, (Robert) Winslow, Sr., (Robert) Winslow, Jr., Jonathan (John) Lalor, Reuben H. Cudlipp, and two highly skilled new play-

ers — Joseph C. Pinckney and Louis F. Wadsworth, both of whom would soon leave the club for greener pastures, perhaps lured by emoluments. Another Gotham with a vagabond temperament was second baseman Edward G. Saltzman, who in the spring of 1856 relocated his jewelry trade to Boston. With Brooklynites Augustus P. Margot and Richard Busteed, Saltzman organized the Tri-Mountain Club to play baseball by New York rules.

On November 7, 1857, correspondent "X" wrote of that year's edition of the club in *Porter's Spirit of the Times:*

Their best men are: Messrs. Vail, Van Cott, Cudlipp, [William] Johnson, [John] McCosker, Wadsworth, Sheriden [Phil Sheridan], Turner, and [Charles] Commerford. Mr. Vail, one of the oldest players in this city, and one of the original members, has had great experience; he has filled the position of catcher since Mr. Burns left (the club miss this player very much). He is a strong bat, and plays with good judgment. Mr. Van Cott stands very high as pitcher, combining speed with an even ball. Mr. Wadsworth formerly belonged to the Knickerbocker [which he joined in 1854, coming from the Gotham], and until the last year or so played in all their matches, but left them through some misunderstanding. It is claimed by his friends that he is the best first base man in any club, perfectly fearless — he will stop any ball that may come within reach — is a good player in any position, as his fielding last Friday will show. McCosker and Johnson are both fine catchers, and remarkably strong batsmen; and of the others it may be said, that if not powerful batters, they are what is termed sure ones, and good catchers.... The Gotham formerly played on the grounds of the Red House, and would probably have played there to this day, had there not some difficulty sprung up with the proprietor or lessee. They play at Hoboken, on grounds but slightly inferior to their old locality.[36]

The Gothams believed they were direct descendants from not only the Washington Club (which they averred to have organized in 1849, not 1850 as Peverelly had it), but also from the primal New York Club. The club limped along through the 1870s as the professionals took hold of the game. In 1871, following the formation of the National Association of Professional Base Ball Players, the first professional league, the Gothams joined with 32 other clubs, including the venerable Knickerbocker and Eagle clubs, hoping to keep top-level amateur play alive. In a last-gasp member-recruitment circular issued at the opening of the centennial year of 1876, the club's directors wrote, "The Gotham Base Ball Club dates its existence from the year 1849; it is, therefore, one of the oldest — if not the oldest — organization of its kind in the country."[37]

A few weeks later, the *New York Times* reported on the meeting of old Gotham players that resulted. It was noted that this club had "turned out more professional players than any other," which oddly may have been true. Buried in the notice was the still, to this day, not fully fathomed heritage of the club — like that of the game itself — in the rough and rowdy crowd that populated Washington Market long before.

The meeting on Monday evening was a large and very harmonious one. Old times were talked over, and a unanimous feeling prevailed in favor of reorganizing and keeping up the old club. Mr. James B. Mingay, a gentleman who has done business in Jefferson Market for over thirty years past, was elected president and Mr. Abraham H. Hummel, of the law firm of Howe & Hummel, at No. 89 Centre street, was made Vice President. [Hummel was the notorious underworld lawyer of his day.] The Secretary is Mr. Melchior B. Mason of No. 32 Chambers Street and the treasurer, Mr. Leonard Cohen, of Washington Market. There were about forty of the old members present; and among those who will take an active part in the new organization are Mr. Seaman Lichtenstein, of No. 83 Barclay street, who has been in business over thirty-five years ... Mr. John Drohan, Mr. James Forsyth, and Mr. Richard H. Thorn, all merchants of Washington Market, of between twenty and thirty years' standing.[38]

CLUB MEMBERS

Cornelius V. Anderson: President of the Washington Club in the early 1850s after being the chief engineer of the Volunteer Firemen from 1837 to 1848. His portrait was prominently displayed at Harry Venn's Gotham Cottage at 298 Bowery, the ballclub's headquarters after 1845. Born in New York City on April 1, 1809, Anderson was a mason by trade. In 1852 he became the first president of the Lorillard Fire Insurance Company. His health began to fail in 1856 and he died on November 22, 1858. He was revered among the city's firemen, who erected an elaborate tombstone in his honor at Brooklyn's Green-Wood Cemetery.

Charles H. Beadle: First baseman and officer of the Gotham Club during and after the Civil War, into the 1870s. Charles's brother, Edward Beadle, was also involved in the club and both brothers later moved to Cranford, New Jersey, where Edward served as mayor in 1885.

Edward Bonnell: Edward Bonnell was recalled by George Zettlein as "one of the players" on the Gothams. Born around 1825, Bonnell was a liquor dealer before becoming a member of the New York Board of Fire Commissioners in 1865. Zettlein reported that Bonnell was living in Philadelphia in 1887.[39]

William F. Burns: A Gotham catcher in 1855–56. According to the *Clipper* article quoted in the profile of Venn, Burns died in the 1857 sinking of the *SS Central America*. Contemporary coverage of that tragedy does indeed list him among the missing: "William Burns of New York City. Had been in California about a year."[40]

C[larence] A. Burtis: The leading Gotham player of 1860, in which his runs-per-game ratio was the third best in the National Association, behind only Grum of the Eckfords and Leggett of the Excelsiors. In a game against the Mutuals on September 4, 1860, Burtis hit two home runs. After playing for the Gotham Club in 1859 and 1860, Burtis was absent from the lineup in 1861. He was back by the summer of 1862 and played through at least 1865. He also played in an 1888 old-timers benefit game for John Zeller, crippled by a gruesome baseball injury. George Zettlein described Burtis (though recalling him as Bustis) as a "boss painter in the Ninth ward," so he can only be Clarence A. Burtis, a painter who was born around 1835 and died in Manhattan on May 16, 1894. Burtis enlisted in the 83rd Regiment, New York Infantry, on May 26, 1861, and was a sergeant-major by the time of his discharge in June of 1862. Like many of his fellow club members, Burtis was also very active in the fire department.

Charles Ludlow Case: Born in Newburgh, New York, in 1818, he was a NYBBC player in the contest of November 10, 1845, when he resided at 7 Murray and was a merchant at 101 Front. He was at one time a butcher at Washington Market. He also played for the New York Club in the two games against the cricketers from the Union Star of Brooklyn on October 21 and 24, 1845. In the game of June 19, 1846, he played with the club designated as the New Yorks. Case arrived in San Francisco for the Gold Rush on February 27, 1849. At a meeting of January 6, 1851, he became a member of the Finance Committee of the newly formed Knickerbocker Association, composed of New York residents living in San Francisco. He was joined on that committee by Edward A. Ebbets and Frank Turk, who had been members of the Knickerbocker Base Ball

Club of New York. It is reasonable to think that they were among the unnamed men reported to have played baseball in Portsmouth Square in 1851.[41] Case returned east and died in Newburgh on March 25, 1857.

Leonard G. Cohen: Officer of the Gotham Club during and after the Civil War; catcher for the ballclub. As of 1869 he was a fruit dealer in Washington Market and living at 144 West Street. Cohen was born around 1839 in New York to a Polish-born father (though one census had Germany). He later moved to Westfield, New Jersey, where he served as the first postmaster and was still living as late as 1910.

Charles C. Commerford: Born in New York City, June 2, 1833; died in Waterbury, Connecticut, February 6, 1920. Played shortstop with Gothams and later the Eagles. Moved from New York to Waterbury in 1864, where he continued to play ball. After some political successes, he was appointed postmaster in Waterbury by President Grover Cleveland in 1886. His father, the chair-maker John Commerford of New York City, was an Abolitionist prominently identified with labor interests, and was a candidate for Congress on the Republican ticket in 1860. See the entry on the Bridgeport Club in *Base Ball Pioneers, 1850–1870* for more details on his life.

John Connell: George Zettlein described this man as a member of the Gothams and added that he "was on the *Herald* for some time, and is still [in 1887] a writer."

Reuben Henry Cudlipp: Reuben Cudlipp was a Nassau Street lawyer who served as vice president of the Gotham Club in 1856 and as one of the vice presidents of the NABBP in 1857. He also played for the first nine until 1858. One of the Gothams' better players, he was proposed for membership in the Knickerbockers on April 1, 1854, the same date as that of Louis F. Wadsworth's similar move.[42] Still active as a New York attorney in 1894, he resided at that time in Plainfield, New Jersey, as did Wadsworth. Cudlipp was 78 when he died at his daughter's home in Yonkers, New York, on December 5, 1899.

C[harles?] Davis: a frequent entrant in the NYBBC box scores, he has been mistaken in print for the celebrated Knickerbocker James Whyte Davis, against whom he played.

William W. De Milt: Like Harry Venn and Seaman Lichtenstein, he was a member of the Columbian engine company, Number 14. As a carpenter and machinist for the Union Square, Brougham's Lyceum (where fellow Gotham George W. Smith worked in 1850) and other New York theatres, he was responsible for producing a wide variety of stage apparatus and special effects. Born 1814, died 1875. Buried at Brooklyn's Green-Wood Cemetery.

Patsy Dockney: Born in Ireland ca. 1844. Catcher with Gotham in 1864–65. Paid under the table to move to Philadelphia Athletics in 1866; according to the *Philadelphia Times*, Dockney "used to play ball every afternoon and fight and drink every night. He was a tough of the toughs."

Andrew J. Dupignac: Andrew Dupignac, Gotham Club secretary in 1860 and 1861, was born around 1828. He later be-

came the president of the New York Skating Club and in 1903 was described as "the oldest living amateur skater."[43] Dupignac died in Brooklyn on November 27, 1908.

James Fisher: Identity not known for certain but after thorough review of the New York City directories and considering other factors, I tentatively conclude that this early player, according to Peverelly, was James H. Fisher. Roughly the same age as the two other prominent players who were named honorary Knickerbockers in June 1846—Col. James Lee and Abraham Tucker (the former born in 1796, the latter in 1793)—Fisher was born in 1798. Like Lee, he had made his fortune by 1850 and in the census lists his occupation as "gentleman." Previously he had listed his profession, with subtlety, as "agent." In 1847, the year of his death, his address was 134 Allen Street, the neighborhood from which Wheaton and his mates had begun their search for lively recreation.

Robert Forsyth: In 1855, the year after the death of the affluent patron of this independent military company, the *Herald* reported: "The Forsyth Cadets, a well drilled company, composed chiefly of butchers belonging to Washington Market, will make their annual parade on the 18th inst."[44] Shortly before his death, the *Clipper* observed: "This organization is named in honor of Robert Forsyth, Esq., a gentleman whose name is a 'Household Word' to all those who have occasion to visit Washington Market, being one of the most extensive dealers connected with that place. He must indeed feel honored at the compliment paid him by the 'Cadets.'"[45] Robert Forsyth was also a member of the Washington Market Chowder Club at the time of his death, which was reported in the *New York Herald* on March 23, 1854. His sons, Joseph and James, were both Gotham Club members. According to the 1887 *New York Sun* article, Joseph was already dead while James was an oyster dealer.

George H. Franklin: George H. Franklin was one of the club's representatives at the 1857 NABBP convention.

Andrew Gibney: Started with Gotham Juniors in 1863, graduated to senior club the following year. Played second base with the Gothams in 1865, then center field with the Nationals of Washington in 1866. Played professionally with Olympics of Washington in 1870. Alfred W. "Count" Gedney played as Gibney with the Keystone club in Philadelphia in his early years, but these two are not the same individual.

John V(an) B(uskirk) Hatfield: Widely regarded as one of the best players of the 1860s, with the Eckford and Mutual clubs, he also played one year with the Gothams, in 1865. See the Active Club of New York for more details.

Johnson: Played in the NYBBC anniversary contest of November 10, 1845. Harold Peterson, in his book *The Man Who Invented Baseball*, names him as a Knickerbocker and calls him F.C. Johnson. However, Francis Upton Johnston was a member of the Knickerbocker and the New-York Academy of Medicine, as were D.L. Adams and Franklin Ransom. One of his sons also practiced medicine for many years at Hyde

Park, where he is buried. The NYBBC Johnson may, however, be neither man but instead William Johnson, named in a reminiscence of the Gotham Cottage by Colonel Thomas Picton in 1878, and a player for the club in the 1850s.

John Lalor: This sturdy New York and Gotham player is surely the Jonathan Lalor listed in the box score published in *Spirit of the Times* on July 9, 1853, detailing a match game between the Knicks and Gothams. He also played in the NYBBC second-anniversary game of November 10, 1845. Harold Peterson, in his book *The Man Who Invented Baseball*, instead identifies the player as Michael Lalor, "Segar Seller." I think it is constable John Lalor, who umpired the Knickerbocker intramural game of June 26, 1846, and signed his name in full this way. This fellow was an up-and-comer in the Whig party in the Fifteenth Ward in 1845, and later its leader in the Seventh Ward. A lawyer by profession, he served in the Civil War, organizing the 15th Regiment, known as McLeod Murphy's Engineers. John Lalor was born in 1819 and died on February 21, 1884. His obituary in the *Herald* noted that he was "a member of the Gotham club." At his death he was chief clerk at Castle Garden.

Col. James Lee: According to Wheaton, he was one of the original Gotham Club members of 1837. Born December 3, 1796, he was a prominent businessman and sportsman. President of the New York Chamber of Commerce, he claimed to have played baseball in New York City ca. 1800. John Ward wrote, in *How to Become a Base-Ball Player* (1888), "Colonel Jas. Lee, elected an honorary member of the Knickerbocker Club in 1846, said that he had often played the same game when a boy, and at that time he was a man of sixty or more years. [In fact he was fifty.] Mr. Wm. F. Ladd, my informant, one of the original members of the Knickerbockers, says that he never in any way doubted Colonel Lee's declaration, because he was a gentleman eminently worthy of belief." In 1907 Ward added to his remarks about Lee a sentence that echoes editor Porter's reason for establishing the New York Cricket Club: "Another interesting tale told me by Mr. Ladd was that the reason they chose the game of Base Ball instead of— and in fact in opposition to — cricket was because they regarded Base Ball as a purely American game; and it appears that there was at that time some considerable prejudice against adopting any game of foreign invention."[46] Lee died on June 16, 1874.

Seaman Lichtenstein: A candidate for the first Jewish player, Lichtenstein began to run with Columbian Engine No. 14 at the age of 15, becoming a member of the company in 1849, at age 24. He began his business career salvaging scraps from the butchers at Washington Market, selling the meat to the Indians who lived in Hoboken and the bones to a manufacturer of glue (Peter Cooper). In the 1880s he owned a trotter named for Gotham Cottage proprietor and archetypal Bowery B'hoy Harry Venn. He died at age 77 on December 24, 1902.[47]

John McCosker: A third baseman, he began play with the Gothams in 1856. Played in Fashion Race Course Game 3

and in many games for the Gothams of the 1850s. Tom Shieber reported in the 1997 *National Pastime*:

> In a match game played between the Gotham and Empire clubs in September of 1857, McCosker hit a home run with the bases full. While he was most probably not the first to accomplish the feat, the description in the New York *Clipper* is the earliest known recounting of what would later be termed a grand slam: "The Gothamites ... scored 4 beautifully in their last innings, chiefly owing to a tremendous ground strike by Mr. McCosker, bringing each man home as well as himself."

George Zettlein described McCosker ("McClosky") as an engineer of the Fire Department, so there can be no question that the ballplayer was John A. McCosker, who was born around 1829 and was a fire department engineer prior to the war. When the war started, McCosker was one of the organizers of the 73rd Infantry — the Second Fire Zouaves — in which he served as a quartermaster until being discharged on August 4, 1862. His whereabouts become much harder to trace after that, but he may have died in 1881.

Dr. John Miller: According to Wheaton, he was one of the original Gotham BBC members of 1837. In 1842 John Miller, physician, is at 74 James Street. In 1845 he is at 186 East Broadway.

James B. Mingay: Entered the poultry business in Jefferson Market in his youth and remained in it until age 72. For 14 years a member of the Volunteer Fire Department with Hose Company 40, the Empire. A member of the Jefferson Market Guard and a judge of its target excursion on Christmas Day 1857. An officer of the Gotham club 1861–64. In 1876 a director of the North River Insurance Company. Born January 6, 1818. Died April 27, 1893, at his 19 Christopher Street residence.

John M. Murphy: According to Wheaton, he was a "hotel-keeper" and one of the original Gotham BBC members of 1837. He played in NYBBC anniversary contest of November 10, 1845, in Hoboken. Murphy's establishment is the Fulton Hotel at 164 East Broadway.

Joseph Conselyea Pinckney: In a celebrated early instance of revolving, or seeming professionalism, Pinckney played a game with the Gothams in 1856 while still nominally a member of the Union of Morrisania. Both the Unions and the Knickerbockers objected publicly. Along with Knickerbocker defector Louis F. Wadsworth, he played with the Gotham in 1857. The next year, back with the Unions, he was one of only three New York players selected for the Fashion Race Course match to play in all three games. Enlisting at the outbreak of the Civil War, he was colonel of the 6th New York Militia. In 1863 he was brevetted brigadier general of volunteers for war service. Afterward he served in New York City politics as an alderman. Born and died in New York City (November 5, 1821–March 11, 1881).

Henry Mortimer Platt: Born July 7, 1822, died December 8, 1898. Played match game in 1854 but otherwise served

Gotham Club as scorekeeper. He merits mention because in 1939 his daughter donated to the Baseball Hall of Fame the sole surviving badge of the Gotham Base Ball Club, featuring three men at sea in a tub.

Dr. Franklin Ransom: In the game of June 19, 1846, Dr. Ransom played with the club designated as the New Yorks. In 1838 Dr. Ransom resided at 44 Wall Street. He was in a medical partnership with Dr. Lucius Comstock but also found time to invent a fire engine with a modified hydraulic system. Dr. Ransom exhibited his fire engine to the City Council in 1841 but came to believe that the city had stolen his design. In 1858 he took a patent infringement lawsuit against the mayor of New York all the way to the United States Supreme Court, but did not prevail. Ransom was born near Buffalo in 1805 and earned his medical degree in 1832 from what was then known simply as the University of New York. He eventually returned to Buffalo, where he continued to file new patents but slipped into obscurity. He died there on March 25, 1873.

Edward G. Saltzman (Salzman, Salzmann, Saltzmann): Born about 1830 in Jefferson County, New York, he was schooled in Hoboken, New Jersey. Saltzman played second base for the Gotham club of New York for five seasons, from 1852 through 1856. Helped to bring the New York Game to Massachusetts via the Tri-Mountain Club. Brought baseball to Savannah, Georgia, in 1865, forming the Pioneer Club. Returned to Boston two years later and resided there until his final year. Died August 14, 1883, in Brooklyn.[48]

T. Seaman(s): Played in NYBBC anniversary match of November 10, 1845. He may be a billiard-room proprietor of that name or, more likely, he is one and the same as the later Gotham player and treasurer Seaman Lichtenstein, discussed earlier.

James Shepard: Played with Gotham, then Alpine BBC in 1860. Pioneer in establishing baseball in San Francisco, beginning in 1861.

William Shepard: Played with Gotham, then Alpine BBC in 1860. Pioneer in establishing baseball in San Francisco, beginning in 1861.

Philip Sheridan: Joined the Gothams in 1854. Frequently umpired. Said by Peter Nash in *Baseball Legends of Brooklyn's Green-Wood Cemetery* to have been buried in Green-Wood Cemetery in Brooklyn, but the Philip Sheridan interred there is not the Gotham player.

George Washington Smith: A member of the Gotham Club after 1845, he was born and raised in Philadelphia. Smith was considered the only male American ballet star of the 19th century. He went on to become ballet master at Fox's American Theater. He also served in this capacity at the Hippodrome, where the costume of a dancer under his instruction caught fire with fatal consequence. In his later years he opened a dancing school in Philadelphia. Born ca. 1820, died February 18, 1899.

Milton B. Sweet: See Excelsior Base Ball Club.

Oscar Teed: Oscar Teed, a celebrated ship's fastener and oarsman as well as a Gotham player. Born in 1828, he died November 4, 1866. A boat named in his honor ca. 1860 continued to race.

Austin D. Thompson: Born in 1820, Austin Thompson was described in his obituary as "a Connecticut Yankee, who came to New York when a youth and opened a coffee house in Pine street, near the old Custom House.... The coffee house, which was called the Phoenix, was frequented by the notabilities of the neighborhood, politicians as well as business men, particularly Democratic politicians, for Mr. Thompson was a Jeffersonian Democrat of the old school." As its proprietor, Thompson was the successor to the famed Edward Windust, 149 Water Street (Wall, corner Water). In 1851 his coffee rooms and restaurant relocated from 13 Pine to 25 Pine. It moved again in 1860, this time to 292 Broadway, where it remained until Thompson's death on June 7, 1892. By then Thompson was "probably the oldest eating-house keeper in the city," which made him "a man who knew nearly everybody and nearly everybody knew him."[49]

Richard H. "Dick" Thorn: Played with Empire Base Ball Club in 1856, yet was a representative of the Enterprise Base Ball Club at the convention of January 22, 1857. With Gotham in 1858; pitched for New York in Game 3 of Fashion Race Course Match that September. Returned to Empire 1859–61. With Gotham again 1862. With Mutual 1865–68. From about 1850 a prominent member and revenue collector of the Washington Market Association, Thorn partnered with Lathrop and then Marcley in his produce business in the 1860s. In 1870s he wholly owned Thorn & Co., 11–13 DeVoe Avenue, west of Washington Street. On January 26, 1889, rode on horseback, with Seaman Lichtenstein, in a parade to mark the opening of the West Washington Market. In that year lived at 233 West 13th Street. Does not appear in New York City directories thereafter, though he did testify at a hearing in 1890. On May 2, 1892, however, the *Riverside* (California) *Daily Press* published a notice that Thorn has purchased a substantial piece of land in the locality. One year later, he is described as an orange grower. He died in Riverside County on May 4, 1901 at the age of 71.

Tooker: Played outfield in Fashion Race Course Game 3. Later played with Henry Eckford Club. In 1871 was a director of the Athletic Base Ball Club of Brooklyn. Possibly this is Theodore, son of William Tooker, ship's carpenter, who joined his brother-in-law George Steers in the shipyards that built the *America*.

Trenchard: Could be Samuel Trenchard, constable or marshal in various years from 1835 until 1861. In 1846 he resided at 86 Ludlow. Played with the club designated as the New Yorks on June 19, 1846. Also played with Washingtons against Knickerbockers in match game of June 17, 1851. Born 1791, died February 15, 1865, in his 75th year. This would make him a bit of a graybeard for active play in the 1840s and

1850s, so perhaps he is billiard-hall proprietor Alexander H. Trenchard, at 139 Crosby Street in 1855.

Tuche: After the 1856 season, *Porter's Spirit of the Times* reported that the Gotham Club had been organized in the early summer of 1852 with "old ballplayer Mr. Tuche" at its head.[50] Other accounts also name Tuche as one of the principals, but his name soon disappeared from the club's annals and nothing more is known about him.

Abraham W. Tucker: Born in 1793, he was named an honorary member of the Knickerbocker Base Ball Club in June 1846, along with another New York Ball Club player, Col. James Lee. In 1822 he operated a "segarstore" at 205 Bowery. In 1837 he resided at 48 Delancey Street. Tucker died in Morristown, New Jersey, on September 10, 1868.

William H. Tucker was a tobacconist in business with his father, Abraham, who was also a player with the New Yorks. They operated at 8 Peck Slip and lived at 56 East Broadway. In 1849–50 he lived in San Francisco. In Alexander Cartwright's journal/address book he is listed as: "Wm. H. Tucker 271 Montgomery st. upstairs, San Francisco, Cal." Tucker appears to have died in Brooklyn, at the home of his son-in-law, on December 5, 1894, in his 76th year, which would conform to a birth year of 1819 recorded in the 1850 census.

Nicholas "Nick" Turner: Played left field in Fashion Race Course Game 2. A shoemaker residing in the Tenth Ward in 1860. Born 1831 in Bavaria. First name supplied by Waller Wallace and Henry Chadwick in *Sporting Life* in 1889.[51]

William Vail: Known affectionately as "Stay where you am, Wail," for his often disastrous derring-do on the basepaths. In later years played with Knickerbocker. There are several candidates by this name, but based upon his age, the most likely one appears to be a tobacconist who was born in 1817 or 1818 and was living at 179 Prince Street in 1849. His wife, Mary, was born in 1822–23, and their children as of 1850 were all sons: William, Francis, Martin, Daniel, George, in descending order of age. This man died on December 12, 1881, age 63, and was described in his obituary as a member of the Exempt Fireman's Association, a good sign that he was our pioneer ballplayer.[52]

Gabriel Van Cott: Acted as umpire for Gothams rather than player. There were a few Gabriels in the Van Cott family, but it appears most likely that this one was a cousin of Thomas and William. Another member of the family, Cornelius C. Van Cott (1838–1904), was the owner of the New York Giants of the National League from 1893 through 1895.

Theodore S. Van Cott: The son of Thomas, Teddy Van Cott later served in the Civil War and died in a home for old soldiers on August 23, 1905.

Thomas Van Cott: Thomas G. (1817–1894), who married Harriet Murphy, was the Gothams' best player in the 1850s, and the great pitcher of all New York ballclubs. The *Elmira Gazette* obituary of December 19, 1894, called him "The Father of Baseball" and the first man to pitch a curved ball. He was a bookmaker in later years, at the Saratoga Track.

William H(athaway) Van Cott: Brother of Thomas; born September 26, 1821, in New York City, died June 30, 1908, in Mount Vernon, New York. Played in Fashion Race Course Games 1 and 2. Elected first president of the National Association of Base Ball Players when it formally organized in 1858. Van Cott, who was a lawyer and justice by profession, continued his family's interest in trotters and began in the stabling business before entering the law. As Justice Van Cott he served 16 years on the bench. His *New York Times* obituary reported that his efforts to rid New York of gangs led to two attempts to burn down his house.[53]

Harry B. Venn: Played in NYBBC anniversary match of November 10, 1845. A noted fireman with Columbian 14 and the proprietor of the venerable (1778) Gotham Saloon beginning in 1830, when he left his porterhouse at 13 Ann Street and took his first lease at the property. His successor in the lease, S.W. Bryham, transformed the cottage in 1836 to become the Bowery Steam Confectionary and Saloon. By 1842, under new ownership, it was renamed the "Bowery Cottage," and was the headquarters for firemen, sporting types, and Bowery B'Hoys. Venn resumed his proprietorship sometime before 1845. Behind the bar at the Gotham was a case with the gilded trophy balls from victorious Gotham Base Ball Club matches. (These survived, amazingly, and were sold to collectors in the 1980s; it would be pleasant to think that the Gotham rules survived too!) The back bar also featured a big gilt "6" taken from the Americus engine (the inspiration for Christy Mathewson's nickname, Big Six). Boss Tweed was a regular patron at the bar. The Gotham Cottage was demolished in 1878, and Venn died a year later, on March 15, 1879. A contemporary wrote that his memorial might be inscribed: "Here lies one whose name was writ in whisky." Much more could be written about Venn and the Gotham Cottage, but suffice for now this snippet from a long paean to the demolished house by Col. Thomas Picton in the *Clipper* on June 1, 1878:

> "The Gotham" became, moreover, extensively known in connection with our national pastime, as beneath its roof was held the first general convention of baseball players, one of the earliest clubs in existence deriving its significant title from this snuggery in the Bowery. "The Gotham" Club [as re-formed in 1852] was a large association from the hour of its inception, organized through the election of Judge William H. Van Cott as president, and Gabriel Van Cott as secretary, with a roll of influential members, principally business men, embracing Harry B. Venn, Seaman Senchenstein [sic], James Forsyth, Joseph Foss, John Baum, George Montjoy, William Johnson, Edward Turner, E. Bonnell, Bates, Tooker, and a host of other notables. Its first playing members distinguishing themselves were Tom Van Cott, Sheridan, McCluskey [McClosky, "an engineer of the Fire Department," as George Zettlein recalled, in fact John McCosker, who played catcher with the Gothams in 1858], Cudliffe [Cudlipp], and William Burns, its pitcher [catcher?], afterwards lost at sea upon the *Central America*, wrecked in the Pacific [sic].

Louis F. Wadsworth: Born in Connecticut in 1825, he commenced to play baseball with the Washingtons/Gothams in 1852. After a few years with the Knickerbockers (1854–57) he returned to the Gothams, whom he represented in Fashion Race Course Games 1 and 3. One of the veteran Knicks, in recalling some of his old teammates for the *New York Sun* in 1887, said:

> I had almost forgotten the most important man on the team and that is Lew Wadsworth. He was the life of the club. Part of his club suit consisted of a white shirt on the back of which was stamped a black devil. It makes me laugh still when I recall how he used to go after a ball. His hands were very large and when he went for a ball they looked like the tongs of an oyster rake. He got there all the same and but few balls passed him.[54][53]

His time with the Knickerbockers, and his crucial role in affixing nine innings and nine men to the rules of baseball, are covered at length in *Baseball in the Garden of Eden*. Dissipating riches and fame, he died a pauper in the Plainfield Industrial Home in 1908.

William Rufus Wheaton: Discussed amply above.

Robert F. Winslow: Robert F. Winslow, a lawyer, played in the NYBBC anniversary game of November 10, 1845, Hoboken. In the game of June 19, 1846, Winslow played with the club designated as the New Yorks. Played center field for Gothams in mid–1850s. He and his son Robert, Jr., played for the Gotham in the match against the Knickerbockers commenced on July 1, 1853 and, after a rain interruption, concluded on July 5. In 1854, an Albert Winslow played with the Knickerbockers. Some evidence points to Robert, Jr.'s earlier demise, but the Robert Winslows are the only father-son pairing of that surname in New York at the time.

George Wright: He joined the Gotham juniors when he was 16, in 1863. One year later he graduated to the senior team and was the club's regular catcher. He also caught for the club in 1866 under the name of "George" before transferring his allegiance to the Union of Morrisania, where he converted to left field and then shortstop. Born in 1847, George Wright was perhaps the greatest player of the 19th century and certainly its first national hero. He died in 1937, four months before his election to the nascent Baseball Hall of Fame. See the Union of Morrisania entry for more on his life.

Harry Wright: The Civil War so decimated the Knickerbockers' schedule that Wright (1835–95) decided to leave them and join the Gothams in 1863–64. But by the next year he had tired of baseball and resumed his 1850s career, as a cricketer, in Cincinnati, Ohio. He had to wait longer than brother George to enter the Baseball Hall of Fame (1953). Leaving his post as the Cincinnati Cricket Club professional in 1867, he was persuaded to take the helm of the Cincinnati Base Ball Club. The rest is history; see the Cincinnati Base Ball Club entry in *Base Ball Pioneers, 1850–1870* for more details.

William P. Wright: With Gothams in 1865, played in five games. Not related to Harry and George. Appears to have gone to Cincinnati with Harry Wright at year's end. With that city's Buckeye club in 1868–69, Live Oak in 1870.

Other Club Members: John Drohan, Joseph E. Ebling, Hackett, J.A.P. Hopkins, N.W. Redmond, Charles S. Riblet, Peter Roe, Albert Squires, Cornelius Stokem, Andrew Whiteside.

Notes

1. For a full discussion of these three individuals, see the present writer's *Baseball in the Garden of Eden* (New York: Simon & Schuster, 2011).

2. His degree from Yale is reported in an untitled article in the *Connecticut Courant*, August 24, 1835, 3. His medical degree is reported in "Harvard University," *The Boston Medical and Surgical Journal*, September 26, 1838, 127. His work as an attending physician in New York is reported in "New York Dispensary," *The New-York Spectator*, February 27, 1840, 1.

3. "Dr. D. L. Adams; Memoirs of the Father of Base Ball; He Resides in New Haven and Retains an Interest in the Game," *The Sporting News*, February 29, 1896, 3.

4. "How Baseball Began: A Member of the Gotham Club of Fifty Years Ago Tells About It," anonymous journalist interviews William Rufus Wheaton, *San Francisco Examiner*, November 27, 1887, 14.

5. "City Intelligence," *New York Herald*, March 2, 1857, 8; Thorn, *Baseball in the Garden of Eden*, 51–53.

6. *New-York Evening Post*, April 13, 1805, 3.

7. *National Advocate*, April 25, 1823, 2.

8. Thorn, *Baseball in the Garden of Eden*, 80–81.

9. Charles A. Peverelly, *The Book of American Pastimes* (New York: Published by the Author, 1866), 340.

10. Col. Thomas Picton, "Among the Cricketers," *Fun and Fancy in Old New York: Reminiscences of a Man About Town*, ed. William L. Slout (San Bernardino, CA: Borgo Press, 2007), 140.

11. *New-York Mirror*, July 15, 1837, 23.

12. Ibid.

13. Ibid.

14. *Commercial Advertiser* [from *New-York Gazette* of that morning], November 13, 1820, 2.

15. Cuyp Obituary, *New York Herald*, July 13, 1871. Also Picton, "The New York Cricket Club," *Fun and Fancy in Old New York*, 133–143.

16. Picton, "Among the Cricketers," *Fun and Fancy in Old New York*, 140.

17. *Spirit of the Times*, March 16, 1844, 37.

18. *New-York Gazette*, March 3, 1803.

19. *New-York Morning Post*, September 19, 1788. Also *New-York Daily Gazette*, April 20, 1789.

20. *American Citizen*, March 7, 1806.

21. Peverelly, *The Book of American Pastimes*, 342–343.

22. Henry Chadwick, *Beadle's Dime Base-Ball Player: A Compendium of the Game, etc.* (New York: Irwin P. Beadle and Co., 1860), 6.

23. "The Military Spirit in New York. The Target Companies on Thanksgiving Day," *New York Weekly Herald*, December 14, 1850, 397; also *The Subterranean*, October 25, 1845, 2.

24. *New York Illustrated* (New York: D. Appleton & Co., 1870), 40–41.

25. Peverelly, *The Book of American Pastimes*, 346.

26. Albert Spalding Baseball Collections, Knickerbocker Base Ball Club of New York, Club Books 1854–1868, New York Public Library.

27. *Spirit of the Times*, October 21, 1848, 414.

28. Randall Brown, "How Baseball Began," *The National Pastime* 24, 51–54.

29. "The Old Atlantics of Fifty Years Ago," 1905 clipped article, perhaps from *Brooklyn Eagle*, otherwise undated. Albert Spalding Baseball

Collections, Chadwick Scrapbooks, vol. 5. Chadwick quotes from a letter he received from Commerford. Also *Auburn Citizen,* September 22, 1911, reprinted from *New York World.*

30. *Auburn Citizen,* September 22, 1911.

31. Albert Spalding Baseball Collections, Knickerbocker Base Ball Club of New York, Game Books 1845–1856, New York Public Library.

32. Tom Melville, *The Tented Field: A History of Cricket in America* (Bowling Green, OH: Bowling Green State University Popular Press, 1998), 168. Melville erroneously cited the game date as October 11.

33. *True Sun,* October 13, 1845, 2.

34. First names were located in Picton, "Among the Cricketers," *Fun and Fancy in Old New York.*

35. "Sporting Intelligence," *New York Herald,* November 11, 1845, 2.

36. *Porter's Spirit of the Times,* November 7, 1857, 148.

37. *New York Herald,* January 7, 1876, 8.

38. *New York Times,* January 23, 1876, 7.

39. *New York Sun,* February 6, 1887, 6.

40. *New York Daily Tribune,* September 21, 1857, 7.

41. Angus Macfarlane, "The Knickerbockers: San Francisco's First Baseball Team?" *Base Ball* 1:1 (Spring 2007), 7–21.

42. Albert Spalding Baseball Collections, Knickerbocker Base Ball Club of New York, Club Books 1854–1868, New York Public Library.

43. *New York Herald,* March 20, 1903, 12.

44. *New York Herald,* October 14, 1855, 1.

45. *New York Clipper,* December 31, 1853.

46. Letter from John M. Ward to A.G. Spalding, stating his "opinion as to the origin of base ball," as Spalding submitted to the Mills Commission, June 19, 1907.

47. *New York Times,* December 25, 1902.

48. *New York Clipper,* August 25, 1883, 365.

49. *New York Sun,* June 8, 1892, 4.

50. *Porter's Spirit of the Times,* January 3, 1857.

51. *Sporting Life,* January 16, 1889, 3.

52. *New York Herald,* December 14, 1881, 8.

53. *New York Times* and *New York Tribune,* July 1, 1908.

54. "Ball Players of the Past," *New York Sun,* January 16, 1887, 10.

❖ *Magnolia Base Ball Club* ❖
(John Thorn)

CLUB HISTORY

NEW YORK MAGNOLIA BALL CLUB — Vive la Knickerbocker. — A meeting of the members of the above club will take place this (Thursday) afternoon, 2nd instant, at the Elysian Fields, Hoboken [N.J.]. It is earnestly requested that every member will be present, willing and eager to do his duty. Play will commence precisely at one o'clock. Chowder at 4 o'clock.[1]

Among the organized groups that played baseball before the Knickerbockers were the Gotham, New York, Eagle, Brooklyn, Olympic, and Magnolia clubs. The last named came into view only recently, as a ballclub composed not of white-collar sorts with shorter workdays and gentlemanly airs but sporting-life characters, from ward heelers to billiard-room operators and bigamists. Why did the game's earliest writers forget to include this club in its histories? One might venture to guess that the Magnolias were too unseemly a bunch to have been covered by a fig leaf, so they were simply written out of the Genesis story.

In 2007, rummaging through the classified advertisement section of the *New York Herald* of November 2, 1843, looking for who knows what, I was astonished to find a notice for a baseball club unrecorded in the annals of the game. Moreover, the notice made clear that this city-based club played its games across the North River at the Elysian Fields, almost two full years before the formation of the "pioneer" Knickerbockers and their lease of playing grounds at Hoboken. That diminutive ad, which also ran in the *New York Sun,* read in full:

NEW YORK MAGNOLIA BALL CLUB — Vive la Knickerbocker. — A meeting of the members of the above club will take place this (Thursday) afternoon, 2nd instant, at the Elysian Fields, Hoboken. It is earnestly requested that every member will be present, willing and eager to do his duty. Play will commence precisely at one o'clock. Chowder at 4 o'clock.

JOHN McKIBBIN, JR., President.
JOSEPH CARLISLE, Vice President
ANDREW LESTER, Sec.
n2 1t*m

The coding at the bottom signaled that the ad was to appear one time only (1t), with that occasion being game day, November 2 (n2). While this may strike modern eyes as a late month for a baseball game, the baseball season of this era typically ran to the very end of November, in part because August, with its fevers and contagions, was regarded as unsuitable for exertion. The mention of chowder signaled the almost sacramental union of those assembled, their like minds symbolized by their partaking of food from a single pot. The chowder was a fixture of political rallies, too; the city's first target company (archery or rifle), arising from the butcher stalls at the westside Washington Market, was the Washington Market Chowder Club of 1818. "Chowder was the national soup," wrote Herbert Asbury, "and in those times chowder was to be more eaten than drunk, for it was not the anaemic liquid which now sloshes so despairingly in restaurant bowls, but a thick and substantial mixture, compounded of eels, fish, clams, lobster, chicken, duck, and all kinds of tempting ingredients. No social function was complete without a great dish of chowder...."[2]

Of the officers named in the ad, the Irish-born president, 29-year-old John McKibbin, Jr., was a U.S. inspector — a patronage position perhaps obtained through the good offices of

In 1836, Colonel John Stevens created Sibyl's Cave at the Elysian Fields by excavating a hollow in the face of the rocky cliff of Castle Point. From a steadily flowing spring that had existed there, "thirsty promenaders drank at one cent a glass."

his father, who in an aldermanic stroke of fortune in 1835 had been named the city's first superintendent of pavements. Seven years after calling the Magnolia Ball Club to muster and chowder, the younger McKibbin found himself a resident of Sing Sing, convicted of bigamy.[3]

The vice president and actual leader of the club, Joseph Carlisle, was the 26-year-old proprietor of the Magnolia Lunch and Saloon at 74 Chambers Street, corner of Broadway, offering "the best of Wines, Liquors, Segars, and every other requisite." Why was this Northern eatery named for a flower symbolic of the South? Perhaps to signal to the sporting crowd that this was a "full-service" house of the sort pleasing to Southerners in New York on business, and to the gamblers

who left New Orleans after it banned gambling in 1835. The Magnolia Lunch advertised in New Orleans as well as in New York.[4]

In the rampant sporting culture of the day, Carlisle was an up-and-comer who went on to run, in addition to the Magnolia Lunch, the Fountain at 167 Walker Street near the Bowery, the Ivy Green in Hoboken, and an unnamed sporting house at 89 Centre Street opposite the Tombs, the city's Egyptianate prison, where all the while he double-dipped as a jailer. The Magnolia Ball Club secretary, Andrew Lester, was a 27-year-old billiard-room proprietor and Tammany Democrat, linked with Isaiah Rynders' Empire Club, the pugilistic arm of the party (which gave its name to the Empire Base Ball Club

1st Annual Ball of the
MAGNOLIA BALL CLUB.

**This engraved ticket to an 1844 soirée is the earliest known image of grown men playing baseball. It depicts the Magnolia Ball Club —
a workingman's aggregation — in action at the Elysian Fields of Hoboken. The Colonnade Hotel is at right.**

in 1854), enforcing discipline on the rank and file and striking fear into undecided voters.

All three Magnolia officers had impeccable working-class, sporting, ruffian, and political associations of the sort that historians have until now presumed to emerge only with the unruly Brooklyn clubs of the mid–1850s, notably the Atlantics. Indeed, the Magnolia Ball Club was precisely the sort of poison for which the gentlemanly Knickerbocker Base Ball Club was created as an antidote ... two years later.

As soon as I saw the Magnolia Ball Club ad in the *Herald* I recalled that some months earlier, historian David Block had pointed me to a puzzling image, one he thought might be suitable to illustrate a scholarly journal article on town ball. Offered as Lot 1600 in a Leland's auction of December 2002, the item was described as a

> signed copper plate engraving of the quality of paper money. The card itself is a heavy stock with a silver mirror finish. This invitation to the "1st Annual Ball of the Magnolia Ball Club" measures 5 × 3.25 [inches]. The image is magnificent. It shows the plantation like Magnolia Club with its main building and a yacht flying the "M" flag.... Magnolia is an area in southern New Jersey and the site of many stately plantations not unlike the one graphically illustrated we see pictured here.[5]

In a Eureka moment, I realized that I knew for certain what that plantation-like building was. It was the Colonnade, at the Elysian Fields, also known as the Colonnade Hotel or McCarty's Hotel, whose proprietor provided the Knickerbockers and other clubs of the 1840s with many a lavish dinner, either after their exertions on the ballfield or in a season-ending banquet.

Engraver William Fairthorne may have been a member of the Magnolia Ball Club; we are unlikely ever to know. The verisimilitude of his art might make one think so; he was, as far as may be claimed at this writing, the first man ever to have depicted *men* playing ball; and if we may judge by the textual record of the early game, he appears to have gotten things largely right. (Of course the vignette could not display all the features of the game, and thus does not address plugging, or the existence of foul ground.)

The auction-house description erred in calling the Magnolia card an invitation. It was in fact, as further digging in the *Herald* revealed, a ticket — providing admission to a ball that would be held on February 8, 1844.[6] It cost a dollar and, given its enamel-coated card stock and its commissioned rather than stock imagery, was intended to be saved as a memento of the event. The baseball scene on the card reveals three bases with stakes, eight men in the field, a pitcher with an underarm delivery, possibly base-stealing, and a top-hatted waiter bearing a tray of refreshments from the Colonnade. Some of the members of the "in" side are arrayed behind a long table; others are seated upon it. The pitcher delivers the ball. A runner heads from first to second base. This is, from all appearances, the original Knickerbocker game, and that of the New York Base Ball Club, and that of the Gothams of the 1830s (shortstop was a position not manned until 1849–1850).

This ticket is the first depiction of men playing baseball in America, and it may also be, depending upon one's taxonomic convictions, the first baseball card. It is also the earliest visual artifact of the New York Game of baseball. But the greater significance of the card is the new understanding that its underlying story affords of how baseball really began in New York, what spin the workingman's culture of that day may have imparted to baseball's growth, and why the story may have been kept under wraps all these years.

Notes

1. Associated with this ballclub is an engraved invitation to its first annual ball, which has the first depiction of men playing baseball, and shows underhand pitching and stakes for bases. Classified advertisement, *New York Herald*, November 2, 1843. For much more on the find and its implications; go to *thornpricks.blogspot.com/2007/11/really-good-find-more-magnolia-blossoms.html*.

2. H. Asbury, *Ye Olde Fire Laddies* (1930), 103; R. Thornton, *An American Glossary: Being an Attempt to Illustrate Certain Americanisms, Etc.*, vol. 1 (New York: F. Ungor, 1912), 173. As to the Washington Market Chowder Club, see "The Military Spirit in New York—The Target Companies on Thanksgiving Day," *New York Weekly Herald*, December 14, 1850, 397; also *The Subterranean*, October 25, 1845, 2 ("Three different parties of whole-souled fellows are going to express their gratitude to Heaven for its manifold blessings, to-morrow, by playing ball and eating chowder").

3. 1850 Federal census and *Subterranean*: December 20, 1845, classified ad for 1845 Holiday Ball of the "Original Empire Club," at Tammany Hall, Tuesday, December 30.

4. When Carlisle and partner Silas Chickering purchased the saloon in 1842 they advertised this fact, suggestively, in the *New Orleans Daily Picayune* of July 16: "*New York Advertisement. MAGNOLIA LUNCH.* CHICKERING & CARLISLE beg leave to inform their New Orleans and other friends that they have purchased that old and favorite resort of Southerners, The Magnolia Lunch, on the corner of Chambers street and Broadway, where they will be always ready to furnish them with every delicacy which the New York market affords. N.B. handsomely furnished private rooms for parties."

5. *www.lelands.com/bid.aspx?lot=1600&auctionid=212*. Link since removed.

6. Classified advertisement, *New York Herald*, February 6–8, 1844. The ad describes the actual event for which the Magnolia card provided admission. It read: "THE FIRST ANNUAL BALL of the New York Magnolia Ball Club will take place at National Hall, Canal st. on Friday evening, Feb. 9th, inst. The Club pledge themselves that no expense or exertions shall be spared to render this (their first) Ball worthy the patronage of their friends. The Ball Room will be splendidly decorated with the insignia of the Club. Brown's celebrated Band is engaged for the occasion. Tickets $1, to be had of the undersigned, and at the bar of National Hall. JOSEPH CARLISLE, Chairman. PETER H. GRAHAM, Secretary. f6 4t*cc." That Carlisle would be the ball's chairman comes as no surprise, but the new name appearing above, that of Peter H. Graham, may point to a fresh area of inquiry. Speeding eight years forward, we come across three notices in the *Herald* about the reorganization of the Unionist Whigs, no longer known as the Knickerbockers. Silas Chickering, Carlisle's partner in the Magnolia Lunch, is cited as a former president of the group and the two secretaries are Peter H. Graham and … Louis F. Wadsworth, the formidable first baseman and mysterious outcast from the Knickerbocker Base Ball Club.

❖ *Active Base Ball Club of New York* ❖ (Gregory Christiano)

CLUB HISTORY

Junior clubs, which were typically composed of players eighteen and under, played an enormous part in the growth and spread of baseball during the 1850s and 1860s. Unfortunately, their stories have proven difficult to do justice to in studies of the era. Most members of junior clubs were anxious to graduate to senior clubs and did so at the earliest opportunity. Competition between junior clubs was commonplace and intense, but was frequently undermined by accusations of using over-aged players and by the indifference of their elders. Accordingly, there is often little record of junior clubs except for scores, dates, and an ever-changing list of players. The Active Base Ball Club of New York was one of the few junior nines to surmount these obstacles, using a talented nucleus to transform itself from a junior to a senior club. Yet even the Active Club's success was short-lived, showing just how difficult a transition that was.

The Active Base Ball Club was organized in October 1856 and remained a junior club until being admitted into the National Association of Base Ball Players (NABBP) at its December 9, 1863, meeting. While a junior club, the Actives did their best to distinguish themselves from the many junior clubs that quickly came and went and were just as rapidly forgotten. The club's members were predominantly drawn from well-to-do families and, in contrast to the many junior clubs that played in tattered non-matching uniforms or even in street clothes, they prided themselves on their neat uniforms.

Star pitcher Charley Walker, in particular, became noted for sporting dapper knickerbockers—a fashion statement that was later popularized by the Red Stockings of Cincinnati.[1] They also established a club room and permanent playing field alongside the notable clubs at the Elysian Fields in Hoboken.

Even so, far less is known about the first seven years of the Active Club's existence than about their shorter tenure as a senior club. Charles A. Peverelly's *Book of American Pastimes*, for example, described how the club once faced "the celebrated Invincible Club, which was deemed something far ahead of any other junior club" and trounced them by a score of 31 to 1. But whether this contest actually took place remains unknown. Another highlight of the Active Club's years as a junior club came after an 1861 contest with the Constellation club. As was customary, the two clubs followed the match by heading to The Study, a Hudson Street saloon that served as headquarters of the Active Club.[2] But what made this evening stand out was that after the usual food, singing, speeches, and assorted merriment, there was a reading of *Romeo and Juliet*.[3] These tantalizing fragments are pretty much all that is known about the Active Club's years as a junior club.

While the club had a strong nucleus of players whose backgrounds enabled them to treat baseball as an amateur recreation, its transition to senior competition in 1864 was not smooth. The heightened level of competition put pressure on the Actives to become less scrupulous in their adherence to the unwritten rules of sportsmanship. Complaints were made about the legality of Walker's lethal delivery (see his profile for details), and talented left fielder John Hatfield, in particular, became a lightning rod for controversy. Hatfield violated NABBP rules in 1864 by playing for the Gothams while still a member of the Actives, then attempted to rejoin the Actives for a September match against the Enterprise Club. The Enterprise Club reluctantly agreed to let him play, but came to regret their generosity when Hatfield made a brilliant catch and also starred with his bat.[4] The Actives won the match but at a cost to their reputation, making it clear that the road to success against senior clubs would not be easy.

By 1865, the Active Club boasted a formidable lineup that was led by the star battery of Charley Walker and catcher Bill Kelley and was filled out by such strong performers as Hatfield, Mahlon Stockman, J. Seaver Page, and brothers William and George Rooney. Their promise came to fruition in August when the young club traveled to Philadelphia and pulled off a stunning upset.

As the *Philadelphia Inquirer* put it, "the Actives took everybody by surprise" with a decisive 28–13 victory over the "hitherto unconquerable Athletic Base Ball Club" in front of an "immense assemblage of ladies and gentlemen." The Athletics took the loss "with becoming dignity and stoicism" and showed good grace during the post-game festivities as Active Club captain J. Seaver Page was presented with the customary baseball. The *Inquirer's* reporter was less generous; while he praised the "superb" play and "splendid use of the bat" by the visitors, he hastened to make these excuses: "Two prominent members of the Athletic were absent through indisposition,

and a favorite ball used by the Club was lost at an early period of the game and while the scores were nearly equal. It is stated that this circumstance affected the playing of the Athletics. This ball was knocked over the fence that separates the Athletic play ground from the premises of the Wagner Free Institute of Science. The Principal of that Institution secured the ball and resolutely declined to give it up to the owners, a circumstance which created considerable indignation."[5]

The 1865 season brought several additional signs that the Active Club was on its way to becoming a legitimate contender for the national championship, including two wins over the Unions of Morrisania. Many accounts in the newspapers lauded the spirited and excellent play of the Actives. "They are young, lively, *Active* players, and real hard hitters," raved one. "They catch well, handle the bases neatly, and field with judgment and care."[6]

The successful campaign culminated with an exciting match against the Mutual Club of New York that was played for a silver ball at an agricultural fair in Kingston, Ulster County, New York. The frenzy of enthusiasm and the unenclosed field meant that the outfielders had to keep an eye out for spectators and for the horses and carriages that "were driven around and across the ball field with perfect impunity, interfering with and delaying the game." One Active Club outfielder even broke into a group of spectators and made a dramatic catch while standing in their midst. The Mutuals defeated the Actives 26 to 20 to win the prize.[7]

The best days of the Active Club seemed to be ahead of them, but that was not the case. Key players were assuming new responsibilities that left them with little time for baseball. The Rooney brothers both gave up baseball entirely at the close of the 1865 season, while Page ceased to be a regular and other members struggled to find time for practice and play. Just as important, with under-the-table professionalism becoming rampant, the strictly amateur Actives could no longer attract top talent.

As a result, the 1866 season proved a disappointment. One reporter offered this tactful summary: "The Actives, though considerably shorn of the strength they possessed when they defeated the celebrated Athletics of Philadelphia in 1865, succeeded in defeating the well-known Irvingtons last season in a game for a silver ball at the Sussex County (N. J.) Fair, but were not so successful with other first-class clubs." The 1867 season began with optimistic reports that the Active Club, "with their playing strength considerably augmented since last season, promises to once more assume a prominent position among our leading ball clubs."[8] Instead the season proved still more lackluster for the Actives, with only a handful of games being played.

A full column article appearing in the Henry Chadwick Scrapbooks (1868) cites *The Actives Club (Of New York)* as a notable organization and a prominent club with a "high social status and playing strength, even when they were juniors." It goes on to mention that the club trophy case contained balls won from the Mutual, Athletic, Union, Excelsior, Eureka, Eckford, all leading clubs with the exception of the Athletics. The article was forecasting the 1868 season predicting the Actives would field one of the strongest nines in the country. However, they had to overcome a problem from a serious breach of rules that occurred in the 1867 season. A few of the Active Club's members, not specifically named, apparently were up to their old tricks again (see the Hatfield incident of 1864). The apparent misconduct was in regard to how the club gained membership of certain individuals, which the article points out, in "certain cases not exactly on the square." As a consequence of this infraction, the team had to vacate Elysian Fields after the 1867 season and take up permanent residence at Union Grounds, where they continued to play their match games in the 1868 season.

The club made up for their indiscretions by demanding a re-entry of these guilty players into the ranks of the club by enforcing Article 3, Section 2 of the club's constitution, which required any prospective member to swear an oath: "I hereby authorize and request you to present my name as a candidate for membership to the Active Baseball Club of the City of New York; and to pledge me, if elected, to the support of the constitution and bylaws of said club. I am not a member of, in arrears, or indebted for any dues, fines, or assessments to any baseball-club belonging to the National Association of Baseball-players, at the time of making the application."

The outstanding battery of Charley Walker and Bill Kelley remained with the Active Club right up until the end, while family ties enabled them to enlist Kelley's two younger brothers. There was thus enough talent to give the Actives a chance in every game, and as late as 1868 the club posted wins over such notables as the Mutuals of New York and the Unions of Morrisania. The Actives also contributed three starters — Walker, Kelley, and Kelley's brother Harry — to an all-star squad of New York's best players that beat its Brooklyn counterparts 13 to 7 on August 8, 1867.[9]

They had premier players like H. Kelley at first, young Hatfield with his strong throwing arm covering second, Theodore Kelley at third. At short stop was M. Stockman fresh from Irvington where he played in 1867. Stockman was also a reliable "change pitcher," (reliever) and an excellent "behind man" (catcher). Among the many outfielders, the best for the 1868 season were Haines in left field, Collins in right and the renowned J. Espe (alias "Muggins") the club captain in center field. Good substitutes were Ebbets, Rogers, Clark and Hebbard.

But the Active Club's continuing inability to recruit talented young players made it unmistakable that its best days were behind it. Despite the two signal victories in 1868, the club lost the majority of its contests that season. In 1869, the Actives lost all six of their known contests, and that appears to have brought an end to this notable pioneer ball club.

Despite its anticlimactic ending, the Active Base Ball Club of New York played a significant role in the development and popularity of the game and was one of the few junior clubs to make the transition to senior competition. It deserves to be remembered for these important contributions during the early years of baseball.

Club Members

Harry Dupignac: Marshall Wright lists an Andrew Dupignac as playing shortstop and third base for the Active Club in 1867 but that appears to be an error. A young man named Harry J. Dupignac died on August 23, 1868, and the Active Base Ball Club suspended play for thirty days in his memory.[10]

George Ebbets: It would be nice to report that the George Ebbets who played for the Active Club was a direct ancestor of Dodgers owner Charles Ebbets. Alas, that does not appear to have been the case. While the man who played the outfield for the Active Club from 1865 to 1867 cannot be positively identified, he was probably a Civil War veteran named George Arcularius Ebbets who soon moved to San Francisco. In 1874, a man identified as George Ebbetts represented the Occidental Club at the Pacific Base-Ball Convention, and this is probably the same man.[11]

John Van Buskirk Hatfield: John V. Hatfield was born in New Jersey in 1847 and had the most significant professional career of any member of the Active Club, but he continued to be tainted by a reputation as an unscrupulous "revolver." After playing outfield, second base, and catcher for the Actives, he moved on to the Mutuals and then joined the Cincinnati club that was to become famous as the Red Stockings. But Hatfield was expelled after one season, with the club going to the trouble of publishing a book to justify his banishment. As a result, he missed the undefeated 1869 campaign. He returned to New York and played for the Mutuals until the middle of the next decade, becoming best known for a pair of record-breaking throws — in 1868 he hurled a baseball some 396 feet, and four years later he bettered that mark by four feet. After retiring from baseball, Hatfield worked as a pool seller. He died in Long Island City on February 20, 1909.[12]

Henry C. Kelley: Harry Kelley was the middle of three brothers who played for the Active Club. Born in Connecticut in June of 1843, he grew up in Yorkville and served in the Civil War. He began playing baseball for the Champion Club of Yorkville, then graduated to the Actives in 1867 and played first base alongside his brothers for the next two seasons. After his ball-playing days ended, Kelley settled in Newark and became a wealthy corn merchant. He died in East Orange on July 11, 1909.[13]

Theodore "Toots" F. Kelley: Ted Kelley was the youngest of the three Kelley brothers, being born in Connecticut around 1845. He began his career with the Mystic Club of Yorkville in 1858 and then played for the Active Club from 1866 to 1868. He then went to work for the post office. He died in Jacksonville, Florida, on February 16, 1884, when he was still young enough for obituaries to mention that he had been one of the ball-playing Kelley brothers.[14]

William J. Kelley: Born in July of 1839 in Connecticut, William Kelley was the eldest and most talented of the three brothers. He was the catcher for the Actives from 1864 through 1868 and it was his skill behind the plate that enabled Charley Walker to become such an effective pitcher. It appears that Kelley continued to play professionally after the Actives disbanded in 1869, but his common name makes it difficult to be certain. At one time, he was thought to be the William Kelly who played in the National Association, but it has now been established that this was a different man. William Kelley had been an electrotyper before his baseball career, and after baseball he worked as a clerk and as a factory superintendent. Following his wife's death in 1904, he retired and moved to Jay, Maine. Kelley was still living there in 1910, but the date and place of his death remain unknown.

James Seaver Page: J. Seaver Page, who was born in New York City in 1844, was the heart and soul of the Active Club. In addition to playing second base and the outfield, he served as President of the Actives for nine years (1856–1864). He also served as Corresponding Secretary for the NABBP in 1863 and as Recording Secretary in 1865 and 1866. The following year, he was elected president of the New York State Association of Base-Ball Players.[15] Page was an 1862 graduate of City College and taught foreign languages during his involvement with the Active Club. He then chose to go into business and became a very successful merchant, also serving as secretary of the Union League. He still retained an interest in sports, as a member of the New York Athletic Club and as one of the speakers at the 1889 Delmonico's banquet for the ballplayers who had gone on the world tour. J. Seaver Page died in New York on March 26, 1920.[16]

Albert H. Rogers: In 1866, H. A. Rogers and Page were the Active Club's two delegates to the national convention. Three years earlier, a man identified as Albert H. Rogers had joined Page at the convention. And a man with the surname of Rogers played for the Actives from 1864 to 1868. There is a good chance this is all the same man, and the most likely candidate is a medical student by that name, but with such a common name it is hard to be certain.

George W. Rooney: The Rooneys were the other brothers on the Active Club, though they only played in 1865. George Rooney was doing work for the Workingmen's Party in Santa Rosa, California, in March of 1880 when he was fatally shot.[17]

William H. Rooney: William Rooney was born in New York City in 1845 and graduated from City College and Columbia Law School. According to his obituary, Rooney "first attracted attention while playing with junior clubs on Hamilton Square, and at 63d street and 3d avenue, the old-

time headquarters of the fraternity of this city, and afterwards secured a wide-spread reputation in 1864 and 1865, when he played with the Active Club in Hoboken, catching the late Charley Walker.... His career was brief but brilliant, as he abandoned the ball-field on being admitted to the bar in 1866."[18] Rooney also later represented the third district in the New York Assembly.[19] He was just past his fortieth birthday when he died in New York on June 11, 1886, of Bright's disease.

Mahlon Stockman: See Irvington Base Ball Club.

Charles D. Walker: Charley Walker was born in Connecticut around 1841, the son of recent emigrants from Scotland. After moving to New York City, he took up the national pastime and became such an expert pitcher for the Actives between 1864 and 1868 that it was said that he "has probably no superior in the country, ranking with McBride for speed and command of the ball."[20] Yet questions were often raised about whether his delivery conformed to the strict rules, with the Unions of Morrisania refusing to finish an 1866 game because Walker was using his patented "underhanded throw."[21]

Walker's style as reported in *The Ball Player's Chronicle* of June 20, 1867, was to throw outside the batters' reach and play a waiting game. It was "either 'too far out,' 'too close,' 'too low,' or 'too high,' in fact, not just within an inch or two of the spot indicated, the batsman would refuse to strike, the Umpire allowing them full liberty to thus delay the game and make it tedious." This "style" no doubt frustrated the fans as well as the batters.

Even Walker's obituary noted the controversy, declaring that, "although he could pitch as fair as anyone when he pleased, he may, in fact, be said to have been the originator of the present style of 'throwing' that marks the play of all the prominent professional pitchers."[22] Walker was also credited with another significant innovation, apparently being the first baseball player to wear knickerbockers. The Red Stockings of Cincinnati popularized this fashion statement a few years later, but Walker seems to have preceded them. Walker also served as club president in 1866 and remained loyal to the Actives when other star players were jumping from club to club. When professional play began and the Active Club finally disbanded, his services were much in demand but he chose instead to retire from baseball and become a provision dealer.[23] Charley Walker died of tuberculosis on June 5, 1881, at the age of 39.[24]

Other Club Members: Collins, Crawford, George Eaton, Tom Haines, E. Hallock, Hibbard, Moran, W. Simonson, Stoutenberg, Edgar Tilton, Vanderwerken, Cornelius T. Williamson.

A player named George also appeared in some of the box scores of the Active Club, but that name was in quotation marks, suggesting that it was not his actual name.

Notes

1. *New York Clipper,* June 11, 1881.
2. William J. Ryczek, *Baseball's First Inning* (Jefferson, N.C.: McFarland, 2009), 62.

3. *Wilkes' Spirit of the Times,* November 2, 1861.

4. *Brooklyn Eagle,* September 4, 1864.

5. *Philadelphia Inquirer,* August 10, 1865, reprinted in *New York Times,* August 12, 1865.

6. *Brooklyn Eagle,* September 4, 1865.

7. *New York Times,* September 24, 1865.

8. *New York Times,* May 29, 1867, 8.

9. Chadwick Scrapbooks.

10. *Brooklyn Eagle,* August 24, 1868.

11. *San Francisco Chronicle,* October 31, 1874, 3.

12. A. H. Spink, *The National Game* (1911; Carbondale: Southern Illinois University Press, 2000), 246.

13. *New York Times,* July 12, 1909, 7.

14. *St. Louis Post-Dispatch,* March 1, 1884.

15. *New York Tribune,* November 14, 1867, 5.

16. *New York Tribune,* March 28, 1920, 19.

17. *New York Clipper,* April 10, 1880.

18. *New York Clipper,* June 26, 1886.

19. *New York Clipper,* April 10, 1880.

20. Chadwick Scrapbooks.

21. Ryczek, *Baseball's First Inning,* 250.

22. *New York Clipper,* June 11, 1881.

23. William J. Ryczek, *When Johnny Came Sliding Home* (Jefferson, N.C.: McFarland, 1998), 62.

24. *New York Clipper,* June 11, 1881; *New York Tribune,* June 6, 1881, 6.

❖ *Eagle Base Ball Club of New York* ❖ (Gregory Christiano)

CLUB HISTORY

"The Eagles rank as the third base ball club of the country in their institution," wrote Charles A. Peverelly in 1866,"and it is no eulogy to say of them that, in all the attributes of a solid, respectable, and honorable organization, they are second to none." By then, the club's best days were in the past, yet the Eagle Base Ball Club's lengthy career lasted into the openly professional era, and the club's influence is incalculable.

The origins of the Eagle Club are rife with contradictions. Although 1854 is the generally accepted date, there are some suggestions that the club may actually have been formed earlier and even hints that it may have preceded the Knickerbocker and Gotham clubs. The most noteworthy piece of evidence is a small book entitled *By-laws and Rules of the Eagle Ball Club,* which was published in 1852 with a cover that states plainly, "organized, 1840."[1] In addition, an 1887 history of the club stated, "A few months after the rise of the Knickerbockers the members of Eagle Hose Cart No. 1 called a meeting and organized a base ball club."[2] Finally in 1871, the Eagle Club made plans to celebrate its eighteenth anniversary on August 25, which suggests that the club was founded in the summer of 1853.[3]

The most plausible explanation for this wide variety of dates is that members of the Eagle Club had been playing ball games for several years prior to 1854, but had not been using the rules devised by the Knickerbockers. The 1852 by-laws, for example, specifically identify the club as the "Eagle Ball Club," and it was not until 1854 that "Base Ball" replaced "ball." And William Wood confirmed that the Eagle Club "originally played in the 'old-fashioned way' of throwing the ball to the batter and at the runner in order to put him out."[4] More support for this view comes from a meeting of the Knickerbocker Club on November 18, 1853, at which a communication was received from the Eagle Club asking for help in devising a set of playing rules.[5]

So it would seem that the members of the Eagle Club had already been playing bat-and-ball games for several years, but it was not until 1853 that they began thinking about using the Knickerbocker Club's rules and not until 1854 that they began to do so. In any event, once the Eagles adopted the new rules, the club had a profound influence that is difficult to overstate. In 1852 and 1853 the Knickerbocker and Gotham clubs had only themselves to play, and there was no indication that their version of ball-playing was about to spread. The addition of the Eagle Club gave the regulation game of baseball new momentum and led directly to its rapid growth. Three, as the saying goes, really is the magic number.

From the start, the Eagle Base Ball Club was a force to be reckoned with. The club began practicing regularly at the Elysian Fields in Hoboken, and on October 24, 1854, it played its first match game. Contests were still being played until one side made 21 "aces," and the Eagles lost to the Gotham Club by a respectable margin of 21–14. The Eagle Club finished the 1854 season with a two-game series with the Knickerbocker Club. In the first contest, played on November 10, the Eagles had scored the required 21 when their opponents had only counted 4. The Knickerbockers were said to have fielded their second nine in this match, but in a rematch held a week later they used seven of the same nine players and the Eagles took advantage of the last turn at bat to eke out another win, 22 to 21.[6]

That concluded a successful season, both for the Eagle Club and the still-young game of "regulation baseball." Some forty-five members of the three clubs commemorated the end of the playing season with a celebratory dinner at Fijux's restaurant on December 15, 1854, at which they "enjoyed themselves in a manner that ball playing does not seriously diminish the appetite, either for physical or intellectual enjoyment."[7] William H. Van Cott of the Gotham Club described the camaraderie and the event in an intriguing letter to *Spirit of the Times* that prefigured some of the changes that would soon reshape the game.

Van Cott began by explaining that the three clubs met

on a semi-weekly basis for "exercise in the old fashioned game of Base Ball." Yet he then added that the "Clubs are composed

REVISED

CONSTITUTION, BY-LAWS

AND

RULES

OF THE

EAGLE BALL CLUB,

ADOPTED 1854.

ORGANIZED 1840.

BL-2A7.56

New-York:

OLIVER & BROTHER, STEAM JOB PRINTERS.

1854.

The constitution and bylaws of the Eagle Club, one of the earliest organizations to form (in 1840) and later to play under the New York rules.

of residents of this city, of various professions, each numbering about thirty members, and their affairs are conducted in such manner, in point of system and economy, as to enable all persons, who can give the necessary time for this purpose, to enjoy the advantages of this noble game. There have been a large

number of friendly, but spirited trials of skill, between the Clubs, during the last season, which have showed that the game has been thoroughly systematized, and that the players have attained a high degree of skill in the game." He closed his letter with a prediction: "The indications are that this noble game will, in the coming season, assume a higher position than ever, and we intend to keep you fully advised."[8] Even in his wildest dreams, Van Cott could not have imagined how much space in American newspapers would eventually be devoted to a game that was still only being played in organized fashion by three clubs.

The influence of the Eagle Club began to be felt almost immediately. One of the spectators who watched the Eagles and Knickerbockers play in the fall of 1854 was a man named John Suydam who was inspired to start a club called the Excelsiors.[9] Other new clubs also sprang up, and by 1857 there were enough adherents to "regulation base ball" for the formation of a governing body, the National Association of Base Ball Players. The foundation of the game was being firmly established in those early years.

Another spectator at an Eagle match game in the fall of 1856 would do even more to encourage the spread of baseball. Henry Chadwick was returning from a cricket match when he "chanced to go through the Elysian Fields during the progress of a contest between the noted Eagle and Gotham Clubs. The game was being sharply played on both sides, and I watched it with deeper interest than any previous ball match between clubs that I had seen. It was not long before I was struck with the idea that base ball was just the game for a national sport for Americans, and, reflecting on the subject, it occurred to me, on my return home, that from this game of ball a powerful lever might be made by which our people could be lifted into a position of more devotion to physical exercise and healthful out-door recreation than they had hitherto, as a people, been noted for."[10] After reaching this conclusion, Chadwick became a tireless advocate of baseball, writing about it for more than half a century.

From the start, the influence of the Eagles extended far beyond those who were able to visit the Elysian Fields and watch them play. During the period when there were still only three active clubs, the Knickerbockers, Gothams, and Eagles engaged in discussions about the rules. There is no way to be sure of how they arrived at their conclusions, but it seems likely that members of all three clubs offered suggestions until a consensus was reached, rather than one man or one club making all the decisions. Interestingly, the Eagles published a new version of their rules in 1854 that closely followed those of the Knickerbockers with one important exception—the Eagle Club prescribed that the pitcher had to stand at least fifteen paces from the batter.[11] The precise distance was changed often in the ensuing years, but the requirement remained an essential part of the baseball rulebook.

The Eagle Club also had a great influence on the development foreshadowed by Van Cott—the intersection of baseball and the newspapers. The club's very first match game in 1854 earned a box score in the *New York Herald*, along with these remarks: "The game of base ball bids fair soon to be as popular as the favorite game of cricket, and right glad are we to see these healthful and manly exercises so frequently indulged in. Many base ball clubs have been recently organized...."[12] This last statement seems to have been an exaggeration, as the Empire Club is the only new club that is known to have entered the field in 1853, meaning that there were still only four organized ball clubs. But it is safe to assume that no enthusiast wrote to the *Herald* to complain!

The Eagle Club continued to receive generous press coverage in 1855. Its first game of the new season was played against the Knickerbockers at Elysian Fields and was recorded on the front page of the *New York Herald*. The description of the contest, which the Knickerbockers won 27 to 15, even mentioned the positions of some of the Eagle players: the "Behind man" (catcher)—Charles Place; the pitcher—Gibbes; and the judge—John W. Mott. The report also critiqued the play and praised the exceptional play of Gibbes.[13]

The exploits of the Eagles were also reported to the press by an anonymous correspondent whose familiarity with the club's doings suggests that he was a member. During 1857 and 1858 the author, who was identified only by the letter X, provided regular updates on the club and lauded individual players. In a typical letter he wrote enthusiastically: "Among the many clubs that have been organized in the last few years, none stand higher than the Eagle, and we hope, will always continue to do so. Shortly after their formation, they did not hesitate to play the first clubs; and if they were defeated, they exhibited such an earnestness to improve, together with physical ability, that their friends were sanguine of their ultimate success. The year 1854 was their first as a ball club. Their rapid improvement since then must certainly have justified the highest expectations of those interested in the welfare of the club."[14]

The Eagle Club had the additional distinction of being portrayed in the earliest known recorded illustration of a baseball game. This woodcut was published in *Porter's Spirit of the Times* on September 12, 1857, and bore the title "Base Ball in America." The caption offered a description of the match:

"The Eagles and Gothams Playing their Great Match at the Elysian Fields on Tuesday September 8th."[15]

By the end of the decade, new clubs with younger players had entered the field, forcing veterans clubs like the Knickerbockers, Empires, and Eagles to take a back seat. There were exceptions, such a contest on July 23, 1861, when the Eagles upset the champion Eckfords 32–23, in a noteworthy upset. But by and large, the members of the first clubs seem to have accepted the new role of elder statesmen who tried to provide an example of sportsmanship to the newer clubs.

This account, for example, appeared following a one-sided 1858 loss to the Excelsiors: "The last man of the Eagles had barely dropped his bat when we were perfectly electrified by some tremendous cheering by the two parties, which we were pleased to observe was not done in an exultant manner by the victors, nor in a dogged one by the defeated, but in a congratulating and jovial spirit, which invariably indicates the gentleman, and gives evidence that our friends of the base-ball fraternity are possessors of noble and generous dispositions."[16] Similarly, another season was launched with the announcement that "The Eagles are going in for fun this year, and will be having 'a real jolly time of it, you know.'"[17]

The Eagle Club was known for being just as gracious in victory. After a surprisingly lopsided 1858 victory over the Knickerbockers, Eagle president Andrew J. Bixby spoke "in terms eulogistic of their opponents' prowess, remarking, also, that the Eagles, while playing the match felt that they were simply contending with friends, and that the great disparity in the score arose from the absence of some of the best of Knickerbocker players. These remarks were well timed, and well rendered, and that he touched the latent chords of some of those fine feeling fellows, was apparent by the way in which their countenances brightened up, and by the thunders of applause which followed them."[18]

But while most members of the earliest clubs strove to be good sports in defeat, there were occasional hints of competitiveness. On July 10, 1860, an 18–18 tie between the Eagles and the Gothams was accompanied by "very hard feelings ... caused by the interference and actions of parties who betted heavily on the result, among whom were alike players and others who are prohibited from betting by the rules of the game."[19]

The heyday of the Eagle Club was before the Civil War. Indeed, those glory days eclipsed the club's post-war activities to the extent that the only known lengthy history of the Eagle Club maintained: "The first gun fired at Fort Sumter seemed to reecho in this city, and the interest in the club died out. A strong effort was made to keep it up, but in vain."[20]

Yet the Eagle Club did continue to play after the war, clad in a uniform that consisted of dark blue flannel pants, a checkered shirt, blue cap with white visor. Wins were few and far between until 1868, when a brilliant catcher named Nat

Hicks led the Eagles to a long string of victories. But Hicks left to join the Star Club during the 1869 season, and the results were disastrous. "Since the secession of Hicks from the ranks of the veteran Eagles," observed one reporter, "they have met with defeat in every game they have played."[21]

The 1869 season was the last year in which the Eagles played an extended series of games, though the club did not immediately disband. In 1871 the Eagles joined other pioneer clubs like the Knickerbockers and Empires in an attempt to organize an amateur rival to the newly formed National Association of Professional Base Ball Players.[22] But, nothing of significance seems to have come of their efforts. So, too, an attempt to celebrate the eighteenth anniversary of the Eagle Club on August 25, 1871, with a "grand reunion and fete" does not appear to have come to fruition. Yet the proposed reunion did occasion this fitting tribute to the club's legacy: "For many years the Eagle Club was foremost in perpetuating and sustaining our national game when it was in its day of glory and integrity, and no association ranks higher as a body or honorable, high-toned, and manly players. May their annual festival be not only one of the happiest of social gatherings, but a pleasant reminder of the days when the Eagle's colors waved proudly in the van, and the first young men of Gotham were proud to acknowledge allegiance to them."[23]

At some point during the next few years, the Eagle Base Ball Club passed out of existence. The exact date of the club's demise, as with the date of the club's origin, may never be known. We can be much more certain that the Eagles left behind a legacy that contributed to the rise and popularity of the cherished game of baseball and helped establish it as our national pastime.

CLUB MEMBERS

Despite the club's significance, even the key members of the Eagle Club remain difficult to identify. In 1871, plans were made for a "grand reunion and fete" on August 25 to commemorate the club's eighteenth anniversary but the event does not appear to have taken place. Similarly, few reminiscences by club members were published in later years. The one notable exception was a lengthy piece in the *New York Sun* on January 16, 1887, which appears to have been based primarily on the recollections of Sam Yates, who worked for the *Sun*.[24] Unfortunately, while that article provided many clues about club members, hardly any of them correspond to listings in the city directories or census. It would appear either that Yates had a poor memory for names or that the author did a sloppy job of transcribing his reminiscences. As a result, there are numerous gaps in these profiles, along with many club members who remain identified by surname alone. Perhaps at some point new information will emerge that will allow firmer identifications.

These problems have made it difficult to find a common thread among club members. The *Sun* article suggested a link to the Eagle Hose Company, but while quite a few members of the ball club were volunteer fire-fighters, only one seems to have belonged to that specific company. As will be seen in the profiles, the common tie appears to have been employment in businesses located on Nassau Street and the vicinity. Since this bond was of a less permanent nature than the ones that joined many ball clubs, it is perhaps not surprising that many club members drifted out of touch.

William W. Armfield: Born in England around 1822, W. W. Armfield was a coal merchant and businessman who served briefly as a Brooklyn alderman. Foreshadowing his career in politics, he served as one of the Eagle Club's three representatives at the 1857 convention and gave a speech in which he declared that the Commissioners of Central Park had allotted room to cricket players "but none for base ball, and he trusted that this convention would put itself in communication with the authorities on the subject."[25] Armfield died in Millington, New Jersey, on September 5, 1903.

Bensel: A man named Bensel or Bensell was a regular for the Eagle Club during its early years. Charles A. Peverelly's book identified him as Walter Bensel, but no man by that name of appropriate age can be found on any census. The 1887 article in the *Sun* said that "Bensall is somewhere in Hoboken," but this clue failed to point to a candidate. It is possible that he was William P. Bensel, who later served as president of the Knickerbockers and is profiled in that entry. Another possibility is John Warner Bensel (1832–1889), who went by his middle name; perhaps "Walter" was confused with Warner.

Andrew J. Bixby: A. J. Bixby was one of the club's first pitchers and was active in its affairs, serving as one of its three representatives at the 1857 NABBP convention and as temporary president of the NABBP in 1858.[26] According to an 1856 game account, "Mr. Bixby, as pitcher, acquitted himself admirably, and has but one fault, that of consuming too much time in preparation, and allowing the men to make their bases too easily."[27] Bixby got "no great speed on the ball" but instead relied upon getting as much twist on his pitches as was possible under the delivery restrictions of the era.[28] Like so many fellow club members, Bixby's involvement with the Eagle Club seems to have ended in 1861. Yet he retained enough interest in the sport to be involved in the 1871 effort to form a strictly amateur association of baseball clubs.[29] In the 1887 article in the *Sun*, he was said to be "if anything ... more fond of base ball than ever." Bixby worked for the brokerage of Fisk and Hatch and later secretary of the Union League. When he died in Fordham, New York, on July 9, 1889, he was working as a bookkeeper for the Sub-Treasury. There is contradictory information about his age, but he was born in the state of New York sometime in the 1820s.[30]

William Crawford Conner: William C. Conner was born in New York on December 4, 1821, the oldest son of James Conner, a pioneer in the type-founding business who was credited with the invention of the electrotyped matrix to replace the use of matrices driven into copper with steel punches. James Conner was also a Tammany Grand Sachem who was elected county clerk in 1843. William Conner graduated from Columbia, and at the outset of the Gold Rush his father sent him to California to serve as his agent. While there he helped a man named Jerome B. Painter to establish the first type foundry in San Francisco. Upon his return, he was named a partner in his father's business, the United States Type Foundry, which eventually became known as James Conner's Sons. Running this very successful business would have been enough to occupy most men, but William Conner also found time for a wide variety of other activities. He was a member of the volunteer fire department, and like many of his fellow fire-fighters, he became involved in baseball. His involvement with the Eagle Club does not seem to have been extensive, but Peverelly identified him as one of its founders. He also followed in his father's footsteps as a Tammany Sachem. After serving two terms as a county supervisor, he was elected in 1865 to his father's former office as county clerk. He was elected sheriff in 1875, and during his term in office Boss Tweed escaped from custody. Though not directly responsible, Conner was deeply embarrassed and spent a great deal of his own money to pursue Tweed, who was eventually recaptured in Spain. William Conner died in New York on April 26, 1881.[31]

Philip J. Cozans: Philip J. Cozans was another Eagle Club founder who served as club president and as an officer in the National Association of Base Ball Players. Cozans was born in Canada in 1828 and established a publishing business at 107 Nassau Street in the early 1850s. He was a very industrious publisher, and he may have written many of the titles he issued. One of the books credited to him was a children's novel entitled *Little Eva: The Flower of the South*, which was a pro-slavery response to Harriet Beecher Stowe's *Uncle Tom's Cabin*. He also used the name of Uncle Philip for such titles as *The Good Child's Own Book of Moral and Instructive Stories*. In addition, he published an 1855 work entitled *Home Games for the People*, which he may have written. But commercial success eluded him, and by the end of the decade he was in financial difficulties and switched his focus to selling stationery and valentines. By 1864 he had set up a new business at 115 Nassau and hired fellow Eagle Club member Andrew Peck (see below) as a clerk. But in May of 1865 he was forced to close his doors. Soon after this Cozans was elected treasurer of the National Association of Base Ball Players, but he was found to have taken money without authorization and was forced to repay it.[32] The decline in Cozans's fortunes continued, and he died in complete obscurity in Manhattan on February 18, 1896. His name was misspelled in both the New York death index and in a brief death notice in the *New York Tribune*; only the fact that the address listed in the *Tribune* was that of Cozans's brother made it possible to confirm that this was indeed the man who had once been president of the Eagle Club.

Frank Fleet: Frank Fleet played for the Eagles after the war and was one of the very few club members to go on to a major league career. He remains, however, one of the most enigmatic and elusive ballplayers in major league history. He played for five major league teams, and obituaries identified him as a former ballplayer when he died on June 13, 1900, in New York City. Yet he has never been identified on any censuses, and nothing whatsoever is known about his life.

Marion E. "Joe" Gelston: Joe Gelston was born in New York around 1839 and by 1857 was a starter for the Eagle Club, playing catcher and shortstop. His stellar fielding prompted one observer to boast that "any ball within his reach is always held."[33] Another described Gelston as "'the little man,' and the finest player of his inches that the city can boast."[34] After the 1859 season he and fellow club member Robert Griglietti left for San Francisco. Gelston soon became captain of a club in that city, which was named the Eagles, purportedly in his honor. By 1863 Gelston was serving as the engrossing clerk of the California State Senate.[35] But in 1866 he was charged with forging $10,550 worth of soldiers' warrants, and he fled California.[36] There were sightings of Gelston in Nevada and Panama, but he was never apprehended, and nothing is known about his subsequent activities.[37]

Robert Griglietti: Robert Griglietti was born in August of 1835 and grew up in Jersey City. He joined the Eagle Club in 1859, but he and Gelston left for San Francisco after that season. A plumber by trade, Griglietti soon returned to the East and was living in Newark as of 1910.

Nathan Woodhull Hicks: Nat Hicks was born in Hempstead, New York, on April 19, 1845. He only took up baseball in earnestness after serving in the Civil War, but soon earned recognition as the greatest defensive catcher of the era. Hicks is sometimes erroneously credited with being the first catcher to station himself directly behind the plate. This was not the case, but he did move close to the plate at a time when catchers still wore no protective equipment and almost all of them were opting to stand farther back. Hicks also played a huge role in the development of the curve ball — he was one of the few catchers skilled enough to handle the pitch, and curve pioneers like Arthur "Candy" Cummings and Bobby Mathews were frequently paired with him. Hicks played for the Eagle Club until the middle of the 1868 season and, as described in the club's history, his departure was a devastating blow to the club. He caught in the major leagues until 1877, earning a reputation for great skill and extraordinary toughness. He then opened a handball club and billiard hall in Hoboken, where he also became noted as a singer. His fearless play was still remembered when he died in Hoboken on April 21, 1907, and numerous papers described his passing as the end of an era in which catchers had demonstrated incomparable skill and courage.[38]

Howe: Howe was an Eagle Club regular for several years and the 1887 article in the *Sun* described him as a member of the Board of Fire underwriters who was also "connected with the fire patrol. He is even more jolly than of old, and is a frequent visitor at the Polo grounds." But he has not been identified.

John W. Mott: John Williams Mott, another of the Eagle Club's founders, served as one of its representatives at the first NABBP convention and was elected as one of two vice presidents of the game's governing body. Mott was born in New York City on March 9, 1822. He founded the brokerage of Mott, McCready & Co. and later served as president of the United States Warehouse Company and as a member of the Produce Exchange. He died in Brooklyn on February 18, 1873.

Andrew Peck: Andrew Peck does not appear to have played any match games for the Eagle Club, but he reported that he joined the club in the late 1850s, and his membership was attested to by his longtime friend Henry Chadwick.[39] Peck was born in New York City on October 15, 1836, but he had no recollections of his mother, and when he was five his father placed him in the Leake and Watts Orphan Home. His father died without being able to reclaim Andrew, who was then "bound out" to an upstate storekeeper at the age of fourteen. After a year and a half of "cruel treatment," Andrew Peck ran away and eventually made his way back to New York and, after working at several menial jobs, he found steady work at the American News Company, located at 121 Nassau Street. While at this job he joined the Eagle Club and began to think about setting out on his own. That dream was interrupted when the Civil War broke out, and Peck enlisted in the 38th New York Volunteers. After ten months' service he was discharged with his left hand and part of his left arm permanently paralyzed.

He returned to New York and began "haunting Nassau street" as an independent salesman of tops, games, and baseball paraphernalia, all of which he made himself. As he later told it:

> "Shortly after my arrival home, I originated and published several games such as the Game of Battles, the Game of Barnum's Museum, and others. The Game of Barnum's Museum I sold to P. T. Barnum at $12 a gross. These I often saw sold in the Museum, which was then located at Broadway, Ann and Fulton streets, by the midgets. I well remember seeing Tom Thumb, Minnie and Lavinia Warring and Commodore Nutt sell them to visitors for $1 a pack.
>
> While engaged in the manufacture of these I took up the making of baseballs.
>
> I would buy old rubber car springs, cut them up into strips, then into small squares about 1 inches in size, round the corners, wind them with woolen yarn, and then give them to some sailor or harness maker to cover with white horse hide. All this was done by hand, and I got $2 to $2.50 each retail and $18 to $24 a dozen for them. I used to go around among the storekeepers with samples of my games and baseballs, take an order one day, and deliver the goods in from two to five days.
>
> I kept this up until 1864 when I clerked it again, working this time for a Phillip J. Cozzens [sic] of 116 Nassau street. All of the time, however, I was pegging away on my own account at baseballs, cheap belts and caps. When my employer gave up

business in May, 1865, I started out at once for myself on the top floor back room of 109 Nassau street, four flights up.

> I started my business with 10 cents in cash, which was all of the money I had. A friend of mine in the building allowed me to use without charge, for my stock, part of a packing table and a three-legged stool. I sold goods for cash only. My plan was to make a general sporting goods store, where outfits and paraphernalia could be bought altogether without the necessity of purchasers buying their needs piecemeal at different stores all over the city.
>
> I remained at 109 Nassau street [sic] until March 1, 1866, when I took into partnership Mr. [Washington I.] Snyder, whose acquaintance I had made when both of us were employed by the American News Company. He was anxious to start in business and we soon came to an agreement. He put in $1,000 cash against my stock and experience and the firm became known as Andrew Peck & Co. In March of 1868 we changed it to Peck & Snyder. During the year 1865 I had brought out the first baseball score book, a small sixteen-page, book, and had it copyrighted as "Peck's Pocket Baseball Score Book." This and other sporting specialties we now began to put out in increased numbers.

During the store's early years, business was slow but on an almost daily basis Henry Chadwick would drop by to offer encouragement and — surprise, surprise — to "discuss the rules of the game." But before long business was booming and the firm made Andrew Peck a very wealthy man. He eventually sold the business to A.G. Spalding and devoted the remainder of his life to other pursuits.[40] He died in Brooklyn on March 21, 1918.

Charles Place, Jr.: Charles Place was born in New York around 1822 and, despite his age, became a regular for the Eagle Club in the late 1850s. The son of a doctor, he worked as a grocer and merchant but then in 1880 was simply listed as a gentleman. He died in Manhattan on November 8, 1893, and by then he was listed as a president, but it is not clear what he was the president of.

James Gilmore Powers: James G. Powers occasionally played for the Eagle Club during their heyday and then served as club secretary in 1861 and as club treasurer in 1866. Powers was born around 1830 and apparently served in the Mexican-American War. A printer by trade, like so many fellow club members he worked on Nassau Street — in 1861, the club's correspondence went to his office at 122 Nassau.[41] He died in Brooklyn on November 2, 1884, and his passing warranted a mention in the *New York Clipper*, though he was erroneously described as a member of the Empire Club.[42]

Tom Smith: Tom Smith was one of the mainstays of the Eagle Club in the 1850s. The 1887 article in the *Sun* stated, "Everyone knows old Tom Smith. Go down Fulton street [sic], and just east of Nassau you will find a large clothing store. The name of Smith is over the door. Once inside, you come face to face with Tom. He has become somewhat older, of course, but not a bit less clear headed." But that description does not match any listing in the city directory.

Thomas Lloyd Thornell: Thomas Thornell, who played shortstop for the Eagle Club, was born in New York City on January 9, 1829. He worked as secretary of the American Fire Insurance Company and died on March 20, 1880.

Van Nice: Van Nice was another of the Eagle Club's regulars in the 1850s. The *Sun* article stated, "If you will go through Washington Market on the West street [*sic*] side you will see a stout, good-natured produce dealer who will acknowledge having been third baseman Van Nice." There is, however, no corresponding listing in the city directory. There was a John Van Nice who was a butcher but whether he is the same man is not known.

Alfred Williams: According to the 1887 article in the *Sun*, "Williams is just as little as ever. He is in the steamboat supply business, and lives in Jersey City." See the entry on the Excelsior Base Ball Club for more details on his life.

Winslow: Winslow was another club mainstay and the *Sun* article said that he had gone to Texas and never returned. It is possible, but by no means certain, that he was a man named Sylvester Atwood Winslow who was born in Ontario County, New York, in 1821 and who died in Annetta, Texas, on February 11, 1893.

Sam Yates: Sam Yates was one of the few Eagles to share memories of the club in later years. He was working for the *New York Sun* in 1887 and was the source of much of what we know about the club's members. The following year he captained a benefit game of old-time players.[43] Yates was born in England in 1826, but immigrated to the United States at a young age — as one reporter put it, "An Englishman by birth, Mr. Yates has lived so long in New York that the very City Hall clock seems to nod to him every day as an old acquaintance."[44] Sam Yates was ninety-two when he died in New York on January 19, 1919, making him one of the last surviving club members.

Other Club Members: Badeau/Radeau, Baker, Benson (?), Bogart, Henry Brinkerhoff (see Pioneer Base Ball Club), Chapin, Chipcase, Clarke, Collins, Charles C. Commerford (see New York Base Ball Club (a.k.a. Washington BBC, Gotham BBC) in *Base Ball Founders* and Bridgeport's 1866 Clubs in *Base Ball Pioneers: 1850–1870*), Cotheal, Colgate, Solomon L. Crosby, Demarest, Samuel Doremus, Ed Duffy (of Mutual and Eckford base ball clubs), Fruin/Bruin (possibly one of the Fruin brothers of the Empire Club of St. Louis), A. Gaughan, T. Gaughan, W. Gallagher, Gibbes, Robert S. Gilman (see Excelsior Base Ball Club), Hazzard, Nick Houseman, Hoyt, Hussey, Hyatt, Conrad Jordan (see Pioneer Club of Jersey City), Kane, Martin A. Kelly, Laker, Leonard, Marsh, Fenton C. McElroy, W. H. Norton, Oliver, Walter A. Pense, Phillips, Reed, George A. Rutzer, Salisbury, Sanger, Schaub/Schwab, John A. Seaman, W. D. Sennard, N. B. Shaffer (president in 1866), W. B. Shaffer, J. Sloat, R. Sloat, Stevens, Vanderbilt, Vitt, Wandell, Norman Welling (see Knickerbocker Base Ball Club), Winicutt/Wintercott, Winterbotham/Winterbottom.

Other Non-Playing Members: James Baskett, W. H. Bennett, Walter J. Billings, Edward H. Bridgham, H. E. Buys or Bays, M.A. Collingwood, Benjamin Farley, Thomas G. Harold, Frank Harper, A. A. McFarlan, John Miller, Edward G. Moore, Simeon Thompson, I. Williams, S.H. Williams, A.D. Wilson.

Notes

1. By-laws and Rules of the Eagle Ball Club; cover reprinted in Irving Leitner, *Baseball: Diamond in the Rough* (New York: Criterion, 1972), 39.

2. *New York Sun*, January 16, 1887, 10.

3. *Spirit of the Times*, undated clipping, July 1871, Old Fulton website

4. William Wood, *Manual of Physical Exercises* (New York: Harper & Bros., 1867), 189–190, quoted on Protoball website.

5. Preston D. Orem, *Baseball (1845–1881) From the Newspaper Accounts* (Altadena, CA: self-published, 1961), 11.

6. *New York Herald*, November 3 and 19, 1854; *Spirit of the Times*, November 25, 1854. The Eagles also seem to have won a rematch against the Gothams on November 3, though the contest is not well documented. See Craig Waff's listing on the Protoball website.

7. "Ball Playing," *New York Herald*, December 19, 1854, 3.

8. William H. Van Cott, "The New York Base Ball Clubs," *Spirit of the Times*, December 23, 1854, 534. The piece in the Herald on the 19th contained almost identical wording, suggesting that Van Cott was also the author of that article.

9. Melvin L. Adelman, *A Sporting Time* (Urbana: University of Illinois Press, 1986), 125.

10. Henry Chadwick, *The Game of Base Ball* (1868; Columbia, S.C.: Camden House, 1983), 10.

11. David Block, *Baseball Before We Knew It* (Lincoln: University of Nebraska Press, 2005), 84.

12. *New York Herald*, November 3, 1854.

13. *New York Herald*, Morning Edition, June 6, 1855.

14. *Porter's Spirit of the Times*, November 7, 1857, 148.

15. *Porter's Spirit of the Times*, September 12, 1857, 17.

16. *New York Clipper*, July 3, 1858; quoted in William J. Ryczek, *Baseball's First Inning* (Jefferson, N.C.: McFarland, 2009), 71.

17. *New York Clipper*, April 16, 1864; quoted in Ryczek, *Baseball's First Inning*, 206.

18. "Eagle vs. Knickerbocker," *New York Clipper*, August 7, 1858.

19. *New York Clipper*, July 21, 1860.

20. "Ball Players of the Past," *New York Sun*, January 16, 1887, 10.

21. *New York Clipper*, August 21, 1869.

22. William J. Ryczek, *When Johnny Came Sliding Home* (Jefferson, N.C.: McFarland, 1998), 249.

23. *Spirit of the Times*, undated clipping, July 1871, Old Fulton Postcard website.

24. "Ball Players of the Past," *New York Sun*, January 16, 1887, 10.

25. *Spirit of the Times*, January 31, 1857, 603.

26. *Spirit of the Times*, March 20, 1858, 65.

27. *Porter's Spirit of the Times*, October 4, 1856.

28. *Porter's Spirit of the Times*, November 7, 1857.

29. Chadwick Scrapbooks.

30. *New York Times*, July 9, 1889.

31. *Inland Printer*, November 1906, 194–195; Wesley Washington Pasko, *American Dictionary of Printing and Bookmaking* (New York: Howard Lockwood, 1894), 113.

32. Ryczek, *When Johnny Came Sliding Home*, 249.

33. *Porter's Spirit of the Times*, November 7, 1857.

34. *Porter's Spirit of the Times*, July 4, 1857.

35. *San Francisco Evening Bulletin*, December 9, 1863.

36. *San Francisco Evening Bulletin*, January 22 and 23, 1866, March 9, 1868, January 12, 1872; *Sacramento Daily Union*, January 1, 1867.

37. *Sacramento Daily Union*, January 1, 1867.
38. Peter Morris, *Catcher: How the Man Behind the Plate Became an American Folk Hero* (Chicago: Ivan R. Dee, 2009), passim.
39. *Sporting News*, December 31, 1904, 7.
40. "Wealthy Brooklyn Man Started on 10 Cents Capital," *Brooklyn Eagle*, June 13, 1915.

41. *New York Sunday Mercury*, October 6, 1861.
42. *Brooklyn Eagle*, November 3, 1884, 3; *New York Clipper*, December 13, 1884.
43. *Brooklyn Eagle*, August 22, 1888.
44. *National Police Gazette*, December 26, 1885, 2.

❖ *Empire Base Ball Club* ❖
(Gregory Christiano)

CLUB HISTORY

Richard L. Haydock, Richard H. Thorne, Henry H.R. Smith, Walter Scott, W. Hart Smith, Thomas Miller, Thomas Leavy, and three men identified only by their surnames: Hearne, Taylor, Campbell. Recognize any of these names? No? It's not surprising, but these gentlemen deserve to be remembered because they formed the core of the Empire Base Ball Club when this pioneer baseball club was founded on October 23, 1854, with a mere eleven members.[1]

By the spring of 1855, the club's membership had grown to "some thirty young men, mostly clerks in the lower wards of the City." They adopted a uniform that consisted of "a white cap and jacket trimmed with crimson, drab pants, buckskin shoes and a black glazed belt, with the letters E.B.B.C. painted on the front." The members began to meet every Wednesday and Saturday afternoon at 4:00 P.M. at McCarthy's Ground in Hoboken, New Jersey, for practice.[2]

The new club got off to an auspicious start with a 21–19 triumph over the Eagle Club at the Elysian Fields on June 15, 1855, in front of a concourse that "was well covered with visitors, especially ladies, who seemed to take great interest in the game."[3] That victory appears to have been the club's only match game win in 1855, but the remainder of the Empire Club's inaugural season saw its members gain valuable experience.[4] For example, on September 5, 1855, the Empire Club returned to the Elysian Fields to face the Gotham Club and were represented by a nine of Haydock, Taylor, Thorne, Smith, Hearne, Scott, Miller, Campbell and Leavy (with John J. Bloomfield acting as the club's "Judge").[5] The outcome was a "terrible defeat" by the score of 25–4 that showed that the Empires were "too young a club for the powerful Gothams."[6] Yet as another reporter tactfully put it, "It showed some little boldness of the Empire Club to challenge the Gothams."[7] The stage was set for the Empire Club to have one of the longest runs of baseball's pioneer era.

The next few seasons saw the club establish grounds on the south side of the Elysian Fields, Hoboken, with Wednesdays and Saturdays at 4:00 P.M. remaining the time for their practices. A number of additional steps were taken to en-sure the permanence of the Empire Base Ball Club. Regular business meetings were held every second Monday at Florence's Hotel, 400 Broadway. A slate of officers was elected, consisting of President Thomas G. Voorhis; Vice President Amedee Spadone; Secretary Thomas Chalmers, Jr.; and Treasurer John J. Bloomfield.[8] Finally, and most importantly, the club sent a three-man delegation of Richard H. Thorne, Walter Scott, and Thomas Leavy to the convention at which the National Association of Base Ball Players (NABBP) was formed.

A twelve-page pamphlet was published by the club titled *Constitution, By-Laws and Rules of the Empire Ball Club* (Oct. 23, 1854), in which the rules and regulations of the organization were established. They played by the Knicker-bocker rules written in 1845, no set number of innings, the game being decided by the first opponent to score 21 aces (or runs). The officers of the club were elected every April for a one-year term. Meetings were held every second Monday of each month at 8:00 PM. The monthly dues were 25¢ for all members. There were plenty of fines to go around requiring strict adherence to the rules:

- 6¼¢ for using profane language
- 25¢ for disputing the decision of the Umpire during games
- 6¼¢ fine for "audibly expressing his opinion on a doubt-ful play before the decision of the Umpire is given (un-less called upon to do so)."
- 50¢ against any member refusing obedience to the Cap-tain
- 10¢ for being late to a meeting.
- 25¢ for being absent without a good excuse.

There was even a fine of 25¢ if a member didn't answer the roll call immediately. The Captain was the man in charge. He directed the playing of the game by designating the position for each player. The player had no say in the matter. The president of the club appointed the umpire. The umpire kept the game book, noted all violations, levied fines, and had the final say in all disputes and differences relative to the game.

The rules were constantly being amended. That same year, 1854, a rule was changed to include, "First base must be vacated by the runner if the batter hits a fair ball; players can be forced out in the same manner as when running to 1B." Rules that we take for granted today were formulated in a slow process over the decades of development and experimentation. One rule that has never changed, however, from the original Knickerbocker list is — if the catcher drops the ball on a called third strike, the batter can run to first. There was a diagram of the baseball field on the last page of the pamphlet.

Many of the clubs that helped form the NABBP had trouble adjusting to the changes wrought by competition, and the Empire Club was no exception. The club's play improved steadily during its first few years, culminating in 1858 when only a one-run loss to the Mutuals stood between the Empires and an undefeated season. But by then the nucleus of the first nine was aging, and many of them chose to retire. Thereafter the Empire Club usually won about half of its match games, but it rarely faced the contenders for the national championship except in 1865.

This awkward transition reflected the reality that the club's original members were upstanding citizens of New York society for whom baseball was a way to amuse themselves and improve their leisure hours. As one reporter put it, they saw the game as a "healthful, manly recreation, improving the physical development without detriment to the morals of our young men."[9] Not only were they amateurs, but it is safe to assume that the idea of professional play never occurred to any of them until after the formation of the NABBP.

Symbolic of the changing times is the tense relationship between the Empire Club and the Atlantic Club of Brooklyn. William V. Babcock, an early president of the Atlantic Club, claimed that he had been a member of the Empire Club before helping to found the Atlantic Club in 1855.[10] Babcock's name does not appear on any list of Empire Club members, but there is no reason to doubt his claim. In further testimony to the ties between the two clubs, Thomas Leavy of the Empires acted as the "referee" in the Atlantic Club's first match game. Yet the two clubs almost immediately took divergent courses, and hard feelings developed. While the Atlantics were emerging as a powerhouse and winning multiple national championships, they did not face the Empires between 1856 and 1864.[11]

Frequent upheaval in the first nine of the Empire Club was another sign of the changes that were transforming baseball. During the 1860s, it was rare for a player to stay with the Empires for more than a season or two, and many seemed to use the club as a stepping-stone to the top clubs. Such notables as Phonny Martin, Fred Waterman, Dick Higham, Nat Jewett, and Joe Simmons played for the Empires at the outset of their professional careers, but none of them remained long. Even the positioning of the players remained in flux; after an 1864 game, a *Brooklyn Eagle* reporter — almost certainly Henry Chadwick — condemned the Empire for "persist[ing] in the stupid plan of placing their men in positions they are not familiar with."[12]

Another vivid example of the changing times was the club's decision to expel James E. Ryder, an infielder on the first nine. Al Spink incorrectly reported that "James E. Roder" was expelled from the Empire Club for being a professional, and other writers have repeated the mistake.[13] In fact, Ryder was expelled on October 9, 1865, for "having collected certain sums of money from members of the said Empire Club under the pretence of paying the expenses of their first nine to Philadelphia, and having appropriated the same to his own use and benefit." The club's members were disgusted to find Ryder playing for the Eclectic Club in 1866 and brought the matter to the attention of the NABBP's Judiciary Committee at that year's convention.[14]

Yet while the Empire Club's transition to the new era of baseball was awkward, they remained an active club long after most of their contemporaries had disbanded. By 1866 the membership had grown to seventy-four, active and honorary. Thomas G. Voorhis continued to serve as club president, alongside vice president Samuel H. Hosford, secretary James Ward, and treasurer Edward Benson. As discussed in the player profile section, although it is not entirely clear that Ward and Benson had been members of the first nine in the 1850s, there is a good chance that they were. If so, that testifies to the ability of the Empire Club to stay true to its original intentions.

The Empire Club also continued to take pride in its uniforms. By 1864 the players were colorfully attired in blue jockey caps, white flannel shirts trimmed with black, white flannel pants trimmed in blue and black belts engraved with the club's initials.[15] Two years later, Charles A. Peverelly reported that the club uniform consisted of white shirts trimmed with red, light grey pants, white caps with a red belt.

In another indication that enjoyable recreation remained at the heart of the Empire Club's activities, its members broke up several dreary winters by playing baseball on ice.[16] The use of ice skates necessitated several changes to the rules, including allowing players to over-skate any base and the use of a tenth player, a right shortstop. Such contests were also tricky to arrange because the ice needed to be thick, yet the temperatures could not be frigid. Fortunately, a perfect mix was achieved on January 16, 1867, when the Empire and Eagle clubs played ice baseball on Sylvan Lake in Hoboken in front of a sizable crowd, as "the presence of ladies in large numbers and a fine band of music added much to the general enjoyment."[17]

Even after the advent of open professionalism the Empire Club continued to compete, playing a full schedule in 1869. By then, however, the club was beginning to fade out. The club again organized for 1870, but after opening its season with a late-April game in Hoboken, it played few if any match games.[18] When the National Association of Professional Base Ball Players was organized in 1871, the Empire Club joined several of the pioneer amateur clubs in forming a rival amateur organization.[19] But the activities of these clubs attracted little interest, and it is likely that they played few if any match games.

The Empire Club left behind a rich legacy, being instrumental in the game's development and ensuring its popularity. The devotion and playing spirit of those young gentlemen who played over a century ago inspired generations to come. They will always be remembered for their part in spreading the game throughout the nation and making baseball an integral part of American culture.

CLUB MEMBERS

Dr. William H. Bell: Dr. William Bell was a colorful and well-known figure on the New York baseball scene, playing for several early clubs in the 1860s despite being close to forty and weighing around 220 pounds.[20] He died in Manhattan on October 19, 1900.

Benson: A player named Benson was a regular for the Empires in the late 1850s and early 1860s and represented the club in the Fashion Race Course all-star game. As of 1866 the club treasurer was a man named Edward Benson, but whether this was the same person is not known.

John J. Bloomfield: John J. Bloomfield, who served as the club's treasurer and "judge," was a stationer who died on August 23, 1907, at the age of 79.[21]

William Culyer: Left fielder William Culyer was the brother of Brooklyn public park supervisor, landscape architect, and civil engineer John Y. Culyer (1839–1924), who was instrumental in maintaining the parks used by local ballplayers. William Culyer was born in England around 1831 and came to the U. S. as an infant. By the time of his death on October 7, 1915, he had served as sexton of the Fifth Avenue Presbyterian Church for sixty-three years.[22]

Richard L. Haydock: Richard Lawrence Haydock, one of the club's organizers and a member of its "Vigilance Committee," was born on Long Island on March 23, 1823. He was thus past thirty when the Empire Club was founded and soon dropped from the first nine. But he remained a frequent substitute with a reputation for hard hitting — an 1857 account noted that, "frequently, when he was about to strike, the fielder may be seen spreading out on the field to the extreme end, as he generally knocks a long ball, unless he tips out."[23] Haydock got married that May, but his twenty-two-year-old wife passed away after only eight months of marriage. He later remarried and moved to Staten Island and was a longtime member of the Republican General Committee of Richmond County. He died at his home in Port Richmond on August 24, 1898, as a result of injuries sustained while falling down the stairs.[24]

Samuel E. Hosford: Samuel E. Hosford was born in Ireland around 1838. As a young man he played for the St. George Cricket Club and played shortstop for the Empire Club, while also serving as club secretary in 1866. A clerk by profession, he stuck exclusively to cricket after becoming captain of the Manhattan Cricket Club of Brooklyn in 1869. He became one of the city's best-known cricketers, belonging to the Manhattan

Cricket Club for more than thirty years and serving four terms as president. In 1910, he retired to Summit, New Jersey, where he died on January 11, 1912.[25]

Monson Hoyt: Monson Hoyt played for the Empires from 1857 to 1859 and was described as having few "equals as a Base Ball Player." In the outfield, he ran "like a deer" in chasing down long hits, and on the bases his speed often enabled him to make "a run home while the ball is passing from the pitcher to the catcher."[26] He is believed to have been a man named Lydig Monson Hoyt, who was born on January 24, 1821, and died in Staatsburgh, New York, on August 8, 1868.

Thomas Leavy: Thomas Leavy was a regular for the Empires until 1860 and, like so many latter-day first basemen, was a left-handed power hitter. According to an 1857 description," Mr. Leavy strikes with his left hand, and when he gets a good ball, he generally knocks it into the river."[27] A marble cutter by profession, Leavy is believed to have died in New York City on October 13, 1900.

Alphonse (Phonny) Martin: Phonny Martin was a nineteen-year-old Civil War veteran in 1864 when he joined the Empire Club. He moved on to more ambitious clubs after two years, and after his departure the Empire Club rarely ventured to take on top clubs. Martin gained renown for a slow pitch that bedeviled batters. Some have claimed it to be the first curveball, but Martin himself maintained that a true curve was not possible under the delivery restrictions of the era. Martin enjoyed a long and successful career and died in Hollis, New York, on May 24, 1933.

Thomas Miller: According to an 1857 account, second baseman Thomas Miller was "once in a while apt to let a ball pass through his fingers, as though it was a hot pan-cake, well buttered. Sometimes he waits for it to bounce and loses it, instead of taking it on the fly. Mr. Miller is a good batter, and frequently makes his run home on a strike."[28] His fielding must have improved as he had one of the longest stints as a club regular, remaining with the first nine through the 1864 season. Due to his common name, he has not been identified.

Richard P. Moore: Richard P. Moore was one of the club's regulars from 1857 through 1861. The only man fitting the known information was an insurance agent named Richard P. Moore who was born in New York City on March 2, 1830. The end of the ballplayer's career corresponds with when this man joined the Union Army and was wounded at Fredericksburg. In common with several Empire Club members, he later became active in the Republican Party. Moore never married and died on November 17, 1893.[29]

Joseph Russell: Joseph Russell was born in Ireland in the early 1830s. He immigrated to New York around 1850 and soon took up baseball, playing shortstop for the Empire Club for several years.[30] He and his wife moved to Hoboken in the early 1860s where he worked as a map engraver and became involved in civic politics. Unlike many of his fellow club members Russell was a Democrat, and in 1875 he was elected to his first of two terms as mayor of Hoboken. After leaving office, he officiated at the 1882 reopening of legendary catcher Nat Hicks's Hoboken handball and rackets court.[31] Russell died in East Orange on May 23, 1908.[32]

James E. Ryder: James E. Ryder played the infield for the Empire Club in the mid–1860s until being expelled, as described in the text. Nothing is known about his subsequent activities.

Walter Scott: Born in New York around 1833, Walter Scott worked as a dry goods clerk while serving as the club's vice president and handling several positions with skill. According to an 1857 account, he "is not afraid to stop a ball, however swift it may come, never waiting for the ball on the bound, if he can possibly reach it on the fly, and is a very sure catcher. He has filled the position of catcher quite often." The writer added that "Mr. Scott's attitude when about to strike, has caused much merriment to outsiders," but he neglected to explain why.[33] He was one of the Empire Club's delegates to the first convention of the National Association of Base Ball Players and was chosen to serve as the assistant secretary of the new organization.[34] Though one of the club's youngest members, he hung up his spikes after the 1857 season. He was married around 1860 and raised a large family. He was living in Hoboken when the 1870 census was taken, and then in Yorkshire, New York, at the time of the 1880 census. His whereabouts after that are not known.

Francis Copeland Sebring: Francis Sebring was born in New York City on April 19, 1829. He was married in 1851 and began a family, but in the late 1850s he took up baseball and played for the Empire Club for several years. In 1866 he created a board game called *"Playing Parlor Base-Ball,"* which he patented on February 4, 1868. The board could be placed either on a tabletop or on the knees of the opposing two players. It was made in the shape of home plate, with a raised rim around the entire border. A baseball diamond was printed on the surface along with foul lines and what Sebring described as 'cavities.' These were depressions in the board designating specific plays. The principle was similar to pinball. The game included a spring-operated batter with a bat that swung around and a spring-operated device for the pitcher to propel the "ball," " a large one-cent piece. The batter, using this spring-operated lever, would swing the bat around to hit the coin. Wherever the coin landed indicated the play on the field, either an out or a base was awarded. Although there were no tokens included in the package, Sebring suggested using pawns from a chess set to represent the players on the bases. Basic New York game rules were used, but it was left up to the discretion of the players to decide what specific rules to follow. Sebring included ways to determine double plays, stolen bases, extra base hits, and so on. This game is a rarity to find today, and the very first board game for baseball. Around 1870, Sebring moved to Bloomington, Illinois, and eventually settled in St. Louis, where he died on October 11, 1910.

Joe Simmons: Joseph Chabriel was born on June 13, 1847, and became a major leaguer in every sense. His career began in 1865 with the Gothams, and by then he had adopted his baseball name of Joe Simmons. He then moved on to the Empire Club in 1867, where he played eleven games as a shortstop, pitcher, and outfielder. He subsequently played for a myriad of teams, including the Unions of Morrisania, Excelsiors of Chicago, Forest City of Rockford, and engagements in Cleveland, Keokuk, Iowa, St. Louis, and Columbus. He managed in Rochester for five years and also managed minor league clubs in Trenton, Wilmington, Richmond, Waterbury, and Syracuse. He eventually retired from baseball and reverted to using his birth name. He died in Jersey City on July 24, 1901.

Henry H. R. Smith: Henry H. R. Smith was one of the club's original members and continued to play for the club through the 1859 season. His fielding at short stop was erratic, but he was a power hitter who gained renown among his fellow ballplayers for his "Sky-Rocket Balls."[35] Smith was listed as a butter dealer at Washington Market in the city directories, but his common name makes him impossible to trace beyond that.

William Hart Smith: W. Hart Smith, another founding member, was born in either New Brunswick or Nova Scotia (sources differ) on January 29, 1833. He began his business career in Charlottetown, Prince Edward Island, before moving to Cincinnati and then New York, where he found work for a copper mining company. He eventually joined the Quincy Mining Company, where he worked his way up to secretary and treasurer. He and another member of that firm then opened a brokerage and Smith remained a successful New York broker until his death at his Lakewood, New Jersey, home on January 31, 1897.[36]

Amadee Spadone: The club's vice president in 1857, Amadee Spadone, was born in Ecours, France, on August 29, 1827, to an Italian father and a French mother. He immigrated to the United States in 1832 and worked in Hoboken and Jersey City as a jeweler before becoming president of the Gutta Percha and Rubber Manufacturing Company. In common with several fellow Empire Club members, he was also active in the Republican Party and the Union League. Business eventually brought Spadone back to New York City, where he died on February 22, 1908.[37]

Richard H. Thorne: Richard H. Thorne was born in New York City on March 15, 1830. He was already married and working as a commission agent when the Empire Club was organized, but he became a founding member and gained a reputation as a premiere pitcher. An 1857 account noted that his "swift ball has caused many a player to strike out; he is not very easily fatigued, but he sometimes lets his feelings get the better of himself." Its author went on to explain that Thorne became understandably frustrated when he made a good pitch and the batter took advantage of the lack of called strikes by making no attempt to swing.[38] It was thus appropriate that it was Thorne who umpired the legendary unfinished third game of the 1860 series between the Excelsiors and the Atlantics.[39] After retiring from baseball, Thorne continued to work as a commission agent and to run a produce stand in Washington Market for many years. In the 1890s, he and his wife moved to a farm in Riverside, California, where this baseball pioneer died on May 4, 1901.

Thomas Griffen Voorhis: Longtime club president Thomas G. Voorhis was born in Manhattan on August 7, 1821. His upholstering firm of Voorhis & Whiteman was located at 632 Broadway and the store also doubled as the club's headquarters. He played for the first nine during the club's first season, but thereafter cheered the club on from the sideline. In 1858, Voorhis was chosen as one of the secretaries of the National Association of Base Ball Players.[40] That October, he married Elizabeth Chalmers, the sister of club vice president Thomas Chalmers, Jr., Voorhis, who remained club president until at least 1866, died in Manhattan on March 13, 1877.

Ward: Along with Tom Miller, a player named Ward spent the longest time on the first nine of the Empire Club, but even his first name remains unclear. As of 1866, the club secretary was a man named James Ward, but Marshall Wright lists the player as Ed Ward. So it's hard to be certain whether there were one or two Wards associated with the club.

Other Club Members: Henry L. Belden, Burd, James Cameron, Campbell, Isaac Carlton, Thomas Chalmers, Jr., Robert L. Clarkson, O. H. Collins, Coulter, George Cox, James Cragin, Dewey, Duncan, Joseph G. Edge, Joseph H. Fanze, Edward V. Fargis, Charles W. Gaunt, Andrew Gedney (see Nationals of Washington in *Base Ball Pioneers, 1850–1870*), Isaac O. Gough, Grady, Griffin, Hart, Hearne, Dick Higham, Nat Jewett, E. C. Johnson, Josephs, Kelly, John Kennard, John Lawton, Wallace Learning, C. Loper, J. P. MacGrath, Andrew Matthews, R. McGown, Joseph H. Merwin, J. Miller, L. Miller, James Mullen, Joseph Murphy, Myers, E. Nestler, M. Nestler, Henry H. Newkirk, William G. Odell, Post, Quinn, Reeves, John D. Robbins, William Saunders, Pete Shreve (see Mutual Base Ball Club), Snow, George Springsteen, Symmes, Taylor, George M. Tice, Vosge, Samuel Waddell, Richard Wandell, Fred Waterman (see Cincinnati Base Ball Club entry in *Base Ball Pioneers, 1850–1870*), Way, Westervelt, Amor Williamson, Wilson.[41]

Notes

1. *Porter's Spirit of the Times,* June 27, 1857; Peverelly's *Book of American Pastimes* has the original figure at 13.

2. *New York Times,* April 26, 1855, 8.
3. "Base Ball: Eagle Club vs. Empire Club," *Spirit of the Times,* June 23, 1855, 223.
4. According to Craig Waff's compilation, the Empire Club initial victory was followed by two losses to the Gothams, one to the Eagles, and a season-ending 12–12 tie with the Atlantics on Thanksgiving Day.
5. *New York Herald,* September 6, 1855.
6. "Base Ball: Empire Club vs. Gotham Club," *Spirit of the Times,* September 8, 1855, 349.
7. "Base Ball: Gotham vs. Empire," *New York Herald,* September 6, 1855, 1.
8. *Porter's Spirit of the Times,* February 7, 1857.
9. *Brooklyn Eagle,* August 21, 1867.
10. *Brooklyn Eagle,* October 9, 1892, 4.
11. William J. Ryczek, *Baseball's First Inning* (Jefferson, N.C.: McFarland, 2009), 201–202.
12. *Brooklyn Eagle,* July 14, 1864, 2.
13. Alfred H. Spink, *The National Game* (1911; Carbondale: Southern Illinois University Press, 2000), 5.
14. *New York Clipper,* December 22, 1866.
15. Chadwick Scrapbooks.
16. Ryczek, *Baseball's First Inning,* 95.
17. *New York Times,* January 17, 1867.
18. *New York Herald,* April 28, 1870.
19. William J. Ryczek, *When Johnny Came Sliding Home* (Jefferson, N.C.: McFarland, 1998), 249–250.
20. Ibid., 12.
21. *New York Times,* August 24, 1907, 7.
22. *New York Times,* October 9 and 10, 1915.
23. *Porter's Spirit of the Times,* February 7, 1857.
24. *New York Tribune,* August 26, 1898, 3; *New York Times,* August 26, 1898, 7.
25. *Brooklyn Eagle,* March 17, 1889, 8; *Brooklyn Eagle,* January 12, 1912, 14; *New York Tribune,* January 12, 1912, 8.
26. *Porter's Spirit of the Times,* February 7, 1857.
27. *Ibid.*
28. *Ibid.*
29. *New York Tribune,* November 20, 1893, 7.
30. *Brooklyn Eagle,* March 17, 1889, 8.
31. *New York Clipper,* January 28, 1882.
32. *New York Times,* May 25, 1908, 7.
33. *Porter's Spirit of the Times,* February 7, 1857.
34. *Spirit of the Times,* January 31, 1857.
35. *Porter's Spirit of the Times,* February 7, 1857.
36. *New York Times,* February 2, 1897; *New York Tribune,* February 1, 1897.
37. *New York Tribune,* February 23, 1908, 7.
38. *Porter's Spirit of the Times,* February 7, 1857.
39. For details on the game, see the entries on those clubs and Ryczek, *Baseball's First Inning,* 141–143.
40. *Spirit of the Times,* March 20, 1858, 65.
41. As far as could be determined, all of these men were active members. George Scott Rose, Henry R. Haydock, and John Lyons were the club's three honorary members in 1854, and there were many more in later years.

❖ *Mutual Base Ball Club* ❖
(William J. Ryczek)

CLUB HISTORY

The Mutual Club of New York was perhaps the most politically connected of the early baseball organizations. The heyday of the Mutuals coincided with the height of Tammany Hall corruption, and a number of Tammany operatives were active in the Mutual Club. Coroner John Wildey served as president for several years, and the infamous William M. Tweed was on the Board of Trustees. At a meeting of the club in April 1866, Tweed was presented with a framed set of resolutions in honor of his contributions to the organization, and in 1869, most likely due to his efforts, the Mutuals received a grant of $1500 from the city treasury. Many of the Mutuals' top players were employed by the coroner's and street sweeping departments, and supposedly did little actual work at either. Their principal occupation was playing baseball for the Mutuals.

Not surprisingly for an organization with such close connections to the seamy side of politics, the Mutuals, particularly in their later years, suffered from a sullied reputation. In 1865, three Mutual players were implicated in the first proven game-fixing incident in the history of baseball. If the club made a number of bad errors, many assumed the fix was on. If they lost a second game of a series after winning the first easily, many thought they did so to force a third game and generate additional gate receipts.

The Mutuals could not have been suspect if they were not a talented team, and the New York club, for nearly its entire existence, fielded one of the top nines in the New York metropolitan area. They won the national championship in 1868, and during an era when Brooklyn clubs like the Excelsiors, Atlantics and Eckfords dominated play, the Mutuals were the one New York nine that could play the Brooklyn clubs on an even basis. When they played on the square, they were a nine to be reckoned with; when they did not, they added to the legend of the club known as the Mutuals.

1857–1858

The Mutual Base Ball Club, according to Charles A. Peverelly, was organized on June 24, 1857, and named after Mutual Hook and Ladder Company #1. They did not play with any other club that first summer, but burst on the scene in 1858 by winning their first eleven games. Included among their victims were well known clubs like the Baltics and Empires. The only loss of the season was to the latter club in the final game of the year. On September 18, the Mutuals had defeated the Empires in a tight 18–17 game, but exactly a month later, the latter club won easily 37–22. Since the Mutuals did not play the Atlantic Club, they did not have an opportunity to win the championship despite their 11–1 record.

1859

The Mutuals played the Atlantics in a best-of-three series in 1859, but were no match for the champions, losing badly in two games. The first defeat was by a score of 39–20 on September 19 in a game of eight innings. The second loss was on October 14 by a score of 15–5 in a game called because of rain after six innings. The Atlantics won the latter contest despite the absence of several of their starters, including pitcher Mattie O'Brien. Mutual catcher John Beard was a particular weak point, as three of the Atlantic runs scored on passed balls.

The Mutuals won only three games against five losses in 1859, a grave disappointment after the fine record of 1858. The three wins were over minor clubs, including two over the Hoboken nine, while the Mutuals lost to every top team they played. Some of the notable Mutual players in 1859 were Simon Burns, Anson Taylor and Billy McMahon. All would be associated with the club for several years, and Taylor served as president, while McMahon was the long time field captain.

1860

If 1859 was a disappointing year, 1860, the year in which baseball made such great strides in popularity, was even worse. The Mutuals finished the season with a sorry record of 1–8–2, beating only the Henry Eckford nine. They also lost to the same team, which had only been formed in late 1859, and never achieved any great renown. Both ties were against the venerable Gothams, once a top club that was beginning to fade from prominence.

The following year, analyzing the Mutuals' 1860 season, *Wilkes' Spirit of the Times* opined, "if they would carry a little more earnestness and effort with them into the field, they would seldom be under the necessity of presenting a ball to their opponents."[1] The Mutuals, *Wilkes'* continued, played for fun and preferred to have a good time rather than make an intense effort to win. They retained their good humor win or lose, the latter being the case in most instances in 1860.

Like several New York clubs, the Mutuals played their "home" games at the Elysian Fields at Hoboken, a venue they shared with several other organizations, each having their designated practice days. There were several fields on the grounds, and often more than one game took place simultaneously.

1861

While most teams were less active in the first war year, the Mutuals lost virtually none of their first nine players to military service. Henry B. Taylor served with the National Guard in Washington during the early weeks of the war, but was back in New York by mid–June. The club played much better than it had in 1860, compiling a fine 8–2 record and even beating the champion Atlantics. They tied the Eckford Club for the most wins of any team.

The first Mutual-Atlantic game drew the largest crowd seen in the New York area in 1861, as neither team had lost a game and the Mutuals had beaten several good Brooklyn clubs earlier in the season. The Mutuals won 23–18[2], and if they could beat the Atlantics a second time, they would be champions of the United States, quite an accomplishment for a club that won just a single game a year earlier.

The second game of the series took place on October 16 at the Atlantic grounds at Bedford, before a crowd estimated at eight thousand. The Mutuals held an 8–7 lead after two innings, but in the third, the Atlantics scored 26 runs, eight players scoring three times each. The Atlantics' batting in that frame was among the best ever seen, and the Mutual outfielding was shaky. The final score was 52–27. A third game was never played, and the Atlantics retained the championship.

1862

The Mutuals had another good year in 1862, finishing with an 8–5 record. They beat the Atlantics again, but the Brooklyn club was no longer the champion by that time, having fallen to the Eckfords. The game was the third of the series carried over from 1861, and had it taken place before the Eckfords took the title away from the Atlantics, the Mutuals would have been champions. The Atlantics were missing some players that day and, according to the *Clipper,* put the remainder in the wrong positions, allowing the Mutuals to take an early lead they never relinquished.[3]

One problem with the club in 1862 was its inability to hold a lead, as the Mutuals often faded in the late innings. "The Mutuals this season have been singularly unfortunate," said one journal. "They have placed a stronger nine in the field than ever before, and still victory has not been with them.... Last season, with an inferior nine, they met with a succession of victories, such as seldom falls to the lot of any organization"[4]

The Mutuals and Eckfords played in early August, with the latter club winning a close 28–24 contest. Billy McMahon hit two homers and William Wansley and Lawrence Bogart one each for the Mutuals, but it was not enough. The Eckfords clinched the series and defended their title with a 28–14 win on the 24th of September. Mutual pitcher Simon Burns was "out of condition,"[5] and Billy McMahon missed the game with an injury.

In late August, the Mutuals traveled to Philadelphia for a series of games against the local clubs. They beat the Olympics and Adriatics but lost to the Athletics. "The Mutuals are a good set of base ball players," said *Wilkes,* "and socially are warm-hearted and courteous."[6] In the game against the Adriatics, the Mutuals displayed a degree of sportsmanship often lacking in their later years. After Wansley ran home on a ball that got by the Adriatic catcher who was interfered with by a couple of spectators, Captain Anson Taylor sent him back to third, declining to profit from an unfair advantage. True to *Wilkes'* prediction, the Mutuals won many friends in Philadelphia with their fine behavior and honorable play.

The Mutuals also displayed their social adeptness following a game against the Harlem Club in early September. The two clubs repaired to a banquet for song, stories, the presentation of the ball by the Harlem Club and, as the grand finale, Billy McMahon finished by "portraying, in his graphic style, the 'lights and shadows' of his trip across the prairies."[7]

By 1862, the Mutuals had added a number of talented players to their nine, including outfielder John Zeller, catcher William Wansley, and powerful first baseman John Goldie. Wansley replaced catcher John Beard, who left for New Orleans and did not return until 1863. When the Mutuals played the

Gothams in August, *Wilkes'* proclaimed, "Wansley, as catcher, was in capital play, and proved himself one of the best players in that position we ever saw."[8]

1863

Once again, the Mutuals tied the Eckfords for most wins, but lost four times while the Eckfords were undefeated and retained the championship. The first game of the Mutual-Eckford series resulted in a 10–9 victory for the champions, in which the winning run scored on a disputed play. Tom Devyr of the Eckfords hit a single with two runners on, but was thrown out trying to stretch his hit into a double. The second runner crossed the plate at almost exactly the same time Devyr was tagged out, and an argument ensued as to whether the run should count. Umpire Bixby of the Eagle Club ruled that the run counted, and the two runs the Mutuals scored in the ninth inning left them one short. The Mutuals were handicapped in the game by the subpar physical condition of catcher Wansley, who'd been assaulted and beaten by toughs in the days before the game.

The second game of the series was not played until October 6, the Mutuals' final game of the season. The Eckfords won 18–10, completing a 10–0 season. *Wilkes'* praised the pitching of the Mutuals' Billy McKeever, but criticized the throwing of his infielders, especially Ed Brown.[9]

In June, the Athletics of Philadelphia visited New York, and on June 16 the Mutuals, reciprocating for the fine treatment they'd received in Philadelphia the previous year, feasted the visitors and drove them around the city. When the game started, the Mutuals were much less hospitable, as leadoff batter Ed Brown hit a home run. Following their 17–11 win, the Mutuals entertained the visitors at Perry's Hotel, and the ball was presented by Colonel DeWitt Moore of the Athletics to William Tweed, who accepted on behalf of the Mutuals.

The Mutuals had a strong battery for the 1863 season. Billy McKeever replaced long time pitcher Simon Burns, who was in and out of the Union Army. Although old catcher John Beard was back from the South, he could not displace Wansley, who continued to shine behind the bat.

1864

Once again, the Mutuals were one of the best teams in the New York area, compiling a 20–3 record, and once more they failed to win the championship, losing twice to the undefeated Atlantics. The first game against the Atlantics took place on June 27 and was the first time the Atlantics had played another club all season. The game was not artistic, with numerous fielding errors on both sides, and Mutual pitcher McKeever was hampered by the new pitching rules instituted during the off-season with the intent of limiting the speed and wildness of hurlers. The Atlantics won 26–16. In the second game the Atlantics overcame a Mutual lead with ten runs in the final three innings en route to a 21–16 victory.

On the 4th of August, the Knickerbockers of Albany came to New York and played the Mutuals at the Elysian Fields before six thousand people. After falling behind 8–0 in the first inning, an occurrence that caused a number of wagers to be placed upon the visitors, the Mutuals won 24–16. The Mutuals also beat the Excelsiors in the first game the two teams had ever played together. At the end of August, the club took an excursion upstate, visiting Albany, Troy, and Newburgh and was victorious at every stop.

The Mutuals were still known as a good-natured group, as after a June game with the Newark Club, a reporter commented, "It was also quite refreshing to see the remarkable good humor with which the grave errors made in fielding at times were received by the club."[10] The Mututals added two very good players during the 1864 season, curly haired, 17-year-old shortstop Tom Devyr, who had played for the champion Eckfords, and infielder Ed Duffy. McKeever, who was never able to adjust to the new rules, pitched sparingly and was replaced by Harris.

1865

The Mutuals compiled a 12–4 record in 1865, but the wins were overshadowed by an event that took place on September 28 during a bad loss to the Eckfords. The Mutuals, who were heavily favored in the betting odds, lost 23–11, as the Eckfords scored 12 runs in the fifth inning, aided by a number of Mutual errors, including several misplays by catcher William Wansley. Wansley's play was so noticeably bad that he was moved to right field in the middle of the inning. He was also very ineffective at the bat, making five outs and not scoring any runs.

After the game, many who'd bet on the Mutuals angrily accused the club, and Wansley in particular, of throwing the game. Whenever a favored team lost badly, gamblers would claim the game had had been fixed, even if there was no palpable evidence. On this occasion, however, they were correct. A few weeks after the game, shortstop Devyr signed a written confession admitting that he, Wansley, and Ed Duffy had conspired with gambler Kane McLaughlin to give the game to the Eckfords. The teenaged Devyr, who was suffering from severe financial problems, was promised $300 (he received only $30) to work in concert with Wansley, who had orchestrated the scandal. Wansley told Devyr and Duffy he would handle the misplays but needed to enlist co-conspirators in order to convince McLaughlin he could deliver.

The players were never given all of the money they were promised, receiving just $100 in total, and after Devyr's confession, all three were dismissed from the Mutual Club. Wansley never played top-flight baseball again, but before long both Devyr and Duffy had been forgiven and were back on the playing field. Duffy was the regular shortstop for the 1871 Chicago White Stockings, while Devyr played for the Mutuals and later became a politician.

The Keystones and Athletics of Philadelphia came to New York in 1865, and the Mutuals defeated the Keystones 31–12. While a number of New York nines went to Philadelphia, the Mutuals stayed close to home, not venturing beyond New York and its suburbs.

On August 3, the Mutuals commenced their quest for the elusive championship by playing the Atlantics at the Elysian Fields before a crowd estimated between fifteen and twenty thousand. That spring, the Mutuals, Actives, and Gothams, the three primary occupants of Edwin Stevens' facility, made several improvements to the playing fields, felling trees, removing rocks, leveling the ground and erecting bleachers to the right of home base. The *Clipper* referred to the Elysian Fields as "the finest free ground in the United States."[11] Free grounds, of course, did not include Brooklyn's two enclosed parks, the Union and Capitoline Grounds.

The Atlantics led 13–12 in the sixth inning when the Mutuals put their first two men on base. At that point the clouds opened, and the ensuing deluge resulted in a called game and an Atlantic victory. The Atlantics took the second game, played at the Capitoline Grounds, with an easy 40–28 victory, eliminating the Mutuals from contention. During the remainder of the season, the Mutuals lost a close game to the Eureka Club of Newark 20–19 and dropped the disgraceful affair to the Eckfords. Following the Eckford loss, the club did not play for more than a month before closing out their season with a relatively easy win over the venerable Eagle Club.

1866

The Mutuals added some prominent players to the nine for the 1866 season. The new pitcher was Alphonse (Phonny) Martin, renowned for his slow pitching. Martin's strategic style endeared him to sportswriter Henry Chadwick, who abhorred the swift pitching that had become prevalent in top-flight baseball. Martin's batterymate was 23-year-old catcher Nate Jewett, a fine receiver who would play for several years, including two NA games with the Eckfords in 1872. Third base was manned by Fred Waterman, who would attain fame three years later as the third baseman on the legendary nine of the Red Stockings of Cincinnati. John Hatfield was a handsome, blond, strong-armed outfielder who later set a record by throwing a ball 396 feet in an exhibition at Cincinnati. Hatfield also nearly set a record for the numbers of teams he played with, for he developed quite a reputation for "revolving," or changing allegiance, often with a cash advance in his pocket. Hatfield might have been part of the 1869 Red Stocking Club had he not been expelled from the nine the previous year for suspicious behavior before a match. Despite the trouble in Cincinnati, the Mutuals took Hatfield back for the 1869 season, and he remained with the club through 1874, often finding himself in the middle of suspicious activity. Despite his reputation, Hatfield served as field captain of the Mutuals and as an umpire on occasion.

For the second straight year, the Mutuals were involved in a scandal, although this time in only tangential fashion. Former Mutual pitcher Billy McKeever was driving a trotting horse in Chicago when someone placed a board across the far side of the track. McKeever, in the semi-darkness, failed to see the board and it crushed his skull, killing him. Betting on the races was undoubtedly the impetus for the crime, and although no one was implicated, the incident pointed out the fact that Mutual players often had questionable associations.

The Mutuals had a good season in 1866, winning ten of fourteen games, but lost twice to the Atlantics, who remained champions for the third straight year. In the club's opening game (against the Unions of Morrisania) there were signs that the liberal good nature of the club and its followers was beginning to wane, for there was a great deal of comment concerning the growling and fault-finding that took place after the Mutuals committed errors. The scorn of the gamblers was expected, but the press reported that some of Mutual players and non-playing members joined in the abuse.

The two losses to the champion Atlantics were no disgrace, but followers of the Mutuals and most knowledgeable baseball observers were greatly surprised when the club lost twice to the Unions of Lansingburgh (aka the Haymakers of Troy). New Yorkers were slow to recognize the fact that men from beyond their city could play good ball, and any loss to a "country club" was bound to elicit shock, especially on the part of the gamblers.

The first defeat, by a score of 15–13 on August 9, was the Mutuals' initial setback of the season. The second loss was by a 32–18 score at Lansingburgh on August 28. The *Clipper* blamed the management of the Mutuals for the first defeat, claiming they had not selected a permanent nine, and needed more quality players, "the members or directors being very remiss in the matter of organizing a regular nine for the season."[12] The second defeat was incurred in unusual fashion. The Mutuals scored nine runs in the first inning and the Unions ten runs in the ninth, aided by some very poor play on the part of the Mutuals. An Albany paper noted the execrable play of the Mutuals and stated,"[H]ad the same sort of play been shown by a 'county club' they would have been put down in the record as third class."[13]

The matches with the Unions were inconsequential to the championship question. On September 13, the Mutuals met the Atlantics in the first game of the series that would give them a chance to gain the title. A large crowd of twelve to fifteen thousand crowded the Elysian Fields and watched the Mutuals once more squander a sizable lead, as the Atlantics scored 14 runs in the last three innings to gain a 17–15 win. Despite the result, the Mutuals apparently kept their poise, even as the runs poured across the plate and their fielding deteriorated. The betting crowd, which had large amounts of money staked on the outcome, was probably not so easygoing. The Mutuals were eliminated from championship contention when they lost a second time to the Atlantics on October 18, by a score of 34–24.

1867

The Mutuals played more games in 1867 than ever before in their history, finishing 23–6–1. Given the number of Mutual players employed by the street cleaning and coroner's departments, it is likely that some streets went unswept that summer. Presumably, there was enough coverage in the coroner's department to make up for the missing ballplayers.

There were very few personnel changes from 1866, the principal one being the return of shortstop Tom Devyr, who missed only one season after confessing to conspiring to fix the Eckford game in 1865. The club held a meeting on April 8, with Devyr's application for re-admission being approved unanimously by the seventy members in attendance, based upon mitigating circumstances and subsequent good behavior. The Mutuals' need for a quality shortstop may have also played a role in the vote.

The Mutuals no longer played at Hoboken's Elysian Fields, which was not adequate for the large crowds that attended big games. Concerned about the prospects of violence and disorder, Edwin Stevens forbade the playing of championship games at the Hoboken site, causing the Mutuals to move their games to the Union Grounds in Brooklyn.

One of the highlights of the early season was a 17–16 win over the Irvington nine at Irvington, a game that was interrupted by a brawl that took place among the crowd during the eighth inning. While the fight raged, pickpockets lifted valuables as liquor-fueled New Jersey roughs battled their New York counterparts. Irvington outfielder Hugh Campbell was injured in the fracas and had to leave the game. Despite the uneasiness created by the fight and the large number of gamblers on the premises, the Mutuals scored the winning run in the ninth inning.

As they had virtually every season, the Mutuals lost twice to the defending champion Atlantics, but there were some notable triumphs, including a second win over Irvington, a victory over the Unions of Lansingburgh, and two wins over the Athletics. One of the wins versus the Athletics was achieved during a tour of the southern segment of the baseball world, which included Baltimore, Washington, and Philadelphia. The Mutuals played five games, beating the Athletics, Nationals of Washington and West Philadelphia clubs while losing to the Pastime Club of Baltimore and the Keystones in Philadelphia. Many non-playing club members accompanied the Mutuals with social activity and camaraderie in high gear in all three cities. The players attended the theater, minstrel shows, billiard halls, and special entertainments held in their honor. While in Washington, the Mutuals visited President Johnson, who the following day was reported to be at the ball game.

Just before the Mutuals left for the South, they were beaten 9–8 by the Unions of Morrisania, who had defeated the champion Atlantics just a few weeks earlier. The defeat by the Unions was followed six days later by another close loss, this time to the visiting Athletics by a score of 18–16.

The Mutuals defeated the eventual champion Unions on September 23, but by the time the Unions beat the Atlantics a second time to claim the title, it was too late in the season for the Mutuals to commence a series to dethrone them. The entire matter became academic when the Unions brought a case before the NABBP's Judiciary Committee claiming that the Mutuals' use of Devyr was illegal. The committee declared the games between the two clubs null and void.

Hatfield and Waterman led the Mutuals in runs scored, while the team was hampered on defense by an injury to pitcher Phonny Martin that caused him to miss several games. The club had no capable hurler in reserve and suffered most of its losses in Martin's absence.

1868

In 1868 the Mutuals finally captured the championship that had eluded them on so many occasions. The nine had to be revamped after the club lost its two top run scorers, Waterman and Hatfield, to the Red Stockings of Cincinnati. Additions to the club were power hitting outfielder Lipman Pike, slick fielding infielder George Flanley, former Atlantic infielder John Galvin and pitcher Rynie Wolters. Wolters, in contrast to Martin, was a swift pitcher who relied on speed rather than cunning.

For most of the summer, the club shuffled players around, and speculation abounded as to who was about to join the Mutuals. "Rumors are firing round every day," said the *Clipper* in mid–August, "as to who will play in the nine and the truth appears hard to arrive at."[14] Late in the season, Ed Duffy rejoined the club, three years after his expulsion for the 1865 incident. Shortly thereafter the Judiciary Committee ruled that the Mutuals had violated the rules by reinstating him, but Duffy was made eligible at the NA Convention in December 1869.

Before the season the Mutuals announced their intention to leave the Union Grounds for their own field on land leased at the Satellite Ground, but political machinations prevented them from doing so. The Mutuals were politically connected, but apparently the connections of William Cammeyer, proprietor of the Union Grounds, were stronger, and he prevented the new site from being developed. The Mutuals would once again play at Cammeyer's facility.

Several teams, including the Atlantics, Athletics, Red Stockings, and Unions of Morrisania, embarked on lengthy tours in the summer of 1868, traveling around the Midwest for up to a month, but the Mutuals stayed close to home, playing a number of second-line New York clubs while their principal rivals were away and taking on the touring teams when they came to New York. The 1868 season was filled with treachery, as the New York and Brooklyn clubs conspired to keep the championship away from the Athletics. The Unions avoided playing them in a full series until after they lost a series to the Atlantics, passing the championship to the Brooklyn club.

The Mutuals and Atlantics split their first two games, each winning a very close affair. The Mutual win was the first time they'd beaten the Atlantics since 1863. On October 26, the Mutuals captured the championship with a 28–17 victory, sparked by 35-year-old veteran Billy McMahon's grand slam during a nine-run sixth-inning rally.

Although the Mutuals were the nominal champions, they were clearly not the best team in the United States. Their 31–10 mark was well behind the Athletics' 47–3, the Atlantics' 47–7, and even the defending Unions' 37–6. The Mutuals lost two of three games to the Haymakers. Yet under the prevailing system, they were entitled to fly the championship banner. Shortly after gaining the crown, the Mutuals were beaten by the Unions, prompting the *Clipper* to declare, "The result of this game, while it does not affect the claim of the Mutuals to the championship, ought to convince our leading clubs of the necessity of taking such action as will in the future prevent such a muddled condition of affairs."[15]

The enigmatic nature of the Mutuals was pointed out by *Wilkes'* just before the club won the championship. "It is a most accommodating organization, playing a first, second or third class game alternately.... They pocket their defeat with an amazing nonchalance, and carry their victories with laudable grace. They are as much at home when beaten as a young monkey on its mother's back, while they are no more elated with victory than a dog possessed of two tails."[16]

1869

The 1869 season began as the previous one had ended. The Mutuals generated a series of excuses for avoiding the Athletics' challenge for a series of games to decide the championship and, instead, allowed the Eckfords the first opportunity at the crown. After splitting their first two games, the teams met on July 3 for the deciding match. The Mutuals were heavily favored, with odds of 100–30, for their loss to the Eckfords had been a rain-shortened game that was the subject of great dispute. Yet the third game was all the Eckfords' way as they won 31–5. Many viewed the Mutual loss with suspicion, first because it was hard to believe the Eckfords won so decisively, and second because it was a convenient way of once again thwarting the Athletics. Further, the Haymakers, who also posed a threat to remove the title from New York, were neatly cast aside by the maneuver.

Even after the Mutuals had been dethroned, the Athletics pursued them with the stated intention of challenging for the championship of 1868, which they claimed they had been deprived of since a series was not played. The Mutuals continued to prevaricate and procrastinate, and managed to avoid the Athletics during a trip to Philadelphia. Eventually, the Mutuals played the Athletics twice and lost both times, but it was irrelevant. In a year in which the Red Stockings of Cincinnati went undefeated, the other clubs continued to bicker over an increasingly meaningless championship. For the year, the Mutuals finished with a 36–16 mark, including a mediocre 11–15 showing against professional teams.

John Hatfield, after his expulsion by the Red Stockings, rejoined the Mutuals for the 1869 season, and the club also added former Atlantic catcher Charley Mills and former Eckford outfielder Dave Eggler. Mills, who was reputed to handle swift pitching well, promised to be a good complement to Wolters. Otherwise, the cast was essentially the same as in 1868, except for the fact that they were now an openly professional nine.

The Mutuals visited several cities during the summer, including a visit to Boston in late May, to New Haven in early June, and a southern swing to Washington, Baltimore, and Philadelphia in late August. Late in the season, they commenced a second series against the Eckfords, some thought in an attempt to pass the championship back to another team from the New York area. It was subsequently announced, however, that the games were exhibitions, another quirk that led to even more questions and disappointed spectators. The long season finally came to an end on November 18, when the Mutuals lost to the Eckfords, who by that time had lost the championship to the Atlantics.

It had been something of a tumultuous season for the Mutual Club, with loose play on the part of the nine leading to conflict between the players and non-playing members and mid-season changes in the nine. The *Clipper* stated that "jealousy and discord have been rife" and the club was deprived of the championship by "thorough bad management."[17]

1870

On December 19, 1869, about twenty members of the Mutual Club boarded a train and reached New Orleans a few days later, the first time any club from the New York area had visited the Deep South. After celebrating Christmas in the city, the Mutuals played their first game the day after, defeating the Southern Club 42–14. The two clubs took the field to the strains of "Dixie," and the New Yorkers received a very warm welcome. They were hosted at an elaborate ball held in their honor and entertained nearly every night of their stay. Despite the rigorous social schedule, the Mutuals managed to play a number of games and won them all. The estimated cost of the trip was $1800, and it was hinted that Mr. Tweed played a role in providing the necessary funds.[18]

The final season before the advent of the professional National Association was an active one and a good one for the Mutuals. They played 88 games, an astonishing workload compared to the schedules of just a few years past. They were 68–17–3 in all games and 29–15–3 against professional clubs. The Mutuals took to the road more than ever before, visiting the

Midwest on two occasions. During one visit to Chicago, Wolters shut out the powerful White Stockings by a 9–0 score, in a game that popularized the term "Chicago," used for years thereafter to describe a shutout.

The notoriously unreliable John Hatfield was named captain of the nine, and gave a forewarning of his future performance by failing to show up for the opening game. Wolters, another whose itinerary was subject to his whim, was also missing. In mid–May, however, the *Clipper* declared that there was newfound harmony on the Mutual nine and that there would be less interference from the directors than had been the case in 1869. None of the officers or directors would be allowed on the field during games.[19]

Once again, the New York clubs engaged in bold chicanery to keep the title in the area. On September 22 the Mutuals beat the Atlantics for the second time to claim the championship. They then announced that they planned to host a tournament in which they would put their newly won title on the line against the top teams in the country. Under their rules, however, each challenging team would be eliminated after a single loss while it would take two losses to eliminate the Mutuals. Further, the New York club would take one third of the proceeds of each game.

The other clubs declined to participate, which led the Mutuals to claim that since their challenge had not been accepted, they were the champions and that any future games they might play would be exhibitions. The *New York Times* referred to the Mutuals as, "our so-called champion nine, a title one would naturally suppose to be a little questionable under circumstances of their having sustained no less than 12 defeats this season."[20] Following their announcement, the Mutuals dropped a number of "exhibition" games. They lost to the White Stockings of Chicago a second time when a hometown umpire gave the White Stockings the game. They then lost a second time to the Red Stockings, who had declared **before** the season that they were not interested in any championship. There followed a dispute with the White Stockings about the site of another game, after which the Mutuals checked out of their hotel and returned to New York. The following March, the Mutuals and White Stockings were still trading angry letters regarding the identity of the champion of 1870. As one writer proclaimed, "It would take a Philadelphia lawyer to find out which was the champion club of 1870."[21]

After the happenings of 1870, it was only fitting that at the December convention, the last one of the old NABBP, William Wansley was ruled eligible to play once more. All three men who had conspired to throw the game to the Eckfords in 1865 were now officially free to play for any team in America. It was a time for a change.

Epilogue

The Mutuals were charter members of the National Association of Professional Base Ball Players when it was formed in March 1871. Alex Davidson, secretary of the Mutuals, was one of the committee that recommended forming a separate professional association. Many of the Atlantic stars of the late 1860s, including Joe Start, Charlie Smith, Bob Ferguson, and Dickie Pearce, joined the Mutuals to create a very strong team.

For the first three years of the new league, the Mutuals were a disappointment, finishing in the middle of the pack and never seriously contending for the championship, often arousing suspicion with losses to inferior teams. By 1873, all of the old Atlantics save Start had departed, and the Mutuals had no dependable leader. Further, they had a number of players with questionable reputations, such as John Hatfield and Richard Higham. The team got off to a horrendous start, displayed some atrocious fielding and quickly dropped out of contention.

In 1874 the Mutuals challenged the Boston Red Stockings for the championship before fading late in the year. The following season, the last of a weak, expanded National Association, was not a good one for the Mutuals. They finished well back in the standings with a 30–38 record, the poorest mark of any established team, and there were a number of rumors circulating about the team's reputed failure to play their best at all times.

Despite the cloud hanging over the head of the New York club, the Mutuals were selected to join the National League when the new circuit began play in 1876. They finished the season with a 21–35 record, good for sixth place in an eight-team league. Believing he would not clear expenses on the club's final road trip, manager William Cammeyer said he would keep his team at home. Many thought there was an unspoken reason for the refusal to make the trip, which could have resulted in the expulsion of the Mutuals from the new league. Toward the end of the season, there were stories that Cammeyer was negotiating with Morgan Bulkeley of the Hartford Dark Blues. The Dark Blues had been an artistic success but a financial failure in Hartford, and Cammeyer allegedly believed they would fare much better in a city the size of New York. If the Mutuals were expelled, the Dark Blues could take their place.

The Mutuals were in fact banished from the league, and the Dark Blues played the 1877 season in Brooklyn. Unfortunately, the prospect of monetary success proved illusory, and the Dark Blues folded after just one year. The entire episode was a fitting conclusion to the murky career of the Mutuals, one of the more colorful and enigmatic teams of early baseball.

CLUB MEMBERS

Compiling profiles of the members of the Mutuals has its share of challenges. In 1885, *Sporting Life* reported that a Mutual pitcher from the 1850s was a Michigan Supreme Court justice, yet none of the judges on that state's Supreme Court match the names of Mutual players, and the only one who was from New York, John Champlin, left the state for Michigan in 1854.[22] Another article thirteen years later stated that the father of Brooklyn pitcher Harry Howell had once played for the Mutuals. But again no record of Howell's father John playing for the Mutuals could be found.[23] That same year it was reported that former Mutual Mark Burns had died in the Connecticut State Hospital for the Insane. This man turned out not to be longtime Mutual pitcher Simon Burns but a player who had reportedly played a few games in the outfield for the Mutuals in 1870—games for which no record seems to exist.[24]

These wild goose chases at least show that the Mutuals were remembered long after the club passed out of existence. Yet paradoxically, several of the club's stalwarts proved impossible to identify. Little could be found about longtime starters such as John Beard and Harris, with the latter player's given name remaining unknown despite six years on the first nine. Others, such as W. Powell, could only be identified by a first initial and surname despite being regulars. No doubt one of the reasons for this was that many of the early members were, as James McConnell put it, "disgusted with the way things went" after the war and no longer wanted their names associated with the team name they had once worn with pride.

John Beard: John Beard was one of the Mutual Club's regulars from 1858 to 1860, mostly as catcher. He then spent two years in New Orleans before playing his final games for the Mutuals in 1863. Nothing is known about his life.

Charley Bearman: See Unions of Lansingburgh (Troy "Haymakers") in *Base Ball Pioneers, 1850–1870*.

Lawrence Hilliard Bogart: A man named Bogart was one of the club's regulars from 1860 to 1862, playing a variety of positions. There was a club director named Lawrence H. Bogart who was likely the ballplayer. Lawrence H. Bogart was born in 1829 and operated a restaurant at 42nd Street and 3rd Avenue.

Thomas W. Bovell: Bovell, a club officer, was working as a lithographer in 1860.

Ed Brown: Ed Brown was the regular second baseman of the Mutuals from 1861 to 1865 (or at least for most of that time). See the Eckford Base Ball Club entry for details on his life.

Simon "Sim" or "Syme" Burns: Simon Burns, who was born in Ireland around 1838, was the Mutuals' primary pitcher from 1858 until the start of the Civil War. A very tall man, he played first base as well, but also had the dexterity to fill in at shortstop when needed. Burns "patriotically went to the war in '61, and was at the battle of Roanoke Island, and since his return he has not taken the position in the club that he once had, that terrible scourge to athletes and ball players, rheumatism, preventing him from being as active in body as he was wont to be in the old days of the club."[25] He rejoined the club in 1862, but that ended his ball-playing career. In 1866 he was granted U. S. citizenship, with John Wildey supporting his application. Burns became very active in billiards and lived for a time in Charleston, South Carolina. In 1890, this obituary appeared: "An eventful life is closed. A note from George E. Phelan tells me that Simon Burns was buried last Thursday. Many men would continue inopulent if they lived a million years and had a million chances for wealth, and Simon was one. Riches never charmed him, for he never cared to get close enough. Content with little, he sometimes missed even that; but he never lacked the mental smartness to get it, and more, had he held his self-respect so cheaply as to give that smartness play. An Anak in size, he was a child in his ways. Odd sometimes in his goodness, he merits the epitaph that he was generally good. He was liberal with his little, sympathetic because familiar with tribulation, and just because he had felt injustice. If he ever wronged anyone consciously he more than squared it in a way by wronging himself twice.

"I first knew him in the early days of the Mutual Base Ball Club, one of whose battery this athlete was. After that he was policeman, detective and special watchman. Coming back from Washington, D. C., after the Civil War, he managed one or two of the largest rooms in this city. Later he conducted a small room for a short time in Philadelphia, and subsequently he had one in the far South. Latterly he had held a position in the Navy Yard, Brooklyn. The sum of principle in Simon's make-up was large. I can pay him no tenderer tribute than to say that in all billiards for forty years I have met but four other men whom I valued so highly, and I valued him because I found him sincere.... [He] was chosen for important billiard missions when shrewder men were passed by. It was he who was commissioned to take Melvin Foster into Canada when he played Joseph Dion in 1870, and he it was also who got Michael Phelan, Hugh W. Collender and Eugene Plunkett safely into a carriage on the night that a rabble virtually took possession of Cooper Institute."[26]

John Carland: John Carland was the first president of the Mutual Club. He was born around 1833, and, like so many of his fellow club members, he was involved in the volunteer fire department and then served in the Civil War. He later ran a saloon and porter house, but what became of him is not known. One note stated that he had become a deacon.

James Leslie Carleton: James Carleton, the Mutuals' regular shortstop in 1869, was born on August 20, 1848, in Clinton, Connecticut. He played professional baseball until 1879, mostly at first base. He lived in Cleveland for some time and made "a pile" by having the foresight to invest in Bell Telephone.[27] He moved to Detroit and worked as a stockbroker until his death on April 25, 1910.

Lawrence Clancy: Lawrence Clancy was the club's secretary in 1858. A man named Clancy was the club's first baseman in 1858 and 1859, then played occasionally during the next two seasons — presumably this is the same person. Lawrence Clancy was born around 1834 and became the city's recording clerk, but no trace of him can be found after the early 1870s.

Warren Davids: Warren Davids served as either club secretary or club treasurer for many years. Davids was born around 1837 and was city weigher as of 1880. He died in New York City on April 28, 1899.

Alexander V. Davidson: Alexander V. Davidson was born in New York City on January 29, 1837, and like so many of the Mutuals was a volunteer firefighter. He became secretary of the Mutual Club in 1870 and was credited with choosing the site of the meeting at which the National Association organized.[28] Davidson also had ties to Tammany Hall and was later elected sheriff of New York.[29] After an investigation by a committee headed by Theodore Roosevelt, he was charged with malfeasance and removed from office, though he was subsequently acquitted. He and his wife moved to Inyo County, California, where he was still living as of 1910. He died between then and 1918.

Thomas Devyr: See Eckford Base Ball Club.

Patrick Dockney: Patsy Dockney earned a reputation as one of the toughest and hardest-drinking ballplayers in an era when these were common attributes. He was born in Ireland around 1844 and grew up in Hoboken after arriving in the United States with his parents on June 14, 1848. After serving for three years in Company I of New Jersey's 21st Infantry Regiment, he took up baseball and quickly gained a reputation as a skilled and fearless catcher. Sam Crane recalled that Dockney also had an old Irish-style mustache and once hit the ball over the pagoda at the Capitoline Grounds.[30] But he also became renowned for the frequency with which he got into knife fights, and in particular for a legendary game that he caught the day after receiving multiple stab wounds.[31] Dockney's playing days had ended by 1870, but he was still listed as an "athlete" on the 1880 census. Trouble continued to follow him around, and he was last heard from in 1885 when he acquired U. S. citizenship. By 1893, he was reported to be dead, but the details remain unknown.

William H. Dongan: William H. Dongan was a Mutual officer who served for several seasons as club secretary. One reporter wrote that Donigan was a "founder of the Mutual Base Ball Club, and was its secretary as long as he believed the Mutuals could not be sold."[32] He died in New York City on May 28, 1889, one day before Wildey, and *Sporting Life* noted both their passings.[33] He was said to have been a descendant of Thomas Dongan, governor of New York in the 1680s.

Ed Duffy: Ed Duffy played third base and shortstop for the Mutuals in 1864 and 1865, before being one of the three players banned for their role in the game-fixing scandal. Born around 1844 in Ireland, Duffy was eventually reinstated and played for several clubs, including a stint in the National Association. He died in Brooklyn on October 16, 1888.

David Daniel Eggler: Dave Eggler played the outfield for the Mutuals in 1869 and 1870, then spent over a decade in the major leagues, earning a reputation "as the finest centerfielder in the country."[34] Born in Brooklyn on April 30, 1849,

Eggler moved to Buffalo after his career to work for the railroad. He died there in an accident on April 5, 1902.

George Henry Flanley: George Flanley was the captain and regular second baseman for the Mutuals in 1868 and 1869 after a long tenure with the Excelsiors of Brooklyn. See that club's entry and the Star Club's entry for details.

John Galvin: See Atlantic Base Ball Club.

P. Gavagan: A man named P. Gavagan was a member of the Mutual Club's first nine from 1858–1860. The only men with that surname and first initial were named Patrick Gavagan, and it seems very likely that the ballplayer was the Patrick Gavagan who served as foreman of the Fulton Engine Company.

John Goldie: John Goldie joined the Mutuals in 1861 and was the club's regular first baseman through the end of the 1866 campaign. Five years later, on July 14, 1871, he died in New York City of tuberculosis at the age of 35. An article about his death in the *Eagle* blamed the disease on his profession, which appears from the city directory to have been electrotype setting. It added, "Goldie informed us shortly before he died that nothing but his playing base ball kept him alive so long, the open air exercise of the ball field mollifying the pernicious effects of the occupation he pursued. Goldie was highly esteemed by the fraternity for his integrity of character."[35]

William C. Gover: William C. Gover was another prominent Tammany Hall figure. Although too old for active involvement with the Mutual Base Ball Club, he and Wildey served as its two delegates to the national convention in 1866.[36] He died on December 14, 1891, at the age of 76.

Harris: A man named Harris was one the Mutual Club's regulars from 1859 to 1864 and played a few more games in 1865, but no clues have been found that would make it possible to identify him.

Anthony Hartman or Hartmann: Tony Hartman was a judge who served as club vice president in 1870. When Billy McMahon's tavern was investigated in 1886, Hartman testified that he had known McMahon for thirty years and that McMahon "had borne an unblemished character and a reputation that ranked 'A No. 1' in an admiring community. Mr. Hartmann had been to the Haymarket some 50 or 60 times to visit Mr. McMahon, but he failed to find anything done that could be called improper or disorderly. Judging by the conduct of the people he saw there, they were orderly and reputable to a degree that was embarrassing to the searcher after pleasure."[37] Born around 1835, Hartman was a grocer's son who went to work as a peddler at age 14 after the death of his father. He served in the 84th New York Regiment during the Civil War, then studied law and passed the Bar in 1868. He was very active in Democrat Party politics and held the offices of alderman and assemblyman; in the latter office, he was best known for his ability to imitate New York Lieutenant Governor Stewart L. Woodford.[38] He died on August 19, 1887, at the age of 52.[39]

John V.B. Hatfield: See Active Base Ball.

Dick Higham: See Union Base Ball Club of Morrisania.

Charles S. Hunt: Charles S. Hunt was born in New York around 1839 and became the regular shortstop of the Mutuals in 1861. An October 3rd win over the Atlantics gave the Mutuals a chance to win the championship by winning the rematch thirteen days later, but Hunt had left to serve in the Civil War in the interim. His replacement's poor play cost the Mutuals their chance.[40] Hunt's military record has been difficult to pin down because of his common name, but he played only sparingly during the next few years. He rejoined the Mutuals in 1865 and played the outfield for the club for the next five seasons. By 1869, he was reduced to a part-time role, and in one of the games he did play he was criticized for playing so deep in center field as to be in the shade of the pagoda.[41] He and his brother switched to the Eckfords in 1870, but he again played sparingly and retired after the season, making him one of the most notable players of the 1860s to not play a single major league game. Like his father and his brother, Charles Hunt was a butcher by trade. He eventually moved across the river to Rutherford, New Jersey, to live with his married daughter. He died in Rutherford on September 1, 1915.[42]

Richard M. Hunt: Dick Hunt was Charles's younger brother and was a semi-regular from 1866 to 1869, then had a brief career in the National Association. Like his brother a butcher by trade, he was born around 1845 and died in New York City on November 20, 1895.

Nathan W. Jewett: Nat Jewett was born in New York City on December 25, 1842. (Some sources suggest an 1844 year of birth, but he was 9 on the 1850 census and his death certificate gives an age consistent with an 1842 year of birth.) After earlier stays with the Henry Eckford and Empire clubs, he joined the Mutuals in 1866 and was the club's regular catcher for three years. He continued his career with the Eckfords in 1869 and 1870 and played two games for that club in 1872 after it joined the National Association. Jewett later worked as a dry goods clerk as he and his wife raised eight children. He died in the Bronx on February 23, 1914.

James Jackson Kelso: James J. Kelso was the original secretary of the Mutual Club. A man named Kelso also played a game for the Mutuals in both 1859 and 1860 and no doubt this is the same man. Kelso was born in New York City on October 31, 1835, and spent several years in the register's office, then joined the Metropolitan Police in 1861 and made his way swiftly up the ranks until being appointed Superintendent in 1870.[43] After he had been in that position for eighteen months, the *Times* published a lengthy editorial explaining why the "misfortune" of retaining Kelso "should be spared the citizens of New York." The *Times* claimed that Kelso had received his appointment because of the influence of people connected to Boss Tweed and had performed his duties in a most "unsatisfactory manner."[44] Kelso was removed from office when the Metropolitan Police system was introduced in 1873, then worked as a stockbroker until being appointed collector of city revenue in 1885. He also remained active in politics until his death in New York on November 26, 1888.[45] After his death, the *Times* published numerous articles alleging that Kelso had used his position as city revenue collector to take bribes from vendors at the Washington Market. One of the men who testified in hearings on the matter was former Mutual pitcher Dick Thorne, who had three stands in the market and acknowledged having "subscribed $25 to the political fund raised in the old market for the use of James J. Kelso in the Twenty-first Assembly District."[46]

P. Kirelin/Kivolein: The shortstop of the Mutuals in 1858 was a man whose surname was misspelled in numerous ways. The original Irish spelling was probably Kivlehan, but this proved too difficult for Americans and was simplified. The ballplayer was probably a Patrick Kivlehan/Kivlin who either left New York or died soon afterward.

Billy Lewis: Billy Lewis joined the Mutuals in 1869 after previously playing with the Irvingtons. He was reported to have returned to Irvington when his career ended. The only William Lewis on the 1900 census who is a good match was a West Orange shoemaker who was born around 1844. We can't be sure he was the ballplayer, but it seems likely.

Robert Lindsay: Robert Lindsay served as vice president of the Mutuals in 1866 and was "one of its most enthusiastic supporters." He died on February 16, 1892, in New York City, at the age of 59.[47]

Phonny Martin: Like many of the Mutuals, "Phonny" or "Farney" Martin went into the billiard business after his baseball career, though a picture of the 1870 Mutuals was on prominent display at his billiard hall.[48] See the entry on the Empire Club for more about his life and career.

James McConnell: James McConnell was a Mutual Club officer in the club's early years and its scorer for many years. A "McConnell" was listed in one 1860 box score, and this is probably James McConnell as well. McConnell, who was born around 1830, was an active member of the Americus Fire Company and the brother-in-law of Justice Edward J. Shandley, another Mutual officer. McConnell was one of the organizers of the Mutual Club in 1857, then served as vice president in 1859 and 1860, and as secretary in 1863. He later worked as a clerk in the tax office and in 1879 was the Democratic candidate for the Assembly in the Eleventh District. When he died in New York on April 18, 1883, his obituary in the *New York Clipper*—undoubtedly written by Henry Chadwick included this commentary: "We had not seen him for some years past, but singularly enough met him on our way to 'The Clipper' office on Wednesday morning and stopped and shook hands with him. He was looking very well. We recommended him to visit the Polo Grounds and witness the fine displays of modern ball-playing to be seen there. His reply was: 'The fact is, I have not been on a ball-ground for years. I became so disgusted with the way things went that I would not go to see the game at all.' 'But,'

we remarked, 'things are different now, and the game is played on the square.' 'Well,' he said, 'I'll try and get up there some day.' And thus we parted. A few hours later and he was dead."[49]

Billy McKeever: Billy McKeever was born around 1837 and pitched for several other clubs before becoming the Mutuals' pitcher in 1863. The following year, Henry Chadwick commented that McKeever's "pitching, like several others, was made effective by his skill in what is called 'dodgy delivery,' that is, the balls he pitched, though apparently for the striker, were not such as he would strike at with any chance of hitting fairly. This style of pitching, and likewise the inaccuracy resulting from efforts to excel in speed, it was that led to the introduction of the new rules in reference to pitching, and hence McKeever's style is this season deprived of all its effect."[50] As described in the club history, McKeever was killed during a harness race in Chicago on September 25, 1866, the result of what may have been an attempt to kill his horse.[51]

William McMahon: Billy McMahon played for the Mutuals from 1859 to 1870, far and away the longest tenure on a club known for frequent changes in its lineup. His career was thus summarized in 1868: "William McMahon is frequently called by his comrades the old veteran. He has been a member of the Mutual and none other for many years, and there is hardly a position he has not filled some time or another and very creditably too. He is 34 years old, weighs 150 pounds, and measures 5 feet 7 inches. He is a great favorite in his club. His position is right field."[52] In 1872, McMahon opened a "dive" known as the Argyle Rooms at Sixth Avenue and Thirtieth Street. Later renamed the Haymarket, it became one of New York's most notorious underworld establishments.[53] Numerous complaints about its "unsavory reputation" spurred an investigation. The business was defended by Tony Hartman (see his entry for his comments) and by a "rather dudish" young man named Robert Osborne, who described McMahon as the "once famous second baseman of the Mutual Baseball Club" whom "he had always heard spoken of as a reputable man."[54] McMahon, who was described as a "small man, with short gray hair and smooth face," also testified that his establishment was a "general place of amusement, with a band and a ballroom, where parties can dance and amuse themselves."[55] In spite of these witnesses the Haymarket lost its liquor license in 1886. According to a later account, "For a time he kept the place open and sold 'soft drinks' to his customers, who clung to the habit of ending the night at the Haymarket. There was no profit in ginger ale, sarsaparilla, and lemonade, however, and after a few months McMahon threw up his lease, $750,000 richer, it was said by his admirers, than when he opened the place."[56] The establishment soon reopened under new management. McMahon passed away on October 22, 1898, at the age of 64.[57] He left an estate of $400,000 that became the subject of prolonged litigation.[58]

Charley Mills: See the Atlantic Base Ball Club for details on the life of Charley Mills, the club's catcher in 1869 and

1870. Charley is not believed to be related to Everitt Mills though he was the brother of Andy Mills, profiled in the piece on the Eckfords.

Everitt Mills: For details on the life of Everitt Mills, the Mutuals' first baseman in 1869 and 1870, see the entry on the Eureka Club of Newark.

Mott: A man named Mott played for the Mutuals from 1859 to 1864, mostly in a reserve role. There was a Daniel Mott who was a club director in 1868 and this could be the same man, but the various Daniel Motts who can be located on the census are not of a plausible age to be the ballplayer.

John W. "Candy" Nelson: Jack Nelson launched a long professional career by playing third base for the Mutuals in 1870. Born on March 14, 1849, in Portland, Maine, Nelson played his last major league game on August 25, 1890. He died in Brooklyn on September 4, 1910.

Michael and Peter Norton: Michael Norton was born in Galway, Ireland, around 1836, while his younger brother Peter was born after the family immigrated to New York. Michael Norton became a well-known boxer and then used Tammany connections to become a state senator in 1867. In January of 1870, he was named to the Mutuals' board of directors.[59] A few days later, his brother Peter died, and obituaries noted that Peter Norton had been a member of the Mutual Base Ball Club (though he does not appear to have ever played for the first nine). The members of the ball club attended his funeral as a group.[60] Michael Norton later became a judge and died on April 23, 1889.[61]

Dan Patterson: Dan Patterson was born in 1838 and was one of the Mutuals' regulars from 1864 to 1866. Two years after his retirement, Patterson's twenty-four-year-old wife died, and the Mutuals cancelled their next game so that players could attend the funeral.[62] His later occupations encompassed three of the club's main themes as he ran both a saloon and a billiard hall and served as an assemblyman.[63] He died in the Bronx on October 16, 1902.

Tom Patterson: See Eckford Base Ball Club.

Lip Pike: See Atlantic Base Ball Club.

W. Powell: W. Powell was a regular for the Mutuals from 1858 to 1860 but changed positions often. This came back to haunt the Mutuals when he replaced Charles Hunt at shortstop in the October 16, 1861, match that could have earned the club the championship. Powell, who had not "practiced since last season" and had never before played shortstop, showed a "want of nerve to stop the swift grounders and pass them to first base."[64] That was Powell's final appearance with the Mutuals, and nothing more is known about him.

Edward J. Shandley: Edward J. Shandley served as the club's vice president during its first two seasons and was one of numerous club officers with strong ties to Tammany Hall. Shandley was born on November 15, 1832, and held the offices of police justice and alderman before his death on July 28, 1876.[65]

Pete Shreves: The rather nomadic career of Pete Shreves included stints with the Gotham, Empire, and Mutual clubs of New York and the Nationals of Washington. Shreves was born in New Jersey around 1844, and when his playing days ended he operated a ball park in Jersey City for a while.[66] He was last heard of living in Hoboken in 1900.

Mahlon Stockman: See Irvington Base Ball Club.

Martin Swandell: See Eckford Base Ball Club.

Anson B. Taylor: Anson B. Taylor was born in Connecticut around 1827. He played a few games for the Mutuals in 1858, then was a regular for the next three seasons. He had served as club treasurer while an active player and began a four-year tenure as club president in 1861. Taylor, who was a partner in a mineral water business, died in New York on June 2, 1884.[67]

Henry B. Taylor: Anson Taylor's younger brother Henry was born in New York in 1836. He was regular in the club's outfield from 1858 to 1861, then played a few more games in 1862 before ending his playing days. According to a family genealogy, he died in Jacksonville, Florida, in January of 1875.

Richard H. "Dick" Thorne: See Empire Base Ball Club.

William M. Tweed: The infamous Boss Tweed's involvement with the Mutuals was greatly exaggerated by Henry Chadwick, who incorrectly claimed that Tweed had been the club's president.[68] But the club was full of Tammany members after the war, and in 1866 Tweed was elected as an honorary member.[69] Then in 1870 Tweed became one of the club's trustees, another position that probably included no real responsibilities, as the Mutuals had a full slate of officers.[70] At the post-season convention, club president John Wildey declared that Tweed "had contributed $7,500 towards the support of the Mutual Base-ball Club during the past year, without any intention of using the Mutual players as gambling instruments."[71] But even if true, this is a far cry from being club president.

William Wansley: William Wansley was the regular catcher of the Mutuals from 1862 to 1865 and was one of the three starters banned from baseball after the game-fixing scandal. Wansley was considered primarily responsible, and, unlike Duffy and Devyr, he never played baseball again (though he was reinstated in 1870). According to an 1879 article, Wansley was already dead.[72] Based on that statement, the ballplayer was almost certainly a William H. Wansley who died in Brooklyn on December 13, 1876, at the age of 37. But his passing was not noted in the sporting press.

Ed Ward: A man named Ed Ward was first baseman for the Mutuals in 1862, also playing for several other clubs. An 1866 note in the *New York Clipper* had Ward living in Hoboken. This suggests that the ballplayer may have been Edward Gender Ward, who was born in 1843 and had a long career in education that included serving as Superintendent of Public Schools for Brooklyn. But when this man died on January 13, 1901, none of the lengthy obituaries that appeared mentioned a connection to baseball, leaving doubt that he is the right man.

Fred Waterman: See Red Stockings of Cincinnati Base Ball Club ("Red Stockings") in *Base Ball Pioneers, 1850–1870*).

John Wildey: John Wildey, onetime coroner of New York City, was probably the most influential member of the Mutual Club. Born around 1824, Wildey, like so many of the Mutuals, was a volunteer fireman, serving for many years as foreman of Engine Number 11. He became an officer in the Mutual Club before the war and seems to have played at least one game in 1860. When the war started, he enlisted in the 11th New York Infantry and earned a reputation for bravery at the First Battle of Bull Run. Upon his return to civilian life, Wildey was elected coroner, a position that he used to the financial benefit of the Mutual Club by arranging patronage jobs for players. He became club president after the war, and was blamed for the club's close association with Boss Tweed and with rumors of "hippodroming" (throwing games). He also served as president of the NABBP and in 1870 tried to convince the convention that, "Boss Tweed had contributed $7,500 towards the support of the Mutual Base-ball Club during the past year, without any intention of using the Mutual players as gambling instruments."[73] Wildey was quite wealthy during his years as coroner, but was broke by the time he died in New York on May 29, 1889.[74]

Reinder Albertus Wolters: Rynie Wolters pitched for the Mutuals from 1868 onward and was responsible for the shutout of the White Stockings of Chicago on July 23, 1870. For more details on Wolters, see the entry on the Irvington Club.

John Zeller: See *Base Ball Pioneers, 1850–1870*s entry on the Excelsiors of Chicago for a profile of Zeller, who roamed the Mutuals' outfield from 1862 to 1867.

Other Club Members: W. Anderson, R. Breslin (officer), Campbell, Henry T. Clark (officer), J. Curtis, Patrick Culkin (officer), Dalton, Dewey, Freeland, one of the Gedney brothers, William L. Green (officer), Greer, Michael Hayes (officer), "Smiling John" Kelly, Bernard Kenney (officer), David Lennox (officer), Lloyd, McCullough, Dan McSweeney, James O'Neill (officer), James Reed, Phineas Smith (officer), Spence, Stephens, Tom Watts, Wismer.

Notes

1. *Wilkes' Spirit of the Times*, June 22, 1861.
2. The umpire for the Mutual-Atlantic game was A.T. Pearsall of the Excelsiors. Although the Civil War had begun six months earlier, Pearsall had not yet left for the South, where he became a surgeon for the Confederate Army, an act for which he was expelled by the Excelsiors.
3. *New York Clipper*, October 11, 1862.
4. *Wilkes' Spirit of the Times*, August 23, 1962.
5. *New York Clipper*, October 11, 1862.
6. *Wilkes' Spirit of the Times*, August 30, 1862.
7. *Wilkes' Spirit of the Times*, October 25, 1862.
8. *Wilkes' Spirit of the Times*, August 9, 1862.
9. *Wilkes' Spirit of the Times*, October 17, 1863.
10. *Wilkes' Spirit of the Times*, July 2, 1864.
11. *New York Clipper*, May 27, 1865.
12. *New York Clipper*, August 18, 1866.
13. Quoted in *Wilkes' Spirit of the Times*, September 8, 1866.
14. *New York Clipper*, August 15, 1868.
15. *New York Clipper*, November 7, 1868.
16. *Wilkes' Spirit of the Times*, September 26, 1868.
17. *New York Clipper*, January 8, 1870.
18. *Wilkes' Spirit of the Times*, December 18, 1869.
19. *New York Clipper*, May 14, 1870.
20. *New York Times*, October 26, 1870.
21. Chadwick Scrapbooks.
22. *Sporting Life*, November 4, 1885.
23. *Sporting Life*, October 29, 1898, 5.
24. *Sporting Life*, January 22, 1898, 1, and March 5, 1898, 9.
25. Chadwick Scrapbooks.
26. Benjamin Garno, *Sporting Life*, November 22, 1890, 12.
27. *New York Sun*, January 2, 1887.
28. *New York Tribune*, January 14, 1870; *Sporting Life*, March 31, 1906, 2.
29. *Louisville Courier-Journal*, reprinted in *Boston Globe*, December 26, 1882.
30. *Washington Post*, August 15, 1909.
31. Peter Morris (Chicago: Ivan R. Dee, 2009), *Catcher*, 175–177.
32. *New York Telegram*, August 29, 1872, 1.
33. *Sporting Life*, June 12, 1889, 1.
34. *Boston Globe*, August 3, 1883.
35. *Brooklyn Eagle*, July 19, 1871.
36. *New York Clipper*, April 21, 1866.
37. "Exceedingly Moral Men," *New York Times*, January 10, 1886, 3.
38. *Utica Observer*, May 10, 1904.
39. *New York Sun*, August 21, 1887, 10.
40. *New York Atlas*, October 20, 1861.
41. *National Chronicle*, May 8, 1869.
42. *New York Times*, September 3, 1915, 9.
43. *New York Times*, October 18, 1870, 8.
44. *New York Times*, April 27, 1872, 4.
45. *New York Tribune*, November 27, 1888, 3.
46. *New York Times*, March 7, 1889, 8; see also February 2, 1889, 2, November 15, 1891, 8, and April 10, 1892, 17.
47. *Sporting Life*, February 13, 1892, 2.
48. *Sporting Life*, June 25, 1892, 1.
49. *New York Clipper*, April 28, 1883.
50. *New York Clipper*, July 9, 1864.
51. William J. Ryczek, *When Johnny Came Sliding Home* (Jefferson, N.C.: McFarland, 1998), 77.
52. *Brooklyn Eagle*, August 15, 1868.
53. Timothy J. Gilfoyle, *A Pickpocket's Tale* (New York: W. W. Norton, 2006), 118–119; Herbert Asbury, *The Gangs of New York* (New York: Alfred A. Knopf, 1927), 162–164.
54. "Exceedingly Moral Men," *New York Times*, January 10, 1886, 3.
55. *New York Sun*, January 10, 1886, 9.
56. "Haymarket Is to Shut Up," *New York Sun*, March 7, 1898, 5.
57. *Sporting Life*, November 5, 1898, 8.
58. *New York Times*, April 13, 1901, 9; *Brooklyn Eagle*, July 2, 1901, 7.
59. *New York Tribune*, January 14, 1870.
60. *Brooklyn Eagle*, January 24, 1870; *New York Clipper*, January 29, 1870.
61. *National Police Gazette*, May 11, 1889, 2.
62. *Brooklyn Daily Times*, September 25, 1868; *New York Herald*, September 24, 1868.
63. *Sporting Life*, July 8, 1885, 7; *New York Sun*, January 2, 1887.
64. *New York Atlas*, October 20, 1861.
65. *New York Tribune*, July 29, 1876, 7.

66. *New York Sunday Mercury*, June 10, 1876.
67. *New York Clipper*, June 21, 1884.
68. *Sporting Life*, October 30, 1897, 10.
69. *New York Clipper*, April 21, 1866.
70. *New York Tribune*, January 14, 1870.

71. *Spirit of the Times*, December 3, 1870.
72. *Brooklyn Eagle*, April 5, 1879.
73. *Spirit of the Times*, December 3, 1870.
74. *Sporting Life*, June 12, 1889, 1; *New York Times*, June 1, 1889, 8.

❖ *Union Base Ball Club of Morrisania* ❖
(Aaron W. Miller)

CLUB HISTORY

For a few brief years in the late 1860s, the Unions of Morrisania were one of the elite teams in baseball. The Unions competed with the best teams in the New York area, as well as the powerful Philadelphia Athletics. In 1867, the Unions became the first team outside of Brooklyn to win the unofficial championship of the United States.[1] The team was the pride of Morrisania, an area of the lower Bronx. Gouvernour Morris, Jr., donated the land for the area in the hopes that it would become an idyllic village for the working class. The town grew up along a newly constructed railroad that cut across the development.

Thomas E. Sutton and five other civic leaders founded the Unions in 1855. Sutton, who also served as the team's first president, was a printer and member of Fire Engine #25. Another founding member was prominent local citizen William Cauldwell, who was the editor and owner of the *New York Mercury* and also owned the Empire Hotel. The other founding members included Edmund W. Albro, of the Knickerbocker Fire Insurance Company, John L. Burnett, a real estate and insurance executive, Henry J. Ford, and Ed White.

The Unions first played their games at a location called the Triangle, near a coal yard and 163rd street. In 1868 or 1869 they moved to their field to Tremont. With one of the first enclosed grounds in baseball, the Unions charged 25 cents for admission. The Unions played their home games at a diamond fourteen miles north of the city near Tremont, Westchester County. The field lacked a grand stand, in favor of simple board seats. Shade trees and embanked railroad tracks surrounded the Unions' outfield. This unusual playing surface provided for tough obstacles for the outfielders, who had to climb the embankments in order to retrieve fly balls hit over them, perhaps providing for a home field advantage. The distance of the Union's field no doubt was an obstacle for those living in the early walking city. This was an era when people walked to most of their destinations in the city; there was not extensive public transportation. But it is also possible that the setting was a respite, free from the unpleasantness of urban life.[2]

Despite the distance from the greater metropolis, the Unions frequently attracted thousands of fans during their heyday. Baseball scholar William Ryczek believed that the Unions were particularly appealing to women, with large numbers of female admirers in the crowd. It is possible that women enjoyed Union games due to the appealing site of their ballpark, away from the city.[3] After the Unions defeated the Eckfords, the *New York Times* recounted, "Quite a large crowd of spectators was present, a number of ladies gracing the scene with their presence."[4] In a game a few weeks later, after the Excelsiors destroyed the Unions 43 to 14, the *Times* noted, "In fact, the Union Ground has become quite a noted resort for the fair patrons of the game in Morrisania, every attention being shown them by the gay gallants of the Union Club, and the accommodations are specially provided for their fair guests on these occasions. Their efforts to induce the attendance of ladies at their matches have been the means of enabling them to surpass every other club in the community in this respect."[5] The *Times* regretted the new, "ungallant" trend: "Once upon a time, the Brooklyn clubs took the lead in having the most numerous attendance of the fair sex at their matches, but of late years they have become the most ungallant set in the country, although they have the facilities for excelling every other locality."[6] The presence of women often calmed the crowd. When the Unions were playing the mighty Philadelphia Athletics, the *Times* credited the women for a well-behaved group of cranks: "The ladies were out in unusual numbers, and by their presence restrained a crowd that would otherwise have been turbulent."[7] Unfortunately, the Unions lost 33 to 20.

The Unions played in patriotically dashing uniforms. The baseballists wore red-trimmed pants, with tri-colored belts around their waists, white shirts adorned with blue and emblazoned with a U on the front, and blue caps.

In the Unions' early years, the team saw some success while not gaining the notoriety and reputation for victory it would have in later years. After another defeat to the Eckfords in October 1856, this time by a score of 22 to 6, the sporting newspaper *Porter's Spirit of the Times* remarked: "A bad closing match this for a young Club like the Union; but if they practice with perseverance before the next season, they can and will do better."[8] The Unions would get better. A few years later, the *New York Times* noted in its September 8, 1860, edition: "One of the best-contested games of Base Ball that has ever taken place in this vicinity, [*sic*] was played yesterday on the Union ground, at Morrisania."[9] The Unions defeated the Excelsiors 7 to 4 in what was an unusually low score for the era. A few days later, after losing to the Putnams of Brooklyn 12 to 6, the *Times* noted that even though the Unions lost," it has been the good fortune of the Union Club to be a participant in some of the best games on record, and though of late quite unsuccessful, yet they always require a strong team to overcome them."[10] On a trip to play the Newarks in the late summer of 1862, after winning a close game 12 to 11, the *Times* commented that it was a "most enjoyable time" and a grand social occasion.[11]

Tragically, the most newsworthy event from the early years of Union play was the death of Jim Creighton. Creighton was an outstanding athlete and perhaps the national pastime's first star. He was multi-talented; the athlete played cricket for the St. George Cricket Club and baseball for the Excelsiors. But on October 14, 1862, Creighton injured himself after hitting a hard home run against the Unions. At the time, players and fans believed that Creighton overexerted himself either playing baseball against the Unions or at a cricket match he had played a few days earlier. Modern theories suggest Creighton died due to a preexisting condition, not the result of his powerful swing. The death of Jim Creighton remains one of early baseball's most enduring mysteries and tragedies.

After the Civil War, the Unions reached their pinnacle. Like the other strong teams in baseball, after the war, the Unions turned to using professional players to win. Baseball was no longer just a social occasion, but a competitive business. The Unions' use of paid players is ironic due to an episode in their early days. In 1856, a Mr. Pinckney (whose identity is discussed in the player profiles) played for the Unions of Morrisania and later for the Gothams in a game against the Knickerbockers. Of course, the Unions objected to Pinckney playing for the Gothams while he was still on their roster.[12] But after the war, the Unions resorted to paid players.

Catcher Dave Birdsall and pitcher Charley Pabor were the key ingredients for the Unions' success in the late 1860s. Birdsall also served as team captain in 1867 and 1868. For a short time, the great shortstop George Wright also played for the Unions. Birdsall was nicknamed the "Old Man" while Pabor was known as the "Old Woman." The April 22, 1870, edition of the *New York Times* noted that despite a loss to the Atlantics, "Pabor and Birdsall work together very nicely."[13] William Ryczek describes Pabor as "an effective, though rather wild, swift left-handed pitcher who apparently threw some type of primitive curve ball."[14] On the field, Pabor was good-natured and friendly while the oft-injured Birdsall was dour in temperament.[15] Birdsall's frequent absences from the lineup hurt the Unions' progress as an elite team. For one example, on July 8, 1870, the Chicago White Stockings easily clobbered the Unions 28 to 12 perhaps due to Birdsall's injuries.

In 1865, the Unions played a busy schedule, earning tough victories over good teams such as the Eckfords, the Ac-

tives, the Stars, and the Olympics. The Eckfords, however, dominated the Unions in another game by a lopsided 43 to 14. Their losses were respectable; they lost to the stronger teams in the area, such as the Atlantics, the Philadelphia Athletics, and the Excelsiors.

The next season, the Unions were even stronger, surprising the Surprise by a score of 52 to 4. Of course, the Unions might have been helped by the fact that they supplied the umpire. In June of 1866, the Unions bravely agreed to play the mighty Philadelphia Athletics, losing 33 to 20. The next month, the Unions toured Connecticut, easily winning all four of their matches by wide margins. The Unions defeated the Waterbury club by a shocking 71 to 11. On the tour, the Unions averaged over 49 runs per match and 6 runs an inning. Despite their wide margins of victory, the Unions "were made the recipients of ovations by various ball clubs at every stopping place, and treated with feeling of profound admiration toward the gentlemen composing the Connecticut base ball fraternity."[16] In October 1866, the Unions also won a decisive victory over the Hudson River Club from Newburgh 43 to 4. The Unions won despite Birdsall's absence. A week later, the Unions defeated the strong Athletics. The Unions finished the season with a 25–3 record, the best record of any team in the National Association of Base Ball Players.

But this did not mean that the Unions would win the 1866 championship. Under the rules of the Association, the championship belonged to whichever team defeated the current champion in a series. The team holding the championship in 1866 was the Atlantics, who scheduled games with the Unions but refused to play. In 1867, the cleat would be on the other foot.

After a slow start in 1867, the Unions defeated the defending champions, the Atlantics, 32 to 19. They subsequently lost to the Athletics but won a close match against the Eckfords. Like other strong teams, the Unions went on tours to play teams in far away places, like rural New York. In July of 1867, the team visited clubs in western New York, concluding with a 25–19 victory over the reputable Niagaras of Buffalo. The Unions' success, though, might have been the result of using an umpire they supplied. Baseball historian Harold Seymour found that "the *Buffalo Express* recommended that the next time the Unions traveled through the state they 'secure the services of an intelligent blind man.'"[17]

On October 10, 1867, the Unions claimed the championship by winning a thrilling second game from the Atlantics 14 to 13. The Atlantics had held the championship since 1864. The Unions finished the season with a record of 21–8. The Unions had not defeated the Atlantics, and hence were not the champions, when the Athletics beat them. Like the Atlantics that refused to face them in 1866, after the Unions won the championship in 1867, they decided not to play another opponent.

The next year, the Unions would flourish again, and included the great George Wright now playing at shortstop. At one point in 1868, the team won 25 games in a row. The Union Club also beat the English professional cricketers in a baseball match in 1868.[18] The following year, 1869, was a rebuilding year after domination in 1867 and 1868. In 1869, the Unions tried to return to a purely amateur team, but struggled in the field. The *New York Tribune* bemoaned the Unions' return to amateur status: "The relapsing of the Union Club of Morrisania and Buckeye of Cincinnati to the full condition of amateurs, threw some dozen first-class players out of employment."[19]

In 1870, the Unions returned to their former glory, turning to professional players by distributing the gate money among the players. Despite paying players, the Unions could not return to championship form.[20] The Unions also played college teams in 1870, defeating Fordham but losing to Manhattan College. The Unions would also use college players in its lineup as substitutes. In May of 1870, the Unions defeated the Athletics by one run, 7 to 6. A few days later, they lost by twenty runs to the Athletics. At least, the *Times* reflected, "the game was very spirited, and the fine play of both clubs elicited much applause from the spectators."[21] Other disappointing losses followed. The Red Stockings of Cincinnati skunked the Unions 14 to zero. The Unions then lost to the Athletics 51 to 20. During the 1870 season, the Unions would manage wins over the Nationals, Haymakers, Resolutes, and Pastimes. But the Unions played so badly in the early innings of a contest against the Mutuals in September of 1870 that the *New York Times* lamented, "Wake up Unions. You are too far behind to make the game interesting."[22] The Mutuals won the game 12 to 1.

Baseball's transition to professionalism ended the Unions time in the sport's spotlight. The Unions played in the National Association until 1870. Despite their flirtation with professional players, the Unions did not continue on to the National Association of Professional Base Ball Players. Unable or unwilling to compete with these full-time professional organizations, the Unions disappeared from baseball.

The Unions' short history in the early years of organized baseball reflected the salient issues of the national pastime. The Unions' failure to win a championship in 1866 while winning one the following year revealed the inequities in the system. The team's transition from paid players to amateurs and back again also highlighted the disparity between teams' access to talent. Lastly, some of the game's greatest early talent, such as George Wright, played for the Unions. Baseball fans and scholars, though, should remember the Unions as a hard-working club that, for a few brilliant years, shone as one of the best in baseball.

CLUB MEMBERS

William Abrams: William Abrams was a regular for the Unions for eight seasons and was the only pre-war member to take part in the championship season. Despite his long tenure, nothing is known about his life.

Albro Akin: Albro Akin played a variety of positions for the Unions in 1866 and 1867. Born into a prominent Dutchess County, New York, family on April 3, 1847, he lived in New York City for most of his life. He and George Wright were reunited in 1924, a year before Akin died in New York City on July 24, 1925.

George H. Albro: George Albro, an early club member, served as the principal of Grammar School #63 and passed away on October 15, 1880.

Henry C. Austin: Henry Austin played for the Unions and fought for the Union. Austin enlisted on June 14, 1861. The veteran played for the Unions from 1865 to 1870; he made the game-ending catch to win the championship for the Unions in 1867. Henry's father Valentine Austin was listed as a "ball maker" on the 1870 census. He was living in Morrisania and his son was playing for the Unions of Morrisania, so it seems likely that he was making the club's baseballs. After his stint with the Unions, Henry Austin played center field for the Resolutes of Elizabeth, New Jersey. Austin later worked as a policeman and served as the chief of police for Elizabeth from 1888–1892. He died in Amityville on November 2, 1904.

John Elias Bass: John Bass played for the Unions in 1870 and went on to play in the major leagues, leading the National Association in triples in 1871. Bass was born around 1848 in South Carolina, the son of a prison chaplain. He lived most of his life in Brooklyn before dying on September 25, 1888, in Denver, where he had gone in hopes of recovering his health.

Thomas Lamb Beals: Tommy Beals was born in August of 1850 in New York. Like Austin, Beals, an outfielder, made an important catch to preserve the Unions' victory over the Atlantics. After playing for the Unions, Beals, a right-handed batter, played second base, catcher, and the outfield for four major league teams. Beals died on October 2, 1915, in San Francisco.

Esteban Enrique "Steve" Bellan: See Unions of Lansingburgh (Troy "Haymakers") in *Base Ball Pioneers 1850–1870*.

David Solomon Birdsall: The backstop for the Unions, Birdsall was one of the key ingredients to the Unions' success in the late 1860s. Birdsall was about 5'9" and weighed around 126 pounds. He was born in either Westchester County or New York City on July 16, 1838. Birdsall died on December 30, 1896, in Boston. The catcher was tough, with a prickly demeanor. Frequently injured, Birdsall sometimes played shortstop to keep his batting talents in the lineup.

William Cauldwell: Cauldwell was one of the founding members of the Unions and also served as the team's secretary. This was convenient for Cauldwell, who also reported on the games for the *New York Sunday Mercury*, which he owned and edited. Cauldwell, the son of one of Morrisania's first settlers, was born in 1824 and went to college. During a distinguished career, he owned the Empire Hotel, was associated with the

Sunday Mercury for close to half a century and eventually became its sole proprietor, served as state Senator from 1868 to 1879, and was elected as supervisor of the Bronx six times. He was also credited with helping to introduce famous writers such as Mark Twain to New York.[23]

Alfred "Al" W. Gedney: Gedney was born on May 10, 1849 in Brooklyn. A left fielder, Gedney died in Hackensack, New Jersey, on March 26, 1922.

Bernard "Berney" J. Hanigan (or "Hannegan"): Hanigan played shortstop, outfield, and pitcher for the Unions. Apparently, Hanigan was quite popular with the ladies. *The New York Atlas* wrote: "'Berney Hanigan,' as he is known in Morrisania, is a great favorite with the Morrisania ball-players, and, what is more, is the most popular player in the club with the belles of the village, who flock in such numbers to the Union grounds when games are in progress, the Union Club mustering a more numerous bevy of pretty girls at their matches than any other club in New York or Brooklyn."[24]

Richard "Dick" Higham: Higham, a second baseman for the Unions in 1870, was born July 24, 1851, in Ipswich, England, the son of a professional cricket player. Higham had a long professional career as a player and umpire before accusations of game-fixing led to his becoming the only umpire ever banned from the major leagues. He died on March 18, 1905, in Chicago.

Wilbur F. Hudson: Hudson played second base for the Unions and worked as a principal and president of the School Teacher's Association of New York.

Dan Ketchum or Ketcham: In addition to playing for the Unions, Ketchum studied law. The well-educated player knew lines from Shakespeare and shared them at the post-game dinner celebrations.[25] Ketchum died in New York City on October 18, 1878.

Alfred D. Martin: Union second baseman Al Martin went on to have a brief major league career. A longtime *New York Times* proofreader, he died in Brooklyn on April 1, 1926.

Abraham R. Lawrence Norton: A. R. L. Norton was a pitcher who first came to prominence on the Red House grounds. He joined the Union Club in 1867 and pitched six games during the championship season. That was the end of his baseball career, and after graduating from the College of the City of New York, he became a successful Wall Street broker. In 1884, he and his partner lost $2 million as the result of the disastrous speculation of the president of the Second National Bank. They could have tried to evade responsibility for the massive loss, but instead they tried in vain to repay the debts. The calamity ruined Norton's health, and he died on February 8, 1887, in the house where he was born. Norton was only 39.[26]

Charles "Charley" H. Pabor: Pabor was a 5'6", 155-pound left-handed pitcher who contributed greatly to the Unions' championship success. He was born on September 24, 1846, in Brooklyn and died on April 23, 1913, in New Haven, Connecticut.[27]

Joseph Conselyea Pinckney: Pinckney was the center of controversy in the early days of the Unions. While a player for the Unions, Pinckney also represented the Gothams. *Porter's Spirit of the Times* reported after a game between the Knickerbockers and the Gothams, "Some dissatisfaction was expressed by members of the Knickerbocker Club and their outside friends, at the introduction of Mr. Pinckney, a superior player, from the Union Club of Morrisania, into the Club of the Gothams for this occasion; but no objection could be made, as it was ascertained that Mr. P. had joined the Gothams on the previous Tuesday." The newspaper reported that Pinckney had not left the Unions: "As, however, it did not appear that he had resigned from the Union, the presumption prevailed that he entered the Gothams for the purpose of this match." The newspaper thought there should be changes: "We do not notice this matter in the way of censure, but to suggest that, from the facility with which good players might be retained at the mere cost of an invitation fee, for any important match, a rule ought to be adopted to prevent such objections in the future. The true interests of sport and association pride require such a rule at once." In a special meeting, the Unions passed two resolutions admonishing Pinckney.[28] Pinckney's first name was long unknown, but John Thorn has identified him as Joseph C. Pinckney and profiles him in the entry on the New York Base Ball Club.

Ed Shelley: Shelley played third base for the Unions. He worked in law enforcement and was also an Assemblyman.

Joe Simmons: Joe Simmons, whose real name was Joseph Chabriel, was born June 13, 1847, in New York City. Simmons initially played for a number of clubs including the Gothams, the Empires, the Excelsiors of Chicago, the Forest Citys of Rockford, Illinois, as well as the Unions. He also played for teams in Cleveland, Keokuk, St. Louis, and Columbus. Simmons went on to work as a team manager for Rochester, Trenton, Wilmington, and a number of other teams. He died in Jersey City on July 24, 1901.

Thomas E. Sutton: Sutton was a founder, and the club's first president. He worked as a printer and was a member of Fire Engine #25.

Charles N. Swift: Swift was a secretary of the Union Base Ball Club of Morrisania.

John Van Horn: Van Horn worked as a cobbler with a store on Second Avenue in New York City. Van Horn made baseballs for the New York clubs along with Harvey Ross, a member of the Atlantic Base Ball Club. The two manufactured some of the best and most popular baseballs in the New York City area.[29] Van Horn played outfield for the Unions.

George Wright: Hall of Famer George Wright and his brother Harry were two of the most influential figures in early baseball. George was born on January 28, 1847, in Yonkers. The right-handed Wright was an innovative shortstop who also played second base, catcher, outfield, and pitcher. In the pioneer years of baseball, Wright played for the Gothams, the

Olympics, the Unions, and the Washington Nationals. Wright would later play for the Cincinnati Reds, Boston Red Stockings, the Boston Red Caps, and the Providence Grays. He also had the honor of being the first batter in National League history. The star athlete started a sporting goods business by the name of Wright & Ditson's, where he worked to develop equipment for other sports. George Wright named his son Beals, probably after Union Club teammate Tommy Beals. Beals Wright would go on to athletic glory in his own right. A terrific tennis player, Beals Wright won two gold medals in the 1904 St. Louis Olympics. He also won the U. S. Open Championship in singles in 1905 and doubles in 1905 and 1906. George Wright passed away on August 21, 1937, in Boston, and was inducted into the Baseball Hall of Fame.

Other club members: William Anner, Baker, Balcolm, Bassford, Charley Bearman, Bennett, Bogle, Booth, Borland, Brandow, Brown, Carsie, Sammy Collins, Dickenson, E. Durrell, F. Durrell, Ferdon, Frisbee, Gaynor, Gifford, John Goldie, Tom Haines, Henry, William Herring, James Holdsworth, Hyatt, Jackson, John Kenney, Kinloch, Lyons, Mallory, Mann, David Milliken, Nicholson, Parker, Reynolds, Rodman, Roosa, F. M. Scott, George Smith, Stearns, Tom Ten Eyke, Todd, Tremper, Valentine, Weidberg, and Whelan

Sources: I used many newspaper articles: *New York Atlas*, September 9, 1860; *New York Times*, September 8, 1860; *New York Times*, September 17, 1860; *New York Times*, August 4, 1862; *New York Times*, June 23, 1865; *New York Times*, July 17, 1865; *New York Times*, June 27, 1866; *New York Times*, April 22, 1870; *New York Times*, July 30, 1866; *New York Tribune*, April 3, 1869; *New York Times*, May 19, 1870; *New York Times*, September 3, 1870; *Porter's Spirit of the Times*, September 13, 1856; and *Sporting Life*, March 13, 1909. For background information on the early days of Morrisania, I used "Old Morrisania Town" by William Wood from August 18, 1938. Wood's article was based on an interview with T. Emery Sutton. This document can be found on the Library of Congress website on American memory. Sutton was the son of Thomas Sutton, the first president of the Unions. Lastly, for general information about early baseball, as well as the Unions, I used the influential and thoroughly researched secondary sources on the first days of baseball. These sources included:

NOTES

1. Harold Seymour, *Baseball: The Early Years* (New York: Oxford University Press, 1960), 25.
2. William J. Ryczek, *When Johnny Came Sliding Home* (Jefferson, N.C.: McFarland, 2006), 31, 34.
3. Ibid., 27.
4. *New York Times*, June 23, 1865.
5. *New York Times*, July 17, 1865.
6. Ibid.
7. *New York Times*, June 27, 1866.
8. *Porter's Spirit of the Times*, October 25, 1856.
9. *New York Times*, September 8, 1860.
10. *New York Times*, September 17, 1860.
11. *New York Times*, August 4, 1862.
12. Seymour, *Baseball*, 51.
13. *New York Times*, April 22, 1870.
14. Ryczek, *When Johnny Came Sliding Home*, 130.
15. Ibid., 130.
16. *New York Times*, July 30, 1866.
17. Seymour, *Baseball*, 44.
18. Melvin Adelman, *A Sporting Time: New York City and the Rise of Modern Athletics, 1820–1870* (Urbana: University of Illinois Press, 1986), 169.
19. *New York Tribune*, April 3, 1869.
20. Ryczek, *When Johnny Came Sliding Home*, 217–218.
21. *New York Times*, May 19, 1870.
22. *New York Times*, September 3, 1870.
23. *New York Times*, December 3, 1907.
24. *New York Atlas*, September 9, 1860.
25. Ryczek, *When Johnny Came Sliding Home*, 181.
26. *New York Clipper*, February 19, 1887; *New York Times*, May 14, 1884, and February 11, 1887.
27. *Auburn Citizen*, May 12, 1913.
28. *Porter's Spirit of the Times*, September 13, 1856.
29. *Sporting Life*, March 13, 1909.

BIBLIOGRAPHY

Adelman, Melvin. *A Sporting Time: New York City and the Rise of Modern Athletics, 1820–1870.* Urbana: University of Illinois Press, 1986.
Kirsch, George B. *Baseball in Blue and Gray: The National Pastime During the Civil War.* Princeton, N.J.: Princeton University Press, 2003.
Morris, Peter. *But Didn't We Have Fun? An Informal History of Baseball's Pioneer Era, 1843–1870.* Chicago: Ivan R. Dee, 2008.
Ryczek, William. *When Johnny Came Sliding Home, The Post–Civil War Baseball Boom, 1865–1870.* Jefferson, N.C.: McFarland, 2006.
Seymour, Harold. *Baseball: The Early Years.* New York: Oxford University Press, 1960.

Chapter Two

Brooklyn

❖ *Introduction* (Peter Morris) ❖

"Verily Brooklyn is fast earning the title of the 'City of Base Ball Clubs,' as well as the 'City of Churches,' " proclaimed *Porter's Spirit of the Times* in 1857. "As numerous as are its church spires, pointing the way to heaven, the present prospect indicates that they may be soon outnumbered by the rapidly increasing ball clubs, both cricket and base."[1] And indeed over the thirteen-year existence of the National Association of Base Ball Players, the national championship rarely left Brooklyn.

"Virginia was the mother of presidents, Brooklyn of ball players," declared a proud resident many years later.[2] Again it is hard to argue — Dickey Pearce, Jim Creighton, Candy Cummings, Joe Start, Joe Leggett, Charley Smith, Al Reach, Joe Sprague, Lip Pike, Bob Ferguson, George Zettlein, Jimmy Wood, Jack Chapman, and a seemingly endless supply of gifted players were produced on the baseball diamonds of Brooklyn.

Those great players were in turn responsible for introducing many of the game's enduring elements and traditions. Pearce transformed the shortstop position from a rover into a key member of the infield, while the left-handed Start revolutionized first-base play and Leggett was one of the first catchers to stand directly behind the plate. Creighton developed a lethal rising pitch while seemingly adhering to the strict delivery restrictions, and then became the game's first martyr at 21. Successors like Sprague and Cummings stunned batters with the first offerings that seemed to curve away from them, while Zettlein was more forthright, sending overpowering fastballs past them at unprecedented speeds. At the bat, Pearce and Tommy Barlow brought baseball the bunt and the "fair-foul," the latter proving so impossible to defend that it was soon banned via rule change. On the other extreme, Pike, the game's first Jewish star, awed onlookers with towering blasts that traveled far over the heads of any outfielder.

Brooklyn's off-the-field contributions were just as impressive. Harvey Ross of the Atlantics, a sailmaker by trade, began manufacturing baseballs; soon, clubs in faraway cities were sending orders to Brooklyn for a "white horsehide ball, just one" and the members were gathering to stare at it and give it "a kindly handling" upon arrival.[3] Henry Chadwick be-

came the first legendary sportswriter and introduced many elements of baseball that are now taken for granted — a strikeout is still a "K," for example, because Chadwick concluded that the "letter K is easier to remember than S." The Excelsior Club of Brooklyn embarked on the first major tour in 1860, a twelve-day, one-thousand-mile tour of upstate New York that was followed by a special trip to Baltimore. The ambassadorial Excelsiors introduced the road trip to baseball and, more importantly, spread the game to regions where it was still unfamiliar.[4]

No Brooklyn innovation changed the game more dramatically than the opening of the first enclosed field used primarily for baseball. The Union Grounds debuted in 1862 and were soon followed by the Capitoline Grounds, giving Brooklyn the first two such sites. Fences made it possible to hit balls out of the ballpark for the first time, but this was an unintended consequence. Their real purpose was to collect admission fees from the scores of spectators anxious to watch the games held within, thereby paving the way for professional baseball.

Manhattan may have been the namesake and birthplace of the New York Game, but it was in Brooklyn that baseball came of age. What was Brooklyn's secret?

It was certainly not because the New York Game got an early start there. The Knickerbockers' version of baseball was ideally suited to be played where space was limited, as was the case on Manhattan Island, where land was already at a premium. That was not the case in Brooklyn, which still had plenty of available space. There was a short-lived 1845 club that tried the new version, but Brooklyn ballplayers had little reason to give up their less formal ways of playing. As a result, "It was not until 1854 that base ball came into vogue in Brooklyn."[5]

The Knickerbockers themselves had run out of room in Manhattan by the mid–1840s and moved across the Hudson River to Hoboken, but the Elysian Fields also had insufficient room.[6] Worse, the site couldn't possibly accommodate all of the clubs that wanted to play there. An explosion of interest

98

Left: William T. Porter was the publisher of *Spirit of the Times* and *Porter's Spirit of the Times,* two of the earliest journals to provide coverage of the emerging sport of baseball. Throughout the 1850s and even after his death in 1858, Porter's papers and the rival *New York Clipper* were the leading sporting publications in New York. *Right:* No journalist did more to promote the game of baseball than English immigrant Henry Chadwick. From the time he discovered baseball in the mid–1850s until his death in 1908 Chadwick wrote tirelessly of the game, promoting integrity, fair play and his favored style of play.

in 1854 led many of them to turn to the "vacant fields then existing in South Brooklyn."[7] Those lots played host to a wave of all ballplayers from all over the surrounding area and they were joined by many of Brooklyn's own. New clubs began to spring up, including the Putnams and Charter Oaks, both profiled here. Three of those clubs were destined for greatness: the Excelsiors, the Atlantics, and the Eckfords.

Of that trio, only the Atlantic Club was an indigenous Brooklyn organization. As described in the entries that follow, both the Excelsiors and Eckfords had strong contingents of outsiders and it took a few years for them to become truly Brooklyn clubs. By 1859, however, all three were distinctively Brooklyn clubs and had established associations with specific neighborhoods: the Atlantics with Bedford, the Eckfords with Greenpoint and Williamsburgh, and the Excelsiors with South Brooklyn. During the last two years before the Civil War they dominated the burgeoning national pastime.

Yet even while Brooklyn was developing peerless ballclubs and exceptional ballplayers, its baseball diamonds continued to be places of joyful diversion. One of the celebrants later recalled with fondness the days "when base ball was a bucolic

pastime ... when the old Atlantics had their grounds on the old corn field adjoining the old Long Island Cricket Club's Field ... and how we played on the old sand lots where the Prospect Park Place now stands."[8] The Eckfords also played at a pastoral setting — the Manor House in Greenpoint, which was "entirely surrounded by cherry trees" and where the games "attracted farmers for miles around."[9]

Later accounts made everything about those years sound idyllic. According to one such reminiscence, "Club matches in these days were meetings which the members gave their whole minds to for the time being. They were important affairs, something that had to be attended to as if the reputation of the club was at stake every time they met in the field. If the day of the match was a fine one then you would see the early birds of the club out on the field hours before the game was to be commenced, tiring themselves out in playing fungo."[10] Yet at the end of the matches, both sides would join together for enthusiastic cheers and then share a bountiful meal. It seemed as though, in Brooklyn at least, baseball could be all things to all people.

Reality, however, was not that simple and even during

those glory years the game had not been as innocent as it appeared. Retrospective accounts suggest that professionalism had already entered baseball by 1860 with the chivalrous Excelsiors being the club most likely to have introduced it. The vacant lots that had once stretched out endlessly were suddenly in short supply; one club obtained a signed document in 1858 that established its right "to occupy the vacant ground on the block between Douglass, Degraw, Hoyt and Smith streets, to the exclusion of any other club, in case any difficulty should arise as to the occupancy of the ground."[11]

The outbreak of the Civil War brought a torrent of changes that transformed baseball forever. In particular, the years after the opening of the Union Grounds saw money impinge upon every aspect of the game. Professional play brought with it the unwelcome trio of gambling, "revolving," and game-fixing. Though officially outlawed until 1869, professionalism was a pervasive force by the end of the war and with it came an end to Brooklyn's dominance.

The Excelsiors announced in 1865 that they would no longer "play any 'Champion' games," while the Eckfords went into such a steep downward spiral that the *New York Clipper* wrote of "the wreck of their former greatness."[12] Meanwhile prewar greats such as Frank Pidgeon and Pete O'Brien turned their backs upon the game and became outspoken critics of professionalism. Even the baseball fields of South Brooklyn, such a boon to the game a decade earlier, had fallen on hard times. "A vacant lot with cobble-stone paved streets on three sides, and the lot a stony and sterile mess," bemoaned the *Brooklyn Eagle* in 1865, was now "the best ground South Brooklyn affords."[13]

The Atlantics also lost talent to raids from other cities and had to take consolation after a loss to the Mutuals of New York City from the fact that three of the members of their vanquishers hailed from Brooklyn.[14] An especially symbolic moment occurred during an 1868 tour. One of the Atlantics' games was played in Buffalo, one of the stops on the legendary Excelsior tour of eight years earlier, and there were the usual expectations that the mighty Brooklyn club was going to "show the uncivilized people of these western wilds how the game is played." Instead the host Niagara Club stunned the Atlantics, and the visiting players "retired from the field with banners ingloriously trailing in the dust."[15]

Yet while the postwar decline of Brooklyn baseball was undeniable, in many ways it was an inevitable symptom of the rapid spread of the game. No city would ever again achieve the baseball preeminence of Brooklyn's prewar trio, but then again how could such dominance continue after clubs like the Excelsiors had introduced the game to so many new regions? Moreover, Brooklyn's clubs remained highly competitive — despite the setbacks, the Atlantics continued to be a national powerhouse, while the Eckfords rebounded and other strong clubs emerged.

The era of open professionalism began in 1869 and posed a new challenge for Brooklyn's standard-bearers. The city's best players were targeted more openly than ever, and in 1870 a newly formed professional club in Chicago was built around Eckford talent. The "City of Base Ball Clubs" did not give up without a fight and in 1870 the legendary winning streak of the Red Stockings came to an end at the hand of the Atlantics. The talent drain continued in 1871 with the formation of the first major league, the National Association, and this time the departures were too much to overcome. Clubs bearing the fabled names of Eckford and Atlantic competed in the first professional baseball league, but both were shadows of their former selves.

The lackluster end, however, does not diminish the glory that was Brooklyn baseball during the pioneer era. In the entries that follow, those great players and clubs receive their due for the contributions they made. We have the Putnam Club, one of the most notable clubs to spring up during the first flurry of excitement in Brooklyn. Then there is the Pastime Club, one of the prewar clubs that came to be better remembered for its spirit than its results. We have the Contest Club, which represents all of the junior clubs that continually renewed local vigor and kept Brooklyn a baseball hotbed. There is also the Star Club, all too often overshadowed by its better-known rivals but a very successful and accomplished club in its own right. Finally, there is the great trio of the Excelsior, Eckford, and Atlantic clubs, each a legend in its own right.

Notes

1. *Porter's Spirit of the Times*, June 20, 1857.

2. *Brooklyn Eagle*, August 5, 1897, 5, letter from G. Smith Stanton of Great Neck.

3. Quoted in Priscilla Astifan, "Baseball in the Nineteenth Century," *Rochester History* LII, no. 3, Summer 1990, 10–11.

4. Baseball firsts are of course often the subject of dispute but there is no question that Brooklyn was at the heart of an extraordinary number of important ones. See my book *A Game of Inches: The Innovations That Shaped Baseball* (Chicago: Ivan R. Dee, 2006) for a discussion of the merits of each of these claims and of many less plausible claims.

5. *Brooklyn Eagle*, July 16, 1873.

6. Peter Morris, *But Didn't We Have Fun?* (Chicago: Ivan R. Dee, 2008), 90–93.

7. *Brooklyn Eagle*, July 16, 1873.

8. Richard Weddle, 1901 letter to Henry Chadwick, *The Sporting News*, January 19, 1901.

9. *Brooklyn Eagle*, June 26, 1885, 1.

10. "Old Boys," *Brooklyn Eagle*, December 2, 1877.

11. "Old Chalk" [Henry Chadwick], "Base Ball Reminiscences," *Brooklyn Eagle*, June 7, 1891, 16.

12. *Brooklyn Eagle*, August 23, 1865, 2; *New York Clipper*, August 31, 1867.

13. *Brooklyn Eagle*, June 26, 1865, 2.

14. *Brooklyn Eagle*, November 5, 1868.

15. Unidentified Cleveland paper, quoted in the *New York Herald*, June 22, 1868, 6.

Excelsior Base Ball Club ❖
(William J. Ryczek and Peter Morris)

CLUB HISTORY

The Excelsior Club of Brooklyn was formed late in 1854 and played serious, competitive baseball for more than a decade. For many years more it functioned as an active social club. Despite its lengthy tenure, however, the Excelsior Club was principally defined by its glorious 1860 season. In that last summer before the start of the Civil War, the Excelsiors made a tour of upstate New York, the first time any baseball nine had ventured far from home for an extended period, and waged a fierce and bitter fight for the championship of the United States with the Atlantic Club of Brooklyn.

Disillusioned by the unfortunate manner in which the battle for the 1860 championship ended, the Excelsiors vowed never again to contest for a title. Many from their ranks, including captain and star catcher Joe Leggett, marched off to war in 1861 and for the next few years the club played a greatly reduced schedule. Pitcher Jim Creighton, perhaps the most famous baseball player in America then, died tragically in 1862 at the age of 21. The club made a brief and ineffective effort to return to prominence in 1866 by enticing a number of the best Atlantic players to join them, but like so many clubs that were prominent in the 1850s the Excelsiors yielded the stage to the professional clubs that dominated the game by the late 1860s.

Early Years

In mid–November 1854, a group of young men, primarily clerks and merchants, observed a game of baseball played by the Knickerbocker and Eagle clubs. They liked what they saw and, led by John H. Suydam, agreed to play a game among themselves on Thanksgiving Day. The players began referring to themselves as the "Jolly Young Bachelors' Base Ball Club" and soon decided to form an official club. On December 8, nineteen of these young men attended a meeting at the Florence Hotel, Broadway and Walker Street in New York City. There a constitution was adopted and a slate of seven officers elected, including Jeremiah Tappan as president. A more solemn name was also deemed necessary, and as a result of a proposal by Charles C. Suydam the club changed its name to Excelsior (the motto of New York State).

According to an article published on the occasion of the club's fiftieth anniversary, its original eighteen members were Elisha Bacon, Edward L. Barnes, J.O. Bartholomew, George T. Dalton, D. Albert Dodge, Frederick G. Eldridge, Alexander P. Fiske, William Herrick, Robert J. Hubbard, F.W. Jones, William H. Ludlow, James Rogers, John H. Suydam, J. Nelson Tappan, James H. Van Nostrand, Peter Van Schaack, Gustavus S. Winston, and A.G. Wood.[1] Since there were reportedly nineteen attendees at the meeting and the name of Charles C. Suy-

dam does not appear among the members, perhaps he declined to join.

The new club's early years contained no hint of impending greatness. During 1855 the Excelsior Club did not play a single match game, an inactivity attributed to "the inaccessibility of its grounds."[2] This seems to have reflected the deeper problem that the members were drawn from both Brooklyn and New York City, making it all but impossible to find a practice site that was convenient to all. The following year they participated in just two interclub matches, both against the Putnams, winning one. The club indeed showed so few signs of life that in the spring of 1857 a new Brooklyn club, apparently unaware of the existence of a forerunner, also took the name of Excelsior.[3]

The 1857 season saw the (original) Excelsior Club play only three match games, splitting a pair of contests with the Unions of Morrisania and losing to the Putnams. An account of the latter match in *Porter's Spirit of the Times* suggested that the defeat was at least partly attributable to a lack of practice. Despite these continued signs of apathy, the 1857 season also witnessed portents of the greatness that lay ahead. The same account that criticized the members' practice habits was quick to note that "Whatever success they may have upon the field, they cannot be beaten in the dispersing of their hospitalities, or in gentlemanly bearing on all occasions."[4] The latter two qualities would become trademarks of the Excelsior Club throughout its existence.

In another sign of growing ambition, the Excelsiors sent delegates to the 1857 convention that standardized the rules of baseball and to the meeting the following year that resulted in the formation of the National Association of Base Ball Players. Dr. Joseph B. Jones, president of the Excelsior Club, was elected first vice president of the Association. Over the next few years, the Excelsiors played an active role in the new organization and, in tandem with the Knickerbockers, led the movement advocating a transition from the bound rule to the more skillful fly game, eventually refusing to play any club that would not agree to play the fly game.

By 1857 the Excelsior Club had established permanent grounds at the corner of Smith and DeGraw streets in South Brooklyn, a site that seems to have alleviated the former difficulty in scheduling matches and practices.[5] At the end of the 1857 season the Excelsiors took another major step by consolidating with the Wayne Base Ball Club of Brooklyn. The merger brought them additional members, the most talented being a catcher named Joseph Bowne Leggett, who was immediately elected vice president. It also stamped the club as unmistakably a Brooklyn club.

With their new reinforcements, the Excelsiors became

The Knickerbocker and Excelsior clubs circa 1859.

much more active in 1858, winning eight of thirteen games. Victories over established teams like the Knickerbockers, Gothams, Unions of Morrisania, and Eagles caused the baseball world to take notice, despite two lopsided losses to the champion Atlantics. "The Excelsiors," the *New York Clipper* wrote in September, "meteor-like, have rushed on to glory, allowing no obstacle to mar the lustre of their escutcheon, their chief delight being to single out the oldest and strongest, accumulate laurel upon laurel in grasping the victory from each, then hold out the right hand of fellowship, in a manner which will not admit of doubt, as to its sincerity, while with the other they point to their best of mottoes, Excelsior."[6] Late that summer Leggett and outfielder John Holder played for the Brooklyn picked nine in the Fashion Race Course series. Holder hit the only home run in the first game.

In 1859 the Excelsiors were even more successful than in the previous year, finishing with a record of 11–3. They had the most wins of any club in the New York area, one more than the Atlantics, but since they didn't play the champion Brooklyn nine, the Atlantics retained the title. The Excelsiors were determined to win the championship in 1860, and during the offseason acquired two new players to strengthen their already formidable nine.

The first addition was infielder George Flanley, a good fielder and light hitter who had played with the Stars the previous year. The second newcomer to the Excelsior Club was the nineteen-year-old pitcher of the Stars, Jim Creighton.

Creighton began his baseball career as a second baseman but had turned to pitching in 1859. Leggett told Creighton to practice throwing an iron ball the size of a baseball during the winter to improve his speed.[7]

The shift of Flanley and Creighton to the Excelsiors caused many to question their motives. Had they been given pecuniary incentives to change allegiance? Although there is no definitive evidence that either player was compensated, many believe that the pair, or at least Creighton, received under-the-table payments from a wealthy patron of the club. If so, Creighton may have been the first player ever paid to play baseball (or perhaps he shares the distinction with Flanley).[8]

The Glorious 1860 Season

If Creighton was paid, he certainly earned his money in 1860, as he led the Excelsiors to one of the most successful seasons in the history of the young game. The opening match of the season, which the Brooklyn club unexpectedly lost to the Charter Oaks, 12–11, gave no indication of the great things that were to come. The Excelsiors later beat the Charter Oaks decisively in the return match, and easily defeated the Stars, from whom they'd taken two of their best players. In all, six former Star players were in the Excelsior lineup.

During the first week of July the Excelsiors did what no nine had ever done previously. They embarked on a lengthy tour of upstate New York, the first time any club had ventured that far from their home base for such an extended period of time. Between July 2 and 11 the Excelsiors played in Albany, Troy, Buffalo, Rochester (twice), and Newburgh, winning all six games easily and outscoring the opposition 194–56. The closest game was a 13–7 win over the Victory Club of Troy. Most "country" teams had been playing baseball for only a couple of years, and the quality of competition was weak. Teams from upstate had begun to develop intracity rivalries and sometimes played clubs from neighboring towns, but most had never seen players like the Excelsiors. A reporter from Buffalo wrote, "It is safe to say that no such ballplaying was ever before witnessed in Buffalo. The manner in which the Excelsiors handled the ball, the ease with which they caught it, the precision with which they threw it to the bases, and the tremendous hits they gave it to the long field made the optics of the Buffalo players glisten with admiration and protrude with amazement."[9]

The Excelsiors had indeed assembled a talented team, including Creighton, Leggett, and Flanley, first baseman A.T. Pearsall, heavy-hitting outfielder Harry Polhemus, and infielder Asa Brainard, who became the star pitcher of the Red Stockings of Cincinnati of 1868–70. The nine was not merely talented; they were gracious and gentlemanly and made a favorable impression at every stop. As was *de rigueur* for antebellum baseball, the Excelsiors were heartily entertained in each city, returning home with full bellies and sore hands, for the nine was unaccustomed to playing so many games in such a brief period of time.

Leggett trained his team to work together in the manner so admired by journalist Henry Chadwick, an untiring advocate of "scientific" team play and wholesome behavior. The players were disciplined on the field and moderate in their habits, and obeyed their captain's orders. Leggett was already 32 in 1860, rather old for a ballplayer, and his maturity, bearing and skill on the playing field gained the respect of his charges.

Upon returning to Brooklyn from their upstate sojourn, the Excelsiors faced the arduous task of wresting the "national" championship from the Atlantics, who had held the title since it was conceived. The first of the best-of-three series between the two clubs took place on July 19 at the Excelsior grounds at the foot of Court Street. Although the weather was oppressively hot, an estimated ten thousand spectators saw the game, including those within the grounds and many who watched from nearby rooftops and the balcony of the Brooklyn Yacht Club.

The Excelsiors dealt the champions the worst defeat in their history, besting them by a 23–4 score. Creighton dominated the famous Atlantic hitters, inducing numerous foul tips and easy chances and causing frustrated Atlantic outfielder Peter O'Brien to complain to Chadwick that Creighton's delivery was an illegal underhand throw.[10] The game was so one-sided, and the Atlantics appeared so helpless against the swift pitching of Creighton, that it seemed almost certain the Excelsiors would be the next champions of the United States.

The Atlantics were not finished, however, and stayed alive with a closely-fought 15–14 victory in the second game. The Excelsiors jumped out to an 8–0 lead, and were in the van by a score of 12–3 after five innings. The Atlantics were known for furious rallies, however, and scored nine times in the seventh inning to take the lead. Creighton was hit so hard by the revitalized Brooklyn club that he was replaced in the pitcher's box by Ed Russell. The game ended when Leggett, carrying the tying run, was thrown out at second base.

As was the custom for a series that lasted three games, the final match, scheduled for August 23, took place on a neutral site, the grounds of the Putnam Club, located between Lafayette and Gates Avenues in Brooklyn. Many were concerned about the selection, for the Putnam Grounds were ill-suited to accommodate a crowd as large as those that attended the first two games.

As they had in the second game, the Excelsiors jumped out to an early lead, scoring five times in the first inning. The Atlantics pecked away, spurred on by a raucous crowd. In the midst of the Atlantic comeback, there were two controversial calls by umpire R.H. Thorne. In the fourth inning Johnny Oliver of the Atlantics hit a foul that bounced off Leggett's neck. Thorne did not see that Leggett caught the ball cleanly on the first bound and ruled Oliver not out. Since it was obvious that Leggett had made the catch, decorum dictated that the Atlantics acknowledge that Oliver was out. The game was for the championship, however, with some serious bets on the line, and the Atlantics insisted that Oliver was not out.

One inning later, Atlantic captain Archie McMahon was called out at third on a close play after he overran the base. McMahon, who had been in the midst of the earlier Oliver fracas, protested vigorously that he had been safe. Although the Excelsiors still led, 8–6, the Atlantics, despite the umpiring calls, clearly had momentum. At that point, the crowd, estimated at as high as fifteen thousand, became louder and more threatening, and was beginning to encroach on the playing field. The game had not begun until after three o'clock, had taken a long time to play, and it was possible that darkness would bring it to a close before nine innings had been completed, if the actions of the crowd didn't cause an earlier termination. Both pitchers had thrown an extraordinary number of pitches, Creighton 331 and the Atlantics' Mattie O'Brien 334.[11]

The Atlantic defense broke down when the Excelsiors next came to bat, committing a series of errors that enraged their fans nearly as much as Thorne's decisions. Leggett said that if the crowd was not put under better control, he would pull his nine from the field. When the disturbances continued, the Excelsior captain made good on his threat and led his club to their carriage. As they left the grounds, Captain Peter O'Brien of the Atlantics spoke with Leggett and the two men agreed to call the match a draw. Umpire Thorne stood on a chair and rendered a decision that left the audience uncertain which team, if any, had won.

The unfortunate episode placed a stain on the image of the game of baseball, in the year it had seemingly come of age. In the days after the debacle, New York and Brooklyn newspapers were filled with letters from the adherents of each team. Atlantic supporters claimed Leggett had been jumpy and unduly concerned and should not have taken his team off the field. Atlantic secretary F.K. Boughton authored a letter absolving his club of blame and naming Leggett as the cause of the game's untimely conclusion. The Excelsiors reaffirmed their decision to terminate play and stated they would never again compete for a championship.

The game was never replayed. Since the championship rules required any challenger to defeat the incumbent in a best-of-three series, the Atlantics remained the champions.

In late September the Excelsiors made a second trip beyond the New York area, visiting Baltimore and Philadelphia. Baseball in Baltimore had an Excelsior pedigree, having been organized by George Beam, a wholesale grocer and a business associate of Harry Polhemus. Beam had learned the game from the Brooklyn club and had recently transported it to his home town of Baltimore. Philadelphia baseball was also in its nascent stages and there was no nine in either city that was expected to provide a serious challenge to the visitors from Brooklyn.

The Baltimore club formed by Beam bore the name Excelsior, but the name was the only thing his club had in common with his friends from Brooklyn, who easily defeated the Baltimore Excelsiors, 51–6. The hosts spared no expense in their entertainment of the visitors and, perhaps a bit worn down from all the social activity, the Brooklyn club was less formidable in Philadelphia, although they defeated a picked nine from the latter city rather handily. The Excelsiors' final record for 1860 was 18–2–1.

Although the Excelsiors did not claim the championship in 1860, they left an indelible imprint on the game of baseball with their groundbreaking tours of upstate New York, Baltimore, and Philadelphia. The games with the Atlantics were probably the most heavily attended and the most exciting series ever played between two clubs.

The Excelsior Club's vow not to challenge for the championship in future years was somewhat hollow, for it was no longer, after 1860, one of the best teams in the country. Their ascent to the top of the baseball world was followed by a gradual descent to mediocrity and eventually oblivion.

The War Years

The Excelsiors, so active and mobile in 1860, did not play a single match with another club in 1861. It was said that ninety members, including Joe Leggett, enlisted in the Union Army, though this may be an exaggeration. At least one, first baseman A.T. Pearsall, joined the Confederate forces as a surgeon and was expelled for doing so, while another member, Charles Etheridge, appears to have fought for the Confederates. (See the player profiles for details on both men.)

The second year of the war resulted in more baseball activity, and the Excelsiors returned to action, playing six games. Summoning up their old wanderlust, they journeyed to Boston for two games in 1862, defeating the Bowdoin and Tri-Mountain teams by large scores. Overall, the Excelsiors won four of their six games and tied another, but the season ended with the tragic death of Jim Creighton. According to legend, the star pitcher ruptured himself while hitting a home run against the Unions of Morrisania, collapsed into his teammates' arms while crossing home plate, and died shortly afterward. More reliable sources attribute his death to the aggravation of a prior injury, which probably resulted in a strangulated intestine. At any rate, Creighton was dead at the tender age of 21.

After the death of Creighton, Leggett, who played just one game in 1862, was the main link to the glory days of the club, and he was but a shadow of his old self. "He must remember," the *Clipper* wrote in 1863, "that he is not nor will ever be again the Leggett of 1860, when he touched the highest point of the ladder. He has been descending since then, and though still a good player, he is not A No. 1 now, his inability to throw weakening his play exceedingly."[12] Leggett was well beyond baseball middle age, and army life must have been hard on him. In addition, he suffered a broken leg prior to the 1864 season that greatly reduced his mobility.

The Excelsiors played a modest schedule for the duration of the war, nine games in 1863 and eleven in 1864. In 1863 the club had its least successful season since 1857, winning five and losing four. Again, the club left the New York area, venturing to Philadelphia to play the Athletics. The latter club was beginning to acquire a reputation as a talented team, and beat the Excelsiors 18–17 in an exciting ten-inning game.

"The Excelsiors," the *Eagle* stated in 1864, "have now come to be regarded as a half dead club,"[13] and "it appears the Excelsiors have gone to sleep again for their ground is nearly deserted now, even the muffins being to [sic] sleepy too [sic] turn out."[14] Although the Excelsiors won eight and lost three, they played only twice against top teams, losing both times to the Mutuals.

The Excelsiors had always been a respected club under the leadership of president Jones and captain Leggett, but with Leggett often absent during the war years, discipline occasionally broke down. In a game they were losing to the Nassau Club of Princeton in 1863, the Excelsiors tried to stall in order to have the match terminated by rain prior to the completion of the fifth inning. Brainard, the club's best pitcher after the death of Creighton, intentionally threw wildly in order to prolong the inning and his teammates declined chances to put out the Nassaus. Henry Chadwick, who deplored such unmanly behavior, declared with certainty that such an episode would never have taken place had Leggett been present.

The Postwar Era

In the years immediately following the end of the Civil War, the Excelsiors were not one of the best teams in New

York, but they remained an important part of the baseball scene. Intercity visits became more common, and whenever a team from Philadelphia, Washington, or Baltimore visited New York, they usually scheduled a game against the Excelsiors, perhaps as much in deference to their reputation as gracious hosts and entertainers as for their skill on the ball field. When the Nationals of Washington visited New York in 1866, the *Clipper* described the occasion as follows: "July the 5th, 1866 will henceforth be a day especially noteworthy in the annals of the National Club, and of the national game itself, for it was one marked by the most splendid reception ever given to one club by another.... This reception surpassed all others of the kind without doubt."[15] If the Excelsiors had slipped a notch on the field, they had lost nothing at the dinner table. They took the Nationals' traveling party to meet the mayor and to visit Creighton's grave, and treated them to a sumptuous feast after the game. In late 1865 the Excelsiors themselves took to the road, visiting Washington and losing to the Nationals 36–30. The following season they played five games on a tour of Philadelphia, Baltimore, and Washington, winning four and playing one tie.

In 1866 the Excelsiors made one final, brief bid for glory, at the expense of their old rivals, the Atlantics. In the winter before the season, in a manner eerily reminiscent of the wooing of Creighton and Flanley from the Stars, the Excelsiors enticed shortstop Dickey Pearce, second baseman Fred Crane, and catcher Frank Norton from the Atlantics. Pearce was perhaps the best shortstop in baseball and Crane and Norton were integral parts of the Atlantic championship nine. Joe Leggett, although 38 and well past his prime, rejoined the club on a full-time basis and played in 16 games.

The new recruits did not vault the Excelsior nine to the top of the list. Norton stayed for the entire season, but Pearce and Crane left after just a few games to return to the Atlantics, the reason for their departure as unclear as what motivated their arrival. On June 1, as the reinforced Excelsiors played a game against the Harvard Club at the Capitoline Grounds, a large number of bitter Atlantic fans showed up and heckled the seceders, threatening for a time to re-enact the violence of the fateful 1860 encounter. Fortunately, the police were able to contain the boisterous members of the crowd and the game was played to a peaceful conclusion.

The Excelsiors played 20 games in 1866, winning 13, losing 6, and playing an 18–18 tie with the Keystone Club of Philadelphia. Like the Stars of Brooklyn, the postwar Excelsiors had the ability to beat second-rate nines but could not compete with top clubs like the Mutuals and the Unions of Morrisania. They lost twice to each without a victory.

While they did not transform the Excelsiors into a championship club, the old Atlantics brought some fighting spirit to the nine. During a game against the Peconic Club in early August, the umpire ruled against the Excelsiors in two questionable decisions. The aggrieved party in the first instance

was James Mitchell, a veteran of the Excelsior Club, who accepted the decision without comment. The second call involved Norton, who, true to his Atlantic roots, protested the incorrect call and persuaded the umpire, George Fox, to change his decision.[16]

The Excelsiors fielded a competitive team in 1867, merging with the Enterprise Club and finishing with an 11–5 record. They employed several players, including pitcher Candy Cummings, outfielders George Hall and Fred Treacy, and infielder Bill Lennon, who would play in the professional National Association. Leggett also played occasionally, although generally at shortstop rather than as the catcher, the position where he had earned his reputation. Again, the Excelsiors posted victories against second-line teams such as Una, Peconic, and Independent, while losing to the better clubs like Lowell, Eckford, Harvard, and Keystone.

The Excelsiors had long been suspected to have been the first club to employ a professional player but, ironically, it was advent of the professional players as the dominant class that relegated the venerable Brooklyn club to secondary status and eventually caused them to disband. By the mid–1860s many teams were quietly paying their players, or compensating them in some manner, and the best players became closet professionals. In 1868, the last season of clandestine professionalism, the Excelsiors, bereft of the best players from the previous year, played just ten times, achieving a record of 4–5–1. In a tribute to days gone by, the veterans of the Excelsiors and Knickerbockers played a match against each other in the old spirit of fun and bonhomie.

The Excelsiors remained an amateur club after the legalization of professionalism and, while some teams played 50 games or more per year, played a modest schedule, finishing 5–7 in 1869 and 5–3–1 in 1870. They withdrew from the NABBP, increasingly dominated by professional clubs, and on December 13, 1870, called a meeting for the purpose of organizing a new amateur association. The new organization was formed on March 16, 1871, in the Excelsior club rooms, just one day before the professionals founded the National Association of Professional Base Ball Players.

During the 1870s the Excelsiors became more of a social club and less of a baseball organization. Social life had always been important and "first nine" matches were just one component of the Excelsior lifestyle. In 1866, the club claimed to have 370 members,[17] most of whom never played in competitive matches. Muffin games were enjoyed nearly as much as the matches between the skilled players. The Excelsiors played occasionally in the 1870s, but they were nothing like the Excelsiors of 1860, when Joe Leggett and Jim Creighton made them one of the best nines in the United States.

In 1878 the club became purely a social club and, dropping the words base ball, became known simply as the Excelsior Club. In the ensuing years, it became known as one of Brooklyn's most exclusive social clubs. Unlike most such clubs, the Excelsior Club kept its membership small and select and its profile deliberately low. As explained in an article published to commemorate the club's 50th anniversary in 1904,"It rarely gets into print. It never 'does' things. There is no handsome big clubhouse to mark it and it seldom formally entertains. Never does it give a famously big dinner for some notable man." The article added that the Excelsiors' club house, at the corner of Clinton and Livingston streets, was "a plain three story brick dwelling house, and it seems like one. Within, it is no less simple, though comfortably equipped. But these four walls of the little house have witnessed through the years a 'chumminess' that city club life almost never attains. The nearest approach to the Excelsior in its real inner significance is a college club."[18]

The club's disinclination for recruiting new members had its advantages, but it led to an aging membership. By 1932 there were only 12 surviving members and they bowed to reality by selling the "old clubhouse at Clinton and Livingston Sts., reminiscent of former glory with gilded baseballs, old scores and photographs commemorating victories of the days before the Civil War." After nearly 78 years, the "oldest existing baseball club in the world" passed out of existence.[19]

CLUB MEMBERS

James W. Andrews: As hard as it can be to reconstruct the playing rosters of pioneer-era clubs, it is still harder to get a sense of which members were responsible for crucial off-the-field decisions. Lists of officers are usually available, but trying to determine which of these men played a key role and which merely attended meetings is all but impossible. At best there are a few hints as to who the decision-makers were, and in many cases we can only guess. (As a result of this uncertainty, most club officers are included in the list of "Other Members," which appears at the end of the profiles.) The Excelsior Club president for 1856 is a perfect example of these difficulties. An account published after that season reported that Andrews had been elected president in May and helped raise the club to "high standing."[20] Someone named Andrews also played for the first nine that year, likely the same man. Then in 1857, Andrews was elected secretary of the newly formed National Association of Base Ball Players. But that's all that is known about him, with the result that even this man's identity cannot be determined with certainty, while the extent of his contributions to building the Excelsior Club is lost to history.

James B. Bach: See Niagaras of Buffalo (in *Base Ball Pioneers, 1850–1870*).

Asa Brainard: See Cincinnati Base Ball Club ("Red Stockings") in *Base Ball Pioneers, 1850–1870*.

Harrison "Harry" Brainard: Asa Brainard's younger brother Harrison was also a longtime member of the Excelsior Club, though he missed the club's best year, playing for it in

1859 and then from 1862 to 1864. Harrison was working as a hotel keeper in Suffolk County in 1870, but is hard to trace after that. His tombstone at Green-Wood Cemetery indicates that he died in 1881, but the details remain elusive.

Peter Remsen Chadwick: Peter Remsen Chadwick was an Excelsior Club officer from 1855 to 1857, including serving as club president in 1857. The first-nine shortstop in 1856 had the surname of Chadwick so the presumption is that this was him as well. He was also involved in the Gotham Club. Born in Brooklyn on June 12, 1831, Remsen Chadwick was a banker by profession. He married in December of 1856 and started a family, which brought an end to his ballplaying days. Despite his young family, Remsen Chadwick enlisted in the 100th New York Infantry Regiment in March of 1861 and served for more than three years. After the war Chadwick and his family settled in Cohoes, New York, up the Hudson from New York City, where he became a partner in Chadwick & Company. He died in Cohoes on March 26, 1891. He was on hand for the Excelsiors' 1875 reunion, but otherwise is not known to have remained involved in baseball. Remsen Chadwick's papers were donated to the New York State Library and an online finding indicates that they contain many documents pertaining to his Civil War service. There is no indication of baseball-related material, but it would certainly be a worthwhile avenue for some researcher to pursue.

Dan Chauncey: Brothers Dan and George Chauncey were stalwarts of the postwar Excelsiors. Daniel Chauncey, the younger of the two, was born in 1850 and joined the first nine in 1867 and played third base, outfield, and first base, among other positions. A 1932 article claimed that Chauncey "had the reputation of being the fastest shortstop in the East. It was said of him that he could be in the clubhouse and all dressed before the outfielders could get in."[21] He later became the senior member of Chauncey & Co. (in partnership with another brother, Michael) and was for many years a member of the New York Stock Exchange. He died on April 26, 1921.[22]

George W. Chauncey: George Chauncey was Dan's older brother but did not join the first nine of the Excelsiors until 1869. Born in Brooklyn on April 17, 1847, he graduated from the Columbia University School of Mines and then became successful in banking and real estate. He eventually became president of the Mechanics Bank, a position earlier held by his father. He was one of the owners of the grounds leased by Brooklyn's Players League entry in 1890 and later a Dodgers shareholder. Chauncey became president of the Excelsior Club in 1887, by which time it was purely a social club, and remained president well into the 20th century. He died in Brooklyn on April 16, 1926, and was described by the *Eagle* as "a never-failing booster of Brooklyn" who "never lived anywhere but on the Heights and firmly declared that he never would live anywhere else as long as he lived."[23]

John Clyne: John Clyne joined the first nine of the Excelsiors in 1863 and remained a regular for five seasons, playing the outfield and all four infield positions at various times. He later played for the Star Club and was described as "a capital general utility man."[24] He is believed to be John H. Clyne, a Brooklyn custom house employee who died on November 20, 1885, at the age of 41.

George W. Cornwell: George Cornwell, who played for the Excelsiors in 1868, was the youngest of three ballplaying brothers who were mostly associated with the Enterprise Club. The best known of the three brothers was John Wesley Cornwell, who was only 23 when he died in Glen Cove Bay on July 4, 1867. George is not buried with his brothers at Green-Wood Cemetery and while a candidate in Westchester County appears on the 1900 census, there is no proof that this is the right man.

Fred Crane: See Atlantic Base Ball Club.

James Creighton: Jim Creighton, destined to become the most celebrated player of the pioneer era, was born in New York City on April 14, 1841, but grew up in Brooklyn. By his teenage years he was showing proficiency in cricket and baseball. In the latter sport he played second base and pitched for the Young America and Niagara clubs before joining the Star Club in 1859. At season's end he became a member of the Excelsiors, a move that Henry Chadwick attributed to financial inducements.[25] His speed, combined with an elaborate delivery that caused spirited debates about whether it was a "fair square pitch" or an illegal "underhand throw," proved lethal. Creighton released his offerings from just above ground level but they rose dramatically and featured enough movement to baffle batters used to straight-arm deliveries. During the Excelsior Club's spectacular 1860 season, which included a historic tour of upstate New York, he secured his legacy as a baseball immortal. Alas, in real life he was all too mortal. The outbreak of the Civil War caused the Excelsior Club to lapse into inactivity in 1861 and Creighton mostly stuck to cricket that year. The Excelsiors played a limited schedule in 1862 and in an October 14 match Creighton sustained a serious internal injury. He died four days later and was buried in Green-Wood Cemetery beneath an enormous monument. The circumstances of his death led to claims that Creighton had swung so hard in hitting a home run that he had ruptured his bladder. The reality appears to have been more prosaic; researcher Tom Shieber has concluded that Creighton most likely had a pre-existing inguinal hernia that was ruptured by one of his mighty swings. Club president Joseph B. Jones meanwhile claimed that the fatal injury had been sustained in a cricket match a few days prior to the baseball game. No matter. Creighton attained a larger-than-life status as baseball's first fallen hero; in 1866, the visiting Nationals of Washington were escorted first to Brooklyn City Hall to meet the mayor and then to Green-Wood Cemetery to pay homage at Creighton's tomb.

Candy Cummings: See Star Base Ball Club.

Tom Dakin: See Putnam Base Ball Club.

A. Dayton: See Pastime Base Ball Club.

Anthony Elmendorf: Anthony Elmendorf played for the Excelsiors in 1866 and 1868. Born in 1840, he enlisted as a captain in the 48th New York Infantry on August 26, 1861, serving until April of 1864. He later moved to Big Springs, Texas, and became a successful sheep rancher. Elmendorf died in Big Springs on November 19, 1886. Even then, his days on the baseball diamond were well enough remembered to warrant a mention the *1887 New York Clipper Almanac*.[26]

C. Etheridge: This man was the pitcher of the first nine of the Excelsior Club in 1856 and he also made appearances for the first nine in 1857, 1858, and 1859. The only candidate in Brooklyn on the 1860 census was a Virginia-born clerk named Charles Etheridge. This man did not remain in Brooklyn and is almost certainly Charles A. Etheredge or Etheridge, a Portsmouth, Virginia, native who served in the Confederate army. This man enlisted in Company C of the 16th Virginia Infantry on April 20, 1861, along with his brother Alexander. He was promoted to sergeant and detailed to the subsistence department, serving until he surrendered at Appomattox. After the war he settled in Columbus, Georgia, where he established a prominent cotton brokerage business and was active in the United Confederate Veterans. He died there on March 3, 1899.

Henry W. Fairbanks: See Star Base Ball Club.

George Henry Flanley: See Star Base Ball Club.

George Horace Elliot Fletcher: See Nationals of Washington in *Base Ball Pioneers, 1850–1870*.

George Hall: See Atlantic Base Ball Club.

John Barrett Holder: See Atlantic Base Ball Club.

Herbert Stuart Jewell: Herbert S. Jewell was born in Rochester on March 4, 1845, and was a substitute for the Excelsiors in 1865 and 1866. In 1867 he became the catcher of the first nine, handling the offerings of Hall of Famer Candy Cummings. Cummings worked with most of the greatest catchers of the era but later said that Jewell "was the pluckiest man I ever saw behind the bat. I often told him he would meet with an accident, but he stood right under the bat with no protection whatever."[27] After the 1867 season both Cummings and Jewell resigned from the Excelsior Club, prompting rumors that they were turning professional. But an article in the *Brooklyn Union* told a different story: "We regret to hear that Mr. Jewell has withdrawn from the Excelsior Club.... Our friend Jewell is wealthy, is his own master, and therefore is not open to the influences in vogue in getting new players into clubs. He can give 'situations,' and does not need them. Whichever club he joins will get a fine player and an ardent supporter of the game."[28] Jewell was indeed the son of Theodore Jewell, a pioneer flour manufacturer who operated mills in Williamsburg and White Plains. Herbert Jewell became very involved in the Jewell Milling Company, eventually becoming its president. He and Cummings joined the Star Club in 1868 and played together for several more years but Jewell turned down opportunities to play professional baseball in favor of business. The family firm later changed its name to the Standard Milling Company and Jewell spent 12 years in Milwaukee supervising the opening of a new mill there. His life was not all business, however, as he found time to serve as an inspector of rifle practice, earning the rank of major. There is no evidence that he retained an active interest in baseball, but he was commodore of the Great South Bay Yacht Club on Long Island, near his summer home. When the 1920 census was taken, the 75-year-old Jewell was living in Buffalo, where he was busy opening yet another mill. But he was soon back in Brooklyn, where he died suddenly on October 1, 1920.[29] Herbert's younger brother Edward M. Jewell (1846–1887) was also a well-known ballplayer during the same years, spending time with both the Enterprise and Excelsior clubs, but does not seem to have played for the first nine of the Excelsiors.[30]

Frank Jones: See Nationals of Washington in *Base Ball Pioneers, 1850–1870*.

Dr. Joseph Bainbridge Jones: Dr. Joseph B. Jones was president of the Excelsior Club during its glory years and also president of the National Association of Base Ball Players (NABBP) in 1860. Born in Manhattan in 1823, the son of a well-known sea captain, he graduated from Columbia College Medical School and later held the offices of Kings County coroner and health commissioner of the City of Brooklyn. A teacher before turning to medicine, he also remained active on the Brooklyn Board of Education. He died in Brooklyn on October 9, 1905.[31]

William B. Kendall: William B. Kendall played for the second nine of the Excelsior Club and then became club secretary. Born on March 1, 1831, he died on January 21, 1898.

Samuel Kissam: See Knickerbocker Base Ball Club.

Joseph Bowne Leggett: Joseph B. Leggett, the celebrated catcher and captain of the Excelsiors, was born in Saratoga, New York, on January 14, 1828. He was vice president of the Wayne Base Ball Club in 1857 when that club merged with the Excelsiors. In 1859 he became the catcher of the Excelsiors' first nine, a position he held until enlisting in the Union Army in 1861. Henry Chadwick confirmed, "It was not until Creighton introduced the swift underhand delivery that catching began to be anything of an arduous undertaking, and then Joe Leggett was found equal to the task of pluckily facing and holding the hot balls sent him, his plan of standing up close behind the bat being then regarded as quite a feat."[32] After completing his tour of duty, he played a few games in 1862 and 1863 before announcing his retirement in 1865 as the result of rheumatism.[33] He came out of retirement in 1866 but that was his last hurrah and he accepted a job at Brooklyn City Hall. In 1877 Leggett was accused of embezzlement and fled.[34] His life after that is cloaked in mystery.[35] Family histories indicate that he died in Galveston, Texas, in 1894 and his widow applied for a Civil War pension in 1899, but definitive evidence has yet to emerge.

William Lennon: See Marylands of Baltimore in *Base Ball Pioneers, 1850–1870*.

Arthur T. Markham (Frank Mordaunt): Anthony Markham made his debut with the Excelsiors in 1857 and was a regular outfielder on the first nine in 1858 and 1859. Markham was born in 1841 in Burlington, Vermont, and engaged in theatrical performances there while growing up. After moving to New York, he retained an interest in acting but also dabbled in many other fields. After having a small part in an 1859 production of *Richelieu* that featured Edwin Booth, he began to focus his attention on acting, adopting the stage name of Frank Mordaunt. This also marked the end of his baseball career. He got his big break in 1862 while watching a performance of Boucicault's *The Colleen Bawn* at Niblo's Gardens. When one of the actors had to leave to visit his dying brother, Mordaunt glanced over the script and used his retentive memory to fill in seamlessly.[36] He became a very famous stage actor, appearing with the likes of Forrest and Booth in such plays as *King Lear*, *Hamlet*, and *East Lynne*. His life offstage, however, was less successful: his marriage to a stage actress ended in divorce, and in 1902 he was institutionalized in a sanitarium in Bedford City, Virginia.[37] He died there in 1906.[38]

Myron Masten: See Putnam Base Ball Club.

Henry Maxwell: Henry Maxwell (1850–1902) was a prominent Brooklyn banker, broker, and philanthropist. Maxwell was president of the Excelsior Club from 1880 to 1883, but by then it was strictly a social club. According to Henry Chadwick, Maxwell was also an officer of the Excelsior Base Ball Club, but the extent of his involvement with the baseball side of things does not appear to have been great and it's possible Chadwick was thinking of the social club.

James Mitchell: James Mitchell played for the Excelsior Club from 1865 through 1868 but little definitive is known about him, a testimony to the diminished status of the postwar Excelsiors (and the perils of having a common name). In 1881, a man named James L. Mitchell was admitted to membership in the social incarnation of the Excelsior Club. Based on this, it is very likely that the ballplayer was James L. Mitchell, who was born in Brooklyn in 1841 and graduated from New York University in 1862. Mitchell worked for the firm of David Dows & Company, a large grain dealer, for more than 40 years. He died in Brooklyn on October 9, 1916, and an obituary confirmed that he was a member of the Excelsior Club.[39]

John Moore: John Moore played for the Excelsiors for several seasons, beginning in 1864. He was reported to be dead by 1896, but little else is known about him.[40]

Tom Morris: See Star Base Ball Club.

William H. Murtha: Senator William H. Murtha was a prominent lawyer, businessman, and politician who was born in Brooklyn on January 3, 1841, and died there on April 15, 1891. In 1883 Murtha was Grover Cleveland's nominee to become emigration commissioner, but the nomination sparked controversy and he was not confirmed.[41] Murtha was a member of the Enterprise Club for several years and then had a brief involvement with the Excelsior Club. Henry Chadwick later produced a box score for an 1869 game in which Murtha played, though Marshall Wright's listings do not credit him with any games played for the first nine.[42] Murtha also served as president of the Excelsior Club after it became purely a social club.

Frank Prescott Norton: See Star Base Ball Club.

Richard Oliver: Richard Oliver was the original president of the Wayne Base Ball Club of Brooklyn when it was formed on July 25, 1857.[43] The Wayne Club merged with the Excelsiors that fall and Oliver became treasurer of the Excelsiors. He also played a major role that year in introducing the Knickerbocker's version of baseball to Buffalo. (See the Niagaras of Buffalo in *Base Ball Pioneers, 1850–1870* for details.) Oliver later served as president of Brooklyn's Excelsior Club in 1868 and again from 1871 through 1877, as the club made a transition from baseball club to social club. It seems safe to assume that the man in question was a British-born jeweler by that name who died in Brooklyn on May 5, 1894, at the age of 67.

Joe Patchen: See Star Base Ball Club.

Dr. Andrew Thustin Pearsall: Though the first baseman of the Excelsior Club in 1859 and 1860 is referred to in many sources as "Aleck Pearsall," this appears to be an error. His actual name was Andrew Thustin Pearsall and, while he often used his initials, there is no evidence that he was ever known as Aleck. Pearsall was born in Florence, Alabama, on April 22, 1839, but his parents were native New Yorkers who returned there when he was 6 years old. He grew up in rural Hooper's Valley, in Tioga County, and was educated at a prep school, then at Hobart College and at the College of Physicians and Surgeons, Columbia's medical school. It was while there that Pearsall began playing first base for the Excelsiors and drawing rave reviews for having "no superior in that position anywhere."[44] When he graduated from medical school in 1861, the Civil War was under way and Pearsall chose to become a surgeon in the Confederate Army. After a chance encounter with an acquaintance from Brooklyn, his fellow club members learned of his allegiance and voted to expel him.[45] After the war Pearsall lived briefly in Richmond, Virginia, and, along with Alexander Babcock of the Atlantic Club of Brooklyn, helped to organize the Pastime Base Ball Club.[46] He then moved to Alabama, where he married and started a family. The marriage was unhappy and Pearsall moved with his daughter to Owego, New York, a town in Tioga County near his boyhood home (not to be confused with Oswego, which lies 110 miles north of Owego). There he served as local doctor for a quarter of a century. In February of 1904, an old-time fan wrote to the *New York Sun* that "old players of baseball in the '60s … have not been seen on the diamond since." He asked rhetorically, "Take Pearsall, first base of the Excelsiors: is such playing ever seen now?" Unwilling to leave the rhetorical question unanswered, he provided a response: "Joe Start is the only peer of Pearsall."[47] Word of the letter eventually made its way to Owego, where the local paper informed its readers, "Dr. A.T. Pearsall of this village is the redoubtable first baseman.... It may be a surprise to the younger element in Owego to know that when Dr. Pearsall witnesses their games they are being watched by one of the greatest amateur ballplayers of the country."[48] He died in Owego on November 17, 1905.

Henry D. Polhemus: In the famous picture of the Excelsiors, outfielder Henry Polhemus is the one who towers over his teammates. He was a larger-than-life figure in other respects as well. He was born around 1829 on the Polhemus farm at Fifth Avenue and President Street in Brooklyn, into a distinguished and wealthy family that traced its ancestry back to the Rev. Johanus Theodosius Polhemus, who emigrated in 1655 and organized the First Dutch Reformed Church in Flatbush. Henry married in 1853 but had no children, leaving him the last male member of his branch of the Polhemus family. He played for the Excelsiors from 1858 to 1862. During the Civil War his firms of Fox & Polhemus and Brinkerhoff & Polhemus had government contracts to manufacture ducking cloth. By the end of the war he was a very wealthy man and he severed his connections with both firms. While he continued to serve as a director of such organizations as the Brooklyn Academy of Music, the Eye and Ear Hospital, the Brooklyn Gaslight Company, the Long Island Bank, the American District Telegraph Company, the Delaware, Lackawanna and Western Railroad Company, the Morris and Essex Railroad Company, and the Long Island College Hospital, he retired from active business and it was as a bon vivant and clubman that he became best known. A noted gourmet, he had a particular fondness for terrapins and ducks and went on regular expeditions in the Adirondacks and in Chesapeake Bay to procure the finest specimens. He was a close friend of President Grover Cleveland and the results of his hunting and fishing trips often ended up being consumed at the White House. Known far and wide as Uncle Harry, Polhemus died in Brooklyn on February 14, 1895.[49]

Thomas Reynolds: Tommy Reynolds was a regular for the Excelsiors from 1858 through 1860 and is included in the most famous photo of the first nine. He was said to have died "years ago" in 1887, and an 1889 article confirmed that he was dead without providing details.[50]

Ed Russell: Ed Russell was the Excelsior Club's regular pitcher in 1859 before relinquishing the position to Creighton and playing the outfield, first base, and shortstop in 1860. He also played a few games for the club in both 1858 and 1862 before retiring from baseball. The English-born Russell became a successful hardware merchant and was involved in several reunion games during the 1870s. When he died in Brooklyn on February 21, 1881, at the age of 52, his baseball exploits were remembered in an obituary in the *New York Clipper*.[51]

John Stagg: John Stagg was the catcher of first nine in 1856 and was said to be a "fine batter."[52]

Charles Crooke Suydam: Charles C. Suydam was the

younger brother of John H. Suydam and is credited with having proposed the name of Excelsior. He was an 18-year-old Columbia College student at the time and it was not clear that he even became a member of the club he had named. Born on June 15, 1836, Charles C. Suydam graduated from Columbia in 1856 and then passed the bar exam. When the Civil War broke out, he enlisted as a private in the 5th New York Cavalry. He later served as a lieutenant colonel in the 3rd New Jersey Cavalry and was twice a prisoner of war. After the war, he became a very successful New York City lawyer. He died on November 19, 1911, in Elizabeth, New Jersey.

John Henry Suydam: John H. Suydam was one of the founders of the Excelsior Club and served as a director that year. The Peverelly sketch described Suydam as "the father of the club" and reported that as of 1866, he was one of two original members who remained connected with the club as honorary members. Aside from that, however, there is no evidence that Suydam played an active role in the club's activities. John H. Suydam was born in New York on February 18, 1832, the son of a grocer. He married around 1855 and soon began a family, which presumably contributed to his limited involvement with the Excelsior Club. Another major factor, no doubt, was that Suydam spent much of his life in New York City rather than Brooklyn. In 1874 Suydam became the manager of the New York store of P. Ballantine and Son. He held this position until his death at his home on East 131st Street on January 8, 1890, as the result of an outbreak of influenza.[53] He is buried in Brooklyn's Green-Wood Cemetery.

Milton B. Sweet: Milton B. Sweet played for the Excelsiors in 1868 and 1870, and was also associated with several other pioneer-era clubs, including the Gothams of New York City. He was primarily a pitcher, but also played the outfield. Sweet was born around 1842 and served briefly in the Civil War. Following in his father's footsteps, he became a well-known hotel proprietor and restaurateur. Several of these ventures were very successful, but Sweet was wiped out by the failure of the Manhattan Hotel. He died suddenly of pneumonia on November 19, 1887. His death merited a brief write-up in *Sporting Life*.[54]

Jeremiah Nelson Tappan: J. Nelson Tappan, the first president of the Excelsior Club, was born in New York City on February 6, 1833. In 1875, he was appointed chamberlain of New York City, a top-level financial position. He resigned in May of 1884 after it was revealed that he had invested over a million dollars of city funds in a bank that had failed. He died a few months later, on September 5, 1884, in Schroon Lake, New York, as the result of a sudden hemorrhage.[55]

Charles W. Thomas: Charles W. Thomas was an early officer. The third baseman of the 1856 first nine was named Thomas and according to an account he was a "good batter, but ought to have his eyes on the ball instead of looking over the field." [56] It seems likely that this was the same man.

Fred Treacy: See Eckford Base Ball Club.

James E. Vail: See Knickerbocker Base Ball Club.

Peter Van Schaack: Peter Van Schaack was an original club member and an early club officer. According to the account in Peverelly, Van Schaack was one of only two original members who were still honorary members in 1866. Van Schaack was a member of a wealthy family who soon afterward moved to Chicago, where he died on December 5, 1904, at the age of 73.

Tom Watts: Tom Watts was the pitcher of the Excelsior Club in 1869 and 1870 and also played for the Mutual Club. He has not been identified.

Frederick Wells: Frederick Wells was an early club officer. Someone named Wells, likely the same man, was the second baseman of the first nine in 1856 and it was said that "any balls that come in his range are almost sure to be caught." [57]

Charles Lowell Whiting, Franklin Phillips Whiting, Frederic A. Whiting, and John Campbell Whiting: See Star Base Ball Club for details on the Whiting brothers, most if not all of whom were associated with the Excelsior Club.

John B. Woodward: General John B. Woodward (1835–1896) was a prominent Civil War soldier, politician, and Brooklyn civic leader. According to Henry Chadwick, Woodward was a member of the Excelsior Club's second nine in 1858 and attended that year's NABBP convention.[58] He was also president of the Excelsior Club after it became a social club.

Van Brunt Wyckoff: Van Brunt Wyckoff was a club officer who was credited with having made major contributions to the club history that appeared in Peverelly. Wyckoff was an 1840 graduate of Columbia College and earned a medical degree from Columbia's medical school. He does not appear to have ever practiced medicine, instead amassing considerable wealth as a merchant only to fall on hard times as a result of bad investments. Wyckoff died in Brooklyn on April 13, 1889, at the age of 68.

William H. Young: William H. Young played for the Excelsiors from 1857 through 1862. He played for the first nine for most of that time but was only a semiregular in 1860 and thus missed out on being included in the famous photo of the club. Young also served as club treasurer. Several references from the 1870s indicate that Young was still in Brooklyn. In 1891 Henry Chadwick reported that he had not seen Young in a year or two. It's possible, but by no means certain, that the ballplayer was a Brooklyn dentist by that name.

Other Club Members: Elisha Bacon (original vice president), Jonathan O. Bartholomew (original treasurer), Benner (1869 substitute), Bergen (1859 substitute), Biggs (this one-game 1859 player is probably Francis Biggs, profiled under the Pastime Club), H.P. Bostwick (1860 and 1862 substitute), George Cole (played from 1857 to 1859), Henry M. Congdon (early officer), George Cook (played between 1862 and 1867, mostly as a substitute), Richard K. Cooke (club officer, including president in 1865), George T. Dalton (early officer), William P. Dean (club's official umpire), Dohrman (1869 and

1870 player), Eddy (1869 and 1870 player), Frederick G. Eldridge (original club secretary), R. Fleet (played in 1857 and 1859), Spencer S. Gregory (scorekeeper), Charles P. Gulick (club officer who played one game in 1860), Gilbert Lawrence Haight (club officer), Charles J. Holt (club officer), William H. Holt (club officer), G. Henry Howell (early club officer), Robert J. Hubbard (original club director), Jerold (1862 substitute), William W. Kelly (club officer), Joseph Ketchum, Jr.,(club officer), B. Kimberley (1860 substitute), Langley (1863–64 player), Lockett (1869 and 1870 player), McKenzie (substitute in 1862–63), John J. McLaren (early officer), C. Miller (1869–70 player), Pomeroy (first baseman of the first nine in 1856), James Rogers (outfielder on the first nine in 1856 and played a few games in subsequent seasons; probably the man of the same name who played for the Pastime Club), Sunderling (1857 player), E. Thompson (1867 player), Whitney (an 1866 player according to Marshall Wright, though it's possible this is one of the Whiting brothers), Le Baron Willard (early officer), John Zuill (1857 player).

Notes

1. "Golden Jubilee of the Old Excelsior Club: Most Exclusive of Brooklyn Organizations Celebrates Fiftieth Anniversary To-morrow," *Brooklyn Daily Eagle*, December 7, 1904, 10.
2. *Porter's Spirit of the Times*, December 20, 1856.
3. *Porter's Spirit of the Times*, May 2, 1857.
4. *Porter's Spirit of the Times*, July 25, 1857.
5. *Porter's Spirit of the Times*, December 20, 1856.
6. *New York Clipper*, September 25, 1858.
7. James Wood, as told to Frank G. Menke, "Baseball in By-Gone Days," part 2, syndicated column, *Marion* (Ohio) *Daily Star*, August 15, 1916.
8. *Brooklyn Eagle*, July 16, 1873.
9. *Brooklyn Eagle*, July 9, 1860.
10. Chadwick Scrapbooks.
11. *New York Clipper*, September 1, 1860.
12. *New York Clipper*, June 27, 1863.
13. *Brooklyn Eagle*, August 10, 1864.
14. *Brooklyn Eagle*, June 13, 1864.
15. *New York Clipper*, July 14, 1866.
16. *New York Clipper*, August 18, 1866.
17. John Freyer and Mark Rucker, *Peverelly's National Game* (Charleston, S.C.: Arcadia, 2005), 61.
18. "Golden Jubilee of the Old Excelsior Club: Most Exclusive of Brooklyn Organizations Celebrates Fiftieth Anniversary To-morrow," *Brooklyn Daily Eagle*, December 7, 1904, 10.
19. "Oldest Baseball Club Takes Third Strike," *Brooklyn Eagle*, August 6, 1932, 1 and 8 .
20. *Porter's Spirit of the Times*, December 20, 1856.
21. "Oldest Baseball Club Takes Third Strike," *Brooklyn Eagle*, August 6, 1932, 1 and 8 .
22. *New York Times*, April 27, 1921.
23. *Brooklyn Eagle*, April 16, 1926, 1; *New York Times*, April 17, 1926.
24. *Brooklyn Eagle*, November 17, 1870.
25. *Brooklyn Eagle*, July 16, 1873.
26. *Brooklyn Eagle*, December 3, 1886; *New York Clipper 1887 Almanac*.
27. *Brooklyn Eagle*, April 26, 1896, 17.
28. *Brooklyn Union*, undated 1867 clipping in the Chadwick Scrapbooks.
29. "Maj. H.S. Jewell; Old Flour Miller," *Brooklyn Eagle*, October 2, 1920, 22.
30. An obituary of Edward M. Jewell in *Sporting Life* on November 23, 1887, 4, suggests that the playing record attributed to him in Marshall Wright's compilation is erroneous.
31. *Brooklyn Eagle*, October 10, 1905, 3; *New York Times*, October 11, 1905, 11.
32. Henry Chadwick, "The Catchers," *New York Clipper*, December 30, 1876.
33. *Brooklyn Eagle*, September 16, 1865.
34. The accusations against Leggett were covered extensively in the *Brooklyn Eagle*, particularly December 20, 1877, 4; December 26, 1877, 4; January 6, 1878, 2; February 9, 1878, 4. According to an editorial on December 22, 1877, 2, Leggett was hired by the city when it was well known that he had previously defrauded the fire department of money.
35. In articles written in 1889 and 1891, Henry Chadwick made clear that Leggett was still alive but added no details. In the first of the two articles, he implied that he had been disgraced but declined, "for old times' sake," to provide details, ("Old Chalk" [Chadwick],"Baseball in its Infancy," *Brooklyn Eagle*, December 15, 1889,"Old Chalk" [Chadwick],"Base Ball Reminiscences," *Brooklyn Eagle*, June 7, 1891, 16).
36. David Beasley, *Mckee Rankin and the Heyday of the American Theater* (Waterloo, Ontario: Wilfrid Laurier University Press, 2002), 451.
37. *New York Times*, July 1, 1884.
38. *New York Times*, October 18, 1906.
39. *Brooklyn Eagle*, October 9, 1916, 19.
40. *Brooklyn Eagle*, February 28, 1896, 9.
41. *New York Times*, April 16, 1891.
42. *Brooklyn Eagle*, February 28, 1896, 9.
43. *Porter's Spirit of the Times*, August 8, 1857.
44. *New York Atlas*, July 31, 1859.
45. *New York Clipper*, July 4, 1863.
46. French Scrapbooks, unidentified clipping from May 1866.
47. *New York Sun*, February 24, 1904, 6, letter signed by (as best can be deciphered) George P. Kygub.
48. *Tioga County Record*, June 16, 1904.
49. "Death of Henry D. Polhemus," *New York Times*, February 15, 1895, 2; *Brooklyn Eagle*, February 17, 1895, 3; *Washington Post*, February 17, 1895; "Oldest Baseball Club Takes Third Strike," *Brooklyn Eagle*, August 6, 1932, 1 and 8 .
50. *Brooklyn Eagle*, January 2, 1887, 15; "Baseball in its Infancy," *Brooklyn Eagle*, December 15, 1889.
51. *New York Clipper*, March 5, 1881.
52. *Porter's Spirit of the Times*, December 20, 1856.
53. *New York Sun*, January 10, 1890, 2.
54. *Brooklyn Eagle*, November 21, 1887; *Sporting Life*, November 30, 1887, 5.
55. *New York Times*, May 30, 1884, and September 6, 1884.
56. *Porter's Spirit of the Times*, December 20, 1856.
57. Ibid.
58. Chadwick Scrapbooks, unidentified clipping.

❖ *Putnam Base Ball Club* ❖
(William J. Ryczek)

CLUB HISTORY

For a decade beginning in the middle of the 1850s and ending in the middle of the 1860s, the city of Brooklyn boasted the best baseball nines in the United States. The battle for the "national" championship was in reality a contest to determine the best club in Brooklyn. The Atlantics and Eckfords won titles, and while the Excelsiors never won, they were probably the best and most renowned baseball club in America in 1860. The Putnams, one of the first clubs to emerge from Brooklyn, never won a title and never came close. They were perhaps better known for their pioneering status, courtly manners, and good sportsmanship than for outstanding skill on the playing field. "It is always a pleasure to witness a match in which the Putnam club are engaged," the *Clipper* said in 1859, "as their courteous conduct is sure to lead to a satisfactory termination of the game."[1] Yet for several years the Putnams played competitively with the Atlantics, Eckfords and other top nines, until the onset of the Civil War caused the venerable club to end its activity on the ball field.

Organization and Early Years

The Putnam Club was formed in May 1855 with James H. Church, Samuel Godwin, Brower Gesner, Daniel Godwin, Edward A. Walton, A. Empie Gibbs, and Albert Davidson, who were described as "most respectable business men," as its officers.[2] Like most clubs of that era, its members played mostly among themselves for recreation and exercise. "The Club being composed of our first citizens," reported the *Brooklyn Times*, "we can only say we wish them the success they so richly deserve, for setting so good an example to others who would find it exceedingly conducive to health, to indulge, like the members of the P.C., in a little of this noble and manly exercise."[3]

The new club gathered at its grounds between Division and Lee avenues in Williamsburgh[4] every Monday, Wednesday, and Friday at 5:00 in the morning for field exercise, which in itself was reason to praise the new club's devotion. During their first summer, the newly minted Putnams played three games against other clubs, two against the Astoria Club and one against the Knickerbockers. After the first Astoria game, which the Putnams lost by 11 runs, the *Brooklyn Times* again praised the players for the "healthful, invigorating and morally unobjectionable" activity, and noted the friendly postgame entertainment and speeches.[5] The Putnams added some skilled new members, practiced a lot, and won the return match handily, scoring the requisite 21 runs in just two innings and holding their opponents to two runs. "There is still room for improvement in their fielding," noted the *Times,* "but we have no doubt that another season will find them prepared to cope with such clubs as the Knickerbocker, Gotham, etc."[6]

The fact that the Knickerbockers, who were extremely particular about whom they would play, ventured from their grounds in Hoboken to play with the Putnams was a great tribute to the latter organization. The Knickerbockers did not arrive with a full nine, and the game was played with a mixture of members of each club opposing each other. The scoring of runs was evenly distributed among the players, a tribute to the skill the Putnams had acquired in a relatively brief period of time. The Knickerbockers had been playing baseball for ten years, and the Putnams had been organized just a couple of months earlier, but it appeared that the players on both sides were relatively evenly matched. The Putnams were so delighted at the respect shown them by the venerable Knicks, said the *Times,* that they were looking forward to giving them a "sound drubbing."[7] The following month, a number of Putnams journeyed to Hoboken to watch the Knickerbockers play the Gothams.[8]

The traditional final day of the baseball season was Thanksgiving, on which most clubs scheduled some kind of activity. On Thanksgiving Day 1855, the Putnams planned to play three complete games, each of which would require, under contemporary rules, 21 runs to be scored by the winning side. The cold weather proved too daunting, and the players adjourned for turkey after 12 innings and 36 runs.

In 1856 the Putnams split two closely contested games with the Excelsiors. The loss was by a 16–15 score, the Excelsiors not making the 21 runs necessary for a win, and given the fact that the game was played in October, it is possible that it had an early termination due to darkness. On the 28th of August the Putnams lost an exciting game to the Continental Club at Wheat Hill by the score of 23–22.[9] The Atlantics challenged the Putnams to a game, but the latter declined. A correspondent to the *New York Clipper*, who styled himself "Spectator," suspected cowardice. "Spectator" referenced a letter praising the ability of the Putnams and calling them the best club in Brooklyn. "Now he has entirely overlooked the existence of the Atlantics of this city," "Spectator" replied, "which club has already challenged the 'Puts.' But it is universally understood that it will not be accepted, *for reasons best known to themselves* [italics in original], but, if upon due consideration, they should summon courage enough to accept the said challenge; I think it will be a one sided affair, as the Atlantics are A No. 1 players."[10]

Although the jab must have stung, the Putnams' 1856 season ended in splendid fashion. On October 25, 1856, the club avenged its earlier defeat by the Excelsiors and then hosted their rivals at a post-game feast at Trenor's Dancing Academy in Williamsburgh. Putnam president Samuel Godwin gave a toast to the "good effects they all experienced, both socially and physically, by the practice of base ball." More toasts and cheers followed, and the entire assemblage joined in a song that paid tribute to the Knickerbockers.

The evening closed with an especially intriguing exchange. In response to a toast to the press, a reporter from the *Sunday Mercury* gave a brief speech in which he suggested that his newspaper deserved the patronage of baseball players because of the space it devoted to their sport. This put the representative of *Porter's Spirit of the Times* on the spot, and in his response he admitted to "being a cricketer, [who] had had but little taste for base ball." He declared, however, that that day's game had changed his mind and that he now intended to join a club. He concluded by pledging that his paper could henceforth be "relied on for doing its part towards furthering the cause of out-door athletic exercises, by publishing reports on base ball as well as cricket or other pastimes, provided the secretaries of clubs would furnish communications of events to come, or which may have come off."[11] On that triumphant note, the curtain came down on the 1856 campaign.

The National Association

In January 1857 the Putnams sent delegates Theodore F. Jackson, James W. Smith, and Edward A. Walton to the convention called to standardize the rules of the New York Game. When the clubs met again a month later, Thomas Dakin of the Putnams was named second vice president of the newly formed National Association of Base Ball Players.

In the spring of 1857, the Putnams left their original site on Lee Avenue and acquired a new ground about one hundred yards from Wheat Hill,[12] and by the middle of the year boasted 86 members.[13] Only a few members, of course, made a difference in the play of the first nine, and in 1857 the Putnams gained the services of two talented players in Dakin and Andrew Burr. Dakin was a competent strategic pitcher, and Burr, who initially played as a catcher, was a strong batter and good fielder. In the pre–Creighton era, the pitcher was not the central figure on a baseball nine, but the catcher's ability to gather foul tips and keep baserunners from stealing at will was critical.

The Putnams played four games that year, following Spectator's prophecy and losing twice to the Atlantics, while defeating the Excelsior and Continental nines. In 1858 their record improved to 4–3, the most notable win being over the Excelsiors, who within a year would be one of the top clubs in New York. The three losses were to the Atlantics (twice) and the Eckfords. The loss to the Atlantics was by a respectable 17–13 score, and the Putnams might well have beaten the champions had they not given them nine runs in the fourth inning by sloppy fielding. During that game they also had the misfortune of having three of their players injured, two being the Putnams' best catchers, Masten and Burr, who had to move to less demanding positions, thereby weakening the club behind the bat. In July, Masten and Burr represented the Putnams on the Brooklyn all-star nine in the first game of the Fashion Course all-star series.[14]

The Putnams and Eagles were two of the oldest baseball clubs in existence, but until 1859 they had never played each other. Previously planned matches had been aborted for various reasons, including inclement weather, but finally, following a challenge issued by the Eagles, the two sides played each other in June 1859. The Putnams won decisively, 28–8. Later in the summer, the Putnams outclassed the inexperienced and butterfingered Oriental club, 47–17, and despite Dakin's absence, soundly defeated the Hoboken Club, 38–8. They finished their

season with a loss to the talented Excelsiors by the narrow margin of 19–17 on a frigid day in late October.

For the season, the Putnams had been 3–3, while among individual players Burr led all New York and Brooklyn players in the average number of runs made per game. Writing years later, Henry Chadwick remembered the battery of Dakin and Masten as the strength of the club. The latter, he said, was "the most graceful catcher of the period."[15] Since Joe Leggett was then at his peak with the Excelsiors and the nimble Waddy Beach was catching for the Eckfords, Chadwick may have indulged in some nostalgic retrospective bias, but Masten was, by all accounts, a very valuable player, and in 1859 the *Clipper* commented, "it is worth a five mile walk to see him play."[16] A year later, it called him "the best catcher in the United States."[17] Dakin was a pitcher from the old school, who relied on strategy rather than the speed Chadwick so detested.

The Final Seasons

At the annual convention in March 1860 Dakin was nearly elected president of the National Association. On the first ballot, he finished one vote behind Dr. Jones of the Excelsiors, and was eventually chosen first vice president. That spring the Putnams moved to a new ground at the corner of Lafayette Avenue and Broadway, and added several new players to the roster, with the intention of providing stiff competition for the Atlantics, Excelsiors, and Eckfords. Before the commencement of the campaign, the *New York Atlas* listed the three aforementioned nines, plus the Putnams, as the four leading contenders for Brooklyn supremacy,[18] which in 1860 meant they would be the four leading nines in the United States.

The first big test of the Putnams' new strength came before a crowd estimated at more than six thousand on June 13 when they played the Eckfords, whose pitcher, the estimable Frank Pidgeon, was on the grounds but unable to pitch due to illness. Pidgeon sat on the sidelines encouraging his men, as did many female Eckford supporters ("more ladies than we have ever seen at a match before"[19]) who "waved their handkerchiefs and cheered as well as their feeble voices were able."[20] The Putnams had never beaten the Eckfords, and the cheering of Pidgeon and the waving of feminine handkerchiefs (in addition to impolite comments several ruffian Eckford supporters directed at the Putnams) sufficiently motivated the Eckfords to add another win, this one by the relatively close score of 36–29. The victors scored 21 runs in the final two innings to overcome a Putnam lead. In early August the Putnams lost to the Excelsiors and Jim Creighton, 23–7, in a game played under the fly rule, in which a ball caught on the first bound was not out. The bound rule, of course, was still the legally accepted standard, and the press generally praised those forward-thinking clubs that played the more skillful fly game.

Baseball was slowly evolving from the bound game to the fly game, stymied by the large number of less skilled clubs who used their votes to defeat the proposed change each year. The art of pitching was evolving much more rapidly, for the rules were more difficult to enforce than the simple fly or bound rule. Creighton was a major factor in changing the role of the pitcher from the passive "feeder" putting the ball into play to being a formidable defensive weapon and the key player on the diamond. Henry Chadwick watched Creighton carefully during the game with the Putnams and declared that, in his opinion, Creighton's controversial delivery was legal.[21]

On June 29, 1860, the Putnams lost to the Atlantics by the very respectable score of 14–11. As in the Eckford game, there were a great number of ladies on hand, and also, as in the Eckford match, there were some unpleasant utterances emanating from the betting crowd. Both sides tried to suppress the vitriol, which was most effectively doused by a six-run eighth-inning rally that gave the Atlantics the game and assured the safety of their backers' wagers.

Perhaps the finest hours of the Putnams' 1860 season were two solid victories over the strong Unions of Morrisania. In the first game Masten was the star with a home run and several excellent fielding plays. The second contest was marred by the "waiting game" during which players of both sides let an interminable number of pitches pass without attempting to strike at them, delaying the game and rendering it very tedious. As was the Putnams' custom, they treated their vanquished opponents to a delightful postgame celebration of food, song, and bonhomie.

The 1860 season was the last in which the Putnams played a meaningful game. It had been a satisfying year, for the nine had held their own with the strongest clubs in the country and drawn large crowds to most of their games. While they did not achieve the lasting renown of the Atlantics and Eckfords, the Putnams made some unique and sometimes indirect contributions to the development of the sport. First, they played a role in the development of baseball in California, for Putnam player E.N. Robinson emigrated to the West and helped organize the Sacramento Club, which wore uniforms nearly identical to those used by Robinson's old mates.

A second incident involving the Putnams was considered somewhat of an oddity. In an 1860 game against the Atlantics, a Putnam player named Brown hit a low pitch from John Price in the same manner in which a cricketer would "block" a pitch he did not particularly like. The ball dribbled out in front of home base, and the players looked to the umpire for a ruling. The umpire decided that the hit had been an accident and ruled no play. The *Clipper* disagreed and thought the ball should have been decided fair, for had a player been on first base at the time, he could have easily made second. Brown had, perhaps unwittingly, been the first player to "bunt" in a baseball game.[22]

The third case in which the Putnam Club contributed indirectly to a significant event was the offer to the Excelsior and Atlantic clubs to use their grounds as a neutral site for the third and deciding game of the hotly contested 1860 champi-

onship series. The site proved inadequate to handle the large crowd and the game ended in an embarrassing row that left the championship question in limbo.

The End

A number of clubs were forced to suspend operations during the Civil War, and the Putnams were one of them, not playing a single game in 1861.[23] Tom Dakin enlisted in the Union Army and became a brigadier general in Brooklyn's 5th Brigade, while many other members of the club also joined the armed forces. Baseball was a popular activity in camp, and a report of one game indicated that Van Valkenburg of the Putnams was one of the prominent players who took part.[24] Back on the home front, the club showed some life as the war ground on, sending delegates to the annual convention in December 1861. They combined with the similarly weakened Brooklyn Club with the intention of taking the field in 1862. "It will not be long," the *Clipper* predicted, "before the club will again occupy the position as a playing club that it possessed in 1860."[25]

In the spring of 1862 William Cammeyer constructed the first enclosed baseball ground in the United States, the Union Grounds, and the Putnams were one of the clubs that intended to play their games at the new facility. The grand opening took place on May 15 and featured a game between sides made up of players from the Eckford, Constellation, and Putnam clubs, the three organizations Cammeyer had selected to use the field that summer. They used the grounds free of charge, and the proprietor retained the right to any admission fees he might charge.

When the Athletics of Philadelphia made their first visit to New York in 1862, the Putnams contributed some players to a picked nine from the Western District of Brooklyn. The 1862 season was the last, however, in which the Putnams were mentioned as an active baseball club. They no longer played top nines like the Atlantics and Eckfords, and, other than the opening of the Union Grounds, there was virtually no mention of them in the sporting press that season. Like so many of the pioneer clubs, they disappeared once competition became more intense and professional teams eventually came to dominate the baseball scene.

CLUB MEMBERS

The "first citizens" and "most respectable business men" who formed the Putnam Club in 1855 were all soon replaced on the first nine by younger men. By the end of the decade, the playing representatives of the nine had no obvious traits in common aside from being athletically gifted men in their mid-twenties. Perhaps that is why the Putnams, unlike many of their contemporaries, never made an effort to re-organize after the war or to stage reunions.

Andrew Eliot Burr: Andrew E. Burr, a carpenter by

trade, was born in New Milford, Connecticut, on August 27, 1833, and was a member of the same family as Vice President Aaron Burr. He died at the Grand Hotel in Manhattan on March 1, 1899.

James H. Church: James H. Church, the club's president in its inaugural year of 1855, was a clerk who was born around 1834. His sister Josephine married fellow club director Empie Gibbs. Church was still in Brooklyn when his wife died in 1871, but he appears to have died a couple of years later.

Thomas Spencer Dakin: Thomas S. Dakin was born on a farm in Orange County, New York, in 1831. At age 17, he walked the seventy-five miles to New York City, where he found work as an office boy and soon earned renown as the pitcher of the Putnams. In 1858 he established his own commission agency, Thomas S. Dakin & Co., yet he continued to find time for baseball and served two terms as vice president of the National Association of Base Ball Players. In 1862, Dakin enlisted in the Union Army, serving in the staff of General George Crook. He entered the oil trade after the war, but in 1870 he retired from business and became a major-general in the National Guard. As a member of the American rifle team, General Dakin led his countrymen in meets against their counterparts in Ireland, Scotland, Australia, and Canada. Yet Dakin never forgot his love of baseball, and in 1878 he offered a "splendid gold mounted willow bat" to the best player on the National League pennant winners.[26] But Dakin died in Brooklyn on May 13, 1878, and the idea of a Most Valuable Player Award did not resurface until the twentieth century. For many years after Dakin's death, members of the local militia paid annual visits to his tomb at Green-Wood Cemetery on Decoration Day/Memorial Day. Dakin's fame was such that when Grover Cleveland Alexander was drafted in 1918, a newspaperman wondered whether "history might repeat itself" by transforming one of the game's best pitchers into a military hero.[27]

John E. Davidson: One of the club directors in 1857 was listed as "John E. Davidson, Jr."[28] This pretty much has to be John Edward Davidson, a Hempstead pharmacist (though he wasn't technically a junior, since his father's name was Dr. John C. Davidson). John E. Davidson was born on August 5, 1831, and spent most of his life in Hempstead, before dying at a ripe old age on November 17, 1917.

Charles Austin Dayton: Charles A. Dayton, a club director in 1857, was born in Williamsburgh on January 19, 1834, and died in Brooklyn on November 7, 1907. Though he earned his living as a clerk and cashier, Dayton's true passion was collecting seashells, and he corresponded with other enthusiasts from all over the world. After his death, his collection of over 20,000 specimens representing 3,700 species was acquired by the Brooklyn Institute of Arts and Sciences.

Brower Gesner: Brower Gesner was born in Parrsboro, Nova Scotia, on November 13, 1834, and moved to New York to study surgery at the College of Physicians & Surgeons of Columbia University. He also found time to play for the Putnam Club in 1855 and serve as the club's first treasurer. When the Civil War broke out, he enlisted in the Union Army as a military surgeon. At the close of the war, he was given the rank of lieutenant colonel as the result of "gallant and meritorious services during the war."[29] Gesner remained in New York and died on November 5, 1874.

A. Empie Gibbs: Born in North Carolina around 1835, Adam Empie Gibbs moved to Brooklyn in the 1850s and married Josephine Church, the sister of fellow Putnam Club member James H. Church. By 1882, Josephine Gibbs was being listed in the Brooklyn city directory as a widow, so it seems a safe assumption that her husband is the A.E. Gibbs who died in Brooklyn on October 14, 1878.

Daniel Godwin, Richard J. Godwin, and Samuel L. Godwin: These three English-born brothers were key members of the Putnam Club during its early years, with Samuel serving as club president in 1856 and Daniel as club treasurer. They operated a successful brokerage at 60 Wall Street for many years. Richard Godwin was quite a wealthy man when he died in Brooklyn on September 19, 1895, age 69.

M. W. Griswold: This club member is almost certainly Merritt W. Griswold, whose role in introducing baseball to St. Louis was discussed in that chapter of the first volume.

George E. Hoyt: After serving as the club's vice president in 1856, George E. Hoyt became president in 1857, the same year in which he served as president of the Union Gymnastic Association of Brooklyn. Born in Albany in 1828, Hoyt was a schoolmate of Senator Roscoe Conkling and the two remained lifelong friends. After moving to Brooklyn in the early 1850s, he became a successful coal merchant and was able to retire in the early 1870s, though he continued to dabble in real estate. Most of his energies, however, were devoted to civic affairs and Nineteenth Ward politics. Hoyt remained loyal to the "Stalwart" faction of the Republican Party until Conkling's death in 1888, but in December 1891 he announced his intention to support Democrat Grover Cleveland in 1892.[30] A month later, on January 12, 1892, Hoyt died suddenly at the age of 63.

Theodore F. Jackson: Born in Rockaway, New Jersey, on November 16, 1830, Theodore F. Jackson was a successful Brooklyn lawyer who served as the first corresponding secretary of the NABBP. He was also active in local civic affairs and politics, serving as Registrar of Affairs and Controller of Brooklyn. In 1889, Henry Chadwick reported that his "old and esteemed" friend Theodore F. Jackson "of the old Putnam Club and the vice president of the old National Association in 1859" had been appointed one of Mayor Chapin's park commissioners and was committed to making the parks available to ball players.[31] By the turn of the century, Jackson and his wife had retired to Westhampton. Theodore Jackson died on June 18, 1913.

Dan Ketcham: see Union Base Ball Club of Morrisania.

Hervey G. Law, John F. Law, and Nathaniel B. Law: Three of the sons of the Rev. Joseph Law, a Methodist clergyman, were involved in both the Putnam and Continental clubs. Hervey Gregory Law operated a wood and willow ware business at 22 Fulton Street. Shortly after his death on March 19, 1872, a thief disguised as Satan broke into the Law home and stole his will, precipitating a long legal battle over the ownership of that highly desirable location.[32] Nathaniel B. Law, Hervey's partner in the wood and willow ware business, was one of the principals in the dispute. He died in Brooklyn on December 17, 1879. There is contradictory information about the ages of Hervey and Nathaniel, but both seem to have been born between 1817 and 1820, so it's not surprising that neither was member of the first nine of the Putnams. The third brother, John F. Law, was considerably younger, having been born around 1827.

Myron P. Masten: Talented catcher Myron Masten was born in 1834 in Ulster County, New York. As described in the club history, during his brief time with the Putnams, he earned a reputation as one of the best catchers in the game. His health soon failed, however, and the family moved to Washington, DC, where Myron Masten died on October 29, 1864.

Ed McKinstry: Ed McKinstry of the Putnams was reported in 1879 to have already died, but the details are not known.[33]

Jeremiah V. Meserole: Jeremiah Meserole was born in New York City on October 23, 1833, into a prominent family that first settled in Williamsburgh in the seventeenth century. As a young man, he played for the Putnams while his older brother Abraham played for the Nassau Club. During those years, Jeremiah worked as a surveyor and helped to lay out many of the streets in Brooklyn's Eastern District. In 1855, he enlisted in the Seventh Regiment as a sergeant, and when the Civil War broke out, he was elected colonel of the Forty-Seventh Regiment. He remained in charge of that regiment until 1868 when he became brigadier general of the Eleventh Brigade. In 1876, Meserole relinquished his military duties and returned to surveying. Fifteen years later, he was named president of the Williamsburgh Savings Bank, a position he held until shortly before his death in Far Rockaway, New York, on August 13, 1908. Despite these many accomplishments, his time as a member of the Putnam Club half a century earlier was mentioned in Meserole's obituaries.[34]

Edward Norman Robinson: Born around 1835, E.N. Robinson was a member of the Putnam Club before emigrating to the West and helping organize the Sacramento Club in 1860.[35] He was head clerk at the state asylum while in Sacramento, but left the city in 1861 to accept a railroad position.[36] Robinson eventually settled in San Francisco and became a prosperous mining engineer. He died on April 28, 1894, during a trip to London, England.[37] He was often referred to as Colonel Robinson, but whether that title was earned or honorary is not known.

David Ryno: David Ryno was a member of both the Putnam and Continental clubs. The 1860 census shows a carpenter named David Ryno, age 30 and a native of New York. This man is believed to be the Putnam Club member, but he cannot be traced after that.

Edward A. Walton: Edward A. Walton was playing for the Putnam Club as early as 1855 and remained a club director for several years. The only person by that name who appears to fit was Edward Attwood Walton, who was born in New York City on May 9, 1836. Walton went to work for the Citizens' Fire Insurance Company in 1850 and in 1874 became its secretary. In 1886 he was named president, serving in that capacity until the company went into voluntary liquidation in 1902. Walton also served on its board along with J. Walter Spalding, brother of Albert, and U.S. Vice President Garret Hobart. He died in Manhattan on March 13, 1913, age 76.

William Wansley: See Mutual Base Ball Club.

Other Club Members: Brown, Chapman, Chichester, Albert Davidson, Gibson, Gillespie, Headford, Kelly, Mermier, J.F. Monsee, John Morrell, G. Oliver, Parmelee, George P. Payson, Pierce, George Sandford, F. E. Smith, James W. Smith, Stimson, Tappan, Van Valkenburgh, Wanzier or Wanzler (quite possibly this is actually William Wansley), M. Wells.

Notes

1. *New York Clipper*, September 17, 1859.
2. *Brooklyn Eagle*, June 25, 1855.
3. *Brooklyn Daily Times*, June 25, 1855.
4. The "h" was officially dropped from Williamsburgh in 1852, but continued to be widely used, so for consistency's sake is used throughout in this piece.
5. *Brooklyn Daily Times*, June 29, 1855.
6. *Brooklyn Daily Times*, October 15, 1855.
7. *Brooklyn Daily Times*, August 6, 1855.
8. *Brooklyn Daily Times*, September 14, 1855.
9. *New York Clipper*, September 6, 1856.
10. *New York Clipper*, July 19, 1856.
11. *Porter's Spirit of the Times*, November 8, 1856.
12. *Porter's Spirit of the Times*, June 13, 1857.
13. *Porter's Spirit of the Times*, June 27, 1857.
14. Dakin had been on the nine initially chosen, while Masten was a substitute. When the team took the field, Masten played and Dakin was absent.
15. Chadwick Scrapbooks.
16. *New York Clipper*, September 17, 1859.
17. *New York Clipper*, May 19, 1860.
18. *New York Atlas*, March 18, 1860.
19. *New York Clipper*, June 23, 1860.
20. *Brooklyn Daily Times*, June 14, 1860.
21. *Brooklyn Daily Eagle*, August 6, 1860.
22. *New York Clipper*, July 14, 1860.
23. Charles A. Peverelly, in his 1866 *Book of American Pastimes*, reported that the Putnams disbanded in 1860, but there is clear evidence that they existed in some form in 1862.
24. *Wilkes' Spirit of the Times*, July 13, 1861.
25. *New York Clipper*, May 31, 1862.
26. *New York Clipper*, January 5, 1878.
27. Paul Purman, "Pitcher of Civil War Days Sets Alexander a Record to Shoot At," *Fort Wayne Journal Gazette*, April 29, 1918, 8.
28. *Porter's Spirit of the Times*, March 21, 1857.

29. *New York Herald*, December 28, 1866.
30. *Brooklyn Eagle*, December 13, 1891, 2
31. *Sporting Life*, July 10, 1889, 5
32. *Brooklyn Eagle*, April 20, 1872, 6
33. *Brooklyn Eagle*, April 5, 1879

34. *New York Evening Post and New York Sun*, August 14, 1908
35. *Stockton Daily Argus*, August 30, 1860; *New York Clipper*, November 17, 1860
36. *Stockton Daily Independent*, September 7, 1861
37. *San Francisco Call*, May 6, 1894; *Chicago Tribune*, May 1, 1894, 2

❖ *Atlantic Base Ball Club* ❖
(Craig B. Waff and William J. Ryczek)

CLUB HISTORY

The Atlantic Club of Brooklyn was probably the best baseball club in the United States during the late 1850s and the 1860s. They entered the 1860s with a dominant nine, and as their players got older and the competition got tougher, the Atlantics replaced their veterans with younger and more talented players, and maintained their position at the top rank. The Atlantics are often used as a contrast with the first clubs such as the Knickerbockers, and used to illustrate the changes that occurred in baseball as the sport got more competitive and the will to win overcame the gentlemanly behavior that characterized the natal years of the sport.

Charles A. Peverelly, in his *Book of American Pastimes* (1866), declared that "the Atlantic Base Ball Club, of Brooklyn, was organized August 14, 1855, and from the day of its entrance upon the base ball field it has occupied and filled a front rank position as a crack playing club. Unlike many of its kindred associations, who place a strong nine in the field for one summer, and perhaps a weak body of players for the ensuing season, the Atlantics have always and at all times had a nine from whom any rival club might almost despair of winning any lasting laurels. It is this extraordinary and unvarying success which has gained for them the title of 'Champion.'"[1]

Formation

Virtually no one would dispute Peverelly's assessment of the Atlantics' pre-eminent position in early baseball, but there is some evidence that the club's members were playing some form of the sport before the start date he noted.

One clue to the origin of the Atlantic club appeared in an interview of John McNamee that was published in the *Brooklyn Daily Eagle* in early 1876. McNamee, a former sheriff of Brooklyn who later moved to Florence, Italy, to pursue a career as a sculptor, suggested to visiting reporter John Clark that he was "one of the originators" of the game of "base ball." Asked to justify that claim, McNamee first queried: "Don't you remember old York street lot, near the station house?" For Clark, mention of the lot brought a smile to his "phiz" because it stimulated "visions of the old battle ground of the boys of the Second and Fifth wards ... and the memory of sundry bloody noses and torn unmentionables, the result of disputes as to the respective merits of old Constitution No. 7, and some other engine company."

McNamee, on the other hand, recalled that "years before the formation of the Atlantic Club, I used to get some of the 'boys' together on a good afternoon, and go in there and play the old game, where you used to 'sock' one another with the ball. My place of business was close by there, in York street, then, and after a while we practiced regularly until the principal of the school (No. 7) complained to the mayor that we interfered with the progress of the scholars in some way, and we had to stop playing there. Shortly after that the Gothams organized, and after them the Atlantic Club was formed."[2] McNamee's mention of the Gothams, a New York City club formed in 1852, is puzzling, and he may have actually had in mind the Excelsiors, a club formed in South Brooklyn on December 27, 1854.

The rest of McNamee's recollection, however, agreed with a separate account published in the *Eagle* on August 24, 1865, which reported on the club's origin: "In the fall of 1854, a body of men used to meet in York street, in an open lot where now stands the Station House, for Base Ball practice. The thought of any future renown never entered their minds, and still this was the nucleus of the present Champion club of the world. In the spring of the year they became associated with many of the Atlantic Market boys of South Brooklyn, among whom were Caleb Sniffen, Lowery, Watson, Peter O'Brien, together with Wm. V. Babcock, George Sexton, Thomas Tassie and others, and they formed April 14th, 1855, what was then and is now known as The Atlantic Base Ball Club."[3]

Two other accounts of the origin of the Atlantics were provided by Babcock, who in the mid–1850s was working as an engraver in New York City but living in Brooklyn. In 1892, while working at Bureau of Engraving and Printing in Washington, D.C., he claimed, on two separate occasions, that he was the chief organizer of the club. In early August, while watching a game between two local amateur clubs, he informed a *Washington Post* reporter, "I played my first match game in 1850.... I commenced my career in the diamond as a member of the old Gotham Club of New York, although I had played the game previously, of course.... Well, the Gothams got a little uppish over their victories, and during a little disagreement one day I left the club, promising to organize another in Brooklyn which would beat them out of their boots. This was in 1855, and according to my promise I organized the old Atlantics of Brooklyn."[4] Two months later, while visiting the Washington bureau of the *Brooklyn Daily Eagle* to look over the newspaper's files, he provided a second recollection in which the name of his pre–Atlantic club was mysteriously changed: "I used to belong to the old Empire base ball club of New York, and in June, 1855, I started the Atlantic base ball club of Brooklyn. I am fully aware that this honor has been claimed by others, but I believe that the record will accord me the credit."[5]

1855

Following their organization, the Atlantics immediately began practicing and played several intraclub games during the summer of 1855. The first club game open to the public and reported in the press was played on August 16, 1855, at the Plank Road Hotel. The box score indicates that the type of game differed in several respects from the one being played by the established Manhattan clubs. Three innings were played, and eleven men played on each side. Caleb Sniffen and W. Whitson formed the pitcher-catcher battery for one side, and J. Loper and Thomas Powers for the other. The latter side was the victor, but the actual final score is uncertain, as the *Spirit of the Times* and an unidentified source, likely the *New York Clipper*, reported 38–31 and 27–26 scores. Two additional intraclub games were played on August 20 and September 17.[6]

In mid–September 1855 the Harmony Base Ball Club of Brooklyn announced its organization and was soon claiming, according to Babcock, that it had "beat every club around town." (No record of any previous games played by the Harmony BBC, however, has been found.) By this time the Atlantics had settled on a first nine that included Sniffen (pitcher), Whitson (catcher), Powers (1b), Tice Hamilton (2b), Loper (3b), Babcock (ss), William Bliss (lf), John Holder (cf), and A. Gildersleeve (rf). They challenged the Harmony club to a best two-out-of-three match. The third game proved unnecessary after the Atlantics won the first two games, 24–22 and 27–10, played in Bedford on October 21 and in Brooklyn on November 5.[7]

One person who claimed to have observed the first game against the Harmony Club was Henry Chadwick, at the time a cricket reporter. In a letter to the editor of the *Eagle* written just over 40 years later, he recalled that the Atlantic field adjoined that of the Long Island Cricket Club, which may explain why he happened to witness this particular base ball game.[8]

The referee for the first Harmony game was Thomas Leavy, president of the Empire Base Ball Club of New York, itself only a year old. Based on what he observed, Leavy must have considered the Atlantics a worthy opponent for the Em-

pires, because the two clubs played, somewhere in East New York, a game on Thanksgiving Day, November 29. The season-ending game was drawn after the clubs fought to a 12–12 tie after an unspecified number of innings.[9]

1856

The inconclusive result of the Thanksgiving Day game led the Atlantics, at a club meeting on July 8, 1856, to issue a challenge to the Empire club for a rematch. The latter accepted the challenge, and the two clubs announced that they would play a "friendly match" on July 24 at the Atlantic grounds, now located in a field opposite Holder's Three Mile House in Bedford, and that "good sport may be anticipated."[10]

The game was attended by a large number of spectators, including not only a number of ladies, but also members of several other New York and Brooklyn clubs. One of these was Louis Wadsworth of the Knickerbockers, who was chosen as referee. On the Atlantic side, Babcock, Whitson, Sniffen, Loper, and Holder were joined by two players named Hunt and Millard, and, most significantly, brothers Peter and Mattie O'Brien, who would be first-nine players for the club for many years to come. Because the game began at 4 o'clock, the two sides had time to play only five innings, with the Empires scoring 19 runs and the Atlantics 15. Because neither side had scored the requisite 21, it was a drawn game, and the clubs eventually agreed to play yet another game on August 13 at the Empire grounds on the Elysian Fields in Hoboken, New Jersey.[11]

Before that occurred, however, the Atlantics made significant changes in the composition of their first nine. These changes may have partially resulted from severe discontent among certain players on the Harmony Club that had played the Atlantics the previous fall and that was now sharing the playing field opposite Holder's. In one of their games, Harmony club president Lem Bergen made a decision, "much against the wishes of most of the members of the Harmony Club," to place an Atlantic member on the Harmony side.[12] And with regard to a second game (against the Continentals), a *Brooklyn Daily Eagle* reporter, while observing that the players appeared in good order and condition "notwithstanding the intense heat," nevertheless severely criticized the quality of play of both clubs: "The play was miserably poor, neither party being entitled to be called good players. Bad, however, as was the play of the Harmony Club, that of the Continentals was worse…. They all require a good deal of practice before again attempting to play a match."[13]

This stinging critique, and second thoughts about an earlier club decision not to have its first nine play in August because of the heat, may have led four Harmony players (Lem Bergen, Folkert Rapelje Boerum, George Phelps, and John Griffith Price) to begin considering whether to continue playing with the club. Disharmony was certainly prevalent among the Harmony players, because on August 13, Bergen and Phelps appeared in the Atlantic line-up in its game with the Empire, which ended in a 5-inning 19–19 tie. It is likely that Bergen, Phelps, Boerum and Price appeared in a fourth Atlantic-Empire game that was played on neutral grounds near the Red House in Harlem.[14] Although their probable presence did not prevent the Empires from winning 24–14 in a twelve-inning game, it likely prompted remarks that appeared in the August 24 issue of the *Sunday Mercury,* which observed that "the Atlantic and Harmony Clubs, in their matches, select men from both clubs to play." This note in turn prompted Bergen, Phelps, Boerum, and Price to respond with a letter in which they declared that the Harmony Club had disbanded and was out of existence and that they were now ex-members of that club which, allowed them to move to another club.[15]

Remaining members of the Harmony Club in return replied, in a mid–September letter to Frank Queen, editor of the *Clipper:* "Now we should like to know when and where they [Bergen, Phelps, Boerum, and Price] became *ex-members* of the Harmony Club, as the club has never received from them any letter of resignation. If these men wish to become ex-members of our club, all they have to do is to send in their resignation, and *plank up,* or they may become *expelled* members."[16]

Whether the Atlantics in any way "encouraged" the movement of the four players may never be known. The episode, however, apparently engendered bitter feelings among certain members of the Atlantic and Empire clubs that prevented any games between them from being played until 1864.

A scheduled game on September 11 with the powerful Gothams of New York was left unfinished due to rain,[17] but later in the month the Atlantics initiated two other series of matches. With all four ex-Harmony players in the line-up, the club narrowly defeated the Baltics of New York, 21–20 in a game played at Bedford on September 18. The game was also notable for the first appearance in the Atlantic line-up of Richard (Dickey) Pearce.[18] The Atlantics had a much easier time nine days later, when they traveled to Williamsburg to meet the Columbia Club of East Brooklyn. The Atlantics won 34–7, and *Porter's Spirit* observed that "this game seems to have been of the slashing order on the part of the winners, and the fielding of the other side not equal, even if they could have made as good batting."[19] The return matches against each of these clubs resulted in similar lopsided scores: 24 or 21 to 7 against the Baltics at the Red House grounds in Harlem on October 13, and 21–3 against Columbia at Williamsburg three days later.[20] These games closed the 1856 season for the Atlantics, whose first nine ended with a record of four wins, one loss, and two draws.

1857

After dispersing for the winter, the Atlantic club members gathered together on Wednesday, April 22, 1857, at Sutton's to elect officers for the coming year. They also resolved to begin practice on the following Monday and continue this activity twice weekly, on Monday and Thursday afternoons.[21] By early July, the club felt ready to play other clubs, and issued challenges to the Putnam and Continental clubs of Brooklyn and the Gothams of New York.[22] On July 24 the Putnams visited the Atlantic grounds. Because the start of the game was delayed, for unknown reasons, until 4:30 PM, the clubs agreed to play only five innings (instead of the standard nine innings approved by a convention of clubs earlier in the year), and the Atlantics were victorious by a score of 19–3.[23] Four weeks later, on August 21, the club was again victorious by a 16-run margin when it defeated the Continentals 37–21.[24]

The long anticipated game between the Atlantics and Gothams suffered another postponement on July 23,[25] but finally took place on September 3 on the Atlantic grounds. Several days before the event, the *Clipper* was predicting that it would be "one of the most exciting and interesting games of base ball witnessed this season." Among the large crowd were quite a number of "critics and adepts," that is, gamblers, who just before the game, according to a *Porter's Spirit* reporter, "were ready to plant their 'tin,' in favor of the Gothamites, at 2 and 3 to 1." After a scoreless first inning, the Gothams edged ahead with three runs, but in the bottom half of the second inning the Atlantics startled their opponents by scoring 10 runs. This explosion, the *Clipper* reporter observed, "caused the Gotham gentlemen to think that they had come to the wrong spot to catch weasels asleep." When the game finally ended with a 41–11 win for the Atlantics, the result "caused the faces of the knowing ones to wear an aspect of wonder."[26]

Following this overwhelming victory, the Atlantics arranged to play matches with three Brooklyn clubs during the next two months. On September 15 they defeated the Eckfords 26–17 on the latter's grounds at the Manor House in Greenpoint, and were victorious over the same club at home on October 22 by a score of 29–11.[27] The Atlantics also engaged the Continental Club in a pair of games at the latter's grounds at Wheat Hill. The first game ended in a 34–34 tie on October 2, while the second, played just four days later, resulted in a 26–13 victory for the Atlantics.[28] The Atlantics were victorious, by a score of 37–15, in a return match on their own grounds against the Putnams on October 20.[29]

The ferryboats to Hoboken carried a large increase in numbers of passengers on Friday, October 30, when the Atlantics and the Gothams engaged in a return match. Won by the Gothams by a score of 24–19, the game featured superb fielding by both sides. The *Clipper* reported that spectators were given "the unequalled treat of witnessing this beautiful game played in its brilliancy and perfection," while the *Sunday Mercury* declared that "it was a day to be remembered, and will no doubt prove one of those occasions which will be looked back upon with the greatest pleasure in after years, by those who took part therein."[30]

The 1857 season was a pivotal one for the Atlantics. In the view of "X.," a *Porter's Spirit* columnist who authored a series of club profiles in the fall of 1857, the club in the space of a year had gone from being considered "not ... very formidable opponents" to standing "unrivalled" among the Brooklyn clubs . He attributed this great improvement to "the care and interest that the members take while playing; their games on practice days are played as particularly as their match games. They never wait for any bound balls, but if they cannot take them on a fly, would almost as soon lose them." He reported a universal opinion that "they are as strong batters as any club in existence, and all seem perfectly fearless of a ball." He also remarked, "I cannot speak too highly in praise of the playing, each one in his position; their throwing from base to base, and short stop to base, is as near perfection as any club has arrived at."

Despite this formidable reputation, the Atlantic club appears to have had some kind of internal dispute as their season neared its end. "X" reported that observers of the second game with the Gothams had perceived that club members, with some exceptions, "did not play the game that they can" and sensed that "some difficulty existed in the Club." Tassie, in a letter to the *Sunday Mercury* editor, stated that the trouble, which he did not specify, had not originated through any match they had played recently. Possibly the dispute may have involved Bergen and John Holder, whom "X" reported had just left the club.[31] They would play for the Excelsiors of Brooklyn in 1858, and one wonders if some under-the-table payment or some significant dispute with fellow club members had encouraged them to switch clubs.

1858

The Atlantic first nine achieved perfection in 1858. Only four clubs challenged them, and each learned just how formidable the club was. The most closely contested game was the first of the season — a match with the Putnams at the latter's grounds near Wheat Hill on June 17. The reporter for *Porter's Spirit* observed that "the strength and science of both parties [was] admirably displayed," but a nine-run fourth inning by the Atlantics put them ten runs ahead. They won the game by a 17–13 score. The pitchers were undoubtedly relieved when the game finally ended; by then, Tom Dakin of the Putnams had pitched 258 balls, and Mattie O'Brien of the Atlantics had delivered 229. Second baseman John Oliver made his first appearance as an Atlantic in this game.[32]

A number of Atlantic players appeared in the Fashion Race Course all-star series late in the summer, including pitcher Mattie O'Brien, first baseman John Price and outfielder Peter O'Brien, who played for the Brooklyn all-stars in the first game. By the third encounter, the Brooklyn nine was comprised entirely of Atlantic and Excelsior players, as Pearce and Boerum were added.

The year 1858 saw the first-ever challenge to the Atlantics from New Jersey, issued by the Liberty Club of New Brunswick. Three days after the final Fashion Course All-Star

game, the two sides met on the latter's grounds, and the score, 24–8 in favor of the Atlantics, was probably not unexpected. When the return match was played on October 11, the Liberty Club increased their run production to 14, but the host Atlantics may have surprised even themselves when they produced an unprecedented total of 61 runs, with Peter O'Brien alone scoring 10; Price, McMahon, and Boerum each crossing home base 8 times, and Mattie O'Brien scoring 7 times.[33] A more typical score of 18–9 in favor of the Atlantics was the result of the return match played with the Putnams on October 18. A crowd estimated at 3,000 attended the game, with quite a number of carriages surrounding the spectators. Third baseman Charley Smith made his first appearance as an Atlantic in this game.[34]

The stage was now set for the home-and-home match between the Atlantics and Gothams. On October 25, an immense crowd gathered at the Atlantic grounds in Bedford, and completely surrounded the players. When the beginning of the game was significantly delayed, pending the late arrival of Mattie O'Brien, the Atlantics pitcher, many friends of the Gothams complained, arguing that this courtesy was "extended" a bit too long and insisting that the rules of the base ball convention should be enforced, that is, the game should have started promptly whether the Atlantics were ready or not.

Once the game began, the Gothams had other reasons to complain. Despite valiant efforts by the Atlantics to control the crowd, which made highly vocal comments in favor of the Brooklyn club to the point of materially interfering with the progress of the game. The *Sunday Mercury* noted that "the Atlantics far excelled the Gothams in their power of striking," but also observed that "their balls were chiefly directed to a specific locality, and though raised high in the air they were invariably safe, from the conduct of persons who preferred the success of the Atlantic Club to their personal honor." By the end of the seventh inning, the crowd's repeated "backing up" of the Atlantics led the Gothams to resign the field in disgust and allow the Atlantics to claim a 31–17 victory. When the Atlantics subsequently gave three cheers for the Gothams, the latter made no response — a dishonorable act in the view of the *Porter's Spirit* reporter, although he clearly understood why the Gothams refused to return the courtesy.

A complaint was also raised regarding the condition of the playing field, which *Porter's Spirit* judged was "a poor one at best, and entirely in favor of the club familiar with its points." The *Sunday Mercury* similarly remarked that the field was "by no means of even surface, and must militate strongly against a strange club." The newspaper added that "within the limits of an ordinary playing field passes a rail fence, enclosing the private property of an individual. He was present inside his own enclosure, in the way of the players, and when desired to leave he declined. This lot should not have been considered a portion of the field, and balls struck there should have been decided *foul*."

Finally, the *Sunday Mercury* reporter characterized the field as being "a public one, where the rights of players are equal." He apparently meant that the Atlantics had little control over who actually watched the game and how these spectators behaved themselves during the course of the game. New York players, unaccustomed to partisan crowds, had little desire to experience it again. According to the *Sunday Mercury* reporter, "The general feeling with the various representatives of New York Clubs, at the termination of the game, was that hereafter they would not play a game with Brooklyn, so long as their grounds are public, and over which they cannot exercise proper police regulations. It is bad enough to go to Brooklyn and be defeated, without being subject to the mockery and derision of infant sepoys."[35] The Gothams carried out that declared intention — they, like the Empires, did not play against the Atlantics again until 1864.

The Atlantics' remaining games in 1858 were played against the Excelsiors of South Brooklyn. After a first attempt was cut short after two innings by rain, the Atlantics and Excelsiors restarted their series on November 9 before an immense concourse of spectators gathered at Carroll Park. The *Porter's Spirit* reporter discerned the contrast with the Gotham-Atlantic game with regard to crowd control: "As the ground is leased by the Excelsior Club, of course they exercised their right to exclude those who at all interfered with the players, and a posse of police effectively attended to the matter, and order reigned throughout." That reporter's rave review of the overall play of the Atlantics — "an excellent exhibition of the skill and ability arrived at this season in the practice of this truly manly and national game" with "every point ... effectively filled" — was matched by that of the *Sunday Mercury* reporter: "to the Atlantics must be awarded the credit of having brought the game to a perfect system — not one single point is lost or escapes their observation, and they are decidedly the hardest club to beat now in existence." The Excelsiors, like the Atlantics' previous opponents, quickly discovered how formidable the Atlantics were. The Atlantics held a 9–0 lead after two innings, and won the game 22–10.[36]

When the clubs met for a rematch at Bedford on November 16, the weather was decidedly more inclement. But despite a piercing wind from the northwest, a crowd of several hundred spectators, including several ladies, "bravely *shivered* through the game, the attraction being sufficiently great to compensate for the unpleasantness of the day." Apparently knowledgeable that most of the Atlantics had outdoor jobs (whether this was correct is not clear), the *Porter's Spirit* reporter argued that the engagement of the majority of the Excelsiors in mercantile pursuits made them "not as fully prepared to withstand the severity of the weather when playing ball, as their more hardy compeers, the Atlantics, whose avocations necessarily oblige them to be more weather-proof." Once again, the reporter placed them in a class above all other clubs: "The Atlantics did not warm up until the third inning, when

they all played as they alone, it would seem, can play. Take the Atlantic's Nine as a whole, and we much doubt if they have their equals, certainly not their superiors. They are practically familiar with every material point of the game, and from always playing the same nine, and always having the players at the same points, they have brought their play to a perfectly harmonious system, and it is to this important fact that they may attribute their invariable success."[37] Invariable, indeed, with a decisive 27–6 victory over the Excelsiors in this game, the Atlantics achieved an unblemished seasonal record of 7–0 and a reputation as the best base ball club in the Greater New York City region.

1859

The Atlantics in 1859 had another excellent season, which included pairs of home-game and return-game victories against the Pastimes, the Baltics, and the Mutuals, and single-game victories against the Star of Brooklyn (a junior club that shortly declared itself senior), the Union of Morrisania, and the Harlem of New York. Their strongest competition was the Eckford of Brooklyn. The Atlantics had won the first game against the Eckfords 25–15 on July 8,[38] and a return-game victory on September 8 would have clinched the series, but the Atlantics were not up to the task. The Atlantics were hampered by the absence of star third baseman Charley Smith, which necessitated a number of position changes, most of which worked out poorly. The *Clipper* noted that a number of the regular first-nine Atlantics, including Pearce, Boerum and Oliver, fielded badly, as did Weber, substituting for Smith.[39] The Eckfords scored nine runs in the first three innings off the pitching of Phelps, who allowed the opposition to run the bases with impunity, before Mattie O'Brien took over. The game was close until the Eckfords broke it open with a six-run rally in the eighth inning, leading to a 22–16 victory over the Atlantics. The crowd, estimated to be about 6,000 spectators, was well behaved, perhaps influenced by the large contingent of the fair sex in attendance.[40]

The two clubs met again on October 12 on the Eckford grounds in Greenpoint before eight to ten thousand spectators, which, claimed the *New York Atlas,* was the largest crowd ever to attend a baseball game save for the Fashion Course Series in 1858. The newspaper concluded that "the gathering of so large a crowd of people, among which there were a large number of ladies, is an unerring and practical indication that the American public, with singular unanimity of feeling and opinion, have decreed for the game of Base Ball, the top niche or head of the column of out-door pastimes."[41] *Porter's* viewed the immense crowd as evidence that "an extraordinary interest was felt in the deciding game for the local championship."[42]

With the Atlantics' 22–12 victory over the Eckfords in this third game and with just one loss in two seasons, the Atlantics were clearly the top nine in the area. The *New York Times* commented, "The Atlantics are now looked upon as the most successful Club of New-York or Brooklyn.... Their first nine are in constant practice, and also enjoy the advantage of having played for a great while together."[43]

One dark note occurred on October 19, when the Atlantics defeated the Stars 15–12 on the grounds the latter shared with the Excelsiors. Not all of the spectators observed the admirable decorum noted in the Eckford games. According to the *Clipper*, "The crowd was a very orderly and well-behaved one, with one prominent exception.... The exception we allude to, was the disgraceful language used by a blackguard who stood in the vicinity of the locality occupied by the ladies who were present; his conduct should have led to his prompt removal from the ground."[44]

1860

The excitement of the 1860 season was the culmination of several years of growing interest in the game of baseball, and the Atlantics were at the apex of the feverish activity of baseball's greatest season yet. The veteran club began the season as the champions, winning their first four games.

The Excelsiors, however, were soon generally perceived as their strongest challenger. The clubs had played each other just twice before, and the Atlantics had won on both occasions, but the Excelsiors had in the off-season added many new quality players, including pitching sensation Jim Creighton from the Stars. In addition, they achieved six straight victories against clubs in Albany, Troy, Buffalo, Rochester, and Newburgh in a pioneering upstate tour in early July.

The first game of the new best-of-three series between the Atlantics and the Excelsiors occurred on July 19 at the latter's grounds in South Brooklyn. Despite oppressively hot weather, the crowd was judged to be at least as large as that for the Fashion Course Series. They saw a masterful performance by the Excelsiors and, in particular, the battery of Creighton and captain Joe Leggett, as the Atlantics were decisively beaten by a score of 23–4, the worst defeat in the club's history. Despite the lopsided loss, the Atlantics acted as sportsmen, and their supporters were controlled and created no incidents.[45]

The second game of the series took place on August 9 at the Atlantic grounds. After five innings, the Excelsiors held a 12–3 lead and looked as though they would claim the championship. But the Atlantics embarked on one of their famous rallies and scored nine runs in the seventh inning to take a 15–12 lead, routing Creighton in the process. An Excelsior rally fell short and the Atlantics held on for a 15–14 win that necessitated a third and deciding game.[46]

The third game was played on August 23 at a neutral site — the Putnam Club's grounds in Brooklyn. In the days before the game, the press speculated on the issue of crowd control, for with neither the Atlantics nor the Excelsiors in control of the facility, with emotions running high from the excitement of the game, and with large amounts of money wagered on the outcome, disturbances were certainly possible.

The Excelsiors jumped out to a 5–1 lead in the first inning, but the Atlantics chipped away and by the fifth inning, the Excelsior margin was reduced to 8–6. Meanwhile, a pair of unpopular calls by umpire R.H. Thorn put the Atlantics' supporters, a number of whom had large wagers on the game, in a foul mood. As the Excelsiors batted in the sixth, the Atlantics made several glaring fielding errors, further agitating the gamblers and roughs in the crowd.

When the crowd, estimated at fifteen thousand, pressed in on the players, Excelsior captain Joe Leggett said he would pull his nine off the field if the crowd weren't restrained. When the catcalls and crowding continued, he made good on his threat. Before the Excelsiors left the ground, Leggett and Atlantic captain Peter O'Brien agreed to call the game a draw.

In the days that followed the aborted match, newspapers were flooded with letters supporting one side or the other. The consensus was that although the Atlantic players had done nothing wrong, it was their supporters who had created the ruckus. The Excelsiors vowed never to play the Atlantics again, and were so upset by the debacle that they never took part in championship contests thereafter. The entire incident placed a stain upon the game that threatened to place it among unsavory sports such as boxing and ruin the greatest season baseball had known.

Their championship intact, although blemished, the Atlantics proceeded to play a series with the Eckfords, also a contender for the crown. The Atlantics beat the Eckfords in a tightly contested three-game series, winning the third game by a 20–11 margin, after the clubs split two close contests. Before the first game, Eckford pitcher Frank Pidgeon told his nine to "go in and play the game just as if they were playing with a common club."[47] The Eckfords did not play well, however, performing more *like* a common club, and a couple of key errors gave the Atlantics a 17–15 victory. Some good batting sparked a four-run rally in the ninth inning for the winning margin. Captain Boerum, returned from a trip to Europe, made his first appearance of the season for the Atlantics and played well, considering his rustiness. Perhaps the most heartening aspect of the afternoon was the fact that the game was completed without incident and the two clubs fraternized sociably following the match.

The Eckfords matched the Atlantics' winning rally in the first game with a seven-run outburst in the second game, played on the Atlantic grounds on October 22, that gave them a 20–15 win in a game called after seven innings.[48] The third game, held at the Putnam Club's grounds on October 29 and won by the Atlantics 20–11, lacked the drama of the first two. In the wake of the Atlantic-Excelsior incident, however, it was good to see a well-behaved crowd of 8,000 spectators, and encouraging to note that Asa Brainard of the Excelsiors served as umpire.

For the fourth season in a row, the Atlantics were champions of the United States. The good crowds for the Eckford series (total attendance for the three games was estimated at seventeen thousand) were an indication that the incident with the Excelsiors had not soured New Yorkers on the game of baseball. The sport would go on.

1861

Like every baseball club in the New York area, the Atlantics were greatly influenced by the onset of the Civil War. While virtually none of their top players entered military service, many non-playing club members trooped off to war, and there was great uncertainty as to whether recreational sport was a suitable activity at a time when the nation was in peril and soldiers were facing enemy fire. The sporting press spoke of how athletic training made good soldiers and how sport had become an integral part of American life, but players were slow to take the field in 1861.

The Atlantics' own first match did not take place until August 5, when they beat the Newark Club, 21–11. The *Clipper* observed that the game was played on a site "beautifully located on a high piece of ground at the corner of High and Court streets, Newark; a fine view of the bay and the surrounding country being had from it."[49] In this game and many others to follow, the club had difficulty assembling the first nine, and often had to use second-nine players as substitutes. The first nine that had been considered the best in the nation over the past several years was decidedly mediocre in 1861, losing two of their seven contests (itself a great reduction from the 16 played in 1860) against outside competition. Shortstop Dickey Pearce and third baseman Charley Smith were the stars of the club, leading the Atlantics with 37 and 33 runs scored, respectively.

Following two victories each against the Newark and Exercise clubs, the Atlantics lost 23–18 to the Mutuals, considered a very strong, up-and-coming organization, on October 3. The *Eagle* reported, "The contest was witnessed by a concourse of persons amounting to at least from six to seven or eight thousand, which filled the fences, the trees, and every available chair and piece of standing ground anywhere near the field."[50] The large crowd was a gathering that would have been heartening even in prewar days. In the return game, on October 13, the Atlantics beat the Mutuals 52–27, but because the clubs did not play a third and deciding game in 1861, the Atlantics remained the unofficial champions, despite their unimpressive showing. The other loss was to the Liberty Club of New Brunswick on October 28 by the embarrassing score of 31–11 in the Atlantics' final game of the season.

1862

The top players of the early Atlantic champions were beginning to cede their places to younger, more talented men. Most of the old Atlantics — the men who'd played in the early years — were no longer active on the first nine, and either played second-nine matches, practice games, or not at all. Some veterans like Pete O'Brien, Pearce, and Smith would

continue to play key roles as a link between the early and later Atlantic clubs. But the season marked the first appearance of first baseman Joe Start and outfielders Jack Chapman and Fred Crane in the Brooklyn nine. All three came from the Enterprise Club, which had shared a field with and been mentored by the Atlantics in the 1850s while the Enterprise was still a junior club. But the latter was now a senior club, and the Atlantics' raid of three additional Enterprise players (in addition to Charley Smith in 1858) permanently soured the Atlantic-Enterprise relationship. The two clubs would not play against each other again. Start, Chapman, and Crane would become stalwarts of the Atlantic Club during the glory years after the war, and all went on to long, successful careers on the diamond.

The second year of war saw the Atlantics delaying practice until mid–May, and playing their first game of the season, against the Eckfords on July 11. The game was an exciting one, as the Eckfords scored the final 11 runs of the game to turn a 14–9 deficit into a 20–14 victory.[51] Ten days later the Atlantics bounced back with a vengeance, beating the Eckfords 39–5 in the second game of the series.[52] The third and deciding match was played on September 18 before a crowd of ten thousand, one of the largest gatherings of the war years. Winning a very well played, low-scoring 8–3 game, the Eckfords received a splendid silver ball (donated by the Continental Club) symbolizing the local Greater New York City championship.[53] The gate proceeds for all three games were donated to the Sanitary Commission, which administered to the needs of wounded and needy soldiers.

The Atlantics played only two other games in 1862, winning 27–12 against the Harlem Club on September 16,[54] and losing 15–10 to the Mutuals on September 22.[55] The latter was the carryover home-and-home game from the match started in 1861, but its occurrence four days after the last Atlantic-Eckford game deprived the Mutuals from making their own claim for the championship.

1863

The Atlantics played more frequently in 1863 than they had the previous year, and finished the season with an 8–3 record. They gained two victories against the Henry Eckfords of New York, and single victories against the Athletics of Philadelphia, the Eurekas of Newark, and the Nassaus of Princeton, New Jersey. They also defeated, 23–8, a side made up of 18 cricketeers from the New York Cricket Club, which required "the Atlantic to put out six for an innings, the Cricketers to put out three for an inning."[56] Two losses to the Eckfords, on September 2 and 8 by lopsided scores of 31–10 and 21–10, however, enabled the Eckfords to retain the crown they'd won in 1862.[57]

The Atlantics also lost to the Mutuals, by the narrow margin of 27–26, in an August 3 game that ended in bizarre fashion. After the Mutuals scored nine times in the ninth inning, the Atlantics began to stall in an attempt to have the game called by darkness before the inning was complete. With two out and the Mutuals' second baseman Ed Brown on second, shortstop John Beard stepped up to home plate. An overthrown pitch allowed Brown to score, tying the game. At this point both clubs apparently believed the umpire would momentarily call the game due to darkness, but he didn't. Beard then missed three pitches. Atlantic catcher Pearce missed the last pitch also, and Beard circled the bases with Pearce making no attempt to throw him out. Beard thus scored what became the winning run. Mutual catcher William Wansley similarly missed three pitches intentionally in an attempt to make the final out. Pearce purposely let the ball pass him. Wansley began walking the bases in order to let someone put him out, which, mercifully, Atlantic third baseman Charley Smith finally did.[58] By defeating the Mutuals in two later games on September 10 and 24 by scores of 15–11 and 42–18, the Atlantics won the best-of-three series over one of the strongest clubs in the New York area.[59]

1864

Playing in a new enclosed field at the Capitoline Grounds, located in the Bedford area of Brooklyn between Marcy, Nostrand, Putnam and Halsey Avenues, the Atlantics in 1864 fielded a dominant club that was clearly the class of the New York area. Meanwhile, the defending champion Eckfords were conspicuously silent. Noticing the lack of play by the latter, the *Eagle* on August 8 inquired, "What are the champions about? They keep pretty quiet now-a-days."[60] The same newspaper on October 10 reported, "Everybody is enquiring whether the match between the [Atlantics and the Eckfords] is to come off or not.... The Atlantics challenged the Eckfords early in the season, and, we believe, received a reply to the effect that the challenge would be accepted as soon as the club was in condition to play such strong opponents."[61] The latter, bereft of many of the star players who led the 1862 and 1863 clubs, virtually abdicated by failing to answer the Atlantic challenge and playing only four games all season.

In 1864 the Mutuals and the Atlantics appeared to nearly everyone to be the best clubs in the metropolis, and it was generally accepted that the winner of their series would be the champion. The first game of the Atlantic-Mutual series took place on June 27. It was the first game of the season for the Atlantics other than a match against a field nine in late May. The Brooklyn club was victorious by a 26–16 score, paced by the fine play of veteran Peter O'Brien.[62] The second game didn't take place until September 12, when the Atlantics clinched the series with a 21–16 win.[63]

The Atlantics were clearly 1864's best nine. They outscored their opponents by a margin of 817–227, an average of 39–11 per game. During a brief upstate tour, the Atlantics played a club from Canada for the first time. In their 75–11 win over the Young Canadian nine of Woodstock, Ontario, played in Rochester, New York, on September 22, they reached

their highest run total ever up to this point.[64] On six occasions they scored more than 50 runs, and never did their opponents tally more than 17. On July 18, they held the Resolute Club of Brooklyn to a single run in an 18–1 win.[65] They played 21 games and won 20. The only blemish on the Atlantics' record was a 13–13 tie with the Empire Club on June 30.[66]

One of the reasons for the Atlantic resurgence was their ability to get their first nine players to come to scratch for virtually every game, despite the increased activity. Seven men appeared in at least 18 of the 21 games, and the two top substitutes were John Oliver and former Eckford pitcher Joe Sprague, both skilled, top-flight players. Charley Smith and Dickey Pearce were again the two leading run scorers, and 20-year-old Tom Pratt was the pitcher in most games, replacing Mattie O'Brien, whose health had been fragile and who would die the following year of consumption. Pratt was a graduate of the Athletic Club of Philadelphia who threw hard and was considered one of the better pitchers in the game. With a strong nine behind him, he was tough to beat, and there was no doubt that Pratt had had a *very* potent club supporting him in 1864.

1865

With the Civil War ended, enthusiasm for baseball was far greater than in any previous season, surpassing even the glorious summer of 1860. More clubs took the field than ever before, and more games were played than in any prior year. Clubs traveled to other cities to play, although admittedly the distance they journeyed was still limited. The Atlantics received numerous challenges from other clubs, including the Empires of New York, the Eureka of Newark, the Eckfords (reconstructed from the weak combination of 1864), the Mutuals, and the Unions of Morrisania. Most significantly, for the first time, a club from beyond the vicinity of New York City, the Athletics of Philadelphia, was considered strong enough to challenge for the "national" championship that had hitherto been held exclusively by Brooklyn clubs.

For the second year in a row, the Atlantics had great stability in their nine. Infielder John Galvin and outfielder Sid Smith were the only additions to the lineup, as holdovers from 1864 filled the remaining positions. Start, Crane and Chapman played in every game. As was their habit, the Atlantics began the season in leisurely fashion, not playing their first game against outside competition until June 21, when they defeated the Empire Club 21–10.[67] Activity picked up with five games in July and eight in August. The most noteworthy July contests were a 15–5 victory over the Union Club on the 24th, a 65–3 drubbing of the Empire Club on the 27th, and a 33–13 victory on the 29th over the Keystone nine that was visiting from Philadelphia.[68]

The first big game of 1865 took place on August 3 against the Mutuals at the Elysian Fields. An immense crowd of fifteen to twenty thousand was on the Hoboken ground, which as an open field was totally incapable of handling such a large gathering. The game was delayed considerably as members of both clubs attempted to herd the spectators from the playing field. The late-starting affair was delayed even further when the ball had to be replaced, and the Mutuals, the host club, had difficulty finding one. Finally, with the Atlantics leading 13–12 on the strength of a three-run home run by Peter O'Brien, the skies opened and a deluge of rain ended the encounter after five innings.[69] The second game between the two clubs took place just eleven days later, at the enclosed Capitoline Grounds, before an attendance estimated at 10,000. The Atlantics won 40–28, ending any hope the Mutuals had of dethroning them.[70]

In late September the Atlantics visited New England for the first time. They had already defeated the visiting Lowells of Boston 45–17 on July 20, and the return game in Boston on September 25 resulted in a 30–10 victory for the Atlantics. Over the next three days, the Atlantics successively defeated the Tri-Mountains of Boston (by the whopping score of 107–16); the Harvard College nine, 58–22; and the Charter Oaks of Hartford, Connecticut, 22–11.[71]

On August 18 and 31 the Atlantics had narrowly escaped with 21–20 and 38–37 victories over the Eurekas.[72] The club also achieved 28–23 and 35–8 victories over the Eckfords on September 21 and October 13, as well as a 58–30 return-game victory over the Unions on October 5.[73] That left only the Athletics as the remaining challenger for the championship. In a preview of the machinations that were to occur over the next several years, the two clubs made accusations, issued invitations, ducked invitations, and generally managed to avoid playing each other for extended periods of time. Mattie O'Brien died in October, and the club announced it would play no more games in 1865, which put an apparent end to their season. The Athletics, however, proclaimed that they intended to show up on their grounds in Philadelphia on October 30 and claim a forfeit if the Atlantics failed to appear. The Atlantics voted to cut the mourning period short and left for Philadelphia by train on the October 29.

The following day the Atlantics came from behind, turning a 9–5 deficit into a 21–15 victory.[74] A week later, on a blustery November day in Brooklyn, the club secured its second straight championship with a 27–24 victory before a crowd estimated at ten to fifteen thousand, a remarkable gathering in uncomfortable weather.[75] Although many nines had greatly improved themselves in 1865, none was the equal of the Atlantics, who went through the season without a loss for the second year in a row. Over the course of the season they played 24 games (including a season-ending contest against a Picked Nine[76]) and won them all. Once again, the Atlantics were the undefeated champions of the United States.

1866

The Atlantics in 1866 didn't appear to be the powerhouse of old. Before the beginning of the season, Dickey Pearce, Fred

Crane, and Frank Norton defected to the Excelsior Club, only to return during the summer. The Atlantics also added strong players like George Zettlein, who shared the pitching chores with Pratt, catcher Charlie Mills and infielder/catcher Bob Ferguson, an excellent fielder who became a key member of the club over the next few years, and eventually assumed the position of captain.

The long Atlantic winning streak came to an unexpected end early in the 1866 season. Within a few years, the Irvington Club of northern New Jersey would come to be regarded as one of the top nines in the metropolitan New York area. In 1866, however, the Irvingtons were derisively referred to as a "country club," an amalgamation of rural bumpkins that only recently had been a junior club. The Irvingtons were not even members of the National Association in early June when representatives of the club appeared on the Atlantic grounds and asked if the champions would visit them to play a game so as to teach their youngsters a thing or two about top-flight baseball.

When the game took place on June 14, the Irvington Club showed the Atlantics a thing or two. The Atlantics had a reputation for toughness and for being a bit rough around the edges, but they yielded nothing to the Irvingtons in that regard. The latter club had its share of "growlers" and fans that weren't afraid to use their fists in support of their club. In addition, the Irvington grounds were difficult to reach, and not particularly well groomed. The Atlantics were so confident that they didn't bring their best players to New Jersey. Their battery consisted of pitcher Potts (recently of the McClellan Junior Club) and catcher George Smith. The Atlantics took an early lead, but the Irvington boys played a plucky uphill game and left the field with a 23–17 victory, the Atlantics' first defeat since a loss to the Eckfords in 1863.[77]

Exactly two months later, on August 14, the Atlantics lost a second game, to another New Jersey club, the fine fielding Eurekas, by the surprising score of 36–10. As in Irvington, field conditions were less than ideal and, as in Irvington, two of the Atlantics' regulars were missing.[78] By late August the Athletics of Philadelphia had beaten the Irvingtons, 77–9 and 18–11, and the Eurekas, 48–8, fostering the impression, given the Atlantics' losses to the two clubs, that it would be difficult for the Atlantics to hold the Athletics off another year. Poised to achieve equality, the Philadelphia nine had a powerful lineup, featuring strong batters like Lipman Pike, Al Reach, Dan Kleinfelder, and veteran Nate Berkenstock. The Athletics averaged 51 runs per game (admittedly many games were played against second-rate competition) and hit numerous home runs.

The first game scheduled between the Atlantics and Athletics, on October 1, resulted in pandemonium in the Pennsylvania city. Many businesses closed down for the afternoon, scalpers plied their trade near the grounds at 15th and Columbia, and a crowd of spectators well beyond the ground's capacity thronged to the area. It was estimated that 40,000 people were within a quarter mile of the field when the game commenced. People climbed trees, rooftops, and anything capable of holding a human body and affording a view of the players. By the time the game started, the police were beginning to lose control of the situation. In the bottom of the first inning, with the Atlantics at bat, an altercation broke out and order disintegrated. In a scene reminiscent of the Atlantic-Excelsior debacle of 1860, people broke through fences, swarmed on the field and made the continuation of play impossible. The game was called.

Two weeks later, the two clubs met at the Capitoline Grounds in Brooklyn. Two hundred Brooklyn police officers were engaged to maintain order, and sixteen gate keepers were employed to see that only those who paid would enter the facility. Although 15,000 attended, order was maintained throughout and the game was played to completion. The Atlantics broke the game open with eight runs in the seventh inning en route to a 27–17 win.[79]

Exactly one week later, the series returned to Philadelphia for the second game. The Athletics spent $1,200 to erect a new fence around the playing field, increased the price of a ticket to one dollar (compared to the traditional twenty-five or fifty cents), and announced their intention to limit ticket sales to 4,000. The high tariff did the job without a limit, and two to three thousand saw the Athletics force a third game by beating the Atlantics handily 31–12 in a 7-inning game.[80]

It is impossible, however, to "force" a game when one party is unwilling. Commercialism had crept steadily into the world of baseball, and crowds of 15,000 or more generated enough money to bicker over. And bicker the Atlantics and Athletics did over the next several weeks. Before splitting the proceeds of the second game, the Athletics had deducted the cost of the fence. On the other hand, the Athletics had paid the travel expenses of their rivals, a courtesy not reciprocated when the Athletics visited Brooklyn. What should have been an exciting championship baseball tussle between the representatives of two major cities degenerated into a vitriolic battle of letters. The third game was never played.

The 1866 season thus ended on an anticlimactic note. Before the year ended, the Atlantics won two games each over the Irvington and Eureka nines, thus taking both series. In the season-ending game on October 29 the pesky Irvingtons took the champions to ten innings before a home run by Fred Crane and an Atlantic seven-run rally gave them a 12–6 victory.[81]

Because no nine had beaten the Atlantics twice, they remained the champion, although the title was certainly tainted by the fact that the deciding game with the Athletics remained unplayed. The Brooklyn club was not as dominant as it had been in 1864 and 1865, as more talented nines emerged and the level of competition escalated. Over the next few years, the battle for the championship would be highly competitive, both on the field and off.

1867

As they had for the past few years, the Atlantics in 1867 retained the core of their nine, while adding a couple of new faces. Charley Smith, a stalwart of the club at third base since 1858, played only 11 games in 1867. George Zettlein pitched nearly every game, as Tom Pratt left for Philadelphia and the newly formed Quaker City nine, taking outfielder Jack Chapman with him. Newcomers John Kenney and Dan McDonald played in the outfield.

Under the informal rules of the era, an uncompleted series in one year was to be finished the following season; therefore the third game of the Athletic-Atlantic series should have been played in 1867, and if the Athletics were victorious, they would be the new champions. The bad blood of the previous season was still boiling, and a series of disagreements, misunderstandings and logistical blunders prevented a meeting of the two clubs for nearly the entire summer.

Finally, on September 16, just a few days before the autumnal equinox, the two clubs played the third game at the Union Grounds in Brooklyn. The Atlantics' easy 28–16 win eliminated the Athletics from championship contention.[82] Although the game was the concluding one of the 1866 series, and theoretically the 1867 series remained to be played, only the most deluded optimist could imagine the two nines arranging two or three games before the end of the season. When the two clubs played a week later in Philadelphia, the Athletics won easily 28–8 before a home crowd estimated at 20,000.[83] Had they done so seven days previous, the Philadelphians would have been the champions. On October 27 the Atlantics informed the Athletics by telegraph that their pitcher (Zettlein) was disabled and four other players (Smith, Mills, Start, and Pearce) were "laid upon the shelf. They thus requested a postponement, which the Athletics refused to grant.[84] When the Athletics appeared at the Union Grounds on September 30 for what they believed would be their shot at the title, the Atlantics at first refused to play, and then presented their "muffin" nine. The Athletics indignantly refused to play the muffins, knowing a win would be meaningless, and the rivalry carried over to 1868. After the Athletics departed, the Atlantics divided into two sides and played a game they felt entitled them to keep the gate money.

Before the first Athletic game, the Atlantics suffered two consecutive losses. One was to the Union Club of Morrisania on July 31, and the other to the Irvington nine, now readily acknowledged as a first-rate organization, on August 5.[85] After weathering the challenge of the Athletics in late September, the Atlantics prepared to play the Unions in a game that, if the latter won, would be their second victory of the series and give them the championship. If the Unions failed, the Irvingtons would have a similar opportunity a few days later.

Ominously, the Atlantics had not been playing well before the game with the Unions. On their trip to Philadelphia, in addition to the loss to the Athletics, the Atlantics tied the Keystones 12 -12 on September 25 and barely beat the Quaker City (24–21 on September 24) and West Philadelphia nines (36–31 on September 26), clubs that were not considered among the top rank.[86] And on October 3 the visiting Keystones beat the Atlantics 21–18 on the Union Grounds.[87]

The second game with the Unions, on October 10, was a very well played match that was tied 9–9 after six innings. When the Atlantics came to bat in the ninth, they trailed 14–12. The Brooklyn club was known for its rallies, and nearly pulled the game out of the fire. They scored one run and would likely have tied the game had it not been for two great catches in the outfield by Tommy Beals and Henry Austin of the Unions. When Austin caught a fly ball for the final out, the Unions were champions, the first time a club other than the Atlantics or Eckfords had held the crown.[88]

The triumph of the nine from Morrisania underscored the weakness of the championship system. The Unions finished their season with a 21–8 record, compared to the Athletics' mark of 44–3. Yet the Unions were the champions, and the Athletics had been foiled once again. The Atlantics, their string of titles at an end, had a final record of 19–5, with one tie.

1868

The Atlantics in 1868 fielded essentially the same squad as they had in 1867, plus Jack Chapman, returning to the club after a year with the Quaker City nine. Given the long association and familiarity, the group of veterans should have worked together harmoniously with each other. The Atlantics, however, were not known for harmony, and continued to court a reputation as a troublesome bunch that often unraveled when things went badly. Still, they remained one of the top clubs in the United States, and would continue to compete for the championship until the establishment of the first professional league.

The Atlantics' 1868 season was noteworthy in a number of respects. First, they played far more games than ever before, finishing with a record of 47–7, a far cry from the five games played in 1862. A second notable achievement was the first lengthy tour in the club's annals. The Atlantics left Brooklyn in mid–June and spent nearly a month on the road, visiting several cities in upstate New York, Ohio, Michigan, Illinois, Wisconsin, Missouri, Indiana, and Kentucky. They ventured into Canada to play the Young Canadians at Woodstock, Ontario. Canadian baseball had apparently improved from the last time the Atlantics had played the Young Canadians, for on June 15 the Brooklyn nine prevailed by the relatively close score of 30–17. Overall, the Atlantics won 16 of the 17 games they played on the road, losing only to the Niagara Club of Buffalo by a 19–15 margin. Among the victories was a convincing 40–17 win over Harry Wright's Red Stocking Club of Cincinnati on July 6.[89] The Atlantics also made a number of brief excursions beyond the New York metropolitan area. Their destinations included upstate New York, Boston, Washington,

and Philadelphia, and the results included a surprising 27–19 loss to the National Club of Albany on August 10.[90]

On September 10 and October 5, the Atlantics decisively defeated the Unions of Morrisania 31–7 and 24–8. The two victories gave them temporary possession of the championship.[91] The glory was short-lived, however, for before the season ended the Atlantics were in turn defeated twice (25–22 and 28–17 on October 10 and 26) by the Mutuals of New York, who ended the year with their first title.[92]

1869

At the annual convention of the National Association in December 1868, the delegates voted to legalize professionalism. It was assumed that the Atlantics and other top clubs had paid some of their players prior to formal legalization, for not many gainfully employed men could play over 50 games per year and leave work for a month to tour the country. With full-time players and an expanded schedule, the season began much earlier than it had earlier in the decade. In some years, the Atlantics had not begun playing regularly until August, but in 1869 they played their first game in April and played nine more in May.

By June 16, the club had played 12 games, won 11 and tied 1 (with the Haymakers of Troy). On that day, the Atlantics faced the Red Stockings of Cincinnati, who were in the midst of their triumphant tour of the East. A year earlier, the Brooklyn nine had beaten the Red Stockings easily, but Harry Wright had added a great deal of talent during the winter, and in 1869 it was the Red Stockings who posted a comfortable 32–10 win.[93]

Although the Red Stockings would not lose a game all season, that did not mean they would win the national championship. They would have to beat the Mutuals twice in three games, or defeat whoever might topple the Mutuals in the meantime.

The club that unhorsed the Mutuals was the Eckfords, champions of 1862 and 1863, who had regained their status as a title contender. As soon as the Eckfords won the title, they began a series with the Atlantics on September 6. The latter club won the first game 45–25 behind a four-home-run game by first baseman Joe Start, who accumulated 21 total bases in the slugfest.[94] The Eckfords won the second game of the series 23–9 on October 9, setting up a decisive third game for the championship.[95] In the meantime, the New York and Brooklyn clubs studiously avoided scheduling the Athletics while any of them held the championship, as they were determined to keep the title out of Philadelphia.

When the Athletics were safely out of the way, the Atlantics and Eckfords met for the third time on the frigid day of November 8.[96] The Atlantics won 16–12 before only a thousand fans and retook the title, a hollow claim in a season in which the Red Stockings had gone undefeated, and the Athletics, with their 45–8 record, were denied a chance to play for the title. The Atlantics, with a 40–6–2 mark, were once again champions of the United States.

1870

Eighteen seventy was the last year the Atlantics were among the elite nines in the United States. It was also the last year of the muddled concept of the championship that had created so much havoc during the post-war era. There were no changes in the Atlantic nine from 1869, and the regulars played in nearly every game, with little need for substitutes. Ferguson was the captain, and often alienated his men with his autocratic manner. The Athletics, after beating the Atlantics twice in May and June, thought they had finally captured the elusive crown. All they had done, however, was initiate another squabble, for the Atlantics claimed the second game had been an exhibition and did not count in the championship race.

The most exciting game of the Atlantics' 1870 season, and one of the most thrilling of the nineteenth century, took place on June 14 at the Capitoline Grounds. The Red Stockings, who had shocked the baseball world by beating the Atlantics and the other New York clubs in 1869, returned to New York without having lost a game since. After nine innings, the Atlantics and Red Stockings each had five runs, and many, including most of the Atlantics, were ready to end the game as a draw. Supposedly, the Atlantics were aware of the monetary potential of playing off the tie on another date. Joe Start estimated that such a game would have meant three or four hundred dollars to be divided among the players.

A game could be ended as a tie, however, only with the consent of both captains, and Cincinnati captain Harry Wright wanted to play on. Umpire Charley Mills called the Atlantics back to the field and ordered the commencement of the tenth inning. There was no scoring in the tenth, but the Reds scored twice in the top of the eleventh. In the Atlantic half of the inning, with a runner on third base, Joe Start lifted a high fly to right field near the foul line. As Red Stocking outfielder Cal McVey pursued the ball, a fan interfered with him, grabbing his arm as he tried to throw, and Start reached third base with the tying run. Captain Bob Ferguson drove in Start with a single, and scored the winning tally on an error by Cincinnati second baseman Charlie Sweasy.[97]

Cincinnati lost five additional games following the loss in Brooklyn, and with top clubs in Chicago, Rockford, and New York, no one club dominated play. With so many nines in contention, the method of determining a champion was clearly inadequate. When the season ended, the Mutuals, the White Stockings of Chicago and the Red Stockings all had claims on the title, depending on who ducked whose challenge, what constituted an official game, and similar issues. The Atlantics were 41–17, and finished the season poorly. In late September and early October, the club lost four straight games, and dropped seven of their last twelve overall.

First baseman Start was the leading hitter for the Atlantics in 1870, pacing the club with 161 hits and 269 total bases. Jack Chapman was second in hits with 150. But the Atlantics were no longer the dominant club they had been five years earlier, despite having a lineup that was probably stronger. The other clubs had caught up to them, and the Atlantics ended the pre-league era in the middle of the professional pack.

Epilogue

The Atlantics chose not to enter the National Association of Professional Ball Players (NA) when it was formed in March 1871. Most of the club's top players, including Pearce, Start, Smith and Ferguson, joined the Mutuals.

The following year, the Atlantics joined the NA, and re-engaged Ferguson to captain the nine. Most of the NA clubs were salaried nines, but some, including the Atlantics, were "coops" in which the players were paid a percentage of the gate. The revenue sharing so coveted by current player unions was not as desirable in the 1870s, and the top players opted for the security of a salaried position. Clubs like the Atlantics were left with lesser players and youngsters. Most of Ferguson's teammates were inexperienced, including 16-year-old pitcher Jim Britt. As might be expected of a young nine among tough competition, the club compiled a poor 8–27 record.

Over the next two years, the Atlantics improved somewhat. They added Dickey Pearce in 1873 and finished 17–37. The following season old Atlantic Jack Chapman, a bit heavier than he'd been in his prime, rejoined old teammates Pearce and Ferguson and the club was 22–33.

The improvement ended abruptly in 1875. Ferguson left to captain the Hartford Dark Blues, and Pearce and Chapman signed with the new Brown Stockings of St. Louis. With a number of new clubs entering the NA, good players were at a premium, and the Atlantics were left with a nine of second- and third-rate performers. All summer long, the club had difficulty rounding up a full complement of players to take the field, and the games were often delayed while the Atlantics scrambled to find substitutes. They employed 35 different men during the season, 14 of whom played just a single game.

The Atlantics beat the New Haven club twice early in the season but, after the second win, remained well back in the standings with a 2–11 record. That was the high-water mark of the Atlantic season. The once proud champions lost their last 31 games, finishing the final NA campaign with a sorry 2–42 record. They didn't make any trips in the latter part of season, lacking the funds to do so, and their home games often drew one hundred fans or less.

The 1875 season effectively marked the end of the Atlantic saga, a sorry finish for a once glorious club. Over the next several years, other clubs took the name "Atlantic," but they had no connection to the one established in 1855. The era of the old Atlantics essentially ended after the 1870 season when the club's top players joined the Mutuals. They would never again be the Atlantics that won five championships in the 1860s.

CLUB MEMBERS

Joshua H. Ackerman: Joshua H. Ackerman was born in New York around 1833. He played in the first and third Atlantic intraclub games in 1855 and served as the club's secretary in 1855 and 1856. An iron dealer by trade, he died in Brooklyn on April 18, 1886. A "T. Ackerman" also played in one of the 1855 intraclub games, but he does not appear to have been a brother.

Alexander G. Babcock: Alec Babcock, the younger brother of William Babcock, was born near Princeton, New Jersey, on April 18, 1835. He played a few games for the Atlantics in 1860 and 1861, but when the war broke out, his sympathies were with the South, and he moved to Richmond, Virginia. Like his brother, he had apprenticed as a bank note printer, and he initially helped print currency for the Confederate government. But he soon was called upon to fight and rose to the rank of captain, serving under Colonel John S. Mosby until being captured and held in Alexandria as a prisoner of war. While a captive he and his fellow Confederate prisoners were often required to ride on the trains carrying Union soldiers so that Mosby would not try to derail them. After the war he remained in Richmond and helped rebuild the city, becoming a successful ice dealer and spearheading the building of a Masonic Lodge. Along with Aleck Pearsall, the former Excelsior Club member who shared his views about the war, Babcock organized the Pastime Base Ball Club in Richmond in 1866 and played for it for several years. He sold his business in 1880 and moved to a large farm outside of Richmond, where Babcock, who never married, died on January 16, 1894.[98]

William V. Babcock: William V. Babcock was born on April 20, 1833, and helped found the Atlantics along with Thomas Tassie, Caleb Sniffen, and Tom Powers. He played shortstop for the Atlantics in 1855 and also did some pitching, but soon relinquished these positions to Dickey Pearce and Mattie O'Brien, respectively. After serving as the club's vice president in 1857, Babcock "got the Western fever and sailed for California." Many years later he recalled that "even in the land of gold I couldn't forget bats and balls, so with some friends I organized two clubs, which played the first regular game of ball on the Pacific coast" in October of 1858. According to Babcock, the game was played "out on the old Mission road, about halfway between the church and the city [of San Francisco]. This started the ball to rolling on the coast; and the result was the formation of the old Pacific nine, to which I gave a ball and the newly adopted rules of the National Association of Baseball Players."[99] He soon returned to Brooklyn and resumed his involvement with the Atlantics, serving another term as vice president in 1863 and then holding the club presidency from 1864 to 1866. An engraver and printer by profession, he was living in Washington in the 1890s and was involved in the printing of bank notes when he provided

his reminiscences about the early days of baseball.[100] Babcock died in Brooklyn on September 8, 1915.

Lem Bergen: Lem Bergen was born on December 30, 1832. Although his first name was sometimes assumed to have been Lemuel, his correct name was in fact Leonard M. Bergen. Bergen began playing base ball in 1855 with the Harmony Base Ball Club, participating in its two matches with the Atlantics that year, and was elected president of the Harmony club in 1856. Midway through the 1856 season, he and three other Harmony Club members — F. R. Boerum, George Phelps, and John Price — joined the Atlantics in a controversial move. Bergen did quite a bit of the catching for the Atlantics over the next two seasons, but he began to lose time to Boerum and moved on to the Excelsiors in 1858. Though close to thirty and newly married, he enlisted in the 10th New York Infantry, Company F, in 1861 and served in the Union Army for more than two years. After the war he worked as a cashier for the Board of Water Rates. He died of tuberculosis on April 2, 1885.[101]

William Bliss: William Bliss played in the Atlantics' three intraclub games as well as in both games against the Harmony club in 1855. He was still playing for the second nine as late as 1860.

Folkert Rapelje Boerum: F. R. "Rap" Boerum was the catcher of the Atlantics from 1857 to 1860 and helped popularize an important innovation. According to sportswriter and historian William Rankin, Boerum began playing close to the batter in the summer of 1859 at the suggestion of Atlantics' president William V. Babcock. Rankin added that the tactic "proved so great a success that it was adopted by all the leading clubs in the vicinity of New York." Boerum was born around 1828 and was a member of a prominent New York family. As of 1877, he was described as "a retired gentleman of wealth and leisure, and quite a patron of the fine arts."[102] His sister married a well-known ballplayer named John Remsen. Boerum died in Brooklyn on November 13, 1903.

Frederick K. Boughton: Fred Boughton was one of the club's reserves in the early 1860s and served as secretary (1860–1861), club president (1862–1863), and as a delegate to the national convention. He was born near Utica on July 13, 1835, and died in Brooklyn on December 5, 1877.

Daniel C. Brayton: Dan Brayton played in several games for the Atlantics in 1855 and 1856. He is believed to be a U. S. Naval officer by that name who was stationed at the Brooklyn Naval Yard for several years but eventually returned to his native Massachusetts.

Oliver E. Brown: Oliver Brown was a member of the Atlantic Club's second nine whose services were often needed by the first nine in 1868. Brown was born in 1849 and was an underage enlistee in the Civil War. When he died in 1932 at the age of 83, Brown was described as "one of the few surviving members" of the Atlantics.[103]

John Curtis Chapman: John Chapman was born in

Brooklyn on May 8, 1843, and, after stints with the Hiawatha and Enterprise clubs he became a fixture in the outfield of the Atlantic Club. He came to be "considered the best left fielder in the country," possessing a rifle arm and being such a sure catch that he was dubbed "Death to Flying Things."[104] Chapman went on to a long major league career, first as a player and then as a manager. When he died in Brooklyn on June 10, 1916, he was the first of several former players to be described as the last surviving member of the Atlantics.[105]

Frederick William Hotchkiss Crane: Fred Crane was born on November 4, 1844, in Saybrook, Connecticut, and began his long tenure with the Atlantics in 1862. Despite weighing a mere 135 pounds, he was known for his "great physical power." He was even better known for his defensive versatility — in 1868, Henry Chadwick wrote that Crane "was at one time second baseman for [the Atlantics], and then it was claimed that none could equal him. Now he is in centre 'garden' as the boys call the field, it is thought that none can play with him."[106] Crane is credited with playing in a few major league games, but accounts of those games suggest it was a different man with the same surname who played them. Crane became president of a printing press manufacturing company. He and his wife were also known for their fine singing voices, and Crane was director of the Apollo Club's choir for many years. He died in Brooklyn on April 27, 1925.[107]

Samuel F. Davenport: Samuel Davenport was one of the Atlantic Club's reserves and the club's secretary in 1870. He had worked in the Brooklyn post office for thirty-three years by the time of his death on March 4, 1895, at the age of 59 and was buried in Cypress Hills Cemetery.[108]

Augustus J. "Gus" Dayton: See Pastime Base Ball Club.

Robert V. Ferguson: Bob Ferguson, who was born in Brooklyn on January 31, 1845, began his career with the junior Frontier Club and then moved on to the Enterprise Club. He joined the Atlantics in 1866 and played third base for three years, then became the club's catcher in 1869 and 1870. It was an appropriate beginning for a career of a ballplayer noted for his ability to adjust to almost any role. Ferguson was the first known switch-hitter, but he chose which side to bat from based on the situation, rather than upon whether the opposing pitcher threw right- or left-handed."[109] At a crucial moment in the game that ended the Red Stockings' winning streak, Ferguson "took the bat, and with commendable nerve batted left hand, to get the ball out of [Cincinnati shortstop] George Wright's hands."[110] Ferguson continued to switch-hit during a fourteen-year major league career with seven teams in the National Association, National League, and American Association.[111] In addition, Ferguson served as a manager, umpire and as president of the National Association while still an active player. When his playing days finally ended, he became an umpire and, typically, was regarded as one of the best. Yet Ferguson's thorny personality had a way of getting him in trouble. When he died in Brooklyn on May 3, 1894, an obituary cap-

tured both his brilliance and his prickly nature: "Of all the bright galaxy of players who flourished in Brooklyn in the sixties and seventies, Ferguson was one of the best known. He had come into this world in the cradle of base ball and he grew up with the first band of professional players. He was unlike that band, however, in many ways. He lacked the dare devil ways of that old company and he was different to them in that he was temperate in all things. He neither touched strong drink nor tobacco and in recent years though long past middle age he was as active as the average athlete and only the grey hairs told that he belonged to the corps of veterans who flourished back in the sixties. Ferguson had few friends among the players. He was a man of too blunt ways to cultivate the friendship of many and he courted the ill rather than the good will of his fellow men. He appeared thoroughly calloused to newspaper criticism and he would not deign to notice a single shaft aimed at either his umpiring or playing. But those who knew him best found beneath the tough exterior a good heart and a liberal spirit. He was honest to a fault and that he had earned that sort of reputation can be imagined when it is stated that in all the years he was devoted to the game his honesty was never once questioned. In the far west he was looked on by base ball crowds as an Ishmaelite. In the east where he was better known he was considered a model player and one ever ready to put forth his best efforts in the support of the national game. Take him all in all Ferguson was an honored representative of the sport he followed and in his death that sport loses one of its ablest and very best exponents."[112] On at least one occasion, Ferguson was referred to as "Death to Flying Things" and that nickname is now credited to him in various baseball reference books, but at the time it was more commonly used to describe Chapman.

John A. Galvin: John Galvin was born around 1841 and played for the Powhatan and Osceola clubs before becoming a regular for the Atlantics from 1863 to 1867. After acquiring a reputation as a hard hitter and a versatile defender, he moved on to the Mutuals and a one-game major league career. Galvin later worked for the city works department and died in Brooklyn on April 20, 1904.[113]

George William Hall: George Hall was born on March 29, 1849, in Stepney, England, and grew up in Brooklyn. After playing for the Stars in 1869, he joined the Atlantics in 1870 and went on to a major league career during which he was known as a splendid hitter and "as good a thrower as ever stepped on the ball-field."[114] During the five years of the National Association, he played for four different teams, including the champion Red Stockings of Boston in 1874. Hall led the National League in home runs with five in 1876, while playing for the Athletics. When the Philadelphia club was expelled from the league at the end of the season, he joined the Louisville Grays. His career ended abruptly when he was banned for life for his role in the 1877 game-fixing scandal. Hall returned to New York and became an engraver like his father. In 1884, the banned player, then 35, attempted to play for a team on Long Island. His identity was discovered, and he was not allowed to continue. Hall died on June 11, 1923, in Ridgewood, New York.

Tice Hamilton: Tice Hamilton played the outfield for the Atlantics from 1857 to 1860. Subsequent notes had him farming in the country, so he is almost certainly a man named Stephen Tyson "Tice" Hamilton who was born in Jamaica, Queens, in 1832 and worked as a milkman before moving to a farm in Mattituck, Long Island. This man raised a large family and was still in Suffolk County at the turn of the century.

William H. Hawxhurst: William Hawxhurst, a reserve in 1859 and 1860 and a regular in 1861, was born in Oyster Bay, Long Island, on September 4, 1835. His family moved to Brooklyn when he was an infant, and he became a volunteer firefighter. After working as a ship carpenter at the Brooklyn Navy Yard, he joined the Building Department and worked his way up to chief inspector. He died in Flatbush on December 10, 1912.[115]

Mike Henry: Mike Henry never played for the Atlantic Club and was never even an officer, although he was named a director in 1870. Nonetheless, his role in the club was considerable, as Jack Chapman explained in 1905: "Mike Henry, before moving up near Boerum place, kept a small place on Fulton street, near York, where several of the players called, but there was no club room or headquarters. For several years the Atlantic Club held its meetings at the old Willoughby Shades, then corner of Willoughby and Adams streets, kept by Paul Mead, and later by Humphrey Hartshorn. The case of baseballs was there on exhibition during these years. It was a most respectable place and run on the same plan as Tom Blankley's old Bank and the old Abbey that were further up Fulton Street in those days. A number of the older members dropped out or died during those years and when the Willoughby Shades gave up business and Mike Henry started a café over on Fulton Street, next to the corner of Boerum place, the members loaned the case and the balls to him. He placed them on exhibition and held them for some time. The Atlantic Club had its rooms and headquarters upstairs."[116] Henry also seems to have played a role in recruiting new players, since Henry Chadwick later claimed that "After Pratt left Mike Henry induced the Eckford battery, Zettlein and Charley Mills to join the Atlantics."[117] In 1889, it was reported that Henry was insane and a benefit game was to be played.[118] He died four months later.[119]

John B. Holder: John Holder was born in Detroit, Michigan, on July 11, 1834, and played second base for the Atlantics in 1857 before joining the Excelsiors. According to Henry Chadwick, he was known as "Easy Going Jack" and was "quite a ball player in his day." Chadwick recalled that during the Fashion Course matches of 1858,"A friend of [Holder's] said to him before he went to the bat in one of the

innings of the games, 'Johnny, I'll bet you'll be put out.' 'I will, eh?' responded John. 'Just you wait and see me make a home run.' At the same moment a bet was made of $100 to $75 that John would make a home run, and, of course, John's play at the bat immediately became deeply interesting. He waited until he got a ball to suit him (in those days the batsman had it all his own way, and he could make the pitcher pitch him 50 or 60 balls before he was suited); getting a nice one, John hit it about two feet from the ground, and away it went flying over the centre fielder's head, John scoring a clean home run and getting $25 for the feat from the friend who had won his bet." But according to Chadwick, like fellow Atlantic Club member John Oliver, Holder "lost his health after he stopped playing ball, and ... died early of consumption induced by neglect of himself."[120] He was only 40 when he died in Brooklyn on September 6, 1874.

Charles Hunt: See Mutual Base Ball Club.

John Henry Ireland: John H. Ireland was elected secretary of the Atlantics in 1858 and played in a few first-nine games and several second-nine games. Ireland was born in New York in April of 1837 and died in Spring Lake, New Jersey on July 30, 1917.

John J. Kenney: John Kenney was a Brooklyn native who was a regular in the Atlantics' outfield in 1867 and a key reserve in subsequent seasons. After playing briefly in the major leagues, he worked for the city as a hydrant inspector. Kenney died in Brooklyn on August 7, 1893.

Stephen A. Mann: Stephen A. Mann was vice president of the Atlantics in 1856 and played several games for both the first and second nine in the late 1850s. He also served as chairman of the arrangements committee for the Atlantics' second annual ball, held at the Musical Hall on December 12, 1859. Mann is presumed to be a sailmaker who was born in New York around 1835. His date of death is unknown.

Frederick Sterling Massey: Fred Massey pitched several games for the Atlantics in 1863. He was born in 1839 in Brownville, Jefferson County, New York, and was a law student while playing for the Atlantic Club. He was also a volunteer firefighter with Pacific Engine Company No. 14, "a 'nobby' organization" that purchased its own fire engine and engine house at staggering prices.[121] In 1869 he became president of the Board of Commissioners that oversaw Brooklyn's first paid fire department. Massey was named president of the board of public works in 1879 and then a justice of the peace four years later. In this position he earned a reputation for embodying "that excellent combination, some law, some business, much intelligence and much heart." He was replaced in 1888 and resumed the practice of law, while also serving as president of the Kings County Inebriates' Home, a position he held until his death on July 19, 1895.[122]

Daniel McDonald: Dan McDonald was born in Brooklyn around 1844 and played for the junior McClellan Club before joining the Atlantics in 1866. He remained the club's right fielder through the end of the 1870 season and then played briefly in the National Association, earning a reputation as "a very heavy batsman, and as fine a fielder as there is in the country."[123] McDonald died on November 23, 1880, in Brooklyn.

Archibald W. McMahon: Archie McMahon was a starter in the Atlantics' outfield from 1857 to 1860. His death in San Francisco was reported in 1869.[124] McMahon's brother lived until 1928 and treasured a picture of his brother playing with the Atlantics until the end.[125]

Charles F. Mills: Charley Mills was a native of Brooklyn, being born there in September of 1844. Despite being six-foot-two, catcher was his natural position, and he was very good at using his long reach to prevent wild pitches. Mills played for the Pacific and Eckford clubs before joining the Atlantics in 1866. He spent three seasons as catcher of the Atlantics, impressing observers like Henry Chadwick both for his skillful play and for "speaking only when necessary."[126] He moved on to the Mutuals and then played briefly in the National Association. Mills was only twenty-nine when he died in Brooklyn on April 9, 1874.

George W. Moore: There is no indication that George W. Moore was much of an athlete, but he was nonetheless involved in numerous club activities, serving as club scorer and on the arrangements committee for the club's annual ball in December of 1859, as well as playing in a muffin-nine game. His involvement with the Atlantic Club ended when he enlisted in the Civil War.[127]

E. C. Morehouse: E. C. Morehouse played on the first nine of the Atlantics in 1855 and 1856 and became club secretary in 1857. He is almost certainly an Edward C. Morehouse who was a founding member of Clinton Hook and Ladder Company No. 2 in 1840. This man was only forty-seven when he died in Brooklyn on May 9, 1867.

James Mowlem: James Mowlem served as club secretary for several years in the mid–1860s. A printer by trade, Mowlem was born on April 10, 1828, in London, England, and died on March 30, 1893, in Flatbush.[128] James Mowlem's brother Gideon was also involved with the club in a non-playing capacity.

Horatio Brinsmade Munn: Horatio B. Munn was born on July 26, 1851, in Newark, New Jersey, and was a reserve for the Atlantics in 1870. He played one major league game and worked as an insurance agent. He died on February 17, 1910, in Brooklyn.

Martin A. O'Brien: Mattie O'Brien was the pitcher of the Atlantics from 1857 to 1862, earning a reputation as "a superior pitcher, an admirable watcher of bases, and withal a gentlemanly and valuable player." Born in Brooklyn around 1831, O'Brien initially worked as an engraver, but later got into the butter and provision business. His death in October of 1865 led the Atlantics to cancel a scheduled game at the Athletics and prompted a heartfelt tribute from his fellow club

members. Six resolutions were adopted at a special meeting, including one stating: "That the case of balls and club room be draped in mourning, and that the flag be hoisted at half mast on every practice day during the remainder of the season." It was also reported that O'Brien's "last thoughts almost were upon his Club, and the game which was to have occurred today, was especially on his mind. He urged upon Charlie Smith, 'to beat the Athletics.'"[129] Henry Chadwick later added that O'Brien was "a thorough gentleman by nature, manly, honorable, kind and considerate, warm hearted and enthusiastic in his friendships and forgiving in his disposition. His enthusiasm in the game knew no bounds. He was completely wrapped up in it."[130]

Peter O'Brien: Peter O'Brien was Mattie's older brother and another of the Atlantic Club's stalwarts, being a fixture in the outfield from 1857 to 1865. He also served as treasurer of the Atlantics from 1856 to 1858. By the time of his brother's death, Pete O'Brien was close to forty and chose to end his ball-playing days. His decision prompted this tribute: "That esteemed member of the Atlantic Club, P. O'Brien, has voluntarily resigned from active service as a playing member of the club, and, at his own request, has been transferred to the list of retired veterans, like Boerum, Price, Oliver, etc., etc. The career of Mr. O'Brien as a ball-player has been one that should be held up as an example to the juniors of the fraternity to follow. As a manly, conscientious player, one incapable of taking an unfair advantage, or of committing a single action on a ball-field in a match not consistent with the most honorable and fair play, P. O'Brien has been without a [peer?] and his reward is a popularity in the fraternity such as any man ought to be proud of. No man who plays ball commands more of the general respect and regard of the members of the metropolitan clubs, and, in fact, of all others who have known him, than this now retired and honored veteran."[131] O'Brien continued to write about the game (under the name "Old Peto Brine") but soon became disillusioned by its post-war growing pains, and in 1868 he observed, "they don't play ball nowadays as they used to."[132] A contractor by profession, Pete O'Brien's life continued to be afflicted with sorrow, most notably the death of his wife. On October 9, 1874, he died of a shotgun wound — whether it was an accident or suicide could not be determined with certainty. Henry Chadwick remembered him as "another of those old fashioned Irishmen, of sterling honesty of character. What a free hearted, outspoken fellow Peter was! What a hearty, firm friend, too."[133]

Joseph Hunter Oliver: Joe Oliver, the younger brother of John, was one of the club's regular outfielders from 1860 to 1864. He was born in Brooklyn on November 25, 1840, and became a retail grocer. He died in Brooklyn on February 9, 1902.

John B. Oliver: John Oliver was born in Brooklyn on October 8, 1838, and seemed destined for stardom when he became the Atlantic Club's second baseman in 1858. According to an 1865 article (probably written by Henry Chadwick), "When John was in full practice, he was considered the best second baseman in the country. He could jump higher, cover more ground than any other baseman and perform all the duties of his position in an unsurpassable manner."[134] But Oliver played less frequently after the 1860 season, and his career ended in 1863. Six years later, on October 12, 1869, he died of tuberculosis in his native Brooklyn. Chadwick later recalled him as "handsome and gentlemanly John Oliver, the most graceful player of the nine, and the model second baseman of his day. John retained his health so long as he engaged in field work during the Summer, but when he relaxed in his exercise he lost health, and finally the seeds of consumption, induced by inattention to proper sanitary rules, led to his early decease."[135]

Dickey Pearce: Many members of the Atlantics had extraordinary careers, but none more so than Dickey Pearce. Pearce was 20 when he joined the club in 1856, which was so early a point in the game's development that he later told Henry Chadwick that the main attraction to him was "plunking the fellows between the bases. I used to enjoy that greatly"[136] One suspects that Pearce was recalling his participation in earlier sandlot play uninformed by the rules adopted by the New York City clubs. He was a mainstay of the Atlantics for the next fifteen years, redefining the shortstop position while also moving behind the plate whenever needed. Yet his lengthy tenure with the Atlantics represented only half of his playing career, which continued in the majors and the high minor leagues until the mid–1880s. Pearce was able to accomplish all this despite standing a mere five feet, three-and-a-half inches because he made up with baseball smarts and determination what he lacked in stature. As William Rankin put it, "No ball player ever displayed his base ball brains to advantage than did Dicky Pearce. It was Dicky who first saw the many possibilities the short field offered, and he was the first to take advantage of them. It was in Dicky's head that many of the 'tricks of the trade' originated, and many of them are in use today. He also invented the bunt in the early '60s, and some years later in trying to draw a bunt away from the third baseman he discovered the fair-foul hit, which was impossible to field, except from foul ground. He also was the first to place the ball in any part of the field he desired."[137] As his playing days were winding down, Pearce did some managing, umpiring, and groundskeeping. He died in Wareham, Massachusetts, on September 18, 1908.

George Palmer Phelps: Born in England around 1829, George Phelps was the pitcher of the Harmony Club in 1855 and was one of the four Harmony players to switch to the Atlantics in 1856. He lost his spot on the first nine in 1857, but played for the club several more times as a reserve and was president of the club. At that point, Phelps enlisted in the 139th New York Infantry and served until 1865, attaining the rank of First Sergeant. Upon his return from service, members and

friends of the Atlantic Club presented him with a light cavalry sword (the sword was auctioned for $37,000 at the Robert Edwards Auctions house in 2005). After the war, he became a letter carrier for the U. S. Postal Service and continued to walk his route until the age of eighty. He died in Harlinger, New Jersey, on June 10, 1915, and an obituary in the *Times* mentioned his time as shortstop of the Atlantics among his many accomplishments.[138]

Boaz Pike: Boaz Pike, the older brother of the much more famous Lipman Pike, was born in New York City on August 27, 1842. He belonged to the second nine of the Atlantics for several years but does not seem to have ever played for the first nine. Even so, he gained a reputation as a power hitter, and in one 1865 second-nine game he "struck the longest ball yet batted on the [Capitoline Grounds], not less, perhaps, than 600 feet straight ahead."[139] Boaz Pike died in New York City on February 14, 1912.

Lipman Emanuel Pike: Lipman Pike was born in New York City on May 25, 1845, and became far and away the best-known Jewish ballplayer of the nineteenth century. Like his older brother, he launched his career with the second nine of the Atlantic Club. He jumped to the Athletics in 1866, but after stints with the Irvingtons and Mutuals, he returned to the Atlantics and played second base for the club in 1869 and 1870. Though not a particularly large man, Pike followed his brother in becoming a noted power hitter. According to an 1868 article while Pike was playing for the Mutuals, "He is the hardest hitter in the nine, and though he does not appear to be strong, he is probably the strongest man in the club."[140] Pike played for eight full seasons in the National Association and its successor, the National League, and continued to embellish his reputation as an outstanding hitter. When he finally retired from baseball, he followed in his father's footsteps as a haberdasher. Pike died in Brooklyn on October 10, 1893.

Thomas S. Powers: Tom Powers helped found the Atlantic Club, served as its first president and treasurer, and played for the first nine in 1855. But in stark contrast to other early members, he was never mentioned in later articles about the club, and his common name makes it impossible to identify him.

Thomas J. Pratt: Tom Pratt was born on January 26, 1844, in Chelsea, Massachusetts, but grew up in Philadelphia and earned a reputation as a first-class cricketer. He also pitched briefly for the Athletics before enlisting in the Civil War. Upon his discharge in 1863, he joined the Atlantics and did much of the club's pitching over the next four years. After returning to Philadelphia in 1867 to pitch for the Quaker City Club, he rejoined the Atlantics in 1868 in a novel role. George Zettlein was now handling the club's pitching, but since substitutions were not allowed under most circumstances, Pratt played the outfield or infield "in matches where it is thought a change pitcher is necessary."[141] After baseball, Pratt became a successful businessman and at one time was said to be a millionaire before suffering financial reverses. He died in Philadelphia on September 28, 1908.

John Griffith Price: John G. Price was one of the four players to switch from the Harmony Club to the Atlantic Club in 1856. Price played for the Atlantics' first nine from 1856 through 1860, mostly at first base, and was occasionally called on as a replacement in subsequent seasons. Price was born around 1834 and became a partner in a firm that made sash hardware. He died in Brooklyn on March 2, 1921, and an obituary in the *Eagle* described him as the last surviving member of the Atlantics.[142] In fact, there were still numerous survivors, including such prominent players as Fred Crane and Joe Start.

Joseph A. Regan: Joseph Regan was one of the Atlantic Club's reserves and served as its corresponding secretary. He was educated at the Seminary of Our Lady of the Angels and died suddenly in 1869.[143]

Harvey H. Ross: Harvey Ross was born around 1820 and was an early member of the Atlantic Club. A man with that surname played one game for the Atlantics' first nine in 1861, and this may have been Harvey. But whether or not it was he, Harvey Ross made a lasting contribution to the club and to the game of baseball. A. J. Reach, one of the first professional players and later a sporting goods magnate, wrote in 1909: "As to the first base balls, my recollection of them dates from about 1855 or '56. The most popular ball in those days was the Ross ball: Harvey Ross, the maker, was a member of the Atlantic Base Ball Club, of Brooklyn, and a sail-maker by trade; his home was on Park Avenue, where he made the balls." According to Reach, Ross and a man named John Van Horn "turned out the best base balls for some years, and they were used in nearly all of the match games that were played up to the early '70s."[144] Ross died in Brooklyn on August 20, 1883.[145]

Frank and George Seinsoth: There were at least two Seinsoth brothers who played for the Atlantics in the early 1860s and possibly more. George was born in Germany around 1827 and was an early volunteer fireman after the family settled in Brooklyn. He worked as a retail produce dealer and died in Brooklyn on April 29, 1892. Frank or Francis was also born in Germany around 1833 and became an ice salesman. He died in Brooklyn on May 24, 1901.

Charles J. Smith: Charley Smith was born in Brooklyn on December 11, 1840, and played for the Atlantics from 1857 to 1870 with only one brief respite. He played only fourteen major league games and is almost entirely forgotten today, but those who saw him play thought him extraordinary. While it is dangerous to put too much weight in the opinions of contemporaries, the assessments of Charley Smith are so uniform and so adulatory that they have to count for something. Smith's versatility enabled him to play several positions, but it was at third base that he really excelled. Henry Chadwick observed that from the time he joined the Atlantics, Smith was "considered a shining light. Charley enjoys the reputation of being the best general player living, and the most reliable in his po-

sition, which is second base. He is captain of the nine, and has an almost magnetic influence over his comrades. He is a general favorite with every one with whom he is acquainted."[146] According to Chadwick, Smith was "an excellent general player; but the moment he sets foot on third base he is what the boys call 'hunky,' that is, 'he's at home.'"[147] Harry Wright similarly called him, "the king of third basemen. He has never had his equal in that position to this day. He was the most graceful and the easiest player I ever saw. Then, too, he was a wonderful all around player. He played well in every position on the diamond, while he was also a great batter and base runner."[148] But Charley Smith walked away from baseball in 1871 and showed so little interest in the game's subsequent development that it was said that he did not know what a bunt was. According to a later account, "In those days, the [Brooklyn] ball tossers played for the fun of the thing and were well taken care of by the politicians. Smith occupied a good berth under Register Billy Barre."[149] (The accuracy of this comment can be confirmed by perusing the other biographies and noting how many of them later worked for the city of Brooklyn.) But eventually he moved outside of city limits and became a farmer. He died on November 15, 1897, in Great Neck.

James E. Smith: James Smith was one of two brothers of Charley Smith who played a few games for the Atlantics. He was born around 1838 and died on May 5, 1867.

Samuel Alpheus Smith, Jr.: S. Alpheus Smith Jr., was another brother of Charley Smith who was one of the Atlantic Club's reserves. Born around 1835, he served in the 28th New York Infantry during the Civil War and died in Brooklyn on July 27, 1912.

Sidney C. Smith: Sid Smith was born on January 6, 1842, and was a reserve in 1862 and 1863, then a starter in the outfield of the Atlantics from 1864 to 1866. He later worked in the city tax office. He died on February 7, 1908, and was reported to be the brother-in-law of Lipman Pike.[150]

Caleb Odell Sniffen: Caleb Sniffen was one of the founders of the Atlantic Club and did much of the club's pitching during its first two seasons. He served as vice president in 1855 and president in 1856 but then "positively declined" to serve another term as president.[151] By then Sniffen was in his mid-thirties, and, as was the case with many of the early members of the Atlantics, his place on the first nine was taken by a younger man. A butcher by profession, Sniffen later moved to Madison, New Jersey, where he died on November 1, 1883. His passing prompted Henry Chadwick to recall Sniffen as "an outspoken, upright veteran, ranking in his peculiarities with those worthy veterans of the old club, the O'Briens.... It is some years since we met him, and he was then the same old lover of the game. Time is rapidly retrieving those ancient landmarks for the path of the national game."[152]

Joseph E. Sprague: see Eckford Base Ball Club.

Joseph Start: Joe Start was born in New York City on October 14, 1842. After a brief stint with the junior Enterprise

Club he joined the Atlantics in 1862, beginning a career that rivaled even Dickey Pearce's for longevity and brilliance. Although of average height and build, Start, because he was left-handed, exclusively played first base. He took advantage to redefine the position, standing off the base before others did (an innovation often incorrectly credited to Charles Comiskey). He also showed an ability to catch poorly thrown balls that was remarkable — especially considering that he did not wear a glove for much of his career. An 1871 article observed, "Start is very effective in taking in low balls, as well as those thrown in over his head, and the hotter they come the more securely they appear to be held; in fact, it is from his being so generally sure in this respect that he derived the soubriquet of 'old reliable.'" Start earned similar praise for his irreproachable integrity at a time when too many players associated with gamblers.[153] After nearly a decade with the Atlantics, Start spent an extraordinary sixteen seasons in the National Association and National League and continued to live up to his nicknames of "Old Steady" and "Old Reliable." Like Charley Gehringer, the epitome of consistency to a later generation of baseball fans, Start married only after many years of caring for his widowed mother. Even so, his marriage lasted for more than four decades. When his playing days finally ended, he and his new wife opened a hotel in Rhode Island. He died in Providence on March 27, 1927.

Thomas Tassie: Thomas Tassie was born in Forres, Scotland, on July 4, 1835, but grew up in Brooklyn, where he became a volunteer fireman for the Engine 14 Company and one of the founders of the Atlantic Club.[154] He played shortstop for the second nine during the club's early years but from the first he was primarily an administrator, serving as club president in 1857, 1858, 1860, and 1869, a delegate to the National Association of Base Ball Players (NABBP) convention in 1866, and as president of the NABBP in 1869. Tassie married Bob Ferguson's half-sister in 1860 and pursued a variety of occupations, running a millinery store, teaching at a truant school, and being a butter dealer in Washington Market. He was also very active in Republican politics.[155] On several occasions there were notes that Tassie had been suffering from a serious illness, and in 1881 he was reported missing from his home, prompting concerns that financial reverses had caused him to take his own life.[156] But he lived a full life, dying in Brooklyn on July 22, 1906.

Augustus C. Tickner: Gus Tickner occasionally played on the first nine of the Atlantics between 1860 and 1863, although his time for baseball during these years was limited because he enlisted in the 84th New York Infantry at the outset of the war and served for a year. Tickner was born in Pennsylvania around 1838, worked as an agent, and died in Brooklyn on May 26, 1924.

Willet P. Whitson: Willet Whitson was the catcher of the Atlantics in 1855. He was already in his mid-thirties, so not surprisingly his playing days ended at that point. Whitson

was a poultry dealer and was reported to be dead in an 1877 article about the Atlantics. In fact, he died in Brooklyn six years later, on December 2, 1883.[157]

George Zettlein: George Zettlein became one of the most celebrated and successful pitchers of the era, being especially well known for the great speed that he was able to generate in spite of the strict delivery restrictions of the era and for "his lasting qualities ... [he] exhibits as much speed in the ninth as in the first innings."[158] Even so, Zettlein's early years remain clouded in mystery (and by the difficulty census-takers had with his German name). He was born in Williamsburgh in either 1843 or 1844, but there is contradictory information about the exact date — a death notice in the *Brooklyn Eagle* implies July 18, 1844, but the 1900 census listing gives July 12, 1843. Zettlein and his two sisters appear to have been orphaned at a young age, but details again have proven elusive. His whereabouts during the war are also difficult to determine. Zettlein would later claim to have "enlisted as a soldier in a company organized by Captain Charles Elliott, of Greenpoint, who was afterward a police justice. He found army life monotonous and early in 1863 he entered the navy and served on Admiral Farragut's flagship in many battles, including those of New Orleans, Vicksburg and Mobile."[159] There is no matching service record, a problem that Zettlein encountered in 1890 when he attempted to collect a pension. But he submitted a wealth of supporting evidence, including hospital records and the sworn affidavits of fellow seamen, and was granted a pension by the U. S. Navy. So it seems safe to assume that he did indeed serve aboard the *US Master Schooner John Griffith*, the *USS N. Carolina*, and the *USS Princeton* from January of 1862 to January of 1865. After pitching for the Star Union and Eckford clubs, Zettlein joined the Atlantics in 1866 and spent the next five years as the club's pitcher. The highlight of his tenure was the 1870 extra-inning thriller in which the Atlantics ended the long unbeaten streak of the Red Stockings. According to one of Zettlein's obituaries, his teammates were willing to call the game a tie after nine innings, but the hard-throwing right-hander insisted, "No, we will play to a finish if it takes us all night. Let it never be said that the Atlantics shirked."[160] He then pitched in the major leagues for six seasons, winning 129 games before retiring after the 1876 campaign. Zettlein then worked for the Brooklyn district attorney for several years and later ran a liquor store. But by the 1890s, failing health made it difficult to work. Zettlein's pension application suggests that the underlying problem may have been a wartime hernia, an injury that forced him to wear a truss for many years. If so, his pitching exploits are all the more impressive. An article written shortly before his death suggested that a baseball injury may have been responsible. Zettlein was known for frequently being hit by line drives during his pitching days. The article reported that "physicians discovered a tumorous growth in the abdomen, which might have been produced by a blow from a swiftly propelled baseball or any hard material. Zettlein for years complained of the big, round hard lump in his abdomen. He said, in answer to the doctors' questions, that he had received many hard raps in the 'bread basket' from baseballs, batted straight out, while he was in the pitcher's box."[161] Zettlein, who never married, died at his sister's home in Patchogue, New York, on May 22, 1905.

Other Club Members: Henry J. Adair, G. W. Benton, P. Bodeman, Brace, John Brown, James Buckley, Butler, Sam Carhart, E. Charman, Chichester, Colyer, Edwin Connor, James H. Cornwell Jr., Delany, Denbigh, Earl, A. Gildersleeve, Haight, C. Haskins, Haywood, J. Irvin or Irwin, Lambert, Edward Lewis, W. H. Lockwood, James Loper, Lowery, Martin, Thomas McGunigle, McIlvane, Thomas R. Mercein, Samuel V. Millard, Samuel H. Mumby, Professor Nichols, O'Flynn or O. Flynn, Owen, Charles W. Peed, Pendleton, Pettibone, George R. Rogers, Seibert, George C. Sexton, Simonson, T. Swalton or Swaltes, Benjamin Van Delft, A. Vilat, Wallsworth, J. Watson, E. Webber, "Ike" Weeks, S. C. Whitehead.

It must be noted that as of 1866 the Atlantic Club had 170 active members and 50 honorary members, which meant that many club members never represented the club in first or second nine matches. The above listing thus only scratches the surface of the club membership and is heavily weighted to those with exceptional athletic skills. The Atlantic Base Ball Club was much broader than that in scope and many members cared more about the social aspects than the wins and losses. There were also several cases in which a man's obituary claimed that he was affiliated with the Atlantic Club but no confirmation could be found, such as Alfred R. Bretell, Hugh Norton, Evans Smith, and Joe Quigley.[162] It is entirely possible that each of these men was an active member of the Atlantic Club even if he never played for the first nine.

Abbreviations

BDE = *Brooklyn Daily Eagle*
NYC = *New York Clipper*
NYDT = *New-York Daily Times*
NYSM = *[New York] Sunday Mercury*
NYT = *New York Times*
PSOT = *Porter's Spirit of the Times*
SOT — *Spirit of the Times*
WSOT = *Wilkes' Spirit of the Times*

Notes

1. Charles A. Peverelly, *The Book of American Pastimes, Containing a History of the Principal Base Ball, Cricket, Rowing, and Yachting Clubs of the United States* (New York: Published by the Author, 1866); reprinted as John Freyer and Mark Rucker, eds., *Peverelly's National Game* (Charleston, S.C.: Arcadia, 2005). The assessment of the Atlantics will be found on p. 61 of the reprint, to which subsequent endnotes will refer.

2. John Clark, "From Milan: A Visit to ex-Sheriff McNamee's Studio at Florence: The Artist Up to His Ears in Work, but Full of Brooklyn Gossip and Reminiscence — Old Times and Old Politics Talked Over — Art Matters Referred to Incidentally," *BDE*, vol. 37, no. 10 (14 Jan 1876), p. 2, cols. 5-6. The article is in the form of a letter dated "Milan, December 28, 1875."

3. "Our National Game: The Game of Baseball: The Atlantic B.B.

Club Champion: Account of the Principal Games: The Play of Ten Years: Brooklyn against the World" [hereafter cited as "Account of the Principal Games"], *BDE*, vol. 25, no. 169 (24 Aug 1865), p. 2, cols. 4-6. The 14 August 1855 founding date is also reported in "Famous Old Times Games," *BDE*, vol. 57, no. 329 (28 Nov 1897), p. 9, cols. 5-6.

4. "Not Like They Used to Play: A Veteran of the Diamond Tells of the Early Days: Baseball 40 Years Ago," *Washington Post*, no. 5,222 (8 Aug 1892), p. 6, cols. 2-3.

5. "Our Washington Letter: The Week's Doings at the National Capital," *BDE*, vol. 52, no. 281 (9 Oct 1892), p. 4, cols. 3-5.

6. The first two games were reported in the news clipping "Base Ball — Atlantic Club" (written by Atlantic Club secretary J. H. Ackerman) and the third in the news clipping "Married vs. Single of the Atlantic Club," both pasted in vol. 1a, p. 4 of The Charles Mears Collection on Baseball, Cleveland Public Library [hereafter cited as Mears Collection]. The publication in which these articles appeared has not yet been identified. The first and third games were also reported in "Base Ball: Atlantic Club," *SOT*, vol. 25, no. 28 (25 Aug 1855), p. 336, col. 2, and "Bedford Club — Married vs. Single," *SOT*, vol. 25, no. 33 (29 Sep 1855), p. 391.

7. "Base Ball — Atlantic versus Harmony Club," undated Oct 1855 *NYC* clipping in Mears Collection, vol. 1a, p. 5; Peverelly, p. 61.

8. Henry Chadwick, "The Old Atlantics: Henry Chadwick Gives Some History," *BDE*, vol. 56, no. 78 (19 Mar 1896), p. 2, cols. 3-4.

9. "Base Ball," *SOT*, vol. 25, no. 43 (8 Dec 1855), p. 511, col. 3.

10. "Base Ball," *BDE*, vol. 15, no. 169 (16 July 1856), p. 2, col. 2; "Long Island," *NYDT*, vol. 5, no. 1508 (19 July 1856), p. 8, col. 2.

11. "The Atlantics and the Empires," *NYC*, vol. 4, no. 15 (2 Aug 1856), p. 115, col. 4.

12. This decision was reported in Letter, Robert Justison, Jr., John H. Graham, Charles B. Wylie, Edward Van Voorhis, William Julian, Jun., and several others, to Frank Queen (editor of the *New York Clipper*), undated, published in "Card," *NYC*, vol. 4, no. 21 (13 Sep 1856), p. 167, col. 3.

13. "Base Ball," *BDE*, vol. 15, no. 169 (16 Jul 1856), p. 2, col. 2. For another account of the game, see "Base Ball," *NYC*, undated Jul 1856 clipping in Mears Collection.

14. The score of this game was recorded in an end-of-the-year listing of games played in 1856 that was initially published in the *Sunday Mercury* and later reprinted in *PSOT*, vol. 1, no. 17 (27 Dec 1856), p. 277, col. 1. No account of this game has yet been found, but it was likely reported in an issue of the *Sunday Mercury* that has not survived.

15. The *Sunday Mercury* remarks and the response of the four players were reported in "Card" (ref. 12).

16. This letter also appeared in "Card" (ref. 12).

17. "City News and Gossip: Base Ball," *BDE*, vol. 15, no. 217 (10 Sep 1856), p. 3, col. 1; "Base Ball: Gotham and Atlantic," *PSOT*, vol. 1, no. 3 (20 Sep 1856), p. 37, col. 3.

18. "Atlantic vs. Baltic," *NYC*, vol. 4, no. 23 (27 Sep 1856), p. 183, col. 2; "Base Ball," *PSOT*, vol. 1, no. 4 (27 Sep 1856), p. 53, col. 2.

19. "Atlantic vs. Columbia," *NYC*, vol. 4, no. 24 (4 Oct 1856), p. 186, col. 4; "Base Ball," *PSOT*, vol. 1, no. 5 (4 Oct 1856), p. 86, col. 1.

20. "Baltic vs. Atlantic" and "Atlantic vs. Columbia," *NYC*, vol. 4, no. 27 (25 Oct 1856), p. 211, col. 4; "Base Ball," *PSOT*, vol. 1, no. 8 (25 Oct 1856), p. 133, col. 2.

21. "Base Ball," *SOT*, vol. 27, no. 11 (25 Apr 1857), p. 126, col. 3.

22. "Base Ball," *PSOT*, vol. 2, no. 18 (4 Jul 1857), p. 276, col. 2; "Base Ball," *BDE*, vol. 16, no. 164 (15 Jul 1857), p. 3, col. 1.

23. "Atlantic and Putnam," *NYC*, vol. 5, no. 15 (1 Aug 1857), p. 115, col. [x]; "Out-Door Sports: Base Ball: Base Ball" *PSOT*, vol. 2, no. 22 (1 Aug 1857), p. 341, col. 2.

24. Peverelly, p. 61. A contemporary account of this game has not yet been found.

25. A Gotham-Atlantic game for this date was announced in "City News and Gossip: Base Ball," *BDE*, vol. 16, no. 164 (15 Jul 1857), p. 3, col. 1.

26. "Match between the Gothams and Atlantics," *NYC*, vol. 5, no.

20 (5 Sep 1857), p. 159, col. [xx]; "Out-Door Sports: Base Ball: The Gotham and Atlantic," *PSOT,* vol. 3, no. 3 (19 Sep 1857), p. 37, col. 2

27. "Eckford vs. Atlantic," *NYC,* vol. 5, no. 23 (26 Sep 1857), p. 183, col. [xx]; "Out-Door Sports: Base Ball: Match between the Eckford and Atlantic Base Ball Clubs," *PSOT,* vol. 3, no. 4 (26 Sep 1857), p. 53, col. 2; Peverelly, pp. 62 and 73. A contemporary account of the second Eckford game has not yet been found.

28. "Continental vs. Atlantic," *NYC,* vol. 5, no. 26 (17 Oct 1857), p. 205; "Atlantic vs. Continental," *NYC,* vol. 5, no. 27 (24 Oct 1857), p. 212.

29. Peverelly, p. 62. A contemporary account of this game has not yet been found.

30. "Gotham vs. Atlantic," *NYC,* vol. 5, no. 27 (24 Oct 1857), p. 212; "Gotham vs. Atlantic," undated *NYSM* clipping in Mears Collection.

31. X., "Base Ball: Base Ball Sketches — No. 5," *PSOT,* vol. 3, no. 12 (21 Nov 1857), p. 180, col. 1.

32. "Out-Door Sports: Base-Ball: Putnam vs. Atlantic," *PSOT,* vol. 4, no. 17 (26 Jun 1858), p. 261, col. 1; "Atlantic vs. Putnam," undated *NYC* clipping in Mears Collection.

33. "Liberty vs. Atlantic," *NYC,* vol. 6, no. 23 (25 Sep 1858), p. 182, col. [xx]; "Base Ball," *BDE,* vol. 17, no. 243 (13 Oct 1858), p. 3, col. 2.

34. "Out-Door Sports: Base-Ball: Atlantic vs. Putnam," *PSOT,* vol. 5, no. 8 (23 Oct 1858), p. 116, col. 3; "Out-Door Sports: Base-Ball: Putnam vs. Atlantic," *PSOT,* vol. 5, no. 9 (30 Oct 1858), p. 134, col. 3.

35. "Out-Door Sports: Base-Ball: Matches to Come," *PSOT,* vol. 5, no. 8 (23 Oct 1858), p. 116, col. 2; "Out-Door Sports: Base-Ball: Atlantic vs. Gotham," *PSOT,* vol. 5, no. 9 (30 Oct 1858), p. 135, col. 1; "Atlantic vs. Gotham," *NYSM,* 31 Oct 1858.

36. "Out-Door Sports: Base-Ball: Atlantic vs. Excelsior," *PSOT,* vol. 5, no. 12 (20 Nov 1858), p. 180, col. 3; a copy of the undated Sunday Mercury clipping is in the Mears Collection.

37. "Out-Door Sports: Base-Ball: Atlantic vs. Excelsior," *PSOT,* vol. 5, no. 13 (27 Nov 1858), p. 197, cols. 1–2.

38. "Base Ball: Atlantic vs. Eckford," *NYT,* vol. 8, no. 2434 (9 Jul 1859), p. 8, col. 1; "Out-Door Sports: Base-Ball: Eckford vs. Atlantic," *PSOT,* vol. 6, no. 20 (16 Jul 1859), p. 308, col. 3 & p. 309, col. 1; "Atlantic vs. Eckford," *NYC,* vol. 7, no. 13 (16 Jul 1859), p. 99.

39. "Eckford vs. Atlantic," *NYC,* vol. 7, no. 22 (17 Sep 1859), p. 173.

40. "Out-Door Sports: Base Ball: Atlantic vs. Eckford," *NYT,* vol. 8, no. 2487 (9 Sep 1859), p. 5, col. 2; "City News and Gossip: Atlantic vs. Eckford," *BDE,* vol. 18, no. 215 (9 Sep 1859), p. 3, col. 1; "Out-Door Sports: Base-Ball: Grand Match in Brooklyn: Atlantic vs. Eckford," *PSOT,* vol. 7, no. 3 (17 Sep 1859), p. 36, cols. 1–2.

41. *New York Atlas,* October 13, 1859.

42. "Out-Door Sports: Base-Ball: Atlantic vs. Eckford," *PSOT,* vol. 7, no. 8 (22 Oct 1859), p. 117, cols. 2–3.

43. "Base Ball: Baltic, of New-York, vs. Atlantic, of Brooklyn," *NYT,* vol. 8, no. 2473 (24 Aug 1859), p. 8, col. 3

44. "Star vs. Atlantic," *NYC,* vol. 7, no. 29 (5 Nov 1859), p. 229.

45. "City News and Gossip: Base Ball — Excelsiors vs. Atlantic," *BDE,* vol. 19, no. 171 (20 Jul 1860), p. 3, col. 1; "Base Ball: Excelsior vs. Atlantic — The Excelsiors Victorious — The Champion Club Beaten," *NYT,* vol. 9, no. 2755 (20 Jul 1860), p. 8, cols. 4–5; "Excelsior vs. Atlantic: The Match for the Championship," *NYC,* vol. 8, no. 14 (21 Jul 1860), p. 108; "Out-Door Sports: Base-Ball: Excelsior vs. Atlantic — The Excelsior Victorious — The Champion Club Beaten," *PSOT,* vol. 8, no. 22 (24 Jul 1860), p. 340, cols. 1–3; "Base Ball — Excelsior vs. Atlantic," *SOT,* vol. 30, no. 25 (28 Jul 1860), p. 304, col. 1; "Grand Match of the Season: Excelsior vs. Atlantic," *NYC,* vol. 8, no. 15 (28 Jul 1860), p. 116; "Out-Door Sports: Base Ball: Match between the Excelsior and Atlantic Clubs," *WSOT,* vol. 2, no. 21 (28 Jul 1860), p. 331, col. 2.

46. "Base Ball: Grand Ball Match at Bedford," *BDE,* vol. 19, no. 189 (10 Aug 1860), p. 2, col. 4; "Out-Door Sports: Base Ball," *NYT,* vol. 9, no. 2773 (10 Aug 1860), p. 8, cols. 3–4; "Out-Door Sports: Base-Ball: Atlantic vs. Excelsior," *PSOT,* vol. 8, no. 25 (14 Aug 1860), p. 388, cols.

2–3; "Grand Base Ball Match: The Atlantics Victorious: Excelsior vs. Atlantic," *NYC,* vol. 8, no. 18 (18 Aug 1860), p. 141; "Out-Door Sports: Base Ball: Atlantic of Bedford vs. Excelsior of Brooklyn," *WSOT,* vol. 2, no. 24 (18 Aug 1860), p. 378, cols. 2–3.

47. *New York Clipper,* October 27, 1860.

48. "Base Ball: Atlantic vs. Eckford," *BDE,* vol. 19, no. 253 (23 Oct 1860), p. 3, col. 1; "Base Ball: Atlantic vs. Eckford," *NYT,* vol. 10, no. 2836 (23 Oct 1860), p. 8, col. 5; "Out-Door Sports: Base Ball: Eckford vs. Atlantic," *PSOT,* vol. 9, no. 9 [*sic:* 10] (30 Oct 1860), p. 149, cols. 1–2; "Grand Match at Bedford," *NYC,* vol. 8, no. 29 (3 Nov 1860), p. 229; "Out-Door Sports: Base Ball: Atlantic vs. Eckford," *WSOT,* vol. 3, no. 9 (3 Nov 1860), p. 133, cols. 1–2.

49. "Base Ball: Newark vs. Atlantic," *BDE,* vol. 20, no. 184 (6 Aug 1861), p. 3, col. 2; "Atlantic, of Brooklyn, vs. Newark, of Newark," undated Aug 1861 *NYC* clipping in the Mears Collection.

50. "Base Ball: Contest for the Championship — The Atlantics Defeated," *BDE,* vol. 20, no. 234 (4 Oct 1861), p. 2, cols. 5–6.

51. "Ball Match for the Aid of the U.S. Sanitary Committee — Ball Players Patriots — Eckford vs. Atlantic — The Champions Defeated" *BDE,* vol. 21, no. 164 (12 Jul 1862), p. 2, col. 6; "Atlantic vs. Eckford," undated Jul 1862 *NYC* clipping in the Mears Collection.

52. "Brooklyn News: Base Ball Match: Atlantic Club vs. Eckford Club," *NYT,* vol. 11, no. 3378 (22 Jul 1862), p. 8, col. 5; "Great Base Ball Match: Second Contest for the Championship Silver Ball: Atlantic versus Eckford — The Atlantic Club Victorious," *BDE,* vol. 21, no. 172 (22 Jul 1862), p. 2, col. 5–6; "The Grand Match for the Championship: The Atlantics the Victors," undated Jul 1862 *NYC* clipping in the Mears Collection.

53. "Base Ball," *NYT,* vol. 11, no. 3429 (19 Sep 1862), p. 3, col. 1; "The Grand Match for the Championship: The Eckfords Victorious and the Champions: A Fine Contest and a Remarkably Small Score: A Fair Field and No Favor Shown," undated Sep 1862 *NYC* clipping in the Mears Collection.

54. "Base Ball: Atlantic vs. Harlem," *BDE,* vol. 21, no. 226 (17 Sep 1862), p. 2, col. 3; "Harlem vs. Atlantic," undated Sep 1862 *NYC* clipping in the Mears Collection.

55. "Base Ball: Another Grand Match — Atlantic of Brooklyn vs. Mutual of N. York — Brooklyn Defeated," *BDE,* vol. 21, no. 226 (23 Sep 1862), p. 2, cols. 5–6; "Atlantic vs. Mutual," undated Sep 1862 *NYC* clipping in the Mears Collection.

56. Peverelly, p. 64.

57. "Atlantic vs. Eckford: The Eckfords the Victors: An Immense Assemblage of Spectators" and "Atlantic vs. Eckford: Eight Thousand Spectators Present: The Atlantics again Defeated," undated Sep 1863 *NYC* clippings in the Mears Collection; "Out Door Sports — Base Ball: The Grand Ball Match at Williamsburgh — Over Six Thousand Spectators Present — The Eckford Club Again Successful," *BDE,* vol. 22, no. 218 (9 Sep 1863), p. 2, cols. 5–6.

58. "Grand Base Ball Match: New York Players versus Brooklyn: 5,000 People Present: The New Yorkers Victorious: Great Excitement at the Close: Almost a Row," *BDE,* vol. 22, no. 156 (4 Aug 1863), p. 2, cols. 5–6; "An Exciting Contest at Brooklyn: The Atlantic vs. Mutual: The Mutuals Victorious by One Run," undated Aug 1863 *NYC* clipping in Mears Collection.

59. "Mutual vs. Atlantic " and "Atlantic vs. Mutual — The Brooklyn Club Victorious," undated Sep 1863 *NYC* clippings in Mears Collection; "Sports and Pastimes: Base Ball — The Grand Matches for the Championship — Atlantic vs. Mutual — Eckford vs. Union — Brooklyn Victorious in Both Games," *BDE,* vol. 22, no. 232 (25 Sep 1863), p. 2, col. 6.

60. "Sports and Pastimes: Base Ball: The Champion Club," *BDE,* vol. 24, no. 184 (8 Aug 1864), p. 2, col. 6.

61. "Sports and Pastimes: Base Ball: Eckford vs. Atlantic," *BDE,* vol. 24, no. 236 (10 Oct 1864), p. 2, col. 6.

62. "Sports and Pastimes: The Grand Base Ball Match at Hoboken — An Immense Assemblage of Spectators Present — The Brooklyn Club Victorious," *BDE,* vol. 24, no. 154 (28 Jun 1864), p. 2, col. 6; "The At-

lantic of Brooklyn vs. the Mutual of New York: The Atlantics the Victors: A Poorly Played Game," undated Jul 1864 *NYC* clipping in Mears Collection.

63. "Sports and Pastimes: Base Ball: Atlantic vs. Mutual," *BDE*, vol. 24, no. 182 (13 Sep 1864), p. 3, col. 6; "Atlantic vs. Mutual," undated Sep 1864 *NYC* clipping in Mears Collection.

64. "The Grand International Match at Rochester: Canada vs. United States — The Yankee Boys Victorious: The Young Canadian of Woodstock, C.W. vs. Atlantic of Brooklyn, New York: The Atlantics the Victors by a score of 75 to 11," undated Sep 1864 *NYC* clipping in Mears Collection.

65. "Sports and Pastimes: Another Grand Base Ball Match — Atlantic vs. Resolute — The Resolutes Distanced — Tremendous Batting of the Atlantics — Score 18 to 1!" *BDE*, vol. 24, no. 172 (20 Jul 1864), p. 2, col. 6; "Atlantic vs. Resolute," undated Jul 1864 *NYC* clipping in Mears Collection.

66. "Sports and Pastimes: The First Grand Base Ball Match at Bedford — The Empires vs. Atlantics — Result, a Tie Game — The Atlantics in a Tight Spot," *BDE*, vol. 24, no. 157 (1 Jul 1864), p. 2, col. 6; "Atlantic vs. Empire," undated Jul 1864 *NYC* clipping in Mears Collection.

67. "Sports and Pastimes: Base Ball: The Champions Again in the Field — They Defeat the Empire Club," *BDE*, vol. 25, no. 118 (22 Jun 1865), p. 2, col. 6; "Empire vs. Atlantic," undated Jun 1865 *NYC* clipping in Mears Collection.

68. "Sports and Pastimes: Base Ball: Atlantic vs. Union," *BDE*, vol. 25, no. 143 (25 Jul 1865), p. 2, col. 6; "Atlantic vs. Union," undated Jul 1865 *NYC* clipping in Mears Collection; "Sports and Pastimes: Base Ball: Unparal[l]eled Game — The Atlantics defeat the Empires by a Score of 65–3," *BDE*, vol. 25, no. 146 (28 Jul 1865), p. 2, cols. 5–6; (2) "Keystone vs. Atlantic — Closing Match of the Philadelphians — Excursion to Coney Island and Welcome by Mayor Wood," *BDE*, vol. 25, no. 146 (31 Jul 1865), p. 2, col. 7; untitled and undated Aug 1865 *NYC* clipping in Mears Collection.

69. "An Exciting Base Ball Match: Contest for the Championship: Atlantics Still Champions: A Close and Exciting Game," *BDE*, vol. 25, no. 152 (4 Aug 1865), p. 2, col. 5; "Mutual of New York vs. Atlantic of Brooklyn: The Best Championship Match on Record: The Atlantics Still the Champions: Twenty Thousand Spectators Present: The Clerk of the Weather Interferes with the Game," undated Aug 1865 *NYC* clipping in Mears Collection.

70. "Base Ball Excitement: Championship Game: 20,000 Spectators: The Atlantics the Champions of the World: Brooklyn Holds the Streamer," *BDE*, vol. 25, no. 161 (15 Aug 1865), p. 2, cols. 4–5; "Mutuals vs. Atlantics: The Second Contest for the Championship: The Atlantics Victorious: A Fine Batting Game but a Poor Display in the Field," undated Aug 1865 *NYC* clipping in Mears Collection.

71. "Sports and Pastimes: Base Ball: The Visiting Club — Atlantic vs. Lowell," *BDE*, vol. 25, no. 140 (21 Jul 1865), p. 2, col. 6; "Lowell vs. Atlantic," undated Jul 1865 *NYC* clipping in Mears Collection; (1) "Our National Game: The Champions in Boston — The Trip to the 'Hub' — Scenes en-Voyage — Reception, Sight-Seeing, Hospitality, etc.," *BDE*, vol. 25, no. 196 (25 Sep 1865), p. 2, col. 5; "The 'Atlantics' in Boston: The Champions Carry Everything Before Them," *BDE*, vol. 25, no. 198 (27 Sep 1865), p. 2, col. 4; "The 'Atlantics' in Boston: Second Days Play — The Atlantics again Victorious — An Unparalelled Game — Score 107 to 16" *BDE*, vol. 25, no. 198 (27 Sep 1865), p. 2, col. 4; "The 'Atlantics' in Boston: Third Day's Game — The College Boys at Base Ball — Brooklyn beats Harvard — Score 58 to 22," *BDE*, vol. 25, no. 100 (29 Sep 1865), p. 2, cols. 6–7; "The 'Atlantics' at Hartford: The Last Day's Play — Continued Victory — The Total Scores 232 to 59," *BDE*, vol. 25, no. 101 (30 Sep 1865), p. 2, col. 5; "Atlantic vs. Boston and Hartford Clubs," undated Oct 1865 *NYC* clipping in Mears Collection.

72. "Base Ball Circles: Atlantic vs. Eureka — Another Exciting Contest — The Atlantic Still Champion — Game 21 to 20," *BDE*, vol. 25, no. 165 (19 Aug 1865), p. 2, col. 4; "The Third Match for the Championship: Eureka of Newark vs. Atlantics: One of the Most Exciting Games of the Season: The Atlantics in a Tight Spot: Score, 21 to 20," undated Aug

1865 *NYC* clipping in Mears Collection; "Sports and Pastimes: An Exciting Championship Game — Atlantic vs. Eureka — The Champions Win by One Run," *BDE*, vol. 25, no. 176 (1 Sep 1865), p. 2, col. 6; "Atlantic vs. Eureka: An Exciting Contest," undated Sep 1865 *NYC* clipping in Mears Collection.

73. "Our National Game: Atlantic vs. Eckford — A Close and Exciting Encounter," *BDE*, vol. 25, no. 194 (22 Sep 1865), p. 2, col. 5; "Eckford vs. Atlantic," undated Sep 1865 *NYC* clipping in Mears Collection; "The Great Championship Game — The Atlantics Defeat the Eckfords — Score, 35–8," *BDE*, vol. 25, no. 213 (14 Oct 1865), p. 2, col. 6; "Eckford vs. Atlantic," undated Oct 1865 *NYC* clipping in Mears Collection; "The National Game: Atlantic vs. Union, of Morrisania," *BDE*, vol. 25, no. 106 (6 Oct 1865), p. 2, col. 6; "Union vs. Atlantic," undated Oct 1865 *NYC* clipping in Mears Collection.

74. Our National Game: Atlantic versus Athletic: Brooklyn Still Champion: Hospitable Treatment of the Keystones: The 'Atlantics' Win the Game: Score Twenty-One Runs to Fifteen," *BDE*, vol. 25, no. 227 (31 Oct 1865), p. 2, cols. 5–6; "Athletic vs. Atlantic," undated Nov 1865 *NYC* clipping in Mears Collection.

75. "Our National Game: Atlantic vs. Athletic — The Details of the Game — An Evening Entertainment — A Visit to Hooley's Minstrels — Speeches, &c., &c.," *BDE*, vol. 25, no. 233 (7 Nov 1865), p. 2, col. 6; "The Championship: The Last Grand Match of the Season: Philadelphia vs. Brooklyn: Athletic vs. Atlantic," undated Nov 1865 *NYC* clipping in Mears Collection.

76. "Our National Game: The Season Formally Closed — Atlantics vs. A Picked Nine — The Champions the Winners," *BDE*, vol. 25, no. 251 (28 Nov 1865), p. 3, col. 5; "Closing Games of the Season," undated Nov 1865 *NYC* clipping in Mears Collection.

77. "Sports and Pastimes: Base Ball: Atlantic vs. Irvingtons — The Champions Defeated — An Experimental Failure," *BDE*, vol. 26, no. 140 (15 Jun 1866), p. 2, col. 7; "The Champions go to Jersey — What Comes of it — They Catch a Tartar," undated Jun 1866 *NYSM* clipping in the Mears Collection.

78. "Sports vs. Pastimes: Base Ball: Atlantic vs. Eureka — The Champions in 'Jersey' Again," *BDE*, vol. 26, no. 174 (15 Aug 1866), p. 2, col. 7; "Atlantic vs. Eureka," undated Aug 1866 *NYSM* clipping in the Mears Collection.

79. "Sports and Pastimes: Base Ball: The Grand Base Ball Match," *BDE*, vol. 26, no. 221 (16 Oct 1866), p. 2, cols. 6–7; "The Grand Match for the Championship — The Atlantic Club Still the Champions — Fifteen Thousand People Present," undated Oct 1866 *NYSM* clipping in the Mears Collection.

80. "Sports and Pastimes: Base Ball: Atlantic vs. Athletic — Defeat of the Champions," *BDE*, vol. 26, no. 227 (23 Oct 1866), p. 3, col. 6; "Atlantic vs. Athletic," undated Oct 1866 *NYSM* clipping in the Mears Collection.

81. "Sports and Pastimes: Base Ball: The Match for the Championship — Brooklyn Again Victorious — Atlantic vs. Irvington," *BDE*, vol. 26, no. 203 (25 Sep 1866), p. 2, cols. 6–7; "Atlantic vs. Irvington," undated Sep 1866 *NYSM* clipping in the Mears Collection; "Base Ball — Match for the Championship — The Eurekas After the Atlantics — The latter Win the Day," *BDE*, vol. 26, no. 206 (28 Sep 1866), p. 2, col. 6; "Atlantic vs. Eureka," undated Sep 1866 *NYSM* clipping in the Mears Collection; "Sports and Pastimes: Base Ball: Another Championship Match: Atlantic vs. Eureka," *BDE*, vol. 26, no. 230 (26 Oct 1866), p. 3, col. 2; "Atlantic vs. Eureka," undated Oct 1866 *NYSM* clipping in the Mears Collection; "Sports and Pastimes: Base Ball: Atlantic vs. Irvington," *BDE*, vol. 26, no. 233 (30 Oct 1866), p. 2, col. 7; "Atlantic vs. Irvington," undated Oct 1866 *NYSM* clipping in the Mears Collection.

82. "The Atlantics Still Champions: Overwhelming Defeat of the Athletics: The Largest Crowd Ever Known at a Base Ball Game: Score Twenty-Eight to Sixteen: History of the Matches between these Clubs — The Atlantics Victors in Six Games out of Seven," *BDE*, vol. 27, no. 221 (17 Sep 1867), p. 2, col. 7; "Defeat of the Athletics: Score, 28 to 16," undated Sep 1867 *NYC* clipping in the Mears Collection.

83. "Sports and Pastimes: Match for the Championship — The Atlantics vs. the Athletics — The Game Played in Philadelphia — Defeat of the Atlantics — Score 28 to 8, &c., &c.," *BDE,* vol. 27, no. 227 (24 Sep 1867), p. 2, cols. 7–8; "The Atlantics in Philadelphia" undated Sep 1867 *NYC* clipping in the Mears Collection.

84. "Sports and Pastimes: Base Ball: Postponement — Atlantics vs. Athletics," *BDE,* vol. 27, no. 231 (28 Sep 1867), p. 2, col. 6; "Local Intelligence: The Base Ball Championship," *NYT,* vol. 17, no. 4906 (30 Sep 1867), p. 8, cols. 4–5.

85. "Sports and Pastimes: Base Ball: Atlantics vs. Unions — The Champions Beaten by the Unions," *BDE,* vol. 27, no. 181 (1 Aug 1867), p. 3, col. 2; "Base Ball: The 'Champions' Again Defeated," *BDE,* vol. 27, no. 185 (6 Aug 1867), p. 2, col. 7; "Irvington vs. Atlantic: The Champions Again Defeated," undated Aug 1867 *NYC* clipping in the Mears Collection.

86. "Sports and Pastimes: Base Ball: Atlantics vs. Keystones," *BDE,* vol. 27, no. 229 (26 Sep 1867), p. 2, col. 7; "The Atlantics in Philadelphia" undated Sep 1867 *NYC* clipping in the Mears Collection.

87. "Sports and Pastimes: Base Ball: Keystones vs. Atlantics," *BDE,* vol. 27, no. 236 (4 Oct 1867), p. 2, col. 7; "Visit of the Keystone Club, of Philadelphia: The Champions Defeated," undated Oct 1867 *NYC* clipping in the Mears Collection.

88. "Base Ball — Interesting to the Unions and Atlantics," *BDE,* vol. 27, no. 242 (11 Oct 1867), p. 2, col. 6; "The Unions Champions," undated Oct 1867 *NYC* clipping in the Mears Collection.

89. "Atlantic vs. Cincinnati," undated Jul 1868 *NYC* clipping in the Mears Collection.

90. "Atlantic vs. National, of Albany," undated Aug 1868 *NYC* clipping in the Mears Collection.

91. "Sports and Pastimes: Base Ball: Union vs. Atlantics — Overwhelming Defeat of the Champions — Score 13 [sic: 31] to 7," *BDE,* vol. 28, no. 213 (11 Sep 1868), p. 2, cols. 6–7; "Atlantic vs. Union — The Champions Defeated," undated Sep 1868 *NYC* clipping in the Mears Collection; "Sports and Pastimes: Base Ball: The Championship Returns to Brooklyn — The Rightful Owners in Possession — The Atlantics Beat the Unions — Score 24–8," *BDE,* vol. 28, no. 235 (7 Oct 1868), p. 2, col. 3; "Atlantic vs. Union," undated Oct 1868 *NYC* clipping in the Mears Collection.

92. "Sports and Pastimes: Base Ball: Defeat of the Champions — Atlantic vs. Mutual — The Mutuals Counted In for the Championship," *BDE,* vol. 28, no. 240 (13 Oct 1868), p. 2, cols. 6–7; "Mutuals, of New York, vs. Atlantics, of Brooklyn," undated Oct 1868 *NYC* clipping in the Mears Collection; "Sports and Pastimes: Base Ball: Defeat of the Champions — Atlantic vs. Mutual," *BDE,* vol. 28, no. 252 (27 Oct 1868), p. 3, col. 7; "Mutuals vs. Atlantics," undated Oct 1868 *NYC* clipping in the Mears Collection.

93. "Base Ball: The Game between the Atlantic and Cincinnati Clubs: Defeat of the Brooklynites: Score 32 to 10: Scenes on the Grounds and at the Atlantic Headquarters," *BDE,* vol. 29, no. 143 (17 Jun 1869), p. 2, col. 5; "Cincinnati vs. Atlantic: Another Victory for the 'Red Stockings'," undated Jun 1869 *NYC* clipping in the Mears Collection.

94. "Base Ball: First Game for the Championship between the Atlantics and Eckfords — The Atlantic Victorious — A Grand Batting Game — 'Old Hocks' Goes In for Four Home Runs," *BDE,* vol. 29, no. 212 (7 Sep 1869), p. 2, cols. 5–6; "Grand Match between the Atlantics and Eckfords," undated Sep 1869 *NYC* clipping in the Mears Collection.

95. "Sports and Pastimes: Base Ball: The Game for the Championship," *BDE,* vol. 29, no. 241 (11 Oct 1869), p. 5, cols. 7–8; "Eckfords and Atlantics: The Latter Badly Beaten," undated Oct 1869 *NYC* clipping in the Mears Collection.

96. "Sports and Pastimes: Base Ball: Atlantic vs. Eckford," *BDE,* vol. 29, no. 266 (9 Nov 1869), p. 2, col. 7; "The Championship: Atlantic vs. Eckford: The Last Grand Match of the Season: The Atlantics Successful. Score, 16 to 12," undated Nov 1869 *NYC* clipping in the Mears Collection.

97. "The Atlantics Triumphant: A Glorious Victory for Brooklyn: The Local Nine Beat the 'Picked Nine' from the West: Gallant, Though Unsuccessful Struggle of the Red Stockings: Fair Field and No Favor — Intense Excitement," *BDE,* vol. 30, no. 141 (15 Jun 1870), p. 2, cols. 4–5.

98. "Captain Babcock Dead," *Richmond Dispatch,* 17 Jan 1894, pp. 1 and 4; French Scrapbooks; *Richmond Dispatch,* 8 Oct 1897, p. 7.

99. "Not Like They Used to Play: A Veteran of the Diamond Tells of the Early Days: Baseball 40 Years Ago," *Washington Post,* 8 Aug 1892, p. 6.

100. "Our Washington Letter: The Week's Doings at the National Capital," *BDE,* 9 Oct 1892, p. 4; "Not Like They Used to Play: A Veteran of the Diamond Tells of the Early Days: Baseball 40 Years Ago," *Washington Post,* 8 Aug 1892, p. 6.

101. *NYC,* 11 Apr 1885; *BDE,* 3 Apr 1885 and 1 May 1885; *St. Louis Post-Dispatch,* 3 Apr 1885.

102. Francis C. Richter, *Richter's History and Records of Base Ball* (1914: Jefferson, N.C.: McFarland, 2005), p. 220; [Chadwick],"Old Stand Bys: Gossip About Veterans of the Ball Field: Where They are and What They are Doing. The Old Atlantic Nine," *BDE,* vol. 38, no. 320 (18 Nov 1877), p. 3, col. 9 (like most articles of the era, this piece was not signed, but its content leaves no doubt that Chadwick wrote it); *NYT,* 14 Nov 1903.

103. *BDE,* 25 Sep 1932, p. A19.

104. "Sports and Pastimes: Base Ball: Atlantic vs. Mutual — Statistics Concerning the Nines which are to Play on Monday Next," *BDE,* vol. 28, no. 190 (15 Aug 1868), p. 2, cols. 7–8 [hereafter cited as "Atlantic vs. Mutual — Statistics Concerning the Nines"]; *Sporting News,* 14 Jan 1909. The nickname is now more commonly associated with Bob Ferguson, and there is evidence that it was applied to him as well, but it appears to have more commonly used to refer to Chapman.

105. *New York Evening Telegram,* 10 Jun 1916, p. 8.

106. "Atlantic vs. Mutual — Statistics Concerning the Nines," p. 2.

107. *BDE,* 28 Apr 1925, p. 2; *BDE,* 1 May 1925, p. 5.

108. "Died," *BDE,* vol. 55, no. 64 (6 Mar, 1895), p. 7, col. 2; "Funeral of S.F. Davenport," *BDE,* vol. 55, no. 65 (7 Mar 1885), p. 5, col. 2.

109. William J. Ryczek, *When Johnny Came Sliding Home* (Jefferson, N.C.: McFarland, 1998), p. 212.

110. "The Atlantics Triumphant," *BDE,* vol. 30, no. 141 (15 Jun 1870), p. 2, cols. 4–5.

111. *NYC,* 21 Aug 1875; *Chicago Tribune,* 31 Mar 1878.

112. *Sporting News,* 12 May 1894, p. 4.

113. "Atlantic vs. Mutual — Statistics Concerning the Nines," p. 2.

114. *Chicago Tribune,* 1 Apr 1894.

115. *BDE,* 10 Dec 1912, p. 18.

116. *BDE,* 1 Dec 1905.

117. "The Old Atlantics: Henry Chadwick Gives Some History," *BDE,* vol. 56, no. 78 (19 Mar 1896), p. 2, cols. 3–4.

118. "'Mike' Henry's Benefit," *BDE,* vol. 49, no. 23 (24 Jan 1889), p. 1, col. 9.

119. "'Mike' Henry: The Death of the Well Known Sporting Man," *BDE,* vol. 49, no. 128 (10 May 1889), p. 6, col. 6.

120. [Chadwick],"Old Stand Bys," p. 3.

121. *Brooklyn Daily Union,* 26 Aug 1876.

122. "Ex-Judge Massey's Death," *BDE,* vol. 55, no. 198 (19 Jul 1895), p. 1, col. 5.

123. "Atlantic vs. Mutual — Statistics Concerning the Nines," p. 2.

124. *NYC,* 10 Apr 1869.

125. *BDE,* 28 Feb 1928, p. 3.

126. "Atlantic vs. Mutual — Statistics Concerning the Nines," p. 2.

127. *BDE,* 7 Jun 1862.

128. "Died," *BDE,* vol. 53, no. 89 (31 Mar 1893), p. 5, col. 2.

129. "Our National Game: The Death and Funeral of Matty A. O'Brien — How Ball Players Honor their Dead — A Large and Imposing Funeral: Meeting, Resolutions, etc.," *BDE,* vol. 25, no. 220 (23 Oct 1865), p. 2, col. 6.

130. [Chadwick],"Old Stand Bys," p. 3.

131. French Scrapbooks.

132. *American Chronicle of Sports and Pastimes*, 9 Jan 1868.

133. [Chadwick],"Old Stand Bys," p. 3.

134. "Account of the Principal Games", p. 2, col. 4.

135. [Chadwick],"Old Stand Bys," p. 3.

136. "Henry Chadwick Gives Some History," *BDE*, vol. 56, no. 78 (19 Mar 1878), p. 2, cols. 3–4.

137. *Sporting News*, 3 Mar 1910.

138. "Obituary Notes," *NYT*, 11 Jun 1915, p. 15, col. 5.

139. "Sports and Pastimes: Base Ball: Atlantic vs. Empire," *BDE*, vol. 25, no. 133 (11 Jul 1865), p. 3, col. 2.

140. "Atlantic vs. Mutual — Statistics Concerning the Nines," p. 2, cols. 7–8.

141. Ibid.

142. *BDE*, 2 Mar 1921, p. 2.

143. "The Late Joseph A. Regan," *BDE*, vol. 29, no. 144 (18 Jun 1869), p. 2, col. 7.

144. *Sporting Life*, 13 Mar 1909.

145. "Died," *BDE*, vol. 44, no. 232 (22 Aug 1883), p. 3, col. 2.

146. "Atlantic vs. Mutual — Statistics Concerning the Nines," p. 2.

147. Henry Chadwick, *The American Game of Base Ball* (1868; Columbia, S.C.: Camden House, 1983), p. 36.

148. "Famous Old Time Games: The Part That the Late Charles Smith Took in Them: Was a Wonderful Player: Harry Wright Said of Him That He Was the King of Third Baseman and That He Never Saw His Equal as an All Around Player — Notable Victories of the Atlantics — Base Ball Notes," *BDE*, vol. 57, no. 329 (28 Nov 1897), p. 9, cols. 5–6.

149. "The Famous Atlantics: Some Ball History Recalled by a Photograph: Every Playing Member of the 1863 Nine Is Still Living — Something About Their Records — The Famous Game With the Red Stockings," *BDE*, vol. 56, no. 74 (15 Mar 1896), p. 22, cols. 3–5.

150. *Sporting News*, 20 Feb 1908.

151. "City News and Gossip: Base Ball," *BDE*, vol. 16, no. 89 (17 Apr 1857), p. 3, col. 1.

152. *NYC*, 10 Nov 1883.

153. *NYC*, 25 Feb 1871.

154. *National Chronicle*, 9 Jan 1869, p. 2.

155. *BDE*, 24 Jul 1906, p. 3; *Sporting Life*, 11 Aug 1906.

156. "Sports and Pastimes: Base Ball: Tassie," *BDE*, vol. 29, no. 172 (22 July 1869), p. 2, col. 8; [Chadwick],"Old Stand Bys," *BDE*, vol. 38, no. 320 (18 Nov 1877), p. 3, col. 9; "City and Suburban News: Brooklyn," *NYT*, vol. 30, (19 Jan 1881), p. 8, col. 4.

157. "Died," *BDE*, vol. 44, no. 335 (4 Dec 1883), p. 3, col. 2.

158. *St. Louis Post-Dispatch*, 2 Jan 1884; "Atlantic vs. Mutual — Statistics Concerning the Nines," p. 2, cols. 7–8.

159. *BDE*, 19 Mar 1905, p. 13.

160. *BDE*, 23 May 1905, p. 22.

161. *BDE*, 19 Mar 1905, p. 13.

162. *NYT*, 6 Jun 1903; *BDE*, 25 Feb 1913, p. 5; *NYT*, 20 Feb 1917: *BDE*, 29 Jun 1918, p. 8.

❖ *Pastime Base Ball Club* ❖
(Peter Morris)

CLUB HISTORY

Like every club of the Pioneer Era, the Pastime Club of Brooklyn began to play baseball with hopes of winning matches and even championships. A few of the club's early matches suggested that such ambitions might be attainable, but it soon became apparent that the players' skill was not on a par with those of the area's top clubs. Although this reality was initially discouraging, the Pastimes ultimately came to symbolize something more important than wins and losses: that early baseball clubs were first and foremost social organizations and that the camaraderie they built was more important than the on-field results. "What jolly fellows they were at that time, one and all of them," Henry Chadwick later recalled, "and how fully they entered into the sport of the game."[1]

Exactly when the Pastimes began playing baseball remains in doubt. The players themselves deemed May of 1858 to be the date when the club was founded.[2] But a club called the Pastime was represented at a February 27, 1858, meeting that led to the formation of the National Association of Base Ball Players. Still, the date remains imprecise because the Pastime Base Ball Club was an offshoot of a group of young men who shared in many leisure pursuits and for whom the camaraderie was more important than the particular activity.

For example, John McNamee later recalled that shortly before the organization of the Gothams in 1852, he "used to get some of the 'boys' together on a good afternoon" on the "old York street lot, near the station house." The game they played was the old-fashioned one in which "you used to 'sock' one another with the ball," and they "practiced regularly until the principal of the school (No. 7) complained to the mayor that we interfered with the progress of the scholars in some way, and we had to stop playing there." McNamee subsequently "helped to organize the Pastimes — the City Hall Club, as it was called." Unfortunately, he does not specify how many of "the 'boys'" who played on the York Street lot became members of the Pastime Club, but it seems likely that there were several holdovers.[3]

A more direct antecedent of the Pastime Club was the Long Island Cricket Club. Precise details are hazy but the Pastimes played their matches on the Cricket Club's grounds in the Bedford section of Brooklyn, and there was some overlap between the two clubs. Moreover, the members of both clubs belonged to the same social circle and often gathered for drinks and dinner at a hotel operated by John Holder, Sr., or at one run by Billy Labon's father.

Henry Chadwick was a member of the Long Island Cricket Club in the mid–1850s and he later recalled that during cricket sessions, "I frequently had my attention attracted to the noisy work of the old Atlantic base ball nines who used to come out there to practice."[4] The Atlantics soon moved to Brooklyn but baseball play on the Bedford grounds continued and it was these players who became known as the Pastime Club. So in essence this was a base ball club that was made up primarily of members of the Long Island Cricket Club who chose to play base ball instead of or in addition to cricket.

By May 1858, the Pastimes had become sufficiently organized to stage their first intrasquad married-single match.[5] Soon they pronounced themselves ready to face outside competition and played home-and-home series against the Osceolas of Brooklyn and the Atlantics of Jamaica (who are not to be confused with the mighty Atlantics of Brooklyn).

Both series proved highly successful. The Pastimes' grounds at the cricket club were described as being "unquestionably the best in Brooklyn. Ample shade is afforded, and a fine green turf renders the field peculiarly attractive to the players, and far superior to the dusty grounds of a majority of the clubs." With the cooperation of the weather, and from the hard work of a committee of club members in making arrangements, the match in which the Pastimes hosted the Osceolas was attended by "a large number of spectators, probably near a thousand altogether, among whom were a large number of the fair sex."[6]

After each of the matches, both clubs joined together to share food, drink, and merriment. The visit of the Atlantics of Jamaica concluded with a trip to Holder's establishment, where the players of both clubs and their guests "partook of the good things the host had made ready for them. Here the best of feeling existed, and speeches made, jokes passed, toasts given, and songs sung, after which the Atlantics started for home."[7]

The Pastimes also acquitted themselves very well on the field, beating the Osceolas twice and splitting the matches with the Atlantics of Jamaica. They also managed victories over a couple of other Brooklyn clubs, the Orientals and the Nassaus. In the latter game, in what may have been a sign of things to come, the Pastimes gave up 12 runs in the first inning before the players "awoke to the consciousness of the fact that the conquest of the Nassau Club was not a matter of so little moment as they had at first supposed," and staged a comeback.[8]

Their success convinced the Pastimes that they should set their sights farther afield. On September 21 the club took a morning train to Trenton, New Jersey, spent the afternoon defeating a picked nine of Mercer and Trenton players, and returned home on the evening mail train.[9] The Pastimes also scheduled three late-season matches against national powerhouses, but these contests proved that they still had plenty to learn. A match against the Adriatics of Newark resulted in a 45–13 thrashing, while two contests against the Excelsiors of Brooklyn also ended in lopsided defeats.

Yet there was no reason for the Pastimes to be demoralized by these setbacks. Their players were still new to baseball and there was every reason to expect that improvement lay ahead. After one of the losses to the Excelsiors, an account in the *New York Clipper* noted, "The Pastime also played well, but when pitted against such a host of talent, it is not to be wondered at that they should come off second best. Practice makes perfect, however, and it is possible that they may regain the laurel ... in their next encounter with the same club."[10]

There was thus reason for optimism in the spring of 1859 that the Pastimes could break through and join the ranks of the elite clubs. The new outlook was shown when matches were scheduled against such strong opponents as the Atlantics and the Excelsiors of Brooklyn and the Eagles and Empires of New York City.

The Pastimes did indeed show improvement in 1859, most notably in closely fought losses to the Atlantics and the Excelsiors in mid–August. The relatively narrow margins (22–13 and 20–12) prompted one sportswriter to comment that the Pastimes "are not to be disposed of by any club without excellent play on the part of their opponents," and another to remark that the Pastimes "have acquired a very high position as players this year, and will soon rank as a first class club.'"[11]

Unfortunately, it also became clear that the improvement of the Pastimes had not been as great as anticipated. The club wasn't able to beat any of the area's top clubs and suffered some embarrassing losses. Each new disappointment made it more obvious that there were now higher expectations that the Pastime players were not going to be able to meet.

An early season home loss to the Neosha Club of New Utrecht in front of a huge crowd raised eyebrows.[12] "The Pastime club has always stood well as an effective playing club," wrote one sportswriter, "and a good many of their friends were a little surprised to hear of their defeat by 'the countrymen.'"[13] In September a loss to the Eagles prompted the *Clipper* to mention that it was the first time all year that a Brooklyn senior nine had been beaten by one from New York City.[14]

The players shared these expectations and began to show their frustrations. One account of the loss to the club from New Utrecht implied that the players were discourteous to the umpire.[15] Even when the Pastimes kept their cool, they had to deal with the disappointment of their supporters. The account of the loss to the Eagles noted that the Pastimes expected to win "and the result was therefore anything but pleasant to them. They took the matter pretty kindly though, and prepared themselves for a thorough roasting when they get home, which they have ere this received."[16]

Such "roasting" was the result of a new perception of the shortcomings of the Pastime Club. In 1858 all losses could be excused by the expectation that better days lay ahead. But the club from New Utrecht had been formed more recently than the Pastimes, making it impossible to blame the loss on inexperience.[17] A new explanation for losses had to be found and the most obvious one was to blame them on a lack of commitment to practice and improve. "The Pastime men," concluded one analysis, "were evidently in want of practice, as their poor fielding at times fully proved. They have the requisite material to fill all points of the field creditably, but on this occasion they failed in doing so."[18]

The disappointments of the 1859 season caused frustration to surface during several matches and it was no surprise that the Pastimes gave up baseball at season's end. As Henry Chadwick later put it, "The club became ambitious of winning matches and began to sacrifice the original objects of the organization to the desire to strengthen their nine for match playing.... After their desire to excel in contests with rival clubs had been aroused, then things changed, and finally the spirit of the club, having been dampened by repeated defeats at the hands of stronger nines, gave out and the Pastimes went out of existence."[19]

Yet while the members of the Pastime Club occasionally exhibited frustration while on the field, it didn't stop them from having fun. A perfect example occurred in August of 1859 when the club hosted the Excelsiors. The members of the host club "had an idea that the Pastimes could 'down' the Excelsiors" and were very disappointed when the match ended in defeat.[20]

Despite the difficult loss, the postgame festivities were even more lavish than usual, as the members of the Pastime Club "were bent upon spreading themselves in the way of a supper on the occasion, and they gave the good Mrs. Holder carte blanche to prepare a feast." Speeches followed the meal, but the delicious food still remained on the mind of the Excelsiors and one gave this speech: "There's one thing, gentlemen, in which you beat us badly to-day, and that is in giving us chicken pot pie." Finally, drinks were called for and the hosts "drank the health of the guests in a bumper of the rosy which nearly filled a celery glass. As the novelists say, 'About two o'clock in the morning a party of jolly roysterers might have been seen issuing from the portals of the hostelry at Bedford.'"[21]

The Pastimes found other ways to exhibit their unique style and sense of fun. A memorable example was the match against the Eagles, which was played at the Elysian Fields. The members of the Eagle Club made their way to Hoboken in parties of two or three and were "waiting for the Pastimes to turn up, when what should they see coming up the roadway from the westward but a line of carriages. Sam Yates [of the Eagles] thought it was a small funeral procession which had lost their way; but it turned out to be the high toned Pastimes, all in carriages."[22]

When the Pastimes stopped playing baseball at the end of the 1859 season, it was not so much a case of a baseball club disbanding as it was of a social club moving on to other leisure activities. The 1861 advent of the Civil War put a halt to most such pursuits, but after the war ended many of the members of the Pastime Club became passionate about harness racing.[23] And of course, as had been the case when these men had played

cricket and baseball, the most enjoyable part was the camaraderie that was shared afterward over food and drinks.

The baseball chapter of the story of the men who made up the Pastime Club ended on a sour note, but these blithe souls soon forgot the wins and losses. One prominent club member, Billy Barre, looked back on those days and commented, "But didn't we have fun though on our practice days?"[24] It was an apt summary of the spirit of the Pastime Club.

Indeed, by 1879 the members of the club recalled their ball-playing days with such fondness that they helped organize a series of reunion games designed to recall "the days when ball-playing was more of a sport and less of a science." Naturally, the highlight of the reunion game was "a grand supper, after the match, at the hotel adjoining the grounds."[25] Just as naturally, everyone who attended had a great time.

CLUB MEMBERS

William Barre: Barre was born in Brooklyn on November 18, 1826. He began working in the office of the register of deeds for Kings County when it was formed in 1853 and became a mainstay at Brooklyn City Hall, ultimately becoming the register and reporting directly to Senator William Murtha. Barre was a widower with three young children when he joined the Pastimes, but remarried in 1859 and began a new family. He died on July 15, 1899, at Babylon, Long Island.

Francis A. Biggs: Frank Biggs was born around 1830 and worked as a broker, street commissioner, county auditor, and paint manufacturer. He died in Brooklyn in March of 1889.

Bill Boyd: Like so many members of the Pastimes, Boyd was connected with Brooklyn City Hall and one account described him as a penitentiary official. He was still alive and living in Brooklyn in 1889, but has not been positively identified.

Brock Carroll: Carroll played first base for the Pastimes and was reported in an 1877 article to be already dead. A note in the *Brooklyn Eagle* on July 23, 1861, said there were reports that Brock Carroll of the 12th Regiment had been killed. Civil War records show a Brock Carroll serving as a private in the 3rd Regiment of the New York Cavalry. But no other trace of this man has been found, suggesting that Brock may have been his middle name or a nickname.

Augustus J. Dayton: Gus Dayton pitched and played the outfield for the Pastimes. He was born around 1829 in New York and grew up in Brooklyn. His father was a real estate broker and Gus initially went into that profession. In 1861, though 32 and married with several children, he enlisted in the Union Army, then re-enlisted for two more tours of duty. He later worked as a clerk, a bookkeeper, and a guard at Sing Sing prison. He appears to have retired in the mid–1880s, and an 1889 article mentioned that Dayton was still in town and had been "building model yachts the past year or two." Dayton died on October 29, 1897, in Brooklyn.

Horatio Eastmead: Eastmead, who played first base for the Pastimes, was born around 1828. He worked as an engraver and was also a member of the Long Island Cricket Club. He died in Brooklyn on November 4, 1878.

Robert Furey: Bob Furey was born around 1832 and became a prominent Brooklyn politician and businessman. Furey served as an alderman and then as street commissioner, a position that at the time had the power to make many patronage appointments. He became a close friend and adviser of Brooklyn Democratic "boss" Hugh McLaughlin, though he was disappointed when McLaughlin did not support his aspirations to become a senator. Furey was also a successful businessman as one of the main shareholders in the Cranford Company, an asphalt contractor. He never married, so in his later years he gave much of his wealth to charity. He died on March 12, 1913, at the age of 81.

Edward Hempstead Holt: Edward Holt was born around 1838 and grew up in Brooklyn, where his father worked as a custom house officer. Edward and his brother Guy both played for the Pastimes and both enlisted in the Civil War. Edward enlisted as a private in the 51st New York Infantry on August 24, 1861, and served for 17 months before receiving a disability discharge. He returned home to Brooklyn, where he died on July 8, 1864, at the age of 26.

Guysbert Vandenbroeck Holt: Guy Holt, the younger brother of Edward, was born on February 17, 1841. He too enlisted in the Union Army and was assigned to the 13th Regiment. On August 11, 1862, while doing picket duty in Suffolk, Virginia, he was shot and killed.

Bill Labon: William Penrose Labon was born in England on September 16, 1822, and immigrated to the United States around 1836. His father was a brewer who operated a roadhouse hotel on the county road that was the site of many of the activities of the Pastimes. The younger Labon was prominent in both the Pastimes and the Long Island Cricket Club. He never married and was known as Bachelor Billy Labon. He eventually retired to Suffolk County and in 1896 Henry Chadiwck reported that he had just spent a "week's sojourn at Mount Pleasant on the Sound just outside of Greenport, this being the home of my old friend William Penrose Labon, whose newly built summer house adjoins the Couklin property, known as the 'Sound View House.'"[26] Labon died in Greenport on January 18, 1913.

John McNamee: McNamee was born in Brooklyn around 1825. During the 1850s, he served as a Brooklyn alderman and was subsequently elected sheriff. He was also a gifted sculptor and around 1870 he moved to Florence, Italy, so that he could sculpt in Italian marble. He also became the owner of the Villa Trollope, where George Eliot stayed while writing the novel *Romola*. Although far removed from his days as a base ball player, he retained a passion for the sport and an obituary stated that "his hobby was to make a statue of a first baseman in the act of receiving a badly delivered ball, so that every muscle could be brought out. He made his model in clay, but for some reason the statue was never attempted in marble." McNamee died in Florence on August 11, 1895.

Frank Quevedo: Francis G. Quevedo was born around 1823 in New York and was described as being the "life of the club and one of its most genial members." He and Barre were the club's delegates at the National Association of Base Ball Players convention of 1860. Quevedo was foreman of one of Brooklyn's volunteer fire departments at a time when that was a high honor. He worked in the railroad business and later was secretary of the park commission. He drowned in October of 1887 at the Coney Island pier.

Bob Story: Stephen Bond "Bob" Story was the catcher of the Pastimes and like so many of his fellow club members he worked at Brooklyn's City Hall as chief payroll clerk. Born on a farm near Gowanus in 1827, Story eventually retired to Freeport on Long Island and died there on January 26, 1910.[27]

Daniel M. Treadwell: Daniel Treadwell was born around 1826 and worked as a hotel keeper, later becoming a lawyer. He was very long-lived, dying in Brooklyn on November 10, 1921, at the age of 95.

Jake Uris: There was only one Uris family in Brooklyn and there was no member named Jacob, so it would seem that this has to be a nickname for John T. Uris, who was born in 1829 and became a dancing master. He died in Brooklyn on December 3, 1904.

Other Club Members: G. Abbott, J. Barnard, Beers (shortstop for the club in a few games but first name never given), Bennett, William A. Brown (a member of the Eckfords who helped organize the Pastime Club), William Cole, Cornish, R. B. Dawson, W. Devine, G. Jenkins, McKenzie, J. McMan, Reynolds (apparently Tommy Reynolds of the Excelsior Club), James Rogers, Saxton, W. G. Tucker, J. Van Wagner, Williams, A. M. Wood.

Sources: Craig B. Waff's summary of game accounts of the Pastimes on the Protoball website was very valuable. A series of later articles added key details, including Henry Chadwick, "Old Boys," *Brooklyn Eagle*, December 2, 1877, and "Our 'Old Boys,'" *Brooklyn Eagle*, December 3, 1877; "Old Chalk" [Chadwick],"Baseball in Its Infancy," *Brooklyn Eagle*, December 15, 1889; *Brooklyn Eagle*, May 11, 1888; *Brooklyn Eagle*, January 14, 1876, interview with John McNamee by John Clark; "Veterans," *Brooklyn Eagle*, May 19, 1879, 2.

Notes

1. "Old Chalk" [Chadwick],"Baseball in its Infancy," *Brooklyn Eagle*, December 15, 1889.
2. *Brooklyn Eagle*, February 27, 1879, noting talk of a reunion game to mark the club's twenty-first anniversary.
3. *Brooklyn Eagle*, January 14, 1876.
4. *Brooklyn Eagle*, May 11, 1888.
5. *Brooklyn Times*, May 26, 1858; "Out-Door Sports: Base-Ball: Pastime Base-Ball Club," *Porter's Spirit of the Times*, June 5, 1858, 212.
6. "Out-Door Sports: Base-Ball: Pastime vs. Osceola," *Porter's Spirit of the Times*, July 31, 1858, 341.

7. "Out-Door Sports: Base-Ball: Pastime vs. Atlantic," *Porter's Spirit of the Times*, August 21, 1858, 388.

8. *Brooklyn Times*, August 17, 1858.

9. *Trenton Daily State Gazette and Republican*, September 22, 1858.

10. *New York Clipper*, undated game account. In another sign that suggests rising ambition, the Pastimes formed a junior club that played a couple of matches in late 1858 and at least one in 1859.

11. "Out-Door Sports: Base-Ball: Excelsior vs. Pastime," *Porter's Spirit of the Times*, August 27, 1859, 404; *New York Atlas*, August 21, 1859.

12. "Brooklyn Intelligence: Base Ball," *New York Times*, May 28, 1859, 8. This article claimed the attendance was nearly 5,000. But that figure should be taken with caution, especially since the writer identified the winning club as the "Oceans."

13. *New York Atlas*, May 29, 1859.

14. *New York Clipper*, September 10, 1859.

15. Clipping of *New York Clipper* account, no date.

16. *New York Clipper*, September 10, 1859.

17. "Out-Door Sports: Base-Ball: Neosho vs. Pastime," *Porter's Spirit of the Times*, June 4, 1859, 213.

18. Clipping of *New York Clipper* account of loss to the Neosha Club of New Utrecht, no date.

19. "Old Chalk" [Chadwick],"Baseball in its Infancy," *Brooklyn Eagle*, December 15, 1889.

20. Ibid.

21. Henry Chadwick, "Old Boys," *Brooklyn Eagle*, December 2, 1877.

22. Ibid.

23. *Brooklyn Eagle*, June 3, 1865, 2, June 4, 1866, 2, April 26, 1873, 2, and December 23, 1888, 10.

24. Henry Chadwick, "Old Boys," *Brooklyn Eagle*, December 2, 1877.

25. *New York Sunday Mercury*, May 3, 1879.

26. *Sag-Harbor Express*, August 20, 1896.

27. *Brooklyn Standard Union*, January 27, 1910.

❖ *Star Base Ball Club* ❖
(Craig B. Waff, William J. Ryczek and Peter Morris)

CLUB HISTORY

The Star Club of South Brooklyn began its existence as one of the most prominent of the "junior clubs" that flourished in Brooklyn in the late 1850s.[1] The membership of such clubs was summed up by the *New York Clipper*'s 1856 description of the Star Club and the Enterprise Club of Bedford as "youths ranging from 15 to 18 years of age, who have organized, like thousands of others, for the purpose of perfecting themselves in the various physical exercises, which are so necessary for a development of the mental faculties."[2] It seems a safe assumption that the pleasures of playing baseball played at least as big a role as the recommendations cited by the reporter.

Junior clubs such as the Stars very quickly became fan favorites, capable of attracting crowds of spectators similar in number to those attending games between senior clubs. They also often forged a special relationship with a prominent senior club. In Brooklyn, many Star players moved on to the senior Excelsior Club, while the rival Enterprise Club became a source of talent for the senior Atlantic Club. Such relationships provided important benefits to these junior clubs. The prestige of association with these two elite clubs made young players eager to join their ranks, so there was never a shortage of talent. There were practical advantages as well—from early in their existence, the Stars shared the Excelsior Club's home field of Carroll Park in South Brooklyn with practice days coordinated so as to allow playing time for both clubs.[3]

Yet being protégés of a senior club was a mixed blessing. The vast majority of pioneer-era baseball clubs were short-lived and the regular loss of key players faced by junior clubs like the Stars made them especially ephemeral. The Star Club, however, was able to defy the odds. In 1859 the club began challenging and playing senior clubs and winning several games against them, and in early 1860 the club declared itself senior and was admitted to membership in the National Association of Base Ball Players (NABBP). As a result, it survived into the 1870s, long after most of the prominent clubs of the 1850s had become distant memories.

The prolonged existence of the Star Club was not without its ups and downs. Even after it became a senior organization, the tendency to develop strong talent and then lose those players to rival clubs continued. This in turn led to the Stars compiling seasonal records that ranged from excellent to mediocre.

While the strength of the first nine varied greatly, the club's longevity helped it to become one of the mainstays of the oft-changing local baseball scene. Always up for a challenge, the Stars played many of the top touring clubs that journeyed to the New York area and they themselves made two tours of Philadelphia. The Stars were also noted for generally being the first club to take the field each spring for practice, because their grounds at Carroll Park dried out more quickly than did those of the clubs with home fields that were used as skating parks during the winter. Thus the opening day of the Star Club was often the event that launched the New York baseball season.[4]

1856

A commentator calling himself "Veritas Amator" (Lover of Truth), writing in late 1857, pinpointed the Stars' date of origin as October 1856. The club's by-laws and constitution, published in 1860, gave the exact date as October 1, 1856.[5]

Within four weeks of forming, the club received its first challenge, from the Enterprise Club of Bedford. The first attempt by the two clubs to play was stymied when, at the appointed time, only four or five of the Enterprise first nine were on the grounds. Although a correspondent partial to the Enterprise claimed that the tardy players were only 15 minutes late, the delay was long enough to cause the Stars, who claimed they had waited a "considerable" amount of time, to leave the field. A second attempt ended in a draw because, with first-to-21 being used in match games, the Stars were clinging to a 7–5 lead when darkness approached.[6] A third try, on November 15, finally produced a winner, with the Stars victorious by a score of 21–16. The Star first nine on this occasion comprised youths with the names of John Van Cleef, Joshua Leavitt Jr., Henry Fairbanks, John Bynner, Robert "Bob" Manly, Tom Morris, F.J. and F.O. Miller, and Creighton.[7] While it is tempting to identify the last player as Jim Creighton, destined to become baseball's first recognized "superstar" before an untimely early death ended his career, it is more likely that he was in fact Henry J. Creighton, whose name appeared on an 1860 list of club members. On November 20 the second nines of the same two clubs played a match, which the Stars won by a score of 22–8. The nine fielded that day included players named Bucklin, John Manly Jr., Latham Fish, Davis, William W. Tracy, Hunter, Crocker, Carter, and George Wheelwright.[8]

So who were the young men who formed the Star Club and what brought them together? As noted in the profiles, the members of the first nine were very young men — the description of them as "youths ranging from 15 to 18 years of age" was a bit generous, as Morris was only 14 and few if any were older than 16. These aspiring ballplayers were closer to boyhood than manhood and posed no immediate threat to Brooklyn's senior clubs. Their main common bond appears to have been that in the mid–1850s they lived near a vacant lot "bounded by Clinton, Livingston and Joralemon streets and Sidney place" where many of the youngsters of the area gathered after school to expend their "surplus energy."[9]

An 1888 retrospective article in the *Brooklyn Daily Eagle* explained that the regulars became known as the "Sidney Place Crowd." These youngsters included Henry Fairbanks, Latham Fish, Tom Morris and his younger brother Charles, and no doubt other future Star Club members.[10] Their boyish activities included footraces, marbles, tops, and "bull in the ring," but there was nothing casual about the nature of their play. For example, the members of the "Sidney Place Crowd" competed in some of "the greatest games of marbles ever played in Brooklyn. More than 200 alleys and agates were often up in the huge ring, and every variety, from the common glazed alley to the expensive glass or pure agate, could be seen in the collection." As the unidentified author of the 1888 article explained, "They played marbles to win; they ran foot races to beat, and when they fought it was to vanquish the enemy."[11]

Proximity and competitive fervor were not the only things

that these adolescents shared. They came from well-to-do backgrounds and seemed to have treasured a sense of exclusivity. Two nearby groups of youngsters, "the Glass House and Furman street crowds," were not welcome visitors to their turf. According to the 1888 reminiscence, these rivals "were low, coarse follows, embryo roughs, in fact, and fights between them and the lads they sought to harass were of so common occurrence that a collision was expected as a part of the regular afternoon diversions."[12] Their exclusivity reflected the privileged backgrounds of many of the young men who made up the "Sidney Place Crowd" and who formed the original core of the Star Base Ball Club. As described in the player profiles, many of these founding members also enjoyed considerable worldly success.

1857

The nine-inning rule went into effect in 1857, which should have made it easier to play contests to successful, nondisputed conclusions. The Star Club's first two games in 1857 were matches involving the second nine, which now included several new players: W.G. Lord, Francis Howland, H.A. Fuller, James Forker, and one of the Whiting brothers. On September 26, despite playing with only eight men until the seventh inning, they once again defeated the Enterprise second nine, this time by a score of 19–14. "An Observer," writing to the editors of *Porter's Spirit of the Times,* declared that the Stars "never played better" and were "all in fine condition and spirits." In his view this showed that "they are not to be despised, if they are small." On October 12 the same nine was also victorious over the first nine of the Union Club of South Brooklyn, winning 18–10 in a game of five innings. The Star second nine also won a rematch with the Unions, 27–19, sometime in November.[13]

The first nine were not as fortunate, as they lost to the Enterprise first nine, 21–11, on October 17. Both sides were hampered by a wind that blew very hard against the bat, making it "impossible for either side to show their batting, for which they are so famous, and few balls went past second base."[14] The Stars had earlier issued a challenge to the Young America Club to play a match on October 20, but the club secretary neglected to include an address. (The challenged club was likely the Young America of Harlem, which the Enterprise had played earlier in the month, rather than the Young America of South Brooklyn.) Thus the members were unaware the Young Americans had accepted the challenge, and on the appointed day almost none of the Stars were present to greet them.

The Star Club secretary caused another problem when, after consulting only one or two members, he scheduled a rematch with the Enterprise Club on October 26. When the other members learned of this arrangement, they claimed "their own arrangements were such that they could not play at all." Rescheduled for November 20, the game, described by one correspondent as "the championship of the junior department of this sport," ended in a draw when the Enterprise players decided to leave the field, "by the advice of our older and more experienced friends." They blamed certain decisions by the referee, who was the brother of a Star player. The aforementioned Veritas Amator responded, "These friends evidently saw how the game was proceeding, and in a very friendly way to the Enterprise, proposed a cessation of the game, to avoid what was likely to have proved anything but a satisfactory termination to the game, as far as they were concerned." The friends, he suggested, were ones who had placed large bets on the game. The Star-Enterprise disputes were aired in the pages of *Porter's* in the late fall of 1857, which led an independent correspondent named "X" to grumble about "the disposition to quarrel that the junior clubs appear to have."[15]

1858

In 1858 the Stars, now boasting some 35 members, manifested a determination to begin their season much earlier than the previous two years. At a meeting held on April 30, the club elected new officers and announced plans to appear within a fortnight in a new uniform, "providing Messrs. P.C. Barnum & Co. are as prompt as usual." New members and promotions from the second nine led to the formation of an almost entirely different first nine, which played together throughout much of the season.[16] It included one of the Tracy brothers as catcher, Henry Fairbanks as pitcher, John Whiting at first base, Sam Patchen at second base, Fuller at shortstop, Fred Whiting at third base, and Charles Whiting, Joshua Leavitt, and Edward Patchen at left, center, and right field, respectively.

The Stars played their first game of the new season on May 28 with their rivals, the Enterprise Club. The reporter for *Porter's* remarked that anyone who witnessed the game would have to admit the Star and Enterprise ranked highest among the junior clubs, and that the two clubs had played the game "as finely, and as many excellent points were made, as will be seen in almost any match of the senior players." The game, which the Stars won by a score of 21–18, was played on the grounds of the Excelsior senior club in Carroll Park in South Brooklyn — a field that had become the grounds of the Star Club as well.[17] This close proximity led, over the next couple of years, to the Stars becoming something like protégés of the Excelsiors, with the senior club offering guidance to their junior counterparts. A similar relationship formed almost simultaneously between the Enterprise and Atlantic clubs, which shared a field in Bedford.

An observer of the 1857 Star-Enterprise first-nine game named "Delta," apparently partial to the Enterprise, asked, "Why don't [the Stars] challenge the Young America, or some other club; for their first nine never played with any club but the Enterprise since they started, now two years?" In 1858, after the opening Star-Enterprise game, the Star first nine did in fact play against no less than four other junior clubs. They

won two games each against the Ashland Club of New York City, the Resolute Club of Brooklyn's Eastern District, and the Lone Star Club of Jersey City. The first nine's only other match was on September 17 against the Champion Club of Yorkville. Because each side went into the game undefeated, both *Porter's* and the *Clipper* anticipated an exciting match and reported great interest in the coming game. The match was in fact closely contested, ending in a Champion victory of 18–15 in eight innings. The Stars thus closed the season with a fine 7–1 record.

1859

Playing with virtually the same lineup, the Stars opened their 1859 season with a match on May 30 against the Charter Oaks of Brooklyn, which two weeks earlier had upset the Excelsiors. That result, plus the fact that the Stars, still characterized as "youths verging on manhood," were challenging a senior club for the first time, attracted a large crowd, estimated at between two thousand and three thousand people, most of whom were strongly in favor of the "boys," even though the match took place on the Charter Oak grounds. The supporters of the underdogs did not go away disappointed, as the Stars used excellent batting and some spectacular fielding plays to upset the Charter Oaks by a score of 26–22. Fairbanks, the Stars' pitcher, was forced to leave the game in the sixth inning after being struck in the face by the ball, but this unfortunate incident did allow "little Manly" to enter the game, and thus begin a long career as a member of the Star first nine. The *Sunday Mercury* reported that Bob Manly's "length of reach and splendid playing was the occasion of much applause and merriment among the lookers-on." The *Porter's* reporter considered the game as one of the most interesting since the Fashion Course All-Star games of the preceding summer. He observed that "a new set of *stars* appear to be rising in the Base Ball firmament," and he advised the Excelsiors "to look to their laurels, for they are in danger."[18]

That warning was apt because a game between the Stars and their mentors was already scheduled for late summer.[19] In the meantime the Stars secured two victories over fellow junior clubs: 26–12 over the Hamiltons of Jersey City on July 8 and 14–8 over the Niagaras of Brooklyn on July 19. The first game attracted few spectators, as an Atlantic-Eckford game was being simultaneously played at Greenpoint. The latter game, however, was seen, according to the *New York Times,* by "an unusually large audience, numbering representations from almost every New-York and Brooklyn Club."[20] They were not disappointed, as all newspapers reported that the game was well contested on both sides, with *Porter's* noting in particular that "every opportunity to catch on the fly was taken advantage of on both sides, and but few misses were made."[21] As for the Stars, the *Sunday Mercury* maintained that they were a junior club in name only, since their players "can take precedence of very many, if not most, of the senior clubs."[22]

The game was also notable as an opportunity for the Stars to see firsthand the play of Jim Creighton, who had played regularly with the Niagaras since the beginning of the 1858 season. (As noted earlier, it is possible that he played for the Stars in single games in 1856 and 1858, but it seems more likely that this was the apparently unrelated Henry J. Creighton.) While the box scores published in the *Clipper, Porter's,* and the *Sunday Mercury* listed Creighton as the Niagara Club's second baseman in the game against the Stars, a biographical note glued to the back of a *carte de visite* depicting him in pitching motion described a memorable event in this game: "On the fifth inning..., when the Stars were a number of runs ahead of the Niagara the pitcher of the latter [Shields] was changed, Jimmy taking that position. Peter O'Brien [of the Atlantics] witnessed this game, and when Creighton got to work something news [sic] was seen in base ball—a low, swift delivery, the ball rising from the ground past the shoulder to the catcher."[23] The Stars had difficulty getting hits off Creighton (they were scoreless for the first time in the game in the sixth inning), and they retaliated, according to the note, by sending in their "wildest" pitcher so as to limit safe hits by the Niagaras. Although the Stars succeeded in winning the game, they took note of Creighton's improvement. By the time of the Excelsior game, they had persuaded Creighton, as well as shortstop George Flanley, to join the Stars. Recruitment of new quality players by the Stars may have become absolutely necessary, for by this time brothers John and Charles Whiting had themselves left the Stars and joined the Excelsiors.

As a Niagara Club member named B.A. Hamilton later recalled, the Star Club's gain proved to be the death knell of the Niagara Club. After the departure of Creighton, "There was hardly room in the same neighborhood for such clubs as the Star and the Niagara, and the Stars gradually absorbed the other, and the 'light blues' faded from the haunts of Smith and Hoyt, Douglass and Degraw streets, leaving a memory of honest playing and wonderful successes."[24]

Heavily anticipated, the Star-Excelsior match attracted a very large crowd of spectators, many of whom were eager to see the club that, despite still being considered "a body of mere youths," had nevertheless, according to a reporter covering the game for both the *New York Times* and *Porter's,* "entered the lists boldly and triumphantly against our best senior clubs." Nevertheless, according to the *Clipper,* they were having difficulty getting acceptances from the many challenges that they had issued to these clubs. Given their close relationship with the Stars, however, the Excelsiors could hardly refuse such a challenge. The attending spectators were not disappointed, as they witnessed a match that the *Clipper* reporter characterized as "unquestionably ... the best played game, and the closest and most exciting contest of the season, the play on both sides, up to the eighth innings, being the finest display of ball playing we have ever seen." There were numerous scoreless innings—five experienced by the Excelsiors, and four suf-

fered by the Stars. At the end of seven innings, the score stood 7–3 in favor of the Stars, who had until then displayed excellent fielding. In the final two innings, however, their fielding deteriorated, epitomized by a collision between Fairbanks and Ed Patchen while trying unsuccessfully to catch a fly ball in right centerfield. By the bottom of the ninth, the Excelsiors held a seemingly insurmountable 12–7 lead. Then the Stars capitalized on shaky fielding by the Excelsiors to stage a ten-run rally in the bottom of the ninth inning. When the winning run was scored by Manly, the reporter observed, "The whole assemblage was excited to a degree of enthusiasm such as is seldom witnessed even on a ball ground." The stirring victory made it clear, in the view of the *Clipper,* that any refusal now to play the Stars by the leading senior clubs could only be interpreted as "evidencing a fear of defeat."[25]

A few weeks later, while reporting on a lopsided 38–4 victory of the Stars over the Hoboken Club of Hoboken, New Jersey, on September 19, *Porter's* characterized the Stars as now being one of the best clubs in the region. Like the *Clipper,* it sensed a reluctance on the part of certain clubs, especially those in New York City, to play the Stars and urged these clubs to accept such a challenge: "The stereotyped excuse of 'or many engagements' should not be put forth in answer to a challenge of the Stars, as it indicates a fear of a successful issue."[26]

One New York club that did accept the challenge was the city's most senior one, the Knickerbockers, which agreed to play a "fly game" on the Stars' grounds on September 13. They apparently had put no credence in the growing reputation of the new Stars pitcher. *Porter's* reported, "The pitching of Creighton ... rather surprised them, his speed and accuracy telling on their batting with considerable effect." Although the Knickerbockers scored three runs in the first inning, all three of their outs were on strikeouts, and Creighton added a fourth in the second inning. The Knicks were then scoreless over the next three innings as the Stars built up a lead of 6–3, at which point rain ended the match. The *Sunday Mercury* praised the play of the entire nine: "The Star Club contains some of the neatest and prettiest players that any club can boast of, and we think that there are few clubs extant which can beat them, with an ordinary run of luck in their favor ... there is no club which plays a more steady and even game than the Stars. Every player seems to be admirably fitted to his position, and fills it well."[27] Nearly two weeks later, on September 26, the Knicks were soundly defeated 33–11, in a game that featured an 18-run eighth inning by the Stars.[28] Two days later, the Stars defeated the Hamilton Club of Jersey City in a return match by a score of 16–10.[29]

On October 8 the Atlantics of Brooklyn, the club that *Porter's* was now characterizing as the "Champion Senior Club," came to the Star grounds for a game. Because both nines had superb records (the Atlantics were undefeated in 1858 and had suffered only a single loss, to the Eckfords, earlier in 1859), the game attracted a large assemblage and the "undoubted favorites" were the Stars. The *Sunday Mercury* reported that "Creighton's pitching somewhat worried the Atlantics, but they are such strong and powerful batters that, we fancy, when they once 'got the hang' of his style of pitching, they would have begun 'putting in the big licks' in their usual style." Nevertheless, when play was suspended after the Atlantic fourth inning, with the visitors narrowly leading, 6–5, the same reporter remarked, "We cannot but think that it was fortunate for the Atlantics that the rain commenced, for they were evidently not in their best playing condition."[30] After a second intervening postponement, the Atlantics returned to the Star grounds on October 19, when, despite extreme cold, more than 4,000 spectators again attended. The game was close throughout and was tied 11–11 after seven innings, but the Atlantics ultimately handed the Stars their first defeat of the season, 15–12, with both *Porter's* and the *Clipper* attributing the Stars' loss to their unsteadiness and lack of judgment in running the bases.[31]

The Stars' first nine closed their 1859 season with a return match against the Charter Oaks on November 10. Rather oddly, the players started the game by not playing in their usual positions; in particular, Fred Whiting was the pitcher, Sam Patchen was the catcher, and Creighton was at shortstop. This experiment did not work well, as the Charter Oaks had a 4–2 lead after the first inning. Most of the Star players then returned to their usual positions, and for the next five innings the Charter Oaks were held scoreless. The *Clipper* reporter left little doubt about who was chiefly responsible for this remarkable feat: the club had "a very material element of success in the person of their pitcher Creighton, who unquestionably stands at the head of the list of players in that position. He is not only unequalled in speed and effectiveness as a pitcher, but is also not surpassed as a fielder, being a fine thrower and an excellent catcher." The Charter Oaks did finally manage to score eight runs in the seventh and eighth innings, as thickening fog and increasing darkness hampered the Stars' fielding. The umpire called the game after eight innings, giving the Stars a 19–12 victory.[32]

1860

The Stars' remarkable 7–1 record in 1859, including four victories over senior clubs and a closely played loss to the mighty Atlantics, led them to apply for and receive membership in the National Association of Base Ball Players (NABBP) in 1860. The Stars' success, however, led several senior clubs (especially those that the Stars had beaten) to cast covetous eyes toward many of their players. By the start of the season the Charter Oaks had recruited Joe and Sam Patchen, while Creighton and Flanley jumped once again, this time to the Excelsiors. A strong suspicion circulated that Creighton's switch had been financially induced, and during the Excelsiors' upstate tour that year, newspapers there published rumors, probably initiated in Brooklyn, that Creighton had been paid

$500 under the table to make the move. The loss of four key players, in any case, severely weakened the Stars, and they understandably struggled through a severe reversal of fortune. Five games against senior clubs all resulted in losses: to the Atlantics, the Charter Oaks, the Excelsiors, and twice to the Eckfords of Brooklyn. Only two games against the Brooklyn Club, which resulted in a 23–6 or 24–6 victory for the Stars on an unknown date and a 12–12 tie on October 6, redeemed an otherwise miserable season.

The on-field struggles were accompanied by signs of internal dissension. So many club officers had resigned during the 1859 season that a special meeting was held at season's end and a new slate elected. Yet the departures continued, and by 1860 an entirely new set of officers was in place, while several club founders allowed their memberships to lapse. Some of the changes were undoubtedly the result of young men approaching adulthood and assuming new responsibilities, but it seems clear that there was also discord in the ranks.

While the Stars were struggling, the Excelsiors were reaping the benefits. After the Excelsiors defeated the champion Atlantics in the first game of their celebrated unfinished series, one newspaper noted that the victorious nine "is composed, principally, of players obtained from the Star Club, five being from that bright luminary."[33] One can imagine the bittersweet emotions that those words must have evoked for the members who had remained loyal to the Stars.

1861

The Stars were among the first clubs to begin practicing in the spring of 1861, and played an intraclub game between the "Lightweights" and the "Heavyweights" on April 3.[34] The outbreak of the Civil War, however, made it difficult for the Stars, as well as other clubs, to recruit enough players, much less schedule games with other clubs. This difficulty was perhaps reflected in the arrangement instead of a game on July 4, on the Charter Oak grounds, between two sides made up of mixture of players — including such first-class players as Creighton, Flanley, and Brainard — from the Star, Charter Oak, Excelsior, Independent, Oriental, and Nassau clubs. The players were chosen in a way to produce sides that were overall fairly even in talent, a course that produced a closely contested game won, 24–23, by the "Star Nine" over the "Charter Oak Nine."[35]

The Stars' first nine participated in only six games, all of which were played in the first month of fall and featured opponents of far less prominence than those encountered in 1859 and 1860. An *Eagle* reporter attributed their 26–15 loss to the Olympics of Brooklyn on September 25 to loose play, but the Stars rebounded the next day with a 32–8 victory over the Powhatans of South Brooklyn.[36] Exactly one week later, excellent play by both the Stars and the Hamilton of Brooklyn clubs led to the very low score of 9–6 in favor of the Stars, inspiring the same *Eagle* reporter to exclaim, "This was one of the best played games of this or any other season."[37] The Stars won easily, 25–4, over the Brooklyn Club on October 12, and then split two games called after six innings because of darkness (a 20–11 loss to the Hamiltons on October 14 and a 12–5 victory over the Powhatans on October 26), thus ending the season with a respectable 4–2 win-loss record.

1862

As the spring of 1862 approached, the Stars and Excelsiors were excited to learn of the completion of a large and commodious clubhouse erected on the southeast corner of the lot that was their shared Carroll Park grounds. Because the grounds were rolled and leveled early, the Stars became the first club in the region to start practicing, and an intraclub match between their first and second nines, on March 26, was the first game played in the Greater New York City region in 1862.[38] Their first interclub match, a decisive 45–11 victory over the Powhatans on May 21, was the first game between senior clubs in the New York area. The *Eagle* did not hesitate in attributing the victory to their constant practice, and to the deficiency of the Powhatans in that regard.[39] After a 17–12 loss to the Charter Oaks (playing their first game since 1860), the Stars achieved three straight victories (over the Resolutes of Brooklyn, the Olympics of South Brooklyn, and the Charter Oaks) before suffering their second loss, coincidentally by the same 17–12 score, to the Henry Eckfords of New York (whose home grounds were at Greenpoint, Brooklyn) on August 1. After a signal 31–4 victory against the Constellations of Brooklyn on August 27, the Stars won three straight return games against the Resolutes, Olympics, and the Henry Eckfords. The Stars' 14–10 loss to the Unions of Morrisania on September 27 was characterized by the *Eagle* as "a tiresome game of nine innings." Both the *Eagle* and the *Clipper* commented on the swift but wild delivery of the Union pitcher Bernie Hannigan, who pitched many balls over the batter's head and few over the plate, thus greatly prolonging the game.[40] The Stars had the intention of closing their season with home-and-home matches against the Charter Oaks and the Henry Eckfords. When the former failed to make an appearance on the scheduled date of October 4, the Stars quickly arranged an impromptu match with the Excelsiors. Excellent fielding on both sides plus a wind that blew against the batters kept the final score low—a 5–5 tie in a six-inning game called because of darkness. Ten days later, however, the Stars achieved another victory, 14–5, against the Henry Eckford, and thus ended with a 9–3–1 record for the year.

1863

After intensive spring practice, including an intraclub match on April 30, the Stars "reaped the reward of their industry and good sense" by opening the 1863 season on June 10 with the sound defeat of a first-class club, the Gothams of New York, by a score of 41–16.[41] The Star Club then, for the first time in its history, played rivals from outside the Greater New York region, losing 37–17 to the Athletics of Philadelphia on June 19 but defeating the Hudson River Club of Newburgh on August 6 by the close score of 8–6. The Stars managed to secure three additional victories in 1863, defeating the Empires of New York, the Resolutes of Brooklyn, and the Gothams again; the last-named game featured the baseball debut, on the Gotham side, of future Hall of Famer George Wright. These victories were offset by two losses to the Mutuals, a defeat at the hands of the Nassaus (a club made up of Princeton College students), and a likely additional defeat by the Resolutes. Despite the disappointing 5–5 record, the Stars earned praise from an *Eagle* reporter who, covering the first game with the Mutuals, observed that "the game throughout was played in the true spirit of ball play, the Stars always playing a gentlemanly game in every match they are engaged in; and good examples like bad ones, being contagious, those they play with generally follow their lead as in the match in question."[42]

1864

On April 1, 1864, prior to the opening of the new season, the Stars held a special meeting in their rooms at the corner of Joralemon and Court streets to deliberate on "considerable business of importance to the welfare of the club." Specifically, two resolutions were debated. The first concerned an issue that had divided the Greater New York City clubs since the late 1850s: whether to continue with the *bound game,* in which any batted ball caught on the first bounce was an out, or to switch to the *fly game,* in which fair balls were outs only if caught in the air. Most of the top clubs, including the Stars but with the notable exception of the Atlantics, favored the more difficult fly game. Seeking to settle the issue once and for all, the Star Club members passed the following resolution:

> Whereas, We the members of the Star Base Ball Club of Brooklyn, having become well satisfied of the superiority in every respect, of what is popularly known as the Fly Game, especially as a rule of play conferring additional advantages for a display of skill, and increasing the attractive features of the game; availing ourselves of the privilege allowed by the proviso of the rules, in reference to the Fly Game, contained in the By-laws of the National Association, hereby
>
> Resolve, That during the ensuing season we shall play all practice games, and also such matches with other clubs that can be so arranged, according to the rules laid down in the proviso above referred to.

The *Eagle,* which published the resolution in full, expressed hope that all other first-class clubs would adopt a similar resolution. The other resolution adopted by the Stars abolished the committee on nines and transferred the power of dismissing any unruly or rebellious player to the captain of the nines. The *Eagle* characterized the second resolution as "a good rule, provided the captain is not one likely to play the tyrant."[43]

There is a good likelihood that the *Eagle*'s kind words were self-serving. No doubt most members of the Star Club, like most top players, favored the fly game. The club's decision to give more power to its captain may have been passed in reaction to the recent dismissal of an unidentified but "well known" member because of some objectionable conduct. Yet at the same time, it is hard not to suspect that Henry Chadwick, the long-serving baseball editor of the *Eagle* and the *New York Clipper*, played a role in both decisions, especially the switch to the fly game.

Chadwick had been awarded an honorary membership in the Star Club in 1863, a tribute he valued enough to preserve the acceptance letter from club secretary Bruce A. Chilton among his scrapbooks.[44] His attachment to the club remained such that when he umpired an 1865 game, the box score in the *Eagle* listed him as "Henry Chadwick, Star Club."[45] Chadwick was an outspoken advocate of the fly game and also a prominent supporter of the importance of having a strong captain, so the Star Club's adoption of these two resolutions may have been the result of lobbying on his part. Alternatively, they could have been an effort by club members to curry favor with the game's most influential reporter. In any event, accounts of the Star Club's games in 1864 make it clear that the club followed up on its resolution to abandon the bound rule by insisting that prospective opponents play by the fly game.

The club, as usual, opened its season early with an intraclub game on April 9, but a chilly easterly wind kept attendance down.[46] The club's next recorded outing took place on May 21 and it too reflected the influence of Chadwick. Opponents of the fly rule contended that the rule change would make it too difficult to record outs, so Chadwick arranged a series of "Union Practice" or "Union Prize" games, which were designed to demonstrate the benefits of both the fly game and another Chadwick proposal — a tenth fielder who would play "right short stop." The first experimental contest pitted ten of the best players from the Star Club against a side of ten composed of three each of the first nines of the Atlantic and Resolute clubs, two from the Eckfords, and one each from the Excelsior and Star clubs. The latter side pulled out a close-fought 21–19 victory, but what was more important was that the modest scores of both sides showed that the proposed rule changes would not lead to interminable scoring. A reporter for the *Clipper*, undoubtedly Chadwick himself, added that the first five innings were played in the "unprecedented" time of 45 minutes and the full game in one hour and 57 minutes, which he claimed proved, in this instance at least, "the assertion that the fly game can be played in less time than that in which the bound catch is permitted."[47]

The Stars played their first match game of the 1864 season on July 5, losing 26–22 to the visiting collegiate Nassau Club from Princeton. The account in the *Clipper* pointedly noted that "the game was played on the fly, the Star refusing, and consistently, too, to play any other."[48] By this time, however,

signs were beginning to surface that this stance was making it harder to schedule match games. On July 20 the *Eagle* published a note, allegedly from the secretary of the Enterprise Club, stating that his club would play a game that day against the Stars at the Capitoline Grounds. One day later, however, William H. Murtha, the recording secretary of the Enterprise Base Ball Club, dismissed the note as a forgery and maintained that the secretaries of the two clubs had not yet made any arrangements for a game and that the challenge from the Stars was still being "held for consideration."[49]

The Enterprise Club never did face the Star Club in 1864, but the Stars' resolve to play only the fly game soon paid off. The Atlantics were the most notable holdout against the proposed rule change, which may have been why a scheduled 1863 Star-Atlantic match had been postponed and never played. At the start of the 1864 season, Dickey Pearce and Charles Smith of the Atlantics refused to play by the fly rule in one of Chadwick's Union Prize Games, forcing the game to be played by the bound rule.[50] But by July the club had had a change of heart and agreed to face the Stars in a fly-game series for the first time in club history. The first contest, played on the Star Grounds on July 30 in front of more than 3,000 spectators, saw the Atlantics win 35–16 and make 12 fly catches, a total that nearly equaled the 13 made by the Stars. The fielding highlight of the game was a rare "treble" (triple) play initiated by Star second baseman Kip — in an unspecified inning, according to the *Clipper*, Kip "took a line ball on the fly in handsome style, put out the player at second base and passed the ball to first base to get the player running back out."[51] Less than a week later, on August 4 at the Capitoline Grounds, the Atlantics won again by a near-identical 35–17 score. The account in the *Eagle* suggested that the result would be enough "to convince the [Atlantic] boys that fly game or bound it was all the same to them, as they were bound to win every game this season no matter who their opponents were, and we think it likely that such will be the result."[52] Indeed, the Atlantics went on to complete an undefeated season in 1864, meaning that these two decisive defeats for the Stars were no cause for dismay.

Yet the crusade for adopting the fly game was not going as well. The Enterprise Club was not alone in showing reluctance to play the Stars, which prompted the *Eagle* to chide: "[The Stars] have challenged nearly all the strong clubs, but they put them off until the latter part of the season on purpose, we presume, to have their full strength against the boys. From the style of play shown in the two Atlantic games all who were present seem to think that there are few clubs that can win a ball from the Stars. Are the other clubs afraid of them, or what is it that leads them to act as if they were? ... Who will give them a chance to win a trophy or be defeated? They can bear both defeat and victory well." The account added that the Stars had issued challenges to the Excelsior, Enterprise, Resolute, Eckford, Eagle, Mutual, Gotham, Eureka of Newark, and Active clubs, and that all but the first two had "accepted" the challenge but then made no effort to schedule games.[53]

With their efforts to schedule fly-game matches having had so little success, the Stars announced, in the *Clipper* report on the second Atlantic game, that "they will play any time and any game, bound or fly."[54] Even this olive branch produced disappointing results — the Eckfords sent the Stars a note expressing a willingness to play, while rumors had the Enterprise Club ready to play a bound game whenever the Stars named a day, but neither of these expressions of interest led to a match game.[55] During the remainder of the 1864 season, the Stars' only match against a local rival was a bound game with the Resolutes on September 26, which the Stars won, 15–12.

With local competition in such short supply, the Stars arranged fly games against two upstate opponents and made their first-ever out-of-town trips. On September 17 the Stars took the morning train upriver to Newburgh, where despite missing the services of several regulars, they generated an 11-run ninth-inning rally to defeat the Hudson River Club, 27–26. After being handsomely entertained that evening at the Newburgh Hotel, the Stars returned to Brooklyn early the following morning.[56] Four weeks later, on October 15, the team traveled even farther to play the Knickerbockers of Albany. The members of the host club, according to an *Eagle* reporter, underestimated their guests: "When the Albanians saw the material the Stars were made of, and what light weights they were in comparison to their own stout party, they felt sanguine of an easy victory and went into the fight confident of success; it was not long, however, before they had their eyes opened to two or three interesting facts of which ... they were not previously aware, viz., that light weights can be far more active and efficient in the field, and at the same time bat the ball as far and as well as the heavy men can. In fact the Knickerbockers found themselves not only out played at every point in the field, but what astonished them most, out batted by these 'youngsters' from Brooklyn, the 'old fellers' like the veterans of the Atlantics being 'nowhere' in the race."[57]

The Stars' 31–7 victory in Albany was the third and final victory in a season that had witnessed great difficulties in scheduling match games, at least in part because of the club's insistence on playing the fly game. As a result, the biggest triumph of 1864 may have come after the season when the membership of the NABBP finally voted to approve the fly game (though foul balls caught on one bounce would remain outs for another two decades).

1865

With the move of the Excelsiors to the Capitoline Grounds, the Stars in early 1865 became the sole occupants of their grounds adjoining Carroll Park in South Brooklyn, a situation that led the *Eagle*'s reporter to remark, "They now have the reputation of all South Brooklyn to keep up, and must work early and late to maintain their honor."[58] As usual, the Stars were the first regional club to play a game — an intraclub match on April 1.[59] By early May the *Eagle* reported that the first nine would be selected from Frank Norton, Tom Mac-Diarmid, Kip, Hope Waddell, Pete Flanders, Sullivan, Herb Worth, Mitchell, Tom Morris, De Camp, and Kelly, and that the club intended to do "big things" in the new season; the *Eagle* itself anticipated that the Star nine would "prove formidable and efficient, and will doubtless worry many of the very best Clubs.[60]

No doubt Star Club member Henry Chadwick was responsible for most of these assessments, which may be why they proved far too optimistic. On May 30 at Hoboken, the Stars lost to the Eagles of New York by a score of 40–31. Heretofore the Stars had been known as "the most stylish and graceful players," but two game accounts probably written by Chadwick emphasized the loose play of the Stars during this game; the wildness of their throws, he wrote in dismay, made for "about as poor a display, as a general thing, as we ever saw the Stars make." He attributed the poor fielding to the fact that they had not once played their nine together, "their practice games being played according to the old fogy style of making up even sides on practice-days rather than playing each member of their nine on their regular positions, and all on one side, so as to make them familiar with each other's play."[61]

A June 24 victory over their old rivals, the Enterprise Club, suggested that the conditions of the Star Grounds had deteriorated as much as the Stars' fielding. The *Eagle* reporter described the field as "a vacant lot with cobble-stone paved streets on three sides, and the lot a stony and sterile waste," and pointed out that "no man can be expected to make much headway with spikes, on pavements."[62]

The highlight of the Stars' season was a visit to the Philadelphia region, where they played four games with local opponents during a 48-hour period centered on Independence Day. After leaving on the 7 A.M. train from the Courtlandt Street station in Manhattan on the morning of July 3 and arriving around noon in Camden, New Jersey, they beat the Camden Club 54–29 that afternoon. The next day, in what may have been the first-ever doubleheader scheduled by a club from Greater New York, the Stars in the morning lost 25–14 to the Athletics of Philadelphia, the champion Pennsylvania team, but beat the venerable Olympics of Philadelphia 31–22 in the afternoon. One day later they concluded the whirlwind tour with a closely contested 32–31 win over the Keystones of Philadelphia, in a game that was called after eight innings because of darkness.

Although the Stars' traditional good fielding was on display in the games in Philadelphia, wild throwing recurred when the Keystones paid a visit to Brooklyn on July 28. The Stars nonetheless escaped with a 37–34 victory, at least in part because the ingestion of a lobster salad the night before at the home of Mortimer Rogers had left many of the Keystone players ill and in no shape to play.[63] The game was also marred by some delaying tactics and other activities "prejudicial to the interests of the game" by Star second baseman and club secretary Tom MacDiarmid. At a special meeting of the club on August 3 the membership condemned his behavior and voted to suspend him from playing in games for the remainder of the season.[64] The suspension seems to have applied only to first-nine games, because his name later appeared in the lineup of a second-nine game.[65]

After another series of postponements, which prompted the *Eagle* to complain that games should not be postponed due to the absence or indisposition of an individual person, a Star-Enterprise return game was played late in the afternoon of August 5.[66] The game, however, was preceded by a rainshower that soaked the grass at the Capitoline Grounds and made the ball clammy. Fielding and batting were thus very poor on both sides in a 47–38 Stars victory.[67] At the same site five days later, the Stars suffered a 26–13 defeat at the hands of the champion Atlantics, which had not lost since the 1863 season.[68]

Soon after these games, several first-nine Star players mysteriously departed from the club. It is tempting to view the departures as fallout from the MacDiarmid suspension, but in fact Captain Tom Morris's formal resignation coincided with his family's return to Philadelphia as the result of his father's failing health. Frank Norton and another longtime starter named Mitchell also left the club without any public explanation, so we can only guess as to their reasons. Whatever the reason, the weakened state of the club led the *Eagle* to observe: "The Star Club, once a formidable and prominent organization, is now subject to almost constant defeat.... A few years ago, the Stars were regarded as a 'crack' club, and no club was entitled to beat them very bad. But other clubs were made strong through the weakness of the Stars, and their best men left them."[69]

Not surprisingly, the Stars lost their final two games of 1865, both lopsided defeats at the hands of the Unions of Morrisania. The losses meant that, despite the success of the Philadelphia trip, the Stars ended the 1865 season with a disappointing 4–5 record. The campaign had also been marred by surprising lapses in fielding and the loss of several first-nine players late in the year. Clearly, the Stars needed to reorganize with a new stock of first-class players.

1866

In contrast to other years, 1866 saw the Stars open their season relatively late, with their first match occurring on June 2 when they hit nine "clean" home runs (that is, ones not aided by poor fielding) to defeat the Independent Club of South Brooklyn 46–24.[70] Their next match, on June 19, was against the revitalized Excelsior nine, which during the winter had acquired not only Star players Norton and Mitchell, but also, at least temporarily, standouts Dickey Pearce and Fred Crane from the Atlantics. The *Sunday Mercury* described the encounter as "not only the finest game they have ever played to-

gether, but [also] the best display the Stars have ever made in a match since they had their old nine together, and it was certainly one of the prettiest games of the season thus far." The *Eagle* similarly described it as "decidedly the best game of Base Ball, that has been played this season." The Excelsiors, however, also "never played better," and a rally in the final two innings enabled the Excelsiors to claim a 27–20 victory.[71]

The Stars' third game was a match with the Athletics of Philadelphia, one of the leading contenders for the national championship. The Athletics were particularly noted for their powerful offense, but the Stars' skillful defense kept the contest close until another late surge gave the Philadelphia club a 37–19 victory. Despite the two consecutive losses, the *Eagle* praised the Stars for having "gained a reputation on which they may well pride themselves — that of being the best fielding club in the country."[72]

The remainder of the 1866 season was a mirror of the first three games. The Stars were consistently victorious against lesser clubs, winning a return game against the Independents and also beating the Unionville Club of Gravesend and Actives of New York (twice apiece), the Monitors of Goshen, and the venerable but still respectable Eagles of New York, 82–19. But they generally lost to the top nines, including the Mutuals and the Atlantics. Their final record was 8–6.

1867

The Stars compiled a 6–4 mark in 1867 and upheld their reputation by beating weaker opponents — the season included a win over the Mohawks of Brooklyn, two victories over the Independents, and a triumph over the visiting Excelsiors of Rochester. There were also two wins over clubs with strong reputations but both came with asterisks. A late-season victory over the Irvingtons was the result of forfeit, while a split with the Eckfords of Brooklyn was less impressive than usual because the Eckfords were struggling through a disappointing year.

Yet while the 1867 season was not a disastrous one for the Stars, it was in almost every way a disappointing one. Other clubs were adding talented young players, but the Stars continued to use the same lineup of veterans, many of whose best days seemed to be behind them. The only notable addition to the first nine in 1867 was future major leaguer Fraley Rogers, and even he had been one of the club's regular reserves in 1866. While most clubs played an increasing number of games in the years immediately following the Civil War, the Stars actually played four fewer contests in 1867 than they had the previous year (including the forfeit victory). After opening the season against the Independents in April, the Stars did not take the field against an outside opponent until July 4, when they lost to the Atlantics at the Union Grounds, 39–21.

At the end of July the Stars were subjected to a 24–10 beating by the strong but cantankerous Irvington, New Jersey, club, which had sprung a remarkable upset against the Atlantics the previous season and featured one of the most talented nines in the metropolitan area. This was followed by another lengthy period of inactivity and the doldrums continued when the Star Club returned to action in September. In a return game against the Atlantics, the Stars suffered their worst loss ever, a 34–7 thrashing.

It was the last straw for Henry Chadwick. Dropping any pretext of anonymity or impartiality, the influential sportswriter described himself as "the first to bring the ability of the Star Club into public notice in 1857" and proceeded to lash out against the club's management. Their lack of judgment and poor arrangement of matches, he argued, meant that "all the advantages naturally accruing from their fine material [i.e., players] is [sic] almost entirely thrown away, and instead of ranking as their individual skill in the game would warrant, they are obliged to occupy a second-rate position." Players were being placed in the wrong positions, he maintained, yet "The men in power in the Club have a prejudiced objection to advice from any quarter, whether made in the interest of the Club or not."[73]

The 1867 season thus ended with a cloud hanging over the Star Club: would its postwar lethargy continue or would the club be able to regain the enthusiasm that had once made it a major force on the Brooklyn baseball scene?

1868

The first game of the 1868 season was intended to be a practice match that would allow the Mutuals to test the skills of their new pitcher, Rynie Wolters. Wolters had been a member of the erratic Irvington nine and in subsequent years was to acquire a reputation for unreliability and temperamental behavior. The Mutuals gained an inkling of what was in store for them when he failed to show up for the game against the Stars. Because the only reason for designating the match a practice game was the desire to test Wolters' ability, the two clubs agreed to play a "regular" match in his absence. Unfortunately, news of the change in plans did not reach several of the Stars' best players, who joined Wolters among the missing. Absent their top talent, the Stars lost, 28–6.[74]

Between June 8 and 20, the Stars were defeated by three powerhouse clubs, the Atlantics, Mutuals, and the defending "national" champion Unions of Morrisania. Despite the outcomes, the Stars had always prided themselves on their fine fielding, and it was an encouraging sign that they were able to hold the Mutuals and Atlantics to 13 runs apiece. The Mutual game was described by the *Clipper* as "one of the best played and most interesting games of the present season." The loss to the Unions was by a less impressive 36–17 score, but that was in part attributable to the absence of some of the Stars' regulars.[75]

Despite significantly less severe competition over the next month, the Stars split their next four games. Both victories came at the Capitoline Grounds against the Independents. On the Fourth of July, the Stars journeyed to New Haven, Con-

necticut, for a holiday match against the nine of Yale University. The game was supposed to be an early affair beginning at 9:00 A.M., but as frequently happened, it was an hour later before play actually commenced. The game was played under a scorching sun, and temperatures reached into the 90s. As noon approached and the heat intensified, the play grew sloppy. Yale scored 12 times in the seventh inning to break open a close game and went on to a 31–14 victory.[76] On July 22 the Stars lost again, this time to the lightly regarded Harlem Club of New York.

Tours were the rage in 1868, and a number of clubs left their home bases and journeyed to other cities. One such club, the Olympics of Washington, D.C., arrived in New York in mid–August, lost decisively to the Atlantics, Mutuals and Eckfords, and fell to the Stars, 15–13. The victory over a club from a distant city was gratifying, but perhaps the most noteworthy aspect of the game was that it marked the first appearances in Star uniforms of former Excelsiors Arthur "Candy" Cummings, catcher Herbert Jewell, and first baseman John Clyne.[77] A fourth former Excelsior, hard-hitting outfielder George Hall, soon joined the threesome. The club that had provided talent to the Excelsiors when the latter was at its zenith was now acquiring talent as the Excelsiors became less competitive and more social.

It is always difficult to determine the reason for pioneer-era player movement, and the manner in which these former Excelsiors joined the Stars seems to have been downright labyrinthine. Each of the four had been Excelsior regulars in 1867, but none of them had played in a single game for any club as of late June of 1868. Some of the mystery surrounding them fell away on June 22, when the *Brooklyn Daily Eagle* revealed that Hall and Cummings had joined the Mohawk Club of Brooklyn, which was "determined to have a first class nine." It was rumored that "two or three others equally as celebrated will join them."[78] Later that week, the Mutuals and Mohawks engaged in a "friendly game, arranged for the purpose of giving practice to the new nines," with Cummings and Hall playing on the Mohawk side and Jewell on the Mutual side.[79]

But something went amiss during the next few weeks. The Mohawks had never been regarded as a strong club, so perhaps promises that other top players would join the former Excelsiors did not come to pass. Under-the-table payments were a major part of the baseball scene by 1868, so money may have also played a role, although the Stars always billed themselves as an amateur club. In any event, Cummings left the Mohawks in mid–July without playing a match game for them, and joined the Stars, where he was soon followed by Hall, Jewell, and Clyne.[80]

The "reconstructed Stars," as the *Clipper* labeled them, brought in several additional reinforcements, including Hy Dollard and Eddie Booth.[81] The new lineup showed signs of improvement, most notably in 57–9 and 76–9 thrashings of the Harlem Club that had earlier handed the Stars an embarrassing defeat. Even with the new lineup, however, the familiar pattern of victories over lesser opponents and losses to the top clubs marked the remainder of the Stars' 1868 campaign. Wins over the likes of the Actives and the Independents were offset by defeats at the hands of the Atlantics, the Unions of Morrisania, and the Unions of Lansingburgh, and when the ledgers were closed, the Stars showed a record of 9–10.

But at least the late-season losses had been by respectable margins, while the increased activity and new additions gave hope that better days were ahead. In the judgment of an *Eagle* reporter, presumably the indefatigable Chadwick, "The Stars have an excellent team, with plenty of first-class reserve, and with practice with each other, and a nine that could be present at each game, there is no reason why they shouldn't rank up with the best of the day. They have always been celebrated as fielders, and in the new nine they have batsmen as well as fielders."[82]

1869

The 1869 season was an eventful one for the Stars, in which the potential of the new players, especially the talented battery of Cummings and Jewell, was realized. Unfortunately, this was the season in which the NABBP allowed open professionalism, a decision that made it very difficult for amateur clubs to remain competitive with the professional clubs. The Stars opted to compete as an amateur club and, given the diminished expectations, their season was an unqualified success.

The club opened play early as usual, ringing in the new season at the Capitoline Grounds on April 10 with "one of the old fashioned jolly days when everybody will take a hand in and enjoy themselves to the best of their 'know how.'"[83] It was two months before the first match game, however, and until August almost all of the Stars' contests were convincing victories over such fellow amateur clubs as the Eagles of Flatbush, the Alphas of Brooklyn, the Powhatans of Brooklyn, the Lowells of Boston, and the Harmonics of Brooklyn.

The occasional contest against a professional rival was also sprinkled in, most notably on June 19, when the Stars stunned the Mutuals, 26–12. It was perhaps the greatest victory in the club's history, as well as one of the most dramatic — the Stars used nine-run rallies in both the seventh and eighth innings to overtake their astonished opponents. It was a victory that the *New York Times* said the Stars should consider as "a feather in their cap," while the *Eagle* concluded that the Mutuals were "outplayed at every point of the game — in the field, at the bat and at pitcher's point." Unfortunately, the Stars did not get the recognition they deserved in many quarters. For one thing, there was only a small crowd on hand, as most baseball aficionados were at the Union Grounds watching the Eckfords defeat the Haymakers. Further, local fans had been satiated with top-flight baseball in the preceding days, for the Red Stockings of Cincinnati, in the midst of their fabulous

tour, had just left the city after defeating each of the top local nines in succession. Worst of all, the Mutuals were a perpetually suspect club and their defeats were followed by speculation as to whether the players had exerted themselves to the fullest. In this case, the Stars' late rally had been aided by dropped fly balls, wild throws, and a change of pitchers by the Mutuals. There is no reason to believe the game was fixed, but the circumstances deprived the Stars of the credit they had earned.[84]

Over the remainder of the 1869 season, wins over openly professional clubs were rare, yet the Stars built a reputation for playing close games with and occasionally defeating their professional brethren. A contest against the Atlantics on July 3 resulted in a close-fought 15–10 defeat. This was followed by a 49–11 drubbing of the visiting Olympics of Washington, D.C., on July 19, a result that led the *Clipper* to declare that "the Stars are one of the strongest amateur clubs in the country, and will trouble some of the strongest professionals before the season is over."[85] A rematch against the Mutuals, played on August 14 at the Union Grounds, ended in a 22–18 loss but brought more acclaim. The *Clipper* compared the 20-year-old Cummings to legendary Excelsior pitcher Jim Creighton, the standard by which all promising youngsters were measured, and commended the pluckiness of catcher Herbert Jewell, who fielded well despite laboring under the handicap of very sore hands.[86] Two weeks later, the Stars dropped another close game to the Atlantics, 27–22, but earned more praise when their stellar fielding of old re-emerged.[87] The club also dropped a rubber game to the Mutuals on October 2 by a 16–6 score — this time it was poor fielding behind Cummings that was blamed for the defeat.

Although their regular series had been completed, the Stars and Atlantics met again on September 25 to raise funds for a worthy cause. Proceeds from this game were donated to a fund for the 110 people (including five boys between the age of 12 and 17 and two volunteer rescuers) who had died on September 6 when a fire broke out in the Avondale Colliery of the Steuben Coal Company mine shaft in Plymouth, Pennsylvania. Sparks, apparently from the ventilating furnace, set fire to the wood-lined shaft, and flames then engulfed the wooden coal-processing plant, or breaker, situated over the shaft, which was the only entrance to the shaft. As a result, all of the miners below were asphyxiated in the anthracite coal industry's deadliest tragedy. Unfortunately, publicity for the game was insufficient, and the proceeds of $120.50 fell short of expectations. To the disappointment of the Stars, the game resulted in yet another closely contested loss, this time by a score of 17–13.[88]

While most of their contests against professional rivals produced only moral victories, it was a different story for the Stars in a late-season series against the Champion Club of Jersey City, New Jersey. The *Clipper* billed the series as being for the amateur championship, pointing out that the Stars "have held the nominal title of champions for a number of seasons, no club, till the present season, disputing their title thereto," while "the Champions have always held a high position as strong players, and 'over in Jersey' were looked upon as almost invincible." [89] The basis for this claim is cloudy, especially since the *Clipper* also billed a Star-Oriental match, held during the season, as being for "the championship of the amateurs." [90] But the Stars removed the doubt by dispatching both opponents, beating the Orientals in a single match and then defeating the Champions in a series that took the full three games to decide.

Although there had been some disappointing losses, the Stars posted a number of impressive victories during the 1869 season and finished with a very good record of 16–6. The *Eagle*, in a summary of the 1869 season, predicted, "If this [Star] nine continues together, it will bother the best professional nines of next year." [91]

1870

The 1870 season saw the Stars again live up to their reputation as the club that made the earliest appearance on the playing field. On a chilly and windy March 26, the Stars defeated a field nine on their old grounds at Carroll Park by a score of 19–7 in a game blessedly ended after five innings. [92] On April 9, in a game played at the Capitoline Grounds, the Stars easily defeated a second field nine, comprising five Atlantics and four other players from the Alpha and Excelsior clubs, by a score of 27–8. [93]

The two exhibition contests prepared the Stars for an early-season schedule in which eight of their first ten opponents were professional clubs. The brutal schedule began at the Union Grounds on May 7 against the Mutuals, who were heavy favorites among the betting fraternity. Instead, the "inimitable pitching of Cummings completely bothered" the Mutuals, whose shaky fielding also contributed to the Stars' 14–3 upset victory. [94] One week later, a crowd of 3,000 spectators packed the Capitoline Grounds to see if Cummings could show the same mastery in a match billed as being between "the champion Atlantics and the Stars — the champion amateurs of the Union." Cummings puzzled plenty of Atlantic batters, but he was outpitched by George Zettlein, who allowed only a single first-inning run as the Atlantics gained an 8–1 victory. [95]

Four days later, on May 18, the Stars took an afternoon train to the Waverly Fair Grounds in Elizabeth, New Jersey, where they secured a 22–9 victory against the amateur Resolutes, who found Cummings' pitching "too troublesome to punish much." [96] The Stars then defeated the professional Eckfords twice by the convincing scores of 15–9 and 24–6. [97] Unfortunately, rain and bad ground conditions terminated the first of these games after eight innings and also washed out a scheduled return game with the Atlantics and terminated a match with the Athletics of Philadelphia before the required five innings were completed. [98] This last event put a damper

on the beginning of a Southern tour by the Stars, which saw them gain 28–7 and 25–18 victories over two Baltimore clubs, the professional Marylands and the amateur Pastimes respectively, and win by forfeit over the Olympics of Washington, before losing 9–5 to the professional Nationals of Washington in a rain-shortened six-inning game.

The Stars then hurried home to prepare for their biggest match of the season. On June 18, four days after their famous long winning streak had been broken by the Atlantics, the Red Stockings of Cincinnati faced the Stars at the Capitoline Grounds before an enormous crowd estimated at over 8,000. The *Times* reported that betting was brisk at the beginning of the game, and that "one gentleman had $40,000 out in different sums." Few anticipated a close contest, but the Stars kept the game close in the early going and trailed only 6–4 after four innings. The visitors added five more in the top of the fifth, seemingly putting the game out of reach, but then the clutch batting of the Stars took even their most devoted followers by surprise. They gained back one run in the bottom of the fifth and followed with a six-run sixth-inning rally to tie the game. Word must have spread about the closeness of the match, as the overflow crowd continued to grow. Alas for the Stars, the Red Stockings used clean home runs by Gould and Harry Wright to counter with five unanswered runs and earn a hard-fought 16–11 victory. Even so, the Stars' loss was certainly a respectable showing against a legendary team of salaried professionals. The *Times* reporter characterized the game as "one of the most exciting ever played at the Capitoline," and he wasn't excluding the aforementioned Atlantic-Red Stockings match. [99]

This completed the toughest part of the Star Club's schedule and the next three weeks were child's play by comparison. The Stars embarrassed the hopelessly overmatched Eagles of Flatbush by a score of 96–0 on June 25 in a game that lasted only seven innings. The newlywed Cummings then departed on his honeymoon, but his absence wasn't missed during a pair of Independence Day games in Connecticut that saw the Stars dispatch the state champion Mansfields of Middletown and the Wesleyan University collegiate nine. [100]

It was back to the grind for Cummings and the Stars five days later when the visitors were the White Stockings of Chicago, a club dubbed the "$18,000 nine" because of the unprecedented salaries that its players received. Yet the high-priced Chicago club had suffered back-to-back defeats at the hands of the Atlantics and Mutuals, and the crowd was limited by the general expectation that the Stars would win with ease. Those who did turn out were treated to an exciting game that saw the White Stockings hang on for a 9–6 win. The Stars actually played the game under protest, complaining that Burns, the new pitcher of the White Stockings, was a recent transfer from another club and therefore ineligible to play. [101]

The game against the White Stockings completed the toughest part of the Star Club's 1870 schedule. During the remainder of the season there were quite a few challenging matches, but also quite a few contests against overmatched amateur clubs such as the Osceolas of Brooklyn and the Warrens of New York City. The highlight was a victory over the Atlantic Club, though the win was tempered by the absence of Zettlein, which forced the inexperienced Jack Chapman to pitch for the Atlantics with only seven fielders behind him during the early innings.[102] On the downside, there were a pair of losses to the Mutuals, which meant that for the second straight season the Stars had lost the season series after winning the first game. The Stars also suffered losses to the Forest City Club of Cleveland and the Harvard College nine and split two more games with the Pastime Club of Baltimore.

Despite the setbacks, the Stars ended the 1870 season with a very respectable 24–9 record. The 33 games represented a significant increase from the activity of any previous season and were indicative of the growing thirst for baseball that was sweeping the entire Northeast quadrant of the country.

1871

The winter following the 1870 season was a tumultuous one, with the growing trend toward professionalism threatening the future of amateur clubs like the Stars. By March of 1871, no fewer than four members of the Stars' "champion nine" of 1870 were reported to have signed with professional clubs. Nevertheless a *Brooklyn Daily Eagle* reporter — undoubtedly Henry Chadwick — predicted that the "prospect is very promising for a great revival of amateur ball playing," led by the Excelsiors and the Stars. He assured his readers that these clubs embodied "the game as played in its integrity, and in a manner which excludes those objectionable features which have become attached to the game through the medium of the worst phases of base ball professionalism."[103]

On the day after the article appeared, the first professional baseball league was organized in New York. The formation of the National Association of Professional Base Ball Players, which became better known as the National Association, meant more turmoil for amateur clubs like the Stars, and a follow-up article in the *Eagle* suggested that four starters would leave for professional clubs — catcher Nat Hicks, first baseman Packer, second baseman Ed Beavan, and pitcher Candy Cummings.[104]

Cummings ended up deciding to remain with the Stars for the 1871 season, but the lure of the professional league wrought havoc on a lineup that had been remarkably stable in 1870. Packer left the club, but never did play professional ball, while Beavan departed to play for Troy, only to soon return to the Star fold. The catching position was the biggest problem — Hicks had succeeded Herbert Jewell during the 1870 season and had proved expert at handling the still-new curveball, but Hicks had now departed and Jewell chose not to rejoin the Stars.

The effects were obvious on April 26 when the Stars opened their season with the customary game against a field nine. The Stars' loss, 13–12, led the *Eagle* reporter to suppose that "the Stars must have thought that with Cummings to pitch they could face any field. But this is not the first time a similar mistake has been made. Creighton himself would have failed but for the excellent support he had." In critiquing the Star Club's lackluster fielding, he pinpointed the glaring need for a catcher, noting, "None have succeeded better than Jewell as yet."[105] After the game against the field nine, the club suffered another loss when Bob Manly, the last player whose career dated back to the Star Club's prewar glory years, left the first nine.

Three new players, named Bennett, Bond, and Fish, had represented the Stars in the field game, but they too soon departed. Yet even with all this turnover, the Stars had a strong returning nucleus that included Cummings, longtime center fielder Herb Worth, the versatile Hy Dollard, dependable John Clyne, Fraley Rogers, and his brother Mort. Eventually the gaps in the lineup were filled, with a newcomer named Breen taking over at second base and another youngster named Tommy Barlow also joining the first nine. Barlow began the season at shortstop but soon was assigned to fill the catching void and was pronounced "the most effective man they have had there since Jewell left, as he is as plucky as the best, and more active in the position than the others."[106]

The majority of the Star Club's games in 1871 were against opponents like themselves that were billed as strict amateurs. In these contests, the Stars compiled a glittering record and came within one run of going through the season unbeaten. The long series of victories included two triumphs apiece over the Amity Club of South Brooklyn, the Mansfields of Middletown, and the Aetnas of Chicago, and single wins over the Athenians of New York, the Actives of Newark, the Brooklyn juniors, a visiting club from Savannah, Georgia, the Harmonics of South Brooklyn, and the Yale College nine. There were several other scheduled matches for which no result was reported. The season's only known blemish against a strictly amateur opponent occurred on June 10, when the Athletics of Brooklyn eked out a ten-inning 14–13 victory. The Stars avenged the defeat three months later and at season's end both the *Times* and the *Eagle* declared the Stars to be the winners of the "amateur championship" for 1871.[107]

The Stars also played six games in 1871 against the openly professional clubs that made up the National Association, but failed to win any of them. Several of these defeats were by the narrowest of margins, such as a 9–8 loss to the Troy Haymakers in a game played in Troy on August 1. An even more agonizing loss took place at home on May 26 when the Stars coughed up a 19–10 lead by allowing the Olympics of Washington to score 11 runs in the eighth inning. Other defeats suggested that there was quite a gap between the amateur champions and their professional brethren. A 23–10 loss to the Forest City Club of Rockford, for instance, was said to show that the Stars were "not yet in condition to cope with first-class professional clubs."[108]

The Stars also played three games in 1871 against their old rivals, the Atlantics. The Atlantics had been paying salaries to their players for several years, but they chose not to join the National Association. As a result, they lost many players to the entrants in the new league and whether they should be considered amateur or professional in 1871 is debatable. In any case, the Atlantics defeated the Stars twice in July, before the Stars rebounded on September 9 to win the final game of a rivalry that dated back to 1859.

While the 1871 season had seen the Star Club retain the amateur championship, professional play had received the lion's share of the attention of both the press and public. As the end of the season approached, even the club's most loyal supporters seemed to sense that it was the end of an era. An *Eagle* reporter—once again, undoubtedly Chadwick—wrote poignantly in October, "As this is the last season that Cummings will play with the Stars, they had better retire on their present laurels, and, leaving ambitious efforts to win future honors as United States amateur champions to other aspirants, go in simply for old time trophies, won on a field where the only incentive is the honor of winning the trophy in a pleasurable contest, and in which gate money receipts and profit and loss are not taken into consideration."[109]

1872

Even before the 1871 season had ended, Candy Cummings was being actively pursued by several National Association teams, and he ultimately joined the Mutuals. The departures to the professional ranks continued over the winter, with Fraley Rogers joining the Boston Red Stockings. An especially crippling blow came when the Atlantics elected to join the National Association and recruited several members of the Stars, including Tommy Barlow.

The extreme difficulty of fielding a strictly amateur team that was competitive against the growing number of salaried professional nines was now inescapable. Under the circumstances, it might have been wisest for the Stars to disband, but instead the club made a few tentative efforts to extend its life. On May 1, 1872, secretary John Sterling announced a meeting to be held on the following day at the Star Club rooms in the Hamilton Building.[110] A June 15 game at the Capitoline Grounds against the venerable Knickerbockers was soon scheduled, prompting the prediction in the *Eagle* that the game would be "one of those pleasant amateur games in which the two nines will go in for recreation and sport instead of to win gate money and bets."[111] Yet such exhibitions no longer held much appeal, and only 100 or so spectators turned out to watch a 49–11 Star victory. In the assessment of the *New York Times*, "never since the primitive days of the game has so complete a display of 'muffinism' been witnessed. The Stars, who once shone as champions, were out of practice and played an

indifferent game. Of the Knickerbockers, the less said the better."[112]

The Stars next scheduled a game against the Atlantics, with the announcement being accompanied by the defiant declaration that "all the gate money [was] going to the Atlantics ... the Stars not sharing gate money this season."[113] No report of the outcome has yet been found. On June 29, 1872, the Stars took the field again to face another club with a rich history, the Gothams of New York. But this ancient club was having an even harder time fielding a competitive nine than the Stars, with the *Eagle* reporting that the Gothams, "apparently unable to collect a representative nine of New Yorkers, have gathered into their fold some Brooklyn players, including Galpin and McCrea, of former nines of the Star Club." The resulting lineup was, with inadvertent humor, described as a "mixed up team" and the Stars won by the lopsided score of 29–12.[114] It was the last known game played by the Stars.

Epilogue

In March of 1873 Fraley Rogers, after one year of professional play, announced his retirement from baseball and expressed his "hope to see my old club retain the championship." An *Eagle* reporter—once again, no doubt Henry Chadwick—observed that the Star Club was an organization that was "not dead but sleeping." With characteristic optimism, he declared, "The Stars intend shining brightly again when that 'revival' is inaugurated. It's bound to come."[115] But it was not to be, and the lack of any reported games, or even any social activity, after 1872 is an indication that the club never awoke after 1872.

In later years, Chadwick often reminisced about his favorite amateur clubs from the 1850s and 1860s. The Pastime Club, in particular, was a regular subject of his recollections. The Star Club had also been a favorite of his and had even awarded him an honorary membership, yet the activities of the Stars figured far less often in his reflections on bygone days.[116] So too the members of the Stars were less inclined than the members of contemporary clubs to gather for reunion games or to publish their recollections. It seems likely that the longevity of the Star Club was at least in part to blame for this absence. The Pastimes, for example, did not survive the war and thus consisted primarily of a single group of members with shared memories. By contrast, the Stars had three distinct nucleuses of talent—the prewar glory years with such players as the Morris brothers, the Patchen brothers and the Whiting brothers; the postwar group of the likes of Waddell, Mitchell, Flanders, MacDiarmid, and Sullivan; and the final years, featuring such players as Cummings, Worth, Jewell, Clyne, Dollard, and the Rogers brothers. Only Bob Manly spanned all three eras and the players from different periods may not have known one another at all, with the result that as time went by it became harder for Chadwick and the players to think of the Star Club as a single entity.

In any event, the Star Base Ball Club of South Brooklyn

left an important legacy. Particularly impressive was the club's ability to evolve from a junior to a senior club and to also survive the transition from amateur to professional play for longer than most of its contemporaries. Despite the loss of top players to senior clubs like the Excelsiors and Charter Oaks in its earlier years, and the later departures of talented players to professional clubs, the club was remarkably successful in recruiting new players and remaining competitive. That success finally came to an end in 1872, when professional play gained such ascendance as to all but obliterate amateur competitors. Nevertheless, the Star Club deserves to be remembered for its many contributions to the pioneer era of baseball.

CLUB MEMBERS

Tommy Barlow: Tommy Barlow caught for the Stars in 1871, then went on to an ill-fated professional career with several major-league clubs. At the end of the 1872 season Henry Chadwick wrote a glowing tribute to Barlow's skill and character, describing him as "a regular, earnest and plucky worker, and one of the most active of catchers, Tommy watching the ball and handling it with the agility of a cat. He was also on the *qui vive* in playing points; in fact he played the position finely throughout the season. A feature of his play was his thorough good humor, and especially his avoidance of that error of catchers, bullying the umpire, one of the greatest mistakes a catcher or pitcher can make. In this respect Tommy Barlow was the model catcher of the season, and when we add that he was thoroughly reliable we give him credit for the best requisite of a professional player."[117] By 1877 he had been arrested for theft and told a sad story of having become a hopeless morphine addict as the result of a severe blow to the head suffered during a game. While some of the details of Barlow's story have been disproved, such mistakes are hardly surprising under the circumstances, and the underlying tale rings true. Barlow was still alive in 1880 but his troubled life had ended by 1888 under unknown circumstances.[118]

E.P. Beavan: E.P. Beavan was a regular for the Stars in 1870 and went on to have a brief major-league career. Though officially unidentified, there is little doubt that he was Edward Price Beavan, who was born in 1845 in Brooklyn, served briefly during the Civil War, and died in Brooklyn on December 28, 1920.

Ed Booth: Ed Booth was a close friend of Candy Cummings who went on to play for four major-league teams, yet he remains one of the most inscrutable players in baseball history. Aside from his friendship with Cummings, not a single biographical fact about him was recorded during his career and subsequent researchers have had just as difficult a time in identifying him. It seems likely that he later worked as a photographer and died in New York City on December 21, 1928, but that remains unproven.

Breen: An unidentified player with this surname joined the Star Club in 1871 and was a regular during that transitional season.

Oliver Brown: See Atlantic Base Ball Club.

John L. Bynner: Born in Brooklyn around 1842, the son of British immigrants, John L. Bynner served as Star Club vice president in 1856 and 1857 and then became president in 1858. By 1860, however, he was no longer a member. Bynner was around 30 when he died in Brooklyn in 1872.[119] His brother Edwin later became a well-known novelist.

Bruce Archibald Chilton: Born in Brooklyn around 1844, Bruce Chilton played for the Star Club in 1862 and served as club secretary in 1863. He later worked as a bookkeeper and was past 90 when he died in Brooklyn on May 23, 1936.

John Clyne: See Excelsior Base Ball Club.

Henry J. Creighton: The only Creighton whose name appears in the 1860 membership listing was Henry J. Creighton, who does not appear to have been a relative of Jim Creighton. Born in Nova Scotia in 1839, Henry Creighton is most likely the Creighton who made appearances for the Star Club in 1856 and 1858. He later became a cotton broker and died in Richmond County on December 3, 1905.

Jim Creighton: See Excelsior Base Ball Club.

Arthur "Candy" Cummings: Candy Cummings is the member of the Stars whose name is most likely to be recognized by today's baseball fans. Cummings' claim to fame is that many sources credit him with having invented the curveball by experimenting with throwing a clamshell as a teenager. Others made competing claims, but Cummings lived until 1924, and was thus able to make his case and defend it over many decades. Born on October 18, 1848, in Ware, Massachusetts, Cummings was a slightly built man, who, although listed as 5-feet-9 in height, weighed only 120 pounds during his playing days. After his family moved to Brooklyn, Cummings began playing baseball at Carroll Park for a club of youngsters known as the Carrolls. Every aspiring ballplayer at Carroll Park dreamed of playing for the Stars or the Excelsiors, and in 1865 Cummings became a member of the Star's junior nine, where, according to his recollection, he led the club to a 37–2 record. The next year he and teammate Eddie Booth were noticed by Joe Leggett and joined the Excelsior Club, once one of the best nines in the country but by then on the downslide.[120] It was around 1867 that Cummings would later claim to have first thrown a curveball in competition (though his version of events changed often). In 1868, Cummings joined the Star first nine, where he remained for the next four years. The young pitcher apparently came from a relatively comfortable background, and was not tempted by the professional offers he undoubtedly received. In 1872, however, he signed with the Mutuals of the National Association. He also signed with the Haymakers of Troy and probably a third club. A lengthy wrangle ensued, after which Cummings ended up with the Mutuals and was one of the best pitchers in the league, winning 33 games. Cummings became a vagabond professional player, moving to the Baltimore Club, the White Stockings of Philadelphia, and the Dark Blues of Hartford during the next three years. He alternated with young Tommy Bond for a fine Hartford club in 1875, finishing 35–12. The following year, his last productive one as a pitcher, Cummings played less frequently with the Dark Blues in their first year in the National League, compiling a 16–8 record. He served as president of the International Association in 1877, and also pitched briefly and ineffectively with the National League club in Cincinnati and played his final game as a professional on August 18, 1877. He played for a number of amateur and semipro teams over the next few years before settling in Athol, Massachusetts, and starting a paint and wallpaper business, which he operated for 30 years. He died in Toledo, Ohio, on May 16, 1924. Based upon his claim to the invention of the curveball, Cummings was elected to the Hall of Fame in 1939.[121]

Henry "Hy" Dollard: Born in Brooklyn in 1849, Henry S. Dollard joined the Stars in 1868 and served as the club's starting shortstop for several seasons. He also earned a reputation as "the crack skater of the Capitoline grounds when the best skaters in the city gathered on its ice in the winter and he won many fine trophies for his fancy work on skates." Dollard never played professional baseball, choosing instead to work as an insurance agent in the New York office of Lloyds of London. In addition, he became known as one of Brooklyn's best whist players. Dollard, who never married, died in Brooklyn in 1920.[122]

Henry W. Fairbanks: Henry Fairbanks was secretary of the Star Club in 1856, vice president in 1858, and pitched for the club during its early years. A *Porter's* correspondent described him as a "very good" pitcher, adding, "(B)ut he loses time in delivering the ball; he bats well, and is a good catcher."[123] In early 1859 he was described as "a cool, collected, and graceful player.... He is a good pitcher, and excellent general player."[124] He did not play for the Stars after 1859 and later joined the Excelsiors. An 1888 article described Henry Fairbanks as a member of the "Sidney Place Crowd" of youngsters, which also included fellow Star Club members Latham Fish and the Morris brothers.[125] Yet his identity remains a very puzzling mystery, as searches of the censuses, city directories and the *Brooklyn Eagle* have not turned up a plausible candidate.

Latham Avery Fish: Latham Fish, who served as club secretary in 1857, was born in Brooklyn on January 21, 1842. Along with the Morris brothers and Henry Fairbanks, Fish was a member of the "Sidney Place Crowd." There he earned a reputation as one of the best marble players, and became "so severe in his fancies as an amateur that he always declined to enter a game where the stakes were not exclusively pure agates."[126] Like several early club officers, Latham Fish was no longer a club member in 1860 when a list of members was published. Fish served in three different Civil War regiments and earned the rank of captain. He later became a prominent

banker and Vice-Commodore of the New York Yacht Club. He died in Greenport, Long Island, on September 21, 1909.

Pete Flanders: Pete Flanders was an infielder who played for the Star Club from 1863 to 1867. There is some mystery about his identity, but a list of club officers during those years included a James P. Flanders, and a later note about the whereabouts of Star Club members reported that Flanders was living in the South. Based on these clues, he is believed to be James Pierpont Flanders, who was born in Macon, Georgia, on September 21, 1845, and was living in Florida when the Civil War broke out. This man's whereabouts during the war are not known, but his father was a native of Connecticut so a temporary relocation to the North seems plausible. James Pierpont Flanders was back in Macon by the time of the 1870 census, and the name Flanders appears in the box score for a Macon club during that year. James Pierpont Flanders was still living in Macon and working as a bookkeeper when the 1900 census was taken. His health failed soon afterward, and he and his wife moved to Gainesville, Georgia, to live with their married daughter. He died at her home on June 29, 1903. An obituary stated that he had been born in Poughkeepsie, New York, and had lived there for many years, but that statement does not correspond to his census listings.[127]

George Henry Flanley: George Flanley is perhaps best known as the shadow of legendary pitcher Jim Creighton. He played with Creighton on the Niagara Club in 1858 and with the Star Club in 1859, and jumped in tandem with Creighton to the Excelsiors for the 1860 season, a move suspected to have been induced by monetary incentives. Born on June 7, 1840, in New York, Flanley was just 5-feet 6-inches tall and weighed less than 150 pounds during his playing days. He was known as a good fielder but a weak batter. After changing clubs twice in two years, as noted above, Flanley settled in with the Excelsiors and played with them until 1868, when he joined the Mutuals. He was a regular infielder with the Mutuals in 1868 and 1869. Flanley was respected for his ability to serve capably as an umpire, and he lived a long and successful life after leaving the ballfield. He was the head of the Brooklyn telegraph system, and later moved to Chicago, where he died on April 10, 1915, at the age of 74.

James Howard Forker, Jr.: James Forker, Jr., played for the Stars from 1857 to 1861 and served as club treasurer in 1859. Born in 1841, he was the oldest of several ballplaying brothers; his brother William was a substitute for the Stars, while another brother, Tom, played for the Excelsiors and Mohawks before enjoying a brief professional career. Tom Forker is profiled in the entry on the Maryland Club of Baltimore. James Forker later worked as a bookkeeper.

H.A. Fuller: A player named H.A. Fuller was a regular for the Stars in 1859–1860. He is presumed to have been Henry Appleton Fuller, who was born in Brooklyn around 1842 and served in the Civil War. Never married, Fuller died in Manhattan on October 17, 1916.[128]

Galpin: It's possible that this player was John A. Galvin, who is profiled in the entry on the Atlantic Club of Brooklyn, but his surname was consistently spelled with a "p" so it seems more likely that the Star player was someone else, identity unknown.

George Hall: See Atlantic Base Ball Club.

Nat Hicks: See Eagle Base Ball Club.

Holt: Someone with the surname of Holt played for the Stars in 1860 and 1861. In 1885 Henry Chadwick identified the Star player as Guy Holt and in 1891 he stated that Holt of the Stars was deceased.[129] However, Marshall Wright identified the 1860 player as "S. Holt" and the club's 1860 constitution and by-laws list "Seymour Holt" as a club member.[130] It thus appears that Chadwick made the understandable mistake of confusing two players with the same surname and that the Star Club member was Seymour Holt. The ballplayer is thus believed to be H.R. Seymour Holt, who was born in Buffalo on June 11, 1842, the son of Horatio Nelson "Henry" Holt and the former Abby Goodman Seymour, a cousin of New York Governor Horatio Seymour. "Henry" Holt was one of the pioneers of doing business along the Erie Canal and the family moved to Brooklyn when Seymour was an infant.[131] Seymour Holt worked as a commission merchant while living in Brooklyn, before eventually settling in Brookline, Massachusetts, where he died on February 21, 1910.[132]

Richard Hunt: See Mutual Base Ball Club.

Herbert Jewell: See Excelsior Base Ball Club.

Joseph Johnson: Joseph Johnson played for the Stars from 1867 through 1869. His identity remains unknown.

Kelly: An unidentified player named Kelly played for the Stars from 1861 to 1864. An 1862 note stated that he was serving in the Civil War, but nothing else is known about him.[133]

Joshua Leavitt, Jr.: Joshua Leavitt, Jr., the original treasurer of the Star Club, was the son of Reverend Joshua Leavitt, one of the most prominent abolitionists of the era. Only months before the birth of his youngest son, Rev. Leavitt was one of the organizers of the Amistad Committee, which raised funds for the mutineers on the slave ship, *La Amistad.* Joshua Leavitt, Jr., was born in Bloomfield, New Jersey, on November 12, 1839. After a successful career as a dry goods merchant, Leavitt took his own life in Manhattan on November 9, 1901.[134]

William H. Lennon: Future major leaguer Bill Lennon was a regular for the Stars in 1863 and 1864. See the entry on the Marylands of Baltimore for details on his life.

Thomas C. MacDiarmid: Tom MacDiarmid, who was born in the state of New York around 1835, appears to have begun his career in 1858 for the Clinton Club of Brooklyn, a club for which his brother William also played. Tom MacDiarmid seems to have first played for the Star Club in 1864. He was Star Club secretary in 1865 when the club felt the need to publicly rebuke him for his actions in a game against the Keystone Club. He returned to the Stars later in 1865, however, and remained a fixture at second base for the club through the end of the 1869 season. He finally lost his spot on the first nine in 1870, but in at least one game "old reliable Tom Macdiarmid" was pressed into duty as a result of injuries.[135] As of 1880, MacDiarmid was farming in Cranford, New Jersey.

John W. Manly, Jr.: John W. Manly, Jr., the brother of Star Club stalwart Bob Manly, enlisted in New York's 159th Regiment and was killed in combat in 1863.[136]

Robert Manly: "Little Bob" Manly played for the Stars for the longest time span. He was a member of the first nine during its glory years in the late 1850s and remained a regular as late as 1870. An 1891 note indicated that he was still in Brooklyn, leaving no doubt that the ballplayer was a clerk by that name who was born around 1841 and was the brother of fellow club member John W. Manly, Jr.[137] This man was not married as of the 1900 census, and he died on May 1, 1901, age 60, and is buried at Green-Wood Cemetery.

F.J. Miller and F.O. Miller: These two original club members pretty much have to be Frederick J. and Frank O. Miller, the twin sons of a Brooklyn fancy goods merchant who were born around 1840. Their common names make them difficult to trace with any high degree of confidence.

Mitchell: A man named Mitchell played for the Star Club's first nine from 1860 to 1865 and later joined the Excelsior and Crescent clubs. Information about him, however, remains in short supply. According to the club's published constitution and by-laws, his first name was James, though at least one note referred to him as Joseph Mitchell.[138] He was reported to still be living in Brooklyn in 1891, but little else is known about him.[139]

Charles Ellis Morris: Charles Morris, Tom's younger brother, was born in Wellsborough, Pennsylvania, on March 7, 1844. He was a regular for the Stars in 1860 and 1864 and played a few games in the intervening years, but as with his brother, his college studies often prevented him from playing. Charles Morris began college at the University of the City of New York (now known as New York University) and concluded his studies at Williams College in Massachusetts. He then returned to Philadelphia with his father and became one of that city's best-known lawyers. When he died in Philadelphia on February 10, 1879, soon after his marriage and the birth of his first child, his grief-stricken friends published a 48-page tribute that stressed both his legal acumen and his many contributions as superintendent of the Hollond Mission Sunday School.[140]

Thomas Burnside Morris: Thomas B. Morris was born in Wellsborough, Pennsylvania, on May 13, 1842. His father, William Morris, was a noted civil engineer and railway builder who moved the family to Brooklyn in 1853 when he became president of the Long Island Railroad Company. Tom and his younger brother Charles were soon prominent members of the group of Brooklyn youngsters known as the "Sidney Place Crowd" in honor of the vacant lot that was their favorite play-ground. Tom earned a reputation for possessing an "accuracy of aim and strength of arm" so great that it was said that he "could 'pot' a man within a 400 foot range" with a stick, stone or snowball any time he desired.[141] Tom and Charles also became fixtures on the baseball diamonds surrounding their new home. Once he was old enough to join a junior club, Tom Morris became the catcher of the Star Club and one of its most prominent players during its prewar glory years. In addition, he and several other members of the Stars, including Sam Patchen and Hope Waddell, were part of a group of Brooklyn cricketers who called themselves the American Cricket Club.[142] Yet sports were never a priority in his life. He was an engineering student at the University of the City of New York (New York University) during these same years, and perhaps it was no coincidence that the university's first baseball club was formed in the spring of 1859.[143] Morris became a Star Club director in 1860 but he earned his B.S. one year later and played little baseball after graduation. He worked briefly for his father's railroad and then spent a couple of years in Panama. He was back in the United States by 1864, but by then failing health had led his father to resign from the Long Island Railroad Company and return to Philadelphia. Tom Morris appears to have split time between the two cities during the next year. In September 1864 he wrote to the *Eagle* and identified himself as captain of the Stars.[144] When the Stars made their 1865 tour of Philadelphia, he reclaimed his old position as catcher, prompting the *Eagle*'s reporter to exclaim, "See what a difference a good catcher makes."[145] But in the end Morris's responsibilities in Philadelphia proved more pressing and he formally resigned from the Stars. In the spring of 1867 there were new reports that Tom Morris was going to rejoin the Stars, but as it turned out his playing days were over.[146] He headed to Utah in 1868 to work as an engineer with the Union Pacific Railroad, then spent several years as a railroad engineer in Ohio and Minnesota. He returned to Philadelphia long enough to marry in 1871, but then in 1874 he and his young family headed west, where Tom Morris went into the coal business. He spent two years in the state of Washington before settling permanently in San Rafael, California, and becoming president of the Renton Coal Company. He held that position until his sudden death in Oakland on November 8, 1885, as the result of an attack of paralysis.[147] The short life of Thomas Burnside Morris was full of accomplishments, and his papers are now housed at the Historical Society of Pennsylvania along with those of his only son, Roland Sletor Morris, the U.S. ambassador to Japan from 1917 to 1921. Yet Morris's ballplaying days were also part of his legacy, and a mention of his passing in the *Brooklyn Daily Eagle* described him as the "old Star Club's catcher."[148]

Frank Prescott Norton: Frank Norton was born on June 9, 1845, in Port Jefferson, New York, and was one of the early players to aggressively change clubs. After playing for the Stars from 1863 to 1865, Norton received an offer to play for the champion Atlantics in 1866. But when he got a better offer from the Excelsiors of Brooklyn, Norton deserted the Atlantics along with Dickey Pearce and Fred Crane. In 1867 he became one of the many members of the Nationals recruited from New York with offers of clerkships, playing catcher, second base, and shortstop over the next two seasons and taking part in the Nationals' famous trans-Allegheny tour in 1867. He then played for the Olympics of Washington in 1870. Norton became a major leaguer by accident, entering Washington's opening day game in 1871 when catcher Doug Allison split his thumb. After baseball he returned to New York and became a successful contractor. He also inherited money, which enabled him to move to Connecticut and live in luxury. By 1920 he was living in a large country house on the Boston Post Road at Greenwich and wintering in South Carolina. Frank Norton died at his home in Greenwich on August 1, 1920.[149]

Packer: A first baseman named Packer became one of the Star Club's regulars in 1870 but even his first name remains a mystery.

Edward F. Patchen: The three ballplaying Patchen brothers were members of an old Brooklyn family that originally owned a large tract of land known as the Patchen farm, in what later became the 1st and 6th wards. All three brothers played for the Stars in 1859, Ed at third base, Sam at shortstop, and Joe in right field. Ed Patchen was also one of several club members to occupy the presidency during the tumultuous 1859 campaign. Sam and Joe Patchen joined the Charter Oak Club in 1860, while Ed alone remained a member of the Star Club, though he did not play for the first nine after 1859. Sam and Ed later ran the Patchen Brothers stock brokerage firm. The oldest of the trio, Ed nonetheless outlived Sam and Joe by almost 40 years, dying in Brooklyn on October 7, 1924, at the age of 86.[150] He is buried with his two brothers at Green-Wood Cemetery in an "imposing granite vault" located near that of Jim Creighton.[151]

Joseph A. Patchen: Joe Patchen, the youngest of the brothers, was a Civil War veteran who was still single when he died in Brooklyn in 1876. Like his brothers, he worked as a Wall Street broker and had been a volunteer fireman with Pacific Engine Company 14 up until the advent of the paid fire department.[152]

Samuel W. Patchen: Sam Patchen was the shortstop of the Stars until leaving for the Charter Oaks in 1860. He also served as a Star Club director in 1858 and as club secretary in 1859. According to Henry Chadwick, Sam was "regarded as the best short stop outside of the Atlantic Club" during those years.[153] He left the baseball diamond after the 1860 season, and operated a stock brokerage with his brother Ed. Sam Patchen remained a regular attendant at local games until his sudden death in 1885 as the result of falling down a flight of stairs at the Brooklyn Club. He was only 44.[154]

Fraley Rogers: Fraley Rogers, a brother of Mort Rogers (captain of the Resolutes of Brooklyn and one of the leaders of the amateur NABBP) and Al Rogers, was born in Brooklyn in 1850. Fraley played with the Stars as an outfielder from 1867 to 1871. In 1872 he was the regular right fielder for the National Association champion Red Stockings of Boston, batting .275 in 45 games. In March 1873 he wrote a letter to the *Eagle* in which he declared, "I have declined all offers, and decided not to play, as my time is engaged otherwise in business."[155] Rogers did, however, come back to play one additional game for the Red Stockings, on July 5, 1873, but never played professionally thereafter. On May 10, 1881, he committed suicide in New York City by shooting himself with a handgun.

Mort Rogers: See Lowell Base Ball Club.

William W. Skaats: William W. Skaats was a Brooklyn composer and professor of music who spent limited time on the first nine of the Star Club, but who nonetheless made important contributions to the club. Skaats was the pitcher and captain of the Star second nine in 1861 and his "indefatigable" passion for baseball did much to keep baseball matters lively in Brooklyn during the gloomy first year of the Civil War.[156] With the Stars often hard-pressed to field a full lineup, Skaats also took part in five of their six first-nine matches. At the close of the 1861 season the "energetic Captain of the Star Second Nine" arranged a "donkey game" of baseball at the Star Club's grounds. The appeal of this scheme, which involved trying not to score runs, is now hard to fathom, yet Skaats managed to enlist the services of many of Brooklyn's best players.[157] Skaats played for the first nine of the Stars in their June 1862 match against the Charter Oaks, beginning the game in center field and ending it as the pitcher, where his work "gave general satisfaction."[158] But it was his final appearance with the first nine, and his enthusiasm for baseball seems to have waned after that. His age may well have been a factor, as he was born in 1830, making him a full decade older than most of his Star teammates. Nonetheless Skaats performed one final important service for the Star Club when he proposed Henry Chadwick for an honorary membership, a token that resulted in no end of free publicity. As of 1900, the widowed Skaats had moved to Nassau County. He is now best remembered as the composer of a patriotic song, "All Hail to the Flag of Freedom."

Sullivan: A player named Sullivan was the Stars' principal pitcher from 1865 until the arrival of Candy Cummings in 1868. In his debut with the Stars on May 30, 1865, Sullivan was described as having "achieved some notoriety as a pitcher in Junior clubs, and in the prize game between New York and Brooklyn played very well. His pitching is not attended with a very rapid delivery, but the balls are very twisty. He takes too much time, however, from the time the ball lodges in his hand until he delivers it again, and this creates a very long game. He batted splendidly, and altogether he is an improvement to the nine as formerly organized."[159] Another report of the game offered the assessment that Sullivan was "unquestionably a valuable acquisition to the club. He is a great bat,

an excellent fielder, runs his bases well, and as a pitcher promises to excel. He has one other merit, and that is steadiness and judgment in delivery. He is perhaps a little too slow in his movements and delivery; but it is better to be slow and sure than quick and inaccurate."[160]

Albert Thake: Outfielder Al Thake played for the Stars for part of the 1871 season and then joined the Athletics of Brooklyn. He played for the Atlantics in 1872 after that club joined the National Association, but on an offday toward the end of the season he took part in a fishing expedition near Fort Hamilton and drowned. Thake, who was only 22, was remembered as "a favorite with his companions [who] stood high in the professional fraternity for integrity of character and genial disposition,... He will be missed by the Atlantic Club both on and off the field."[161]

Frank Thompson: A player or players named Thompson represented the Star Club from 1862 through 1868. At least part of this record belongs to Frank Thompson, a well-known Brooklyn player whose career lasted well into the professional era. Frank Thompson was described in one later account as now being "in mercantile life" in the city. But it seems unlikely that Frank Thompson was playing for a senior club as early as 1862, so part of the record may belong to a different man by the same surname. Adding to the confusion, a man named William J. Thomson was president of the Star Club in 1865 and later a club director.

Gus Ticknor: See Atlantic Base Ball Club.

George Douglas Tracy and William Wolcott Tracy: Brothers George D. (born November 26, 1839) and William W. Tracy (born September 29, 1842) were both Star Club officers during the club's early years and one of them played for the club's first nine until the end of the 1860 season. George's age makes it seem more likely that he was the one who played for the first nine, but the evidence is not conclusive. William died in Manhattan on December 1, 1886; the details of George's life remain unknown.

John S. Van Cleef: John S. Van Cleef was the original president of the Star Club, filling that position in both 1856 and 1857. There were two young men in Brooklyn by that name at the time, so it is not possible to identify Van Cleef with absolute certainty, but all signs point to the Star Club's first president having been John Schenck Van Cleef, a lifelong resident of Brooklyn who was born around 1841 and died in 1916. A member of a prominent Dutch family, Van Cleef's home was on Livingston Street, one of the four streets that surrounded the vacant lot that was home to the "Sidney Place Crowd." He enrolled in the first class of Brooklyn's Polytechnic Institute, also located on Livingston Street, when it opened in 1855. At the outset of the Civil War, although newly married, Van Cleef enlisted as a lieutenant in Company H of New York's Thirteenth Regiment, serving alongside General Thomas S. Dakin, one of the major figures of baseball's pioneer era and later to become Van Cleef's brother-in-law. After the war he went into the hat and cap business, becoming the senior partner in the Manhattan firm of Van Cleef & Nutman. After the death of his father-in-law, wealthy Brooklyn builder Daniel A. Robbins, Van Cleef became the executor of Robbins's extensive holdings, a task that consumed most of his energies for the remainder of his life. Though he was 75 when he died at his Brooklyn home on September 28, 1916, he was still in such vibrant health that it was reported that "his many friends were shocked at the news of his sudden death." John Schenck Van Cleef is buried at Green-Wood Cemetery.[162]

Hope M. Waddell: Hope Waddell played first base for the Star Club from 1861 until 1868. Born in Ireland around 1841, he worked as a civil engineer in Brooklyn and also ran a business with his father. He disappeared from the city directory in the mid–1880s and his whereabouts after that are not known.

W. Weeks: A man by this name played for the Stars during the 1860 and 1861 seasons, but without knowing his full name he can't be identified with certainty. It seems likely that the man in question was Washington W. Weeks, a Civil War veteran who died in Rockville Centre, Long Island, on June 17, 1916, age 75.[163]

Charles Lowell Whiting, Franklin Phillips Whiting, Frederic Augustus Whiting, and John Campbell Whiting: The Whiting brothers are a bit difficult to keep straight, as there were seven in all and at least three played for the Stars. Fred, Charles, and John are believed to have been the brothers who played for the Stars in 1858, with Fred and John also playing in 1859. A man identified as "F.P. Whiting" was club president in 1859, which has to be a fourth brother, since P was Frank's middle initial. Meanwhile, John served as a club director that year. John and Charles moved on to the Excelsiors in 1860, with John being featured in the famous picture of that club's nine. Their playing careers ended with the outbreak of the Civil War, with the exception that one brother — it's not clear which one — played for the Excelsiors in 1863. As will be clear from the sketches that follow, they left baseball behind because they had more serious concerns. Charles Lowell Whiting, the oldest of the ballplaying brothers, was born in 1835. In 1863 he married Lucy Tifft, a member of a prominent Buffalo family. Lucy's brother, George Harrison "Harry" Tifft, was killed two years later in the American Hotel fire, and Whiting took over the management of the Tifft family business, a steam-engine foundry and boiler works. Lucy Whiting died in 1869, leaving him with two young children. Charles Whiting remarried but stayed in Buffalo and continued to manage George W. Tifft & Sons until the business closed in the mid–1890s. Charles died of Bright's disease on Christmas Day in 1898.[164] Franklin Phillips Whiting was born in 1837 and took over the family business when his father, George, a print and lithograph dealer, died in 1862. Frank Whiting closed that business around 1869 and later became a carpet wholesaler. He remained in Brooklyn until his death on November 8, 1918. Frederic Augustus Whiting was born in 1840 and became an investment broker. He lived in Tennessee and New Jersey before settling in Framingham, Massachusetts, where he and his wife were still living when the 1920 census was taken. He apparently died later that year. His son Frederic Allen Whiting, Sr., became the first director of the Cleveland Museum of Art. John Campbell Whiting was born in 1842 and fought in the Civil War in the same regiment as Joe Patchen. He became a Brooklyn investment broker, and Chadwick reported seeing him at a ballgame at Washington Park in 1891.[165] John Whiting was 87 when he died at his daughter's home in Lanesboro, Massachusetts, on September 26, 1929.[166]

Herbert Worth: Herb Worth joined the Star Club in 1863 and remained a fixture in the club's outfield through the end of the 1871 season. He then enjoyed a brief major-league career. Born on May 2, 1847, Worth later worked as a bookkeeper and died in Brooklyn on April 27, 1914.

Other Club Members: F.S. Aymar, G. Allen Jr., Anderson, Bancroft, Barnett, S. Barstow Jr.,(vice president, 1859), John E. Beale (vice president, 1867), Charles H. Belknap (director and substitute, 1859), Bennett, Bond, John C. Boyd, Henry Bradish, Harrison Brainard (Asa's brother; see Excelsior Base Ball Club for details), Brown, Bucklin, E.L. Carpenter, Carter, Chappell, W.H. Condit (one of several men to serve as president in 1859), D. Crocker, E. Curtis, James S. Cushman, A.M. DaCosta, David, DeCamp, Doty, H. Ferris, William Forker, P.C. Garrison, James Gayler, R. Gignoux, J. Kimball Gordon (captain of second nine in 1867), Greenwood, Mason Griffith (captain of second nine in 1866), Alfred Hammatt (president, 1867), Charles A. Hammatt, Henry, Francis H. Howland (treasurer in 1859), Richard Hunt (see Mutual Base Ball Club), W.R. Hunter, Jackson, Jerome, Simon F. Johnson, Kip, F.W. Lawrence, R.B. Lawrence (club secretary in 1859), T. Lennington, W.G. Lord, S.E. Lounsbury, William R. MacDiarmid (club member by 1860, club secretary in 1867 and occasional first-nine substitute; brother of Thomas), McCrea, McCullogh, McKenzie, E. McMannus, Merwyn, Mudge, Mumby, Charles B. Peck (vice president in 1866), Clifford Pierson, Povie, Price, Reeve, J.M. Robins, James Scott, C.H. Seaman, M. Seaver, James Smieton, Toby Smith, John Sterling (club secretary in 1871–1872), T.F. Stoddard, J.S. Story, Thomas, William J. Thomson, W. Watson, Frederick B. Weeden (club vice president in 1859 and subsequently treasurer, but no longer a member by 1860), George Wheelwright, Samuel Wheeler, Whitney, Wickham, A. Wilson, R.B. Woodward, W. Woodward.

Notes

1. The word "South" was not part of the club's official name, which, according to the club constitution, was "Star Base Ball Club of Brooklyn."

2. *New York Clipper*, November 22, 1856, 247.

3. The August 22, 1857, issue of *Porter's Spirit of the Times*, for instance, specified that the Stars would be practicing on Tuesdays and Fridays and the Excelsiors on Wednesdays and Saturdays.

4. *Brooklyn Eagle,* March 14, 1864, 2.

5. *Constitution and By-Laws of the Star Base Ball Club of Brooklyn* (New York: Mann, Stearns & Beale, 1860).

6. Veritas Amator, "The Base-Ball Controversy," *Porter's Spirit of the Times,* December 12, 1857, 228; Square, of the Enterprise, "The Enterprise Dispute," *Porter's Spirit of the Times,* December 19, 1857, 244.

7. "Base Ball," *Porter's Spirit of the Times,* November 22, 1856, 197; "Ball Play: Enterprise vs. Star," *New York Clipper,* November 22, 1856, 247.

8. "Base Ball: Match between the Star Club, of Brooklyn, and the Enterprise Club, of Bedford," *Porter's Spirit of the Times,* November 29, 1856, 213; "Ball Play: Base Ball — Star vs. Enterprise," *New York Clipper,* November 29, 1856, 255.

9. "The Sidney Place Crowd," *Brooklyn Daily Eagle,* January 15, 1888, 11.

10. According to the article, "Conspicuous in the clan were Latham Fish, George and Dan Chauncey, John Scrymser, James B. Bach, Tom and Charley Morris, sons of the president of the Long Island Railroad; Henry Fairbanks, Joe Bostwick, Charles Ely, Charley Sproule, Tom, Sam and Will Cochrane and many others." Four of these fourteen were also members of the first or second nine of the Star Club, while Bach was a prominent member of the senior Excelsior Club and was one of the founders of the Niagara Club of Buffalo. See *Base Ball Pioneers, 1850–1870* for a profile of Bach.

11. "The Sidney Place Crowd," *Brooklyn Daily Eagle,* January 15, 1888, 11. The author's initials were given as "P.M.B." but the author was not necessarily the source of the reminiscences, which appear to have been the result of a gathering of several former members of the "Sidney Place Crowd."

12. "The Sidney Place Crowd," *Brooklyn Daily Eagle,* January 15, 1888, 11.

13. An Observer, "Out-Door Sports: Base Ball: Enterprise vs. Star," *Porter's Spirit of the Times,* October 3, 1857, 77; "Out-Door Sports: Base Ball: The Union, vs. The Star," *Porter's Spirit of the Times,* October 17, 1857, 101; "Out-Door Sports: Base Ball: Star vs. Union," *Porter's Spirit of the Times,* December 5, 1857, 212.

14. Delta, "Out-Door Sports: Base Ball: Enterprise vs. Star," *Porter's Spirit of the Times,* October 24, 1857, 117.

15. "Out-Door Sports: Base Ball: Star vs. Enterprise," *Porter's Spirit of the Times,* November 21, 1857, 180; Square of Enterprise Club, [letter to editor dated 39 [*sic*] Nov 1857], *Porter's Spirit of the Times,* December 5, 1857, 212; Veritas Amator, "The Base-Ball Controversy," *Porter's Spirit of the Times,* December 12, 1857, 228; X, "Out-Door Sports: Base Ball: Base Ball Sketches –No. 6," *Porter's Spirit of the Times,* November 28, 1857, 196; X, "Out-Door Sports: Base Ball: Base Ball Sketches –No. 8," *Porter's Spirit of the Times,* December 12, 1857, p. 228.

16. One of the Constellation, "Out-Door Sports: Base-Ball: Star Base-Ball Club," *Porter's Spirit of the Times,* May 15, 1858, 164.

17. "Out-Door Sports: Base-Ball: Enterprise vs. Star," *Porter's Spirit of the Times,* June 5, 1858, 212.

18. "City News and Gossip: Base Ball," *Brooklyn Daily Eagle,* June 2, 1859, 3; "Out-Door Sports: Base-Ball: Star vs. Charter Oak," *Porter's Spirit of the Times,* June 4, 1859, 213; "Star vs. Charter Oak," *New York Clipper,* June 4, 1859, 51; "Out-Door Sports: Base Ball: Charter Oak vs. Star," [New York] *Sunday Mercury,* June 5, 1859, 8.

19. The match was originally scheduled for August 27, but for reasons unknown was postponed to September 3.

20. "Base Ball: Star Club vs. Niagara," *New York Times,* July 20, 1859, 5.

21. "Out-Door Sports: Base-Ball: Star vs. Niagara," *Porter's Spirit of the Times,* 341.

22. "Out-Door Sports: Base Ball: Star vs. Niagara," [New York] *Sunday Mercury,* July 24, 1859, 5.

23. The *carte de visite,* which was probably issued in the mid–1860s, was found in the Culver Studio in 1983 by John Thorn and Mark Rucker.

24. "Old Brooklyn Ball Players," *Brooklyn Daily Eagle,* April 26, 1905, 4.

25. "Out-Door Sports: Base Ball: Star vs. Excelsior," [New York] *Sunday Mercury,* September 4, 1859, 5; "Base Ball: Star Club vs. Excelsior," *New York Times,* September 5, 1859, 1; "City News and Gossip: Base Ball," *Brooklyn Daily Eagle,* September 8, 1859, 3; "Out-Door Sports: Base-Ball: Star vs. Excelsior," *Porter's Spirit of the Times,* September 10, 1859, 20; "Star vs. Excelsior — An Exciting Contest," *New York Clipper,* September 10, 1859, 164.

26. "Out-Door Sports: Base Ball: New Jersey vs. Brooklyn," *Porter's Spirit of the Times,* 69.

27. "City News and Gossip: Knickerbocker vs. Star," *Brooklyn Daily Eagle,* September 14, 1859, 3; "Sporting News: [B]ase Ball: Knickerbocker of New-York, vs. Starr [*sic*], of Brooklyn," *New York Times,* September 15, 1859, 8; "Out-Door Sports: Base Ball: Star vs. Knickerbocker," *Porter's Spirit of the Times,* September 24, 1859, 53.

28. "Out-Door Sports: Base Ball: Knickerbocker of New York vs. Star of South Brooklyn," [New York] *Sunday Mercury,* October 2, 1859, 5.

29. "Out-Door Sports: Base Ball: Hamilton (of Jersey City) vs. Star (of South Brooklyn)," [New York] *Sunday Mercury,* October 2, 1859, 5.

30. "Out-Door Sports: Base Ball: Star (of South Brooklyn) vs. Atlantic (of Bedford)," [New York] *Sunday Mercury,* October 9, 1859, 5.

31. "City News and Gossip: Base Ball — Match between the Atlantic and Star Clubs," *Brooklyn Daily Eagle,* October 20, 1859, 3; "Out-Door Sports: Base-Ball: Atlantic vs. Star," *Porter's Spirit of the Times,* October 29, 1859, 132 & 133; "Star vs. Atlantic," *New York Clipper,* November 5, 1859, 229.

32. "Base Ball: Charter Oak vs. Star," [New York] *Sunday Mercury,* undated clipping in Chadwick Scrapbooks, vol. 8; "Star vs. Charter Oak," *New York Clipper,* November 19, 1859, 245.

33. "Defeat of the Atlantics," *Brooklyn Times,* July 20, 1860.

34. "Base Ball Season," *Brooklyn Daily Eagle,* April 3, 1861, 3.

35. "Star vs. Charter Oak," undated *New York Clipper* clipping in Mears Collection.

36. "Out-Door Sports: Base Ball: Star vs. Olympic," *Brooklyn Daily Eagle,* September 28, 1861, 2.

37. "Out-Door Sports: Base Ball — Star vs. Hamilton," *Brooklyn Daily Eagle,* October 5, 1861, 3.

38. "Out-Door Sports: Base Ball: Star First Nine vs. Second Nine," *Brooklyn Daily Eagle,* March 27, 1862, 2.

39. "Out-Door Sports — Base Ball: Powhattan [*sic*] vs. Star," *Brooklyn Daily Eagle,* May 23, 1862, 2.

40. "Base Ball: Union, of Morrisania vs. Star, of Brooklyn," *Brooklyn Daily Eagle,* September 29, 1862, 2; "Union vs. Star," *New York Clipper,* undated clipping in Mears Collection.

41. "Star" and "The Gotham vs. Star," undated *New York Clipper* clippings in Mears Collection.

42. "Out-Door Sports — Base Ball: An Interesting Match at South Brooklyn — Star vs. Mutual," *Brooklyn Daily Eagle,* September 5, 1863, 2.

43. "Sports and Pastimes: Base Ball: The Star Club," *Brooklyn Daily Eagle,* April 2, 1864, 2.

44. Chadwick Scrapbooks, letter to Chadwick from Star Club secretary Bruce A. Chilton, dated February 5, 1863.

45. *Brooklyn Daily Eagle,* August 18, 1865, 2.

46. "Sports and Pastimes: Base Ball: First in the Field," *Brooklyn Daily Eagle,* April 11, 1864, 2.

47. "Ball Play: The Union Prize Match on the Star Grounds," *New York Clipper,* undated clipping in Mears Collection; "Sports and Pastimes: The Prize Base Ball Game at South Brooklyn: Over 2,000 Spectators Present: A Lively and Well-Played Game," *Brooklyn Daily Eagle,* May 23, 1864, 2.

48. "Nassau vs. Star," *New York Clipper,* undated clipping in Mears Collection.

49. "Sports and Pastimes: Base Ball: Enterprise vs. Star," *Brooklyn Daily Eagle,* July 20, 1864, 2; "Sports and Pastimes: Base Ball: Enterprise vs. Star," *Brooklyn Daily Eagle,* July 21, 1864, 2.

50. "Capitoline: The End of the Old Ball Grounds," *Brooklyn Daily Eagle*, April 2, 1880, 1.

51. "Atlantic vs. Star," *New York Clipper*, undated clipping in Mears Collection.

52. "Sports and Pastimes: Base Ball: Another Large Assemblage on the Capitoline Grounds," *Brooklyn Daily Eagle*, August 5, 1864, 3.

53. "Sports and Pastimes: Base Ball: The Star Club," *Brooklyn Daily Eagle*, August 8, 1864, 2.

54. "Atlantic vs. Star," *New York Clipper*, undated clipping in Mears Collection.

55. "Sports and Pastimes: Base Ball: The Star Club — A Letter from their Captain," *Brooklyn Daily Eagle*, September 21, 1864, 2. As the title implied, the article included a letter, dated September 9, 1864, from Thomas B. Morris, the captain of the Stars, to the *Eagle* editor.

56. "Sports and Pastimes: Base Ball: Star of Brooklyn vs. Hudson River of Newberg [sic]," *Brooklyn Daily Eagle*, September 19, 1864, 3; "Star, of Brooklyn, vs. Hudson River, of Newburgh," *New York Clipper*, undated clipping in Mears Collection. The two articles are identical, indicating a common author, presumably Henry Chadwick.

57. "Sports and Pastimes: Base Ball: The Star vs. Knickerbocker," *Brooklyn Daily Eagle*, October 17, 1864, 2.

58. "Opening of the Base Ball Season: What the Different Clubs Purpose: Brooklyn Still to Keep the Lead in the National Game: The Organization of the Clubs for 1865," *Brooklyn Daily Eagle*, March 27, 1865, 2.

59. "Out-Door Sports: Base Ball," *New York Times*, March 28, 1865, 2.

60. "Sports and Pastimes: Base Ball: The Star Club," *Brooklyn Daily Eagle*, May 6, 1865, 2.

61. "Sports and Pastimes: First Base Ball Game of the Season: Eagle versus Star Club," *Brooklyn Daily Eagle*, May 31, 1865, 2; "Star vs. Eagle," *New York Clipper*, undated clipping in the Mears Collection.

62. "Sports and Pastimes: Base Ball: Enterprise vs. Star — The Star Club Victorious," *Brooklyn Daily Eagle*, June 26, 1865, 2.

63. "Base Ball: Keystone vs. Star," *New York Times*, July 29, 1865, 8; "Sports and Pastimes: Base Ball: Star vs. Keystone," *Brooklyn Daily Eagle*, July 29, 1865, 2; "The Visit of the Keystone Club of Philadelphia to the Metropolis," *New York Clipper*, undated clipping in Mears Collection.

64. "Sports and Pastimes: Base Ball: Well Deserved Rebuke," *Brooklyn Daily Eagle*, August 8, 1865, 3.

65. "Sports and Pastimes: Base Ball: Resolute vs. Star," *Brooklyn Daily Eagle*, September 4, 1865, 2.

66. "Sports and Pastimes: Base Ball: Is it Justifiable?" *Brooklyn Daily Eagle*, July 15, 1865, 2.

67. "Out-Door Sports: Base Ball: Star vs. Enterprise," *New York Times*, August 7, 1865, 8; "Sports and Pastimes: Base Ball: The Star and Enterprise Game — Another Def[e]at for the Enterprise Club," *Brooklyn Daily Eagle*, August 7, 1865, 2.

68. "Sports and Pastimes: Base Ball: Atlantic vs. Star," *Brooklyn Daily Eagle*, August 11, 1865, 2.

69. "Base Ball: Star vs. Union," *Brooklyn Daily Eagle*, October 16, 1865, 2.

70. "Star vs. Independent," [New York] *Sunday Mercury*, June 3, 1866 (clipping in Mears Collection).

71. "Sports and Pastimes: Base Ball," *Brooklyn Daily Eagle*, June 20, 1866, 3; "Base Ball: Excelsior vs. Star," *New York Times*, June 20, 1866, 5; "A Fine Game in Brooklyn — Star vs. Excelsior," [New York] *Sunday Mercury*, undated clipping in both the Mears Collection and the Chadwick Scrapbooks, vol. 8.

72. "Sports and Pastimes: Base Ball: Athletic vs. Star — The Philadelphians Win Another Victory," *Brooklyn Daily Eagle*, June 28, 1866, 2; "Out Door Sports: Base Ball: Athletic vs. Star — A Handsome Fielding Game in Brooklyn," *New York Times*, June 29, 1866, 8; "Athletic vs. Star," [New York] *Sunday Mercury*, undated clipping in both the Mears Collection and the Chadwick Scrapbooks, vol. 8.

73. "Sports and Pastimes: The National Game: Atlantic vs. Star," unidentified clipping, Chadwick Scrapbooks, vol. 8.

74. "Sports and Pastimes: Base Ball: Star vs. Mutual," *Brooklyn Daily Eagle*, June 1, 1868, 3; "Mutual vs. Star," *New York Clipper*, undated clipping in Mears Collection.

75. "Atlantic vs. Star," *New York Clipper*, undated clipping in Mears Collection; "Sports and Pastimes: Base Ball: Star vs. Mutuals," *Brooklyn Daily Eagle*, June 15, 1868, 2; *New York Clipper*, June 20, 1868; "Sports and Pastimes: Base Ball: Star vs. Union," *Brooklyn Daily Eagle*, June 22, 1868, 2; "Base Ball: The Champion Unions vs. Star of Brooklyn," *New York Times*, June 21, 1868, 5; "Sports and Pastimes: Base Ball: Star vs. Union," *Brooklyn Daily Eagle*, June 22, 1868, 2; "Union vs. Star," *New York Clipper*, undated clipping in Mears Collection.

76. "Star, of Brooklyn, vs. Yale College: The Collegians Victorious," *New York Clipper*, undated clipping in Mears Collection.

77. "Tour of the Olympic Club, of Washington, D.C.," *New York Clipper*, undated clipping in Mears Collection.

78. "Sports and Pastimes: Base Ball: Personals and Sundries: Hall and Cummings," *Brooklyn Daily Eagle*, June 22, 1868, 2.

79. "Sports and Pastimes: Base Ball: Mohawk vs. Mutual," *Brooklyn Daily Eagle*, June 29, 1868, 2.

80. "Sports and Pastimes: Base Ball: Cummings," *Brooklyn Daily Eagle*, July 13, 1868, 2.

81. "Star vs. Harlem," *New York Clipper*, undated clipping in Mears Collection.

82. "Sports and Pastimes: Base Ball: Star vs. Peconic," *Brooklyn Daily Eagle*, August 31, 1868, 2.

83. "City News and Gossip: The Star Club," *Brooklyn Daily Eagle*, April 9, 1869, 3.

84. "Base Ball — Star vs. Mutual," *New York Times*, June 20, 1869, 8; "Sports and Pastimes: Base Ball: Star vs. Mutuals," *Brooklyn Daily Eagle*, June 21, 1869, 2; "Starr [sic] vs. Mutual," *New York Clipper*, undated clipping in Mears Collection.

85. "Star vs. Olympic: A Splendid Victory for the Amateurs," *New York Clipper*, undated clipping in Mears Collection.

86. "Mutual vs. Star," *New York Clipper*, August 21, 1869.

87. "Sports and Pastimes: Base Ball: Star vs. Atlantics," *Brooklyn Daily Eagle*, August 30, 1869, 5; "Atlantic vs. Star," *New York Clipper*, undated clipping in Mears Collection.

88. "Base Ball: Atlantics vs. Stars — Benefit for the Avondale Sufferers," *New York Times*, September 26, 1869, 8; "City News and Gossip: The Avondale Relief," *Brooklyn Daily Eagle*, September 28, 1869, 3; *New York Clipper*, October 2, 1869. The most thorough history of the Avondale event is Robert P. Wolensky and Joseph M. Keating, *Tragedy at Avondale: The Causes, Consequences, and Legacy of the Pennsylvania Anthracite Industry's Most Deadly Mining Disaster, September 6, 1869* (Easton, PA: Canal History and Technology Press, 2008).

89. "Champion vs. Star," *New York Clipper*, undated clipping in Mears Collection.

90. "Star vs. Oriental," *New York Clipper*, undated clipping in Mears Collection.

91. "Sports and Pastimes: Base Ball: The Season Just Passed," *Brooklyn Daily Eagle*, November 11, 1869, 2.

92. "Base-Ball — The Opening Game of the Season at Carroll Park," *New York Times*, March 27, 1870, 8; "Opening Game of the Season," *New York Clipper*, undated clipping in Mears Collection.

93. "Base-Ball: The Star Nine against the Field," *New York Times*, April 10, 1870, 8.

94. "Base-Ball — Star vs. Mutual — Severe Defeat of the Mutuals," *New York Times*, May 8, 1870, 6; "Sports and Pastimes: Base Ball: Mutual vs. Star," *Brooklyn Daily Eagle*, May 9, 1870, 2.

95. "Base-Ball — Atlantic vs. Star," *New York Times*, May 15, 1870, 5.

96. "Base-Ball — The Stars at Elizabeth — A Pretty Game with the Resolutes," *New York Times*, May 19, 1870, 2.

97. "Base-Ball: Eckford vs. Stars — Stars Victorious," *New York Times*, May 22, 1870, 5; "Base-Ball: Eckford vs. Star," *New York Times*, June 5, 1870, 8.

98. "Base-Ball," *New York Times,* May 30, 1870, 2.

99. "Base-Ball: The Great Contest of the Red Stockings and Stars: An Immense Attendance — Victory of the Reds," *New York Times,* June 19, 1870, 8.

100. "Base-Ball — The Stars in Connecticut," *New York Times,* July 6, 1870, 8.

101. "Base-Ball: The White Stockings Defeat the Stars — A Pretty Fielding Game," *New York Times,* July 10, 1870, 8.

102. "Defeat of the Atlantic Club," *New York Times,* October 9, 1870, 5.

103. "Out-Door Sports: The Coming Season: The Poor Policy of All Work and No Play: The Base Ball and Cricket Fields: The Quoiting Grounds: Yachting and Racing: Shooting and Fishing," *Brooklyn Daily Eagle,* March 16, 1871, 2.

104. "Sports and Pastimes: Base Ball: The Star Club," *Brooklyn Daily Eagle,* March 24, 1871, 2.

105. "Base-Ball: Base-Ball Notes," *New York Times,* April 25, 1871, 8; "Sports and Pastimes: Base Ball: Star vs. Field," *Brooklyn Daily Eagle,* April 26, 1871, 2.

106. "Sports and Pastimes: Base Ball: A Splendid Game on the Capitoline Grounds," *Brooklyn Daily Eagle,* June 21, 1871, 2.

107. "Sports and Pastimes: Base Ball: Star vs. Etna," *Brooklyn Daily Eagle,* October 9, 1871, 2; "Out-Door Sports: Etna, of Chicago, vs. Star," *New York Times,* October 9, 1871, 5.

108. "Base-Ball: The Star Ball Club Beaten by the Rockfords," *New York Times,* June 4, 1871, 5.

109. "Sports and Pastimes: Base Ball: Star vs. Etna," *Brooklyn Daily Eagle,* October 9, 1871, 2.

110. Advertisement, *Brooklyn Daily Eagle,* May 1, 1872, 3.

111. "Sports and Pastimes: Base Ball: Amateur Notes," *Brooklyn Daily Eagle,* June 15, 1872, 2.

112. "Base-Ball: Star vs. Knickerbocker — Revival of the 'Old Amateur Days,'" *New York Times,* June 16, 1872, 5.

113. "Sports and Pastimes: Base Ball: Amateur Arena," *Brooklyn Daily Eagle,* June 24, 1872, 3.

114. "Sports and Pastimes: Base Ball: The Amateur Arena," *Brooklyn Daily Eagle,* July 1, 1872, 3.

115. "Sports and Pastimes: Base Ball: Gossip and Notes," *Brooklyn Daily Eagle,* March 20, 1873, 3.

116. There were exceptions, such as two articles after Sam Patchen's death (reference 135) and "Old Chalk" [Henry Chadwick],"Base Ball Reminiscences: Old Chalk Talks About an Old South Brooklyn Team," *Brooklyn Daily Eagle,* June 7, 1891, 16. But clubs such as the Pastimes and Excelsiors were mentioned more often in Chadwick's reminiscences.

117. *New York Clipper,* December 21, 1872.

118. Peter Morris, *Catcher* (Chicago: Ivan R. Dee, 2009), 177–178; David Arcidiacono, "The Curious Case of Tommy Barlow," *Elysian Fields Quarterly,* Winter 2004, 31–44; David Arcidiacono, *Grace, Grit and Growling* (East Hampton, CT: n.p., 2004), 95–101.

119. *Brooklyn Daily Eagle,* March 8, 1872.

120. "He Pitched the First Curve Ball," *Brooklyn Daily Eagle,* April 26, 1896, 17.

121. Much of the information on Candy Cummings was obtained from the biography written by David Fleitz and posted on the SABR BioProject site. An extended discussion of the various claims for the invention of the curveball, including Cummings', can be found in Peter Morris, *A Game of Inches,* vol. 1, pp. 118–136.

122. *Brooklyn Daily Eagle,* May 1, 1920, 2.

123. *Porter's Spirit of the Times,* November 28, 1857, 196

124. *Porter's Spirit of the Times,* June 4, 1859, 213.

125. "The Sidney Place Crowd," *Brooklyn Daily Eagle,* January 15, 1888, 11.

126. "The Sidney Place Crowd," *Brooklyn Daily Eagle,* January 15, 1888, 11.

127. *Atlanta Constitution,* July 1, 1903.

128. *Brooklyn Daily Eagle,* October 18, 1916, 4.

129. "Sports and Pastimes: A Base Ball 'Tempest in a Teapot,'" *Brooklyn Daily Eagle,* December 20, 1885, 6; "Old Chalk" [Henry Chadwick],"Base Ball Reminiscences," *Brooklyn Daily Eagle,* June 7, 1891, 16.

130. *Constitution and By-Laws of the Star Base Ball Club of Brooklyn* (New York: Mann, Stearns & Beale, 1860).

131. "Horatio Nelson Holt," *New York Times,* May 21, 1894.

132. *Brooklyn Daily Eagle,* February 24, 1910, 18.

133. "A Ground Match on the Union Grounds," *Brooklyn Daily Eagle,* June 7, 1862, 2.

134. "Leavitt Kills Himself," *Brooklyn Daily Eagle,* November 10, 1901, 1.

135. *Brooklyn Daily Eagle,* August 22, 1870.

136. *Brooklyn Daily Eagle,* May 5, 1863.

137. "Old Chalk" [Henry Chadwick],"Base Ball Reminiscences," *Brooklyn Daily Eagle,* June 7, 1891, 16.

138. *Constitution and By-Laws of the Star Base Ball Club of Brooklyn* (New York: Mann, Stearns & Beale, 1860).

139. "Old Chalk" [Henry Chadwick],"Base Ball Reminiscences," *Brooklyn Daily Eagle,* June 7, 1891, 16.

140. *Memorial: Charles E. Morris* (Philadelphia: J.B. Lippincott, 1879); available on Google Books.

141. "The Sidney Place Crowd," *Brooklyn Daily Eagle,* January 15, 1888, 11.

142. "Sporting Reminiscences: The Old Cricket and Base Ball Clubs," *Brooklyn Daily Eagle,* July 16, 1873, 4.

143. *Spirit of the Times,* April 9, 1859, 102.

144. "Sports and Pastimes: Base Ball: The Star Club — A Letter from their Captain," *Brooklyn Daily Eagle,* September 21, 1864, 2.

145. "Sports and Pastimes: Base Ball: The Star Club in Philadelphia," *Brooklyn Daily Eagle,* July 6, 1865, 2.

146. *The Bat and Ball,* May 1, 1867.

147. *Daily Alta California,* November 10, 1885, 8.

148. "Sports and Pastimes: A Base Ball 'Tempest in a Teapot,'" *Brooklyn Daily Eagle,* December 20, 1885, 6.

149. "Obituary Notes: Frank Prescott Norton," *New York Times,* August 3, 1920, 9.

150. *New York Clipper,* December 10, 1885, 634; "A Fatal Fall: The Sudden Death of Mr. Samuel W. Patchen," *Brooklyn Daily Eagle,* December 11, 1885, 6; "Sports and Pastimes: A Base Ball 'Tempest in a Teapot,'" *Brooklyn Eagle,* December 20, 1885, 6; "Patchen Funeral Service Thursday," *Brooklyn Daily Eagle,* October 29, 1924, 5.

151. Glenn Collins, "Ground as Hallowed as Cooperstown; Green-Wood Cemetery, Home to 200 Baseball Pioneers," *New York Times,* April 1, 2004; Peter J. Nash, *Baseball Legends of Brooklyn's Green-Wood Cemetery* (Charleston, S.C.: Arcadia, 2003), 63.

152. "Obituary: The Death of Mr. Joseph Patchen," *Brooklyn Daily Eagle,* May 3, 1876, 4.

153. "Sports and Pastimes: A Base Ball 'Tempest in a Teapot,'" *Brooklyn Eagle,* December 20, 1885, 6.

154. *New York Clipper,* December 10, 1885, 634; "A Fatal Fall: The Sudden Death of Mr. Samuel W. Patchen," *Brooklyn Daily Eagle,* December 11, 1885, 6; "Sports and Pastimes: A Base Ball 'Tempest in a Teapot,'" *Brooklyn Eagle,* December 20, 1885, 6.

155. "Sports and Pastimes: Base Ball: Gossip and Notes," *Brooklyn Daily Eagle,* March 20, 1873, 3.

156. "Out-Door Sports: Base Ball: Match on the Star Grounds," *Brooklyn Daily Eagle,* November 30, 1861, 2.

157. "Out-Door Sports: Base Ball: The Match on the Star Grounds To-Morrow," *Brooklyn Daily Eagle,* November 14, 1861, 11.

158. "City News and Gossip: Base Ball — Star vs. Charter Oak," *Brooklyn Daily Eagle,* June 12, 1862, 3.

159. "Sports and Pastimes: First Base Ball Game of the Season: Eagle vs. Star Club: The New Yorkers Victorious," *Brooklyn Daily Eagle,* May 31, 1865, 2.

160. Undated clipping in Mears Collection.

161. "Sports and Pastimes: Base Ball: Death of a Base Ball Player," *Brooklyn Daily Eagle*, September 2, 1872, 2.

162. "John S. Van Cleef Dies in 76th Year," *Brooklyn Daily Eagle*, September 19, 1916, 2

163. *Brooklyn Daily Eagle*, June 19, 1916.

164. *Buffalo Morning Express*, December 26, 1898, 6.

165. "Old Chalk" [Henry Chadwick],"Base Ball Reminiscences: Old Chalk Talks About an Old South Brooklyn Team," *Brooklyn Daily Eagle*, June 7, 1891, 16.

166. *Brooklyn Daily Eagle*, September 26, 1929, 1.

❖ *Eckford Base Ball Club* ❖
(William J. Ryczek and Peter Morris)

CLUB HISTORY

From the time the world of baseball began recognizing a champion club, through 1866, the Atlantics of Brooklyn held the title in all but two years. The only organization other than the Atlantics to capture the title was the Eckfords, who did so in 1862 and 1863.

The Eckfords are often linked with the Atlantics as workingmen's clubs that represented a departure from the gentlemanly style of play and organization that characterized early clubs like the Knickerbockers, Eagles, and Gothams.[1] It's a distinction that is misleading at best. Members of the latter three clubs were generally merchants and clerks who were engaged in white-collar work, but few of them were of elevated social status. Meanwhile the Atlantics and Eckfords were very far from being unskilled laborers and, as we shall see, the class status of the Eckfords is especially misunderstood.

On the field, the Eckfords boasted one of the strongest nines in the country by the early 1860s. The glory days seemed to end with the departure of many players in 1864, but there was an unexpected resurgence in 1869, when the venerable Brooklyn club was a contender in a very muddled battle for the championship. After that, however, the decline was precipitous and the final year of the Eckfords was downright embarrassing, as they were perhaps the feeblest team in a weak 1872 National Association.

Nevertheless, the Eckford nine had many proud moments during their nearly two-decade existence as a baseball club and such fine players as Jimmy Wood, Waddy Beach, Al Reach, Joe Sprague, and George Zettlein donned their uniform. The leader of the club in its earliest days was the estimable Frank Pidgeon, a good pitcher and one of the most respected voices in the councils of the National Association of Base Ball Players. For several years the Eckfords were a big fish in the very small pond that was top-flight baseball, and they played a major role in the sport's early years.

Formation and Early Years

The Eckford Base Ball Club was formed on June 27, 1855,[2] and established grounds at the Manor House in Greenpoint, near Newtown Creek. Originally a private residence, the Manor House had been converted into a public inn around 1840 and soon became very popular among sportsmen. Newtown Creek provided an abundance of striped bass for fishermen, while hunters found plenty of prey in a dense wood located nearby. When the Eckford Club selected the Manor House as its headquarters, a new wing was built on the building for the exclusive use of club members. This picturesque setting, which was entirely surrounded by cherry trees, remained the home base of the Eckfords until the opening of the Union Grounds in 1862.[3]

Like most early clubs, the Eckford Club initially spent the overwhelming majority of its time gathering for exercise and dividing the players into two sides for practice. The best-known early clubs typically held three or more practices each week, but the Eckford players' work schedules meant that these sessions could be held only once a week, on Tuesdays at 2 P.M.,[4] and the members of the Eckfords believed that they would be hopelessly overmatched against these well-drilled clubs. For more than a year after organizing, the Eckfords did not play a single first-nine match against another club. "Still," as Pidgeon memorably recounted, "we had some merry times among ourselves; we could forget business and everything else on Tuesday afternoons, go out in the green fields, don our ball suits, and go at it with a perfect rush. At such times, we were boys again."[5]

The boys longed to be men, however, and prove their mettle against other nines. Pidgeon said the Eckfords decided to challenge another club, and were granted the right to play the winner of a game between the Baltics and the Union Club of Morrisania. Pidgeon and his mates turned out to witness that match and the sight of the mighty Unions beating the Baltics convinced them that they had been far too rash. As the big day approached, the players remained certain they would be annihilated and the reputation of the club destroyed.

Game day finally arrived on September 17, 1856, and its events were recounted in dramatic fashion by Frank Pidgeon. "No use trying to win;" he wrote, "do the best we can however." When the club scored its first run, some of the excited players "ran to the Umpire's book to see how it looked on paper." The Eckfords won handily, 22–8, to their amazed delight. "About seven o'clock that evening," Pidgeon continued, "nine peacocks might have been seen on their way home, with tail-feathers spread." For good measure, the Eckfords beat the

Unions a second time a month later, by the nearly identical score of 22–6.

In January of 1857 the Eckfords sent Pidgeon, Charles Welling, and James Gray to represent the club at the important meeting of the leading clubs at which the rules of the game were standardized. The Eckfords now had a firm place on the baseball map, leading many to wonder who these newcomers were. *Porter's Spirit of the Times* described them as "mostly ship-builders from the Eleventh Ward," while Pidgeon referred to them as "shipwrights and mechanics," comments that have led others to portray them as members of the working class.[6]

The club was named in honor of a celebrated shipbuilder, Henry Eckford, and its early members did indeed share close ties to the East River's prosperous and bustling shipyards. Frank Pidgeon, James M. Gray, and Joseph Vanderbilt were all shipbuilders, while William Logan is presumed to have been a ship carpenter by that name, and Henry Metzler was a wood carver who sculpted ships' figureheads. As described in the member profiles, many others worked at the shipyards or had business dealings with that thriving industry. Some of these men no doubt did demanding physical work as shipwrights, but they were nonetheless skilled tradesmen whose work, as Sean Wilentz explains, "could not be placed in ordinary mechanics' hands or be directed by men new to the trade."[7] Even more important, they worked in one of the two major New York industries identified by Wilentz as having continued to function in the old artisan tradition long after the Industrial Revolution had introduced class-based divisions into most worksites.[8]

While most if not all of the original men who enjoyed "merry times among ourselves ... on Tuesday afternoons" shared close ties to the shipyards, by the time the Eckfords became a formidable baseball club they had begun to draw members from a new source. The new members were active in the civic affairs of the nearby Eastern District of Brooklyn, with most of them belonging to the volunteer fire department. The new recruits brought more talent, new energy, and a sense that the Eckfords belonged to a specific region, but at the same time they weakened the club's connections to the shipbuilding craft. Intriguingly, three of the most prominent of these players — brothers John and George Grum and Henry Manolt — had all been apprenticed as butchers, the other major craft that Wilentz singled out as having successfully resisted the pressures of industrialization until several decades after class division had transformed other industries.

The tendency to view the Eckfords as being of rougher-hewn quality than the Knickerbockers and Gothams is thus a misconception. In the Eckfords' early years, Frank Pidgeon was the acknowledged leader of the organization and he was the antithesis of the uncultured, brawling workingman. A shipbuilder, inventor, and entrepreneur as well as a skilled musician and a student of art, science, and literature, Pidgeon was a fierce opponent of professional ballplaying in any form. In 1859 he sent a letter to *Porter's Spirit of the Times* in response to the *Spirit's* criticism of the National Association of Base Ball Players' stance against compensating players in any manner. The *Spirit* had stated that there was nothing wrong with helping out club members who could not afford to pay their dues, and that doing so would make the game more egalitarian. Pidgeon took great umbrage, arguing that any man who could pay dues and didn't do so was not to be trusted and that anyone who could not afford dues should spend his time working rather than playing baseball.[9] It is striking that such a vehement defense of amateurism came not from the purportedly courtly Knickerbockers or Gothams, but from the supposedly working-class Eckfords. Meanwhile, one of Pidgeon's first batterymates was Joseph L. Vanderbilt, a man described by his granddaughter, etiquette maven Amy Vanderbilt, as "one of those striped-pants, silk-hat ancestors who liked the game so much, he never dreamed of making it pay."[10]

On the field the Eckfords were more active in 1857 but not as successful, losing five of seven games, coming home with their tails between their legs more often than with tail feathers spread. They played the Atlantics twice, losing convincingly both times, and garnered their only two victories against the Empire Club. The disappointing season seems to have cast a damper on the mood of the members, as the Eckfords did not play their first match game in 1858 until August 31. When they did at last take the field, however, it was with a younger and more skillful lineup. They won five of six games that year, losing only to the Gothams. They did not play the champion Atlantics, and thus did not have a chance to win the title, but it was a breakthrough season.

In 1859 the Eckfords, like most clubs, were more active, finishing the season with a record of 11–3, including a spirited series against the Atlantics. The Atlantics won the first game in July, but on September 8 the Eckfords rallied for six runs in the eighth inning to gain a 22–16 victory, the first time the Atlantics had been defeated since 1857 and the only defeat they would suffer in 1859. If they could defeat the Atlantics in the third game, the Eckfords would be the champions. Pidgeon's crew was unequal to the task, losing 22–12 on October 12 before a crowd estimated at 6,000 to 10,000, a tremendous gathering for the antebellum era. Although the Eckfords were unable to dethrone the Atlantics, it was clear that Brooklyn had unhorsed New York as the city with the best baseball clubs (Brooklyn was an independent city until it became a borough of New York City in 1898). The Atlantics, Eckfords, and Excelsiors were probably the best teams in the country and all three hailed from Brooklyn.

Not all of the members of the Eckford Club lived in Brooklyn, however, and this became a source of friction within the ranks. On August 23, 1859, as a result of "some difficulty among the members," a disenchanted faction led by Dr. William Bell formed the Henry Eckford Club.[11] We can only speculate as to the exact nature of the dispute but it certainly seems to have divided club members by city of origin. A later account in the *New York Sun* maintained, "Although the [Eckford] club always practiced in Brooklyn, they were organized as a New York club. For a number of years their meetings were held in this city. About 1860, a majority of the members being residents of Brooklyn, the club went over there."[12]

The splinter Henry Eckford Club was very much a New York City club and it played for several years but never achieved any lasting distinction. Meanwhile the defections of these members left the original Eckford Club a distinctively Brooklyn organization. In the years that followed, new members almost always came from Brooklyn's Eastern District and most of them had begun their careers with the junior Marion Club of Williamsburg, which effectively became the farm club of the Eckfords. In addition, new players were less likely to come from the shipbuilding industry, which was already beginning to struggle by the start of the Civil War and which experienced a catastrophic postwar decline. Jimmy Wood, who joined the Eckfords in 1860, declared that the club "represented Williamsburg, then a separate town, but now part of Brooklyn."[13] (Williamsburg in fact was annexed into Brooklyn in 1855.)[14]

As a sign of an increased focus on winning baseball games, the Eckfords ended the 1859 season by making the first real road trip in club history. On Thanksgiving Day the players headed up the Hudson River to face the Newburgh Base Ball Club. "The day was rather too cold for the full enjoyment of ball playing," reported the *New York Clipper*, "but, nevertheless, the warmth of the reception was such as to compensate for the unpleasant weather. At the conclusion of the match, which resulted in the defeat of the Newburgh Club, all parties adjourned to the hotel, where they sat down to a splendid dinner provided for them by their hospitable entertainers. After full justice had been done to the good things placed before them, and after duly responding to the friendly sentiments of their hosts, the whole party of visitors returned to the city highly gratified with the day's proceedings."[15]

It was a fitting end for the season and set the stage for an even more exciting season in 1860. In the first week of the new year, members of the club announced plans to hold a fancy invitation-only ball at the Odeon on January 24. The club earned praise for the obvious care that had gone into the arrangements, including the "tasteful and appropriate get up of their invitation cards."[16] The annual ball became a regular event and was another important reminder that the Eckford Club was not a working-class organization.

The 1860 campaign saw the eyes of the baseball-watching populace focused on the Excelsiors and Atlantics as they waged a bitter struggle for the championship. When the third contest between the two clubs ended in an inconclusive draw, the Eckfords challenged the Atlantics to a series. The three games, played in rapid succession on October 15, 22, and 29, were closely contested and well played. Fortunately, after the fiasco

of the third Atlantic-Excelsior game, there were no untoward incidents in the Eckford-Atlantic contests, a circumstance attributed to diminished interest on the part of gamblers.[17] The Atlantics scored four times in the ninth inning of the first game to pull out a 17–15 victory but it was a different story a week later. When his club, losing 9–6, came to bat in the fourth inning, Pidgeon told them, "Now, boys, just think that you're playing a common club, and forget that these fellows are the Atlantics."[18] So inspired, the Eckfords scored four runs to take the lead, then fought back a second time with seven runs in the ninth inning to win the game, 20–15, and even the series. The rubber match saw the Atlantics, aided by exceedingly loose fielding on the part of the Eckfords, win 20–11 and earn the championship.

Five thousand spectators were on hand for the second game and that impressive figure was surpassed by a throng estimated at 6,000 to 8,000 that turned out to watch the deciding game. It was an indication that the troubles of the Atlantics and Excelsiors had not destroyed the game of baseball in the metropolis, something that was welcomed by all of the game's devotees. It was also a sign that there was enough public interest to support professional play, a development that many viewed less favorably.

The Championship Seasons

The Eckford Club's 1861 season opened in elegant fashion with the club's second annual ball, held at the Odeon on January 20.[19] In a ballroom that was "elegantly and profusely decorated with an abundance of bunting," Frank Pidgeon "officiated ... in regular Parisian style" and the "dancing was kept up with great animation and spirit until 'daylight did appear.'" An account in the *New York Clipper* declared the ball an "entire and perfect success" and expressed the "hope that the Club and their 'troops of friends' will long live to arrange and indulge in the joys of many similar festive occasions."[20]

Alas, the Civil War commenced that spring and brought an end to such merriment. Like most clubs, the Eckfords played a fairly light schedule in 1861, finishing with an 8–4 record. They won more games than the 5–2 Atlantics but didn't play them, and so had no chance to win the championship. Before the season, the Continental Club had commissioned a silver ball as emblem of the championship, "but the war breaking out, interfered with the arrangement, and the ball was left at the manufacturers, Messrs. Ball and Black, N.Y."[21]

The following year, the two clubs did meet in a best-of-three series that took place in a new and very different venue. The Eckford Club finally left the picturesque Manor House in the spring of 1862 and began playing at the newly opened Union Grounds, the first enclosed field designed for baseball.[22] The enclosure made it possible to capitalize on the excitement generated by baseball by collecting admission fees for the first time, but there was still great resistance to the whole concept of paying to watch a baseball game. To alleviate these concerns, it was announced that the proceeds of the relatively modest ten-cent admission fee for the first Atlantics-Eckfords game were going to be donated to the Sanitary Commission, an organization established to care for wounded soldiers.

Even so, it was reported that more than half of the 3,000 to 4,000 attendees on July 11 watched from beyond the confines of the field as the Eckfords beat the Atlantics in dramatic fashion. Trailing 14–9 after five innings, the Eckfords scored 11 unanswered runs in the last four frames and pulled out a thrilling 20–14 victory. The spectators responded with so much enthusiasm that they had to be reminded afterward that "indecorous language ... is against the laws of the ground, and will not be permitted."[23]

The series continued ten days later. The proceeds were again dedicated to the Sanitary Commission and attendance at the Union Grounds was approximately 6,000, almost equally divided between those within and outside the enclosure. It was hardly an unqualified success, but it did represent progress and it raised $104 for a worthy cause.[24] The game itself, in a pattern reminiscent of the Atlantic-Excelsior series of 1860, saw the Atlantics overwhelm the Eckfords by the score of 39–5 to even the series. "[I]n all our experience," wrote one journalist, "we never saw the out field of a match played in such an execrable manner as the Eckford's was yesterday. It was 'awful to behold.'"[25]

After the contest, it was reported that the third and deciding game was going to be played "in a week or two."[26] Instead, the game did not take place until September 18, which allowed the Eckfords the services of hard-throwing pitcher Joe Sprague, who had just returned from serving three months in Virginia in the 13th New York Regiment.[27] The delay was no coincidence, according to the *New York Clipper*, which reported that "[Andy] Mills was the pitcher on the Eckford side [in the first two games], and though he discharged the duties of the position ably, nevertheless, the club determined to await the return of Sprague, the regular pitcher, before they played the third game."[28] What the Atlantics thought of this delay can only be guessed at, but the once friendly rivalry between the two Brooklyn powerhouses soon became noticeably chillier.[29]

A crowd of at least 10,000 "by a very moderate estimate" turned out for the big game, one of the largest of the wartime era. "For an hour or more before the time appointed for commencing the game," reported the *Clipper*, "all the avenues leading to the grounds were occupied with streams of people proceeding to witness the match, every car on the routes that passed near by being crowded to excess with passengers." As game time approached, the crowd was abuzz with the news that brilliant young Eckford second baseman Jimmy Wood would be "absent through mistaking the date of the match." The members of the "betting fraternity" were sent into a tizzy, with the Atlantics becoming 3-to-1 or even 2-to-1 favorites as

the word of Wood's absence spread. It looked as though the Eckfords had outsmarted themselves by maneuvering for a more advantageous date.[30]

Instead, the Eckfords won 8–3 in a game as well played as the low score would indicate. Sprague's pitching received the lion's share of the credit but it was very much a collective effort, with Al Reach moving to second base and filling Wood's shoes capably. "The Eckfords never played a better game," declared the *Eagle*, "and considering all, every man did his whole duty." For the first time, a team other than the Atlantics was the champion club of the United States. After the game both clubs were entertained by William Cammeyer, proprietor of the Union Grounds, and the Eckfords were presented with the silver ball donated by the Continental Club the previous year. The ceremony concluded on a patriotic note: "Toasts were drunk, and the Union and the Constitution vehemently cheered, after which the parties separated in the best of spirits."[31]

The composition of the Eckford nine had changed since the early days, and in 1862 the club was bolstered by a number of reinforcements. Frank Pidgeon rarely appeared in the first nine; the game he played on July 29 was his first appearance since 1860. Andy Mills did much of the pitching until the dramatic return of Sprague from his second tour of duty in the Union Army. Catcher Waddy Beach was perhaps the club's best player, a quick, agile backstop who possessed all the skills needed for that difficult position. Al Reach played a number of positions, his left-handedness proving no obstacle to his performance at several infield spots. Splitting time between shortstop and third base was young, curly-haired Tom Devyr, an excellent infielder who within three years would gain infamy as one of the three members of the Mutuals who were the first baseball players proven to have conspired to throw a game. The talented Jimmy Wood, a mainstay of the club since moving up from the junior ranks in 1860, was the second baseman. Andy Mills, Josh Snyder, and the mysterious Campbell also saw action in the infield, with Josh Snyder and Harry Manolt being the mainstays of an ever-changing outfield.

In late October 1862 the champion Eckfords went to Philadelphia to play a series of games. Clubs from the latter city were still learning the game, and the Brooklyn club was very successful, winning all four games, playing as champions should and teaching the Philadelphia clubs that the best baseball was still played in New York — more specifically, in Brooklyn!

The 1863 season brought a repeat of the championship and an undefeated season, as the Eckfords won all ten of their match games. They repulsed the Atlantics with two easy victories, ending any chance of the latter reclaiming the title. The Mutuals, the only other formidable challengers, were vanquished in two straight, although both games were close (10–9 and 18–10).

With the passage of time, the Eckfords' 1863 campaign

became more famous, as journalists pointed out that the club had not lost a first-nine, second-nine, or muffin match, although the latter two accomplishments involved more coincidence than skill. A victory of one's muffin nine was hardly reason to claim superiority. Jimmy Wood embellished the club's record still further, maintaining that the Eckfords won 144 straight games and, with one notable exception, beat "every team of strength and importance in New York, Brooklyn, Philadelphia, Troy, Syracuse, Albany, Washington, and the smaller cities." Wood explained, "The single exception was the Excelsior team of Brooklyn. We wanted to play them, issuing repeated challenges. But their captain, Joe Leggett, refused for the sole reason that he had become angered during the summer of 1862 when our captain, who was captain of a picked nine on which Leggett played, was presented with a souvenir ball. Leggett thought he was entitled to it and vowed afterward that so long as he was leader of the Excelsiors he never would permit them to play the Eckfords. He kept his word."[32]

How Wood arrived at the figure of 144 straight wins is not clear and there's no way the Eckfords played anywhere near that many games. Still, as the *Brooklyn Daily Eagle* pointed out, "[Their] record is one that any club might feel proud of, and it is one that unquestionably entitles them to the honor of being considered the champion club of the season, as they were last year."[33]

Decline and the Postwar Years

Before the 1864 season began, the Eckfords lost both members of their championship battery — Sprague defected to the rival Atlantics, while Beach was badly injured in a fistfight and then left town for most of the year. Nevertheless, the *Eagle* spoke optimistically about the club's chances for a third straight title. "[T]hough they will not have the services of Beach or Sprague," the paper stated, "they have nevertheless a sufficiency of first class players on their roll to supply their places. The pitcher's position is not the important one this year that it was last, and instead of the best player on the club being required for it, any one of the Nine can fill it creditably."[34]

The attrition continued, however, with infielders Tommy Devyr and Ed Duffy joining the Mutuals. With so much talent gone, the Eckfords were very dilatory in taking the field to defend their title. "What are the champions about?" Henry Chadwick lamented. "They keep pretty quiet now-a-days."[35] He thought the guiding enthusiasm of Frank Pidgeon "was needed at the Eckford helm, for they appear to be drifting on a lee shore very rapidly at present."[36]

Pidgeon, however, was not interested. As early as 1859 he had angrily demanded, "We will suppose, sir, you belong to a club composed mostly of mechanics and you had taken great interest in helping to build it up.... How would you like to see those you depended upon to uphold the name of the club bought up like cattle, or if not bought, would like to see

the bribes repeatedly offered to them to desert their colors."[37] Baseball had gone much further down the road to professionalism in the intervening five years and Pidgeon was done with the sport. "Frank would have nothing to do with the Eckford club," wrote Chadwick, "when its nine became professional, as they did in the sixties."[38]

On July 21 the Eckfords played their first game of the season, defeating the Newark Club easily, although their performance was sloppy. The *Eagle* wrote optimistically that if they could beat the Newark nine while playing poorly, the Eckfords would surely equal their record of 1863 once they rounded into shape.[39] But it was not to be. The Eckfords played only three more games the rest of the year, losing them all. When the Atlantics challenged them for the championship, they declined, allowing the former champions to regain the crown by default. The bad blood between the Eckfords and Atlantics had grown after the Atlantics had failed to give a customary postgame cheer and declined to participate in any social activity.[40] The Eckfords, with their weakened nine, had no desire to play the vastly superior 1864 Atlantics and were content to let the bad feelings continue.

Perhaps the final humiliation of the proud Brooklyn club came when they lost to the venerable Eagles, an old organization that hadn't been taken seriously as a contender for years. "We could scarcely realize," said the *Brooklyn Eagle,* "that it was the same club that had gone through last season in such brilliant style."[41]

The departures continued in 1865, with both Jimmy Wood and Al Reach leaving the area, the latter agreeing to take a salary to play for the Athletics of Philadelphia and beginning his long association with the city as a player, executive, and manufacturer of sporting goods. The loss of so much talent led one sportswriter to observe, "The Eckfords once led all, having beaten the champions, but last season their main players left for other clubs, and the star of the Eckford nine set, — as a leading club."[42]

That gloomy assessment was a bit extreme, as the Marion Club continued to produce an abundance of talent, much of which made its way into the lineup of the Eckfords. The most important additions were the talented young duo of catcher Charley Mills and pitcher George Zettlein, who was known as George the Charmer after a renowned minstrel performer.[43] With these reinforcements playing alongside the holdovers and returnees from the glory years, the Eckfords posted a respectable 8–6 record in 1865 and were no easy mark. They lost twice to the champion Atlantics, but one defeat was by the close margin of 28–23. They split a pair of games with the powerful Mutuals and lost twice to the Unions of Morrisania. The win over the Mutuals was tainted, however, for that was the game in which William Wansley persuaded two of his Mutual teammates, both of whom were former Eckford players, to join him in throwing the game. The most shocking defeat of the 1865 season was an 18–16 loss to the visiting Keystones of Philadelphia, in which the Eckfords dissipated a 13–1 lead.

For the remainder of the "amateur" period that preceded the formation of the openly professional National Association, the fate of the Eckfords continued to parallel that of the shipyards that had originally produced the club. New York's shipbuilding industry had been devastated by high protective tariffs on iron that led iron to be substituted for wood, the emergence of steamers, the high value of the land occupied by the East River shipyards, and the U.S. Navy's decision to sell off many of its ships at the end of the war. A stunning government report found that in November 1866, "there was but a single vessel in the course of construction in the ship-yards of the city of New York."[44] Many of the proud members of the trade were not yet ready to admit defeat, but stark reality forced all too many of these highly skilled artisans to make midlife transitions to less rewarding lines of work.

Similarly, the Eckford Base Ball Club wasn't the best club in the New York area, but it remained competitive, generally losing to contenders like the Atlantics and Mutuals and beating second-line opponents. The late '60s witnessed the development of top-flight baseball in other areas of the country, and when the Western and Southern clubs toured New York, they almost always played the Eckfords.

In 1866 the Eckfords finished with a 9–8 record, but did not defeat a single top club. The 1866 lineup included such stalwarts from the glory years as Waddy Beach, Marty Swandell, and both Grum brothers, but while other clubs had grown stronger, the Eckfords seemed to be treading water. With baseball fever having swept Brooklyn, the best players of 1862 and 1863 were rarely the equal of the stars of the postwar era and while the Eckford Club brought in plenty of talented young players, all too often they didn't stay very long. George Zettlein and Charley Mills both departed after the 1865 campaign to join the Atlantics, making it look as though the star of the Eckford Club had indeed set for good.

The decline of the former champions continued in 1867, as the Eckfords posted a sorry 6–16 mark that led the *Clipper* to refer to "the wreck of their former greatness."[45] Swandell and the Grums remained, and the Eckfords added 18-year-old infielder Jack Nelson, who would play major-league baseball through the 1890 season, but in 1867 Nelson was still an unpolished youngster. The club's best effort of the year was a 20–20 tie with the Mutuals in early July, but the season also included a 41–9 loss to the Atlantics and a number of other lopsided defeats.

The 1868 season was marked by a renewed spirit that yielded a significant turnaround from the nadir of 1867. The season was launched on May 29 when 70 club members gathered at the Union Grounds to raise a new flag. A short practice session was then held, after which "the club entered the dining room and partook of Capt. Lewis's chowder. Speaking and singing followed, and all departed well pleased."[46] Although many clubs undertook extensive tours, the Eckfords stayed close to home and posted a 23–12 record that included wins over the Mutuals and Atlantics, capping the best Eckford season in several years.

One of the keys to success was the addition of noted slow-ball pitcher Alphonse "Phonney" Martin. In an era of pitchers whose main goal seemed to be throwing as hard as their catcher was able to stand, Martin was a "strategic" pitcher, the type so admired by Henry Chadwick. Martin threw slow lobs, relying on placement and varying speeds, and a "sinker" that dropped from lack of velocity. Like relief pitcher Stu Miller of the 1960s, Martin threw in a manner so different from his contemporaries that batters were often unable to time his delivery well enough to hit it effectively. Martin put a spin on the ball that frequently resulted in easy popups and foul tips which under the rules of the day were outs if caught on the fly or first bound.

Martin had plenty of support, as the 1868 roster was the most formidable the Eckfords had fielded since the championship years. Jack Nelson returned from the 1867 club and second baseman Jimmy Wood was back in the fold. In addition, the Eckfords added strong young players like outfielder Dave Eggler and catcher Charley Hodes. Eggler played major-league ball through 1885, while Hodes unfortunately died at the age of 27 after playing three seasons in the professional National Association.

In 1869, the first year of open professionalism, the Eckfords posted an outstanding 47–8 mark, and were a contender for the national title in a season where the championship race was as murky as any in history. The Red Stockings of Cincinnati won 57 games without a loss and yet were not considered the official champions of the United States, as the New York and Brooklyn clubs vied with each other to win the title and conspired to keep the flag away from any aspirant from outside the New York area.

The Eckfords lost twice to Cincinnati, including a 24–5 defeat during the Red Stockings' triumphant visit to New York in June. The Eckfords made the first extensive tour in their history in August of that year, traveling to upstate New York, Cleveland, Cincinnati, and Detroit. On August 20 the club crossed the border to Woodstock, Ontario, where they defeated the Young Canadians, 29–16.

The Mutuals had won the 1868 "championship" and the Eckfords were given a chance to wrest it from them early in the season. In the first game of the series they beat the Mutuals 6–1 in a game that was called after five innings because of rain. Umpire Charley Walker indicated that he had intended only to suspend the game, not to call it, but the Eckfords insisted that under the rules five innings had been completed and the game was official. The Mutuals won the second game, 24–8, and on July 3 the Eckfords won the third game decisively, 31–5, giving them, for the time being, their first championship since 1863. The Mutuals were always a suspect nine, and the fact that they lost so badly to a team they had beaten easily just a few weeks earlier led many to believe the fix was in, especially since betting odds favored the Mutuals by 100 to 30. The suspicion was heavy that the Mutuals had lost intentionally to prevent the Haymakers of Troy from winning the title. The Haymakers had beaten the Mutuals previously and had a game coming up that could make them the champions. Better to lose to the Eckfords and keep the title in New York.

In early August, the new champion club played an exhibition against the Eckford nine of 1862. Frank Pidgeon was on hand, although he didn't play, as were Waddy Beach, Al Reach, Joe Sprague, and other veterans. With the championship streamer in their possession, the Eckfords were not eager to give another team the opportunity to take it away, as their August tour took them away from the New York area — and prospective challengers — for a lengthy period. Upon their return the Eckfords agreed to play a three-game series with the Atlantics. The teams split the first two games, then took a hiatus while the Atlantics finished their series with the Athletics. The sequence was important, for if the Atlantics beat the Eckfords, they would be champions and the Athletics, by beating the Atlantics, would take the banner to Philadelphia.

After the Atlantics defeated the Athletics rather easily in two straight games, the Atlantics and Eckfords played the decisive game of their series. The three games had been stretched over more than 60 days, the first played September 6, the second October 9 and the deciding game on November 8. The first game was a slugfest, a 45–25 Atlantic win in which Atlantic first baseman Joe Start had seven hits, including four home runs, and 21 total bases. The Eckfords won the second game, 23–9, and the Atlantics the clincher by a 16–12 score. The win gave the venerable Brooklyn club yet another national championship, for whatever it was worth at that point. The chicanery of the Brooklyn and New York clubs had so offended fans, journalists, and virtually everyone outside the metropolitan area that few cared which club called itself the champion. During a year in which the Red Stockings of Cincinnati won every game, it seemed laughable to refer to the Atlantics as the best nine in the country.

During the winter before the 1870 season, the Chicago White Stockings were formed with great fanfare, sizable financial resources, and lofty ambitions. Jimmy Wood was hired as manager and he in turned signed outfielder Fred Treacy and catcher Charley Hodes from the 1869 Eckford first nine, along with former Eckfords Ed Pinkham and Ed Duffy. The latest spate of departures prompted the *New York Times* to refer to "the Chicago branch of the old Eckford club, known as the White Stockings."[47] Others dubbed the team the "$18,000 nine."

With such devastating personnel losses, the Eckfords played much less frequently and far less effectively in 1870. For the season, the club finished 13–16–1 and was never a serious contender for any championship. Their victories were against second-rate clubs and virtually every game against an opponent like the Mutuals or Atlantics resulted in defeat. When the Cincinnati nine toured New York in June, the Eckfords were pleased to have held them to just 24 runs in a 24–8 defeat. Fittingly, they finished the season with a loss to the White Stockings, the high-priced Chicago team that had taken their best players. The Eckfords were a professional club, but they were unable or unwilling to match the expenditures of teams like Chicago and Cincinnati, and with their subpar performance, suffered at the gate, often drawing crowds of just 200 or 300. Among the players who replaced the departed stars were former Eckford infielders Tom Devyr and Ed Duffy, both of whom had been implicated in the Mutual scandal of 1865. Fittingly, Duffy jumped to the White Stockings in the middle of the season and by the fall Devyr was more focused on a different campaign — he was running for Supervisor in the Seventeenth Ward.

Epilogue

It could be argued that the history of the Eckford Base Ball Club ended at the close of the 1870 season. Professional clubs used that name for two more years, but bore hardly any relationship to the club led by Frank Pidgeon. Even Phonney Martin, one of the few stars, admitted as much when he later commented about one of these seasons that "the Eckford Club had not organized that year, so we called ourselves the Eckfords."[48]

When the amateur and professional clubs parted company prior to the 1871 season, the Eckfords did not join the professional National Association, although they sent a delegate to the March 17 meeting at which the Association was formed. The Eckfords played many exhibition games against teams from the new league and played competitively, scoring a number of victories. Not all of the National Association entries made it to the finish line that year, and when the Kekiongas of Fort Wayne ceased operations in August, the Eckfords agreed to play out their schedule. While the games would generate much-needed gate receipts, they would not count in the official standings. The 1871 fight for the pennant was a confusing one, with forfeits, illegal players, and a lack of clarity about the standard that would be used to determine the championship. The late entry of the Eckfords did nothing to alleviate the confusion, although in the end their games were not counted. The public were understandably confused and crowds for the Eckfords' games were invariably smaller than those between teams that had entered the race at the start.

The Eckfords decided to invest the $10 entry fee and compete for the National Association championship in 1872, despite losing their battery of Phonney Martin (to the Haymakers of Troy) and catcher Nat Hicks (to the Mutuals). The old Brooklyn club had two strikes against it when it entered the championship arena. First, the Eckfords were a cooperative organization, which meant that players shared gate money rather than receiving a regular salary. The best players went to the salaried clubs and co-ops were left with the remainders. Second, the Eckfords had signed a number of players with reputations as malcontents, and when times got tough, the players began to bicker on the field.

Not surprisingly, the Eckfords got off to a terrible start, losing their first 11 games. Two defeats (against Boston) were by embarrassing 20–0 and 24–5 scores. On multiple occasions the *New York Times* described their play as "indifferent." When the club lost 17–11 to the Haymakers of Troy, the *Times* commented that everyone was astonished by the Eckfords' good showing.[49] After a 15–3 defeat at the hands of the Haymakers, the *Clipper* noted that the Eckfords' 13 errors were the fewest of the season and added, "If the Eckfords can get this team into working trim, they will soon offset their defeats with noteworthy displays."[50] The *Clipper* deemed a 24–6 loss to the Mutuals "unworthy of a detailed report."[51] Perhaps the nadir was a 24–5 loss to a Cleveland club that had only eight players. The turnover on the Eckfords was tremendous and, in an era of limited rosters, the club wound up using 25 different players.

In late July, the Haymakers of Troy folded. Many of the Troy players hailed from the New York area, and they petitioned the league for the right to finish the Eckfords' schedule. Several of the defunct Haymakers were former Eckfords and came to Brooklyn to play for the reorganized nine. It was like the 1860s again at the Capitoline Grounds, as old stalwarts Jimmy Wood, George Zettlein, Phonney Martin, and Jack Nelson donned Eckford uniforms and took their former positions with the nine. Catcher Doug Allison, of Cincinnati Red Stocking fame, came from Troy as the catcher. Wood served as captain.

The "new" Eckfords played better than the cooperative nine that stumbled through the beginning of the season, but could manage just three wins. With Zettlein and Martin supplying quality pitching, the horrendous runs totals of the early season were reduced, but the club still suffered consecutive 20–1 and 18–1 defeats. The team's final record was 3–26. One of the losses was a forfeit to the Athletics incurred when acting captain Martin pulled his team off the field in protest of an umpire's decision. The Eckfords didn't come close to completing their quota of games against the other clubs in the Association.

When the 1872 season ended, so did the career of the Eckfords as a competitive baseball nine. The best players joined salaried organizations for the 1873 campaign and the rest played with semipro and amateur teams in the New York area. It was a sorry finish for a club that had won the national title twice and a poor ending for the nine led by the estimable Frank Pidgeon in its formative years.

The Eckford Base Ball Club began humbly, rose to the top of the list, sank, rose again in 1869, and finally collapsed

in pile of losses near the foot of the 1872 National Association standings. Ironically, the only team with more losses that year was the Atlantics, against whom the Eckfords had fought so intensely for championships throughout the early 1860s. Brooklyn was no longer the center of the baseball universe and the amateur ideals of Frank Pidgeon had long since been replaced by a quest to win at all costs. The era of the Atlantics and Eckfords, which had succeeded that of the Knickerbockers and Gothams, was over.

The shipyards that had given birth to the Eckfords experienced an even more dramatic decline. The postwar slump deepened and before long it was hard to find any signs of life in the once-thriving industry. An 1882 article in *Harper's Magazine* about "The Old Ship-Builders of New York" presented the contrast in especially bleak terms. The article quoted an account from a New York newspaper from around 1852 that boasted, "New York is one of the great ship-yards of the world. Our clippers astonish distant nations with their neat and beautiful appearance, and our steamers have successfully competed with the swiftest-going mail packets of Great Britain. In the farthest corners of the earth the Stars and Stripes wave over New York built vessels." That article was followed by this passage from an 1881 article: "Passengers on the Brooklyn ferries between 9 and 10 A. M. on Tuesday saw something which made them stare. The curious object was a new trim-built clipper ship, fresh from the shipwright's hand, and flying the American flag at the fore. The old flag has become such a novelty and a new-built clipper such a rarity that as she sailed leisurely down the East River, old-timers recalled the days when such objects were common and ship-building was at its zenith. Many looked upon the sight as an omen of better days to come."[52]

By then, the "shipwrights and mechanics" who had formed the Eckford Base Ball Club had almost all been forced to move on to other lines of work. As described in the member profiles that follow, some of them made the transition successfully but those men were far outnumbered by the club members who struggled in later life. No doubt those struggles had much to do with why the erroneous depiction of the Eckfords as members of the working class became common. It was also why later reminiscences about the Eckford Club were rare and abounded in errors, with some even referring to club namesake Henry Eckford as "John Eckford."[53]

In another poignant reminder of the club's heyday, the Manor House was torn down in 1885 after several years of standing vacant.[54] That meant that the last legacy of the Eckfords was a social club that had been formed on September 16, 1865, by members of the baseball club. After the 1873 demise of the baseball nine, "the base ball section of the club dropped away" and none of the old-time ballplayers are known to have remained members of the social club.[55]

Nevertheless, the Eckford social club was still alive as late as 1961, more than a century after Frank Pidgeon and some fellow shipyard workers had decided to found a baseball club.[56] The social club's ties to baseball were rarely emphasized, but every so often there was a reminder of those origins. John L. Smith, a minority owner of the Dodgers during the late 1940s, was an Eckford Club member and in 1946 the club secretary wrote to the *Brooklyn Eagle* and provided an unusually accurate listing of the names of some of the club's earliest members.[57]

Most important, the Eckford social club retained souvenirs of the glory years of the Eckford Base Ball Club. In 1888 the club relocated to a "cozy" new building near the East River and decorated it with baseball memorabilia, including "a large steel engraving of what was known as the Eckford base ball nine in the year 1858.... The picture has been hung in the hallway on the first floor, where its position at once attracts the attention of visitors." Also featured was a glass case in which the 164 balls won in match games were stacked in pyramid form: "It is customary for a stranger to the club to have them shown and their value explained to him, and while a pleasant hour is thus spent a good deal of knowledge in regard to the past history of the club is obtained in a very interesting form. At the close of every game which the club won the ball used was gilded. The names of both competing nines, the scores, and the date of the playing of the game has been painted on each ball. The leading trophy in the stand is a silver ball won by the Eckford club from the Atlantic club, September 18, 1862, and it denotes the winners of the championship for that year."[58] The glass case was later donated to the National Baseball Hall of Fame in Cooperstown, where it remains on display in the exhibit "Taking the Field: the 19th Century" and provides a vivid reminder of one of the greatest baseball clubs of the pioneer era.

CLUB MEMBERS

Andrew Kent Allison: Andy Allison became the first baseman for the Eckfords in 1867 and continued in that role until the Eckfords' disastrous 1872 season as a National Association club. Allison's brother William (1850–1887) also played a few games for the 1872 club. (They were not related to the more famous Allison brothers from Philadelphia, Art and Doug.) Andy was born in New York City around 1848, the son of Scottish immigrants. He began playing baseball in 1864 for the Marions, the junior club that developed many players for the Eckfords. After three years he moved up to the Eckfords and never played for another club. Allison's father was a shipwright and his brother a ship joiner, so he came by his allegiance naturally. According to an 1869 sketch, Allison was "a remarkably safe player, and very rarely errs in judgment. He is one of the best if not the best batter of the nine, and generally makes his base on a safe hit. He is noted for hitting what is termed 'fair fouls,' the ball striking just outside the fair line and bounding foul to the field between the third and home bases. In one game this season he struck eight of these balls in

succession, making his first on three of them and his second on the remainder."[59] A compositor by profession, Andrew Allison remained in Brooklyn after finishing with baseball, where he raised a family and took part in at least one old-timers game. His name vanished from the city directory in 1897 and until very recently his date and place of death were unknown. At last researcher Bob Bailey discovered that he had died in Brooklyn on March 21, 1897, but that his surname was recorded as Ellison, making it impossible to locate him.

Waddy Beach: Waddy (or Watty) Beach was a great catcher for the Eckfords in the early 1860s and a great mystery ever since. In 1887 he was said to have "disappeared" and a 1906 article indicated that Beach was alive but with "whereabouts unknown."[60] Later researchers could find no such player by that name and were forced to give up. One part of the mystery has been resolved by the discovery of an 1869 article about an ugly incident in a Brooklyn bar that referred to the instigator as "Washington B. Clark ... familiarly known as Waddy Beach."[61] Subsequent research determined that this man's full name was Washington Beach Clark, and with his age fitting the ballplayer there can be little doubt that he is the right man. Washington Beach Clark was born around 1839 and grew up in Brooklyn. He played for the Eckfords from 1859 through 1863, earning a reputation as one of the game's best catchers. According to one of the reporters who followed his play, "Every effective fielder must of necessity be, to an extent, graceful in movement, but there are some we know of, who rank as first-class players, that lack this quality considerably, but Beach has it to perfection. Watch him, when playing in his regular position as catcher, when he is in right condition to play, and has his work before him to do, and observe how skillfully and yet with what comparative ease he handles the ball, whether a grounder from a low pitch, a swift fly tip, or high foul, pretty well out of reach; no such a thing as awkwardness to be seen in any motion he makes. Lithe and agile as a cat, his sharp eyes eagerly on the look-out for all chances, and with a smile that displays his fine ivories, we have before us the beau ideal of a ball player, cool, plucky and skillful."[62] Beach was a fireman with Brooklyn's Engine Company Number 1 during these years, but had been expelled by January of 1864 when he was badly injured in a fistfight with an active fireman.[63] When he recovered, he went to Tennessee and did not return until August.[64] He played only one known game for the Eckfords that year and is not known to have played at all in 1865, but then rejoined the club in 1866. After another year away from baseball, he played for the Olympics of Washington in 1868, then retired. His first child was born that year and a second son followed four years later, but the marriage did not last. Waddy also got in trouble with the law in the 1869 incident alluded to earlier, which saw him throw a beer stein at a saloonkeeper and hit the man's daughter instead, seriously injuring her. He becomes difficult to trace in the ensuing years, but resurfaced in 1887 when he applied for an umpiring job. National League president Nick Young, a teammate on the Olympics, described Beach as the "king of catchers" and helped him get a job as a Southern League umpire.[65] According to Young, Beach was living in Gloversville, New York, at the time. He cannot be traced after that, though as noted earlier, he was reported to be alive in 1906.

William H. Bell (club officer): See Empire Base Ball Club.

Edmund Brown: Edmund Brown was a mainstay of the Eckfords and later accounts clearly identify him as having become a Brooklyn police captain. This man was a native of New Jersey who retired from the police force in 1903 and died on October 29, 1908, at the age of 72. An obituary noted that "in his youth he was one of the best semi-professional baseball players in Brooklyn, and up to the time he retired he was known throughout the department as 'Pincher' Brown. He was a veteran of the Civil War, having served in the Ellsworth Zouaves, and was one of the guard of honor at the funeral of President Lincoln. He was also a veteran volunteer fireman." The article was accompanied by a picture of Brown, who sported a remarkable set of sideburns.[66] While there is no doubt about Brown's identity there are some questions about the exact length of his career with the Eckfords. According to Marshall Wright's compilations, a player or players named Brown played for the Eckfords from 1857 through 1862 and then again in 1866 and 1868. Most of the record belongs to Edmund Brown, but it's possible that some of it belongs to another man with the same surname. We know that both Ed Brown and his brother Billy were regulars on the club in 1856. Marshall Wright credits a player named Brown with playing the outfield for the Eckfords in both 1857 and 1858. An 1896 article about a picture of the 1858 first nine indicated that Ed was on the first nine that year, but it's possible that some of the games from these years belong to Billy.[67] Ed became the club's regular catcher in 1859 but then left the Eckfords during the 1860 season and joined the Putnams.[68] Henry Chadwick later referred to Billy playing the outfield for the Eckfords in 1860, so it would seem that that year's games belong entirely to him or are a combination of the two brothers.[69] A player named Brown was again a regular for the Eckfords in 1861, but beginning that year the Mutuals also had a regular named Brown and Edmund Brown is known to have played for the Mutuals for several seasons. More to the point, Edmund Brown's service record in Ellsworth's Fire Zouaves (the 11th New York Infantry) shows that he enlisted on April 20, 1861, and was discharged due to disability on December 27, 1861, meaning that it is very likely that he didn't play for either club in 1861. So it would seem that the 1861 Eckford was either Billy Brown or some unrelated man with the same surname. Edmund Brown was definitely with the Mutuals for several seasons beginning in 1862, even umpiring the match between the Eckfords and Atlantics that decided the 1862 championship.[70] He left the Mutuals and rejoined the Eckfords

in 1866.[71] There's a good chance that the 1868 Eckford player is him as well, but it's hard to take anything for granted with a player named Brown. At least we can be sure that Edmund Brown was a longtime member of the club and had a sensational pair of sideburns.

William A. Brown: William Brown, a club officer, was the older brother of Edmund Brown and was an integral part of the club during the early years. He also helped organize the Pastime Club. He was a good friend of Henry Chadwick, who reminisced about standing beside " 'Dear old Billy Brown,' of the Eckfords."[72] Chadwick indicated that Billy Brown played the outfield for the Eckfords during their early years, so it appears that at least some of the games usually credited to his brother belong to him.[73] Since Chadwick later referred to Billy playing the outfield for the Eckfords in 1860, he probably deserves credit for all of that season's games.[74] In addition, the man who was a regular for the 1861 club is almost certainly not Edmund, then off at war, and the logical inference is that this is also Billy. Born in Rahway, New Jersey, around 1835, Brown worked at Brooklyn City Hall for over 50 years, celebrating his golden anniversary on January 2, 1906. Along with his brother, he had been deeply involved in the volunteer fire department and was credited among other accomplishments with helping to organize Brooklyn's first paid fire department.[75] Brown died at his son's home in Glen Ridge, New Jersey, on December 1, 1913.[76] There is contradictory information about Brown's middle initial, but most sources give it as A.

Butler: A player with this surname was a regular in 1865 and 1866 but it says much about the fortunes of the club during those years that his first name remains unknown.

William H. Butts: William Butts, an early club member, was born in Rochester, New York, in 1839. Butts appears in the famous 1858 picture of the Eckford Club because he was scorer at the time. A ship carpenter by trade, he became a detective during the war and worked in that line of work until failing health forced him to resign in 1881. He died in Greenpoint on June 12, 1883.[77]

Hervey Chittenden Calkin: A man identified as "H.C. Calkins" was the club's vice president in 1857 and it seems a safe assumption that he was also the man with that last name who played in a couple of games for the club that year. An 1858 game account listed "Harvey Calkins" as the scorer of the Eckfords.[78] That seems to point to Hervey Chittenden Calkin, a congressman from New York City from 1869 to 1871 who had Tammany connections, and indeed an 1893 article in the *New York World* confirmed that this was the case.[79] According to his congressional biography, Calkin had business interests in the shipping industry, which probably accounts for his involvement with the Eckford Club.[80] Calkin died in the Bronx on April 20, 1913, at the age of 85.

Campbell: A man with the surname of Campbell played a variety of positions for the Eckfords between 1860 and 1862, then joined the Mutuals.[81] An 1879 article stated that he was a fish merchant in the Fulton Market.[82] That article gave his name as West Campbell, while a later article gave it as Ivy Campbell. Neither name appears in the city directory or the censuses, so he remains a mystery. Whoever he was, he was still alive in 1885 when he was scheduled to play in an old-timers game.

James Carleton: See Mutual Base Ball Club.

Charles Coon: See Nationals of Washington in *Base Ball Pioneers, 1850–1870.*

Samuel Davenport: Sam Davenport pitched for the 1868 Eckfords when Phonney Martin was unavailable, after having previously pitched for the Contest Club. Davenport was born in New Jersey but lived in Brooklyn or the vicinity from infancy onward. A painter by trade, Davenport was only 40 when he died in Flatbush in 1888.[83]

Thomas Devyr: Born in Brooklyn in 1844, Thomas Devyr was the son of noted Irish journalist and political reformer Thomas Ainge Devyr (1805–1887), who was facing the threat of imprisonment for his involvement with the Chartist movement when he fled England in 1840. Upon arrival in New York, the elder Devyr became the editor and proprietor of the *Williamsburgh Democrat.* Thomas Ainge Devyr was eventually forced out of that position for refusing to follow the party line and in 1847 became editor of the *Williamsburgh Morning Post,* the first daily ever published in that town (which discarded the h from its name in 1852). He was also an Anti-Rent leader, a friend of many of the leading American reformers, and an influential writer.[84] There is contradictory evidence as to whether his son was given the same middle name; some sources list him as Thomas A. Devyr and others as Thomas H. Devyr. In any event, he began playing shortstop for the Marion club, the junior club that supplied the Eckfords with so much talent, and soon impressed observers as being as "active and agile as a cat."[85] Although slight of stature at 5-feet-8½ and 140 pounds, Devyr was also able to generate surprising power when batting. He joined the Eckfords in 1862 and was the starting shortstop on the two consecutive national championship winners. Devyr became a member of the Mutuals of New York in 1864 and it was during his second year with the Mutuals that he became a central figure in baseball's first scandal. The Mutuals were playing Devyr's old club the Eckfords in a best-of-three series, with the Mutuals having won the first game, when Mutuals catcher William Wansley approached Devyr and asked him if he'd like to make an easy $300. Wansley told him that gamblers were offering to pay them to intentionally lose that day's game and assured Devyr that "We can lose this game without doing the club any harm, and win the home and home game." He even promised that he would make all the misplays necessary to ensure defeat. Fatally, Devyr agreed to the scheme, only to have nothing go as planned. Devyr received only $30 and the errors made by Wansley, Devyr, and a third conspirator, Ed Duffy, were so blatant as to raise suspicions. When confronted, Devyr immediately confessed and humbly expressed his re-

morse, claiming that he only agreed to the scheme because he was broke. All three players were expelled by the Mutuals and banned from baseball. There was almost unanimous sentiment that Devyr's repentance was genuine and that he was "more sinned against than sinning," with the result that he was reinstated after only one year.[86] He played shortstop for the Mutuals from 1867 to 1869 and never gave the club any reason to regret giving him another chance. He rejoined the Eckfords late in the 1869 season and played for them for part of the 1870 campaign, but retired from baseball for good that fall after being elected Supervisor in the Seventeenth Ward in an exciting election that saw him win by a mere 23 votes.[87] He remained active in civic politics and held several prominent positions in city government. He died in Brooklyn on January 22, 1896. According to an obituary, "At winning prizes [Devyr] was also very successful, the most valuable being a handsome gold badge, for the best general play, during the Masonic benefit tournament between the picked nine, New York vs. Brooklyn. He played on the New York nine, which won the series, the minor prizes awarded him at the same time being a pair of ball shoes for the best home run, and a statuette of 'The Pitcher,' for the best fly catch. Of all the many prizes he received, none remained in his possession at the time of his death, save a book of poems bestowed on him by Colonel Fitzgerald, president of the Athletic club of Philadelphia."[88]

Ed Duffy: See Mutual Base Ball Club.

David Eggler: See Mutual Base Ball Club.

John Eggler: Dave Eggler's brother John played for the Eckfords in 1869. He was considered a substitute rather than a member of the first nine, but ended up playing regularly. He had begun his career playing second base for the Junior Green Mountains of Williamsburg, then played for the Jefferson Juniors, the Independents, the Amitys of Brooklyn and the Putnam Juniors of East New York. In light of his long career, it's not surprising that he was described as being "about 23" when he joined the Eckfords.[89] In fact, he was Dave's younger brother and was not yet born when the 1850 census was taken, so was still a teenager. The 1870 census reported that he was only 17, but that seems far-fetched and it's more likely he was born shortly after the 1850 census-taker's visit. Eggler was a glass-blower by trade and seems to have played no more baseball after 1869. In 1875 he was accused of murder after the drowning death of a friend, which he described as an accident.[90] No account of the verdict has been found, but he must have spent little if any time behind bars as he had several children born during the next few years. By 1900 he was a widower raising several children, two of whom he was training as glass-blowers. A John J. Eggler, age 54, died in Kings County on March 26, 1904. No obituary has been located, but it seems almost certain that this was him.

George Fox: See Nationals of Washington (in *Base Ball Pioneers, 1850–1870*).

James M. Gray: James M. Gray was one of the Eckford

Club's three representatives at the 1857 NABBP convention. Somebody named Gray played the outfield for the Eckford in 1857 and this is probably the same man. Like so many of the Eckfords, Gray worked at the East River shipyards. As was also the case with so many club members, the decline of the shipbuilding industry brought hard times for Gray. Fortunately for him, wealthy shipbuilder William Webb had created the Webb Academy and Home for Shipbuilders (now known as the Webb Institute), which provided instruction to students and a free home for elderly shipbuilders. Gray spent his last years there, dying on November 7, 1915, at the age of 87.

George L. Grum: The sons of a New York City butcher who moved the family to Brooklyn during the 1850s, the Grum brothers were mainstays of the Eckford Club from the late 1850s through 1868, with the exception of the war years. George was the younger brother but according to Marshall Wright's listings he joined the Eckfords first, taking a regular turn in the club's lineup as early as 1857, when he was only 17. That seems unlikely and is probably a mistake, as an obituary of Peter Tostevin listed John Grum as the brother who played for the club during those years.[91] An obituary of John Grum also confirmed that he began playing shortstop for the Eckfords in 1856.[92] In any event, both brothers were playing for the club by 1859 and so was Henry Manolt, their father's apprentice. George Grum served in the 9th New York Infantry during the war and then followed in his father's footsteps as a butcher, as did his brother. George moved to Hastings-on-Hudson, New York, after this father's death. According to Civil War pension records, he died on May 12, 1901, though his passing did not attract the attention given to his brother's death 12 years later.

John J. Grum: John Grum was the older of the two Grum brothers — an obituary stated that he was born in New York City on December 7, 1837, but the 1850 census listed him as 15, suggesting he was a few years older than that. Like his father and brother, John Grum was a butcher by profession, working in the Washington Market until retiring in 1907 and moving to Pittsfield, Massachusetts. He died there on December 8, 1913, and his passing was noted in an obituary that bore the headline, "Old Baseball Star Dead."[93]

Louis Guillaudeu: Louis Guillaudeu was president of the Eckford Club in 1859 and was a key part of that year's revolt by discontented members. He became president of the newly formed Henry Eckford Club of New York, which was organized on August 23.[94] Guillaudeu was born in New York State in 1831 and was the son of French-born Emile Guillaudeu, a Columbia graduate who worked as a taxidermist at P.T. Barnum's American Museum. Louis was living in New York City and listed a machinist when the 1850 census was taken. He was listed in subsequent city directories as a clerk and an accountant but soon becomes hard to trace, probably because of the difficulties Americans had with his French surname. It appears that he may have ended up in New Jersey.

William H. Haight: William H. Haight was club pres-ident in both 1856 and 1857 and one of the club's two delegates at the 1858 convention. There's only one plausible candidate in the city directories and censuses: a New York City man by that name who was born in Canada around 1824 and who operated a tinning and galvanizing business. Presumably the shipyards provided much of his business and accounted for his involvement with the Eckford Club. Like many club members, his fortunes suffered after the decline of the shipbuilding business. He was forced into bankruptcy in the late 1850s. He started a new business, but the firm disappeared from the city directory around 1871 and his whereabouts cannot be traced after that.

Charles Hodes: Charley Hodes was originally a member of the rival Atlantics but was unable to crack their first nine. He joined the Eckfords in 1868 and was a regular in 1868 and 1869, showing himself "competent to fill any position in the Nine with the exception of pitcher."[95] Jimmy Wood recruited him to join Chicago's $18,000 nine in 1870 and he remained in Chicago for the first season of the National Association. He played two more seasons in baseball's first major league and continued to show great versatility, playing almost every position on the diamond. He was a compositor by trade but that's pretty much all that is known about his life outside of the game, as efforts to find him in the censuses and city directories have been unsuccessful. In November of 1874 a benefit game was staged for the bedridden Hodes.[96] His far-too-early death occurred in Brooklyn three months later, on February 14, 1875.[97]

Charles Hunt: See Mutual Base Ball Club.
Richard Hunt: See Mutual Base Ball Club.
Nat Jewett: See Mutual Base Ball Club.
Richard H. Ketcham (and perhaps a second player with the same surname): A man named Ketcham or Ketchum was a semi-regular on the 1862 championship squad and Marshall Wright lists the player as being Dan Ketchum, a well-known ballplayer profiled in the Union of Morrisania entry, but it's not entirely clear that this is the correct man. A fish dealer named Richard H. Ketcham died on April 6, 1885, at the age of 62 and an obituary in *Sporting Life* identified him as an original member of the Eckford Club.[98] In light of his age and the fact that he was already a father of four, it's unlikely that he returned to the first nine in 1862. Thus the 1862 player may indeed be Dan, but no clear-cut evidence has been found.

Adam Klein: Adam Klein was a regular for the Eckfords from 1865 through 1867, playing first base and third base. Born in Germany in March of 1842, Klein immigrated to the United States around 1860. After an 1866 game Klein was cited as an example of the conduct of the Eckford Club having deteriorated. When the umpire called a strike on Klein for being "overly particular," Klein declared that he "wasn't going to stand any of his nonsense any more!" The comment elicited this scolding of both Klein and Eckford captain Waddy Beach: "This is the first time in our recollection that we ever knew the decision of an umpire disputed by an Eckford player, and for the credit of a club having such a good name as the Eckfords, we trust never to see it occur again. The excuse that Klein is a man who 'doesn't know better' is valid to a certain extent; but Beach, who partly countenanced him, is too old a player not to know that a dozen victories would not offset the discredit of disputing an umpire in the way in which Klein did. Here was a club which, knowing that they could not proceed in their game without a referee, and who, after asking a man whom they knew to be a thoroughly impartial player and one holding an honorable position in the National Association, to oblige them by acting as umpire, returned his kindness by disputing his decisions, and rating him all the way home — as one of the Eckfords did for his 'lack of judgment' and 'partiality.' Why, the thing is simply disgraceful, and if it is allowed to go unrebuked by the club whose members thus disgraced it, it will soon be difficult to get any man to serve as umpire in a match in which the Eckfords play."[99] Klein later worked as a saloonkeeper and bridge policeman. He was 80 when he died in Brooklyn on June 13, 1923.

George S. Lanphear: George Lanphear played second base for the Eckfords from 1859 through 1861. (His surname was usually spelled "Lamphear" in newspaper articles, but it appears that Lanphear was the correct spelling.) Born in Rhode Island in 1829, Lanphear worked as a fish dealer in Fulton Market along with Ben West and the mysterious Campbell. He died on May 11, 1889, and a front-page article in the *Brooklyn Eagle* later that week recorded, "George has played and done his work manfully in the game of life, but he could not avoid being struck out by that great pitcher, King Death."[100]

William Logan: William Logan was the original vice president of the Eckford Club. A man named Logan played third base for the club in 1857, likely the same person. His name is too common to identify with a high degree of confidence but there is an obvious candidate: a ship carpenter who was born around 1829.

Malone: A man named Malone played for the Eckfords in 1867, 1868, and 1870. He is believed to be Martin Malone, an enigmatic ballplayer who also had a brief major-league career but who had eluded all efforts to identify him.

Henry A. Manolt: Harry Manolt was born in New York City on March 11, 1828, and apprenticed as a butcher in the household of Lewis Grum, father of John and George. Like the Grum brothers, he was a club mainstay from the days at the Manor House until after the war, meaning that one-third of the Eckford lineup in many games came from a single household. Manolt was a member of Engine Company No. 1 of the Brooklyn Volunteer Fire Department from 1849 until being honorably discharged in 1863. By then he was married with two children, yet Manolt continued to play baseball for several years after the war. Despite apprenticing as a butcher, he worked for many years as a foreman at the Brooklyn Navy Yard. Manolt then moved to Toms River, New Jersey, in 1877,

where he became a farmer. Around 1901, he returned to Brooklyn, where he died on October 2, 1908.[101]

Alphonse "Phonney" Martin: See Empire Base Ball Club.

D.J. McAuslan: D.J. McAuslan was club secretary in 1861 and a man with that surname appeared in one match game in 1862. McAuslan was a very rare name in the United States at that time, so it's a safe assumption that this was David J. McAuslan, who was born in Scotland around 1836 and immigrated in 1860, then did some baseball reporting for the *Brooklyn Times* after the war. He also appeared in several games for the Eckfords' muffin club and for a reporters' nine. A printer by trade, McAuslan's interests seem to have soon changed to a different sport. Henry Chadwick reported in 1885 that McAuslan was the bowling reporter for the *Brooklyn Times*.[102] He also edited a publication called the *National Bowler*.[103] McAuslan was still alive in 1900 and even gave testimony to the Mills Commission a few years later, but appears to have died soon afterward.[104]

McDermott: A mysterious man named McDermott became the Eckford Club's regular pitcher in 1870. McDermott was described as being "heretofore unknown to fame," and glowing reports of his ability caused a decent-sized crowd to show up for his debut. Unfortunately, according to a reporter who was on hand, "This unwise pre-laudation of their pitcher placed him in a false position by raising expectation too high, instead of allowing the new-comer a fair chance to win his own laurels, and stand for what he was worth; too much was consequently expected of him at the outset, and his efforts being but fair, there was considerable disappointment. He sends a ball with rapidity, but wildly, and his endurance, judging by his play yesterday, is not great."[105] After the Eckfords' disappointing 1870 season, McDermott agreed to join the Atlantics in 1871. When the Fort Wayne Kekiongas of the newly formed National Association beckoned, McDermott jumped at the chance, but he lasted only two games. He pitched seven games for the Eckfords in 1872, losing all of them, and his career tapered off after that. He is generally listed in reference works as "Joseph McDermott" but that appears to be the result of misreading "Jas. McDermott," the usual abbreviation for James McDermott, as "Jos. McDermott." James McDermott is believed to have worked as a clerk at Brooklyn City Hall in the mid–1870s, but efforts to trace him after that have been unsuccessful.

Henry Frederick Metzler: Henry F. Metzler was the club secretary from 1855 to 1857. Born around 1828, Metzler was a wood carver by trade and most of his work adorned ships, which explains his involvement with the Eckford Club. Metzler is best known for creating Atlas, the famous clock sculpture that still adorns the front of the Tiffany Building in Manhattan. Like many early members of the Eckfords, Metzler struggled after the East River shipyards fell on hard times. He started a business that involved hobby horses and baby carriages, but the firm went bankrupt in 1868. Metzler moved to New Jersey, then returned to Brooklyn, and finally died in Cedar Grove, New Jersey, on May 2, 1912, at the age of 82. He is buried at Green-Wood Cemetery.

Andrew Hodges Mills: Andrew H. Mills was one of the mainstays of the Eckfords, playing a variety of positions for the club between 1857 and 1866. Born around 1837, he was the older brother of Charley Mills, who joined the Eckfords in 1865 and had a stellar career with several clubs. The Mills brothers grew up in Williamsburg, where their father, Samuel D. Mills, started the first local private academy. Their mother, the former Charlotte Hodges, was the daughter of Alfred Hodges, a prominent Williamsburg businessman who operated the first ferry between Williamsburg and New York. No doubt that connection had something to do with Andy Mills joining the Eckfords, as did his involvement with the volunteer fire department. Mills in turn was credited with recruiting Al Reach. After leaving baseball, Mills became a policeman, working at the Bedford Avenue station until his retirement around 1884. He died unexpectedly at his home in East Rockaway on June 21, 1899.[106]

Charley Mills: See Atlantic Base Ball Club.

John W. "Candy" Nelson: Born in Maine on March 14, 1849, Jack Nelson was the son of a sea captain who moved the family to Brooklyn around 1860. Jack began playing baseball for the junior Sheridan Club in 1861 as a catcher. He joined the Eckfords in 1867 and spent three seasons with them, playing shortstop, third base, and catcher. A profile described Nelson as a shipping agent, but he didn't have to practice that profession, as his stint with the Eckfords was the start of a professional baseball career that lasted until 1890.[107] Although then 51, his occupation on the 1900 census was still listed as "ball player." Nelson died in Brooklyn on September 4, 1910.

Thomas W.H. Patterson: Tom Patterson was born around 1845 and grew up in Williamsburg, where his Scottish-born father was a mariner. Living two doors away was Marty Swandell, later an Eckford teammate. Like so many of the Eckfords, Patterson began playing baseball with the junior Marion Club of Williamsburg. He put baseball and life on hold on February 9, 1864, when he made a one-year enlistment in the Navy as a landsman. His enlistment record reveals that he stood 5-feet-7-inches tall, had hazel eyes, brown hair, a florid complexion, and a tattoo with the initials "T.P." on his right forearm.[108] He began his time in the Navy aboard the USRS (U.S. Receiving Ship) North Carolina and was then transferred on March 8 to the USS Niagara, which was stationed in Antwerp. After being honorably discharged on September 22, 1865, Patterson played for the Enterprise Club, then joined the Eckfords in 1867 and spent three seasons playing second base and the outfield and proving himself "competent to play in almost any position in the field."[109] He moved on to the Mutuals in 1870 and then spent four years in the National Association, which made him the first known

major leaguer to sport a tattoo. He ended his career with the Atlantics in 1875 and by then was described unkindly as "an antiquated fossilized player who was once considered the prince of outfielders, but who is not now fit to play on a second-rate amateur nine. Indeed, there are not many amateur clubs in [New York City] who would have him in their ranks. He was never a respectable batter, and is now too old to learn. If he ever sees first base this season it will be on three balls only."[110] After a first marriage ended in divorce, Tom Patterson remarried in Jersey City in 1878 and later worked as a painter and as a compositor or printer. He began collecting a Navy disability pension in the 1890s as the result of rheumatism, bronchitis, neuralgia, and an assortment of other ailments that prevented him from doing manual labor. His wife reported that he needed her constant attention, making it impossible for either of them to work. Tom Patterson was, however, listed as a clerk in the city directories. They moved from Brooklyn to New York City in the middle of the decade and that was where Tom Patterson died on May 31, 1900. His widow filed for a pension but she died 46 days after her husband while the application was still being processed.

Francis Pidgeon, Sr.: Frank Pidgeon was born in New York City on February 11, 1825, which meant that he was already past the ideal age for baseball when he took up the sport. He went to California during the Gold Rush but was back in New York and newly married by the time the 1850 census was taken. He thereafter devoted himself to dock-building and became a close friend of George Steers, a member of a legendary family of shipbuilders and the man who built the racing yacht America that became the namesake of the America's Cup. In 1855, though now 30 and having already begun a family, Pidgeon helped to found the Eckford Club. He served as its first president and was later described as "the moving spirit among the shipbuilders and was practically the father of the movement and under his guidance the Eckford nine achieved much of the power it enjoyed in his time."[111] He was also the club's primary pitcher for the next five years, earning a reputation for headiness and for carefully studying the weak points of opposing batters. "In finesse and the general management of a game," wrote one reporter, "we think Pidgeon has no equal."[112] Frank Pidgeon gave up baseball after the 1862 season, during which the club he had helped build captured its first of two consecutive national championships. He became an outspoken opponent of professional play and moved to Saugerties, New York, where he built his dock-building trade into a prosperous business. He also cultivated a wide range of interests, becoming known for his discerning tastes in art and literature, his skill as a musician, and for creating paintings that hung in the homes of his friends. He was also said to have invented the first successful steam traction plow. The 1870s brought reversals in his business, however, and by 1881 he was forced into bankruptcy. Pidgeon spent the next few years working for his son but then on June 12, 1884, he was struck and killed while walking along the tracks of the Hudson River Railroad. Many suspected suicide, but his friends preferred to believe that he had been too deep in thought to hear the approaching train.[113]

Edwin B. Pinkham: Ed Pinkham was born in New York in August of 1846 and grew up in Williamsburg. He and his older brothers played for several clubs in the area while growing up and Ed, a left-hander, was the best of the lot. He sometimes pitched, making him one of the first prominent southpaw pitchers, but more often played the infield. After serving briefly in the 47th New York Infantry as an underage enlistee during the Civil War, he played for the Eckford Club in 1864 and 1865. He then saw time with several clubs, including the Enterprise, the Excelsiors, and the Orientals of Greenpoint, before rejoining the Eckfords as their full-time shortstop in 1869. He joined Jimmy Wood's new Chicago nine in 1870 and was the club's primary pitcher, displaying a "quick, ugly delivery of the ball that has often bothered many of the heaviest batters of the country to hit."[114] He remained with the White Stockings during the first year of the National Association, mostly playing third base, but also taking an occasional turn at pitching. The Great Chicago Fire caused the White Stockings to disband after the season but Pinkham remained in Chicago for the next two years, playing for semipro clubs. In 1874 a Brooklyn paper reported that Pinkham, "a former resident of this city, but more recently of Chicago has turned Granger and will devote what little energy he has to raising beets."[115] He pitched for an amateur club in Hempstead, on Long Island, in 1875 but created controversy because of his status as a professional.[116] That seems to have ended his baseball career and his whereabouts become extremely difficult to trace in the years that follow. An 1876 article reported that he had last been heard of living in New Jersey, and another piece that year stated ominously that he was "living (if at all) in Hoboken."[117] The following year two baseball medals, one of which bore the name Ed Pinkham, turned up in a New York pawnshop.[118] On the 1892 New York state census, he is listed as living in Brooklyn with a wife and two young children and working as a blind-maker. A third child followed around 1894, but his son seems to have died in 1896 and the family split up. His older daughter was living with Ed's sister when the 1900 U.S. census was taken, while his younger daughter had been adopted by an unrelated family. His wife was nowhere to be found and Ed appears to have been living in the state of Washington and working as a fisherman. By the time of the New York state census of 1905, Ed was again living with both daughters in Brooklyn and working as a painter. He died in Brooklyn on December 19, 1906.

Al Reach: See Athletic Base Ball Club.

James Snyder: James Snyder became the regular catcher of the Eckford Club in 1870. The obvious supposition is that he was a brother of John and Josh but no brother by that name appears in the family listing on the 1860 census. He does not seem to have ever played baseball before or afterward, so he remains a mystery.

John H. Snyder: John H. Snyder played for the Eckfords from 1859 to 1862 and again in 1865 and was the older brother of Josh Snyder. The Snyder brothers were the sons of John Snyder, Sr., an undertaker and Brooklyn alderman, and the former Eliza Varian, whose family traced their ancestry back to the Huguenots.[119] After finishing with baseball, the younger John Snyder followed in his father's footsteps, succeeding him as 15th Ward alderman and also taking over his undertaking business. He was also elected a Supervisor during the 1870s but then got out of politics and devoted most of his energies to his business. Born in New Jersey around 1839, John H. Snyder died in Brooklyn on March 19, 1911.

Joshua M. Snyder: Josh Snyder was said to have been "quite a boy" when he joined his brother on the Eckford first nine in 1860.[120] The encyclopedias indicate that he was only 16 at the time, though census listings suggest he was actually a year or two older. He was one of the club's mainstays for the next decade, even playing a few games for the 1872 National Association club, though as with most Eckford players there were a few gaps. He too worked as an undertaker after baseball and died in Brooklyn on April 21, 1881.[121]

Peter Spence: Peter Spence played several games for the Eckfords during their first championship season in 1862. It seems very likely that the ballplayer was a man by that name who served in the 13th New York Regiment, Joe Sprague's regiment. This man is very hard to trace but probably died in 1893, when his wife filed for a Civil War widow's pension.

Joseph E. Sprague: Though he now languishes in obscurity, the enigmatic and gifted Joe Sprague has every bit as strong a claim as Jim Creighton to be remembered as the pioneer era's greatest legend. The grandson of an early Brooklyn mayor, Sprague led the Eckfords to two consecutive championships—even returning home from serving in the Civil War to pitch the Eckfords to their first championship. He then joined the Atlantics for another championship, only to walk away from baseball for good at the tender age of 22. It is the stuff of which legends are born and, to top everything off, several teammates credited him with throwing the first curve. Born in Brooklyn in 1843, Joseph E. Sprague was the son of Major Horace Sprague and the former Margaret McKenzie, both members of distinguished Brooklyn families. His grandfather and namesake served five terms as president of the village of Brooklyn and then became the city's second mayor. Sprague made his first-known appearance on a baseball diamond on Thanksgiving Day in 1857, pitching the National Club of Brooklyn to a 41–5 victory over the Montauks of Bedford in a portent of the dominance that was to follow.[122] He remained with the Nationals in 1858 and 1859, then played for the Exercise and Oriental clubs in 1860 and the Exercise Club in 1861. All of these clubs were junior clubs, but Sprague's prodigious talents were already attracting the attention of senior clubs and in 1860 he provoked controversy by briefly playing for the Atlantics of Jamaica, a senior club that is not to be confused with the more famous Brooklyn club that bore the same name.[123] He finally moved up to the senior ranks in 1862 by joining the Enterprise Club, but soon switched allegiances to the Eckford Club. Not long after joining the Eckfords, he enlisted in the 13th New York Regiment for a three-month tour of duty in Virginia.[124] Upon his return, he was pressed into duty to pitch the September 18 game against the Atlantics that was to decide the championship. While Sprague was away at war, the two rivals had split two high-scoring affairs — a 20–14 win by the Eckfords had been followed by a 39–5 win for the Atlantics. With the large, powerfully built Sprague pitching, however, the rubber match took on an entirely different tenor with the Eckfords winning by the astonishing score of 8–3. As one later account put it, "Few people could understand how it was that the Atlantics had scored only three runs."[125] Another eyewitness subsequently recalled that "[the Atlantics'] defeat was solely due to Joe Sprague, the pitcher of the Eckfords. Joe had just returned from the army. He was the swiftest pitcher that ever wore a uniform. He pitched a ball as swift as it is thrown to-day. The result was that the Atlantics' batsmen generally struck out. I remember the remark of Fred Massey to his fellow players after his striking out: 'why, that ball was in [catcher] Waddy Beach's hand before I struck at it!' Beach was forty feet behind the plate."[126] Joe Sprague pitched the Eckfords to an undefeated season and their second straight championship in 1863. The Eckford Club lost many key members after the 1863 season and Sprague chose to join the rival Atlantics, yet he never pitched a game for his new club. He appeared in six games for the Atlantics at shortstop and first base in 1864 and three more games in 1865, both seasons in which the Atlantics were undefeated national champions. Sprague had still not lost a game since returning from service in the war — baseball, it would seem, was simply too easy for him. He became interested in cricket that year and on August 17, 1865, made his last appearance with the Atlantics.[127] He joined the Manhattan Cricket Club and then the Staten Island Cricket Club, bowling for the latter eleven for many years. In 1873 he returned to baseball and pitched 17 games for the Staten Island Base Ball Club of Tompkinsville, a strictly amateur club that played against the likes of the Knickerbockers and Gothams. Sprague became a partner in the tea brokerage of Lewis & Sprague. When Sprague died obituaries described him as a bachelor who was the last surviving male member of his family and who had retired from business in the early 1890s. Rarely leaving the family home at 156 Adelphi Street, where he lived with his mother and sister, he devoted most of his time to reading and the weight of the once-great athlete increased to over 250 pounds. On June 26, 1898, he died of apoplexy in the same room that he had lived in since childhood.[128] The portrayal omits a number of key details. Sprague was listed as married to a young woman named Phoebe (nee Ryerson) when the 1880 census was taken. She sued for divorce and alimony in 1882, alleging that he had

failed to support her and had "acted in an improper manner with several women," one of whom had successfully sued him after becoming pregnant. Sprague disputed most of her contentions, maintaining that they were never legally married because he had a prior marriage that had ended in divorce with the stipulation that he could not remarry during that woman's lifetime. He also described himself as being destitute and without enough means to support his aging mother, let alone pay alimony. Charges and countercharges continued to fly for two years and it's not clear how the matter was resolved.[129] In any case, by the time of Sprague's death, his legacy had been forgotten by many, but by no means all. Teammate Jimmy Wood declared Sprague the "greatest pitcher of all times" and made another surprising claim on his behalf. "Sprague threw a curve ball — that was back in 1862 — which means that Sprague, not Arthur Cummins [sic], of the Brooklyn Stars of 1863–64, or Bobby Mathews, of the Baltimores of 1866–67 was the original curve ball pitcher," Wood maintained. "We always noticed that some of Sprague's deliveries took a sharp twist, sometimes turning in and sometimes turning away from the batter. All of us used to remark about the peculiar gyrations of the ball that he threw. It was not until some years later, however, when curved balls became an established fact, that we recognized the delivery, then called a curve as the same kind of ball that Sprague had thrown in 1862 and 1863."[130] Sprague's catcher, Waddy Beach, also affirmed that Sprague "could and did curve the ball while pitching for the Eckfords in 1863."[131]

Martin Swandell/Schwendel: Marty Swandell was born in Germany in 1841 with the surname of Schwendel and moved with his family to Williamsburg in 1847. There he grew up two doors away from Tom Patterson, who would later play alongside him in the Eckford outfield. He sometimes used the anglicized version of his surname, but his father, a baker, retained the Schwendel spelling until his death. The encyclopedias list Martin's full name as John Martin Swandell, but there's no source for the John and an 1868 profile referred to him as "George M. Swandel." In any event Martin was always the name that he used. He began playing baseball for a junior club called the Benicia Boy Club, moving up to the Eckfords in 1863 and earning a reputation as a stellar center fielder and "an excellent general player, playing well in every position. He is a still player and it is very seldom a word is heard from him."[132] He joined the Mutuals in 1868 and spent three years with that club. He played outfield in his first two years with the Mutuals, then moved to second base in 1870 so that his old neighbor Tom Patterson could have a place in the club's outfield. Swandell was now nearing 30 and his career wound down, but he did see action for the Eckfords and Resolutes in the National Association. With the former club, he played alongside Patterson. After baseball, Swandell became a baker like his father and raised a large family. He remained in Brooklyn until his death on October 25, 1906. One obituary described him as having been "one of the best center fielders that ever put on a uniform" and as having "started his baseball career with the Eckford team, when the rivalry between the baseball nines was intense. The Eckfords were the representatives of the old Williamsburg district, the Mutuals came from Manhattan and the Atlantics were the Brooklyn team."[133]

Peter Tostevin: Peter Tostevin played first base for the Eckfords in 1856 and 1857 and third base in 1858. He served as club president during the latter year and was also said to have helped organize the club.[134] Born in France in the mid–1820s, he was already well past the normal age for baseball by then and he relinquished his position to a younger man in 1859. He was a wealthy Brooklyn master builder and architect with a wife and eight children when he died at his Brooklyn home on December 8, 1879. The *New York Times* reported his death as a suicide, though this detail was omitted from references to his death in the *Brooklyn Eagle* and the *New York Clipper*.[135] Money was not a factor as Tostevin left an estate valued at over $100,000 and the business was continued under the name Peter Tostevin's Sons. In 1902 his two oldest sons committed suicide within the space of three months, the second being Henry Tostevin, now the president of the family business. Once again, thoughts that business problems were responsible were quickly put to rest. Henry Tostevin's son noted that his grandfather had also taken his own life and friends blamed "a life long pessimism which appears to be the inheritance of the sons from the father."[136]

Fred Treacy: Like many of the Eckfords, Fred Treacy began his career with the junior Marion Club of Williamsburg, but his path was not predictable after that and he became one of the most notorious "revolvers" of the era. After stints with the Franklins, Excelsiors, and Mohawks of Brooklyn, he left for Chicago in the middle of the 1868 season to play for that city's Excelsiors (see volume one). He spent the entire 1869 campaign with the Eckfords, then started the 1870 season with the Atlantics, only to return to Chicago in the middle of season to play for Jimmy Wood's $18,000 nine. He remained in Chicago in 1871 and tied for the National Association lead with four home runs. His wandering ways continued over the next five seasons as he roamed the outfields of a variety of major-league teams, finishing up with the Mutuals in 1876. He kept a low profile after leaving baseball but several newspaper articles had him back in Brooklyn. Based on that, there's only one viable candidate: a man named Frederick B. Treacy who was born in County Carlow, Ireland, around 1848, grew up in Brooklyn and died there on January 26, 1891. This man had several different occupations in the Brooklyn city directories and was listed in the 1880 census as a ship's carpenter, another intriguing link to the Eckfords.[137]

Joseph Leviness Vanderbilt: Joseph Vanderbilt was born in New York City on September 19, 1821, the son of Oliver Vanderbilt and the former Sarah Leviness. His father was a first cousin of shipbuilding magnate Cornelius Vanderbilt but there was no love lost between the two men. After several earlier disputes, Oliver Vanderbilt bought a small ferry business in 1839, prompting his wealthy cousin to take legal action against him, and initiated a price war. Oliver Vanderbilt persevered for several years but was finally forced out of business and ruined.[138] Joseph began his business career working as a broker, and then his brother-in-law, Charles M. Simonson, hired him as bookkeeper and general clerk of Simonson Brothers Shipbuilding Company, which operated out of one of the large shipyards on the East River. He thrived in this position and was also an active member of the New York Volunteer Fire Department, Engine Company No. 18, giving him connections with both of the Eckford Club's core groups. Simonson died in 1855 and in 1857 Joseph Vanderbilt's wife died, leaving him a widower with two young children. The two families had already been living in the same house, so Vanderbilt and his widowed sister amalgamated the two families — she raised the children from both families, while he devoted himself to the family business. Although now in his mid–30s, Vanderbilt also found time to play at least one game for the Eckfords in 1857 and became Frank Pidgeon's regular catcher in 1858. That same year, he and a partner began the Ingelson & Vanderbilt Ship Building Company, which may have been why he played no more baseball. Vanderbilt's new firm was destroyed in a fire a few years later. He remarried and moved from New York City to Brooklyn and took a position with the National Bank of Commerce, where he worked until retiring shortly before the turn of the century. After his move to Brooklyn, Vanderbilt renewed his ties with the Eckfords and served as club treasurer in 1866. He moved to New Brighton, Staten Island, in 1875 and continued to live there after retirement. In 1900 Vanderbilt was struck by a wagon while trying to cross the road in New Brighton and run over, breaking two of his ribs. But the old catcher shrugged off the injury, refused to press charges, and lived for another 16 years.[139] After the death of his second wife, he moved to the Westerleigh, Staten Island, home of his son, Joseph Mortimer Vanderbilt. When he died there on February 20, 1916, he was described as "the oldest volunteer fireman of New York," but his connection to the pioneer era of baseball had been largely forgotten.[140] His only granddaughter, however, was living with Joseph Vanderbilt at the time of his death and though she was only 7 years old at the time she was well aware of his days on the baseball diamond. Amy Vanderbilt went on to give etiquette advice to millions of Americans and in 1952, after the publication of her *Complete Book of Etiquette*, she told an interviewer, "If my grandfather, Joseph L. Vanderbilt, had had the foresight to patent his invention of the double-8 cut-of-leather with which all baseballs are covered today, I might not have written this book. I'd be far too rich to bother four years about a book, as I have with this one, plus an additional year to edit it. But he was one of those striped-pants, silk-hat ancestors who liked the game so much, he never dreamed of making it pay. He was a life member of the Baseball Hall of Fame, lived to be 96 and attended ballgames till he died, always bringing his folding seat with him."[141] In one of her syndicated columns she wrote that her grandfather "lived to be 96 years of age and was very active until his final days."[142]

William Webster: William Webster was a regular outfielder for the Eckfords in 1857 and 1858 but the name is too common to be certain of his identity. Intriguingly, there is a William Webster of plausible age (born around 1832) who is listed on the same page of the 1892 Brooklyn census as early Eckford player Benjamin West (see below). This William Webster operated a restaurant, so it's possible that he kept up his connection to West and the other Eckford members associated with the Fulton Market. But there is not enough information to be certain that this is the correct William Webster.

Charles Welling: Charles Welling was a regular for the Eckfords in 1857 and 1858 and was one of the three men who represented the club at the 1857 National Association of Base Ball Players convention. He has not been definitively identified, but the name is not common and it seems very likely that he was a Brooklyn printer by that name. Born in Brooklyn around 1825, the man in question apprenticed in the office of the *Long Island Farmer* and then became that newspaper's longtime editor and proprietor. Presumably that brought him into regular contact with the East River shipyards and accounts for his involvement with the Eckford Club. Welling died at his Clarenceville home on August 9, 1891.

Benjamin W. West: Ben West played for the Eckfords in 1861 and despite his short tenure was mentioned in several retrospective articles about the club. West joined George Lanphear and other club members in organizing and running the Fulton Market Fish-Mongers' Association. After giving up baseball, he became known as one of Brooklyn's best trapshooters.[143] West is believed to have died in 1894, but details have proven elusive.

James Leon Wood: Jimmy Wood was a giant of early baseball whose playing career came to an abrupt end when his leg had to be amputated. As a result, until very recently, even when and where he died remained unknown, and his many accomplishments are also forgotten. Wood was born to English immigrants on December 1, 1842, most likely in Canada. He and his family soon settled in Brooklyn, where Wood apprenticed with the junior Harlem and Marion clubs before joining the Eckfords in 1860. Though still only 17, Wood played right field in the decisive October 29 loss to the Atlantics and earned rave reviews for his play. He became the Eckfords' starting second baseman in 1861 and was an anchor of consecutive national championships in 1862 and 1863. The 1863 campaign saw Wood average 3½ runs scored per game — the best mark on any of the clubs that kept records — despite playing with a heavy heart. Jimmy's only brother, Rufus, had enlisted in the Union Army and was sent to Louisiana, where he suffered fatal wounds at the Battle of Port Hudson. Rufus Wood was only 25 when he died on June 26, 1863, leaving a young widow

named Sarah. By 1864 the Eckfords were in transition and so was their brilliant second baseman. He left the club at season's end and he and his new wife spent the next three years in Ohio, where they began a family. His new bride was named Sarah and it appears that she was his brother's widow. Wood was back in Brooklyn in 1868 and he rejoined the Eckfords, where he continued to swing a ferocious bat and to cover as much ground "as three ordinary players."[144] In one reporter's estimation, Wood "has no superior. His play is a rare combination of shrewdness, courage and activity. He covers the great part of the in-field and has been known to put out men on all three bases, although the second was his position. His stopping and throwing are superb. He faces every ball that comes near him, never flinching, no matter how hot it may come. He is also very efficient at the bat, generally getting his bases on clean hits."[145] He also served as captain and helped the Eckfords return to national prominence in 1869 with a 47–8 record. That December a newly formed stock syndicate in Chicago hired Jimmy Wood as captain and offered him an unprecedented bankroll to try to dethrone the Red Stockings of Cincinnati. Wood commanded the then-princely salary of $2,500 and he raided the Eckfords to sign Charley Hodes, Ed Pinkham, and Fred Treacy (along with former Eckford Ed Duffy) to contracts with the club that became known as the White Stockings or as the "$18,000 nine." It soon became clear, however, that writing big checks did not guarantee championship-level baseball. The club struggled in the early going and hit rock-bottom with a humiliating 9–0 loss to the Mutuals of New York — the first time that a notable club had ever played an entire game without scoring a run. Rumors had Wood's job in jeopardy, but instead he initiated a rebuilding project that produced astonishingly rapid results. The White Stockings improved dramatically and the 1870 season culminated with a long winning streak and two dramatic wins over the Red Stockings. At year's end there was no clear consensus as to which club was the national champion, with each contender having at least four losses, but the White Stockings had one of the strongest claims. Wood now had a national reputation as an outstanding captain and as someone who was equally at home with his fellow ballplayers and with the higher class of spectators that professional clubs needed to cultivate. Among the latter, Wood was known as "a thorough gentleman." But as soon as he stepped on the baseball diamond, he became a "good-natured, square, jolly ball-player and a capital second baseman. To look at him as he roils on the field like a sailor just off a long voyage, no one would suppose him to be the player he is; but 'country' as he looks, he's as sharp as a steel-trap the moment the ball is in motion."[146] As a result, his services were in demand throughout the five-year run of the National Association. In the circuit's inaugural season of 1871 he again led Chicago's White Stockings and had the club in the thick of the pennant race until the Great Chicago Fire devastated the city and the club. Chicago did not field a professional club for the next two seasons, so Wood split the 1872 season between Troy and Brooklyn. In 1873 he was signed as player-manager for a new club in Philadelphia that had been assembled to rival the Athletics. Wood's new charges led the pennant race for much of the year, until word came that Chicago was going to again field a club in 1874 and had signed most of the club's players. Those players soon began to show little interest in their work and the remainder of the season was marred by suspiciously bad performances. Wood had also signed to again serve as Chicago's player-manager, but his return was delayed by an accident that led to an abscess in his leg. Eventually came the terrible news that the leg would have to be amputated, bringing Wood's splendid playing days to an end. Few baseball clubs could afford the luxuries of a nonplaying manager, so he was let go after the 1875 season. Wood was trained as a machinist, but a one-legged man would face enormous challenges in that profession as well. Undaunted, Wood embarked on a series of new ventures that included running a saloon in Chicago, supervising orange orchards in Florida and running minor-league ball clubs in the South. In a sad testimony to the neglect of the great players of the pioneer eras, the encyclopedias for many years listed Wood as having died in 1886. In fact, he was still alive more than four decades after that. He split his time between Florida, New York, and New Orleans, and his ties to baseball deepened when his daughter married businessman William Chase Temple, part owner of the Pittsburgh Pirates and sponsor of the Temple Cup. Their daughter in turn married a major-league ballplayer named Del Mason. Wood even found time in 1916 to write a six-part memoir of "Baseball in the By-Gone Days" that was published in serial form in many newspapers. By all accounts, his life was a busy and productive one despite a series of adversities — on top of the loss of his brother and spending more than 50 years with only one leg, he endured the deaths of his wife and both his children.

By 1927 he was living in New Orleans when he decided to travel to San Francisco for cataract surgery. There were complications and one of the pioneer era's greatest players and captains died there on November 30, 1927, one day shy of his 85th birthday.

George Zettlein: See Atlantic Base Ball Club.

Other Club Members: Burr (likely Andy Burr of the Putnams), Coleman, Comstock, Coniglan, Courtney, Curtis, John Farrell, Fesler, Guyon F. Gosman, Holmes, E.F. Jenkins, R.W. Kenyon, Laing, Lynch, M.L. Mann, McCutchen, McVoy, Moss, E.N. Orr, W.C. Patterson, George Price, William H. Ray, Ryan, M.M. Simonson, C.C. Smith (and probably one or two other men named Smith), Southworth, Squires, Charlie Van Dyke, William J. Watson, George Wildey, James E. Wilson.

Notes

1. Melvin Adelman's *A Sporting Time*, 125–326, contains the most detailed analysis of the class status of the Eckfords and rejects the simplistic distinction between the Eckfords and clubs such as the Knickerbockers. Adelman attempted to identify 18 members of the 1855 Eckfords by means of city directories, but was able to identify only eight. As he acknowledges in an appendix, using city directories is a very imprecise approach to the subject. The identifications in this entry make use of the far greater resources now available, though even with them there are many players who cannot be identified with any confidence.

2. *Porter's Spirit of the Times*, June 20, 1857.

3. *Brooklyn Eagle*, June 26, 1885, 1. That article stated that the Manor House was located on Meeker Avenue, but that may have been a later name for the road as other sources suggest that at the time it was called Woodpoint Road.

4. *Porter's Spirit of the Times*, June 20, 1857.

5. Pidgeon's account originally appeared in *Porter's Spirit of the Times*, January 10, 1857, and has since been reproduced in numerous sources, including Albert G. Spalding, *America's National Game* (1910; Lincoln: University of Nebraska Press, 1992), 60–61.

6. *Porter's Spirit of the Times*, September 27, 1856, and January 10, 1857.

7. Sean Wilentz, *Chants Democratic* (New York: Oxford University Press, 1984), 135.

8. Ibid., 134–140.

9. *Porter's Spirit of the Times*, March 26, 1859.

10. *Corning Evening Leader*, October 14, 1952, 4.

11. *New York Atlas*, September 4, 1859.

12. *New York Sun*, February 6, 1887, 6.

13. James Wood, as told to Frank G. Menke, "Baseball in By-Gone Days," part 3, syndicated column, *Indiana* (Pennsylvania) *Evening Gazette*, August 17, 1916.

14. Williamsburg was spelled with an h until 1852. For simplicity's sake, the later spelling is used throughout this entry, except in the title of the newspapers of the 1840s edited by the elder Thomas Devyr.

15. Quoted in *Sporting Life*, December 23, 1911, 16.

16. *Brooklyn Eagle*, January 7, 1860, 3.

17. *Brooklyn Eagle*, October 30, 1860.

18. Chadwick Scrapbooks, unidentified clipping.

19. Charles A. Peverelly, *The Book of American Pastimes* (New York: Published by the Author, 1866), 438–439. According to the account in Peverelly, the Eckford Club's next three balls were held on January 25, 1864, at Union Hall, on January 26, 1865, at Union Hall, and on January 4, 1866, at the Odeon. The *New York Clipper* of January 17, 1863, however, reported that an "Invitation Hop" was scheduled for the 26th of that month. Whether they continued after 1866 is not known.

20. *New York Clipper*, February 2, 1861, 330.

21. *Brooklyn Eagle*, July 12, 1862, 2.

22. See Philip Lowry, *Green Cathedrals* (Reading, MA: Addisen-Wesley, 1992), 33–34, for a description of the site of the Union Grounds and a brief history. Some sources confuse the Union Grounds with the Capitoline Grounds and list them as a single ballpark, but they were in fact two separate parks.

23. *Brooklyn Eagle*, July 12, 1862, 2.

24. Ibid.

25. Chadwick Scrapbooks, unidentified clipping.

26. *Brooklyn Eagle*, July 22, 1862, 2.

27. *Brooklyn Times*, September 19, 1862.

28. *New York Clipper*, September 27, 1862.

29. Intriguingly, a 1919 article claimed that "the Eckfords knew that Sprague had kept on practicing pitching while in the army and that if they could get him back to Brooklyn before the third and deciding game of the series they would have the championship. William Wall, owner of a ropewalk in Brooklyn, was the member of Congress from the Williamsburg district at that time and in response to frantic appeals from his constituents he called on President Lincoln to ask for Sprague's release. The President asked General Grant to release the Eckford pitcher, and Sprague received his discharge immediately. His team managed by the

use of a series of excuses to postpone the third game until his arrival" (*Philadelphia Inquirer*, September 7, 1919). The idea that Wall, Lincoln, and Grant had nothing better to do than to scheme for Sprague's release is highly implausible and the article's credibility is further damaged by other misstatements of fact. Nonetheless, it's very suggestive of the fact that the Eckfords' stalling tactics were still remembered 57 years after the fact. It strongly implies that these stalling tactics were a bone of contention between the Atlantics and Eckfords and accounted for the less cordial relationship between the two clubs that ensued.

30. *New York Clipper*, September 27, 1862.

31. *Brooklyn Eagle*, September 19, 1862, 2.

32. James Wood, as told to Frank G. Menke, "Baseball in By-Gone Days," part 3, syndicated column, *Indiana (Pennsylvania) Evening Gazette*, August 17, 1916.

33. *Brooklyn Eagle*, October 3, 1863.

34. *Brooklyn Eagle*, May 13, 1864.

35. *Brooklyn Eagle*, August 8, 1864.

36. *Brooklyn Eagle*, August 31, 1864.

37. Letter from Frank Pidgeon to *Porter's Spirit of the Times*, March 26, 1859; reprinted as Appendix A of William J. Ryczek's *Baseball's First Inning* (Jefferson, N.C.: McFarland, 2009).

38. "Old Chalk's Reminiscences: The True Story of the Old Eckford Club," *Brooklyn Eagle*, January 18, 1891, 16.

39. *Brooklyn Eagle*, July 22, 1864.

40. Chadwick Scrapbooks, unidentified clipping.

41. *Brooklyn Eagle*, August 31, 1864.

42. *Brooklyn Eagle*, August 23, 1865, 2.

43. *Brooklyn Eagle*, January 21, 1871, 2, which noted that the nickname "clings to [Zettlein] like a chestnut-burr."

44. Quoted in George William Sheldon, "The Old Ship-Builders of New York," *Harper's New Monthly Magazine* 65 (1882), 241.

45. *New York Clipper*, August 31, 1867.

46. *New York Tribune*, May 30, 1868, 5.

47. *New York Times*, May 30, 1871.

48. *Brooklyn Eagle*, December 22, 1889, 2. Martin offered several other comments on the last two seasons of the Eckfords but is badly confused about the sequence of events and many related details.

49. *New York Times*, May 8, 1872.

50. *New York Clipper*, July 20, 1872.

51. *New York Clipper*, May 25, 1872.

52. George William Sheldon, "The Old Ship-Builders of New York," *Harper's New Monthly Magazine* 65 (1882), 241. The newspapers Sheldon cites are not identified.

53. "Old Chalk's Reminiscences: The True Story of the Old Eckford Club," *Brooklyn Eagle*, January 18, 1891, 16. Chadwick repeated the mistake in several other articles so it is clearly not just a typographical error.

54. *Brooklyn Eagle*, June 26, 1885, 1.

55. *Brooklyn Eagle*, April 12, 1896.

56. "Guide to the Eckford Social Club Scrapbook," Brooklyn Historical Society finding aid.

57. *Brooklyn Eagle*, June 16, 1946, 12.

58. *Brooklyn Eagle*, April 12, 1896.

59. *New York Tribune*, August 6, 1869, 8.

60. *Brooklyn Eagle*, January 7, 1906, 9.

61. *New York Herald*, September 15, 1869, 8. The *Brooklyn Eagle* of February 25, 1864, 2, reported that Beach's real name was "Wallace Beach Clark."

62. Chadwick Scrapbooks, circa 1861.

63. *Brooklyn Eagle*, February 25, 1864, 2.

64. *Brooklyn Eagle*, August 23, 1864, 2.

65. *Sporting Life*, December 28, 1887, 5.

66. *Brooklyn Eagle*, October 30, 1908.

67. *Brooklyn Eagle*, April 12, 1896.

68. *Brooklyn Eagle*, April 5, 1879.

69. *Brooklyn Eagle*, June 15, 1884.

70. *New York Clipper*, July 11, 1898, 311.

71. *Brooklyn Eagle*, April 24, 1866.

72. *Brooklyn Eagle*, January 7, 1906, 9.

73. "Old Chalk's Reminiscences: The True Story of the Old Eckford Club," *Brooklyn Eagle*, January 18, 1891, 16.

74. *Brooklyn Eagle*, June 15, 1884.

75. *Brooklyn Eagle*, December 24, 1905, 8; *Brooklyn Eagle*, January 7, 1906, 9.

76. *Brooklyn Eagle*, December 1, 1913, 1.

77. *Long Island Star*, June 16, 1883.

78. *New York Times*, September 1, 1858.

79. *New York World*, February 2, 1893, 3.

80. http://bioguide.congress.gov/scripts/biodisplay.pl?index= C000047.

81. *Brooklyn Eagle*, August 25, 1863.

82. *Brooklyn Eagle*, April 5, 1879.

83. *Sporting Life*, December 19, 1888, 2.

84. *Brooklyn Eagle*, May 28, 1887, 1.

85. *Brooklyn Eagle*, August 15, 1868.

86. *Brooklyn Eagle*, September 30, 1868, 2.

87. *Brooklyn Eagle*, December 3, 1870.

88. *Brooklyn Eagle*, February 2, 1896, 3.

89. *New York Tribune*, August 6, 1869, 8.

90. *Brooklyn Eagle*, September 9, 1875.

91. *New York Clipper*, December 20, 1879, 309.

92. *Sporting Life*, December 13, 1913, 2.

93. *Boston Globe*, December 9, 1913. See also *Sporting Life*, December 13, 1913, 2.

94. *New York Atlas*, September 4, 1859.

95. *New York Tribune*, August 6, 1869, 8.

96. *New York Herald*, November 11, 1874, 4.

97. *New York Clipper*, February 27, 1875, 379.

98. *Sporting Life*, April 22, 1885, 6.

99. Phonney Martin Scrapbook, National Baseball Hall of Fame, unidentified clipping.

100. *Brooklyn Eagle*, May 17, 1889, 1.

101. *Brooklyn Eagle*, October 6, 1908, 3.

102. *Brooklyn Eagle*, October 25, 1885.

103. *Brooklyn Eagle*, May 10, 1885, 10.

104. John Thorn, *Baseball in the Garden of Eden* (New York: Simon & Schuster, 2011), 103.

105. *Brooklyn Eagle*, April 21, 1870.

106. *Brooklyn Eagle*, June 23, 1899, 8; *Newtown Reporter*, June 29, 1899, 2; *New York Times*, June 23, 1899.

107. *New York Tribune*, August 6, 1869, 8.

108. United States, Naval Enlistment Rendezvous records, 1855–1891, from familysearch.org (https://www.familysearch.org/search/image/ show#uri=https percent3A percent2F percent2Fapi.familysearch.org percent2Frecords percent2Fpal percent3A percent2FMM9.3.1 percent2 FTH-1-14732–31390–77 percent3Fcc percent3D1825347).

109. *New York Tribune*, August 6, 1869, 8.

110. *Chicago Tribune*, April 24, 1875, 7, New York correspondent.

111. *Brooklyn Eagle*, April 12, 1896.

112. *New York Atlas*, August 28, 1859.

113. *New York Clipper*, June 21, 1884, 213.

114. Chadwick Scrapbooks, unidentified 1870 clipping.

115. *Brooklyn Daily Times*, June 2, 1874.

116. *Brooklyn Eagle*, June 24, 25 and 28, 1875.

117. *Chicago Tribune*, October 8 and December 31, 1876 .

118. *Chicago Tribune*, December 2, 1877.

119. *Brooklyn Eagle*, August 24, 1883.

120. *Brooklyn Eagle*, April 5, 1879.

121. *New York Clipper*, May 14, 1881.

122. *New York Clipper*, July 11, 1898, 311.

123. Chadwick scrapbooks, unidentified clippings.

124. *Brooklyn Times*, September 19, 1862.

125. *New York Clipper*, July 11, 1898, 311.

126. *Brooklyn Eagle*, August 5, 1897, 5, letter from G. Smith Stanton of Great Neck, New York.

127. *New York Clipper*, July 11, 1898, 311.

128. Ibid.; *Brooklyn Eagle*, June 27, 1898, 16.

129. *Brooklyn Eagle*, February 12, 1882; *Newtown Register*, May 4, 1882, 6; *Brooklyn Eagle*, January 12, 1884.

130. Wood, as told to Menke, "Baseball in By-Gone Days," part 3, syndicated column, *Indiana* (Pennsylvania) *Evening Gazette*, August 17, 1916.

131. Quoted by William Rankin in *Sporting News*, May 25, 1901; Rankin cites it as originating in the *New York Clipper* in the summer of 1883 but does not provide an exact date.

132. *Brooklyn Eagle*, August 15, 1868.

133. *Syracuse Journal*, October 26, 1906.

134. *New York Clipper*, December 20, 1879, 309.

135. *New York Clipper*, December 20, 1879, 309; *New York Times*, December 17, 1879; *Brooklyn Eagle*, December 16, 1879, 4.

136. *Brooklyn Eagle*, September 3, 1902, 3; *New York Times*, September 3, 1902, 16; *New York Sun*, June 21, 1902, 1.

137. *Brooklyn Daily Times*, March 18, 1870; *New York Tribune*, August 6, 1869, 8.

138. Edward J. Renehan, Jr., *Commodore: The Life of Cornelius Vanderbilt* (New York: Basic Books, 2007), 140–141.

139. *New York Times*, May 6, 1900.

140. *New York Evening Post*, February 21, 1916, 6; *New York Sun*, February 21, 1916, 7.

141. *Corning Evening Leader*, October 14, 1952, 4; see also "Manners: The Guider," *Time*, March 1, 1963.

142. *Paris* (Texas) *News*, August 13, 1958, 6.

143. *Brooklyn Eagle*, July 31, 1892, 12.

144. *Chicago Tribune*, July 15, 1870.

145. *New York Tribune*, August 6, 1869, 8.

146. Chadwick Scrapbooks, unidentified clippings.

❖ *Contest Base Ball Club* ❖
(Peter Morris)

CLUB HISTORY

Junior clubs, typically made up of players 21 and younger, made an enormous contribution to the explosion of baseball activity in Brooklyn in the 1850s and 1860s. Henry Chadwick was an especially ardent champion of their cause, regularly urging the senior clubs to pass used equipment along to them and even suggesting that the senior clubs adopt them as feeders. "[U]nless we have plenty of junior clubs in our midst," Chadwick implored, "we may look in vain for a perpetuity of the game of ball, for unless ball play is learnt in early life, no great degree of skill can ever be acquired at it."[1]

Yet history has not been kind to junior clubs. It is in the natural order of things for junior clubs to be short-lived and thus unable to forge an enduring identity. Making matters worse, the most talented junior players were gobbled up by senior clubs, which robbed the first nines of continuity. Finally, junior clubs rarely documented their activities with the diligence of their older counterparts. Without an enduring identity, continuity or a written record, history becomes all but impossible to preserve.

This is especially true of the Contest Club of Brooklyn, a junior club that claimed several notable distinctions. Despite the claimed achievements, the Contest Club soon sank into such obscurity that the accuracy of those claims is very difficult to either confirm or refute. The club does not warrant even a mention in *Long Before the Dodgers*, James Terry's history of early baseball in Brooklyn. As a result, the Contest Club is being included in this volume, not because its history can be re-created with much certainty, but as a reminder of how much remains unknown.

According to the club's entry in Peverelly's *Book of American Pastimes*: "The Contest Base Ball Club, of Brooklyn, was organized in 1857, being the first junior club organized in Brooklyn. They held the championship of the juniors from 1857 to 1861, when they were defeated by the Mohawks, being the first and only defeat in a home-and-home game that they suffered since organization."[2]

It seems safe to assume that the club secretary was the source of this information, which raises suspicion. No reference book or history of early baseball provides confirmation that the Contest Club was Brooklyn's first junior club. Nor can the claim that the club held the junior championship for four years be verified from these sources. As a result, it's hard not to wonder whether the club secretary was indulging in some unwarranted boasting. At the same time, given the lack of readily available information, it could also be that everything he said was true.

Fortunately, we do have Craig Waff's tabulation of prewar games — which is available on the Retrosheet.org website — and it sheds some light.[3] Waff's compilation shows a Brooklyn junior club, the Columbia Club of East Brooklyn, playing a couple of games in 1856, one season before the Contest Club claimed to have become the city's first such organization. Waff's listing also show the Contest Club playing five games in 1858: three wins, then a loss to the Superior Club, followed by a season-ending victory over the same club. At least four more games were scheduled in 1859, including a win and an unreported result against a New Jersey club, and two games against the Mohawks. The first produced a narrow 11–9 loss and the second, played on Thanksgiving and billed as being "for the championship of their size," also ended in defeat.[4]

It thus seems clear that the claims made on behalf of the Contest Club in Peverelly were not strictly true. Yet many questions linger, most of which may never be answered. Was the declaration of being Brooklyn's first junior club a deliberate falsehood, or had the Columbia Club been so short-lived or negligible that its existence was not known or remembered by the writer?

Similarly, while the claim to have held the junior championship until 1861 is clearly mistaken, it too could be either an innocent mistake or a deliberate fabrication. Junior clubs were not allowed to be members of the National Association of Base Ball Players (NABBP), so there could be no formal championship until the juniors formed their own association in 1861. In addition, while Waff's tabulation is meticulous, it cannot be assumed to include all games.

Some match results were never reported at all, others appeared in sources no longer extant or readily available, and even outcomes that were reported were not always reliable. Clubs were known to report victories after being defeated and reporters with more pressing concerns tired of trying to settle such issues. One such harried Chicago journalist wrote with dismay in 1870, "It became customary last season to publish the scores of games played between the less known clubs of this city — clubs with barbaric, comic, stupid or overridiculous names, and whose scorers did write most villainously, and spelt at random.... A report of one of these games would be left at the office, stating that the Young Americas had beaten the Hopefuls by a gigantic score. The next day the Captain of the Hopefuls, aged 4 to 9, after climbing our 80 stairs with great difficulty, would appear panting, and claim that his organization had the great score, and the others, the small one. He would frequently argue for half an hour as to the vital importance of a correction, and would denounce the unscrupulous mendacity of the Young Americas. Repressing a strong inclination to give him five cents to buy marbles with, we promised to correct, and he went downstairs exultant."[5]

The claims for distinction made on behalf of the prewar Contest Club thus are demonstrably untrue, but the reasons and extent remain matters of conjecture. The club seems to have been one of Brooklyn's best junior clubs, but whether it ever had a legitimate claim to being the junior champion is murky. Given the passage of time, the turnover of membership, and the absence of a formal championship set-up, it's quite possible that the Contests were generally regarded as champion up until their loss to the Mohawks in the fall of 1859, yet there is no specific evidence to confirm it. So we're back where we started: with another indicator that the doings of junior clubs received little attention.

The later history of the Contest Club is a little easier to trace, though again the main source is the less-than-reliable account published by Peverelly. There's a strong hint of boasting in its version of events, which has the club remaining inactive throughout the Civil War. At the war's end,"... (T)he Club was reorganized by the old members, and in the latter part of 1865 they stood at the head of the juniors. They played

eight home-and-home games,—each time carrying off the ball as a memento of victory. The Unknowns and Monmouths received challenges from them, which they refused to accept, so that the Contests think their title as champions of the juniors could easily be substantiated if they desired to claim it, but they do not, as they now belong to the seniors. They have upwards of forty members, and are in an extremely flourishing condition. They practice every Tuesday, Thursday, and Saturday on the Contest grounds, corner of Twelfth street and Third avenue."[6]

So we are left with another imponderable: did the Contests have a legitimate basis for believing themselves Brooklyn's best junior club or was that another exaggeration? In light of the club's decision to abandon junior play and relinquish any claim to the junior championship, it seems best to waste no additional ink on that question.

What is clear is that the Contest Club's transition to senior play was not successful. Despite the "flourishing" condition of its membership and the regular practices, the 1866 season brought lopsided defeats at the hands of the Excelsior and the Irvington (New Jersey) clubs. There were also a few victories, but none against notable opposition, and after the season the club seems to have passed out of existence. In an intriguing twist, the final blow may have come in the spring of 1867 when the Contest Club's battery — pitcher Samuel Davenport and catcher Janes — joined the club's old rival, the Mohawks.[7]

In 1871 the old name was revived by a junior club known as the Contest Club of South Brooklyn, which announced that its "club-house, which is handsomely furnished, is situated on Twelfth street, South Brooklyn, second door from Fifth avenue."[8] The members included three with familiar surnames, so it was probably formed by the younger brothers of the earlier players. But its existence seems to have been a brief one. The Contest name was recycled by a few subsequent Brooklyn baseball clubs, but there is no reason to believe that there was a meaningful link.[9]

The Contest Club thus has an ambiguous legacy. After leaving the junior ranks in 1865, it accomplished nothing of note, while its achievements as a junior club were at best exaggerated. Perhaps it is best to remember the club as an embodiment of the spirit that junior clubs brought to the pioneer era, a spirit that brought much-needed enthusiasm but that often muddied the historical record.

CLUB MEMBERS

The identities of the members of the Contest Club are even more difficult to determine than the club's history. With little more than surnames to go on, it makes more sense to present what is known than to try to use the format of other entries.

The only available prewar box score, from an 1859 game,

lists these players: Brockett, Dillon, Doheny, Donohue, Geoghagan, Janes, Jaques, Van Pelt, Wilson. (They didn't bat in alphabetical order; that was my doing.) There are a few more box scores available after the war, making it possible to compile this list of 1865–66 players (again alphabetized): Boerum, Boone, Davenport, Garvey, Gibson, Hough, Janes, Kennelly, Leet, Shannon, Tompkins, Van Pelt. As will be noted, only Janes and Van Pelt overlap, shedding doubt on the claim in Peverelly that the club was reorganized by its original members. Pitcher Samuel Davenport can at least be solidly identified because he went on to pitch for the Eckfords and had a brief obituary in *Sporting Life*; see the Eckford Club entry for details.

A listing of officers provides a few clues about the others. While a senior club's officers cannot be assumed to be players, that's a pretty safe assumption in the case of junior clubs. The officers of the Contest Club in 1866 were: President, Charles Hough; Vice President, George Tompkins; Secretary, J. Boerum; Treasurer, Silas Boone; Corresponding Secretary, F. Boone.[10] It would be nice to report that Charles Hough was a pioneer knuckleball pitcher, but in fact he turns out to have been an infielder and catcher.

Even with the benefit of a handful of initials and first names, there is no way to do more than guess at the identities of most of these players. George Tompkins may have been a George P. Tompkins who was born in 1847 and became a clerk, but there are other candidates. Charles Hough appears to have been Charles Alexander Hough, who became a successful Brooklyn businessman and died in Long Island in 1913, but I wouldn't bet the farm on it. J. Boerum was probably a young man named John Boerum (who does not seem to be an immediate relative of the far more accomplished Folkert R. Boerum, catcher of the Atlantics). If any of these men reminisced about their days with the Contest Club in later years, what they recalled has been lost to history.

But there is one club member whose name was unusual enough that there can be little doubt of his identity and that of his brother. Silas Ilsley Boone served as treasurer of the Contest Club and is believed to have been one of the first nine, mostly playing first base. He was born in Brooklyn on March 26, 1846, and had a younger brother named Frederick Howard Boone, who was born on August 21, 1848.

Frederick Boone does not seem to have played for the Contests — no initial was given for the ballplaying Boone, but given their ages it seems more likely that it was Silas who played for the first nine. Yet he too is a significant figure, because as corresponding secretary he is the person most likely to have composed the exaggerated club history that was sent to Peverelly. If so, the misstatements become still easier to understand because Frederick Boone would have been 8 or 9 when the Contest Club was formed and 11 when it was defeated by the Mohawks on Thanksgiving Day of 1859.

Frederick Boone's life was unremarkable: he worked as a shipping clerk, raised a large family, and died in his native Brooklyn on December 2, 1916. It was not so with his older brother. By the 1870s Silas Boone had graduated from treasurer of the Contest Base Ball Club to deputy collector of Brooklyn's Internal Revenue Office. He also had a wife and young family, taught Sunday school, and seemed well on the path to success. But he was charged with embezzlement in 1880 and, while the missing money was being investigated, he fled.

Over the next twelve years, local gossip placed him in a variety of far-flung locations. In 1883 a Brooklyn man who had known Boone well was shocked to run into him while traveling in Haiti. "I would have known him," reported the traveler, "if he had changed even more than he has, which is scarcely possible. Boone in the days of his good repute was a trim, clean cut, gentlemanly looking fellow, quiet and self possessed and not easily disturbed. He has evidently gone to pieces. I did not place him for the moment, with his full grown beard and slovenly appearance, but I was perfectly clear as to his identity before he was ten feet away." But before the traveler could say anything, Boone gave a start of recognition and hurried away.[11]

Then in February of 1892, the Brooklyn superintendent of police received an intriguing letter from the sheriff of Empire City, Oregon. "Dear Sir," wrote the sheriff, "A medal was found in the mountains here bearing the inscription: 'Volunteer Fire Association, Brooklyn City, W.D.' Close by it a man camped who acted very strange; would not allow himself to be seen, but ran and hid on the approach of anyone. As well as can be ascertained from appearance and what is found in his camp he has been in good circumstances, wears good clothes, etc. Now, if you can throw any light on this matter, I would be obliged for the information. The medal has on it hook and ladder, fireman's cap, etc. The owner of it has been in the mountains but a short time."

Inquiries were made and the letter was published in several local newspapers. When the letter was shown to an old-time volunteer firefighter, a plausible candidate emerged. "Why, that must be Si Boone," he exclaimed. "I felt when I took that letter in my hand that he was in it somehow. Si has been wandering over the land since he lost his place as cashier in the internal revenue office here. He belonged to [Fire Engine] No. 1, and I think was a member of the association after the volunteer force disbanded. He left Brooklyn under a cloud years ago, although he was not to blame for the hole he got into and he has been away from here ever since. I don't believe that even his family knows what has become of him. He was a great fisherman and hunter and this is just about what he would be doing if he were to lose his bead. Before he went away he used to play the races, but I don't believe that he was dishonest. Why, I used to go off on fishing excursions with him, and we had jolly times together. Since he has been away he has been all over. A couple of years ago, he was in Sydney, N.S.W. [Australia], and only last summer I learned that he had turned up in Oregon. He was well dressed then, but the chances are his head has gone wrong. Now that this letter has been shown me I am convinced that he is the [sic] man spoken of. Nobody else that I know has gone wandering with any of the old volunteer badges. I think if you hunt this thing up you'll find that Silas Boone is the man."[12]

Other old acquaintances were also inclined to believe that Silas Boone was the mysterious camper. But if so, he soon moved on and was not heard from again.

Sources: William Ryczek's *Baseball's First Inning*, 59–60, and George B. Kirsch's *The Creation of American Sports*, 64–65, are good sources of information on the largely neglected subject of early junior clubs. The description of the club's activities comes from Charles A. Peverelly's *Book of American Pastimes*. Otherwise, this entry relies entirely on the newspaper accounts that are cited in the notes and on Craig Waff's tabulation of pre–Civil War games.

Notes

1. *New York Clipper*, September 4, 1858.
2. Peverelly, *The Book of American Pastimes*,(New York: Published by the Author, 1866), 439.
3. http://www.retrosheet.org/Protoball/GamesTab.htm.
4. *Brooklyn Eagle*, December 2, 1859, 3.
5. *Chicago Times*, November 27, 1870; quoted in Robert Pruter, "Youth Baseball in Chicago, 1868–1890: Not Always Sandlot Ball," *Journal of Sport History*, Spring 1999.
6. Charles A. Peverelly, *The Book of American Pastimes*, 439–440.
7. *Brooklyn Eagle*, May 7, 1867, 2
8. *Brooklyn Eagle*, July 19, 1871; *New York Evening Telegram*, August 14, 1871
9. The *Brooklyn Eagle* had references to clubs calling themselves the Contest Club on April 27, 1876, and July 16, 1884, but the surnames of the players did not match those of earlier clubs by that name and there is no reason to believe that there was a link.
10. *Brooklyn Eagle*, April 21, 1866; Peverelly, *The Book of American Pastimes*, 440
11. *Brooklyn Eagle*, June 18, 1883, 4
12. "Who Is He?" *Brooklyn Eagle*, February 20, 1892, 6; see also "A Wild Man from Brooklyn," *New York Sun*, February 21, 1892.

CHAPTER THREE

NEW JERSEY

❖ *Introduction* (John G. Zinn) ❖

A lack of adequate playing facilities in Manhattan may have challenged baseball's growth in New York City, but it probably spurred the game's antebellum beginnings in New Jersey. The frequent use of Elysian Fields in Hoboken by New York and Brooklyn clubs certainly brought baseball to the attention of young men in the Garden State before it could have reached other parts of the country. This geographic good fortune, sufficient population levels, and necessary transportation and communication systems facilitated the formation of New Jersey's first baseball clubs.[1]

It is no surprise, therefore, that at least 130 New Jersey clubs were founded between 1855 and 1860. Two-thirds were in Newark and Jersey City, where it seemed "nearly every ward, neighborhood or even street organized at least one club." Orange, Bloomfield, and Paterson also had nines as early as 1855. New Jersey's first baseball players were predominantly native born (84 percent in one sample) with immigrants not playing a major role until after 1861. Club members were drawn largely from the middle and upper classes, which had sufficient leisure time for the new sport. A study of early players from Newark, Jersey City, and Orange concluded that over 45 percent came from white collar occupations, particularly merchants and clerks. The next largest group was skilled laborers, who made up over one-third of the total.[2]

Baseball became popular so quickly in New Jersey that its redeeming features were publicly praised within a month of the first match between New Jersey clubs. On June 26, 1855, the *Newark Daily Advertiser* endorsed the game as "beneficial to young men who are confined by business during the day." Less than two years later, the game's popularity was so widespread, Newark police forbade play in Military Park while permitting the game in South Park (today's Lincoln Park). In this latter locale, "every afternoon is filled by a crowd of boys and young men indulging in this favorite pastime." Apparently, the "new" game was, to some extent, co-existing with the "old fashioned" version since at least one "old style" match with 16 on a side took place in 1857. That game most likely took place under the auspices of the Knickerbocker Club, which was still

in existence in the 1870s after the majority of New Jersey's pioneer nines had faded from the scene.[3]

The new game also quickly took hold in New Jersey's African American population. Only a few months after the first documented game between New Jersey clubs, the *Newark Daily Mercury* reported on a game between "the St. John's and Union Clubs (colored)." Although African American clubs received very little media recognition at least one other club (the Hamilton Club of Newark) played throughout the Civil War era.[4]

Although a significant number of baseball clubs were formed in antebellum New Jersey, they did not always last long. An exception to this quick start/quick finish pattern was the Newark Base Ball Club which was founded on May 1, 1855, and is believed to be New Jersey's first baseball club. The club grew quickly with some 26 members just 90 days later and continued to play for a dozen years. There were at least three other clubs in Newark that year, and the Newark Club's earliest match was an inter-city contest with the Oriental Club on June 13, 1855. Newark Club members included "a variety of skilled craftsmen, petty proprietors, clerks and bookkeepers of moderate worth." Some 75 percent lived in the "old core" center city of Newark. Not surprisingly for a club with an average age of almost 34, a significant number were married, leading to a social aspect that included boat trips and annual dances.[5]

Unfortunately, in spite of being pathfinders, the Newark Club never enjoyed any real competitive success. Over a 12-year period, the Newarkers won only 22 matches, while losing 40 and tying one. This included only one winning season (5–3 in 1861). To their credit, the Newark Club joined the National Association of Base Ball Players (NABBP) in 1860 and took on many clubs from the baseball hotbeds of New York City and Brooklyn. The 1864 season also saw the beginning of an exodus of the club's better players when Everett Mills went to the Eureka Club. After a 1–5 season in 1865, there were mass defections as Isaac "Joe" Terrill and Osborne joined Mills on the Eureka, while Alexander Bailey, Billy Lewis, and Thomas Buckley joined the Irvington Club.[6]

While the Newark Club was not very successful in its own right, they nonetheless played an important role in the development of baseball in New Jersey. As one of New Jersey's first baseball clubs, their social and professional status helped to make the new game respectable. Also unlike clubs that did not last long, they provided continuity and a place for local talent to develop. This became especially important after they joined the NABBP in 1860. Along with the Eureka, they provided opportunities for the best players in the state's largest city to play against the best competition. The Newark Club's development of talent paid off when its alumni moved on to make important contributions to the Eureka and Irvington Clubs — the best New Jersey clubs of the period.

Another interesting early club was the Washington Junior Club of Newark. Surviving records indicate that this club began play in 1857 with a series of matches against the Union Club of Bloomfield. The Washington Club played through at least 1859, mostly against lower-level New Jersey clubs with some matches against New York City rivals. The significance of the club, however, comes not from its on-field results, but rather from how it developed young talent. Of the nine players listed in an 1859 box score, at least seven went on to play with the Eureka and Irvington Clubs, the premier New Jersey clubs of the period. Included in the group were Charles Thomas, considered one of the best shortstops of the era, James Linen, the Eureka's first pitcher, and R. Heber Breintnall, another mainstay of the Eurekas.[7]

Understandably, the beginning of the Civil War in 1861 limited New Jersey baseball activity. Some like the Liberty Club of New Brunswick shut down entirely while others such as the Eureka and Newark clubs played fewer matches. Some New Jersey players volunteered for military service and took the game with them. Reports of at least five matches between New Jersey regiments were reported to the Newark newspapers, including in some cases full box scores. The 2nd New Jersey regiment went so far as to form its own baseball club, the Excelsior. Two New Jersey baseball players, Horace Smith and James Conklin of the Newark Club, made the ultimate sacrifice at Gaines Mill in June of 1862.[8]

Whether due to fewer available players because of military absences or a desire to support good causes, the Civil War period also saw matches between select nines. At least two select games took place between New Jersey and Philadelphia clubs, with the New Jersey boys coming out on top both times. In the first match at the High Street grounds in Newark on June 2, 1862, a nine made up of Eureka and Newark Club players defeated a Philadelphia squad, 13–4. Almost two years later, the Pennsylvanians hosted a more broadly representative New Jersey side at the Olympic Club's grounds at Jefferson and 25th Street for the benefit of the United States Sanitary Commission. A crowd estimated at over 2000 fans braved threatening weather and paid 25 cents each to see the New Jerseyans prevail 18–10. Two members each from the Eureka

(Thomas and Henry Northrop) and Newark Clubs (Billy Lewis and Joe Tyrell) joined players from the Nassau, Camden, and Bridgeton Clubs to make up the New Jersey nine. One of the representatives of the Camden Club was Weston Fisler, who would go on to play in the first game in National League history.[9]

After the Civil War ended in the spring of 1865, baseball grew rapidly in New Jersey as it did throughout the rest of the country. In addition to new clubs and expanded schedules, New Jersey experienced its share of what might be called "special interest" games. One such match took place in July of 1867 between the saloon keepers of Newark's 1st and 4th wards. Almost all of the participants supposedly weighed in at 200 pounds with the rival shortstops reportedly closer to 300. In a match that was "novel if not very scientific," the 4th ward bar owners prevailed 38–34. Later that same year Newark's proximity to New York and Brooklyn facilitated a match between a nine of Newark sportswriters and a combined squad from Brooklyn and New York City. Anticipating that the players they so often criticized would see turn about as fair play, the scribes acknowledged ahead of time that it was "easier to preach than practice." As with the select games with Philadelphia sides, the Newark group emerged triumphant by a 27–23 score. Among the New York-Brooklyn writers listed in the box score was one Chadwick of the *Ball Players' Chronicle*, suggesting that for once, the legendary Henry Chadwick appeared in a box score instead of keeping one.[10]

While most of those involved in New Jersey baseball in 1867 were focused on the future of the relatively new game, there was apparently significant nostalgia in Paterson for the "old-fashioned" game. Beginning in August, no fewer than 12 different sides took part in what could arguably be called the first vintage base ball league. Entrants like the "Never Sweats" and "Unknowns" played against squads representing Paterson's many manufacturing businesses in games with 11 on a side and no foul territory. Reportedly more than 1000 people witnessed a contest between the "Never Sweats" and the "Unknowns."[11]

In their efforts to preserve the "old-fashioned game," the Paterson clubs were only following what the Knickerbocker Antiquarian Base Ball Club of Newark had been doing since at least 1857. By the post-war years, the club was playing an annual match featuring bats that looked like "miniature bread shovels," 15-inch stakes for bases and between 11 and 19 players on a side. The annual match continued through at least 1875, and one participant who played in 1857 was still playing in 1874. The games were apparently popular social events attended by a number of political and civic leaders.[12]

Although baseball grew after the Civil War, changes in the game at the end of the 1860s caused leading New Jersey clubs like the Eureka, Irvington, and Champions either to go out of existence or fall from prominence. Three other nines, the Resolute Club of Elizabeth, and the Active and Amateur clubs of Newark tried to fill the vacuum at the state level. Organized as a senior club in 1867, the Active club seems to have been a gathering place for Eureka alumni. At least two former Eurekas, Charles Faitoute and Albert Beans, appeared in the Active lineup as early as May of 1867. Despite playing a competitive schedule, they did not enjoy significant success. More successful was the Amateur Club, which after the Resolute, had the best 1870 record among New Jersey members of the National Association of Base Ball Players. The Resolutes also took two out of three head-to-head matches and won the New Jersey state championship.[13]

Apparently the 1870 state championship contests had more than a little controversy since the state association decided not to endorse such matches in the future due to the "ill-feeling and rivalry" they generated. It is hard not to believe that at least some of the "ill-feeling" was attributable to the Resolutes. In May of 1870, *The Evening Journal* of Jersey City, after reminding readers of the Resolutes' 1869 unsportsmanlike conduct against the Champion Club, quoted a report of similar behavior from the *Newark Evening Courier*. This time, the Elizabeth club was supposedly using players from other clubs. Whatever else can be said about the Resolutes, they must have been confident in their masculinity, since they wore pink stockings in an 1870 match.[14]

Although the Elizabeth club had existed since at least 1865, their later rise to prominence was concurrent with the arrival of three former members of the Irvington Club — Hugh and Mike Campbell, and William Greathead. The connection to the Irvingtons most likely explains the Resolute's opportunity to play (and lose to) the famed Cincinnati Red Stockings in June of 1870. Opposing their "brothers," now with the Resolute, were "old Irvingtons" Charles Sweasy and Andy Leonard. On their way to the New Jersey state championship, the Elizabeth club compiled a 14–11 record, but five of the losses came at the hands of the Red Stockings, Mutuals, and Atlantics. In one of the losses to the Atlantics, the Resolute suffered the dubious distinction of being on the wrong end of the first shutout in the Brooklyn club's long and distinguished history. That experience probably should have taught the Resolute something about competing at the proper level. It must not have, however, because in 1873 they made the ill-fated decision to join the National Association, suffering a 2–21 record before disbanding in August.[15]

Notes

1. George B. Kirsch, "The Rise of Modern Sports: New Jersey Cricketers, Baseball Players, and Clubs, 1845–60," *New Jersey History*, Spring-Summer 1983.

2. Ibid.; James Diclerico and Barry J. Pavelec, *The Jersey Game* (New Brunswick: Rutgers University Press, 1992); *Newark Daily Advertiser*, August 6, 1855; George B. Kirsch, *The Creation of American Team Sports: Baseball and Cricket, 1838–72* (Urbana: University of Illinois Press, 1989), 146.

3. *Newark Daily Advertiser*, June 26, 1855, April 7, 1857, October 31, 1857.

4. *Newark Daily Mercury*, October 25, 1855; *Newark Daily Advertiser*,

September 30, 1862, September 29, 1866. According to John Thorn, official historian of Major League Baseball, of this writing, the October 23, 1855, match is the earliest documented game between "colored" clubs (John Thorn e-mail, September 7, 2011).

5. Kirsch, *The Creation of American Team Sports*, p.160, Diclerico and Pavelec, *The Jersey Game*, 25; *Beadle's Dime Base-Ball Player—1860*; *Newark Daily Advertiser*, June 16, 1855, June 26, 1855, August 11, 1855.

6. *Newark Daily Advertiser*, March 14, 1860, *New York Herald*, March 18, 1860.

7. *Newark Daily Advertiser*, November 16, 1857, November 23, 1857, September 6, 1859.

8. *Newark Daily Advertiser* November 21, 1861, December 4, 1861, September 26, 1862, April 15, 1863, April 28, 1863, June 6, 1863.

9. *Newark Daily Advertiser*, June 3, 1862; *Philadelphia Inquirer*, May 26, 1864; *New York Clipper*, June 4, 1864, William J. Ryczek, *Baseball's First Inning: A History of the National Pastime Through the Civil War* (Jefferson, N.C.: McFarland, 2009), 116–17; www.19cbaseball.com.

10. *Newark Daily Advertiser*, July 24, 1867, July 26, 1867, September 12, 1867, September 14, 1867.

11. *Paterson Daily Press*, July 31, 1867, August 2, 1867, August 8, 1867, August 10, 1867, August 21, 1867, August 26, 1867, August 28, 1867, September 4, 1867, September 7, 1867.

12. *Newark Daily Advertiser*, November 6, 1857; *Newark Evening Courier*, May 25, 1869; *Newark Daily Journal*, May 30, 1873, May 22, 1874, May 25, 1875.

13. *New York Times*, May 31, 1867, November 11, 1870; Marshall D. Wright, *The National Association of Base Ball Players, 1857–70* (Jefferson, N.C.: McFarland, 2000), 313, 315, 324.

14. *New York Times*, July 14, 1870, November 10, 1870; *The Evening Journal*, May 20, 1870.

15. *New York Times*, May 14, 1870, June 17, 1870; Wright, *The National Association of Base Ball Players 1857–70*, 313.

Bibliography

Books

Diclerico, James, and Barry J. Pavelec. *The Jersey Game: The History of Modern Baseball From Its Birth to the Big Leagues in the Garden State.* New Brunswick: Rutgers University Press, 1993.

Kirsch, George B. *The Creation of American Team Sports: Baseball and Cricket, 1838–72.* Urbana, University of Illinois Press, 1989.

Peverelly, Charles A., *American Pastimes.* New York: Published by the Author, 1866.

Ryczek, William J. *Baseball's First Inning: A History of the National Pastime Through the Civil War.* Jefferson, N.C.: McFarland, 2009.

Wright, Marshall D. *The National Association of Base Ball Players, 1857–70.* Jefferson, N.C.: McFarland, 2000.

Periodicals

Kirsch, George B. "The Rise of Modern Sports: New Jersey Cricketers, Baseball Players, and Clubs, 1845–60." *New Jersey History*, Spring-Summer 1983.

Proceedings of the New Jersey Historical Society, 2nd Series, Vol. VIII, No. 2, 1884.

Newspapers

Brooklyn Daily Eagle
The Evening Journal
New York Clipper
New York Times
Newark Daily Advertiser
Newark Daily Journal
Newark Evening Courier
Paterson Daily Press
Philadelphia Inquirer

Other Sources

www.19cbaseball.com

❖ *Pioneer Base Ball Club of Jersey City* ❖
(John G. Zinn)

CLUB HISTORY

While Brooklyn Heights sometimes claims to be New York City's first suburb, Jersey City also served in that capacity during the 1850s. The city's proximity to Manhattan led to regular interaction between the two municipalities so that young men in Jersey City were among the first outsiders to be exposed to the "New York" game. Not surprisingly, the convenience of both Manhattan and Hoboken's Elysian Fields facilitated the formation of Jersey City's first baseball clubs. Unfortunately, it also contributed to their quick demise.[1]

By 1855 matches between New York and Brooklyn clubs were such a regular feature in Hoboken that the *Jersey City Daily Sentinel* was already praising baseball as an "old fashioned and healthful game." Citing the game's benefits for "the man of sedentary habits," the paper hoped a Jersey City baseball club might soon join the five Brooklyn and New York clubs playing at Elysian Fields.[2]

Someone was paying attention because less than a month later, not one, but two clubs "were on the tapis" for Jersey City. Initially known simply as "the base ball club," the Pioneer Club began inter-club play in June of 1855. The club's roster included members of some of Jersey City's leading families such as Dudley S. Gregory, Jr., the son of the city's first mayor and Henry Brinkerhoff, a judge's son. There also seemed to be a close connection between the club and Empire Hook and Ladder Company, Number 1, a prominent Jersey City fire company. The names of eleven men, including Gregory and Brinkerhoff, appear on both rosters. Since the Empire Company was reportedly made up of "men who would not associate with the rough element," there was no inconsistency between firefighting and social position. The makeup of the Pioneer Club was also somewhat different from the "average" pre-war Jersey City baseball club. All of the identified members were born in the United States compared to a Jersey City club average of 82 percent. More significantly, all of the identified Pioneer players were in white-collar professions, more than twice the Jersey City average. Pioneer Club members were also somewhat older with an average age of just over 27. Given their social standing and professions, no one could question the character of the men taking up the "new" game.[3]

After several months of intraclub contests, the Pioneer Club played their first match game with the Excelsior Club, Jersey City's other charter baseball club, on August 15, 1855, at "the field between this city and Hoboken." In announcing the match, the *Jersey City Daily Telegraph* reported there would be 11 Pioneers against 11 Excelsiors. This comment and the game account itself indicate the two clubs hadn't quite adopted all of the "New York" game rules. Before a crowd that included

members of New York and Brooklyn clubs, the Excelsiors won two games by scores of 21–16 and 46–19. Each game consisted of eight innings, and the *Daily Telegraph* noted that both clubs were missing two players for the first contest, but had a full complement of 11 for the second.[4]

Although defeated twice, the Pioneer Club wasn't discouraged, and a return match was scheduled for less than a week later. This contest was played at the Hamilton Square grounds, making it in all likelihood the first match between Jersey City clubs played within the city boundaries. Anticipating interest even from across the Hudson River, the *Daily Telegraph* announced that stages would run directly from the ferry to the grounds. Regardless of where they came from, "a large number of spectators" watched as the Excelsiors easily won the rematch, 49–25. Once again it was 11 on a side in a game that lasted 11 innings.[5]

While the Pioneer Club continued match play after the Excelsior defeats, they also took time for a social event where "the Married men took those they had married, while the Single men took those they wished to marry." The occasion featured a single/married game which gave one writer the chance to criticize the Pioneers' play. After noting the need for more fielding practice, the commentator advised that "smoking while playing must be stopped especially with the stri[k]er."[6]

Although the players may have taken a more casual approach to the latter game, they certainly took a series of matches with the Columbia Club of Brooklyn seriously enough. After losing the initial contest, the Pioneer Club won the return match in Jersey City on September 19. The *Daily Sentinel* raved about the play of Jordan and Brinkerhoff and boldly predicted that "by this time next year," the Pioneer Club "will be able to frighten the best of clubs." Fully embracing the sport, the paper proudly proclaimed baseball "our national game," and "much superior to cricket." Further praise for the Pioneer players came from a more neutral source when the Jersey City club journeyed to Brooklyn for the deciding match with the Columbia Club. After the Pioneers won by a comfortable 23–8 margin, the *Brooklyn Times* commented that the visitors from New Jersey "played admirably for so young a club."[7]

The Pioneer Club certainly seemed poised for the bigger things in the future and, along with the Excelsiors, began practice in the spring of 1856. Unfortunately, it was not to be; by July the *Daily Sentinel* was bemoaning an apparent lack of interest by both clubs. Finally in early September, the paper reported the two clubs were "virtually defunct." While blaming the "sudden demise" on the loss of two playing sites, the *Daily Sentinel* also noted that three unnamed players from both the Pioneer and Excelsior clubs would play the next day for the

Eagle Club of New York City. In fact, the paper emphasized the six were now "bona fide" members of the New York club. The paper's account of that match between the Eagle and Empire Clubs mentions Jordan, Bixby, and Brinkerhoff, all of whom has previously played for the Pioneer Club. Losing its grounds must have hurt the Pioneer Club, but the departure of some of its best and probably most committed players may have been even worse. The ease with which good Jersey City players could move to New York clubs was the downside to the advantages of early exposure to the game. Although the club existed for only one season, they were pioneers in spirit as well as in name. They showed that gentlemen from New Jersey could form a club and play the "New York" game competitively against rivals from outside the state. Along with the Excelsiors, they got things started, and it wouldn't take long to fulfill the *Daily Sentinel*'s wish for new clubs to take their place.[8]

CLUB MEMBERS

Andrew J. Bache: Born in Peekskill, New York, about 1829, Andrew J. Bache was one of a number of Pioneer players who was also a member of Empire Hook and Ladder Company Number 1. An exchange broker in 1850, Bache apparently left Jersey City during the 1860s. By 1870, he was living in Plainfield, New Jersey, working as a wine importer with total assets of over $60,000 (over $1 million today). A decade later, Bache had changed both his residence and his occupation. Bache's father was from the Morristown, New Jersey, area and by 1880 Bache had moved there with his second wife and their five children. During this period Bache was working as a theatrical manager including being the manager of Niblo's Theater in New York City. According to Bache's obituary, "in this venture he failed." At the time of his death in 1899, the former Pioneer player was active in real estate "in a small way." Bache died of a stroke suffered while on the way to a real estate closing in Pennsylvania.[9]

Andrew J. Bixby: Andrew J. Bixby was born in New York in the 1820s. He apparently moved to Jersey City sometime between 1850 and 1855. In 1860, he was working as a bookkeeper, and by 1870 Bixby had advanced to the position of bank clerk with personal assets of $17,000. He joined the Eagle Base Ball Club of New York during the 1856 season and more details about his life can be found in that club's entry. Bixby was still living in Jersey City in 1883 before moving to Fordham, New York, where he died on July 9, 1889. At the close of his career, he was chief bookkeeper at the Sub-Treasury in New York City. He also worked for the Union League Club and Fisk & Hatch, a prominent government securities broker.[10]

Henry H. Brinkerhoff: Born in Bergen City, New Jersey, about 1834, Henry Brinkerhoff was the eldest son of John B. Brinkerhoff, a wealthy farmer and judge. Brinkerhoff was an-

other member of Empire Hook and Ladder Company, Number 1 who played for the Pioneer Club. Like A. J. Bixby, Brinkerhoff is believed to have moved on to the Eagle Club of New York and may have also played briefly for the Nassau Club of Princeton. Listed as a merchant on the 1860 census, Brinkerhoff served two brief periods in the Union army during the Civil War. At one point, Brinkerhoff and his family moved to Somerset County, New Jersey, for a five-year stint in farming. Back in Jersey City by 1880, he was a clerk in the Register's Office in 1884. Brinkerhoff was a member of Van Houten GAR post as well as Rathbone Lodge, Knights of Pythias. Brinkerhoff died on February 13, 1899.[11]

Thomas C. Brown: Brown was born in Paterson, New Jersey, in 1826 and moved to Jersey City in 1847 where he opened a dry goods store. Brown enjoyed considerable success in this field as his total assets increased more than ten-fold between 1860 and 1870. In 1868 Brown's company became T. C. Brown and Van Anglen with the addition of the latter individual as a partner. Van Anglen's name also appears in one Pioneer box score. In addition to his dry goods business, Brown was active in Republican politics and musical organizations, and was a trustee of the Provident Savings Institution. Brown's death on June 16, 1893, from heart disease was accompanied by some unwanted publicity. Due to a series of strokes, the former Pioneer had been an invalid for several years, but three weeks before his death Brown elected to be baptized by immersion "in the bay at Greenville, New Jersey by faith curists." Both Brown's widow and his doctor denied the experience had anything to do with his death, which was said to be inevitable owing to his long-term illness.[12]

Dudley S. Gregory, Jr.: Gregory, who was born in New York City in 1831, was the son and namesake of one of Jersey City's most prominent citizens. Born in Connecticut in 1800, the elder Gregory made a large fortune in the lottery business in New York and in Jersey City real estate. In 1850 he valued his real estate holdings at $400,000 ($11.5 million today) and at the time of his death in 1874, his estate was estimated to be worth $1 million (almost $20 million today). Gregory, Sr. also had a long political career, serving as Jersey City's first mayor and in the U. S. House of Representatives.

Given his father's wealth, it's not surprising that Dudley, Jr. had no stated occupation in 1850. During the Pioneer Club's brief existence, he was a regular in the club's lineup, typically at catcher. After the Pioneer Club disbanded, Gregory, Jr. may have been a member of the Eagle Club of New York. He was also another of the Pioneer Club members who belonged to the Empire Hook and Ladder Company, Number 1. Gregory was reportedly appointed a Colonel in the New Jersey State Militia in 1849. Although two obituaries claimed he served with the 2nd New Jersey Militia during the Civil War, his name does not appear on state records. A Dudley S. Gregory did serve for three months with the 71st New York State Militia in 1862.

Like his father, the younger Gregory was active in politics, serving in the state assembly and on the boards of finance and the fire department of Jersey City. He was also very active in musical affairs, serving as President of the Jersey City Harmonic Society. At his father's death in 1874, Gregory inherited a large fortune and supposedly became "one of the leading spirits of Jersey City society." However, the later years of his life were troubled, especially after he was separated from his wife and exhibited bizarre behavior such as trying to jump from a ferry boat and shooting himself in the side. Gregory died on February 1886 at the age of 55. In reporting his death, the *New York Times* claimed Gregory and his brothers "wasted" the "large fortune" left to them by their father.[13]

Conrad Jordan: Jordan was born in New York City in 1830 and by 1850 was living with his parents in Jersey City, working as a printer. He played in all the Pioneer Club's matches and pitched for the club in their win over the Columbia Club of Brooklyn on September 19, 1855. He appears to have joined Brinkerhoff and Bixby in moving to the Eagle Club in 1856. By 1860 Jordan had left the printing business and begun a long career in banking and finance. He was credited with sorting out the affairs of the Gold Exchange Bank when it failed during the panic of 1880. A "staunch" Democrat, he was appointed Treasurer of the United States in June of 1885 by Grover Cleveland and served for just over two years. After another period in banking and railroad finance, Jordan was appointed Assistant Treasurer of the United States by Grover Cleveland and re-appointed by William McKinley at "the urgent request of leading bankers" of New York City. He remained in that position until his death on February 26, 1903.[14]

Philip B. Marsh: Marsh was born about 1830. Like other Pioneer players, he was a member of Empire Hook and Ladder Company, Number 1. Marsh played in the majority of the club's 1855 matches. In 1870 Marsh was a grocer with assets of $10,000 ($172,000 today). By 1880 Marsh and his family had moved to Brooklyn, where he worked as a wholesale grocer. After 1880 Marsh apparently moved back to New Jersey and became a traveling salesman, dying on the road in 1901 at the age of 71.[15]

Adrian Reynolds: Adrian Reynolds was born in New York in 1822. He moved to Jersey City in 1850 and "embarked in the crockery business." Reynolds was a fireman in New York City and continued his service in Jersey City as part of Empire Hook and Ladder Company, Number 1. According to *The Evening Journal*, he had a "flourishing business" even though he "never made a large fortune." In addition to service as Assistant Engineer of the Fire Department, he was interested in civic affairs without getting involved in politics. Reynolds was also very active in the Jersey City Yacht Club and was known for his storytelling prowess regarding the city's early history. Adrian Reynolds died of heart failure on May 11, 1897.[16]

Other Club Members: J.J. Boyce, J.E. Brown, J.J. Burgess, Crangle, E.O. Dummer, George Dummer, Fox, Hart, Hathaway, Henderson, Hyde, Hooker, Hutton, Kirkpatrick, Pringle, Quaife, P. Rogers, Scudder, Selden, Sellow, Shasdy, Shane, Sillman, W. Smart, Taylor, Thompson, Tilley, Van Anglen, Varick, Young.

Notes

1. George B. Kirsch, "The Rise of Modern Sports: New Jersey Cricketers, Baseball Players and Clubs, 1845–60," *New Jersey History*, Volume 101, Numbers 1–2, Spring-Summer 1983, 56.

2. *Jersey City Daily Sentinel*, May 26, 1855.

3. *Jersey City Daily Sentinel*, June 16, June 25, 1855; Alexander McLean, *History of Jersey City, N.J.: A Record of its Early Settlement and Corporate Progress Compiled for the Evening Journal* (Jersey City: Press of the Jersey City Printing Company, 1895), 115: *The Evening Journal*, December 16, 1882; Kirsch, "The Rise of Modern Sports," *New Jersey History*, Spring-Summer 1983, 62–63.

4. *Jersey City Daily Telegraph*, August 15, August 16, 1855.

5. *Jersey City Daily Telegraph*, August 20, August 22, 1855.

6. *New York Daily Tribune*, September 13, 1855.

7. *Newark Daily Advertiser*, October 18, 1855; *Jersey City Daily Sentinel*, September 20, 1855; *Brooklyn Times*, October 18, 1855.

8. *New York Times*, May 1, 1856; *Jersey City Daily Sentinel*, July 12, 1856, September 9, September 11, 1856.

9. U. S. Census 1850, 1870, 1880; McLean, *History of Jersey City, N.J.*, 115; Chalmers Hall Bache Family Tree, www.ancestry.com; *The Democratic Banner*, July 6, 1899; *The Jerseyman*, June 30, 1899; www.measuringworth.com.

10. U. S. Census 1860 and 1870; www.measuringworth.com; *Gopsill's Jersey City and Hoboken Directory for the Year Ended, April 30, 1883*, 60; *New York Times*, July 9, 1889.

11. U. S. Census, 1850, 1860, 1870, 1880; McLean, *History of Jersey City, N.J.*, 115; *The Evening Journal*, February 14, 1899; Frank Presbrey and James Hugh Moffat, *Athletics at Princeton* (New York: Frank Presbrey Company, 1901), 72.

12. U. S. Census, 1860 and 1870; *The Evening Journal*, June 17, 1893; *New York Times*, June 17, 1893; *Jersey City Daily Sentinel*, July 12, 1855.

13. U. S. Census, 1850, 1860, 1870; Hamilton Club of Jersey City Minute Book, A. Bartlett Giamatti Research Center, National Baseball Hall of Fame, Cooperstown, New York; www.itd.nps.gov/cwss/soldiers.cfm; William S. Stryker, *Record of Officers and Men of New Jersey in the Civil War, 1861–65, 2 vols.* (Trenton: John L. Murphy, 1876); McLean, *History of Jersey City, N.J.*, 70, 115; *New York Herald*, December 9, 1874, January, 25, 1875, July 2, 1881, February 16, 1886; *The Evening Journal*, February 16, 1886; *New York Times*, February 16, 1886.

14. U. S. Census 1850, 1860, *New York Times*, October 17, 1897, February 27, 1903; *New York Daily Tribune*, February 27, 1903; *Jersey City Daily Sentinel*, September 20, 1855.

15. U. S. Census, 1850, 1870, 1880; www.measuringworth.com; McLean, *History of Jersey City, N.J.*, 115; *Red Bank Register*, April 18, 1900.

16. U. S. Census, 1850, 1860, 1870, 1880; McLean, *History of Jersey City, N.J.*, 115; *New York Times*, May 12, 1897; *The Evening Journal* May 11, 1897.

Bibliography

Books

McLean, Alexander. *History of Jersey City, N.J.; A Record of Its Early Settlement and Corporate Progress Compiled for the Evening Journal.* Jersey City: Press of the Jersey City Printing Company, 1895.

Stryker, William S. *Record of the Officers and Men of New Jersey in the Civil War, 1861–65, 2 vols.* Trenton: John L. Murphy, 1876.

Periodicals
Kirsch, George B. "The Rise of Modern Sports: New Jersey Cricketers, Baseball Players and Clubs, 1845–1860." *New Jersey History*, Volume 101, Numbers 1–2, Spring-Summer, 1983.

Newspapers
Brooklyn Times
The Democratic Banner
The Evening Journal
Jersey City Daily Sentinel
Jersey City Daily Telegraph
The Jerseyman
New York Daily Tribune
New York Herald

New York Times
Newark Daily Advertiser
Red Bank Register

Other Sources
Gopsill's Jersey City and Hoboken Directory for the Year Ended 1883.
Hamilton Base Ball Club of Jersey City Minute Book, A. Bartlett Giamatti Research Center, Baseball Hall of Fame and Museum Library, Cooperstown, New York.
www.ancestry.com
1850, 1860, 1870 and 1880 U.S. Census
www.measuringworth.com
www.itd.nps.gov/cwss/soldier.cfm

❖ *Excelsior Base Ball Club of Jersey City* ❖
(John G. Zinn)

CLUB HISTORY

Noting in June of 1855 that two baseball clubs were supposed to be "on the tapis" for Jersey City, the *Daily Sentinel* reported that an unnamed club met the previous evening at the City Recorder's office. Since Jersey City Recorder George E. Cutter was a member of the Excelsior Club, this group of more than 25 "well-known citizens" was most likely the Excelsiors. About a month later came news of the club's formal organization with Cutter as President; Isaiah Hutton, Vice President; Benjamin Haines, Secretary; and Levi Towle, Treasurer. The report further noted the club would play on Tuesdays and Thursdays at Hamilton Square.[1]

Like their fellow Jersey City charter club, the Pioneers, the Excelsiors were primarily native born with only one immigrant among the nine identified players, slightly higher than the 82 percent average for Jersey City clubs. However, unlike the white-collar Pioneers, the Excelsior players were primarily skilled artisans employed as blacksmiths, whitesmiths, engravers, and the like. The Excelsior players were also older than the Pioneer players (31 to 27 average ages) and well over the Jersey City club average of almost 26.[2]

Actual play had begun at least a few days before the organizational announcement as a squad of 13 captained by Charles J. Farley defeated another 13 led by Charles Van Brunt, 21–19. Among the participants were three men with the same last names as some Pioneer Club members, suggesting that initially players may have gone back and forth between the two clubs. At least one other intraclub match took place before the first Excelsior-Pioneer matches of August 15. Extra incentive was added to that intraclub match by a local "gentleman" who offered a pair of boots to the player making the most runs. William Taylor responded to the challenge by scoring eight times.[3]

While the Pioneer Club appears to have gotten on the field first, the Excelsiors were clearly superior. After a relatively close 21–16 win in their first match, the Excelsiors dominated the next two, scoring over 40 runs in each contest. After the three August victories over the Pioneer Club, the Excelsiors continued to dominate Hudson County competition in September. A September 6, 83–18 rout of the Pavonia Club was followed by a 27–7 win over the Fear-Not Club of Hudson City. While the latter club may have been courageous, they were clearly no match for the Excelsior Club which, "as usual," "was impregnable." In October the Jersey City club moved outside the county to take on the state's first baseball club, the Newark Club. The Excelsiors continued to be "impregnable," winning both matches, 24–6 and 22–12.[4]

Surviving newspaper accounts indicate the Excelsior Club finished a perfect 7–0 in its inaugural 1855 season. It was no wonder that "many experienced players" believed "there are few if any of the older clubs that can beat them." Based on its 1855 performance, the club had even more reason than the Pioneer Club to be optimistic about the future. Unfortunately, like their fellow charter club, it didn't happen as the Excelsior Club failed to survive its initial season. Given their stellar record, it is unfortunate that the Excelsiors didn't stay together longer as they could have been one of New Jersey's premier pre-war clubs. As with the Pioneer Club, loss of their grounds had to hurt, but losing players to the more prestigious Eagle Club of New York must have seriously damaged an older group that may have already been hard-pressed to find time for competitive baseball.[5]

CLUB MEMBERS

George E. Cutter: Cutter was born in New York about 1815 and served as a Justice of the Peace and Recorder in Jersey City. A Democrat, Cutter was the first Recorder of Jersey City and served as a justice of the peace from 1850 to 1880. At the time of his death in April of 1890, he was reportedly the oldest justice of the peace in the state. Cutter was also active in other civic affairs in Jersey City, serving as Tax Assessor, President of the Board of Health and Collector of Tax Arrears. In addition, he was active in Masonic lodges.[6]

Charles J. Farley: Born near Albany, New York, about 1822, Farley was working as an iron moulder in Jersey City in 1850. Farley was also a member of Washington Engine Club, Number 4. In 1852 he was appointed Assistant Captain of the Watch, moving up to Captain two years later. Farley had a troubled tenure as Captain of the Watch. In late 1854, his assistant accused him of "misconduct and neglect of duty," but the charges were "not sustained." Two years later however, "ugly charges" against him surfaced in "certain New York papers." In response, Farley asked for an investigation, which resulted in his dismissal in September of 1856. By 1858 Farley was calling himself an independent police detective. During that year he became involved in further controversy and was jailed for supposedly stealing the watch of a Jersey City alderman. When the Civil War broke out in 1861, Farley volunteered for the 5th New York Cavalry Regiment, becoming a captain in the fall of 1862. He had a leg amputated due to a war wound and was granted a pension after the war. Farley and his wife Sarah lived in Manhattan until his death in 1888.[7]

Robert S. Gilman: Gilman was born about 1822 in New York, and by 1850 he, his wife, and two young daughters were living in Jersey City. Gilman was working as a pencil case maker at that point. During the 1850s, he served as Comptroller of Jersey City and was also a Street Commissioner. He was also a member of Phoenix Hose Company Number 2. At the end of the decade, Gilman had moved to New York City, and by 1870 he was working as a house painter. Gilman appears to be one of three Excelsiors who left the club to play for the Eagle Club of New York. His death date is unknown.[8]

Benjamin Haines: Haines, who was born in Massachusetts around 1830, was the Treasurer of the Excelsior Club when it was organized in July of 1855. Although born in Massachusetts, Haines was living in New York about 1850, moving to Jersey City sometime before 1855. Like other members of the Excelsior Club, Haines was active in the police force, serving as Chief from 1857 to 59. In 1860 he was in the fancy goods business, sharing a house and an occupation with William S. Taylor, who may also have been a member of the Excelsior Club. Haines apparently had musical gifts, as his singing talents were praised in the media. His death date is unknown.[9]

William C. Hutton: Like many of his teammates, Hutton was born in New York in the early 1820s. In 1850 he was living in Jersey City and working as a blacksmith. Hutton was the catcher for the Excelsiors. By 1860 he was a shipsmith with total assets of $12,000, a ten-fold increase from 1850. Whether by this time or later, Hutton owned his own business. By 1880 the former Excelsior had moved out of physical labor and become a real estate agent. Things didn't always go smoothly for Hutton's business ventures since in 1867, he lost a lawsuit to Thomas Lacy, a former teammate, for $217.62 (just over $3300 today). Hutton was also active in politics, serving as a County Freeholder. When he died in 1892, the *Jersey Journal* described him as "one of the most popular members of a popular family."[10]

Thomas T. Lacy: Unlike most of his teammates, Lacy was born in New Jersey about 1817. Like his teammate, William Hutton, Lacy was a blacksmith in 1850 and a shipsmith in 1860. Lacy reported total assets similar to Hutton's in both census returns, which along with their being neighbors in 1860 suggests they may have been business partners. If so, the subsequent litigation and probable estrangement is even sadder. As with the rest of the Excelsiors, Lacy didn't ignore civic affairs, serving on the school board from 1855 to 1866. By 1870, Lacy was a boilermaker, but he eventually left both Jersey City and the East Coast as the 1880 census found him farming in Michigan. His death date is unknown.[11]

Charles Tanner: One of the more elusive members of the Excelsior Club, Charles Tanner was not living in Jersey City in 1850 and has not been located elsewhere. By the time he was playing for the Excelsiors, however, the Connecticut native had been appointed Assistant Captain of the Watch. In 1860 he was living in Jersey City with his wife and two children. Tanner has not been found on the 1870 census, and since his wife was remarried by 1880, he may have been dead by 1870.[12]

Charles Van Brunt: Born in New Jersey about 1830, Charles Van Brunt was a whitesmith and silversmith in Jersey City. He captained and pitched for one of the sides in the July 1855 intraclub match. He was also the pitcher for the Excelsior in all of their match games for which a box score survives. Van Brunt was active in fire companies, serving as a member of both the Americus and Protection Fire Companies. Van Brunt must have died fairly young, as his family appears without him in the 1870 census.[13]

Alfred Williams: Williams is the only identified immigrant member of the Excelsior Club as he was born in England about 1829. In both 1850 and 1860, he was working as an engraver, by 1870 he had become a bookkeeper. He was also active at St. Paul's M.E. church, teaching a class that earned him a surprise party from grateful church members in 1870. His exact death date has not been determined, but he was alive in 1880, and his widow died in August of 1886. Williams is believed to be another member of the Excelsiors who left the club for the Eagle Club of New York.[14]

Other Club Members: Barry, Baum, Bennett, Bogardus, Boyce, Chapsin, Dummer, Gopsill, Gourley, Harris, Hiersted, Hunt, C. Hutton, Joseph Kittle, Lindsley, J. Marshall, C.C. Martindale, Meeker, Randall, Reynolds, Roosevelt, W. Savage, William Taylor, Tilden, Levi W. Towle, Traverse, M. Travis.

Notes

1. *Jersey City Daily Sentinel*, June 16, 1855; *New York Times*, July 20, 1855.

2. George B. Kirsch, "The Rise of Modern Sports: New Jersey Cricketers, Baseball Players and Clubs, 1845–60," *New Jersey History*, Volume 101, Numbers 1–2, Spring-Summer 1983, 62–63.

3. *Jersey City Daily Sentinel*, July 20, 1855; *Jersey City Daily Telegraph*, July 25, 1855.

4. *Jersey City Daily Telegraph*, August 16, 1855, August 22, 1855, September 7, September 26, 1855, November 17, 1855; *Newark Daily Advertiser*, October 26, 1855.

5. "Base Ball Pavonia vs. Excelsior," undated article in the Mears Collection; *Jersey City Daily Sentinel*, September 9, 1856.

6. United States Census, 1850, 1860; *New York Times*, June 1, 1866, April 20, 1890; *The Evening Journal*, March 19, 1880; March 22, 1881, October 7, 1884; *New York Daily Tribune*, October 13, 1858.

7. U. S. Census, 1850, 1870, 1880; June 15, 2011, e-mail from Ruth Hankins; *Commercial Advertiser*, November 15, 1858; *New York Daily Tribune*, November 24, 1858; *New York Times*, May 17, 1854; Alexander McLean, *History of Jersey City, N.J.: A Record of its Early Settlement and Corporate Progress Compiled for the Evening Journal* (Jersey City: Press of the Jersey City Printing Company, 1895), 113, 125–26; A.E. Costello, *History of the Police Department of Jersey City from the Reign of the Knickerbockers to the Present Day* (Jersey City: The Police Relief Association Publication Company, 1891), 49, 51–52, 57; www.ancestry.com, Headstones Provided for Deceased Union Veterans.

8. U. S. Census, 1850, 1860, 1870; *The Evening Journal*, January 10, 1896; *New York Times*, May 17, 1854; McLean, *History of Jersey City, N.J.*, 117; Marshall D. Wright, *The National Association of Base Ball Players, 1857–1870* (Jefferson, N.C.: McFarland, 2000), 19.

9. United States Census, 1850, 1860; *The Evening Journal*, February 13, 1872; *The Jersey Journal*, October 30, 1918.

10. United States Census, 1850, 1860, 1880; *The Evening Journal*, October 9, 1867, November 16, 1867; June 25, 1872; May 14, 1886, January 15, 1892; www.measuringworth.com.

11. United States Census, 1850, 1860, 1870, 1880; McLean, *History of Jersey City, N.J.*, 146.

12. United States Census, 1850, 1860, 1870, 1880; McLean, *History of Jersey City, N.J.*, 126.

13. United States Census, 1850, 1860, 1870; McLean, *History of Jersey City, N.J.*, 114, 116.

14. United States Census, 1850, 1860, 1870, 1880; *The Evening Journal*, March 23, 1870, August 30, 1886; Wright, *The National Association of Base Ball Players, 1857–1870*, 19.

Bibliography

Books

Costello, A.E. *History of the Police Department of Jersey City From the Reign of the Knickerbockers to the Present Day*. Jersey City: The Police Relief Association Publication Company, 1891.

McLean, Alexander. *History of Jersey City, N.J.: A Record of Its Early Settlement and Corporate Progress Compiled for the Evening Journal*. Jersey City: Press of the Jersey City Printing Company, 1895.

Wright, Marshall D. *The National Association of Base Ball Players, 1857–1870*. Jefferson, N.C.: McFarland, 2000.

Periodicals

Kirsch, George B. "The Rise of Modern Sports: New Jersey Cricketers, Baseball Players and Clubs, 1845–60." *New Jersey History*, Volume 101, Numbers 1–2, Spring-Summer 1983.

Newspapers

Commercial Advertiser
The Evening Journal (1867–1909)
Jersey City Daily Sentinel
Jersey City Daily Telegraph
The Jersey Journal (1909–Present)
New York Herald Tribune
New York Times
Newark Daily Advertiser

Other Sources

www.ancestry.com
The Cleveland W. Mears Collection on Baseball, Scrapbook 1a.
Headstones Provided for Deceased Union Veterans
www.measuringworth.com
U. S. Census, 1850, 1860, 1870, 1880

❖ *Liberty Base Ball Club of New Brunswick* ❖ (John G. Zinn)

CLUB HISTORY

While New Brunswick, New Jersey, is deservedly known as the "Birthplace of College Football," even earlier it played an important role in the development of baseball in the Garden State. New Brunswick was the home of the Liberty Base Ball Club, the first non-New York club to join the National Association of Base Ball Players (NABBP). Possibly taking its name from a local fire company, the club was founded in 1857. A year later the Liberty Club led the way as the NABBP took its first steps towards a more national presence.[1]

Although the Liberty Club was at the forefront of NABBP membership, they were apparently not so up to date with major changes to the rules of the game. One of the first newspaper accounts of the Liberty Club listed rules it followed in 1857. The rules seem to mirror the 1845 Knickerbocker rules and don't reflect 1857 NABBP revisions, such as the winner no longer being the first side to score 21 aces. Regardless of how the game was played, the reporter found the 20–25 young men "picturesque" in their "dashing uniforms." Analysis of 1857 box scores indicates a group of young men ranging in age from 18 to 27, almost all of whom were born in New Jersey. The players held a wide array of occupations including construction and retailing plus a bartender and a cigar dealer. The club's grounds were near the "Catholic cemetery," which one source names as today's Commercial Avenue between Sudaym and Townsend Streets.[2]

During their first season, the Liberty Club seemed to limit itself to intra-squad contests with only one surviving account of a match game — "a friendly game" with the Union

Club of Elizabeth. That game, played on the Liberty grounds, appears to have had some resemblance to a cricket match as the clubs played two innings, the Liberty Club winning 21–2 and 25–6 for a combined final 46–8 score. The club's playing rules continued to evolve as the next game (an intra-squad contest) required the first nine to score 30 times before the second nine reached 15. The game was played for an oyster supper ultimately provided by the second nine, who were on the short end of a 30–6 score. The easy triumph must have boosted the first nine's confidence as they offered to take on any nine players from New Brunswick. The challenge was reportedly accepted for something bigger than an oyster supper — a $25 purse. If the match against an unnamed opponent ever took place, no record survives.[3]

The Liberty Club's confidence in its ball-playing ability continued to grow in 1858. The first step was joining the NABBP in March, thereby becoming the first non-New York club to do so. Then after winning four straight matches against local rivals, the New Brunswick club took a quantum step up in class, playing two matches against the Atlantics of Brooklyn. Both games resulted in defeats, one by the "decisive" score of 61–14, a match that saw the Liberty Club trail 16–0 after one inning and 26–1 after two. At least the New Brunswickers did no worse than other clubs as the Atlantics enjoyed an undefeated (7–0) season. There were descriptions of the members of the Liberty Club as "country boys" who played barefoot, but this account appeared some seven years later, which along with the absence of any similar contemporary report makes this later claim somewhat questionable.[4]

No matter how "decisive" the 61–14 defeat, the Liberty Club clearly was not intimidated as it embarked on a more aggressive schedule in 1859 — all against New Jersey rivals. The New Brunswick men compiled a 7–1 record, with their only defeat coming at the hands of the Newark Club — considered to be the oldest club in the state. The defeat was reportedly the first match of a series for the New Jersey championship. Undeterred by the opening loss, the Liberty Club won the second match and then took the final and deciding game at a neutral site in Rahway. There was every reason to be optimistic as the new decade began.[5]

Early in the 1860 season, the Liberty Club suffered its second defeat to a New Jersey club, a 29–24 loss to the Hamilton Club of Jersey City. Playing primarily local clubs that year, the New Brunswick club won four matches before renewing its acquaintance with the Atlantics of Brooklyn. The first contest took place in New Brunswick and saw the upstart New Jersey club take a 16–11 lead into the ninth inning. Dreams of what would arguably have been the greatest upset of the pre-war period ended when Brooklyn tallied five times in their last at-bat. However, there was no further scoring, so the match ended in a 16–16 tie. Although ties are seldom satisfactory results to either side, the Liberty Club reportedly felt "like victors, because they were not beaten" by an opponent that

"seldom fails of success." The Atlantics themselves "gracefully" admitted their opponents were "worthy competitors." No doubt a 15–10 Atlantic victory about 10 days later further increased the Brooklyn club's respect for the Liberty Club and the New Brunswickers' good opinion of themselves.[6]

The coming of the Civil War in April of 1861 put a damper on baseball activities throughout New Jersey. Especially hard hit was the Liberty Club, which played only one game that season, but it was a match to remember. After coming close twice the prior year, the New Brunswickers pulled off the big upset on October 28, 1861, decisively defeating the Atlantics, 30–12. While lamenting the loss to a "so called country club," the *Brooklyn Daily Eagle* acknowledged the "thrashing," in what was described as the "total defeat of the Atlantics." It was the Brooklynites' first loss to a club from outside of New York, the last such loss until the Irvington Club pulled off what was arguably an even greater upset in 1866. Played at the grounds of the Newark club before "a numerous assemblage," the match was close until the fourth inning when the Liberty Club broke things open and coasted from there.[7]

Although it does not appear that a significant number of the Liberty Club served in the military during the Civil War, the club "disbanded" for the duration of the conflict. With the coming of peace, they reorganized in September of 1865 with 50 active and 25 honorary members. Sporting uniforms of blue pants, white shirts, and blue caps, the Liberty Club had another successful season with a 4–2 mark. Four of the six matches were against out-of-state foes; the Liberty Club beat the Gothams of New York twice and fell to the National Club of Washington and the Athletic Club of Philadelphia. Since the latter two clubs went 33–7 in 1866, the Liberty Club was still clearly a competitive club. In spite of an almost five-year gap, five of the leading players of the pre-war period returned in 1866.[8]

Given this continued success and the rapid expansion of the game in the post-war period, it would have been reasonable to expect the club to continue to be quite active. However, that was not the case, as surviving records reflect only two games over the next two years. One possibility is that the core players who had returned in 1866 gave up active participation thereafter. For some reason, baseball did not fare well in New Brunswick in 1867 and 1868. In June of 1869, the *New Brunswick Daily Fredonian* reported that most clubs in the city had disbanded with only the Liberty Club having "a complete organization." The Liberty Club supposedly acquired some players from the disbanded clubs, allowing them to become more active. In addition to the new players, the Liberty Club also had new grounds on Trenton Avenue.[9]

Playing mostly local clubs, the Liberty Club had another winning record in 1869. Both losses came against the Resolute Club of Elizabeth, one of the premier New Jersey clubs at the end of the 1860s. In addition, there was a notable win against the Resolutes. The following year saw the Liberty Club suffer its only losing season, winning only twice against six losses. The losses included defeats by the Amateur Club of Newark and the Champion Club of Jersey City, two other prominent New Jersey clubs of the era. The Liberty Club ended the 1870 season with two losses to the Rutgers College nine. At least one of the games was played on the "Old Bishop ground, near College Avenue," reportedly the same site where Rutgers had defeated Princeton in the first intercollegiate football game some eleven months earlier. In November of 1870, the *Daily Fredonian* reported plans to consolidate the Liberty and Rutgers clubs in 1871. However, the Rutgers *Targum* makes no mention of such plans, and the 1871 Rutgers squad did not include any members of the Liberty Club. It appears the Liberty Club went out of existence after 1870; no subsequent game accounts have been found and by early 1873, the *Daily Times* asked plaintively (and probably rhetorically), "Are the Liberty Base Ball Club to reorganize this year?"[10]

From 1855 to 1860 baseball in New Jersey enjoyed considerable growth and expansion. Four years of Civil War disrupted almost every club, but probably none suffered more than the Liberty Club. In five years it had grown from a small-town club, playing out-of-date rules, to one capable of contending with one of the era's best squads. Indeed by 1860 the *Daily Fredonian* grouped the Liberty Club with the Eurekas as one of the state's "well known Clubs." Between its founding in 1857 and its Civil War sabbatical, the club recorded a 17-5–1 mark. Although some of the premier players returned after the war, the club soon dropped back into the lower levels of New Jersey clubs. However, the Liberty Club's history is still noteworthy due both to the club's early membership in the NABBP and its on-the-field success.[11]

CLUB MEMBERS

Abram Cortelyou: Born in New Vernon, New Jersey, on June 17, 1834, Cortelyou was a founding member of the Liberty Club, playing the outfield and second base. He was one of the pre-war players to return for the 1866 season. The Cortelyou family has a long history in the New Brunswick area, and at some point Abram purchased the jewelry business of his uncle John Cortelyou. Abram died on May 14, 1924, at the end of his 90th year.[12]

William H. Cortelyou: The older brother of Abram, born at Six Mile Run, New Jersey, on November 26, 1826. William joined the Liberty Club for their second season in 1858, playing through 1866. He was the club's pitcher from 1860 through 1866. Like his brother, William was active in the jewelry business; he is listed in various New Brunswick directories as a watchmaker and silversmith as well as being a jeweler. He died on May 28, 1871.[13]

John V. Conover: Born in New Jersey on July 29, 1826, Conover was a founding member of the Liberty Club who played for three seasons through 1859 at third base. During and after his baseball career, he was a mason and builder. He died on September 11, 1899.[14]

Isaac L.F. Elkin: Born in New Brunswick on May 15, 1836, Elkin apparently only played one season with the Liberty Club, but he was the club's founding secretary. Like his teammate Jarvis Wanser, Elkin enlisted in the Union Army, serving in the 1st New Jersey Regiment from the beginning to the end of the conflict including a period as a prisoner of war. After the end of the war, Elkin returned to New Brunswick, going into the liquor business with his brother-in-law. He subsequently became the proprietor of the Macom hotel in New Brunswick, a position he held until his death on February 14, 1908.[15]

Matthew Hildebrandt: The first president of the Liberty Club, Hildebrandt was the club's catcher through the 1861 game with the Atlantic. Born about 1833 in New Jersey, he was a carpenter and builder. By 1880, Hildebrandt and his family had moved to Bethlehem, Pennsylvania. He died sometime between 1880 and 1900 as his wife is listed as a widow on the 1900 census.[16]

Elias R. Sturges: A founding member of the Liberty Club, Sturges played first base and right field for the club through the 1860 season. Although born in New Jersey about 1834, he apparently moved back and forth between New Brunswick and Brooklyn as he lived in the latter city both prior to and after the Civil War. Another Liberty in the construction trade, he was a mason, a profession he shared with his father and brother. By 1900 Sturges was out of the building trade, living in Brooklyn and working as a candy and sugar dealer. He died on February 25, 1905.[17]

Martin Vannuise: Like William Cortelyou, Vannuise joined the Liberty Club for the 1858 season and stayed with the club through 1866, playing catcher and third base. Born in New Jersey about 1836, Vannuise was a carpenter who was still living in New Brunswick in 1895.[18]

Jarvis Wanser: Another founding member of the Liberty Club, Wanser played shortstop for the club through the 1866 season. Wanser was born in New Jersey on March 20, 1838, the son of an inn-keeper and was working as a bartender in 1860. One of the few club members whose military service is clearly documented, he enlisted in the 14th New Jersey, rising to the rank of Captain. After the war he worked in various retail businesses including a bowling alley and an eating house and billiard parlor. At some point around 1880, Wanser and his family moved from New Brunswick to Vineland in southern New Jersey. During this period, he was active in Republican politics and veterans affairs while working in the real estate field. In 1906 he was appointed to a commission to erect at monument at Monocacy, Maryland, where the 14th regiment suffered heavy casualties. In 1899 he was elected commandant of the Home for Aged and Indigent Soldiers and their Wives in Vineland. He also authored a book about Vineland. The old soldier and ball player died on January 22, 1908.[19]

Charles S. Williams: Born in New Jersey in 1821, Williams was one of the oldest members of the Liberty Club. He played first and third base for the club for three years, 1859–61. He is listed in city directories as being in the grocery and fruit and vegetable businesses. Williams appears in the 1868 directory as an express man, but by 1870, his wife is listed as a widow, so he must have died in the interim period, making him one of the first club members to die.[20]

Founding Officers: Isaac L.F. Elkin — Secretary; Matthew Hildebrandt — President; William Shooks — Vice President; John Van Nest — Treasurer

Notes

1. Charles A. Peverelly, *The Book of American Pastimes* (New York: Published by the Author, 1866), 460; *New Brunswick Daily News*, July 22, 1857, www.baseballchronology.com.

2. *New Brunswick Daily News*, July 22, 1857, David Block, *Baseball Before We Knew It: A Search for the Early Roots of the Game* (Lincoln: University of Nebraska Press, 2005), 80–93, www.baseballchronology.com; 1860 Census; www.ancestry.com.

3. *New Brunswick Daily News*, August 20, 1857, August 24, 1857, August 26, 1857.

4. Marshall D. Wright, *The National Association of Base Ball Players, 1857–1870* (Jefferson, N.C.: McFarland, 2000), 16, 19, *New Brunswick Daily News*, October 13, 1858; *Brooklyn Daily Eagle*, August 24, 1865.

5. *New Brunswick Fredonian*, September 15, 1859, November 17, 1859; *Newark Daily Advertiser*, October 7, 1859.

6. *New York Times*, July 3, 1860; *New Brunswick Daily Fredonian*, September 28, 1860, October 9, 1860.

7. *Brooklyn Daily Eagle*, October 31, 1861.

8. Peverelly, *The Book of American Pastimes*, 460–61, Wright, *The National Association of Base Ball Players, 1857–1870*, 114, 117.

9. Wright, *The National Association of Base Ball Players, 1857–1870*, 173, *New Brunswick Daily Fredonian*, June 10, 1869.

10. *New Brunswick Daily Fredonian*, October 20, 1870, November 2, 1870; *The Targum*, January 1871, March 1871, www.baseballchronology.com; *New Brunswick Daily Times*, March 11, 1873.

11. *New Brunswick Daily Fredonian*, August 31, 1860.

12. 1860 and 1870 U. S. Census; New Brunswick City Directories, 1880, 1890, 1900, and 1910; *New Brunswick Daily Times*, May 16, 1900; www.familysearch.org.

13. 1860 and 1870 U. S. Census; New Brunswick Directories 1855, 1868; www.familysearch.org.

14. 1870 U.S. Census; New Brunswick Directories 1855, 1870, 1880, 1890 and 1900; www.familysearch.org; *New Brunswick Daily Times*, September 12, 1899.

15. U.S. Census 1860, 1900; *New Brunswick Daily Times*, February 14, 1908.

16. 1860, 1870, 1880, 1900 U.S. Census.

17. U.S. Census 1850, 1860, 1870, 1880, 1900; New Brunswick Directories 1856, 1865, 1866, 1870, 1880; www.familysearch.org.

18. U. S. Census 1860, 1870; New Jersey Census 1895.

19. U. S. Census, 1860, 1870, 1880, 1900; *Trenton Evening Times*, January 24, 1893; *Philadelphia Inquirer*, May 17, 1899, May 28, 1906.

20. U. S. Census 1860; New Brunswick Directories, 1855, 1865, 1866, 1868, 1870.

Bibliography

Books

Block, David. *Baseball Before We Knew It: A Search for the Roots of the Game.* Lincoln: University of Nebraska Press, 2005.

Peverelly, Charles A. *The Book of American Pastimes.* New York: Published by the Author, 1866.

Wright, Marshall D. *The National Association of Base Ball Players, 1857–1870.* Jefferson, N.C.: McFarland, 2000.

Newspapers

Brooklyn Daily Eagle
New Brunswick Daily Fredonian
New Brunswick Daily News
New Brunswick Daily Times
New Brunswick Fredonian
New York Times
Newark Daily Advertiser
Philadelphia Inquirer
The Targum
Trenton Evening Times

Other Sources

www.ancestry.com
www.baseballchronology.com
www.familysearch.org
New Brunswick City Directories, 1855, 1856, 1865, 1866, 1868, 1870, 1880, 1890, 1900, 1910
United States Census 1860, 1870, 1880, 1900

❖ *Nassau Base Ball Club of Princeton* ❖
(John G. Zinn)

CLUB HISTORY

As the New York game spread across New Jersey in the late 1850s it was only a question of time before it took root on college campuses. One school where baseball got an early start was the College of New Jersey — today's Princeton University. Baseball activity got underway in the fall of 1857 when a group of freshmen formed the Nassau Base Ball Club even though few of them had ever played or even seen a game. Like freshmen everywhere, their lack of experience didn't intimidate them, as they challenged the even less experienced sophomore class to a game. The sophomores must have been quick learners as they won the game by "twenty-one rounds." Since the contest lasted only five innings with 15 on a side, it isn't clear what rules were in use.[1]

If nothing else, the late 1857 inter-class match generated enough interest for the formation of a number of baseball clubs the following spring. However, all of this activity was merely a prelude to the introduction of "baseball proper" in the fall of 1858. Among the incoming class of 1862 were three young men with significant baseball experience. Lewis Mudge, Henry Sampson, and Henry Butler, all of whom came from Brooklyn, brought bats, balls and uniforms, but most especially their passion for the game. Mudge, who became known as the Father of Base Ball at Princeton, had played for the Hiawatha Club of Brooklyn. They were joined by about 20 other young men, almost all from the north, half from New Jersey, with only three coming from the Deep South. [2]

After playing on Saturdays throughout the fall, the young men formed the "Base Ball Club of the Class of 1862, Nassau Hall" on March 14, 1859. Initiation dues of 50 cents and monthly fees of 10 cents covered the first year's operating expenses of $9.43 for bats and balls. Regular fees were supplemented by the typical array of fines ranging from 3 cents for voicing an "opinion on a doubtful play" before the umpire had spoken to 10 cents for "profane or impious language." Since at least ten club members, including the three Brooklyn boys, were preparing for the ordained ministry, the higher fine for inappropriate language is not surprising. The future vocations of so many club members may also have facilitated a series of bi-weekly matches in the fall of 1859 against students from Princeton Seminary in which the collegians "were usually the victor." [3]

Although club membership was technically only open to the Class of 1862, honorary memberships for upperclassmen quickly helped get the best players on the field. In 1860 the club took over the title of the now-defunct Nassau Club and played twice a week on the "field back of Edwards." No record of faculty/administration concerns over the time devoted to athletics survives, but there was apparently plenty of debate when the club wanted to play its first road game. The college students were invited to come to Orange, New Jersey, to play an amateur opponent headed by Dr. Edward Pierson, Class of 1854. Reportedly it took "much persuasion" before faculty permission was obtained. The match took place on October 22, 1860, with the younger collegians taking an early lead before the home side tied it at 42–42 in the ninth. By that point it was growing dark, and the two sides were probably worn out from running the bases so they agreed to accept a tie. The experience apparently moved Mudge to issue challenges to Yale, Columbia, and Rutgers. All declined, claiming their school was still playing the "old Connecticut game" and didn't have a baseball club. [4]

Whether it was because of the lack of college opposition and/or the outbreak of the Civil War, the initial Nassau Club was limited to playing against the Seminary through the Class of 1862's graduation. With a heavy percentage of Southerners in its student population, the College of New Jersey suffered serious disruption during the early 1860s. The Class of 1862, which was more than halfway through their college careers when the war broke out, was especially hard hit. Lewis Mudge wrote that there were 100 in the class at the beginning of their sophomore year, 40 percent of whom were Southerners. By

graduation less than half that number remained to receive their diplomas. Among them were all of the members of the Nassau Club, including the three Southerners (Alexander Marks, Alexander Morse, and Charles Petrie), who didn't leave with their "countrymen." [5]

Although they stayed through graduation, the three Southerners did go on to serve in the Confederate army. Interestingly only three of their northern teammates appear to have served in the Union army and then only for a brief period. That may be partially due to the large number preparing for the ordained ministry at Princeton Seminary. While they were no doubt working hard in their seminary classes, the former Nassau Club members still had time for important things. Henry Butler, one of the Brooklyn three, told classmate Joseph Munn that they were "not so busy however that we cannot play ball every day at noon." [6]

The original Nassau Club was important in the development of early baseball in particular and college athletics in general because they showed participation in sports wasn't incompatible with high academic performance. Seven members of the club finished in the top ten academic places of their class, including two of the Brooklyn boys who finished second (Mudge) and tenth (Butler). College President John MacLean had to be mindful of this in the fall of 1862 when he allowed not just the club, with an entirely new set of players, but other students to travel to New Brunswick for a match with the Star Club of New Brunswick. The Nassau Club members occupied the 17-mile railroad journey with "songs, shouts and visions of a jolly day." After being welcomed by Star Club representatives, the collegians visited a billiards saloon (probably not what President MacLean had in mind) and "spent the rest of the morning examining the beauties of the rustic village." Setting a time-honored precedent for all collegiate road trips, the young men took special notice of "a few pretty girls with skirts fastened (enchantingly) up to avoid the wet." The "wet" was symptomatic of the rainy conditions, but the two clubs got six innings in as the Nassau Club won, completing a sweep of two games from the New Brunswick Club. Although some publications later claimed this made the Nassau Club New Jersey champions, the Stars were a junior club and the contemporary claim was limited to a willingness to take on all New Jersey comers at that level. [7]

By the spring of 1863, however, the members of the Nassau Club were ready to step up in class. Led by Captain Henry Millspaugh (or Milspaugh), they journeyed to Philadelphia in May, where they split two games with Philadelphia clubs. Since there was no competition from football or other fall sports, baseball resumed in the fall with almost 25 percent of the student body joining the Nassau Club or one of the two other clubs active on campus. Among the 30 members of the Nassau Club was one graduate, who apparently had eligibility left, Lewis Mudge, then a student at the seminary. Members of the first nine continued to be almost entirely from the Northeast. [8]

After defeating the Athletics of Philadelphia and the Irvington Club at Princeton, the collegians decided to use a "Quarterly Week" fall academic break for a road trip to Brooklyn. Since this was long before athletic department budgets, the players paid their own expenses, but lodging costs were limited since a majority of the club members reportedly lived in the City of Churches. Resplendent in new uniforms of white shirts, blue pants and "a thin white ribbon with the word NASSAU printed on it," the college club more than held their own, winning three of the four matches. Of special note was a dramatic come-from-behind victory over the Excelsior Club and an honorable 18–13 loss to the Atlantic. Things apparently got a little tense at the end of the former game as "a little excitement among a few members of both clubs" disrupted "the pleasure of the game" before "true harmony was restored." In the latter match special mention was made of the pitching of Frederick Henry which "bothered the Atlantics exceedingly." This combined with comments from the September 26th match with the Athletics that Henry pitched a "slow ball with a heavy twist" has led to speculation that the Princeton pitcher may have been intentionally throwing a curve ball. Apparently the club was not met by cheering students on its triumphant return to campus as "the majority of students preferred to write an essay for the *Lit* than knock down flies on the diamond."[9]

Testifying to the ability of the Princeton players was the selection of Millspaugh and Henry to a New Jersey all-star squad that defeated a Pennsylvania opponent in a May 1864 match for the benefit of the United States Sanitary Commission. The choice of Henry as pitcher gives added evidence of his effectiveness, curve ball or not. Aggressive scheduling continued that spring as the club traveled to Philadelphia, New York, Hoboken, and Newark. While it is unlikely that the club ever brought in paid players, a few players who were not college students did play for the Nassau Club. This included a brother of captain Millspaugh and a "Mr. Brinkerhoff" who took over for an injured player in the June 30, 1864, loss to the Athletics in Philadelphia. Brinkerhoff appears to be Henry Brinkerhoff who played for the Pioneer Club of Jersey City in 1855 and the Eagle Club of New York thereafter. Less of an exception was Lewis Mudge (now two years out of college), who played in matches during the summer of 1864. The high point of the summer was a 19–10 victory over the New York Mutuals, which lost only two other games all year, both to the Atlantics. The collegians and others had a rematch with the Atlantics, who quickly ended any Nassau upset plans with a resounding 42–7 victory. The resumption of the academic year in the fall saw the Princetonians play their first intercollegiate contest against Williams. Apparently the Nassau players no longer had their uniforms as their 27–16 victory in "shirt sleeves" added to the "bitterness of the defeat" for the uniformed New Englanders.[10]

Baseball suffered a downturn at Princeton over the next few years, especially after some "alumni and tutors" formed the Princeton Base Ball Club in the spring of 1867. The wealthier newcomers were able to arrange better grounds and bring in better opposition which apparently helped them attract undergraduates as players. Things changed dramatically, however, in the fall of 1868 when the new president, Dr. James McCosh, "astounded the whole College" by actually attending a game only three days after being inaugurated. The new president's public witness made baseball "an acknowledged factor in college life." By the next spring, the Princeton Club went out of business and turned its grounds and equipment over to the Nassau Club, now appropriately known as the Princeton University Base Ball Club, which has represented the University on the diamond ever since.[11]

The Nassau Club made a major contribution to baseball's acceptance as a legitimate activity for young men. Participation by a group of good students, many headed for the ministry, made it almost impossible to oppose the new game as inappropriate for young men. This had to help baseball's growth in general, but especially at the college level. Without the positive examples of the Nassau Club, it would have been more difficult for the game to gain acceptance at institutions of higher learning. Intercollegiate sports owe no small debt to the three young men from Brooklyn and those who joined them on the Nassau Club.

CLUB MEMBERS

Leroy Anderson: born in New York City in 1841, Anderson was one of two members of the Class of 1861 to play in the October 1860 game in Orange. After college, Anderson became a lawyer and settled in Princeton, where he lived for the rest of his life. Anderson held a number of important positions in his new community including mayor and positions on the Boards of Health and Education. Professionally, Anderson worked in the railroad industry, serving as Secretary and Treasurer of the United Railways of New Jersey and as a Director of the Pennsylvania Railroad. Teammate Lewis Mudge officiated at Anderson's funeral in December of 1905.[12]

William Baldwin: Baldwin was a member of the original first nine although he didn't play in the Orange match. Born in Newark in 1841, Baldwin attended Princeton Seminary after graduation from college. He was ordained a Presbyterian minister and served churches in Illinois, Michigan, New Jersey, Massachusetts, and Washington, D. C. Baldwin died on May 16, 1930, as one of Princeton's oldest alumni.[13]

Henry Butler: one of the Brooklyn three, Henry Butler was born in New York City in 1840. After graduation from Princeton, he taught school before attending Princeton Seminary. Butler was ordained to the Presbyterian ministry in 1866 and served churches in New York, New Jersey, and Pennsylvania. He was awarded a Doctor of Divinity Degree from Lafayette College and died on September 11, 1923, at the age of 83.[14]

Edward A. Condit: While almost all of the Nassau Club members went on to respectable post-baseball careers, Condit was a glaring exception. A native of East Orange and a member of the class of 1866, Condit was the club's regular first baseman from 1862 through his graduation. At some point after leaving college, Condit embarked on a long career of white-collar crime. In 1876 he was arrested for sending a "bogus telegram" with false reports of Cornelius Vanderbilt's death which "materially affected affairs in Wall Street." This was followed by additional arrests for defrauding a group of stock brokers.

Clearly identified in newspaper accounts as a former Princeton baseball player, Condit was arrested again in Jersey City in 1884 for forgery. Visitors to the jail smuggled in saws and other tools that enabled Condit to attempt a jail break which failed. The former first baseman was sentenced to four years at hard labor by Judge McGill, who was a Princeton classmate (apparently conflict of interest standards were more flexible then). At the very least Condit put up a good front as he "smiled" and "received the sentence with a good deal of composure." Condit reportedly had a lot of experience inside a prison which extended into the 20th century. In 1903 a Boston judge sentenced him to 10–15 years for forgery and swindling under an assumed name. Condit's date and place of death remain unknown.[15]

David W. Guy: Shortstop in the 1860 game, David Guy was born in Cincinnati in 1842. After graduation from Princeton, he returned to Ohio and earned a law degree. Guy practiced law for the rest of his life, dying in 1902.[16]

Frederick Porteous Henry: Pitcher for the Nassau Club for the 1863 and 1864 seasons before leaving college for unexplained reasons in the fall of 1864 halfway through his sophomore year. Although he was born in Middlesex, New Jersey, in 1844, Henry's family was actually from Mobile, Alabama. He did, however, live in New Jersey before college while his parents were abroad. Former teammates and others at Princeton supported the claim that Henry was the first pitcher to intentionally throw a curve ball. Henry himself said, "There is no doubt that the ball I pitched had a very decided outcurve." Among former teammates supporting Henry's claim was John McPherson, a Federal Judge. Although Henry never graduated from Princeton, he went on to become a doctor in Philadelphia, where he died on May 24, 1919.[17] See the profile of Henry in the entry on the Excelsior/Pastime Club of Baltimore in volume one for a more detailed summary of his life.

William W. Knox: William Knox was born in Utica in 1842. Like many of his 1862 classmates, he followed graduation by enrolling at Princeton Seminary and becoming a Presbyterian minister. Knox served churches in New York and New Jersey, especially First Presbyterian Church of New Brunswick, where he was pastor for 24 years and pastor emeritus until his death in 1929. Knox received a Doctor of Divinity degree from Rutgers College in 1894. He played third base in the 1860 game in Orange and apparently maintained his love of baseball in

seminary as classmate and teammate Henry Butler wrote in 1865 that Knox was "doing big things in the base ball line."[18]

Henry C. Milspaugh or Millspaugh: Born in Montgomery, New York, in 1842, Henry Millspaugh was captain of the Nassau Club in both 1863 and 1864. His surname was generally spelled with one "l" during his time at Princeton, but the second "l" was used in his hometown of Newburgh, New York. Millspaugh was the Nassau Club's regular left fielder beginning in the 1862 season. Along with Henry, he was one of the two players picked for the New Jersey nine which took on a Pennsylvania squad in May of 1864 for the benefit of the United States Sanitary Commission. After graduation and during summer recesses Millspaugh and teammate Lewis Halsey played for the Hudson River Club of Newburgh for several seasons. Awarded an A.M. degree from Princeton in 1867, the former outfielder went on to become a lawyer and justice of the peace in Newburgh. Sadly Millspaugh died of consumption in 1883 at the age of 41.[19]

Lewis W. Mudge: The Father of Baseball at Princeton was born in New York City in 1839 and moved with his family to Brooklyn in 1841. Mudge became a member of the Hiawatha Base Ball Club of Brooklyn and took his love of the game to Bloomfield Institute in Bloomfield, New Jersey, in 1857 where he prepared for Princeton. Mudge actually returned to the Hiawatha Club shortly before starting his studies at Princeton, throwing over 200 pitches in a July 1858 victory over the Osceola Club. At Princeton, Mudge organized the Class of 1862 Club along with Butler and Sampson. He was captain of the nine and both pitcher and catcher. Mudge was also an exemplary student-athlete, finishing second in his class. In a note in Mudge's alumni file in the Princeton archives, classmate John DeWitt described Mudge as the "only student he ever knew who could work out a mathematical problem, lay plans for winning a base ball game and carry on a conversation at the same time."

Mudge also attended Princeton Seminary and not surprisingly went on to a long (47 years) and distinguished career in the Presbyterian ministry. This included almost 20 years at the Second Presbyterian Church in Princeton. In 1895, Mudge selflessly gave up his position in order to facilitate the merger of the two Presbyterian churches in Princeton. During his time there, he was reported to be "deeply interested" in students at both the college and the seminary. In 1902 he became the Pastor of Central Presbyterian church in Downingtown, Pennsylvania, where he served until his death in 1914.[20]

Joseph Munn: Born in East Orange, New Jersey, in 1840, Munn was the second baseman in the 1860 game. After college, he studied law with Amzi Dodd, Princeton Class of 1842. Munn went on to serve in the State Assembly and as Essex County Surrogate. He continued to live in his hometown, where he was President of the Board of Education. The old second baseman died in 1914.[21]

Nehemiah Perry: Perry, along with Leroy Anderson, was

one of the two members of the Class of 1861 who played in the 1860 game in Orange. Perry, who was the Nassau catcher in that game, was born in Newark in 1840. Like a number of his classmates, he became a lawyer after college, but died young at the age of 35 in 1875.[22]

Edward P. Rankin: Born in India in 1845 while his father was a missionary, Rankin was the second baseman for the Nassau Club and captain of the 1865 squad. Following in his father's footsteps, he became a minister, serving Presbyterian congregations in Illinois and Wisconsin. After retiring, Rankin moved to California, where until age 85, he celebrated his birthday by climbing 5000-foot-high Monrovia Peak. At the time of his death in 1937, he was one of Princeton's oldest living alumni. After his death, Monrovia Peak was renamed Rankin Peak in his honor.[23]

Henry L. Sampson: The third of the three Brooklynites who initiated baseball at Princeton, Sampson was born in Brooklyn in 1843. He played first base in the 1860 game and planned to join Butler and Mudge in the Presbyterian ministry. However, on graduation from Princeton, Sampson was too young for the ministry, so he began studying law until he reached the appropriate age. Sadly, he died in 1863 at the age of 20 before he could pursue either career.[24]

William H. Wickham: Wickham was the Captain of the 1866 squad, playing primarily at catcher beginning in the 1862 season. As Fred Henry's battery mate, he backed up the latter's claim of throwing a curve ball. After years of watching Princeton baseball, one longtime fan said that Wickham "is still my ideal" catcher. Born in Brooklyn in 1846, Wickham went into the drug and chemical business in New York City becoming the head of McKesson & Robbins before his death on November 21, 1925.[25]

Henry Young: The center fielder in the 1860 game, Young was born in Newark in 1844. After college he became a lawyer and served as a prosecutor and Assistant U.S. District Attorney. Young died in his hometown of Newark in 1908.[26]

Other Club Members: Edward Atwater (who is not the man by the same man who starred for the Niagara Club of Buffalo), Henry A. Boardman, Edward Brewster, Edward Burkhalter, Walter Butler, James Coale, Ellis Freeman, James Green, Lewis B. Halsey (see the entry for the Hudson River Club of Newburgh in *Base Ball Pioneers, 1850–1870*), Samuel Jacobus, Robert F. Little, Joseph McIlvaine, Alexander Marks, William Mershow, Alexander Morse, Charles Nassau, Charles Petrie, Charles Remington, Henry Robinson, Reuben Van Pelt, Charles Young.

Notes

1. Frank Presbrey and James Hugh Moffat, *Athletics at Princeton* (New York: Frank Presbrey Company, 1901), 67.

2. Ibid., 67; *Brooklyn Daily Eagle*, February 2, 1913; Princeton University Class of 1862 Alumni Files, Boxes 121–22, Department of Rare Books and Special Collections, Princeton University Library; *New York Clipper*, August 21, 1858.

3. Presbrey and Moffat, *Athletics at Princeton*, 67.

4. Ibid., 67–68.

5. Ibid., 67; Lewis Mudge to Mr. Collins, November 27, 1912; Princeton University Class of 1862 Alumni Files, Boxes 121–22, and Princeton University Class Records, Box 6, 1862–66, Department of Rare Books and Special Collections, Princeton University Library.

6. Princeton University Class of 1862 Alumni Files, Boxes 121–22, Department of Rare Books and Special Collections, Princeton University Library; Henry S. Butler to Joseph Munn, March 22, 1865, Princeton University Class Records, Box 6, 1862–66, Department of Rare Books and Special Collections, Princeton University.

7. Princeton University Class Records, Box 6, 1862–1865, Department of Rare Books and Special Collections, Princeton University; Presbrey and Moffat, *Athletics at Princeton*, 68; George B. Kirsch, *Baseball in Blue and Gray: The National Pastime During the Civil War* (Princeton, N.J.: Princeton University Press, 2003), 74, *New York Sunday Mercury*, September 20, 1862 and October 19, 1862; *Nassau Literary Magazine*, March 1863, 23, 6, p. 281.

8. Presbrey and Moffat, *Athletics at Princeton*, 68–70; Princeton Alumni records list 359 members of four classes, while the Presbrey and Moffat list 87 members of the three clubs, http://www.princeton.edu–mudd/databases/alumni.html; Princeton University Class of 1864, 1866 and 1867, Alumni Files, Boxes 124–129, Department of Rare Books and Special Collections, Princeton University.

9. Presbrey and Moffat, *Athletics at Princeton*, 70–72, 84; *New York Herald*, October 21, 1863; Princeton's athletic representatives did not begin using black and orange until 1867. The tiger did not become the school mascot until 1880, http://www.Princeton.edu/mudd/news/faq/topics/tigers:shtml.

10. *New York Clipper*, June 6, 1864; Presbrey and Moffat, *Athletics at Princeton*, 72–75; Marshall D. Wright, *The National Association of Base Ball Players, 1857–1870* (Jefferson, N.C.: McFarland, 2000), 85. Although Henry Brinkerhoff lived in Jersey City for most of his life, he did spend five years farming in Rocky Hill, New Jersey, near Princeton.

11. Presbrey and Moffat, *Athletics at Princeton*, 80, 86.

12. Princeton University Class of 1861 Alumni Files, Box 119, Department of Rare Books and Special Collections, Princeton University Library, Presbrey and Moffat, *Athletics at Princeton*, 67; *Jersey Journal*, December 15, 1905; *Trenton Evening Times*, December 18, 1905.

13. Princeton University Class of 1862 Alumni Files, Box 121, Department of Rare Books and Special Collections, Princeton University Library, Presbrey and Moffat, *Athletics at Princeton*, 67.

14. Princeton University Class of 1862 Alumni Files, Box 121, Department of Rare Books and Special Collections, Princeton University Library.

15. Presbrey and Moffat, *Athletics at Princeton*, 70–75; *New York Sunday Mercury*, September 29, 1862; Princeton University Class of 1866 Alumni Files, Box 127, Department of Rare Books and Special Collections, Princeton University Library; *Elkhart Daily Review*, December 3, 1884; *New York Herald*, December 17, 1876, December 18, 1876; *New York Times*, March 3, 1883; *Jersey Journal*, January 20, 1885; *Duluth News Times*, September 24, 1903.

16. Princeton University Class of 1862 Alumni Files, Box 121, Department of Rare Books and Special Collections, Princeton University Library; Presbrey and Moffat, *Athletics at Princeton*, 67.

17. *New York Clipper*, June 4, 1864; Presbrey and Moffat, *Athletics at Princeton*, 70–75; Princeton University, Class of 1866 Alumni Files, Box 127; *Princeton Alumni Weekly*, Vol. XVI, No. 34; *Philadelphia Inquirer*, May 25, 1919.

18. *Trenton Evening Times*, May 4, 1929; Presbrey and Moffat, *Athletics at Princeton*, 67; Princeton University Class of 1862 Alumni Files, Box 121, Department of Rare Books and Special Collections, Princeton University; Henry S. Butler to Joseph Munn, March 22, 1865, Princeton University Class Records, Box 6, 1862–66, Department of Rare Books and Special Collections, Princeton University.

19. Presbrey and Moffat, *Athletics at Princeton*, 70–75; *New York Clip-*

per, June 4, 1864; Princeton University Class of 1864 Alumni Files, Box 125 — William Kelly to J.L. Collins, January 20, 1917, Department of Rare Books and Special Collections, Princeton University; Wright, *The National Association of Base Ball Players, 1857–1870,* 88, 102; *New York Sunday Mercury,* September 29, 1862.

20. *Princeton Seminary Bulletin,* Vol. VIII, No. 3, November 1914; *Trenton Evening Times,* April 11, 1895; Princeton University Class of 1862 Alumni Files, Box 122, Department of Rare Books and Special Collections, Princeton University; *New York Clipper,* August 21, 1858.

21. Princeton University Class of 1862 Alumni Files, Box 122, Department of Rare Books and Special Collections, Princeton University; Presbrey and Moffat, *Athletics at Princeton,* 67.

22. Princeton University Class of 1862 Alumni Files, Box 120, Department of Rare Books and Special Collections, Princeton University; Presbrey and Moffat, *Athletics at Princeton,* 67.

23. Presbrey and Moffat, *Athletics at Princeton,* 70–75; Princeton University Class of 1865 Alumni Files, Box 126, Department of Rare Books and Special Collections, Princeton University.

24. Princeton University Class of 1862 Alumni Files, Box 122, Department of Rare Books and Special Collections, Princeton University; Presbrey and Moffat, *Athletics at Princeton,* 67.

25. Presbrey and Moffat, *Athletics at Princeton,* 70–75; Princeton Class of 1866 Alumni Files, Box 128, Department of Rare Books and Special Collections, Princeton University; *New York Sunday Mercury,* September 29, 1862; *Princeton Alumni Weekly,* Vol. XVI, No. 34.

26. Princeton University Class of 1862 Alumni Files, Box 122, Department of Rare Books and Special Collections, Princeton University; Presbrey and Moffat, *Athletics at Princeton,* 67.

Bibliography

Books
Kirsch, George. *Baseball in Blue and Gray: The National Pastime During the Civil War.* Princeton, N.J.: Princeton University Press, 2003.

Presbrey, Frank, and James Hugh Moffat. *Athletics at Princeton, A History.* New York: Frank Presbrey Company, 1901.
Wright, Marshall D. *The National Association of Base Ball Players, 1857–1870.* Jefferson, N.C.: McFarland, 2000.

Periodicals
"Death of Dr. L. W. Mudge." *Princeton Seminary Bulletin,* Volume VIII, Number 3, November 1914.
Herring, Donald Grant. "The Pioneer of Curved Pitching Comes Back." *Princeton Alumni Weekly,* Volume 16, No. 34.
P. B. "Nassau vs. Star" — The Trip of Our Nine." *Nassau Literary Magazine,* March 1863.

Newspapers
Brooklyn Daily Eagle
Duluth News Times
Elkhart Daily Review
Jersey Journal
New York Clipper
New York Herald
New York Sunday Mercury
New York Times
Trenton Evening Times

Other Sources
Princeton University Alumni Records, Princeton Archives, Princeton University
Princeton University Class Records, 1862–66, Princeton Archives, Princeton University.
http://www.princeton.edu~mudd/databases/alumni.html
http://www.Princeton.edu/mudd/news/faq/topics/tigers:shtml

❖ *Eureka Base Ball Club of Newark* ❖
(John G. Zinn)

CLUB HISTORY

During the winter of 1859–60, a group of young men formed the Eureka Base Ball Club of Newark. That the Eureka Club had high goals was clear early on when its formation was followed by application for membership in the National Association of Base Ball Players. A similar application was made by the more senior Newark Base Ball Club, giving New Jersey's largest city two clubs in the quasi-national organization.[1]

While no records survive regarding the number of founding members, 19 different young Newarkers took the field for the Eureka Club at least once during the 1860 season. Roughly one-third of that group had been members of the Washington Base Ball Club the prior year, including R. Heber Breintnall and Charles Thomas, who played for the Eureka Club throughout the club's existence.[2] It seems clear that the new club was an enthusiastic group of young men who wanted to test their abilities against the strongest adversaries in the region.

The original Eurekas included 11 who played in at least half of the 1860 matches and/or played an active part in the club's future. With one exception, all were under 20, with Henry Northrop, Breintnall, and Albert Littlewood the youngest at 16. The senior citizen was Ichabod Dawson (28), who played only one season for the first nine, but remained involved in leadership positions with both the Eurekas and the NABBP. In addition to being young, the Eurekas did not have a lot of work-related responsibilities since only three of them listed occupations on the 1860 census. Littlewood was an English immigrant, but the rest were born in the United States, mostly in New Jersey. More than half of the members were living in households with servants, indicating they came from the upper levels of Newark society. The comfortable financial positions of their families came from manufacturing professions and the law, but also included a portrait painter. Social standing came from Edward R. Pennington, who was descended from two New Jersey governors and one of Newark's founding families.[3]

Match games in New Jersey during this period did not typically begin until June, and the Eurekas wasted no time, starting their inaugural season on June 7, 1860. The first match was played against the Hamilton Club of Jersey City at the Eureka Club's grounds on Railroad Avenue, a "short distance below the Chestnut Street Depot." It was to be the first of at least four different home grounds occupied by the club. Perhaps not surprisingly, the Eurekas lost their initial match, 35–18, as well as their next two matches, to the Harlem (New York) and Union (Elizabeth, New Jersey) clubs. On August 3, 1860, however, the club broke through with its first win, a 34–18 road victory over the Harlem Club. Not only was it the Eureka Club's initial win, it was the first 1860 triumph for any Newark club and the first victory ever for a New Jersey club over a NABBP club from outside of the state. Reports of "brilliant fielding and successful batting" augured well for the club's long-term future.[4]

After their 0–3 start, the Eureka Club went 4–3–1 for an inaugural season's overall record of 4–6–1. Highlights included a victory over the Enterprise Club of Brooklyn and wins over two intra-city rivals, the more experienced Adriatic and Newark clubs. The victory over the Enterprise Club earned the Eurekas high praise from both the *New York Times* and the *Brooklyn Daily Eagle*. Clearly the newcomers were off to a good start and looked forward to the 1861 season.[5]

Although members of the Eureka Club and their fellow New Jersey ballists may have been optimistic about the future, they also had to be aware of the looming threat of the Civil War. Added emphasis was provided when president-elect Abraham Lincoln stopped briefly in Newark on the way to his inauguration. Even so, the outbreak of war shortly thereafter had only a limited impact on the club's 1861 season, which saw the Eurekas go 6–2, again defeating both the Newark and Adriatic clubs. The victories also included an easy triumph over the Irvington Club, a far cry from what would occur later in the decade. Two new members, Stephen Plum and Fred Callaway, who would become mainstays of the club, saw their first game action in 1861. Both had backgrounds similar to their teammates, with Plum coming from a very wealthy family and being descended from another of the city's founders. Further evidence of the Eureka Club's dominance of Newark baseball became clear in October when an "all Newark nine" was chosen to play a similar elite group from New York City. Six of the first nine were Eurekas, and at least two more were on the second nine.[6]

For the 1862 season, the Eureka Club changed grounds, renting the facilities of the Newark Club at High and Court streets. They did not have much chance to use the new site, however, as the war limited the Eurekas to only three games in 1862 and five in 1863. By September of 1862, the *Newark Daily Advertiser* was lamenting that the Eureka and Newark clubs had "almost entirely suspended play" due to the number of players serving in the military. Slight as their usage was, the leasing of the Newark Club's grounds apparently didn't work out, and the Eurekas moved to the old Newark Cricket Club grounds on Railroad Avenue for the 1863 season. The move included plans to build dressing rooms, permanent seats, and other facilities, but for some reason, possibly the war, this never happened. Even with the limited 1863 schedule, the Eurekas managed a winning season (3–2). They lost to the Atlantics of Brooklyn and the Mutuals, but defeated two Philadelphia opponents, and, once again, the Newark Club.[7]

The Eureka Club's visit to Philadelphia in September of 1863 suggests a greater insulation or separation from the Civil War than claimed by the *Daily Advertiser*. Throughout the summer of 1863 the threat of the draft led to intensive efforts in Newark (including the payment of large cash bonuses) to recruit volunteers for the 33rd New Jersey which left Newark on September 9, 1863. At almost the exact same time, members of the Eureka Club of prime military age were making a trip to Philadelphia to play baseball. The fact that no member of the Eurekas was enticed by cash bonuses close to a working man's annual income supports the notion of the players' relatively secure financial status.[8]

While the war would not end for another year, the Eurekas began to return to pre-war levels of activity in 1864. In early February the club hosted their first annual dinner at the Park House featuring a display of 30 balls won in matches. There were two significant additions to the 1864 roster, one home grown with the other being the first player to join the Eureka Club from outside of New Jersey. Everett Mills (who would go on to play professionally) came over from the Newark Club and Theodore Bomeisler (who would become a professional umpire) came all the way from the Olympic Club of Philadelphia. No explanation of Bomeisler's move survives, but it is reasonable to believe it was facilitated by contact during the Eureka Club's 1863 visit to Philadelphia. The grounds on Railroad Avenue had not worked out as the club was back on High Street and ultimately completed a 5–4 season. This may not have been an ideal facility since the *New York Clipper* commented that "the bound [bounce] being very uncertain in all parts of the field," the players had little alternative, but to play "the fly game." Although the Eurekas finished just over .500, three of the losses came at the hands of the Atlantics of Brooklyn and Mutuals of New York, who had a combined 1864 record of 40–3–1.[9]

The spring of 1865 saw the end of the war and the beginning of the Eureka Club's best season. Symbolic of the post-war expansion of baseball, the club opened their own new grounds. Located at the corner of Ferry and Adams streets in what is now called the "Ironbound" section of Newark, the new facilities were inaugurated in fine fashion on June 12 when the Eureka Club hosted the Athletics of Philadelphia. While the visitors prevailed 12–9, the Eurekas finished the 1865 season with a 10–5 record. As in 1864, their performance is even more impressive given the level of competition, since the five losses were to three clubs that had a combined record of 45–7. The season also saw the Eurekas become a truly regional club, playing only four of their 15 contests against New Jersey opponents. In addition to playing clubs from New York, Brooklyn, and Philadelphia, the Newarkers journeyed to southern New England, where they defeated the Charter Oak Club of Hartford.[10]

Of special note were the two 1865 matches with the Atlantic Club of Brooklyn, who would finish the season with a perfect 18–0 record. On August 18, the Atlantics came to Newark for a match with the Eurekas before a crowd estimated at 5,000. The onlookers must have been roaring when their local heroes jumped out to a 9–1 second inning lead. The Atlantics, however, were too experienced to be discouraged by a bad start and rallied for a 21–15 lead going to the bottom of the ninth. The Eurekas were not done, cutting the margin to one run with one out, making it seem that "all Newark was wild." Unfortunately, it was not to be as the Atlantics got the last two outs to hold on for a hard-fought victory.[11]

A return match at Brooklyn's Capitoline Grounds took place on August 31 before a crowd also estimated at 5,000. Although the *Brooklyn Daily Eagle* claimed the Atlantics were "jaded out" from their recent trip to Washington, they still took a 10–1 first inning lead. The advantage lasted only an inning when the Eurekas tied the contest at 10 in the 2nd, but then fell behind, 27–23, with seven innings complete. Another rally generated a 37–34 lead heading to the ninth, but once again they came away empty as the Atlantic scored four times for a 38–37 win. As disappointing as this had to be, the Eureka Club was not demoralized, closing the season with seven straight wins. One of the club's strengths was its fielding, evidenced by 17 fly put outs in a low-scoring 6–5 victory over the Active Club of New York. The game was reported to be the shortest of the 1865 season, taking only one hour and forty-five minutes, far shorter than the norm for the era.[12]

After the successes of 1865, the Eureka Club and its supporters were probably optimistic about the future, but their best days were behind them. Symbolic of the impatience to start the season was a January 23 game played on ice with the Active Club of Newark "between the bridges" over the Passaic River. Osborne and Terrill had joined the Eurekas from the Newark Club, no doubt due to a desire to be part of a more successful club. On the other hand, the addition from Philadelphia of pitcher Harry Lex, formerly of the Keystone Club, was most likely a sign of the growing professionalism that would contribute to the death of the Eureka Club. Other negative signs included newspaper criticism of a fall-off in the play of the first nine, comments about the need for "proper management," and prominent players being absent from matches. Still on a day when they were reportedly without four members of their first nine, the Eurekas finally defeated the Atlantics, 36–10. Three of the four were absent due to being "detained by business." Missing "one of the most important base ball

matches of the season" for business reasons may offer a clue as to how increased personal responsibilities also contributed to the death of the Eureka Club. As the season continued, the *Newark Evening Courier* criticized the club's "chronic affection [*sic*]" of missing players. Controversy also arose when a Morris County, New Jersey, club was accused of improperly adding players from the Eurekas. In addition, the Newarkers were accused of being unwilling to compete in a state tournament in Newton. In spite of all these storm clouds, the Eureka Club completed a successful season, finishing 9–7 primarily against rivals from Brooklyn, Philadelphia, and New York City.[13]

If the Eurekas were aware that their days were numbered, it certainly wasn't indicated by their off-season activities, including incorporation and making plans to buy or lease an enclosed ground. It was announced that practice rules for the first nine would be "stringent and rigidly enforced," showing that the club intended to address the attendance issue. Furthermore, new uniforms had been selected, hardly a sign of a club in decline. Major roster changes included the addition of Albert Beans from the Active Club of Newark and another import, catcher Patsy Dockney.[14]

Historically, the Eureka Club had dominated its New Jersey rivals, but that changed in 1867. The resurgent Irvington Club, soon to contribute two of its players to the famed Red Stockings of Cincinnati, beat the Eurekas twice. Those losses cost the Newarkers their seventh consecutive winning season as they finished at 6–8. No contests were played with Philadelphia opponents, but the Eurekas did make the arduous journey to Lansingburgh, New York, to play the Union Club (the future Troy Haymakers). Fan interest in Newark was certainly not lacking since a crowd reminiscent of those looking for news of Civil War battles gathered outside the city's telegraph office waiting in vain for the final score. When the news did come the following day, it wasn't good as the Eurekas had suffered a 42–21 defeat. About a week later, the Eureka Club hosted and defeated the Charter Oak Club of Hartford, followed by a tour of the city and a lavish banquet at the Park House.[15]

The next day the *Newark Evening Courier* bemoaned the fact that the Eureka Club did not have the funds to regularly host opponents in this manner. This was attributed to the lack of an enclosed ground, which prevented the club from charging admission. The article stressed the economic benefits the Eureka Club brought to the city and suggested that citizens invest in the newly formed joint stock company. According to the paper, the additional funds could be used to support club social events and toward the high cost of land which was apparently thwarting the acquisition of an enclosed ground. Although all of this was probably accurate, one has to wonder if the unspoken financial issue was the cost of paying players, especially the Philadelphia imports. Player attendance also continued to be a problem in 1867 as evidenced by a comment in the *Clipper* that at a September 28 match, the Eurekas were "short handed as usual." This deteriorated to the point that the Eurekas had to "borrow" three players for their October 3rd game against the Mutuals.[16]

Few details were made public, but 1867 had clearly not been a positive experience for the Eurekas. In March of 1868, the *Daily Advertiser* worried that betting, the negative influence of "roughs" at games and other abuses could bring baseball down to the level of boxing and cock fighting. In response to these issues the newspaper reported that the "gentlemanly fellows" of the Eureka Club were "wisely returning to the old Eureka stock." Specifically, Philadelphia imports Harry Lex and Patsy Dockney had moved on to Indianapolis and Cincinnati, respectively. Simultaneously, Beans and Mills joined the Irvingtons. In the midst of this, the *Evening Courier* reported the Eureka would play only amateur matches in 1868 and would have no professionals on the first nine. The *New York Clipper* confirmed the changes, which were attributed to the club's "having tried the 'professional' system one season and becoming disgusted with it." Since construction of some kind was underway on their old field, the Eureka Club arranged to play their matches at the New Jersey Agricultural Society property at Waverly on the Newark/Elizabeth border.[17]

In spite of their stated intention to play only amateur matches in 1868, the Eurekas opened the season against their old rivals, the Atlantics of Brooklyn, who were not amateurs in any sense of the word. This was supposedly done as a favor to the Atlantic, who were preparing for a tour. Exactly how the "professionals" benefited from thrashing the Eurekas, 46–8, remains to be seen, but it clearly illustrated the decline in the competitive balance between the two clubs. The situation was once again not helped by the absence of some of the Eureka Club's best players. The *Clipper* commented on the lack of familiar names in the lineup, suggesting that the "others have evidently become disgusted with the huckstering now going on among clubs and players." As a result the former regulars had apparently "given up a pastime which is not as it used to was [sic]." Player attendance problems continued throughout a limited four-game schedule that saw the club finish at 2–2. Interestingly, the two 1868 victories were over the Champion Club of Jersey City and the Resolute Club of Elizabeth, two of the clubs vying to replace the Eurekas as the standard-bearer for New Jersey. Things finally hit rock bottom when not a single member showed up for a scheduled game against the Active Club of Brooklyn. No record of other games survives, and as the 1869 season opened, it was announced that the Eureka Club would play only practice games. One such contest was reported in the press with a number of the old standbys on hand, but no records of any other matches have been found. Nor has any documented evidence of a formal decision to disband the club been discovered, but by June of 1870, the *Newark Evening Courier* referred to "the demise of the Eureka Club."[18]

What happened to the Eureka Club? It was most likely a combination of factors. The financial issues raised in 1867 appear to be evidence of the difficulty the club had competing for paid players with rivals in New York City, Brooklyn, and Philadelphia. In addition, the original well-to-do members of the Eureka Club may have had difficulty relating to paid players with a working-class background. That is the sense one gets from the newspaper accounts of early 1868. In any event, it would have been difficult to continue as a top amateur club. The veteran players were now mostly in their late twenties with greater personal and professional responsibilities. Younger members who did want to continue were probably better advised to join the Amateur and Active clubs of Newark.

Despite their decline and death, the Eurekas were an important part of baseball's amateur era, both at the state and regional level, compiling an overall 47–37–1 record. After going only 2–3–1 against New Jersey clubs in their first season, the club won 14 straight matches from state rivals over a seven-year period. While the streak ended with two losses to the Irvington Club in 1867, the Eureka Club still compiled an overall 20–5–1 record against New Jersey clubs. Although the Irvington Club enjoyed a shorter period of arguably greater success, the Eureka Club was clearly the dominant New Jersey nine. The Eurekas were not, however, satisfied with being the best club in their home state. They were willing and able to take on all comers between Connecticut and Philadelphia. Against New York City opponents, the Newarkers finished over .500 with an 18–15 mark and finished at .500 (3–3) in six matches against Philadelphia clubs.

The best baseball of the era, however, was played not in New York City or Philadelphia, but rather in the then independent city of Brooklyn. Again, the Eurekas did not duck anyone, but were able to win only three out of 16 contests against clubs from the City of Churches. The most noteworthy of the Brooklyn clubs was the Atlantics; the Eurekas took them on nine times, but managed only one win. However, this was hardly unusual since the Brooklyn juggernaut rolled up a 148–25–4 total record over the same period. In fact, of the Eureka Club's 37 total match-game losses, 40 percent came against two opponents, the Atlantics and the Mutuals of New York. Like the Atlantics, the Mutuals were a dominant force with an overall record of 123–44–3 during the same period. Taking those results out of the equation, the Eurekas were an impressive 44–22–1 over their nine seasons, dominating play in New Jersey and more than holding their own outside of the state.

CLUB MEMBERS

Theodore Bomeisler: Born on December 9, 1836, in St. Louis, to a prominent Jewish family, Bomeisler joined the Eurekas for the 1864 season from Philadelphia and played second base, shortstop and the outfield through 1866. He was elected vice president and director for the latter season. After his playing career was over, he went on to umpire 15 professional games in the National Association between 1871 and 1875. An 1873 game account in *The Spirit of the Times* implied he had taken money from gamblers in a previous contest. It is noteworthy that his former Eureka teammate, Everett Mills, played in at least one 1873 game umpired by Bomeisler. After leaving baseball, he lived in East Orange, New Jersey, and was reportedly very active in Democratic politics. Bomeisler died on November 16, 1891, and is buried in East Orange.[19]

R. Heber Breintnall: Born on August 18, 1843, in Philadelphia. Breintnall joined the Eureka Club at the age of 16 in the club's inaugural season and played in at least one game in each of the club's nine seasons, in addition to serving as an officer and director. Although Breintnall's primary position was catcher, he also played second and third base. During the Civil War, he served with the New Jersey militia in the summer of 1863 and with the 39th New Jersey in 1865. Breintnall remained in the reserves immediately after the war, beginning a career in the New Jersey National Guard that lasted through at least 1910. With the rest of the 1st New Jersey Regiment, he volunteered for service in the Spanish American War. The former Eureka Club member became the Adjutant General of New Jersey (the state's top National Guard position) in 1902. He was legislatively forced to retire in 1905, but subsequent litigation returned him to office. Breintnall was also active in veteran's affairs, including membership in Phil Kearny Post 1 of the GAR. He died on July 3, 1925, and is buried in Newark's Mt. Pleasant Cemetery. Sadly, none of his obituaries make reference to his play for the Eureka Club.[20]

Henry Burroughs: Born in Newark in 1845, Burroughs played the infield and outfield for the Eureka Club during the 1862 and 1864 seasons. The young Newarker then headed west to Detroit, where he became captain of the Detroit Base Ball Club and probably Michigan's first paid player. Burroughs continued to play in Michigan through 1866, returning to the Eurekas for the 1867 season. He was back in Michigan in 1868, returning to the East after that season. Burroughs went on to play professionally for the Washington Olympics in 1871 and '72, competing in 14 games. He worked as a clerk in the tax office in Newark and in the Treasury Department in the nation's capital, most likely during his stint with the Olympics. Tragically, he died of consumption (tuberculosis) on March 31, 1878, at the age of 33. The report of his death in the *Newark Daily Advertiser* mentions his role with the Eureka Club.[21]

Frederick C. Callaway: Fred Callaway was born in 1842 in New Jersey. After missing the Eureka Club's inaugural season, he joined the first nine in 1861 and played in at least one game each year through 1867. Primarily the club's left fielder, he also served as an officer and director. An 1868 game was postponed and apparently cancelled due to his wife's death. In 1870, Callaway was living with his young son, suggesting his wife may have died in childbirth. He followed his father into the sash and blind manufacturing business, which was operating from four locations by 1891. Callaway subsequently re-married and died sometime in 1919.[22]

John W. Collins: Born in New Jersey in 1843, Collins was a founding member of the Eureka Club. He played four other seasons with the club, primarily as an outfielder—in 1860 his play in center field was praised by the *New York Times*. Of all the Eurekas, Collins had the most extensive Civil War experience, serving in the 2nd New Jersey from 1861 through June of 1864, thereby missing the entire 1862 and 1863 seasons. His name appears in box scores of games played by New Jersey regiments in Virginia late in 1861. Following the war, he went into the real estate business with his father and died on February 3, 1902.[23]

Ichabod Dawson: Born in 1832 in New York, Dawson was a founding member of the Eureka Club, but played only one season. However, he continued in club leadership positions, serving as president at least three times and also as vice president of the National Association of Base Ball Players. Dawson came from a very wealthy Newark family in the patent leather business, and formed his own patent leather manufacturing business, I.W. Dawson & Co. By 1870, he owned almost $40,000 in total assets. Dawson died sometime between 1900 and 1903.[24]

Charles W. Faitoute: Born in New Jersey in 1843, Faitoute pitched for the Eurekas from 1862 to 1863, and then again during the 1865 and 1866 seasons. In 1867, he pitched for the Active Club of Newark, before returning to the Eurekas in 1868 after the departure of Harry Lex. After the demise of the Eurekas, Faitoute returned to the Active Club. Like other members of the Eureka Club, Faitoute came from a family with deep roots in New Jersey history. His great-grandfather served in the American Revolution, entitling Faitoute to membership in the Sons of the American Revolution. Although Faitoute was living in Newark in 1860, by 1870 he was living with his parents on a farm in Union County while employed in a hat shop. He apparently followed in his father's footsteps as subsequent census returns show him as a farm owner, living in Summit, New Jersey. The old ball player died sometime between 1920 and 1930. Faitoute apparently had a distinctive delivery which was found to be funny by fans, but less so by opposing batters. His reputation survived long after his playing career, as in 1957 *Baseball Digest* commented on his unusual delivery, which made it look as if he was "winding up a clock."[25]

James Linen: Born on June 23, 1840, in what is now Lackawanna, Pennsylvania, James Alexander Linen was a member of the Eurekas for their first four seasons both as a player and club officer. Linen was the club's first pitcher and in 1860 his play was highly praised by the *New York Times* on two separate occasions. He volunteered for the Union Army, serving as an officer with the 26th New Jersey from September 1862 to June 1863. After leaving the 26th New Jersey, Linen apparently stayed in the army, joining the Quartermaster Department in Kentucky. After his military service, Linen returned to his native Pennsylvania to work as a bank teller in the First National Bank of Scranton. He stayed with the bank for almost 50 years, serving as president from 1891–1913 and then chairman of the board. Linen also continued his baseball career in Scranton, helping in 1865 to found the Wyoming Base Ball Club, the city's first prominent nine. He was captain and pitcher in both 1867 and 1868. Linen died in Scranton on May 29, 1918. His name was passed along for several generations and his grandson, James Alexander Linen III, was the publisher of *Time* in the 1950s.[26]

Albert Littlewood: Born in England in 1841, Littlewood was apparently the only member of the original Eurekas born outside of the United States. Like Breintnall and Charles Thomas, he played in at least one game in each of the club's nine seasons, primarily in the outfield. Littlewood was a jeweler and had died by 1900.[27]

Everett Mills: Born in Newark on January 20, 1845, Mills moved to the Eurekas from the Newark Club for the 1864 season. He subsequently left for the Irvington Club after the 1867 season. Mills began his career with the Eurekas at third base, but then switched to first for the rest of his tenure, probably due to his 6'1" height. After his time with the Irvington Club, Mills played for the New York Mutuals in 1869 and 1870. He then played professional baseball with the Washington Olympics, the Baltimore Canaries, and the Hartford Dark Blues from 1871 to 1876. In 1876, Everett played in the inaugural season of the National League, hitting .260 with Hartford. Mills, who continued to play first base, had a lifetime professional batting average of .289. When his baseball career was over, Mills was appointed Sergeant at Arms at the quarter sessions court in Newark, a position he held until his death on June 22, 1908. His obituary in the *Newark Evening News* mentions his baseball career, but incorrectly says that he was a member of the Cincinnati Red Stockings. There was no mention of his play for the Eurekas or any New Jersey club.[28]

Henry D. Northrop: Born in 1844 in New York City, along with Breintnall and Littlewood, Northrop was one of the three youngest of the founding members of the club. Other than 1866, Northrop appears to have played in at least one match in every season also serving as vice president in 1864. He was a first baseman until Mills joined the club, leading Northrop to switch to the outfield. His play was praised by the *New York Times*, the *New York Herald*, and the *Brooklyn Daily Eagle* on three different occasions. Although one of the youngest of the club founders, Northrop was one of the few with an occupation listed on the 1860 census — clerk. Like many of his teammates, he worked in the financial field, both in banking and in municipal government. One of the low points of his banking career had to be presiding over the voluntary liquidation of a New York bank in 1894. Northrop was also well known in musical circles, serving at one time as Vice President of the Orpheus Club of Newark — a glee club that still exists. Northrop died on June 30, 1926. According to his

obituary in the *Newark Evening News*, Northrop was a member of the Lincoln Post of the G.A.R. because of his service with the 22nd New York State Militia. The obituary mentions his role with the Eurekas and stated that he was the last surviving member of the club.[29]

Edward Riggs Pennington: Born on February 28, 1841, in Newark, Pennington was the son and grandson of governors of New Jersey, as well as a descendent of one of Newark's founding families. Also a founder of the Eureka Club, he played for the club in 1860 and 1861 before missing the 1862 season due to Civil War service as a Captain in the 12th Regiment of the Regular Army. After returning to Newark at the end of 1862, Pennington played with the Eureka Club through the 1865 season, also serving as president and director during that period. Exclusively a second baseman, Pennington's play was praised by the *New York Times* and *Brooklyn Daily Eagle*. A lawyer by profession, he was elected a Newark City Alderman as well as a State Assemblyman, but lost an election for Essex County Register. In addition to his distinguished New Jersey heritage, Pennington was a member of the New Jersey Chapter of the Society of Cincinnatus, open only to those descended in the male line from Revolutionary War officers. He died suddenly and tragically on June 14, 1884, after a brief illness, apparently contracted at the 1884 Republican Convention in Chicago.[30]

Stephen Plum: Born on November 12, 1842, in Newark, like his teammate Edward Pennington, Plum was also a descendent of an original settler of Newark. He joined the Eureka Club in 1862 and was a member of the first nine through 1865, playing both third base and the outfield. Plum's father was extremely wealthy, leaving a fortune estimated at between $1.5–$2 million when he died in 1890. Plum was working as a bank clerk in 1870, but by 1900 his occupation was simply listed as "capitalist." He was reportedly "one of the most philanthropic citizens" of Newark, active in both the Peddie Memorial Baptist Church and the New Jersey Historical Society. He died on May 31, 1906.[31]

Charles Thomas: Born on October 9, 1841, in Newark, Thomas was the third founding member of the Eureka Club to play in at least one game in each of the club's nine seasons. A shortstop who also did some pitching, Thomas was the club's vice president during its final season in 1868. A highly regarded shortstop, he was profiled in *Frank Leslie's Weekly Newspaper* in 1866, which favorably compared his fielding and batting to the top shortstops of the era. Thomas was further described as "ever gentlemanly in word and action." After working for a Newark bank from 1859 to 1865, Charles Thomas joined a New York bank that ultimately became part of Chemical National Bank. His New York banking career lasted some 50 years until his retirement in 1915. He obviously did well financially, owning some $30,000 in assets in 1870 and living in a household with one servant. Thomas died on March 26, 1926, leaving Henry Northrop as the last of the Eurekas.[32]

Other Club Members: Osborne, Isaac "Joe" Terrill.

Notes

1. *Newark Daily Advertiser*, February 8, 1860; *New York Herald*, March 18, 1860.

2. *Newark Daily Advertiser*, September 6, 1859.

3. 1860 Census; *Newark Daily Advertiser*, December 19, 1860, November 14, 1861, December 11, 1862, December 23, 1862, December 15, 1864, *Newark Morning Register*, June 16, 1884; *Harper's New Monthly Magazine*, Vol. LIII, June–November 1876, 663.

4. *Newark Daily Advertiser*, June 8, 1860, June 30, 1860, July 20, 1860, August 4, 1860; *New York Times*, August 4, 1860.

5. *Newark Daily Advertiser*, August 23, 28, 1860, September 27, 1860; *Brooklyn Daily Eagle*, August 28, 1860; *New York Times* August 28, 1860.

6. *Newark Daily Advertiser*, June 5, 1861, August 9, 1861, September 5, 1861, September 27, 1861, October 7, 1861; 1860 Census; *New York Times*, April 23, 1890; *Biographical and Genealogical History of the City of Newark and Essex County, New Jersey* (New York: Lewis Historical Publishing Company, 1898).

7. *Newark Daily Advertiser*, September 26, 1862, January 21, 1863; Charles Eckhardt and Robert MacAvoy, *Our Brothers Gone Before*, 2 vols., (Hightstown, N.J.: Longstreet House, 2006), www.ancestry.com, Linen, Pennington, Northrop and Collins were all in the Army at this time. After 1862, R. Heber Breintnall served two tours, one with the New Jersey militia during the summer of 1863 and at the very end of the war with the 39th New Jersey.

8. John Zinn, *The Mutinous Regiment: The Thirty-third New Jersey in the Civil War* (Jefferson, N.C.: McFarland, 2005), 5–19; *Newark Daily Advertiser*, September 15, 17, 18 and 21, 1863.

9. *Newark Daily Advertiser*, February 3, 1864, June 16, 1864, July 5, 1864; *Brooklyn Daily Eagle*, September 15, 1864; Marshall D. Wright, *The National Association of Base Ball Players, 1857–1870* (Jefferson, N.C,: McFarland, 2000), 85, *New York Clipper*, November 1, 1862, July 16, 1864.

10. *Newark Daily Advertiser*, June 10, June 13, October 14, 1865; Wright, *The National Association of Base Ball Players*, 98–99, 101.

11. *Newark Daily Advertiser*, August 19, 1865; *Brooklyn Daily Eagle*, August 19, 1865.

12. *Newark Daily Advertiser*, September 1, 1865; *Brooklyn Daily Eagle*, September 1, 1865; *New York Clipper*, October 28, 1865.

13. *Newark Daily Advertiser*, January 24, March 26, June 28, August 15, 1866; *Newark Evening Courier*, June 29, July 6, July 28, August 22, September 8, 1866, October 1, 1866; *New York Clipper*, September 22, 1866; *New Jersey Herald and Democrat*, September 13, 1866.

14. *Newark Daily Advertiser*, February 11, June 17, 18 and 24, 1867; *Newark Evening Courier*, April 8, May 6, and July 9, 1867.

15. *New York Times* May 17, 1867; *Newark Daily Advertiser*, August 7, 15, 1867.

16. *Newark Evening Courier*, August 16, September 11 and October 3, 1867; *New York Clipper*, October 5, 1867; *Newark Daily Advertiser*, September 11, 1967.

17. *Newark Daily Advertiser*, March 25, April 18, May 5, 1868; the paper linked Beans' departure with that of Lex and Dockney, suggesting he may have been part of the problem in 1867. *Newark Evening Courier*, March 25, 1868; *New York Clipper*, April 11, 1868.

18. *Newark Daily Advertiser*, May 29, June 5, June 23, 1868, May 19, 1869; *Newark Evening Courier*, May 19, 1869, June 7, 1870; *Brooklyn Daily Eagle*, July 17, 1868; *New York Clipper*, June 6, 1868.

19. Bomeisler family tree; 1891 passport application; *The Spirit of the Times*, June 7, 1873, www.retrosheet.org; *New York Times*, November 18, 1891.

20. www.virtualnewarknj.com; *New York Times*, March 5, 1890, September 26, 1902, March 5, 1905, January 7, 1910; John Urquhart, *A History of the City of Newark* (New York: Leslie Historical Publishing, 1913), 834.

21. www.retrosheet.org; *Newark Daily Advertiser*, April 1, 1878; Peter Morris, *Baseball Fever: Early Baseball in Michigan* (Ann Arbor: University of Michigan Press, 2003), 91–92, 103, 113, 214.

22. U.S. Census 1860, 1870, 1880, 1900; Newark Directory 1891; *Newark Daily Advertiser*, September 21, 1868.

23. *Newark Daily Advertiser*, November 11, 21, December 4, 1861; U. S. Census, 1860, 1870, 1900; Newark Directory 1891; *New York Times*, August 4, 1860; Eckhardt and MacAvoy, *Our Brothers Gone Before*.

24. Newark Directory 1890–91; U. S. Census 1860, 1870, 1880; Urquart, *History of the City of Newark*, 137.

25. U.S. Census, 1860, 1870, 1880, 1900, 1910, 1920; "Official Bulletin of the National Society of the Sons of the American Revolution," Vol. I, No. 1, June 1916; *Newark Evening Courier*, May 31, 1867, July 26, 1867; *Baseball Digest*, January 1957.

26. U.S. Census 1860; *New York Times*, August 4, August 28, 1860; www.ancestry.com; *Newark Daily Mercury*, July 8, 1863; Col. George L. Hitchcock, *History of Scranton and Its People* (New York: Lewis Historical Publishing Company, 1914), 411, Nicholas E. Petula, *A History of Scranton Professional Baseball, 1865–1913*; "Old-Time Local Base Ball Players," *Scranton Tribune*, May 26, 1897, 2.

27. U.S. Census, 1870, 1880, 1900.

28. www.retrosheet.org; U.S. Census, 1860, 1870, 1880, 1900; *Newark Evening News*, June 22, 1908; Wright, *The National Association of Base Ball Players*, 247, 290.

29. U. S. Census, 1860, 1870, 1880, 1900, 1910, 1920; *New York Times*, August 4, 1860, July 1, 1926; *New York Herald*, June 21, 1863; *Brooklyn Daily Eagle*, August 28, 1860; *Newark Evening News*, July 1, 1926; *New York Times*, July 23, 1894; www.orpheusnewark.org.

30. U. S. Census, 1860, 1870, 1880; *New York Times*, July 6, 1880; *Newark Evening News*, June 16, 1884; *Newark Morning Register*, June 16, 1884; www.ancestry.com.

31. U. S. Census, 1860, 1870, 1880, 1900; *New York Times*, April 23, 1890; "Proceedings of the New Jersey Historical Society," Third Series, No. 1, 1908, 27.

32. U. S. Census 1860, 1870, 1880, 1900, 1910, 1920, 1930; *Frank Leslie's Weekly Newspaper*, November 3, 1866; *Newark Evening News*, March 28, 29, 1926.

Bibliography

Books

Biographical and Genealogical History of Newark and Essex County, New Jersey. New York: Lewis Publishing Company, 1898.

Eckhardt, Charles, and Robert MacAvoy. *Our Brothers Gone Before*, 2 vols. Hightstown, N.J.: Longstreet House, 2006.

Hitchcock, George. *History of Scranton and Its People*. New York: Lewis Publishing Company, 1914.

Morris, Peter. *Baseball Fever: Early Baseball in Michigan*. Ann Arbor: University of Michigan Press, 2003.

Petula, Nicholas E. *A History of Scranton Professional Baseball, 1865–1953*. Scranton, PA: n.p, 1989.

Urquhart, John. *A History of the City of Newark*. New York: Lewis Historical Publishing Company, 1913.

Wright, Marshall D. *The National Association of Base Ball Players, 1857–1870*. Jefferson, N.C.: McFarland, 2000.

Zinn, John. *The Mutinous Regiment: The Thirty-third New Jersey in the Civil War*. Jefferson, N.C.: McFarland, 2005.

Newspapers

Brooklyn Daily Eagle
New Jersey Herald and Democrat
New York Clipper
New York Herald
New York Times
Newark Daily Advertiser
Newark Daily Mercury
Newark Evening Courier

Newark Evening News
Spirit of the Times
Periodicals
Baseball Digest
Frank Leslie's Weekly Newspaper
Harper's New Monthly Magazine, Vol. LIII, June–November 1876.
Official Bulletin of the National Society of the Sons of the American Revolution, Vol. XI, No. 1, June 1916.
Proceedings of The New Jersey Historical Society, Third Series, No. 1, 1908.

Other Sources
www.ancestry.com
www.orpheusnewark.org
www.retrosheet.org
U.S. Census 1860, 1870, 1880, 1900, 1910, 1920
www.virtualnewarknj.com

❖ *Irvington Base Ball Club* ❖
(John G. Zinn)

CLUB HISTORY

Early New Jersey baseball clubs frequently consisted of members of trade organizations, fire companies, or even the employees of a business. Many such clubs existed for a few years with little real impact either locally or nationally. The major exception was the Irvington Base Ball Club, which was formed in the early 1860s by the employees of the Belcher Rule Company. Irvington, formerly called Camptown, was then a small village bordering on the city of Newark. The Irvington Club or the Irvingtons, as they were often called, played at least one intraclub game in 1860 and were playing matches with other New Jersey clubs as early as 1861.[1]

By 1864, the Irvingtons had developed into a top junior club, winning a state junior championship match from the Champion Club of Jersey City. Junior clubs were supposed to consist of players aged 16 or younger, but these two clubs were apparently considered juniors because they were not members of the National Association of Base Ball Players (NABBP). In spite of this success, the Irvington Club might still have labored in relative obscurity, but their ultimate fate was quite different due an extraordinary series of events in the years immediately following the Civil War. An article in the June 23, 1866, issue of the *New York Clipper*, most likely by Henry Chadwick, reported that after winning the 1864 state junior championship, the best Irvington players moved to the Newark and Pioneer clubs for the 1865 season. However, by 1866 they had returned to an Irvington Club that was now a member of the NABBP.[2]

The *Clipper* story suggests the Irvington Club broke up for the 1865 season, and then reassembled in 1866. Further analysis suggests a more complicated story. The few surviving 1865 box scores for the Newark and Pioneer clubs confirm that most of the key members of the 1866–67 Irvingtons played at least once in 1865 for one of the two Newark clubs. What is not clear is how many of these players actually began their careers with the Irvington Junior Club. This is difficult to determine since only one box score for the latter club has been found, but certainly Alexander Bailey, Thomas Buckley, Billy

Lewis, and Mahlon Stockman played for the Newark Club before 1865. This suggests they may have only joined the Irvington Club after their time with the old-line Newark Club. In effect, the famous 1866–67 Irvingtons may have been a consolidation of players from several clubs, especially the Irvington Juniors and the Newark Club. This is significant because it suggests that like the Eureka, the Irvingtons were ballplayers who came together to compete at a high level. In other words, this was not a group of unknowns with little or no experience.[3]

That the Irvingtons were no novices was established beyond a doubt when they engineered a coup that secured the club a place in baseball history. Early in the 1866 season, representatives of the Irvington Club traveled to Brooklyn on one of the prominent Atlantic Club's practice days. Apparently knowing the Brooklyn club president was a "good natured" man who liked to help younger clubs, they appealed to his good nature. Claiming to be only "a mere country club," they asked the Atlantics to come to Irvington and "teach them a few points" in what would, no doubt, be an easy Brooklyn victory. So taken in were the Atlantics by this ploy, they made the journey without three of their regulars.[4]

Upon their arrival the Brooklynites, or at least the *Clipper* correspondent, were shocked to see some familiar faces formerly from the Newark Club. At the same time, the Atlantics were still the Atlantics and got off to an early lead. Although Irvington tallied six times in the third to take a 7–4 lead, Brooklyn rallied for 11 runs and a 15–9 advantage after five innings. At this point, the Irvingtons made a pitching change, inserting Alexander Bailey, the "renowned slow pitcher of the Jersey nine" (probably the Newark Club). He allowed only two more runs the rest of the way in a 23–17 Irvington victory that was as historic as it was unlikely.[5]

The defeat was the Atlantics' first since 1863, ending a three-year, 43-game winning streak. Proving the win was no fluke, the Irvingtons swept home-and-home matches from the Eckfords, the last club to beat the Atlantics. In their first year in the National Association of Base Ball Players, the Irvingtons went on to post a 10–6 record — not bad since four of their losses came at the hands of the Atlantics and the Athletics of Philadelphia, who had a combined 1866 record of 40–5. There were, however, some embarrassing moments along the way, including a 77–9 rout in Philadelphia at the hands of those same Athletics. In a classic understatement, the *Newark Evening Courier* found the score "slightly one sided." Also embarrassing was a 20–16 loss to the Olympic Club of Paterson, an opponent they had previously humiliated, 77–6.[6]

The Irvingtons had the opportunity to avenge the latter defeat in the first, and, perhaps only, New Jersey silver ball championship (a tournament or game played for a trophy in the form of a silver baseball). Scheduled in conjunction with the Sussex County Fair, the tournament offered separate competitions for local clubs, New Jersey clubs in the NABBP, and NABBP clubs from any state. Irvington played for both the state and "national" championships, defeating the Olympic Club of Paterson for the New Jersey title and an appropriate measure of revenge. In the other title match, the Irvingtons faced the Active Club of New York. Apparently there was a distinct lack of good feeling between the two clubs as the umpire was constantly resolving disputes. As the *Clipper* reporter (again probably Chadwick) euphemistically put it the clubs "did not manifest the best of feelings to each other." The hard feelings were probably somewhat due to Mahlon Stockman's presence in the Active Club's lineup. Stockman had somehow managed to play for both clubs in 1866, and Irvington protested to the NABBP, claiming he should not have been playing for the New York club. The protest was ultimately dismissed on a technicality because the New Jersey club failed to provide the Actives with a copy of the written protest.[7]

The match was close until the Actives, by "the sharpest piece of play we have seen for a long time past," killed off an eighth-inning Irvington rally. The New York club then broke the contest open with seven runs in the ninth. The bad feelings generated in the 19–10 Active triumph spilled over into the post-match ceremonies. After the Actives cheered their opponents, the Irvington players failed to return the compliment, walking off the field "like a party of beaten school boys." Critical comments like this regarding the Irvingtons were not uncommon but do not appear to be the whole story. Although such behavior obviously did not reflect well on the New Jersey nine, on at least three other occasions reporters commented favorably on the club's hospitality toward its opponents. This included the Irvingtons' treatment of the Eckford Club of Brooklyn on July 2, which one reporter said proved the Irvingtons "to be not only good ball players but gentlemen as well."[8]

Other negative comments about the Irvington Club included the difficulty of getting to their grounds and the quality of the field. Even the *Newark Evening Courier* joined the chorus, labeling the grounds "the worst we ever visited." Access to the village of Irvington was also apparently difficult because

of the limited number of cars traveling the relatively short distance from Newark to Irvington. The latter issue immediately resurfaced at the beginning of the 1867 season when the first match saw the Irvingtons take on the Eurekas of Newark, to that point New Jersey's pre-eminent club.[9]

The contest was scheduled for May 7, and the cars were "swarming with young men," while many others opted for the pedestrian route. Those unable to attend were advised to look for the result at "Briggs' Base Ball Emporium" in Newark. Unfortunately, the weather failed to cooperate, and rain ended the match after only two innings with Irvington ahead 17–12. In addition to whatever other issues there were with the Irvington grounds, there were also some unusual ground rules. Isaac "Joe" Terrill of the Eureka hit a ball that "cleared the fence on the fly, but was unfortunately stopped by hitting a horse on the other side." Somehow, even after clearing the fence, the ball was still in play, and Terrill was held to a triple. The match was rescheduled for May 16 and played before an even larger crowd, estimated by the *New York Times* at 3000–4000. A holiday atmosphere prevailed as "farmers poured into town with their families all dressed in holiday attire." On a more ominous note, it was reported that "considerable money has been staked on the result by outsiders."[10]

It was another big day for the Irvington Club, which handed the Eureka its first loss to a New Jersey opponent since 1860. In the lineup for the Irvingtons was "Lip" Pike, who had joined the club from the Athletics of Philadelphia. He was not in New Jersey for long, however, moving on to the Mutuals in New York after reportedly receiving a $1,200-per-year clerkship from "Boss" Tweed. This was an example of the double-edged sword that would quickly curtail the Irvingtons' success. Good players were attracted to the club because of its success, but those same players continued to seek new opportunities at even higher levels of competition and corresponding remuneration.[11]

The upstart New Jersey club completed another successful season in 1867, compiling a 17–7 mark against some of the best competition in the country. Included in those 17 wins was a second triumph over the Eurekas, two wins over the Union Club of Morrisania, as well as victories over the Atlantics of Brooklyn and the Nationals of Washington. The Irvingtons also managed to take two out of three from the Unions of Lansingburgh — another upstart club with high ambitions. Except for two disappointing losses to the Mutuals by a total of only four runs, there was much reason for satisfaction.

Perhaps the club's most dramatic 1867 win was a triumph over the Atlantics of Brooklyn on August 5. Once again large crowds made the difficult journey with the cars crowded by 11:00 A.M., since fans knew it was "impossible to get too early on the ground." Irvington tallied eight times in the first inning but fell behind 15–10 after four. The Jersey men rallied, however, to take a seemingly safe 28–18 advantage, especially after Brooklyn had two out and no one on in the eighth. Suddenly, though, the visitors erupted for eleven runs and a 29–28 lead as the match moved to its last inning. The Irvingtons were un-fazed; "there was no fear in them" as they came up with "a de-termination to do or die." With their fans cheering wildly, the home side scored six times and held on for a 34–32 win.[12]

That match was played before another large crowd esti-mated between 4000–5000, which was reported to be well be-haved other than a few "mock fights" intended to facilitate pick-pocketing. The *Clipper* praised improvements to the grounds that would shortly provide "all the necessary buildings for the use of the public." "Necessary" is probably the key word in this context. Improved security may have been due to an ugly scene at the June 28 match with the Mutuals. Fights in the crowd, also reportedly faked to create pick-pocketing opportunities, spilled onto the field, temporarily halting play. Henry Chadwick praised the efforts of the Irvington Club president to restore order, while Hugh Campbell of the Irv-ingtons was injured so badly that he could not continue trying to break up the fight. Although the *Newark Daily Advertiser*'s claim that the blame rested with New York "roughs," is prob-ably somewhat self-serving, similar complaints about the crowd at the return match, at a neutral site in Brooklyn, sug-gests the comment had some merit.[13]

From these accounts it appears the fault on the Irvington side was inadequate crowd control, which was certainly not the responsibility of the players. That the players themselves knew how to behave was demonstrated by their treatment of the National Club of Washington later that season. When those two nines met at Irvington on October 25, the New Jersey club provided all of the courtesies expected of the host club, beginning with meeting the visitors in Newark with a six-horse omnibus. After the match the club provided a "bountiful" col-lation, followed by speeches, cheering and a trophy presenta-tion. Hospitality did not extend to the match itself, as the tro-phy remained in Irvington. After being down 9–7 in the fourth, the Irvingtons rallied to earn a 29–23 victory. The Irv-ingtons had completed another very successful season, but un-fortunately their best days were now behind them.[14]

The player losses that doomed the club began before the start of the 1868 season. In March, it was reported Charles Sweasy and Andy Leonard had left to join the Buckeye Club of Cincinnati. It was also rumored that Buckley, Wolters, and Campbell would move to the Mutual Club, although this was denied by members of the Irvington Club. In fact, the rumor was one-third accurate as Wolters did go to the Mutuals. While Buckley and Campbell did not accompany him, Mahlon Stockman did. In an attempt to rebuild their roster, the Irv-ingtons added George Lines from the Actives and Everett Mills from the rapidly disintegrating Eurekas. Mills, however, became the Lip Pike of 1868, moving to the Mutuals in August, although he did return for some games with Irvington.[15]

Not surprisingly, losing almost half of their first nine hurt the Irvingtons a great deal. After winning their first two

matches against New Jersey clubs, they played seven of their next eight matches against the Atlantics, Mutuals, and Eckfords. In those encounters, the Irvingtons managed only one win, a 14–12 victory over the Eckford Club. Unfortunately, on-field problems were accompanied by continued problems on the grounds. A closer-than-the-score-indicated 13–6 defeat to the Atlantics on September 11 was marred by a fight in the crowd that deteriorated into a brawl on the return train journey. The *Brooklyn Daily Eagle* blamed "a party of Newark roughs" who had become a chronic problem. While noting the ruckus, the *Newark Daily Advertiser* distinguished it from the players' behavior, claiming "the game was played, as between the clubs, in the utmost good nature." How far the Irvingtons had fallen was demonstrated by their final game of the season, a 16–13 loss to the Seton Hall college nine.[16]

Things got even worse in 1869 when the Irvingtons lost all seven games they played against what were now professional clubs from Brooklyn and New York. One loss with honor came against the fabled Red Stockings of Cincinnati, who were on their way to a 57–0 record. The reason for the contest, of course, was the presence of two former Irvingtons, Leonard and Sweasy, in the visitors' lineup. For one last time a large crowd, estimated at 3000, arrived at the Irvington grounds to see the Red Stockings prevail, 20–4. Whether it was the pres-ence of the celebrated Red Stockings or better crowd control, three separate accounts noted the crowd "maintained perfect order."[17]

Another 1869 defeat was at the hands of the Resolute Club of Elizabeth. Perhaps something in the encounter sug-gested that the Resolutes were on the rise. In any event, in 1870, the Campbells, along with another 1869 Irvington reg-ular, joined the Elizabeth club. This was the death knell for the Irvingtons' ability to compete at a high level. While they continued to play matches, detailed reports of their games dis-appeared from the local newspapers. Along with the Eurekas, the Irvington Club was one of the pre-eminent baseball clubs of the pioneer period. Because of the changing nature of the game, the club did not compete at a high level for long, but still helped prove that New Jersey boys could play with any-one.[18]

CLUB MEMBERS

Alexander Bailey: Born in 1843 in New Jersey, Bailey joined the Irvington Club in 1866 after playing for the Newark Club in 1865. He played the outfield and pitched for the Irv-ingtons through at least the 1869 season. After his baseball playing days were over, he lived in Newark, working as a book-keeper and clerk. Bailey died sometime between 1900 and 1910.[19]

Thomas Buckley: Born in 1841 in New Jersey, he played for the Newark Club in 1864 and 1865, before joining Irvington in 1866 where he played third base and catcher. Like former Newark Club teammate Alexander Bailey, he remained with the Irvington Club through 1869. In 1860 Buckley was living in Newark working as a salesman. He could not be located on any census after that year.[20]

Hugh Campbell: Born in Ireland about 1846. Along with his brother, Mike, Campbell was a member of the Irvington Junior club prior to 1865. He played the outfield and first base for the Irvingtons through 1869 when he joined the Resolute Club of Elizabeth. Campbell remained with his new team through its horrendous 1873 professional season. He was the club's primary pitcher that year and registered a record of 2–16. Amazingly, of the 213 runs Campbell allowed in 1873, only 52 were earned. As a result, his 2.84 ERA was 6th best in the league. Sadly, he died on March 1, 1881, from tuberculosis at the age of just 35.[21]

Michael Campbell: Born in 1850 in Ireland, Campbell was living in Irvington in 1860 with his mother and two brothers, both of whom were rule makers. This suggests he had connections to the original founding of the club by Belcher Rule Company employees. Campbell did play at least one game for the Newark Club in 1865 before returning to the Irvingtons the following year. He played first base and the outfield through 1869 before joining the Resolutes for the 1870 campaign. Like his brother, he took part in the disastrous 1873 season, hitting just .143 in 21 games. Campbell lived in Elizabeth after his baseball career, working for many years for an express company. He was married and had at least seven children. Campbell died on January 12, 1926, and was probably the last surviving member of the club.[22]

Andrew J. Leonard: Born in Ireland on June 1, 1846, Leonard played catcher and third base during his two years with the Irvingtons, leaving after the 1867 season to join the Buckeye Club of Cincinnati. In 1869 he moved again, joining the cross-town Red Stockings for their legendary 57–0 season. After playing with the Red Stockings in 1870, Leonard declined Harry Wright's offer to join him in Boston, moving instead to the Olympic Club of Washington in 1871. Leonard subsequently moved to Boston, where he played through 1878, before finishing his playing days in 1880 in Cincinnati. Leonard had a career .298 batting average, hitting over .300 four times. On the 1880 census, he listed his occupation as "base ballist." Once his playing career was over, Leonard lived in Massachusetts with his wife and children, working for some of that time in a sporting goods store. Leonard died in Boston on August 21, 1903.[23]

Mahlon Stockman: Born in New Jersey in 1848. While he was a long-time Irvington resident, Stockman played his first significant baseball in New York with the Active Club. This apparently continued into 1866, when he managed to play for two clubs during the same year. A shortstop, Stockman appears to have played exclusively for Irvington in 1867 before moving to the Mutuals in 1868 along with Rynie Wolters. That move apparently did not work out as Mahlon returned to Irvington in 1869 and was probably out of baseball thereafter or at least not with a prominent club. By 1870 Stockman was working as a bookkeeper. Sometime after 1880, he became Irvington's town clerk, a position he still held in both 1900 and 1910. Stockman died sometime after 1911.[24]

Charles Sweasy: Born on November 2, 1847, in Newark, Sweasy was another member of the Irvington Junior club in 1864. He may also have played for the club in 1865 since there is no record of his being with another club that year. Like Andy Leonard, Sweasy played for Irvington in 1866 and 1867, moving with him to the Buckeyes and Red Stockings from 1868–70. After the break-up of the Red Stockings, he played for six other professional teams through 1878. Sweasy remained in baseball after that, playing for teams in New England until 1882, when rheumatism forced him to retire. He returned to New Jersey and in 1900 was the watchman at the Irvington town hall. Sweasy may have been helped into this position by his former teammate Mahlon Stockman, then town clerk. Sweasy died of consumption (tuberculosis) on March 30, 1908, at the age of 61.[25]

Reinder Albertus Wolters: Born in Holland on March 17, 1842, Wolters was another member of the Irvington Junior club. He pitched for Irvington in 1866 and 1867 before moving to the Mutuals of New York, where he played from 1868 to 1871. This was followed by one season with Cleveland and a final appearance for the ill-fated Elizabeth Resolutes in 1873. After baseball, Wolters was in the produce business in Newark. He died on January 3, 1917, at the age of 70.[26]

Other Club Members: J. Campbell, Harry Crawford, George Eaton, William Greathead, William Lewis, George Lines, Everett Mills, and "Lip" Pike. Club officers included David Anderson, C. Belcher, John Campbell, Chalmers Chapman, F. Elyea, Walter Kimber, Major D. A. Peloubet, Peter Shenck, Dr. D. S. Smith, Joseph Snyder, Alex Williams, and E. K. Williams.

Notes

1. James M. DiClerico and Barry Pavelec, *The Jersey Game: The History of Modern Baseball From Its Birth to the Big Leagues in the Garden State* (New Brunswick: Rutgers University Press, 1991), 35. *Newark Daily Advertiser*, August 19, 1860, July 1, 1861, and July 12, 1861.

2. *New York Clipper*, June 23, 1866; *Newark Daily Advertiser*, August 5, 1864.

3. *New York Clipper*, July 8, 1865, July 30, 1864, September 2, 1865.

4. *New York Clipper*, June 23, 1866.

5. Ibid.

6. Marshall Wright D. *The National Association of Base Ball Players, 1857–1870* (Jefferson, N.C.: McFarland, 2000), 77, 85, 98, 115); *Newark Evening Courier*, July 17, 1866.

7. *New Jersey Herald*, August 16, 1866; *New Jersey Herald and Sussex County Democrat*, October 11, 1866; William Ryczek, *When Johnny Came Sliding Home: The Post-Civil War Baseball Boom, 1865–70* (Jefferson, N.C.: McFarland, 1998), 106; *New York Clipper*, December 6, 1856, October 13, 1866.

8. *New York Clipper*, October 13, 1866, June 23, 1866; *Newark Evening Courier*, June 30, 1866, July 3, 1866.

9. *Newark Evening Courier*, June 21, 1866.

10. *Newark Evening Courier*, May 6, 1867, May 8, 1867; *Newark Daily Advertiser*, May 7, 1867, May 16, 1867; *New York Times*, May 17, 1867.

11. *Newark Daily Advertiser*, March 30, 1867, May 17, 1867, July 15, 1867; *Newark Evening Courier*, May 17, 1867.

12. *Newark Daily Advertiser*, August 6, 1867; *New York Clipper,* August 10, August 17, 1867.

13. *Newark Evening Courier*, August 6, 1867; *New York Clipper* August 17, 1867; Henry Chadwick, *The Game of Base Ball: How to Learn It, How to Play It, How to Teach It* (New York: George Munro, 1868); *Newark Daily Advertiser*, June 29, 1867, September 5, 1867.

14. *New York Clipper*, November 2, 1867.

15. *Newark Daily Advertiser*, March 25, 1868, March 27, 1868, April 18, 1868, August 10, 1868, August 25, 1868; *New York Clipper*, April 11, 1868, June 27, 1868, August 1, 1868, August 29, 1868.

16. Wright, *The National Association of Base Ball Players, 1857–1870,* 226, *Newark Daily Advertiser*, July 7, 1868, August 25, 1868, September 12, 1868, September 21, 1868; *Brooklyn Daily Eagle*, September 12, 1868.

17. Wright, *The National Association of Base Ball Players, 1857–1870,* 253; *Jersey City Times,* June 19, 1869; *Newark Evening Courier*, June 19, 1869; *Newark Daily Advertiser*, June 19, 1869.

18. Wright, *The National Association of Base Ball Players, 1857–1870,* 253, 313; *Newark Daily Advertiser*, July 1, 1870.

19. U.S. Census, 1880, 1900; Wright, *The National Association of Base Ball Players, 1857–1870,* 121, 151, 226, 253.

20. U. S. Census 1860; Wright, *The National Association of Base Ball Players, 1857–1870,* 121, 151, 226, 253.

21. www.retrosheet.org; *New York Clipper,* June 23, 1866; www.the deadballera.com.

22. *New York Clipper*, July 8, 1865; www.retrosheet.org; Wright, *The National Association of Base Ball Players, 1857–1870,* 121, 151, 226, 253; U.S. Census, 1860, 1880, 1900, 1910, 1920.

23. U. S. Census, 1860, 1880, 1900; Wright, *The National Association of Base Ball Players, 1857–1870,* 88, 102, 126, 196; Warren N. Wilbert, *Opening Pitch: Professional Baseball's Inaugural Season, 1871* (Lanham, MD: Scarecrow Press, 2008), 116.

24. Wright, *The National Association of Base Ball Players, 1857–1870,*

100, 121, 151, 194, 226, 255; U.S. Census, 1850, 1860, 1870, 1880, 1990, 1910; *Trenton Times*, October 23, 1911.

25. *New York Clipper*, June 23, 1866; Wright, *The National Association of Base Ball Players, 1857–1870,* 121, 151, 196, 243, 292; *New York Times*, March 31, 1908; U. S. Census 1900.

26. Wright, *The National Association of Base Ball Players, 1857–1870,* 121, 151, 194, 247; www.retrosheet.org; U.S. Census 1900 and 1910.

Bibliography
Books

Chadwick, Henry. *The Game of Base Ball: How to Learn It, How to Play It, How to Teach It.* New York: George Munro, 1868.

DiClerico, James M., and Barry Pavelec. *The Jersey Game: The History of Modern Baseball From Its Birth to the Big Leagues in the Garden State.* New Brunswick: Rutgers University Press, 1991.

Ryczek, William. *When Johnny Came Sliding Home: The Post–Civil War Baseball Boom, 1865–1870.* Jefferson, N.C.: McFarland, 1998.

Wilbert, Warren N. *Opening Pitch: Professional Baseball's Inaugural Season, 1871.* Lanham, MD: Scarecrow Press, 2008.

Wright, Marshall D. *The National Association of Base Ball Players, 1857–1870.* Jefferson, N.C.: McFarland, 2000.

Newspapers

Brooklyn Daily Eagle
New Jersey Herald
New Jersey Herald and Sussex County Democrat
New York Clipper
New York Times
Newark Evening Courier
Newark Daily Advertiser
Trenton Times

Other Sources

U. S. Census 1860, 1880, 1900, 1910, 1920
www.retrosheet.org
www.thedeadballera.com

❖ *Olympic Base Ball Club of Paterson* ❖
(John G. Zinn)

Club History

Founded in 1792 as a center for American manufacturing, Paterson was home to baseball clubs as early as 1855. However, the city's premier club of the pioneer period, the Olympic Base Ball Club, did not take the field until July of 1864. Unfortunately, Paterson newspapers provided extremely limited baseball coverage during the Civil War, so little information survives about the club's first two seasons. What is known is the Olympic Club was founded in July of 1864 and enjoyed immediate success with a perfect 3–0 record in their inaugural season. Things were not quite as easy in 1865 when the record dropped to 2–6–1. Home matches were played at the Red Woods, a recreational facility near the famous Paterson Falls. Perhaps inspired by patriotic wartime feelings, the club's uniforms featured blue pants and white shirts, topped off with red and blue caps.[1]

Like other prominent New Jersey clubs, the Olympic en-

joyed their best seasons immediately after the Civil War. In 1866 they finished 8–4, which was followed by an 1867 record of 9–4. The Olympic played rivals from both New Jersey and New York, with one extended 1867 road trip to Connecticut. For the most part, the Olympic's opposition consisted of middle-level clubs, although they did face some of the best nines of the era. This included matches with the two leading New Jersey clubs, the Eureka and Irvington, as well as contests with the Atlantics of Brooklyn and Union Club of Morrisania. Interestingly, all four came to Paterson, while the Olympics' only visit was to Irvington.[2]

Unquestionably, the Olympics' greatest triumph came on September 5, 1866, in what was thought to be a return match against the Irvington Club. This was the same season the club from the tiny village bordering Newark burst on to the national scene by upsetting the Atlantic and the Eckford. If those accomplishments were not sufficiently intimidating, the Olympic Club already had first-hand knowledge of the Irvington Club's

The Olympics of Philadelphia organized to play town ball, absorbing other clubs in the period 1831–33. Until 1860 they played their own antique game, mostly across the river in Camden, New Jersey. They built this clubhouse in Philadelphia in 1860.

ability. Earlier in 1866, the Irvingtons humiliated the Olympics by an incredible 77–6 mark. Things were different on the Red Wood grounds in what the *Paterson Daily Press* described as "the great match." A back-and-forth contest saw Irvington leading 12–11 after six innings. That advantage ended abruptly and decisively when the Olympic erupted for nine runs in the seventh and a 20–12 lead. Although the Paterson club did not score again, they limited Irvington to four runs over the final three innings for a 20–16 win. Defense and pitching were the keys to the victory as the Olympic recorded 13 fly outs and retired eight other Irvington batters on fouls. The latter statistic was a tribute to the pitching of Mike Toomey and the fielding of his battery mate, Sam McKiernan. In addition to the fouls he caught, McKiernan allowed only four passed balls. Given both the turn around from the first match and Irvington's overall 1866 success, it was no wonder that the *New York Clipper* used the game as an example of the "uncertainties of base ball."[3]

The Olympic and Irvington clubs were not done with each other, however, as both entered the state tournament held in Newton, New Jersey. On October 5 they met again for what was billed as the "great match for the championship of the state." Hampered by injuries to three starters and a supposedly "unfavorable" ground, the Olympic fell 25–9. Interestingly, it turned out the Irvington Club's earlier 77–6 victory in the first

1866 match did not count in the home-and-home series since the umpire, supposedly neutral, was, in fact, a member of the Irvingtons. True or not, it is more than a little difficult to imagine how an umpire could produce a 71-run differential.[4]

The high point of the 1867 season was the Olympics' four-day, four-game trip to Connecticut. Traveling by boat and rail, including "the rudest cars and the ruggedest railroad to be found anywhere," the Patersonians visited Waterbury, Hartford, and New London. The Olympics split the four games, the high point being a 50–21 trip-ending win in New London over the Pequots, supposedly the "champions of the State of Connecticut." The victory was followed by an overnight boat trip that got the party to New York City by 6:00 the next morning, and on to Paterson some two hours later, no doubt tired but happy.[5]

Earlier in 1867, the Olympic lost to the Eurekas in a "friendly match" after which the Newark club declined to accept the game ball. As with the Eureka, it probably seemed the Olympic were on their way to bigger and better things. Unfortunately, like the Eureka, the club's best days were behind them. There was a clear indication of this the following year when the Olympics played only five matches, going 2–3. The clouds on the horizon may have been somewhat obscured because two of the five matches were against the highly regarded

Union (Morrisania) and Atlantic (Brooklyn) Clubs. Both games were played in Paterson, the first with the Union Club on June 1, which the *Paterson Daily Guardian and Falls Register* called "a gala day in Paterson." Since the match took place on an obscure holiday (Pfingster Monday — the day after Whit-Sunday/Pentecost — a German/Dutch holiday), a crowd estimated at 2000–3000, and perhaps as many as 5000, was in attendance. Also present were a number of the New York sporting press, along with gamblers who were betting 2–1 against the Olympics.[6]

As with many New Jersey matches during the period, there was a large female presence, including some standing on "long high benches" who "were watching the maneuvers of the players more closely than their own footing." No doubt pushing the boundaries of contemporary newspaper propriety, the *Daily Guardian* reporter commented on "some 20–25 young ladies (a good looking set by the way)," standing on one bench that tipped backward throwing them to the ground. More embarrassed than hurt, the young women displayed "Colby skirts," blushes, and "scrambling, screeching and laughing" as they regained "a more natural perpendicular." How much effort it took to get this account past the editor is not clear. Although the Union Club prevailed 30–16, there was apparently little disappointment since the Olympics' goal was not so much to win, but to test themselves against the best players of the day. A similar attitude governed a 28–5 loss to the Atlantic on July 27. That match was witnessed by a much smaller crowd, estimated at 500, partially because it was not a holiday, but also because the game was played at the enclosed Paterson race track. The enclosed grounds enabled the club to charge 25 cents admission, supposedly more than twice the norm. In another ominous note for the Olympics' future, the *Paterson Daily Press* noted that the club "had but little practice."[7]

The 1868 season also marked the departure of one of the Olympics' best players, first baseman Milt Sears, for what he hoped were greener pastures with the Union Club. The Olympics played only two more matches in 1868, a forerunner of their demise the following year. The post-war baseball expansion in New Jersey apparently had a negative economic impact in Paterson. In July of 1869, the *Daily Press* observed that both baseball and cricket "were carried to excess last year, and the year before, causing heavy loss to our industries by the negligence of their employees." Whether due to a negative reaction from employers and/or personal financial loss, the Olympics had pretty much "abandoned any idea of playing" during 1869. They did come together to suffer a 53–25 loss to the Union Club of Poughkeepsie in which their lack of practice was evident. Unlike the Eureka, however, this was not the end of the Olympics. In 1874 the club was reborn, apparently in large measure through the efforts of some of the "old" Olympics, particularly Arthur Fitzgerald and Milt Sears. The revival was conditional upon the players receiving "pecuniary support for the time they lose in practicing." This comment,

along with the 1868 editorial, suggests economics had much to do with the end of the original Olympic Club.[8]

At first glance, the original Olympics don't appear to have had a prominent role in baseball's early days in New Jersey. Founded in 1864, they played for only five-plus seasons, a shorter lifespan than other premier clubs of the era. During that time they did take on some of the best clubs, but other than their 1866 victory over the Irvingtons, they had no great success. Yet their achievements during those years created enough interest in the relatively new game to put it on a firm foundation in Paterson.

The first evidence of this is seen in the rebirth of the Olympics in early 1874, led to some degree by members of the original club. The new team went on to play into the 1880s, taking on some of the best teams in the area, including one game against a National League team. During the period four future major leaguers played at least one game for the Olympic Club. In this group were major leaguers William "Blondie" Purcell, Edward "The Only" Nolan, and Jim McCormick, the last of whom won 265 major league games. The most noteworthy, however, was Michael "King" Kelly, arguably the most colorful player of the era. Kelly had a lifetime .300 batting average and was elected to the Hall of Fame in 1945. The significance of four members from one team going on to play in the majors can be better appreciated with the knowledge that in 1880, for example, only about 135 players appeared in a National League game.[9]

Baseball continued to be popular in Paterson into the 1890s as evidenced by the decision of another future Hall of Famer, Ed Barrow, to purchase the Paterson franchise in the Atlantic League for the 1896 season. Barrow was not the only one who believed a minor league team could succeed in Paterson since he convinced prominent Patersonian (and future Vice President of the United States) Garret Hobart to invest $4000 in building a ball park for the team. Aptly known as Olympic Park, the new facility was reportedly "surpassed as the class of the east coast by only the Polo Grounds." Important as an attractive ballpark was to drawing crowds, the caliber of play on the field was obviously even more important. Barrow had this covered, and then some, with a young ball player named Honus Wagner. Playing in his last full season in the minors, Wagner hit .349 for a club that claimed to have won the pennant in a disputed race that was never completely resolved. The future Hall of Fame shortstop returned to Paterson for the 1897 season, hitting .379 before he was purchased by Louisville of the National League.[10]

Future Hall of Famers continued to appear in Paterson in the early 20th century in exhibition games against a noted semi-pro team, the Paterson or Doherty Silk Sox. Although their home field was technically in neighboring Clifton, they were treated by media and others as a Paterson team. On a number of occasions major league teams like the Boston Red Sox (with Babe Ruth), Philadelphia Athletics, New York Yankees, and New York Giants came to play the Silk Sox. On October 1, 1916, a crowd estimated at 10,000 saw their local heroes play and shut out a New York Giant team that had just won 26 straight games — a record that still stands. Paterson in the twentieth century was also not finished producing its own Hall of Famers as Larry Doby starred at Eastside High School before going on to break the color barrier in the American League and earn his own rightful place in Cooperstown.[11]

All of this baseball tradition, no doubt, played some part in another baseball classic — the "Who's on First?" routine immortalized by Bud Abbott and Paterson's own Lou Costello. Looking carefully at the routine in their movie *The Naughty Nineties*, one can see the name Paterson printed on the outfield wall. Close to 100 years after the Olympics took the field in Paterson, baseball's popularity had been well established. While it was not solely their doing, the members of the original Olympic Base Ball Club had truly been pioneers.[12]

CLUB MEMBERS

Arthur Fitzgerald: Born in Ireland in 1841, Fitzgerald played second base for the Olympic, also serving as club secretary and as captain of the nine. A sign painter by trade, he was reported to be "the pioneer in that line of business." After the club was revived in 1874, he served as manager, helping to develop two future major leaguers, Jim McCormick and Hall of Famer Michael "King" Kelly. Reportedly, early in their careers both players consulted with Fitzgerald before signing contracts. A volunteer fireman, elected municipal official, and active in Democratic politics, he was renowned for having a "fund of wit and humor that appeared to be inexhaustible." Fitzgerald died on April 21, 1918, at the age of 77.[13]

Samuel McKiernan: Born in Paterson on November 19, 1839, McKiernan appears to be one of the few members of the Olympic Club who took part in the Civil War, serving with the 25th New Jersey. Kiernan was promoted to sergeant and then lieutenant before being mustered out with his regiment in 1863. His older brother, John, was captain of the same company. After the war, Samuel became an "ardent" member of Farragut GAR post. McKiernan was the Olympics' regular catcher throughout its existence and club president in 1866. Originally a clerk in a dry good store, he became a general contractor, forming a well-known regional company called McKiernan and Bergen. Throughout his life, he was very active in both the Roman Catholic Church and various charities. McKiernan died at the age of 88 on May 11, 1928. His obituary in *The Morning Call* said he "was proud of Paterson and was always ready with his time and money for anything that was for the best interests of the city." This included an anonymous donation at the very end of his life when the local hospital was in great need. The obituary also noted McKiernan's baseball career, calling him an "expert player" and "one of the first to promote baseball."[14]

Milton Sears: Born in Paterson on March 10, 1847, Sears was probably the best player on the original Olympic Club. He played right field and then first base from 1866 to 1869, with a hiatus for an unsuccessful tryout with the Union (Morrisania) Club. Following that stint, Sears played with teams in Portsmouth and Mansfield, Ohio, before returning to Paterson in 1874. Along with Fitzgerald and others, he helped to revive the Olympics. Sears and his brother, Samuel, took over his father's book and stationery store called "The Sears Brothers." Milton's 1871 wedding to Emma Oates at St. Paul's Episcopal Church, then in downtown Paterson, was reportedly the social event of the season. In the late 1880s, ill health forced him to retire, and he was a "partial invalid" until his death on April 2, 1909.[15]

Michael Toomey: was the pitcher for the Olympics from 1865 through 1869, also serving as club treasurer in 1865 and 1866. Although a prominent member of the club, no information has been found about him on the U.S. Census or in other sources. References in the Paterson Directory list him as a saloon keeper in 1890, and then list his wife as a widow in 1891–92. In contemporary game accounts there are references to post-game celebrations at Toomey's, probably his saloon.[16]

Founding Officers: Simon J. Carroll, President; James McMannus, Secretary; Michael Morris, Vice President; James Rossiter, Treasurer.

Notes

1. Charles A. Peverelly, *The Book of American Pastimes* (New York: Published by the Author, 1866), 458; *Newark Daily Advertiser*, August 6, 1855, August 22, 1855; *Paterson Daily Press*, July 20, 1865, July 17, 1866.

2. *Paterson Daily Press*, September 6, 1866, July 13, 1867; *Paterson Daily Guardian and Falls Register*, June 2, 1868, July 28, 1868.

3. *Paterson Daily Press*, July 14, 1866, September 6, 1866; *New York Clipper*, September 15, 1866; *Newark Daily Advertiser*, July 14, 1866.

4. *Paterson Daily Press*, October 6, 1866.

5. *Paterson Daily Press*, September 23, 1867.

6. *Paterson Daily Press*, July 13, 1867; *Paterson Daily Guardian and Falls Register*, June 2, 1868; www.germanabout.com.

7. *Paterson Daily Guardian and Falls Register*, June 2, 1868, July 28, 1868; *Paterson Daily Press*, July 28, 1868.

8. *Paterson Daily Press*, July 11, 1868, September 10, 1868, October 1, 1868, July 6, 1869, July 22, 1869, June 17, 1874.

9. *Paterson Daily Press*, June 16, 1875, June 18, 1875, May 27, 1876, June 17, 1876; *Sporting Life*, April 24, 1909; www.retrosheet.org.

10. Dennis DeValeria and Jeanne Burke DeValeria, *Honus Wagner: A Biography* (New York: Henry Holt, 1995), 30–31, 38, 43.

11. Paul Zinn and John Zinn, *The Major League Pennant Races of 1916: The Most Maddening Baseball Melee in History* (Jefferson, N.C.: McFarland, 2009), 229; *New York Times* June 20, 2003.

12. The Naughty Nineties, dir. Jean Yarbrough, prod. John Grant, perf. Bud Abbott and Lou Costello, Universal Pictures, 1945.

13. Peverelly, *The Book of American Pastimes*, 458; *The Morning Call*, April 22, 1918.

14. U. S. Census, 1860, 1870, 1880, 1900, 1910, 1920; www.ancestry.com; Peverelly, *The Book of American Pastimes*, 458; *The Morning Call*, May 12, 1928.

15. U. S. Census, 1850, 1860, 1870; *Paterson Morning Call*, April 3, 1909.

16. Peverelly, *The Book of American Pastimes*, 458; www.ancestry.com.

Bibliography

Books

DeValeria, Dennis, and Jeanne Burke DeValeria. *Honus Wagner: A Biography.* New York: Henry Holt, 1995.

Peverelly, Charles A. *The Book of American Pastimes.* Published by the Author, 1866.

Zinn, Paul, and John Zinn. *The Major League Pennant Races of 1916: The Most Maddening Baseball Melee in History,* Jefferson, N.C.: McFarland, 2009.

Newspapers

The Morning Call

New York Clipper

New York Times

Newark Daily Advertiser

Paterson Daily Guardian and Falls Register

Paterson Daily Press

Paterson Morning Call

Sporting Life

Other Sources

www.ancestry.com

www.germanabout.com

The Naughty Nineties. Dir. Jean Yarbrough. Prod. John Grant. Per. Bud Abbott and Lou Costello, Universal Pictures, 1945.

www.retrosheet.org

United States Census 1860, 1870, 1880, 1900, 1910, 1920

❖ *Champion Base Ball Club of Jersey City* ❖
(John G. Zinn)

CLUB HISTORY

While some of New Jersey's first baseball clubs were formed in Jersey City as early as 1855, the city's most competitive club of the pioneer period, the Champion Club, took the field during the Civil War. A junior club, many of their players would have been too young to serve in the war. Moreover, avoiding service wasn't overly difficult in New Jersey, and most of the men who served did so as volunteers. The earliest surviving documented reference to a Champion match is from late in the 1863 season, when they played as a junior club. The Jersey City club was clearly competitive at that level since they played in at least one 1864 state junior championship match with the Irvington Club. As with the Irvingtons, the Champions were apparently considered a junior club because they had not joined the National Association of Base Ball Players (NABBP).[1]

After posting a 4–2 record in 1864, the Jersey City club was even more successful in 1865, compiling a 9–5 mark, primarily against other New Jersey clubs. The Champions remained outside the NABBP, publicly offering to take on all clubs "outside the convention." Their nine wins included a pair of routs—66–22 over their inter-city rival, the Aetna Club and 75–25 over their future competition for state honors, the Resolute Club of Elizabeth. These easy wins may, however, have led to a less than gentlemanly attitude toward their fellow Jersey clubs. Whatever the cause, the Champions were accused of "contemptible action" against both the Aetna and Resolute Clubs on the same day, November 1, 1865.[2]

On that date, the Resolutes and Aetnas arrived at the Champions' grounds at the head of Erie Street to play a previously scheduled match. The Champions were bad hosts, refusing to vacate the premises, and continued their unmanly behavior when the match was moved to grounds opposite Hamilton Square. A "mob of half grown loafers" plus members of the Champion Club harassed the two sides until the Cham-

pions finally relented and ungraciously allowed the match to return to Erie Street. The Champion Club members then watched the game and "gave frequent expressions of their ignorance and ill will." According to the *Jersey City Daily Times,* this was hardly a one-time occurrence, and the Aetna would reportedly "shun their society" in the future. This behavior was more than a little inconsistent with the Champions' publicly stated desire to take on "respectable clubs."[3]

Unlike their counterparts in Irvington, the Jersey City club remained outside of the NABBP again in 1866. Playing a combination of New Jersey and Brooklyn clubs, the Champions won eight of nine matches, falling only to the Friendship Club of Brooklyn. The season also saw another triumph over the Resolutes of Elizabeth, apparently without any carryover from the ungentlemanly incident of the previous season.[4]

After their successful 1865 and 1866 campaigns, the Champions joined the National Association of Base Ball Players in time for the 1867 season. Before beginning match play, the first nine played a practice contest against the second nine, where in order to make the game more competitive, they spotted the second stringers 20 runs and five outs an inning. In recognition of their new status, the Champions added seats at the Erie Street grounds and erected club rooms. A more competitive schedule not withstanding, the Jersey City club had another successful season, recording an 11–5 record. All told, the Champions had the second-best record of any New Jersey club in the Association, trailing only the Irvingtons.[5]

Although it was one of their five losses, a highlight of the season was a visit from the Mutual Club of New York. Before the largest baseball crowd ever in Jersey City (estimated at 2000–3000), the Champions fell 52–14. Like other New Jersey clubs in similar situations, the Champions claimed they "had not the remotest idea of winning." Instead, their goals were to score as many runs as possible and give the Jersey City fans an opportunity to see the Mutuals play. From a competitive perspective, the season's high point was a 42–30 triumph over the Active Club of New York. This was apparently an upset as *The Evening Journal* claimed "the result of this game is gratifying to the members and friends of the club as it was unexpected."[6]

The Champions' on-field success, along with the status of NABBP membership, generated increased excitement for 1868. The most tangible evidence was the "new" grounds at the head of Erie Street, which had been "improved at great expense." The enhancements included seats for 300 fans, plus the delicately phrased "every convenience necessary for a club." The club rooms had also been expanded, providing sufficient space for four clubs. Mention was made in the press of the Champions' uniforms, which consisted of "dark blue pants, white flannel shirt, blue trimming, blue meribo cap and red waist band."[7]

But with success came the risk of losing players to other clubs, probably due to financial enticements. At various times during 1868, Charles Bliven, William Willis, and William Snowden were reportedly with or headed to other clubs. While they may have flirted with such possibilities, the three players remained with the Champion Club for 1868 and beyond. Whether due to higher expectations, possible player losses or other issues, the Jersey City club got off to a slow start, losing three of their first four matches. This included a 17–4 rain-shortened loss to the famous Eureka Club of Newark, now in its final season of match play. The loss was exacerbated by complaints the Champions had delayed the contest in an unsportsmanlike manner, hoping a rainout would save them from defeat. This was not the Jersey City club's first offense of this nature and prompted criticism in both the Newark and Brooklyn newspapers. Succinctly contrasting the spirit of earlier days with the new realities of 1868, the *Newark Daily Advertiser* said the Eureka "would be justified to have nothing further to do with ball players who think more of their bets than their reputation as gentlemen."[8]

The easy, albeit abbreviated, win by the Eurekas was attributed to their having a nine "of the old Eureka stock" on the field, something that had become increasingly problematic. Similar problems were also afflicting the newer Champion Club. After a June 30th loss to the Athlete Club of Brooklyn, *The Evening Journal* commented critically that the Champions' lineup was "what we suppose they call their first nine," although there "is room for some of them in the muffins." The paper placed the responsibility on "the management of the club," concluding "we never saw the Champions so completely demoralized." However, as always in baseball, nothing was so bad that a few wins couldn't cure, and after a 22–17 victory over "the famous Olympic Club of Paterson," the paper felt the Champions had "redeemed themselves."[9]

The win marked the beginning of a turnaround that saw the Jersey City club go 12–4 over the rest of the 1868 season. Also of note in the Olympic match was the return of Willis to the lineup as the Champions pitcher. Since the club had been forced to break in Reynolds as a replacement, the Champions now had the unexpected and unusual blessing of pitching depth. By August, the club's play had **so** improved that *The Evening Journal* now claimed the Champions "should certainly be champions of the state," if not that year then in 1869. Perhaps the high point occurred on October 6 when the club defeated the previously unbeaten Eagle Club of New York, handing them their sole loss of 1868. The Champion's overall record of 14–7 was by far the best of any New Jersey club in the National Association of Base Ball Players. In fact, they were the only member of the NABBP from New Jersey to enjoy a winning season.[10]

Whether it was confidence from their 1868 success or coincidence, the Champions opened 1869 with a very aggressive schedule. After a third consecutive loss to the Mutuals (39–14), the Jersey City club traveled to Brooklyn to take on the fabled Atlantics. Only a small crowd was on hand, supposedly because the Champions were unpopular in Brooklyn since they had failed to appear for two prior "announced" matches with the Atlantics. Regardless of how people in Brooklyn felt about it, there must have been more than a few Champions who saw the wisdom of those absences after absorbing a 52–2 thrashing. There was little to be said about this disaster, and none of it was good. Although William Willis scored both Champion runs, he was in trouble with his teammates, due to "very careless fielding," to the point he was "threatened with expulsion from the club." One New York paper even labeled the Champions "muffin players of the country" but added more kindly they shouldn't get discouraged, it was just too early in the season to take on the Atlantics.[11]

Wisely, the Champions did not dwell on the loss, recording a 17–6 record over the balance of the 1869 season, including separate four-, five-, and six-game winning streaks. On August 4, the Jersey City club hosted the Resolutes for the opening of a series to determine the championship of New Jersey. Before a crowd estimated at 3000–4000, the home side took a 7–1 lead after one inning, increased it to 18–5 after three innings on the way to an easy 45–21 win. About a month later, the two clubs met again for the return match at the Resolutes' grounds. The Champions led 10–5 after two innings when rain interrupted play. By the time the rain stopped, three Resolutes had left the premises, and the Elizabeth club refused to continue without them. Although the Champions agreed to wait, the absent players never returned, and the match was never completed. Understandably, the Jersey City press condemned the "extraordinary and unprofessional conduct of the Resolutes." Feelings were so strong that the two clubs did not meet again for almost two years.[12]

Another highlight of the 1869 season was "a series for the amateur championship of the United States" with the Star Club of Brooklyn. The Stars won a close 16–13 decision in the opener at Jersey City. Unlike most newspaper accounts of the period which praised the umpires, the *Daily Evening Times*, not so subtly, said, "it very much looked like the umpire favored the visitors." Whether motivated by revenge or because this time they had their first nine out, the October 9 rematch saw the Champions play their "finest game" of 1869, a 24–9 victory. Unfortunately, the Brooklyn club captured the deciding match on October 26th. The Champion Club lost their last three matches of the season, so in between a 0–2 start and a 0–3 finish, they recorded a 17–3 record. Once again the Champions had the best record of any New Jersey club in the National Association of Base Ball Players.[13]

The 1870 season saw a changing of the guard in New Jersey baseball, both in the NABBP and in the state. While the Champions had a commendable overall record of 24–6, their standing against Association clubs put them well behind the Resolutes, the Amateur Club of Newark, and the Trenton Club. Furthermore, although there was no New Jersey championship series with the Resolutes, the Champions did lose a similar series to the Amateur Club. Another match of a very different nature took place on August 30, although it had no official standing. Eight members of the Champion Club went to their grounds to watch a match between two other clubs. For some reason the match did not take place, so the Champions played against another nine recruited "without respect to age or *color*" (my italics.) The uniqueness of this event was confirmed by the coverage in the local media. The *American Standard* considered it the practical result of the fifteenth amendment to the Constitution and provided several paragraphs of commentary, which were either critical or positive in a highly sarcastic manner. Among other things, the writer commented that "the crime these young men have been guilty of, is an enormous one," so that it would require "a long season of repentance." The writer also hoped that the experience would not have a negative impact on the club's future success. *The Evening Journal*, on the other hand, simply called it "a game extraordinary."[14]

Less pleasant was a controversy surrounding veteran William Willis. There had been questions about Willis's play in the Atlantic match early in the 1869 season. In reviewing the Champion first nine a month later, the *Daily Evening Times* said of Willis, "we cannot say much in his favor," his only "redeeming feature" apparently being his "slow twisty" pitching. Now over a year later, after a 26–10 loss to the Star Club on August 9, 1870, *The Evening Journal* accused him of "treason" and a "sell-out" which led to his resignation from the club. Equally critical was the *American Standard*, which blamed the loss on Willis' "school-boy play," including "refusing to run to his base after striking the ball."

While confirming that he did submit a written resignation, the *Jersey City Times* defended Willis, blaming his failure to run on an injury and the unsportsmanlike refusal of the Star Club to permit a replacement runner. In any event, the club ultimately cleared Willis of any wrongdoing, but this still did not completely satisfy *The Evening Journal*. In any

event Willis continued to play for the Champions as he had since the club's early days.[15]

The Champion Club continued to play and play well after the end of the pioneer period. In 1871 they won ten straight before losing a September 27 re-match to the Resolutes, 34–16. The defeat cost the Champions any chance they had for the state championship. Both performance and participation began to fall off the following year. After winning their first four matches, the Champions lost four of their last five to finish 5–4. This was most likely due to fading interest since *The Evening Journal* reported that the Champions never practiced and played only about once every two weeks. Like most of New Jersey's amateur nines, the Champions had a difficult time surviving past the first generation. The Jersey City club, however, still played an important role in the pioneer period. Coming into prominence as the Eureka and Irvington Clubs faded or failed, the Champions represented New Jersey well against amateur competition both in New Jersey and in the New York metropolitan area.[16]

CLUB MEMBERS

Unfortunately, relatively little information has been found on the individual Champion players. In addition to the standard problem of having only last names, most of those names are so common that there are multiple candidates.

Charles Bliven: Born about 1846 in Connecticut, Bliven was the catcher for the Champion club from 1864 to 1870. In 1870, he was working as a clerk in a store. Bliven was probably deceased by 1880.[17]

John T. Denmead: Denmead was born about 1840 and played second base for the Champions in 1868 and 1869. Denmead had a long career with the Jersey City Fire Department; throughout the 1880s and 1890s, he was Assistant Engineer of the department. A veteran of the 2nd and 13th New Jersey Civil War regiments, Denmead was the President of the Veterans Association of New Jersey in 1896. He died on October 22, 1898.[18]

Peter Donnelly: Donnelly was born about 1849 and played infield and outfield on the Champions from 1867 to 1870. Beyond baseball, Donnelly worked as a plumber, but also became very active in Democratic machine politics in Jersey City. He won election as a Jersey City alderman (1888), state legislator (1889), and finally as a Hudson County freeholder (1889) in what was described as a "bitter fight." During this period the *New York Times* described him as "a famous ringster," referring to a political machine that dominated Jersey City and Hudson County politics for many years. Donnelly's political career was cut short by death from bronchial troubles on October 1, 1890, at the age of only 41.[19]

Henry and John McMahon: Henry was born about 1843; John was two years younger. The brothers were members of the Champion Club from 1865–1868, playing both the infield and outfield. Both brothers worked as butchers after their baseball playing days were over.[20]

William Willis: born about 1844, Willis played for the Champions from 1864 to 1872, primarily as the club's pitcher. Interestingly, in 1870 Willis had no stated occupation, simply being "at home." By 1880, he was a boatman and by 1900 a steward. Willis apparently never married and probably died before 1910.[21]

Other Club Members: Johnson, Reynolds, William Snowden.

Notes

1. George B. Kirsch, "The Rise of Modern Sports: New Jersey Cricketers, Baseball Players and Clubs, 1845–60," *New Jersey History*, Spring–Summer 1983; *Newark Daily Advertiser*, August 5, 1864; *American Standard*, November 24, 1863.

2. *Jersey City Daily Times*, September 2, 1865, October 7, 1865, November 2, 1865.

3. *Jersey City Daily Times*, September 2, 1865, November 2, 1865.

4. *Jersey City Daily Times*, September 10, 1866.

5. *The Evening Journal*, June 15, 1867, July 10, 1867; Marshall D. Wright, *The National Association of Base Ball Players, 1857–1870* (Jefferson, N.C.: McFarland, 2000), 180.

6. *The Evening Journal*, August 6, 1867, August 14, 1867.

7. *The Evening Journal*, June 3, 1868, June 5, 1868.

8. *The Evening Journal*, June 5, 1868, August 1, 1868, August 4, 1868, September 1, 1868; Wright, *The National Association of Base Ball Players, 1857–1870*, 197; *Newark Daily Advertiser*, June 23, 1868; *Brooklyn Daily Eagle*, June 25, 1868.

9. *Newark Daily Advertiser*, June 23, 1868; *The Evening Journal*, July 1, 1868, July 15, 1868.

10. *The Evening Journal*, July 15, 1868, August 6, 1868, October 7, 1868; Wright, *The National Association of Base Ball Players, 1857–1870*, 197, 205, 229.

11. *Daily Evening Times*, May 18, 1869 (includes quotations from article in the *New York Tribune*), Wright, *The National Association of Base Ball Players, 1857–1870*, 259.

12. *Daily Evening Times* August 5, 1869, August 12, 1869; September 10, 1869, *New York Times*, July 22, 1871; Wright, *The National Association of Base Ball Players, 1857–1870*, 259.

13. *Daily Evening Times*, September 16, 1869, October 11, 1869; Wright, *The National Association of Base Ball Players, 1857–1870*, 259, 280.

14. *The Evening Journal*, June 3, 1870, June 24, 1870, July 29, 1870; September 1, 1870, *American Standard*, September 1, 1870; Wright, *The National Association of Base Ball Players, 1857–1870*, 324.

15. *Daily Evening Times*, June 12, 1869; *The Evening Journal*, August 11, 1870; August 13, 1870, *American Standard*, August 10, 1870; *Jersey City Times*, August 12, 1870; Wright, *The National Association of Base Ball Players, 1857–1870*, 324.

16. *New York Times*, July 22, 1871; *Jersey City Times*, September 29, 1871; *The Evening Journal*, July 26, 1872.

17. U. S. Census 1870.

18. W. H. Boyd, ed., *Gopsill's Jersey City and Hoboken Directory* (Washington, D.C.: W. H. Boyd, 1879, 1881–82, 1883, 1885–86, 1898); www.ancestry.com (record of headstones for Union veterans); *New York Times*, September 17, 1896.

19. U. S. Census 1880; www.ancestry.com; *The Evening Journal*, October 2, 1890; *New York Times* September 26, 1889, October 30, 1889.

20. U.S. Census 1860, 1870, 1880.

21. U.S. Census 1870, 1880, 1900.

Bibliography

Books

Gopsill's Jersey City and Hoboken Directory 1879, 1881–82, 1883, 1885–86, 1898, Washington, D.C.: William H. Boyd.

Wright, Marshall D. *The National Association of Base Ball Players, 1857–70*. Jefferson, N.C.: McFarland, 2000.

Newspapers

American Standard
Brooklyn Daily Eagle
Daily City Times
The Evening Journal
Jersey City Daily Times
Jersey City Times
New York Times
Newark Daily Advertiser

Journals

Kirsch, George B. "The Rise of Modern Sports: New Jersey Cricketers, Baseball Players and Clubs, 1845–60." *New Jersey History*, Spring-Summer 1983.

Other Sources:

www.ancestry.com

CHAPTER FOUR

PHILADELPHIA

❖ *Introduction* (John Shiffert) ❖

It is only right and appropriate that the distinguished senior member of the (virtual and unofficial) Philadelphia Society of Baseball Historians David Quentin Voigt said it best, in speaking to a symposium on Philadelphia's Baseball History, held at the estimable Historical Society of Pennsylvania in February of 1990: "[If] you wanted to learn the history of nineteenth century baseball, you had better visit Philadelphia. Philadelphia was in the thick of things, it was innovative. Things were happening in Philadelphia that were significant to the growth of the game."[1]

Voigt, who could well also be called the Father of Philadelphia Baseball Historians, was absolutely correct. Philadelphia, and Philadelphia bat-and-ball clubs, were significant to the growth of the game. Such notable milestones, admittedly not always positive ones, as a pioneering club, a dominant national power in the first 15 years of the game, the first player to change cities in the pursuit of baseball professionalism, the first club to be specifically targeted by the Color Line, and the first instance of a team purchasing player contracts from another team, belonged to Philadelphia and Philadelphia bat-and-ball clubs. These particular distinctions all belonged to clubs profiled in the coming pages of this history: the Olympic, Athletic and Pythian clubs.

Note, however, the qualifier, "bat-and-ball" clubs, as opposed to referring to these pioneers as baseball clubs, because they weren't all baseball clubs. The distinction is important, since the first such organization in Philadelphia, the Olympic Club, was not initially a baseball club, and wouldn't be a baseball club for close to 30 years after its founding. While research still continues as to both the game played by these pioneers, and the organization of bat-and-ball clubs in other cities, the Olympics, who apparently played their first game as an organized club on July 4, 1833,[2] were one of the first American organizations devoted to the bat-and-ball games that would eventually evolve into baseball. Although the Olympic Club originally played a game called town ball, which in Philadelphia was a game marked by an interesting amalgam of plugging, overhand throwing to the bat, and the entire side being put out before having to take the field,[3] the greatest significance was the fact of their organization.

The first decades of the 19th century in the northeastern part of the United States were a period of explosive growth of cities, with resulting change in much of American society. No longer was what had been the neighborhood street life of smaller communities always the norm. Many more people, many of them recent immigrants from the British Isles, now lived in the first "modern" big cities, of which Philadelphia, starting around 1830, was one. While this may have been a key step towards the future, it also led to understandable social upheaval. To deal with this feeling of a lack of familiar social norms, people created the closest approximation possible to their old small neighborhood associations, such entities as clubs or fraternal groups, or associations built around a variety of commonalities, such as politics, fire companies, lodges, benefit clubs, just plain gangs, and, yes, social and athletic clubs.

In the years between 1830 and 1860, Philadelphia more than tripled its population, from 161,000 to 565,000. These new citizens were predominantly from the British Isles, which was also the home of rounders, English base ball, cricket and other bat-and-ball games—all games from which the American pastime would evolve. And they did indeed show a propensity to join clubs, whether they were town ball enthusiasts like the Olympic Club or, a singing organization like the Handel and Haydn Society. Thus, Philadelphia, with its heavily ethnic British population, and its explosive growth in the key years following 1830, was the ideal place to find what we would now call "yuppies," those individuals who had the most free time, joining together in organizations dedicated to what had originally been a child's pastime.

However, following the formation of the Olympic Club, new Philadelphia bat-and-ball clubs, at least ones with staying power, were pretty scarce. It wasn't until the latter part of the 1850s that additional such organizations began to prosper and proliferate. The reasons for this are unclear, although they encompass both a certain degree of social pressure along with Philadelphia's infamous "Blue Laws," which prohibited just about anyone from doing anything fun, both on the Sabbath and in some cases, during the rest of the week as well. Aside from the restrictions of the Blue Laws, it is also easy to picture proper Philadelphians wondering what these young men were doing playing a kids' game, a pastime that had little redeeming social value. Maybe worse, bat-and-ball games also proved to be a threat to window panes, at a time when glass was neither cheap nor terribly easy to obtain. No less a near-contemporaneous observer of the 1840s to 1850s baseball scene, Charles A. Peverelly, noted the "bravery" of the Olympics in dealing with what he referred to as the prejudice against the game. Of course, in point of fact, the Olympic Club dealt with the Blue Laws and the prejudice by playing their games in Camden until 1857.[4]

Fortunately for Philadelphia, baseball history, and baseball players, the Blue Laws relaxed, apparently in 1857, leading both to the Olympics returning home to play, and to the formation of other ball clubs, notably the Minervas in 1857, the Keystones in 1859, and the Pennsylvania, Mercantile, Benedict, Penn Tiger and United clubs around that same time. At least four major clubs—Athletic, Equity, Hamilton and Winona—followed in 1860, when the Olympics switched over to baseball. According to Peverelly, this was the "first active ball season in Philadelphia," by which he meant that 1860 was the first year in which Philadelphia clubs generally played interclub contests of what Peverelly considered baseball, that is, the New York game.[5] It is enlightening to note how one of those clubs was formed, as a direct outgrowth of the Handel and Haydn Society. Not content with just singing, some of the members felt the need for something more "athletic" in their club. And thus came about the first name in Philadelphia Baseball—the Athletic Club, the first and longest-lived Philadelphia baseball dynasty, and eventually a major player in the national scene, with a heyday from 1860 to 1875. Athletic would also prove to be a name that would dominate Philadelphia baseball for the first half of the 20th century.

Formed by members of the Handel and Haydn Society in 1860, the Athletic Club's blue, Gothic "A" dominated play on the field, and was worn by such noted early figures as Hicks Hayhurst, Dick McBride, and Al Reach, who was lured to Philadelphia from the Eckfords of Brooklyn in 1865, the first clear case of a professional player changing cities for fiduciary incentives. The Athletic Club had other distinctions as well— for example, they played their home games on what became the city's most noted early baseball grounds, at 17th Street and Columbia Avenue, a venue that came to be unofficially known as the Athletic Grounds. Later in their history, the Athletics became the first team to purchase player contracts from another team, buying George Bechtel and Bill Craver from the Philadelphia Centennials in 1875, thus paving the way for every other professional player transaction ever made.

Playing in the Athletics' shadow during these years was the Keystone Club, generally a solid aggregation that played top flight, Greater New York-based, teams as far back as 1862 and featured some fine players like Ned Cuthbert and Fergy Malone. The Keystone Club was also notable for its staying power during the Civil War, when so many clubs went on hiatus due to a lack of players. The Keystones first joined the National Association of Base Ball Players (NABBP) in 1863, right in the middle of the war, and stayed until the association folded after 1870, eventually becoming a professional team in 1869.

Although the Athletics and Keystones joined the pro ranks, by far the more common turn of events among the majority of Philadelphia clubs in the 1860s and early '70s was to stay non-professional. The continuing amateur trend, though possibly overlooked by historians studying the sport's rush to professionalism, was epitomized by the Marion Club, which was formed in 1871 as a baseball club. The formation of new amateur baseball clubs, as well as the older clubs remaining amateur, were symbolic and significant steps in the development of the game; no longer were social clubs playing baseball on the highest level. Instead, the majority of the clubs were baseball clubs, devoting their time to playing the game and serving as something along the lines of primordial farm clubs for the pros. Although the Marion Club was short-lived, founder Jack Smith put together a pretty fair squad, headed by captain Jim Devlin. He was a pitcher who could have been one of the top professional players on the 1870s and 1880s, if he hadn't thrown a series of games, and the National League pennant, for Louisville in 1877.

Among the pros, the addition of players like Reach, in tandem with home-grown stars like McBride, would help the Athletics lead the way on the field between 1860 and 1875. Hayhurst, an early center fielder who later became a key administrator and leader on and off the field, was the seminal figure in the game's development in Philadelphia in the middle years of the century. Long-associated with the Athletics, Hayhurst nearly had the distinction of being Branch Rickey, 14 years before The Mahatma was born. In 1867 Hayhurst attempted to integrate the NABBP when he proposed that a top-drawer Philadelphia baseball team, the Pythian Club, comprised solely of what are now called African Americans be admitted as members. First he tried to get Pythian into the Pennsylvania chapter of the NABBP, and then to the national organization. While Hayhurst's advocacy of this radical move failed, resulting in the drawing of baseball's first Color Line, his leadership in this regard, and the spotlight it threw—even 140 years later—on the team he championed, are a remarkable moment in, not just Philadelphia baseball history, but history in general.

That's partly because the team he was championing, the Pythian Club, was arguably the first great African American baseball team. While the team's greatness may be debated, the greatness of their leader cannot. Octavius Valentine Catto was Jackie Robinson, Booker T. Washington, and Martin Luther King all in one, a 19th century Renaissance Man. Catto was an educator, baseball star and organizer, civil rights leader, and radical. His too-short life and varied careers, including being the leader, captain, shortstop, and second baseman of the Pythians, was indicative of the social upheaval that took place in the North in the years following the Civil War. While, as John Thorn has pointed out, the pervasive attitudes towards African Americans in the nation in the years following the Civil War do not prove that those who drew the first Color Line were "racist"[6] by modern definitions, it is no less true that Catto's life mirrored the societal struggle of those years. Catto was the exemplification of those years, right up to the moment he was shot in the back and killed at the age of 32 on a Philadelphia street on Election Day 1871, an election that was open to African American males, thanks in part to Catto's efforts in support of the 15th Amendment. Philadelphia was indeed in the thick of things, in both societal changes and base-ball, which were inevitably intertwined, in the middle years of the 19th century.

To know those years, you need to know Philadelphia.

Notes

1. David Voigt, *Proceedings from Philadelphia's Baseball History* (Philadelphia: Historical Society of Pennsylvania, 1990), 6–7. Remarks at symposium held on February 24, 1990.

2. Research is still on-going as to the origins and the organizational date of the Olympic Club. Some place the date of their first game as being on July 4, 1831. It is also possible that they evolved from a group of rope-makers who were asked to stop playing on a field adjacent to the grounds of the Philadelphia Orphans Asylum in 1829.

3. John Thorn, *Baseball in the Garden of Eden: The Secret History of the Early Game* (New York: Simon & Schuster, 2011), 32.

4. Ibid., 46.

5. John Shiffert, *Base Ball in Philadelphia: A History of the Early Game* (Jefferson, N.C.: McFarland, 2006), 25.

6. Ibid., 55.

❖ *Olympic Base Ball Club* ❖ (Richard Hershberger)

CLUB HISTORY

The Olympic Ball Club of Philadelphia[1] holds a unique position in the history of early baseball. It was the oldest club during the glory days of early baseball, and outlived its contemporaries, with a history of over a half-century.

Its history falls conveniently into the traditional three periods: (1) town ball (1833–1859); (2) the baseball mainstream (1860–1872); and (3) genteel retirement (1873–1889).

Town Ball: 1833–1859

The Olympic club was created in 1833 through the merger of two groups of ballplayers.[2] One of these had been playing in Camden, New Jersey, since 1831. The other, which took the name Olympic, organized to play on the Fourth of July, and occasionally on other days. The association with the national holiday persisted throughout the club's history, for many years including a picnic, the singing of national songs, and the reading of the Declaration of Independence by the club's president.[3] The two groups played a match, which in turn led to their union.

At that time baseball was a family of innumerable regional versions, some played by formally organized clubs but most as informal schoolyard games. These also went by several names, depending on the region. Philadelphia used one of the most widespread names: town ball.[4] The direct ancestor of modern baseball arose somewhat later in New York City, and spread outward in the late 1850s. The version the Olympics played was a somewhat formalized version of the local schoolyard game.[5]

While the club was invariably identified as a Philadelphia organization, during most of this period it actually played across the Delaware River in Camden, New Jersey. The New York City clubs would later follow the same pattern, playing in Hoboken, New Jersey, for the same reason. Public transportation was very rudimentary in this era. Convenient room to play was difficult to find in the city itself, but there was a ferry to New Jersey. Camden at this time was scarcely more than a village, with available open space.

During most of this period the Olympics were the only formal club. Its history somewhat vaguely records two other groups that briefly played independently before joining the Olympics. A solitaire ballclub seems odd today, but was perfectly natural at the time, and typical of the early clubs. Their purpose was not to compete with other clubs, but to provide a structure for the members to gather regularly to divide into teams and play ball for exercise and recreation. In 1838 they met but once a month, on the second Thursday. In later years they were more active, playing twice a week.

The Olympics were also typical of early ballclubs in their social makeup, consisting mostly of doctors, lawyers, and merchants. At the club's founding the members were typically in their mid–20s to early 30s, and therefore comparatively early in their careers. William E. Whitman was a founding member and for many years its president, through 1873. He was a prominent attorney, for two terms a member of the Pennsylvania legislature, and secretary of the Library Company of Philadelphia.[6] Other notable founders included Charles Gilpin, who went on to be mayor of Philadelphia from 1850 to 1854, and Thomas Firth, who was an officer of the Pennsylvania Railroad in the 1850s. It is sometimes claimed that the Olympics drew its membership from the social elite, but this is largely untrue. Its members were of the up-and-coming class, with a few exceptions. Among them were Hartman Kuhn, listed as a "gentleman" in census records and a grandson of Dr. Adam Kuhn, one of the leading physicians in Philadelphia during the Revolutionary War period.

During this period the club established ties with the Philadelphia cricket community. Cricket clubs played in Camden (though not at the same site as the Olympics) from the 1840s, crossing the river for the same reason as the Olympics. They also recruited members from the same social class, in some cases sharing members. A Hartman Kuhn (probably the cousin of the Olympics member) was a prominent member of the Philadelphia Cricket Club. It was also later claimed that the Olympics had defeated the Philadelphia Cricket Club in cricket, but with no details provided it is impossible to judge this claim.[7]

The Olympics' competitive isolation came to an end in 1857, with the establishment of the Camden Club. By 1859 there were four town ball clubs: the Olympic, Camden, Excelsior, and Athletic. Inevitably, the various clubs would test their mettle against one another. Records of matches are sparse, but it is clear that the clubs each played several a year, and that the Olympic first eleven (i.e., their best players) were unbeaten. (The only loss on record was by the second eleven to the first eleven of the Athletics in 1859.) The Olympics were the acknowledged champions of Philadelphia.

The club moved from Camden to Philadelphia proper in 1859. The new home was at Camac's Woods, an estate centered roughly on the modern site of Temple University. At that time it was on the outskirts of the developed area of the city, and conveniently close to the new Germantown Passenger Railway.[8] Camac's Woods was the home ground of the St. George's Cricket Club, and sublet to the Olympics. In years following it would be similarly rented by several of the top Philadelphia baseball clubs.

For town ball, 1859 was the peak season. The following year the baseball (i.e., New York game) craze would hit Philadelphia, and within a few years town ball was completely abandoned as an organized adult activity.

The Baseball Mainstream: 1860–1872

At its regular meeting in May of 1860, the Olympic club voted to adopt the New York game. This version had been introduced to Philadelphia in late 1858, with the formation of the "Pennsylvania Tiger's [sic] Social Base Ball and Quoit Club" (later renamed the Winona Club).[9] The second club would not form until the fall of 1859. The baseball craze struck the following spring. By May there were no fewer than nine baseball clubs in Philadelphia, including two converts from town ball, the Olympics and the Athletics. The first match game of

baseball in Philadelphia, between the Winona and the Equity Clubs, soon followed, in June.[10]

The decision to adopt the New York game was made "setting aside their time-honored play, endeared by the memories of thirty years, to pass on in the race of progress." There was a generational split: "An honorable retirement of most of their old members was ... the immediate consequence."[11] This account can be fleshed out by observing Theodore Bomeisler, who had joined the Olympics in 1853. In 1859 he began to appear in Winona (then still named the Penn Tigers) intramural games, played in their matches of 1860, and was a member of their ground committee. The following year he was once again back with the Olympics.[12] He is the only clear defection, but his activities suggest that the future of baseball was clear. The club had to choose between adopting the New York game and alienating its older members, or maintaining the status quo and losing its younger members, and, worse, abandoning hope of recruiting new members. The latter choice would have amounted to slow organizational suicide. The club wouldn't have lasted as long as it already had without an institutional understanding of the need to recruit new members, so there really was no other option but to go with the times.

This did not mean the Olympics had to immediately abandon town ball entirely. It likely means that their club days were spent playing under the new rules, but despite this they played a town ball match against the Excelsiors, winning 87–71.[13] They played town ball occasionally over the next few years, participating in a "union game" combining with players from the Excelsiors and Camdens in 1861 and announcing a town ball game in 1862 where the "old members will be present."[14] This suggests an effort to heal the rift with the old members and restore at least the social ties. This is the last clear evidence of the Olympics playing town ball, but there is a curious claim two years later by Henry Chadwick, the New York baseball journalist, that they "favor [town ball] almost entire; and but for a few members would not play Base Ball at all." The claim is absurd on its face. The Olympics were a thoroughly mainstream baseball club in 1864. The probable explanation lies in an incident that took place a few days before he wrote that article. Charles Bomeisler (brother of Theodore) had captained the Olympics in a match with the visiting Resolute club of Brooklyn. Chadwick criticized Bomeisler's conduct, leading Bomeisler to accost Chadwick and threaten him, which seems to have colored, if only temporarily, Chadwick's opinion of the club.[15] It is clear, however, that there was a kernel of truth. Unclear is whether this kernel is that the Olympics had until fairly recently played town ball, or that to some extent it still did. In any case, any town ball activity was vestigial and short-lived.

The Olympics played just two match games of baseball in 1860. One was a "friendly game" with their landlord, the St. George's Cricket Club. The more serious match was to defend their championship of Philadelphia, held over from town ball, against the Hamilton Club. The Olympics held firm, winning 18–16.[16] The other notable event of the season was the visit by the Excelsior club of Brooklyn. They played a "picked nine" of players from the leading Philadelphia clubs, including John Kuen and Frederick DeBourg Richards of the Olympics.

They would continue to successfully defend their local championship for several years. The rising challenger was their old rival the Athletics. The Athletics soon became the undoubted premier club in Philadelphia, but as late as 1862 the Olympics split two games with them, winning 19–18 and losing 19–10. That year also saw the first visit of a Philadelphia team (a picked nine like the team that played the Excelsiors two years previously), composed of players from the Olympic, Athletic, and Adriatic clubs. As late as 1864 the Atlantics of Brooklyn, one of the top clubs anywhere, visited Philadelphia as the guests of the Olympics, playing them and other local clubs at the Olympics' new grounds at Twenty-Fifth and Jefferson Streets. These would be acknowledged as the finest in Philadelphia and were the site of most major matches with visiting clubs.[17]

Baseball went through a boom immediately after the Civil War. The Olympics participated fully in this, taking in more than new members in 1865 alone. They were never again dominant on the field. The Athletics surged past them by aggressively recruiting top players; it was an open secret that many were paid. The Olympics abstained from this practice through the 1860s. The resulting disparity on the field is shown by the scores of the annual matches with the Athletics. Where formerly they played as equals, by 1865 the Athletics were thrashing them with scores such as 57–9 and 93–26.[18]

The Olympics were never again to be a top club, even locally, but they remained in the tier immediately below the Athletics, and were a part of the larger baseball community. Visiting clubs routinely played them, including the Red Stockings of Cincinnati on their undefeated tour of 1869. The Olympics were never keen on touring themselves, and largely let out-of-town clubs come to them.

One game from this period stands out for historical interest: It was played against the Pythian club of Philadelphia, winning 44–23.[19] The Pythians were a prominent black club. Baseball in the immediate postwar years was completely segregated. Not only were there no mixed-race clubs, but black and white clubs did not play each other. The Pythians actively sought a white club willing to break this barrier, and the Olympics' agreeing to this was a political act. This was not without some controversy. Later in the month the (white) Olympic Club of Washington played the (black) Alert Club, resulting in a subsequent refusal by the Maryland Club of Baltimore to play the Olympics.[20] This resistance soon faded, and for all of baseball's later history of racism, black and white teams at least could play against each other.

The social character of the club largely remained steady.

William Wheaton was re-elected president every year. Frederick DeBourg Richards stands out as a notable member. He joined in 1859, but it was during the baseball years that he rose to prominence, both as an outfielder and as an organizer. Richards was an early photographer, taking numerous architectural photos of Philadelphia during the 1850s. (A photo of the Olympics' clubhouse and members in the 1860s may be his work, but there is no proof of this.) He was a member of Philadelphia's Academy of Fine Arts, painting primarily landscapes.[21] He maintained his connection with the Olympics for many years, being an active member into the 1880s. The club's ties with the cricket community continued. George Wright was hired by the Philadelphia Cricket Club as a professional for the 1865 season. Wright played baseball with the Olympics in his spare time, appearing in several matches. (There is no evidence that he was paid for this.) The following season he committed his career to baseball rather than cricket, becoming the leading shortstop of his day. George Wright is the only Hall of Famer to play with the Olympics. Further ties with cricket can be found in the membership of George and Gilbert Newhall. The Newhalls were an extended family famous in cricketing circles.

Genteel Retirement: 1873–1889

In early 1873 the Olympics "determined to rest upon the laurels of the last season, and merely organize as a club for social play."[22] This was a withdrawal from competitive baseball, returning to the old pattern of club days devoted to exercise in intramural games. With only minor exceptions, the club maintained this pattern through the end of its existence.

To understand this decision, we need to look at those laurels of 1872. By this time organized baseball was divided into professional and amateur teams. Professionalism had entered baseball due to competitive pressures. Any club that wanted to win matches was tempted to recruit members for playing ability rather than social compatibility, and to offer inducements to prospective recruits. The paying of salaries was banned by the National Association of Base Ball Players, but this ban was not enforced well. In 1869 the National Association acceded to reality and permitted clubs to declare themselves to be professional.

The Olympics never declared themselves professional, but the "amateur" distinction was not wholly straightforward. The competitive pressures did not disappear simply because a club was not professional, and the cycle of inducements to recruits began anew. For the early 1870s it is safe to assume that any top team of "amateurs" were in reality paid to play. The Olympics succumbed to these pressures in 1872. They fielded a strong team, but an examination of their lineups shows players recruited from elsewhere. Six of their starting nine had played the previous season with a single club, the Expert.

The problem this created was that the goal of fielding a competitive team of nine good players was fundamentally incompatible with the structure of a club of many members gathering for exercise and camaraderie. In its pure form, the old club had played entirely internally, with ad hoc teams chosen for the day. Athletic ability didn't really enter into the matter. As soon as matches were played with other clubs, this created a division between the first team and everyone else, but early on match games were rare, and there were opportunities for a second team to compete as well. What, however, was a club member to make of the 1872 team, with most of its members taken wholesale from another club and paid to play for the Olympics? And what of club days? Are they for members to take their exercise, or for the team to practice? The club changes from a group of sociable ballplayers to a group of enthusiasts sponsoring a team. This is not necessarily a bad thing, but it is a different thing.

None of the old amateur clubs successfully made this transition. The oldest baseball organizations surviving in the 21st century date from the 1870s, and were businesses rather than social clubs from the start. The old amateur clubs tried various strategies in response to the changing competitive environment. The Olympics' was the most straightforward: They chose to return to the older model. The problems of competition were solved by opting to be noncompetitive.

This strategy did not require the complete abandonment of match games, but they became much rarer and took on the character of "friendly" matches. An 1873 match against the Germantown club hints at this, with an Olympics member acting as umpire and the Germantown club winning, 21–5. Several players in the Germantown lineup had been Olympics members in years past, suggesting that this match was an act of reconciliation like the town ball games of ten years before.[23]

The Olympics maintained close relations with the Athletics, continuing for several years to share the Jefferson Street grounds. They did not take in gate receipts, paying the rent from club dues. Olympics members acted as umpires in Athletics games from time to time. This produced the odd (to modern eyes) phenomenon of a major-league club having to ask if it could borrow its ballpark on the Olympics' day. The Olympics granted permission for a National League game, but denied it for a mere amateur match.[24] They played a rare match with a much-reduced Athletic club, losing 33–12, on the Fourth of July 1877. Their status is summed up by the report of the "once celebrated" club, "which once had considerable renown, but is now out of practice."[25] They then virtually dropped out of sight, but there are occasional reports of their meetings. In 1878 they were still renting a professional ground, now the Oakdale grounds at Eleventh and Cumberland, two days a week.[26]

The club continued steadily for the next several years, with 35 members in 1882, but with an increasingly backwards-looking air: The note that its members "are constantly relating incidents that took place in contests when the national game was known as 'town ball'" was not one to inspire young men

to join.[27] The members celebrated the club's 50th anniversary that year with a "reunion" game of old members, playing 13 on a side, followed by a speech relating "several instances of the old town ball days."[28]

The realization that the club was moribund spurred two of the old members to seek out new recruits, "gentlemen connected with ... prominent mercantile, insurance and manufacturing companies," and in the season of 1884 the Olympics fielded a competitive team for the first time in a dozen years. They played 22 games against area amateur clubs, with a record of 12–8–2. This flurry of activity was short-lived, however. The only record of play the following season was of a match with the University of Pennsylvania, which was rained out.[29]

The club celebrated its 53rd anniversary with a banquet in Atlantic City. There was no mention of any game play. The state of the organization was such that by 1887 Dr. Neil, an old member of 20 years "when a game cannot be arranged ... gets a number of boys together and bats the ball to them. He never goes without his exercise," showing that however dedicated the good doctor was, he had trouble finding compatriots to join him. The last report of the club is from 1889, another reunion at the banquet table of some 20 members with "appropriate speeches and reminiscences of the earlier days of our national game, and the former triumphs of the club."[30]

This era was backward-looking, so it is fitting that the most notable addition to the club's membership was an old player, E. Hicks Hayhurst. Hayhurst had played town ball with the Excelsiors and baseball with the Winonas as early as 1860. He soon moved to the Athletics, where he was a regular player, usually on the second nine, for several years in the mid– and late-1860s. He served as the club's business manager in the early 1870s. He eventually joined the Olympics, giving him a chance to return to the playing field, and was elected president in 1882. Apart from baseball, he was trained as a chair maker but made his living as a produce merchant. He was elected to the Philadelphia Common Council, serving for four years. He contracted typhoid fever in late 1882 and died a week later, at the age of 56.[31]

The sporting world had made obsolete the old model of the fraternal club gathering for exercise. Baseball was no longer the game associated with the respectable professional class. Indeed, no one game was. The 1880s saw the rise of the multisport country club. In Philadelphia several cricket clubs took on this role. The Philadelphia Cricket Club, the Olympics' old neighbor in Camden, moved in 1883 into a permanent facility in the fashionable Chestnut Hill neighborhood, on land donated by the area's developer, Henry Houston. They already sponsored lawn tennis, and in 1895 added a golf course. The different fate of the cricket and baseball clubs derived from baseball's descent down the social ladder, to the staus of a working-class sport. Cricket, in the meantime, was adopted by the professional class in Philadelphia, inspiring Houston to regard a cricket club as an amenity adding value to his development. (A similar dynamic would apply in other cities, but apart from Philadelphia not centered on cricket.) The old model of the fraternal baseball club had become obsolete, unable to attract new members.

The club went out quietly, but its final period deserves respect. The group wanted to gather for exercise and fellowship. Other clubs who strove for championships might have won plaudits, but only fleetingly. The Olympics played the game they loved the way they wanted to, for longer than any of their contemporaries.

CLUB MEMBERS

The unique history of the Olympic Club makes it impossible to distinguish which of its many members were of central existence. As a result, this sequential list of members is all that can be offered.

1833

William E. Whitman; Edward E. Law; Edward Hathaway; Lewis Cooper; George Emlen; John H. Diehl; Samuel Branson; Joseph Reeves; Charles Gilpin; Isaac C. Jones; Samuel Robb; Robert P. Desilver; Joseph M. Thomas; Samuel Carpenter; Charles Desilver; Robert P. McCullagh; Joseph T. Hillborn; George W. Watson; Edward Gaskill; William Hart Carr; Edward Bowlby; John G. Brenner; Samuel S. Bowlby; Kirk Wells; William A. Blanchard; Charles J. Thomas; Nicholas Newlin; Thomas Robb; Peter O. Ellmaker; Robert Lindsay; James G. Edwards; Edward John Fox; George P. Herse; Samuel Hufty; John R. James; Frederick S. Ellmaker; Thomas T. Firth; Joseph Saxton; George W. Wharton; Joseph Mort; Thomas Clark; Joseph Lewis; James R. Garrigues; Marcellus Coxe; William H. Dunlap; George Schober; Charles C. Dunn

1841

Hartman Kuhn; Charles Kuhn; William H. Hazeltine; O. Reeves; Marmaduke Moore

1842

F.C. Jones; Philip P. Steiner; John Trucks; Clifford Phillips; Samuel Goldey; Charles Gibbons; Jesse Lee; J. Warner Johnson; Edward N. Wright; Edmund Draper

1843

Henry S. Camblos; Samuel H. Smith

1844

George Helmbold

1845

Daniel M. Zimmerman; Henry Sawtell; John W. Whetham; John W. Sexton; William D. Jones

1846

Morris Keen; Peter Sparks

1847

Merchant Malsby; Bettle Paul; Elliston Perot; William H. Neville; E.T. Mort; James W. Harrison; James A. Wright; Benjamin M. Dusenberry; John A. Ellison; Edward M. Davis; Enos Gandy; Jacob H. Fisler; Edwin W. Payne; Robert Forsyth; Caleb S. Hunt

1849

Louis D. Senat; James L. Rahn; Edward C. McClure; Ambrose Hunt; William Hunt; John E. Neal; Charles W. Wright; Matthew F. Hagen

1850

Edward T. Parker; Henry S. Paul; Charles Parker; C. Eugene Claghorn

1851

James H. Bulkley; Thomas B. Simpson

1852

Peter T. Wright; George M. Rush; Jacob S. Hess; Daniel Neall; John S. Kuen; James C. Boyd; Andrew Mason; William Ernst; Edwin L. Bomeisler

1853

Charles S. Lincoln; John H. Weeks; A. Theodore Chur; John R. McCurdy; Felix Traner; Emerson G. Elkinton; William Gillam; Theodore Bomeisler

1854

William M. Hayes

1855

John W. Hurn; G. Alfred Fletcher

1856

N. Longmire; Thomas Helm

1857

Henry C. Alexander; Thomas Alexander; John M. Caldwell; Charles McGill; Philip E. Kelly; Charles M. Bomeisler

1858

Frank L. Neall; Walter Chur; Charles S. Clampitt; E. Rutledge Toole; Charles Boric; Carles G. Phillips; William D. Stroud, M.D.

1859

F. DeB. Richards; Charles E. Anspach; John T. Tagg; A. M. Austin; Theo. B. Woodward; Edwin A. Johns; Edwin A. Kelley

1860

Alfred Willis; Isaac Vandusen; John F. Warner; William C. Vinyard; E. Tracey; Charles H. Hamrick

1861

Henry B. Ashmead; M. Hall Stanton; Emmor S. Kimber; A.M. Spangler; Wes Fisler; Edward B. Kimber; Joseph B. Smith; William F. Warburton; John J. Heisler

1862

Nathan T. Mulliner; Edward Woods; Michael W. Smith; N. Clement Hunt; H.B. McCauley; John N. Wilkins

1863

B.R. Crosdale; A. Charles Barclay; E.M. Davis, Jr.

1864

Duffield Ashmead; James L. Bispham; George M. Newhall; Gilbert A. Newhall; William G. Clarkson; William G. Huey

1865

D. Dodson; John E. Addicks; H.E. Williams; Wilson M. Jenkins; E.B. Ferris; Courtland F. Jenks; W.W. Allen; Joseph Bull; C.E. Whittaker; J. McCahan; J.T. Graff; Benjamin Wharton; Isaac Shaner; H.C. Cochran; R.H. Adams; William N. Weightman; Smedley Darlington; Thomas P. Parry; W.R. Stewart; William Turner; Arthur Thatcher, Jr.; John S. Capp; David Gratz; John L. Redner; W.L. Dubois; Samuel J. McMullen; Robert B. Knight; William H. Taber; G.W. Marsh; Levi Dickson, Jr.; Caleb Pearce; E.H. Webb; George W. Harmer; F.M. Dixon, M.D.; J.H. Partt, M.D.; Thomas B. Morris; Edward T. Emory; H. Graffen; E. B. Douredoure; W.C. Barnes; Edward Hopper; H.G. Clement; Joseph S. Meyers, M.D.; Charles P. Coane; John V.C. Clarke; William Harvey; John Case, Jr.; H.L. Humphrey; Joseph J. Redner; W.J. Whittaker; S.H. Bell; H.C. Haines; William H. Howell; Henry Shaner; J. Hayes Carson; E.S. Heston; E.D. Mullin; C.T. Yerkes, Jr.; William H. Piersol; E.F. Poulterer; L.L. Webster; Oliver Saylor; Daniel Saylor; Robert Glendenning; John Sensenderfer; Conrad Waldie; C.F. Lipp; George Wright; P. Dockney; Joseph E. Parker; R.C. Coane

1866

W.S. Mason; Richard L. Willing; J.D. Higgins; John C. Browne; J.M. Barker; Thomas Browne; J.M. Baker; S.P. Darlington; Enoch Lewis; Charles H. Addicks; B.W. Miller; W.L. Fox; Edgar E. Cuthbert; Henry Tolman; T. Moran; H.J. Lex; Samuel T. Potter; A. Witmer; J.E. Gillette; Thomas C. Porter; Thomas D. Watson; Henry Avery; Charles H. Morgan; S. Mason Graffen; Charles E. Morris; M. Marshall; J.W. Cooper; Silas George; J.W. Gilbough; James Hoyt; Joel Woolman; William Milward; S. Moore, Jr.; Eugene Scott; Douglas Hubbard; George B. Pharo

Notes

1. Some sources name the organization the Olympic Base Ball Club or, for the earlier period, the Olympic Town Ball Club. The official designation throughout the organization's existence was the Olympic Ball Club.

2. The two important sources for the early history of the Olympics are pamphlets printed by the club, one in 1838 and the other in 1866. These pamphlets were typical of clubs of all sorts in that era. The 1838 pamphlet includes the club constitution, bylaws, and membership roster. The 1866 pamphlet added to these the contemporary rules of baseball and, most importantly for our purposes, a brief history of the club and historical membership roster from its founding to that day. Most later accounts of the club are based on this, sometimes with additional reminiscences.

3. *Sunday Dispatch* (Philadelphia), January 14, 1872.

4. For a description of how town ball was played in Philadelphia, see R. Hershberger, "A Reconstruction of Philadelphia Town Ball," *Base Ball: A Journal of the Early Game* 1, no. 2 (Fall 2007): 28–43.

5. The *Press* (Philadelphia) of November 11, 1858, assured its readers that the game "is the one many have delighted in during school-boy days, somewhat elaborated, but in all its essential features the same."

6. *Philadelphia Inquirer*, August 4, 1875.

7. *New York Clipper*, May 24, 1862.

8. The exact timing of the move is unknown, but press reports of 1858 place the Olympics' home ground in Camden, while the *Press* (Philadelphia) of November 9, 1859, announced an upcoming match against the Athletics to be held at the Olympics' home ground at Camac's Woods. An advertisement in the *Press* on October 11, 1859, for a cricket match at that site noted the convenient railway access (actually about three-quarters of a mile away).

9. *New York Clipper*, November 27, 1858.

10. *Morning Pennsylvanian* (Philadelphia), May 28, 1860; *Wilkes' Spirit of the Times*, March 30, 1861.

11. *Wilkes' Spirit of the Times*, March 2, 1861.

12. *New York Clipper*, August 20, 1859, June 30, 1860; *Wilkes' Spirit of the Times*, March 30, 1861; *Press* (Philadelphia), June 29, 1861.

13. *New York Clipper*, August 11, 1860. This game resulted in one of the finest town ball box scores, reprinted in Charles A. Peverelly, *Peverelly's National Game*, eds. John Freyer and Mark Rucker (Charleston, S.C.: Arcadia, 2005), 99. Two similar box scores were published the same year, both involving the Excelsior and therefore probably the product of that club. They may have been an attempt at pushing back against the incursion of the New York game into Philadelphia.

14. *Philadelphia Inquirer*, June 29, 1861; *North American & U.S. Gazette*, May 21, 1862.

15. *Brooklyn Eagle*, August 2, 1864, August 3, 1864, August 5, 1864.

16. The match was widely reported. The *Press* (Philadelphia), November 8, 1860, has a fine example of the extended box score accorded to particularly important matches.

17. Peverelly, *Peverelly's National Game*, 99, 101; *Brooklyn Eagle*, June 3, 1862; *Press* (Philadelphia), August 9, 1864, August 10, 1865.

18. *Philadelphia Inquirer*, November 20, 1865, November 27, 1865.

19. The match was widely reported. See the *Philadelphia City Item*, September 11, 1869, for a particularly extensive account.

20. *The Critic* (Washington, D.C.), September 20, 1869, September 23, 1869.

21. The Library Company of Philadelphia has a large collection of his photographs. Unlike his contemporary Thomas Eakins, he did not paint any baseball subjects.

22. *Sunday Dispatch* (Philadelphia), March 16, 1873.

23. *Philadelphia Inquirer*, September 15, 1873.

24. *Philadelphia Sunday Mercury*, May 21, 1876; *Philadelphia Item*, June 7, 1876.

25. *Times* (Philadelphia), July 2, 1877, July 5, 1877.

26. *Philadelphia Weekly Times*, March 23, 1878.

27. *New York Clipper,* April 1, 1882; *New York Times,* March 29, 1883.

28. *Philadelphia Inquirer,* June 30, 1883.

29. *The Sporting Life* (Philadelphia), December 31, 1884; *Philadelphia Inquirer,* May 25, 1885.

30. *Brooklyn Eagle,* June 6, 1886; Chadwick Scrapbooks, vol. 2; *Philadelphia Inquirer,* March 22, 1889.

31. *Philadelphia Inquirer,* December 19, 1882; *New York Clipper,* December 23, 1882.

❖ Athletic Base Ball Club ❖
(Richard Hershberger)

CLUB HISTORY

The Athletic Base Ball Club came out of the first flush of baseball mania in Philadelphia and went on to be the unquestioned premier club of Pennsylvania. In the years immediately after the Civil War the Athletics were the only outside club that could face as equals the best New York area clubs. They went on to win the first official national championship pennant, in 1871, and were one of the original members of the National League in 1876. They faded from the scene soon afterwards, but their name survives, via a succession of later clubs, in the modern Oakland Athletics

The Athletic club was founded on May 31, 1859. This rather mundane fact is subject of a minor controversy, since the usual date given for the foundation of the club is April 7, 1860. The confusion arose as early as 1861, when the date was given as June 12, 1860.[1]

This confusion is not accidental. In 1859 the Athletics were playing not the New York game (the direct ancestor of modern baseball), but the Philadelphia version of town ball, a cousin of the New York game. The club's president in 1860, William Ernst, was an old town-ball player who had joined the Olympic club in 1852.[2] The event of April 7, 1860, was their voting to switch to the New York game, which was sweeping the Philadelphia ballplaying community.

The first members came from Philadelphia's Handel and Haydn Musical Society.[3] This seems an odd connection today, but the musical society and baseball clubs recruited from the same social class, typically professionals and merchants. The early clubs were as much social as they were competitive, providing the members with a vehicle for taking their exercise together. It made sense that a group of friends would remain together to play ball. According to a club scrapbook now housed at the Baseball Hall of Fame the 15 founders were William Ernst, William H. Cunningham, Nathan Berkenstock, Charles A. Denney, Colonel Thomas Fitzgerald, John J. Heisler, Dr. A.G. Heston, Colonel D.W.C. Moore, G.H. Troutman, John Conard, B. Croasdale, W. Coulston, H. Bartine, H.W. Karchner, and C. Warner.

The Athletics were like other early clubs in that they were oriented inward, typically playing intramural games. Matches against other clubs were rare highlights of the calendar, with

only three played in 1860.[4] The classic pattern was to have some 30 or 40 members, meeting twice a week during the season. Match games involved nine players on a side, but intramural games were more flexible, allowing all members who wished it a chance to play. The Athletics were slightly larger than was typical, with a reported 50 members after the 1860 season.[5] They initially played in West Philadelphia, but soon moved to Camac's Woods (near the present site of Temple University), subletting grounds from the St. George's Cricket Club.

They were from the start prominent in the Philadelphia ballplaying community, but they would not dominate it for several years. The Excelsior Club of Brooklyn visited Philadelphia late in 1860 and played a "picked nine" of top local players. The Athletics' vice president, D.W.C. Moore, was in charge of the arrangements, but only one Athletic played on the team, second baseman Nate Berkenstock. Two years later a picked nine visited New York City, the first tour of Philadelphia players to New York, with the trip organized by Moore.[6]

The club's rise to dominance began in 1863 as shown by two trips, to New York and to Altoona, Pennsylvania. They played six matches over six successive days against New York and Brooklyn clubs, winning two and keeping the score respectable in the other four. The trip to Altoona is in some ways more remarkable. The Civil War years were a pause and retrenchment period in the spread of baseball. This trip, a mere two months after central Pennsylvania had been invaded by the Confederacy's Army of Northern Virginia, was as far west as any Eastern club had yet traveled. Predictably, the Athletics soundly defeated the Mountain Club of Altoona, 73–22.[7]

By 1865 the Athletics were clearly the premier club in Philadelphia, and their competitive focus turned toward New York and the national championship. This championship was unofficial but widely acknowledged. The usual pattern was to challenge the championship club to a best-of-three series. The champions were the Atlantics of Brooklyn. They had visited Philadelphia in 1864 and beaten the Athletics 43–16, but this was actually the best score by any Philadelphia club that visit.[8] They visited again in 1865, winning by a much closer 21–15. The return match in Brooklyn a week later was closer yet, the Atlantic winning in a comparative squeaker by 27–24. The game in Philadelphia brought out an estimated 12,000 spectators. This number should be regarded with skepticism, as the game was played on an open field with no tickets, much less turnstiles, but it is clear that the game produced great excitement. Meanwhile, matches with local teams became one-sided, with the Athletics beating the Olympics twice that season, 57–9 and 93–26.[9]

This improvement in play was not achieved merely by members getting together twice a week for club days. It required concerted effort and outside help in the person of Alfred J. Reach. This era saw the rise of professionalism, despite this being against the rules of the National Association of Base Ball Players. Al Reach, an accomplished player in Brooklyn, was at the forefront of this trend. The circumstances of his recruitment are not entirely clear, but the fact of his being paid was an open secret. Over the next few seasons more and more of the club's first nine would be paid. Soon a newspaper would print the team's planned itinerary under the matter-of-fact heading "A Professional Trip."[10]

This change to the character of the first nine was accompanied by change to the character of the club membership. Its size had been steadily growing: Prior to the 1866 season the club added some 50 new members, bringing the total to more than 400.[11] Obviously these 400 members weren't meeting twice a week to take their exercise, if for no other reason than physical limitations of space. What motivated them to join the club and pay dues was not to play baseball, but to watch it and to support their favorite team. The organization was no longer a club of ballplayers, but a social club sponsoring a team. This pattern persisted through the rest of the club's existence. This also explains how the club could afford to pay players several years before it played games on an enclosed ground, which in turn allowed it to charge admission. It was even prosperous enough to rent the Academy of Music (a fixture of Philadelphia to this day, and not cheap) for its annual ball; an event that was praised for having "no more tickets disposed of than the capacity of the building would warrant."[12] This separation of the club from the team was taken to an extreme in 1874, when the "Athletic Baseball Association" formed "entirely distinct from the Athletic Baseball Club, although a large majority of its members belong to that organization" with a clubhouse including "reception parlor, billiards-room, dressing rooms with marble-top wash stands." This was intended as a classic Victorian gentleman's club.

Whatever the benefits of such a membership base, it could also be the source of problems. They were not merely a booster club. They were voting sponsors of the team. Usually management questions were left to the officers, but in what must be a manager's nightmare they occasionally took a more direct interest. The meeting of May 1876 included a vote of 66–12 against hiring Fergy Malone as the catcher. No suggestion was made as to who should fill the position, and Malone was hired anyway, leading to a complaint at the June meeting.[13]

These changes to the club were not without controversy.

In the summer of 1866 there was a falling out and Thomas Fitzgerald, the club's president of several years, resigned his office and later from the club. The reasons for this are not clear. They seem to be a personality dispute with a faction led by the vice president, D.W.C. Moore. But the dispute soon took on a moralistic tone, and since Fitzgerald published a newspaper and therefore bought ink by the gallon, the disagreement was very public. "Nincompoops" was one of the kinder characterizations. Tellingly, he advised the club to say, "Gentlemen, we have broken every law of the game, and we have defied public opinion. Six of our nine are regularly paid — are 'Hired Men,' in fact."[14] There is a distinct element of hypocrisy here, since certainly the hiring of Reach occurred under Fitzgerald's presidency, but the fact that the charge of using "hired men" was made shows that the practice was controversial.

A portent of darker matters was Fitzgerald's adding that the club should also say, "We are in the hands and under the control of Gamblers, Pickpockets, Profane Swearers, and Ruffians generally." This was written in the heat of anger, and so perhaps should not be taken at face value. But two years earlier he himself had addressed this very issue: "The President of the Athletic has requested us to state that the club has no knowledge of the individual who offers to bet five hundred dollars to two hundred and fifty dollars that they can beat any club in America. The Athletics disapprove of betting, and do not permit the practice on their grounds; neither is anyone permitted to play who is interested in a bet."[15] The status of betting in either 1865 or 1867 is impossible to determine, but the significant fact is that the issue was raised. With it come doubts, which are harder to erase than betting itself.

The Athletics never won the national championship during the 1860s. The challenge system was showing its weakness. There are suggestions that the New York clubs collaborated to manipulate the system to keep the championship in metropolitan New York. Regardless of whether or not this is true, the system worked only when the serious contenders were close to one another. In 1869 the National Association acceded to reality and legalized openly professional teams. That year also saw the rise of the Red Stockings of Cincinnati, who toured the country undefeated, playing all the top teams. It was obvious that they were the best team in the county, yet they weren't playing for the national championship, with its best of three matches. The system was broken. In 1871 the professional clubs formed a new association, the National Association of Professional Base Ball Players, with the great innovation of the championship season, with every club playing every other club a set number of games. They were the first sporting organization to use this system, which in its essence survives to this day.

In the first year of the professional association the Athletics finally won the pennant, taking the first official national championship of baseball. The pennant race was not without controversies, with the final record determined by arguments about forfeited games due to ineligible players, but the fact remains that the Athletics of 1871 were as good a team as any in the country.

The season of 1871 was the club's peak, but it was more than respectable for the next four years, with a winning record every year and finishes from third to fifth in the standings. The 1876 season saw the new National League, with the Athletics a charter member. It also saw their collapse, posting a dismal 14–45 record, being financially unable to complete the season, and being expelled from the League the following December.

The club's leaders regrouped over the winter and fielded a team in 1877. It played in the League Alliance, a sort of minor auxiliary to the National League. They entered 1877 with high hopes of re-establishing themselves and eventually rejoining the National League. They began the season fielding a re-spectable minor team, playing an active schedule against other minor professional teams and local amateur clubs, plus 18 games against National League clubs, winning two, and taking an extended tour of New York state and Canada in May and another of New England in June. These tours lost money, and the team made no major trips after June. It also started releasing players in a salary dump (possibly the first in professional baseball), most notably with Dave Eggler going to the Chicago club, but also dropping others such as Levi Meyerle and Johnny Ryan, both going to Cincinnati. The roster was unstable through the rest of the season.[16]

The situation becomes progressively more obscure in following years. Through the end of the 1870s and into the 1880s there was always be a team playing in Philadelphia under the name "Athletic" but the actual connection with the old club gradually attenuated. The team of 1878 was under the management of Al Wright, who had managed the 1876 team, and bore a connection with Al Reach.[17] It played almost entirely locally, with only one short trip to Washington, D.C. Several minor professional clubs visited, but no National League clubs made the trip. By 1879 the Athletics were effectively a local semiprofessional team, with no obvious connection with its predecessors beyond a handful of old players who couldn't get signed elsewhere.

So it was that the former premier club of Philadelphia, the only first-rate club outside of New York, and the winner of the first professional pennant, disappeared. How was it that the organization could fall so quickly? There is no single explanation, but a combination of factors both local and national.

The biggest national factor was that the economy was in a depression after the financial Panic of 1873. It took a few years for the effects to percolate into the general economy, and the late 1870s were a difficult time to run a professional baseball club. This would be reflected in the turnover rate of National League franchises, with as many as half the clubs changing from one year to the next. This was especially true in New York City and Philadelphia, the old heartland of baseball in the 1860s. Professional baseball died out in both cities, to be revived in the early 1880s.

A factor specific to Philadelphia was local competition. In the early 1870s it was not clear whether this was a net asset, due to local competitive rivalries stimulating attendance, or a liability, with attendance spread between the clubs. The answer was that it was a liability, and the National League instituted territorial rights sacrosanct in organized baseball to this day. Philadelphia was the proving ground, with the Philadelphia club forming in 1873 and the Centennial club in 1875. The Centennials didn't last long, but the Philadelphias played into the 1876 season, and revived Philadelphias played in succeeding years. This split the attention of the shrinking base of potential attendees.

A widespread contemporary explanation for waning interest was the influence of gamblers. Gambling was a part of organized baseball since the mid–1860s, with gamblers often operating openly at ballparks. At best, this gave the affair an air of disreputability, discouraging some potential spectators. In the most extreme instances, gamblers paid players to deliberately lose games. The number of documented occurrences is small, but the perception existed that games were not necessarily honest. When baseball was revived in the early 1880s, honest play and the expulsion of gamblers was a constant drumbeat in the press. Why were gamblers allowed in, if this was widely considered disreputable? There are some hints that the gamblers were members of the club. Its reorganization for the 1877 season included extraordinary measures to "prevent a certain element from getting into our association."[18] While the idea was sound, it came too late.

An underlying fact is that none of the old fraternal clubs survived the transition to the modern professional era. Greater than any local factor was the inability to adapt. They began as social clubs of men gathering for exercise and occasionally playing against other, similar clubs. As match games by the first nine became the primary purpose of the club, the best players inevitably became separated from the rest of the club. As the clubs began hiring professionals, first covertly then openly, the division grew, with a club sponsoring a team. In many instances the club became irrelevant to the team, and died off.

The Athletics early on went a different route, with the club becoming effectively a booster organization. This arrangement had some advantages. It provided a built-in fan base, their membership dues a source of capital. But the dues were only a minor source of income. In the 1873 season the club's proceeds were $22,073.34, with only $3,390 of this from the 226 members. The bulk of income, over $17,000, was from gate receipts.[19]

The final balance sheet for 1873 showed a small profit. Two years later the club, with a similar income, ran a small deficit.[20] Underlying this, however, was the subtext that player salaries were kept down by letting key players be signed by other clubs. The most notable was Adrian Anson, who went on to be a star player for Chicago. The Athletics also lost pitcher Dick McBride to Boston and catcher John Clapp to St. Louis. They were unable to find effective replacements for either position.

A new model for a professional baseball club arose in the 1870s: the stock company. This model, standard today, has investors buying stock rather than members paying dues. It allows for a small number of shareholders holding different numbers of shares, lending itself to more concentrated raising of capital and centralized direction of the organization.

The Athletics attempted to solve their financial problems by converting to a stock organization, but the project was a failure. The initial proposal was to sell 200 shares at $50 each. It immediately became apparent that they would have difficulty finding buyers at this price, so the issue was changed to 400 shares at $25 each. (By way of comparison, the 1873 financial figures showed about 200 members paying annual dues of $15.) By mid–January less than half of the shares were subscribed. The final sales figures were not published, but it is likely that not many more were sold. The leadership had tried to raise new capital while maintaining the flavor of the old club, even emphasizing how little changed the new organization was from the old. The result was that the problems were left unchanged.[21]

The following season, 1876, saw the collapse of the team, both on the field and financially. The economics of limited initial capitalization required that expenses be met through gate receipts, but as it became obvious that the team was outclassed, attendance dropped. By mid–August the balance in the treasury was reduced to $20.84. Payroll wasn't being met, leading to embarrassments like the cancellation of an exhibition game in Harrisburg because only seven players showed up at the train station. By late September it was apparent that the money wasn't there for the team to travel west to finish its schedule, and its season was announced over.[22]

Ultimately the Athletics failed because they were unable to adapt in time to the changing competitive conditions of the 1870s, with stock clubs in other cities more effective at raising capital needed to field a winning team, and were unable to maintain the confidence of the public. There was an entrenched baseball establishment that would not or could not change its ways and which included individuals with interests at odds with those of the club. By 1877 the leaders seem to have understood this, but in the weak economy they were unable to effect the necessary changes.

CLUB MEMBERS (1870 AND EARLIER)

George Bechtel: See Keystone Base Ball Club.

Richard W. Benson: Richard W. Benson was secretary of the Athletic Club from 1862 to 1873. A grocer's clerk, Benson was 45 when he died suddenly on June 26, 1875.[23]

Nathan Berkenstock: Nate Berkenstock was one of the founding members of the Athletics and, after serving briefly in the Civil War, he played first base on the first nine through the end of the 1866 season. The following year he became so dismayed by the club's use of "revolving" players that he submitted his resignation.[24] But he patched up his differences and even played a single game for the Athletics after they joined the National Association. Berkenstock has two distinctions that differentiate him from all of the game's other "cup of coffee" major leaguers. One is that his 1831 year of birth makes him the first-born major leaguer. The other is that Berkenstock's one major league appearance came in the final game of the season and his game-ending catch in right field clinched the pennant for the Athletics. In 1886 Berkenstock was described as one of the last four surviving founders of the Athletic Club.[25] A hat store owner by profession, Nate Berkenstock died in Philadelphia on February 23, 1900.

Thomas Haney Berry: Tom Berry joined the Athletics in 1867 and was one of the outside players whose additions caused dissension within the club. For more on his career, see the entry on the Chester Club.

William H. Cunnington: William Cunnington was born in England around 1829 and became a journalist after settling in Philadelphia. He was one of the 15 founders of the Athletic Club and is credited with coming up with the club's name.[26] He covered the Civil War for the *Philadelphia Inquirer* and was associated with several Philadelphia newspapers after the war, also writing several books. He was described in 1886 as one of the last four surviving founding members of the Athletic Club.[27] Cunnington died in Philadelphia on February 6, 1897.[28]

Ned Cuthbert: See Keystone Base Ball Club.

Charles A. Denney: Charles A. Denney was one of the founders of the Athletic Club. In 1886 he was described as a "celebrated checker-champion" and as one of the last four surviving founding members of the Athletic Club.[29] The only possible person he could be is Charles Augustus Denney, a leather dealer who was born in Germany on April 15, 1833, and died in Philadelphia on September 23, 1906.

Patsy Dockney: See Buckeyes of Cincinnati in *Base Ball Pioneers, 1850–1870.*

William Ernst: William Ernst was an Athletic Club founder and its initial president. Ernst was a lawyer who died in his native Philadelphia on February 14, 1891, at the age of 65.

Wes Fisler: Wes Fisler was a rare example of a player who fit in with the old style of middle-class social baseball club, and fully made the transition to the later model of baseball professional. He is also notable as a similarly rare example of a player from this period with a nickname both colorful and unquestionably authentic: Icicle.

Born in either 1841 or 1843, he was the son of Lorenzo Fisler, a physician and mayor of Camden, New Jersey. As a teenager he played town ball with the Camden Club.[30] He quickly adapted to the introduction of the New York game and joined the Equity Club. His playing stood out enough that he was selected to be the catcher on the Philadelphia squad in 1860 when the Excelsior Club of Brooklyn made its historic first visit of a New York club to Brooklyn.

He played with various clubs through the Civil War, but was with the Athletics from 1866 through the end of his playing career. The story is told that he was the last of the Athletic first nine to play for free. This may or may not be true, but would be consistent with his social standing. A common version of the story is that he was persuaded by his teammates to ask for a salary.[31] In any case he clearly was a paid professional from some time in the late 1860s through 1877.

Fisler was a good, though not great, player, mostly playing first base and second base. His place in baseball historical trivia is secure by virtue of his having scored the first earned run in National League history.[32]

After his retirement from playing he opened a haberdashery in Philadelphia and lived in the family home in Camden. He remained active in baseball, managing various minorleague entries from Camden. He spent his last years living in a rooming house in Philadelphia, dying in 1922.

Thomas Fitzgerald[33]: Thomas Fitzgerald led the Athletics and was president during their rise to pre-eminence in Philadelphia. He was born in New York City in 1819. He entered journalism as a teenager, holding editorial positions with various newspapers. He moved to Philadelphia in 1844 and in 1847 established his own paper, the *Item*. This was his main employment, and was very successful. He is said to have died a multimillionaire.

Fitzgerald's interests included the arts. He wrote several successful plays. He left his art collection to the Pennsylvania Academy of Fine Arts. He was a director of the Musical Fund Society and while serving as a controller he introduced music instruction in the public schools. It is likely this musical connection that led him to the Athletics, via the Handel and Haydn Society.

He was older than most players on amateur clubs. While it is likely that he took his exercise with the club, there is no record of his playing in any competitive match games. He served as umpire in various matches in the late 1860s and into the 1870s.

Fitzgerald campaigned for Abraham Lincoln. His progressive racial politics carried over into baseball. He was the umpire for (and probably helped arrange) the first game between a colored and a white club, in 1869 between the colored Pythian club and the white Olympic club.[34] Later that season he arranged a match between the Pythians and his own newspaper team, the City Items.

He was elected vice president of the Athletics in 1860, and president from 1861 to early 1866. He oversaw its rise to prominence. He and the club had a falling-out, for reasons which are not fully clear. He printed denunciations of the club and its practice of paying professionals — a practice that began during his tenure with the hiring of Al Reach. He and the club eventually reconciled, but he no longer took a major leadership role in baseball. Fitzgerald died on June 25, 1891, during a trip to London, England.

James H. Foran: Jim Foran was a regular for the Athletics in 1868 and played in the National Association's inaugural season. Foran later moved to California and is listed in the encyclopedias as dying in Los Angeles on January 30, 1928, but there is no proof that this man was the ballplayer. Former teammate Eddie Cuthbert reported in 1904 that "Forran is in jail in California for killing a man."[35] His whereabouts after that are difficult to trace.

Charles Merwin Gaskill: Charles Gaskill was born in New Jersey on August 14, 1838, and he and his brother Edward were well-known Philadelphia ballplayers. Charles was one of the Athletics' regular oufielders through the end of the 1868 season but he had died by 1870, leaving a wife and several children.[36]

Edwin A. Gaskill: Edwin Gaskill, Charles's younger brother, played occasionally for the Athletics in 1865. A lumber merchant by profession, he also served on Philadelphia's board of harbor commissioners. Edwin Gaskill was born in New Jersey around 1842 and died in Philadelphia on May 1, 1894.

Hicks Hayhurst: Elias Hicks Hayhurst — invariably known as Hicks — was a fixture of the Philadelphia baseball scene for over two decades. He was born probably somewhere from 1826 to 1830. Even his obituaries disagree on his age. He was trained as a chairmaker but later in life made his living as a wholesale grocer.[37]

He played town ball in the late 1850s with the Excelsior Town Ball Club and in 1860 took up the New York game with the Winona Base Ball Club.[38] He joined the Athletics the following year and was a regular in the outfield of the first nine for six years, and a backup player as late as 1869. It is a remarkable achievement that at a relatively advanced age he was able to adapt to the new game and play at the top level.

While still an active player Hayhurst served as an officer of the club, and after retiring from active play he assumed the managerial role. (In the era the manager was the business manager. The functions of the modern field manager were carried out by the team captain.) In this role Hayhurst led the Athletics to the 1871 pennant and through the tumultuous early years of the new professional league.

In 1867, while vice president, he served as the Athletic Club's delegate to the Pennsylvania State Association meeting in Harrisburg. There he sponsored for membership the Pythian Base Ball Club of Philadelphia, a colored club. The application was withdrawn after it became apparent that it would be rejected. This set the pattern for baseball and racial politics for nearly the next century.

While the fight was lost, Hayhurst stands out as being

not merely on the right side, but in the forefront. This was an era when baseball and broader politics could intersect. The attempt to integrate a colored club into organized baseball was a direct result of this. In 1874 Hayhurst entered politics as a Republican and served four years as a city councilman.

Hayhurst left the Athletics (apparently amicably) in 1875 to form a new professional club, the Centennials. This was ill-advised, and the club was short-lived. He dropped out of professional baseball after that and eventually joined the old Olympic Club, whom he had played town ball against 20 years before. He was the Olympic Club president at the time of his death, which occurred on December 19, 1882, in Philadelphia.

John J. Heisler: According to an 1886 obituary, John J. Heisler was one of the 15 members of the Handel and Haydn Musical Society who helped organize the Athletic Club. He played second base for the club during its inaugural season and continued to take a prominent role in its activities. Born in Maryland around 1830, Heisler took his own life on May 12, 1886, an act that a coroner's jury attributed to temporary insanity.[39]

George Heubel: See Forest City Base Ball Club of Cleveland in *Base Ball Pioneers, 1850–1870*.

George Daniel Kleinfelder: Dan Kleinfelder was a long-time regular for the Athletics who played a variety of positions before retiring in 1868. A butcher by profession, he died in Philadelphia on August 2, 1894, at the age of 54.

Gus Luengene: Gustav "Forest" Luengene played for the Athletics in 1864 and 1865. He soon moved to New York and worked as a tobacconist. He had returned to Philadelphia by 1915, when he reminisced about the days when "the players had to give their services without receiving a cent from the gate receipts in return."[40]

Fergy Malone: See Keystone Base Ball Club.

John Dickson McBride: Dick McBride was born in Philadelphia on November 30, 1844, and became well known on the local cricket scene while still a teenager. His decision to take up baseball was one of the key factors in the Athletic Club's rise to prominence, as he was soon recognized as one of the game's best pitchers. In the words of Henry Chadwick, "What Dick doesn't know about the tricks and dodges of strategic pitching isn't worth knowing."[41] Tim Murnane credited McBride with being the "first man to work the raise ball successfully."[42] McBride remained a star when the National Association came into being, winning 149 games and losing only 74 in five seasons. But he played only a few National League games in 1876 before retiring from baseball. McBride remained in Philadelphia as a postal clerk, but he lapsed into such obscurity that no notice was paid of his death on January 20, 1916. To this day, many reference books list an incorrect date of death and first name for McBride.

John F. McMullin: John McMullin was born in Philadelphia around 1849 and played for the Athletics in 1869. He then put in five seasons in the National Association. McMullin died

in Philadelphia on April 11, 1881. Tim Murnane credited him with being the first left-handed pitcher to throw a curveball and with being one of the masters of the fair-foul hit.[43]

Levi Samuel Meyerle: Born in 1845 in Philadelphia, Levi Meyerle was a very large man by the standards of his time at 6-feet-1 and 177 pounds. He was a regular for the Athletics in 1869 and then played eight major-league seasons. In 1871 he batted .492, a batting average that has never been topped in major-league history. More than four decades later, a Cleveland writer expressed the opinion that "if there be any one third baseman that will be known as long as base ball is played and records kept, that player is Meyerle."[44] Instead the hard-hitting early star is all but forgotten today. Levi Meyerle died on November 4, 1921, in Philadelphia.

DeWitt Clinton Moore: Colonel DeWitt C. Moore was the president of the Handel and Haydn Society and was one of several members of that organization who helped found the Athletic Club.[45] He was the field captain of the Athletics during their early years. His playing days soon ended, but he remained deeply involved in the club's activities, serving as both vice president and as president. He was also chosen vice president of the National Association of Base Ball Players in 1861. Moore was born in Ewing, New Jersey, on December 22, 1825, and graduated from Lafayette College. He worked as a commission merchant with the firms of F.V. Krug & Co. and Colladay, Trout & Co. He was also a colonel in the Pennsylvania State Guard. He died in Philadelphia on May 29, 1875, of kidney cancer.[46]

Lip Pike: See Atlantic Base Ball Club.

John Y. Radcliffe: John Radcliffe was born on June 29, 1846, in Philadelphia and was a regular for the Athletics from 1867 through the end of the 1870 season, primarily playing catcher and shortstop. Radcliffe played in the National Association in all five of its seasons and then became a successful produce merchant. He died in Ocean City, New Jersey, on July 26, 1911.

Al Reach: Al Reach is credited with being the first professional baseball player: a distinction he shares with several other candidates. Professionalism was outlawed by the National Association of Base Ball Players, and so was initially kept quiet. If Reach's professionalism was any first, it was that his was an open secret.

He was born in London, England, in 1840 and was raised in Brooklyn, where he was a star with the Eckford Club. After the Civil War he semi-openly marketed his skills. He reputedly was offered a position in Baltimore, but accepted a lower offer from the Athletics so as to be closer to home.[47] He became a fixture of the Philadelphia sporting scene.

Reach stayed with the Athletics through the rest of his career, mostly playing second base. (This despite his being left-handed, since the disadvantage of left-handedness in the position was still outweighed by the need for a skilled fielder.) He retired after the 1875 campaign and thereby missed playing in the National League. He came out of retirement for 1877, but withdrew as the Athletics faded into history.

He is best known for his contributions to baseball on the business and manufacturing side. While still playing, he opened a cigar store which soon became a gathering spot for the Philadelphia baseball community. As his playing career wound down he moved into retail sporting goods. In the early 1880s he took as partner an expert leather worker, Benjamin Shibe, and moved to the manufacturing side.

In 1882 Reach took another partner, a local real-estate and corporate lawyer named John Rogers, and formed a new baseball team: the Philadelphia Ball Club. They joined the National League the following year, and are today's Phillies.

He went on to become a grand old man of baseball well into the 20th century. He finally retired in the early 1920s, and died in Atlantic City, New Jersey, in 1928.

Harry C. Schafer: Harry Schafer played for the Athletics in 1868 and went on to have a very successful major-league career — in eight seasons in Boston, he played for four National Association champions and two National League pennant winners. He was born in Philadelphia on August 14, 1846, and died there on February 28, 1935.

John Phillips Jenkins Sensenderfer: "Count" Sensenderfer was a regular for the Athletics from 1866 to 1870 and was described in one account as the "model outfielder of the country."[48] He played in the major leagues for four seasons and then launched a successful political career, serving three terms as a Philadelphia city commissioner. A lifelong Philadelphian, Sensenderfer was born on December 28, 1847, and died on May 3, 1903.

Michael W. Smith: Third baseman and outfielder Mike Smith played on the first nine of the Athletics through the end of the 1865 season. He was a brother of John J. Smith of the Eastons and was a medical student.[49] Smith was only 25 when he died in Philadelphia on December 10, 1868, after what was described as a "severe illness."[50]

Isaac P. Wilkins: Ike Wilkins was born in Philadelphia around 1842 and graduated from Philadelphia's Central High School in the same class as early sportswriter Alfred H. Wright. He had already earned a reputation as a skater, cricketer, and town ball player before baseball caught on in Philadelphia in 1860. He played for a club called the Uniteds before that club merged with the Athletics. He became one of the mainstays of the Athletics, playing on the first nine until 1869, usually at shortstop. Wilkins later became the treasurer of the Schuylkill Navigation Company. He died in Bethayres, Montgomery County, Pennsylvania, on September 27, 1884.[51]

Other Club Members: Charles W. Bacon, H. Bartine, R. Bartine, Collom, John Conard, W. Coulston, B. Croasdale, R. Croasdale, W. Deal, Gratz, Dr. A.G. Heston, Kahmar, H.W. Karchner, Lipp, McCleary, F. Mudie, Patterson, Paul, Pharo, Potter, Reyer, G.H. Troutman, C. Warner, George Wilson, Woolman

Notes

1. The 1859 date is given in the *New York Clipper*, May 10, 1862; the April 1860 date is given in Charles A. Peverelly's 1866 *Book of American Pastimes*; the June 1860 date is given in *Wilkes' Spirit of the Times*, February 9, 1861. For an 1859 mention of the Athletics, see *Fitzgerald's City Item* (Philadelphia), October 22, 1859.

2. See the entry on the Olympic Base Ball Club for a discussion of town ball and the Olympics' membership roster. Peverelly misidentified Ernst as "William Emot" in what is likely a transcription error. See *Wilkes Spirit*, February 9, 1861, for the officers of the Athletics. No known record exists of the officers of 1859.

3. Versions of this origin story would be recounted for many years. The earliest known is in the *New York Clipper*, October 5, 1861, which presents the connection with the musical society as a contemporary fact.

4. Some sources list four matches, with one of October 31, 1862, vs. the Olympics incorrectly assigned to 1860. This confusion dates at least from 1868, in an unidentified article in the Chadwick scrapbooks vol. 1, citing Athletics scorer A.H. Wright. The origin of this confusion is not known.

5. *Wilkes' Spirit of the Times*, February 9, 1861.

6. *New York Clipper*, October 6, 1860; June 7, 1862.

7. Charles A. Peverelly, *Book of American Pastimes* (New York: Published by the Author, 1866), 480.

8. Ibid., 424.

9. *Philadelphia Inquirer*, October 31, 1865, November 7, 1865, November 20, 1865, November 27, 1865.

10. *North American and United States Gazette* (Philadelphia), May 25, 1868.

11. Chadwick scrapbooks, vol. 10.

12. *North American and United States Gazette* (Philadelphia), February 23, 1866.

13. *New York Clipper*, May 20, 1876; *Philadelphia Item*, June 13, 1876.

14. *Philadelphia City Item*, June 9, 1866, July 14, 1866, October 19, 1867.

15. *Philadelphia City Item*, October 19, 1867; *Press* (Philadelphia), August 26, 1865.

16. The club's performance is compiled from various Philadelphia newspapers. For Eggler, *Chicago Tribune*, July 1, July 8, and July 15, 1877; for Meyerle, *Philadelphia Sunday Dispatch*, July 22, 1877; for Ryan, *Philadelphia Weekly Times*, July 14, 1877.

17. *Philadelphia Sunday Item*, March 10, March 31, 1878.

18. Quoted from a letter written by Charles Cragin, secretary of the Athletics, in a letter from Harry Wright of the Bostons to William Hulbert, president of the National League, dated March 10, 1877, found in the Spalding Collection of the New York Public Library.

19. *New York Clipper*, November 22, 1873.

20. *Philadelphia Sunday Mercury*, November 14, 1875.

21. *Philadelphia Sunday Mercury*, November 28, 1875, January 16, 1876, April 16, 1876.

22. *Philadelphia Item*, August 15, 1876; *Philadelphia Sunday Mercury*, August 27, 1876, September 24, 1876.

23. *North American and United States Gazette* (Philadelphia), June 29, 1875.

24. *Ball Players' Chronicle*, June 20, 1867.

25. *New York Clipper*, May 22, 1886.

26. Athletic Scrapbook, National Baseball Hall of Fame.

27. *New York Clipper*, May 22, 1886.

28. *Philadelphia Inquirer*, February 9, 1897, 2.

29. *New York Clipper*, May 22, 1886.

30. The *West Jerseyman* of June 23, 1858, has two box scores of matches between the first eleven of the Camden and the second eleven of the Olympic clubs. The Camden roster includes "W. Fisler" and "L. Fisler," undoubtedly Wes and his brother Lorenzo.

31. John Shiffert, *Base Ball in Philadelphia* (Jefferson, N.C.: McFarland, 2006), p. 203, has a version that clearly is not entirely correct, as

it has him going to Thomas Fitzgerald for the salary two years after Fitzgerald had left the club.

32. Some modern sources incorrectly credit him with the first run. The game was played on April 22, 1876, between the Bostons and the Athletics in Philadelphia. The Bostons batted first — not a given for the visiting team in that era — and scored an unearned run in the second inning, and the Athletics an earned run. See the *New York Clipper*, April 29, 1876, for an account and box score.

33. The major source for Fitzgerald's non-baseball-related biography is Charles Morris, *The Makers of Philadelphia: An Historical Work Giving Sketches of the Most Eminent Citizens of Philadelphia from the Time of William Penn to the Present Day* (Philadelphia: L.R. Hamersley & Co., 1894), 122.

34. *Philadelphia Inquirer*, September 4, 1869, has a box score and full account of this match.

35. *Washington Post*, August 14, 1904.

36. *North American and United States Gazette* (Philadelphia), May 16, 23, and 30, 1870.

37. Obituary in the *Philadelphia Inquirer*, December 19, 1882, for his occupation, described as "a produce commission merchant." The 1880 census lists him as an "agent" and the 1870 census as a "bookkeeper."

38. Obituary in the *New York Clipper*, December 23, 1882; he appeared in a town ball game box score in the *New York Clipper*, August 11, 1860.

39. *New York Clipper*, May 22, 1886.

40. "Gus Luengene Is Among the Select; One of Only 3 Players Still Living Who Were Members of Athletics in 1864," *Philadelphia Inquirer*, October 10, 1915, 2.

41. *New York Clipper*, December 28, 1872.

42. *Boston Globe*, February 22, 1900.

43. *Boston Globe*, February 6, 1910, and March 7, 1915.

44. *Sporting News*, November 28, 1912.

45. *Dwight's Journal of Music*, October 2, 1858.

46. "Death of Colonel D.W.C. Moore," *Harrisburg Patriot*, June 1, 1875, 1; Selden Jennings Coffin, *Record of the Men of Lafayette: Brief Biographical Sketches of the Alumni of Lafayette College from Its Organization to the Present Time* (1879), 177.

47. This story is not universally accepted. See Shiffert, *Base Ball in Philadelphia*, 238.

48. Chadwick Scrapbooks, unidentified article.

49. *New York Clipper*, January 26, 1884.

50. *Philadelphia Inquirer*, December 12, 1868.

51. *Philadelphia Inquirer*, September 29, 1884, 8; *St. Louis Post-Dispatch*, September 30, 1884; *Sporting Life*, May 6, 1905; Chadwick Scrapbooks, obituary in unidentified source; E.F. French Scrapbooks.

❖ *Equity Base Ball Club* ❖
(Peter Morris)

CLUB HISTORY

The Athletic Club was Philadelphia's preeminent baseball nine during the 1860s and in retrospect its dominance of the city's baseball scene may seem inevitable. In fact, when the eventful 1860 season ended it was the now-forgotten Equity Club that seemed better positioned to emerge as Philadelphia's premier baseball club. Instead, the Civil War intervened, and as a result of the war and other factors the Equity Club was never again a serious contender.

A great deal of what is known about the Equity Club comes from a club history that appears in Charles A. Peverelly's 1866 *Book of American Pastimes*. Peverelly was a New York journalist who contributed to the profiles of that city's clubs, but in the case of out-of-town clubs he seems to have solicited a history from the club and published whatever was submitted. Thus the author of this history is most likely Equity Club corresponding secretary Eugene Armitt Burling Brown, which may explain why it begins with the startling declaration that the Equity Club "claims to be the Pioneer Base Ball Club of Pennsylvania."[1]

The explanation that follows, however, suggests that there is little basis for that boast. As the writer acknowledges, the Equity Club was not formed until April 21, 1860, when at least three "mere ball clubs" were already in existence in Philadelphia. By "mere ball club" a distinction clearly is being drawn between baseball and town ball, the game of preference

of the Olympics and of most of the Philadelphia clubs of the 1850s. Yet while most pre–1860 Philadelphia clubs played town ball, several seem to have experimented with the New York Game, with the Pennsylvania Base Ball Club adopting this version at the end of the 1859 season.[2]

The Equity Club does, however, deserve credit for being one of the Philadelphia clubs that sparked a major shift from town ball to baseball that took place in 1860. As Peverelly's correspondent put it, "Several clubs went to work 'with a will,' and made the inaugural season of 'our National Game' one long to be remembered." While no one club ought to be singled out as the leader of this groundswell, it can safely be said that none participated in it more heartily than the Equity Club. The author of an early 1861 article on the club in *Wilkes' Spirit of the Times*, after summarizing the 1860 season, recalled that "The Equity was organized with the determination to subdue, if possible, that lagging spirit which was very manifest among the base ball organizations of the Quaker City, and they look back with pride at having accomplished even more than they anticipated."[3] The club also took the significant step of joining the National Association of Base Ball Players (NABBP) and sending two delegates, Richard Fowler Stevens and Benjamin F. Shantz, to its 1860 convention.

Grounds were established between Ridge and Columbia avenues and 24th and 25th streets. After the war, this location was known by several different names and eventually became the site of Recreation Park, the first home of the Philadelphia

Phillies. In 1860, however, it was so central to the city's baseball activity that one newspaper account referred to it simply as "the Ball Ground, corner of Columbia and Ridge Avenue."[4] As John Shiffert explains, Ridge Avenue was one of the rare Philadelphia roads that followed the old Indian trails, which gave the field an odd shape that was not well suited to baseball. That disadvantage, however, was offset by the enormous recommendation of being located next to a trolley terminal, which made it possible for players from all over the city to congregate. As a result, the site was also the 1860 home of the Winona, Swiftfoot, and Pennsylvania clubs.[5]

For the purpose of the Equity Club this location had the even more important recommendation of easy access from New Jersey, where about half of the club's original first nine lived. That first nine, proudly listed in the account sent to Peverelly, "consisted of R.F. Stevens, pitcher; W.H. Litzenburg [sic], catcher; B.F. Shantz, first base; Frank Knight, second base; J.B. Daniels, third base; Harry Shantz, short stop; C. Fackler, right field; Weston Fisler, centre field; B. Loughery, left field." Of these, the Shantz brothers are definitely Philadelphians, while Litzenberg hailed from Pennsylvania and Daniels and Loughery seem to be from Pennsylvania. But Fisler was the son of a former mayor of Camden, New Jersey, and Fackler, Knight, and Stevens also are believed to have been living in New Jersey while they played for the Equity Club of Philadelphia.

The Equity Club played its historic first match game on June 11, losing 39–21 to the Winona Club.[6] This contest is now also generally given the distinction of being the first match game ever played in Philadelphia under the New York rules. Yet the club history in Peverelly, as well as a summary of the club's 1860 season published in Wilkes' Spirit of the Times in March 1861, fail to so much as mention this game, stating instead that the club's first game took place at the end of the month and resulted in a win over the Pennsylvania Club.[7] It's a puzzling contradiction.

The 1866 article was almost certainly the work of a club officer and the 1861 article may have been as well, so one possibility is that pride prevented them from admitting that the club's debut had ended in defeat. It is also possible that the Equity Club had some legitimate reason for not considering the June 11 contest to be a match game, such as a prior agreement between the two sides, but if so there is no mention of it. A different 1861 profile of the Winona Club in Wilkes' Spirit of the Times acknowledged the existence of this game, but its author recalled, "There was not much good playing exhibited in this match by either Club."[8] Perhaps this led the Equity Club to come to regard the game as a friendly practice, rather than an official match between the clubs. It seems unlikely that we will ever know for sure.

The remainder of the Equity Club's 1860 season is at least well documented. On June 25 the club earned its first match-game victory by defeating the Pennsylvania Club, 65–52, on the ground shared by the two clubs. The two sides were tied after eight innings of play, but Equity outscored its opponent 18–5 in the final inning.[9] Next up was a July 5 match against the Winonas that included among the spectators the president of the Atlantic Club of Brooklyn. The Equity Club emerged victorious, 59–39, and the match warranted a lengthy write-up in the New York Clipper, whose reporter expressed pleasure that, "This manly pastime has become a fixed institution in Philadelphia, there being already twelve regular clubs organized." The account, however, described the home field of the Equity Club as "a very poor ground" and one that would not be improved "even if the high grass with which it is surrounded were removed."[10]

A rematch between the two clubs took place on July 23 and resulted in a decisive 58–21 victory for the Equity Club.[11] This was followed by a second triumph against the Pennsylvania Club, 49–23, on August 25.[12] On September 19 the Equity Club won again, defeating the Keystone Club by a score of 42–20. The result, a fifth straight match victory, moved the Wilkes' reporter to observe that the Equity Club had in the 1860 season "enjoyed an almost uninterrupted tide of victory, notwithstanding they have engaged in an unusual number of games."[13]

As a result of their impressive performance, two Equity Club members, Wes Fisler and Richard Stevens, were selected to play for a Philadelphia picked nine in a September 24 match against Jim Creighton and the visiting Excelsiors of Brooklyn. To nobody's surprise, the Excelsiors won 15–4 in a contest played at Camac Woods (a site that became famous after the war as the home of the Athletics).[14] Despite the defeat, the respectable margin of victory and a crowd of some 1,500 spectators showed that baseball had made huge inroads in Philadelphia.

The much lower score for the contest between the picked nine and the Excelsiors suggested that the conditions at the Equity Club's home grounds were responsible for the relatively high scores of their matches. That supposition was confirmed on October 23 when the Equity Club traveled to West Philadelphia for what proved to be a low-scoring and tightly fought contest against the Hamilton Club. When the last out was made, the Hamilton Club had earned a 15–11 victory, ending the Equity Club's five-game winning streak.[15]

It looked as though the loss would also end any hopes of the Equity Club's being 1860 champions of Philadelphia. The Hamilton Club, although "the youngest organized club in the city," now boasted victories over the Pennsylvania, Athletic, and Equity clubs and had yet to suffer defeat.[16] Two weeks later, however, the Hamilton Club was beaten 18–16 by the Olympic Club, which had only just switched from town ball to baseball.[17] Once again, recognition as Philadelphia's top club was up for grabs.

The Equity Club staked its claim on November 12 in a contest played against the soon-to-be-famous Athletic Club at Camac Woods. After eight innings, with the Equity Club ahead 29–17, the Athletic Club elected to concede defeat. According to an account in the *Clipper*, "A little ill feeling was noticeable, throughout the game, and too strongly exhibited in the eighth innings. But at the end of the game, the clubs cheered each other ... the parties left the field, many of them arm in arm with each other — thus exhibiting that the ire displayed was absolutely temporary."[18]

That was the last match of the year for the Equity Club (though its second nine did play once more)[19] and the result left no clear champion for 1860. Including the June 11 loss to the Winona, the Equity Club boasted a 6–2 record but the Hamilton Club had an equally impressive 3–1 mark that included a win over the Equity Club. What it did mean, however, was that the 1861 season was anxiously awaited. Would one of those two clubs clearly establish itself as Philadelphia's best? Or would one of the additions to the rapidly growing baseball scene surpass both of them?

The account in Peverelly offers this description of the Equity Club's sophomore season: "In the spring of 1861, just as preparation was being made for an active season, the war drew most of the Equity Club to a different field, and, as a natural sequence, the organization of the club was for the time suspended."[20] The assertion was confirmed by an article at the war's conclusion explaining that the Equity Club was "obliged to suspend operations until the close of the war" when "many of its members" enlisted in the Union Army.[21] Another piece went still further, declaring that the Equity Club had been "unsurpassed" before the war, but then "almost all of its members enlisted in the service of their country."[22]

This last claim sounds like an overstatement but in fact at least six of the club's nine starters seem to have seen combat duty during the Civil War, with another serving in the New Jersey Militia. The loss of so many starters meant that only one game is known to have been scheduled in 1861, and it is not clear whether it was played.[23] The Equity Club had no recorded activity at all from 1862 through 1864, not even electing officers, which made for a four-year hiatus from baseball.

Careful analysis, moreover, shows just how much the Civil War upset the balance of power in Philadelphia baseball. While the Equity Club was far from dominant in 1860, it had a strong claim to the local championship and could well have solidified it if the war had not intervened. Of course the Civil War brought hardships to all of Philadelphia's baseball clubs, but not in the same measure. Many ballplayers from the Athletic and Keystone clubs also served in the Civil War, but the most notable ones were in the hundred-day regiments of 1864 (and even then managed to arrange furloughs to play baseball). In stark contrast, not only did the Equity Club lose almost its entire first nine but those enlistees served from near the start of the war until its conclusion, with most of them serving multiple tours of duty.

The result was that the Athletic Club grew stronger while the Equity Club and Philadelphia's other prewar clubs stood idle. By the end of the war, the Athletics had the benefit of five years of growth, while the members of the Equity Club were four years removed from any baseball competition. To make matters worse, the Equity Club's most talented player, Wes Fisler, had temporarily given up baseball and would eventually join the Athletic Club. These developments ensured the postwar dominance of the Athletics.

It would be silly to argue that the Equity Club *would* have been Philadelphia's preeminent club if only somehow the Civil War had been averted. Alternative histories are fun topics for debate, but in the end they rarely amount to much more than guesswork. Yet there is more than enough evidence to conclude that matters *might* have been very different. A few members of the Equity Club's first nine were past the ideal age for baseball in 1860, but the rest were young enough that new players could have been gradually introduced and the club's strength maintained. If the club had been successful in attracting the best players from talent-laden Philadelphia, the Equity Club might have vied with the top Brooklyn and New York City clubs for the national championship. At the least, the dominance of the Athletic Club — with the Keystones a distant second and the rest of the local clubs far behind — might have been transformed into a far more competitive situation.

Instead, when the war ended in 1865, there was little of the Equity Club's 1860 first nine left to preserve. Stevens and Daniels were now well into their thirties and both gave up baseball. They were joined in retirement by Ben Shantz, who was approaching thirty, and Frank Knight, who married as soon as he left the Army. Loughery seems to have left town and with Fisler inactive, the only remaining starters were Litzenberg, Fackler, and Harry Shantz.

Despite the severe losses, the Equity Club made an effort to rebuild in May of 1865. Despite the loss of so many starters, the reorganized club included several familiar faces, with Litzenberg serving as club secretary and handling the catching duties, Harry Shantz playing shortstop and acting as captain, and longtime treasurer J.H. Beitel again handling financial matters. Abandoning its prewar grounds, the club announced that its "play days are Tuesday and Friday afternoons of each week, at Fairmount Park, permission having been granted by Mr. Charles Dixey, the Commissioner of City Property."[24]

Nothing more was heard from the Equity Club in the months that followed, suggesting that its survival was in jeopardy. Eventually the club was forced to amalgamate with a younger club. According to the history in Peverelly, "a number of gentlemen connected with the Philadelphia and Reading Railroad, having formed themselves into a kind of mutual exercise club, for ball-playing and general exercise, overtures were made them by the Equity, with privilege of an equal distribution of officers. This proving agreeable, a consolidation was effected, and they once more began to play, securing, temporarily, the grounds attached to the Saunders Institute in West

Philadelphia. Subsequently, they secured their present fine grounds at Forty-first street and Lancaster avenue."

A new club president was duly elected and several intrasquad games were staged. By November, a new first nine had been chosen and the Equity Club's first match game in five years was scheduled for the new grounds. The Bachelor Club was the opposing side and it emerged victorious by a 32–17 score.[25]

The Equity Club's first post-war match game was also its final recorded contest. The club remained ominously silent in the spring of 1866 and by that summer all appearances were that it had died a natural death. Then came another flurry of activity.

In the fall the club sent representatives to the conventions of both the state baseball association and the National Association of Base Ball Players.[26] Corresponding secretary E.A. Burling Brown was one of the Equity delegates at the state baseball convention, which may account for the rosy picture of the club's status that was sent to Peverelly. According to the account, "The [Equity] club was not engaged in many games during the season of 1866, neither do they claim to be very strong at present; but with Colonel Fitzgerald, of the *City Item*, at their head, united with the fine material of which the organization is composed, they are certain to take high rank at an early day as one of the prominent clubs of the country."

That claim was, to put it kindly, rather fanciful, as were so many others apparently made by Burling Brown. So what was the background of the Equity Club's corresponding secretary? Appropriately enough, he was the grandson of Charles Brockden Brown, the Philadelphian whose elaborate gothic tales have led many literary critics to judge him America's first major novelist. There is no evidence that Burling Brown inherited his grandfather's literary skills but it might be argued that he followed in his distinguished ancestor's footsteps as a writer of imaginative works.

In any event, the Equity Club was not heard from again and soon faded into oblivion. That is a shame, as the club has a strong claim to having been Philadelphia's best prewar club and might well have remained a major force on the city's baseball scene if not for the intervention of the Civil War.

CLUB MEMBERS

The original first nine of the Equity Club, accorded the honor of being listed in Peverelly, "consisted of R.F. Stevens, pitcher; W.H. Litzenburg [*sic*], catcher; B.F. Shantz, first base; Frank Knight, second base; J.B. Daniels, third base; Harry Shantz, short stop; C. Fackler, right field; Weston Fisler, center field; B. Loughery, left field." Here is what is known about those nine men.

J.B. Daniels: The only man by this name in the 1860 Philadelphia city directory was a watchcase maker named James B. Daniels. Research determined that this man was the

business partner of Equity Club president Lawrence Mann and that the two men and their families also shared a house, so there can be little doubt that this is the ballplayer. Daniels was born in Pennsylvania around 1831 and he and his wife had been living in New York state in 1855 when their first child was born. By 1880 they were living in Brooklyn, where Daniels continued to work as a watchcase maker until his death on December 22, 1901.

C. Fackler: The only man by this name of plausible age is Charles F. Fackler, the son of a Camden merchant. Fackler was born around 1839 and enlisted in the first regiment of Camden volunteers that was formed after the outbreak of the Civil War. By war's end he had served in four different New Jersey regiments. He returned to Camden after the war and again played for the Equity Club in 1865. After his father's death Charles F. Fackler moved his family to a farm in Lawrence Township. He died there on March 13, 1926.

Weston Dickson Fisler: Wes Fisler, whose father served several terms as mayor of Camden in the 1840s and 1850s, was the only member of the Equity Club to go on to a professional career. His life is discussed more fully in the entry on the Athletic Club.

Frank Knight: There was no man by this name in Philadelphia in 1860, so the supposition is that he was Franklin L. Knight of Camden. Knight was born around 1838 and fought in the Civil War, first in the 3rd New Jersey Infantry and then as a lieutenant colonel in the 24 New Jersey Infantry. Knight returned home at war's end and was married in Camden in November of 1864. He later worked as a bookkeeper and clerk and died in Camden on November 16, 1895.

William H. Litzenberg: William H. Litzenberg is believed to have been the youngest member of the first nine, having been born around 1843. During the Civil War he served in two Pennsylvania regiments, the 29th and 124th infantries. He rejoined the Equity Club in 1865, also serving as club secretary. Litzenberg married in 1869 and soon left Philadelphia. A bookkeeper by profession, he died in Wilkinsburg, Pennsylvania, on April 21, 1911.

B. Loughery: It's always a challenge to identify a man whose first name is not provided, but in this case there's an obvious candidate: Bernard Loughery, who like fellow club members James B. Daniels and Lawrence Mann was a watchcase maker by profession. Census records reveal that this Bernard Loughery was born in Ireland around 1841. He appears to be a Bernard Loughery who served in the 116th Pennsylvania Infantry during the Civil War and died on July 1, 1899, but little more is known about him.

Benjamin F. Shantz: Brothers Ben and Harry Shantz were two of the mainstays of the Equity Club. Ben was born in Philadelphia in March of 1836 and his baseball career ended when he enlisted in the 197th Pennsylvania Infantry. After the war, he married and raised two children and worked as a clerk. Shantz died in Atlantic City on August 6, 1900.

Harry Shantz: Ben Shantz's younger brother's full name may have been William Henry Shantz, but if so he went by his middle name. Born in Philadelphia on May 12, 1838, Harry served in three different Pennsylvania regiments, including the 197th alongside his brother. He was one of the few members of the Equity Club to continue playing after the war, becoming club captain. Shantz never married and worked as an engine turner. He died in Philadelphia on December 27, 1913.

Richard Fowler Stevens: Equity Club pitcher R.F. Stevens can only be Richard Fowler Stevens, a member of the famous Stevens family. Born in Hoboken, New Jersey, in July of 1832, Stevens was the grandson of Colonel John Stevens III, the steamboat inventor who pioneered ferryboat excursions between New York City and Hoboken, and the nephew of John Cox Stevens, the sportsman who capitalized by administering the Elysian Fields, home of the Knickerbockers and most of the other important early baseball clubs. Richard Fowler Stevens graduated from Columbia in 1852 and became involved in several of the family's railroad holdings and other businesses. By 1856 he was pitching for the Knickerbockers at Elysian Fields and attracting attention for his use of an early version of the curveball. According to an account, Stevens "sends the ball with exceeding velocity, and he who strikes it fairly must be a fine batsman. It is questionable, however, whether his style of pitching is most successful, many believing a slow ball curving near the bat, to be the most effective."[27] Stevens married Emily Gouverneur Dickinson in 1857 and the couple settled in Gloucester, New Jersey, where they began a family. Stevens, however, still found time to pitch for the Equity Club until the outbreak of the Civil War, when he became brigadier-general of the 1st Brigade of the New Jersey Militia, a rank he held until the war's end. Stevens continued his business activities after the war but never again was involved in baseball. By 1896 he was living in South Orange, New Jersey. Richard Fowler Stevens died on September 2, 1914.[28]

Postwar Additions to the First Nine: Dunkel; C. Hancock (presumably Clinton G. Hancock (1845–1896), who served as club secretary in 1866); Schelenberg; Scott; Wood.

Nonplaying Club Officers: J.H. Beitel (club treasurer in 1860, 1861, 1865, and 1866); Eugene Armitt Burling Brown (corresponding secretary in 1865 and 1866); Edgar Darrach (1842–1913; one of two men who served as club president in 1865); Col. Thomas Fitzgerald (club president in 1866; see Athletic Club); James A. Lewis, Jr.,(club vice president in 1860); Lawrence K. Mann (born 1832 England; club president in 1860 and 1861); Charles R. Shantz (one of two men who served as club president in 1865; not a brother of Ben and Harry, though perhaps a cousin); H.L. Shillingford (club vice president in 1865); Benjamin Tithian (club secretary in 1861).

SOURCES: This piece is based upon contemporaneous newspaper sources and three major sources: Charles A. Peverelly's *Book of American Pastimes*; John Shiffert's *Base Ball in Philadelphia* (Jefferson, North Carolina: McFarland, 2006);

and "Pre-Civil-War 'Base Ball'- Related Games Played in Greater Philadelphia Region," a compilation by Craig B. Waff that is currently found on the Retrosheet.org website.

Notes

1. Charles A. Peverelly, *Book of American Pastimes* (New York: Published by the Author, 1866), 486–488.
2. "Pennsylvania Base Ball Club," *Porter's Spirit of the Times*, November 26, 1859, 196. John Shiffert, in *Base Ball in Philadelphia* (Jefferson, N.C.: McFarland, 2006), pages 21–26, discusses several other Philadelphia clubs that may have used the New York Rules prior to 1860.
3. "Out-Door Sports: Base Ball: Equity Base Ball Club of Philadelphia," *Wilkes' Spirit of the Times*, March 9, 1861. This article was one of a series profiling Philadelphia clubs that were published in *Wilkes'* throughout the winter of 1860–1861.
4. *Philadelphia Inquirer*, August 24, 1860, 1.
5. Shiffert, *Base Ball in Philadelphia*, 25–26.
6. "Winona and Equity," *New York Clipper*, undated 1860 clipping in Mears Collection, Cleveland Public Library; "Philadelphia Base Ball Clubs," [New York] *Sunday Mercury*, June 24, 1860, 5; "Equity Base Ball Club, of Philadelphia," *Wilkes' Spirit of the Times*, June 30, 1860, 260.
7. Peverelly, *Book of American Pastimes*, 486; "Out-Door Sports: Base Ball: Equity Base Ball Club of Philadelphia," *Wilkes' Spirit of the Times*, March 9, 1861, 5.
8. "Out-Door Sports: Base Ball: Winona Base Ball Club of Philadelphia," *Wilkes' Spirit of the Times*, March 30, 1861, 52.
9. "Out-Door Sports: Base Ball: Base Ball in Philadelphia," *Porter's Spirit of the Times*, July 10, 1860, 309. Both the 1861 summarizer and Peverelly ascribe a date of June 26 to this game.
10. "Winona vs. Equity," *New York Clipper*, undated 1860 clipping in Mears Collection. Other shorter accounts of the game include "Out-Door Sports: Base-Ball: Equity vs. Winona," *Porter's Spirit of the Times*, July 17, 1860, 325, and "Out-Door Sports: Base Ball: Base Ball in the Quaker City — Equity Ball Club vs. Winona," *Wilkes' Spirit of the Times*, July 21, 1860, 315.
11. "Out-Door Sports: Base Ball: Equity vs. Winona," *Wilkes' Spirit of the Times*, August 4, 1860, 347, and "Winona vs. Equity," *New York Clipper*, undated 1860 clipping in Mears Collection. Other brief accounts include Clio, "Out-Door Sports: Base-Ball: Base Ball in Philadelphia — Equity vs. Winona," *Porter's Spirit of the Times*, July 31, 1860, 357, and "Equity vs. Winona (of Philadelphia), [New York] *Sunday Mercury*, July 24, 1860, 5.
12. Identical articles discussing the game appeared in "Out-Door Sports: Base Ball: Base Ball among the 'Keystone Boys,' " *Porter's Spirit of the Times*, September 4, 1860, 436 and 437, and "Out-Door Sports: Base Ball: Base Ball in the Quaker City — Equity vs. Pennsylvania," *Wilkes' Spirit of the Times*, September 8, 1860, 5.
13. "Out-Door Sports: Base Ball: Base Ball in Philadelphia — Equity vs. Keystone," *Wilkes' Spirit of the Times*, September 29, 1860, 53.
14. For the most detailed description of the game itself (including some brief commentary on Fisler's catching), see "Interesting Match in Philadelphia, between the Excelsior, of Brooklyn, and Nine Philadelphians," *New York Clipper*, undated September 1860 article in the Mears Collection.
15. "Out-Door Sports: Base-Ball: Base Ball in Philadelphia — Hamilton vs. Equity," *Porter's Spirit of the Times*, November 6, 1860, 165; [untitled article], *New York Clipper*, undated 1860 clipping in Mears Collection; "Out-Door Sports: Cricket [sic]: Base Ball in the Quaker City — Equity vs. Hamilton," *Wilkes' Spirit of the Times*, November 10, 1860, 149.
16. *Philadelphia Inquirer*, November 8, 1860, 1.
17. "Base Ball," *Philadelphia Inquirer*, November 8, 1860, 1; "Out-Door Sports: Base Ball: Hamilton vs. Olympic," *Porter's Spirit of the Times*, November 13, 1860, 197; "Base Ball Matches, Trotting and Running at Point Breeze," *New York Clipper*, undated November 1860

clipping in the Mears Collection; "Out-Door Sports: Base Ball: Base Ball in Philadelphia," *Wilkes' Spirit of the Times,* November 24, 1860, 180.

18. "Base Ball — Equity vs. Athletic," *New York Clipper,* undated November 1860 clipping in the Mears Collection. A short account also appeared in "Equity vs. Athletic (of Philadelphia)," [New York] *Sunday Mercury,* November 25, 1860, 5.

19. The Equity Club second nine played two known games in 1860. The first was a 63–27 loss to the Winona second nine on September 21, 1860, which was reported in "Winona vs. Equity (of Philadelphia)," [New York] *Sunday Mercury,* October 7, 1860, 5. The second was a 32–19 loss to the same club on November 29, 1860, which was reported in an untitled *New York Clipper* clipping in the Mears Collection.

20. Peverelly, *Book of American Pastimes,* 487.

21. "The Equity Base Ball Club," *Philadelphia Inquirer,* June 1, 1865, 2.

22. *Philadelphia Illustrated New Age,* August 25, 1865, 2.

23. The *Philadelphia Inquirer,* June 8, 1861, 2, reported that the Equity Club would play the Atlantic Club of Philadelphia that afternoon, but no record of the game has been found.

24. "The Equity Base Ball Club," *Philadelphia Inquirer,* June 1, 1865, 2.

25. *Philadelphia Inquirer,* November 27, 1865.

26. *Philadelphia Patriot,* October 18, 1866, 3; *Philadelphia Inquirer,* December 13, 1866, 8.

27. *Porter's Spirit of the Times,* December 6, 1856.

28. *Trenton Times,* September 6, 1914, 6.

❖ Keystone Base Ball Club ❖
(Peter Morris)

It was the fate of the Keystone Club of Philadelphia to become the city's second best club and yet to lag well behind the Athletics. This status had its advantages, as it provided the club with regular opportunities to play against top-flight rivals that came to town to challenge the Athletics. But it also meant that the Keystones often found themselves overshadowed and had a difficult time retaining players.

The Keystone Base Ball Club of Philadelphia was organized on November 30, 1859, amid a flurry of activity that saw many town-ball clubs switch to baseball and many new clubs form. The Keystones played three known games in 1860, losing two of them. The 1861 season got off to an early start, with the club's first and second nines playing each other in late March at the club's grounds at the lower terminus of the Second and Third street railroads.[1] But then came the outbreak of the Civil War, bringing an abrupt end to many of the new clubs.

The Keystones survived, although they played only three recorded games during the next 2½ years. Things picked up again in September of 1863 as the club began playing at Eleventh and Wharton and took advantage to host the Eurekas of Newark and play two games against the Athletics. All three contests ended in defeat for the Keystones, but that was no surprise considering the high quality of the opposition. More important were the signs of improvement that were evident in the second game against the Athletics — after a 25–5 loss in the opener, the Keystones were nosed out 14–13 in the rematch. The encouraging season ended with a match in late November.

Another outburst of interest followed in 1864, despite the ongoing war. The governor of Pennsylvania had issued a call for 30,000 new enlistees and the resulting "hundred-day" regiments meant the "absence from the city of nearly all the young and best players, none but the older members being left." The Keystones were especially hard hit; for one game, "they were not only minus the services of some of their best players, but

had neither an organized nine to play with [nor] had they been benefited by practice together."[2]

Even so, the Keystones played quite a busy schedule for wartime, including two games apiece against the Camden Club and the Athletics and playing host to two Brooklyn clubs, the Resolutes and the Atlantics. The visits of the Brooklyn clubs were big events in Philadelphia. The Atlantics arrived in Philadelphia on August 7, 1864, and "registered at the American Hotel. On the ninth, the club and friends were invited to a supper given by the Keystone Club, at the St. James's Hotel. On the tenth, the Club and friends were taken in charge by the Olympic Club, and by stages proceeded to the Schuylkill Falls, and there partook of a supper. On the twelfth, they were invited to a fruit supper provided by Mrs. Col. Moore."[3]

The 1864 season was less successful on the field for the Keystones, as the club lost six of its seven recorded games.[4] This was understandable in light of the disruption of the lineup that the war brought and the quality of the opponents, but it didn't show the hoped-for improvement. Even so, there were encouraging signs.

An article in the *Brooklyn Eagle* described the Athletic and Keystone clubs as "the two strongest and most prominent Base Ball clubs of Philadelphia." Its author, almost certainly Henry Chadwick, dismissed the other three Philadelphia-area clubs, noting that the Camden Club was still "a new organization, who never played before last Spring," that "the Mercantile Club merely practice the game for exercise at irregular periods," and that the venerable Olympic Club "having played Town Ball for nearly thirty years, favor that game almost entirely; and but for few members would not play Base Ball at all."

But when he turned to the Keystone Club, he was rhapsodic: "the hospitable whole souled players composing this now flourishing club are in a fair way to become the leading club in Philadelphia and take equal rank with the strongest in the country. The Keystones number nearly *two hundred* members and have three good nines."[5] The stage, it would seem, was set for the emergence of the Keystones as a national power.

When the Civil War ended in the spring of 1865, the club was able to present a younger and improved first nine. In the 1864 contest against the Resolutes, the Keystones had fielded this lineup: Dick, c; Mulholland, 1b; Coady, ss; E. Cope, p; Deal, lf; Frazier, 2b; H. Cope, cf; Duffy, rf; McIntyre, 3b.[6] In 1865, only Dick, Elias Cope, Mulholland, and Deal were still in the first nine. Frazier now filled a reserve role, while the others had been replaced by promising young players such as William Wallace, Eddie Woods, Ned Cuthbert, and Fergy Malone.

This younger incarnation of the Keystones played at least twenty games in 1865, highlighted by an ambitious tour that saw the club leave Philadelphia on the Camden and Amboy Railroad on the morning of July 24 and play six games in seven days in Newark, Hoboken, and Brooklyn.[7] The trip gave the ballplayers of Brooklyn a chance to repay the hospitality they had received in Philadelphia.

"THE KEYSTONE CLUB COMING — GIVE THEM A WORTHY RECEPTION," urged a headline in the *Brooklyn Eagle*. The article, again undoubtedly written by Chadwick, described the Keystones as "a splendid set of fellows, and when the Atlantics visited Philadelphia, last summer, treated the Brooklyn boys like princes. Drives, sails, banquets, etc., in abundance, and anything that the heart could wish or tongue express was ever before them. The Atlantic Club haven't forgotten these hospitalities, nor can they remove them from their memory. It is a perpetual green spot in their recollection, fruitful with gratitude and earnest respect."[8]

A worthy reception did indeed await the Keystones. The players were escorted to Coney Island and given a series of banquets during their weeklong stay. On their final night in Brooklyn, Mayor Fernando Wood and the heads of many city departments were among the party of 75 that dined at the Oceanic House. The songs, toasts, and merriment went on so late that only half of the visitors made the midnight train on which they were scheduled to return home.[9]

Such moments made the 1865 season a memorable one for the Keystones, yet the results on the field were disappointing. With a stable lineup of much younger players, there were victories over such renowned clubs as the Resolutes and Eckford of Brooklyn and the Empires of New York City. But none of these clubs had impressive seasons in 1865 and these triumphs were offset by a much longer list of defeats. Especially disheartening was a pair of losses to the Athletics, the second of which was a season-ending 49–5 debacle.

Perhaps that was why the 1866 campaign got off to a very slow start, with the Keystones having played only a few games by the end of the summer. Things finally perked up in September, when the Excelsiors of Brooklyn came to town and the Keystones again outdid themselves in entertaining their guests. According to an account in Charles A. Peverelly's *Book of American Pastimes*, the Excelsiors were met in Philadelphia "by a delegation of the Keystone Club. After a dinner at the Continental, the party left for the scene of action." At the conclusion of the game, which ended in a draw, "the Keystones took the Excelsiors to Carncross & Dixie's Minstrel Hall, and paid them courteous attention."[10]

Visits from a number of other strong out-of-town clubs followed that fall, and the Keystones upheld their reputation as Philadelphia's second strongest club. In a season-ending series for local supremacy, however, the Keystones were once again beaten by the Athletics. Another blow followed a few days later with the death of 27-year-old Francis A. Frazer, the club's secretary since its inception and a former member of the first nine.

At the outset of the 1867 season, there was reason to be optimistic that better days were ahead. Frazer's replacement as secretary informed Charles A. Peverelly that the club boasted eighty-two active members (seventy contributing and twelve honorary), practiced on Mondays and Thursdays at the parade ground at Eleventh and Wharton streets, and had a uniform consisting of a white shirt trimmed with blue, blue pantaloons, an elastic belt, and a white cap bearing the word "Keystone."[11]

Philadelphia was now challenging New York for the title of the country's baseball capital. One sportswriter observed that baseball was now "strictly" the "national pastime," explaining:

> As late as the year 1860, base ball was confined to one or two of the middle states — New York being the centre. Now it is played in every state in the union, from Maine to Oregon. New York has in a measure lost its ascendancy in the game, Philadelphia now being the base ball centre of the country. There are ten clubs in the Quaker City to one in the metropolis, and last year the best record made by any club in the United States was made by the champion club of Pennsylvania — the gallant Athletics of Philadelphia.[12]

Just as important as the geographic expansion of the game was the increasing participation of first- and second-generation immigrants, and in this area the Keystones also played a leading role. Its roster included Irish-born players Fergy Malone, Hugh McLarnan, Francis Frazier, and many others of Irish heritage, while its list of directors was also dotted with surnames like Duffy, Mahony, and McCarthy. Identifiably German names like Halbach and Kulp were also represented on the club.

Befitting the sterling quality of play in Philadelphia, the 1867 season saw the Keystones post impressive wins over the Atlantics, Eckfords, and Excelsiors of Brooklyn and the Mutuals of New York. This last victory was especially exhilarating, as it came two days after the visiting Mutuals had rallied to hand the Athletics their first defeat of the season. But when they faced the Keystones, the Mutuals "had things all their own way for eight innings," only to be shocked in the ninth when their hosts "treated the New Yorkers to a 'whitewash,' and batting for double figures, scored eleven runs, which performance won the Mutual ball 'like a mice.'"[13]

Yet in spite of such signal triumphs, the Keystone Club was finding it harder to maintain its status in Philadelphia. In addition to losing to the Athletics once again, the Keystones also lost to two other local rivals, the Arctics and the West Philadelphia Club. The latter defeat prompted a sportswriter to warn, "The Keystones must look out for their laurels, originally the champions of the State, they yielded the palm to the Athletics, but since then have had the reputation of being second best in the State."[14]

In addition to the threat posed by the improvement of other Philadelphia clubs, the Keystones were also facing the danger of losing star players to other clubs. Fergy Malone had moved on after the 1865 season and Cuthbert had followed suit one year later, joining the crosstown Athletics. More defections occurred after the 1867 campaign, with Billy Dick, Eddie Woods, and Elias Cope all joining Malone on the Olympic Club of Washington. During the Keystone Club's second game of the 1868 season, "the staging gave way, precipitating a number of people to the ground."[15] There were no serious injuries, but no doubt the Keystones were able to relate to the feeling of having the ground fall out from beneath them.

With a largely new roster, the Keystones won only five of the sixteen recorded games they played in 1868. Despite the poor record, the club did manage signal victories over the Unions of Morrisania and the Cincinnati Base Ball Club — the club that was to go undefeated in 1869 and become universally known as the Red Stockings.

Billy Dick and Eddie Woods returned to the Keystones in 1869 and their addition, coupled with the availability of several longtime diamond stalwarts, prompted the club to turn professional. The club's new beginning was greeted with optimism in some quarters. "The Keystones," noted one sportswriter, "under the inspiring influence of [Theodore] Bomeisler, [Dan] Kleinfelder, and other new members, are making arrangements for a season of brilliancy and success. Their meeting last week was the largest and most enthusiastic they have held. Arrangements were made for an early spring, and challenges were directed to be issued to all leading clubs. A complimentary benefit was tendered the Keystones, April 8th, at Fox's American Theatre. A mammouth [sic] bill was offered, most of the prominent artists of the city volunteering, in addition to the full strength of the regular company."[16] Another publication also predicted a strong season for the Keystones, but criticized the club having "foolishly hired [John] Radcliffe, the man expelled from the Athletic Club, to catch for them."[17]

Yet the 1869 season proved a disappointing one, as Radcliffe lasted only a few games and the Keystones won only three of twenty contests against professionals. On that dismal note, the club's history came to an apparent end. After being one of at least eighteen baseball clubs represented at a meeting in No-

vember of 1869, the Keystone Club faded out of view.[18] Over the next few years, many former Keystone players showed up in the lineup of another Philadelphia club called the Experts, offering apparent confirmation that the Keystone Club was defunct.

But then in 1877, this note appeared in the *New York Sunday Mercury*: "The Keystones, of Philadelphia, have been reorganized, and propose placing the following team in the field: Morris, pitcher; Ritterson, catcher; Samson, Fisher, and Firth on the bases; Shaw, short stop; with Bartlett, McBride and McCartney in the out-field, the last named acting as change catcher. The Keystones in 1875 were prominent contestants for the amateur championship."[19] But were the 1875 and 1877 incarnations of the Keystone Club in fact a continuation of the original club or just a new one recycling an old name?

Seven years later, the Keystone Club of Philadelphia was admitted into the Union Association, prompting the *Philadelphia Inquirer* to write, "The Keystone Club held a prominent place in the base ball fraternity years ago, but dropped out of sight at the time the national game fell off in the patronage bestowed by the public."[20] The wording certainly suggests that this club was seen as a continuation of the original Keystone Club.

Whether the 1884 club was in fact directly connected to the original Keystones is debatable, and cannot be determined with certainty based on the evidence now available. But there are at least two suggestive facts that point to some connection. The chairman of the 1884 club was Tom Pratt, who had been a star pitcher for the Athletics in the 1860s. In addition, Fergy Malone, eight years after his last major-league appearance, came out of retirement to catch for the Keystones in the first game of the 1884 campaign.

CLUB MEMBERS

George M.D. Albertson: George Albertson was born in Philadelphia in November of 1847 and played first base for the Keystones in 1869. He worked as the foreman of a car shop and tube works. He died in Philadelphia on July 1, 1905.

Samuel L. Barnes: Samuel L. Barnes was club president in 1860 and 1861.

George W. Bechtel: George Bechtel was born in Philadelphia on September 2, 1848. He began playing baseball with clubs in West Philadelphia, then joined the Keystones for the 1868 and 1869 seasons. He moved on to the Athletics in 1870 and then played for several years in the major leagues. He later worked as a blacksmith and then as a baseball manufacturer. While there is some doubt, he probably died on April 3, 1921, in Philadelphia.

Edward "Ned" Connor: Ned Connor was born in New York State around 1850. He played for the Keystones in 1867 and 1868, and again in 1870, then had a brief major-league career. He later worked as a plasterer and became very active in Fourth Ward Republican politics, running unsuccessfully for the state legislature in 1882. He died in Philadelphia on January 28, 1898.

Elias P. Cope: Elias Cope was born in Philadelphia around 1845. He enlisted in the 104th Pennsylvania Infantry, Company D, in February of 1862 and received a disability discharge seven months later. He played for the Keystones from 1864 to 1867, being the primary pitcher for most of that time. In 1868 he followed batterymate Fergy Malone to the Olympics of Washington, and then he joined the Marylands of Baltimore in 1869. Already married and with two young children, Cope retired from baseball in 1870 and returned to Philadelphia, where he became a butcher like his father and raised six children. On the 1900 census, Cope's wife is listed as married but Elias was not living with her.

Philip Culp: See Philip Clark Kulp.

Edgar Edward Cuthbert: Eddie Cuthbert was born in Philadelphia on June 20 1845, and served in the 196th Pennsylvania Infantry, a 100-day regiment, in 1864. He then had a long baseball career as an outfielder, playing for the Keystones in 1865 and 1866, the Athletics from 1867 to 1869, the White Stockings of Chicago in 1870, and then for a variety of major-league teams between 1871 and 1884. When his playing days ended, he worked as a butcher, a saloonkeeper, and as an ambulance driver, as well as umpiring in the National League and managing a minor-league team. He died in St. Louis on February 6, 1905.

William Deal: William Deal was the center fielder of the Keystones in 1865 and 1866 and a pallbearer at the 1886 funeral of Eddie Woods.

William "Billy" Dick: Second baseman Billy Dick was one of the mainstays of the Keystones, playing for the club from 1865 to 1867 and again in 1869. He also had stints with the Olympics of Washington in 1868 and the Haymakers of Troy in 1870, before retiring. His identity is not well established, but he may be a man who was born in New York in 1839 and died in Manhattan on July 22, 1903.

James Duffy: James Duffy served as club president from 1862 to 1864 and then as vice president in 1866. He was also part of a delegation that welcomed Brooklyn clubs to the city in July of 1862.[21]

George W. "Shorty" Ewell: Shorty Ewell was born in Philadelphia on October 29, 1850. He caught for the Keystones and then for the Olympics of Washington and was listed as a "base ballist" in the 1870 census. But his career pretty much ended at that point and he later worked as a sailor and an oysterman. He died in Philadelphia on October 20, 1910.

Charles Richard "Dickie" Flowers: Dickie Flowers was born in Philadelphia around 1849 and played shortstop for the Keystones in 1868 and 1869. He joined the Haymakers of Troy in 1870 and then had a brief major-league career before becoming a Philadelphia fireman. He died in Philadelphia on October 5, 1892.

Francis A. Frazer: Francis Frazer was born in Ireland around 1839 and worked as a bookkeeper. He was the club's secretary every year from 1860 to 1866 and played second base in 1864 and 1865. He died in Philadelphia on November 9, 1866.

Charles John "Chick" Fulmer: Chick Fulmer was born in Philadelphia on February 12, 1851. He claimed to have been a drummer boy during the Civil War (a claim that may well be true but is impossible to verify from Civil War records). He began playing for a Philadelphia club called the Logans and then spent the 1869 and 1870 seasons with the Keystones, pitching in 1869 and playing shortstop in 1870. He then had a long major-league career that included being one of the founders of the American Association in 1881. By the 1930s he was recognized as one of the oldest living former major leaguers. He died in Philadelphia on February 15, 1940.

Harris N. Graffen: Harris Graffen was born around 1842 and served in the 6th Pennsylvania Cavalry (70th Volunteers) during the Civil War. Pension records indicate that he also served in the 15th Pennsylvania Cavalry under the alias Harry Walters. After the war he became the recording secretary of the Keystone Club (with Frazer remaining as corresponding secretary) and also played on the club's muffin nine. His brother Mase also became involved in baseball, later moving to St. Louis and managing that city's National League club. Harris Graffen made a name for himself in Camden real estate circles and served as secretary of the Camden Board of Trade. But he struggled with an addiction to laudanum and took his own life in Camden on June 6, 1901. After his death an erroneous desertion charge on his Civil War record was expunged by an act of Congress.

Joseph Gwynn: Joseph Gwynn was born in Philadelphia in February of 1850. He pitched for the Keystones in 1867 and played the outfield the following year. He became a lawyer and died in Philadelphia on August 8, 1886.

Alfred C.N. Halbach: Al Halbach was born around 1842 in Upper Saucon, Pennsylvania, and served in the 5th Pennsylvania Cavalry from July of 1861 to July of 1864. After the war he played center field for the Keystones in 1869 and umpired several National Association games. He had been a jeweler before the war but after the war was hired as a post-office clerk. He retained an interest in the military and attended the 26th National Encampment of the Grand Army of the Republic in 1892. He died in Philadelphia on December 27, 1895.

Philip Clark Kulp: Philip Kulp, whose name was often given as Culp, was born in 1849. His death certificate lists Germany as his place of birth, but he was already in Trenton, New Jersey, on the 1850 census and the censuses always gave New Jersey as his birthplace. He played third base for the Keystones in 1868 and 1869 and then played the same position for the Olympics of Washington in 1870. He later worked as a brickmaker and served on the Trenton City Council from 1885 to

1892. He was also a member of the National Guard. He died in Philadelphia on January 29, 1902.

Harry Lex: See Excelsiors of Chicago, Postwar, in *Base Ball Pioneers, 1850–1870.*

Leonard Walker "Len" Lovett: Len Lovett was born in Little Britain, Lancaster County, Pennsylvania, on July 17, 1852, and grew up in Philadelphia. After pitching for the Keystones in 1870, he played baseball for several more years, including very brief stints with two major-league teams. He was a dentist at one point, but eventually settled in Newark, Delaware, where he sold furniture and was elected to four terms as a magistrate. He died on November 18, 1922, in Newark.

J.H. Mahony: J. H. Mahony was the club's president in 1866.

Fergus G. "Fergy" Malone: Fergy Malone was born in August of 1842 in County Tyrone, Ireland. After serving in a 100-day regiment during the Civil War, he became the catcher of the Keystones in 1865. He went on to a long career that saw him catch in the major leagues from 1871 to 1876. In 1902 he gave this summary of his career: "I started out as a cricketer with the Oxford Club. In 1863 I joined the Athletics as pitcher. After two years' service in the Army I returned and played with the Keystone Club. From there I went to the Diamond State Club of Wilmington, Delaware. This was a gentleman's organization and included such afterwards famous men as Ambassador and Secretary of State Thomas F. Bayard, United States Senator Anthony Higgins, the great Bancroft, W.J. Pussey and the Rev. Mr. Thomas. 1867 found me back in Philadelphia. After playing a time with the noted Olympics, of Washington, I returned to the Athletics and helped defeat the champion Atlantics, of Brooklyn, in what was destined to be a memorable series of games. It was the first club that bore the name 'Philadelphia.' This was in 1873 and we trimmed the Athletics eight times out of nine. I was captain of the team and trained it until 1886. I continued as a player, then I quit the game and sought other means of livelihood."[22] Fittingly, before retiring for good, Malone played one final major-league game in 1884—for the Keystone Club, the Philadelphia entry in the new Union Association. After retiring, Malone worked in Philadelphia as a baker, a grocer, and a policeman before receiving a United States Customs Service appointment and moving to Seattle. That is where he died on January 18, 1905.

D.F. McCarthy: D.F. McCarthy was club treasurer in 1862–63 and its president in 1865.

Hugh McLarnan: Hugh McLarnan was born in Ireland in May of 1848 and played right field for the Keystones in 1869. He became a laborer and his last job was with the Board of Water. He died in Philadelphia on June 27, 1919.

John F. McMullin: John McMullin was born in Philadelphia on April 1, 1849, and played the outfield for the Keystones in 1867. That was the first season of a career that saw him become one of the first well-known left-handed pitchers and participate in the Athletics' 1874 trip to England. He died in Philadelphia on April 11, 1881.

Mulholland: A man named Mulholland was the Keystone Club's first baseman from 1864 to 1866. Two men with that surname were officers in the club—F.P. Mulholland was vice president in 1860, while H.D. Mulholland was vice president in 1863 and treasurer in 1864 and 1865. Most likely they were brothers named Hugh and Felix.

Robert Reach: Bob Reach was born in Brooklyn on August 28, 1843, and was the younger brother of A.J. Reach, famed ballplayer and sporting goods manufacturer. Bob Reach served in the Civil War before playing baseball for several clubs, including being the second baseman of the 1868 Keystones. He later ran one of his brother's stores. He died in Springfield, Massachusetts, on May 19, 1922.

William Wallace: William Wallace was the second baseman of the Keystones in 1865 and its catcher in 1866 before joining the Quaker Citys in 1867.

Charles Weaver: Charley Weaver was born in Philadelphia around 1845. He first played for the Keystones in 1866 and then spent the 1867 season with the West Philadelphia club, before rejoining the Keystones for 1868 and 1869. He later worked as a painter and died in Philadelphia on May 27, 1909.

Edward P. "Eddie" Woods: Eddie Woods was born in Philadelphia around 1838. According to his obituary, "'Neddy' Woods took part as catcher in the initial game of baseball in the Quaker City, which was played on Thanksgiving-day, Nov. 18, 1858, and from 1859 to 1870, inclusive, with the exception of one season, he was one of the nine of the famous Keystone Club." During the war, he served in the 196th Pennsylvania Infantry, a 100-day regiment. Then, "On Aug. 21, 1864, at the formal inauguration of the grounds—a portion of which is now used by the Athletic Club—Woods represented the Keystones, and played second-base for the Pennsylvania nine that contended unsuccessfully with a nine selected from New Jersey clubs." He remained the shortstop of the Keystones until he joined the Olympics in 1868. He returned to the Keystones in 1869 and then retired to help raise his young family. He worked as a police officer, then a watchman at the Philadelphia Navy Yard, and finally a painter. His wife died in 1881, leaving him to raise eight children. On November 15, 1886, Woods was painting one of the city's public buildings when he slipped and fell to his death. His funeral drew a large crowd that included several Keystone teammates, with William Deal serving as one of the pallbearers. Many politicians also attended, with Congressman Samuel J. Randall and Councilman William McMullen sending flowers.[23]

Other Club Members: Allen, Hugh Barr (vice president in 1861), Bratton, Brown, Burleigh, George W. Butler (vice president in 1862), Clinton, Coady, H. Cope (1864 player, probably Elias's brother Henry), Gibboney, Grattan, Hatfield, Henry, Dan Kleinfelder (see Athletics), Mackie, Thomas J. Martin (officer in 1860), John McGinnis (vice president in 1865), McIntyre, McKenna, Myers, Outerbridge, John Radcliff, Robinson, W. Shane, Mike Smith (see Athletics), Strang, Job T. Williams (treasurer, 1860–1861).

SOURCES: This piece is based primarily on contemporaneous newspaper accounts, which are listed in the notes, and on the account in Charles A. Peverelly's *Book of American Pastimes*. Also helpful were William Ryczek's *When Johnny Came Sliding Home* and *Baseball's First Inning*, John Shiffert's *Base Ball in Philadelphia: A History of the Early Game, 1831–1900*, and Francis Richter's *Richter's History and Records of Baseball*.

Notes

1. *Philadelphia Inquirer*, March 21, 1861.
2. *Brooklyn Eagle*, August 6, 1864, 2.
3. Charles A. Peverelly, *The Book of American Pastimes* (New York: Published by the Author, 1866), 424.
4. Marshall Wright, *The National Association of Base Ball Players, 1857–1870* (Jefferson, N.C.: McFarland, 2000), 93.
5. *Brooklyn Eagle*, August 6, 1864, 2.
6. *Philadelphia North American*, July 30, 1864.
7. *Philadelphia Inquirer*, July 24, 1865.
8. *Brooklyn Eagle*, June 19, 1865, 2.
9. William J. Ryczek, *When Johnny Came Sliding Home* (Jefferson, N.C.: McFarland, 1998), 60–61; *Brooklyn Eagle*, July 28, 1865, 2.
10. Peverelly, *The Book of American Pastimes*, 415.
11. Ibid., 479.
12. *Chicago Times*, April 7, 1867, apparently reprinted from the *New York Tribune*.
13. *National Police Gazette*, September 7, 1867.
14. *Philadelphia Patriot*, July 4, 1867.
15. *Philadelphia North American*, May 13, 1868.
16. *National Chronicle*, April 10, 1869.
17. *Oliver Optic's Magazine: Our Boys and Girls*, June 5, 1869.
18. *Philadelphia North American*, November 18, 1869.
19. *New York Sunday Mercury*, April 7, 1877.
20. *Philadelphia Inquirer*, March 22, 1884.
21. *Philadelphia North American*, July 3, 1862.
22. *Philadelphia Inquirer*, May 18, 1902.
23. *New York Clipper*, November 20, 1886, 571.

❖ *Pythian Base Ball Club* ❖
(Jared Wheeler)

CLUB HISTORY

On January 31, 1865, the United States Congress called for the abolition of slavery with the passing of the 13th Amendment. The amendment was ratified later that year, marking the end of the Civil War Era. Reconstruction began, and the newly freed slaves were required to assimilate into a society that rejected them. In the North, African Americans were seen as threats to the immigrant worker. The struggle for work and territory created tension among the races. African Americans established and unified institutions such as schools and churches. These strong social units helped strengthen the development of the African American community and created an escape from the social tension of the time.

Following the ratification of the 13th Amendment, the city of Philadelphia had the second largest urban African American community. Philadelphia's dense African American population brought about a strong resistance against racial injustice, becoming a centralized location for civil rights activists. Those who spent their days fighting in the realm of social reform and racial inequality often sought out activities of interest for their personal enjoyment.

In 1866, the Philadelphia Pythians Base Ball Club was established as a form of competitive recreation within the African American community. Many successful doctors, educators, and activists took to the club, using the skills they attained from playing town ball or cricket. Baseball, as did cricket, quickly circulated in popularity among the African American community. Both the Pythians and the lesser-known Excelsior held competitive demonstrations of the game. Racial tension caused the Pythians to avoid playing at the Parade Grounds, which was located in an Irish-populated section of Philadelphia. "Apparently, there was a turf boundary, and the Irish tried to keep the blacks of the inner-city wards from venturing south of Bainbridge Street. According to reminiscence, Bainbridge was the 'dead line' and any movement beyond meant contention."[1] They hosted their games on the other side of the Delaware River in Camden, New Jersey. On October 3, 1866, the Pythians played their first match at the Parade Grounds, standing firm against the racial objections of the Irish.

The Pythians found great success on the field and played other African American teams from cities such as Washington and Albany. In connecting with other African American teams the Pythians were able to form a unified bond in the fight for civil equality. It also allowed them to discuss issues concerning the imposed intimidation their race was experiencing in post–Civil War society.

However, the Pythians' importance goes far beyond their success on the diamond. Their desire to emerge as a recognized amateur organization led to the first form of segregation within the game of baseball. A color line would be drawn, barring African Americans from playing with whites at the professional level.

In October of 1867 the Pythians submitted an application to the Pennsylvania Association of Amateur Baseball Players at their conference in Harrisburg. The Pythians sent R.S. Bun to serve as their delegate among the members of the association. The Pythians had the support of the Philadelphia Athletics' vice president, E. Hicks Hayhurst, and the President of the association. However, the majority of the delegates voted against the admission of the Pythians on the grounds of race. R.S. Bun informed the members of the Pythians in a letter: "The majority of the delegates were opposed to it and they would advise me to withdraw my application, as they thought it were better for us to withdraw than to have it on record that we were black balled."[2]

Later that year, the National Association of Base Ball Players (NABBP) added a clause to their constitution prohibiting the admission of African American clubs. Reconstruction, racism, and the desire to maintain the status quo influenced the passing of this clause. "They [NABBP] worried about the possible political ramifications of allowing entry to African American teams. This concern came at a time when the nation was attempting to recover from the devastation of the Civil War. One of the major concerns for the government was the reconstruction of the nation and getting the 14th and 15th amendments ratified. Blacks in significant numbers were moving into northern cities and factories, and there were concerns about how these new demographics would affect the recently reunited union."[3] The Pythians' application for admittance within the Pennsylvania Association of Amateur Baseball resulted in a strictly drawn color line, segregating the baseball diamond.

The Pythians had been a viable club for some time before their fateful meeting with the Pennsylvania Association. On Seventh and Lombard Streets, just south of Philadelphia's center square, the members of the Pythians met to discuss the orders and matters concerning the club. They met at the Banneker Institute, a school that supported academic growth in the African American community, within Liberty Hall. The first recorded meeting was held in March 1867. Rules were laid out concerning the behavior of the member during the time in which meetings were held. Members were to refrain from alcohol and gambling while in the meeting hall. The dues of membership were established at $1.00 a year, and the appointing of officers took place. Educator and political activist Octavius Catto was named the club's field captain.

In 1867, the Pythians played their first full season with a 13-game schedule. They finished with a record of 8 wins, 3 losses, and 2 unrecorded outcomes. The games were scheduled by the club secretary, Jacob White, a school friend of Catto and a well-known advocate for civil rights. White would see to the matter of reserving a field and getting an umpire. One of the more celebrated clubs which the Pythians played was the Washington Alert. Activist Frederick Douglass, whose son played third base for the Alert, attended the game. Douglass evoked discussions of strengthening the African American race and their onward fight for civil rights as well as the competitive entertainment that played out before their eyes. The Pythians defeated the Alert, and the game was followed by an entertaining evening. Jacob White would direct a grand event to follow the match. Food was bought, hotels booked, and travel expenses documented. The Pythians picked up the entire tab for the event. The Pythians would host social events after their games, bringing together the African American community.

In 1868, the Pythians continued to grow in number, fielding 4 units of 9 players each. The club played 11 games, 8 with unknown results. The Pythians were led by Catto and John Cannon, a well respected power-hitting pitcher. In 1869, the Pythians played 14 games, 10 of whose results are unknown. This was the strongest year of their existence, as teams began accepting their challenge based upon their success on the field. Despite the fact that they couldn't contend with clubs of the amateur status, the Pythians scheduled games against prominent, non-affiliated, white baseball clubs. The Pythians played the Olympics, Philadelphia's oldest ball club, on September 3, 1869. This was the first meeting between the Pythians and an opposing white club. The Olympics defeated the Pythians 44–23. The game received strong support from the members of the Philadelphia Athletics as their founding president served as the game's umpire. The Pythians went on to play other white clubs throughout the area during the 1869 campaign.

The 15th Amendment was ratified on February 3, 1870, giving African Americans the right to vote. Whites resorted to violence to prevent African Americans from going to the polls. The racial tension caused by the 15th Amendment may have resulted in a lost season for the Pythians. There is no record of the Pythians playing during 1870. Death threats were made and carried out. This fear could have kept the club from traveling, hosting other clubs, or playing in a public setting. Playing was too dangerous and the attention of the players, such as Catto and White, was needed on the front of social reform. The Pythians resumed play in 1871 with a light 4-game schedule. The highlight of the season came in a series of two games played against the Unique Baseball Club from Chicago. The Unique defeated the Pythians by a score of 19–7. A few days later, the Pythians got their revenge, winning 24–16 against the Unique.

Racial tension flared in the fall of 1871 as African Americans continued to fight for their legal right to vote. On October 10, Election Day, fights erupted throughout the African American sections of the city as whites inflicted racial intimidation. The violence spread into the neighborhood of the Institute for Colored Youth. Octavius Catto, who by now was considered the most prominent African American in Philadelphia, left his post for the day to exercise his right to vote. Catto encountered several threats on his life while on his way to cast his vote. These threats prompted him to purchase a gun from a local store for his protection. As he continued along his way Catto encountered. "...a white man with a bandage on his head came up from behind and called out to him [Catto]."

Catto moved away from the man, later identified as Frank Kelly, cognizant of the gun held in his hand ... Kelly fired three shots into Cato killing him instantly. Kelly ran from the scene while numerous citizens stood staring at the bleeding body lying in the street."[4]

Catto's death was mourned deeply within the African American community. The students in his school spent weeks focusing on the importance of his life. Catto was given a military funeral. The impact he had on the citizens of Philadelphia, white or African American, was seen during the day of his burial. "Octavius Catto's funeral was on October 16. City offices and businesses closed out of respect. The procession was comparable to Lincoln's cortege. Thousands of people, black and white, lined Broad Street to pay their respects to this martyred leader."[5] Frank Kelly was never convicted of the murder of Octavius Catto.

The Pythian Baseball Club wouldn't field another nine after the death of their beloved captain Octavius V. Catto. Their brief history within the game of baseball formed the segregated structure in which the game was played. On April 15, 1947, Jackie Robinson took the first-base position at Ebbets Field in Brooklyn, breaking the color line that was drafted as a result of the Pythians' desire to play baseball within an equal society.

Octavius Catto

Octavius Catto was born free in Charleston, South Carolina, on February 22, 1839. His father, William Catto, served as a minister in the Presbyterian Church. In 1844, William Catto moved his family to Philadelphia to provide Octavius with a better education. William Catto was a strong advocate of education, and his conviction greatly influenced and shaped the growth and development of Octavius. "William Catto's intellectual curiosity and emphasis on scholarly pursuits provided a model for Octavius to pursue in later life. This, coupled with his father's belief in individual responsibility and a life anchored by deep religious convictions, formed the basic principles by which Octavius would live. Every individual had a responsibility to contribute to the progress of mankind, never to be pushed aside by the will of the masses."[6] Octavius carried out these principles throughout his life, making them the foundation of his work in unifying the black race.

When Octavius Catto arrived in Philadelphia, the educational leadership within the African American community was strengthening. Catto was enrolled in school and progressed through several different academies, including a white academy in New Jersey. In 1854, Catto began attending the new Institute for Colored Youth. This was originally founded as a Quaker vocational academy in 1842. Catto's father, among other African American community leaders, urged reform in the teachings in the Quaker-based academy. It was within this successful restructuring that the school dismissed the trade development curriculum and began standing upon the higher learning of mathematics, literature and philosophy under the name Institute of Colored Youth.

During Catto's time at the Institute for Colored Youth

Octavius Catto was captain of the Pythian Club and one of the most prominent African Americans in postwar Philadelphia. He was murdered on Election Day 1871 during the violence resulting from the grant of suffrage to African Americans.

he was introduced to the ideals of racial equality, civil liberties, and freedom from enslavement. Catto also became familiar with the game of cricket and joined the debating society. He graduated with high honors from the Institute of Colored Youth in 1858, their fourth graduate. He finished his education with the highest honors and went to Washington, D.C., for another year of study. Upon his return, Catto was hired to serve on the faculty at the Institute for Colored Youth.

Catto's status as an educator and lecturer brought him high praise within the African American community. In 1863, Catto volunteered his services to the Pennsylvania militia to defend against the advancement of General Robert E. Lee's northward push. Catto inspired several of his students to join the fight and was named the leader of the company. However, upon their arrival in Harrisburg, they were denied admittance into the militia upon the refusal of General Darius N. Couch. Catto and his unit were enlisted as an emergency unit. Couch, who didn't want African American troops, used this as an excuse to relieve them of their duty. Upon Catto and his troops' arrival back in Philadelphia, a protest against Couch's unfair treatment began. Couch was reprimanded for his decision to send them home, and the growth of African American involvement in the defense of the Union grew. Catto, who served a key roll in the protest, served in the Pennsylvania National Guard during the Civil War.

Catto emerged as a leader within the black community as he continued fighting for equal rights and civil liberties. Catto served as the corresponding secretary for the Pennsylvania State Equal Rights League, which was founded in 1864 to support the growth of the African American community. Catto was also a strong force in the Equal Rights League. He used his status within the league to eliminate the segregation of street cars in Philadelphia. "While some blacks tried to force the local street car companies to change their policies, Catto took a different approach. Appointed to lead a three man committee from the Equal Rights League, he went to Harrisburg to solicit the support of legislators in ruling against the segregation of street cars throughout the state.... Catto's tactics won the day, for despite local foot dragging by city officials, the state legislature, under pressure from Radical Republicans, passed on 22 March 1867 a bill that desegregated the street cars of the state."[7] Catto fought tirelessly for the advancement of the African American community in a segregated society, even during his time in recreation.

Catto was named the team captain of the Pythian Base Ball Club in 1867. His baseball skills were developed during his time playing cricket at the Institute for Colored Youth. Catto viewed his time on the field as competitive and recreational, but he also saw its strong role in uniting the African American community. "It [baseball] provided Catto with a status that allowed him to circulate among the northeastern African American communities that fielded baseball teams."[8] Catto was the Pythians' most successful player, building on his status as a community leader. This status made him a target of racial hate.

On October 10, 1871, Catto faced immense danger in ex-ercising his 15th Amendment right to vote. Racial violence spread throughout the city as whites tried to prevent African Americans from voting. As Catto was en route to vote he was assassinated at point blank range by a white Irish man named Frank Kelly. Catto's life was celebrated on October 16 in a large observance. Catto's emergence as a civil rights leader, educator and political voice has, and will always, influence the history of our society.

Jacob White

Jacob C. White, Jr., was a prominent African American educator in the Philadelphia public school system. White served as the principal of the Roberts Vaux Consolidated School from 1864–1896, the highest position held by an African American. White came from an affluent African American family and he engaged in many business ventures such as the Benezet Joint Stock Association of Philadelphia and the Lebanon Cemetery Company. White also served as the secretary of the Pythians Base Ball Club. White scheduled games, organized events, and collected member dues during the time of their existence. White died in Philadelphia on November 11, 1902.

Notes

1. Jerrold Casway, "Philadelphia's Pythians," *The National Pastime* (1995), 121.
2. American Negro Historical Society collection, 1790–1905, Wilmington, DE.
3. Leslie Heaphy, *The Negro Leagues 1869–1960* (Jefferson, N.C.: McFarland, 2003), 10.
4. Harry Silcox, *Nineteenth Century Black Militant: Octavius V. Catto* (University Park: Penn State University Press, 1977), 73.
5. Jerrold Casway, "Octavius Catto and the Pythians of Philadelphia" (Philadelphia Historical Society, 2007), 8.
6. Silcox *Nineteenth Century Black Militant*, 54.
7. Ibid., 65.
8. Casway, "Philadelphia's Pythians," 121.

❖ *Chester Base Ball Club* ❖
(Peter Morris)

CLUB HISTORY

The city of Chester, Pennsylvania, is located only fifteen miles from Philadelphia, with the result that it is now increasingly impinged upon by that metropolis's suburban sprawl. The difficulties of living in the shadow of Philadelphia also played a major role in the demise of Chester's first prominent baseball club. Fortunately, several retrospective articles in the *Chester Times* preserved some details about that pioneer club. These reminiscences are the source of almost everything known about the Chester Base Ball Club, and they provide a fascinating window into one of the many clubs that sprung up during the post-war flurry of baseball activity.

Even the dates of the Chester Base Ball Club's existence cannot be pinpointed exactly, but a 1910 article reported that the club was organized in the fall of 1865.[1] Meanwhile an 1883 reminiscence maintained that the club was active from 1866 to 1868. That sounds like an estimate, but several factors confirm that it is pretty close to being accurate. Many club members were Civil War veterans who were still serving in 1864, so the club could not have formed before 1865. On the other end, star player Tom Berry joined the Athletics early in the 1867 season, an event that marked the end of the Chester Club. So it seems that the club was organized in the fall of 1865 and disbanded in the spring of 1867.

Despite the short existence, Chester's first baseball club had two different playing fields. According to the unidentified player who reminisced in 1883,"We used to play on the grounds along Chester creek adjoining the Friends burial grounds near the Beale House — Seventh street now runs right through the lot — and when the street was cut through we went to the lot in front of what is now Patterson's row."[2]

The new club soon proved to be "the crack team of these parts" and elicited a rabid local following.[3] David M. Johnson served as club secretary and had his hands full keeping track of a membership that swelled to include 116 Chester baseball enthusiasts. "If a person did not belong to the Chester Base Ball Club in those days," he later recalled, "he was behind the times and showed a lack of enterprise and public spirit."[4] According to Johnson, the club was undefeated until it boldly challenged the mighty Athletics of Philadelphia.[5]

What came next was predictable. The player who reminisced in 1883 offered this account: "The Athletic club came down to play the Chester boys one day and I'll never forget that game. It was the biggest picnic the Athletics ever had. They batted the balls almost out of sight and made as many home runs as our boys did runs. Nine innings were played and they scored eighty runs to twelve for Chester."[6]

Johnson similarly recalled, "This club defeated all comers until it made up its mind to try conclusions with the professional Athletic Club of Philadelphia, which it invited to come down to Chester and be added to the other sacrificial offerings to the athletic gods. The score was Chester 14, Athletics 80. Dick McBride pitched for the Athletics; W.B. Broomall for the Chester. Tom Berry was catcher for Broomall. The Athletics were so pleased with our Tom that they adopted him."[7]

While the lopsided defeat at the hands of the Athletics undoubtedly hastened the end of the Chester Club, it was not their final game. In the words of the player who reminisced in 1883,"It was not long after this that our club broke up. 'Billy' Broomall, the pitcher, had a fashion of running up on a ball after his delivery when there were runners on base, and we were playing in Philadelphia one afternoon when the batter hit a ball that the pitcher followed up that way, and 'Billy' was hit in the stomach. He was plucky and held the ball putting the man out, but it made him spit blood and with Tom Berry going with the Athletics and our pitcher leaving, it broke the club up."[8]

Though the end wasn't pretty, the members of the Chester Base Ball Club retained fond memories of their hometown's first such club. "They don't play ball now like they used to," Tom Berry declared in 1902. "Talk about your men playing first base. I have seen the best of them in that position for the past few years and I tell you we had a man on our team who has them all beat. None of your modern players begin to touch him. And another thing, just while I am on that subject. We didn't use any mattresses for gloves in those days either. If a player hurt his hand and wanted to wear a rag or some other protection, he was called to the centre by the umpire and he wanted to see what that hand looked like." He concluded his comments with another now-familiar complaint: "Pitchers in those days pitched every day in the week and thought nothing of it. Now if a pitcher tosses the ball one or two games a week he thinks he is worked hard. Yes, those were great days."[9]

Nostalgia also suffused the recollection of the 1883 player, whose comments are similar enough to those of Tom Berry to suggest that he may have been the source of that article as well. "Base ball is not what it used to be," that early Chester player maintained. "If it has been brought down to a science you don't see a bit better playing than you used to in the old time days. Then we had the lively ball and straight out round arm pitching. There was none of this curved throwing balls at the batter, but the batsman could stand up to the plate and know that he was going to get a ball where he wanted it before he had to strike at it or be called out."[10]

CLUB MEMBERS (FIRST NINE, PLUS ONE)

Tom Berry: Tom Berry was born in Chester on December 31, 1842, and during the Civil War served in Company A of the 197th Pennsylvania Volunteers along with future teammates Minshall and Wilson. He caught for the Chester Base Ball Club and then joined the Athletics in 1867. According to James H. Conahan, who umpired briefly in the National League as the result of Berry's recommendation, his mentor was working at Chester shipyard until he laid down his tools and declared to his coworkers, "Boy, I'll never sling another hammer again."[11] Berry's arrival caused internal dissension among the Athletics, but he remained a regular for the next four seasons, mostly playing third base. He even had a one-game major league career with the Athletics in 1871. Berry then returned to Chester and eventually became the chief of police. He was also active in the Hanley Hose Company. Dick McBride, the star pitcher of the Athletics, remained in touch and paid several visits to Chester to see his old friend. Berry became a Chester alderman in 1912, an event that was made official by the governor's signature. The Pennsylvania governor at the time was former major leaguer John K. Tener, who expressed pleasure that the new alderman was also a former professional ballplayer. In later years, Berry often reminisced about his days on the baseball diamond and was adamant that later players were no better than the ones of his generation.[12] He died in Chester on June 6, 1915.

William Booth "Billy" Broomall: William B. Broomall was born in Chester on January 30, 1843, the son of Judge John Broomall. After graduating from Haverford College in 1861 at the age of 18, he began studying law at his father's office. He put his studies on hold to enlist in the Union Army, seeing combat duty at the battles of Antietam and Chancellorsville, before being called to the Bar in 1864. He opened a law practice in Chester, but also found time to pitch for the Chester Base Ball Club. He earned a reputation as a "rattler" of a pitcher who could also "everlastingly bat a ball."[13] Like his father,

Broomall became a judge, and in 1914 he celebrated his golden anniversary as a practicing lawyer. Failing health finally forced him to step down from the bench in 1925, and he died on March 3, 1927.

Geoffrey P. Denis: G.P. Denis was born in Philadelphia around 1842 and served in the Civil War, spending two months as a prisoner of war after the battle of Murfreesboro. He settled near Chester after the war and became owner of the Yeadon Mill.[14] Though not a regular member of the first nine, he often substituted, and there reportedly was "not a better man on the nine."[15] First base was his natural position, which was appropriate since it was said later that Denis "was a man whose heart was as large as his body, and that is saying a great deal, because 'Jeff' was a giant in stature and of huge physical proportions."[16] During the 1880s local star pitcher Hamilton Dutton worked at Denis's mill.[17] Denis later expanded his business interests, becoming president of the Eureka Cast Steel Company of Chester and vice president of the Johnston Railroad Frog and Switch Company. He died in Chester on February 15, 1897.

Dr. H.W. Farrington: First baseman Harvey W. Farrington was only 21 and a recent graduate of the Homoeopathic Medical College of Pennsylvania when he arrived in Chester in 1865. After practicing briefly in Chester, Farrington moved to Beverly, New Jersey, and was later reported to have moved to California. His younger brother, Dr. Edward Albert Farrington, became a celebrated physician, but little is known about Harvey Farrington.

Job L. Green: Job Green, the club's shortstop, was born in Marcus Hook, Delaware County, in 1846. He married around 1866 and eventually moved back to Marcus Hook, where he became a successful merchant and raised four children. Green died there on June 10, 1919.

Stephen C. Hall: Outfielder Stephen C. Hall was considerably older than most of his teammates, having been born around 1834. A sugar refiner, he is believed to have died in Chester in 1885.

Callender Irvine Leiper: General Leiper's younger brother "Cal," who was born in 1846, also played the outfield for the Chester Base Ball Club. Their paternal grandfather was an early Delaware County land owner who laid out one of the country's first private railways. The family holdings included several profitable stone quarries. Their maternal grandfather was a member of the Lewis family of Virginia, which produced the famed explorer Meriwether Lewis. Cal Leiper took over management of the family quarries and remained at Avondale until his death on August 28, 1928.[18]

General Charles Lewis Leiper: Charles L. Leiper, who was born in Avondale, Delaware County, on Christmas Day in 1842, enlisted in the Union Army at the outset of the Civil War. He served first as a private in the Pennsylvania Militia, experiencing combat duty during the First Battle of Bull Run. Leiper was then commissioned as an officer in the 6th Pennsylvania Cavalry, better known as "Rush's Lancers." His bravery in leading his troops' saber charges earned him a series of promotions, and after serving as commander of the unit, he was brevetted Brigadier General on March 13, 1865. After the war, he developed a passion for baseball and played the outfield for the Chester Base Ball Club along with his brother "Cal." Chester Mayor David M. Johnson later recalled: "The name of General Leiper stirs up old memories. Many times have I seen him playing backstop for the Chester Baseball club to the pitching of William B. Broomall on the Beale lot back of the Friend's Burying ground in Chester."[19] General Leiper later moved to Philadelphia and was successful in the textile business. He died there on May 14, 1899, and his wartime heroism was commemorated in a granite monument erected by the surviving members of Rush's Lancers.

Jesse D. Minshall: Third baseman Jesse Minshall served in both the 124th and 197th Pennsylvania Volunteers, fighting alongside Berry and Press Wilson in the latter regiment, as well as the 40th New Jersey. He married in 1879 and moved to Washington, D.C. His wife filed for a widow's pension in 1890, but his exact date of death is not known.

Preston E. "Press" Wilson: Press Wilson, the club's second baseman was born in 1845. During the Civil War he served in Company A of the 197th Pennsylvania Volunteers along with Berry and Minshall. He also served in the 2nd Pennsylvania Infantry. He remained in the area, working for a local print works and as a bank and hotel clerk. He died in Chester on April 5, 1922.

Other Club Members: David M. Johnson, later the mayor of Chester, served as club secretary and Thomas Appleby as club president. In 1910 Mayor Johnson provided this list of additional club members: Samuel Anderson, David Appleby, Edward Barton, James Barton, Jr., John H. Barton, General E.F. Beale, James S. Bell, Theodore J. Bell, A.J. Benjamin, James B. Berry, J. Frank Black, John W. Black, Christopher Blakeley, J.H.T. Blois, Bartram Booth, Robert Booth, Daniel Brown, John Brown, James Carrick, Dr. Theodore J. Christ, J. Edward Clyde, Joseph R.T. Coates, I. Engle Cochran, Thos. V. Cooper, Charles E. Creamer, Alfred O. Deshong, John O. Deshong, Jr., Maurice W. Deshong, Julius A. Dutton, John E. Dyer, John G. Dyer, Samuel A. Dyer, Caleb Emlen, Frederick Engle, J. Edgar Engle, Peter Hill Engle, William H. Eves, Caleb Eyre, N. Walter Fairlamb, Dr. J.L. Forwood, Thomas Garrett, Amos Gartside, Lewis Geoltz, George Geoltz, Peter Goff, John Goff, John P. Green, John P.M.M. Greig, Bethuel T. Hall, Robert E. Hannum, Jr., Orlando Harvey, John Hinkson, W. Alfred Hughes, Col. Theodore Hyatt, Thomas James, D.M. Johnson, Jonathan R. Johnson, Thomas Kean, Walter G. Keen, General Joseph Ladomus, William B. Lambson, Alonzo W. Lear, Albert Lees, Charles E. Lenny, D. Jackson Lenny, Daniel Lewis, S.P. Lindsay, Charles Longbotham, Edward M. Lyons, John S. Marshall, Archibald Martin, William McCall, John McFall, Robert McKay, G. McKinley, Thurlow McMullin, Richard

Miller, Edward R. Minshall, David W. Morrison, Robert Morrow, Benjamin N. Morton, John R. Nowland, William G. Oglseby, Charles D. Pennell, J. Wade Price, John Pyle, David S. Quinn, C.M. Rathbun, George Robinson, Samuel H. Seeds, James Shedwick, William L. Simpson, George L. Smedley, Edward C. Smith, Samuel N. Smith, Jeremiah Stevenson, Alfred Taylor, William R. Thatcher, John Thomson, D.A. Vernon, Y.S. Walter, Harrison Wheaton, Nelson Wilde, George Wilson.

SOURCES: "Old Time Base Ballists," *Chester Times*, September 6, 1883, 3; "Playing Ball in the Days Gone By," *Chester Times*, July 17, 1902, 7; "Reminiscences of an Old Ball Player," *Chester Times*, May 7, 1913, Page 6; a transcription of a speech by D.M. Johnson in the *Chester Times*, June 25, 1912, 7.

Notes

1. "Chester Baseball Club of Long Ago," *Chester Times*, November 17, 1910, 6.
2. "Old Time Base Ballists," *Chester Times*, September 6, 1883, 3.
3. Ibid.
4. "Chester Baseball Club of Long Ago," *Chester Times*, November 17, 1910, 6. I have changed the spelling of the word Baseball, which was one word in the original.
5. *Chester Times*, June 25, 1912, 7; "Chester Baseball Club of Long Ago," *Chester Times*, November 17, 1910, 6.
6. "Old Time Base Ballists," *Chester Times*, September 6, 1883, 3.
7. *Chester Times*, June 25, 1912, 7.
8. "Old Time Base Ballists," *Chester Times*, September 6, 1883, 3.
9. "Playing Ball in the Days Gone By," *Chester Times*, July 17, 1902, 7.
10. "Old Time Base Ballists," *Chester Times*, September 6, 1883, 3.
11. *Chester Times*, June 24, 1915, 10.
12. "Reminiscences of an Old Ball Player," *Chester Times*, May 7, 1913, 6; "Playing Ball in the Days Gone By," *Chester Times*, July 17, 1902, 7. As noted in the text, there is a good chance that the unidentified player who reminisced in 1883 was also Berry.
13. "Old Time Base Ballists," *Chester Times*, September 6, 1883, 3.
14. *Chester Times*, November 22, 1932, 8.
15. "Old Time Base Ballists," *Chester Times*, September 6, 1883, 3.
16. *Chester Times*, November 22, 1932, 8.
17. *Chester Times*, April 28, 1885, 3.
18. *Chester Times*, August 30, 1928, 6.
19. *Chester Times*, June 25, 1912, 7.

❖ *Marion Base Ball Club* ❖
(Richard Hershberger)

CLUB HISTORY

A new kind of baseball club arose in the 1870s. The old clubs had originally been turned inward. Their members met during the season to take their exercise and to socialize. Baseball was the forum selected for both. The vast majority of baseball played by these clubs was internal, with only a handful of match games each year against other clubs.

Over the years these match games took on more and more importance, and the clubs adapted by placing more emphasis on their "first nines." In earlier days new members were recruited for social compatibility. Gradually, members came to be recruited for playing ability. Professionalism was, inevitably, introduced. The rest of the club gradually took on a supporting role.

The new kind of club of the 1870s took this to its logical conclusion, and eliminated nearly all of the old club structure other than the team of nine players. At the top professional level, there were owners, salaried players, and a rudimentary front office. At the amateur level, there could be merely the nine players, with one taking on the leadership role as field captain and business manager. Gone were the old club days, meeting once or twice a week to play together. Gone were most of the social rituals: any social activity among the players was incidental. Whether the club was a business or recreation, the essential purpose was to play and win match games against other clubs.

The Marion was one such club. It existed for just a few months in 1871, but for that season rose to be one of the most prominent amateur clubs in Philadelphia, stocked with future professionals. It is also unusually well documented, primarily in the *Philadelphia Sunday Dispatch*. It provides a picture of the new face of organized baseball.

The Marion club was organized on June 22, 1871, representing "a very reputable down-town circle."[1] The driving force behind it was 23-year-old John J. Smith (invariably referred to either as "J.J. Smith" or "Jack Smith"). Smith was a member of the Marion Hose Company of the Philadelphia Volunteer Fire Department, and he named his new baseball club after it.

After some practice, the new Marions played their first match game on July 10 against the George M. Roth Club, an established local amateur club, winning 19–18. This immediately made their reputation, and they had no shortage of challenges. They even made a brief tour in September, defeating clubs in Harrisburg and Lancaster, Pennsylvania. Their sole loss was their one game against a professional club, the Athletics, at the end of the season. The remaining gap in their record was that they did not play the two best amateur clubs in Philadelphia, the Experts and the Olympics. The *Sunday Dispatch* looked forward to seeing the Marions challenge these clubs the following season, but it was not to be. Jack Smith accepted an offer to captain the Neptune Club of Easton, Pennsylvania, and the Marion Club never returned.

In its short existence, Smith managed to put together a remarkable collection of future professional ballplayers. The best remembered today is James Devlin, who was captain and played third base. He was one of four players banned from baseball for throwing games while with Louisville in 1877. The scandal should not obscure the fact that he was a very good player, converting later in his career to pitcher. The catcher, Tommy Miller, is mostly remembered for the controversy characteristic of the era when he signed with both Hartford and St. Louis for the 1875 season. In the end he caught for a good St. Louis club, but while his defensive work was universally praised, he couldn't hit professional pitching. He was retained by St. Louis as a utility infielder for 1876, but died of a sudden illness without getting into a game. William Hague would have a journeyman career, including playing for the pennant-winning Providence club of 1879.[2] John Donnelly and John Abadie played briefly as professionals. George Ewell was a reverse situation: he played one game in 1871 for the professional Cleveland club, going 0-for-3, then returned home to Philadelphia, where he joined the Marions.

This raises the question of the role of money. The Marions were an amateur club, but in this era that was not the same thing as the players not receiving payment. Amateur and professional were competitive categories that did not necessarily correspond to the question of payment. Top-level amateur clubs often charged admission for important games, with the profits divided among the players. As a rule of thumb, games played at enclosed parks usually fell into this category. The Marions' home field was the Parade Ground, an open public common in South Philadelphia formerly used for militia musters. There would be no way to charge admission on such a site. Some of the later games were played on the Athletic ground, as the club received enough attention that spectators would be willing to pay to watch. The likeliest interpretation is that they were what would later come to be called semipro, taking in what money they could but not expecting to earn a living wage.

Smith was able to collect a team including six players who would have at least a taste of a professional career, all in their early 20s and from South Philadelphia, who joined more than a month into the season. He had an eye for talent, knew all the players in his age group and section of the city, and had powers of persuasion. That he also had the opportunity to exercise these abilities was due to the changes in the baseball community. In earlier years, when the clubs had a strong fraternal, social element to them, changing clubs had a sense of abandoning one's comrades. Both the formal and informal structures worked to discourage this, at least during the season. With the loss of the social underpinnings, the individuals' ties to their clubs weakened and it became acceptable to "revolve" to a different club as opportunities presented themselves. The clubs still had some social function. The Marions went boating on the Delaware River in late August.[3] But this had a different character from the old clubs. A social function of the old club would have been a large, involved affair with speeches and meals and toasts. The Marions' expedition was more in the way of a group of similar ages and interests taking a sailing trip together. More like the old clubs, there was a "reunion" in October and a "complimentary benefit given them" in December — it is not clear by whom — with singing and eating.[4] The difference is that the old clubs held such banquets for themselves and guests. The dozen or so who had played on the Marion club would have made for a small party. The clue to the event is that at the "reunion," "Many notables of the base ball world were present." This was not a party for club members, but for the local baseball fraternity generally.

Not only was there no membership in the old sense, but the formal club structures were in clear decline. Newspapers formerly had routinely reported on club officers and directors. The Marions probably had these, but they were vestigial. Smith officially was the club secretary, putting him in position to arrange match games. There is no mention of who was the president, vice president, or treasurer, and there is merely a passing mention that Charles Grampher was a director as well as substitute player. Three nonplayers are mentioned as having great credit for the "notable energy with which the Marion Club has been conducted." They likely were officers or directors, but this is just a guess.

The clear sense is that Smith was the driving force behind the club. The rapid creation of the club was made possible by the new organization of the game. So was its equally rapid disappearance. With Smith in Easton, there was no organization to keep the rest together.

The old clubs didn't disappear right away. The Olympics of Philadelphia and the Knickerbockers of New York both carried on into the 1880s. The new clubs, however, were the competitive center of the game. The future was for managers and, on the higher levels, financial backers putting together teams, which lasted only as long as times were good.

Jack Smith

Jack Smith is forgotten today, not appearing in any baseball record books and barely being a footnote in baseball history. This is unfortunate, as he is one of the more interesting baseball figures no one has ever heard of, as much for what he didn't do as what he did.

Smith was born on February 22, 1848, son of Patrick W. Smith, an Irish immigrant.[5] While in Philadelphia he was a member of the Marion Hose Company of the Philadelphia Volunteer Fire Department, and was a private in the Pennsylvania National Guard. He is listed in the 1870 census as a laborer with no estate given; his father is described as working in a store, and there were a younger brother, Charles, and sister, Mary. None of this suggests wealth, though there was also a housekeeper, so they also seem not to have been impoverished.

Like many men of his generation, he was caught up in the baseball fever. He pitched for a series of obscure clubs, the Mozart, Jr. Arctic, Durego, Malvern, and Mutual, before making his appearance on the historical record.[6] In 1871 he organized and led the Marion Club of Philadelphia, which made his reputation. The following winter he was recruited by William Hullick and George Reeder of the Neptune Club of Easton, soon renamed the Easton Club. Over the next three years he built up the Eastons, recruiting from the ballfields of Philadelphia, and in 1874 the Easton club was arguably the best amateur club in the country.

The 1874 Eastons were too good to survive. The players were recruited by various professional clubs, with several forming the core of the new St. Louis Brown Stockings. The Easton Club did not field a team in 1875, and played only local amateur games later in the decade. The city hosted minor-league clubs over the years, but would never again be a baseball stronghold.

Smith remained in Easton, living there the rest of his life. George Reeder was the editor of the *Easton Express* and had hired Smith as a reporter, presumably as part of the inducement to relocate. He continued with the *Express* for several years. He married a local girl, Susan Bonstein, joined a local volunteer fire company, and was a founding member of the Easton Grays militia. When Easton converted to a professional fire department in 1879 he was appointed chief engineer, with the appointment renewed in 1885. This was considered something of an achievement, as the original appointment was by a Republican city council and the second by a Democratic council. A post like chief engineer was a plum position, and his reappointment a testament to his competence overcoming the usual imperative of political patronage. Even so, this could not last forever and in 1891 he lost the position. He returned to journalism for several years, then was once again made chief in 1896. He suffered a stroke the following year and died a week later, at the age of 49.

There is every reason to believe that Smith could have made a career in professional ball. It is difficult to tell how good a player he really was, as the statistical record is largely meaningless with wildly varying opposition. He was a pitcher most of his days, apparently with a good fastball but no curve (still rare in those days). He moved to the outfield for 1874, as he had recruited George Bradley, who would be one of the top professional pitchers in 1875–1876. Smith's move to the outfield is not a sign of inadequacy, but of sensible management. More than as a player, he clearly was management material. This was the era of the rise of the professional baseball managers (more like a modern general manager than the field manager). The 1874 Eastons stand as proof that Smith was more than competent for this job.

While he could have been a professional manager, he could not do it in Easton. We can guess that local ties trumped baseball. He did not abandon the game entirely. He played in local matches in the late 1870s. The *Express* also occasionally carried insightful coverage of Philadelphia baseball affairs, suggesting that he maintained his contacts in his home town. The only formal connection he made was when he was appointed an umpire in the minor Eastern League in 1884. He resigned the position before the season began. This might have been due to his commitment as fire chief, but the report of an exhibition game he umpired, where "his decision gave rise to considerable dissatisfaction, but his mistakes operated against both teams about equally," hints that officiating was not his strength.[7]

Smith's funeral included a long procession including city officials, the police department, a band, and multiple fire companies.[8] It is unlikely that he would have remained a laborer regardless of what path he took, but the fact remains that baseball was the reason he went to Easton, and the original source of his position in the community. Smith's family continued this upward mobility. His son Clarence followed him into journalism, eventually becoming managing editor and part-owner of the *Allentown Morning Call* as well as the rank of lieutenant colonel in the Pennsylvania National Guard.

Smith's main interest to baseball history is that he was that rare bird who used baseball to raise his social and economic position. Most ballplayers, even if well paid professionals, tended to revert to their origins once their baseball career ended. Most of the exceptions were men who continued in baseball in other capacities, such as equipment manufacturers or managers, and in a very few instances owners. Smith took a different route, abandoning baseball almost entirely, and with it his chance for an entry in *The Baseball Encyclopedia*.

Notes

1. *Sunday Dispatch*, December 31, 1871. In the context of Philadelphia, downtown should be understood not as the central business district, which is called Center City, but as the district to the south of Center City, now usually called South Philadelphia.

2. Hague's surname was actually spelled Haug but Hague is what he generally used for baseball and how he is known today.

3. *Sunday Dispatch*, September 3, 1871.

4. *Sunday Dispatch*, October 15, 1871, December 24, 1871.

5. Most of the nonbaseball biographical information comes from obituaries in *Easton Express*, May 22, 1897; *Sunday Call* (Easton, Pennsylvania), May 23, 1897; *Free Press* (Easton, Pennsylvania), May 25, 1897; and *Semi-Weekly Argus* (Easton, Pennsylvania), May 25, 1897.

6. *Sunday Dispatch* (Philadelphia), December 31, 1871.

7. *The Sporting Life* (Philadelphia), April 23, 1884, May 7, 1884.

8. *Semi-Weekly Argus*, May 28, 1897.

CHAPTER FIVE

MASSACHUSETTS

❖ *Introduction* (Peter Morris) ❖

CLUB HISTORY

The definitive history of early baseball in Massachusetts remains to be written. At first blush, that seems surprising but on closer examination it begins to make sense. Victors usually write history, especially baseball history, which too often is reduced to a list of the exploits of great teams and players. Massachusetts, however, produced few of either during the 1850s and 1860s and as a result its early history defies the usual formulations.

Massachusetts' early baseball history also differed from those of other states in substance. "Which is the best club?" was the question that occupied the minds of baseball fans in most locales, but in Massachusetts it was more often "What version of the game are we going to play?" Further complicating efforts to arrange competition was the large role played by students at colleges like Amherst, Williams, and, in particular, Harvard. These collegians brought great enthusiasm to the state's baseball scene but their summer recesses were a scheduling nightmare that eventually led to the decision to melt down the silver ball that was the emblem of New England baseball supremacy.

In other states, clubs representing the largest city dominated the landscape, but here too Massachusetts was unusual. The Olympics were initially viewed as Boston's top club but in 1858 they were upended by the Massapoags of Sharon, which was still a rural town. The Tri-Mountains of Boston, as the first Massachusetts club to adopt the New York rules, were next looked upon as the state's standard-bearer. A landmark 1860 contest against the crosstown Bowdoins, however, proved the Tri-Mountains to be "generally older and heavier men than the Bowdoins, and not so spry."[1] In turn, the Bowdoins traveled to Springfield expecting to make easy work of their country cousins and were instead handily defeated by that city's Pioneer Club. For most of the decade, baseball in Massachusetts continued to exhibit what writers of the era liked to call the game's "glorious uncertainty." Spectators found the unpredictability exhilarating, but historians have struggled to make sense of it.

In recognition of that regional diversity, the entries in this chapter include one from Boston, one apiece from the nearby towns of Stoughton and Stoneham, one from Lowell, two from Harvard, one from Cape Cod, one from North Brookfield in central Massachusetts, and one apiece from Springfield and Florence in western Massachusetts. Other clubs could just as easily have been substituted, especially ones from Boston, but it is fitting that the entries span the entire state instead of clustering in one region.

The decentralized competition also created yet another challenge for historians. With so many potential sources of information, new details about Massachusetts' first clubs have continued to surface, especially in recent years as a result of the Protoball Project and the work of Massachusetts Games experts such as Richard Hershberger. Each new tidbit necessitates a re-examination of the entire era.

The early history of Massachusetts baseball thus followed a different course from that of other states, making it at once unusually messy and extraordinarily interesting. Let's take a look at some of the highlights.

Disorganized Ball (Prior to 1857)

Numerous after-the-fact accounts, along with the occasional contemporaneous description, establish that bat-and-ball games were being played in Massachusetts during the first half of the nineteenth century. We can be just as certain that many more such games were played but not recorded for posterity. Beyond that, little can be said with confidence. Larry McCray, in a survey of pre–1850 bat-and-ball games in all six New England states, concludes:

> [A]bout two-thirds of our references fail to name the game played, using terms like "game of ball," "playing at ball," and the like. The games that are specifically named, in order of their relative frequency of appearance, are (1) round ball, found mostly in Eastern Massachusetts, (2) bat-and-ball, mostly to the north and east of Boston, including Maine, (3) one of the old cat versions, (4) base, or base ball, and (5) goal, or goal ball. But we are given very few clues whether these labels attached

to identical, similar, or dissimilar games, let alone what their playing rules were.... Ours is not a rich field of anecdotes.[2]

One of the young men who played ball during those years offered a similar assessment. "Previous to the year 1854," he wrote half a century later, "the game of bat and ball was played in a 'scrub' way, and there were too many differences of opinion on rules to allow the game to proceed smoothly."[3]

By midcentury the various games were beginning to coalesce into a single game, known as round ball or the Massachusetts Game. According to almost all sources, it was in 1854 that Massachusetts' first known club, the Olympic Club, came into being. Some of those sources go further. "The first organized ball club in New England," declared Troy Soos, "was the 1854 Olympic Club of Boston."[4] The word organized suggests a new era of more uniform and orderly competition, but in fact the next few years were anything but organized.

A dozen of the young men who became members of the Olympic Club began meeting on the Boston Common in 1854 for games among themselves. There is, however, no indication that they recorded any of their activities or that anyone else saw fit to do so. By the following year, a second group, known as the "Elm Trees," had emerged. The two sides reportedly played one undocumented game in 1855 and the result was such a lopsided victory for the Olympics that it caused the Elm Trees to disappear forever. That September brought one of the state's first published references to baseball, which read: "Ball Players on the Common. The first game of ball for the autumnal season, was played this morning by the Olympics. The club consists mostly of young men from the States of Maine, New Hampshire and Vermont. They will continue their manly performances every morning during the season."[5] But no more was heard that year.

It was much the same story in 1856. The Olympic Club did show new signs of seriousness of purpose by officially organizing, electing team officers, and scheduling regular times for practices. They also had new rivals in the "Green Mountain Boys," a group of Pearl Street vendors who had begun playing in April of that year and who had little use for efforts to impose greater structure. "We did not recognize [the Green Mountain Boys] as an organization," one early ballplayer later recalled. "They furnished much merriment to bystanders from their disregard of rules, which was inexcusable, to say the least."[6] The new rivalry was thus contentious, with a three-game series between the two clubs featuring complaints about rule violations and accusations of gamesmanship.[7] Curiously, although the Massachusetts game usually featured many players in the field, these games were contested with eight or fewer per side.

The heated series of games between the Olympics and the Green Mountain Boys are the earliest documented matches played in New England, but it must always be kept in mind that the games we know about may be just the tip of the ice-

berg. "Barre has for many years been famous for its ball players," declared the *Barre Gazette* in 1858.[8] In how many other Massachusetts cities were similar boasts made?

While Massachusetts ball play displayed little organization between 1854 and 1856, there was plenty of enthusiasm. "In the 50s," recalled one early ballplayer, "it was customary to commence game at 5 A.M. on the Common, and after play of an hour and a half repair to Braman's excellent system of bath houses at the foot of Chestnut street for a swim of fifteen minutes, and then get home in time for breakfast."[9] He added, "The Olympic club was the most popular club in this section and was classed as the champion. They had games in the morning before breakfast, in the afternoon and on holidays and drew crowds of admirers."[10]

Competition Between Rival Versions: 1857–1860

Organization finally arrived in Massachusetts in 1857, along with a rash of new clubs. Among them was the Bay State Club, "a fine set of young men" who formally organized on May 1, 1857, and promptly challenged the Olympics.[11] Five games were played on the Boston Common over the next month, and while the new club won only once, the contests did much to promote baseball in Massachusetts. An account in the *Boston Daily Courier* provided quite a few details and was even reprinted in the *New York Clipper*.[12]

The baseball fever also spread to Sharon, twenty miles south of Boston, where the Massapoag Club was organized in early June. After besting the nearby South Walpole Club, the Massapoags arranged to play the Olympics on June 29. More than two thousand spectators were on hand at the Boston Common on the big day to watch "the most exciting game of ball ever played in Boston."[13] The home side was confident of victory and en route to the ball field the visitors were "a mark for the street gamins, who nudged one another and cracked wicked jokes upon the farmer lads from 'Shannon,' who came to play the Olympics."[14] Instead the large crowd was treated to the first of several noteworthy upsets of the state's pioneer era: In a best-of-five series of games to twenty-five runs the Massapoag Club defeated the Olympics 25–21, 25–24, and 25–19.

In addition to the surprising outcome, the match produced another unforeseen result. A typographical error in the *Boston Herald* led to the Massapoag name being rendered as "Wassapoag." The error was corrected in the next day's issue but the damage had been done.[15] The *New York Clipper* picked up and repeated the original mistake and it has been repeated in many subsequent articles and books.[16]

That was not the only indignity suffered by the members of the Massapoag Club. According to an article published in 1907 to commemorate the club's fiftieth anniversary, there were no passenger trains scheduled to run after 4 P.M. and railroad superintendent Daniel Nason initially refused to add a special passenger car. Only the intervention of businessman William

Rufus Mann persuaded Nason to change his mind and enabled the triumphant ballplayers to return safely back to Sharon.[17]

Other new clubs that emerged in Boston's surrounding towns in 1857 included the Bunker Hill Club of Charlestown, the American Club of South Dedham, Rough and Ready Club of South Walpole, the Winthrop Club of Holliston, and the Unions of Medway. At the end of the eventful season, the *New York Clipper* published the Olympic Club's eighteen "Rules for Playing Base Ball," adopted by the club that season.[18]

By then, however, their version of baseball had competition. In 1856 watch case-maker Edward G. Saltzman and two business associates, Augustus P. Margot and Richard Busteed, relocated from New York City to Boston. Saltzman had been a member of the Gotham Club while living in New York and he soon began to try to convince Bostonians of its merits.[19] His efforts were met with skepticism, with one of the ballplayers later recollecting that "the implements used seemed very strange to us.... The game was not popular at that time." Nevertheless, the "newcomers continued to play it" and on June 16, 1857, they organized the Tri-Mountain Club, Boston's first New York-rule club.[20]

As a minority of one, the Tri-Mountains had nobody to compete against and were limited to playing intrasquad games. Their isolation continued in 1858 and was underscored by Massachusetts' first baseball convention. Held at the Phoenix House in Dedham on May 13, 1858, the convention brought together ten baseball clubs: three from Boston and one apiece from Charlestown, South Dedham, Walpole Center, South Walpole, Sharon, Medway, and Holliston.[21]

The goal of the convention was simple: "preparing the way ... for the rapid and systematic formation of clubs for the enjoyment of the manly and healthful game of Base-Ball" by agreeing to a uniform set of rules.[22] The delegates did succeed in unanimously approving a constitution and by-laws for the "Massachusetts Association of Base Ball Players" (which was expanded into the New England Association of Base Ball Players two years later). But when it came time to codify the rules, the differences proved too great. After two hours of debate, Tri-Mountain president Benjamin Franklin Guild made a graceful speech in which he congratulated his fellow delegates on their progress but reaffirmed his club's commitment to the New York version and withdrew it from the newly formed association.[23]

This outcome had a predictable effect on baseball in Boston in 1858. There was lively competition among the vast majority of clubs that had opted for the Massachusetts Game, including a historic contest between sides from Amherst College and Williams College on July 1, 1859. (Amherst won both the ballgame and the following day's chess match.)[24] Meanwhile the Tri-Mountains continued to search in vain for competition until finally they played a club from Portland, Maine, on September 9 on the Boston Common. After waiting for nearly fifteen months to find an opponent willing to play by the New York rules, the Tri-Mountains were defeated, 47 to 42.

Though it appeared that the Massachusetts Game was still firmly in control of the state, its grip was in fact beginning to loosen. As described in the entry on the Lawrence Base Ball Club, Harvard's first baseball club was organized in 1858 and it adopted the New York version. Western Massachusetts was also becoming a hotbed for the Knickerbockers' rules, for reasons explained in the entry on the Pioneer Club of Springfield.

While a solid majority of the state's clubs were still playing the Massachusetts Game, that wasn't enough.[25] The New York Game was sweeping the country and gaining acceptance in regions where town ball or another variant had prevailed, while the Massachusetts Game had gained no adherents outside of New England. As a result, the clubs that stuck to the state's traditional version began to look more and more like holdouts against a nationwide trend.

Pressure on the traditionalists mounted in 1859 and 1860 as more Massachusetts clubs opted for the New York Game. In 1859 an instructional book published in Boston declared that the New York version "may now be considered as firmly established in New England, and we trust the day is not far distant when the rules of the National Association will govern all matches played in the country."[26] One year later a periodical for Massachusetts farmers reported: "(T)he motto of the Tri-Mountain was 'Success,' and from time to time during the past two years, there have been similar clubs organized, until at the present time the number is quite flourishing; and the New York Game bids fair to supplant all others."[27]

The Massachusetts Game did not go down without a fight. In the final years before the Civil War the state continued to have far more adherents to the old game, many of whom were adamant that they would never switch. And even in other states, there were those who believed the New York Game to be just a passing fad. "The so-called 'Base Ball' played by the New York clubs — what is falsely called the 'National' game," wrote one of the naysayers, "is no more like the genuine game of base ball than single wicket is like a full field of cricket. The Clubs who have formed what they choose to call the 'National Association,' play a bastard game, worthy only of boys ten years of age. The only genuine game is known as the 'Massachusetts Game.'"[28]

Nonetheless the devotees of the New York Game were clearly in the ascendant as the 1850s drew to a close. The Tri-Mountain Club even began experimenting with the fly game in 1859, five years before it was adopted by the National Association for Base Ball Players.[29] It seemed that the battle over how to play baseball in Massachusetts was turning, just as the country itself plunged into civil war.

Wartime Baseball: 1861–1864

As was the case everywhere, the Civil War brought the rapid growth of baseball to a skidding halt. After four seasons that saw little activity, however, Massachusetts' soldiers returned home and found the New York Game solidly ensconced in their home state. The factors that had pushed the Massachusetts Game to the verge of extinction remain the subject of debate among historians.

As described in the entry on the Lowell Club of Boston, John Lowell's 1864 decision to offer a silver ball to the best New York Game club undoubtedly played a role. So too did an 1862 tour by the legendary Excelsiors of Brooklyn, whose visit to Boston demonstrated the need for a single uniform rulebook. The choice of the New York Rules by a club formed at Harvard by members of the Class of 1866 was another factor. Yet a compelling case can also be made that the Massachusetts Game was already doomed before the Civil War's first shots were fired. Whatever the reason, the war began with the Massachusetts Game still the state's most popular version and ended with it on its last legs.

The Postwar Years: 1865–1870

Even in 1865, the Massachusetts Game endured in several parts of the state. Several of the entries that follow discuss the doings of the ballplayers who remained loyal to the old way of playing. For most, however, the issue had already been resolved and youngsters in particular seemed to have opted for the now national "New York" version without giving the matter much thought. In November of 1865 the New England Association of National Base Ball Clubs was formed as an official body for clubs playing by the New York rules.[30]

With the nagging question of "What version of the game are we going to play?" finally settled, attention returned to the question of "Which is the best club?" This question, however, proved perplexing.

Lowell's silver ball was supposed to provide clarity but it failed to do so and was finally melted down in 1867. The particular squabble that led to its incineration involved the troublesome issue of Harvard's summer break but there were also the broader concern that the challenge system was ill-equipped to determine the state championship. In other states a few powerhouse clubs dominated play, which gave the challenge system a chance to be effective. In Massachusetts, by contrast, the "glorious uncertainty" of baseball prevailed and it made Lowell's silver ball largely irrelevant: the Harvard Club and the Tri-Mountain and Lowell clubs were the only clubs to hold it, but others were of comparable strength and might easily have claimed it if given the opportunity.

In addition to the parity that existed among the top postwar Massachusetts clubs, all of them were prone to mystifying ups and downs. The Tri-Mountains in particular were wildly unpredictable, some years looking like the state's best clubs and at others like a venerable elder statesman whose best years were long in the past. The Lowells put together several strong years and then fell off so precipitously that longtime star Jimmy Lovett later acknowledged that it "would have been for the

best interests of the club to have disbanded either in the spring or fall of 1869, when it was at its best."[31] Harvard's nine was of course forced to replace graduated players each season, which inevitably caused inconsistent performances. Meanwhile strong clubs from elsewhere in the state would surface each year, yet none of them remained a force for very long.

The one thing that did remain consistent was that no Massachusetts club emerged as a true contender for the national championship (though by 1870 the Archie Bush-led Harvard nine was very formidable). Touring clubs that passed through Massachusetts were never quite sure whom to schedule and the national press was just as perplexed. Some found this state of affairs discouraging and in 1868 one such commentator observed, "Several base ball clubs at Boston have disbanded and more are to follow. The furor is evidently subsiding. It is hoped it will not break out again this summer."[32]

Despite the disappointments and setbacks, enthusiasm for baseball in Massachusetts never flagged for long and whenever it reached a nadir a revival soon followed. Mort Rogers, for example, moved from Brooklyn to Boston in 1867 after making a name for himself with the Resolute Club. He cast his lot with the Lowells and helped to breathe new life into the local baseball scene by co-founding the weekly *New England Base Ballist*, which featured profiles of pioneers such as Saltzman alongside of the exploits of up-and-coming players. Rogers was far from alone and this chapter features profiles of many of the other ballplayers who helped keep interest in baseball during these pivotal years.

In 1871 Harry Wright arrived in Boston and the long and distinguished (if sometimes agonizing) history of professional baseball in Massachusetts began. That history has often obscured the state's pioneer era, but it is hoped that the entries that follow will stimulate long-overdue interest in those fascinating years.

Notes

1. "Base Ball in Boston," *New York Clipper*, undated clipping apparently from May 1860; cited in Craig Waff's *Pre–Civil-War "Base Ball"–Related Games Played in Massachusetts* on the Protoball website.

2. Larry McCray, "The Rise and Fall of New England–Style Ballplaying," *Base Ball* 5:1 (Spring 2011), 70.

3. *Boston Journal*, February 27, 1905.

4. Troy Soos, *Before the Curse: The Glory Days of New England Baseball, 1858–1918*, rev. ed. (Jefferson, N.C.: McFarland, 2006), 13.

5. *Boston Herald*, September 3, 1855.

6. *Boston Journal*, February 27, 1905.

7. *New York Clipper*, May 24, 1856.

8. *Barre Gazette*, October 1, 1858, 2.

9. *Boston Journal*, March 6, 1905.

10. *Boston Journal*, February 27, 1905.

11. *Boston Journal*, March 6, 1905.

12. *Boston Daily Courier*, May 15, 1857; *New York Clipper*, May 23, 1857.

13. *New York Clipper*, July 11, 1857, 92.

14. "Base Ball Years Ago," *Boston Globe*, March 27, 1888, 5.

15. *Boston Herald*, June 29 and 30, 1857.

16. *New York Clipper*, July 11, 1857, 92.

17. *Sharon Advocate*, June 7, 1907.

18. *New York Clipper*, October 10, 1857.

19. *New England Base Ballist*, August 6, 1868.

20. *Boston Journal*, February 20, 1905. The Tri-Mountain name paid tribute to the three former hills that stood around what became the Beacon Hill section of the city.

21. The ten clubs represented were the Olympic, Bay State and Tri-Mountain clubs (all from Boston), the Bunker Hill Club of Charlestown, the American Club of South Dedham, the Rough and Ready Club of South Walpole, the Neponset Club of Walpole Center, the Massapoag Club of Sharon, the Union Club of Medway, and the Winthrop Club of Holliston.

22. *Dedham Gazette*, May 29, 1858.

23. See Dean Sullivan, *Early Innings* (Lincoln: University of Nebraska Press, 1997), 15–16, for the twenty-one rules that were adopted, as originally published in *The Base Ball Player's Pocket Companion* (Boston: Mayhew and Baker, 1859.

24. See Sullivan, *Early Innings*, 32–34, for details on the game.

25. According to an unidentified clipping, as of 1859 Massachusetts had 37 clubs that used the rules of the Massachusetts Game and 13 that played the New York Game.

26. *The Base Ball Player's Pocket Companion*, 26.

27. *Farmers' Cabinet*, vol. 58, no. 42 (May 16, 1860), 2. Thanks to Joanne Hulbert for discovering and sharing this article.

28. *New York Tribune*, October 18, 1859, 5; discovered by George Thompson and featured on the Protoball website.

29. *Boston Journal*, March 6, 1905.

30. *Boston Daily Advertiser*, November 8, 1865.

31. James D'Wolf Lovett, *Old Boston Boys and the Games they Played* (Boston: Riverside Press, 1907), 149.

32. *Barnstable Patriot*, May 12, 1868.

❖ *Lowell Base Ball Club* ❖
(Benjamin Dettmar)

CLUB HISTORY

In the spring of 1861 members of the Bowdoin Base Ball Club, led by John A. Lowell, set out to form a junior base ball club — the result of this was the creation of the Lowell Club of Boston. The Bowdoin Base Ball Club had been one of the first in the New England region to switch from the Massachusetts version of baseball to the New York version of the game. The Massachusetts version was much closer to cricket in that it had no foul territory, allowed overhand pitching, had fewer innings with more outs per inning, and featured more players on each side. It also allowed runners to be retired by throwing the ball at them, rather than being tagged or called out at the base as is the case in the New York version. James D'Wolf Lovett, one of the stars of the Lowell Club, explains the switch:

> It was evident that this new type [the New York game] was "catching" and that many present were in that condition when they are said to "take things." There were points about the new game which appealed to them. The pitching, instead of swift throwing, looked easy to hit, and the pitcher stood off so far, and then there was no danger of getting plugged with the ball while running bases; and the ball was so lively and could be batted so far! Yes, decidedly, there were points about this new game which pleased many who had never played ball before, and who thought they would like to try it.... In 1859 the Bowdoin Club was formed in Boston with the intention of playing ball in the good old Massachusetts way; but, just for the fun of the thing, they tried the new rules to see how they worked and, behold! The whole nine proved to be in the receptive condition above alluded to, and were promptly infected with the new germ.[1]

March 18, 1861, saw the first meeting of the club in the offices of John Lowell. Lowell was the driving force and financial backer behind the creation of the club, and it was subsequently named in his honor. Along with several members of the Bowdoin Base Ball Club, who left with the blessing of that club, the Lowell Club consisted of base ball players from Latin High School, English High School, and Chauncey Hall Schools.

The Lowell Club played their first game on October 16, 1861, beating Medford 17 to 10 in front of a sizable crowd. The game highlighted many of the stellar qualities of the Lowell Club, with George B. Wilder having a faultless game as catcher, Gat Miller's pitching being "swift and to the mark," and James Lovett excelling at shortstop — missing no balls for the duration of the game.[2] Although they lost their second game to the Bowdoins by a 23 to 14 score, the Lowell Club continued to be successful in its formative years, going on to regularly beat local clubs such as Trimountain, whom the Lowells defeated 37 to 1 on May 29, 1863, and the Hampshire Club of Northampton, Massachusetts, whom the Lowells defeated on October 18, 1864.

Some of the Lowell Club's most memorable games were with local rival Harvard. The geographic locales of the two clubs ensured a competitive rivalry, but this was increased immensely by the social status of the clubs' players. Harvard captain Daniel Putnam ("Put") Abercrombie summed up the difference between the two clubs: "There was considerable talk among the spectators of 'town' as represented by the Lowells and 'gown' as represented by Harvard."[3] The Lowell Club initially included several players who were members of the social elite along with several who went on to study at Harvard, but they clearly were a mixed group, as befitted the schools from which they came. The makeup of the club shifted gradually throughout the 1860s, with several early members entering

Harvard and being replaced by young men of less distinguished backgrounds.

July 9, 1864, saw the two clubs meet in a highly anticipated match that the Lowell nine won, 55 to 25. The rivalry between the two clubs was already evident with Harvard having a scouting report for the Lowell nine — Harvard player "Put" Abercrombie later admitted to having a "card or memorandum of instructions which Capt. [Frank] Wright gave me as centerfield as to where the Lowells were likely to hit."[4]

Later that year John Lowell commissioned a Silver Ball as a trophy for games between clubs in New England. Created to pique interest in the game in Boston, the Silver Ball trophy was first awarded on September 27, 1864, and would go on to be a highly sought-after prize, especially in games between Lowell and Harvard.[5] The Ivy Leaguers won the Silver Ball on occasion, but the Lowell Club, especially in its early years, usually had the edge over the Harvard nine.

The Silver Ball could be won by any club in the Boston area who defeated the current holders of the trophy. The Lowells won the ball more than any other club. Sadly, the trophy came to an ignominious end in 1867 when, after 17 games — the results of which were engraved on the ball — the trophy was unceremoniously destroyed by the Boston base ball authorities. It was felt, somewhat understandably, that the trophy was creating a spirit of competitiveness that was leading to hard feelings and animosity amongst local clubs.

One of the highlights of the Lowell Club's history was a tour to New York City in July 1865. The Lowells played three Brooklyn clubs: Resolute, Atlantic, and Excelsior. The New Yorkers were happy to welcome purveyors of their game from the Massachusetts area, wining and dining the Lowells during their stay in the Empire State. Though the Lowells lost handily to their more experienced opponents, and though they encountered local rule variations and some dubious umpiring, they were in no way disgraced as they put up a good fight in all three games. Indeed, much of the talk after the three-game series focused on John Lowell's stolen base during the game with Atlantic. Lowell, realizing that Atlantic catcher "Dickey" Pearce had a habit of leisurely rolling the ball back to the pitcher, took second base with ease as Pearce languidly returned the ball. Lowell stole the base "amidst much laughter and applause" from the New York crowd, and as such a feat was a rare occurrence at the time, it ensured that the Lowell Club lived long in the memory of many who witnessed the game.[6] Later that year the Atlantics of Brooklyn came to Boston for a return match. Undefeated for two years, the Atlantics drew a crowd reported as exceeding 5,000 people to the Boston Common, the home field for the Lowell Club, and defeated the Lowells 30 to 10.[7] Despite their defeat, the Lowells showed the same hospitality to the Atlantics that they had received in New York, escorting the Atlantics to the Fair of the Massachusetts Charitable Mechanics' Association at Faneuil and Quincy Halls.

Meanwhile, the Lowells' heated rivalry with Harvard continued throughout the fall of 1865 with both clubs beating each other to win the Silver Ball. The Lowell Club narrowly beat the Harvard nine 40 to 37 in a game that saw Lovett's debut as pitcher. The Lowell club's former pitcher Miller was now a student at Harvard, and as such he played for neither side and actually umpired the game. Harvard player "Put" Abercrombie was glowing in his praise of Lovett, although he could not resist a slight dig at his controversial action: "'Jimmy' Lovett played in that game as pitcher, a new place for him, and he was very successful then and later. He had a sort of twist to the ball, and he really had an under-hand throw. Under the rules the under-hand throw was not allowed, and 'Jimmy' cleverly escaped it although he and the umpire had some sharp disputes."[8]

Their retention of the Silver Ball was short-lived, however, as just three weeks later Harvard defeated Lowell 73 to 37 to ensure that they wintered with the trophy. This game, on October 20, saw one of the most remarkable occurrences in games between the two nines. "Nelson's Great Strike" was a home run hit by Harvard player Tom Nelson that caught a high west wind and flew over the Flagstaff Hill in the direction of West Street. Nelson walked around the bases, and the ball was never retrieved — rumors abound that the ball bounced down West Street into a passing horse-car and ended up at Norfolk House! The Lowells were now recognized as one of the premier clubs of the city, and baseball was fast becoming embedded in the culture of the area, as a Boston journalist acknowledged in 1865:

> All over the city lads are forming clubs to practice baseball, so that it promises to grow into a fashionable amusement. It is becoming an object of ambition, we are told, among the young men of our most cultivated families, to gain admission into the Lowell club. The number is limited to 50 and there are more applications for membership than can be received. One word more in regard to the morally as well as physically beneficial tendency of these sports. This thing is so well understood in New York that the merchants in that city encourage the young men in their employ to engage in them by becoming honorary members of their clubs, contributing liberally to their funds, granting them many afternoon hours for this particular recreation and often attending their games themselves. Is not this spirit worthy of imitation? Think where many of these young men might be in their leisure hours were it not for these games and then give the answer.[9]

Eighteen sixty-six was the Lowells' greatest season as they regained the Silver Ball from the Harvard Club and went on to successfully defend the trophy all year long. Victories included a massive 121 to 14 win over the Flyaways of East Boston and a 33 to 23 victory over the Eons of Portland. The most memorable on-field moment of 1866, however, came in front of over 10,000 spectators as the Lowells played Harvard on July 14 — beating their rivals 37 to 27.[10]

The game's "memorable moment" came in the form of

Lovett's extraordinary catch of a ball hit by James B. Ames, the future Dean of Harvard Law School. Lovett, the pitcher that day, pitched the ball to Ames, "which he struck with such force that, before any eye in the crowd could mark its flight, it had returned to my hand as the latter was in the act of swinging back after delivery." The ball was struck so hard, according to the somewhat hyperbolic account given by Lovett, that no one except Lovett and Ames knew where the ball had gone.[11]

Off the field, 1866 also proved a memorable year for the Lowell Club as they opened their club-room on the corner of West and Mason Streets. Most famously of all, 1866 was the year the club found themselves playing a game on July 4 within hitting distance (of Nelson's Great Strike at least) of the Great Portland Fire. In typical fashion Lovett explains how the club helped to save a local jewelry company during the blaze.

> We went to Portland on July 4 and played the Eons, whom we beat 33 to 23, upon a park a mile or so outside the city limits. While playing we could see that there was a good-sized fire raging in the city, and when we returned thither found ourselves in the midst of the "big Portland fire." We had intended returning home that evening, but stayed and worked nearly all night in assisting to save the jewelry stock of Messrs. Lowell & Senter, who very handsomely acknowledged our efforts in the newspapers.[12]

The *Boston Daily Advertiser* backs up Lovett's story:

> The Lowell Base Ball Club of Boston, who had finished their successful game with the Portland Eons just as the fire began to assume a serious aspect, rendered valuable assistance in combating the flames and saving property. The president of the club, Mr. William C. Page, for a time directed the operations of a hand engine, and subsequently joined other members of the club in the work of removing the valuable stock of Lowell & Senter, jewelers, to a place of safety.[13]

Interestingly, the Bangor newspaper the *Daily Whig & Courier*, in a special issue entitled "Burning of Portland: Full Account of the Great Conflagration in Portland, July 4, 1866," reports that "the exertions of a base-ball club" saved the house of a prominent resident; this turned out to be the house of the Lowell family.[14] John Lowell was actually born in Portland and trained there as a silversmith; furthermore, the company saved by the Lowell Club, Lowell & Senter, was founded in 1836 by Abner Lowell and William Senter. John Lowell was the eldest of Abner's five children.

The fortunes of the Lowell Club began to decline in 1867. They lost 53 to 5 (in only five innings) to the visiting Atlantics of Philadelphia. More agonizingly for the Lowells, their old rivals Harvard beat them two games to one in a best-two-out-of-three match-up for the Silver Ball. This series was one of the final hurrahs for the great rivalry. The Lowells won the first game on Boston Common in front of around five thousand fans, many of whom were ladies dressed in the team colors of either the magenta of Harvard or the blue and white of the

Lowells. The second game was not as memorable for the Lowells, as they lost to their cross-town rivals again in front of around five thousand fans, many of whom were students who had been requested to put their studies first, on the much smaller venue of Harvard's Jarvis Field:

> We are desired to state that the Nines request their fellow-students not to absent themselves from recitations during the match with the Lowell nine on Friday. The Faculty were very kind in accomodating [*sic*] the College about the last match; and this is the opportunity for showing our appreciation of their conduct.[15] ...From 2 to 3 P.M., there was a steady flow of humanity of all forms and sizes toward the Jarvis Field.[16]

Harvard won the third game quite convincingly by eleven runs. The game was, however, a contentious affair that was played on the neutral venue of Medford with a neutral umpire — Hicks Hayhurst of the Athletic Club of Philadelphia, who was brought in as no man in New England was deemed to be neutral enough for the occasion. Many partisans of both clubs came to watch the game and according to a report by the *Boston Globe* the "feeling between the players was not the best," and "it was about as hot a game as was ever witnessed in the 'no-admittance fee' days."[17]

Adding to the anguish of the Lowell Club, rumors circulated freely that some of the club's players had accepted bribes to deliberately lose the second game of the series. Believing that they had "lost many friends in consequence" of the innuendos, the members appointed a seven-man committee to investigate. After taking testimony under oath, the committee found no evidence of wrong-doing and exonerated all involved. The club also adopted a new by-law calling for the expulsion of any member who bet on a game. The findings were published in the Boston papers, along with secretary Charles L. Fuller's expression of hope "that the judgment of the public against this club, so long and so recently the favorites of Boston, will be suspended; and that the Lowell Base Ball Club may not be prevented by any suspicions or coldness of treatment from winning its way back again to the hearty support of its former friends, and so maintaining its right to the title which has been the object of its ambition — that of the Model Base Ball Club."[18]

There is of course no way to be certain whether the game in question was fixed. Gambling had already become a big problem for baseball and when fixes did occur they usually took place in the second game of a three-game series, since this set up an exciting rubber game. Yet unsubstantiated rumors were far more common than actual fixes and there is little reason to believe that there was anything untoward in this instance. Gamblers would need to bribe multiple members of the club to ensure defeat and it is unlikely that such a conspiracy would have taken place among the members of the Lowell Club and still more unlikely that such a scheme would have survived the internal investigation.

The animosity between the two clubs continued as the

Lowells managed to exact a revenge of sorts on the Harvard nine when they regained the Silver Ball in the summer of 1867 without actually playing a game. The Lowell Club challenged Harvard during the school's summer vacation, when the majority of the Harvard team was "scattered over the country," thus forcing the Harvard team to forfeit the game and return the trophy to the Lowells.[19]

The Lowells went on to have limited success that year as they easily beat the Rockinghams of Portsmouth, New Hampshire, scoring 107 runs, and the celebrated Excelsiors of Brooklyn (29 to 21), becoming the first club from New England to beat a prominent New York nine. The game against the Excelsiors saw former pitcher Gerrit S. Miller, now a Harvard student, rejoin the club and get a victory against Excelsior pitcher Arthur "Candy" Cummings, the Hall of Fame pitcher usually credited with originating the curveball. But their year ended on a sour note as they lost in a best-two-out-of-three match for the Silver Ball, this time to the Trimountain Club. The Silver Ball was destroyed later that fall.

It must have been some consolation to the Lowells that they did capture another Silver Ball at a September tournament in Keene, New Hampshire, sponsored by the Connecticut River Valley Agricultural Association. In the championship game, the heavy batting of the Lowells allowed them to defeat the Star Club of Greenfield, Massachusetts, and capture this new trophy.[20]

Eighteen sixty-eight saw the Lowells embark on a "neighborly" tour of New England. The Lowells had mixed success on their travels, as they defeated clubs such as the Rollstones of Fitchburg, the Yale nine, and the Charter Oaks of Hartford. The Lowells, however, lost the final game of the tour 22 to 19 to the skillful Brown University nine that included the great Frank Herreshoff. They went on to split a July home-and-home series with the Harvard Club before losing a best-two-out-of-three series with Harvard in October. The July series with Harvard was notable because three prominent members of the Lowell team were sick and unable to play, so the Harvard nine insisted on playing an exhibition game only. The Lowells passed a resolution thanking Harvard for "this polite and gentlemanly act"; thus, perhaps, showing that civility had returned to the rivalry following the shenanigans of the previous year.[21]

The 1869 season again saw mixed fortunes for the Lowell Club. They avenged their defeat to Brown on June 17, winning by a margin of 40 to 13. However, during the spring of 1869, Boston Common was plowed up, leaving the Lowells with no chance to practice and nowhere to play. It is at this time in the club's history that James D'Wolf Lovett says:

> It would have been for the best interests of the club to have disbanded either in the spring or fall of 1869, when it was at its best; for, although we afterwards won games occasionally ... '70, '71, and '72 were regrettable years to the original members and their friends, and would much better have been forestalled by non-existence of the club.[22]

The Lowells did continue, however, and after a political battle they were allotted a portion of the lower end of Boston Common. Visits by the Mutuals of New York and the renowned "Red Stockings" of Cincinnati saw the Lowells defeated, and, despite subsequent victories over the Trimountain and Harvard Clubs, the spirit of the Lowell Club was beginning to suffer as some influential members began to join the now professional Boston Club. The club's fans and the local media began to notice a change in the club's play, and a *Boston Journal* report noted that "the Lowells' play was not equal to that of three-quarters of the junior organizations in this locality. Muffs and wild throws were frequent, and what was worse, a spirit of carelessness prevailed among a majority of the nine throughout the game."[23] December 12, 1873, saw the official end of the Lowell Club as the few remaining original members decided it was time to wind up the club for good.[24]

The Lowells were one of the most important clubs in the early history of baseball in New England. During their heyday they had about one hundred members and were probably the most successful club in the region. Large crowds often turned out on Boston Common to watch the Lowell Club, playing in their distinctive uniform of white cap trimmed with blue, white flannel shirt, and dark blue pants with scarlet stripes.

CLUB MEMBERS

While not necessarily "blue collar," the members of the Lowell Club were generally from a different social background to that of their fierce rival Harvard, and many of the following members fit the description of "Put" Abercrombie's "town" and "gown" description of the two clubs.

Thomas Spencer Adams, Jr.: T. Spencer Adams was born in Massachusetts around 1844, the son of a police officer. He was the first baseman of the Lowells when the club made its 1865 tour of New York, and his play led one New York paper to remark, "Adams is an A1 player at first base."[25] With that, however, his involvement with the club seems to have ended. He died on September 29, 1878.

Captain William Henry Alline: William Henry Alline, who was known by his middle name, was born in 1843 and served in the Civil War. He appears to have been a close friend of Lovett, who describes the two sledding together in his book. When Alline's wife died on February 1, 1923, a lengthy obituary appeared in the following day's *Boston Globe*. According to Civil War pension records, Captain Alline died three months later on May 4, 1923, but the *Globe* made no mention of his passing.

George B. Appleton: George B. Appleton was born around 1845 and was the longtime scorer of the Lowells. He became a partner in the sporting goods firm of Appleton & Bassett and was a close friend of longtime Boston National League franchise owner Arthur Soden. It was Appleton who first got Soden involved in the club's ownership by selling him three of his shares. An 1888 article in the *Boston Globe* described Appleton as someone "who thinks of base ball in his waking hours and dreams of it when asleep."[26] He died on September 22, 1921.

Edward Lincoln "Ned" Arnold: Arnold was primarily associated with the Tri-Mountains but also served as vice president of the Lowells in 1865. He was also a teammate of three Lowell Club members — Lovett, Miller and Peabody — on the Oneida Foot Ball Club. He was born in Cambridge on December 8, 1845, and was still alive in 1925, when he attended the dedication of the monument on the Boston Common.

William M. "Met" Bradbury: William Bradbury was born in 1849 and became well known as the principal catcher of the Lowells from 1868 to 1870. He also played for several other Boston amateur clubs. He got married in 1876 but died of tuberculosis on December 30 of that year. A lengthy obituary chronicled his career and tragic death and claimed, implausibly, that "The primary cause of his death was thought to be the force of the balls which struck his chest while catching."[27]

Samuel Bradstreet, Jr.: Sam Bradstreet, the club's vice president in 1861, enrolled in Harvard in 1865, but left after one year to become a Boston stock broker. Born in Dorchester on December 21, 1844, he played with Lovett on a junior club called the Hancocks in 1857. Although Bradstreet's stay at Harvard was brief, he lived long enough to attend the fiftieth anniversary of what would have been his graduating class in 1918. He died at his home in Marshfield, Massachusetts, on October 4, 1927, and an obituary described him as the last descendant of Simeon Bradstreet, the Colonial Governor of Massachusetts.[28]

Hazen James "Jim" Burton: H. J. Burton was born in Roxbury on July 14, 1847, and graduated from Boston English High School with multiple firsts at the age of 15. He began working in the wholesale clothing manufacturing business while also taking courses at the newly founded school that became known as the Massachusetts Institute of Technology. He also played shortstop for the Lowell Base Ball Club until he made a lengthy tour of Europe in 1867. After graduating from MIT and gathering a dozen years' worth of experience in the clothing business, he moved to Minneapolis in 1880 and founded the Plymouth Clothing House, which soon became very successful. In his later years, he wrote extensively about the U.S. tax system. He died in Deephaven, Minnesota, on September 21, 1934.

Dudley Richards Child: Dudley Child was born in Hillsboro, Illinois, on June 23, 1845, and attended Boston English High School. He served as the club's vice president in 1862. He devoted himself to the study of old coins and other antiquarian pursuits and was a member of the New England Historic Genealogical Society. His health began to fail in the 1880s. He went to Oakland, California, in hopes of regaining his health but died there on May 12, 1883.

Henry Beals Dennison: Henry B. Dennison was born in Bath, Maine, on May 2, 1846, and was a regular for the Lowells in 1867, then a substitute in 1868 and 1869 as his increasing role in the family business made it difficult for him to find time for baseball. He eventually became president of the Dennison Manufacturing Company. Dennison died at his home in Roxbury on March 17, 1912. (Note: Dennison is not to be confused with his near exact contemporary and fellow New Englander, Henry Willard Denison, who was a member of the Olympics of Washington. Henry Willard Denison, who was nine days younger, played for the Olympics while a college student in Washington and then became a renowned diplomat, living in Tokyo from 1880 until his death in 1914. Among his many accomplishments was representing Japan at the drafting of the 1905 peace treaty with Russia, which occurred in Denison's former home state of New Hampshire. Denison was profiled in *Base Ball Pioneers, 1850–1870* in the entry on the Olympic Club.)

Charles Lyman Fuller (club scorer): Charles Lyman Fuller was born in Boston in January of 1844 and, like Lovett, went into the insurance business. He died in Somerville, Massachusetts, on June 17, 1896.

William Burt Joslin: William B. Joslin was born in Massachusetts in October of 1842 and played cricket with Lovett before turning to baseball. In the club's 1864 win over Harvard a newspaper account credited him with making "the most beautiful one hand catch at left field which we have ever witnessed."[29] Joslin later moved to the infield but remained a starter for the Lowells throughout their existence. His father was a globe maker, and William joined the business in 1874, continuing to run it well into the twentieth century.

James D'Wolf Lovett: James D'Wolf Lovett was the author of *Old Boston Boys and the Games they Played* (1907), which is the source of much of the information in this entry. Born in Boston on May 31, 1844, Lovett played sports of all kinds from early boyhood and was one of the mainstays of the Lowell Club. He became a life insurance agent and lived to a ripe old age, dying on September 29, 1935, in Cambridge, Massachusetts.

John Adams Lowell: John A. Lowell, the club's namesake, was born in Portland, Maine, on July 29, 1837. After apprenticing as a silversmith, he moved to Boston and began his own engraving firm, which he ran for 57 years. In addition to the huge role he played in popularizing the New York Game in New England, Lowell also played the outfield for the club named in his honor for several years. He was also credited with helping to invent the halftone engraving process. In 1911, an article in the *Boston Globe* referred to him as "the late John A. Lowell," prompting a bemused Lowell to challenge anyone who thought he was dead to run a hundred-yard dash.[30] He died on December 23, 1915.

Gerrit S. Miller: Gerrit Smith Miller was born on January 30, 1845, and named in honor of his grandfather, a wealthy social reformer and abolitionist who ran for president three times. He grew up on the family's large estate near Peterboro, New York. In 1860, he was sent away to Boston to attend Epes Sargent Dixwell's School. While there, Miller organized the Oneida Foot Ball Club, which played its games on the Boston Common. According to a monument erected at the Common in 1925, this pioneer club took on all comers between 1862 and 1865, never losing a game and never having its goal line crossed. The ball used by the club is now displayed at the National Soccer Hall of Fame in Oneonta and Miller has occasionally been referred to as "the father of American soccer." The problem with this, however, is that descriptions by Oneida Foot Ball Club member James D'Wolf Lovett make it clear that the game they played borrowed generously from rugby, with the result that Miller is sometimes claimed as a football pioneer as well. Along with Lovett, Miller was also a member of the Lowell Base Ball Club. He entered Harvard in 1865 and during the next few years played for the Harvard nine and the Lowells. On October 4, 1867, he pitched the Lowells to victory over the famed Excelsiors, which James D'Wolf Lovett described as the first-ever win by a New England club against a prominent New York club. One month later, he married Susan Dixwell, the daughter of his former schoolmaster. His grandmother died shortly thereafter, and Miller decided to leave Harvard and attend to the estate. His return also allowed him to pitch for the Ontarios of Oswego, although the Central Citys of Syracuse protested his involvement in the gold-ball match on September 15, 1868. One later account maintained that "for three years [Miller] pitched for the Ontarios and did not lose a game. The only trouble was it was very difficult to find a catcher who could hold his terrific speed." While the statement that he was never beaten seems very unlikely, the claim that his pitches were hard to corral seems more plausible. Miller continued to attend to the estate for the rest of his life, but his farming practices were far from routine. He established the first registered American herd of Holstein cattle, later describing his "interest in 'making two blades of grass grow where one grew before' and in producing two quarts of milk where one was produced before. In October, 1869, I established a herd of Holstein cattle imported from Holland on my farm, with the intention of improving the dairy cattle of the country. At that time a cow that would give six thousand pounds of milk per year and twelve pounds of butter per week was considered a good cow. We now have Holstein cows which under official tests have given over thirty thousand pounds of milk per year, one thousand pounds in seven days, one hundred and fifty pounds in one day, over fifty pounds of butter in seven days, and fifteen hundred pounds in three hundred and sixty-five days. Most of the cows making the above-named records trace back to my herd."[31] Miller's son and namesake inherited this fascination with the Holstein cattle. Gerrit Smith Miller, Jr., was educated at Harvard and became one of the country's best-known zoologists and mammalians. He was perhaps best known for his involvement in

the Piltdown Man controversy. Gerrit Smith Miller, Sr., died on his beloved Peterboro estate on March 10, 1937, at the age of 91.

Dr. Francis Greenwood Peabody: F. G. Peabody was born in Boston on December 4, 1847, and was treasurer of the Lowell Club in 1864. His father, a Unitarian minister, died when he was nine, but his former congregation provided the funds for Francis's education. He enrolled in Harvard College, Class of 1869, where he played first base for the school nine. After receiving his undergraduate degree, he remained at Harvard and earned additional degrees from the Divinity School and the Graduate School. Peabody served as a chaplain and teacher at Antioch College in Ohio, then returned home and became the minister at the First Church (Unitarian) in Harvard Square. In 1880, he joined the faculty of the Harvard Divinity School and remained on it for twenty-six years, eventually becoming its dean. He wrote many books, including *Jesus Christ and the Social Questions* (1900), *Jesus Christ and the Christian Character* (1905), *The Approach to the Social Question: An Introduction to the Study of Social Ethics* (1909), and *The Church of the Spirit* (1925). He died in 1936 at the age of eighty-nine.

George G. Richards: George G. Richards, the club's initial president in 1861, was born in Massachusetts in December of 1844 and became a financial clerk.

Maxson Mortimer "Mort" Rogers: Mort Rogers was born in Brooklyn around 1848, one of three sons of fish dealer Albert Rogers, Sr., By the 1860s, Mort and his two brothers, Albert, Jr. and Fraley, were all playing for a Brooklyn club called the Resolutes. According to fellow club member G. Smith Stanton, the Resolute Club was known as "oul man Rogers and Sam Storer's fish chowder nine" and did not take themselves too seriously: "The Resolutes played ball merely to work off the effects of rich dinners the night before. We were the Seventh Regiment, I might say, of the base ball fraternity."[32] On behalf of the Resolute Club, Mort Rogers met the Lowells at the station on their 1865 trip to New York, and a lasting friendship formed.[33] He ended up moving to Boston and becoming the center fielder for the Lowells during their prime years, while he and C. Ruthven Bryan edited a short-lived baseball journal called the *National Chronicle*. In the 1870s, he wrote for the *Sunday Mercury* and produced the scorecards of Boston's National Association club, for which his brother Fraley played. The scorecards he produced were the first to include photographs of players. Mort Rogers died in New York City on May 13, 1881, three days after the suicide of his brother Fraley. Fraley Rogers reportedly killed himself while temporarily insane as a result of malaria, while Mort's death was said to have been hastened by the shock of his brother's passing.[34]

Marshall Paddock Stafford: Marshall Paddock Stafford, a club director in 1861, was born in Brattleboro, Vermont, on October 14, 1845. After moving to Boston, he attended the Mayhew Grammar School and then studied at the English

High School and the Boston Latin School. He enrolled at Harvard in 1862 and then wrote a biography of James Fisk, Jr., He also passed the bar exam and practiced law in New York and Washington. He died in Bellingham, Washington, on October 29, 1904.

Other Club Members: Bentley, Briggs, G.H. Burditt, Frederick Conant, (Albert?) Crosby, Dillingham, William H. Eayrs, William French, J. Frank Gardner, Gorham, Henry Hawes, Edward B. Kimball, Jewell (Marshall Wright identifies him as Hebert Jewell's brother Edward, but this is an error), (Philip?) Mason, Mellen, A. M. Newton, William C. Page, Frank H. Perkins, C.H. Porter, Reed, George R. Rogers, Simmons, George S. B. Sullivan, Frank H. Sumner, Thompson, Troupe, (R. Clifford?) Watson, George B. Wilder, J. Wilder, Frank A. Winn.

SOURCES: The most important source on the Lowell Base Ball Club is the memoirs of club member James D'Wolf Lovett, *Old Boston Boys and the Games They Played* (Boston: Riverside Press, 1907). A number of articles about the Harvard Base Ball Club help clarify the Lowell Club's most intense rivalry: "Harvard's First Ball Team," *Boston Globe*, June 8, 1902, 46; "73 to 37," *Boston Globe*, February 14, 1897, 15; J. Mott Hallowell, "American College Athletics: 1. Harvard University," *Outing*, December 1888; and contemporaneous game accounts in the *Harvard Advocate*. Also helpful was Charles A. Peverelly's *American Pastimes, Containing a History of the Principal Base Ball, Cricket, Rowing, and Yachting Clubs of the United States* (New York: Published by the Author, 1866). Other sources are noted in the citations.

Notes

1. James D'Wolf Lovett, *Old Boston Boys and the Games They Played* (Boston: Riverside Press, 1907), 142–143.
2. Ibid., 147.
3. "Harvard's First Ball Team," *Boston Globe*, June 8, 1902, 46.
4. Ibid.
5. *New England Base Ballist*, August 13, 1868; *New England Base Ballist*, November 5, 1868.
6. Lovett, *Old Boston Boys and the Games They Played*, 165.
7. *New York Times*, October 26, 1865; *Hartford Courant*, October 26, 1865.
8. "Harvard's First Ball Team," *Boston Globe*, June 8, 1902, 46.
9. Ibid.
10. "73 to 37," *Boston Globe*, February 14, 1897, 15.
11. Lovett, *Old Boston Boys and the Games They Played*, 179–180.
12. Ibid., 177.
13. *Boston Daily Advertiser*, July 7, 1866, 5.
14. *Bangor Daily Whig and Courier*, August 18, 1866.
15. *Harvard Advocate*, May 24, 1867, 88.
16. *Harvard Advocate*, June 6, 1867, 108.
17. "73 to 37," *Boston Globe*, February 14, 1897, 15.
18. *Boston Daily Advertiser*, June 25, 1867.
19. *Harvard Advocate*, September 25, 1867, 152–155.
20. *Hartford Courant*, September 20, 1867.
21. *Boston Journal*, July 18, 1868.
22. Lovett, *Old Boston Boys and the Games They Played*, 149.
23. *Boston Journal*, June 28, 1870.
24. Lovett, *Old Boston Boys and the Games They Played*, 204.
25. Ibid., 164.
26. *Boston Globe*, October 21, 1888.
27. *Fitchburg Sentinel*, January 8, 1877.
28. *Boston Globe*, October 5, 1927.
29. Quoted in Lovett, *Old Boston Boys and the Games They* Played, 161.
30. *Boston Globe*, November 19, 1911.
31. *Report of Harvard University, Class of 1869* (1919), 181.
32. *Brooklyn Eagle*, August 5, 1897, 5.
33. Lovett, *Old Boston Boys and the Games They* Played, 165.
34. *New York Clipper*, May 21, 1881.

❖ *Pioneer Base Ball Club of Springfield* ❖
(Peter Morris)

CLUB HISTORY

"Baseball historians could make no worse mistake," cautioned the *Springfield Republican* in 1911,"than to overlook Springfield's contribution to the game, now national, but then only in its infancy."[1] The article went on to spell out the impressive accomplishments and claim to fame of the city's first New York Rules club, formed in 1858. Despite the newspaper's warning, that is exactly what has happened: Springfield is now thought of as the birthplace of basketball and its role in baseball history is forgotten. It is time to right that wrong.

The Tri-Mountain Club of Boston has the distinction of being the first Massachusetts club to adopt the New York rules, making that historic choice upon being organized by trans-planted New Yorker E.G. Saltzman on June 16, 1857. By 1859 the New York version had made so much progress that a Boston guidebook declared, "It may now be considered as firmly established in New England, and we trust the day is not far distant when the rules of the National Association [of Base Ball Players] will govern all matches played in the country."[2]

The claim that the New York Game was "firmly established" was a bit premature, but the prediction did indeed come to pass. The Tri-Mountains understandably receive much credit for that development, but it takes two to play a game and Boston clubs were unwilling to join them in using the New York Rules. After trying unsuccessfully to find a local rival, the club finally played its first match game on September 9, 1858, against an opponent from Portland, Maine. Instead it was western Massachusetts that was the site of the state's first match game by the New York Rules and the first in-state series, so those clubs deserve at least a share of the credit. At the heart of that activity was the aptly named Pioneer Club of Springfield.

Three accounts of the origins of the Pioneer Club were published many decades later in the *Springfield Republican* and they agree on several key facts. All of them agree that the club was formed in 1858 and that it was one of the first clubs in Massachusetts to choose the New York Game over "round ball," also known as the Massachusetts Game. They are also unanimous that, like the Tri-Mountains, Springfield's first club was founded by two recent arrivals from New York, H.M. Griswold and John E. Selden (though one of the accounts erroneously gives the latter's name as Sheldon).

The accounts differ, however, on many key details. How, for example, was the crucial decision to play by the New York Rules made? One version of events records that, in contrast to the resistance that met the efforts of the Tri-Mountains, the young men of Springfield readily "forsook their rude but pleasurable strife at round ball" in favor of the New York Game.[3]

Another article, however, painted an entirely different picture. According to it, the city's "young men of athletic inclination and outdoor habits began to gather day by day on a vacant lot just back of the building on the north side of Lyman street, near Main" to play the Massachusetts Game. Then came the arrival of Griswold and Selden, who moved the action to Hampden Park and demonstrated the rival version. The round-ball players were not pleased with the elimination of soaking, the rule by which a baserunner could be retired by hitting him with the ball while he was between bases. They found, however, that "there were many compensations for even this loss, not least of which was the ability to bat the new hard ball 'over the left-field fence' for a home-run." That was enough to convince them, and after that nothing could "prevent the new game from taking amazingly."[4]

The three retrospective accounts also differ about many of the details. According to one of them, Griswold and Selden "gathered their candidates on a lot back of Main and Lyman streets and there explained and demonstrated this game of baseball."[5] In another version, on a July day in 1858, the two New Yorkers simply "went out to Hampden park, measured off a diamond, set stones for bases and started in. Then they organized with Sheldon [sic] as president and Griswold as captain."[6] The third account, the one that had the two New Yorkers moving the action from the vacant lot to the park, stated that the "first game under the new rules was played July 4, 1858, on Hampden park, with flat stones for bases and under other disadvantages."[7] Yet one of the articles pinpointing July as the month of origin also described a club medallion that gives the date of organization as "April 30, 1858."[8]

There's no way to entirely reconcile these discrepancies, which are not surprising since all three accounts were published

more than three decades after the fact and two of them in the twentieth century. Fortunately, however, enough contemporaneous accounts were published in the *Springfield Republican* to give a clearer picture. The medallion, it turns out, is far closer to being accurate than the retrospective accounts.

The first intimations came on Friday, April 23, 1858, with this intriguing note: "About thirty young men — clerks in our stores and offices and students at law — have formed a 'Pioneer Ball Club' and will play their initiating game on the Park this afternoon. Some dozen of an older generation — including leading members of the bar, clergymen, state senators, railroad presidents, poets, editors, historians and 'other sich' — have indulged in a weekly game there for several Saturday afternoons, and we trust will organize themselves into a permanent institution for exercise and sport of this character."[9]

There were no more updates about the doings of the railroad president and poets, but plenty of news about the Pioneers. The following day brought word that "notwithstanding the rain and clouds of yesterday, about twenty members of the 'Pioneer ball club,' or a little more than half the whole number, assembled on Hampden Park and played a matched and very exciting game — the first they have had. The game is conducted under regularly established rules, taken from the most approved authorities, and it is the intention of the members to make the club a permanency. They meet next Monday evening to choose officers and pass finally upon their constitution and by-laws."[10]

The historic meeting did indeed occur on Monday, April 26, 1858, and on the following day the *Republican* provided this account: "The members of the new 'Pioneer ball club' met at the Russell House, last evening, and made a permanent organization with J.E. Selden, president; George B. Smith, vice president; and E. Morgan secretary and treasurer. The rules to regulate the game are drawn from the crack clubs of New York, where two or three members of this club have played."[11] So it seems that the date on the medallion was also a few days off, though the Pioneer Club did schedule its first practice session as a formally organized club for the afternoon of April 30.[12]

The next order of business was to secure playing grounds and that proved easy. The following week brought word that "the 'Pioneer ball club' have [sic] arranged with the directors of Hampden Park for the use of two or three acres of the land for a weekly game during the summer, merely paying the value of the grass so destroyed. Their second game will come off this afternoon, at half past 2 o'clock, and all members will of course be promptly in attendance."[13]

The weather was less cooperative, however, as was conveyed by a wry note a week later. "The Pioneer boys," its author remarked, "are reminded of their weekly game of base ball at Hampden Park, at 3 o'clock this afternoon, and if it doesn't rain, as has been the case at all former games, there will be an interested crowd of spectators."[14]

The rain at last let up and before long the Pioneer Club was reported to be "in 'the full tide of successful experiment,' and its weekly games will be a decided attraction to the Park during the summer."[15] Soon it was time to choose a first and second nine. Griswold conducted the tryouts and selected Hamilton Downing as the club's pitcher for an intriguing reason. Round ball, also known as the Massachusetts Game, featured overhand pitching, so most of the players were unfamiliar with the strict underhand motion required by the New York Game. Not so with Downing, who used his expertise at the not dissimilar art of pitching quoits (a game similar to horseshoes) to impress Griswold. The captain himself took the important duty of catching Downing's offerings. Rounding out the first nine were Em Hawks, Joe Stevens, Dr. Henry Collins, Marsh Frost, Bliss Vinton, Abner Trask, and Cortes Fairbanks.[16]

A second nine was also selected, which made it possible to hold lively practice sessions on Thursday and Friday afternoons.[17] One of the later accounts even claimed that there were enough players to form a third nine.[18] But intrasquad contests are only fun for so long, and there were increasing signs that there was time for a test against an outside rival. "Why won't some of the 'down town' boys get up an opposition club for an occasional match game?" wondered the *Republican*.[19]

Fortunately, the Atwater Club of nearby Westfield had also been formed that spring and "adopted the New York Rules and Regulations for playing Base Ball."[20] The Nonotucks of Northampton soon followed suit, though no indication was given of what version it intended to use.[21] At least one other Northampton club was formed that year and the *Springfield Republican* and *Massachusetts Spy* brought word of half a dozen clubs in the Worcester area.[22] Worcester is about forty-five miles from Springfield, not so far away that competition was out of the question. There were now more than enough clubs for a memorable and historic season of competition.

Matters got started in earnest in August when the Atwaters of Westfield challenged the Nonotucks of Northampton to a match game.[23] On August 11, a sizable contingent from Springfield made its way to Northampton, where a crowd of over two thousand turned out at the "beautiful green in the meadows, near the large elm tree at Hockanum Ferry" to watch the Atwaters win by the remarkable score of 36–2.[24] The historic event was followed by "three hearty cheers" for the victors and "a sumptuous repast ... which received ample justice from all present."[25]

It seemed a promising beginning for the New York Game in Massachusetts, but it soon started to look more like an ending. Five days after the match in Northampton, the *Republican* ran an advertisement advising members of the Pioneer Base Ball Club that an "important business" meeting would be held that evening at the Russell House, with a "full attendance ... desired."[26] To all appearances, the Pioneer Club was on the verge of challenging the Atwaters, but then there was ominous silence. The challenger would lose home-field advantage, so a cat-and-mouse game ensued in which each club waited "for the other to throw down the glove."[27]

In addition, it became clear that the contentious issue of what set of rules to use was far from being resolved. In the spring the zest for playing baseball had been enough that clubs weren't too particular about what rules were being used — all that really mattered was that each region adopt a common set of rules so that match games could be held. In western Massachusetts that was the New York version, while Boston and the rest of eastern Massachusetts, round ball was chosen. The situation in Worcester and the rest of central Massachusetts was confusing, as we shall see.

In May of that year, the eastern clubs had met to agree upon those rules and form a statewide association. The meeting, in Dedham, a town outside Boston, is often given great significance by baseball historians, but it doesn't appear to have seemed very important by the ballplayers of the time. The *Springfield Republican* had only this to say: "Six base ball clubs of Boston and vicinity met at Dedham on Thursday last, and organized the Massachusetts association of base ball players. Now we shall have base ball annual conventions, with banners, music and prizes."[28] No mention at all was made of the rules chosen, and much of the state went on happily playing the New York version.

Once a few match games had been played, however, that changed. The version used by the Nonotucks had never been clear and the lopsided defeat at the hands of the Atwaters strongly suggested that the Northampton club had been playing "round ball," perhaps with some modifications. An account in the *Hampshire Gazette* of Northampton observed that "there seemed to be some considerable difference of opinion upon vital points of the rules ... the 'Nonotuck' [had] to adopt to an entirely diverse mode of playing."[29] After scoring only two runs in the match game, they seem to have lost interest in playing baseball by any version.

It was a similar story in central Massachusetts, where the summer had seen the birth of numerous clubs, most of them in or near Worcester. The difference in rules used was not enough to prevent match games between these clubs, but once those contests had been played the differences suddenly seemed very important. After one game had been played between clubs from Barre and North Brookfield, efforts to arrange a rematch devolved into an argument about the merits of each version. The latter club eventually declared that "one out–all out" (the Massachusetts Game) was the "game played by all organized clubs" and passed a resolution "*never to play the game* 'one out one out.'"[30]

Even in western Massachusetts, allegiance to the New York Game was wobbling. The demolition of the Nonotucks had sapped Northampton's enthusiasm and even the commitment of the Pioneers was in doubt. The club continued its weekly practice sessions but the only detailed summary that appeared in the *Republican* suggests that hybrid rules may have been used. According to that description, "The 'Pioneer' boys have reached a high state of perfection in their ball playing on Hampden Park, and now that they understand one another are enabled to make such divisions as result in very exciting games. Last Friday afternoon, in twenty-seven innings, a side of ten players made 17 tallies, and a side of twelve only 13. It is harder to make one tally in this game than almost a dozen in the 'old base.'"[31]

The last sentence of the account makes it clear that a serious attempt had been made to follow the New York Rules, but the twenty-seven innings and the ten- and twelve-player sides sound much more like the Massachusetts Game. The most plausible explanation is that modifications were made during the sessions so that every member who showed up could play. Nevertheless, after witnessing the ease with which the Atwaters had defeated the Nonotucks, it seems likely that members of the Pioneers wondered about the wisdom of facing them in a version of the game that differed from the one used at the club's weekly practices.

Meanwhile the Atwaters and Pioneers continued to wait for the other to issue a challenge. Perhaps other factors, such as the harvest, also contributed to the prolonged standoff. Just when it was beginning to look as though cold weather would come before either side made a move, the Atwaters at last threw down the gauntlet. The first game of the three-game series that "had been anticipated all summer" was scheduled to begin on Monday, October 4, at Hampden Park.[32] The contests were to feature "the same mode of playing as is practiced by the New York Clubs."[33]

Although the Pioneers had gained the home-field advantage by outwaiting their opponents, there were still grumbles that "the expected challenge came at a time when the Springfield club looked for it least, and felt still less prepared to meet it, because the constant use of the park for several weeks past had badly interfered with their regular practice. The Pioneers accepted the proposition, therefore, with many misgivings, but firmly resolved to give their antagonists a manly fight."[34]

The game began at 3:20 P.M. with five hundred spectators on hand, an impressive turnout considering that Hampden Park had no grandstand, forcing each spectator to bring "his own chair or camp stool."[35] After four tightly fought innings, the Pioneers broke the game open with an eight-run fifth-inning outburst and they widened the gap during the later innings to win 29–15. Captain H.M. Griswold was the hero of the day, scoring a game-best six runs without being retired. Matters concluded at 5 P.M. with the obligatory cheers and the presentation of the game ball.[36]

Despite the convincing margin of victory, nobody was taking the result of the game for granted. The *Republican*'s verdict was that the two sides were very "evenly matched" and

that "the Pioneers were best at the bat and the Westfield boys best in fielding, and a reason for this may exist in the fact that the play ground at Westfield is not so open and level as Hampden Park, requiring the Atwaters to be expert in catching the ball as it flies through the air, while the Pioneers have full swing for a long knock. The tables may therefore be turned with a change in the field of contest."[37]

The return game in Westfield was delayed until the 20th, apparently by inclement weather. After two scoreless innings, the Atwaters seized a small lead and gradually increased it to 8–2 after six innings. Then the Pioneers staged a dramatic nine-run seventh-inning rally and surged to the lead. They were on the verge of sweeping the series, but then their bats fell cold again and the Atwaters tied the game in the eighth and scored once in the ninth to pull out a dramatic 12–11 victory. Griswold, who had been the star of the first game, had a game-high five outs and was the only member of the Pioneers who failed to score a run.

Reported the *Republican*, "The game was played on the village green, a little south of the old church, and the Springfield boys, although they find no fault, ascribe their defeat in great measure to the fact that the neighboring elms gave Westfield all the advantages of their long knocks." Home field advantage was, obviously, more than just an abstract concept. As the account noted, the stage was now set for a third contest, to "be had in Hampden Park whenever the Westfield boys decide to come over. The result will be watched with great interest, and there will unquestionably be a very large crowd in attendance at their final meeting. We do not believe there are two clubs in the state more evenly matched."[38]

With winter fast approaching, it was essential to conclude the series as soon as possible. So the third game took place only five days after the second contest on an afternoon "so blustering that but few ladies were present. Overcoats and mittens were decidedly comfortable, and the players had to work sharp to keep warm." Nonetheless, around a thousand spectators were on hand from towns all over the area, including Longmeadow, West Springfield, Chicopee, and Palmer.[39]

The Pioneers jumped to an early lead, but the Atwaters kept matters close and the outcome remained in doubt. Tension continued to build until a late surge by the home nine put the game out of reach. After the final out, the players and spectators gathered around scorer M.A. Wood, who announced that the Pioneers had won, 18–9. The announcement was no mere formality as Wood's score "conflicted somewhat with the private reckonings, because the spectators, not being able to hear all the rulings of the umpire, were uncertain about several doubtful tallies on either side. These, if allowed, would have made the score stand about 21 to 11." Cheers were then offered and the victors treated the vanquished to dinner at the Russell House.

In the end, the Pioneer Club's unwillingness to issue the challenge may have made the difference. They had won the series by winning the two games played on their home field and even the hometown *Republican* acknowledged that that advantage had been crucial. The Atwaters, according to its reporter, seemed to feel "that the Pioneers were invincible on their native heath; while the Springfield boys, on the other hand, felt confidence of success for about the same reason."

That was it for the Pioneer Club's first season, except for a planned married-single game that, if played, was not reported on by the *Republican*.[40] Expectations were high that 1859 would see the rivalry with the Atwaters continue and be enlivened by the emergence of new contenders. New clubs were indeed formed, in Pittsfield, North Adams, South Adams, Chicopee, Cheshire, Northampton, and Westfield, creating the possibility for a lively summer of ballplaying in western Massachusetts.[41] Accounts rarely specified the rules by which these clubs were playing, but a description of the newly formed Hampden Base Ball Club of Chicopee indicated that the club had adopted "the general rules of the Pioneer, Atwater, and other clubs in the vicinity."[42] Since the Pittsfield Base Ball Club traveled to New York State for a match game against the Champion Club of Albany, it seems safe to assume that the New York version was still the game of choice in western Massachusetts.[43]

Yet the two clubs responsible for the area's first series played under the New York Rules were not part of the fun, as baseball pretty much went into hibernation in both Westfield and Springfield.[44] Pioneer Club captain H.M. Griswold seems to have already left Springfield by the spring of 1859, while co-founder John Selden soon followed, leaving a leadership void. In August the *Republican* announced a practice between the first nine of the Pioneer Club and its other members, but aside from that there were no signs of life at all.[45] The paper regularly carried accounts of baseball in other cities, so journalistic priorities were not the problem. By the end of 1859, it was hard to tell whether the Pioneer Base Ball Club was still in existence.

The spring of 1860 brought a few signs of revival. The first practice was greeted with the hope that the Pioneer Club was going to "re-organize for the campaign with full strength."[46] This was followed by tantalizing hints that the club planned to adopt a new uniform and intended to stage a novel contest between the supporters of Abraham Lincoln and those loyal to Stephen A. Douglas.[47] But nothing seems to have come of these plans and even the organization of a second Springfield club, the Massasoits, didn't stir the Pioneers from their lethargy. In August the *Republican* issued this rebuke: "Neither [the Pioneer Club] nor the Massasoit club have contested for honors outside their associations this season. It is time they had whipped other clubs, or vice versa."[48]

The call to action was not heeded immediately but before long the Pioneer Club was beginning to show signs of life. An exhibition contest was played against the crosstown Massasoits and there was a concerted effort to arrange match games.[49]

Most of the area's newer clubs proved far too weak to compete with the Pioneers, so games were instead played between their first nines and the second nine of the Pioneer Club. At last, however, after considerable "trouble and expense" the efforts paid off.[50] On August 31, 1860, the first nine of the Pioneers faced the Pittsfield Base Ball Club in the Pioneers' first match game in nearly two years. Despite the lengthy absence from formal competition, a very familiar lineup was used by the Pioneers: Griswold had been replaced at catcher by a young newcomer named Lucius Warner and Emory Hawks was now handling the pitching duties, but the infield and outfield positions were almost all manned by holdovers from 1858.[51]

The Pioneers won the first game of the series, 18–8, in Pittsfield. Then the series moved to Hampden Park, where the visitors evened the series by eking out a 16–14 victory. The *Republican*'s account of the second game stated that both sides had "covered themselves with honor" by their fine play and also expressed pleasure at the "interchange of civilities provoked by the coming together of the two clubs."[52] Nonetheless, it appears that the Pioneer Club had taken their rivals too lightly after the comfortable road win. Abner Trask, usually the club's left fielder, was behind the plate for this game and Downing did the pitching, suggesting overconfidence.

No complacency was on display in the rubber game, played at Hampden Park on September 24.[53] With Hawks and Warner again forming the battery, the Pioneers jumped to a 6–3 lead after two innings and then turned the game into a rout with three unanswered runs in the third inning, four more in the fourth, sixteen in the fifth, and twelve in the sixth. Meanwhile, "[l]ike pins on a bowling alley the Pittsfield boys were no sooner set up than they came down; or, no sooner came in, than they went out." The game ended with an extraordinary final score of 51–4.[54]

After the postgame festivities, the Pioneer Club made the electrifying announcement that it would close the 1860 playing season with a single match game at Hampden Park against the Bowdoin Club of Boston. This was a very exciting piece of news, probably brought about by Ham Downing, who in May had umpired a game on the Boston Common in which the Bowdoins had defeated the Tri-Mountains. At the same time, it was a cause for concern. The Pioneers had beaten the best clubs that western Massachusetts had to offer but were they ready to face a club from Boston? The Bowdoins, formally known as the Bowdoin Square Base Ball Club, had been formed in 1859 as a Massachusetts Rule club but quickly switched over to the New York Game and already boasted a pair of wins over the Tri-Mountains. So the anticipation of the big game was accompanied by anxiety that it might result in an embarrassing defeat.

One of the retrospective accounts described how the Bowdoin Club "challenged Springfield to play for the championship of New England. Boston's attitude toward Springfield at that time had much in common with that of the town mouse toward the country mouse, and the offer was regarded as a great condescension. The Springfield boys had not practiced nearly as much as the metropolitan players, but they gamely accepted the challenge, asking only that the decision should rest on the result of three games." But the Bowdoins "refused to consider" that proposal, so only a single game was played.[55]

The "great game of base ball" was played on Saturday, October 6, a "cold and blustering" day that was "more like December than any weather we have yet had this fall." Nevertheless a crowd estimated at between 1,200 and 1,500, including a significant number of women, braved the elements. Initial appearances suggested that an overwhelming defeat might indeed await the home side: "The Pioneers are rather the larger men in size, but the Bowdoins are a muscular and well trained set of fellows, some of them boasting of a physical development that it would do [physical activity advocate Thomas Wentworth] Higginson good to see. The Bowdoins came here confident of victory, although confessing it would have to be worked for, and never entertained a suspicion that their unvaried success hitherto would now sustain a check. The Pioneers enter in less confidently but not less determinedly, prepared for defeat, if it must come, but not to be beaten bad."

All of the apprehension proved unfounded. The Pioneers grabbed an early lead with a six-run second inning and were able to withstand several rallies by the visitors. When the final score was announced, the home club had beaten their rivals from the big city, 22–13. The members of the two clubs shared a supper at the Massasoit House, where Bowdoin captain John Lowell presented the game ball to counterpart Ham Downing "with words of congratulations and assurances of perfect good feeling." The disappointed Bowdoins returned to Boston on the night express and the *Republican* declared the Pioneer Club to be the "champion base ball club of Massachusetts."[56]

The excitement of the big win carried over to the winter. A Springfield die sinker named J.A. Bolen was commissioned to create club medallions. One side depicted a young man in a baseball uniform batting a ball, along with the inscription "Pioneer Base Ball Club," decorated with several stars. On the other side could be seen a few bats and balls, along with the words "Organized April 30, 1858" and "Play-ground on Hampden Park, Springfield, Mass." As we have seen, it was possible to quibble about the exact date, but there was no gainsaying the elegance of the design.[57] The medallions became "cherished possessions" of club members and Ham Downing kept his with him at all times.[58]

There were also regular meetings and eager discussions about how to improve upon a season that had been "so great a credit and success" to the Pioneer Club.[59] Two grand balls were even staged at Springfield's Union Hall in February.[60] By March, the members were discussing the possibility of leasing a new lot near Main Street that was said to be far more convenient and "far better than Hampden Park."[61]

One month later, shots were fired at Fort Sumter and the nation's attention was turned to much more serious matters than baseball. The three retrospective accounts in the *Republican* all made it sound as though the Civil War also brought an end to the Pioneer Club. According to one of them, "The game was at the summit of its popularity when an unforeseen obstacle killed its local development. In other words, the civil war broke out, and there was other business for young men of strong body and bubbling enthusiasm. And when Johnny came marching home, so many things had happened and the ordinary hum-drum aspect of life had undergone such a sudden and violent transformation that base-ball was little thought of again for many a year, save as a pastime of the good old days when secession was only a theory and blood and iron were mere abstractions to be found in the worm-eaten pages of bygone history books."[62]

In fact the end was not nearly that neat or sudden. While the outbreak of war delayed the start of the 1861 season, by July of that year there were signs that the Pioneer Base Ball Club intended to persevere.[63] The end of the month brought concrete proof in the announcement that "the Pioneer base ball association of this city, of such renowned fame last summer, has not been extinguished or paralyzed by the present national calamities, as many may suppose; but, on the contrary, the club is more lively and enterprising than ever. It meets on the play-ground, on Hampden park, for practice, every Friday afternoon, at 3 o'clock, and will continue through the season. The members of the club have recently obtained handsome uniforms, which they will wear on all occasions when out in a body. It consists of a fine flannel white shirt, trimmed with blue and blue pants with red stripes."[64]

Before long the uniforms were set off by a "new style of base ball shoes.... They are a pretty combination of fine white canvass and uncolored calf-skin, substantially and tastefully made, and among ball clubs, fire companies, and local military organizations, are becoming quite popular. They are original with Cutler & Warner, shoe dealers and manufacturers opposite Massasoit block, and at this time form one of the principal features of their business, as did the sale of army shoes several weeks since."[65]

The signs of revival continued when a challenge was received from the Bowdoin Club for a rematch on the Boston Common.[66] Several practice sessions and meetings were held, but in the end the obstacles to wartime baseball proved too great to surmount.[67] The Pioneer Club gradually lapsed into inactivity and baseball in Springfield was left to adolescents, including the newly formed Pioneer Juniors.[68]

If the Civil War had been short-lived, as was generally expected at its outset, the Pioneers would probably have sprung back into action. Instead the war dragged on year after year and the passage of time rendered the days on the baseball diamond increasingly remote. After two years with little being heard from the club, the spring of 1864 brought word that

"The old Pioneer ball club is dead, but a new organization with the same name has just been started with the following organization: President, Michael Hennefick; secretary, John Shay; treasurer, Richard Fitzgerald; captain, John Ludden. Members of the club will meet for practice at Hampden Park every pleasant afternoon, and in a few weeks will be in a good challenging condition, when matched games of base ball may be expected."[69] The new club showed a few signs of life that year, but even the end of the war in 1865 was not enough to sustain it.

The spring of 1866 was accompanied by the news that the "old Pioneer base ball club, formerly the Champion club of the valley, is getting in working order again, and propose to hold a meeting in the course of a few evenings for the purpose of reorganizing."[70] The "old members" of the club were "earnestly requested to be present" at the organizational meeting.[71] A first nine was soon chosen and it included at least a couple of prewar players. Catcher Lucius Warner and the venerable Dr. Henry Collins, though he turned 40 that year, both returned as starters. The new lineup also included players with the surnames Frost and Trask; these men may have been prewar players Marsh Frost and Abner Trask, but it's also possible that they were younger men with the same surnames.[72]

So was the celebrated prewar club back in business or was this essentially a new club using that now-familiar name? Probably the latter, but the question was rendered pretty much moot by the lackluster course of the new Pioneer Club. Within days of the organizational meeting, it amalgamated with another local nine with an eyebrow-raising name: the Smith & Wesson Club.[73] Even this injection of fresh blood produced limited results and the summer brought few signs of life.

As had been the case in several previous years, the approach of fall brought increased activity.[74] In early September the new Pioneer Club challenged the Eagles of Florence to play for the silver ball that symbolized the championship of western Massachusetts.[75] It was a promising sign, but the game itself produced a dispiriting 68–20 defeat and play that was of so little interest that "a large portion of the spectators retired without waiting to see the last innings played." Lucius Warner's work behind the plate was singled out for praise, but the fielding of his teammates, "was weak, and they lacked precision and force in throwing to the bases."[76]

The club's 1866 playing season closed soon afterward and by the following spring it was again beginning to look as though the Pioneer Club had passed out of existence. Baseball fever was raging all over the state and indeed all across the country, but it was a very different picture in Springfield. "Base-ball seems under a cloud in Springfield," the *Republican* bemoaned. "While there were a dozen clubs, young and old, all eager for the fray, at this date last year, there are now only two, and seem likely to be only one.... Now that the Pioneer club has hopelessly gone under, the Union might become its legitimate successor, but is now in a way to imitate it only in

dying. The base-ball season opened with May, and clubs in other places are stripping for work. 'Wake up!' and don't let Springfield be caught napping longer."[77]

After a great deal of additional prodding from the *Republican*, the Pioneer Club of Springfield did indeed reorganize for the 1867 season.[78] The summer was an eventful one for the latest incarnation of the club but not a distinguished one, with the members exhibiting an apathy that the efforts of the local newspaper were only occasionally able to lift. It is arguable whether this club was truly the same one as the antebellum trailblazers by the same name, and it is easy to understand why the retrospective accounts in the same paper maintained that the Civil War ended the club's history.

Yet while most clubs of the pioneer era went out with a whimper, that was not the case with the postwar version of the Pioneers of Springfield. On July 4, 1867, the club hosted the Hampden Club of Chicopee, which had succeeded the Eagles of Florence as the champions of western Massachusetts. As explained in the next day's account, the contest itself soon seemed unimportant:

> [A]fter each club had played one inning, the Chicopee boys had made one tally and the Springfield boys three. At this juncture a tremendous tornado, which ominous black clouds had been threatening for some time, came sweeping over the park bearing an immense cloud of dust. The thousands and tens of thousands on the park fled like frightened sheep, and the rush for the south gate was fearful. On came the storm of dust, filling the air so densely that breathing was laborious. There was a terrible jam at the gate and the screams of women, who feared being crushed to death, added to the general excitement. A baby's carriage was trodden under foot, and torn to pieces, but the baby was rescued and held above the crowd by a brave man. The people, once out of the park, filled every available nook and place that had roofs above them, the great mass, however, going to the depot and filling its vast area full. A dirtier crowd was probably never gathered there, for the dust had for a time completely enveloped them. A little rain followed this most remarkable tornado, which must have done considerable damage to vegetation in its course.[79]

The game was completed the following week and the Pioneers were defeated 46–34.[80] According to a later account, the loss was described as being "not so bad a beat as the Pioneers had expected."[81] Obviously it was time for the club to call it quits.

Rather than simply disbanding, however, the Pioneer Club began negotiating to "consolidate" with the club that had just beaten it: the Hampden Club of neighboring Chicopee.[82] It was a strange move to say the least. Chicopee was within a few miles of Springfield but this was not a trivial distance to travel in the nineteenth century, meaning that the merger was going to create major logistical problems. More importantly, the merger was a troubling development that seemed to suggest that winning baseball games had become more important to the members of the two clubs than civic pride. Which town's name would the new club bear? Where would it practice? Would it retain the silver ball earned by the Chicopee club?

After prolonged negotiations, the two clubs announced that the first nine of the amalgamated nine was going to consist of four members of each club, with the ninth player then being selected by a vote of the other eight. With Lucius Warner having recently married and apparently finished with baseball, the new club included no members of the prewar Pioneers. The Pioneer name was also given up in favor of the Hampden nickname, which was appropriate, since both Chicopee and Springfield were part of Hampden County.[83] Settling on the other half of the club's name was more difficult — the club was usually referred to as the Hampden Club of Chicopee, occasionally as the Hampden Club of Springfield, and its doings in general were a source of confusion.

The arrangement proved just as awkward and bewildering, and the following spring brought word that the "Hampden base-ball club has been reorganized by the Chicopee players, or rather a new club has been formed."[84] All connection to the old Pioneer Club and to Springfield now seemed to have been severed, yet when the Hampdens beat the famed Tri-Mountains of Boston the *Springfield Republican* claimed it as a victory for "the Hampden club of this city and Chicopee."[85] Even that win, however, was not particularly impressive, as the Tri-Mountains were far better known for helping to introduce the New York Game to Massachusetts than for strong play. If the Chicopee-Springfield fusion club had been formed with the intention of being a regional and perhaps national powerhouse, as seems to have been the case, it fell far short of its goal. In 1869 yet another amalgamation took place and the Comet Club of Chicopee subsumed what was left of the Hampdens.[86]

By then the long series of mergers had left no trace of the original Pioneer Club. Its members were left with only memories of their days on the baseball diamond, but that was more than enough to sustain them. "The jolly rides to and fro in the six-horse coaches of that day," one of the retrospective accounts recalled, "are still a fragrant memory in the dusty chambers of the survivors' recollections." It added, "In those days there was never a thought of professional players — the man who wouldn't give all his old boots to get on the nine just for the fun of it, being the rare exception and a person for whom the old-time players, in the language of this degenerate day, had no use. But there was good play all the same, and plenty of fun, and the idea that a game might have been sold out was a conception that never so much as crossed the minds of the game's ante-bellum patrons."[87]

CLUB MEMBERS (PREWAR)

Dr. Henry A. Collins: Right fielder Henry Collins was born on August 27, 1826, in nearby South Hadley. He gradu-ated from Yale with a medical degree in 1850. After a few years of practice in Conway, he began "drifting toward homeopathy" and decided to move to Springfield to open a homeopathic practice. Widowed in 1855, he had recently remarried when the Pioneer Club was formed. Later accounts had him being on the first nine in 1858, but he didn't play in any of the three games against the Atwaters. He did see action for the club in all of its games in 1860 and was again a regular on the 1866 incarnation of the club, though he turned 40 that summer. During one practice, his medical expertise came in handy as he administered to a bleeding teammate named Moody.[88] After practicing medicine in Springfield for thirty years, he contracted blood poisoning and died on May 13, 1884, after an illness of five months. An obituary noted that "his habit of driving rapidly through the streets made him one of the best known men of the town, and illustrated his character. He was magnetic and hopeful in the sick room, and this buoyancy of spirit was often of the highest value.... More vacations would probably have carried Dr. Collins beyond the age of 58, but like so many active natures, it was difficult for him to step out from under the load and he bore it with too little relief."[89]

Hamilton F. "Ham" Downing: Hamilton Downing used his experience tossing quoits to become the pitcher of the Pioneers. Downing was also a heavy hitter and, according to Stevens, once hit a long drive in a game in Westfield that went through the slats of a church steeple and stayed there while four runs crossed the plate.[90] In May of 1860 he umpired a game in Boston in which the Bowdoins had defeated the Tri-Mountains, so he was probably responsible for the subsequent visit of the Bowdoins to Springfield.[91] Born in Preston, Connecticut, on October 29, 1828, Downing was eighteen when he moved to Springfield. He went to work for a wholesale grocer and before long became a partner in the business. The firm gradually expanded and eventually he became president and treasurer of Downing, Taylor & Co., a large wholesaler. For many decades he was one of Springfield's most prominent businessmen. Downing died on October 16, 1906, in Tolland, Connecticut, where he had been stricken ill while attending his brother-in-law's funeral. An obituary that recounted his many accomplishments also found time to mention that Downing "was a member of the Pioneers, and always carried with him a souvenir which was given the team at the close of the season."[92] The souvenir in question was of course the medallion described in the club history.

Cortes Fairbanks: First baseman Cortes Fairbanks was later described as having been "a wizard ... how he could scoop in the low throws and jump for the high ones!"[93] Fairbanks was born around 1836 and grew up in Chicopee. He became a conductor for the New York, New Haven, and Hartford Railroad and moved to New Haven, Connecticut, where he was still living in 1920. A couple of accounts refer to him as Scott Fairbanks, so perhaps this was a nickname, but it may simply be a mistake.

Marshall S. "Marsh" Frost: Third baseman Marsh Frost was born on Auburn Street in Springfield in 1836 into a family that had lived in the city since 1689. He lived on that same street for his entire life. At nineteen he went to work for the Boston and Albany Railroad and eventually became a locomotive engineer. Frost married at the start of the Civil War and during the war years he "guided many a troop train on its way South, with the soldiers standing up all the way in wooden cars." Frost died on February 17, 1919.[94]

H.M. Griswold: A New Yorker named Griswold was Pioneer Club founder and captain, as well as the club's first catcher and leadoff hitter, but his identity is a puzzle. One box score gave his name as H.M. Griswold and there is a Henry Griswold listed in the Springfield city directory. He seems to have left town by 1859 and where he came from and where he headed remain mysteries. There are no plausible candidates on the census and the *Springfield Republican* gave no clue to his identity aside from one unlikely claim that he had previously been a member of the Gotham Club of New York.[95]

Julius Francis Hartwell: Julius Hartwell was not listed as a member of the first nine but played center field in the first game against the Atwaters. He also played for the club's second nine in at least one 1860 contest. Born in Berry, Ohio, in 1838, Hartwell had married Mary J. King on September 14, 1858, so was a newlywed when he played against the Atwaters. Hartwell worked for the Agawam Bank of Springfield and later earned a trusted position in Boston with the U.S. Treasury. In 1867 he was accused of participating in a major embezzlement scheme and in June 1870 he was sentenced to five years in prison and fined $100,000 for embezzlement. He received a presidential pardon in February 1872 as a result of a petition whose signees maintained that Hartwell "had been sufficiently punished, while others who had profited by his error had escaped ... [and] that after his first offense [Hartwell's course] had been manly and honorable."[96] Hartwell then moved to Providence, where he died on February 26, 1906.

Emory H. "Em" Hawks (or Hawkes): Em Hawks was born on August 12, 1827, in Charlemont, Massachusetts, the youngest of fifteen children. His exact name was a source of considerable confusion. The spelling of his surname varied, but there is no "e" on either his birth record or death certificate so that is presumed to be correct. His middle name is also unclear; his birth record lists it as Hart but his death certificate gives it as Houghton. In any event, Hawks moved to Springfield around 1849. He was a member of the Pioneer Club's first nine, usually playing the outfield but also serving as the other pitcher. During the Civil War, he served in the 34th Massachusetts Infantry Regiment. Hawks worked as a brick mason, but was already listed as being retired when the 1880 census was taken. He later ran a billiard room that was a popular gathering spot for the local sporting men. As late as 1937, Hawks was still remembered as having been able to

"throw a ball farther than anyone else in the city."[97] He died in Springfield on October 18, 1904.[98]

John E. Selden: Club president and co-founder John E. Selden was born in Connecticut on February 22, 1828, and moved to Springfield from New York state to accept a position as a telegraph operator with the American Telegraph Co. He played right field in all three 1858 match games. Selden soon moved to Providence and then on to New Orleans before returning to his home state and finally ending up in Chicago, where he died on October 30, 1912.

Joseph Arthur Stevens: Second baseman Joe Stevens was born in Chester, about 30 miles west of Springfield, in 1839 and moved to Springfield in 1854. Within the next three years, he took a position as a machinist for the Boston and Albany Railroad and became a "torch boy" for the Ocean fire engine. Stevens was not alone, as an account of the third game between the Pioneers and Atwaters noted the "singular circumstance that three of the Westfield players should be members of the Rough and Ready fire company, while three of the Springfield boys are members of Ocean No. 3."[99] He remained with the railroad for forty-six years and was an engineer with the fire department for over half a century, before a fall finally led to his retirement from firefighting in 1908.[100] In 1911 Stevens was described as being "a hot baseball rooter to-day and always has been since he first heard of the game."[101] Joe Stevens died at his Springfield home on December 10, 1919.[102]

Abner Trask: Abner Trask was born around 1830 and was raised in Springfield. He played left field for the Pioneers in all of their recorded prewar games except for the one in which he moved behind the plate. A player named Trask was on the postwar Pioneers, but whether this is the same man is not known; the Trasks were a fairly large Springfield family. While still a young man, Abner Trask purchased a large piece of land in East Hartford, Connecticut, and turned it into a profitable tobacco farm. He married Julia Roberts in 1877 in East Hartford — though not that Julia Roberts! When he died in 1912, he was still well remembered in Springfield and his time with the Pioneer Club was prominently featured in his obituary.[103]

Edward Bliss Vinton: Bliss Vinton played shortstop for the Pioneers in all of their recorded first-nine games and usually batted leadoff in 1860. His was a most unhappy life. Born in Northampton on August 18, 1832, Edward Bliss Vinton was the middle of three sons of Joshua and Mary Vinton. Joshua Vinton soon moved his young family to Springfield, where he worked as a hotel clerk and then became manager of the Hampden House. In 1842 he relocated to New York and started a Wall Street brokerage firm; within two years, he had amassed enough money to return to Springfield and retire. Nonetheless, he continued to dabble in real estate and built one of Springfield's best-known mansions in an affluent area known as Prospect Hill. His eldest son had died in an accident and the two surviving sons could have enjoyed lives of leisure as well. Instead Bliss Vinton went to work as a clerk for the Boston and Albany Railroad and married a young Vermont woman. Then began a long series of tragedies and misfortunes. Bliss Vinton's young wife died, leaving him a widower with a sickly young son, and his father had to be committed to a private institution for the insane, where he died in 1869. Bliss Vinton remarried in 1871 and his new wife, Emma Goodrich, was a member of another prominent Springfield family that lived in a neighboring Prospect Hill mansion. The couple inherited this mansion, but did not have long to enjoy it. Emma Vinton suffered burns in a mysterious fire, rumored to have taken place while her husband was distilling alcohol. Bliss Vinton in turn became afflicted by a series of physical ailments and by the mental illness that ran in the family. In 1876, a court pronounced him legally insane and his affairs were in receivership until he died in Springfield on January 29, 1882, of Bright's disease. That was only the beginning of the family's woes. Bliss's younger brother — "plagued by the burden of his unproductive property, the fact of his father's insanity and the melancholia it attached to his mother" — committed suicide on the day before the first anniversary of Bliss's death. During Bliss Vinton's final years, his wife had hired a stableman and brought him into the household; their relationship soon became a local scandal. Bliss's only son died in 1887 and his widow became a recluse. When she died, she seemingly confirmed the local gossip by leaving the estate to her former stableman. Family members tried to break the will, but they were forced to withdraw their suit when the key witness, a servant, also died. By 1962 the mansion built by Joshua Vinton had been converted into a rectory, while the one in which Bliss Vinton spent his final years was abandoned and generally believed to be haunted.[104]

W. Walker: A man identified as W. Walker in one box score (and just as "Walker" in others) played in most of the club's match games in both 1858 and 1860, though he does not seem to have been a member of the first nine. The name is too common to be sure of his identity, though one interesting clue surfaced. In 1933 one of the Pioneer Club medallions was donated to the Connecticut Valley Historical Society by Dr. Emma Walker, who reported that it had belonged to her father, Henry Walker.[105] So perhaps Henry Walker was a member of the same family as "W. Walker" or perhaps he was the ballplayer and the initial listed was in error.

Lucius Porter "Loosh" Warner: Nineteen-year-old catcher Lucius Warner breathed new life into the Pioneer Club when he joined the first nine in 1860. Born in Springfield on October 8, 1840, Warner married in October 1866 and moved to Hartford in 1878 and worked as a steel polisher. In 1916, the *Springfield Weekly Republican* reported that Warner had celebrated his golden wedding anniversary; the article described him as "[o]ne of the members of the famous old-time baseball club, the Pioneers" and claimed that Warner "played baseball professionally prior to his wedding and about a year there-

after."[106] Warner died in Hartford on May 30, 1917, and was described in an obituary as having been "formerly a baseball player with the Pioneers of Springfield, one of the crack teams of this part of the country in the late 70s."[107]

Other Prewar Club Members: J.B. Wood (second nine member), M.A. Wood (club scorer).

SOURCES: This piece is based primarily upon contemporaneous coverage in the *Springfield Republican* and on three retrospective pieces that appeared in that newspaper: on January 5, 1890 (page 5), September 13, 1903 (page 20), and August 6, 1911 (page 13). A fourth retrospective article, published in the *Springfield Republican and Union* on June 22, 1930 (page 15A), added a few new details about the later years but was largely repetitive. Brian Turner and John S. Bowman's *The Hurrah Game* (Northampton: Northampton Historical Society, 2002) provided valuable coverage of the 1858 series against the Atwaters. Helpful background material on baseball in Massachusetts came from Troy Soos's *Before the Curse: The Glory Days of New England Baseball, 1858–1918*, rev. ed. (Jefferson, N.C.: McFarland, 2006); *The Base Ball Player's Pocket Companion* (Boston: Mayhew and Baker, 1859); the Protoball website; and several articles on the Massachusetts Game by Richard Hershberger in *Base Ball*.

Notes

1. *Springfield Republican*, August 6, 1911, 13.
2. *The Base Ball Player's Pocket Companion* (Boston: Mayhew and Baker, 1859), 26.
3. *Springfield Republican*, September 13, 1903, 20.
4. *Springfield Republican*, January 5, 1890, 5.
5. *Springfield Republican*, August 6, 1911, 13.
6. *Springfield Republican*, September 13, 1903, 20.
7. *Springfield Republican*, January 5, 1890, 5.
8. *Springfield Republican*, September 13, 1903, 20.
9. "Ball Playing on Hampden Park," *Springfield Republican*, April 23, 1858, 4.
10. *Springfield Republican*, April 24, 1858, 8.
11. *Springfield Republican*, April 27, 1858, 4.
12. *Springfield Republican*, April 30, 1858, 4.
13. *Springfield Republican*, May 7, 1858, 4.
14. *Springfield Republican*, May 13, 1858, 4.
15. *Springfield Republican*, May 22, 1858, 8.
16. This was the first nine given in the 1911 article, except that the writer gave the wrong first name for Trask. The 1903 article was rather vague about the make-up of the first nine, explaining that the "first nine had the privilege of drafting players from the second" and listing eleven members of the "major organization": those nine plus Selden and someone named Walker. None of the contemporaneous articles listed the first nine, though they did provide box scores for the three contests against the Atwaters. Collins played in none of the 1858 games, so this may have been an error, but it's also possible he was unavailable and Selden took his place.
17. *Springfield Republican*, June 4, 1858, 4. The practices alternated between Thursdays and Fridays, an unusual arrangement.
18. *Springfield Republican*, January 5, 1890, 5.
19. *Springfield Republican*, May 22, 1858, 8.
20. "Base Ball in Massachusetts," *New York Clipper*, August 21, 1858, 143; *Springfield Republican*, June 3, 1858, 4.
21. *Springfield Republican*, June 23, 1858, 4.

22. *Massachusetts Spy*, June 23 and July 7, 1858; *The Base Ball Player's Pocket Companion*, 26; *Springfield Republican*, September 10, 1858.

23. *Springfield Republican*, August 2, 1858, 4.

24. Game account from the *Northampton Courier* reprinted in Brian Turner and John S. Bowman, *The Hurrah Game* (Northampton: Northampton Historical Society, 2002), 5; *Springfield Republican*, August 12, 1858, 4. As Turner and Bowman point out, the elm tree in question was one mentioned by Oliver Wendell Holmes, Sr., in *The Autocrat of the Breakfast Table*, which by coincidence was also published in 1858.

25. Game account and box score reprinted in Turner and Bowman, *The Hurrah Game*, 4.

26. *Springfield Republican*, August 16, 1858, 3.

27. *Springfield Republican*, October 5, 1858, 4.

28. *Springfield Republican*, May 19, 1858, 2.

29. Quoted in Turner and Bowman, *The Hurrah Game*, 5.

30. *Barre Gazette*, September 17, 1858, 2, and October 1, 1858, 2.

31. *Springfield Republican*, June 22, 1858, 4.

32. *Springfield Republican*, October 5, 1858, 4.

33. *New York Clipper*, October 16, 1858, 206.

34. *Springfield Republican*, October 5, 1858, 4.

35. *Springfield Republican*, September 13, 1903, 20.

36. *Springfield Republican*, October 5, 1858, 4; *New York Clipper*, October 16, 1858, 206; *Porter's Spirit of the Times*, October 16, 1858, 100.

37. *Springfield Republican*, October 5, 1858, 4.

38. *Springfield Republican*, October 21, 1858, 4.

39. *Springfield Republican*, October 26, 1858, 4.

40. *Springfield Republican*, November 6, 1858, 8.

41. *Springfield Republican*, April 4, June 10, June 22, and July 23, 1859; *Pittsfield Sun*, July 21, August 18, September 15, and October 27, 1859.

42. *Springfield Republican*, April 4, 1859, 4.

43. *Pittsfield Sun*, October 27, 1859, 2. The Albany club won the game, 11–8, so there can be no doubt it was played by New York rules.

44. The Atwater Club of Westfield was not entirely defunct and news of its doings occasionally were reported during the next few years, but it played very few match games and like the Pioneers seems to have played none at all in 1859.

45. *Springfield Republican*, August 12, 1859, 4.

46. *Springfield Republican*, May 10, 1860, 4.

47. *Springfield Republican*, July 16 and 17, 1860.

48. *Springfield Republican*, August 3, 1860, 4.

49. *Springfield Republican*, August 29, 1860, 4.

50. Ibid.

51. Dr. Henry Collins now played right field in place of Selden, but the later accounts suggest that Collins had been the first-nine right fielder all along so Selden may have been filling in for him in the 1858 games.

52. *Springfield Republican*, September 11, 1860, 4.

53. Newspaper coverage originally indicated that the third game was going to be played in Pittsfield, but after several delays it was finally played in Springfield. According to the *Republican* of September 24, 1860, page 4, the Pioneers had earned the home-field advantage by virtue of scoring the most total runs in the first two games. This was an unusual and possibly unique arrangement, if indeed the *Republican*'s explanation was correct.

54. *Springfield Republican*, September 25, 1860, 4.

55. *Springfield Republican*, September 13, 1903, 20. The account refers to the Bowdoin Club as the Lowell Club, an understandable mistake since the Lowell Club was an offshoot of the Bowdoin Club.

56. *Springfield Republican*, October 8, 1860, 4.

57. *Springfield Republican*, July 31, 1861, 4.

58. *Springfield Republican*, September 13, 1903, 20.

59. *Springfield Republican*, January 29, 1861, 4.

60. *Springfield Republican*, February 2, 13, 19, and 26, 1861.

61. *Springfield Republican*, March 13, 1861, 4.

62. *Springfield Republican*, January 5, 1890, 5.

63. *Springfield Republican*, July 26, 1861, 4.

64. *Springfield Republican*, July 31, 1861, 4.

65. *Springfield Republican*, August 8, 1861, 4.

66. *Springfield Republican*, August 14, 1861, 4.

67. *Springfield Republican*, August 23 and September 3, 1861.

68. *Springfield Republican*, September 24, 1861, 4.

69. *Springfield Republican*, May 24, 1864, 4.

70. *Springfield Republican*, May 8, 1866, 4.

71. *Springfield Republican*, May 11, 1866, 4.

72. *Springfield Republican*, September 10, 1866, 4.

73. *Springfield Republican*, June 6, 1866, 8.

74. *Springfield Republican*, August 27, 1866, 4.

75. *Springfield Republican*, September 3, 1866, 4.

76. *Springfield Republican*, September 10, 1866, 4.

77. *Springfield Republican*, May 7, 1867, 4.

78. *Springfield Republican*, May 18, June 4, and June 5, 1867.

79. *Springfield Republican*, July 5, 1867, 2.

80. *Springfield Republican*, July 13, 1867, 2.

81. *Springfield Republican and Union*, June 22, 1930, 15A.

82. *Springfield Republican*, August 7, 1867, 8.

83. *Springfield Republican*, August 7, 9, 12, and 13, 1867.

84. *Springfield Republican*, June 1, 1868, 8.

85. *Springfield Republican*, September 21, 1868, 8.

86. *Springfield Republican*, August 18, 1869, 6.

87. *Springfield Republican*, January 5, 1890, 5.

88. *Springfield Republican*, September 19, 1866, 8.

89. *Springfield Republican*, May 14, 1884, 6.

90. *Springfield Republican*, September 13, 1903, 20.

91. The 1903 account made this claim about the game in Boston umpired by Downing: "[I]t is believed that from an arbitrary ruling of his originated the present three-strike regulation. The Boston team set no limit to the number of balls that could be pitched to a single batter, and Mr. Downing consequently found them consuming three and four hours in a match. At Springfield he had been used to a limit, and at the outset of the contest which he was to umpire he said to the Lowell [*sic*] and Trimountain players, 'If you don't strike at the good balls I shall call strike, gentlemen. There is no need for dragging a match through three hours in Boston which we country people can finish in an hour and a half.' The Bostonians did not demur, and as other contemporaneous clubs were playing without a limit rule it is reasonable to suppose that Mr. Downing's arbitrary dictum is responsible for the present method of persuading the batsman to try all the 'good ones'" (*Springfield Republican*, September 13, 1903, 20).

92. *Springfield Republican*, October 17, 1906, 4.

93. *Springfield Republican*, August 6, 1911, 13.

94. *Springfield Republican*, February 20, 1919, 11.

95. *Springfield Republican*, January 5, 1890, 5. That article also claimed that Selden had been a member of the Knickerbocker Club, another highly unlikely assertion.

96. *Pittsfield Sun*, February 15, 1872, 2.

97. *Springfield Republican*, April 4, 1937, 17.

98. *Springfield Republican*, October 19, 1904, 8.

99. *Springfield Republican*, October 26, 1858, 4.

100. "Joseph A. Stevens Resigns," *Springfield Republican*, February 6, 1908, 4.

101. *Springfield Republican*, August 6, 1911, 13.

102. "Old-Time Fireman Dies," *Springfield Republican*, December 11, 1919, 4.

103. "Abner Trask Dies; Was Member of Famous Pioneer Baseball Club," *Springfield Union*, July 16, 1912, 6.

104. "Abandoned Franklin St. Mansion Holds Dramatic Memories in Empty Rooms," *Springfield Union*, November 11, 1962, 8A; *Springfield Republican*, January 25, 1908, February 29, 1908, February 13, 1910, and April 29, 1911.

105. *Springfield Republican*, March 24, 1933, 3.

106. *Springfield Weekly Republican*, October 26, 1916, 14.

107. *Hartford Courant*, May 31, 1917, 12.

❖ *Lawrence Base Ball Club of Harvard* ❖
(Peter Morris)

CLUB HISTORY

A number of references suggest the presence of "various games of bat and ball" on the Harvard campus prior to 1850, but not surprisingly, these didn't coalesce into anything formal.[1] The school's first organized ballplaying club was the Lawrence Base Ball Club, founded in the fall of 1858 at the Lawrence Scientific School, a special branch of Harvard that provided instruction in engineering and applied science. The club did not play a match game that fall and its activities after 1858 are murky, yet it has several claims to our attention beyond being the first of its kind at Harvard.

The Lawrence Scientific School opened in 1847 as the result of a $50,000 endowment from industrialist Abbott Lawrence (1792–1855). Lawrence left another $50,000 to the school in his will, enabling it to attract a faculty and student body that included many gifted minds. Even so, the study of applied sciences did not fit easily into the traditional conception of a liberal-arts college. As a result, the Lawrence Scientific School remained separate from Harvard College, though the two branches of the University shared the Cambridge campus.

No doubt this division contributed to the failure of many histories of baseball at Harvard to recognize the Lawrence Base Ball Club as the school's first organized club. There were other factors, however, most notably the club's short existence and the fact that all of its doings were recorded in notebooks that soon became buried among more important artifacts. Indeed, the entire history of the Lawrence Club might still be forgotten if not for records that were unearthed from among the papers of one of the club's two secretaries, Harvard Professor Frederic Ward Putnam, upon his death in 1915. Those records in turn provided the basis for a 1917 article in the *Harvard Graduates' Magazine*.[2] Now housed at the Harvard Archives, they remain the main source of what we know about this pioneer club.

The records compiled by Putnam and fellow secretary Eulogio Delgado, which are now part of the Harvard University Archives, show that the club adopted a formal "Constitution, By-Laws, Rules and Regulations" on November 3, 1858. Among the articles were one that designated the club's name as "the Lawrence Base Ball Club" and one that specified that the club would play the "New York Game of Base Ball" and that "in no case shall any other Game be played by this Club."[3] The choice of the New York Game is an intriguing one and it is unfortunate that nothing is known about how the members reached this decision.

The standard rules of the National Association of Base Ball Players are written out in longhand and are augmented with several intriguing bylaws. One of these specifies a fifty-cent "Entrance fee" for members, but an entry adopted only fifteen days later doubled the amount. Evidently, the club's expenses exceeded initial expectations.

Another bylaw called for a ten-cent fine for being absent without justification and a three-cent fine for offenses that, alas, are not entirely legible.[4] The club also adopted a rule making it possible to expel a member if two-thirds of his peers found him guilty of "behaving in an ungentlemanly manner, or rendering himself obnoxious to the Club." On a more pleasant note, it was decided to hold regular practices on Mondays and Thursdays at 2:30 P.M., weather permitting, and that "any twelve members wishing to use the apparatus of the Club, may do so at other than the regular hours of Play."[5]

In all, thirty-five young men became club members, though not all of them did so at the initial meeting. The members did not belong to a particular class. After consulting the school catalogue, the author of the 1917 article in the *Harvard Graduates' Magazine* concluded: "College standing seemed to have little to do with membership. Some were graduates; some few may not have been connected with the College at all; several were Freshmen when the Club was started."[6]

It does not appear that any faculty members belonged to the Lawrence Club. (Putnam, later a longtime Harvard professor, was still an undergraduate in 1858.) The club did, however, confer honorary membership status upon Professor Eben N. Horsford, who had the delightful title of Rumford Professor and Lecturer on the Application of Science to the Useful Arts. Horsford acknowledged the tribute with a note expressing his "obligations to the Lawrence Base Ball Club for the honor they have conferred upon me in electing me an honorary member."[7]

There were also two very notable names among the thirty-five members. Eulogio Delgado, who shared the secretary duties with Putnam, was a native of Peru, while Primitivo Casares hailed from Mexico. Did their membership in the Lawrence Base Ball Club play any role in the introduction of the New York version of baseball in those countries? At this point, there is no direct evidence that it did, and Casares died only five years after returning to Mexico, but perhaps future research will find such a link.

The club's painstaking record-keeping makes its activities sound less than enjoyable. Putnam even missed church one Sunday to assist as Delgado transcribed the club constitution into the notebook in elegant handwriting.[8] Yet the members saw it differently, with Albert W. Edmands, one of the surviving members, stating in 1916 that he didn't "recall much about the organization of the Club" but indicating that he remembered its meetings as "very jolly affairs. The members indulged in fencing, boxing, single stick, and various athletic games."[9]

Once all the business was completed it was time to take to the playing field and, with winter fast approaching, there was no time to lose. Four intrasquad games were played between November 8 and November 18 and, as mandated by one of the club's bylaws, the results were dutifully recorded in the club's notebook. The respective scores were 27–9, 33–11, 39–32, and 54–39, with Francis Washburn and Albert Gould serving as captains during the first two outings. The third contest was cut short by snow after eight innings, so it's impressive that the club held another session before adjourning for the winter.[10]

The snow-shortened game had another distinction. At its close, secretary Putnam wrote as follows to thank a young woman named Adelaide Edmands for her assistance:

> *Lady*: At a meeting of the Lawrence Base Ball Club held this day, the following resolutions were passed unanimously:
>   Resolved:— That the Lawrence Base Ball Club tender their thanks to Miss Edmands for her kindness in making the Flags and Bases for the Club.
>   Resolved:— That the Secretary be requested in behalf of the Club, to forward a Copy of these resolutions to Miss Edmands.
>   Yours respectfully.[11]

Putnam and Edmands married six years later. While the 1917 article carried no byline, it was apparently written by their only son, Eben. Adelaide Putnam passed away when Eben was only ten, so he must have felt a tug at the heart upon reading this letter from his father to his mother.

Another document attests both to the meticulousness of the clubs' secretaries and to the high hopes of a sizable membership. The club arranged for the printing of a neat document to be used to welcome new members. Beneath the letters "L.B.B.C." and a space for the exact date, appears this message: "Sir: I have the honor, in behalf of the Lawrence Base Ball Club, to inform you that, at a regular meeting of the Club, held this day, you were duly elected a member. Yours, respectfully." There follows a space for the secretary's signature and an excerpt from the club constitution that explains the need to pay the membership fee.

So where did the Lawrence Base Ball Club play its intrasquad games? The club's records make no mention of this detail but according to Edmands, "The practice ground of the Club was usually on the ground where now stands the University Museum, opposite Divinity Hall, and the matches were played on the Common, at the north end, over by the Elm. The Common was larger than it is now." Edmands added that the club's meetings were held in the Zoological Hall, which was also where equipment was stored.[12]

Details of the club's doings after November of 1858 are even more difficult to pin down. Frederic Putnam's son believed that the club remained active for a few years, but if so why did the careful record keeping cease?[13] The 1917 article, probably also written by Putnam's son, speculated that "the books with scores and accounts of meetings between 1859 and the dissolution of the Club are probably lost."[14] This is certainly possible, but there's no way to be sure. As Harry Lewis points out, the meticulous record-keeping of the fall of 1858 came to an end and only a few shards of evidence establish that the Lawrence Base Ball Club remained in existence.[15] The result is that until recently it's been unclear whether the club lapsed into inactivity in 1859 or whether the apparent inactivity just reflects a gap in the written record.[16]

Fortunately, a partial answer to that intriguing question has now emerged. As Lewis notes, the last member to sign the constitution did so on September 22, 1859, proving that the club was still then at least nominally in existence.[17] Another important clue is that, after the first four games in the fall of 1858, three additional games are recorded in the notebook in much more abbreviated fashion. No dates appear and it does not even appear that two complete nines could be assembled, as the names of as few as six players per side appear. In contrast to the impressive penmanship of Delgado, the writing is in a messy scrawl and at the bottom of one page appears the notation "In hand writing of F W Putnam — EP." Obviously Eben Putnam was very familiar with the challenge of deciphering his father's scribbling.

Both of these clues strongly suggest that the club remained in existence in 1859 but that it was struggling to stay alive. The inability to get together enough players for intrasquad games implies that there was widespread apathy among the membership. It seems just as plausible, however, to attribute the lack of a written record to diminished interest on the part of its secretaries — Delgado in particular. Most likely, the two factors worked in tandem.

Two recent discoveries shed additional light on the state of the club in 1859. At the Harvard Archives, Harry Lewis found a separate folder containing a bank deposit slip. On the back of the bank deposit slip there is a handwritten note with the words, "Sept 15, 1859. We had a meeting of the LBBC tonight and have put Albert in as a director of the Club, we tried to get a speech out of him but it was no go." It's another piece of evidence that raises more questions than it resolves — with three members named Albert, we can't even be sure which of them had been selected as a club director. Nonetheless, it leaves no doubt that the Lawrence Base Ball Club was still in existence in the fall of 1859.[18]

An even more exciting find establishes that the club played at least one match game that year. One of the last surviving members, Albert Edmands, claimed in 1917 that the club "played regular matches with a Club formed by men in the Law School."[19] There is natural suspicion about putting much weight on a statement made nearly sixty years after the fact, but a new discovery by researcher Joanne Hulbert confirms the basic accuracy of Edmands's recollections. On July 2, 1859, the following note appeared in the *Boston Atlas & Bee*:

Match Game of Base Ball. A match game of Base Ball, according to the rules of the National Association of New York, was played at Cambridge, Thursday afternoon, between the Lawrence Club and the Dane Club of Cambridge, the Lawrence Club being the challenging party. The Lawrence Club was organized last September, and is composed of students from the Lawrence Scientific School; the Dane about two months, and is composed of students of the Dane Law School. The game commenced at 3–½ o'clock, was finished at 6 o'clock, and was won by the Dane Club....

The names of the players followed, along with their respective positions and scores.[20]

Much remains unknown about the activities of the Lawrence Base Ball Club but this new discovery brings the club's activities into clearer focus. It can now be said with certainty that the members continued to use the equipment stored in the Zoological Hall in 1859. Perhaps further research will discover evidence of even more extensive activity.

In any event, the club's members soon moved on to more serious pursuits. As described in the profiles that follow, at least two of them died in the Civil War, while others led lives of distinction in the burgeoning fields they had studied at the Lawrence Scientific School. Did the members retain an interest in baseball and try to introduce the New York version in any of the far-flung places their work took them to? At this point, we cannot say so with any certainty but new evidence continues to emerge and perhaps future research will produce proof that they did. It seems unlikely that the passion they showed in the fall of 1858 went away entirely.

CLUB MEMBERS

There is little way to know which of the thirty-five members played the most important roles in the brief history of the Lawrence Base Ball Club, so seven members with special claims to significance are profiled and the remainder are listed at the end.

Primitivo Casares (Galera): Primitivo Casares (Galera) was born in 1836 and graduated from the Lawrence Scientific School in 1861. He returned to his native Mexico, but died five years later in Mérida, in the Mexican state of Yucatán.

José Eulogio Delgado: José Eulogio Delgado, who was known by his middle name, shared the secretary duties with Frederic Putnam and was known for his elegant penmanship. Delgado returned to his native Peru after graduating in 1858 and became chief engineer of the Oriental Rail Road Company in Lima. According to his obituary, Delgado became "one of the most distinguished of Peruvian engineers. He was minister of the treasury under General Caceres from 1890 to 1892, was for years the head of the Associated Charities of Lima, and had been conspicuously identified with almost every permanent improvement carried out in that city in the past 50 years." Delgado died on February 14, 1912, at his estate outside of Lima. At his funeral, Harvard was represented by Charles Lyon

Chandler, a member of the Class of 1905 who was then serving as United States vice consul general at Callao.[21]

Albert William Edmands: Albert W. Edmands was born in Charlestown, Massachusetts, on September 9, 1840, and was the brother of Adelaide Edmands, the future wife of Frederic Putnam. Upon graduation in 1862 Edmands enlisted in the 44th Massachusetts Regiment. After the war he settled in Somerville and became a teller for the Bunker Hill National Bank, also serving as an alderman. Edmands died on October 13, 1918, little more than a year after contributing his memories of the Lawrence Base Ball Club for the article in the *Harvard Graduates' Magazine*. He was still working for the same bank that he had joined in 1865, though it had become a branch of the American Trust Company.

Albert Gould: Albert Gould, who captained one of the two sides in at least the first two intrasquad games, was born in North Bridgton, Maine, on February 18, 1830. He graduated from Bowdoin College in 1851 and then from Harvard Law School the following year, but doesn't appear to have ever practiced law. After teaching in Norwich, New York, for four years, he returned to Harvard and earned a degree from the Lawrence Scientific School in 1859. Gould then returned to North Bridgton and worked as a chemist and photographer until his death on February 1, 1874.

Simon Newcomb: The extent of Simon Newcomb's role in the Lawrence Base Ball Club is unknown and was probably limited, as he was the last member to join the club in 1858. Newcomb, however, rivals Frederic Putnam as its most distinguished member. Born in Wallace, Nova Scotia, on March 12, 1835, Newcomb had a haphazard education before entering the Lawrence Scientific School. After graduation, he took a position at the Naval Observatory in Washington and became one of the country's most respected authorities on astronomy. Among his many accomplishments, Newcomb was a founding member and the first president of the American Astronomical Society, and president of the American Mathematical Society. He is credited with numerous important contributions to astronomy and the measurement of time, while also dabbling in a wide variety of other fields. Newcomb died in Washington on March 11, 1909.

Frederic Ward Putnam: Born in Salem, Massachusetts, on April 16, 1839, Frederic W. Putnam began his studies at the Lawrence Scientific School with the intention of becoming a physician. By the time he graduated in 1862, however, renowned Harvard Professor Louis Agassiz had redirected his interest to zoology and related fields of inquiry. The types of research that most interested Putnam were not then generally recognized as academic disciplines in the United States but Putnam did much to help them achieve that status. After working at two Salem museums, he returned to Harvard in 1874 to become curator of the Peabody Museum of Archaeology and Ethnology. He held that position until 1909 and directed many archaeological digs in the United States, Mexico, and

Central and South America, prompting one colleague to describe him as "the father of American archaeology." His contributions to the burgeoning study of anthropology were just as impressive, with another fellow scholar referring to him as the "father of municipal anthropological research institutions in America."[22] In 1864 Putnam married Adelaide Edmands, the young woman who had made the Lawrence Base Ball Club's flags and bases; sadly, she died in 1879 after bearing three children, and Frederic Putnam eventually remarried. He died in Cambridge on August 14, 1915, and the papers of the Lawrence Base Ball Club were excavated from among his many learned writings.

Francis Washburn: Francis Washburn, who captained one of the sides in the first two intrasquad games, was fatally wounded in one of last battles of the Civil War, waged for control of a bridge over the Appomattox River. He died in a Worcester, Massachusetts, hospital on April 22, 1865, thirteen days after Robert E. Lee's surrender. He was not the only club member to die in the war: North Carolina native Elijah Graham Morrow fought for the Confederates and died at Gettysburg in 1863.[23]

Other Club Members: Francis Higginson Atkins, Frederick William Bardwell, Charles Henry Barrett, Nathaniel Bowditch, George E. Boyden, Calvin Choate, William Charles Cleveland, Sergeant S.P. Coe, James Mason Crafts, Bryan Croom, James G.C. Dodge, H.J. Doolittle, Francisco Weld Evans, Samuel F. Eveleth, Farwell F. Fay, Julius Allen George, Francis Booth Greenough, Clemens Herschel, Herbert Eager Johnson, Elijah Graham Morrow, Albert Ordway, Henry A. Perkins, John Gardner Perry, Warren Rawson, Edward J. Reynolds, Samuel Hubbard Scudder, William F. Stetson, and F. Henry Whitman.

SOURCES: The primary source of this entry is the original notebook of the Lawrence Base Ball Club, which now resides at the Harvard Archives. Two important articles have added greatly to our knowledge of the club's activities. The first was "The Lawrence Base Ball Club," *Harvard Graduates' Magazine*, March 25, 1917, 346–350. The author of this article is not identified but is likely Eben Putnam, the son of Frederic Putnam. In addition, this article includes the recollections of club member Albert Edmands, who was Eben Putnam's uncle. Also extremely valuable is Harry Lewis, "Protoball at Harvard: From Pastime to Contest," *Base Ball* 5:1 (Spring 2011), 41–45. Harold and Dorothy Seymour's *Baseball: The People's Game* (New York: Oxford University Press, 1990), p. 133, offers a good overview of the club's brief history. Special thanks are due to Harry Lewis for sharing photographs of the club notebook

and for providing a great deal of assistance in compiling this entry and to Joanne Hulbert for generously sharing her exciting find of proof that the club played at least one match game in 1859.

Notes

1. Harry Lewis, "Protoball at Harvard: From Pastime to Contest," *Base Ball* 5:1 (Spring 2011), 41–43.

2. "The Lawrence Base Ball Club," *Harvard Graduates' Magazine*, March 25, 1917, 346–350.

3. Ibid., 346.

4. According to the 1917 article, "Inserted in pencil after the words 'any regular meeting' are the words 'and one of 3 [cents] for not atd. or for being dr******'" — here the words are illegible, but probably refer to the costume or to the conduct of the players. The last seems likely, both on account of the initial letters of the lost word and because Section IV reads, "'Any member of the Club behaving in an ungentlemanly manner, or rendering himself obnoxious to the Club, may be expelled from the Club by a vote of two thirds of the members present at a meeting specially called.'" Harry Lewis and I have also examined the scribbled insertion, which appears to be in Frederic Putnam's hand, and we too have been unable to determine what it says.

5. "The Lawrence Base Ball Club," *Harvard Graduates' Magazine*, March 25, 1917, 347.

6. Ibid., 348.

7. Ibid., 349.

8. Harry Lewis, "Protoball at Harvard: From Pastime to Contest," *Base Ball* 5:1 (Spring 2011), 44.

9. "The Lawrence Base Ball Club," *Harvard Graduates' Magazine*, March 25, 1917, 349.

10. Ibid., 348–349.

11. Ibid., 350.

12. Ibid., 349.

13. Harry Lewis, "Protoball at Harvard: From Pastime to Contest," *Base Ball* 5:1 (Spring 2011), 44.

14. "The Lawrence Base Ball Club," *Harvard Graduates' Magazine*, March 25, 1917, 350.

15. Harry Lewis, "Protoball at Harvard: From Pastime to Contest," *Base Ball* 5:1 (Spring 2011), 44.

16. The Lawrence Club's existence was also recorded in *The Base Ball Player's Pocket Companion* (Boston: Mayhew and Baker, 1859); this may be a sign that the club showed signs of life in 1859 but it seems more likely that the mention was based upon the club's lively doings in the fall of 1858.

17. Harry Lewis, "Protoball at Harvard: From Pastime to Contest," *Base Ball* 5:1 (Spring 2011), 45 (note 24).

18. Harry Lewis, email correspondence, September 26, 2011.

19. "The Lawrence Base Ball Club," *Harvard Graduates' Magazine*, March 25, 1917, 349.

20. *Boston Atlas & Bee*, July 2, 1859. Thanks to Joanne Hulbert for sharing this exciting find.

21. *Harvard Alumni Bulletin*, Volume 14 (1911), 577.

22. Both quoted in David L. Browman, "The Peabody Museum, Frederic W. Putnam, and the Rise of U.S. Anthropology, 1866–1903," *American Anthropologist* 104:2 (new series), June 2002, 508.

23. Harry Lewis, "Protoball at Harvard: From Pastime to Contest," *Base Ball* 5:1 (Spring 2011), 45 (note 25).

❖ Harvard Class of '66 Base Ball Club ❖
(Peter Morris)

CLUB HISTORY

College clubs played a crucial role in baseball's pioneer era, but the rapid turnover of the student body makes it very difficult to tell their stories in a coherent fashion. A prominent school such as Harvard, in particular, had many noteworthy clubs and accomplishments. By the end of the nineteenth century, the school nine had played nearly one thousand match games and been involved in many significant events.[1] Rather than trying to do justice to every season of this rich history, this piece will be limited the first club to represent the school in match games. Founded in 1863 by freshmen George A. Flagg and Frank Wright, that club was originally restricted to members of the freshman class. While that was to change, for our purposes, it will be considered to have ended in the summer of 1866 with the graduation of the students who formed it.

As described in the entry on the Lawrence Base Ball Club, there were quite a few references to "various games of bat and ball" being played on campus prior to 1850, but no effort at organization.[2] Harvard's first organized club was founded in the fall of 1858 at the Lawrence Scientific School, which was a part of Harvard. The members displayed a considerable amount of interest that fall, but there were few signs of life in the years that followed and the club never played a match game.[3]

Five years later Flagg and Wright revived the idea with more success. The pair had played many sports as prep students at Phillips Exeter Academy and began talking about the need for a baseball club shortly after arriving on campus in the fall of 1862.[4] We are fortunate to have Wright's account of the club's origins: "One afternoon in March of 1863 a classmate of mine, during Professor Lane's Latin recitation, passed a slip of paper to me asking if I would help him in starting a baseball club. We had talked of this before, and I adopted the suggestion and wrote upon a slip of paper and passed it round, asking the fellows to meet in Flagg's room in Stoughton [Dormitory] at eight that evening and form a baseball club. After the recitation the hint was given out to men of other divisions."[5]

A slightly different version of events was given by Daniel Putnam Abercrombie, another freshman who became deeply involved in the baseball club. After being approached by Wright and Flagg, Abercrombie agreed to serve as club secretary, and his fellow classmates soon received a card bearing his signature. "You are hereby notified," began the historic document, "to attend the meeting of the '66 base ball club to be held at the room of Mr. Flagg, S [Stoughton] 19, on Monday, May 11, 1863, at 9 o'clock."[6]

According to Wright, the "room was well-filled at the appointed hour."[7] But neither he nor Abercrombie is specific about the number of attendees and that is a shame because it would give us a better sense of how some important decisions were made. The Harvard Class of 1866 originally comprised 135 young men, so Flagg's dormitory room could easily have been packed to overflowing with baseball enthusiasts. Yet the three originators of the club are the only students who are actually known to have been there, so it's quite possible that they were joined by only a handful of stragglers.

Far and away the most important decision to be made was whether to play the Massachusetts Game, usually known as round ball, or the rival New York version that had been popularized by the Knickerbocker Club. The Massachusetts Game would seem the logical choice for a club based at Harvard, but this was far from inevitable. The New York version had already begun to spread at an impressive rate and made important inroads into Massachusetts.

"In 1859 the Bowdoin Club was formed in Boston with the intention of playing ball in the good old Massachusetts way," explained James D'Wolf Lovett, "but, just for the fun of the thing, they tried the new rules to see how they worked and, behold! The whole nine ... were promptly infected with the new germ."[8] Other area clubs also began to opt for the New York Game, with added impetus coming when a Boston jeweler named John Lowell became a strong advocate for this version. By the end of the Civil War, the New York Game had vanquished the Massachusetts Game, but as of 1863 that result was far from inevitable. If a club from as venerable an institution as Harvard had opted for the "good old Massachusetts way" the history of baseball might have been different.

So how was the crucial issue resolved? Frank Wright related that "the question of the kind of baseball was discussed [at the initial meeting]. A majority of the fellows wished to form a club to play Massachusetts baseball, which was then in vogue, a game slightly improved upon town ball, which was an improvement upon the old English game of rounders, but a few of us who hailed from New York state carried the meeting in favor of the new game, then called the 'Brooklyn' game."[9]

In fact, state of origin may have been less important than prep school attended. Wright, who hailed from Auburn, New York, and Flagg, a native of Millbury, Massachusetts, had both played baseball while attending Phillips Exeter Academy in New Hampshire. Accounts suggest that they played the New York version and no doubt that is why they pressed for Harvard's first club to do the same.

But this still leaves the question of how the advocates of the New York Game persuaded the majority to go along with them. Neither Wright nor Abercrombie offers insight into the debate that ensued, but Abercrombie's recollections do suggest a possibility. Abercrombie had done his prep studies at Highland Military Academy in Worcester, Massachusetts, where the Massachusetts version remained universal. "In those early days the old-fashioned round ball was the game played," said a 1902 article about Abercrombie, "and he had a taste for it."

Having never played the New York Game, Abercrombie might have been expected to be adamantly opposed to its incursion into the heart of Brahmin Massachusetts. Yet as a slightly built freshman who never weighed more than 125 pounds during his student years, Abercrombie made up for his lack of size with scrappiness and New England pluck. As such, he seems to have raised little objection to the switch and allowed Wright and Flagg's preference to carry the day. "Undoubtedly the boys had played round ball but none of us knew anything about baseball," he later explained. But as he immediately added, "For that matter we knew as much as anyone, for the national game was then in its first days."[10]

The club was now well on its way to becoming a reality but there were still many details to arrange. "A committee of two was appointed," recalled Wright, "consisting of George A. Flagg and myself, to arrange the preliminaries and to suggest a uniform."[11] The "committee of two" traveled to Boston in search of a uniform, where they met up with John A. Lowell, the president of the Lowell Club of Boston. It proved to be a fateful trip.

As Wright recalled, the three men first "went to Hovey's in Summer Street to select cloth for a uniform. At that time all the baseball clubs wore a fierce, fireman-like uniform of red or blue flannel shirts with any kind of trousers and a gaudy leather belt. We decided to try some quiet color and selected a gray French flannel, to be trimmed with crimson, with a crimson 'H' to be embroidered upon the shirt front. We bought flannel enough for one shirt, and it was decided that I was 'to bell the cat' and have the first shirt made for me. Mr. Lowell steered me to a seamstress in Essex Street, who made uniforms for his club, and she took the order for a shirt to be embroidered with an old English 'H' in crimson. When the shirt was sent to me a note came from the seamstress that she had taken the liberty to embroider my 'H' in magenta instead of crimson, as magenta was much more fashionable and much prettier than crimson. I was of course disgusted, but the shirt was there and the magenta 'H' looked fine. I called a meeting of the club and appeared in my outfit. Every one liked the shirt and the color, and it was decided to adopt it. The crew could wear crimson if they liked, but the baseball color should be magenta."[12]

The question of a playing ground was settled when the city of Cambridge granted the club use of part of the city common. The club's new practice ground was located near the "Washington Elm," the tree under which George Washington purportedly took command of the American Army in 1775. With assistance from James Lovett and other members of the Lowell Club of Boston (an offshoot of the Bowdoins), the bases were laid out with the catcher facing west and practice began.[13]

Bats, balls, and bases also needed to be procured, but this does not seem to have proved much of an obstacle. Abercrombie served as club treasurer and probably collected a fee from each player for such expenses, but the amount was small enough that he couldn't remember the details by the time of his 1902 reminiscences. "Masks, mittens and all that sort of thing were unknown," he related. "There was, to be sure, an organization of members of the class and I presume there was an initiation fee and dues. The players, however, had the glory and fun, and they paid for it."[14]

Soon the members were itching to test themselves against outside competition, but this was not easy to arrange. For one thing, the college's schedule was not conducive to arranging matches, since the students were on summer vacation during the prime months for baseball. For another, the Cambridge Common does not appear to have been considered suitable for hosting matches. Most dauntingly, there were very few other clubs in existence, especially at the other colleges that were Harvard's natural rivals.

A challenge sent to Yale's Class of 1866, for instance, yielded the response "that the game was not played by them, but that they hoped soon to be in a condition to meet Harvard on the ball-field."[15] It was beginning to look as though Harvard's first club would play nothing but scrimmages and practice games until one day when the postman at last brought an encouraging response.[16] "The '65 base ball club of Brown university," read the reply, "hereby accept the challenge of the '66 base ball club of Cambridge, Mass., to play a match game of first nines, which shall take place in this city on the Dexter training ground, June 27, at 15 minutes to 3 o'clock P.M."[17] The document was signed by Miner Rudd Deming, the secretary of the club from Brown.

When the day of the big match arrived, the members of the Harvard Class of '66 Base Ball Club made the trip to Providence along with a small party that included Gerrit Smith Miller, president of the Lowell Club, and John J. Mason. Mason served as scorer and Miller as umpire, but neither man's responsibilities were very onerous. "I have a copy of the original score," Abercrombie reported thirty-six years later. "There were no such things in those days as score cards."[18] Presumably Mason used a notebook of some sort to record the runs and "hands out," but he kept track of no other details and his main function was to make sure that players batted in the correct order. Miller had even less to do, as it was customary for the players to make most if not all of the rulings, with the umpire intervening only when a disputed point arose.

No such disputes are known to have occurred and, when the contest ended, Harvard was the winner by a score of 27–17. Frank Wright was the star of the day, handling the pitching duties and scoring five runs. First baseman Alfred Irons and second baseman Charles Fiske chipped in with four runs apiece. The day wrapped up with the Brown students treating their visitors to a festive supper at the City Hotel in Providence.

There is no indication that the players received a hero's welcome when they returned to campus. Indeed, there may well have been no reception at all, and it seems likely that most of the congratulations were received from fellow members of the Class of '66 since this was still very much a class club. But according to Wright, in the wake of this victory, "Our success attracted the attention of the college, our girl friends began to wear our magenta colors, and by the time the boat-races were on at Worcester, magenta was talked of as the Harvard color. In those days the crew rowed in the 'buff,' but with crimson silk handkerchiefs about their heads. When Horatio Curtis of

'65 and his crew appeared on Lake Quinsigamond with magenta handkerchiefs, magenta as Harvard's color was established."[19] Magenta remained the color of Harvard for eight years before crimson was restored.

School adjourned for the summer soon after the victory over the Brown sophomores, but when the new school year began, the Class of 1867 formed its own baseball nine and gave the Class of 1866 a handy opponent. According to *The Harvard Book*, which used Flagg as a source, the two clubs played "many an unrecorded contest."[20] But the distance of the Cambridge Common from campus, the class schedule, and the ongoing war were all imposing obstacles, with the result that no more match games were played until July of 1864, when the club returned to action by playing three games.

The comparative flurry of activity began with an Independence Day contest against Bowdoin College. The Harvard students were the challengers, yet the match was played in Portland, Maine, because the city of Portland had offered a $100 prize to the winning side, an unusual gesture in an era when amateurism generally prevailed. The Harvard Class of 1866 claimed the prize with a convincing 40–13 victory.[21]

Five days later, the club faced the Lowell Club of Boston in the first match of what was to become a very heated rivalry. The contest was scheduled for a section of the Boston Common known as the Parade Ground, a site that brought its own challenges.[22] Under the Knickerbocker Rules, any batted ball caught on the first bounce counted as an out. But the "bound rule" was unpopular in many quarters, because it allowed fielders to make easy snags of balls that had already bounced, rather than attempting the far more difficult feat of catching the ball on the fly.

The peculiarities of the Parade Ground made the issue especially problematic. As explained in *The Harvard Book*, the field there "was destitute of turf, and within the bases and about the catcher's position was as hard as a stone-pavement. When the Ross ball, so popular from 1865 to 1868, was used, it was no uncommon occurrence for a ball from the bat to strike the ground within the bases, and yet to be caught on the first bound by one of the out-fielders."[23] In an effort to avoid such farcical outs and reward skillful play, the two sides decided before the game to waive the "bound rule" and count an out only when a batted ball was caught on the fly.

Yet this was far from ideal because it deprived fielders — who did not yet wear gloves — of their best method of recording outs. The Class of 1866 kept the score close during the early innings, but the Lowells kept piling up the runs, tallying six or more times in seven of the nine innings. The Harvard students were far less successful at hitting the offerings of the Lowell pitcher, who was none other than Gerrit Smith Miller, the future Harvard student who had umpired the 1863 contest in Providence. The match ended with the Lowells the winners by a lopsided 55–25 score.

While the high score by the Lowells could be justified by the change of rules, both clubs had played under the same conditions and rules, so this was not much of an excuse. Even fewer excuses could be offered twenty days later when Harvard's first club was defeated by the Williams College Class of 1866 nine, 12–9. The contest was played on the Agricultural grounds a mile from Worcester on the morning of the annual Harvard-Yale regatta and failed to generate a fraction of the enthusiasm of the main event.

Only a few hundred made the long trek to watch the game and the one reporter who is known to have done so was unimpressed. "The New York game was played, much to the disappointment of many," he recorded. "There can hardly be a youth in any considerable town of New England who is not more or less familiar with the old-fashioned game of 'round' ball, which is so admirably adapted to develop the activity of those who practice it. The New York game is less familiar here, and the game yesterday was therefore lacking in the usual interest." After describing the key differences between the two versions, he concluded, "The Massachusetts game requires more activity. There was not much science displayed yesterday, although some of the playing was very good."[24]

The turnout of players was just as disheartening. First baseman Ben Banker had obtained a special leave of absence from his war duties so that he could play in the match, but even so there were not enough members of the Class of '66 on hand to field a nine. The Williams captain granted permission for F.P. Stearns of the Class of '67 to take the place of one of the absent players, while H.P. Parker, another member of the Class of '67, and William Tiffany, a member of the Class of '66 who played in no other match games, also had to be pressed into service. It was becoming very clear that something needed to be done to enable the ballclub to field a regular nine.

The need became even more urgent in the fall of 1864 when the members of the Class of '66 reassembled for their junior year at Harvard. Three of the students who had played in the historic game against Brown — Charles Fiske, Alfred Irons, and T.F. Wright — were no longer in school, and it was going to be a challenge to find nine juniors with the available time and the necessary skill. On October 12, 1864, the players bowed to the inevitable and formed a "University Nine" that was open to members of all classes. Three days later, a contest was played between the Classes of '66 and '67, which the Class of '66 won, 13–10.

As the ground was thawing in the spring of 1865, word came of the end of the Civil War. The Harvard campus generally shrugged off news from afar; as F.P. Stearns put it, "The undergraduates were too much absorbed in their own small affairs to pay much attention to politics, even in those exciting times."[25] But this was different: "Everywhere there was joy and exhilaration. To many it was the happiest day they had ever known. President Hill was seen holding a long and earnest conversation with [Professor] Agassiz on the path towards his house. The professors threw aside their contemplated work.

Every man went to drink a glass of wine with his best friend, and to discuss the fortunes of the republic. The ball-players set off for the Delta, where Memorial Hall now stands, to organize a full match game; the billiard experts started a tournament on Mr. Lyon's new tables; and the rowing men set off for a three-hours' pull down Boston harbor."[26]

The news of President Lincoln's assassination followed within days and plunged the campus back into gloom. Before long, however, the ball playing resumed and it became clear that the University Nine would be very different from its predecessor. Flagg and Wright remained in firm control of the club's activities, as they would until their graduation, and the sudden availability of four times as many candidates enabled them to enforce a new level of discipline and the club to show newfound purpose.

As explained in *The Harvard Book*, "The old ground on Cambridge Common was abandoned, and the 'Delta,' now covered in part by Memorial Hall, was taken possession of by permission of the Faculty. It was properly graded, and the field laid out with the striker facing the east. The uniform adopted consisted of gray pantaloons, gray shirts, and caps trimmed with magenta. This proved very serviceable and becoming and — with slight changes — is still worn. Regular and systematic practice was daily had during the fall, and continued at the Gymnasium during the winter.... Fines were imposed for absence from practice, and tardiness; and systematic training was carried to an extent that has perhaps not been surpassed by any Nine of subsequent years."[27]

At length a first nine was selected that consisted of five holdovers from the Class of '66 — Flagg, Wright, Abercrombie, Banker, and Thomas Nelson — supplemented by four underclassmen: H.P. Parker, T.H. Gray, and W.F. Davis of the Class of '67 and Arthur Hunnewell of the Class of '68. These are the nine young men who appear in a well-known picture of Harvard's 1865 club. The plethora of candidates, however, allowed a luxury never before possible. The first nine prepared itself for competition that spring with daily contests, weather permitting, against "a Second Nine composed of candidates for the University."[28] Each of the four classes also continued to field its own nine, and according to the account of the club in Charles A. Peverelly's *Book of American Pastimes*, "the Class Clubs ... generally comprise about one-half of each class — fifty or sixty in number."[29]

The University Nine began match play on June 17 and showed the benefits of the new dedication. Two convincing victories over the Tri-Mountains of Boston, one on Boston's South End fairgrounds and one on the Boston Common, were followed by an Independence Day trip to Holliston that produced an easy win over that city's Granite Club. This set up a match against the Lowell Club of Boston for a silver ball donated by John Lowell as an emblem of the championship of New England. The big match was played at the Boston Common on July 15, 1865, in front of several thousand anxious spectators, with the symbolic silver ball displayed prominently. When the game concluded, Harvard had earned an exciting 28–17 victory and the coveted trophy.

Two more matches were played before the students dispersed for the summer. On July 19 the University Nine traveled to Williamstown for a rematch against Williams College, the only collegiate club to have accepted one of the numerous challenges that had been issued. Harvard eked out a 35–30 victory, enabling the players to consider themselves "entitled in a measure to the title of Champion of College Nines."[30] Play wrapped up on Regatta Day with a 35–13 win over the Charter Oak Club of Hartford. It was the club's sixth straight victory without defeat and a sign of how much progress had been made since the discouraging loss on Regatta Day one year earlier.

The excitement spilled over into the fall term of the senior year of the Class of '66. On September 27, 1865, Harvard played a historic match against the national champion Atlantics of Brooklyn on the Boston Common. To nobody's surprise, the Atlantics won a score of 58–22, but there was no embarrassment in such a defeat at the hands of a club concluding its second straight undefeated season. As explained in *The Harvard Book*, "The University Nine had been out of practice for some two months, and in the game that followed naturally played below its standard. The game was exceedingly interesting, however, notwithstanding the disparity in the scores, and added to, rather than detracted from, the prestige of Harvard. The large number of runs made by the Atlantics may in part be accounted for by the fact that a very lively ball was used."[31]

Three days later there was another silver-ball match between the Harvards and the Lowell Club, again held on the Boston Common. It was a close and heatedly contested game with "considerable talk among the spectators of 'town' as represented by the Lowells and 'gown' as represented by Harvard." Adding to the excitement were some "sharp disputes" between Lowell pitcher James D'Wolf Lovett and the umpire over the legality of Lovett's deliveries.[32] The match ended with the Lowell Club squeaking out a 40–37 win and reclaiming the championship trophy.

The University Nine issued an immediate challenge for one more contest before winter fell and the match was scheduled for October 20. Then came word that Lovett was bedridden and the college nine offered to postpone the contest. But the Lowells gamely declined and Harvard battered their pitching for nine home runs, including a massive drive by Thomas Nelson that was said to have been the "longest 'hit,' perhaps, ever seen on the Common."[33] In Lovett's picturesque account, "There occurred in this game a most remarkable hit made by Tom Nelson, which is to-day often referred to as 'Nelson's great strike.' There was a high west wind blowing during the game and Tom caught the ball square on the nose with the full swing of his great strength and away it soared, truly, upon the wings of the wind. Over the Flagstaff hill it flew and bounded down the other side, in the direction of West Street. There are numerous legends extant as to where it was finally picked up. One was that it was stopped while trying to get through West Street gate. Another, that it went down West Street, bounced aboard a passing horse-car and went out to the Norfolk House. As I was confined at home, I do not know anything about it, but anyway Nelson wandered around the bases, and then 'waited patiently about until it did appear,' and often laughed about it in after years."[34] Harvard won 73–37 and earned the right to keep the silver ball all winter.

While the coming of winter ended active play, it did not end thoughts of baseball. Members of the University nine made an ambitious attempt "to arrange a base-ball tournament between all the eastern colleges; such a tournament to be held every year at Worcester, and to have a silver ball as the prize for that college which should beat the most games." The idea was greeted with enthusiasm on other campuses and plans were begun for a tournament that would comprise at least six colleges. But when Yale, Princeton, and Williams all backed out, leaving only Harvard, Dartmouth, and Hamilton, the scheme had to be abandoned.[35] Undeterred, the Harvard ballplayers began making arrangements for an ambitious tour of New York City and vicinity during the May recess.

The spring of 1866 saw the students who had organized Harvard's first important ball club approaching graduation. The looming changes in their lives made starters unavailable for some games and one starter gave up baseball for a very different reason — the deeply religious W.F. Davis had concluded over the winter that "participation in College sports ... encouraged betting, and that vice he would do nothing to promote. Thus he remained an elusive and mysterious companion in his College generation, contributing much skill to teaching and advising players on the ball-field, but refusing to compete, or even to witness, an intercollegiate competition."[36] Fortunately, a talented young trio was on hand to fill the gaps: sophomore James Barr Ames, destined to succeed Wright as captain of the Harvard Base Ball Club and later become dean of the Harvard Law School, and freshmen Gerrit Miller and Nathaniel Smith.

Thus reinforced, the club began preparations for the tour of New York, New Jersey, and Connecticut scheduled for the May recess. The first nine warmed up with easy victories over the Tri-Mountain and Orient clubs of Boston, though sloppy play in these games and several losses to the Harvard second nine caused alarm.[37] Another ominous portent was the neglected state of the campus baseball diamond. "Would not some real, bona-fide bases on our ball-ground be an improvement?" asked the student newspaper. "Certainly we need something more substantial than the imaginary ones that have so long supplied their place. The pitcher's stand, too, has all the appearance of having been lately inhabited by woodchucks, and we should think, would be an uncomfortable position for any one to play at, especially after rainy weather, when the holes

are full of water. The strikers stand is but little better; and so uneven is the ground there, that for the striker to assume 'a firm, impressive attitude' is next to impossible. The broom of reform might sweep away much dust and many cobwebs from the Delta."[38]

The players left for New York from the Worcester depot on the afternoon of May 28 and arrived the next morning, setting up headquarters at the Brevoort House on Fifth Avenue.[39] It was an establishment known for hosting heads of state and was not cheap; according to Putnam Abercrombie, his expenses for the brief trip amounted to $75, no small sum of money at the time.[40] Needless to say, these expenses were paid by the players.

The collegians were escorted to the famed Capitoline Grounds on the following afternoon for a rematch with the Atlantics, who were starting their pursuit of a third straight national championship. The Atlantics were easy winners, 37–15, but the courage and skill of the college players impressed a New York reporter. According to his account, "The chief point of interest in the playing was the general fielding of the Harvards; Smith in the left field being particularly efficient. Wright's pitching was good, and his general play good likewise; except that once or twice he was a little wild in throwing to bases. As captain he was unexceptional. We cannot close our remarks without commending in the highest terms the ability, spirit, and endurance of Flagg. With both hands used up, a battered face, and a half blinded eye, he stood up to his post as unflinchingly as if he had been Casabianca on the traditional burning deck [in a poem by Felicia Dorothea Hemans]."[41]

The beating that Flagg had taken had a lingering effect on the tour. Harvard's next game was played in Newark the following afternoon against the Eureka Club and "Flagg, all battered and torn by the buffets he received the day before, was finally forced to reluctantly abandon his important stand behind the bat."[42] Ames filled in, but this forced several other players to move to unfamiliar positions, which may have been decisive in a close-fought 42–39 defeat. The match was played in front of an immense crowd and the field was entirely surrounded by "hundreds of vehicles of every description from the elegant private carriage, through the whole range of hack, hotel-coach, street omnibus, etc., to the 'old mare and buggy,' driven by a young man from the country."[43] At one point, the game was briefly interrupted by the amusing spectacle of a "fat 'Jersey' pig, making full trot for the pitcher's stand."[44]

It was back to the Capitoline Grounds the next day to take on the Excelsiors of Brooklyn, the legendary prewar club. Alas, the "Harvards were evidently suffering from the wounds and fatigue of the two previous days, and were unable to reach that pitch of excellence in their action which won them so much applause in their game with the Eurekas."[45] Miller took over for Wright as pitcher and Ames did the catching in a disappointing 46–28 loss. At the conclusion of the match, the "usual routine of chowder and lager was gone through"—the presentation of the ball, cheers for both sides, and speeches—along with a couple of special awards. Excelsior captain Joe Leggett gave a "beautifully inlaid bat" to the Harvard club, while Arthur Hunnewell received an elegantly polished bat of his own from a spectator for scoring the most runs.[46]

One day later, the Harvard students traveled to the legendary Elysian Fields in Hoboken to take on the Active Club of New York. Once again they were forced to use a makeshift lineup, with center fielder Abercrombie being the only player who was stationed in the same position as in the game against the Atlantics. The batting of the Harvard players proved their undoing this day, as they were baffled by the offerings of Active pitcher Charley Walker. Harvard trailed 17–2 after five innings and it took a late rally to make the final score a more respectable 24–15. The tour was scheduled to conclude in Hartford with a game against the Charter Oak, but weather forced its cancellation and the students returned to campus with four defeats to show for the first tour in school history.

The players did their best to put a positive spin on the excursion. An account in *The Harvard Book*, based on George Flagg's notes, observed that "as the object of the Nine 'was not to win balls and a great reputation, but simply to get practice, and let it be known that there was such a Nine in existence as the Harvard,' the result may be considered a success."[47] Abercrombie added, "We played a number of professional teams. We did not expect to win a game and were not disappointed.... You see we could generally play and defeat the swift amateur teams, but we were not in it with the professionals."[48]

It's hard not to be suspicious of these claims. The Atlantics were still a national powerhouse and the Harvard nine knew itself to be outclassed, but the college nine had a fighting chance against its other three opponents and the losses undoubtedly stung. Abercrombie's excuse that the Harvard players were amateurs and their opponents professional is also suspect; there certainly were professional players by 1866 and the Atlantics and Excelsiors both featured at least a few such players, but the other two opponents were mostly if not entirely made up of amateurs. Yet while the trip failed to produce any victories, it gave the members of the University Nine the chance to play against legendary clubs and on hallowed ball fields, memories they no doubt cherished. They also made a positive impression in the metropolis, with one reporter writing, "These gallant New England youths leave behind them hundreds of well-wishers, their plucky and skillful play, and their gentlemanly conduct on and off the field, winning them hosts of admirers."[49]

Graduation was now fast approaching for the 113 members of the Class of 1866 who had fulfilled all of Harvard's requirements. One final silver-ball match against the Lowell Club had been scheduled, however, so the University Nine went into daily practices against its second nine. They also were victorious in three warm-up games, two of them against

the Beacons of Boston and one in Hartford on Independence Day against the Charter Oaks.

On July 14 the big day finally arrived and the Class of 1866 members of the Harvard ballclub faced their old rival the Lowell Club on the Boston Common for one last time. A huge crowd was on hand, but the college students did not rise to the challenge. The Lowells won 37–27 and reclaimed the silver ball.

The seniors' last match game was played in Worcester on Regatta Day, July 27, 1866, against another frequent opponent, the Williams College nine. Williams emerged victorious, 39–37, and the *Harvard Advocate* groused that the Williams rooters "had a way of crowing over any bad luck on our side with a Yi! Yi! Yi! and a howl" that made them sound like a group of New York "professionals, firemen and roughs."[50] It was Harvard's first loss to a college rival since the formation of the University Nine and, according to *The Harvard Book*, it would be the last such loss for seven years.[51]

The *Harvard Advocate*'s reporter attributed the two defeats to "over confidence on the part of the Harvard nine," who "relied on their previous records too much."[52] He also cited the lack of "systematic practice," explaining, "Harvard was the first college to take up base-ball and consequently easily distanced her sister colleges, and also wrested the championship from the Lowell Club in the first attempt. Defeat taught the vanquished the necessity of discipline. The Williams College nine was under the care of two professional trainers for several weeks before the match at Worcester, and the powerful batting of the Lowell nine was the result of faithful attendance at the gymnasium last winter. Success on the other hand blinded the Harvard nine to the necessity of exertion before it was too late."[53]

On this discouraging note, Harvard's Class of 1866 ended its four years at Cambridge. The Harvard baseball nine became a firmly rooted institution in the years that followed. Play moved to Jarvis Field in 1867 and the competition for the silver ball soon became so intense that the trophy was melted down. In its place, Harvard initiated rivalries with schools such as Yale, Dartmouth, and Princeton that continue to this day. In 1869 and 1870, the club featured such a strong lineup that it defeated the likes of the Athletics of Philadelphia and the Mutuals of New York. The club almost pulled off an even bigger upset in Cincinnati, leading the Red Stockings 17–12 in the ninth inning before that legendary nine rallied for a 20–17 victory. Later years brought many great moments that included the introduction of the catcher's mask, exciting triumphs over archrival Yale, a celebrated 24-inning game, and the exploits of many players who became campus heroes.

The members of the Class of 1866 could only participate in these exciting moments vicariously. They must, however, have derived satisfaction from the knowledge that they had played a crucial role in establishing Harvard's baseball tradition.

CLUB MEMBERS

For reasons explained in the club history, the profiles are restricted to men who either played for the Class of 1866 nine or for the University Nine prior to 1867.

Daniel Putnam Abercrombie (Class of 1866): Daniel Putnam Abercrombie was born in Lunenberg, Massachusetts, on January 25, 1844, the son of a doctor who died when he was seven. He was generally known by his middle name, which was the maiden name of his mother, a descendant of General Israel Putnam of Battle of Bunker Hill fame. He studied at the Highland School in Worcester before enrolling in Harvard as part of the Class of 1866. According to the class secretary, while at Harvard Abercrombie "was a diligent student, but was particularly distinguished for his work in baseball. He was a member of the first Nine ever organized at Harvard, and played centre field in both his Class and College Nines with marked ability and success."[54] Though he weighed only 125 pounds when he graduated, Abercrombie was one of the stalwarts of the nine, playing in every known game up until he earned his degree. He then spent a few years in Michigan before returning to Massachusetts and settling in Millers Falls. In 1876 he became cashier of the Crocker National Bank, a position he held until becoming president of that bank in 1915. Abercrombie died at his home in Turners Falls, Massachusetts, on December 20, 1919.

James Barr Ames (Class of 1868): James Barr Ames was a member of the Class of 1868 who played several games for the University Nine in 1865 and 1866. After the graduation of the class that launched the club, he became a regular and the club's second captain, a position he held during his junior and senior years. Born in Boston on June 22, 1846, Ames remained at Harvard as a law professor and is credited with popularizing the case-study method of teaching law. He became the dean of Harvard Law School in 1895 and held that position until his death on January 8, 1910, in Ipswich, New Hampshire.

Benson Beriah Banker (Class of 1866): Ben Banker was born in Peasleeville, New York, on March 19, 1843, and moved with his family to Roxbury ten years later. After graduating from the local high school, he did prep studies at the Roxbury Latin School, where he "was particularly distinguished in athletics. Of tall stature, robust build, and more than usual physical strength, he early delighted and excelled in outdoor sports. When motoring by Jamaica Pond on our Fortieth Anniversary, he proudly pointed out to us where in boyhood he swam that sheet of water." At Harvard Banker's interest in sports continued: "he rowed and played ball, but it was to baseball, introduced into Harvard by Frank Wright, that he was most devoted, and it was on what is now known as 'the diamond,' and particularly on first base, that he won his laurels."[55] On May 9, 1864, he enlisted as a hundred-day man in Massachusetts 12th Infantry but this did not interfere with his playing baseball. For the contest against Williams College,

Banker "obtained leave of absence from Fort Warren, in Boston Harbor, where he was doing duty as a three-months volunteer."[56] He also played in both of the club's other games that summer and was mustered out in August, in time to resume his studies. Banker's family had relocated to Chicago during his time at Harvard, and he joined them there after graduation, playing for the Excelsior Base Ball Club during that nine's tumultuous 1867 season. That ended his connection with baseball. Banker taught school in Chicago and LaColle, Quebec, before settling in Boston. He eventually became the accountant at the law firm of Charles E. Stratton, class secretary of Harvard's Class of 1866. Banker died on February 28, 1913.

William Franklin Davis (Class of 1867): A man named Davis became the club's left fielder when the University Nine was formed and played in six games in 1865. As was common, his first name was never given, but his membership in the Class of 1867 was stated in multiple sources and there was only one Davis in that year (and none in the Class of 1866). This can only be William Franklin Davis. Born in Attica, New York, on August 21, 1840, Davis was older than most of his classmates and became a Baptist minister in Rhode Island after graduation. He gave up his church in 1875 and devoted the remainder of his life to missionary work in such places as the Boston North End Mission and the lumber camps of northern Michigan. He was also a prolific writer of religious tracts.

Intriguingly, Harvard first baseman Francis G. Peabody later described Davis as a "robust young giant" who "might have been an athletic hero had he not been inhibited by rigid evangelical convictions from all participation in College sports. These contests, he had observed, encouraged betting, and that vice he would do nothing to promote. Thus he remained an elusive and mysterious companion in his College generation, contributing much skill to teaching and advising players on the ball-field, but refusing to compete, or even to witness, an intercollegiate competition. The same protesting spirit led him later as an 'Evangelist' to defy the police regulations of Boston, which required a license for speaking on the Common."[57]

The statement seems to bring the identity of the Harvard left fielder into doubt, but in fact there is no question that it was indeed William Franklin Davis. Peabody was a member of the Class of 1869 so was not on campus when Davis played for the Harvard nine, as he played no games after 1865. In addition, an obituary written by his college friend Silas Parsons Cook stated very specifically that Davis played six games for the Harvard Club in June and July of 1865. So there can be no doubt that Davis was a member of the ballclub for one season and then his religious convictions caused him to step aside.

Beginning in 1886, Davis was arrested on numerous occasions for preaching on the Boston Common without a license. He adamantly maintained his constitutional right to do so, eventually spending a year in jail after refusing to pay the resulting fine. He continued to preach the gospel with fervor until his death in Everett, Massachusetts, on May 26, 1916.

Charles Fiske (Class of 1866, nongraduate): Born in Buffalo, New York, on February 25, 1845, Charles Fiske played second base for the Class of 1866 in its first-ever game against Brown. He played two more games for the club in 1864 but left Harvard that year without earning his degree. He wrote for several newspapers, including the *New York Times*, before moving to San Francisco and going into business. He was only 30 when he died in Los Angeles on January 28, 1876.

George Augustus Flagg (Class of 1866): George A. Flagg was born in Millbury, Massachusetts, on May 2, 1845, and was one of the two Harvard students who started the school's first baseball club. He was the catcher throughout his time at Harvard and earned renown for his courage. As his time at Harvard was drawing to a close, the school newspaper wrote: "We think it but just to pay some tribute to the spirit and skill with which Mr. Flagg has fulfilled the duties of his position as Catcher in this match as well as in the whole course of games played last year. Brilliant in his action, cool and collected in every emergency, he has likewise shown himself the most watchful and attentive of all to the interests of each individual player, and to the game as a whole. We fear it will be a long time ere Harvard College is to see again his equal or superior."[58] Flagg went into business after leaving Harvard, eventually becoming the secretary and treasurer of the Calumet & Hecla Mining Company and also having an interest in a cotton manufacturer. He sat in the Massachusetts House of Representatives in 1877 and remained active in Republican politics. Flagg was the last surviving member of the club when he died on June 11, 1929.

Thomas Herbert Gray (Class of 1867): T.H. Gray earned a spot on the first nine when the University Nine was formed and was one of the nine young men who appear in the photo that appeared in the *Boston Globe* article. But he played in only seven known match games with the club, none after the fall of 1865. Born on November 14, 1844, in Walpole, Massachusetts, Gray became a successful wool dealer. He died in Boston on November 8, 1928.

Eugene Douglass Greenleaf (Class of 1866): Gene Greenleaf represented the Class of 1866 in its 1863 game against Brown and played several more games in 1864, but did not compete for Harvard after the formation of the University Nine. Born in Boston on August 19, 1844, after leaving Harvard he went into the iron business and eventually became a member of the Boston Stock Exchange. Greenleaf, who never married, died in Boston on November 16, 1914.

Dr. Francis Augustine Harris (Class of 1866): Frank Harris played several games in 1864 but did not play in the historic contest against Brown or in any games after 1864. Harris was the scorekeeper in one game, making him the only playing member of the club known to have also kept score. Born in Ashland, Massachusetts, on March 5, 1845, Harris be-

came a prominent Boston doctor whose distinctions included a long tenure as medical examiner of the Northern District of Suffolk County and teaching surgery at the Boston Dental College. Harris also found time to write several plays. He died in Winthrop, Massachusetts, on January 18, 1911.

Arthur Hunnewell (Class of 1868): Arthur Hunnewell, who was born in Boston on December 1, 1846, was the only member of the Class of 1868 selected to the first nine when the University Nine was formed. He remained a fixture at shortstop while the original members were still in school, then became the club's pitcher after Frank Wright's graduation. Hunnewell joined his father's banking firm after graduation from Harvard and died in Wellesley, Massachusetts, on October 17, 1904. An obituary suggested that Hunnewell's devotion to college sports was not matched by a similar interest in his studies: "In College he achieved prominence in athletics, especially in baseball and in rowing. He rowed in two races. In baseball he belonged to the Harvard Nine for four years; as a swift pitcher and runner he maintained leadership, and played in every club match during his college course, as well as in several other matches. His interest and dexterity in athletic exercises continued through life. He was a member of the Institute of 1770, of the Hasty Pudding Club, and of the Porcellian Club. As a student he did not aim for or attain noticeable rank."[59]

Alfred Brayton Irons (Class of 1866, nongraduate): Alfred Irons played in the 1863 game against Brown and a few 1864 contests, but left Harvard that year. Born in Rhode Island on November 28, 1842, Irons studied at Phillips Exeter Academy before enrolling at Harvard. After dropping out he returned to Providence and went into business. He died there on April 8, 1894.

Dr. Charles McBurney (Class of 1866): Charles McBurney was a member of the Harvard crew and played baseball only in the game between the classes of 1866 and 1867. Born on February 18, 1845, in Roxbury, Massachusetts, McBurney became a prominent surgeon in New York City. He retired in 1905 and died in Brookline, Massachusetts, on November 7, 1913.

Edward Windsor Mealey (Class of 1867): Mealey played only one recorded game for the University Nine, though the school newspaper listed him as the right fielder of the first nine prior to the 1866 tour. (Confusingly, he was also listed as the shortstop and captain of the second nine.)[60] He was born in Hagerstown, Maryland, on August 23, 1846, and entered Harvard in 1865 as a junior. He went on to graduate from Harvard Law School and then returned to Hagerstown, where he practiced law for several years. His interests then turned to business and civic affairs and he became one of Hagerstown's most prominent citizens and a generous benefactor. Mealey died in Hagerstown on April 28, 1911.

Gerrit Smith Miller (Class of 1869): Miller made his debut for the University Nine against the Atlantics in September of 1865, shortly after beginning his freshman year. Before enrolling at Harvard, he had served as umpire of the Class of '66's historic game against the Brown sophomores. Miller left Harvard without his degree when the death of his grandmother made it necessary for him to attend to the family estate. His life is described in considerable detail in the entry on the Lowell Club of Boston.

Thomas Nelson (Class of 1866): Along with Flagg, Frank Wright, Abercrombie, and Banker, Thomas Nelson was one of the five Class of '66 players who formed the core of Harvard baseball between 1863 and 1866, though he missed more games than the other four combined. He also rowed for Harvard, which may be the reason he missed several matches. Nelson's strength was such that two decades later he was still remembered as "the man who used to visit freshmen's rooms and twist the knobs off the doors in his hand."[61] James Lovett similarly recalled a football game in which another player sprang "upon the back of Tom Nelson, who was running with the ball; no doubt he thought thereby to down Tom and get the ball away from him. Nelson, who, by the way, was one of the most powerful men who ever entered Harvard College, continued placidly upon his way, apparently unconscious of the other's presence, and, when he got ready, calmly shook the passenger from off his back much as a mastiff might get rid of a troublesome pup, and proceeded to kick the ball according to original intentions."[62] He was also long remembered for his tremendous home run against the Lowell Club in the fall of 1865. "The old-timers to this day," declared Abercrombie in 1902,"will tell of a famous hit made by Nelson over Flag-staff hill on Boston Common."[63] Born in Boston on March 4, 1845, Nelson went into the mining business with his father after graduation. He died in Boston on November 19, 1897.

Henry Boynton Parker (Class of 1867): Despite his being one of the nine players in the photograph, there has been some confusion about Parker's identity, with James D'Wolf Lovett referring to him as "George Parker." But this was clearly a slip on Lovett's part, as there was no Harvard student by that name. Parker was referred to as a member of the Class of 1867 in many accounts, and Henry Boynton Parker was the only student with that surname in that class. In addition, one account referred to the ballplayer as "H.B. Parker," the student newspaper identified Henry B. Parker as the third baseman of the first nine, and an obituary of Henry Boynton Parker in the *Harvard Graduates' Magazine* made prominent mention of his baseball exploits. Indeed, after the graduation of the Class of 1866, Parker emerged as the star of the club, clouting "three magnificent home runs" in the first game of the 1867 season. In the next game, Parker's play prompted the school's reporter to write: "(B)esides performing his usual course of circus-feats to amuse the spectators and the 'muckers,' and turning over the fence on his head, he made four stunning home runs, and played his base perfectly."[64] Born in Boston on March 5, 1846, Parker became a successful businessman, working first as a

commission merchant and then as a civil engineer for several railroad companies before joining the Calumet & Hecla Mining Company, where he was reunited with George Flagg. Parker, who never married, died of pneumonia in Baldwinsville, Massachusetts, on January 24, 1898.[65]

Nathaniel Stevens Smith (Class of 1869): Nat Smith was one of two freshmen who joined the University Nine in 1866, along with Gerrit Miller. He remained a club mainstay until his graduation, playing in more than 70 games for Harvard, most often at third base. He was born in Southwick, Massachusetts, on July 4, 1847, and grew up in Kingston, New York. He practiced law in New York City after completing his studies. Smith died in New York City on March 22, 1912. His death led Gardner Willard, a Harvard classmate and baseball teammate who later played for the Excelsiors of Chicago, to recall the "halcyon years of Harvard athletics in the competitive sports of our College times, the times when Harvard just couldn't be beaten in anything. Nat was on the Nine from the beginning to the end. Excepting only Archie Bush of glorious memory, he was perhaps the best player in it most of the time. I recall reading in Wilkes' 'Spirit of the Times,' in June, 1869, a ranking of the then great ball-players of the country, where Nat and two professionals were rated together as the three greatest third basemen. All his heart and soul were in every game he played. His first thought was for the 'Honor of Harvard,' as we youths of that time rather frenziedly, but sincerely enough, held victory."[66]

Edward Everett Sprague (Class of 1868): Ned Sprague first played for the University Nine as a freshman in 1865, but saw limited action during his first two years on campus. After the graduation of the Class of 1866, he became the club's regular center fielder and had played more than 30 games for Harvard by the time he earned his degree. Sprague was born in Albany, New York, on January 3, 1848, and studied at Albany Law School after graduating from Harvard, then practiced law in New York City. Sprague died in Flushing, New York, on October 3, 1924.

Frank Preston Stearns (Class of 1867): F.P. Stearns was a member of the Class of 1867 who played only three recorded games for the University Nine. He was the son of George Luther Stearns, a prominent Boston Abolitionist who was one of the "Secret Six" supporters of John Brown. F.P. Stearns became a prominent Abolitionist in his own right, as well as the author of numerous books, including several books on Italian art and biographies of Bismarck, Nathaniel Hawthorne, and his own father. Baseball is rarely mentioned in his books, but *Cambridge Sketches* does include a few passages about the school nine. Born in Medford, Massachusetts, on January 4, 1846, Stearns died in Arlington, Massachusetts, on January 21, 1917.

William George Tiffany (Class of 1866): William Tiffany played only one known game, the July 29, 1864, contest against the Williams College Class of 1866. Born in Baltimore on March 26, 1844, Tiffany spent much of his early years in Europe and began his education in Switzerland. He later lived in California and France among other places and made little effort to keep in touch with his classmates. He died in New York City on April 23, 1905.

John Henry Watson (Class of 1866): John Watson was a member of the Class of 1866 but did not play for the baseball club until his appearance in two games in July of 1866, as he was preparing for graduation. Perhaps that was no coincidence, for Watson seems to have been as focused on his studies as Hunnewell was on extracurricular activities. A classmate recalled of Watson, "During our four years at Harvard, while taking his part in different college societies and in the usual social activities, he was a faithful student and maintained high rank in scholarship."[67] Born in Boston on December 18, 1845, Watson was the son of John Lee Watson, an Episcopal minister who also served as a U.S. Navy chaplain. After graduating from Harvard, John Henry Watson followed in his father's footsteps, studying divinity at the Berkeley Divinity School in Middletown, Connecticut, and being ordained in 1872. Watson then led churches in Hartford, Long Island, Philadelphia, and New York City, among other places. He died in New York City on October 31, 1913.

Edward Tuckerman Wilkinson (Class of 1866): Like Charles McBurney, Wilkinson concentrated on rowing while at Harvard and played baseball only in the single game between the Class of 1866 and the Class of 1867. Wilkinson was born in Boston on October 14, 1844, and had an older brother who died of tuberculosis while a student at Harvard. Soon after graduation, Wilkinson's own health failed and he died on December 27, 1873, while en route from England to New York on the steamship Cimbria. He was the first of two ballplaying members of the Class of 1866 to die at sea.

Frank Wright: Frank Wright, pitcher and captain of the club, was born in Auburn, New York, on November 12, 1844. He was the son of David Wright, a lawyer, and Martha Coffin Wright, the sister of famed Abolitionist and women's rights activist Lucretia Mott. It was during an 1848 visit to the Wright home in Auburn that the two sisters joined with Elizabeth Cady Stanton, Jane Hunt, and Mary Anne McClintock to organize the historic Seneca Falls Convention on women's rights. Martha Coffin Wright was also very active in the Underground Railroad and in 2004 she was the subject of a full-scale biography: Sherry H. Penney and James D. Livingstone's *A Very Dangerous Woman: Martha Wright and Women's Rights* (Amherst: University of Massachusetts Press, 2004). Frank was educated at Englewood Academy in New Jersey and Phillips Exeter Academy before entering Harvard, where he was known for being "not a hard student, but he was popular, companionable, manly, clean, and athletic." He returned to Auburn after graduation and briefly studied law, but soon chose instead to marry and take a position with an Auburn harvester manufacturer, a job that required him to spend con-

siderable time in England. In 1873 he moved to Florida and invested heavily in orange plantations, but heavy frosts plagued this initiative. At last he ran for county clerk of Putnam County, serving in that capacity "until a change in the political complexion of the County and State rendered him no longer persona grata to the party in power." He also found time to start the Harvard Club of Florida. Frank Wright left Florida in 1890 and became involved in the telephone business, working for both the American Bell Telephone Company and the American Telephone and Telegraph Company. His work with the latter company took him to St. Louis in 1898 and that was where Wright died on June 16, 1903. Wright's life was not the success that many expected of him — in addition to his other misfortunes, his wife died of a brain tumor at the age of 43. Yet according to a friend from Harvard, "His sanguine temperament made it easy for him to bear the disappointments which are sure to come to all of us; and, if fortune sometimes went against him, he did not repine, but turned to some new field of activity and usefulness. He was persevering and industrious, and, had favorable opportunities come to him, he would have achieved greater success."[68]

Theodore Francis Wright (Class of 1866): T.F. Wright played in the club's historic first match game against Brown University, which was also his only official appearance in a Harvard uniform, for reasons that will soon become clear. Wright was born on August 3, 1845, in Dorchester, Massachusetts, into a family that could trace its lineage back to the earliest settlers of Plymouth Colony. His mother imbued a deep religious sense in her son and urged him to keep a journal from a very young age. That journal revealed an interest in a wide range of topics, including baseball and other sports. After enrolling at Harvard, he continued the journal and on the train trip home after the victory at Providence he wrote that he was "inexpressibly happy." Wright turned 18 shortly after that contest and became convinced that it was his duty to leave school and serve in the Union Army. He soon wrote in his journal, "I have for some time been deliberating about leaving college to go to the war, and have, at last, with the consent of my parents, determined to study for a commission in the colored troops." His classmates all turned out to bid him a fond farewell as he left Cambridge to become a lieutenant in the 108th U.S. Colored Infantry. Wright returned to Harvard after the war's end and took extra classes so as to graduate with his class. He then studied divinity at the New Church Theological School and became a minister in the Church of the New Jerusalem, one of several churches with roots in the writings of Emanuel Swedenborg. He remained involved in the church for the remainder of his life, as both a preacher and as dean of its theological school. In 1889, he re-enrolled at Harvard and received a Ph.D. In 1907, as a result of failing health, he and his wife decided to spend a year in Egypt and Palestine. On the journey there, he became unwell and they chose to return home. They left Naples on November 13 aboard the Schleswig and that evening he followed his wife back to their cabin. She was only a few steps ahead of him, but when she reached the cabin, he had vanished. His body was never found, making him the second ballplayer from the Class of '66 to die at sea.[69]

Other Club Members: The above is a complete listing of the students who represented either the Class of 1866 or the University Nine prior to 1867. In addition, several students served as club scorer for at least one game, including Arthur Brooks, E.H. Clark, G.F. Emery, and J.J. Mason.

SOURCES: A rich crop of sources on this pioneer club made my job very easy. Frank Wright's reminiscences were originally published in the *Harvard Bulletin* on October 15, 1902, and were reprinted in James D'Wolf Lovett, *Old Boston Boys and the Games They Played* (Boston: Riverside Press, 1907), 156–158. Lovett's entire book is of considerable value as he was a friend of many members of the Harvard Club. Daniel Putnam Abercrombie's reminiscences appeared in "Harvard's First Ball Team," *Boston Globe*, June 8, 1902, 46. The best source on the club's entire history was the section on baseball in *The Harvard Book: A Series of Historical, Biographical, and Descriptive Sketches* (accessed via the Harvard University Archives). The baseball portion appears in volume 2, pages 268–340 (the part on the years covered in this entry on 268–279), and was written by William Delano Sampson, with founding member George A. Flagg being credited with providing much of the data. "Twenty Years of Harvard Base-Ball," a four-part series on Harvard baseball that appeared in the *Harvard Crimson*, beginning on February 9, 1887, was useful, though it mostly focused on later years. Conversely, Harry Lewis's "Protoball at Harvard: From Pastime to Contest," *Base Ball* 5:1 (Spring 2011), 41–45, has much on baseball at Harvard prior to the Civil War but little on this club. The *Harvard Advocate* was, as far as I can tell, the only student newspaper during these years. Available issues have been cited; others quoted from the later series in the *Crimson*, whose author had access to far more issues. Frank Preston Stearns's *Cambridge Sketches* (New York: J.B. Lippincott, 1905) has much on life at Harvard during those years and a few mentions of the baseball club, for which Stearns played three games. Charles A. Peverelly's 1866 *Book of American Pastimes* has a brief entry that provided several details. J. Mott Hallowell's "American College Athletics: 1. Harvard University," *Outing*, December 1888, is a good overview of the history of Harvard baseball, but adds little new about the early years. George Walton Green, "Clippings from a College Scrap-Book," *Harvard Monthly*, vol. 24 (March 1897), 91–100, is similarly devoted almost entirely to later years. *Base Ball at Harvard*, privately published by the 1903 Harvard baseball team, is helpful, but is primarily a reference guide. The various class secretaries' reports on the doings of alumni are the primary source of biographical information. Fortunately, Class of 1866 secretary Charles E. Stratton was especially diligent in doing his duties. Most of his reports can be accessed via Google Books.

Notes

1. *Base Ball at Harvard*, privately published by the 1903 Harvard baseball team, lists 980 games played by the school between 1865 and 1903: 654 wins, 312 losses, and 14 ties.

2. Ibid., 41–43.

3. Ibid., 43–45.

4. According to a history of Phillips Exeter, Flagg and Wright were also among a group of five who introduced baseball there: "Most enthusiastic of these early players was Mr. Flagg, who abandoned the Massachusetts style of baseball for the New York style. The ball then used was a small bag of shot wound with yarn, and could be batted much further than the present baseball. The men just named played among themselves and with town teams. Mr. Wright, of Auburn, New York, was perhaps more responsible than anyone else for bringing the game to New England" (Laurence M. Crosbie, *The Phillips Exeter Academy: A History* [Exeter: The Academy, 1923], p. 233, discovered by researcher George Thompson and posted on the Protoball website). Crosbie's source is unknown.

5. *Harvard Bulletin*, October 15, 1902; reprinted in James D'Wolf Lovett, *Old Boston Boys and the Games They Played* (Boston: Riverside Press, 1907), 156–158.

6. "Harvard's First Ball Team," *Boston Globe*, June 8, 1902, 46. The *Globe*'s transcription of the historic card renders "baseball" as one word, but the word was invariably spelled as two words at the time so I have restored that spelling.

7. *Harvard Bulletin*, October 15, 1902; reprinted in Lovett, *Old Boston Boys and the Games They Played*, 156–158.

8. Lovett, *Old Boston Boys and the Games They Played*, 143.

9. *Harvard Bulletin*, October 15, 1902; reprinted in Lovett, *Old Boston Boys and the Games They Played*, 156–158.

10. "Harvard's First Ball Team," *Boston Globe*, June 8, 1902, 46.

11. *Harvard Bulletin*, October 15, 1902; reprinted in Lovett, *Old Boston Boys and the Games They Played*, 156–158.

12. *Harvard Bulletin*, October 15, 1902; reprinted in Lovett, *Old Boston Boys and the Games They Played*, 156–158.

13. *The Harvard Book*, vol. 2, 269; Lovett, *Old Boston Boys and the Games They Played*, 154.

14. "Harvard's First Ball Team," *Boston Globe*, June 8, 1902, 46.

15. *The Harvard Book*, vol. 2, 269.

16. Frank Wright reports that a victory over the Tri-Mountains preceded the contest against the Brown University sophomores, but no other source lists such a game, so my presumption is that either this was a practice game or, more likely, that Wright's memory was faulty.

17. "Harvard's First Ball Team," *Boston Globe*, June 8, 1902, 46. As elsewhere, I have restored the word "base ball" to two words.

18. "Harvard's First Ball Team," *Boston Globe*, June 8, 1902, 46.

19. *Harvard Bulletin*, October 15, 1902; reprinted in Lovett, *Old Boston Boys and the Games They Played*, 156–158.

20. *The Harvard Book*, vol. 2, 270.

21. Ibid.

22. The precise location, according to *The Harvard Book*, vol. 2, 271, was as follows: "The batsman stood about one hundred and fifty feet from the Beacon Street Mall, facing the south; nearly opposite No. 54 Beacon Street.".

23. *The Harvard Book*, vol. 2, 270–271.

24. "College Regatta at Worcester," *Boston Daily Journal*, July 30, 1864, reprinted in *Sixth Report of the Secretary of the Class of 1865* (1885).

25. Frank Preston Stearns, *Cambridge Sketches* (New York: J.B. Lippincott, 1905), 22.

26. Ibid., 15–16.

27. *The Harvard Book*, vol. 2, 272.

28. *The Harvard Book*, vol. 2, 272.

29. Charles A. Peverelly, *The Book of American Pastimes*, 466.

30. *The Harvard Book*, vol. 2, 273.

31. *The Harvard Book*, vol. 2, 273–274.

32. "Harvard's First Ball Team," *Boston Globe*, June 8, 1902, 46.

33. *The Harvard Book*, vol. 2, 275.

34. Lovett, *Old Boston Boys and the Games They Played*, 171–172.

35. *Harvard Advocate*, quoted in "Twenty Years of Harvard Base-Ball" (part 1), *Harvard Crimson*, February 9, 1887.

36. Francis G. Peabody, "The Germ of the Graduate School," *Harvard Graduates' Magazine*, vol. 27, 177–178.

37. *Harvard Advocate*, May 25, 1866, 22.

38. *Harvard Advocate*, May 11, 1866, 2.

39. *Harvard Advocate*, May 25, 1866, 23; *Brooklyn Eagle*, May 31, 1866, 2.

40. "Harvard's First Ball Team," *Boston Globe*, June 8, 1902, 46.

41. Unidentified article, quoted in *The Harvard Book*, vol. 2, 275.

42. Ibid., 276.

43. *Brooklyn Eagle*, June 1, 1866, 2.

44. *Harvard Advocate*, quoted in "Twenty Years of Harvard Base-Ball" (part 1), *Harvard Crimson*, February 9, 1887.

45. Unidentified article, quoted in *The Harvard Book*, vol. 2, 277.

46. *Brooklyn Eagle*, June 2, 1866, 2.

47. *The Harvard Book*, vol. 2, 278; the quotation is from an article in the *Harvard Advocate* that appeared before the tour.

48. "Harvard's First Ball Team," *Boston Globe*, June 8, 1902, 46.

49. *New York Tribune*, June 4, 1866, 5.

50. *Harvard Advocate*, quoted in "Twenty Years of Harvard Base-Ball" (part 1), *Harvard Crimson*, February 9, 1887.

51. *The Harvard Book*, vol. 2, 278–279.

52. *Harvard Advocate*, quoted in "Twenty Years of Harvard Base-Ball" (part 1), *Harvard Crimson*, February 9, 1887.

53. *Harvard Advocate*, quoted in "Twenty Years of Harvard Base-Ball" (part 2), *Harvard Crimson*, February 10, 1887.

54. *Harvard Graduates' Magazine*, vol. 28 (1920), 495–496.

55. *The Thirteenth Secretary's Report of the Class of 1866 of Harvard College* (1916), 10–11.

56. *The Harvard Book*, vol. 2,.

57. Peabody, "The Germ of the Graduate School," *Harvard Graduates' Magazine*, vol. 27 (1919), 177–178.

58. *Harvard Advocate*, May 11, 1866, 12.

59. *Harvard Graduates' Magazine*, vol. 13 (1905), 315.

60. *Harvard Advocate*, May 25, 1866, 22–23.

61. "Twenty Years of Harvard Base-Ball" (part 2), *Harvard Crimson*, February 10, 1887.

62. Lovett, *Old Boston Boys and the Games They Played*, 88–89.

63. "Harvard's First Ball Team," *Boston Globe*, June 8, 1902, 46.

64. "Twenty Years of Harvard Base-Ball" (part 4), *Harvard Crimson*, February 15, 1887.

65. *Harvard Graduates' Magazine*, vol. 6 (1898), 417.

66. *Eleventh Report of the Class of 1869 of Harvard College* (1919), 259.

67. *The Thirteenth Secretary's Report of the Class of 1866* (1916), 67.

68. *The Eleventh Report of the Class of 1866 of Harvard College* (1906), 55–57.

69. The profile of T.F. Wright is based upon two profiles written after his death: Horace Winslow Wright, "Theodore Francis Wright," *The New-Church Review*, vol. 15 (April 1908), 161–212, and a tribute by a classmate in *Twelfth Secretary's Report of the Class of 1866 of Harvard College* (1911), 60–66.

❖ *Eagle Base Ball Club of Florence* ❖
(Brian Turner and John S. Bowman)

CLUB HISTORY

Northampton lads played games of bat and ball as early as anyone, as a 1791 ordinance banning "bat-ball" near the courthouse shows. But the city's first championship team emerged after the Civil War during the "base ball fever" that swept the Northeast. An account by "one of the players" claims that, in 1865, as the war wound down, a young man in Florence, a section of Northampton, received a letter from an army friend. The friend boasted that his regiment (sources vary as to which one) had the championship ball club of the Army of the Potomac. With their return home imminent, the letter said, the soldiers would welcome an opportunity to play a team from Florence.

A group of young men, mostly from Florence, formed the Eagle Base Ball Club and defeated the army veterans 30–3 on August 1, 1865. Emboldened, the Eagles challenged other local teams — including nearby Amherst College. Before season's end, the Eagles had won all six matches recorded in the official team scorebook, only just rediscovered in 2009 in the possession of William F. Stevens of Cambridge, Massachusetts, a descendant of John B. O'Donnell, Eagle second baseman. Given that official NABBP rules printed in the scorebook were

not approved until December 1865, the first six games must have been transcribed into the book the following season, after which the scoring shows clear evidence of being entered in real time.

The principal players in 1865 were Henry H. Bond, Edward S. Bottum, Arthur G. Hill, Michael H. Dunn, Philip J. Mara, John McGrath, John B. O'Donnell, Patrick Whalen, and Luther B. Askin. Hill and Bond were sons of the town's "upper class," but others were mill workers and common laborers, many of them Irish Catholics from recent immigrant families. The most unexpected player of the 1865–1866 seasons was Luther B. Askin, an African American. Askin started at first base the first season and several games into the second season. So the claim is made — yet to be disputed — that Askin is the earliest known case of an African American on a formally organized adult ball club.

Over the winter, the Eagle first nine expanded to include Edmund Connell, Edward Hammond, Jonas Polmatier, and Andrew Robertson. Some of these players had appeared in a game or two in 1865; most had played on a regular basis for the second nine. The Eagles also acquired uniforms: long-sleeve white shirts with two vertical stripes in front (in one team photo the players' shirts bear American flag shields), dark pants, and leather belts with metal buckles stamped Eagle BBC above a pair of crossed bats. An original Eagle belt is on display at the Baseball Hall of Fame in Cooperstown.

The Eagles won their first three games in 1866, only to suffer their first loss against the reigning western Massachusetts champions, the Hampdens of Chicopee. As the season went on, the Eagles beat the Hampdens in a re-match; won a third meeting; then lost to the Hampdens in a final match. In so doing the Eagles also lost the silver ball that went with the championship. The Florence lads chose never again to compete for the silver ball, in part because they suspected the Hampdens of using a significantly lighter ball, with which the Hampdens had practiced in secret for weeks.

The Eagles were not disheartened; indeed, their ambition knew no bounds. In November they went down to New York to take on the most powerful teams of the day, the Excelsiors and the Atlantics. As was to be foreseen, the Eagles lost both games.

In 1867, the Eagles defeated teams from western and central Massachusetts and Connecticut. But the lads overextended themselves again by playing the Troy (New York) Haymakers twice, and losing both times. Their overall record earned them an invitation to travel to Boston in September to vie with four other teams for the championship of New England. They beat three of these and then came up against the Tri-Mountain Club of Boston. Convinced that the umpire was biased in favor of the Tri-Mountains and after several disputed calls, the Eagles forfeited the game with two out in the sixth inning.

The Eagles did not reorganize for '68. Many faced demands on their time — law school, jobs, travel, families. Other teams would emerge in Florence and Northampton, but the Eagles retain the luster of pioneers. Over three seasons, they played as many as 40 matches and lost but seven. Perhaps their more significant achievement was to include an African American, Luther Askin, on an old New England town's team.

Askin was present at the home of Judge John B. O'Donnell, first in 1915 to celebrate the team's founding, and again in 1916 to celebrate the winning of the silver ball, which the Judge had tracked down in Chicopee and borrowed for the occasion. Nothing was said of Askin's race, nor did he appear in the reunion pictures. Yet he did address the gathering on the evolution of Two Old Cat and Round Ball to the modern game. Askin's reticence about mentioning his integration of the Eagle club may have been due to long habits of deference, a survival skill for African Americans. Also, his son and namesake, a bandleader in New York State, was passing for white at the time, which may have been another factor in his decision to remain silent.

Let us remember the Eagles at their zenith, the moment of their first victory over the Hampdens, as depicted in *The History of Florence, Massachusetts* (1895): "When Ed Hickey of the Hampdens planted a fly ball in Bottum's hands, the game was won by the Eagle nine and the excitement culminated.

The players and the crowd went crazy; Dunn came in from the field turning handsprings, Hammond stood on his head on the third base, Polmatier and O'Donnell were yelling themselves hoarse, Hill and Bond were on the shoulders of enthusiasts going around the 'Patch' at a little less than forty miles an hour, while Whalen to this day cannot tell what happened to him. The arrival home was an ovation from the Northampton railroad station to the homes of the boys, a brass band parade and an illuminated village giving them a great welcome."

CLUB MEMBERS

Luther B. "Bushel Basket" Askin: Askin was born in 1843 in Pittsfield, Massachusetts, died in 1929 in Brooklyn, New York. Askin came to Florence when he was six and worked for 56 years in the Florence Brush Shop, rising to foreman. In 1870 Askin joined the Nonotuck volunteer fire brigade on which he served for 20 years. Askin, an African American, played first base in every Eagle match until the club's first loss in June 1866. "'Old Bushel Basket' was his pet name, for, until his sickness, the balls seemed to drop into his fingers and stay there as if a basket held them." The "sickness," left unspecified, did not prevent Askin from playing several games for the second nine that same season. During his tenure with the first nine, Askin was a top offensive performer, with 2.20 more runs scored per game than "hands lost" (outs made); furthermore, he hit three home runs in 10 games, a rate of one every 3.33 games. (He hit another home run with the second nine.) Yet a reference to Askin's "heavy hitting" in the original handwritten manuscript of the Eagles' history was edited out, so the version published in 1895 emphasized only his fielding. Even so, the case for a racial factor in his demotion remains largely circumstantial.

Henry Herrick "H. H." Bond: Born in 1847, the Eagles' star pitcher and club president made a "scientific study of the art of pitching," compiling a 19–7 career record. Bond did his share of hitting, including three home runs in 26 games. In 1869 Bond graduated from Columbia Law School and entered practice in Northampton, until ill health forced him to retire in 1878. He moved to the South so that the milder climate might enable his recovery, but died in 1881 at the age of 34.

Edward S. "Batt'em" Bottum: Born in 1847, played outfield: "Bottum, though small, was cordy [i.e., wiry, yet muscular] and resolute, never afraid, a strong batter and a sure catch." In spite of Bottum's three home runs in 33 games, he made so many outs that he finished his career with only .70 more runs scored per game than hands lost. (During the 1866 season, Bottum made *more* outs than runs, even though Eagle batters reached base more than 80 percent of the time.) Bottum was a salesman for the Florence Furniture Company, the Florence Tack Company, and the J. M. Carpenter Tap and Die Company of Pawtucket, Rhode Island. "A genial man, interested in everyone, and always having a good word for those he met," he served as the club secretary. He died in 1925.

Arthur G. "Prince" Hill: Born in 1841 in the Northampton Association of Education and Industry, a utopian community that his father, S. L. Hill, helped found. From the community's failed enterprises, the senior Hill built Nonotuck Silk Company. Arthur attended Harvard, then entered the silk business. He played shortstop for the Eagles and was team captain. Elected Northampton's second mayor in 1887 and 1888 on the Republican-Temperance ticket, Hill spent a month in the Massachusetts legislature. His service was brief because his fellow legislators attached an amendment to a bill that he had introduced calling for police to search drunkards for alcohol. The amendment mockingly proposed that inebriates have their stomachs pumped for evidence. Offended, Hill resigned his office. (Such stiff-necked behavior may be reflected in Hill's tenure as team captain, when, based on perceived slights, the Eagles removed themselves from competition.) Hill was a leader of the Florence Dramatic Society, along with Bond and Bottum. Like Askin, Hill belonged to the Nonotuck fire brigade. Hill involved himself in entrepreneurial schemes that only occasionally turned a profit; in 1892, in spite of his inheritance, he was forced to file for insolvency. Hill died in 1926.

John B. O'Donnell: Born in Ireland in 1846, moved to Florence when he was eight and left school to work in the mills when was 12. With the Eagles, O'Donnell played second base. The leading batsman, he scored 2.55 more runs per game than hands lost; he also hit seven home runs, a rate of one every 4.7 games. In 1871, O'Donnell turned to his education, earning his degree from Boston University Law School in 1877. He was admitted to the bar in Massachusetts in 1878. He entered politics, and was twice elected mayor of Northampton in 1892 and 1893, running as a Democrat in a Republican stronghold. In 1915 he was appointed Judge of the District Court, a position he held until his death in 1927 at the age of 80.

Jonas S. Polmatier: Polmatier was born in Florence in 1840, the oldest of all Eagle players. His name appeared in local box scores as early as 1860. During the Civil War, Polmatier served in Massachusetts 27th Regiment. Upon discharge, Polmatier joined the Eagles, appearing in the first game of 1865, then with the second nine the rest of the season. In 1866, after the Eagles' first loss, he became the starting first baseman. "Polmatier, long of arm and large of frame, was the easiest player on the team, sometimes a bit too easy for the best results." In 29 games he hit three home runs, including one against the Excelsiors of New York. He made his living as a tailor and in middle age moved to upstate New York. He died in 1928, having returned to Florence in his last years.

Andrew "Little Andie" Robertson: Robertson was born in 1848 in Scotland, came to America when he was nine. While still a teen, Robertson worked in the oil fields of Pennsylvania before joining the Eagles in 1866; after two seasons with the

Eagles, he worked on the Transcontinental Railroad and served as a "Mormon scout," guiding wagon trains to Utah. During the 1880s he worked the mines of Idaho. In 1886 he moved to Springfield, Massachusetts, where he coached youth baseball. "Without mask or protector he stood up to the bat when there was a man on base. His throwing was quick, swift and straight to the mark." Another source reported, "His favorite habit was to take off his shoes and stockings and play in his bare feet." Robertson died in 1924, and was hailed in his obituary as "one of the few 'old timers' remaining in Springfield."

Patrick E. "Whale'em" Whalen: Whalen, like O'Donnell, was born in Ireland, probably in 1848. He came to America as infant. After playing outfield for the Eagles, Whalen moved to New Haven, Connecticut. "Whalen was thoroughly reliable, no steadier or more graceful player appeared on the field. His 'daisy cutters' were sent with such power that rarely were they stopped." Whalen played 34 games, the most of any Eagle. He hit four home runs and was second only to O'Donnell in scoring production, averaging 2.27 more runs scored per game than hands lost. Whalen attended the team reunions in 1915 and 1916, and was reported to be one of the surviving members as late as 1926.

OTHER CLUB MEMBERS

Edmund F. Connell played shortstop during the periods when Hill was injured. He was also a reserve pitcher in 1867, starting four games, winning three. He pitched the final game that the Eagles played, a 21–21 tie against the Hampdens. He "generally did heavy batting," yet Connell's career numbers show that he scored .73 more runs per game vs. hands lost. Only Bottum (.70) and Edward H. "Ned" Hammond (.50) did worse. Hammond played third base, as did several others, among them James Meehan (or "Mehan" or "Mahan"). Third base was generally regarded as the weakest position on the team. John McGrath, "the pitcher of the first year," was 5–0 in six games pitched. Philip Mara, starting catcher of 1865, became the first Eagle to die — in 1873, the cause, "a congestion of the lungs." Michael H. Dunn, outfielder, "was always in the right place, seemingly by accident." Dunn played 30 games, hit four home runs. Relatively little is known of his life, though he may have been born in Ireland in 1845, since a Michael Dunn appears in Northampton's 1860 census, age 15. His fellow players at the 1915 team reunion regretted that Dunn was too ill to attend.

Bibliography

Daily Hampshire Gazette, Northampton.
Daily Herald, Northampton.
"The Eagle Base Ball Club." *History of Florence, Massachusetts.* Ed. Charles A. Sheffeld. Florence: privately published, 1895, 179–186.
Florence Eagle Base Ball Club Scorebook, 1865–1867.
Free Press, Northampton.
The Republican, Springfield.

Turner, Brian. "America's Earliest Integrated Team?" *The National Pastime*, vol. 22 (2002): 81–90.

_____, and John S. Bowman. *The Hurrah Game*. Northampton: Northampton Historical Society, 2002.

❖ *Lightfoot Base Ball Club of North Brookfield* ❖
(Peter Morris)

CLUB HISTORY

In 1904 the members of the Lightfoot Base Ball Club of North Brookfield, Massachusetts, staged a memorable reunion that included most of the men who had played baseball there some 50 years earlier. The aged pioneers were issued badges that read "Lightfoot Base Ball Club, North Brookfield, 1850," and were given the "freedom of the town," which they took advantage of by making stops at the Essex House and the West Brookfield Tavern. The players also found plenty of time to reminisce about those long-ago days and while their memories may have included some inaccuracies, they do paint a vivid portrait.

The Lightfoot Club dated its origin to 1850 and was so named "because the members were specially active and agile on their feet. They used to run up and down North Brookfield's main street every night for practice."[1]

The game played by the Lightfoots for most of their history was known at the time as round ball and later became known as the Massachusetts Game. The members of the Lightfoots claimed to have never lost while playing by those rules, earning them recognition as champions of Western Massachusetts. At the reunion, club member David Earle gave a talk on the history of the club from its inception, but unfortunately none of the accounts saw fit to recap Earle's remarks. As a result, we have no idea of how many matches they played or of many other key details.

Another club member did, however, provide a description of the rules followed by the Lightfoots. "The rules of the old Massachusetts game," recalled Henry Hibbard, "called for not less than nine and not more than fourteen players on a side. But there was invariably a full complement of men. The ball field was in the form of a square, not the diamond shape of the present day, the batter standing in a four-foot circle. The first base was thirty feet to the right of the batter and the fourth base, or home, thirty feet to his left. The bases were sixty feet apart, forming three sides of the square. The thrower stood thirty-five feet in front of the batter, the catcher, of course, being behind him. The referees were seated ten feet behind the thrower. The ball was to be thrown anywhere over the four-foot ring, provided it went to the right of the batter, or to his left in case he was left-handed. It was stipulated that the ball used must not weigh more than two and three-quarters ounces, or less than two and one-half ounces. Batted balls must be caught on the fly to put the player out. One hundred runs constituted a game. The other positions in the out-fields were 'first behind' and 'second behind,' two shortstops, one to the right, the other to the left of the batter and about twenty feet from him, one on each of the four bases, one each behind second and third bases, one farther back between these men and one to the right of the 'first' and 'second behind.'"[2]

According to a 1904 article, Hibbard became so well known as an authority on the rules of the Massachusetts Game that he was invited to referee and to make the baseballs for a historic 1859 match played between Amherst College and Williams College.[3] It's a nice story, but unfortunately a game account states that a man named William Plunkett served as referee.[4]

When the Civil War broke out, the Lightfoot Club disbanded and about half of the players enlisted in the Union Army, many of them serving together in the 25th Massachusetts Infantry. The club reorganized at the war's end and in August of 1865 it met a rival from Brookfield in a match billed as being for the championship of Central and Western Massachusetts. It was the 39th anniversary of this match that was being celebrated by the 1904 reunion.

The big contest was scheduled to begin on Friday, August 18, 1865, and since a round-ball match was played until one club had scored 100 runs, it was to continue for as many days as necessary. The site was the West Brookfield Common and anticipation was at such a fever pitch that business in all of the Brookfield villages was put on hold until the match was concluded. As if added incentive was needed, each side put up a stake of $250.

Play began on the 18th but runs proved difficult to come by and the match was still being contested on the 21st with the Lightfoots ahead by 24–14 but with the requisite 100 runs still very far off. At that point, however, "a batted ball rolled under a carriage and was picked up by a girl and handed to a Brookfield player, who was thus enabled to put out the North Brookfield player."

Referee Seth Wetherbee ruled the runner safe because of the extra help, prompting a dispute. Eventually, the Brookfield players refused to play any further, ending the match. This left the stakeholder in a dilemma, and an effort was made to persuade him not to pay the North Brookfield side their winnings, but in the end he chose to do so.[5]

That was the final match the Lightfoots played by the

Massachusetts rules. Though it was not the last time that once-popular version was ever used, it is not too much of a stretch to describe the game as the swan song of round ball. By the end of the Civil War, the New York Game was well on its way to sweeping aside all rivals and become truly the national game. There were still a few pockets of resistance, but the specter of a round-ball game that could go on for days and be ended only by dispute made that mode of play look like a relic of a bygone age. Thereafter, that version's demise was very swift and in 1867 a national publication reported that every single club that had played the Massachusetts game had either switched to the New York game or disbanded.[6]

To some this was a great loss, but others were less sympathetic. In 1879, David Earle, who had played the outfield for the Lightfoots, took part in an exhibition of the Massachusetts Game that involved such members of the local professional team as Charley Bennett, Doc Bushong, George Wood, and Harry Stovey. The throwback contest had some memorable moments, such as when Earle attempted "to knock the ball over the second catcher's head. He failed in the attempt and got 'patched' in the back before reaching the first goal." Yet according to an account in the *Worcester Spy*, the novelty soon wore off. "One game of round ball will do for a long time," the *Spy*'s reporter sniffed, "it has been 20 years since a match game was played in this city until yesterday, and it will be several years before the experiment is tried again.... The game furnishes amusement for two or three innings and then becomes monotonous, especially after the people have been accustomed to witness skillful base ball play."[7]

Symbolically, the Lightfoots switched to the New York rules and played by them in 1866 and 1867. The results are largely unknown and perhaps that is just as well — in one of the few recorded games the club lost to the Pioneers of Springfield, 78–5.[8] After the 1867 season, the Lightfoot Base Ball Club of North Brookfield gave up the sport for good and the players moved on with their lives.

Nevertheless, their days on the ballfield must have remained very fond memories, as all but one of the surviving members returned to North Brookfield in 1904 for the reunion. Also invited to the reunion was Seth Wetherbee of Warren, the man who had refereed the famous 1865 match. In honor of his service, Wetherbee was presented with a silver fruit dish.

As described in the player profiles that follow, the members of the Lightfoot Club had more in common than baseball, with many of them having worked as shoemakers and with around half of them having served in the Civil War. They also were uncommonly long-lived, as only Charles Torrey died before the age of 50 and ten of the fourteen men lived to celebrate their seventieth birthdays. No more reunions are known to have been held, but it was not for lack of surviving members: in 1917 there were still five members still alive and as late as 1928 there were still three survivors. It was not until August 16, 1935, two days shy of the seventieth anniversary of the fa-mous contest that Henry Hibbard, the last of the Lightfoots, passed away.

CLUB MEMBERS

James Brackenridge Cummings: Baseman James B. Cummings was born in North Brookfield on July 31, 1844. He enlisted when the Civil War broke out and served for three years in the 36th Massachusetts. He married soon after the war and went to work at a North Brookfield shoe factory. By 1872, the marriage had soured "on account of his intemperate habits and his wife's alleged intimacy with Timothy Spooner, who boarded with the family." Upon finding the two walking together, Cummings shot at Spooner four times, wounding him in the shoulder with the last bullet, and then surrendered to a police officer. The outcome of his trial is not known and James Cummings and his wife were still married when the 1880 census came out, but eventually divorced. James Cummings died in Brookfield on May 17, 1901, so missed out on the reunion. Hall of Famer William Arthur "Candy" Cummings was born in nearby Ware in 1848 and was his second cousin.[9] The Cummings name had been prominent in Ware since 1691.[10] "Candy" Cummings moved with his family to Brooklyn in the late 1850s but by then was very familiar with the "old Massachusetts game" and probably witnessed the games of the Lightfoot Club.[11] His familiarity with overhand throwing likely influenced his development of the curveball.[12]

David Matthews Earle: David M. Earle, an outfielder for the Lightfoots, was born in North Brookfield on August 15, 1838. He served for three years in the 15th Massachusetts Infantry during the Civil War, along with his brother Henry and several of his Lightfoot teammates. He was wounded at Antietam and received several promotions, eventually earning the rank of captain. After the war he farmed in North Brookfield, then served as warden of the state prison from 1881 until being removed by the governor in 1883.[13] He later moved to Worcester and became a deputy sheriff. Around 1902, he was appointed doorkeeper on the Republican side of the U.S. Senate. At the time of the 1904 reunion, he was dividing his time between Washington and Worcester. Earle died in Worcester on January 29, 1917.[14]

Albert Henry Foster: The "second behind" of the Lightfoots, was born in New Braintree, Massachusetts, on November 12, 1839. By 1860 he had settled in North Brookfield and had a job stitching boots. He enlisted in the 15th Massachusetts on May 1, 1861. Taken prisoner at Ball's Bluff in October 1861, he was held as a prisoner of war at Richmond, Virginia, for four months. After being exchanged, he served until July 1864. After the war Foster became a coal dealer and lived in North Brookfield until his death on November 5, 1928.

Francis Babbitt Hibbard: Outfielder Frank Hibbard was born on March 27, 1842, and was one of three brothers to play for the Lightfoots. He worked as a shoemaker in North

Brookfield, but by the 1880s he had moved to Nebraska and become a farmer. His farm, Evergreen Farm at Irvington-on-the-Papio, became well known around Omaha. He was still living on his farm near Omaha in 1917 when he was described as "one of the rugged, sterling characters of pioneer record in Nebraska.... He has been active as a citizen and in politics, never seeking office but serving as state oil inspector under Governor Poynter. A prominent populist in the hey day of that party, he was the friend and advisor of governors and United States senators, with wide personal acquaintance among the leading men."[15] Hibbard died within days of that article and left a unique will in which he requested no funeral, instead asking his loved ones to "Think of me as having gone on a long journey!"[16]

Henry A. Hibbard: Henry Hibbard, the first behind, was born on May 16, 1839. He became a dentist and moved to Missouri before settling in Fort Worth, Texas. Despite the distance, he and his brother Frank both came back to North Brookfield for the 1904 reunion. He lived to great old age, dying in Fort Worth on August 16, 1935.

John Lawton Hibbard: Infielder John Hibbard was the oldest of the three brothers, being born on April 6, 1833, in West Brookfield. In 1856, he married Abigail Poland, the sister of fellow club member Anson Poland. When the war broke out, he enlisted in the 34th Massachusetts, serving as a musician and joining in Sherman's March to the Sea. He then settled in Worcester, where he worked as a schoolhouse janitor. He died in Worcester on June 2, 1908.

James Needham ("Kirkham"): One of the club's outfielders was the only surviving member who missed the 1904 reunion. He was identified as James Kirkham in several articles, but nobody by that name seemed to fit. One article listed him as James Needham of Coldbrook.[17] There was a James Walker Needham living in Oakham on the 1900 census, a stone's throw from Coldbrook Springs, so this is very likely the man in question. Needham was born in New Braintree on April 7, 1837, worked as a farm laborer and gardener, and died in Oakham on June 8, 1910. He was buried in Coldbrook Cemetery.

James Nichols: Baseman James Nichols was reported to be dead when the 1904 reunion was held. It's always hard to be positive about the identity of someone with a common name, but there's one candidate that is almost certainly the man in question. James S. Nichols was born in Princeton, Massachusetts, on May 23, 1842, and his family had moved to Brookfield by the time of the 1850 census. James became a shoemaker and, along with three other members of the Lightfoot Club, enlisted in the 15th Massachusetts Infantry in 1862. He was wounded at the Battle of Ball's Bluff in October 1861 and, like Albert Foster, was taken prisoner. Exchanged in January 1862, he was discharged from service three months later due to disability. James Nichols returned to working as a shoemaker and married in 1867. He died in Pepperell, Massachusetts, on October 17, 1899.

Anson Barnet Poland: Anson Poland, an outfielder, was born in North Brookfield on September 20, 1835. He worked as a shoemaker and later as a farmer, while also being a long-serving road commissioner of North Brookfield and a member of its Board of Selectmen. He was still living in North Brookfield at the time of the 1904 reunion. He died there two years later, on October 10, 1906.

Benjamin "Ben" Stevens: Ben Stevens, the third behind of the Lightfoots, was born in Andover, Massachusetts, on June 18, 1840. He worked as a shoemaker before the Civil War, then enlisted in the 15th Massachusetts Infantry, the regiment in which several of the Lightfoots served. Also serving alongside Stevens was his future father-in-law, William Babbitt. Stevens was wounded at Antietam and the Battle of the Wilderness. After the war he married Babbitt's daughter and worked at a North Brookfield shoe factory. He later moved to Boston and worked as a prison officer. Stevens died in Auburn, Massachusetts, on April 25, 1928, and was survived by his wife of 61 years.

George Washington Stone: George W. Stone, the "thrower" of the Lightfoots, was living in Oakham, Massachusetts, at the time of the 1904 reunion. Tim Murnane's *Sporting Life* article specifically identified him as "ex-Representative George W. Stone."[18] Identifications are always tricky with common names, but these clues leave no doubt that he was a man named George Washington Stone who was born in Spencer, Massachusetts, on August 1, 1840, and who served in the Massachusetts legislature in 1901. Stone came from a prominent Oakham family: his great-great-grandfather, Isaac Stone, arrived in Oakham in 1765 and fought in the Revolutionary War. George himself served in the 25th Massachusetts Infantry for nearly four years during the Civil War and was wounded at the Battle of Cold Harbor. He inherited the family farm and was also very active in civic affairs, serving as a selectman and on many municipal committees in addition to his time in the Massachusetts legislature.[19] He died in Oakham on October 16, 1914.

Charles and Henry Torrey: The Torreys were both basemen and were reported to have died by the time of the 1904 reunion.[20] It seems highly likely that they were brothers Charles Adams Torrey and Henry Augustus Torrey, who were born in Ware on September 19, 1840, and September 25, 1842, respectively. The sons of a shoemaker, both were living in North Brookfield when the 1860 census was taken and were also listed as shoemakers. Charles died on September 1, 1878. Henry died under mysterious circumstances fourteen years later — his frozen body was found in a North Brookfield pasture on December 21, 1892, two days after he had been last seen alive.[21]

John J. Upham: Infielder John Upham was born in North Brookfield on May 22, 1836. He was a shoemaker before the war, then enlisted in the 42nd Massachusetts and served for a year. After the war he moved to Worcester and worked in clothing sales. He died in Worcester on April 13, 1910.

SOURCES: "A Famous Old Team: The North Brookfield Lightfoots, Baseball Heroes of the 50s, Who Held a Reunion Last Week," *Springfield Republican*, August 28, 1904, 20; "The Most Unique Base Ball Reunion on Record," *Omaha Sunday World-Herald*, September 25, 1904; "Reunion of Old Ball Team," *Springfield Republican*, August 24, 1904, 3; Tim Murnane, *Sporting Life*, September 10, 1904.

Notes

1. "A Famous Old Team: The North Brookfield Lightfoots, Baseball Heroes of the 50s, Who Held a Reunion Last Week," *Springfield Republican*, August 28, 1904, 20.

2. "The Most Unique Base Ball Reunion on Record," *Omaha Sunday World-Herald*, September 25, 1904.

3. "A Famous Old Team: The North Brookfield Lightfoots, Baseball Heroes of the 50s, Who Held a Reunion Last Week," *Springfield Republican*, August 28, 1904, 20.

4. *Pittsfield Sun*, July 7, 1859; reprinted in Dean Sullivan, *Early Innings* (Lincoln: University of Nebraska Press, 1995), 32–34.

5. A brief summary of the article appeared in the *Boston Herald* on August 23, 1865, but otherwise all of these details come from the 1904 accounts of the reunion.

6. *The Ball Player's Chronicle*, June 6, 1867.

7. *Worcester Daily Spy*, October 17, 1879, 4.

8. *Springfield Republican*, August 6, 1866, 4.

9. *The Cummings Memorial: A Genealogical History of the Descendants of Isaac Cummings, an Early Settler of Topsfield, Massachusetts* (1903).

10. *Springfield Union*, August 24, 1961, 55.

11. *The Sporting News*, February 20, 1897; *Boston Globe*, April 6, 1896.

12. See the lengthy entry on the curveball in my *A Game of Inches* for details.

13. *Worcester Daily Spy*, February 12, 1883, 1.

14. *Springfield Republican*, February 1, 1917, 11.

15. *Omaha World Herald*, April 9, 1917, 1.

16. *Omaha World Herald*, April 14, 1917, 1.

17. "Reunion of Old Ball Team," *Springfield Republican*, August 24, 1904, 3.

18. Tim Murnane, *Sporting Life*, September 10, 1904.

19. Henry Parks Wright, *Soldiers of Oakham, Massachusetts, in the Revolutionary War, the War of 1812 and the Civil War* (New Haven: The Tuttle, Moorehouse and Taylor Press, 1914), 197–198.

20. "Reunion of Old Ball Team," *Springfield Republican*, August 24, 1904, 3.

21. *Boston Globe*, December 22, 1892, 5.

❖ *Chemung Base Ball Club of Stoughton* ❖ (Peter Morris)

CLUB HISTORY

In 1909 Billy de Coster, a member of the second nine of the Chemungs of Stoughton in the late 1860s, gave this history of the club:

We used to play what was called the Massachusetts game. That was where we had a square, instead of a diamond, and ran four bases. We had a small ball and a small bat, and the ball could be thrown at a base runner and if it hit him before he got to the base he was out.

It was in 1866, not long after the war, when Halsey J. Boardman, who was president of the Tri-Mountains of Boston, got us interested in the present game, which we called the New York game. Boardman lived in Stoughton, and showed us boys how to play the new game and coached us right along until we organized the Chemungs and got some uniforms.

There were so many of the boys in Stoughton interested that we had a first, second and third nine, and we would have some kind of a game on our grounds every night when the weather permitted. Everyone played for the love of the game, and we began to play some of the teams from other towns. There were teams then from Foxboro, Mansfield and the King Philips of East Abington, what is now known as Rockland, and in Weymouth and Boston.

The Chemungs were successful from the very start, and in '68 were the champions of the county. Norfolk county had a fair in Dedham, and the Chemungs and the Mechanics of East Weymouth were the teams that played for the championship. That was a great game. We had seven or eight home runs in

that game. You see the ball had to be delivered straight, and not above the hips, so it was easier to get home runs than it is now.

The towns were divided into districts and at the close of the season the champion of each district would play the other champions. I remember there was a team called the Eurekas of Cambridge and the Winthrops of Boston and I think the Shields of Chelsea. It finally came down to the Tri Mountains of Boston and the Chemungs to play for the silver ball that was the trophy of the champions of the state. The Chemungs won the championship, but never got the silver ball.

All of the Chemungs were still alive in 1909 and remained fans of the game who loved nothing better than recounting memories of their ballplaying days. One favorite recollection was of a game against the Tri-Mountains on the Boston Common during which one of the Chemungs knocked the ball over a building on Tremont Street. The ball could not be found and a home run was the result.

Another much-told anecdote involved a game umpired by a minister who did not have a firm grasp on the game's rules. One of the opposing players clouted a ball clear out of sight and over a house. But when the outfielder ran back clutching the ball, the minister called the batter out.

Naturally, the players loved most to reminisce about the triumph over the Tri-Mountains. Archie McDonald gave this account: "We had got friendly with the Tri Mountains through Halsey Boardman, who was their president. He ran for mayor of Boston afterward. Well, we had beaten them once and they had one on us, and we were the two best teams in the state. We had played them once on the Boston Common, but this deciding game was to be played in Medford.

> Well, a few days before the deciding game they got a pitcher, Del Linfield, away from us and we asked for a little more time so as to get a pitcher ready for the game, but they answered and said the game was scheduled for a certain day and they should expect us there on time. We were there all right, but it was raining some and then for some reason they wanted us to wait and said that the grounds would be all wet, but Dick Seeley had been to sea some and he said that we would play if we had to get a boat or swim for the ball.
>
> They wouldn't postpone for us, and so we wouldn't postpone for them, so we went ahead. Linfield was the best pitcher in the league, but besides him they had a professional player named O'Brien, from New York, who was supposed to be a wonder. Well, we went in and batted O'Brien out of the box and then they put in Linfield and we batted him just as bad as we did O'Brien. We had taken Capen Brown, the pitcher on our second team, and he proved to be a star and they couldn't do a thing with him. We won the game, but did not get the silver ball. I don't know just why it was, but we were the champions just the same.

CLUB MEMBERS

Berthier Richmond Ballou: B.R. "Bob" Ballou was born on December 8, 1836, in Stoughton. He worked as a trader in livestock, but lost his eyesight around 1895. After that, his wife supported the family by keeping a boarding house in Stoughton, while Berthier continued to make his way downtown each day to talk to his friends. He died on January 7, 1915, in Stoughton, and his front-page obituary mentioned his long-ago involvement with the Chemung ballclub. *Sporting Life* even noted his passing in its January 16 issue, describing him as a "heavy hitter" of baseball's early days.

James Leighton Belcher: James Belcher was born in Canton, Massachusetts, on February 19, 1840. He enlisted in the Union Army and fought in more than 20 Civil War battles, including Gettysburg, the Wilderness, and Antietam. Upon returning home, he got married in 1866 and started a family the following year. He worked in a boot factory and then for many years at the Stoughton last factory of his brother, George Belcher. James Belcher became a skilled last maker and had worked his way up to foreman by 1907. He died at his Stoughton home on May 30, 1910, which appropriately enough was Memorial Day. His obituary took up much of the front page of the next day's Stoughton paper, with lengthy coverage of his Civil War service but no mention of his days on the baseball field. The Belchers were such prominent citizens in Stoughton that the death of James Belcher's widow 20 years later was also featured on the front page.

Capen Brown: Capen Brown, who "became the proud boast of the Chemungs because of his victory over the Tri-Mountains," was born in 1848. Like so many of the Chemungs, he worked for a while in a Stoughton boot factory, but even-

tually moved to Brookline, where he continued to work in the shoe business. He died in Boston on October 19, 1925.

William Henry DeCoster: Billy DeCoster of the second team was born in Stoughton in May of 1852 and also found work at a Stoughton boot factory. His mother's maiden name was Record and she was from Buckfield, Maine, so he must have been a cousin of teammate Wellington Record. He moved to South Dakota for a while, then returned to Stoughton and was living in Boston as of 1920. He died on August 10, 1920, at his daughter's house in Dorchester.

Isaac L. Gay: Isaac Gay was born in 1847 and was also working in a boot factory at the time of the 1870 census. He later worked as a clerk and as a chef in hotels and restaurants in Stoughton and nearby Brockton. He and his brothers were still running a lunchroom in Stoughton as late as 1915. Gay died of acute alcoholism in Stoughton on October 24, 1916.

Charles H. Jaques: Charles Jaques was born in 1845 and served for three years in the 12th Massachusetts Infantry during the Civil War, being wounded at Antietam. He later worked as a bootmaker and a laborer. He passed away in Stoughton on October 15, 1931.

Adelbert Moses Linfield: Linfield was born in 1842. Unlike most of the Chemungs, he left Stoughton soon after his ballplaying days ended, moving to Worcester, then to Philadelphia, and finally to Newport, Rhode Island. There he and his second wife, Lizzie, kept a hotel. He died on April 22, 1916, in Cranston, Rhode Island, and his obituary mentioned that he had once been a ballplayer.

Archibald H. McDonald: Archie McDonald was born on March 4, 1848. He worked at same bench at the Stacy Adams shoe factory in Brockton for more than 40 years. He died in Stoughton on March 20, 1921.

Francis Raymond: Frank Raymond was born in December of 1842. During the Civil War he served with future teammate Charles Jacques in the 12th Massachusetts Infantry. He was captured at Gettysburg on July 1, 1863, and was exchanged on March 8, 1864. He was married in 1867 and worked as a bootmaker and a mason. He died on September 20, 1919.

Wellington W. Record: Wellington Record was the youngest member of the team, having been born on August 10, 1852, in Buckfield, Maine. He became a physician and practiced in Quincy and became the first doctor to actually live in the Wollaston section of the city. He died on November 11, 1912, when, after treating a patient, he tried to board a train but slipped under it. The quantity of flowers at his funeral was the greatest ever seen in Wollaston.

Dick Seeley: Seeley's real name was Alden A. Seeley and he was born in Old Town, Maine, in 1845. He married in 1866 and as of 1870 he too was working at a last factory in Stoughton. Eventually he moved to Leominster and worked as a factory engineer. He died on January 20, 1927, at the War Veterans Hospital in Chelsea, Massachusetts.

SOURCE: *Boston Globe*, June 27, 1909.

❖ *Kearsarge Base Ball Club of Stoneham* ❖
(Peter Morris)

CLUB HISTORY

The Kearsarge Base Ball Club of Stoneham, Massachusetts, you say? Where is Stoneham and what's the story behind that odd nickname? And why on earth would anyone care about that club a century and a half after the fact?

The first two questions are fairly simple to resolve. Stoneham today is a modest-sized town of 20,000 in Middlesex County described on its official website as "a residential suburban community situated less than 10 miles to the Northwest of the city of Boston." In the mid-nineteenth century, however, Boston's suburban sprawl had yet to reach that close and Stoneham was still a sleepy town whose agricultural past was slowly giving way to an economy based upon shoe factories and other byproducts of the Industrial Revolution. As for the nickname, it was a tribute to the USS Kearsarge, a Civil War Union Navy sloop that became famous for sinking the CSS Alabama.

The significance of the Kearsarge Base Ball Club is a more complicated question. The best place to begin is with two retrospective articles in the *Boston Globe* that recounted the exploits of this pioneer club.

According to a 1900 article, the Kearsarge Club was "the acknowledged peer of any nine in Massachusetts" in the years immediately after the Civil War as the New York version of baseball came to the fore in the state. In 1869 the club joined forces with a Stoneham junior nine called the Atalantas and the resulting lineup went through the 1870 season without losing a series, beating such well-regarded clubs as the Lowells, Tri-Mountains, and Reds of Boston, Live Oaks of Lynn, King Philips of Weymouth, Clippers of Lowell, Fairmounts of Marlboro, and the Newton and Waltham clubs.

The 1900 article went on to explain that the Kearsarge Club was eventually succeeded by the General Worths, a club that sent Sid Farrar, Arlie Latham, and Billy Annis to the major leagues. Even so, according to the article, the "memory of the old 'Kearsarges' occupies the chief place in the affections of the old-time baseball fan." The club's captain, Charlie Tay, particularly enjoyed telling about a win in Marlboro. Afterward, the account reported, "there was no barge to be found to carry the victors to South Framingham; nothing daunted, the walk of 12 miles was covered and enjoyed, as the game had been won." All nine regulars on the undefeated squad were still living in the area in 1900 and they expressed their willingness to take on all comers — of their age.[1]

A noticeably different description of the club's claim to fame was given in an 1894 article summarizing a recent reunion. In this version, the Kearsarge Club was "the champion of New England, both in the old Massachusetts and the modern game." Stories were told at the reunion about the rules

of the days and of "an all-day game at Danvers." The highlight of the club's existence was a win over the Alphas of Ashland on the Boston Common that made the Kearsarge Club the state champion, prompting a memorable reception when the players returned home to Stoneham.[2]

While both accounts relate the Kearsarge Club of Stoneham's ascendance to state supremacy, in many ways they sound as though they are describing different clubs. The 1900 article pinpoints 1870 as the pinnacle of the club's success and is vague about whether the club ever played the Massachusetts Game. The 1894 piece, in contrast, made it sound as though the Kearsarge Club was predominantly a Massachusetts Game club that reached its peak in 1866 when it won the championship on the Boston Common. Which of these versions of events is accurate? Or are both instances of the exaggerations that men of a certain age are prone to making about their younger days?

None of the immediate postwar Massachusetts clubs was a national contender, so the state's clubs received little attention in the national press. Accordingly, it will take access to primary source material, particularly local newspapers, in order to recreate the history of the Kearsarge Club in great detail. There is, however, enough readily available material to establish the basic veracity of the claims made in both of the retrospective articles.

Stoneham seems to have had a prewar Massachusetts Game club but even its name is lost to history. Like so many clubs, the Civil War brought a halt to its activities but they picked up again at war's end and the Kearsarge name was adopted. By then the Massachusetts Game was losing favor in the state and was in grave danger of extinction, but it was nonetheless the version of choice in Stoneham. They were not alone, as an "association of base-ball players, who play the old Massachusetts game, was formed" at the Parker House in Boston on September 15, 1866. Eleven clubs joined the organization and the officers included Daniel A. Caskin of Danvers as president and Richard Park of Stoneham as secretary.[3]

The organization had its work cut out for it, beginning with the choice of a name. It opted for the New England Association of Base Ball Players, a name previously used by a prewar association that had lapsed into inactivity. This risked confusion, however, as Massachusetts now had a state association for players of the New York version with a virtually identical name: the New England Association of National Base Ball Players.

Adding to the challenges faced by the new association, its rival had a larger membership and offered a silver ball for the New York Game championship of the state. Western Massachusetts had its own silver ball for the championship of that region — again restricted to clubs playing by the New York version. Not surprisingly, the new association had a hard time getting much attention for a version of baseball that struck many of the state's young ballplayers as outdated.

In an effort to overcome these challenges, plans were announced to hold a state championship of the Massachusetts Game, to be played on the Boston Common on Saturday, October 6, 1866, between the Alpha Club of Ashland and the Kearsarge Club. This of course was the contest that was remembered so fondly at the 1894 reunion.

Unfortunately, while the match was an understandable source of pride in Stoneham, it failed miserably in its ostensible purpose of showing that the Massachusetts Game was alive and well. To begin, there was no clear indication of how the Alpha and Kearsarge clubs had been selected as the two opponents. The Kearsarge Club had recently defeated the host Peabody Club of Danvers (in what may have been the day-long game referred to at the 1894 reunion).[4] Perhaps this match and other similar ones provided the justification for choosing the two opponents, but since no explanation was given, the legitimacy of the "championship" match was open to question.

Worse, the contest itself revealed the least appealing aspects of the Massachusetts Game. Accounts were published in at least two newspapers and both noted the significance of the version used. A report in the *Springfield Republican* noted that the "old Massachusetts game" was used, while one in the *Boston Journal* explained that the "game played was the 'New England,' and differs considerably from the 'New York' game." Both accounts, however, devoted only a single sentence to the actual play. "The game was to have been for fifty tallies," reported the *Republican*, "but at the end of four hours' playing, it was terminated by a disagreement between the umpire and referees, when the score stood, Kearsarge 18, Alpha 9." In the *Journal*'s version of events, "Owing to a disagreement between one of the Clubs and the Umpire the playing was discontinued, with the score as follows: Kearsarge 18, Alpha 9." The *Journal* actually devoted a comparable space to a description of a game between the *second nines* of the Lowell and Harvard clubs.[5]

Clearly, the match had been a complete failure at showing the Massachusetts Game to still be a legitimate rival to the New York version. The game-ending dispute was bad enough, but there was also the damning reality that four hours had been nowhere near enough to determine a winner. As a result, the match that brought the state championship to Stoneham was effectively the swan song of the Massachusetts Game. Little more was heard from the New England Association of Base Ball Players (though the 1894 article claimed that it held one final convention in April of 1867). Even the Kearsarge Club soon switched to the now national version, joining the other association in the fall of 1868.[6]

For the next three years, little was heard from the club and the few results that were recorded were defeats. A less re-

silient club would have given up, but the Kearsarges kept working on the nuances of the New York version and continued to improve. The merger with the younger Atalanta Club, which apparently took place after the conclusion of the 1869 season, brought a much-needed infusion of young talent. By the spring of 1870 Stoneham once again had a formidable baseball club.

Details on the Kearsarge Club's 1870 season are again difficult to nail down. The championship silver ball had been the subject of so many disputes that it had been melted down — by coincidence, at the same meeting in which the Kearsarges were accepted as members, the association reported that $19.46 had been realized from the sale of the silver from the melted ball.[7] The squabbles soured many on the whole notion of trying to determine a champion. Those who still cared found it hard to keep track of the championship after the demise of the silver ball, since the results of matches often received little attention. Baseball's growing professionalism was the biggest hindrance of all — most Massachusetts clubs were still amateur or semipro entities and their doings were overshadowed by the professional powerhouses from New York, Philadelphia, and the Midwest. As a result, by 1870 it was hard to tell which club was Massachusetts's best.

Adding to the confusion, Harvard probably boasted the state's finest club. The college nine handily defeated all of the Massachusetts clubs that it played and was very competitive in a grueling schedule of matches against top professional nines such as the Red Stockings of Cincinnati, Mutuals of New York, and White Stockings of Chicago. The summer recesses taken by colleges, however, posed a daunting problem for formal competition, so collegiate nines were often left out of consideration.

All of these factors mean that there was no clear-cut state champion in 1870. Yet the Kearsarge definitely had a legitimate claim and, if the Harvard Club is left out, seem to have had the strongest claim. In October, with the season nearing an end, the *Lowell Daily Citizen and News* wrote, "The Kearsarge club of Stoneham are to play with the Clippers of this city tomorrow afternoon, on the Fair Grounds. This nine stands in the front rank of base ball clubs, having played with every club of note in New England, save the Harvards, and having been victors in every game, with the exception of that played with the Fairmounts of Marlboro, when they were beaten by a score of 24 to 9."[8] The Kearsarges then split two games with the Clippers, and, having also beaten the Fairmounts once, had every right to later boast that they had gone the entire season without losing a series.[9]

The Kearsarge Club seems to have faded out quickly after its stellar 1870 season and, as noted in the 1900 article, was succeeded as Stoneham's standard-bearer by the General Worth Club. As described in the player profiles, many members of the first nine were getting to the age where other priorities took precedence. Massachusetts got its first openly professional club in 1871, the Red Stockings of Boston, and the attention that this club received while winning four National Association pennants left little for the state's amateur and semipro clubs.

Yet the Kearsarge Club deserves to be remembered. Asterisks must be attached to any assertion that the club won a state championship in either 1866 or 1870, but the simple fact that such a claim could be made on behalf of a club from a town the size of Stoneham is impressive. The fact that one of these was accomplished under the Massachusetts rules and the second under the New York rules is quite remarkable. Who can blame the members for bragging about those accomplishments when they gathered in 1894 and 1900?

CLUB MEMBERS (1870 FIRST NINE)

Elbridge Mason Annis: First baseman Elbridge Annis was born in Benton, New Hampshire, on May 1, 1848. He moved with his family to Sheffield, Vermont, before settling permanently in Stoneham around 1856. His younger brother Billy, a future major leaguer, was born the following year. Elbridge Annis left Stoneham soon after his own baseball career ended but didn't move too far away. He eventually settled in Pittsfield, in western Massachusetts, where he served as a deputy sheriff. He died of sudden heart failure on December 15, 1906, while on a fishing trip in Hinsdale. An obituary recalled that Annis was "formerly a well-known baseball player."[10]

Asa G. Hill: Two of the members of the 1870 club shared the surname of Hill, but they were not brothers and may not have been related at all. It was a fortunate coincidence for researchers because it meant that box scores gave initials for both men (instead of the usual practice of publishing only surnames). The third baseman was listed as A.G. Hill and since Asa Hill was one of the attendees at the 1894 reunion there can be little doubt that he was the ballplayer in question. Asa G. Hill was born in November of 1841 and worked in a Stoneham shoe factory as a young man. He married in 1872 but he and his wife had no children. He later worked in a jewelry store and was still in Stoneham in 1910.

Henry F. Hill: The club's shortstop was identified as "H.F. Hill" so is presumed to be Henry F. Hill, who was born on June 27, 1848, and grew up in Stoneham. Henry Hill worked as a shoe cutter in a local shoe factory and never married. He died in Danvers on February 15, 1901.

Amasa Albert Holden: The Kearsarge left fielder is believed to have been A. Albert Holden, who was born in nearby Billerica on April 29, 1847. Holden moved to Stoneham in 1865 to learn the shoemaking trade. In 1871 he went to work in the provision shop of Kittredge and Tweed and eventually became its co-owner, along with his brother George. Holden died at a ripe old age in 1939 and is buried in Lindenwood Cemetery in Stoneham.

Smith: The center fielder of the Kearsarge Club first nine was named Smith and is unidentified.

Charles O. Tay: Charlie Tay, the second baseman and captain of the 1870 Kearsarges, was born in December of 1847 and grew up in Stoneham. As a young man he worked in one of the local shoe factories and also made a name for himself as a billiards player. He later ran a billiard hall in Stoneham but had to close it after being prosecuting for selling liquor without a license. As of 1910, he was still in Stoneham and was associated with a grocery store. Tay died in Lyndeborough, New Hampshire, on April 6, 1919.

Samuel Emmons Tweed: The pitcher's name was usually given as Tweed, though one box score had it as Weed. The only man in Stoneham by that name who seems to fit was Samuel Emmons Tweed, who, in an odd coincidence, married Eliza Weed in Stoneham on November 28, 1867. Tweed was born in Providence on January 24, 1843, and apparently served in the U.S. Navy during the Civil War, though the details have not been pinned down. He and his wife welcomed their first child on August 26, 1870, meaning that he was a new father when he pitched the Kearsarge Club to its big wins that fall. Perhaps that new responsibility had something to do with the fact that little more was heard from the club. Tweed remained in Stoneham and worked as a trader. He died on October 9, 1915, at the old soldiers' home in Chelsea, Massachusetts.

Peter H. Wilkins: The right fielder was named Wilkins and it seems very likely that he was Peter H. Wilkins, a neighbor of Elbridge Annis. Born in 1846, Wilkins worked in a shoe factory and was foreman of the General Worth fire company. He was still living in Stoneham in 1920.

Young: The catcher had the surname of Young and has not been identified.

Other Club Members: The above players were the first nine of the 1870 club. The make-up of the 1866 nine is, unfortunately, unknown, though it presumably included several of the same players. The 1894 article mentioned William H. Marden and Myron J. Ferren as early members of the club. The article listed forty or so of the attendees at the reunion but not all of them seem to have been club members. In addition, even those who had been members may not have played for the club; according to the article, the club had 150 members during its prime.

SOURCES: "Famous Old Club," *Boston Globe*, March 23, 1894, 13; "Heroes of 40 Years Ago," *Boston Globe*, March 19, 1900, 9; contemporaneous newspapers.

Notes

1. "Heroes of 40 Years Ago," *Boston Globe*, March 19, 1900, 9.
2. "Famous Old Club," *Boston Globe*, March 23, 1894, 13.
3. *Boston Daily Advertiser*, September 17, 1866; *Springfield Republican*, September 18, 1866, 4; "Famous Old Club," *Boston Globe*, March 23, 1894, 13. According to the *Advertiser*, the eleven clubs were Excelsior of Upton, Wyoma [?] of Lynn, Liberty of Danvers, Alpha of Ashland, Active of Salem, Wencehuse [?] of Lynn, Union of Danvers, Warren of South Danvers, Warren of Randolph, Peabody of Danvers, and Kearsarge of Stoneham.
4. *Boston Daily Advertiser*, September 11, 1866.

5. *Springfield Republican*, October 9, 1866, 4; *Boston Journal*, October 8, 1866, 4.

6. *Boston Herald*, November 11, 1868, 6.

7. *Ibid.*

8. *Lowell Daily Citizen and News*, October 14, 1870.

9. *Boston Journal*, August 16, 1870, 1.

10. "Deputy Sheriff Annis Dead," *Springfield Republican*, December 16, 1906, 12.

❖ *Clipper Base Ball Club of Lowell* ❖
(Peter Morris)

CLUB HISTORY

"In 1864 and 1865 base ball [in Lowell] was almost un-known, 'round ball' and cricket being the only games of ball played at that time, besides foot ball. In 1865 base ball again began to attract the attention of lovers of athletic sports, it having recovered somewhat from the 'set-back' which the great rebellion caused, and the game became quite popular in New York, and it also began to excite somewhat a local interest; and in 1866 the first genuine nine in this city was organized, and was known as the 'Clippers.' This nine was the pioneer nine of this city. It was run on what is called now the co-operative plan, each man receiving an equal amount of the receipts. This team was composed of young men whose only time they could practice was a few hours every week, but for all that it was a decidedly stiff team for those times, and attracted much at-tention among sporting men, both local and otherwise."[1] So wrote the *Lowell Courier* in 1877 and that account provides a good summary of the club's early years and is unusually specific about its financial arrangements.

Longtime Clipper catcher Ben Whitney later recalled that the club was founded when Josiah W. White "got it into his head to organize a ball nine to play a game which would be livelier than cricket." A meeting was called at which the club was formally organized and Whitney was elected captain. A first nine was also reportedly chosen at this meeting, though the accompanying list of the players who made up that first nine included so many obvious errors that its veracity remains doubtful.[2]

Neither of these articles provided specific dates, but the club itself recognized March of 1866 as its date of origin.[3] The Clipper Base Ball Club is not known to have played any match games that spring or summer, apparently sticking to practice sessions. That may have been appropriate if we are to believe the assessment of the author of the 1877 account, who wrote dismissively: "In those days a player could make five or six square muffs in a game and nothing be thought of it."[4]

Nevertheless the Clippers worked hard at mastering the game and made steady progress. A few other baseball clubs were formed in the Lowell area in 1866 and that fall witnessed the town's first significant series of match games.[5]

The opposing nine was the Centralville Club, which had been formed so recently that the Clippers were now amusingly described as an "old" club.[6] Centralville, now best known as the birthplace of beat poet and baseball board game enthusiast Jack Kerouac, had been annexed by Lowell in 1851 but remained a distinct community. Perhaps that was why the games were surprisingly contentious.

The Clippers won all three contests handily, but instead of accepting the outcomes philosophically, as new clubs of the era usually did, the losses came "as a surprise to the Centralville boys." Particularly surprising is that the men who umpired the games had their rulings regularly second-guessed by the players. "We were very sorry to see so much fault finding with the Umpire's decisions," chastised the *Courier* after the second game, "and hope it will not occur again. Abide by his judgment always, and the game will be far pleasanter. We hope he will not think members of either club an ungentlemanly set, for none would have done so had they thought a moment."[7]

The rebuke seems to have been taken to heart by some, but not all, of the players. After the final game, they were again reminded: "We are glad to see that both clubs were not so severe in their denunciations of the Umpire as in former games. We hope they will still continue to improve. Let each one of our ball players strive to abide by his decisions, whether right or wrong, and the game will prove far more interesting."[8]

On that note, the first season of the Clipper Base Ball Club of Lowell came to a close. Over the following two years, the club did not host any notable clubs and stayed close to home on the few occasions when it ventured outside of Lowell. Yet while the club remained anonymous on the national baseball scene, these were years of great activity spurred by the emergence of several notable local rivals.

There was, for example, a club formed at the Bartlett grammar school that was "was known by the name of the Unions. Although they were quite young yet they played a good game of ball and had several hot skirmishes with the Rockets of Belvidere [another Lowell neighborhood that had been independent until being annexed in 1834]." Another Belvidere nine, "the Fearless club ... superseded the Rockets and the games between them and the Unions were hot and closely contested for those times." Belvidere also boasted the Lightfoot club, whose "chief competitors were the Hopes, a club of young men from the South common." Lowell, mean-while, produced the Eurekas, the Shamrocks and no doubt many other clubs whose names are lost to history.[9]

Yet another new club, the Sheridans, carried on the quarrelsomeness of the series that ended the 1866 season. The Sheridan Club was later described as being "a rattling club, composed of boys from St. Patrick's parish. The boys could fight as well as play ball, and many a game on the North common was settled by a 'scrap.'" According to Ben Whitney, "whenever the score was close the kicking became general and the umpire had to take the consequences. The rumpus oftentimes approached the riot point."[10]

The most formidable of all of the Clippers' rivals was the Salmons, organized in June of 1867 by employees of the Lawrence Manufacturing Company.[11] Lowell was one of the first American cities to spring up as a direct result of the Industrial Revolution, so it was appropriate that it also featured one of the first company baseball teams. Taking advantage of Lowell's flourishing mills, the Lawrence Manufacturing Company was incorporated in 1831 and manufactured textile products such as shirtings, sheetings, and printing cloth. The vast majority of its employees were female, but there were also enough men to form the Salmon Club, which was named in honor of William F. Salmon, the firm's principal agent.[12]

The rash of new clubs in 1867 and 1868 made Lowell the site of many exciting games. According to one of the retrospective pieces, those clubs "played ball in those days for glory and not for cash. There were some hotly contested games, as soon as the principles of the game were understood. Games were played for no better a prize than a ball. The prize was kept on exhibition in Joe White's store. In a glass case were a number of brackets in the shape of gilded hands, and in the hand belonging to the winning club was placed the ball after a game. It was a good bulletin of a game for the crowd outside could tell if the prize had changed hands. Then in this case was a miniature diamond and on it was placed from time to time the prize balls of several clubs for during that summer many nines were organized."[13]

The Clippers were especially eager to spur on such rivalries, joining the New England Association of National Base Ball Players and proclaiming themselves willing to play any Lowell club for the city championship.[14] Everything was in place for vibrant local competition except for one thing — clubs that were evenly enough matched for there to be suspense about the outcome.

At the Agricultural Fair in September 1867 the Clippers and Salmons met in a highly anticipated contest for a prize offered by the Middlesex North Society.[15] The game, however, ended with the Clippers victorious by the overwhelming score of 66–9 and the local press published only brief accounts.[16]

The Eurekas and the argumentative Sheridans were not quite as strong as the Salmons, yet they "had good individual players" and boldly took on the "crack Clippers." Predictably, each challenger "came out second best, as the Clippers were determined to be 'king pins.' Their main strength, however, lay in the perfect harmony with which they played their games,

each man playing to win. To this important feature the Clippers owed many of their victories."[17]

The clear supremacy of the Clippers helped to maintain a healthy gap between the city's pioneer club and its local rivals. The champions "continued to strengthen themselves by picking up good players from all over the city," making it even harder for other Lowell clubs to keep pace.[18] It soon became necessary for the Clippers to look outside of Lowell to find well-matched opponents.

The first such rivalry of note was with the Rollstone Club of nearby Fitchburg in an 1867 best-of-three series billed as being for the "championship of the Fifth Base Ball District."[19] This designation puzzled a reporter for the Courier who wanted to know why clubs from the state's 7th and 4th Congressional districts were contesting for this title. The answer was provided by the *Citizen and News*, which explained, "the base-ballites are not politicians and do not apportion their clubs as such. The fifth base ball district of New England includes, among others, a club from Providence, R.I., and another from Portland, Me."[20] No explanation was given of how the dividing lines had been drawn.

The Clippers won the first game of the series on their home grounds. The Rollstones rebounded to win the second contest, a loss that was blamed on the Fitchburg ballpark's "uneven ground, to which the Rollstone club were [sic] well accustomed."[21] No such excuses, however, could be offered after the third game, which was played in Boston and which resulted in a 45–35 triumph for the Rollstones.

The Clippers also scheduled match games against the likes of the Shields of East Cambridge, the Lawrence Base Ball Club, and the Independents of Leominster in 1867. The playing season wrapped up with a planned series against Harvard's baseball nine. The first game, played on the Boston Common in early October, ended with the collegians on the long end of a 45–27 score. A second game was scheduled to be played in Lowell and elaborate plans were made to entertain the visitors, but the Harvard students were forced to cancel at the last minute.[22]

The fall of 1867 also brought the somber news of the sudden death of club member Clarence Lovejoy. The Clippers responded by holding a special meeting, at which they passed resolutions of condolence for Lovejoy's parents and vowed that "the members of this association will throw around his memory a halo of pleasant recollection."[23] Lovejoy was only 20 years old.[24]

In 1868 the Clippers continued their gradual trend toward looking outside of Lowell for suitable opponents. While continuing to face local opponents, they also played matches against the Websters of North Woburn, Kearsarges of Stoneham, Mishawaums of Woburn, Eagles of Natick, Unions of Lynnfield Centre, and the Harvard nine.

The July 16 visit of the Harvard nine, postponed from the previous fall, was an especially big event for the Clipper

Club. The match was played at the local fairgrounds and a ten-cent admission fee was charged in order, it was explained, to "defray expenses."[25] It was likely the first time that anyone paid to watch a baseball game in Lowell.

The spectators were treated to a "spirited match" and some "fine playing" by the home side, but in the end the Harvard Club prevailed, 27–15. Both sides shared in a postgame meal and things appeared to have gone well, though no doubt the Clippers were disappointed by the outcome.[26] There was no way to anticipate what was going to happen next.

On the following afternoon, Clipper player Amos Blake committed suicide by jumping into the Suffolk Canal. Blake had in his possession some of the club's bats and balls, which he had carefully marked as belonging to the Clippers. He left a suicide note but it gave no explanation of his motives, stating only: "I'm in the water, back of the house; see that I am got out." Friends of the dead man suspected that too much exposure to the sun, perhaps during the previous day's game, had "exhausted his energies and impaired his reasoning facilities."[27] According to another account: "The deceased has exhibited evidence of insanity at times since the 4th of July when he became heated in playing a base ball match as a member of the Clipper Club, and being of a nervous temperament, the defeat of the club on Thursday is believed to have aggravated his disease."[28] For the second time in less than a year, a special meeting of the Clipper Club was held and resolutions of sympathy were unanimously adopted.[29]

The Clippers bounced back, however, and in August its members were commended for their courage in helping to extinguish a dangerous fire at a Lowell mill. The players, according to a Lowell newspaper, "made themselves particularly useful by their united exertions, working in a body, and illustrating in a quiet way the advantage of training as athletes."[30]

September brought one of the most memorable games in club history. Trailing the Eagles of Natick 6–3 after seven innings, the Clippers put together an eight-run eighth-inning rally and pulled out an 11–7 victory. In an era when "close games ... were something like 57 to 48," the efficient fielding of both sides caused a great stir in Lowell.[31] The next day's paper recorded: "It was conceded by all 'ballists' present that this was the sharpest game ever played on the grounds."[32] Nearly a decade later, the match was still remembered as having been "probably the best game played in the country at that time."[33]

For the still-young national pastime and for amateur clubs like the Clippers, 1869 was a year of transition. After years of preaching the virtues of amateurism, the National Association of Base Ball Players had at last sanctioned openly professional play during the off-season. This brought new levels of press coverage to clubs like Cincinnati's Red Stockings and made it possible for top players to earn a living without subterfuge, but it was a daunting problem for the many clubs in cities and towns that were not yet ready to support professional ball and

where the players were not skilled enough to compete against professional nines. A club like the Clippers could of course try to hire professionals of their own but that would represent an enormous leap of faith that might not be rewarded.

It was quite a dilemma and it dogged the Clippers throughout the 1869 season. There were early-season reports that the first nine had been improved by the recent arrival in town of new talent, suggesting that the club may have been considering professionalism. If so, however, it soon reconsidered. The first nine eventually selected — George Conway, p; Whitney c, White, ss; Temple 2b; Carter 1b; Cooledge 3b; Hill rf; Church cf; Davis lf— consisted almost entirely of familiar names, while the entire Lowell baseball scene was lethargic.[34]

"The interest in base ball," the *Lowell Courier* complained in early August, "does not appear to be so great among leading clubs as in years previous. We learn that the Clipper Club is to be re-organized. An unusually small number of games with out of town clubs have been played this season."[35]

This may have had more to do with the new era of open professionalism than with a lack of interest on the part of the Clippers. With clubs like the Red Stockings hogging the headlines, matches against fellow amateur clubs from neighboring towns had suddenly lost much of their luster, but bringing in a top professional nine to compete against was sure to result in an embarrassing loss. What to do?

In mid–August, the Clipper Club sprang back to life and began trying every possible means of addressing a seemingly intractable dilemma. Among those efforts was an attempt to bring one celebrated professional club, the Eckfords of Brooklyn, to Lowell. The negotiations eventually fell through, however, and the explanation given was illuminating. According to a Lowell newspaper, "The Eckford base ball club ... expressed a willingness to come here and play with the Clippers for the guarantee of $100 and expenses — rain or shine, but the members of our home clubs were not anxious enough to be beaten to pay that sum for the privilege."[36]

As a result, the Clippers faced no truly professional clubs in 1869. Curiously, however, the first game of a home-and-home series against the Tri-Mountains of Boston was billed as being just such a David-versus-Goliath struggle. A Lowell reporter informed his readers that the visiting club was the state champion and added: "It will be remembered that the Tri-mountain club has a salaried nine, every one of whom is a crack player."[37]

It's a puzzling claim, to say the least. There is of course no way to prove that a club was not professional, but there is no credible evidence that the members of the Tri-Mountains were receiving salaries. The claim that each of them was a "crack player" can be categorically dismissed; none of them had a national reputation and the Tri-Mountain Club lost by a lopsided margin whenever it faced an actual professional nine that season. So perhaps the reporter was misinformed or maybe he was trying to drum up local interest by exaggerating the strength of the visitors. If the latter, the ploy may have backfired by intimidating the Clippers, who lost both games to the supposedly professional Tri-Mountains though the two sides seem to have been evenly matched.

The Clippers' efforts to bring strong competition to Lowell were not restricted to professional nines (real or imagined). Several attempts were made to schedule another visit by the Harvard nine, which was probably the only amateur club with enough prestige to draw a large crowd in Lowell. A match was arranged, but to the considerable disappointment of their hosts the collegians canceled at the last minute. The contest was rescheduled for October 2 and this time the Harvard nine did indeed appear, only to leave after five innings with the score tied in order to catch a train.[38]

Even matches against amateur clubs from neighboring towns were not always easy to arrange. A challenge to a club in Chicopee elicited the response that that town's nine "declined to play with so renowned a club as the Clippers."[39] A victory in Salem over the Lightfoot Club revealed that visiting clubs could no longer expect much in the way of hospitality. "On arriving at Salem," grumbled a Lowell reporter, "the Clippers were received by an enthusiastic crowd of bootblacks and escorted to the base ball grounds, none of the Salem boys making their appearance."[40]

Despite these setbacks, the Clippers rebounded from the sluggish start to the 1869 season and showed great energy during its last few months. The revival started on September 1 with the introduction of a "very neat uniform of gray throughout, trimmed with purple, with a shield on which the letter 'C' is worked on the shirt fronts. The uniforms attracted much attention and were generally admired." New belts, specially ordered from New York, were expected to arrive any day and complete the outfit.[41]

Attired in these dapper new uniforms, the Clippers played a grueling fall schedule and finished the 1869 season with 14 wins and the tie against Harvard in 19 match games, totals that far surpassed those of previous seasons.[42] "The Clipper Club have [sic] had a very successful season this year in their match games," wrote a Courier reporter in a summary, "although it has been seldom that an opportunity has been offered for all the members to get together for practice. Their first nine has never been better, and has not changed during the season."[43]

Viewed through the more exacting lens of history, however, it is impossible to arrive at such a rosy outlook on the Clippers' 1869 campaign. Even during the bustle of the final months, it remained evident that the club was caught in the middle of baseball's rocky transition to professionalism. This reality was vividly demonstrated by an effort to stage a major tournament in Lowell in October.

The original plans, announced in mid–September, were as follows: "A great base ball tournament, to which all the well-established clubs in the state — over one hundred in number —

are to be invited, is to take place at the Lowell Riding Park on Monday and Tuesday, Oct. 4th and 5th. The first prize to be played for is a silver ball valued at $100 for the best club in the state, and the second prize is to be a ball valued at $50 for the best in this city. The arrangements for the game will be made by representatives of the different clubs on the first morning of the tournament."[44]

Early reports had a significant number of clubs from around the state planning to attend. Then, however, it was announced that the tournament would last for four or five days, possibly longer if necessary.[45] It was an ill-advised change since few baseball nines consisted entirely of men who could afford to be away from home for that long. In addition, the era when club members were excited about competing for a silver ball had passed — Massachusetts had in fact recently had such a trophy that had been melted down because it caused too many disputes. These problems were compounded by a bad storm on the first day and turned the tournament into a disaster.

When the weather finally cleared, there were only four clubs on hand: three Lowell clubs, the Salmons, Eurekas, and Clippers, along with the Atalantas of Stoneham. "It is a matter of regret," observed the Courier's reporter, "that only one out of town club is yet here prepared to play for the state ball," though he maintained that "the non-appearance of others is not in consequence of a lack of proper notice and effort on the part of the management."[46]

Whatever the reason, the outcome of the tournament was now "regarded as a foregone conclusion."[47] As everyone anticipated, the Clippers earned both the prize balls by defeating the Salmons and Atalantas once apiece and the Eurekas twice. Just as predictably, attendance was disappointing, creating a financial loss for the owner of the local racetrack at which the event was staged.[48]

After the final game of the tournament an extraordinary scene took place:

> At the conclusion of the match the members of the different clubs present were drawn up in a semi-circle, near the base ball grounds, and the award of the beautiful balls made, the Clippers winning both, according to the published rules governing the tournament. The presentation was made by W.F. Salmon, esq., on behalf of the management, in an address quite appropriate to the occasion. He referred to the fact that the Clipper club had won both city and State balls, a victory creditable to the club, although but one club out of the city had contended for the State ball. He expressed gratification at witnessing the growing interest in base ball in our city. He took this occasion, however, to make one suggestion to members of the different clubs. They should recollect that others were present on the playing grounds beside themselves. Much depends upon the manner in which a game is played. The ball players should be careful about their language, as many ladies are often present, but will not continue to lend the benefit of their influence if improper language is used. Those engaged in the game will have different classes or spectators to witness their proficiency, according as

they conduct themselves. The game will be made additionally popular if the members of the different clubs conduct themselves properly. We have clubs in Lowell of which we may well feel proud. These balls (the speaker addressing himself to Mr. Whitney, captain of the Clippers) are not champion balls, but are the property of the Clipper club, to dispose of as they see proper. If they are content afterward to enter them for competition they can do so at their option.

The game yesterday afternoon had been a source of gratification to the spectators, and there was much good playing on both sides. He concluded by expressing the hope that next year the Clippers would prove themselves worthy of continuing to hold the ball as champions of the state, and that the clubs of the city would continue to hold as honorable a position as they do at present.

The city and state balls being presented to Capt. Whitney on behalf of the Clippers he responded briefly. He acknowledged the propriety of the remarks made in the presentation address upon the subject of the conduct of members of the contesting clubs upon the baseball field, and expressed his feeling that there was often a lack of caution in this particular. The members of the club which he represented had endeavored during the tournament to do no discredit to themselves or the city, and should continue the effort to be worthy of commendation. In conclusion he thanked the management of the tournament for kindnesses and courtesies received, and expressed the feeling that his club would offer the ball for competition. Cheers were given for the members of the competing clubs, for Mr. Davis of the Riding Park and others who had participated, in one form or another in the tournament, and the members of the different clubs then dispersed.[49]

The bizarre scene spoke volumes about the plight of amateur clubs during baseball's new era of openly professional play. After four seasons of steady improvement, the Clippers had become, as one later account put it, "a decidedly stiff team and one not easily defeated" and were too good for meaningful rivalries with other local amateur clubs.[50] Yet there still seemed to be an insurmountable gap separating them from their professional brethren. Clubs such as the Clippers seemed to have no viable course open to them and it would have been understandable if they had chosen that moment to disband.

Instead, after having had a winter to mull over their future, the members made a conscious decision to play against the "leading clubs of the country" in 1870.[51] In early May the city of Lowell was electrified by the news that the celebrated Red Stockings of Cincinnati and several other noted clubs would be paying visits to the Riding Park.[52]

The Clipper Base Ball Club did not bring in any outside professionals to augment its first nine, but it did take some subtle steps in that direction. In March, the club's bank account was enhanced by throwing a "grand party" at a local dance hall, with music provided by a quadrille band.[53] The Clippers also began enlisting "honorary members" whose dues were to be used "to establish a fund, to help the 'nine' to defray incidental expenses incurred by them in their games."[54]

There was such an encouraging initial reception to this plan that, with the visit of the Red Stockings rapidly approaching, the "honorary members of the Clipper base ball club ... decided to make an effort to increase the number of honoraries and thereby secure the co-operation of as many of the lovers of the national game of base ball as possible. Circulars have been issued, extending invitations for honorary membership, the amount required of each honorary being $3. This amount being paid, he is entitled to a badge, which will admit him to all matches played this season, and games are to be played with the leading clubs of the country. It is hoped that this circular will meet with a cordial and general response."[55] It did indeed, according to a follow-up piece that noted: "The new feature of introducing honorary members into the Clipper Club is working well, quite a number of people having sent in their names. All who become honorary members before Wednesday noon will receive a badge, and can therefore have free admittance to witness the game against the Redstockings, on that day."[56]

The excitement continued to build, but concerns also began to surface. To begin with, there was the unprecedented admission fee being charged to spectators. "Some complaint is made that the price for the base ball match (50 cents) tomorrow is too high," noted the *Courier* on the eve of the match. It explained apologetically that "The price is fixed by the Red Stockings, who wouldn't hear of anything less, and is not the fault of any of our own people, who wanted it reduced."[57] Then too, how would the crowd react if the mighty Red Stockings pinned a humiliating loss on the home side? Hoping to lower expectations, the *Lowell Daily Citizen and News* explained to its readers: "It is not supposed that the Clippers will play the Redstockings an even game, but the contest will be interesting."[58]

Plans were made to meet the famous ballplayers at the depot on the morning of the game and give them a tour of Lowell's renowned mills.[59] Then it was on to the Riding Park, where the Clippers would have their chance to face a club in the midst of one of baseball's greatest winning streaks. (Only six days after the game in Lowell, the Red Stockings were destined to meet their first defeat since 1868.)

Of course the visitors won the game with ease, 32–5. An account in the *Courier*, written by a "special base ball reporter ... in the original base ball dialect," noted that the Clippers' "batting was weak — very weak." Consolation was taken, however, from the home side's fine play in the field: "The game was a very neatly played one, the Clippers playing better in the field than any of their most sanguine friends had anticipated.... The Clippers ... kept their opponents' score down to thirty-two, which is less than they have made against most clubs this year."[60]

The *Daily Citizen and News* offered a similar verdict. Its reporter concluded that "where the Clippers failed most was in their batting; the swift balls they received [from Cincinnati pitcher Asa Brainard] puzzling them all through." But he had praise for the fielding done by several local players and noted that the Clippers' "defeat is not as decisive as in the case of four-fifths of the clubs who play with the Cincinnati nine."[61]

Most encouraging of all was the "large crowd of spectators, many of whom were ladies.... The receipts were quite gratifying, the gross amount received by the Red Stocking from the admittance money being about $140, in addition to the amount realized by the Clippers. The match will doubtless have an influence toward increasing the interest in base ball in this city."[62]

The "celebrated Mutual base ball club of New York" followed the Red Stockings to Lowell less than two weeks later.[63] In hopes of attracting another big crowd — and perhaps in acknowledgment of the previous grumbling — the admission fee was reduced to twenty-five cents for men, while female spectators were "free, and ... especially invited to be present."[64] Nonetheless the turnout was only half as large, with unseasonably cold weather undoubtedly keeping some away.[65]

After four innings the Mutuals were clinging to a narrow 8–7 lead and it looked as though a major upset might be in the offing. But then the visitors pulled comfortably ahead and "the game commenced to wane, the Clippers seemingly losing the greater share of their interest, and consequently their good play."[66] The final score was 34–14.

Nobody seems to have enjoyed the afternoon very much, least of all the miserable spectators, who "could scarcely keep comfortable without frequent change of position."[67] The Mutuals had been scheduled to stay until the following morning and go on a tour of several Lowell factories, but they elected to catch an early train instead.[68]

The recent contest against the Red Stockings had brought predictions of a great increase in baseball activity in Lowell, but the Mutuals' visit elicited less optimistic assessments. "The Clippers of course did not expect to take the laurels from this 'professional' nine, nor did anyone expect them to, and perhaps they did as well as could be hoped," wrote the *Daily Citizen and News*. "What has been said before is equally true now, and that is, that the Clippers, with practice, will make one of the best clubs in New England."[69]

It was a realistic appraisal and the members of the Clippers seemed to have recognized its wisdom. A previously announced visit by the professional Olympics of Washington was quietly canceled and for the balance of the 1870 season the Clippers confined their energies to games against New England rivals.[70] Instead of taking on national powerhouses such as the Mutuals, they defeated the Athletics of Manchester, New Hampshire, on the Fourth of July for a $30 prize.[71] Rather than playing the likes of the Red Stockings in front of a huge crowd, they faced the inexperienced Nichols Club of Sandwich, whose players were said to lack "one important element of success, and that is their fielding. In this part of the game there must necessarily be considerable 'running around,' and if all stand motionless in their field positions, as though

rivited [sic] to the spot, their success as a nine, will be small indeed."[72]

There was no glory to be obtained from such matches, but there was plenty of opportunity for camaraderie and fun. Best of all, the results of the games were not foregone conclusions and playing to the best of one's ability could mean the difference between victory and defeat. The previous fall had seen the Clippers win a silver ball that was supposed to represent state supremacy, but now that emblem seems to have been entirely forgotten and Massachusetts' best clubs played for less tangible rewards. As described in the entry on the Kearsarge Club of Stoneham, that club had the strongest claim to the state championship of 1870 but the question attracted little attention.

While the Clippers were not New England's best club, they did win more often than not. A season-ending summary noted, "The total number of runs made Clippers are 469, and by their opponents 429, notwithstanding the fact that they played with many leading clubs of the country. As will be observed the Clippers won 10 games and lost 8 during the season."[73]

A particular source of pride was the club's steady improvement, which culminated in very strong play in September and October. The final four matches resulted in a split with the Kearsarge Club and victories over Boston's two best-known clubs, the Lowells and the Tri-Mountains. The latter victory was earned in particularly dramatic fashion — after a nip-and-tuck affair, the two sides were tied at 21 apiece after nine innings and "it was decided to play an extra inning to settle the matter."[74] The Clippers scored three times in their half of the extra frame and then held the Tri-Mountains to two runs, thereby claiming the win by the narrowest of margins.[75] The heart-stopping conclusion to this "famous game" was still remembered in vivid detail seven years later by a witness who added that the Tri-Mountains had "three men left on bases as the last man retired on a foul bound to left field."[76]

Another wrap-up of the 1870 season noted that "the Clipper base ball club has played sixty-three match games of base ball" during its five years of existence and won all but seventeen of them.[77] It sounded a bit like a eulogy and, with the amateur era now a thing of the past, it might have been best for the Clippers to make the 1870 campaign their final one. Instead the club reassembled for another season.

The 1871 Clippers adopted a uniform modeled upon that of the Red Stockings — indeed the "white flannel knickerbocker pants, loose jacket, blue stockings, and a cap of the same material as the jacket" were said to be virtually identical except for the color of the stockings.[78] But if the hope was that the new uniforms would enable the Clippers to play like the Red Stockings, such did not prove to be the case.

The Red Stocking name had been transferred from Cincinnati to Boston along with manager Harry Wright and many star players. The club's new incarnation paid two visits to Lowell in 1871, but the resulting 19–2 and 29–3 trouncings of the Clippers were of interest to few.[79] A game against the Eckfords of Brooklyn was even more discouraging. A member of the formerly supportive local press wrote that the contest was "a 'jug-handle' game" and added that the play of the Clippers was "never poorer, their fielding and striking being weak and unsatisfactory."[80]

Little more was heard from the Clippers in 1871 and to all intents and purposes that was the end of Lowell's first known baseball club. Baseball as a whole "was a little quiet in Lowell" in 1872 and the Clippers lapsed into inactivity.[81] Some club members made a serious "effort ... to awaken a renewed interest" in the spring of 1873.[82] Several meetings were held, but in the end nothing came of them.

One year later, "the Lowells were thoroughly organized, and so also were the Bartletts. The former club embraced most of the old Clipper stock" and that pioneer ball club gave up baseball.[83] In place of their former sport, the Clippers "formed a social club, with rooms at the corner of Middle and Central street, in the old Sanborn block. They held parties and balls in the winter, and upon their reputation as the 'Clippers of '67' had a long and successful life."[84]

Lowell's subsequent clubs experienced greater success and often overshadowed the accomplishments of the Clippers. The Lowells had especially great seasons in 1875 and 1877, putting the town on the national baseball map for the first time. The Clippers' principal rivals, the Salmons, had started another important tradition of company baseball teams sponsored by Lowell's factories and mills. This too continued to build up strength and in 1886 the champion company team was the Hoods, made up of the employees of C.I. Hood, an "extensive dealer in Hood's Sarsaparilla and other health-giving concoctions." According to a write-up of the club's achievements, "Mr. Hood has allowed the men in his employ to practice ball playing on Saturday afternoons during the warm weather for three years, giving them their pay and encouraging them in many ways. His generosity has had its effect in making the ball players persevering at play and at work, and they do nobly at both.... All of the Hoods drink the Sarsaparilla of their employer and affirm that it helps them win."[85]

But while the Clippers came to be overshadowed by these later Lowell clubs, they were not entirely forgotten. There were still many in town who recalled with fondness the days when the Clipper Base Ball Club had been the "pride of Lowell" and when every player "was a king pin and the small boys worshipped them like 'tin gods.'"[86]

CLUB MEMBERS

Henry J. Boynton: Center fielder Henry Boynton was born around 1850; it is not clear whether he was actually born in Lowell but he lived there for most of his life. Boynton joined the Lowell fire department in 1869 and remained a fixture there

for many decades, becoming known to one and all as "Deacon" Boynton. Boynton died in Lowell on November 28, 1924.[87]

Fred Appleton Buttrick: Fred Buttrick was born in Lowell on January 10, 1848. He pitched for the Clippers in 1867 and was said to have been "quite a pitcher ... until George Conway proved himself more competent for this responsible position."[88] Buttrick began his career as a bank clerk and worked his way up to treasurer and then president of the City Institution for Savings. After giving up baseball Buttrick switched to playing cricket. He died in Lowell on January 13, 1914.[89]

Daniel Stanley "Stannie" Carter: First baseman Stannie Carter was born in New Jersey around 1849. He remained in Lowell after his playing days ended and married Mary White, the sister of Clipper shortstop Joe White. Carter worked as a machinist until losing an eye in a workplace accident. He was later employed by a grocery firm. Carter's death on August 8, 1900, merited a front page obituary in the *Lowell Sun* that observed: "The deceased will be remembered by old-time lovers of the national game of baseball, when the Clipper Baseball club was the crack team of Lowell, if not of New England. Carter, who was familiarly known as 'Stannie,' covered first base and was a 'cracker-jack' in high thrown balls and grounders while attending the initial bag. He was also a clever batsman and was idolized by the local cranks of the latter '60s."[90]

George A. Conway: George and James Conway were the two eldest of at least twelve children born to Joseph and Hannah Conway. George was born in Pawtucket, Rhode Island, on May 19, 1846, and arrived in Lowell with his family around 1856. He was usually the pitcher for the Clippers, but sometimes played other positions. He married around 1868 and briefly left the Clippers in 1870 to pursue a professional career with the Mutual Club of Springfield.[91] Two of George's younger brothers, Dick and Bill Conway, both played major-league baseball and are among only a dozen brother tandems to form a big-league battery.[92] George worked as a cotton operator and was still living in Lowell in 1932 when another old-time ballplayer, James B. Russell, declared that "Mr. Conway, with his straight, fine physique today is a tribute to the game, as a sporting occupation for young men."[93] Conway died in Lowell on October 19, 1936.

James Conway: James Conway, younger brother of George and older brother of two major leaguers, was born in Pawtucket on July 24, 1848. An iron molder by trade, he was still living in Lowell in 1915.

Martin J. Cooledge: Third baseman Martin Cooledge was born in Ireland around 1848. He worked as a machinist, a bartender, and a clerk before his premature death of tuberculosis in Lowell on July 12, 1883.

David W. O'Brien: Dave O'Brien was born around 1846 and worked as a shoe dealer. He was an original member of the first nine but soon moved down to the second nine. O'Brien was still living in Lowell in 1910.

Charles Temple: Later accounts referred to this player as both Edward Temple and George "Goboy" Temple, but it's clear from contemporaneous reports that he was in fact Charles Temple, who also served as club secretary.[94] Charles was born in Lowell on November 16, 1847, and left the state in the mid–1880s to move to Montana, where he farmed and raised a large family.

George B. "Ben" Whitney: Catcher Ben Whitney was born around 1844. The catching position was tremendously demanding in the years before protective equipment and in 1871 the club held a benefit game for Whitney as the result of unspecified injuries.[95] Nevertheless, he returned to action later that season. Whitney joined the Lowell fire department as a driver and worked his way up to being its chief electrician. He was still in that position when he died on December 11, 1895, after a bout with typhoid fever.[96]

Josiah W. "Joe" White: Shortstop and club founder Joe White was born on January 17, 1849, and grew up in Lowell. He opened a clothing business at about the same time as organizing the Clipper Club. According to a later account, "White was credited with being the crack short stop in this section of the country, and at times his backing up of basemen was almost activity itself."[97] White married on July 20, 1870, but his baseball career continued; he was a starter on a celebrated professional club in 1875 and was prominently involved in the management of several Lowell professional clubs during the next few years. His clothing business was also thriving and he branched out into selling baseball paraphernalia. He was also a prominent volunteer firefighter with the Hope Hose Company. In the mid–1880s White's business failed and his marriage came to an end — whether due to death or divorce has not been ascertained. In any case, he left Lowell for Boston and remarried in 1889. White returned to the Lowell area during the 1892 and 1896 presidential campaigns to sell "campaign suits."[98] But he soon returned to Boston, where he was still living as of 1920.

Other Club Members: Bailey, Blaisdell, Amos B. Blake, Blood, Britton, Brown, Butler, H. Church, Clisby, Dr. Cook, Davis, E. Dickey, (Joseph?) Grey, (Horace?) Grover, Hicks, Hill, Lamson, Lane, Clarence Lovejoy, Lowe, Moore, F. Parker, F.T. Parker, Pierce, George Proctor, George A. Roper (scorer), Stewart, Ted Wentworth, Woodward

SOURCES: Retrospective club histories appeared in the *Lowell Courier* on December 8, 1877, page 1, and the *Lowell Sun*, July 20, 1893, page 4. Helpful season summaries appeared in the *Lowell Courier* on November 6, 1869, and November 16, 1870. Otherwise this piece is based upon contemporaneous newspaper coverage, as cited in the notes.

Notes

1. *Lowell Courier*, December 8, 1877, 1.
2. *Lowell Sun*, July 20, 1893, 4.
3. *Lowell Daily Citizen and News*, March 24, 1870, 2.
4. *Lowell Courier*, December 8, 1877, 1.
5. In addition to the Centralville Club, the *Lowell Daily Citizen and News*, May 29, 1866, page 2, reported the formation of the Amateur Club of Lowell and the *Lowell Courier*, October 16, 1866, noted that the Andover Club intended to challenge the Clippers (though there is no indication that the two clubs played that season).
6. *Lowell Daily Citizen and News*, September 28, 1866, 2.
7. *Lowell Courier*, October 16, 1866.
8. *Lowell Daily Citizen and News*, November 30, 1866.
9. *Lowell Courier*, December 8, 1877, 1.
10. *Lowell Sun*, July 20, 1893, 4.
11. *Lowell Daily Citizen and News*, June 20, 1867, 2.
12. *Lowell Courier*, December 8, 1877, 1.
13. *Lowell Sun*, July 20, 1893, 4.
14. *Lowell Daily Citizen and News*, April 29 and May 20, 1867; *Lowell Courier*, April 29, 1867.
15. *Lowell Daily Citizen and News*, September 24, 1867, 2.
16. *Lowell Courier*, September 27, 1867.
17. *Lowell Courier*, December 8, 1877, 1.
18. Ibid.
19. *Lowell Daily Citizen and News*, August 9, 1867, 2.
20. *Lowell Daily Citizen and News*, September 3, 1867, 2.
21. *Lowell Daily Citizen and News*, August 13, 1867, 2.
22. *Lowell Courier*, October 10 and 18, 1867.
23. *Lowell Courier*, September 5, 1867.
24. *Lowell Daily Citizen and News*, August 31, 1867.
25. *Lowell Daily Citizen and News*, July 14, 1868.
26. *Lowell Daily Citizen and News*, July 17, 1868.
27. *Lowell Daily Citizen and News*, July 18, 1868; *Lowell Courier*, July 18, 1868.
28. *Lowell Courier*, July 18, 1868.
29. *Lowell Courier*, July 20, 1868.
30. *Lowell Daily Citizen and News*, August 4, 1868.
31. *Lowell Courier*, December 8, 1877, 1.
32. *Lowell Daily Citizen and News*, September 12, 1868.
33. *Lowell Courier*, December 8, 1877, 1.
34. *Lowell Daily Citizen and News*, August 23, 1869.
35. *Lowell Courier*, August 2, 1869.
36. *Lowell Courier*, October 25, 1869.
37. *Lowell Daily Citizen and News*, August 28, 1869.
38. *Lowell Daily Citizen and News*, October 4, 1869. According to its account, "Before the game opened, the splendid practice catching of the Harvards somewhat prejudiced the spectators in their favor, and intimations were made 'that the Clippers stood no chance; they weren't anywhere.'"
39. *Lowell Daily Citizen and News*, September 9, 1869.
40. *Lowell Courier*, September 24, 1869.
41. *Lowell Courier*, September 2, 1869; *Lowell Daily Citizen and News*, September 2, 1869.
42. The *Courier* gave the club's record as 15–4–1 but that included a muffin game that certainly did not belong in the total.
43. *Lowell Courier*, November 6, 1869.
44. *Lowell Courier*, September 16, 1869.
45. *Lowell Courier*, September 24, 1869; *Lowell Daily Citizen and News*, September 22, 1869.
46. *Lowell Courier*, October 7, 1869.
47. Lowell Courier, October 9, 1869; *Lowell Daily Citizen and News*, October 6, 1869.
48. *Lowell Daily Citizen and News*, October 6, 1869.
49. *Lowell Courier*, October 9, 1869. The same day's *Lowell Daily Citizen and News* offered a similar but much briefer description in which Salmon counseled the players, "You will have around you those whom your conduct warrants."
50. *Lowell Courier*, December 8, 1877, 1.
51. *Lowell Courier*, November 16, 1870, in a detailed summary of all of the club's 1870 games.
52. *Lowell Daily Citizen and News*, May 4, 1870.

53. *Lowell Daily Citizen and News*, March 8, 1870.
54. *Lowell Daily Citizen and News*, May 28, 1870.
55. *Lowell Courier*, May 31, 1870; *Lowell Daily Citizen and News*, June 1, 1870.
56. *Lowell Daily Citizen and News*, June 4, 1870.
57. *Lowell Courier*, June 7, 1870. The *Lowell Daily Citizen and News* of the same date added that the fifty-cent fee was "owing to the expense of bringing the club to the city.".
58. *Lowell Daily Citizen and News*, June 4, 1870.
59. *Lowell Daily Citizen and News*, June 7, 1870.
60. *Lowell Courier*, June 9, 1870.
61. *Lowell Daily Citizen and News*, June 9, 1870.
62. *Lowell Courier*, June 9, 1870. The same day's *Daily Citizen and News* described it as "the largest crowd that has ever witnessed a base ball game in this city.".
63. *Lowell Courier*, June 21, 1870.
64. *Lowell Daily Citizen and News*, June 20, 1870.
65. *Lowell Courier*, June 22, 1870.
66. *Lowell Daily Citizen and News*, June 22, 1870.
67. *Lowell Courier*, June 22, 1870.
68. *Lowell Courier*, June 21 and 22, 1870.
69. *Lowell Daily Citizen and News*, June 22, 1870.
70. *Lowell Daily Citizen and News*, May 4, 1870.
71. *Lowell Daily Citizen and News*, July 5, 1870.
72. *Lowell Daily Citizen and News*, June 27, 1870.
73. *Lowell Courier*, November 16, 1870.
74. *Lowell Daily Citizen and News*, September 26, 1870.
75. *Lowell Courier*, September 26, 1870; *Lowell Daily Citizen and*

News, September 26, 1870. Though the game was played in Lowell, the visitors batted last, as was often the case in that era.
76. *Lowell Courier*, December 8, 1877, 1.
77. *Lowell Courier*, October 20, 1870.
78. *Lowell Daily Citizen and News*, May 29 and 31, 1871.
79. *Lowell Courier*, December 8, 1877, 1.
80. *Lowell Daily Citizen and News*, July 1, 1871.
81. *Lowell Courier*, December 8, 1877, 1.
82. *Lowell Daily Citizen and News*, May 1, 1873.
83. *Lowell Courier*, December 8, 1877, 1.
84. *Lowell Sun*, July 20, 1893, 4.
85. *Lowell Sun*, September 25, 1886, 1.
86. *Manchester* (N.H.) *Mirror*, reprinted in the *Lowell Daily Citizen and News*, June 1, 1871; *Lowell Sun*, July 20, 1893, 4.
87. *Lowell Sun*, November 29, 1924, 48.
88. *Lowell Sun*, July 20, 1893, 4.
89. *Lowell Sun*, January 14, 1914, 2, and January 24, 1914, 3.
90. "Stannie Carter; Old First Baseman of the Clippers," *Lowell Sun*, August 9, 1900, 1.
91. *Lowell Daily Citizen and News*, July 6, 1870, 2.
92. Charlie Bevis, "Bill Conway," SABR BioProject, http://bioproj.sabr.org/bioproj.cfm?a=v&v=l&bid=1372&pid=2778.
93. *Lowell Sun*, September 7, 1932, 9.
94. *Lowell Daily Citizen and News*, April 29, 1867, 2.
95. *Lowell Daily Citizen and News*, April 24, 1871.
96. *Lowell Sun*, December 11, 1895, 5.
97. *Lowell Sun*, July 20, 1893, 4.
98. *Lowell Sun*, August 12, 1896, 8.

❖ *Cummaquid Base Ball Club of Barnstable* ❖
(Peter Morris)

CLUB HISTORY

The Cummaquid Base Ball Club of Barnstable, formed in 1867, didn't introduce baseball to Cape Cod. There can be no doubt that "round ball" — the Massachusetts version of the game — was played on the Cape before the Civil War. Though such games were not as a rule documented, in 1857 a Fourth of July game was played in Falmouth "in which some of the principal men of the place participated."[1] Unquestionably, many more games were played but never recorded for posterity.

The rival New York Game had swept Massachusetts by the end of the war, but even if we restrict our search to the new version, the Cummaquid Club still has no claim to being earliest. That distinction may belong to a group of young men who played a game on School Street in Sandwich in November 1865, but it is more likely that the true identity of those pioneers is lost in the mists of history.[2]

The Cummaquid Club was not even the first organized baseball club on the Cape. Barnstable's earliest known club was preceded by the Nichols Club of Sandwich, founded in 1866 and named in honor of Captain Edward Nichols. As the story goes, Nichols, a retired sea captain, allowed the ballplayers to use his lot without charge when none of the local farmers were willing to rent a suitable ground to them.[3]

For that matter, the Cummaquid Club had a brief history, experienced limited success, earned no renown outside of Cape Cod, and was little remembered in later years. So why is it the only Cape Cod club included in this volume?

That comes down to two simple reasons. First, the Cummaquids received abundant coverage in the *Barnstable Patriot* because two regulars were the sons of editor Sylvanus B. Phinney. Second, the *Patriot* is now freely available and text-searchable on the internet thanks to the historic Sturgis Library's *Barnstable Patriot* digital newspaper archive.[4] There is much truth in the old saying that history is written from the perceptive of victors, but it's often just as true that history is written from the perspective of those who take the trouble to record it.

By 1867 Cape Cod had already started to take shape as a summer resort community. For the last eight or ten weeks of every summer, towns like Barnstable were swollen by an influx of "visitors who ... enjoyed the luxuries of fishing, bathing, boating and the charming afternoon [carriage] drives over the Cape, rendered so refreshing by the ever present pure, real sea air."[5] Then the out-of-towners departed and Barnstable returned to being a sleepy community populated by a small but hardy coterie of year-rounders.

Tourism had yet to be recognized as a legitimate industry

that needed to be cultivated, so Barnstable responded to the annual flood of summer tourists in ad hoc fashion. Then, as now, most of the seasonal residents had been "successful in the grand scramble for money," so there was plenty of "refinement and culture." The appreciation for the finer things meant that "Barnstable boasts, what too many of our small towns cannot, a public library."[6] The library in question was the Sturgis Library, housed in a building first constructed in 1644 for use by Barnstable's founder, the Reverend John Lothrop, and reconstituted as a public library in 1867.[7] Still standing today, the Sturgis Library is now the host of the digital archive that made this piece possible.[8]

Practical needs, however, were sometimes overlooked. As one bemused tourist remarked, visitors to Barnstable could choose from more than 1,200 books but couldn't obtain a shave at any price. "It is a somewhat curious fact," he observed, that "Barnstable ... boasts no professor of the tonsorial art, and the traveler must either take the next train, carry his own barberous instruments, or go unshaven."[9]

The Cummaquid Club took its name from a historic village that had been subsumed by the town of Barnstable. The exact date of the club's formation is not known, but in mid–October 1867 it was reported to be only two months old.[10] There was no mention of the club prior to August of that year, so it seems safe to assume that that was indeed its month of origin. Barnstable's pioneer ballclub was thus yet another product of the bustle of the last two months of summer.

Right from the start, the activities of the Cummaquids were recorded by the *Patriot* in considerable detail. Many new baseball clubs of the era spent months in practice before playing a match game, but Barnstable's representatives were made of sterner stuff: a match against the more experienced Nichols Club was arranged for Saturday, August 10.

On that historic day, the eager players made the twelve-mile trip to Sandwich on the afternoon train, accompanied by a "large number of the friends" of the club, all sporting the club badge. The train dropped the party off at "a beautiful site" selected for the purpose, a short distance from the Sandwich Glass Company's works. There they found that a "tent had been erected and seats prepared in a shady place, for a large number, and all the arrangements — including even 'lemonade' for the crowd — was bountifully supplied."

When the match began, according to the *Patriot*, "it was very soon discovered that several of the finest players in the State were members of the Clubs, and the greatest interest was manifested throughout on both sides." After four innings, the more experienced Nichols Club led by eight runs but then there was a surprising reversal of fortune. When play concluded after the sixth inning, the Cummaquids had won by a score of 25–19!

Next came a "mutual shaking of hands, all round." The home club offered "three hearty cheers for the 'Cummaquids,' which was responded to by them and their friends with a good will." Similar cheers had been freely given during the match itself and, all in all, the afternoon had afforded a perfect "interchange of good feeling between the citizens of Barnstable and Sandwich."

But why were only six innings played? Oddly, no explanation of this significant detail was offered in the *Patriot*'s account. It was said to be "late in the afternoon" when the visiting party headed back to Barnstable so darkness seems an unlikely reason. The most plausible explanation is that the train's schedule accounted for the foreshortened match.[11]

Over the next few months, there was a mention of the Cummaquid Base Ball Club in most of the weekly issues of the *Patriot*. Two weeks after the first match, it was the Nichols Club's turn to visit Barnstable. This time nine innings were played, though it took three hours and forty minutes to do so "and before its close, the players had evidently become quite exhausted." When the grueling contest finally did end, the club from Sandwich had earned a 34–21 victory.[12]

The stage was set for an exciting deciding game, which took place one week later at a neutral site in West Barnstable. After eight innings and another three hours and twenty minutes, the Cummaquids emerged triumphant, 50–17. In the judgment of the *Patriot*'s reporter, "few towns in the State or country can boast of better Clubs: Tilden, Fay, Bacon, Shaw and Baker, of the Cummaquids received the plaudits of the crowd, as did also Dalton, Swansey and Montague, of the Nichols, and there were others deserving of praise for the admirable manner in which they performed their parts.... They would all of them do honor to the best organized Club, not excepting the Atlantic, of Brooklyn."[13]

Was this high praise truly deserved or just a case of a club member gushing about his teammates? No doubt the latter, but if the accomplishment of the Cummaquid Club was exaggerated, the enthusiasm it created was very real.

The second and third Cummaquid-Nichols games had been witnessed by large parties "from this and adjoining villages" and they provided the stimulus for some of those visitors to form clubs of their own.[14] Soon New Bedford boasted the Wamsutta and Onward clubs, Hyannis was the home of the Iyannough Club, Yarmouth took pride in the Mattakeesett Club, and a club known as either the Masketuketts or Moskeetukget had been launched in West Barnstable.[15] Meanwhile Sandwich alone featured four clubs, with the Independents, the Shawmes, and the Americans all having joined the Nichols Club.[16]

With winter approaching, there was no time to lose and the ensuing weeks saw a flurry of baseball activity on Cape Cod, led by the Cummaquids. On September 7 the members traveled the forty-five miles to New Bedford to play a "friendly game" against the Wamsutta Club. They came up on the short end of a 38–13 decision (in seven innings), but the hospitality was exemplary and "the excursionists returned in the evening train delighted with their visit."[17] The Mattakeesetts of

Yarmouth were next up for the Cummaquids and the two sides proved to be a very evenly matched, with a 24–23 Mattakeesett win being followed by a 32–27 victory for the Cummaquids.[18]

The two nailbiters made those clubs ideally suited to taking part in an exciting event. The county's annual agricultural fair was scheduled for October 8–9 and the organizers decided to capitalize on the local baseball fever by arranging a game. The Mattakeesetts and Cummaquids were invited to play for an impressive prize: a "beautiful silver mounted carved black walnut bat, costing $15."[19]

A visitor to Barnstable who was under the mistaken impression that the prize was a cup was moved to observe: "The mania for base ball playing has penetrated even to the Cape, and flourishing clubs are in daily practice both here and at Yarmouth, in anticipation of the contest for a silver cup, a prize offered to the victors by the managers of the Barnstable County Agricultural Fair, to be held here on the 8th of October. I believe this is the first instance in which base ball has ever been treated as an agricultural product. Doubtless the cup is offered on the principle of encouraging domestic industry."[20]

The anxiously awaited game took place on the first day of the fair and proved surprisingly lopsided, with the Cummaquid Club winning, 30–13. After the final out there was an "interchange of compliments between the two clubs" and the trophy bat was presented "to the winning club, in behalf of the Society, in a brief complimentary speech." The Cummaquid Club played again later the same day, losing to the Onward Club of New Bedford.[21]

It seemed that baseball had been smoothly integrated into the county fair but controversy swirled in the days that followed. An article in the *Sandwich Gazette* complained that an "unwarranted slight was put upon the Nichols Club in leaving them entirely out of consideration." Its angry author demanded to know why the Cummaquid Club saw fit to "send out of the county" for an opponent and declared that "there was something wrong in their management of the base ball games at the Fair."[22]

The *Patriot* leapt to the Cummaquids' defense, maintaining that its members "have always endeavored to treat the Nichols Club with courtesy and attention, and accept their challenges whenever tendered." The response pointed out that the matchups at the fair had been arranged by officials of the Agricultural Society and were out of the control of the ballclub. The article closed by listing all twenty-five members of the Cummaquid Club, a seemingly unnecessary gesture but one that proved extremely helpful in compiling the player profiles that follow this history.[23]

The Cummaquid Club remained active in the ensuing weeks. The players traveled fifty miles to Middleboro a few days after the Fair and won a close game from the Monitors.[24] They closed a successful inaugural season with two victories over the Masketuketts/Moskeetukgets of West Barnstable, played on Election Day and Thanksgiving.[25]

After those few months of considerable industry, however, very little was ever heard from the Cummaquid Base Ball Club again. The club did not disband and the *Patriot* published a few brief references to its activities in both 1868 and 1869, but each mention was followed by another long silence.[26] No explanation for these gaps was provided and in 1870 the *Patriot* at last acknowledged that "Base Ball has somewhat 'played out' in these parts."[27] There is no trace of the club after that, though in the mid–1870s a new Barnstable club of young players adopted the name of "Cummaquids Jr." in tribute to their predecessors.

Did the controversy over the agricultural fair create a lasting bitterness that broke up the Cummaquids? Had the players lost interest and moved on to other pursuits? Or did the club remain active only to have the *Patriot* stop reporting its activities because the editor's sons were no longer involved?

As implausible as it may sound, the latter possibility cannot be entirely dismissed. In 1867, the *Patriot* had been unfailingly supportive of the Cummaquid Club but by the spring of 1868 there had been a very noticeable shift in its attitude. According to an openly hostile note, "Several base ball clubs at Boston have disbanded and more are to follow. The furor is evidently subsiding. It is hoped it will not break out again this summer."[28] By 1869 a new editor had taken over from Sylvanus B. Phinney and references to baseball became even less frequent. So it's conceivable that the Cummaquid Club was alive and well for several years after its inaugural season but that its doings were not reported in the local newspaper.

On the whole, however, it seems most likely that the Cummaquid Club was struggling to stay alive during these years. The *Patriot* did publish articles about other baseball clubs on a fairly regular basis, and in the fall of 1868 it mentioned that the Nichols Club had joined the New England Association of Base Ball Players.[29] While the newspaper's coverage was not usually substantive, neither did the hostility continue. So it would appear that both the Cummaquid Club and the editors of the local newspaper simply lost interest in baseball.

Once gone, Barnstable's first baseball club slipped into oblivion. No doubt it was fondly remembered by some of its members, but even in a town that puts an emphasis on preserving history, no retrospective articles about the Cummaquids are known to have appeared during the lifetime of the players.[30] But while there were no reminiscent pieces, the *Patriot* did publish this poem in the summer of 1868 and it serves as a perfect eulogy of Barnstable's pioneer baseball club:

Base Ball
The noon-day sun was pouring down
Upon a meadow, sere and brown,
Where stood a youth, with bat on high,
Loud to his comrades rang the cry,
"Base Ball!"

He hopes to win himself a name,
By playing soon "a great match game."
For him 'twill be the greatest fun,
To hear the words "Cummaquids have won."
     "Base Ball!"

His brow was bumped, his eye was black;
His coat was torn from off his back;
But still, like battered bugle, rung
The accents of that swollen tongue,
     "Base Ball!"

Around the field he saw the light
Of friendly faces, beaming bright.
Just by his head a ball has flown,
And from this lips escapes a groan,
     "Base Ball!"

"Now stop this game," the old man said,
"The 'second base' has smashed his head;
The 'pitcher,' too, has sprained his wrist;
The umpire's brain is in a mist;
     "Base Ball!"

"Oh! Drop that bat," the maiden said,
"And make a long 'home run' instead;
A "hot ball" hit him in the eye,
But still he answered, with a sigh,
     "Base Ball!"

"Beware! you'd soon be out on foul!"
This was the fielder's awful howl;
But still there echoed in his ear,
In that deep voice, so thick and queer,
     "Base Ball!"

"Used up," he sinks upon the ground,
While pitying comrades gather round,
And in the awful throes of death,
He murmurs, with his latest breath,
     "Base Ball."

There, on the cool earth, drear and gray,
To perfect jelly, smashed, he lay;
While o'er the autumn fields afar,
Was heard the victor's loud huzza,
     "Base Ball."[31]

CLUB MEMBERS

Note: As befits the summer resort town that Barnstable was already becoming, the Cummaquid Club did not use a stable lineup in the relatively few games for which box scores are available. The following are the players who appeared in at least one game and could be identified with a reasonable degree of confidence based upon the listings in box scores and the list of club members that appeared in the *Barnstable Patriot* on October 22, 1867.

Davis Annable: Center fielder Davis Annable was born in New Orleans on September 2, 1846, the son of Freeman and Mehitable Annable, and grew up in Barnstable. He became a sailor and lived for some time in New York, then moved on to San Francisco, where he was first officer of the steamship City of Paris when he died on December 17, 1898, of pyaemia.[32]

Francis W. Bacon: The younger of one of a number of brother tandems on the Cummaquid Club, Frank Bacon was born in Boston in October of 1849. He became a stockbroker and lived in San Francisco and then New York City, where he was reunited with his brother. He was only 54 when he died in Manhattan on February 11, 1904.

Horace Bacon: Horace Bacon, Frank's older brother, was the club's pitcher in its first game. Born in Boston around 1845, he became a Wall Street real-estate agent. He died in Manhattan on April 9, 1915.[33]

James Clagg: Second baseman James Clagg was born on February 27, 1841, and appears to have served in the Civil War. He was appointed postmaster of Barnstable in 1866 and served for fourteen years, being succeeded by teammate Alfred Crocker. He lived in Barnstable until his death on May 20, 1925.

Alfred Crocker: Third baseman Alfred Crocker, Sr., was born on November 3, 1844, and lived in or near Barnstable for his entire life. He was in the salt manufacturing business with his father until around 1873, when he became a railway postal clerk. In 1880, he succeeded James Clagg as postmaster at Barnstable. He continued to serve the city in many capacities, including clerk of the Superior Court, deputy sheriff, and as a member of the school committee, as well as working as an undertaker. Crocker died on October 31, 1930, a few days shy of his 86th birthday.

Joseph Story Fay, Jr.: Joseph Fay was born into a prominent and wealthy Boston family in 1847. His father, Joseph Fay, Sr., played a significant role in establishing Cape Cod as a popular summer resort for Boston's elite, so Joseph, Jr. split his early years between that city and Barnstable.[34] He was still completing his preparatory studies when he played first base for the Cummaquid Club in 1867. He enrolled directly in Harvard Law School in 1868 and during the next two years earned a reputation as one of the country's best single scullers. In 1869 Fay was part of the Harvard Varsity Crew that beat Yale and also went to England with the Harvard crew to row against Oxford. He then entered the iron trade and became president of the Champion Iron Company and treasurer of the Lake Superior Iron Company. In later years, his love of sports shifted to horse racing and yachting. Joseph Fay died in Boston on February 4, 1912.[35]

E.B. Hallett: Third baseman E.B. Hallett appears to be Edward B. Hallett, though he was quite a few years older than the other players. Born in April of 1834, Hallett died of tuberculosis on May 1, 1875.

Charles A.C. Harris: Right fielder Charles Harris was born on June 15, 1841, and was the brother of shortstop Marcus Harris. Charles Harris became a mariner and lived all over the country, but eventually returned home and died in Barnstable on May 24, 1922.[36]

Marcus N. Harris: Shortstop Marcus Harris, the younger brother of Charles, was born in September of 1848. While his brother was roaming the high seas, Marcus never left Barnstable and became a successful coal merchant. After an extremely long life, he died in Barnstable on December 28, 1942.

Robert John Walker Phinney: Catcher Robert Phinney was born on April 10, 1847, and was one of two sons of *Patriot* editor Sylvanus Phinney to play on the Cummaquid Club. Robert Phinney worked as a cotton mill agent and a bookkeeper and died in Woburn, Massachusetts, on September 28, 1900.

Theodore Warren Phinney: Left fielder Theodore Phinney was Robert's older brother, born on July 13, 1845. He worked for his father at the *Barnstable Patriot* from 1860 to 1868, and no doubt had much to do with the paper's generous coverage of the club's activities. After marrying in 1873, he left Barnstable for West Virginia but eventually returned to his native state. He was living in Malden, Massachusetts, a suburb of Boston, when the 1920 census was taken.

E.F. Smith: The first baseman was listed as E.F. Smith. It's always a challenge to identify a man named Smith, but it seems likely that our man was Ebenezer Franklin Smith, Jr., who was born in nearby Harwich on December 20, 1845. His later whereabouts have not been determined.

Other Club Members: R.N. Baker, W. Chipman, Dehon, Drew, F.I. Gray, Frank Hallett, H.A. Hinckley, Dolly Huckins, Melchin Kramer, Frank Low, Parker, E.P. Percival, Perkins, O. Shaw, Orlando Smith, George Tilden, Fred Whelden

SOURCES: David Still II, "Play Ball! An Incomplete History of Baseball on Cape Cod," *Barnstable Patriot*, June 25, 2009; James H. Ellis, "Cape Cod League a Talent Showcase," *Baseball Research Journal* 15 (1986), 56–59; contemporaneous accounts in the *Barnstable Patriot*, as cited in the notes and as retrieved from the Sturgis Library's *Barnstable Patriot* Digital Newspaper Archive.

Notes

1. *Barnstable Patriot*, July 7, 1857, 3. Another article about baseball appeared in the *Patriot* on April 17, 1860 (page 1).

2. James H. Ellis, "Cape Cod League a Talent Showcase," *Baseball Research Journal* 15 (1986), 57, citing a reminiscence in an unspecified 1926 issue of the *Sandwich Independent*.

3. David Still, II, "Play Ball!: An Incomplete History of Baseball on Cape Cod," *Barnstable Patriot*, June 25, 2009; James H. Ellis, "Cape Cod League a Talent Showcase," *Baseball Research Journal* 15 (1986), 57.

4. Sturgis Library's *Barnstable Patriot* Digital Newspaper Archive (http://digital.olivesoftware.com/Default/Skins/Sturgis/Client.asp?Skin=Sturgis&AW=1230806469283&AppName=2).

5. "Letters from the Cape," *Pawtucket Chronicle*, reprinted in the *Barnstable Patriot*, October 15, 1867, 1.

6. Ibid.

7. *Barnstable Patriot*, July 30, 1867, 2. The library was named in honor of William Sturgis, who had made it possible by means of a generous endowment in his will.

8. The Sturgis Library today boasts several notable distinctions, including being part of the oldest U.S. building that houses a public library. Since Reverend Lothrop also used part of the building for worship services, the library is also the only building still in active use that was regularly used for religious services that long ago. See the library's website, *http://www.sturgislibrary.org/general/history*, for details.

9. "Letters from the Cape," *Pawtucket Chronicle*, reprinted in the *Barnstable Patriot*, October 15, 1867, 1.

10. *Barnstable Patriot*, October 15, 1867, 2.

11. *Barnstable Patriot*, August 13, 1867, 2.

12. *Barnstable Patriot*, August 27, 1867, 2.

13. *Barnstable Patriot*, September 3, 1867, 2.

14. *Barnstable Patriot*, August 27, 1867, 2.

15. *Barnstable Patriot*, September 10, October 8 and 22, November 12, and December 3, 1867.

16. *Barnstable Patriot*, September 3, 1867, 2.

17. *Barnstable Patriot*, September 10, 1867, 2.

18. *Barnstable Patriot*, September 24 and October 1, 1867, 2.

19. *Barnstable Patriot*, October 15, 1867, 2.

20. "Letters from the Cape," *Pawtucket Chronicle*, reprinted in the *Barnstable Patriot*, October 15, 1867, 1.

21. *Barnstable Patriot*, October 15, 1867, 2.

22. Quoted in "The Cummaquid Club," *Barnstable Patriot*, October 22, 1867, 2.

23. "The Cummaquid Club," *Barnstable Patriot*, October 22, 1867, 2.

24. *Barnstable Patriot*, October 22, 1867, 2.

25. *Barnstable Patriot*, November 12 and December 3, 1867.

26. *Barnstable Patriot*, June 30, July 7 and August 4, 1868, and August 31, 1869; *Provincetown Advocate*, September 1, 1869, 2.

27. *Barnstable Patriot*, May 31, 1870, 2.

28. *Barnstable Patriot*, May 12, 1868, 2.

29. *Barnstable Patriot*, November 17, 1868.

30. An apparent exception was a note in the *Patriot* on September 22, 1891 (page 3), indicating that J. Edward Mullen of Boston was visiting Barnstable. It added, "Mr. Mullen coached our boys in base ball playing when the fever first reached this village and through him the old Cummaquid Club gained an enviable reputation." Mullen, however, turned out to have been far too young to have been associated with the original Cummaquids and the note probably referred to the Cummaquid Jrs. of the mid–1870s.

31. *Barnstable Patriot*, August 11, 1868, 1.

32. *San Francisco Chronicle*, December 18, 1898, 30; *Barnstable Patriot*, December 26, 1898, 3.

33. *Barnstable Patriot*, April 12, 1915, 2.

34. James C. O'Connell, *Becoming Cape Cod: Creating a Seaside Resort* (Hanover, N.H.: University Press of New England, 2003), 12.

35. *Boston Evening Transcript*, February 5, 1912, 16; *The Harvard Graduates' Magazine*, Volume 20 (1912), 544.

36. *Barnstable Patriot*, May 29, 1922, 5.

General Bibliography

Each entry in this work contains a listing or discussion of specific sources used by the author. The following titles are, however, national in scope and are listed here instead of being repeated entry after entry.

Adelman, Melvin L. *A Sporting Time: New York City and the Rise of Modern Athletics, 1820–70.* Urbana: University of Illinois Press, 1986.

Bingham, Dennis, and Thomas R. Heitz. "Rules and Scoring," in John Thorn and Pete Palmer with Michael Gershman, eds., *Total Baseball: The Official Encyclopedia of Major League Baseball,* 4th ed. New York: Viking, 1994.

Block, David. *Baseball Before We Knew It.* Lincoln: University of Nebraska Press, 2005.

Chadwick, Henry. *The American Game of Base Ball* (a.k.a. *The Game of Base Ball. How to Learn It, How to Play It, and How to Teach It. With Sketches of Noted Players*). 1868. Columbia, S.C,: Camden House, 1983.

_____. *Beadle's Dime Base-Ball Player.* 1860. Morgantown, PA: Sullivan Press, 1996.

Charlton, James, ed. *The Baseball Chronology: The Complete History of Significant Events in the Game of Baseball.* New York: Macmillan, 1991.

Church, Seymour R. *Base Ball: The History, Statistics and Romance of the American National Game from Its Inception to the Present Time.* 1902. Princeton, N.J.: Pyne Press, 1974.

Deming, Clarence. "Old Days in Baseball." *Outing,* June 1902, 357–360.

Dickson, Paul, ed. *The Dickson Baseball Dictionary: The Revised, Expanded, and Now Definitive Work on the Language of Baseball,* 3d ed. New York: W.W. Norton, 2009.

Fox, Stephen. *Big Leagues: Professional Baseball, Football, and Basketball in National Memory.* New York: William Morrow, 1994.

Goldstein, Warren J. *Playing for Keeps: A History of Early Baseball.* (Ithaca: Cornell University Press, 1989.

Henderson, Robert W. *Ball, Bat, and Bishop: The Origin of Ball Games.* 1947. Urbana: University of Illinois Press, 2001.

"How Baseball Began — A Member of the Gotham Club of Fifty Years Ago Tells About It." *San Francisco Examiner,* November 27, 1887, 14 (interview with William Wheaton).

Ivor-Campbell, Frederick, Robert L. Tiemann, and Mark Rucker, eds. *Baseball's First Stars.* Cleveland: Society for American Baseball Research, 1996.

Kirsch, George B. *The Creation of American Team Sports: Baseball and Cricket, 1838–72.* Urbana: University of Illinois Press, 1991.

Levine, Peter. *A.G. Spalding and the Rise of Baseball: The Promise of American Sport.* New York: Oxford University Press, 1985.

Lowry, Philip J. *Green Cathedrals: The Ultimate Celebration of All 271 Major League and Negro League Ballparks Past and Present.* Reading, MA: Addison-Wesley, 1992.

Melville, Tom. *Early Baseball and the Rise of the National League.* Jefferson, N.C.: McFarland, 2001.

Morris, Peter. *But Didn't We Have Fun: An Informal History of Baseball's Pioneer Era, 1843–1870.* Chicago: Ivan R. Dee, 2008.

_____. *A Game of Inches: The Stories Behind the Innovations That Shaped Baseball. Volume 2: The Game Behind the Scenes.* Chicago: Ivan R. Dee, 2006.

_____. *A Game of Inches: The Stories Behind the Innovations That Shaped Baseball. Volume 1: The Game on the Field.* Chicago: Ivan R. Dee, 2006.

Nash, Peter. *Baseball Legends of Brooklyn's Green-Wood Cemetery.* Portsmouth, N.H.: Arcadia, 2003.

Nemec, David. *The Rules of Baseball.* New York: Lyons & Burford, 1994.

Nucciarone, Monica. *Alexander Cartwright: The Life behind the Baseball Legend.* Lincoln: University of Nebraska Press, 2009.

Peverelly, Charles A. *Book of American Pastimes.* New York: Published by the Author, 1866.

Orem, Preston D. *Baseball (1845–1881) from the Newspaper Accounts.* Altadena, CA: Self-published, 1961.

Protoball website, *http://www. retrosheet.org/Protoball/index.htm.*

Richter, Francis C. *Richter's History and Records of Base Ball.* 1914. Jefferson, N.C.: McFarland, 2005.

Ryczek, William J. *Baseball's First Inning: A History of the National Pastime Through the Civil War.* Jefferson, N.C.: McFarland, 2009.

_____. *Blackguards and Red Stockings: A History of Baseball's National Association, 1871–1875.* Jefferson, N.C.: McFarland, 1992.

_____. *When Johnny Came Sliding Home: The Post-Civil War Baseball Boom, 1865–1870.* Jefferson, N.C.: McFarland, 1998.

Seymour, Harold, and Dorothy Seymour Mills. *Baseball: The Early Years.* New York: Oxford University Press, 1960.

Shieber, Tom. "The Evolution of the Baseball Diamond," originally in *Baseball Research Journal* 23 (1994), 3–13; reprinted in an expanded version in John Thorn and Pete Palmer with Michael Gershman, eds., *Total Baseball: The Official Encyclopedia of Major League Baseball,* 4th ed. New York: Viking, 1994, 113–124.

Spalding, Albert Goodwill. *America's National Game: Historic Facts Concerning the Beginning, Evolution, Development, and Popularity of Base Ball, with Personal Reminiscences of Its Vicissitudes, Its Victories, and Its Votaries.* 1910. Lincoln: University of Nebraska Press, 1992.

Spink, Alfred H. *The National Game.* 1911. Carbondale: Southern Illinois University Press, 2000.

Sullivan, Dean A., comp, and ed., *Early Innings: A Documentary History of Baseball, 1825–1908.* Lincoln: University of Nebraska Press, 1995.

Thorn, John. *Baseball in the Garden of Eden: The Secret History of the Early Game.* New York: Simon & Schuster, 2011.

_____, and Pete Palmer. *The Hidden Game of Baseball.* Garden City, N.Y.: Doubleday, 1984.

Tiemann, Robert L., and Mark Rucker, eds. *Nineteenth Century Stars.* Kansas City: Society for American Baseball Research, 1989.

Wood, James Leon, as told to Frank G. Menke. "Baseball in By-Gone Days." Syndicated series, Indiana (PA) *Evening Gazette,* August 14, 1916; *Marion* (OH) *Star,* August 15, 1916; Indiana (PA) *Evening Gazette,* August 17, 1916.

Wright, Marshall D. *The National Association of Base Ball Players, 1857–1870.* Jefferson, N.C.: McFarland, 2000.

Zoss Joel, and John Bowman. *Diamonds in the Rough: The Untold History of Baseball.* New York: Macmillan, 1989.

About the Contributors

John S. Bowman is co-author, with Brian Turner, of *The Hurrah Game*, a history of the early years of baseball in his hometown, Northampton, Massachusetts, and was co-author, with Joel Zoss, of *Diamonds in the Rough*. He has also written about the game in the 19th century.

Gregory Christiano is a published author, freelance writer, and researcher. As a retired cartographer, he has produced a series of maps of the New York City area pinpointing locations of many of the mid-nineteenth century sandlots of the earliest baseball clubs.

Benjamin Dettmar is a Ph.D. candidate in American studies at Michigan State University, where he also works for the *Journal of Popular Culture* and the University Archives & Historical Collections. His research interests include the Olympic Games and the impact they have on host cities and the attitude toward homosexuality in contemporary sport.

A retired English professor and a member of SABR since 1994, **Jan Finkel** has contributed to several collective biographies, the *Baseball Research Journal*, *NINE*, and the SABR Biography Project for which he is chief editor.

Richard Hershberger is a paralegal in Maryland. He has written numerous articles on early baseball, concentrating on its origins and its organizational history. He is a member of the SABR 19th Century and Origins committees.

Leonard Levin, who would be happy to watch a baseball game in any century, is a retired newspaper editor who keeps his brain sharp by working on SABR-sponsored publications. He has been a member of SABR since 1977, and has been a national officer twice.

Now retired from work as a picture framer, **Richard Malatzky** joined SABR in 1976 and has worked with Bill Haber through SABR's Biographical Committee researching missing players. He enjoys traveling throughout the United States and abroad visiting art museums and seeing the sights.

Aaron W. Miller is a history teacher in Columbus, Indiana. His dissertation, "Glorious Summer: A Cultural History of Nineteenth-Century Baseball," focused on the influence the rise of the national pastime had on the dynamic late 1800s. He has also published on Zane Grey's baseball literature and baseball on *Seinfeld*.

Peter Morris is a baseball historian whose books include *A Game of Inches*, *Baseball Fever*, *But Didn't We Have Fun?*, and

Catcher: How the Man Behind the Plate Became an American Folk Hero. He won SABR's prestigious Henry Chadwick Award in 2010.

William J. Ryczek has written a trilogy (*Baseball's First Inning*, *When Johnny Came Sliding Home* and *Blackguards and Red Stockings*) covering the history of baseball from its beginnings through 1875. He has also written on New York baseball in the 1960s.

A native Philadelphian, **John Shiffert** has been writing about baseball in various venues and media since 1970. His "19 to 21" e-column has been running since the 2003 season, and he has had four baseball history-themed books published, including *Base Ball in Philadelphia*.

Robert Tholkes has written several articles for SABR publications, edits and writes for *Originals*, the newsletter of SABR's Committee on the Origins of Baseball, and operates a vintage baseball team in Minnesota.

John Thorn is the official historian of Major League Baseball and author of *Baseball in the Garden of Eden*. He maintains a baseball history blog, "Our Game," and writes frequently on the early game. He founded the journal *Base Ball* and co-founded SABR's 19th century baseball research committee.

Brian Turner has published his baseball research in *The National Pastime*, the *African-American National Biography*, and *Base Ball: A Journal of the Early Game*. Along with John S. Bowman, he co-authored *The Hurrah Game: Baseball in Northampton*.

Craig B. Waff, a member of SABR since 1992, was the creator of the Protoball's "Games Tabulation" and the author of essays on six games for the Greatest Games of 19th-Century Base Ball project. He was a senior historian at the Air Force Research Laboratory at Wright-Patterson Air Force Base who passed away in July 2012.

Jared Wheeler, a Temple University graduate with a B.A. in social American history, served as the book review editor for *Black Ball*. He has contributed to Sports Illustrated's *Baseball Book* and *Basketball Book*, and his research appeared on the cover of the October 9, 2006, issue of *Sports Illustrated*.

John G. Zinn is an independent historian with special interest in both the Civil War and baseball. He is the author of *The Mutinous Regiment* and *The Major League Pennant Races of 1916* (with Paul Zinn), and the editor (also with Paul Zinn) of *Ebbets Field: Essays and Memories of Brooklyn's Historic Ballpark, 1913–1960*.

Index

Abadie, John 258
Abbott, Bud 221
Abercrombie, Daniel Putnam "Put" 264–265, 267, 285–286, 288–291
Abrams, William 95
Ackerman, Joshua H. 129
Active Club of Brooklyn 210
Active Base Ball Club of Newark 192–193, 209–211
Active Base Ball Club of New York City 65–69, 83, 94, 151–152, 154, 156, 209, 215–217, 223, 290
Adair, Henry J. 136
Adams, Doc 2, 7, 11–14, 16–18, 24, 29–30, 46, 50, 57
Adams, Thomas Spencer 267
admission fees 3, 4, 93, 98, 114, 169–170, 209, 220, 235, 258, 309, 311, 312
Adriatic Base Ball Club of Newark 141, 208
Adriatic Base Ball Club of Philadelphia 82, 230
Aetna Base Ball Club of Chicago 156
Aetna Base Ball Club of Jersey City (NJ) 222
African Americans 40, 191, 226, 227–228, 238, 251–254, 296–297
Agassiz, Louis 283
Akin, Albro 95
Albany Knickerbocker 21
Albertson, George, M.D. 248
Albro, George 95
alcohol 22, 34, 56, 60, 63, 84, 88, 135, 140, 142, 175, 195, 201, 252, 279, 288, 298, 303, 306
Allentown (PA) Morning Call 259
Alline, William Henry 267
Allison, Andrew 175
Allison, Art 175
Allison, Douglas 175
Allison, William 175
all-star teams 67
Alpha Base Ball Club of Ashland (MA) 304–306
Alpha Base Ball Club of Brooklyn 154–155
Amateur Club of Newark 192–193, 201, 224
American Base Ball Club of Sandwich (MA) 316
American Base Ball Club of South Dedham (MA) 262, 264
American Cricket Club 161
American Fire Company 90

American News Company 74
The American Phrenological Journal 33
American Standard 224
American Star 48
Ames, James 266, 289, 291
Amherst College Base Ball Club 260, 262, 296, 299
Amity Base Ball Club of South Brooklyn 156, 177
Anderson, Cornelius V. 56
Anderson, Leroy 204
Andrews, James W. 106
Annable, Davis 318
Annis, Billy 304, 306
Anthony, David H. 18
Anthony, Edward 19
Anthony, Henry T. 17–20
Anthony, Jacob Sr. 18
Appleton, George 267
The Approach to the Social Question 269
Armfield, William W. 72
Arnold, Edward Lincoln "Ned" 268
Askin, Luther B. 296–297
Astor, John Jacob 31
Atalanta Base Ball Club of Stoneham 304, 310
Athenian Base Ball Club of New York 156
Athletic Base Ball Club of Brooklyn 67, 156, 162
Athletic Base Ball Club of Manchester (NH) 312
Athletic Base Ball Club of Philadelphia 10, 57, 59, 66, 82–86, 93–95, 104, 114, 123–128, 130, 132–133, 149, 151–152, 155, 171, 173–174, 177, 185, 200, 204, 208, 215, 226–227, 229–231, 234–252, 254–255, 257–258, 266, 290
Atlantic Base Ball Club of Brooklyn 1, 3, 7, 17, 51, 64, 67, 77, 80–86, 89, 92, 94–96, 98–105, 109–114, 117–140, 141, 144, 146–157, 161–162, 167–176, 178–184, 189, 193, 200–201, 204, 208–210, 214–216, 218, 220, 223–224, 230, 234, 242, 246–247, 250, 265–266, 288–290, 292, 297, 316
Atlantic Base Ball Club of Jamaica (NY) 141, 181–182
Atwater, Edward 206
Atwater Base Ball Club of Westfield (MA) 272–274, 277–280
Austin, Henry C. 95
Austin, Valentine 95
Avery, Amelia Titus 19

Avery, Catherine Reynolds 28
Avery, Deborah Lothrop 26
Avery, Ephraim 26
Avery, John Smith 19
Avery, Walter 17, 19–20, 26

Babbitt, William 301
Babcock, Alexander G. 129
Babcock, William V. 77, 117, 119
Bache, Andrew 195
Bacon, Elisha 101, 110
Bacon, Francis W. 318
Bacon, Horace 318
Bailey, Alexander 191, 214, 216–217
Baldwin, William 204
Ball Players' Chronicle 192
Ballou, Berthier 303
Baltic Base Ball Club of New York 8, 81, 119, 121, 167
Banker, Benson Beriah 291
bankers 30, 106, 108, 159
banquet 16, 28, 35, 64, 68, 82, 209, 231, 247, 258
Bansel, Walter 72
Baptis, John 48
Barlow, Tommy 98, 156–158, 163
Barnes, Edward 101
Barnes, Samuel L. 248
Barnstable County Agricultural Fair 316
Barnstable Patriot 315–317
Barre (MA) Gazette 261
Barre, William 142
bartenders and saloon keepers 22, 54, 60, 63, 88, 91, 179, 185, 192, 199, 201, 221, 249, 313
Bartholomew, Jonathan 101, 110
The Baseball Encyclopedia 259
Baseball in the Garden of Eden 46, 61
Baseball Legends of Brooklyn's Green-Wood Cemetery 59
base stealing 3, 65, 79, 113, 265
Bass, John Elias 95
bat (trophy) 16, 52, 317
Bay State Base Ball Club of Boston 261, 264
Bayard, Thomas F. 250
Beach, Waddy 113, 170, 172–173, 175, 178, 182
Beadle, Charles H. 56
Beadle, Edward 56
Beadle's Dime Base Ball Player 3, 50
Beals, Tommy 95, 97, 124
Beam, George 104
Beans, Albert 193
Beard, John 81, 82, 87
Bearman, Charley 87

Beavan, E.P. 158
Bechtel, George 227, 237, 248
Beitel, J.H. 243
Belcher, James 303
Belden, Henry 80
Bell, William H. 78, 176
Bellan, Steve 95
Bellevue Hospital (New York City) 26
Belloni, Louis, Jr. 19
Benedict Base Ball Club of Philadelphia 227
Bennett, Charley 300
Bensel, William P. 19
Benson, Edward 77–78
Benson, Richard W. 237
Benton, G.W. 136
Bergen, Lem 118–119, 129
Berkenstock, Nathan 234, 237
Berry, Thomas 237, 254–255
Bibby, Edward 19–20, 26, 29, 35
Bibby, Justine 35
Bibby, Thomas 19
Biggs, Francis 110, 142
Birdsall, Dave 94, 95
Birdsall, Edward H. 20
Birdsall, Samuel 20
Birney, Charles H. 17, 20
Bixby, Andrew J. 71–72, 195
Blake, Amos 309
Bliss, William 118, 129
Bliven, Charles 223–224
Block, David 63
Blomfield, John J. 76,78
Boardman, Halsey 302
Boardman, Henry 206
boating craze 47–49
Boerum, Folkert Rapelje 118–119, 129
Bogart, Ann S. 20
Bogart, Lawrence 82, 87
Bogart, Rachel 20
Bolen, J.A. 275
Bomeisler, Charles 229
Bomeisler, Theodore 208, 211, 232, 248
Bond, Henry H. 296–297
Bonnell, Edward 56
Book of American Pastimes 11, 47, 55, 66
Boone, Silas 189
Booth, Edwin 108, 153, 158
Boston Daily Courier 261
Boston Stock Exchange 292
Bottum, Edward S. 296–297
bound rule 4, 41, 101, 113–114, 150, 287
Bowdoin Square Base Ball Club of

Boston 104, 260, 264, 274–275, 277, 280, 285–286
Bowell, Thomas 81
Boyd, Bill 142
Boyd, Theodore 36
Boyle, John A. 20
Boynton, Henry 313
Bradbury, William M. 268
Bradley, George 259
Brainard, Asa 41, 103, 106, 311
Brainard, Harry 106
Brainard, Redelia 41
Brayton, Daniel 129
Breitnall, R. Heber 192, 207, 211
Brennan, Matt 22
Bretell, Alfred R. 136
Brewster, Edward 206
Bridgeton (NJ) Base Ball Club 192
Brinkerhoff, Henry 194–195, 204
Broadstreet, Samuel, Jr., 268
Brodhead, George 20
Brodhead, Reverend John 20
Brodhead, Captain Luke 20
Brodie, George 21
brokers 19, 20, 21, 22, 23, 25, 26, 28, 29, 30, 31, 33, 35, 37, 39, 41, 42, 50, 51, 72, 74, 79, 88, 90, 96, 107, 108, 115, 142, 158. 161, 163, 182, 183, 195, 205, 268, 278, 318
Brooklyn Eagle 100, 183, 200, 208, 212, 216
Brooklyn Times 112, 179, 194
Broomall, William B. 255
Brotherson, Benjamin 21, 30
Brotherson, Philip 21
Broughton, F.K. 104, 129
Brown, Aaron 29
Brown, Anna Mary 29
Brown, Capen 303
Brown, Charles Brockden 244
Brown, Edmund 82, 84, 87, 124, 176
Brown, Eugene Armitt Burling 241, 244
Brown, George A. 21, 28
Brown, John 136, 293
Brown, Dr. Joseph 101, 108
Brown, Oliver 129, 158
Brown, Randall 52
Bryan, C. Ruthven 269
Bryham, S.W. 60
Buchanan, General George B. 30
Buckley, James 136
Buckley, Thomas 191, 214, 216–217
Bulkeley, Morgan 87
Bunker, William J. 22
Bunker Hill Base Ball Club of Charlestown (MA) 264
bunt 98, 114, 133, 134
Burkhalter, Edward 206
Burlock, Esther 22
Burns, Mark 87
Burns, Simon 81, 82, 87
Burns, William 55–56
Burr, Thomas 113
Burroughs, Henry 211
Burtis, Clarence 56
Burton, Hazen James "Jim" 268
Bush, Archie 263, 293
Bushong, "Doc" 300
Busteed, Richard 55, 262
butchers 48, 50–51, 52, 56, 57, 58, 62, 75, 89, 134, 168, 178, 179, 225, 239, 249
Butler, Benjamin F. 20
Butler, Henry 22, 203–204

Butler, Walter 206
Buttrick, Fred 313
Butts, William H. 176
By-Laws and Rules of the Eagle (NY) Ball Club 69
By-Laws and Rules of the Empire (NY) Ball Club 76
Bynner, John 145

Callaway, Frederick 208, 211
Camac's Woods 229, 233, 234, 242–243
Cameron, James 80
Cammeyer, William 85, 87, 114, 170
Campbell, Alexander 52
Campbell, Hugh 84, 216–217
Campbell, Mike 193
Campbell, Sarah 21
Cannon, John 252
Cape Cod baseball clubs 315–319
Capitoline Grounds (Brooklyn) 7, 98, 105, 124, 126–128, 133, 150–155, 157, 159, 174, 209, 289
Carhart, Sam 136
Carl, Andrew J. 22
Carland, John 88
Carleton, James 88, 177
Carlisle, Joseph 62, 63
Carlton, Isaac 80
Carroll Park (Brooklyn) 121, 144, 146, 149, 151
Carter, Daniel Stanley 313
Cartwright, Alexander 1, 7, 10–12, 18, 22, 25–26, 34–35, 46, 60, 321
Cartwright, Alfred DeForest 22
Casares, Primitivo 281, 283
Case, Charles Ludlow 56
Caskin, Daniel 304
Cassio, George D. 22
Catto, Octavius Valentine 227, 252–253
Cauldwell, William 4, 95
Central Park 7
Centralville (MA) Base Ball Club 307
Chadwick, Henry 31, 38, 50, 53, 60, 70, 74, 83, 90, 98–99, 103–104, 107–108, 110, 113–115, 118, 130–134, 140, 142, 150–153, 156, 158, 160–162, 171–176, 179, 187, 192, 194, 214, 216, 229, 239, 246
Chadwick, Peter 76
Chalmers, Thomas, Jr. 76, 80
Chambers, John 48
Champion Base Ball Club of Albany (NY) 274
Champion Base Ball Club of Jersey City (NJ) 154–155, 192–193, 201, 210, 214, 222–225
Champion Base Ball Club of Yorkville (NY) 67, 146
Champlin, John 87
Chapman, Jack 98, 123, 126–128, 131, 156
Chapman, John Curtis 129
Charter Oak Base Ball Club of Brooklyn 99, 102, 146, 148–149, 158, 161–162
Charter Oak Base Ball Club of Hartford (CT)125, 209, 267, 288, 290
Chauncey, Dan 106
Chauncey, George 106
Chemung Base Ball Club of Stoughton (MA) 302–303

Chester (PA) Base Ball Club 237, 254–257
Chicago Fire, Great 181, 184–185
Chicago White Stockings 83, 94, 173, 305
Child, Dudley Richards 268
Chilton, Bruce 150, 158, 163
Church, James H. 112, 115
The Church of the Spirit 269
City Fire Insurance Company (New York City) 24
Clagg, James 318
Clancy, John 22
Clancy, Lawrence 88
Clapp, John 237
Clare, Joseph 23
Clark, Edward 49
Clark, Leila 40
Clarke, Beverly 23
clerks 10, 20, 21, 22, 23, 27, 29, 30, 32, 33, 34, 37, 38, 39, 40, 41, 42, 28, 58, 68, 73, 74, 76, 78, 79, 88, 89, 90, 101, 197, 115, 116, 142, 143, 160, 161, 178, 179, 180, 183, 189, 191, 195, 211, 212, 215, 216, 217, 221, 224, 238, 239, 244, 249, 256, 269, 271, 278, 279, 294, 302, 313, 318
Cleveland, Grover 57, 108–109, 115, 196
Clipper Base Ball Club of Lowell (MA) 304–305, 307–315
Clyne, John 106, 153, 156, 158
Coale, James 206
cobblers *see* shoemakers, cobblers and bootblacks
Coffin Wright, Martha 294
Cohen, Herman 23
Cohen, Leonard G. 56–57
Colden, Cadwallader 39
Cole, George 110
Collender, Hugh 88
Collins, Dr. Henry 272, 276–277
Collins, John 211
Collins, Mary Stacy 34
Columbia Base Ball Club of Brooklyn 194, 196
Columbia Base Ball Club of East Brooklyn 119, 187–188
Comet Base Ball Club of Chicopee (MA) 277
Comiskey, Charles 135
Commerford, Charles 53, 57
Committee to Revise the Constitution and By-Laws (Knickerbockers) 12
Conahan, James 255
Conard, John 234
Condit, Edward 205
Cone, Edward W. 23
Congdon, Henry M. 110
Conklin, James 192
Connecticut River Valley Agricultural Association 267
Connell, Edmund 296
Connell, John 57
Conner, James 73
Conner, William Crawford 72
Connor, Edwin 136
Connor, Ned 248–249
Conover, John 201
Conover, Richard S. 23
Constellation Base Ball Club of Buffalo 66, 114, 149
Contest Base Ball Club of Brooklyn 100, 177, 187–190

Conway, Dick 313
Conway, George 313
Conway, James 313
Cooke, Richard 110
Cooledge, Martin 313
Coon, Charles 177
Cope, Elias 247–249
Cornwell, George 107
Cornwell, James H., Jr. 136
Cornwell, John 107
Cortelyou, Abram 201
Cortelyou, John 201
Cortelyou, William H. 201
Costello, Lou 221
Couch, General Darius N. 253
Cox, George 80
Cozans, Phillip J. 73–74
Cragin, James 80
Crane, Fred 105, 107, 123, 125–126, 130, 134, 152, 161
Craver, Bill 227
Creighton, Jim 94, 98, 101, 102, 104, 105, 107, 113, 122, 145, 147, 154, 158, 159, 161, 181, 242
cricket 4, 8, 9, 10, 11, 35, 47, 49–50, 51–54, 56, 58, 61, 70, 71, 72, 78, 94, 95, 96, 98, 99, 107, 112, 114, 118, 123, 133, 136, 140–141, 142, 161, 182, 194, 206, 220, 226, 229, 230, 231–232, 239, 240, 245, 250, 251, 262, 264, 268, 307, 313
Crocker, Alfred 318
Crooke, Phillip S. 33
Cudlipp, Reuben 55, 57
Culyer, William 78
Cummaquid Base Ball Club of Barnstable (MA) 315–319
Cummings, Albert "Candy" 78, 98, 105, 107, 153, 156–158, 162, 267, 300
Cummings, James Brackenridge 300
Cunnington, William 234, 237
Cuppaidge, James F. 49
Curry, Duncan 11, 13–15, 17, 23, 24, 38, 50
Curtis, Horatio 287
curveball 78, 156, 158–159, 239, 245, 267, 300
Cushman, Paul, Jr. 30
Cuthbert, Ned 227, 237–238, 247–249
Cutter, George 197–198

Dakin, Tom 107, 114, 120
Dalton, George T. 101, 110
Dark Blue Base Ball Club of Brooklyn 87
Dark Blues of Hartford 159
Dartmouth College Base Ball Club 289–290
Davenport, Samuel F. 130
Davids, Warren 88
Davidson, Albert 112, 116
Davidson, Alexander 87–88
Davidson, John E. 115
Davis, Charles 57
Davis, Harriet 25
Davis, James Whyte 12, 17, 24–25, 30, 32, 35, 37, 54, 57
Davis, John 25
Davis, William Franklin 289, 291
Dawson, Ichabod 207, 211
Dayton, Augustus 130, 142
Dayton, Charles Austin 107, 115

De Milt, William W. 57
Deal, William 249
DeBost, Charles 12, 25, 30, 35
DeCoster, Billy 302–303
Delgado, Jose Eulogio 281–283
Deming, Miner Rudd 286
Denis, Geoffrey P. 256
Denison, Henry Beals 268
Denmead, John 224
Denney, Charles A. 234, 237
Dennison, Henry Willard 268
Devlin, Jim 227, 258
Devoe, George 25
Devyr, Tom 82–84, 88, 171
DeWitt, Alfred 27
DeWitt, Peter 25–26
DeWitt, Theodore 26
Dick, Enoch 26
Dick, Thomas W. Jr. 26
Dickinson, Emily Gouverneur 245
Dion, Joseph 88
Dixey, Charles 243
Dixon, John D. 26
Dixwell, Susan 269
Doby, Larry 221
Dockney, Patrick "Patsy" 25, 57,
   88, 209–210, 237
Dodge, D. Albert 101
Dollard, Hy 153, 156, 159
Dongan, William 88
Donnelly, John 258
Donnelly, Peter 224
Dorsett, Robert 26
Doubleday, Abner 10, 50
Doughty, Epentus 25
Douglas, Stephen A. 274
Douglass, Frederick 252
Dowling, Joe 22
Downing, Hamilton 272, 275, 277
Drohan, John 56, 61
Drummond, Alexander 14, 26, 29,
   35
Duffy, Ed 83, 85, 88, 171, 173
Duffy, James 249
Dunn, Michael H. 296, 298
Dupignac, Andrew J. 57
Dupignac, Ebenezer 17, 26, 50
Dupignac, Harry 67
Duyckinck, Evert A. 20

Eager, William Blake, Jr. 26–27
Eagle Base Ball Club of Flatbush
   (Brooklyn, NY) 154–155
Eagle Base Ball Club of Florence
   (MA) 260, 276, 296–299
Eagle Base Ball Club of Natick
   (MA) 308–309
Eagle Base Ball Club of New York
   City 7, 10, 12–13, 51, 56–57, 69–
   77, 80, 82–83, 101–102, 113, 141–
   142, 151–152, 167, 171, 195–198,
   204, 223
Earle, David 299–300
Eastern League 259
Eastmead, Horatio 143
Ebbets, Arthur M. 27
Ebbets, Daniel, Jr. 27
Ebbets, Daniel, Sr. 27
Ebbets, Edward A. 27, 56
Ebbets, Elizabeth Kip 27
Ebbets, George A. 67
Ebling, Joseph F. 61
Eckford, Henry 168–169
Eckford Base Ball Club of Brooklyn
   1, 4, 7, 12, 17, 56–57, 61, 67, 71,
   81–86, 89, 93–94, 99–100, 105,

112–114, 119, 121–125, 127, 131–
   132, 135, 143, 146–148, 150–155,
   167–187, 189, 214–216, 218, 227,
   239, 247, 309, 313
Eclectic Club (New York City) 77
Edge, Joseph 80
Edmands, Adelaide 282, 283
Edmands, Albert 281, 283
Eggler, Dave 86, 88, 172, 177, 236
Eldridge, Frederick G. 101, 111
Elkin, Isaac 201
Ellis, Henry C. 27
Elm Tree Base Ball Club of Boston
   261
Elmira (NY) Gazette 60
Elysian Fields (Hoboken, NJ) 7–12,
   16, 31, 41–42, 47, 49, 53–54, 62–
   67, 69–71, 76, 81, 83–84, 98, 118,
   124–125, 142, 191, 194, 245, 290
embezzlement 21, 30, 108, 189, 278
Emmet, Robert 48
Empire Base Ball Club (New York
   City) 10, 22, 58–59, 63, 71, 72,
   74, 76–80, 81, 89–91, 96, 118–
   119, 121, 124, 141, 149, 168, 176,
   179, 195, 247
Empire Base Ball Club (St. Louis)
   75
Empire Club (social club affiliated
   with the Democratic Party) 22–
   23, 63–64
Empire Hook and Ladder Company
   (Newark) 194–196
Empire Hotel (New York City) 93.
   95
enclosed baseball grounds 4, 7, 8,
   83, 93, 98, 114, 124, 125, 169,
   209, 220, 235, 258, ; *see also*
   Capitoline Grounds *and* Union
   Grounds
Enterprise Base Ball Club of Bed-
   ford/Brooklyn 59, 105, 107–108,
   123, 130, 134–135, 144–146, 150–
   152, 180–182, 208
Equity Base Ball Club of Philadelphia 38, 227, 229, 238, 241–246
Ernst, William 234, 237
Etheridge, Charles 104, 107
Eureka Base Ball Club of Cambridge (MA) 302
Eureka Base Ball Club of Lowell
   (MA) 307–308, 310
Eureka Base Ball Club of Newark
   67, 83, 91, 123–126, 150, 191–193,
   201, 207–216, 218–220, 223–224,
   246, 289
Ewell, George 249, 258
Excelsior Base Ball Club of Brooklyn 3, 7, 12, 17, 21, 41, 56, 67,
   70–71, 80–81, 83, 89, 93–94, 98,
   101–114, 117, 120–123, 125–126,
   129, 131, 141–142, 144, 146–156,
   158–161, 163, 168–171, 181, 188,
   197, 204, 230–231, 234, 238,
   242, 247, 263, 265, 267, 269,
   289–290, 297–298
Excelsior Base Ball Club of Baltimore 104
Excelsior Base Ball Club of Chicago
   79, 291, 293
Excelsior Base Ball Club of Jersey
   City (NJ) 194–195, 197–199
Excelsior Base Ball Club of New Jersey's 2nd Regiment 192
Excelsior Base Ball Club of Philadelphia (town ball club) 229, 238

Excelsior Base Ball Club of Philadel-
   phia (African-American club) 251
Excelsior Base Ball Club of Upton
   (MA) 306
Exercise Base Ball Club of Brooklyn
   123, 181

Fackler, Charles 242–244
Fairbanks, Cortes 272, 277
Fairbanks, Henry 107, 145–146, 159
fair-foul hitting 98, 133, 175, 239
Fairthorne, William 63
Faitoute, Charles 193
Fanze, Joseph 80
Fargis, Edward V. 80
Farley, Charles J. 197–198
Farrar, Sid 304
Farrington, Dr. Edward Albert 256
Farrington, Harvey W. 256
Fashion Race Course Games 3, 78,
   113, 120, 121, 122, 131, 146
Fay, Joseph 318
Fearless Base Ball Club of Belvidere
   (MA) 307
Fear-Not Base Ball Club of Hudson
   City (NJ) 197
Ferguson, Bob 87, 98, 125, 130, 135
Ferren, Myron J 306
Fijux, Charles 28
Fijux, Francis 28
Fijux, Jules 28
fines 15
firefighters 3, 19, 41, 49, 56, 60, 72,
   73, 131, 134, 135, 143, 161, 175,
   176, 179, 180, 189, 193, 194, 196,
   198, 199, 214, 221, 224, 226, 249,
   257, 258, 259, 263, 275, 278,
   290, 297, 298, 306, 309, 313, 314
Firth, Thomas 228
Fish, Latham 145, 159, 164
Fisher, James 17, 28, 50, 57
Fiske, Alexander 101
Fiske, Charles 286–287, 292
Fisler, Lorenzo 237
Fisler, Wes 192, 237, 242
Fitzgerald, Arthur 220–221
Fitzgerald, Richard 276
Fitzgerald, Colonel Thomas 234–
   235, 238
Flagg, George A. 285–290, 292–
   293
Flanders, Pete 151, 159
Flanley, George 85, 89, 102, 147,
   159
Fleet, Frank 73
Flender, Henry C. 28
Flender, Thomas 28
Fletcher, George 107
fly rule 4, 41, 101, 113–114, 150
Foran, James 238
Forest City Base Ball Club of Cleve-
   land 156, 239
Forest City Base Ball Club of Rock-
   ford (IL) 79, 96, 156
Forker, James 145, 159
Forman, Theodore 54
Forsyth, James 56
Forsyth, Robert 57
Foster, Albert Henry 300
Foster, Melvin 88
foul territory 11, 64, 120, 128, 151,
   192, 264, 312
Franklin, George H. 57
Frazer, Francis 247, 249
Freeman, Ellis 206
Fronk, Edwin C. 28

Frost, Marsh 272, 276, 278
Fuller, Charles 266, 268
Fuller, H.A. 145, 159
Fulmer, Chick 249
Furey, Robert 143

Galvin, John 85, 89, 124, 130
gambling 4, 21, 47, 63, 91–92, 100,
   236, 252, 266
Gaskill, Charles 238
Gaskill, Edwin 238
Gaunt, Charles 80
Gavagan, Patrick 89
Gay, Isaac 303
Geary, John W. 40
Gedney, Alfred 96
Gedney, Andrew 80
Gehringer, Charles 135
Gelston, Marion E. "Joe" 73
General Worth Base Ball Club of
   Stoneham (MA) 304–305
Gesner, Brower 112, 115
Gibbs, A. Empie 112, 115
Gibney, Andrew 57
Gilman, Robert 198
Gilmore, William 54
Gilpin, Charles 228
Godwin, Daniel 112, 115
Godwin, Samuel 112
gold ball (trophy) 60, 269
Goldie, John 86, 89
*The Good Child's Own Book of
   Moral and Instructive Stories* 73
Goodspeed, William Benson 28
Gordon, J Kimball 163
Gotham Base Ball Club of New
   York City 1, 7–8, 10–13, 21, 28,
   34, 39–42, 46–62, 65–66, 69–
   72, 75–76, 79–83, 91, 94, 96,
   102, 106, 110, 112, 117–121, 136,
   140, 149–150, 157, 167–168, 174,
   182, 200, 262, 278
Gotham Cottage *see* Gotham Inn
Gotham Inn 55
Gotham Saloon *see* Gotham Inn
Gough, Isaac 80
Gould, Albert 282, 283
Gould, George 39
Gourlie, Archibald 28
Gover, William 89
Graffen, Harris 249
Grampher, Charles 258
Granite Base Ball Club of Holliston
   (MA) 288
Grant, Ulysses S. 33
Graves, Abner 50
Gray, James 168
Gray, Thomas 292
Greathead, William 193
Green, James 206
Green, Job L. 256
Green Mountain Base Ball Club of
   Williamsburg (Brooklyn, NY)
   177
Green Mountain Boys Base Ball
   Club of Boston 261
Greenleaf, Eugene Douglass 292
Gregory, Dudley 194
Gregory, Spencer 111
Grenelle, William H. 14, 19, 26, 29
Grierson, Thomas 29
Griffith, Mason 163
Griglietti, Robert 73
Griswold, H.M. 271–274, 278
Griswold, Merritt W. 36, 115,
Grum, George 168, 179

Grum, John 168, 179
Guild, Benjamin Franklin 262
Guillaudeu, Emile 178
Guillaudeu, Louis 178
Gulick, Charles 111
Guy, David 205
Gwynn, Joseph 249

Hague, William 258
Haight, Gilbert L. 111
Haight, William 178
Haines, Benjamin 197–198
Haines, Tom 67
Halbach, Alfred 249
Hall, George 105, 107, 130, 153, 160
Hall, Stephen C. 256
Hallett, E.B. 318
Hamilton, B.A. 147
Hamilton, Tice 118, 131
Hamilton Base Ball Club of Jersey City (NJ) 208
Hamilton Base Ball Club of Philadelphia 227, 230
Hamilton Club of Newark, 191
Hammond, Edward 296
Hampden Base Ball Club of Chicopee/Springfield (MA) 274, 276–277, 297
Hampshire (MA) Gazette 272
Handel and Haydn Society 226–227, 238–239
Hanigan, Berney 96, 149
Hardy, John 54
Harlem Base Ball Club of New York City 8, 82, 121, 123, 153, 184, 208
Harmonic Base Ball Club of South Brooklyn 154, 156
Harmony Base Ball Club of Brooklyn 118–119, 129, 133–134
Harper's Magazine 174
Harris, Charles 319
Harris, Dr. Francis Augustine 292
Harris, Joseph Smith 21
Harris, Marcus 319
Hart, Bernard 29
Hart, David 29
Hart, Emanuel Bernard 29
Harte, Bret 29
Hartman, Anthony 89, 90
Hartwell, Julius 278
Harvard Advocate 290
The Harvard Book 287, 288, 290
Harvard Base Ball Club 32, 105, 125, 156, 260, 263–270, 284–296, 305, 308–310, 314
Harvard Graduates Magazine 281
Harwood, Maria 25
Hatfield, John 57, 67, 83, 85–86, 89
Havemeyer, William 19
Havemeyer, Frederick 19
Havemeyer, Kate 19
Hawks, Emory 272, 274, 278
Hawthorne, Nathaniel 293
Hawxhurst, William 131
Haydock, Richard 76, 78
Hayhurst, Hicks 227, 231, 238–239, 251, 266
Haymakers of Troy (NY) 84, 156, 209, 297
Haymarket (saloon) 89, 90
Hayward, Abner 29
healthfulness 3, 47, 70, 71, 77, 112, 194, 262
Heisler, John 234, 239

Hempstead Inquirer 36
Henderson, Peter S. 29
Hennefick, Michael 276
Henry, Frederick 205
Henry, Mike 131
Henry Eckford Base Ball Club of New York City 59, 81, 89, 123, 149, 168–169, 178
Herrick, William 101
Hershberger, Richard 260, 323
Heston, Dr. A.G. 234
Heubel, George 239
Hiawatha Base Ball Club of Brooklyn 130, 203, 205
Hibbard, Frances Babbitt 300
Hibbard, Henry 299–301
Hickey, Ed 297
Hicks, Nathaniel Woodhull ("Nat") 73, 156, 160, 173
Higginson, Thomas Wentworth 275
Higgins, Anthony 250
Higham, Dick 77, 80, 89, 96
Hildebrandt, Matthew 201
Hill, Arthur G. 296, 298
Hill, Asa G. 306
Hill, Henry F. 306
Hill, S.L. 298
Hines, John 54
Hinsdale, Richard H 29
The History of Florence (MA) 297
Hobart, Garret 116
Hoboken Turtle Club 50
Hodes, Charles 172–173, 178, 184
Hodge Mills, Charlotte 180
Hoffman, Ogden 48
Holden, Amasa 306
Holder, John 102, 107–108, 118, 120, 131, 140
Holt, Charles 111
Holt, Edward 143
Holt, Guy 143, 160
Holt, William 111
Home Games for the People 73
Hope Base Ball Club of Belvidere (MA) 307
Hopkins, J.A.P. 61
Horsford, Eben 281
Hosford, Samuel 77–78
Hosmer, Stephen 29
Hosmer, Titus 29
Hough, Charles 189
How to Become a Base-Ball Player 58
Howe, William 34
Howell, Harry 87, 111
Hoyt, George E. 115
Hubbard, Robert J. 101, 111
Hudson River Base Ball Club of Newburgh (NY) 94
Hudson, Wilbur 96
Hulbert, Joanne 282
Hullick, William 259
Hummel, Abraham H. 56
Hunnewell, Arthur 288, 290
Hunt, Charles 89, 131, 178
Hunt, Jane 294
Hunt, Richard 89
Hutton, Isaiah 197–198
Hyannis Base Ball Club of Iyannough (MA) 316

Independent Base Ball Club of South Brooklyn 105, 148, 152–154, 177
Independent Base Ball Club of Leominster (MA) 308

Independent Base Ball Club of Sandwich (MA) 316
Invincible Base Ball Club of New York City 66
Ireland, George, Jr. 29
Ireland, John 131
Irons, Alfred 286–287, 292
Irving, Washington 16
Irvington (NJ) Base Ball Club 66–68, 84, 90–92, 125–126, 133, 152–153, 188, 191–193, 200, 204, 208–209, 210, 212, 214–220, 222, 224
Ivy Green (saloon) 22–23, 64

Jackson, Andrew 34
Jackson, Theodore 113, 115
Jacobus, Samuel 206
Jaques, Charles 303
Jay, John 30
Jefferson Junior Base Ball Club of Brooklyn 177
Jersey City (NJ) Evening Journal 193
Jersey City (NJ) Telegraph 194
Jersey (NJ) Journal 198
Jesus Christ and the Christian Character 269
Jesus Christ and the Social Questions 269
jewelers 22, 79, 109, 201, 212, 249, 285
Jewell, Herbert 107, 153–154, 156, 160
Jewett, Nat 77, 80, 83, 89
Jewish players 29, 58, 98, 133, 210
Johnson, Andrew 84
Johnson, David M. 255–256
Johnson, William 57–58
Johnston, Dr. Francis Upton, Jr. 29, 57–58
Johnston, Dr. Francis Upton, Sr. 29, 57–58
Jones, Dr. Joseph Bainbridge 108
Jones, F.W. 101
Jones, Frank 108
Jordan, Conrad 196
Joslin, William Burt 268
Joyt, Monson 78
judges *see* lawyers and judges

Kearsarge Base Ball Club of Stoneham (MA) 304–308, 312
Keeler, David, Jr. 15, 30
Kelley, Henry 67
Kelley, Theodore 67
Kelley, William J. 66, 67
Kelly, Michael "King" 220–221
Kelso, James J 89
Kennard, John 80
Kenney, John 126, 131
Kerouac, Jack 307
Ketcham, Dan 96, 115, 178
Ketcham, Richard 178
Ketchum, Joseph, Jr. 111
Keystone Base Ball Club of Philadelphia 57, 83–84, 105, 124, 127, 151, 160, 209, 227, 239, 242–243, 246–251
King, Martin Luther 227
King Philip Base Ball Club of Weymouth (MA) 304
Kirby, W.H. 30
Kissam, Benjamin 30
Kissam, Catherine 21
Kissam, Peter 30
Kissam, Samuel 24, 30, 38, 108

Kittel, Jeffrey 37
Klein, Adam 178
Kleinfelder, Dan 239
Knickerbocker Antiquarian Base Ball Club of Newark 192
Knickerbocker Base Ball Club of Albany (NY) 83, 151
Knickerbocker Base Ball Club of New York City 1, 3–4, 7, 10–46, 47–48, 50–62, 64–65, 69–70, 72, 94, 96, 98, 101–102, 105, 108–110, 112, 117, 118, 147, 157, 167, 168, 174, 182, 185, 191, 242, 245, 248, 285
Knickerbocker Boat Club 47–48
Knight, Frank 242, 244
Knox, William W. 205
Kuen, John 230
Kuhn, Dr. Adam 229
Kuhn, Hartman 229, 232
Kulp, Philip 249

Labon, Bill 143
Ladd, William F. 13–14, 30–31
Lalor, Jonathan 54–55, 58
Langworthy, John 31
Lanphear, George 179, 184
Lansdown, James P. 31
Lask, Edgar 31
Latham, Arlie 304
Law, Hervey G. 116
Law, John F. 116
Law, Nathaniel B. 116
Lawrence Base Ball Club (Harvard) 262, 281–285
Lawrence Scientific School 32, 281, 283, 285
Lawton, John 80
lawyers and judges 23, 25, 33, 35, 36, 52, 56, 57, 58, 60, 61, 89, 91, 108, 110, 115, 143, 160, 204, 205, 206, 212, 228, 237, 240, 249, 256
League Alliance 6
Leake and Watts Orphan Home 74
Learning, Wallace 80
Leavitt, Joshua, Jr. 145–146, 160
Leavitt, Rev. Joshua, Sr. 160
Leavy, Thomas 76–78, 118
Lee, Benjamin C. 31
Lee, Colonel James 17, 31, 50–51, 57–58
Lee, General Robert E. 253
Leggett, James 31
Leggett, Joe 98, 101, 104–105, 108, 113, 122, 158, 171, 290
Leiper, Cal 256
Lennon, William 105, 108, 160
Lester, Andrew 62
Leveridge, John 23, 51
Lewis, Billy 90, 191–192, 214
Lewis, Edward 136
Lex, Harry 209–211, 250
Liberty Base Ball Club of Danvers (MA) 306
Liberty Base Ball Club of New Brunswick (NJ) 120, 123, 192, 199–202
Lichtenstein, Seaman 57–59
Lightfoot Base Ball Club of Belvidere (MA) 307
Lightfoot Base Ball Club of North Brookfield (MA) 299–302
Lightfoot Base Ball Club of Salem (MA) 310
Lincoln, Abraham 208, 238, 274

Lindsay, Robert 90
Linen, James 192, 211
Lines, George 216–217
Linfield, Adelbert Moses 303
Lippincott, William 31
Little Eva 73
Little, Robert F. 206
Littlewood, Albert 207, 211
Litzenburg, W.H. 242, 244
Live Oak Base Ball Club of Lynn (MA) 304
Livingston, Charles L. 48
Livingstone, James D. 294
Lockwood, Gershom 31
Logan, William 168, 179
Long Before the Dodgers 187
Long Island Cricket Club 49, 99, 118, 140–141, 143
Lord, David 29
Lord, W.G. 145, 163
Lothrop, John 316
Loughery, Bernard 242–244
Lovejoy, Clarence 308
Lovett, James D'Wolf 263–269, 285–286, 288, 293
Lovett, Len 250
Lowell Base Ball Club of Boston 32, 105, 125, 154, 263–270, 280, 286–288, 290, 293, 304
Lowell (MA) Daily Citizen and News 305, 311
Lowell, Abner 266
Lowell, James Russell 32
Lowell, John 263–266, 275, 285, 288
Lowell, John Adams 268
Ludden, John 276
Ludlow, Wiliam H. 101
Luengene, Gus 239

MacDiarmid, Tom 151–152, 162
MacLean, John 203
Magnolia Base Ball Club of New York City 1, 7, 10–11, 47, 62–65
Magnolia Lunch and Saloon 63, 65
Malone, Fergy 227, 235, 239, 247–249, 250
Maltbie, William D. 31
The Man Who Invented Baseball 57–58
Manhattan Cricket Club 78
manliness 10, 11, 15, 37, 47, 71, 72, 77, 104, 112, 121, 132, 167, 222, 242, 261, 262, 273, 294
Manly, Robert 145–146, 160
Mann, Stephen 131
Mann, William Rufus 261–262
Manolt, Henry 168, 178
Manor House, Greenpoint (NY) 99, 119, 167, 169, 174, 179, 185
Mansfield Base Ball Club of Middletown (CT) 155–156
Mara, Philip 296
Marden, William H. 306
Margot, Augustus 55, 262
Marion Base Ball Club of Brooklyn 169, 171, 175, 177, 180, 183–184
Marion Base Ball Club of Philadelphia 227, 257–259
Markham, Arthur 108
Marks, Alexander 203, 206
Marryat, Frederick 47
Marsh, Philip 196
Martin, Alfred D. 96
Martin, Alphonse "Phonney" 77–78, 83, 90, 172–174, 179

Masketukett/Moskeetukget Base Ball Club of West Barnstable (MA) 316–317
Mason, Charles 286
Mason, Del 185
Mason, Melchior B. 56
Massachusetts Association of Base Ball Players 262
Massachusetts Game 1, 10, 47, 260–263, 271–273, 285, 287, 299, 300, 302, 304–305
Massachusetts Rules *see* Massachusetts Game
Massachusetts Spy 272
Massapoag Base Ball Club of Sharon (MA) 260–261, 264
Massey, Frederick 131, 182
Masten, Myron 108, 116
Mathews, Bobby 73, 182
Mathewson, Christy 60
Mattakeesett Base Ball Club of Yarmouth (MA) 316–317
Matthews, Andrew 80
Maxwell, Henry 108
McAuslan. D.J. 179
McBride, Dick 227, 237, 239, 255
McBurney, Dr. Charles 292, 294
McCarthy, D.F. 250
McCarty, Michael 31
McCarty's Hotel 49
McClellan Base Ball Club of Brooklyn 131
McClintock, Mary Anne 294
McCloud, James 51
McConnell, James 90
McCormick, Jim 221
McCosker, John 58
McCutcheon, Hugh 32
McCutcheon, William 31
McDonald, Archie 302–303
McDonald, Dan 126, 131
McDonald, William Ogden 32
McGunigle, Thomas 136
McIlvane, Joseph 206
McKeever, Billy 82, 84
McKibbin, John, Jr. 62
McKiernan, Sam 219, 221
McKim, Charles F. 32
McKinstry, Ed 116
McLarnan, Hugh 247, 250
McLaughlen, Napoleon 32–33
McLaughlin, Kane 83
McMahon, Archie 103, 132
McMahon, Billy 81–82, 85, 89
McMahon, Henry 224
McNamee, John 117, 140, 143, 224
McVey, Cal 128
Mealey, Edward Windsor 292
Mechanic Base Ball Club of East Weymouth (MA) 302
Melville, Tom 54
Mendes, Rabbi Henry Pereira 29
Menke, Frank 30
Mercantile Base Ball Club of Philadelphia 227
Mercein, Thomas R. 136
Merwin, Joseph 80
Mesrole, Jeremiah 116
Metropolitan Base Ball Club of New York City 10
Metzler, Henry 168
Millard, Samuel 136
Miller, Gerrit Smith, Jr. "Gat" 264, 267–269
Miller, Dr. John 53, 58
Miller, Thomas 76, 78, 80, 258

Mills, A.G. 10, 180
Mills, Charley 86, 90–91
Mills, Everitt 91
Mills, Samuel 180
Millspaugh, Henry 203–205
Minerva Base Ball Club of Philadelphia 227
Mingay, James B. 56, 58
Minshall, Jesse 256
Mishawaum Base Ball Club of Woburn (MA) 308
Mitchell, James 105, 108
Moncrief, James 33, 39
Monitor Base Ball Club of Goshen (NY) 152
Monitor Base Ball Club of Middleboro (MA) 317
Monroe, James 19
Montgomery, James L. 33
Moore, Clement 36
Moore, DeWitt C. 82, 234–235, 239
Moore, John 108
Moore, Richard P. 78
Morehouse, Edward 132
Morgan, Henry T. 33
Morning Star Club (St. Louis, town ball club) 37
Morrill, Augustus C. 33–34
Morrill, Elisha 33
Morris, Charles 145, 160
Morris, Mary G. 19
Morris, Tom 108, 145, 151–152, 161
Morse, Alexander 203, 206
Morse, Samuel 19
Mott, Daniel 91
Mott, John 74
Mowlem, James 132
Mudge, Lewis 203–205
Mullen, James 80
Mulliken, Nancy 18
Mullin, John F. 250
Mumby, Samuel H 136
Mumford, J. Paige 34
Mumford, John 34
Munn, Horatio 132
Munn, Joseph 205
Murphy, Harriet 60
Murphy, John 34, 53, 58
Murphy, Joseph 80
Murray, John Jr. 34
Murray, Lindley 34
Murray, Mary Lindley 34
Murray, Robert 34, 35
Murtha, William 108, 142
Mutual Base Ball Club of New York City 4, 7, 10, 12, 59, 66–67, 75, 77, 80–93, 95, 100, 104–105, 110, 121, 123–125, 127–128, 130–133, 149–150, 152–160, 170–174, 176–177, 180, 182–184, 193, 204, 208, 210, 212, 215–217, 222–223, 247–248, 267, 290, 305. 312
Mutual Base Ball Club of Springfield (MA) 313

Nash, Peter 59
Nason, Daniel 261–262
Nassau Base Ball Club of Brooklyn 116, 141, 148
Nassau Base Ball Club of Princeton (NJ) 104, 123, 149–150, 192, 195, 202–207
Nassau, Charles 206
National Association 15, 17
National Association of Base Ball

Players (NABBP) 3, 65, 70–72, 77, 86, 98, 101, 106, 108, 113, 135, 140, 143–144, 148, 167–168, 184, 188, 191, 193, 199, 207, 211, 214, 222, 224, 227, 230, 235, 239, 241, 244, 252, 281, 309
National Association of Professional Base Ball Players (NA) 56
National Chronicle 269
National League 6, 10, 60, 87, 97, 115, 130, 133, 135, 159, 175, 192, 212, 220, 227, 231, 234, 236, 238–240, 249, 255
National Pastime 52, 58
National Soccer Hall of Fame 269
National Base Ball Club of Washington 84, 105, 107, 155, 177, 215
National Guard 19, 81, 115, 211, 249, 254, 258, 259
Needham, James 301
Nelson, Edward 221
Nelson, Jack 172, 174, 180
Nelson, John Candy 91
Neponset Base Ball Club of Walpole Center (MA) 264
New Brunswick (NJ) Daily Fredonian 200–201
New England Association of Base Ball Players 262–263, 304–305
New England Base Ballist 263
New England Game *see* Massachusetts Game
New York Atlas 97, 113, 116, 121
New York Base Ball Club *see* Gotham Club of New York City
New York Boat Club 48
New York Clipper 52, 60, 74, 82–83, 85–86, 90–91
New York Club *see* Gotham Club of New York City
New York Cricket Club 47, 49–50, 52, 58, 123
New York Game 3, 7, 10, 47, 98, 113, 194–195, 202, 227, 229, 234, 238, 241 262–264, 268, 270–272, 274, 277, 281, 285, 287, 300, 302, 304–305, 315
New York Herald 54, 62, 71
New York Illustrated 51
New York Leader 22
New York Mirror 47
New York Morning News 54
New York Rules *see* New York Game
New York Sporting Club 50
New York Stock Exchange 20, 25, 30–31, 39, 106
New York Sun 16, 72
New York Sunday Mercury 3, 35, 95, 269
New York Times 3, 21, 56, 86, 93
New York Tribune 22, 51, 73
New York World 3, 53
Newark Daily Mercury 191
Newark Evening Courier 193, 209–210, 215
Newcomb, Simon 283
Newkirk, Henry 80
Niagara Base Ball Club of Brooklyn 107, 146–147, 159
Niagara Base Ball Club of Buffalo 94, 100, 106, 109, 127, 164, 206
Nichols Base Ball Club of Sandwich (MA) 312, 315–316
Nichols, Edward 315
Nichols, James 301

Nichols, Samuel 35
Niebuhr, Fraley C. 17, 35
Nonotuck Base Ball Club of Northampton (MA) 272–273
Northrop, Henry 192
Norton, Abraham R. Lawrence 96
Norton, Frank 105, 109, 125, 151–152, 161
Norton, Hugh 136
Norton, Michael 91
Norton, Peter 91
Nucciarone, Monica 11, 22

O'Brien, David 313
O'Brien, John 35
O'Brien, Mattie 81, 103, 118, 120–121, 124–125, 129, 132
O'Brien, Peter 100, 117, 120, 122–125, 130, 132, 143
O'Brien, Thomas J. 35
O'Brien, William 35
O'Donnell, John B. 296–298
Oakley, Walter 35
occupations see bankers; bartenders and saloon keepers; brokers; butchers; clerks; firefighters; jewelers; lawyers and judges; policemen and sheriffs; physicians and surgeons; produce merchants; shipbuilders; shoe-related professions
Odell, William 80
Old Boston Boys and the Games They Played 268
Oliver, John 103, 120, 124, 131–133
Oliver, Joseph 132
Oliver, Richard 109
Olympic Base Ball Club of Boston 260–262, 264
Olympic Base Ball Club of Brooklyn 94, 148–149
Olympic Base Ball Club of Paterson (NJ) 215, 218–223
Olympic Base Ball Club of Philadelphia (originally a town ball club) 62, 82, 151, 192, 208, 226–235, 238–242, 246, 252, 257–258
Olympic Base Ball Club of Washington, D.C. 57, 97, 153–156, 161, 175–176, 211–212, 217, 248–250, 268, 312
Onderdonk, Rev. Benjamin 35
Onderdonk, Henry 35
Ontario Base Ball Club of Oswego 5
Onward Base Ball Club of New Bedford (MA) 316
Oriental Base Ball Club of Brooklyn/Greenpoint 113, 141, 148, 155, 181, 191
Osborne, Robert 90
Osceola Base Ball Club of Brooklyn 130, 141, 156, 205
Ottignon, Charles F. 33
Owen, Major Edward 26

Pabor, Charley 94, 96
Page, J. Seaver 66, 67
Page, William 266
Painter, Jerome B. 73
Palmer, Anson S. 36
Palmer, Pete 18
Parisen, C.H. 36
Parisen, Otto 36
Park, Richard 304
Parker, Henry 287, 292–293

Pastime Base Ball Club of Brooklyn 100, 107, 109–111, 121, 130, 140–144, 157, 176
Pastime Base Ball Club of Baltimore 84, 95, 155–156
Pastime Base Ball Club of Richmond (VA) 129
Patchen, Edward 146–147
Patchen, Joe 109, 161, 163
Patchen, Sam 146, 148, 161
Paterson (NJ) Daily Guardian 220
Paterson (NJ) Daily Press 219–220
Patterson, Dan 91
Patterson, Thomas 91, 180, 182
Paulding, John 36
Pavonia Base Ball Club of Jersey City (NJ) 197
Peabody, Dr. Francis Greenwood 269
Peabody Base Ball Club of Danvers (MA) 305–306
Pearce, Dickey 87,98, 105, 119, 123–125, 128–129, 133, 135, 150, 152, 161, 265
Pearsall, A.T. 92, 103–104, 109
Peck, Andrew 73, 74
Peconic Base Ball Club of Brooklyn 105
Peed, Charles W. 136
Peirson, Charles H 36, 37
Pell, Miriam 28
Pell, Sir John 28
Penn Tiger Club see Winona Base Ball Club of Philadelphia
Penney, Sherry 294
Pennington, Edward 207, 212
Pennsylvania Base Ball Club of Philadelphia 227
Pennsylvania blue laws 227
Perry, Nehemiah 205
Peterson, Harold 20, 22–23, 28, 41, 57–58
Petrie, Charles 203, 206
Peverelly, Charles A. 2, 11, 18, 47, 55, 66, 69, 72, 81, 117, 121, 227, 241, 288
Peverelly, William 50
Phelan, George 88
Phelan, Michael 88
Phelps, George 118–119, 129, 133
Philadelphia Athletics 94, 220
Philadelphia Inquirer 66
Philadelphia Phillies 5
Philadelphia Times 57
Phillips Exeter Academy 20, 285, 292, 294–295
Phinney, Robert 319
Phinney, Sylvanus 315
Phinney, Theodore 319
physicians and surgeons 18, 26, 29–30, 37, 52, 53, 58, 92, 104, 209, 225, 256, 292, 303
Pickwick Papers 40
Picton, Colonel Thomas 48–50, 58, 60
Pidgeon, Frank 100, 103, 122, 167–171, 173–174, 180, 183
Pike, Boaz 133
Pike, Lipman 85, 91, 98, 125, 133
Pike, Mary R. 21
Pinckney, Joseph C. 55, 58, 96
Pinkham, Edwin 171, 173, 178, 181
Pioneer Base Ball Club of Jersey City (NJ) 75, 194–197, 204, 214
Pioneer Base Ball Club of Savannah (GA) 59

Pioneer Base Ball Club of Springfield (MA) 260, 262, 270–280, 300
Pittsfield (MA) Base Ball Club 274
Place, Charles, Jr. 74
Platt, Henry Mortimer 58
Playing Parlor Base-Ball 79
plugging see soaking
Plum, Stephen 208, 212
Plunkett, Eugene 37, 88, 299
Poland, Abigail 301
Poland, Anson 301
Polhemus, Harry 103–104, 109
Policemen and sheriffs 73, 88, 89, 91, 95, 117, 135, 143, 176, 179, 180, 198, 250, 255, 300, 306, 318
Polmatier, Jonas 296, 298
Poole, Bill "The Butcher" 51
Portland (ME) Fire, Great 266
Powers, James Gilmore 74
Powers, Thomas 118
Powhatan Base Ball Club of South Brooklyn 130, 148–149, 154
Pratt, Tom 124, 126, 133, 248
Price, John Griffith 118–119, 134
produce merchants 19, 25, 50–51, 59, 75, 80, 134, 217, 231, 239
Purcell, William 220
Purdy, Dr. James W. 37
Purdy, R.F. 37
Putnam, Eben 282, 284
Putnam, Frederick Ward 281–284
Putnam, General Israel 291
Putnam Base Ball Club of Brooklyn 17, 26, 94, 99–101, 103, 111–117, 119–120, 122, 124, 176, 185
Pythian Base Ball Club of Philadelphia 226–228, 230, 238, 251–254

Queen, Frank 119
Quevedo, Frank 143
Quigley, Joe 136

Radcliffe, John Y. 239
Rankin, Edward P. 206
Rankin, William 24, 129
Ranney, William Tylee 49
Ransom, Dr. Franklin 57, 59
Raymond, Francis 303
Reach, Al 98, 125, 134, 167, 170–171, 173, 180, 227, 235–236, 238–239, 250
Reach, Bob 250
Record, Wellington 303
Red House Grounds in Harlem 8, 51, 55–56, 96, 119
Red Stockings of Cincinnati 66, 86, 162, 212, 305, 311–312
Reeder, George 259
Regan, Joseph A. 134
Remington, Charles 206
Republic Fire Insurance Company 24
Resolute Base Ball Club of Brooklyn 95, 146, 149, 151, 161, 229, 246–247, 263, 265, 269
Resolute Base Ball Club of Elizabeth (NJ) 95, 155, 182, 192–193, 200–201, 210, 216–217, 222–224
revolving 58, 83, 100, 237, 258
Reynolds, Adrian 196
Reynolds, Thomas 109
Riblet, Charles S. 61
Richards, Frederick DeBourg 230
Richards, George G. 269

Rickey, Branch 227
Righter, Charles 37
Robbins, John 80
Robertson, Andrew 296, 298
Robinson, Anna 21
Robinson, E.N. 114, 116
Robinson, Henry 206
Robinson, Jackie 227
Rocket Base Ball Club of Belvidere (MA) 307
Rockinghams of Portsmouth (NH) 267
Roe, Peter 61
Rogers, Albert H. 67
Rogers, Fraley 152, 156–157, 161, 269
Rogers, George R. 136
Rogers, James 101, 111
Rogers, John 240
Rogers, Mortimer 151, 263
Rollstone Base Ball Club of Fitchburg (MA) 267, 308
Rooney, George W. 66, 67
Rooney, William 66, 67
Ross, Harvey 96, 98, 134
Rough and Ready Base Ball Club of South Walpole (MA) 262, 264
rowing 288, 292, 294
Russell, Ed 103, 109
Russell, Joseph 78
Rutherford, Walter 37
Ryczek, William 93
Ryder, James E. 77, 79
Ryno, David 116

St. George Cricket Club 49, 94
St. John's Base Ball Club of Newark 191
St. Louis Brown Stockings 259
Salmon, William F. 308
Salmon Base Ball Club of Lowell (MA) 308, 310
saloon keepers see bartenders and saloon keepers
Saltzman, Edward G. 55, 59, 262–263, 270
Sampson, Henry L. 206
San Francisco Examiner 52
Sandwich Gazette 317
Saunders, William 80
Schafer, Harry C. 240
Scott, Walter 76, 79
Sears, Milt 220–221
Sebring, Francis 79
Seeley, Dick 303
Seinsoth, Frank 134
Seinsoth, George 134
Selden, John 271, 274, 278
Sensenderfer, John 240
Senter, William 266
Sexton, George 117, 136
Shamrock Base Ball Club of Lowell (MA) 307
Shandley, Edward J 90, 91
Shantz, Benjamin F. 241–244
Shantz, Harry 242, 244
Sharp, William H. 54
Shawme Base Ball Club of Sandwich (MA) 316
Shay, John 276
Shelley, Ed 96
Shepard, James 59
Shepard, William 59
Sheridan, Phillip 59
Sheridan Base Ball Club of Lowell (MA) 308

sheriffs *see* policemen and sheriffs
Shieber, Tom 58
Shield Base Ball Club of East Cambridge (MA) 308
Shield Base Ball Club of Chelsea (MA) 302
shipbuilders 59, 131, 168, 169, 172, 174, 175, 176, 178, 179, 180, 183, 189, 198, 255
shoe-related professions 60, 90, 96, 300, 301, 303, 306, 310
Shreve, Pete 80, 91
Sickles, General Dan 22
silver ball (trophy): Greater New York City championship 123, 169–170, 175; New England championship 260, 263, 265–267, 288–290, 302–303, 310, 312; New Jersey championship 175, 215; New York Game championship of Massachusetts 304; presented to James Whyte Davis 24, 43; presented to Samuel Kissam 30; Sussex County (NJ) tournament 66; Ulster County (NY) tournament 66; Western Massachusetts championship 276–277, 297, 304–305
Simmons, Joe 77, 79, 96
Simonson, Charles 183
Simpkins, John 37
Simpkins, John, Jr. 37
Simpkins, Nathaniel 37
Skaats, William W 162
Slote, Alonzo 37, 38
Slote, Daniel, Jr. 37
Slote, Henry 38
Smith, Charley 98, 120–121, 123–124, 126, 134
Smith, Cornelius 31
Smith, D.D., 38
Smith, E.F. 321
Smith, Evans 136
Smith, George B. 271
Smith, George W. 57, 59
Smith, Henry 76, 79
Smith, Horace 192
Smith, J. Connor 38
Smith, Jack 227, 257–258
Smith, Joseph 134
Smith, Michael 240
Smith, Nathaniel 289, 293
Smith, Samuel 134
Smith, Sid 124, 134
Smith, Tom 74
Smith, W. Hart 76, 79
Smith & Wesson Base Ball Club of Springfield (MA) 277
Sniffen, Caleb 117–119, 134
Snowden, William 223, 225
Snyder, James 181
Snyder, John H. 181
Snyder, Joshua 181
Snyder, Washington 74
soaking 11, 64, 117, 140, 226, 264, 271, 302
Soden, Arthur 267
Sons of Diagora 47
Soos, Troy 261
South Walpole (MA) Base Ball Club 261
Southern Base Ball Club of New Orleans 86
Spadone, Amedee 76, 79
Spalding, Albert 17, 50
Spalding, J. Walter 116

Spence, Peter 181
Spirit of the Times 48–51, 55, 71, 81, 85, 93
Sporting Life 5, 87
Sprague, Joe 98, 124, 167, 170, 173, 181–182
Springfield (MA) Republican 270–272, 277–278, 281
Springsteen, George 80
Squires, Albert 61
Stafford, Marshall Paddock 269
Stagg, John 109
Stansbury, Daniel 15, 38
Stanton, Elizabeth Cady 294
Stanton, John 38
Star Base Ball Club of Brooklyn 72, 94, 100, 102, 105, 107, 121–122, 130, 144–167, 182, 223–224
Star Base Ball Club of Greenfield (MA) 267
Star Base Ball Club of New Brunswick (NJ) 203
Star Cricket Club of Brooklyn 52–53
Star Union Base Ball Club of Brooklyn 135
Start, Joe 87, 98, 109, 123, 127–128, 134–135, 173
Staten Island Base Ball Club of Tompkinsville (NY) 182
stealing *see* base stealing
Stearns, George Luther 293
Steers, George 59
Stevens, Edward A. 47, 49
Stevens, Edwin 84
Stevens, Joe 272, 278
Stevens, John 48
Stevens, John Cox 23, 245
Stevens, Richard Fowler 38, 241–245
Stevens, Robert L. 48
Stevens, William 296
Stewart, Thomas 41
Stockman, Mahlon 66–67, 91, 214–217
Stokem, Cornelius 61
Stone, George Washington 301
Storm, John G. 38
Story, Bob 143
Stovey, Harry 300
Stowe, Harriet Beecher 73
The Study (saloon) 66
Sturges, Elias R. 201
Sunday Mercury see *New York Sunday Mercury*
surgeons *see* physicians and surgeons
Sutton, Thomas 93, 96
Suydam, Charles 101
Suydam, John 70, 101
Suydam, Lambert 38
Swandell, Martin 91, 172, 180, 182
Sweasy, Charles 128, 130
Sweeney, Peter 22
Sweet, Milton 59, 110
Swift, Charles 96
Swiftfoot Base Ball Club of Philadelphia 242

Talcott, Edward B. 25
Tallmadge, Daniel B. 33, 39
Talmadge, Thomas 39
Talman, Edward 39
Talman, William 19, 26, 29, 39
Tanner, Charles 198
Tappan, Jeremiah 101, 110

Tassie, Thomas 117, 129, 135
Tay, Charlie 304, 306
Taylor, Anson 81–82
Taylor, Asa 39
Taylor, Henry B. 81, 90
Taylor, William 39
Teed, Oscar 59
Temple, Charles 314
Temple, William Chase 185
The Tented Field 54
tenth player 150
Terrill, Joe 191, 209, 212, 215
Terry, James 187
Thake, Albert 162
Thomas, Charles 110, 192, 207, 292
Thomas, Henry A. 39
Thompson Austin 39, 59
Thompson, Frank 162
Thorn, John 1, 7, 96, 228
Thorn, Richard 56, 59, 76, 79, 89, 91, 103
Thorne, William S. 39
Thornell, Thomas 75
Tibbits, Hall J. 27
Tice, George 80
Tickner, Augustus C. 135
Tiffany, William George 287, 293–294
Tiger Base Ball Club of New York City 8
Tompkins, George 189
Tooker, Theodore 59
Tooker, William 59
Toomey, Mike 219, 221
Torrey, Charles 300–301
Tostevin, Peter 178, 183
Towle, Levi 197
Tracy, Cadwallader Gilbert Colden 39, 40
Tracy, George Douglas 162
Tracy, Harriet 39
Tracy, Uriah 39
Tracy, William Wolcott 162
Trask, Abner 272, 274, 276, 278
Treacy, Fred 105, 110, 173, 183–184
Treadwell, Daniel 143
Tredwell, Alanson 38
Trenchard, Samuel 59
Tri-Mountain Base Ball Club of Boston 55, 59, 104, 125, 260, 262–264, 268, 270–271, 274, 277, 288–289, 295, 297, 302–304, 309–310, 312
trophies *see* bat; gold ball; silver ball
Troutman, G.H. 234
Tucker, Abraham 17, 40, 50, 52, 57, 60
Tucker, Fanning C., Sr. 28
Tucker, William H. 11, 16–17, 40, 50–51, 54, 60
Turk, Francis 40, 56
Turner, Nicholas 60
Turney, James 40
Twain, Mark 96
Tweed, Samuel 306
Tweed, William M. ("Boss") 10, 63, 73, 81–82, 89, 91
two old cat 297
Tyron, Frank 40
Tyson, William 40

umpires 3, 28, 39, 53, 68, 76, 80, 83, 86, 94, 96, 103–104, 114, 122, 128, 141, 148, 158, 172, 174, 178–179, 219, 223–224, 231, 238,

255, 259, 265, 286, 297, 302, 305, 307, 308, 318
Una Base Ball Club of Brooklyn 105
Uncle Tom's Cabin 73
Underhill, Anthony 34
uniforms 53, 65, 77, 93, 114, 153, 174, 199, 200, 203, 204, 209, 218, 223, 275, 286, 296, 302, 310, 312
Union Base Ball Club of Bloomfield (NJ) 192
Union Base Ball Club of Danvers (MA) 306
Union Base Ball Club of Lynnfield Centre (MA) 308
Union Base Ball Club of Medway (MA) 262, 264
Union Base Ball Club of Morrisania (NY) 7, 10, 58, 61, 66–68, 79, 84–85, 93–100, 104–105, 114, 121, 124, 126–127, 149, 152–154, 167, 178, 215, 218, 220–221, 248
Union Base Ball Club of Lansingburgh *see* Haymakers of Troy (NY)
Union Grounds (Brooklyn) 7 98, 100, 114, 126–127, 152, 154–155, 167, 169–170, 172
Union Grounds (Tremont, NY) 93–95, 96
Union Star Cricket Club of New York City 54, 56
Unionville Base Ball Club of Gravesend (NY) 152
United Base Ball Club of Philadelphia 227
Upham, John 301
Uris, Jake 143
US Master Schooner *John Griffith* 135
USS *North Carolina* 135
USS *Princeton* 135
Utica Club 5

Vail, James 40
Vail, William 41, 55, 60
Van Brunt, Charles 197–198
Van Buren, Martin 20
Van Cleef, Charles 163
Van Cleef, John 145, 162, 163
Van Cott, Gabriel 60
Van Cott, Theodore 60
Van Cott, Thomas 55, 60
Van Cott, William H. 55, 60, 69
Van Delft, Benjamin 136
Van Horn, John 96
Van Nice, John 75
Van Nostrand, James H 101
Van Pelt, Reuben 206
Van Schaack, Peter 101, 110
Van Wie, Eliza 22
Vanderbilt, Amy 168
Vanderbilt, Joseph 1, 168, 183
Vanderbilt, William H. 30
Varian, Eliza 181
Venn, Harry 54, 56–58, 60
A Very Dangerous Woman 294
Victory Base Ball Club of Troy (NY) 103
Vinton Goodrich, Emma 279
Vinton, Edward Bliss 272, 278–279
Vinton, Joshua 278
Vinton, Mary 278
Voigt, David Quentin 226

Voorhis, Thomas 76, 77, 80
Vredenburgh, Alfred 41

Waddell, Hope 151, 161, 163
Waddell, Samuel 80
Wadsworth, Louis F. 13–14, 41,46, 55, 57–58, 61
Waff, Craig 187
Wagner Free Institute of Science 66
Walker, Charley 65, 67, 290
Walker, Dr. Emma 279
Wallace, Waller 60
Wallace, William 247, 250
Walsh, Mike 22
Walton, Edward 112, 113, 116
Wamsutta Base Ball Club of New Bedford (MA) 316
Wandell, Richard 80
Wansley, William 82–83, 86, 91, 116, 124, 171, 177
Ward, Ed 91
Ward, James 77, 80
Ward, John Montgomery 11, 30, 58
Warner, Lucius 274, 276–277, 279
Warren Base Ball Club of New York City 156
Warren Base Ball Club of Randolph (MA) 306
Warren Base Ball Club of South Danvers (MA) 306
Washburn, Francis 282, 284
Washington Base Ball Club see Gotham Club of New York City
Washington Junior Base Ball Club of Newark 192
Washington Market 31, 50–51, 52, 56, 57, 58, 59, 62, 75, 79, 80, 90, 134, 178

Washington Market Chowder Club 50, 57, 62
Washington, Booker T. 227
Waterman, Fred 77, 80, 83, 85, 92
Watson, John Henry 294
Watson, John William 294
Weaver, Charles 250
Webster, William 184
Webster Base Ball Club of North Woburn (MA) 308
Welling, Charles 168, 184
Welling, Norman 15, 41
Wenman, James 41, 42
Wenman, Uzziah 41
Wesleyan College Base Ball Club 155
West, Benjamin 184
Westervelt, William 20, 42
Wetherbee, Seth 299–300
Whalen, Patrick 296, 298
Wheaton, William 2, 7, 11, 17, 27, 42, 46–47, 49–52, 54, 57–58, 61, 230
Wheeler, John 38
Wheelwright, George 145, 163
White, Josiah "Joe" 307, 313–314
White, Mary 313
Whiteside, Andrew 61
Whiting, Charles 146–147, 163
Whitman, William 228
Whitney, Ben 307–308, 314
Whitson, Willet 118, 135
Wickham, William 206
Wilder, George B. 264
Wildey, John 80, 88, 92
Wilkes' Spirit of the Times 98, 118, 145, 168, 211, 242, 293
Wilkins, Isaac 240

Wilkinson, Edward Tuckerman 294
Willard, Gardner 293
Willard, Le Baron 111
Williams College 160, 287–288, 290–291, 293, 299
Williams College Base Ball Club 260, 262, 287–290
Williams, Alfred 75, 199
Williams, Charles S 202
Williamsburgh (NY) Democrat 187
Williamson, Cornelius T. 67
Willis, William 223–225
Wilson, Press 256
Windust, Edward 59
Winne, James 21
Winona Base Ball Club of Philadelphia 227, 229, 231, 238, 242–243
Winslow, Albert 61
Winslow, Robert 55, 61
Winslow, Robert, Jr. 55
Winslow, Sylvester 75
Winslow. Albert 42
Winston, Gustavus S. 101
Winthrop Base Ball Club of Boston 302
Winthrop Base Ball Club of Holliston (MA) 264
Wolters, Reinder "Rynie" 85, 92, 153, 217
women as specators 33, 66, 76, 77, 93, 96, 113, 114, 118, 121, 122, 203, 220, 266, 273, 275, 276, 310, 312
Wood, A.G. 101
Wood, Fernando 22–23, 247
Wood, George 300
Wood, Jimmy 98, 167, 169–174, 178, 181–184

Wood, M.A. 273–279
Wood, William 69
Woodford, Stewart 89
Woodhull, William 37, 42
Woods, Eddie 247–250
Woodward, John 110
Wooldridge, George 22
Worcester (MA) Spy 300
Worth, Herbert 163
Wright, David 294
Wright, Frank 265, 285–286, 291–294
Wright, George 61, 94–97, 130, 149, 230, 233
Wright, Harry 12, 41, 43, 61, 127–128, 134, 155, 217
Wright, Marshall 28, 67, 80, 111, 176, 178
Wright, Theodore Francis 296
Wright, William P. 61
Wyckoff, Van Brunt 110

Yale College Base Ball Club 153, 156, 203, 267, 286, 289, 290
Yates, Sam 43, 75, 142
Young, Henry 206
Young, Nick 176
Young, William H. 110
Young America Base Ball Club of Harlem 145
Young America Base Ball Club of South Brooklyn 107, 145–146

Zeller, John 56, 82, 92
Zettlein, George 56–58, 98, 125–126, 133, 135, 155, 167, 171–172, 174